Administrative Medical Assisting

Administrative Medical Assisting

A Workforce Readiness Approach

Helen J. Houser, RN, MSHA, RMA (AMT)
Phoenix College
Phoenix, AZ

Terri D. Wyman, CPC, CMRS
Financial Applications Analyst
Wing Memorial Hospital
Palmer, MA

ADMINISTRATIVE MEDICAL ASSISTING: A WORKFORCE READINESS APPROACH
Published by McGraw-Hill, a business unit of The McGraw-Hill Companies, Inc., 1221 Avenue of the Americas, New York, NY, 10020.

Some ancillaries, including electronic and print components, may not be available to customers outside the United States.

This book is printed on acid-free paper.

1 2 3 4 5 6 7 8 9 0 QDB/QDB 1 0 9 8 7 6 5 4 3 2 1

ISBN 978-0-07-340215-4
MHID 0-07-340215-X

Vice president/Editor in chief: *Elizabeth Haefele*
Vice president/Director of marketing: *Alice Harra*
Publisher: *Kenneth S. Kasee Jr.*
Managing development editor: *Christine Scheid*
Editorial coordinator: *Jenna Skwarek*
Marketing manager: *Mary B. Haran*
Lead digital product manager: *Damian Moshak*
Digital development editor: *Katie Ward*
Director, Editing/Design/Production: *Jess Ann Kosic*
Lead project manager: *Susan Trentacosti*
Buyer II: *Sherry L. Kane*
Senior designer: *Anna Kinigakis*
Lead photo research coordinator: *Carrie K. Burger*

Photo researcher: *Pam Carley*
Digital production coordinator: *Brent dela Cruz*
Media project manager: *Cathy L. Tepper*
Outside development house: *Triple SSS Press—Alexis Breen Ferraro*
Cover design: *Alexa R. Viscius*
Interior design: *Laurie J. Entringer*
Typeface: *10/12 Slimbach*
Compositor: *Laserwords Private Limited*
Printer: *Quad/Graphics*
Cover credit: *(clockwise starting with Administrative Medical Assistant):* © *Jack Hollingsworth/Getty Images;* © *Tom Grill/Corbis;* © *Jose Luis Pelaez Inc/Getty Images;* © *TRBfoto/Getty Images*

Credits: The credits section for this book begins on page 743 and is considered an extension of the copyright page.

Library of Congress Cataloging-in-Publication Data
Houser, Helen J.
    Administrative medical assisting: a workforce readiness approach / Helen J. Houser,
Terri D. Wyman.
       p. ; cm.
    Includes index.
    ISBN-13: 978-0-07-340215-4 (alk. paper)
    ISBN-10: 0-07-340215-X (alk. paper)
    1. Medical assistants. 2. Medical offices—Management. I. Wyman, Terri D. II. Title.
    [DNLM: 1. Allied Health Personnel—United States. 2. Practice Management, Medical—
United States. 3. Career Choice—United States. 4. Medical Secretaries—United States. W 80]
    R728.8.H668 2012
    610.73'7092--dc22
                                                    2010054443

WARNING NOTICE: The clinical procedures, medicines, dosages, and other matters described in this publication are based upon research of current literature and consultation with knowledgeable persons in the field. The procedures and matters described in this text reflect currently accepted clinical practice. However, this information cannot and should not be relied upon as necessarily applicable to a given individual's case. Accordingly, each person must be separately diagnosed to discern the patient's unique circumstances. Likewise, the manufacturer's package insert for current drug product information should be consulted before administering any drug. Publisher disclaims all liability for any inaccuracies, omissions, misuse, or misunderstanding of the information contained in this publication. Publisher cautions that this publication is not intended as a substitute for the professional judgment of trained medical personnel.

The Internet addresses listed in the text were accurate at the time of publication. The inclusion of a Web site does not indicate an endorsement by the authors or McGraw-Hill, and McGraw-Hill does not guarantee the accuracy of the information presented at these sites.

www.mhhe.com

HELEN J. HOUSER, RMA, RN, BS, MSHA

Ms. Houser is a registered medical assistant and a registered nurse. She also holds a master of science in health care administration from the University of Colorado. For 10 years she served as the Director of the Medical Assisting Program at Phoenix College and consults on health care and educational issues. Her experience in health care spans over 30 years with various positions involving medical assisting, including Vice President of Phoenix General Hospital, Deer Valley, where she opened and managed medical practices in rural areas. Ms. Houser is a national speaker on topics such as Immunization Education for Medical Assisting Students and is the recipient of several awards, including the National Institute of Staff and Organizational Development Excellence Award and two Arizona Governor's Awards for Excellence. She worked on the Navajo Reservation, where she established school-based health services and a prenatal clinic. As a teacher and a health-care provider, she has extensive experience working with diverse populations. Houser continues to serve the community as a board member of Adelante Healthcare, a federally qualified community health center with several locations in the Phoenix area.

TERRI D. WYMAN, CPC, CMRS

Terri started her medical career as a CMA for a solo internal medical practitioner with a sub-specialty in hematology/oncology. Her interest in the administrative side of medicine blossomed when she accepted a position as home care coordinator for a home care/DME provider. After 18 years in the medical field, a teaching opportunity presented itself and she began her career as an educator of medical assisting students, eventually becoming the director of the program. She then assisted with the creation, development, and supervision of medical billing and coding programs at two separate technical schools in Massachusetts and Connecticut. She currently has returned to the medical field as the financial applications analyst at Wing Memorial Hospital in Palmer, Massachusetts. She is delighted to have had the opportunity to work with McGraw-Hill and their author teams on several projects. She would like to thank Dale, Mom, Mari Lou, and all of her extended family for their continued love and support.

Brief Table of Contents

Table of Contents

unit **2** The Medical Office **118**

Chapter 20   CPT AND HCPCS CODING   566

Chapter 21 FINANCIAL PRACTICES 597

unit 7   Workforce Readiness   694

CAAHEP Correlation Chart

FOUNDATIONS FOR CLINICAL PRACTICE	CHAPTER #
I. C. Cognitive (Knowledge Base)	
I. Anatomy & Physiology	
11. Identify the classifications of medications, including desired effects, side effects and adverse reactions	16
I. P Psychomotor (Skills)	
I. Anatomy & Physiology	
6. Perform patient screening using established protocols	8
11. Perform quality control measures	8
I. A. Affective (Behavior)	
I. Anatomy & Physiology	
1. Apply critical thinking skills in performing patient assessment and care	4, 23
2. Use language/verbal skills that enable patients' understanding	4
3. Demonstrate respect for diversity in approaching patients and families	4
II. A Affective (Behavior)	
II. Applied Mathematics	
2. Distinguish between normal and abnormal test results	16
III. C Cognitive (Knowledge Base)	
III. Applied Microbiology/Infection Control	
1. Describe the infection cycle, including the infectious agent, reservoir, susceptible host, means of transmission, portals of entry, and portals of exit	9
2. Define asepsis	9
3. Discuss infection control procedures	9
4. Identify personal safety precautions as established by the Occupational Safety and Health Administration (OSHA)	9
7. Match types and uses of personal protective equipment (PPE)	9
11. Describe Standard Precautions, including:	9
a. Transmission based precautions	
b. Purpose	
c. Activities regulated	
12. Discuss the application of Standard Precautions with regard to:	23
a. All body fluids, secretions and excretions	
b. Blood	
c. Non intact skin	
d. Mucous membranes	
13. Identify the role of the Center for Disease Control (CDC) regulations in healthcare settings.	9

III. P Psychomotor (Skills)

III. Applied Microbiology/Infection Control

1. Participate in training on Standard Precautions	9
2. Practice Standard Precautions	9
3. Select appropriate barrier/personal protective equipment (PPE) for potentially infectious situations	23
4. Perform handwashing	9

APPLIED COMMUNICATIONS

IV. C. Cognitive (Knowledge Base)

IV. Concepts of Effective Communication

1. Identify styles and types of verbal communication	4
2. Identify nonverbal communication	4
3. Recognize communication barriers	4
4. Identify techniques for overcoming communication barriers	4
5. Recognize the elements of oral communication using a sender-receiver process	4, 24
6. Differentiate between subjective and objective information	15
7. Identify resources and adaptations that are required based on individual needs, i.e., culture and environment, developmental life stage, language, and physical threats to communication	4, 5, 8
8. Recognize elements of fundamental writing skills	13, 24
9. Discuss applications of electronic technology in effective communication	7, 10, 11, 12, 13, 24
10. Diagram medical terms, labeling the word parts	Appendix I
11. Define both medical terms and abbreviations related to all body systems	Appendix II
12. Organize technical information and summaries	13
13. Identify the role of self boundaries in the health care environment	4, 2
14. Recognize the role of patient advocacy in the practice of medical assisting	2, 5
15. Discuss the role of assertiveness ineffective professional communication	4
16. Differentiate between adaptive and non-adaptive coping mechanisms	4

IV. P Psychomotor Skills

IV. Concepts of Effective Communication

1. Use reflection, restatement and clarification techniques to obtain a patient history	15
2. Report relevant information to others succinctly and accurately	7, 8, 15
3. Use medical terminology, pronouncing medical terms correctly, to communicate information, patient history, data and observations	15
4. Explain general office policies	7, 8, 9, 22
5. Instruct patients according to their needs to promote health maintenance and disease prevention	4
7. Demonstrate telephone techniques	11, 16
8. Document patient care	15
9. Document patient education	5, 15

10. Compose professional/business letters	13
11. Respond to nonverbal communication	4
12. Develop and maintain a current list of community resources related to patients' healthcare needs	5
13. Advocate on behalf of patients	2, 4

IV. A Affective (Behavior)

IV. Concepts of Effective Communication

1. Demonstrate empathy in communicating with patients, family and staff	4, 11
2. Apply active listening skills	4
3. Use appropriate body language and other nonverbal skills in communicating with patients, family and staff	4
4. Demonstrate awareness of the territorial boundaries of the person with whom communicating	4
5. Demonstrate sensitivity appropriate to the message being delivered	4
6. Demonstrate awareness of how an individual's personal appearance affects anticipated responses	2, 4, 24
7. Demonstrate recognition of the patient's level of understanding in communications	4
8. Analyze communications in providing appropriate responses/feedback	4, 11, 15
9. Recognize and protect personal boundaries in communicating with others	4
10. Demonstrate respect for individual diversity, incorporating awareness of one's own biases in areas including gender, race, religion, age and economic status	4, 22

MEDICAL BUSINESS PRACTICES

V. C Cognitive (Knowledge Base)

V. Administrative Functions

1. Discuss pros and cons of various types of appointment management systems	12
2. Describe scheduling guidelines	12
3. Recognize office policies and protocols for handling appointments	12
4. Identify critical information required for scheduling patient admissions and/or procedures	12
5. Identify systems for organizing medical records	14, 15
6. Describe various types of content maintained in a patient's medical record	14, 15
7. Discuss pros and cons of various filing methods	14
8. Identify both equipment and supplies needed for filing medical records	14
9. Describe indexing rules	14
10. Discuss filing procedures	14
11. Discuss principles of using Electronic Medical Records (EMR)	8, 14, 15
12. Identify types of records common to the healthcare setting	14, 15, 22
13. Identify time management principles	12
14. Discuss the importance of routine maintenance of office equipment	10

V. P Psychomotor (Skills)

V. Administrative Functions

1. Manage appointment schedule, using established priorities	12
2. Schedule patient admissions and/or procedures	12

4. Describe how to use the most current HCPCS coding	20
VIII. P Psychomotor (Skills)	
VIII. Procedural and Diagnostic Coding	
1. Perform procedural coding	20
2. Perform diagnostic coding	18, 19
VIII. P. Psychomotor (Skills)	
VIII. Procedural and Diagnostic Coding	
1. Work with physician to achieve the maximum reimbursement	18, 19, 20

MEDICAL LAW AND ETHICS

IX. Cognitive (Knowledge Base)	
IX. Legal Implications	
1. Discuss legal scope of practice for medical assistants	6, 24
2. Explore issue of confidentiality as it applies to the medical assistant	4, 6, 7, 14, 22, 24
3. Describe the implications of HIPAA for the medical assistant in various medical settings	4, 6, 7, 8, 14, 24
4. Summarize the Patient Bill of Rights	6
5. Discuss licensure and certification as it applies to healthcare providers	1, 6, 22
6. Describe liability, professional, personal injury, and third party insurance	6, 17
7. Compare and contrast physician and medical assistant roles in terms of standard of care	3, 6
8. Compare criminal and civil law as it applies to the practicing medical assistant	6
9. Provide an example of tort law as it would apply to a medical assistant	6
10. Explain how the following impact the medical assistant's practice and give examples:	6
a. Negligence	
b. Malpractice	
c. Statute of Limitations	
d. Good Samaritan Act(s)	
e. Uniform Anatomical Gift Act	
f. Living will/Advanced directives	
g. Medical durable power of attorney	
11. Identify how the Americans with Disabilities Act (ADA) applies to the medical assisting profession	6, 8, 22
12. List and discuss legal and illegal interview questions	6, 22
13. Discuss all levels of governmental legislation and regulation as they apply to medical assisting practice, including FDA and DEA regulations	6, 16
14. Describe the process to follow if an error is made in patient care	6, 15
IX. P Psychomotor (Skills)	
IX. Legal Implications	
1. Respond to issues of confidentiality	6
2. Perform within scope of practice	1, 3, 6, 24
3. Apply HIPAA rules in regard to privacy/release of information	6, 15, 24

4. Practice within the standard of care for a medical assistant	1, 6, 24
5. Incorporate the Patient's Bill of Rights into personal practices and medical office policies and procedures	6
6. Complete an incident report	6, 22
7. Document accurately in the patient record	8, 15
8. Apply local, state, and federal health care legislation and regulation appropriate to the medical assisting practice setting	6, 22

IX. A Affective (Behavior)

IX. Legal Implications

1. Demonstrate sensitivity to patient rights	6
2. Demonstrate awareness of the consequences of not working within the legal scope of practice	6
3. Recognize the importance of local, state and federal legislation and regulations in the practice setting	6, 22, 8

X. C Cognitive (Knowledge Base)

X. Ethical Considerations

1. Differentiate between legal, ethical, and moral issues affecting healthcare	6
2. Compare personal, professional and organizational ethics	6
3. Discuss the role of cultural, social and ethnic diversity in ethical performance of medical assisting practice	4
4. Identify where to report illegal and/or unsafe activities and behaviors that affect health, safety and welfare of others	6
5. Identify the effect personal ethics may have on professional performance	2, 6

X. P. Psychomotor (Skills)

X. Ethical Considerations

1. Report illegal and/or unsafe activities and behaviors that affect health, safety and welfare of others to proper authorities	6
2. Develop a plan for separation of personal and professional ethics	6

X. A. Affective (Behavior)

ETHICAL CONSIDERATIONS

1. Apply ethical behaviors, including honesty/integrity in performance of medical assisting practice	2, 6, 22, 24
2. Examine the impact personal ethics and morals may have on the individual's practice	2, 6
3. Demonstrate awareness of diversity in providing patient care	4, 6

SAFETY AND EMERGENCY PRACTICES

XI. C. Cognitive (Knowledge Base)

XI. Protective Practices

1. Describe personal protective equipment	9
2. Identify safety techniques that can be used to prevent accidents and maintain a safe work environment	7, 23
3. Describe the importance of Materials Safety Data Sheets (MSDS) in a healthcare setting	22
4. Identify safety signs, symbols and labels	23
5. State principles and steps of professional/provider CPR	23

ABHES Correlation Chart

COMPETENCY	CHAPTER
1. GENERAL ORIENTATION	
a. Comprehend the current employment outlook for the medical assistant	1
b. Compare and contrast the allied health professions and understand their relation to medical assisting	1, 3, 7, 9, 22
c. Understand medical assistant credentialing requirements and the process to obtain the credential; comprehend the importance of credentialing	1, 22
d. Have knowledge of the general responsibilities of the medical assistant	1, 3, 4, 7, 8, 9, 14, 24
e. Define scope of practice for the medical assistant, and comprehend the conditions for practice within the state that the medical assistant is employed	1, 3, 24
2. ANATOMY AND PHYSIOLOGY	
a. Comprehend and explain to the patient the importance of diet and nutrition; effectively convey and educate patients regarding the proper diet and nutrition guidelines; identify categories of patients who require special diets or diet modifications	5
3. MEDICAL TERMINOLOGY	
a. Define and use entire basic structure of medical words and be able to accurately identify in the correct context; i.e., root, prefix, suffix, combinations, spelling, and definitions	Appendix I
b. Build and dissect medical terms from roots/suffixes to understand the word element combinations that create medical terminology	Appendix I
c. Understand the various medical terminology for each specialty	3, Appendix I, Appendix II
d. Recognize and identify acceptable medical abbreviations	16, Appendix II
4. MEDICAL LAW AND ETHICS	
a. Document accurately	6, 7, 8, 24
b. Institute federal and state guidelines when releasing medical records or information	6, 14, 15, 16
c. Follow established policies when initiating or terminating medical treatment	6, 7
d. Understand the importance of maintaining liability coverage once employed in the industry	6
e. Perform risk management procedures	6, 22
f. Comply with federal, state, and local health laws and regulations	6, 8, 16, 22
5. PSYCHOLOGY OF HUMAN RELATIONS	
a. Define and understand abnormal behavior patterns	4
b. Identify and respond appropriately when working/caring for patients with special needs	4, 8
c. Use empathy when treating terminally ill patients; identify common stages that terminally ill patients go through and list organizations/support groups that can assist patients and family members of patients struggling with terminal illness	4
d. Identify common stages that terminally ill patients go through and list organizations/support groups that can assist patients and family members of patients struggling with terminal illness	4
e. Advocate on behalf of family/patients, having ability to deal and communicate with family	2, 4
f. Identify and discuss developmental stages of life	4
g. Analyze the effect of hereditary, cultural, and environmental influences	4

6. PHARMACOLOGY

b. Properly utilize *PDR,* drug handbook, and other drug references to identify a drug's classification, usual dosage, usual side effects, and contraindications	16
c. Identify and define common abbreviations that are accepted in prescription writing	16
d. Understand legal aspects of writing prescriptions, including federal and state laws	16
e. Comply with federal, state, and local health laws and regulations	14, 16, 22

7. BASIC KEYBOARDING/COMPUTER CONCEPTS

a. Perform basic keyboarding skills including:	7, 10, 14
(1) Locating the keys on a keyboard	
(2) Typing medical correspondence and basic reports	10, 7, 14
b. Identify and properly utilize office machines, computerized systems, and medical software such as:	7, 10, 13, 14, 15, 22
(1) Efficiently maintain and understand different types of medical correspondence and medical reports	
(2) Apply computer application skills using variety of different electronic programs including both practice management software and EMR software	

8. MEDICAL OFFICE BUSINESS PROCEDURES/MANAGEMENT

a. Perform basic clerical functions	7, 8, 10
b. Prepare and maintain medical records	7, 14, 15
c. Schedule and manage appointments	12
d. Apply concepts for office procedures	7, 8, 10, 13, 14, 22
e. Locate resources and information for patients and employers	5
f. Schedule inpatient and outpatient admissions	12
g. Prepare and reconcile a bank statement and deposit record	21
h. Post entries on a day sheet	21
i. Perform billing and collection procedures	17
j. Perform accounts payable procedures	21
k. Perform accounts receivable procedures	17, 21
l. Establish and maintain a petty cash fund	8
m. Post adjustments	21
n. Process credit balances	21
o. Process refunds	21
p. Post non-sufficient funds (NSF)	21
q. Post collection agency payments	21
r. Apply third-party guidelines	17
s. Obtain managed care referrals and pre-certification	17
t. Perform diagnostic and procedural coding	18, 19, 20
u. Prepare and submit insurance claims	17
v. Use physician fee schedule	17

11. CAREER DEVELOPMENT

a. Perform the essential requirements for employment such as résumé writing, effective interviewing, dressing professionally, and following up appropriately — 24

b. Demonstrate professionalism by: — 1, 2, 3, 4, 5, 7, 8, 12, 14, 15, 22, 24

    (1) Exhibiting dependability, punctuality, and a positive work ethic

    (2) Exhibiting a positive attitude and a sense of responsibility

    (3) Maintaining confidentiality at all times

    (4) Being cognizant of ethical boundaries

    (5) Exhibiting initiative

    (6) Adapting to change

    (7) Expressing a responsible attitude

    (8) Being courteous and diplomatic

    (9) Conducting work within scope of education, training, and ability

Procedures

Preface

Why THIS Text?

This decade brings with it many challenges for health care—the full implementation of the electronic health record, the ICD-10, the Red Flags Rule, new health-care legislation, the rise in corporate-owned medical practices, the necessity for bioterrorism and other disaster preparedness, the threats of pandemics, the increase of English language learner (ELL) staff who are from countries with very different health-care systems, and more. These realities place increasing responsibilities and demands on the administrative medical assistant. It is our goal to ensure that graduates are educated professionals and **workforce ready.**

We all look for a text that is accurate, up-to-date, and user friendly. Our reviewers tell us this book accomplishes that goal. The comments include:

This is good!!!; Quality; Text material flows in a realistic manner; There are no missing topics; I have described this text to my colleagues as direct, friendly, and real time; AWESOME coverage; The lists at the beginning for each credentialing agency are wonderful! The health-care team info—perfect! Professionalism aspect, perfect!; I did not find a single error; No equivalent; An updated user-friendly text that both students and instructors can both enjoy and learn from this book; This is a very well-written text.

What Is Unique about This Text and How Does It Promote Workforce Readiness?

In addition to accurate treatment of the ABHES/CAAHEP topics, competencies, and the CMA (AAMA), RMA (AMT), and CMAS (AMT) certification content, some of the unique inclusions are:

- **Aseptic technique** specifically for the administrative areas; the H1N1 influenza outbreak brought to light the importance of patient screening at the point of entry and patient and staff education. A reviewer commented: *the information is pertinent to the time.*

- Major **emphasis on professional behaviors** in each chapter and a behavioral assessment rubric for instructors and students. A reviewer says: *I do not have a chapter that is equivalent to the chapter in comparison. I feel that the new chapter is very detailed and I am extremely excited to see how this chapter plays a role in my program.*

- The chapter, **Appointment to Payment**, helps students to understand their many functions as administrative medical assistants and how they "fit" in the integration and flow of the medical office. Using this as one of the

opening chapters is especially helpful to schools on the modular wheel curriculum. A reviewer felt: *it was important to tie the whole visit together.*

- **Disaster preparedness,** with a universal color coding chart. A reviewer's words: *(The) Chart of disasters and responses is excellent.*

- A **chapter on practice management** featuring models of practice ownership and the chain of command; a reviewer commented: *Good exposure to risk management and corporate ownership in the medical field; I have not seen this before.*

- A **chapter on the personal health record** that includes information on state immunization registries with required reporting and extensive information on the EHR; when asked for a strength of the chapter, a reviewer answered: *The informative information on the Electronic Health Records within the chapter.*

- The **chapter on the externship** includes the responsibilities of the school, the practice, and the student. A reviewer's opinion: *This chapter is good enough to adopt the book.* Another reviewer states: *Text covers all aspects of the externship—very informative; I really enjoyed the Guidelines for a successful externship table.*

- An **entire chapter on ICD-10** is included. Two reviewers' thoughts: *This is a thorough explanation of Official ICD-10 Coding Guidelines; I like the transition from ICD-9 to ICD-10.*

- The **human resources chapter** follows an employee through the hiring and employment process; a reviewer stated: *It gives a clear view on policies and procedures.* Another said: *Interesting presentation of material– following the job applicant. This is a good overview of HR management and employment laws.*

What Are the Pedagogical Features?

The chapters are purposefully written in a manner that accommodates both the linear and the modular wheel curricula. Each is basically "freestanding" but references other chapters where topics overlap. They may be utilized out of sequence to accommodate your program design. Previous reviewer comments emphasize the pedagogical strength of the text. Special features are designed to reinforce instruction and to provide real-world workforce readiness. These include:

- **Preparation for Success** unit-opening interviews are based on true experiences of graduates and they offer advice to current administrative medical assisting students.

- **Learning Outcomes,** based on the revised Bloom's taxonomy, are tied to major chapter topic headings and review questions providing the instructor and student with a clear roadmap of what needs to be studied in each chapter.

- **EHR Readiness** provides tips for working with the electronic health records that apply to the specific chapter being studied—not only in the medical records chapters.

- **Working with the Health-Care Team** introduces students to the various health-care team roles and their interface with the administrative medical assistant.

- **Checkpoint Questions** are a stopping place in the chapter, following each learning outcome, to reinforce the material that has just been read.

- **Practice Readiness** is an example of how the chapter information is used and applied in the medical office.

- **Procedures** list the goal, materials needed, and method for all 87 administrative procedures.
  - The procedures include asepsis for administrative areas, ICD 10, EHR, and more.
  - The procedures are up-to-date with both electronic and paper considerations.
  - The procedures provide students with the opportunity to use an experiential (or "realistic" or both) approach to workforce readiness. They promote the concept of workforce readiness, addressing the cognitive (knowledge) as well as the psychomotor (skills) and behaviors (attitude) required to successfully enter the administrative medical assistant workforce.
- **Case Study** is the answer to many reviewer requests and is a forthright, true-to-life case study that relates to a professional behavior appropriate to the chapter, and ends with critical-thinking questions.
- **Professional Readiness** is included as part of the Case Studies to remind students of professional dress, etiquette, and ethics.
- **Practice Applications** are hands-on activities that provide a closer look into the medical office procedures and practices.
- **Exam Readiness** questions relate to the national certification exams and the chapter's learning outcomes.
- **CAAHEP and ABHES Competencies** are listed at end of each chapter for student and instructor reference, showing how this text aligns with national standards.

What Are the Electronic Assets?

The text would not be state-of-the-art without the appropriate technological features to also help students in their pursuit of workforce readiness and, in addition, have some fun. We think you will like the following:

- **Administrative Medical Assisting Student DVD-ROM,** which includes
  - Video vignettes
  - Drag and drop activities
  - Matching activities
  - Chapter tests
  - Games
  - Audio glossary
- **McGraw-Hill** *Connect Plus* which includes
  - More than 500 CMA- and RMA-style questions correlated to learning outcomes and CAAHEP and ABHES competencies
  - Twenty-five (25) videos showing some of the most important procedures performed by the administrative medical assistant
- **LearnSmart: Medical Assisting**
- **Instructor's Manual** with lesson plans, teaching tips, answer keys, lecture outlines, discussion topics, Internet activities, written assignments, and group activities
- **PowerPoint Presentations** with talking points
- **EZTest** questions correlated to Learning Outcomes, Difficulty Levels, Revised Bloom's Taxonomy, and CAAHEP/ABHES competencies

What Ancillary Print Material Is Available?

The **Student Study Guide** provides additional activities, procedure check-off forms, and a variety of questions.

- **Test Your Knowledge** includes: Vocabulary Review, Multiple-Choice Certification Questions, True or False Questions, Sentence Completion
- **Apply Your Knowledge** includes: Short Answer, Problem-Solving Activities, Thinking Critically Case Studies
- **Demonstrate Your Knowledge** includes: Procedure Check-Offs noting CAAHEP and ABHES competencies achieved
- **Application Activity Forms** include: Work Products needed for various Procedures

What Every Student Needs to Know

Many tools to help you learn have been integrated into your text.

PREPARATION FOR SUCCESS

interviews are based on true experiences of medical assisting graduates who offer their advice to current administrative medical assisting students.

LEARNING OUTCOMES

present the key points you should focus on when reading the chapter. They are tied to each major chapter topic heading and review question. Consider this your roadmap to the knowledge and skills you will acquire upon studying this content.

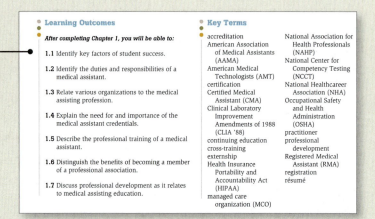

Learning Outcomes

After completing Chapter 1, you will be able to:

1.1 Identify key factors of student success.

1.2 Identify the duties and responsibilities of a medical assistant.

1.3 Relate various organizations to the medical assisting profession.

1.4 Explain the need for and importance of the medical assistant credentials.

1.5 Describe the professional training of a medical assistant.

1.6 Distinguish the benefits of becoming a member of a professional association.

1.7 Discuss professional development as it relates to medical assisting education.

Key Terms

accreditation
American Association of Medical Assistants (AAMA)
American Medical Technologists (AMT)
certification
Certified Medical Assistant (CMA)
Clinical Laboratory Improvement Amendments of 1988 (CLIA '88)
continuing education
cross-training
externship
Health Insurance Portability and Accountability Act (HIPAA)
managed care organization (MCO)
National Association for Health Professionals (NAHP)
National Center for Competency Testing (NCCT)
National Healthcareer Association (NHA)
Occupational Safety and Health Administration (OSHA)
practitioner
professional development
Registered Medical Assistant (RMA)
registration
résumé

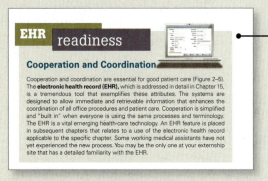

EHR readiness

Cooperation and Coordination

Cooperation and coordination are essential for good patient care (Figure 2–5). The **electronic health record (EHR)**, which is addressed in detail in Chapter 15, is a tremendous tool that exemplifies these attributes. The systems are designed to allow immediate and retrievable information that enhances the coordination of all office procedures and patient care. Cooperation is simplified and "built in" when everyone is using the same processes and terminology. The EHR is a vital emerging health-care technology. An EHR feature is placed in subsequent chapters that relates to a use of the electronic health record applicable to the specific chapter. Some working medical assistants have not yet experienced the new process. You may be the only one at your externship site that has a detailed familiarity with the EHR.

EHR READINESS

offers tips for working with the electronic health record that applies to the specific chapter—not only in the medical records chapters.

WORKING WITH THE HEALTH-CARE TEAM

introduces you to various health-care team roles and their interface with the administrative medical assistant.

Working with the Health-Care Team

MEDICAL ASSISTING EDUCATOR (INSTRUCTOR, PROFESSOR)

Duties and Skills

Typical skills required of the medical assisting educator, instructor, or professor are expertise in the area of instruction, ability to teach and train, a courteous and respectful manner with students and staff, strong organization skills, good time-management skills, demonstrated evidence of growth and academic currency, good communication skills, and knowledge of relevant technology.

Workplace Settings

The medical assisting educator may teach in a post-secondary private school or community college medical assisting program. In addition, large organizations, such as a community health center with multiple sites, may employ the educator to assess skills of newly hired medical assistants and to provide in-service training for new and updated skills.

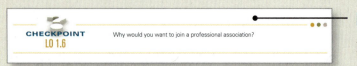

CHECKPOINT
LO 1.6

Why would you want to join a professional association?

CHECKPOINT QUESTIONS

provide a stopping place in the chapter after each learning outcome to reinforce the chapter material that you have just read.

PRACTICE READINESS

PRACTICE readiness

Recycling in the Medical Office, Hospital, Laboratory, or Clinic

You may easily incorporate recycling procedures into the daily routine of a medical office, hospital, laboratory, or clinic. Recycling may be required by state law. Some states levy large fines for noncompliance with recycling regulations. Purchase paper products that can be recycled, or those made of postconsumer recycled materials, and take care in disposing of them. Care should be taken to ensure HIPAA compliance when recycling paper. Shredding is the most effective way to comply with HIPAA regulations.

There are two essential aspects of recycling: disposal and purchasing. To create a complete recycling program, ensure that materials are disposed of properly and that pur-

the product or package is made up of recycled materials or that the product or package is recyclable. Check with your town's recycling center to ensure proper disposal.

Unless the package is made of 100% recycled materials, the law requires the package to display how much.

PRACTICE READINESS presents examples of how the chapter information is used in the medical office.

PROCEDURES

list the Goal, Materials needed, and Method for all 87 administrative procedures.

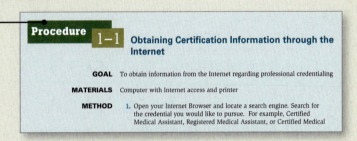

Procedure 1–1 Obtaining Certification Information through the Internet

GOAL To obtain information from the Internet regarding professional credentialing

MATERIALS Computer with Internet access and printer

METHOD 1. Open your Internet Browser and locate a search engine. Search for the credential you would like to pursue. For example, Certified Medical Assistant, Registered Medical Assistant, or Certified Medical

PROFESSIONAL READINESS

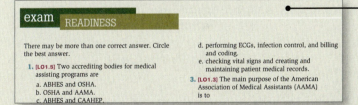

Case Study

PROFESSIONAL READINESS

Growth
Continual striving to improve and learn new materials

Debbie is a 23-year-old administrative medical assistant. She is mainly responsible for phone reception and patient check-in and check-out. A 29-year-old female patient calls complaining of lower back pain. As Debbie listens to the patient describe her condition, she determines the severity of the patient's

PROFESSIONAL READINESS reminds students of professional dress, etiquette, and ethics in the medical office and is included as part of the Case Study.

PRACTICE APPLICATIONS

provide a closer look into the common activities of the medical office.

practice APPLICATIONS

1. Chose a mentor who displays the personal attributes listed in this chapter and write a few sentences to explain why these attributes apply to her or him.

2. A. Think of all the personal qualifications you possess. List those that will help you as an administrative medical assistant.

B. List all of the personal qualifications you need to develop or improve in order to work successfully in the career of an administrative medical assistant.

EXAM READINESS

exam READINESS

There may be more than one correct answer. Circle the best answer.

1. **[LO1.5]** Two accrediting bodies for medical assisting programs are
   a. ABHES and OSHA.
   b. OSHA and AAMA.
   c. ABHES and CAAHEP.

d. performing ECGs, infection control, and billing and coding.
e. checking vital signs and creating and maintaining patient medical records.

3. **[LO1.3]** The main purpose of the American Association of Medical Assistants (AAMA) is to

EXAM READINESS questions correlate to the style of the national CMA and RMA certification exams and the chapter's learning outcomes.

CAAHEP AND ABHES COMPETENCIES

are listed at end of each chapter for student reference.

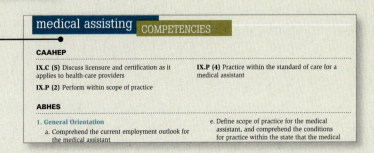

medical assisting COMPETENCIES

CAAHEP

IX.C (5) Discuss licensure and certification as it applies to health-care providers

IX.P (2) Perform within scope of practice

IX.P (4) Practice within the standard of care for a medical assistant

ABHES

1. General Orientation
   a. Comprehend the current employment outlook for the medical assistant

e. Define scope of practice for the medical assistant, and comprehend the conditions for practice within the state that the medical

Acknowledgments

Every area of the text was reviewed by practitioners and educators in the field. Their insights helped shape the direction of the book.

Text Consultant

Kathryn A. Booth, MS, RN, RMA (AMT), RPT, CPhT
Facilitator/Instructor, Military to Medicine
INOVA Health System, Falls Church, Virginia
VP, Total Care Programming, Inc.
Palm Coast, FL

Special Acknowledgments

Richard Bradley, Arizona Department of Health Services, Arizona State Immunization System.
Maricopa Community College, Tempe, AZ, for permission to use HIPAA confidentiality form.
Jack Smyth, Spring Medical Systems, Inc. for permission to use screen captures of SpringCharts® Electronic Health Records.

Chapter Contributors and Supplement Writers

Deborah D. Eid, CBCS, DiHOM, MHA
Program Director, Medical Billing & Coding Program
Carrington College

Tiffany Heath, CMA (AAMA), CMAS (AMT), AHI (AMT), CS
Porter and Chester Institute

Cheryl D. Jerzak, BSHA, CMA (AAMA)
Four-D College

Noreen Semanski, LPN, ASB, CHI, Medical Program Director
McCann School of Business & Technology

Janet Sesser, RMA (AMT), BS Healthcare Management, MS Health Education
Eastern Division Corporate Director of Education
Anthem Education Group

Administrative Medical Assisting Symposium Attendees

Rhonda Church, CMA (AAMA), CPC
Rockford Career College

Sue Coleman, LPN, AS
National College

Courtney M. Conrad, MBA, MPH, CMA (AAMA)
Robert Morris University

Diane Gryglak, BS, CMA (AAMA)
College of DuPage

Cheryl D. Jerzak, BSHA, CMA (AAMA)
Four-D College

Barbara Kalfin Kalish, AAS, BS, CMA (AAMA)
Palm Beach State College

Wilsetta McClain, NRCMA, RMA, EMT-B, NCICS, NCPT, MBA, ABD
Baker College

Tamara E. Mottler, B.A., CMA (AAMA)
Daytona State College

Linda Spang
Davenport University

Jamie Wyatt, CMA, NREMT-B
Brown-Mackie College

Reviewers

Judie L. Alessi, CMA (AAMA) RMA
Stautzenberger College

Elizabeth Aschwege, MM, BBA, CMT, AHDI-F
Davenport University

Kaye F. Bathe, CMA (AAMA), BSHA
Tri County Technical College

Cynthia Boles, CMA
Bradford School

Beverly Brunson Horton, MHA
Kings College

Rhonda Church, CMA (AAMA), CPC,
Rockford Career College

Jennifer Claire, Professor of Health Sciences, MSHS, MPH
Kaplan

Sheila Clark, RMA, RPT
Lincoln Technical Institute

Sue Coleman, LPN, AS
National College

Beth Collis, CMA (AAMA)
Globe Education Network

Courtney M. Conrad, MBA, MPH, CMA (AAMA)
Robert Morris University

Patricia Davis Christian, MS
Southwest Georgia Technical College

Sharon S. Dayton RMA, CPT
Professional Skills Institute

Denise J. DeDeaux, MBA
Fayetteville Technical Community College

Dean A. Delp, Sr., CPC, CMAA, CBCS
Lincoln Technical Institute

Linda H. Donahue, RHIT, CCS, CCS-P, CPC
Delgado Community College

Amy Ensign, CMA (AAMA), RMA (AMT)
Baker College

Mark A. Everett, DHA, MBA
Brown-Mackie College

Cindy Feldhousen, MSBE, CMA (AAMA)
Manchester Community College

Deanna Head, LPN
(Founder/CEO) Unitech Training Academy

Rose Hecht, CMA-C (AAMA), BS
Southern California Regional Occupational Center

Elizabeth Hoffman, MA Ed., CMA (AAMA), CPT (ASPT)
Baker College

Faraneh Javan, MD
West Valley College

Cheryl D. Jerzak, BSHA, CMA (AAMA)
Four-D College

Barbara Kalfin Kalish, AAS, BS, CMA (AAMA)
Palm Beach State College

Sharon Kelsey, CMA (AAMA), AS
Lincoln Technical Institute

Ruby D. King, CMA (AAMA)
Lincoln Technical Institute

Linda LaGrange
Career Institute of Florida

Kristin Maguire NCMA, NCPT, NCVT
Anthem Institute

Barbara Marchelletta, AS, BS, CMA (AAMA), CPC (AAPC)
Beal College

Tracy Martin, RN, MSN, Ed.
YTI Capital Region

D. P. Martinez, MD, MPH
Florida Career College

Wilsetta McClain, NRCMA, RMA (AMT), EMT-B, NCICS, NCPT, MBA, ABD
Baker College

Nancy Measell, BS, CMA (AAMA)
Ivy Tech Community College

Lane Miller, MBA/HCM
ECPI College of Technology

Marcia Morse, MBA Health Care, BS, RMA (AMT)
Davenport University

Tamara E. Mottler, BA, CMA (AAMA)
Daytona State College

Mary Nichols, RMA (AMT), Director of Healthcare Programs
Heald College

Patricia Nicelli
Jamestown Business College

Gail Pieronski Orr
National College

Rhonda L. Pruitt, MPH
National College

Dr. Carol Qare Carcar, DPM, CPT, RMA (AMT)
Heald College

Angela M. Reed, MA, NCMOA
Kaplan College

Adrian Rios EMT, CPT-1, RMA (AMT) NCMA, MA
Newbridge College

Janette Rodriguez, BS, RN, RMA (AMT)
Wood-Tobe Coburn School

Andrea B. Ross, BA, RHIT, CMA (AAMA)
Chabot College

Rosemarie Scaringella, MA Dept. Director
Hunter Business School

Noreen Semanski, LPN, ASB, CHI, Medical Program Director
McCann School of Business & Technology

Tammy L. Shick, CPC
Great Lakes Institute of Technology

Debra L. Smith, MPA
Davenport University

Kimberly Ann Thorpe CCMA, CBCS, PCT
Florida Career College

Marilyn M. Turner, RN, CMA (AAMA)
Ogeechee Technical College

Janice Vermiglio-Smith, RN, RMA, PhD
Central Arizona College

Karon G. Walton
Augusta Technical College

Lori Warren Woodard, MA, RN, CPC, CPC-I, CCP, CLNC
Spencerian College

Pam Williams, RN, MSN
Antonelli College

Camille Wright RMA, BS
Lincoln Technical Institute

Jamie Wyatt, CMA, NREMT-B
Brown-Mackie College

Patti Zint, Certified Healthcare Instructor, Certified Medical Administrative Assistant
Apollo College

Administrative Medical Assisting

Foundations and Principles of Administrative Medical Assisting

If you are not learning, you are not growing. If you are not growing, you are not really living.

Crash Taylor, Photographer

Preparation for Success

Each unit opens with a success story based on real graduates from schools around the country. As you begin your educational journey to becoming an administrative medical assistant, these graduates share their experiences and offer advice to help you on your path.

Interviewer: Benjime, you are from Sierra Leone in Africa and came to this country as a refugee in 2003. Would you tell us what you decided to do when you came to the United States and why?

Benjime: I wanted to get into a career that was pretty secure and I wanted to learn about health care in the United States. With the advice of the social service agency that sponsored me and the community college advisor, I went into administrative medical assisting.

Interviewer: Tell us what happened next.

Benjime: I completed a certificate program, found a job in a medical office, and married Zaria, who is also from Sierra Leone. We had our first son during this time.

Interviewer: What is your current position?

Benjime: I am the practice manager for a large cardiology practice.

Interviewer: Would you share with the students how that happened?

Benjime: I found the health-care system in the United States very complex but very interesting. With the encouragement of the doctors I worked with and one of my former teachers, I went back to school for my associate's degree and then a bachelor's degree in health administration.

Interviewer: You really worked hard and your family must be very proud of you. As a graduate and as a person who hires administrative medical assistants, do you have some advice for students?

Benjime: There are such wonderful opportunities to get an education in this country. People that are born here do not always appreciate the chance. My advice is to take the gift of being in the administrative medical assisting program and do your best every day. Also, keep a smile on your face.

Interviewer: That is great advice and I can tell from your wonderful smile that it would be an asset. Thank you.

unit 1

Medical Assisting as a Career

1

Learning Outcomes

After completing Chapter 1, you will be able to:

1.1 Identify key factors of student success.

1.2 Identify the duties and responsibilities of a medical assistant.

1.3 Relate various organizations to the medical assisting profession.

1.4 Explain the need for and importance of the medical assistant credentials.

1.5 Describe the professional training of a medical assistant.

1.6 Distinguish the benefits of becoming a member of a professional association.

1.7 Discuss professional development as it relates to medical assisting education.

Key Terms

accreditation
American Association of Medical Assistants (AAMA)
American Medical Technologists (AMT)
certification
Certified Medical Assistant (CMA)
Clinical Laboratory Improvement Amendments of 1988 (CLIA '88)
continuing education
cross-training
externship
Health Insurance Portability and Accountability Act (HIPAA)
managed care organization (MCO)
National Association for Health Professionals (NAHP)
National Center for Competency Testing (NCCT)
National Healthcareer Association (NHA)
Occupational Safety and Health Administration (OSHA)
practitioner
professional development
Registered Medical Assistant (RMA)
registration
résumé

Preparation for Certification

RMA (AMT) Exam
- Professional development
- Licensure, certification, registration

CMAS (AMT) Exam
- Professionalism

CMA (AAMA) Exam
- Displaying professional attitude
- Professional communication and behavior

Introduction • • •

Health care is changing at a rapid rate. Advanced technology, implementation of cost-effective medicine, and the aging population are all factors that caused the growth in the health-care services industry.

As the health-care services industry expands, the U.S. Department of Labor projects that medical assisting will be the fastest-growing occupation between 2008 and 2018. The growth in the number of physicians' group practices and other health-care practices that use support personnel will in turn continue to drive up demand for medical assistants. The medical assistant is the perfect complement to this changing industry.

Administrative medical assistants, a subset of medical assistants, perform a variety of medical assisting duties that make them well-qualified to enter a variety of job openings in the health-care industry. This chapter introduces the professional standards that are required in medical assisting, specifically administrative medical assisting.

LO 1.1 Your Success as a Student

The world of administrative medical assisting is an exciting and rewarding career path. Opportunities are numerous but your success is determined by the path that you take toward your goal of becoming an administrative medical assistant. As a new student in this field, there are several key factors that will assist you while embarking on this great career. These factors include:

1. *Organizational skills.* Students who are disorganized waste a great deal of time locating assignments and other materials before they get started on their work. Organizational skills are crucial to your success. Prepare in advance. Make sure you purchase a binder, notebook, or folders that have your homework assignments in them, reminders about upcoming tests, your course syllabus, and other pertinent information such as your instructor's office hours and phone, and classmates' information for study sessions. Obtain access to a computer with an Internet connection at home, through your school, or at the local library.

2. *Study habits.* Study habits will assist you with concentration and retention of the materials. Make sure you study in a quiet area away from distractions; find a study "buddy" who is just as committed and focused on success as you are; and prepare flashcards to assist you with independent studying. Most formal classroom courses require at least as much work time outside of class as inside of class to prepare. Budget your time between school and other responsibilities. Set aside time for study by making yourself a study schedule.

3. *Set goals.* By setting goals for yourself, you can take responsibility for the results of your efforts. You must take ownership toward your success as a student. Your overall goal is to complete this course. To succeed you must first create smaller daily, weekly, or course-specific goals to accomplish the overall goal. You can generate on the computer or in writing a goal-setting sheet such as the one in Table 1–1.

• • •
_____

Identify one goal for yourself and create a sample goal-setting sheet to meet that goal.

CHECKPOINT
LO 1.1

GOAL(S)	STUDY STRATEGIES	WHO? (PERSONS INVOLVED IN CARRYING OUT YOUR STRATEGIES)	SPECIFIC CONCERNS?	COMPLETION DATE?
To make an "A" in my Medical Terminology class.	1. Flashcards and note cards 2. Study with Andrea (my study buddy) on Thursday nights before each test.	1. Shania (myself) 2. Shania and Andrea	1. I can't remember the prefixes and suffixes of medical terms 2. Finishing my presentation on time 3. I feel I am lacking the typing skills to finish my presentation	June 28, 2011 (the day before final exam)

table 1–1

Sample Goal-Setting Sheet

LO 1.2 The Responsibilities of the Medical Assistant

As a medical assistant, you will be an allied health professional trained to work in a variety of health-care settings such as medical offices, clinics, and ambulatory-care facilities. Your specific responsibilities will likely depend on the location and size of the facility as well as its medical specialties.

Medical assistants may choose to work in an administrative, clinical, or laboratory capacity. This textbook focuses on administrative medical assisting. The following list of duties is provided to help you understand the various duties of a medical assistant.

Entry-Level General Duties

Your general duties may vary according to state law. In an entry-level position, they may include:

- Recognizing and responding effectively to verbal, nonverbal, and written communications
- Explaining treatment procedures to patients
- Educating patients within scope of practice
- Facilitating treatment for patients from diverse cultural backgrounds and for patients with hearing or vision impairments, or physical or mental disabilities
- Acting as a patient advocate
- Maintaining medical records

Entry-Level Administrative Duties

In an entry-level position, your administrative duties may include the following:

- Greeting patients
- Handling correspondence
- Scheduling appointments
- Answering telephones
- Creating and maintaining patient medical records
- Handling billing, bookkeeping, and insurance processing
- Performing medical transcription
- Arranging for hospital admissions/outpatient diagnostic testing

Advanced Administrative Duties

Your advanced administrative duties may vary according to the practice and may include:

- Developing and conducting public outreach programs to market the physician's professional services
- Negotiating leases of equipment and supply contracts
- Negotiating nonrisk and risk managed care contracts
- Managing business and professional insurance
- Developing and maintaining fee schedules
- Participating in practice analysis
- Coordinating plans for practice enhancement, expansion, consolidation, and closure
- Performing as a HIPAA compliance officer
- Providing personnel supervision and employment practices
- Providing information systems management

If you choose to expand your knowledge and skills into the clinical or laboratory aspect of medical assisting you may perform additional duties. These duties, listed in Table 1–2, vary according to state law.

table 1–2

Medical Assisting Clinical and Laboratory Duties

ENTRY-LEVEL CLINICAL DUTIES	ADVANCED CLINICAL DUTIES	ENTRY-LEVEL LABORATORY DUTIES	ADVANCED LABORATORY DUTIES
• Assisting the doctor during examinations • Asepsis and infection control • Performing diagnostic tests, such as spirometry and ECGs • Giving injections (state laws and work setting will determine ability to perform) • Phlebotomy including venipuncture and capillary puncture • Disposing of soiled or stained supplies • Performing first aid and cardiopulmonary resuscitation (CPR) • Preparing patients for examinations • Preparing and administering medications as directed by the physician and following state laws for invasive procedures • Recording vital signs and medical histories • Removing sutures or changing dressings on wounds • Sterilizing medical instruments • Instructing patients about medication and special diets • Authorizing drug refills as directed by the physician	• Initiating an IV and administering IV medications with appropriate training and as permitted by state law • Reporting diagnostic study results • Assisting patients in the completion of advanced directives and living wills • Assisting with clinical trials	• Performing Clinical Laboratory Improvement Amendments (CLIA)–waived tests, such as a urine pregnancy test, on the premises • Collecting, preparing, and transmitting laboratory specimens • Teaching patients to collect specific specimens properly • Arranging laboratory services • Meeting safety standards (OSHA guidelines) and fire protection mandates	• Performing as an OSHA compliance officer • Performing moderately complex laboratory testing with appropriate training and certification

CHECKPOINT
LO 1.2

Identify three duties from the entry-level and advanced administrative duties that you would like to know more about. Research these duties and describe them in the space below.

LO 1.3 Medical Assisting Origins and Organizations

With the emergence of formal training programs for medical assistants and the continuous changes in health care today, the role of the medical assistant has become dynamic and wide ranging. These changes have raised the expectations for medical assistants. The knowledge base of the modern medical assistant includes:

- Administrative and clinical skills
- Patient insurance product knowledge (specific to the workers' geographical locations)
- Compliance, especially of OSHA and HIPAA guidelines
- Exceptional customer service
- Practice management
- Current patient treatments and education

The medical assisting profession requires a commitment to self-directed, lifelong learning. Health care is changing rapidly because of new technology, new health-care delivery systems, and new approaches to facilitating cost-efficient, high-quality health care. A medical assistant who can adapt to change and is continually learning will be in high demand.

American Association of Medical Assistants

American Association of Medical Assistants (AAMA)
The professional organization that certifies medical assistants and works to maintain professional standards in the medical assisting profession.

The seed of the idea for a national association of medical assistants—to be later called the **American Association of Medical Assistants (AAMA)**—was planted at the 1955 annual state convention of the Kansas Medical Assistants Society. The next year, at an American Medical Association (AMA) meeting, the AAMA was officially created. In 1978 the U.S. Department of Health, Education, and Welfare declared medical assisting an allied health profession. Figure 1–1 shows the pins worn by medical assistants who are certified by the American Association of Medical Assistants (AAMA) and by those registered by the American Medical Technologists (AMT).

AAMA's Purpose The AAMA works to raise standards of medical assisting to a more professional level. It is the only professional association devoted exclusively to the medical assisting profession. Its creator and first president, Maxine Williams, had extensive experience in orchestrating medical assisting projects for the Kansas Medical Assistants Society. She also served as co-chair of the planning committee that formed the AAMA.

AAMA Creed To maintain the professional standards of the medical assisting profession, the AAMA has developed the following creed, which is reprinted here with the permission of the organization:

I believe in the principles and purposes of the profession of medical assisting.

I endeavor to be more effective.

figure 1–1

The pin on the left is worn by medical administrative specialists registered by the American Medical Technologists and the pin in the middle is worn by medical assistants registered by the American Medical Technologists. The pin on the right is worn by members of the American Association of Medical Assistants.

I aspire to render greater service.

I protect the confidence entrusted to me.

I am dedicated to the care and well-being of all people.

I am loyal to my employer.

I am true to the ethics of my profession.

I am strengthened by compassion, courage, and faith.

AAMA Code of Ethics The AAMA has also established a code of ethics, which is reprinted here with the permission of the organization:

The Code of Ethics of AAMA shall set forth principles of ethical and moral conduct as they relate to the medical profession and the particular practice of Medical Assisting.

Members of AAMA dedicated to the conscientious pursuit of their profession, and thus desiring to merit the high regard of the entire medical profession and the respect of the general public which they serve, do pledge themselves to strive always to:

A. render service with full respect for the dignity of humanity;
B. respect confidential information obtained through employment unless legally authorized or required by responsible performance of duty to divulge such information;
C. uphold the honor and high principles of the profession and accept its disciplines;
D. seek to continually improve the knowledge and skills of medical assistants for the benefit of patients and professional colleagues;
E. participate in additional service activities aimed toward improving the health and well-being of the community.

AAMA Occupational Analysis In 1996 the AAMA formed a committee whose goal was to revise and update its standards for the accreditation of programs that teach medical assisting. The committee's findings were published in 1997 as the "AAMA Role Delineation Study: Occupational Analysis of the Medical Assistant Profession." The study included a new Role Delineation Chart that outlined the areas of competence to be mastered as an entry-level medical assistant. The Role Delineation Chart of the CMA (AAMA) was further updated in 2003 to include additional competencies and in 2009 was updated again and was renamed the Occupational Analysis of the CMA (AAMA).

The Medical Assistant Occupational Analysis provides the basis for medical assisting education and evaluation. Mastery of the areas of competence listed in this Occupational Analysis is required for all students in accredited medical assisting programs. The Occupational Analysis shows three areas of competence: administrative, clinical, and general. Each of these three areas is divided into two or more narrower areas, for a total of ten specific areas

of competence. Within each area, a bulleted list of statements describes the medical assistant's role.

According to the AAMA, Occupational Analysis may be used to:

- Describe the field of medical assisting to other health-care professionals
- Identify entry-level areas of competence for medical assistants
- Help **practitioners** assess their own current competence in the field
- Aid in the development of continuing education programs
- Prepare appropriate types of materials for home study

practitioner
One who practices a profession.

Additional Organizations that Influence the Medical Assisting Profession

Many other organizations influence the medical assisting profession. In addition to the AAMA, which provides the CMA credential, other organizations provide certification testing and medical assisting credentials. Different organizations provide accreditation or approval for the educational program. As a student, you should know what organization approves your school and program of study as well as what test you may take and what credential you will receive once you have completed your study.

American Medical Technologists (AMT) The **American Medical Technologists (AMT)** is a nonprofit certification agency and professional membership association representing over 45,000 individuals in allied health care. Established in 1939, AMT began a program to register medical assistants at accredited schools in the early 1970s. The AMT has been providing allied health professionals with professional certification services and membership programs to enhance their professional and personal growth. Upon certification, individuals automatically become members of AMT and start to receive benefits. You will read more about the benefits of joining a professional organization later in the chapter. The AMT provides many certifications including the Registered Medical Assistant RMA (AMT) credential as well as the Certified Medical Assistant Specialist CMAS (AMT) credential.

American Medical Technologists (AMT)
The registering organization for medical assistants that provides online continuing education, certification information, and member news.

Other Certification Agencies The **National Healthcareer Association (NHA)** was established in 1989 as an information resource and network for today's active health-care professionals. They offer a variety of certification exams including Billing and Coding Specialist, Medical Transcriptionist (CMT), and Medical Administrative Assistant (CMAA). Some of the programs and services of the NHA include:

National Healthcareer Association (NHA)
An organization that provides certification and continuing education services for health-care professionals as well as curriculum development for education institutions.

- Certification development and implementation
- Continuing education curriculum development and implementation
- Program development for unions, hospitals, and schools
- Educational, career advancement, and networking services for members
- Registry of certified professionals

The National Healthcare Association certification exams are developed by health-care educators working in their various fields of study. The NHA is a member of The National Organization of Competency Assurance (NOCA).

The **National Center for Competency Testing (NCCT)** is another independent agency that certifies the validity of competency and knowledge of the medical profession through examination. Medical assistants and medical office assistants receive the designation of National Certified Medical Assistant (NCMA) and National Certified Medical Office Assistant (NCMOA) after passing the certification examination.

The **National Association for Health Professionals (NAHP)** (www.nahpusa.com) offers multiple credentials for health-care professionals. The organization, which has been in existence for 25 years, prides itself in making the process of

National Center for Competency Testing (NCCT)
An independent, third-party organization that certifies individuals through examination and avoids any allegiance to a specific organization or association.

National Association for Health Professionals (NAHP)
An organization dedicated to assisting students in the health-care field to obtain a credential in the most proficient manner possible.

obtaining a credential an accessible, affordable, and obtainable goal for those individuals who wish to show commitment to their chosen profession. Having multiple credentials with one agency makes maintaining continuing education easier for the practicing health-care professional. The NAHP offers many credentials including the Nationally Registered title of Certified Administrative Health Assistant (NRCAHA) and the Nationally Registered title of Certified Coding Specialist (NRCCS).

CHECKPOINT
LO 1.3

What agency do you plan to receive certification from when you complete your administrative medical assisting training?

LO 1.4 Medical Assistant Credentials

Medical assisting credentials such as **certification** and **registration** are not always required to practice as a medical assistant. You may practice with a high school diploma or equivalent, although opportunities for this type of on-the-job training are becoming less common. Employers today are aggressively recruiting medical assistants who are credentialed in their field.

This section explains why obtaining and maintaining a professional credential is so important for a medical assistant's entry into and advancement within the health-care field. More detailed information about how to obtain these credentials is provided as well.

Malpractice

The United States continues to be one of the most litigious nations in the civilized world. Disputes that used to be settled by discussion and mediation are now being referred to attorneys and ending up in courts of law. Lawsuits are particularly acute in the world of health care. Employers of allied health professionals have correctly concluded that having credentialed personnel or staff will lessen the likelihood of a successful legal challenge to the quality of work of employees.

An accredited medical assisting program is competency based; this means that standards are set by the accrediting body, such as the Accrediting Bureau of Health Education Schools (ABHES) or the Commission on Accreditation of Allied Health Education Programs (CAAHEP), for administrative and clinical competencies. It is the duty of the educational institution to ensure that all medical assisting competencies are learned by medical assisting students and that evidence is clearly documented for each student. Periodic evaluations are performed by the accrediting agencies to ensure the effectiveness of the program. The theory of the competencies as well as the proficiency assessments are components of the CMA (AAMA) examination. For example, administering medications is a competency required of accredited medical assisting programs and is a component of the CMA (AAMA) examination. The CMA (AAMA) credential and the affiliation with a professional organization demonstrate competence and provide evidence of training. They will also lessen the likelihood of a legal challenge to the quality of a medical assistant's work. Additional information about school accreditation will be discussed in more detail later in this chapter.

Managed Care Organizations

Managed care is a growing trend in today's health-care industry. The cost limitations imposed by **managed care organizations (MCOs)** are causing mergers and buyouts throughout the nation. Small physician practices are being consolidated or merged into larger providers of health care, such as by hospitals or for-profit organizations, which result in decreased operating expenses. These larger health-care providers can make the delivery of health care more cost-effective.

certification
Confirmation by an organization that an individual is qualified to perform a job to professional standards.

registration
Granting of a title or license by a board that gives permission to practice in a chosen profession.

managed care organization (MCO)
A health-care business that, through mergers and buyouts, can deliver health care more cost effectively.

Human resource directors of MCOs place great importance in professional credentials for their employees and therefore are more likely to establish certification or registry as a mandatory professional designation for medical assistants.

State and Federal Regulations

Certain provisions of the **Occupational Safety and Health Administration (OSHA)** and the **Clinical Laboratory Improvement Amendments of 1988 (CLIA '88)** are making mandatory credentialing for medical assistants a logical step in the hiring process. Presently, OSHA and CLIA '88 do not require that medical assistants be credentialed, but there are various components of these statutes and their regulations that can be met by demonstrating that medical assistants in a clinical setting are certified. For example, some physician offices perform moderately complex laboratory testing on-site. The medical assistant can perform moderately complex tests if she or he has the appropriate training and skills.

CMA Certification

The **Certified Medical Assistant (CMA)** credential is awarded by the Certifying Board of the AAMA. The AAMA's certification examination evaluates mastery of medical assisting competencies based on the Occupational Analysis of the CMA (AAMA) and is available at www.aama-ntl.org/resources/library/OA.pdf. The National Board of Medical Examiners (NBME) also provides technical assistance in developing the tests.

CMAs (AAMA) must recertify the CMA (AAMA) credential every 5 years. To be recertified as a CMA (AAMA), 60 contact hours must be accumulated during the five-year period: 10 in the administrative area, 10 in the clinical area, and 10 in the general area, with 30 additional hours in any of the three categories. In addition, 30 of these contact hours must be from an approved AAMA program. The AAMA also requires you to hold a current CPR card. This mandate requires you to learn about new medical developments through education courses or participation in an examination. Hundreds of **continuing education** courses are sponsored by local, state, and national AAMA groups. The AAMA also offers self-study courses through its continuing education department. As described in the AAMA's publication *CMA Today*, the advantages of CMA (AAMA) certification include respect and recognition from peers in the medical assisting profession.

As of June 1998, only applicants of medical assisting programs that were granted accreditation by CAAHEP and ABHES are eligible to take the certification examination. The AAMA offers the *Candidate's Guide to the Certification Examination* to help applicants prepare for the examination. This guide explains the test format and test-taking strategies. It also includes a sample examination with answers and information about study references. Some schools even offer test preparation reviews that they have incorporated into their programs due to the changes passed down from the accrediting agencies that now have applied pass rates of the exams in order for the schools to keep their accreditation. As of January 2009, the CMA (AAMA) examination is computerized. While previously this exam was offered only at selected times during the year, the computerized test may now be taken any time at a designated testing site in your area. You may search the Internet for an application and test review materials. Once you have successfully passed the CMA (AAMA) examination you have earned the right to add that credential to your name such as: Tiffany Heath, CMA (AAMA).

American Medical Technologists (AMT) Credentials

The American Medical Technologists (AMT) organization credentials medical assistants as **Registered Medical Assistants (RMA)** or Certified Medical Assistant Specialists (CMAS).

The AMT sets forth certain educational and experiential requirements to earn the RMA (AMT) credential. These include:

- Graduation from a medical assistant program that holds programmatic accreditation by ABHES or CAAHEP, or that has institutional accreditation by a Regional Accrediting Commission or by a national accrediting organization approved by the U.S. Department of Education, or a formal medical services training program of the United States Armed Forces.
- Alternatively, employment in the profession of medical assisting for a minimum of five (5) years, no more than two (2) years of which may have been as an instructor in the postsecondary medical assistant program.
- Passing the AMT examination for RMA (AMT) certification. RMAs (AMT) must accumulate 30 contact hours for continuing education units (CEU) every three years if they were certified after 2006. RMAs (AMT) who were certified before this date are expected to keep abreast of all the changes and practices in their field through educational programs, workshops, or seminars. However, there are no specific continuing education requirements. Once a medical assistant has passed the AMT exam, he has earned the right to add RMA (AMT) to his name: James Wood, RMA (AMT).

As stated on the AMT Web site (www.amt1.com), to qualify for the CMAS (AMT) the applicant must be of good moral character and meet at least one of the following requirements:

- Applicant shall be a graduate of (or scheduled to graduate from):
  - A medical office administrative program that holds programmatic accreditation by (or is in a postsecondary school or college that holds institutional accreditation by) the Accrediting Bureau of Health Education Schools (ABHES).
  - A medical office administrative program in a postsecondary school or college that has institutional accreditation by a Regional Accrediting Commission or by a national accrediting organization approved by the U.S. Department of Education, which program includes a minimum of 720 clock-hours (or equivalent) of training in medical office administrative skills (including a practical externship). Training program must have been structured to include at least the following content areas: (1) medical records management, (2) health-care insurance processing, coding, and billing, (3) office financial responsibilities, and (4) information processing.
- Applicant shall be certified as a Registered Medical Assistant (RMA) (or equivalent) and possess a minimum of two (2) years experience working as a medical office administrative specialist.
- Applicant shall have been employed as a medical office administrative specialist for a minimum of five (5) years.

Once a medical office administrative specialist passes the CMAS exam, he can add the credentials CMAS (AMT) to his name, for example, John T. Haddix, CMAS (AMT).

The RMA (AMT), CMA (AAMA), and CMAS (AMT) Examinations

The RMA (AMT), CMA (AAMA), and CMAS (AMT) qualifying examinations are rigorous. Participation in an accredited program, however, will help you

learn what you need to know. The examinations cover several distinct areas of knowledge. These include:

- General medical knowledge, including terminology, anatomy, physiology, behavioral science, medical law, and ethics
- Administrative knowledge, including medical records management, collections, insurance processing, and the **Health Insurance Portability and Accountability Act (HIPAA)**
- Clinical knowledge, including examination room techniques, medication preparation and administration, pharmacology, and specimen collection

Each of the three certification examinations is based on a specific content outline created by the certifying organization. In order to assist you in preparing for any of these examinations, each chapter introduction includes a feature titled "Preparation for Certification." This feature correlates content from each of the exams with the chapter content. You should also research the Internet to gain additional information regarding any of these certifications. See Procedure 1–1, Obtaining Certification Information through the Internet.

Health Insurance Portability and Accountability Act (HIPAA)
A set of regulations whose goals include the following: (1) improving the portability and continuity of health-care coverage in group and individual markets; (2) combating waste, fraud, and abuse in health-care insurance and health-care delivery; (3) promoting the use of a medical savings account; (4) improving access to long-term care services and coverage; and (5) simplifying the administration of health insurance.

CHECKPOINT
LO 1.4

What three reasons cause employers to seek credentialed medical assistants?

LO 1.5 Training Programs

Formal programs in medical assisting are offered in a variety of educational settings. They include vocational-technical high schools, postsecondary vocational schools, community and junior colleges, and 4-year colleges and universities. Vocational school programs usually last 9 months to 1 year and award a certificate or diploma. Community and junior college programs are usually 2-year associate's degree programs.

Accreditation

accreditation
The documentation of official authorization or approval of a program.

Accreditation is the process by which programs are officially authorized. There are two national entities recognized by the U.S. Department of Education that accredit medical assisting educational programs:

1. The Commission on Accreditation of Allied Health Education Programs (CAAHEP). CAAHEP works directly with the Medical Assisting Educational Review Board (MAERB) of Medical Assistants Endowments to ensure that all accredited schools provide a competency-based education. CAAHEP accredits medical assisting programs in both public and private postsecondary institutions throughout the United States that prepare individuals for entry into the medical assisting profession.

2. Accrediting Bureau of Health Education Schools (ABHES). ABHES accredits private postsecondary institutions and programs that prepare individuals for entry into the medical assisting profession.

Accredited programs must cover the following topics: anatomy and physiology; medical terminology; medical law and ethics; psychology; oral and written communications; laboratory procedures; and clinical and administrative procedures. High school students may prepare for these courses by studying mathematics, health, biology, keyboarding, office skills, bookkeeping, and information technology. You may obtain current information about accreditation standards for medical assisting programs from the AAMA.

Medical assisting programs must also include an externship. An **externship** (or practicum) is practical work experience for a specified timeframe in an ambulatory-care setting, such as physicians' offices, hospitals, or other health-care facilities.

Additionally, the AAMA lists its minimum standards for accredited programs. This list of standards ensures that all personnel—administrators and faculty—are qualified to perform their jobs.

The AAMA requires that administrative personnel exhibit leadership and management skills. They must also be able to fully perform the functions identified in documented job descriptions. Faculty members must develop and evaluate lesson plans, assess student progress toward the program's objectives, and be knowledgeable regarding course content. They must be qualified through work experience and be able to effectively direct and evaluate student learning and laboratory experiences.

The AAMA also has accreditation requirements for financial and physical resources. Each program's financial resources must meet its obligations to students. Schools must also have adequate physical resources—classrooms, laboratories, clinical and administrative facilities, and equipment and supplies.

Graduation from an accredited program helps your career in three ways. First, it shows that you have completed a program that meets nationally accepted standards. Second, it provides recognition of your education by professional peers. Third, it makes you eligible for registration or certification. Students who graduate from an accredited medical assisting program, such as ABHES or CAAHEP, are eligible to take the CMA (AAMA) or RMA (AMT) immediately.

externship

A period of practical work experience performed by a medical assisting student in a physician's office, hospital, or other health-care facility.

Externships

In an externship you will obtain work experience while completing a medical assisting program. This is an extension of the classroom learning experience. You will apply skills learned in the classroom in an actual medical office or other health-care facility. Because of this professional experience, you also earn the right to include your externship on your résumé under job experience, as long as you title it as "Medical Assistant Externship." Externships are mandatory in accredited schools. The length of your externship will vary, depending on your particular program. Familiarize yourself with the program requirements as soon as possible because as a mandatory part of the program, no matter how good your grades are in class, if the externship is not completed you will not graduate from the program. The "Externship and Employment Search" chapter (Chapter 24) further explains externship.

CHECKPOINT
LO 1.5

1. Why is accreditation of your medical assisting program important?
2. What is the purpose of the externship?

LO 1.6 Membership in a Medical Assisting Association

Professional associations set high standards for quality and performance in a profession. They define the tasks and functions of an occupation. In addition, they provide members with the opportunity to communicate and network with one another. They also present their goals to the profession and to the general public. Becoming a member of a professional association helps you achieve career goals and further the profession of medical assisting. Joining as a student is encouraged and some associations even offer discounted rates to the student for a specified amount of time after graduation.

figure 1-2

In this picture, a representative is giving information concerning certification to students and instructors at a local chapter meeting of the AAMA.

Professional Support for CMAs (AAMA)

When you become a member of the AAMA, you will have a large support group of active medical assistants. Membership benefits include:

- Professional publications, such as *CMA Today*
- A large variety of educational opportunities, such as chapter-sponsored seminars and workshops about the latest administrative, clinical, and management topics (Figure 1-2)
- Group insurance
- Legal information
- Local, state, and national activities that include professional networking and multiple continuing education opportunities
- Legislative monitoring to protect your right to practice as a medical assistant
- Access to the Web site at www.aama-ntl.org

Professional Support for RMAs (AMT) and CMASs (AMT)

The AMT offers many benefits for RMAs (AMT) and CMASs (AMT). These include:

- Professional publications
- Membership in the AMT Institute for Education
- Group insurance programs—liability, health, and life
- State chapter activities
- Legal representation in health legislative matters
- Annual meetings and educational seminars
- Student membership
- Access to the Web site at www.amt1.com

CHECKPOINT
LO 1.6

Why would you want to join a professional association?

LO 1.7 Professional Development

Professional development refers to skills and knowledge attained for both personal development and career advancement. During your training you should strive to improve your knowledge and skills. This will help you transition into your first job with ease. You can gain valuable knowledge and skills through volunteering prior to or in addition to an externship.

Once you have entered the world of work as a medical assistant you will want to continue to develop in your profession. This can be done by gaining more knowledge and skills through additional training, cross-training, and/or other forms of continuing education. During training and practice as a medical assistant you must know and work within your scope of practice and network to improve yourself professionally.

professional development
The skills and knowledge attained for both personal development and career advancement.

Volunteer Programs

Volunteering is a rewarding experience. Before you even begin a medical assisting program, you can gain experience in a health-care profession through volunteer work. As a volunteer, you will get hands-on training and learn what it is like to assist patients who are ill, disabled, or frightened.

You may volunteer as an aide in a hospital, clinic, nursing home, or doctor's office, or as a typist or filing clerk in a medical office or medical record room. Some visiting nurse associations and hospices (homelike medical settings that provide medical care and emotional support to terminally ill patients and their families) also offer volunteer opportunities. These experiences may help you decide if you want to pursue a career as a medical assistant.

The American Red Cross also offers volunteer opportunities for the student medical assistant. The Red Cross needs volunteers for its disaster relief programs locally, statewide, nationally, and abroad.

As part of a disaster relief team at the site of a hurricane, tornado, storm, flood, earthquake, or fire, volunteers learn first-aid and emergency triage skills. Red Cross volunteers gain valuable work experience that may help them obtain a job.

Because volunteers are not paid, it is usually easy to find work opportunities. Just because you are not paid for volunteer work, however, does not mean the experience is not useful for meeting your career goals.

Include information about any volunteer work on your **résumé**—a computer-generated document that summarizes your employment and educational history. Be sure to note specific duties, responsibilities, and skills developed during the volunteer experience. Refer to the "Externship and Employment Search" chapter (Chapter 24) for examples of résumés.

résumé
A typewritten document summarizing one's employment and educational history.

Continued Training

Continuing education and training are essential to your career as a medical assistant. As discussed earlier, continuing education is mandatory for maintaining your certification or registration. In addition, you may want to become *multiskilled.*

Many hospitals and health-care practices are embracing the idea of a multiskilled health-care professional (MSHP). An MSHP is a cross-trained team member who is able to handle many different duties.

Reducing Health-Care Costs   As a result of health-care reform and downsizing (a reduction in the number of staff members) to control the rising cost of health care, medical practices are eager to reduce personnel costs by hiring multiskilled health professionals. These individuals, who perform the functions of two or more people, are the most cost-efficient employees.

Recycling in the Medical Office, Hospital, Laboratory, or Clinic

You may easily incorporate recycling procedures into the daily routine of a medical office, hospital, laboratory, or clinic. Recycling may be required by state law. Some states levy large fines for noncompliance with recycling regulations. Purchase paper products that can be recycled, or those made of postconsumer recycled materials, and take care in disposing of them. Care should be taken to ensure HIPAA compliance when recycling paper. Shredding is the most effective way to comply with HIPAA regulations.

There are two essential aspects of recycling: disposal and purchasing. To create a complete recycling program, ensure that materials are disposed of properly and that purchased products have been made from recycled materials.

You may easily call the town's recycling center for guidelines for packaging recycled materials and for a pickup schedule. The recycling center may also provide containers for recyclable materials and a list of paper materials that can and cannot be recycled. You must fulfill all town and state legal recycling requirements.

You must also research disposal techniques for biohazardous materials and follow regulations listed in the office policy manual and OSHA guidelines. These materials cannot be recycled and must be disposed of properly. They must not be mixed with recyclable waste. Follow the office policy manual and OSHA guidelines for hazardous medical wastes. These materials must be disposed of following OSHA guidelines and in a specially designed protective container.

Use the following guidelines to assist you when purchasing items for recycling.

This is the universal recycling symbol. It has three chasing arrows. It could mean that

the product or package is made up of recycled materials or that the product or package is recyclable. Check with your town's recycling center to ensure proper disposal.

Unless the package is made of 100% recycled materials, the law requires the package to display how much.

An office copier that is labeled "recycled" because it was rebuilt, reconditioned or remanufactured must state whether the recycled content came from rebuilt, reconditioned, or remanufactured parts. That's because it may not be obvious that it contains used parts.

Watch out for claims that do not mean anything. Claims that a product or service is "environmentally friendly," "environmentally safe," "environmentally preferable," or "eco-safe" or labels that contain environmental seals are unhelpful. These phrases alone do not provide the specific information you need to compare products, packaging, or services on their environmental merits. If you want to go "green," look for claims that give some substance and additional information that explains why the product is environmentally friendly or has earned a special seal.

For more about recycling and green advertising, check the Web sites of the Federal Trade Commission (www.ftc.gov) or the Environmental Protection Agency (http://epa.gov).

Expanding Your Career Opportunities Career opportunities are vast if you are self-motivated and willing to learn new skills. If you continue to learn about new administrative techniques and procedures, you will be an important part of the health-care team.

Following are several examples of positions for medical assistants with additional experience and certifications:

- Office manager
- Medical transcriptionist
- Medical biller
- Hospital admissions coordinator
- An administrative assistant at insurance companies
- Medical assisting instructor (with a specified amount of experience and education)

If you are multiskilled, you will have an advantage when job hunting. Employers are eager to hire multiskilled medical assistants and may create positions for them.

You can gain multiskill training by showing initiative and a willingness to learn every aspect of the medical facility in which you are working. When you begin working within a medical facility, establish goals regarding your career path and discuss them with your immediate supervisor. Indicate to your supervisor that you would like **cross-training** in every aspect of the medical facility. Begin your mastery of the department that you are currently working in and branch out to other departments once you master the skills needed for your current position. This will demonstrate a commitment to your profession as well as a strong work ethic. Cross-training is a valuable marketing tool to include on your résumé.

cross-training
The acquisition of training in a variety of tasks and skills.

Scope of Practice

Medical assistants are not "licensed" health-care professionals and most often work under another licensed health-care provider, such as a nurse practitioner or physician. Licensed health-care professionals may delegate certain duties to a medical assistant, providing she or he has had the appropriate training through an accredited medical assisting program or through on-the-job training provided by the medical facility or physician. Questions often arise regarding the kinds of duties a medical assistant can perform. There is no universal answer to these questions. There is no single national definition of a medical assistant's scope of practice. Therefore, the medical assistant must research the state in which he or she works to learn about the scope of practice. In general, a medical assistant may not perform procedures for which he or she was not educated or trained. The AAMA and AMT are good resources to assist you in your research. The AAMA Occupational Analysis is also a good reference source that identifies the procedures that medical assistants are educated to perform. Professional development includes knowing your scope of practice and working within it.

Networking

Networking is building alliances, socially and professionally. It starts long before your job search. By attending professional association meetings, conferences, or other functions, medical assistants generate opportunities for employment and personal and professional growth. Networking, through continuing education conferences throughout your career, keeps the doors open to employment advancement.

 What is professional development and why is it important?

 **CHECKPOINT**
LO 1.7

Procedure 1-1 Obtaining Certification Information through the Internet

GOAL To obtain information from the Internet regarding professional credentialing

MATERIALS Computer with Internet access and printer

METHOD 1. Open your Internet Browser and locate a search engine. Search for the credential you would like to pursue. For example, Certified Medical Assistant, Registered Medical Assistant, or Certified Medical

Assistant Specialist. If you are unsure of the credential you would like to pursue, you may just want to search for "Medical Assisting Credentials."

2. Select the site for the credential you are pursuing. Avoid sponsored links. These links are paid for and will not typically bring you to the site of a credentialing organization.

3. Navigate to the home page. For the CMA (AAMA) credential, enter the site www.aama-ntl.org. For the RMA (AMT) or CMAS (AMT) credential, enter the site www.amt1.com.

4. Determine the steps you must take to obtain the selected credential.

   a. For CMA (AAMA) go to the drop-down menu "CMA (AAMA) Exam" and select the link "How to Become a CMA (AAMA)."

   b. For RMA (AMT) go to the drop-down menu on the left, click "Certification" and then select "Medical Assistant" for RMA (AMT) or "Medical Administrative Specialist" for CMAS (AMT). Navigate to the tab "Qualifications."

5. Print or write down the qualifications you must obtain.

6. Once you have met the qualifications you will need to apply for the examination or certification. Download the application and the application instructions for the RMA (AMT) or the CMAS (AMT) or the candidate application and handbook for the CMA (AAMA).

7. To view or print these instructions you may need to download Adobe Reader. You can click on a link to download Adobe Reader after you click on the "Apply for Certification" link for AMT or the "Apply for the CMA (AAMA) Exam" for AAMA.

8. Before or after you apply for the examination you will need to prepare for the examination. Select the link "Prepare for the CMA (AAMA) Exam" on the AAMA site or the "Prepare for Exam" link under the "Medical Assistant" or "Medical Assistant Specialist" drop-down menus on the AMT site.

9. Prepare for the exam by reviewing the content outline, obtaining additional study resources, or taking a practice exam online.

10. Print or save downloaded information in a file folder on your desktop labeled "Credentials" or something that you can recognize. To print, click the printer icon found at the bottom of the Web page or just simply click the printer icon in your browser.

11. Return to the appropriate site if you have additional questions. For the CMA (AAMA) site you may want to check the "FAQs on CMA (AAMA) Certification" link. On the AMT site for RMA or CMAS click the "Take Exam" link and download the FAQs regarding the testing process.

12. Any questions you have that are not addressed on the sites can be e-mailed to the organizations. For CMAS send an e-mail to the link cmas@amt1.com. For RMA send an e-mail to the link rma@amt1.com. On the AAMA site for the CMA credential, click the "Contact" link on the top right-hand side of the screen.

Case Study

PROFESSIONAL READINESS

Growth
Continual striving to improve and learn new materials

Debbie is a 23-year-old administrative medical assistant. She is mainly responsible for phone reception and patient check-in and check-out. A 29-year-old female patient calls complaining of lower back pain. As Debbie listens to the patient describe her condition, she determines the severity of the patient's

discomfort and schedules a same-day appointment. When the patient arrives at the office, Debbie greets her at the front desk, verifies her address and insurance information, and escorts her to an exam room. After the physician completes the exam, the patient is instructed to see Debbie on the way out. Debbie reviews the patient's prescriptions and schedules a diagnostic test and laboratory work for the patient at another facility. Debbie then collects the patient's co-pay and gives the patient a receipt. After the patient leaves, Debbie prepares the insurance forms for reimbursement and files the patient's chart.

Thinking Critically

1. Why should Debbie maintain a credential and membership to a professional organization?
2. What could Debbie do to improve her knowledge and skills as she performs her duties?

practice APPLICATIONS

1. Chose a mentor who displays the personal attributes listed in this chapter and write a few sentences to explain why these attributes apply to her or him.

2. A. Think of all the personal qualifications you possess. List those that will help you as an administrative medical assistant.

   B. List all of the personal qualifications you need to develop or improve in order to work successfully in the career of an administrative medical assistant.

exam READINESS

There may be more than one correct answer. Circle the best answer.

1. [LO1.5] Two accrediting bodies for medical assisting programs are
   a. ABHES and OSHA.
   b. OSHA and AAMA.
   c. ABHES and CAAHEP.
   d. CAAHEP and CLIA.
   e. CAAHEP and NHA

2. [LO1.2] Entry-level administrative duties for a medical assistant include
   a. patient education, drawing blood, and negotiating leases.
   b. taking vital signs and prescribing medicine.
   c. creating and maintaining patient medical records and billing and coding.
   d. performing ECGs, infection control, and billing and coding.
   e. checking vital signs and creating and maintaining patient medical records.

3. [LO1.3] The main purpose of the American Association of Medical Assistants (AAMA) is to
   a. raise the standards of professionalism.
   b. assist with malpractice lawsuits.
   c. provide externships.
   d. use their resources to support CMAs' (AAMA), RMAs' (AMT), and CMASs' (AMT) continuing education.
   e. provide accreditation for medical assisting programs.

4. **[LO1.3]** The increase in job opportunities for medical assistants is due to
   a. population increase, wage increases, and increases in births.
   b. the growth of outpatient clinics and HMOs.
   c. patient education and professional membership.
   d. the ability to handle patients' privacy.
   e. the regulations set forth by CLIA and OSHA.

5. **[LO1.7]** Which of the following is best description of networking?
   a. Building alliances that generate opportunities
   b. Practical work experience during training
   c. Official authorization of medical assisting educational programs
   d. Training in every aspect of the medical facility
   e. Using the Internet

6. **[LO1.1]** Which of the following is most likely the best practice to ensure student success?
   a. Study in the cafeteria during lunch
   b. Maintain a paper or electronic calendar with assignments and tests
   c. Work with a large group of students
   d. Prepare for the test right before it so you can remember
   e. Keep yourself motivated by avoiding goals

7. **[LO1.4]** Which of the following is most likely the best reason for you to cross-train?
   a. Reduction of health-care costs
   b. Learning of new skills

c. Increased employment opportunities
d. Ability to work two jobs
e. Reduced wages

8. **[LO1.6]** You have become a member of the AAMA. Which of the following is most likely one of your benefits?
   a. Medical transcription
   b. Accreditation
   c. Cross-training
   d. Increased wages
   e. Group insurance

9. **[LO1.2]** Which of the following would you be expected to do as an entry level administrative medical assistant?
   a. Develop public outreach programs
   b. Be a HIPAA compliance officer
   c. Arrange laboratory services
   d. Arrange outpatient diagnostic tests
   e. Sterilize medical instruments

10. **[LO1.3]** When you have the credentials CMAS (AMT) you are considered a
    a. Certified Medical Administrative Specialist.
    b. Certified Medical Assistant Specialist.
    c. Certified Administrative Medical Assistant Specialist.
    d. Community Medical Assistant Specialist.
    e. Credentialed Medical Administrative Specialist.

learning outcome SUMMARY

LO 1.1 The key components to student success include organizational skills, study habits, and goal setting.

LO 1.2 The responsibility of an administrative medical assistant varies from entry-level administrative duties to advanced administrative duties.

LO 1.3 Many organizations provide certification and support to the medical assisting profession. The AAMA and AMT are the organizations most recognized.

LO 1.4 Certification and registration provide recognition of your education by peers and for advancement in your career.

LO 1.5 Professional training for medical assistants includes formal training in a variety of educational settings (i.e., postsecondary vocational schools, four-year colleges).

LO 1.6 Professional membership affiliation provides networking opportunities and access to potential employers.

LO 1.7 Cross-training is an important part of professional development. Medical assistants are much more marketable if they are multiskilled.

medical assisting COMPETENCIES

CAAHEP

IX.C (5) Discuss licensure and certification as it applies to health-care providers

IX.P (2) Perform within scope of practice

IX.P (4) Practice within the standard of care for a medical assistant

ABHES

1. General Orientation

a. Comprehend the current employment outlook for the medical assistant
b. Compare and contrast the allied health professions and understand their relation to medical assisting
c. Understand medical assistant credentialing requirements and the process to obtain the credential; comprehend the importance of credentialing
d. Have knowledge of the general responsibilities of the medical assistant

e. Define scope of practice for the medical assistant, and comprehend the conditions for practice within the state that the medical assistant is employed

11. Career Development

b. Demonstrate professionalism by:
   (1) Exhibiting dependability, punctuality, and a positive work ethic
   (4) Being cognizant of ethical boundaries
   (9) Conducting work within scope of education, training, and ability

2 Professional Behaviors

Learning Outcomes

After completing Chapter 2, you will be able to:

2.1 Understand the importance of professionalism in medical assisting.

2.2 Explain the professional behaviors exhibited by medical assistants.

2.3 Discuss strategies for success in the medical assisting education program.

Key Terms

attitude
communication
compensation time
comprehension
continuing education
  units (CEU)
constructive criticism
cooperation
coordination
critical thinking
cultural diversity
electronic health record
  (EHR)
empathy
hard skills

integrity
judgment
knowledge
organization
patient advocacy
persistence
professional
professionalism
prioritizing
punctuality
self-confidence
soft skills
time management
work ethic
work quality

Preparation for Certification

RMA (AMT) Exam
- Human relations

CMAS (AMT) Exam
- Professionalism

CMA (AAMA) Exam
- Recognize and respect cultural diversity

Introduction ● ● ●

A **professional** is a member of a vocation requiring specialized educational training. **Professionalism** is behavior that exhibits the traits or features that correspond to the models and standards of that profession which, in this case, is medical assisting (Figure 2–1). Models and standards are developed by professional organizations such as the American Association of Medical Assistants (AAMA) and the American Medical Technologists (AMT) and, in some states, by governmental entities. Community needs and cultures also play roles in developing standards of professionalism. When discussing the traits and features of a profession, there are two major areas:

1. **Hard skills**—specific technical and operational proficiencies
2. **Soft skills**—personal attributes or behaviors that enhance an individual's interactions, job performance, and career prospects

Hard skills are taught with relative ease and represent the minimum proficiencies necessary to do the job. Examples of hard skills for administrative medical assisting are appointment scheduling, insurance coding, and medical records management. The ability to perform hard skills is readily observable. The hard skill set is the first screen employers use to determine if applicants are qualified for the position.

Soft skills are more elusive and less concrete. These are the characteristics, attributes, or **attitudes** that people develop throughout their lives and bring with them to their educational programs and jobs. Examples are respect, dependability, and integrity. While these are generally personal attributes, when they are sought after and significant for specific jobs they are also professional attributes or behaviors. This chapter discusses the professional behaviors necessary for medical assisting and provides the student an opportunity to evaluate himself or herself in these areas. Tips for success in your medical assisting educational program and the importance of keeping current in your field as an expectation of being a professional are also included.

LO 2.1 The Importance of Professionalism in Medical Assisting

A medical assisting credential and the technical skills associated with it are the reasons most graduates are hired. However, the lack of a specific soft skill or professional behavior is the reason for most terminations. Weakness in the soft skills is also the major reason that students do not successfully complete their medical assisting education.

In the previous chapter, the role of the medical assistant was discussed. Much of this role involves dealing with other people, whether a patient, a patient's family member, a co-worker, an insurance agent, a pharmaceutical sales representative, a laboratory staff member, or others. The majority of soft skills are about working with people. It only makes sense that someone going into a profession that constantly deals with people would need these skills or behaviors to do a good job. Professional behaviors for medical assisting are described in many ways and have many facets. The ones that will be discussed in this chapter are: comprehension, persistence, self-confidence, judgment, knowledge, organization, communication, integrity, growth, cooperation, acceptance of constructive criticism, relations with others, work quality, punctuality and attendance, and professional appearance.

professional
A member of a vocation requiring specialized educational training.

professionalism
Exhibiting the traits or features that correspond with some model of that profession.

hard skills
Specific technical and operational proficiencies.

soft skills
Personal attributes that enhance an individual's interactions, job performance and career prospects.

attitude
A disposition to act in a certain way.

figure 2-1

The medical assistant must exhibit professionalism when working with others.

Together they produce what is called a good **work ethic,** which is what employers seek. You will continually experience assessment of your professional behaviors in the following environments:

- Classroom
- Externship
- Hiring process
- Workplace performance evaluation
- Promotion consideration

Here is an example to further emphasize the importance of professionalism in the workplace. The medical assistant, who did not know the proper instructions to give a patient regarding a diagnostic test, was too shy (lacked self-confidence) to ask. Consequently, instructions were given based on what she thought might be appropriate (lacked knowledge). The probability is high that the patient would not be adequately prepared for the test. The results might be:

- Difficulty in performing the test
- Cancellation of the test, wasting time and resources
- Repetition of the test, incurring increased costs which may not be reimbursed by insurance or, most importantly, inaccurate results of the test leading to incorrect diagnosis and treatment and a poor patient outcome
- Potential litigation against the medical practice

The issue is not that the medical assistant did not know the correct instructions but that the medical assistant did not use the correct behaviors (communication, cooperation, knowledge, persistence, work quality) to obtain and give the correct instructions. While this scenario seems exaggerated, it has unfortunately occurred. The importance of professional behaviors cannot be overemphasized. The following chapters in this text each contain a case study associated with a professional attribute that is relevant to the topic of the chapter.

**CHECKPOINT
LO 2.1**

Explain the difference between hard skills and soft skills.

LO 2.2 Professional Behaviors in Medical Assisting

You now have an overview of professionalism and the desired professional behaviors for medical assisting. Let's examine each one (Table 2–1).

Comprehension

Comprehension is the ability to learn, retain, and process information. In order to function as a medical assistant you must comprehend your responsibilities and role. This means to not only have information but to be able to analyze that information and know how to use it. The information must also be retained. You must remember it, even if used infrequently. An example of comprehension is learning the different methods of appointment scheduling and then going to your externship and remembering the basics of the system they use. The final step is to correctly schedule appointments.

Persistence

Persistence is continuing in spite of difficulty; being determined, and overcoming obstacles. Another word for persistence is tenacity. The slang is "stick-to-itiveness." This attribute ensures that you will finish the job no matter how

BEHAVIOR	DEFINITION
Comprehension	Learning, retaining, and processing information
Persistence (tenacity)	Continuing in spite of difficulty; determined; overcomes obstacles
Self-confidence	Believing in oneself; assured
Judgment	Evaluating a situation and coming to an appropriate conclusion, then acting accordingly; critical thinking
Knowledge	Understanding gained through study and experience; putting theory into practice
Organization	Planning and coordinating information and tasks in an orderly manner to efficiently complete the job in the given time
Communication	Giving and receiving accurate information
Integrity (honesty)	Adhering to the appropriate code of law and ethics, trustworthy
Growth	Ongoing efforts to learn and improve
Cooperation	Working with others in the best interest of completing the job
Acceptance of criticism	Willing to consider feedback and suggestions to improve; taking responsibility for one's actions
Relations with others	Getting along with people
Work quality	Striving for excellence in doing the job; pride in one's performance
Punctuality and attendance	Showing up on appointed days and times
Professional appearance	Adhering to the standards and codes of dress, including rules on body art, and practicing good personal hygiene

table 2-1

Professional Behaviors

difficult or boring or annoying or time-consuming. One example that is not uncommon in the medical office is trying to reach a patient whose contact information is not up-to-date. The issue may be an abnormal laboratory report that requires follow-up or another vital matter. The practitioner must be able to count on you and know that you will follow through. The patient's well-being often depends on it.

Self-Confidence

Self-confidence is believing in oneself. It is a trait that puts people at ease. The patient and the physician and others are more comfortable when they feel that you know what you are doing. The self-assured medical assistant is generally the one that the patient and the physician prefer to work with (Figure 2–2). This self-assured medical assistant is also the one who remains calm in an emergency. The popular television commercial slogan "Never let them see you sweat" relates to displaying self-confidence even in tense or difficult situations.

self-confidence
Believing in oneself; assured.

Judgment

Judgment is evaluating a situation, reaching an appropriate conclusion, and acting accordingly. It is also referred to as **critical thinking,** which is defined as purposeful decisions resulting from analysis and evaluation. An example is observing a patient in the reception area who appears to have difficulty breathing. You evaluate the situation and realize the patient is in distress, and then immediately bring the patient to the treatment area and alert the practitioner. Other patients may become upset that they were not seen first. This requires you to use further judgment by providing an explanation or rationale for your decision and actions without violating any confidentiality involving the other patient.

judgment
Coming to an appropriate conclusion and acting accordingly; critical thinking.

critical thinking
Purposeful judgment resulting from analysis and evaluation.

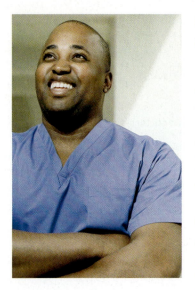

figure 2-2

Expressing self-confidence is an important professional behavior.

knowledge
Understanding gained through study and experience; associating theory with practice.

organization
Planning and coordinating information and tasks in an orderly manner to efficiently complete the job in a given time.

time management
Utilizing time in effective manner to accomplish the desired results.

prioritizing
Sorting and dealing with matters in the order of urgency and importance.

communication
Giving and receiving accurate information.

integrity
Adhering to the appropriate code of law and ethics; trustworthy and honest.

compensation time
Time off given for working extra time without pay.

Knowledge

Knowledge is understanding gained through study and experience. Medical assisting is a profession that requires understanding the theory or cognitive base and then applying psychomotor skills or hands-on experience. You will acquire knowledge by learning the principles and then performing the procedures. Students who do not establish a cognitive base and only learn the rote procedure are not able to apply critical thinking or judgment. They usually have difficulty performing when equipment varies or if a procedure is done differently but also correctly at the externship site. These students are often unable to function when the procedure does not go as planned. Be sure you understand the rationale or "why" for what you are doing. Do not just memorize steps.

Organization

Organization is planning and coordinating information and tasks in an orderly manner to efficiently complete the job in a given time frame. This attribute has many aspects including **time management** and **prioritizing.** A medical assistant must have good organizational skills to function in a busy practice. The phone may be ringing at the same time a patient is trying to schedule a follow-up appointment while the physician is inquiring about the results of a diagnostic report and a coworker is asking for information on a specific insurance plan. Organization is required to know how to prioritize the issues and tasks while addressing them all in an efficient and timely manner. You are probably noticing that professional behaviors are not isolated but are integrated. This means they fit together. Knowledge, comprehension, judgment, and other skills are all necessary for effective organizing.

Communication

Communication is giving and receiving accurate information. The key word is accurate. If a person is a bad communicator, it means that he or she cannot communicate or provide information that is accurate or understandable. Sometimes the patient leaves the office confused because he or she did not understand medical terms that were used and did not communicate that he or she did not understand. Sometimes the student leaves class confused because he or she did not understand the assignment and did not communicate to the instructor that he or she did not understand. In these scenarios, communication was poor from the sender since it was not understood. It was also poor from the receiver since lack of understanding was not communicated back to the sender. Effective communication is a two-way process with a responsibility on both sides. It impacts every aspect of health care and is discussed in-depth in Chapter 4, Professional Communication.

Integrity

Integrity is adhering to the appropriate code of law and ethics and being honest and trustworthy. This behavior involves relatively simple matters such as not taking pens home from the workplace to more complex matters such as always being truthful with patients. It also deals with subjects that are punishable and illegal such as taking cash or cheating on an exam or falsifying a time card. Falsifying a time card is clearly dishonest but knowingly extending breaks or lunches demonstrates a lack of integrity. The employee is not working the full time that he or she is paid to work. The same applies for externship time since the student is receiving credit. This does not refer to **compensation time,** which is time off given for working extra without pay or credit. Knowing that a coworker or a classmate is doing something dishonest is another area of integrity (Figure 2–3). If you do not report your facts or suspicion of the act, you could be considered an accomplice or an abettor and also be subject to a penalty. Besides causing

harm, once a person is involved in a dishonest act or is seen as lacking integrity, it is very difficult to regain the trust of others.

Growth

Growth is an ongoing effort to learn and improve. Being a professional brings with it an obligation to keep up with new standards, methods, procedures, and technologies in the field. Throughout this text you will learn up-to-date material in the areas of administrative medical assisting. Examples are the electronic health record which is still an unknown to some working professionals and the new diagnostic coding system which will be fully implemented in 2013. As discussed in the previous chapter, once you graduate, you should join one or more of the medical assisting professional organizations such as the AAMA and AMT. Besides the benefits, you are expected to earn a specific amount of **continuing education units (CEU)** within a specified time frame. These are credits given by the organization for participating in approved professional educational offerings. Examples are attending seminars, reading articles, taking courses, and completing CEU modules which may be online, on a DVD, or in print (Figure 2–4). These processes include the most pertinent, interesting, and current information in the field and keep you up-to-date. Crash Taylor, a photographer, wrote: *If you are not learning, you are not growing. If you are not growing, you are not really living.*

Cooperation

Cooperation is working with others in the best interest of completing the job. Chapter 3 describes portions of the large, complex health-care team. Like any other team, if its members work together and cooperate with each other, the likelihood of achieving the goal increases. Also, studies show that in workplaces where staff cooperate and help each other, job satisfaction and patient (client) satisfaction are high.

Imagine what would happen to a soccer team if each player was going in his or her own direction and no one knew where the real goal was! In the medical practice, the overall goal should be providing good patient care. Imagine the following example where your role is to confirm that a visit or procedure is covered by the patient's insurance. Appointments fill quickly and there is concern that an opening may not be available by the time the insurance confirmation is received. You and the scheduler work together (cooperate). Your coworker will schedule the first available appointment. When you receive approval, you will confirm it with the scheduler who will then confirm the appointment with the patient. This may not be considered a formal part of your jobs but you are working as a team to ensure care for the patient, which is the primary concern. Cooperation may also require **coordination,** which is the integration of activities (Figure 2–5). Today's typical patient may have three or more physician specialists, several prescriptions, home health care, routine blood work, physical therapy, hospital care, and outpatient procedures. This requires multiple appointments, insurance companies, medical claims, prior authorizations, and other processes which you will learn in future chapters. Frequently, the coordination of patient care activities is the role of the administrative medical assistant and requires cooperation with other staff and members of the health-care team outside of the office.

Acceptance of Criticism

Acceptance of criticism is the willingness to consider feedback and suggestions to improve; it is taking responsibility for one's actions. In this context,

figure 2-3

There are consequences for cheating.

continuing education units (CEU)
Credits given by a professional organization for participating in approved educational offerings to maintain membership.

cooperation
Working with others in the best interest of completing the job.

coordination
Integration of activities.

figure 2–4

This medical assistant is attending a seminar to stay current in the profession.

constructive criticism
A type of critique that is aimed at giving an individual feedback about his or her performance in order to improve that performance.

empathy
Feeling and understanding another's experience without having the experience yourself.

figure 2–5

Cooperation in the medical office is essential for good patient care.

constructive criticism is what is addressed. It is defined as counseling or advice that is intended to be useful with the goal of improving something. Earlier, the professional attribute of growth was discussed. It is difficult to grow and understand the areas in which improvement is needed if you do not receive feedback or constructive criticism. This may come from medical assisting educators, classmates, preceptors, physicians, other coworkers during your externship, and even patients. Throughout your education and workplace experience you will be evaluated. As human beings, no one is perfect and improvements can always be made. Be open to accepting criticism and suggestions. Offer your own thoughts on what you may do to improve. Do not be defensive and do not blame others. It is not about what your classmate or coworker does, it is about you.

Relations with Others

Relations with others is the ability to get along with those around you. This involves treating everyone with respect and caring even when it is difficult. This sometimes includes **empathy,** feeling and understanding another's experience without having the experience yourself. In the health-care environment the medical assistant works with many patients who are experiencing great loss. It may be the loss of their own health or function or a terminal diagnosis. It may be a personal loss such as death of a spouse. As in any other workplace, coworkers also experience losses and unfortunate events. Sometimes medical assistants are very kind to patients but do not exhibit the same behaviors with coworkers. They may become involved in gossip and pettiness or display impatience and rudeness. Two additional concerns frequently arise with people that go into helping industries such as health care: confusing caring with enabling and lacking professional boundaries.

Caring and Enabling   Caring is showing concern and appropriate attention. Enabling or codependency in this context is doing for others the things that they should be doing for themselves. When you enable, you become part of the disease process. A young medical assistant learned this early in her career when she became attached to a 10-year-old juvenile diabetic patient of an indigent family. Every time the child came into the office, the MA gave her a stuffed animal or cute T-shirt or other gift. The patient started to have more and more problems and the office visits became more frequent. An experienced medical assistant pointed out that the child was being rewarded for not managing her illness. This exemplifies enabling or codependency. Instead of giving a gift (reward) for not managing the disease and becoming ill, the two medical assistants developed a reward system for the patient if her diabetes was kept under control. This system became a model for all juvenile diabetics in the practice.

Professional   Boundaries   Having professional boundaries or limitations means always treating a patient as a client and not becoming involved in issues of his or her private life that do not directly relate to the health care. This is often difficult, especially with patients that you see often and particularly enjoy, and with patients you feel you may be able to help in addition to providing care in the medical office. Generally,

the guidelines for maintaining professional boundaries are:

- Address the patient only by his or her last name unless first asking permission to use his or her first name (children are an exception)
- Avoid offering advice on personal matters
- Use only tasteful, appropriate humor
- Avoid becoming *excessively* friendly
- Decline meeting a patient outside of the workplace unless you were acquainted prior to taking your position
- Avoid giving a patient money

If you are in doubt concerning a situation involving professional boundaries, consult your medical assisting educator, practice manager, or other supervisory personnel.

Patient Advocacy   As an administrative medical assistant, you may be in a situation to speak or to act on behalf of the patient or the patient's family. This is called **patient advocacy.** Understanding *enabling* and *boundaries* helps you in determining when it is appropriate to advocate for the patient. Be sure you have all the facts before you act, and include the physician when suitable. Tables 2–2 and 2–3 provide additional guidelines.

Respect and Cultural Diversity   Relations with others include respect for the individual and the individual's culture. Today's health-care facilities serve

EHR readiness

Cooperation and Coordination

Cooperation and coordination are essential for good patient care (Figure 2–5). The **electronic health record (EHR),** which is addressed in detail in Chapter 15, is a tremendous tool that exemplifies these attributes. The systems are designed to allow immediate and retrievable information that enhances the coordination of all office procedures and patient care. Cooperation is simplified and "built in" when everyone is using the same processes and terminology. The EHR is a vital emerging health-care technology. An EHR feature is placed in subsequent chapters that relates to a use of the electronic health record applicable to the specific chapter. Some working medical assistants have not yet experienced the new process. You may be the only one at your externship site that has a detailed familiarity with the EHR.

electronic health record (EHR)
A computerized system of the patient's medical record allowing tracking and transmission of documentation of histories, care, orders, results, reports, and administrative functions.

patient advocacy
The act of speaking and acting on behalf of the patient's needs and well-being.

table 2-2

Guidelines for Patient Advocacy

CIRCUMSTANCE	EXAMPLE	SUGGESTED ACTION
Concern for the individual's safety	You suspect an elderly patient is being abused	Discuss with physician; follow legal requirements and office protocols for reporting suspected elderly abuse (Chapter 6 discusses your legal responsibilities)
A complex situation requires your level of expertise	A patient is having difficulty with an insurance claim	Assist the patient as needed
A potentially untoward situation exists that your knowledge may help avoid or resolve (you will learn about HIPAA and patient confidentiality in coming chapters)	You are aware that a patient will not fill a prescription for an expensive drug because he cannot afford the insurance copay	Inform the physician who may prescribe a generic version of the drug; if that is not in the patient's best interest, with the physician's approval, contact the drug company (sometimes protocols are available for people who cannot afford the medication)
Giving extra attention is likely to benefit the patient	You are reviewing a one-year-old patient's demographic profile and notice that she is probably eligible for the Women, Infants, and Children (WIC) nutritional program.	Take the time to explain the program to the mother and provide the information for her to enroll (Chapter 5, Patient Education, discusses community resources)

CIRCUMSTANCE	EXAMPLE	SUGGESTED ACTION
The patient is capable of advocating for himself or herself	The patient does not want to tell the physician that he does not understand why he needs a proposed procedure	Encourage the patient to talk to the physician and assure him it is not unusual for patients to not fully understand the first time information is presented
Anything that can be considered medical advice or a medical recommendation should be avoided	The patient is asking your telephone advice regarding his symptoms	Avoid saying anything that involves a potential diagnosis such as "that sounds like the flu"; follow the office protocol for scheduling an appointment
The action interferes with your job duties or presents a potential liability	A patient asks you to keep an eye on her children during her exam	Suggest the patient reschedule when she can arrange childcare; if needed, provide a contact number for a facility close to the office
There are reasonable options	A patient forgets to fill his monthly prescriptions and is consistently asking for an emergency refill. The office policy is that refills will be processed in three business days. He wants you to call and remind him each month.	Suggest to the patient that many pharmacies provide a monthly automatic refill or a monthly reminder

table 2–3

Guidelines for Caution

cultural diversity
The variety of human social structures, belief systems, and strategies for adapting to situations in different parts of the world.

patients from many countries who speak many languages (Figure 2–6). The variety of human social structures, belief systems, and strategies for adapting to situations in different parts of the world is referred to as **cultural diversity.** As you proceed through your education, you will learn the majority of customs were practical responses to issues faced by the various groups of people. For example, the traditional older Navajo or Dineh consider it rude to look you in the eye. This custom came from living in the dwelling called a hogan that is a large five-sided open room. To allow privacy, family members kept their eyes down and avoided looking directly at each other as a sign of respect. Chapter 4, Professional Communication, discusses cultural diversity. Showing respect to all individuals regardless of culture or socioeconomic standing is a highly valued professional attribute that impacts your relations with others.

figure 2–6

Health-care facilities care for patients of many cultures.

Working with the Health-Care Team

MEDICAL ASSISTING EDUCATOR (INSTRUCTOR, PROFESSOR)

Duties and Skills

Typical skills required of the medical assisting educator, instructor, or professor are expertise in the area of instruction, ability to teach and train, a courteous and respectful manner with students and staff, strong organization skills, good time-management skills, demonstrated evidence of growth and academic currency, good communication skills, and knowledge of relevant technology.

The duties of the medical assisting educator include teaching and instruction; revising and updating curriculum and course content; meeting with, advising, and counseling students as appropriate; and promoting and maintaining positive relationships with externship sites and other community partners. The medical assisting educator is also expected to attend department and other meetings, to serve on committees, and to participate in the school's accreditation and evaluation processes. Other responsibilities may include managing the skills laboratory and laboratory assistants and ordering textbooks and materials.

Educational Requirements

The educational requirements are specific to the institution. Generally, the minimum of an associate's degree or higher in medical assisting or a related field is required with a minimum amount of employment in the health-care setting, for example, five years. Also, a credential, such as CMA (AAMA), RMA (AMT), CMAS (AMT), or RN is necessary along with current cardiopulmonary resuscitation (CPR) certification.

Workplace Settings

The medical assisting educator may teach in a post-secondary private school or community college medical assisting program. In addition, large organizations, such as a community health center with multiple sites, may employ the educator to assess skills of newly hired medical assistants and to provide in-service training for new and updated skills.

The Medical Assistant Educator as a Team Member

The medical assistant educator works closely with medical practices to ensure the curriculum reflects the community needs and to provide availability of quality externship sites for students. This person may also be employed in the health-care setting as an MA while teaching. Medical practices participate on the medical assisting program's advisory committee and precept its externs who are monitored by the educator. This role may also facilitate employment placement for graduates. Medical assisting education and the medical practice are an example of a win-win partnership.

For more information, visit the Web sites of the following organizations, which are available on the Online Learning Center at www.mhhe.com/houseradminmedassist

American Association of Medical Assistants

American Medical Technologists

Work Quality

Work quality means striving for excellence in doing the job and having pride in your performance. If you feel you need improvement in an area or would like to learn a new skill, consider taking a course, asking your supervisor or a coworker for help, or spending more time in that area. If you have an idea to improve a work process, make a suggestion. If you see something that is a potential risk, report it. Never say "it is not my job." If it is not your job, simply state that you will get the person who can help and then get that person. Being flexible is another part of work quality. If a staff member is absent or the schedule changes, the important thing is to get the job done. Again, do not worry about whose job it is as long as you are staying within your scope of practice. In striving for excellence within your own job performance, this may also involve assisting your teammates in *being the best that they can be*. People who perform quality work want to be employed in a place where everyone exemplifies quality and does a good job. Quality in the workplace will be discussed in Chapter 22.

work quality
Striving for excellence in doing the job; pride in one's performance.

Punctuality and Attendance

Being on time—**punctuality**—and coming to work every day that you are scheduled is essential for maintaining your job. Poor attendance is a frequent reason for termination. This is a behavior that speaks for itself. You are expected to be

punctuality
Showing up on appointed days and times.

The Invaluable Medical Assistant

The medical assistant who exhibits the professional behaviors discussed in this chapter is invaluable to the medical office. To assist you in becoming an invaluable medical assistant, the chapters of this book contain the Practice Readiness feature. It will present a topic related to each chapter that aids you in preparing for your role in the medical practice. Becoming practice ready is a huge asset in your externship and in obtaining a job.

---

figure 2-7

Tobacco smoke may intensify nausea and allergies.

at your duty station or in your classroom ready to work at the given time. Ready to work means no breakfast at your desk, no personal telephone calls during duty or class time, no gossiping with coworkers or classmates, and no excuses. Whether you are late or absent as a result of poor planning or an emergency, it still means that either your job is not getting done or you created additional work for your teammates. Patient care is impacted when you are not present.

Professional Appearance

In most medical practices, a type of uniform is required for all employees. Health-care employers generally have a standard of dress that may include restrictions on body art such as tattoos, body piercings, and unnatural colors for hair. Patients tend to lack confidence in staff that do not have an appropriate appearance for their role. Good personal hygiene is an absolute must. Patients with immunocompromised systems cannot afford to be around someone whose dirty hair or hands contain bacteria. Body odors related to hygiene issues are offensive. This includes the smell of tobacco smoke (Figure 2-7). However, even pleasant odors such as hairspray, perfumes, lotions, and so on may trigger nausea or allergies in some patients and should be avoided. Artificial nails, gels, and wraps are usually restricted in the direct patient care areas but, where allowed, should be clean and tasteful and not impair the ability to carry out the job. You may be the first point of contact for the patient. Ensure you are a good representative for the practice.

CHECKPOINT
LO 2.2

Select one of the professional behaviors discussed in this chapter. Give an example of why that behavior is important in medical assisting.

LO 2.3 Strategies for Success in the Medical Assisting Program

Incorporating professional behaviors in the workplace will result in your becoming an invaluable medical assistant. These behaviors or attributes will also contribute to success in medical assisting education. Some schools use a tool similar to the rubric found in Figure 2-8 to evaluate students' readiness before beginning the externship. It may also be utilized throughout the training program. In addition to the professional behaviors, the following strategies for success in your medical assisting educational program may be offered:

- Make your administrative medical assistant program a priority; it is a relatively short amount of time and worth it.
- Keep up with class work.

figure 2–8

Professional behaviors assessment rubric.

PROFESSIONAL BEHAVIORS ASSESSMENT
Student's Name: _____
Be honest as you complete this self-assessment. It is for your benefit.
Rate yourself on each behavior. Create an improvement plan for behaviors that are questionable or unacceptable.
Decide on specific time intervals to review your progress, for example every week or every month.
You may ask a classmate to assess you and compare that student's ratings with your own.

BEHAVIOR	1 *Unacceptable*	2 *Questionable*	3 *Acceptable*	4 *Super*	5 *Rating*	6 *Comments*
COMPREHENSION Ability to learn, retain, and process information in a reasonable time	Responds slowly and with poor understanding or does not retain information.	Is inconsistent in learning or retaining information. Sometimes does well and other times not.	Learns information in reasonable time. Retention is adequate.	Understands all concepts and details; learns new things easily. Retention is excellent.		
PERSISTENCE Ability to continue in spite of difficulty; determined; tenacious	Fails to finish work on time, gives up easily, or puts forth little effort.	Sometimes does not finish work as assigned or has a tendency to give up easily.	Follows through on assignments.	Follows through on assignments despite challenges; never gives up.		
SELF-CONFIDENCE Believes in oneself; assured	Overconfident; unaware of own limitations or inability to act Independently.	Indecisive, cannot proceed without reassurance.	Generally acts independently with minimal reassurance.	Approaches assignments with full knowledge and no hesitation; checks when appropriate.		
JUDGMENT Ability to evaluate, come to appropriate conclusion, and act; critical thinking	Frequently does not evaluate, reach appropriate conclusion, or act; never or seldom thinks critically.	Does not consistently evaluate or come to appropriate conclusion; limited critical thinking.	Evaluates, reaches appropriate conclusion, and acts; uses critical thinking.	Consistently analyzes situations; performs well in complex situations.		
KNOWLEDGE Understanding through study and experience; associating theory with practice	Poor understanding or difficulty associating theory with practice.	Inadequate understanding or inability to consistently associate theory with practice.	Possesses adequate understanding; associates theory with practice.	Demonstrates superior understanding and ability to associate theory with practice.		
Comment Section:						

(Continued)

figure 2-8 *(Continued)*

BEHAVIOR	1 *Unacceptable*	2 *Questionable*	3 *Acceptable*	4 *Super*	5 *Rating*	6 *Comments*
ORGANIZATION Independent tasks are planned and completed properly and orderly in a given time	Poor or no planning with extra steps. Improper performance. Delay. Work area in disorder.	Occasional poor planning or performance. Delay. Work area in disorder.	Sequences steps as directed. Ability to coordinate more than one task. Work area in order.	Anticipates future work. Performs multiple tasks simultaneously and systematically. Work area impeccable.		
COMMUNICATION Ability to give and receive clear, accurate Information	Difficulty due to inability to encode, decode; language or other barriers.	Does not consistently communicate adequately or clearly.	Standard communication.	Consistently uses good encoding and decoding with extreme tact and professionalism.		
INTEGRITY Sound and honest decision making within acceptable code of values*	Likely to make poor decisions or inability to function within acceptable code of values.	Actions suggest personal considerations may outweigh code of values.	Trustworthy. Makes appropriate decisions.	Role model for code of values.		
GROWTH Continual striving to improve and learn new material	Puts forth little effort or interest in improving or personal Responsibility.	Tries to improve when asked to do so; content with passing grades but can do better.	Consistently puts forth effort to learn and Improve. Accepts criticism.	Always striving for improvement; seeks feedback; has career plan.		
COOPERATION Appropriately and willingly works with others in the best interest of the work	Uncooperative when asked to perform a task; irritates others; is inclined to be quarrelsome.	Does not consistently cooperate with others.	Cooperates with others in agreeable manner.	Always appropriately helpful; others enjoy working with him/her; uses tact in getting job done.		
ACCEPTANCE OF CRITICISM Willing to consider suggestions and observations	Frequently rejects or is defensive of appropriate criticism. Demonstrates hostility.	Sometimes defensive of appropriate criticism from faculty or peers.	Accepts most criticism.	Accepts and appreciates appropriate criticism. Offers suggestions for correction.		

* Code of values refers to student handbook, catalog syllabus, other guidelines.

Comment Section:

(Continued)

figure 2-8 *(Concluded)*

BEHAVIOR	1 *Unacceptable*	2 *Questionable*	3 *Acceptable*	4 *Super*	5 *Rating*	6 *Comments*
RELATIONS WITH OTHERS Ability to appropriately get along with others	Shows lack of respect or patience or avoids others or disruptive.	Has occasional difficulty in routine program relationships.	Gets along with others; handles routine interactions appropriately.	Has superior ability to deal with others; is respected by peers and faculty; respects all.		
QUALITY OF WORK Striving for excellence in performing work	Work contains an unacceptable % of errors or shows evidence of minimal effort.	Does not seem to have quite enough concern about the quality of his/her work.	Quality of work is adequate.	Work is consistently close to perfection.		
PUNCTUALITY AND ATTENDANCE Coming to work/ class on appointed days and times	Chronically late or absences excessive to expectations* or takes "extended" breaks.	Occasionally late or absent or takes "extended" break.	Never late or absent with the exception of a rare emergency; takes appropriate breaks.	Never late or absent; takes appropriate breaks.		
PROFESSIONAL APPEARANCE Adherence to dress code; practices good hygiene	Very untidy. Doesn't follow dress code. Has hygiene issues or inappropriate body art.**	Sometimes untidy and careless about appearance or hygiene. Problem with body art.	Generally neat and clean. Adheres to dress code. Body art appropriately covered.	Always impeccable personal appearance. Properly attired all of the time. No body art.		

*Expectations are defined in syllabi and policies and procedures.
**As described in program policies.

Comments:

Reviewed _____ Date: _____

Reviewed _____ Date: _____

Reviewed _____ Date: _____

- Organize class and study materials on the first day of each course.
- Ask for clarification if you do not understand material or assignments.
- Plan your study time and stick to it.
- Select a "buddy" in class and exchange phone numbers; in the event you must be absent or late your buddy can provide missed material.
- Seek support of family and friends to help you stay on track.
- Avoid family and friends that are not supportive.
- Make flashcards to study (they help you memorize concepts by writing the cards and also provide the opportunity for family and friends to quiz you).
- Consider joining a study group.
- If you are an English language learner, study with a student who is a native English language speaker to ensure correct understanding of material.
- Look for physical exercise opportunities; take stairs instead of the elevator; use the furthest parking spot from the building.
- Make a strong effort to eat properly and avoid fast food; this endeavor is more successful when the entire class is involved.
- Buy a small book of motivational thoughts and read daily.
- Plan a celebration when you reach your goal.

CHECKPOINT
LO 2.3

Think about what area of your life might impede you from completing your medical assisting education. What is it and what will you do to "fix it"?

Procedure 2-1 Professional Behavior Self-Assessment

GOAL To conduct a self-assessment of professional behaviors as a baseline for personal and professional growth and development

MATERIALS Professional behavior rubric (Figure 2–8), pen or pencil

METHOD
1. Rate yourself according to the four possible choices on the professional behavior rubric (Figure 2–8).
2. Create a self-improvement plan for any of your behaviors that are unacceptable or questionable (ask your instructor or the program director for assistance if needed).
3. Tell an instructor, classmate, family member, or friend the areas you are focused on improving. Research demonstrates that telling someone, especially in public, increases the chances of success.
4. Review your original self-assessment at specific intervals selected by you to monitor your improvement (mark your calendar now for the interval you chose; suggestions are weekly, monthly, or by class).
5. (Optional) Ask a colleague or instructor to rate you using the rubric one month into your medical assisting program.
6. File the rubric in a safe place for further use prior to your externship.

Case Study

Donesha is a medical assisting student. She does well with the "hands on" skills and gets along fairly well with her teachers and classmates; however, Donesha's problem is getting to school on time. Her reasons generally show a pattern of poor planning, such as missing the bus, forgetting to set the alarm, and returning home for an assignment she forgot. The school has a strict policy on punctuality and attendance. Following the fourth time she was late, Donesha was placed on a performance improvement plan. The plan states that if she is late again she may not proceed to her externship as scheduled. Donesha feels this is unjust since she believes that she makes an effort to be on time and when she has been late it has not been her fault. Donesha also shared with the Medical Assisting Program Director that it would be different when she went to her externship.

Thinking Critically

1. Why do you think the school has a strict policy on punctuality and attendance?
2. Should tardiness be excused if it is not the student's fault?
3. Do you think Donesha's inability to be on time would change during her externship?

practice APPLICATIONS

1. Role play the following scenario with another student in your class:

   Two medical assistants are sitting in the staff lounge having lunch. One medical assistant begins to gossip about a staff member who is not present. The other medical assistant does not like to gossip. She is reluctant to stop her lunch companion since she is afraid it may upset her but she also does not want to be a partner in this discussion.

   What do they say? Act out the conversation.

2. Ask five people outside of your medical assisting program what gives them confidence in the staff in their doctors' office. Inform them they are not to include technical skills.

exam READINESS

There may be more than one correct answer. Circle the best answer.

1. **[LO2.2]** An indication that a person lacks integrity would be exhibited by

   a. being rude to a coworker.
   b. coming into work late.
   c. ignoring the dress code.
   d. taking money from the cash drawer.
   e. gossiping.

2. **[LO2.2]** Good communication is primarily the responsibility of the

   a. physician and practice manager.
   b. physician and medical assistant.
   c. patient and insurance company.
   d. medical educator and student.
   e. sender and receiver.

3. **[LO2.1]** The primary reason an employee is hired is usually associated with their

   a. hard skills.
   b. soft skills.
   c. references.
   d. punctuality.
   e. cooperation.

4. **[LO2.2]** An example of a hard skill is

   a. making an appointment.
   b. keeping your work area orderly.
   c. having self-confidence.
   d. being persistent.
   e. lacking good judgment.

5. **[LO2.2]** A significant part of critical thinking is

   a. memorizing.
   b. analyzing.
   c. being tenacious.
   d. empathizing.
   e. criticizing.

6. **[LO2.2]** Adhering to the dress code and good personal hygiene demonstrates

   a. persistence.
   b. growth.
   c. respect.
   d. knowledge.
   e. organization.

7. **[LO2.2]** If a medical assistant is not self-confident, this may lead to the patient feeling

   a. confident.
   b. neglected.
   c. apprehensive.
   d. ignored.
   e. ill.

8. **[LO2.2]** An example of enabling or codependency would be

   a. providing a wheelchair for a patient who is weak.
   b. helping a patient identify a community resource.
   c. scheduling the patient's next appointment.
   d. offering cookies to a morbidly obese patient.
   e. calling a taxi for a patient.

9. **[LO2.1]** Maintaining professional boundaries involves

   a. showing the patient you care by being personal.
   b. being friendly but not excessively affectionate.
   c. avoiding any touch with the patient.
   d. babysitting for the patient.
   e. buying the patient lunch.

10. **[LO2.3]** When the practice manager points out to the medical assistant that he is not scheduling the patients correctly resulting in long waiting times, this is referred to as

    a. bashing.
    b. being insensitive.
    c. disciplining.
    d. relating with others.
    e. providing constructive criticism.

learning outcome SUMMARY

LO 2.1 Professionalism is behavior that exhibits the traits or features corresponding to the standards of that profession which, in this case, is administrative medical assisting. Standards are developed by professional organizations and, in some states, by governmental entities. The skills are placed in two broad categories: hard skills and soft skills. Hard skills are specific technical and operational proficiencies. Soft skills are personal attributes or behaviors that enhance an individual. Professional behaviors are needed to function at a high level in medical assisting and produce what is called a good work ethic. You will continually experience assessment of your professional behaviors in the classroom, externship, hiring process, workplace performance evaluation, and consideration for promotion.

LO 2.2 The professional behaviors described in this chapter include comprehension, persistence, self-confidence, judgment, knowledge, organization, communication, integrity, growth, cooperation, acceptance of criticism, relations with others, work quality, punctuality and attendance, and professional appearance. Table 2–1 provides a description of each.

LO 2.3 Professional behaviors also contribute to success in medical assisting education. Some schools use a behavioral tool to evaluate students' readiness before beginning the externship. Other strategies for successful program completion involve planning, keeping up with the work, and using methods and family and friends to stay motivated.

medical assisting COMPETENCIES

CAAHEP

IV. C (13) Identify the role of self boundaries in the health-care environment

IV. C (14) Recognize the role of patient advocacy in the practice of medical assisting

IV. A (6) Demonstrate awareness of how an individual's personal appearance affects anticipated responses

IV. A (9) Recognize and protect personal boundaries when communicating with others

X. A (1) Apply ethical behaviors, including honesty/integrity in performance of medical assisting practice

X. A (2) Examine the impact personal ethics and morals may have on the individual's practice

ABHES

5. Psychology of Human Relations
   e. Advocate on behalf of family/patients, having ability to deal and communicate with family

11. Career Development
   b. Demonstrate professionalism by:
      (1) Exhibiting dependability, punctuality, and a positive work ethic

      (2) Exhibiting a positive attitude and a sense of responsibility
      (5) Exhibiting initiative
      (6) Adapting to change
      (7) Expressing a responsible attitude

3 The Health-Care Team

Learning Outcomes

After completing Chapter 3, you will be able to:

3.1 Identify medical specialties and specialists certified by the American Board of Medical Specialties (ABMS).

3.2 Explain the duties of various allied health professionals with whom medical assistants may work.

3.3 Distinguish the organization structure of various health-care practice settings.

3.4 Differentiate the professional associations that may help advance an administrative medical assistant's career.

Key Terms

acupuncturist
allergist
American Board of
    Medical Specialties
    (ABMS)
anesthetist
autopsy
biopsy
cardiologist
chiropractor
dermatologist
doctor of osteopathy
endocrinologist
family practitioner
gastroenterologist
gerontologist
gynecologist
internist
massage therapist

nephrologist
neurologist
oncologist
orthopedist
osteopathic
    manipulative
    medicine (OMM)
otorhinolaryngologist
pathologist
pediatrician
physiatrist
plastic surgeon
podiatrist
primary care physician
proctologist
radiologist
surgeon
triage
urologist

Preparation for Certification

RMA (AMT) Exam
- Ethical conduct
- Licensure, certification, registration

CMAS (AMT) Exam
- Participate in appropriate continuing education

CMA (AAMA) Exam
- Professionalism

Introduction • • •

Administrative medical assistants are an integral part of a health-care delivery team. As such, you should recognize the many different physician specialists and allied health professions. Administrative medical assistants work in various roles and must be in contact with multiple other health-care team members on an ongoing basis. For example, administrative medical assistants are asked to call and process insurance referrals to different specialties and diagnostic departments. A working knowledge of the different specialties and allied health professionals demonstrates professionalism and competence and assists the administrative medical assistant in developing a spirit of cooperation.

LO 3.1 Medical Specialties

Since the beginning of the 20th century, some physicians have specialized in particular areas of study. According to the **American Board of Medical Specialties (ABMS),** there are now approximately 24 major medical specialties approved in the United States. The primary purpose of the ABMS is to maintain and improve the quality of medical care and to certify doctors in various specialties. This organization helps the member boards develop professional and educational standards for physician specialists.

Within each medical specialty are several subspecialties. For example, cardiology is a major specialty; pediatric cardiology is a subspecialty. As advances in the diagnosis and treatment of diseases and disorders unfold, the demand for specialized care increases and more medical specialties emerge.

As an administrative medical assistant, it is helpful to understand the education and licensing process any medical doctor must undergo to become a board-certified physician.

American Board of Medical Specialties (ABMS)
An organization of different medical specialty boards. Its primary purpose is to maintain and improve the quality of medical care and to certify doctors in various specialties. This organization helps the member boards develop professional and educational standards for physician specialists.

Physician Education and Licensure

The educational requirements for physicians are rigorous and take several years to complete. To earn the title MD (doctor of medicine), thereby qualifying as a licensed physician, a student must complete a bachelor's degree with a concentration typically in the sciences. Then she must attend a medical school accredited by the Liaison Committee on Medical Education (LCME). Upon completing medical school, she is awarded the degree of MD, but this is not the end of her required medical training. She must also pass the U.S. Medical Licensing Examination (USMLE). This examination, commonly known as medical boards, has three parts. Part 1 is usually taken after the second year of medical school, part 2 during the fourth year of medical school, and part 3 during the first or second year of postgraduate medical training.

After medical school an MD begins a residency—a period of practical training in a hospital. The first year of residency is known as an internship. Once it is completed an MD can become certified by the National Board of Medical Examiners (NBME). After completing an internship and passing her medical boards, the MD becomes certified as an NBME Diplomate. If she wishes to specialize in a particular branch of medicine, she must complete an additional 2 to 6 years of residency. She also will apply to the ABMS to take an examination in her specialty area. After passing the examination, she will be board-certified in her area of specialization. For example, a physician who specializes in pediatrics would receive certification from the American Board of Pediatrics.

Family Practice

Family practitioners (sometimes called general practitioners) are MDs or DOs who are generalists and treat all types of illnesses and ages of patients. They do not specialize in a particular branch of medicine. Family practitioners are called

family practitioner
A physician who does not specialize in a branch of medicine but treats all types and ages of patients; also called a general practitioner.

primary care physician
A physician who provides routine medical care and referrals to specialists.

oncologist
A specialist who identifies tumors and treats patients who have cancer.

biopsy
The removal and examination of a sample of tissue from a living body for diagnostic purposes.

allergist
A specialist who diagnoses and treats physical reactions to substances including mold, dust, fur, pollen, foods, drugs, and chemicals.

anesthetist
A specialist who uses medications to cause patients to lose sensation or feeling during surgery.

cardiologist
A specialist who diagnoses and treats diseases of the heart and blood vessels (cardiovascular diseases).

dermatologist
A specialist who diagnoses and treats diseases of the skin, hair, and nails.

primary care physicians (PCPs) by insurance companies. The term refers to individual doctors who oversee patients' long-term health care. Some people, however, have internists or OB/GYNs as their primary care physician.

A family practitioner sends a patient to a specialist when the patient has a specific condition or disease that requires advanced care. For example, a family practitioner refers a patient with a lump in her breast to an **oncologist,** a specialist who treats tumors, or to a general surgeon. Either of these doctors may order a mammogram or an ultrasound (if these have not already been done). A needle **biopsy** of the lump is done by the specialist to determine if the lump is malignant.

Working in a general practice, you will encounter patients with many different conditions and illnesses. As in any medical setting, you must become knowledgeable about preventing the transmission of disease. This important topic is discussed in Chapter 9, Asepsis for Administrative Areas.

If you work for a general practitioner, you will often be responsible for arranging patient appointments with specialists. It is important, therefore, for you to know about the duties of each medical specialist.

Allergy

Allergists diagnose and treat physical reactions to substances, including mold, dust, fur, and pollen from plants or flowers. An individual with allergies is hypersensitive to substances such as drugs, chemicals, or elements in nature. An allergic reaction may be minor, such as a rash; serious, such as asthma; or life-threatening (capable of producing anaphylactic shock), such as swelling of the airways or nasal passages.

Anesthesiology

Anesthesiologists and **anesthetists** use medications that cause patients to lose sensation or feeling during surgery. These health-care practitioners administer anesthetics before, during, and sometimes even after surgery. They also educate patients regarding the anesthetic that will be used and its possible postoperative effects. An anesthesiologist is an MD. A certified registered nurse anesthetist (CRNA) is a registered nurse who has completed an additional program of study recognized by the American Association of Nurse Anesthetists.

Bariatrics

Bariatrics is the specialty of medicine that deals with the medical and surgical treatment of obesity. Bariatric surgery may be recommended for extremely obese patients who may suffer impaired health as a result of their weight. Prior to undergoing any type of bariatric surgery, candidates must first undergo counseling and other treatment options for weight management. Therapy before and after bariatric surgery is necessary for successful weight loss and improved health. There are several options available in bariatric surgery, such as gastric banding and gastric bypass.

Cardiology

Cardiologists diagnose and treat cardiovascular diseases (diseases of the heart and blood vessels). Cardiologists also read electrocardiograms (ECGs, which are sometimes referred to as EKGs) for hospital cardiology departments. They educate patients about the positive role healthy diet and regular exercise play in preventing and controlling heart disease.

Dermatology

Dermatologists diagnose and treat diseases of the skin, hair, and nails. Their patients have conditions ranging from warts and acne to skin cancer. Dermatologists

treat boils, skin injuries, and infections. They remove growths—such as moles, cysts, and birthmarks—and they treat scars and perform hair transplants.

Doctor of Osteopathy

Doctors of osteopathy, who hold the title of DO, practice a "whole-person" approach to health care. DOs believe that patients are more than just a sum of their body parts, and they treat the patient as a whole person instead of concentrating on specific symptoms. Osteopathic physicians understand how all the body's systems are interconnected and how each one affects the other. They focus special attention on the musculoskeletal system, which reflects and influences the condition of all other body systems.

One key concept that DOs believe is that structure influences function. If a problem exists in one part of the body, it may affect the function in both that area and other areas. DOs focus on the body's ability to heal itself and they actively engage patients in the healing process. By using **osteopathic manipulative medicine (OMM)** techniques, DOs can help restore motion to these areas of the body, thus improving function and often restoring health.

Emergency Medicine

Physicians who specialize in emergency medicine work in hospital emergency rooms and outpatient emergency care centers. They diagnose and treat patients with conditions resulting from an unexpected medical crisis or accident. Common emergencies include trauma, such as gunshot wounds or serious injuries from car accidents; other injuries, such as severe cuts; and sudden illness, such as alcohol or food poisoning. Emergency medicine practitioners stabilize their patients so they can then be managed by their PCP or other specialist.

Endocrinology

Endocrinologists diagnose and treat disorders of the endocrine system. This system regulates many body functions by circulating hormones that are secreted by organs and glands throughout the body. An example of a disorder treated by an endocrinologist is hypothyroidism, or a less than normal amount of thyroid hormone. This common disorder can cause a variety of symptoms including fatigue, weight gain, dry skin, and constipation.

Gastroenterology

Gastroenterologists diagnose and treat disorders of the gastrointestinal tract. These disorders include problems related to the functioning of the stomach, intestines, and associated organs.

Gerontology

Gerontologists study the aging process. Geriatrics is the branch of medicine that deals with the diagnosis and treatment of problems and diseases of the older adult. A specialist in geriatrics may also be called a geriatrician. As the population of older adults increases, there is a greater need for physicians who specialize in diagnosing and treating diseases of the elderly.

Gynecology

Gynecology is the branch of medicine that is concerned with diseases of the female genital tract. **Gynecologists** perform routine physical care and examination of the female reproductive system. Many gynecologists are also obstetricians.

Internal Medicine

Internists specialize in diagnosing and treating problems related to the internal organs. The internal medicine subspecialties include cardiology, critical care

doctor of osteopathy
A doctor who focuses special attention on the musculoskeletal system and uses hands and eyes to identify and adjust structural problems, supporting the body's natural tendency toward health and self-healing.

osteopathic manipulative medicine (OMM)
A system of hands-on techniques that help relieve pain, restore motion, support the body's natural functions, and influence the body's structure. Osteopathic physicians study OMM in addition to medical courses.

endocrinologist
A specialist who diagnoses and treats disorders of the endocrine system, which regulates many body functions by circulating hormones that are secreted by glands throughout the body.

gastroenterologist
A specialist who diagnoses and treats disorders of the entire gastrointestinal tract, including the stomach, intestines, and associated digestive organs.

gerontologist
A specialist who studies the aging process.

gynecologist
A specialist who performs routine physical care and examinations of the female reproductive system.

internist
A doctor who specializes in diagnosing and treating problems related to the internal organs.

medicine, diagnostic laboratory immunology, endocrinology and metabolism, gastroenterology, geriatrics, hematology, infectious diseases, medical oncology, nephrology, pulmonary disease, and rheumatology. Internists must be certified as specialists in these areas.

Nephrology

nephrologist
A specialist who studies, diagnoses, and manages diseases of the kidney.

Nephrologists study, diagnose, and manage diseases of the kidney. They may work in either a clinic or hospital setting. A medical assistant working with a nephrologist may assist in the operation of a dialysis unit for the treatment of patients with kidney failure, known as end stage renal disease (ESRD). In a rural setting a medical assistant might help a doctor operate a mobile dialysis unit that can be taken to the patient's home or to a medical practice that does not have this technology.

Neurology

neurologist
A specialist who diagnoses and treats disorders and diseases of the nervous system, including the brain, spinal cord, and nerves.

Neurology is the branch of medical science that deals with the nervous system. **Neurologists** diagnose and treat disorders and diseases of the nervous system, such as strokes. The nervous system is made up of the brain, spinal cord, and nerves that receive, interpret, and transmit messages throughout the body.

Nuclear Medicine

Nuclear medicine is a fast-growing specialty related to radiology. Nuclear medicine and radiology use radiation to diagnose and treat disease, but radiology beams radiation through the body from an outside source, whereas nuclear medicine introduces a small amount of a radioactive substance into the body and forms an image by detecting radiation as it leaves the body. The radiation that patients are exposed to is comparable to that of a diagnostic x-ray. Radiology reveals interior anatomy whereas nuclear medicine reveals organ function and structure. Noninvasive, painless nuclear medicine procedures are used to identify heart disease, assess organ function, and diagnose and treat cancer.

figure 3-1

Obstetricians who are part of a private practice are usually connected with a specific hospital where they help their patients through labor and delivery.

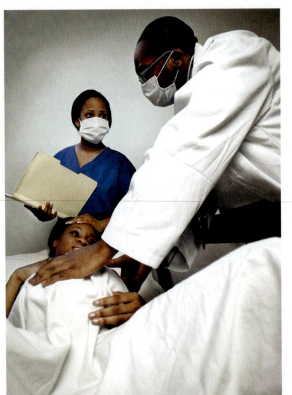

Obstetrics

Obstetrics involves the study of pregnancy, labor, delivery, and the period following labor called postpartum (Figure 3–1). This field is often combined with gynecology. A physician who practices both specialties is referred to as an obstetrician/gynecologist, or OB/GYN.

Oncology

Oncologists determine if tumors are benign or malignant, and treat patients with cancer. Treatment may involve chemotherapy, which is the administration of drugs to destroy cancer cells. Treatment may also involve radiation therapy, which kills cancer cells through the use of x-rays. Newer therapies include immune therapy and transplant techniques to urge the body to create healthy tissues to replace those affected by cancer. Oncologists treat both adults and children.

Ophthalmology

An ophthalmologist is an MD who diagnoses and treats diseases and disorders of the eye. This physician specialist examines patients' eyes for poor vision or disease. Other responsibilities include prescribing corrective lenses or

medication, performing surgery, and providing follow-up care after surgery. The specialty of ophthalmology includes two other practitioners who are not MDs. An optometrist obtains the credential of OD (optometric doctor). An optometrist specializes in diagnosing and treating visual defects with glasses and contacts. An optician is the specialist who works with ophthalmologists and optometrists by filling the prescriptions written by them for glasses and contact lenses.

Orthopedics

Orthopedics is a branch of medicine specializing in maintaining the function of the musculoskeletal system and its associated structures. An **orthopedist** diagnoses and treats diseases and disorders of the muscles and bones. Some orthopedists concentrate on treating sports-related injuries, either exclusively for professional athletes or for nonprofessionals of all ages. They are called sports medicine specialists.

orthopedist
A specialist who diagnoses and treats diseases and disorders of the muscles and bones.

Otorhinolaryngology

Otorhinolaryngology involves the study of the ear, nose, and throat. An **otorhinolaryngologist** diagnoses and treats diseases of these body structures. This physician specialist is also referred to as an ear, nose, and throat (ENT) specialist. Otorhinolaryngology is also called otolaryngology according to the American Academy of Otolaryngology.

otorhinolaryngologist
A specialist who diagnoses and treats diseases of the ear, nose, and throat.

Pathology

Pathology is the study of disease. It provides the scientific foundation for all medical practice. The **pathologist** studies the changes a disease produces in the cells, fluids, tissues, and processes of the entire body. These samples often come from biopsies, cultures, and tissue samples, but some pathologists also perform **autopsies,** examinations of the bodies of the deceased, to determine the cause of a patient's death and to advance the clinical practice of medicine.

There are two basic types of pathologists. Governments and police departments use forensic pathologists to determine facts about unexplained or violent crimes or deaths. Anatomic pathologists often work at hospitals in a research capacity, and they may read biopsies (samplings of cells that could be malignant).

pathologist
A medical doctor who studies the changes a disease produces in the cells, fluids, and processes of the entire body.

autopsy
The examination of a cadaver to determine or confirm the cause of death.

Pediatrics and Adolescent Medicine

Pediatrics is concerned with the development and care of children from birth until 18 (in some practices, up to 21) years and the diseases and conditions that affect children and adolescents. A **pediatrician** diagnoses and treats childhood diseases and teaches parents skills to keep their children healthy.

pediatrician
A specialist who diagnoses and treats childhood diseases and teaches parents skills for keeping their children healthy.

Physical Medicine

Physical medicine specialists **(physiatrists)** are physicians who specialize in physical medicine and rehabilitation. They are certified by the American Board of Physical Medicine and Rehabilitation to diagnose and treat diseases and disorders such as sore shoulders and spinal cord injuries. Physiatrists offer an aggressive, nonsurgical approach to pain and injury. Physical medicine specialists' patients include both adults and children.

physiatrist
A physical medicine specialist, who diagnoses and treats diseases and disorders with physical therapy.

Podiatry

Podiatry is practiced by a licensed doctor of podiatric medicine (DPM). A **podiatrist** is a podiatry professional devoted to the study and treatment of the foot and ankle. A podiatrist's education consists of an undergraduate degree

podiatrist
A physician who specializes in the study and treatment of the foot and ankle.

plus a doctoral level 4-year program followed by a 2- or 3-year residency. Podiatrists may independently diagnose, treat, prescribe medication, and perform surgery for disorders of the foot and, in some states, the ankle and leg. There are three board certification possibilities for podiatrists. The Board of Primary Care and Orthopedics is a nonsurgical Board Certification. The Surgical Board of Certification is divided into foot surgery and rear foot and ankle reconstruction surgery. The rear foot and ankle Board Certification requires at least a 3-year residency to qualify.

Plastic Surgery

A **plastic surgeon** performs the reconstruction, correction, or improvement of body structures. Patients may be accident victims or disfigured due to disease or abnormal development. Plastic surgery includes facial reconstruction, face-lifts, and skin grafting. Plastic surgery is also used to repair problems like cleft lip and cleft palate, as well as disfigurement and restrictive scarring due to trauma.

Proctology

Proctology is the branch of medicine that diagnoses and treats disorders of the anus, rectum, and intestines. **Proctologists** treat conditions such as colitis, hemorrhoids, fistulas, tumors, and ulcers. Proctologists often work closely with urologists.

Radiology

Radiology is the branch of medical science that uses x-rays and radioactive substances to diagnose and treat disease. **Radiologists** specialize in taking and reading x-rays.

Sports Medicine

Sports medicine is an interdisciplinary subspecialty of medicine that deals with the treatment and preventative care of amateur and professional athletes. Sports medicine teams consist of specialty physicians and surgeons, athletic trainers, and physical therapists. Sports medicine is more than treating injuries to the musculoskeletal system. Sports medicine can include an array of treatments, such as prevention and nutritional health.

Surgery

Surgeons use their hands and medical instruments to diagnose and correct deformities and treat external and internal injuries or disease (Figure 3–2). They work with many different specialists to surgically treat a broad range of disorders. General surgeons may, for example, perform operations as diverse as breast lumpectomy and repair of a pacemaker. There are also subspecialties of surgery, such as neurosurgery, vascular surgery, and orthopedic surgery.

Urology

A **urologist** diagnoses and treats diseases of the kidney, bladder, and urinary system. A urologist's patients include infants, children, and adults of all ages. Urologists also treat male reproductive diseases.

plastic surgeon
A specialist who reconstructs, corrects, or improves body structures.

proctologist
A physician who diagnoses and treats disorders of the anus, rectum, and intestines.

radiologist
A physician who specializes in taking and reading x-rays.

surgeon
A physician who uses hands and medical instruments to diagnose and correct deformities and treat external and internal injuries or disease.

urologist
A specialist who diagnoses and treats diseases of the kidney, bladder, and urinary system.

figure 3–2

Most surgeons specialize in a particular type of surgery, such as heart surgery or eye surgery.

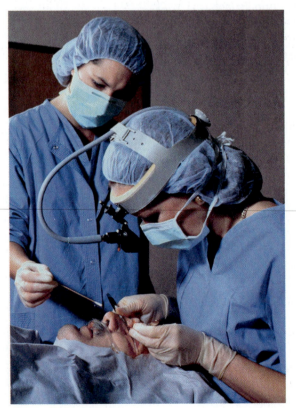

In which medical specialist's office would you most likely encounter the following patients?

1. A pregnant female

2. A patient over the age of 65

3. A patient under the age of 21

4. An athlete with an injury

5. A patient diagnosed with cancer

LO 3.2 Working with Other Allied Health Professionals

An administrative medical assistant is a member of a health-care team. That health-care team will include doctors, nurses, specialists, and the patients themselves. Contact with other members of the team will occur in person, electronically, or by telephone. You should recognize and understand the duties of other allied health professionals in order to be effective in your role as an administrative medical assistant. Following is an introduction to some common allied health professionals. Chapter 22 will discuss how health-care practices are organized.

Acupuncturist

Acupuncturists treat people with pain or discomfort by inserting thin, hollow needles under the skin. The points used for insertion are selected to balance the flow of *qi* (pronounced *chee),* or life energy, in the body. The theory of acupuncture relates to Chinese beliefs about how the body works. Qi is composed of two opposite forces called yin and yang. If the flow of qi is unbalanced, insufficient, or interrupted, then emotional, spiritual, mental, and physical problems will result. The acupuncturist works to balance these two forces in perfect harmony. Although there are variations in types of acupuncture—Chinese, Korean, and Japanese—all practitioners will focus on many pulse points along different meridians, the channels through which qi flows.

acupuncturist
A practitioner of acupuncture; an acupuncturist uses hollow needles inserted into the patient's skin to treat pain, discomfort, or systemic imbalances.

Chiropractor

Chiropractors treat people using manual treatments, although they may also employ physical therapy treatments, exercise programs, nutritional advice, and lifestyle modification to help correct problems causing the pain. The manual treatments, called adjustments, realign the vertebrae in the spine and restore the function of spinal nerves. Chiropractors use diagnostic testing such as x-rays, muscle testing, and posture analysis to determine the location of spinal misalignments, also called *subluxations.* Using their findings they develop a treatment plan that may require several adjustments per week for several weeks or months.

chiropractor
A physician who uses a system of therapy, including manipulation of the spine, to treat illness or pain. This treatment is done without drugs or surgery.

Electroencephalographic Technologist

Electroencephalography (EEG) is the study and recording of the electrical activity of the brain. It is used to diagnose diseases and irregularities of the brain. The EEG technologist (sometimes called a technician) attaches electrodes to the patient's scalp and connects them to a recording instrument. The machine then provides a written record of the electrical activity of the patient's brain. EEG technologists work in hospital EEG laboratories, clinics, and physicians' offices.

Electrocardiograph Technician

The electrocardiograph (ECG/EKG) technician is a trained professional who operates an electrocardiograph machine, as pictured in Figure 3–3. An ECG

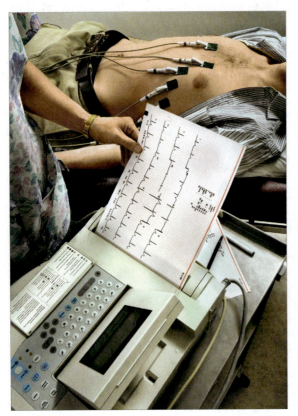

records the electrical impulses reaching the heart muscles. Physicians and cardiologists use the readings from this machine to detect heart abnormalities and to monitor patients with known cardiac problems. Electrocardiograph technicians generally work in hospitals and large clinics.

Massage Therapist

Massage therapists use pressure, kneading, stroking, vibration, and tapping to promote muscle and full-body relaxation as well as to increase circulation and lymph flow. Increasing circulation helps remove blood and waste products from injured tissues and brings fresh blood and nutrients to the areas to speed healing. Massage is one of the oldest methods of promoting healing and is used to treat strains, bruises, muscle soreness or tightness, lower back pain, and dislocations. It can also relieve muscle spasms, restore motion and function to a body part, and decrease edema.

Medical Technology

Medical technology is an umbrella term that refers to the development and design of clinical laboratory tests (such as diagnostic tests), procedures, and equipment. Two types of allied health professionals who work in medical technology are the clinical laboratory technician and the medical technologist.

figure 3–3

The electrocardiograph (ECG) technician is responsible for operating an electrocardiograph machine, which detects heart abnormalities and monitors patients with cardiac problems.

massage therapist
An individual who is trained to use pressure, kneading, and stroking to promote muscle and full-body relaxation.

Clinical laboratory technicians (CLTs) have 1- to 2-year degrees and are responsible for clinical tests performed under the supervision of a physician or medical technologist. They perform tests in the areas of hematology, serology, blood banking, urinalysis, microbiology, and clinical chemistry. Medical technologists examine specimens of human body tissues and fluids, analyze blood factors, and culture bacteria to identify disease-causing organisms. They also supervise and train technicians and laboratory aides. Medical technologists have 4-year degrees and may specialize in areas such as blood banking, microbiology, and chemistry.

Mental Health Technician

A mental health technician, sometimes called a psychiatric aide or counselor, works with emotionally disturbed and mentally challenged patients. This health professional assists the psychiatric team by observing behavior and providing information to help in the planning of therapy. The mental health technician also participates in supervising group therapy and counseling sessions. This technician may work in a psychiatric clinic, specialized nursing home, psychiatric unit of a hospital, or community health center. Other places of employment include crisis centers and shelters.

Nuclear Medicine Technologist

A nuclear medicine technologist performs tests to oversee quality control, to prepare and administer radioactive drugs, and to operate radiation detection instruments (Figure 3–4). This allied health professional is also responsible for correctly positioning the patient, performing imaging procedures, and preparing the information for use by a physician.

Occupational Therapist

An occupational therapist works with patients who have physical injuries or illnesses, psychological or developmental problems, or problems associated

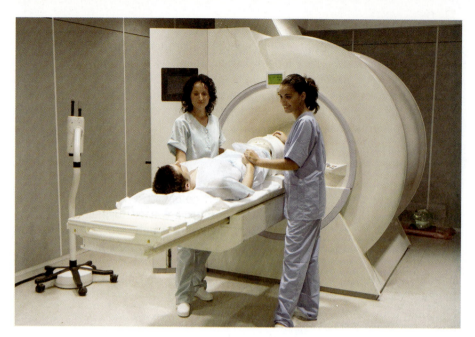

figure 3–4

A nuclear medicine technologist positions the patient, performs imaging procedures, and prepares the information for use by a physician.

with the aging process. This health professional helps patients attain maximum physical and mental health by using educational, vocational, and rehabilitation therapies and activities. The occupational therapist may work in a hospital, clinic, extended-care facility, rehabilitation hospital, or government or community agency.

Pharmacist

Pharmacists are professionals who have studied the science of drugs and who dispense medication and health supplies to the public. Pharmacists know the chemical and physical qualities of drugs and are knowledgeable about the companies that manufacture drugs.

Pharmacists inform the public about the effects of prescription and nonprescription (over-the-counter) medications. Pharmacists are employed in hospitals, clinics, and nursing homes. They may also work for government agencies, pharmaceutical companies, privately owned pharmacies, or chain store pharmacies. Some pharmacists own their own stores. A pharmacy technician (CPhT) can typically receive on-the-job training. Formal training, although not yet required by most states, includes certificate programs and 2-year college programs offering associate degrees in science. Voluntary certification is by examination. A registered pharmacist (RPh) requires 5 years of college training with a bachelor's degree in science. Pharmacists must be registered by the state and must pass a state board examination. A doctor of pharmacy (PharmD) requires 6 to 7 years of college training, which may be followed by a residency in a hospital setting.

Phlebotomist

Phlebotomists are allied health professionals trained to draw blood for diagnostic laboratory testing. They work in medical clinics, laboratories, and hospitals. Although medical assistants are also trained to draw blood for standard types of tests, phlebotomists are trained at a more advanced level to be able to draw blood under difficult circumstances or in special situations. For example, if a blood sample is needed for an ammonia-level test, it must be drawn and stored in a particular manner that only phlebotomists are trained to do. In most states phlebotomists must be certified by the National Phlebotomy Association or registered by the American Society of Clinical Pathologists.

Physical Therapist

A physical therapist (PT) plans and uses physical therapy programs for medically referred patients. The PT helps these patients to restore function, relieve pain, and prevent disability following disease, injury, or loss of body parts. A physical therapist uses various treatment methods, which include therapy with electricity, heat, cold, ultrasound, massage, and exercise. The physical therapist also helps patients accept their disabilities.

Radiographer

A radiographer (x-ray technician) is one of the most common positions for individuals whose education is in radiologic technology. The radiographer assists a radiologist in taking x-ray films. These films are used to diagnose broken bones, tumors, ulcers, and disease. A radiographer usually works in the radiology department of a hospital. The x-ray technician may, however, use mobile x-ray equipment in a patient's room or in the operating room. A radiographer may be employed in a hospital, laboratory, clinic, physician's office, government agency, or industry.

Registered Dietitian

Registered dietitians help patients and their families make healthful food choices that provide balanced, adequate nutrition particularly when disease or illness makes knowing what to eat to help fight the disease difficult. Dietitians are sometimes confused with nutritionists. Where a dietician has specialized training to assist ill patients with their nutritional needs, a nutritionist's goal is for those of us who are healthy to maintain a lifestyle of healthful eating. Dietitians may assist food-service directors at health-care facilities and prepare and serve food to groups. They may also participate in food research and teach nutrition classes. Dietitians work in community health agencies, hospitals, clinics, private practices, and managed care settings. They may also teach at colleges and universities, and they serve as consultants to organizations and individuals.

Radiologic Technologist

A radiologic technologist is a health-care professional who has studied the theory and practice of the technical aspects of the use of x-rays and radioactive materials in the diagnosis and treatment of disease. A radiologic technologist may specialize in radiography, radiation therapy, or nuclear medicine. Radiologic technologists generally work in hospitals; some work in medical laboratories, medical practices, and clinics.

Respiratory Therapist

A respiratory therapist evaluates, treats, and cares for persons with respiratory problems. The respiratory therapist works under the supervision of a physician and performs therapeutic procedures based on observation of the patient. Using respiratory equipment, the therapist treats patients with asthma, emphysema, pneumonia, and bronchitis. The respiratory therapist plays an active role in newborn, pediatric, and adult intensive care units. The therapist may work in a hospital, nursing home, physician's office, or commercial company that provides emergency oxygen equipment and services to home-care patients.

Nursing Aide/Assistant

Nursing aides assist in the direct care of patients under the supervision of the nursing staff. Typical functions include making beds, bathing patients, taking vital signs, serving meals, and transporting patients to and from treatment areas.

Nursing assistants are often employed in psychiatric and acute care hospitals, nursing homes, and home health agencies. On-the-job training can range from 1 week to 3 months. Certification as a certified nursing assistant (CNA) is available and is required by many health-care facilities, especially long-term care facilities.

Practical/Vocational Nurse

Licensed practical nurses (LPNs) and licensed vocational nurses (LVNs) are different names for the same type of nurse. Their duties involve taking and recording patient temperatures, blood pressure, pulse, and respiration rates. They also include administering some medications under supervision, dressing wounds, and applying compresses. LPNs and LVNs are not allowed, however, to perform certain other duties, such as some intravenous (IV) procedures or the administration of certain medications. LPNs/LVNs can obtain additional training to become certified in IV therapy.

Practical/vocational nurses assist registered nurses and physicians by observing patients and reporting changes in their conditions. LPNs/LVNs work in hospitals, nursing homes, clinics, and physicians' offices and in industrial medicine. To meet the needs of the growing aging population in this country, employment opportunities for LPNs and LVNs in long-term care settings have increased.

LPNs/LVNs must graduate from an accredited school of practical (vocational) nursing (usually a 1-year program). They are also required to take a state board examination for licensure as LPNs/LVNs.

Registered Nurse

A nurse who graduates from a nursing program and passes the state board examination for licensure is considered a registered nurse (RN), indicating formal, legal recognition by the state. The RN is a professional who is responsible for planning, giving, and supervising the bedside nursing care of patients. An RN may work in an administrative capacity, assist in daily operations, oversee programs in hospital or institutional settings, or plan community health services. Registered nurses work in hospitals, nursing homes, public health agencies, industry, physicians' offices, government agencies, and educational settings.

There are three types of nursing education programs that qualify an individual to take a state board examination to become an RN. These include Associate Degree Nurse, Diploma Graduate Nurse, and Baccalaureate Nurse.

Associate Degree Nurse   Associate degrees in nursing (ADNs) are offered at many junior colleges and community colleges and at some universities. These programs combine liberal arts education and nursing education. The length of the ADN program is typically 2 years.

Diploma Graduate Nurse   Diploma programs are usually 3-year programs designed as cooperative programs between a community college and a participating hospital. The programs combine course work and clinical experience in the hospital.

Baccalaureate Nurse   A baccalaureate degree refers to a 4-year college or university program. Graduates of a 4-year nursing program are awarded a bachelor of science in nursing (BSN) degree. The curriculum includes courses in liberal arts, general education, and nursing courses. Graduates are prepared to function as nurse generalists and in positions that go beyond the role of hospital staff nurses. Some RNs with a BSN will continue their education to earn master's or doctoral degrees.

Nurse Practitioner

A nurse practitioner (NP) is an RN who functions in an expanded nursing role. The NP usually works in an ambulatory patient care setting alongside physicians. An NP may work in an independent nurse practitioner practice without physicians. An independent nurse practitioner takes health histories, performs physical exams, conducts screening tests, and educates patients and families about disease prevention.

An NP who works in a physician's practice may perform some duties that a physician would, such as administering physical exams and treating common illnesses and injuries (Figure 3–5). For example, in an OB/GYN practice the NP can perform a standard annual gynecologic exam, including taking a Pap smear or a culture to test for yeast infection or a bacterial infection. The nurse practitioner usually emphasizes preventive health care.

The NP must be an RN with at least a master's degree in nursing and must complete 4 to 12 months of an apprenticeship or formal training. With specific formal training the student may become a pediatric nurse practitioner, an obstetric nurse practitioner (midwife), or a psychiatric nurse practitioner.

CHECKPOINT
LO 3.2

The health-care team includes many types of members that perform nursing care. List each of these members starting with the least to the most amount of education time required.

LO 3.3 Specialty Career Options

As an administrative medical assistant you will find opportunities to advance in the fields of medical billing and coding, medical records technology, medical transcription, administration, and practice management. Careers such as a compliance officer, transcriptionist, hospital admissions clerk, health-care administrator, registered health information technician (RHIT), billing and insurance specialist, medical coder, certified medical reimbursement specialist (CMRS), electronic claims professional, clearinghouse claims representative, and payroll specialist are all possibilities. These careers will be discussed in the "Working with the Health-Care Team" feature throughout this book.

Clinical medical assistants may specialize in the clinical area. As an administrative medical assistant you may find yourself working with the following members of the health-care team. Most of these careers require mostly clinical skills; however, many also include administrative skills.

Anesthetist's Assistant

Anesthetist's assistants provide anesthetic care under an anesthetist's direction. Hospitals and high-technology surgical centers frequently employ anesthetist's assistants. These assistants gather patient data and assist in evaluation of patients' physical and mental status. They also record planned surgical procedures, assist with patient monitoring, draw blood samples, perform blood gas analyses, and conduct pulmonary function tests.

Dental Assistant

A dental assistant can practice without formal education or training. In this case, on-the-job training is provided. A dental assistant performs many administrative and laboratory functions that are similar to the duties of a medical assistant.

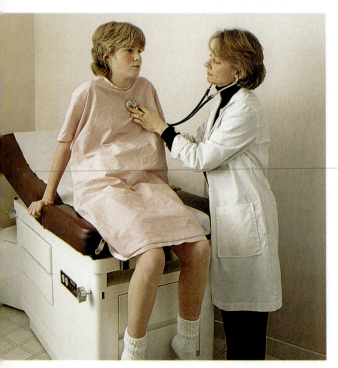

figure 3–5

Many nurse practitioners work in physicians' offices and are trained to perform routine examinations.

For example, a dental assistant may serve as chair-side assistant, provide instruction in oral hygiene, and prepare and sterilize instruments. To perform expanded clinical and chair-side functions such as those of a hygienist, a dental assistant must have at least 1 year of training in theory and clinical application. This formal education also requires work experience in a dental office.

Emergency Medical Technician

An emergency medical technician (EMT) works under the direction of a physician through a radio communication network. This health professional assesses and manages medical emergencies that occur away from hospitals or other medical settings, such as in private homes, schools, offices, or public areas. An EMT is trained to **triage** patients (to assess the urgency and type of condition presented as well as the immediate medical needs) and to initiate the appropriate treatment for a variety of medical emergencies. While transporting patients to the medical facility, an EMT records, documents, and radios the patient's condition to the physician, describing how the injury occurred. An EMT may work for an ambulance service, fire department, police department, hospital emergency department, private industry, or voluntary care service. Training requirements vary by state.

triage
A process of determining the level of urgency of each incoming emergency and how it should be handled.

Occupational Therapist Assistant

Occupational therapist assistants work under the supervision of an occupational therapist. They help individuals with mental or physical disabilities reach their highest level of functioning through the teaching of fine motor skills, trades (occupations), and the arts. Duties include preparing materials for activities, maintaining tools and equipment, and documenting the patient's progress. Occupational therapist assistants must earn a 2-year degree (OTA).

Pathologist's Assistant

Pathologist's assistants work under the supervision of a pathologist. Pathologist's assistants sometimes work with forensic pathologists—professionals who study the human body and diseases for legal purposes, in cooperation with government or police investigations. They may prepare frozen sections of dissected body tissue. Assistants working for anatomic pathologists (professionals who study the human body and diseases in a research capacity) may maintain supplies, instruments, and chemicals for the anatomic pathology laboratory. Pathologist's assistants perform laboratory work about 75% of the workday. Assistants also perform a variety of administrative duties. They work in community hospitals, university medical centers, and private laboratories.

Physical Therapy Assistant

A physical therapy assistant (PTA) works under the direction of a physical therapist to assist with patient treatment. The assistant follows the patient care program created by the physical therapist and physician. This health professional performs tests and treatment procedures, assembles or sets up equipment for therapy sessions, and observes and documents patient behavior and progress (Figure 3-6). A physical therapy assistant may practice in a hospital, nursing home, rehabilitation center, or community or government agency.

figure 3-6

Physical therapy assistants provide guidance and support to patients who are recovering from a physical injury or from surgery on a limb or joint.

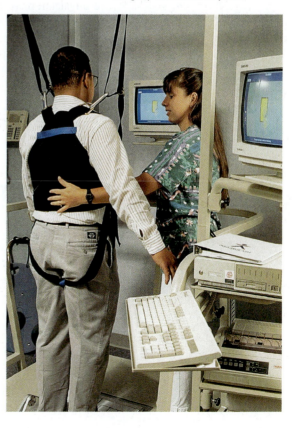

Radiation Therapy Technologist

A radiation therapy technologist assists the radiologist. He may, for example, assist with administering radiation treatment to patients who have cancer. He may also be responsible for maintaining radiation treatment equipment. The technologist shares responsibility with the radiologist for the accuracy of treatment records. A radiation therapy technologist may work in a hospital, laboratory, clinic, physician's office, or government agency. Training requires a high school diploma and graduation from a 2-or 4-year program in radiography.

Respiratory Therapy Technician

Respiratory therapy technicians work under the supervision of a physician and a respiratory therapist. Respiratory therapists perform procedures such as artificial ventilation. They also clean, sterilize, and maintain the respiratory equipment and document the patient's therapy in the medical record. Respiratory therapy technicians work in hospitals, nursing homes, physicians' offices, and commercial companies that provide emergency oxygen equipment and therapeutic home care.

Speech/Language Pathologist

A speech/language pathologist treats communication disorders, such as stuttering, and associated disorders, such as hearing impairment. This health professional evaluates, diagnoses, and counsels patients who have these problems. A speech/language pathologist may work in a school, hospital, research setting, or private practice or may teach at a college or university.

Surgical Technician

A surgical technician provides patient services under the direction, supervision, and responsibility of a licensed surgeon. This health professional's tasks include obtaining a patient's history and physical data. She then discusses the data with a physician or surgeon to determine what procedures to use to treat the problem. A surgical technician may also assist in performing diagnostic and therapeutic procedures. She must be calm and have good judgment in the high-pressure environment of the operating room. Surgical technicians work primarily in hospitals and outpatient surgery centers.

CHECKPOINT
LO 3.3

Explain the difference between a physical therapy assistant and an occupational therapy assistant.

LO 3.4 Professional Associations

Membership in a professional association enables you to become involved in the issues and activities relevant to your field and presents opportunities for continuing education. It is a good idea to become informed about such associations, even those, such as the American Medical Association, that are open to physicians only. The physician you work for may ask you to obtain information about the group's activities and meetings. Table 3–1 summarizes some of the professional associations related to the field of medicine and medical assisting.

American Association of Medical Assistants (AAMA)

The American Association of Medical Assistants (AAMA), as described in Chapter 1, was created to serve the interests of medical assistants and to further

table 3-1

Professional Medical Organizations

PROFESSIONAL ORGANIZATION	MEMBERSHIP REQUIREMENTS	ADVANTAGES OF MEMBERSHIP
American Association of Medical Assistants (AAMA) www.aama-ntl.org	Interested individuals, including medical assisting students and those who practice medical assisting, may join the AAMA	Offers flexible continuing education programs; publishes *CMA Today;* offers legal counsel, professional recognition, and various member discounts
AAPC (American Association of Professional Coders)	All persons interested in coding profession. Student membership also available for those currently in a coding program, as are corporate memberships for six or more employees	Training, continuing education, multiple certifications for specialties, including compliance, job board, networking, local and state chapter memberships, discounts on coding books, educational materials
Association of Healthcare Documentation Integrity (AHDI) www.ahdionline.org	Interested individuals and those who practice medical transcription may join the AHDI	Educates and develops medical transcriptionists as medical language specialists; offers advice and support for self-employed medical transcriptionists
American College of Physicians (ACP) www.acponline.org	Physicians and medical students may join	Provides education and information resources to the field of internal medicine and its subspecialties
AHIMA (American Health Information Management Association)	Members may be students (of approved AHIMA programs only), AHIMA credentialed members, and noncredentialed members interested in HIM and willing to abide by their code of ethics	Subscription to *Journal of AHIMA,* legislative advocacy, professional development, discounts on services/programs, job postings, members-only Web site, automatic enrollment in local and/or state chapter.
American Hospital Association (AHA) www.aha.org	Institutional health-care providers and other individuals may join	Provides consultant referral service and access to health-care information resources
American Medical Association (AMA) www.ama-assn.org	Physicians and medical students may join	Provides large information source; publishes *Journal of the American Medical Association (JAMA);* offers AMA/Net
American Medical Technologists (AMT) www.amt1.com	Medical assistants, medical technologists, medical laboratory technicians, dental assistants, and phlebotomy technicians may join	Offers national certification as Registered Medical Assistant (RMA); offers certification to other health-care professionals, publications, state chapter activities, continuing education programs
American Pharmacists Association (APhA) www.pharmacist.com	Pharmaceutical professionals and physicians may join	Helps members improve skills; active in pharmacy policy development, networking, publishing, research, public education
American Society of Clinical Pathology (ASCP) www.ascp.org	Any professional involved in laboratory medicine or pathology may join	Resource for improving the quality of pathology and laboratory medicine; offers educational programs and materials; certifies technologists and technicians
American Society of Phlebotomy Technicians (ASPT) www.aspt.org	Interested individuals and those who practice phlebotomy may join	Offers national certification as a phlebotomy technician and continuous education programs
Health Professions Network www.healthpronet.org	Health-care professionals or students in health-care fields	Explores current issues and advances allied health professions. Provides networking benefits to members.
National Healthcareer Association (NHA) www.nhanow.com	Individual or student in allied health career	Health-care job search assistance, free seminars and workshops for continuing education and certification of administrative and clinical medical assistants

the medical assisting profession. The AAMA offers self-paced continuing education classes; workshops and seminars at the local, state, and national levels; and job networking opportunities. Other benefits include legal counsel, group health insurance, professional recognition, and member discounts.

The Association for Healthcare Documentation Integrity (AHDI)

The Association for Healthcare Documentation Integrity (AHDI) is the professional organization for the advancement of medical transcription. The AHDI also educates medical transcriptionists as medical language specialists. The AHDI offers advice and support to the many medical transcriptionists who are self-employed.

American College of Physicians (ACP)

Founded in 1915, the American College of Physicians (ACP) is the largest medical specialty organization in the world. It is the only society of internists dedicated to providing education and information resources to the entire field of internal medicine and its subspecialties.

American Hospital Association (AHA)

The American Hospital Association (AHA) is the nation's largest network of institutional health-care providers. These providers represent every type of hospital: rural and city hospitals, specialty and acute care facilities, free-standing hospitals, academic medical centers, and health systems and networks. The AHA works to support and promote the interests of hospitals and health-care organizations across the country. Organizations as well as individual professionals may join the AHA. Membership benefits include use of the AHA consultant referral service, accessed, for example, by hospitals that need experts in areas not addressed by in-house personnel. Members also have access to AHA's health-care information resources, including teleconferencing and AHA database services.

The Joint Commission (TJC)

The Joint Commission (TJC), is a U.S.-based nonprofit organization with the goal of maintaining and elevating the standards of health-care delivery through the evaluation and accreditation of health-care organizations. TJC employs surveyors who are sent to health-care organizations to evaluate their operational practices and facilities. Healthcare organizations are highly motivated to do well during a survey because accreditation by TJC is a significant factor in gaining reimbursement from Medicare and managed care organizations. In addition to hospitals, TJC evaluates and accredits ambulatory care, behavioral health care, home care, laboratory service, long-term care and office-based surgery facilities. Starting in 2003 TJC established safety requirements, known as National Patient Safety Goals, to help accredited health-care organizations address issues of patient safety that can lead to adverse events that can result in lawsuits. The purpose of the Goals, found at www.jointcommission.org, is to improve patient safety. The Goals focus on problems and how to solve them. (See Table 3–2.)

Council of Ethical and Judicial Affairs (CEJA)

The Council of Ethical and Judicial Affairs (CEJA) develops ethics policy for the AMA. It is composed of seven practicing physicians, a resident or fellow, and a medical student. The Council prepares reports that analyze and address timely ethical issues that confront physicians and the medical profession. CEJA maintains and updates the AMA Code of Medical Ethics. This code is widely

table 3-2

2010 Ambulatory Care National Patient Safety Goals

Identify patients correctly	Use at least two ways to identify patients. For example, use the patient's name and date of birth. This is done to make sure that each patient gets the medicine and treatment meant for them.
	Make sure that the correct patient gets the correct blood type when they get a blood transfusion.
Use medicines safely	Label all medicines that are not already labeled. For example, medicines in syringes, cups, and basins.
	Take extra care with patients who take medicines to thin their blood.
Prevent infection	Use the hand cleaning guidelines from the Centers for Disease Control and Prevention or the World Health Organization.
	Use safe practices to treat the part of the body where surgery was done.
Check patient medicines	Find out what medicines each patient is taking. Make sure that it is OK for the patient to take any new medicines with their current medicines.
	Give a list of the patient's medicines to their next caregiver. Give the list to the patient's regular doctor before the patient goes home.
	Give a list of the patient's medicines to the patient and their family before they go home. Explain the list.
	Some patients may get medicine is small amounts or for a short time. Make sure that it is OK for those patients to take those medicines with their current medicines.

Source: The Joint Commission: www.jointcommission.org.

recognized as the most comprehensive ethics guide for physicians who strive to practice ethically.

American Medical Association (AMA)

The American Medical Association (AMA) was founded in 1847. Its members include physicians from every medical specialty. The AMA promotes science and the art of medicine and works to improve public health. The AMA is the world's largest publisher of scientific and medical information and publishes 10 monthly medical specialty journals. The AMA also accredits medical programs in the United States and Canada.

The AMA provides an online service called AMA/Net for physicians and medical assistants, offering up-to-date information about current medical topics. To use the AMA/Net, the medical office must have a computer, telephone, and modem.

American Medical Technologists (AMT)

American Medical Technologists (AMT) was established in 1939 as a not-for-profit organization. The AMT offers national certification as a Registered Medical Assistant (RMA) to medical assisting practitioners. It also offers certification to medical technologists, clinical laboratory technicians, dental assistants, medical administrative specialists, and phlebotomy technicians. Membership benefits include continuing education classes, workshops and seminars, and job networking opportunities.

American Pharmacists Association (APhA)

The American Pharmacists Association (APhA), the national professional society of pharmacists, was founded in 1852. The APhA represents the interests of pharmaceutical professionals, and it strives to help individual members improve

their skills. The APhA works to advance the field of pharmacy and the safety of patients. The APhA is active in pharmacy policy development, networking, publishing, research, and public education.

CHECKPOINT
LO 3.4

Explain why you should join a professional association.

Case Study

PROFESSIONAL READINESS

Cooperation
Appropriately and willingly works with others in the best interest of the work

Natalie, the receptionist at the Total Care Clinic practice, takes her break exactly as scheduled every day regardless of the workload. She does not inform other staff members when she is leaving her duty station, assuming they should know. When a patient calls to cancel an appointment, Natalie usually does not notify other staff members unless they specifically ask. In addition, Natalie refuses to convey any complaints, concerns, or requests that patients may express to her when they are signing in. Even though she has been asked to do so, she feels this is not her job. Natalie was surprised and angry when she heard one of the other staff members say she was uncooperative.

Thinking Critically

1. Does Natalie work with others in the best interest of the practice?
2. When a staff member is not being a "team player" what are some possible problems for the patient and the practice?
3. What should you do if you are having issues with a coworker?

practice APPLICATIONS

1. Interview a medical assistant who has chosen an advanced administrative career option. What additional education or training did she need to obtain the position? What are her additional administrative duties? What does she like about her job? What does she find most challenging?

How did she come to choose her career? Report your findings to the class.

2. Invite a guest speaker who is currently working in an allied health career to talk to your class about his or her job duties, certifications, and overall involvement in the medical community.

exam READINESS

1. **[LO3.1]** _____ are medical specialists that deal with the medical and surgical treatment of obesity.
   a. Gastroenterologists
   b. Allergists
   c. Gynecologists
   d. Bariatric surgeons
   e. Neurologists

2. **[LO3.1]** The abbreviation for a licensed doctor of podiatric medicine is
   a. DPM.
   b. DVM.
   c. MD.
   d. OD.
   e. LDPM.

3. **[LO3.4]** The Joint Commission (TJC) is a U.S.-based organization that
   a. offers continuing education for medical assistants.
   b. provides credentialing for physicians.
   c. maintains and elevates the standards of health-care delivery through credentialing and accreditation.
   d. obtains information for medical groups.
   e. ensures safety to employees in all facilities.

4. **[LO3.1]** The first year of residency for a new physician is known as
   a. student practice.
   b. credentialing of medical training.
   c. diplomatic certification.
   d. an internship.
   e. an externship.

5. **[LO3.1]** An _____ is an MD who diagnoses and treats diseases and disorders of the eye.
   a. optometrist
   b. orthopedist
   c. ophthalmologist
   d. optician
   e. otorhinolaryngologist

6. **[LO3.4]** Which professional medical organization offers continuing education for medical assistants?
   a. ACP
   b. AHA
   c. APhA
   d. AAMA
   e. AMA

7. **[LO3.2]** Which specialty career medical assistant would most likely be working outside of a health-care facility?
   a. Occupational therapist assistant
   b. Emergency medical technician/paramedic
   c. Anesthetist's assistant
   d. Physical therapy assistant
   e. Surgical technician

8. **[LO3.2]** Which health-care team member can work independently, performing examinations and treating common illnesses?
   a. Associate degree nurse
   b. Radiologic technologist
   c. Physical therapist
   d. Medical records technologist
   e. Nurse practitioner

9. **[LO3.1]** Which physician specialist would most likely perform an autopsy?
   a. Radiologist
   b. Proctologist
   c. Pathologist
   d. Urologist
   e. Oncologist

10. **[LO3.3]** Which specialty career medical assistant would most likely be working within the operating room?
    a. Surgical technician
    b. Speech/language pathologist
    c. Pathologist's assistant
    d. Anesthetist's assistant
    e. Certified laboratory assistant

learning outcome SUMMARY

LO 3.1 The American Board of Medical Specialties (ABMS) certifies 24 major medical specialties. Within these specialties are several subspecialties. Medical specialties range from cardiology to oncology. A subspecialty in the area of cardiology is pediatric cardiology. As new medical advances occur, the demand for more specialty areas will emerge.

LO 3.2 Medical assistants are members of a health-care team. The health-care team includes doctors, nurses, physical therapists, other allied health professionals, and patients. Understanding other health-care professionals' duties will assist the medical assistant as a professional. Even if you do not work with some of the team members directly, you may

have to contact them on the telephone or through written correspondence.

LO 3.3 A variety of medical specialty careers are available for the practicing administrative or clinical medical assistant. These careers require additional training or education.

LO 3.4 Membership in professional associations enables medical assistants to become involved in activities relevant to their field. These organizations were created to further the careers and education of those in the medical assisting field. The American Association of Medical Assistants is a key professional organization for medical assistants.

medical assisting COMPETENCIES

CAAHEP

IX.C (7) Compare and contrast physician and medical assistant roles in terms of standard of care

IX.P (2) Perform within scope of practice

ABHES

1. General Orientation

b. Compare and contrast the allied health professions and understand their relation to medical assisting
d. Have knowledge of the general responsibilities of the medical assistant
e. Define scope of practice for the medical assistant, and comprehend the conditions for practice within the state that the medical assistant is employed

3. Medical Terminology

c. Understand the various medical terminology for each specialty

11. Career Development

b. Demonstrate professionalism by:
   (4) Being cognizant of ethical boundaries
   (9) Conducting work within scope of education, training, and ability

4 Professional Communication

Learning Outcomes

After completing Chapter 4, you will be able to:

4.1 Identify elements of the communication circle.

4.2 Understand human relations and the correlation with professional relationships.

4.3 Model examples of positive and negative communication.

4.4 Model ways to improve your communication and interpersonal skills.

4.5 Model the difference between assertiveness and aggressiveness.

4.6 Model examples of effective communication strategies with patients in special circumstances.

4.7 Carry out ways to establish positive communication with coworkers and management.

4.8 Differentiate how stress relates to communication and identify strategies to reduce stress.

Key Terms

active listening
aggressive
assertive
body language
boundaries
burnout
closed posture
conflict
feedback

hierarchy
homeostasis
hospice
interpersonal skills
open posture
passive listening
personal space
rapport

Preparation for Certification

RMA (AMT) Exam
- Interpersonal skills
- Cultural diversity
- Oral and written communication

CMAS (AMT) Exam
- Communication
- Professionalism

CMA (AAMA) Exam
- Recognizing and responding to verbal and written communication
- Patient interviewing techniques
- Professional communication and behavior

Introduction ● ● ●

The ability to recognize human behaviors and the ability to communicate effectively are vital to a medical assistant and the pursuit for success. This chapter has taken a psychological approach to understanding human behavior and the challenges that influence therapeutic communication in a health-care setting. Patients will often have more interaction with the administrative medical assistant than with any other health-care practitioner in the facility. It is important that patients develop a good rapport and feel confident in the care they are receiving from your office. The medical assistant sets the tone for the communication circle and must be aware of all the obstacles that can affect human communication. As a medical assistant, you are often exposed to all kinds of patients. You will see patients from different cultures, socioeconomic backgrounds, educational levels, ages, and lifestyles. You must be able to communicate with each patient with professionalism and diplomacy.

Think about the last time you had a doctor's appointment. How well did the staff and physicians communicate with you? Were you greeted cordially and pleasantly invited to take a seat, or did someone thrust a clipboard at you and say, "Fill this out"? If you had a long wait in the reception area or examination room, did someone come in to explain the delay? Did you become frustrated and angry because nobody told you what was happening?

As an administrative medical assistant, you are a key communicator between the office and patients and families. The way you greet patients, explain procedures, ask and answer questions, and attend to the individual needs of patients forms your communication style. Your interaction with the patient sets the tone for the office visit and can significantly influence how comfortable the patient feels in your practice. Developing strong communication skills in the medical office is just as important as mastering administrative and clinical tasks.

Customer service is the most important part of communication to families and patients. Your mastery of clinical and administrative skills is only a portion of your skills; customer service and communication skills are the other 70%.

A definition of customer service includes the following two points:

1. The patient comes first
2. Patient needs are satisfied

In today's health-care environment, patients are consumers and are more educated than ever before. Patients have more options in choosing a physician or a health-care facility. Patients who feel that they were not given exceptional customer service will choose another physician or facility to meet their needs. Another reason a facility must strive for exceptional customer service is that a medical facility grows rapidly from referral business. A medical facility that acquires a reputation for having an "unfriendly" staff will feel the negative impact from that reputation.

Listed here are some examples of customer service in the physician's office:

- Using proper telephone techniques
- Writing or responding to telephone messages
- Explaining procedures to patients
- Expediting insurance referral requests
- Assisting with billing issues
- Answering questions or finding answers to patient questions
- Ensuring that patients are comfortable in your office
- Creating a warm and reassuring environment

From a business perspective, exceptional customer service is vital to a medical facility's success. Any business that does not provide exceptional customer service will not grow and thrive in today's business economy.

LO 4.1 The Communication Circle

As you interact with patients and their families, you will be responsible for giving information and ensuring that the patient understands what you, the doctor, and other members of the staff have communicated. You will also be responsible for receiving information from the patient. For example, patients will describe their symptoms. They may also discuss their feelings or ask questions about a treatment or procedure. The giving and receiving of information forms the communication circle.

Elements of the Communication Circle

The communication circle involves three elements:

1. a message
2. a source
3. a receiver

Messages are usually verbal or written. (As you will see later in the chapter, some messages are nonverbal.) The source sends the message, and the receiver receives it. The communication circle is formed as the source sends a message to the receiver and the receiver responds (Figure 4–1).

Feedback **Feedback** is verbal or nonverbal evidence that the receiver got and understood the message. When you communicate information to a patient or ask a patient a question, always look for feedback. If you are providing the patient with instructions, a common feedback method is to ask the patient to repeat the instructions back to you or to explain what he or she will do. Good communication in the medical office requires patient feedback at every step.

feedback
Verbal and nonverbal evidence that a message was received and understood.

Noise Anything that distorts the message or interferes with the communication process can be referred to as noise. Noise refers not only to sounds, such as a siren or jackhammer on the street, but also to room temperature and other types of physical comfort or discomfort, such as pain, and to emotions, such as fear or sadness. If patients are feeling uncomfortable in a chilly or hot room, upset about their illness, or in great pain, they may not pay close attention to what you are saying. Conversely, if you are feeling upset about a personal problem outside work or if you are unwell or preoccupied with all the things you have on your to-do list, you may not communicate well.

As you deal with each patient, try to screen out or eliminate both literal and figurative noise. For example, before you start a conversation with a patient, you might ask, "Are you too chilly or too warm? Is the temperature in here comfortable for you?" If there is construction going on outside the building, see if there is a less noisy inner room or office that you might be able to use. If a patient seems nervous or upset, address those feelings before you launch into a factual discussion. These actions are part of being an advocate or supporter of the patient.

If you are feeling stressed or out of sorts, that feeling constitutes a type of noise. Try to take a "breather" between patients or a break from desk

figure 4–1

The process of communication involves an exchange of messages through verbal and nonverbal means.

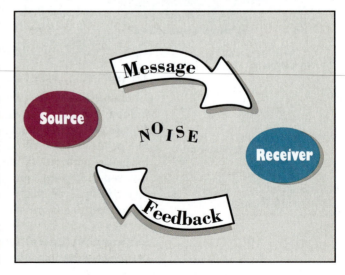

work—walk downstairs, get some fresh air, stretch your legs. Leave your personal problems at home.

Humanizing the Communication Process in the Medical Office As highly structured health-care organizations and technological advances rapidly change the face of health care, many patients feel that health care is becoming impersonal. Every time you communicate with patients, you can counteract this perception by playing a humanistic role in the health-care process. Being humanistic means that you work to help patients feel attended to and respected as individuals, not just as descriptions in a chart. Good communication supports this patient-centered approach.

Make a point of developing and using strong communication skills to show patients that you, the doctors, and other staff members care about them and their feelings. Taking care to treat patients as people helps humanize the communication process in the medical office (Figure 4–2).

CHECKPOINT
LO 4.1

Think of the first conversation you had when you came to class today. Identify the message, the source, and the receiver.

figure 4–2
Greeting the patient with a smile demonstrates a caring attitude.

hierarchy
A term that pertains to Abraham Maslow's hierarchy of needs stating that human beings are motivated by unsatisfied needs that must be satisfied before higher needs are met.

LO 4.2 Understanding Human Behavior and How It Relates to the Provider-Patient Relationship

Understanding human behavior is important when you are communicating with patients. Medical assistants are exposed to many different personality types in addition to different illnesses. When you understand why a person is behaving in a certain way, you can adjust your communication style to adapt to that person.

The Developmental Stages of the Life Cycle

Understanding the stages of human growth and development will enable you to enhance your communication skills, such as patient education, with patients of all age groups, cultures, and religions. Human growth includes physical, psychological, and emotional growth. Many scientists and behaviorists have studied and researched the developmental stages of human life and have developed guidelines to assist us in our patient communication skills. Table 4–1 is an example of a lifespan development model created by Erik Erikson (1902–1994). He is best known for his personality development research regarding children.

Maslow's Hierarchy of Human Needs

Abraham Maslow, a well-known human behaviorist, developed a model of human behavior known as the **hierarchy** (i.e., a classification) of needs (Figure 4–3). This hierarchy states that human beings are motivated by unsatisfied needs and that certain lower needs have to be satisfied before higher needs, like self-actualization, are met. Maslow felt that people are basically trustworthy, self-protecting, and self-governing and that they tend toward growth and love. He believed that humans are not violent by nature, but are violent only when their needs are not being met.

Deficiency (Basic) Needs According to Maslow, there are general types of needs—physiological, safety, love/belonging, and esteem—that must be

LIFE STAGE	EXPECTED DEVELOPMENT
I. Infant (years 0–1)	**Trust vs. Mistrust.** The newborn begins to experience a degree of familiarity and begins to trust the world around her. She also begins to trust her own body.
II. Toddler (years 2–3)	**Autonomy vs. Shame and Doubt.** The child will begin to explore the environment at home and everywhere else. He will begin to gain autonomy (independence) and develop self-control. He also can begin to feel shame and doubt in his abilities. Firm but tolerant parenting is the best practice during this stage.
III. Preschooler (years 3–6)	**Initiative vs. Guilt.** A child begins to learn new things, and has an active imagination and curiosity about everything. As she grows older, she begins to feel guilt for actions taken, which is a sign that she is developing the capacity for moral judgment.
IV. School Age (years 7–12)	**Industry vs. Inferiority.** The child becomes exposed to people other than family members, such as teachers and peers, who contribute to his development. He begins to experience feelings of success that can arise from sports, academics, or social acceptance. Failure to experience success at this stage can result in inferiority feelings.
V. Adolescence (years 12–18)	**Ego Identity vs. Role Confusion.** An adolescent begins to discover who she really is as a preadult human being. She begins to realize how she fits into society (ego identity). When an adolescent is confused about who she is and where she fits in society, role confusion results. Role confusion develops "follower" personality traits, which can lead to inappropriate decision making.
VI. Young Adult (20s)	**Intimacy vs. Isolation.** A young adult begins to think about marriage, family, and career responsibilities. These issues can come into conflict with the isolation that is an issue in modern society; careers often move people to different cities, and working at home has become more common.
VII. Middle Adult (late 20s to 50s)	**Generativity vs. Stagnation.** This stage is primarily devoted to raising children. Middle adults have a desire to help future generations and will often teach, write, or become involved in social activism.
VIII. Old Adult (60s and older)	**Integrity vs. Despair.** Older adults are usually retired and live without children in the house. They tend to question their usefulness at this stage. They begin to notice changes in their physical health and begin to become concerned about these changes. They begin to experience the deaths of relatives, friends, spouses, and, in some cases, their children.

table 4–1

Lifespan Development

satisfied before a person can act unselfishly. He called these needs *deficiency (basic) needs.*

Physiological Needs   Physiological needs are very basic needs, such as air, water, food, sleep, and sex. When these needs are not satisfied, we may feel sickness, irritation, pain, and discomfort. These feelings motivate us to alleviate them as soon as possible to establish **homeostasis** (that is, a state of balance or equilibrium). Once those feelings are alleviated, we may think about other things or move to the next level of Maslow's hierarchy.

homeostasis
A balanced, stable state within the body.

Safety Needs   People have the need and desire for establishing stability and consistency. These basic needs are security, shelter, and existing in a safe environment.

Love/Belonging Needs   Humans have a desire to belong to groups: family, clubs, work groups, religious groups, and so on. We need to feel loved and accepted by others. Humans are like pack animals—we place great importance in belonging to society.

Esteem Needs   Humans like to feel that they are important and have worthiness to society. There are two types of self-esteem. The first results from competence or mastery of a task, such as completing an educational program. The second is the attention and recognition that comes from others.

Self-Actualization   The need for self-actualization is finding self-fulfillment and realizing one's own potential. To reach this level, a person utilizes many

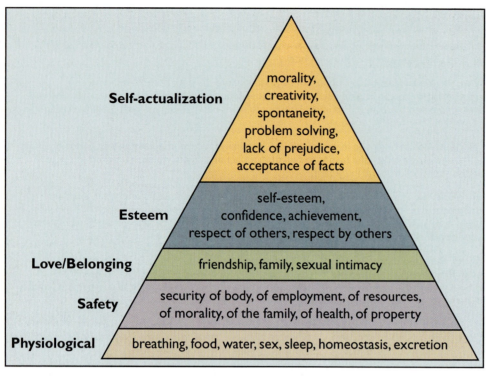

figure 4–3
Maslow's hierarchy of needs.

tools to maximize potential, such as education, a fulfilling career, and a balanced personal life.

When working and communicating with patients, remember this hierarchy of human needs and observe what need a patient is deficient in. For example, if an elderly patient has recently lost her husband, she may feel lonely and deficient in the love need. You may see homeless patients who are deficient in their physiological and safety needs. You may have a young girl as a patient who is overweight and has low self-esteem. On the other hand, you may have a high-level executive as a patient who has reached self-actualization. Each of these scenarios would require a communication style adjustment in order for you to effectively communicate with these patients.

CHECKPOINT
LO 4.2

The physician informed a single mother of five children who recently lost her job that she is at risk for a stroke. To avoid it she must exercise more, eat healthier foods, and get more rest. Where do you think she is on Maslow's hierarchy and what do you think might motivate her to follow the physician's instructions? As an administrative medical assistant, how could you help?

LO 4.3 Types of Communication

Communication can be positive or negative. It can also be verbal, nonverbal, or written, which also includes electronic methods. To help ensure effective communication with patients, familiarize yourself with these different modalities. (Chapter 13 discusses written communication.)

Positive Verbal Communication

In the medical office, communication that promotes patients' comfort and well-being is essential. Treating patients brusquely or rudely is unacceptable in the health-care setting. It is your responsibility—not the patient's—to set the stage for positive communication.

When information—even bad news—is communicated with some positive aspect, patients are more likely to listen attentively and respond positively themselves.

Examples of positive communication are:

- Being friendly, warm, and attentive ("It's good to see you again, Mrs. Armstrong. I know you're on your lunch hour, so let's get started right away.")

- Verbalizing concern for patients ("Are you comfortable?" "This paperwork won't take long at all.")
- Encouraging patients to ask questions ("I hope I've explained the procedure well. Do you have any questions, or are there any parts you would like to go over again?")
- Asking patients to repeat your instructions to make sure they understand
- Looking directly at patients when you speak to them
- Smiling (naturally, not in a forced way)
- Speaking slowly and clearly (enunciate). Be sure to pronounce words correctly.
- Listening carefully

Negative Verbal Communication

Most people do not purposely try to communicate negatively. Some people, however, may not realize that their communication style has a negative impact on others. Look for and ask for feedback to help you curb negative communication habits. Ask yourself, "Do the physicians and my other coworkers seem glad to speak with me? Are they open and responsive to me?" "Do patients seem at ease with me, or are they very quiet, turned off, or distant?" (Note that some patients may respond this way because of the way they feel, not because of the way you are communicating with them.) Here are some examples of negative communication:

- Mumbling
- Speaking brusquely or sharply
- Avoiding eye contact
- Interrupting patients as they are speaking
- Rushing through explanations or instructions
- Treating patients impersonally
- Making patients feel they are taking up too much of your time or asking too many questions
- Forgetting common courtesies, such as saying please and thank you
- Showing boredom

A good way to avoid negative communication is to open your eyes and ears to others in workplace settings. The next time you buy something at a store, call a company for information over the phone, or eat out at a restaurant, take note of the way the staff treats you. Do they answer your questions courteously? Do they give you the information you ask for? Do they make you feel welcome? What specifically makes their communication style positive or negative? Remember, you can always improve your communication skills.

Nonverbal Communication

Verbal communication refers to communication that is spoken or written. Nonverbal communication is also known as **body language** and it includes facial expressions, eye contact, posture, touch, and attention to personal space. In many instances, people's body language conveys their true feelings, even when their words may say otherwise. A patient might say, "I'm OK about that," but if she is sitting with her arms folded tightly across her chest and avoids looking at you, she may not mean what she says.

body language
Nonverbal communication, including facial expressions, eye contact, posture, touch, and attention to personal space.

Facial Expression Your face is the most expressive part of your body. You can often tell whether someone has understood your message simply by his

facial expression. For example, when you are explaining a procedure to a patient, look at his expression. Does he seem puzzled? Is his brow wrinkled? Does he look surprised? Facial expressions can give you clues about how to tailor your communication efforts. They also serve as a form of feedback.

Eye Contact   Eye contact is an important part of positive communication. Look directly at patients when speaking to them. Looking away or down communicates that you are not interested in the person or that you are avoiding her for some reason.

There may be cultural differences in the way patients react to eye contact. In some cultures, for example, it is common to avoid eye contact out of respect for someone who is considered a superior. Thus, children may be taught not to look adults in the eye.

Posture   The way you hold or move your head, arms, hands, and the rest of your body can project strong nonverbal messages. During communication, posture can usually be described as open or closed. Posture may also indicate self-confidence or lack of self-confidence.

Open Posture   A feeling of receptiveness and friendliness can be conveyed with an **open posture.** In this position, your arms lie comfortably at your sides or in your lap. You face the other person, and you may lean forward in your chair. This demonstrates that you are listening and are interested in what the other person has to say. Open posture is a form of positive communication.

Closed Posture   A **closed posture** conveys the opposite, a feeling of not being totally receptive to what is being said. It can also signal that someone is angry or upset. A person in a closed posture may hold his arms rigidly or fold them across his chest. He may lean back in his chair, away from the other person. He may turn away to avoid eye contact. Slouching is a kind of closed posture that can convey fatigue or lack of caring. Watch for patients with closed postures that may indicate tension or pain. Avoid closed postures yourself—they have a negative effect on your communication efforts.

Touch   Touch is a powerful form of nonverbal communication. A touch on the arm or a hug can be a means of saying hello, sharing condolences, or expressing congratulations. Family background, culture, age, and gender all influence people's perception of touch. Some people may welcome a touch or think nothing of it. Others may view touching as an invasion of their privacy. In general, in the medical setting, a touch on the shoulder, forearm, or back of the hand to express interest or concern is acceptable (Figure 4–4).

Personal Space   When communicating with others, it is important to be aware of the concept of personal space. **Personal space** is an area that surrounds an individual. By not intruding on patients' personal space, you show respect for their feelings of privacy.

In most social situations, it is common for people to stand 4 to 12 feet away from each other. For personal conversation, you would typically stand between 1½ and 4 feet away from a person. Some patients may feel uncomfortable—and may become anxious—when you stand or sit close to them. Others prefer the reassurance of having people close to them when they speak. Watch patients carefully. If they lean back when you lean forward or if they fold their arms or turn their head away, you may be invading their personal space. If they lean or step toward you, they may be seeking to close up the personal space.

figure 4–4

The nonverbal communication of a frowning physician may indicate concern, confusion, or other emotion.

Indicate whether you think each of the following exhibit positive or negative communication and consider exceptions to your rationale:

1. Frowning

2. Writing while someone is speaking

3. Looking directly at the person

LO 4.4 Improving Your Communication Skills

Sharpening your communication skills should be an ongoing effort and will help you become a more effective communicator. Good communication skills can enhance the quality of your interaction with patients and coworkers alike. Among the skills involved in communication are listening skills, interpersonal skills, therapeutic communication skills, and assertiveness skills.

Listening Skills

Listening involves both hearing and interpreting a message. Listening requires you to pay close attention not only to what is being said but also to nonverbal cues, such as those communicated through body language.

Listening can be passive or active. **Passive listening** is simply hearing what someone says without the need for a reply. An example is listening to a news program on the radio; the communication is one-way. **Active listening** involves two-way communication. You are actively involved in the process, offering feedback or asking questions. Active listening takes place, for example, when you interview a patient for her medical history. Active listening is an essential skill in the medical office.

There are several ways to improve your listening skills:

- Prepare to listen. Position yourself at the same level (sitting, standing) as the person who is speaking and assume an open posture (Figure 4–5).
- Relax and listen attentively. Do not simply pretend to listen to what is being said.
- Maintain eye contact.
- Maintain appropriate personal space.
- Think before you respond.
- Provide feedback. Restate the speaker's message in your own words to show that you understand. This is also referred to as paraphrasing.
- If you do not understand something that was said, ask the person to repeat it.

Interpersonal Skills

When you interact with people, you use **interpersonal skills.** When you make a patient feel at ease by being warm and friendly, you are demonstrating good interpersonal skills. In addition to warmth and friendliness, valuable interpersonal

passive listening
Hearing what a person has to say without responding in any way.

active listening
Part of two-way communication, such as offering feedback or asking questions.

interpersonal skills
Attitudes, qualities, and abilities that influence the level of success and satisfaction achieved in interacting with other people.

figure 4–5

Active listening requires two-way communication and positive body language.

skills include empathy, respect, genuineness, openness, and consideration and sensitivity.

Warmth and Friendliness   A friendly but professional approach, a pleasant greeting, and a smile get you off to a good start when communicating with patients. When your approach is sincere, patients will be more relaxed and open.

Empathy   The process of identifying with someone else's feelings is empathy. When you are empathetic, you are sensitive to the other person's feelings and problems. For example, if a patient is experiencing a migraine headache and you have never had one, you can still let her know you are trying to imagine, or relate to, her situation. In other words, you can acknowledge the severity of her pain and show support and care. You must, however, always remain objective in your interaction with patients.

Respect   Showing respect can mean using a title of courtesy such as "Mr." or "Mrs." when communicating with patients. It can also mean acknowledging a patient's wishes or choices without passing judgment.

Genuineness   Being genuine in your interactions with patients means that you refrain from "putting on an act" or just going through the motions of your job. Patients like to know that their health-care providers are real people. In a medical setting, being genuine means caring for each patient on an individual basis, giving patients the full attention they deserve, and showing respect for them. Being genuine in your communication with patients encourages them to place trust in you and in what you say.

Openness   Openness means being willing to listen to and consider others' viewpoints and concerns and being receptive to their needs. An open individual is accepting of others and not biased for or against them.

Consideration and Sensitivity   You should always try to show consideration toward patients and act in a thoughtful, kind way. You must be sensitive to their individual concerns, fears, and needs.

Therapeutic Communication Skills

Therapeutic communication is the ability to communicate with patients in terms that they can understand and, at the same time, feel at ease and comfortable in what you are saying. It is also the ability to communicate with other members of the health team in technical terms that are appropriate in a health-care setting. Therapeutic communication techniques are methodologies that can improve communication with patients.

Therapeutic communication involves the following communication skills:

- Being Silent. Silence allows the patient time to think without pressure.
- Accepting. This skill gives the patient an indication of caring. It shows that you have heard the patient and follow the patient's thought pattern. Some indicators of acceptance include nodding; saying "Yes," "I follow what you said," and other similar phrases; and body language.
- Giving Recognition. Show patients that you are aware of them by stating their name in a greeting or by noticing positive changes. With this skill, you are recognizing the patient as a person or individual.
- Offering Self. Make yourself available to the needs of the patient.
- Giving a Broad Opening. Allow the patient to take the initiative in introducing the topic. Ask open-ended questions such as "Is there something you'd like to talk about?" or "Where would you like to begin?"

- Offering General Leads. Give the patient encouragement to continue by making comments such as "Go on" or "And then?"

- Making Observations. Make your perceptions known to the patient. Say things like "You appear tense today" or "Are you uncomfortable when you . . . ?" By calling patients' attention to what is happening to them, you encourage them to notice it for themselves so that they can describe it to you.

- Encouraging Communication. Use open-ended questions asking. Ask patients to verbalize what they perceive. Make statements such as "Tell me when you feel anxious" or "What is happening?" Patients should feel free to describe their perceptions to you, and you must try to see things as they seem to the patients.

- Mirroring. Restate what the patient has said to demonstrate that you understand.

- Reflecting. Encourage patients to think through and answer their own questions. A reflecting dialogue may go like this:
  - Patient: Do you think I should tell the doctor?
  - Medical Assistant: Do you think you should?

  By reflecting patients' questions or statements back to them, you are helping patients feel that their opinions about their health are of value.

- Focusing. Focusing encourages the patient to stay on the topic.

- Exploring. Encourage patients to express themselves in more depth. Try to get as much detail as possible about a patient's complaint, but avoid probing and prying if the patient does not wish to discuss it.

- Clarifying. Ask patients to explain themselves more clearly if they provide information that is vague or not meaningful.

- Summarizing. This skill involves organizing and summing up the important points of the discussion and gives the patient an awareness of the progress made toward greater understanding.

Ineffective Therapeutic Communication In the previous section, the focus was on how to communicate effectively in a therapeutic environment. Oftentimes people think they are communicating thoroughly, but they are not. Here are some roadblocks that can interfere with your communication style:

- Reassuring. This type of communication indicates to the patient that there is no need for anxiety or worry. By doing this, you devalue the patient's feelings and give false hope if the outcome is not positive. The communication error here is a lack of understanding and empathy.

- Giving Approval. Giving approval is usually done by overtly accepting a patient's behavior. approving a patient's behavior. The perception of approval for negative behavior impedes true progress.

- Disapproving. Being disapproving is done by overtly disapproving a patient's behavior. This implies that you have the right to pass judgment on the patient's thoughts and actions. Find an alternate attitude when dealing with patients. Adopting a moralistic attitude may take your attention away from the patient's needs and may direct it toward your own feelings.

- Agreeing/Disagreeing. Overtly agreeing or disagreeing with thoughts, perceptions, and ideas of patients is not an effective way to communicate. When you agree with patients, they will have the perception that they are right because you agree with them or because you share the same opinion. Opinions and conclusions should be the patient's, not yours. When disagreeing with patients, you become the opposition to them instead of

Improved Communication

One of the disadvantages of the hard copy medical record is that it can only be viewed by one person at a time. The EHR can be viewed by several staff members at once. In addition, the physician may e-mail a consultant, send a prescription, or find a lab report—all while in the exam room with the patient. These capabilities improve communication and efficiency.

their caregiver. Never place yourself in an argumentative situation regarding the opinions of a patient.

- Advising. If you tell the patient what you think should be done, you place yourself outside your scope of practice. You cannot advise patients.

- Probing. Probing is discussing a topic that the patient has no desire to discuss.

- Defending. Protecting yourself, the institution, and others from verbal attack is classified as defending. If you become defensive, the patient may feel the need to discontinue communication.

- Requesting an Explanation. This communication pattern involves asking patients to provide reasons for their behavior. Patients may not know why they behave in a certain manner. "Why" questions may have an intimidating effect on some patients.

- Minimizing Feelings. Never judge or make light of a patient's discomfort. It is important for you to perceive what is taking place from the patient's point of view, not your own.

- Making Stereotyped Comments. This type of communication involves using meaningless clichés when communicating with patients. An example of a stereotypical comment is "It's for your own good." These types of comments are given in an automatic, mechanical way as a substitute for a more reasonable and thoughtful explanation.

Defense Mechanisms When working with patients, it is important to observe their communication behaviors. Patients often will develop defense mechanisms (also known as coping strategies), which are unconscious, to protect themselves from anxiety, guilt, and shame.

The following are some common defense mechanisms that a patient may display when communicating with the doctor, medical assistant, or other healthcare team members. The mechanisms may be adaptive (ability to change or adjust) or nonadaptive (inability to change or adjust).

- Compensation: Overemphasizing a trait to make up for a perceived or actual failing
- Denial: An unconscious attempt to reject unacceptable feelings, needs, thoughts, wishes, or external reality factors
- Displacement: The unconscious transfer of unacceptable thoughts, feelings, or desires from the self to a more acceptable external substitute
- Dissociation: Disconnecting emotional significance from specific ideas or events
- Identification: Mimicking the behavior of another to cope with feelings of inadequacy
- Introjection: Adopting the unacceptable thoughts or feelings of others
- Projection: Projecting onto another person one's own feelings, as if they had originated in the other person
- Rationalization: Justifying unacceptable behavior, thoughts, and feelings into tolerable behaviors
- Regression: Unconsciously returning to more infantile behaviors or thoughts

- Repression: Putting unpleasant thoughts, feelings, or events out of one's mind
- Substitution: Unconsciously replacing an unreachable or unacceptable goal with another, more acceptable one

CHECKPOINT
LO 4.4

You are making a follow-up appointment for a patient who is frowning and looking uncertain. What do you say?

LO 4.5 Assertiveness Skills

As a professional, you need to be **assertive,** that is, to be firm and to stand by your principles while still showing respect for others. Being assertive means trusting your instincts, feelings, and opinions (not in terms of diagnosing, which only the doctor can do, but in terms of basic communication with patients) and acting on them. For example, when you see that a patient looks uneasy, speak up. You might say, "You look concerned. How can I help you feel more comfortable?" versus asking the patient "What is the matter with you?"

Being assertive is different from being aggressive. When people are **aggressive,** they try to impose their position on others or try to manipulate them. Aggressive people are bossy and can be quarrelsome. They do not appear to take into consideration others' feelings, needs, thoughts, ideas, and opinions before they act or speak.

To be assertive, you must be open, honest, and direct. Be aware of your body position: an open posture conveys the proper message. When you communicate, speak confidently and use "I" statements such as "I feel . . ." or "I think . . ." (Assertiveness is also discussed later in the chapter in the section on communicating with coworkers.)

Developing your assertiveness skills increases your sense of self-worth and your confidence as a professional. Being assertive will also help you prevent or resolve conflicts more peacefully and increase your leadership ability. People look up to and respect professionals who are assertive in the workplace. See Table 4–2 for a comparison of assertive, nonassertive, and aggressive behaviors.

assertive
Being firm and standing up for oneself while showing respect for others.

aggressive
Imposing one's position on others or trying to manipulate them.

table 4–2

A Comparison of Nonassertive, Assertive, Aggressive, and Nonassertive Aggressive Behavior

	NONASSERTIVE BEHAVIOR	ASSERTIVE BEHAVIOR	AGGRESSIVE BEHAVIOR	NONASSERTIVE AGGRESSIVE BEHAVIOR
Characteristics of the Behavior	Emotionally dishonest, indirect, self-denying; allows others to choose for self; does not achieve desired goal	Emotionally honest, direct, self-enhancing, expressive; chooses for self; may achieve goal	Emotionally honest, direct, self-enhancing at the expense of another, expressive; chooses for others; may achieve goal at expense of others	Emotionally dishonest, indirect, self-denying; chooses for others; may achieve goal at expense of others
Your Feelings	Hurt, anxious, possibly angry later	Confident, self-respecting	Righteous, superior, derogative at the time and possibly guilty later	Defiance, anger, self-denying; sometimes anxious, possibly guilty later
The Other Person's Feelings Toward You	Irritated, pity, lack of respect	Generally respected, tactful	Angry, resentful, lacks tact	Angry, resentful, irritated, disgusted
The Other Person's Feelings About Her/Himself	Guilty or superior	Valued, respected	Hurt, embarrassed, defensive	Hurt, guilty or superior, humiliated

Source: Adapted from Alberti, Robert E., and Emmons, Michael, *Your Perfect Right: A Guide to Assertive Behavior,* San Luis Obispo, California: Impact, 1970.

CHECKPOINT
LO 4.5

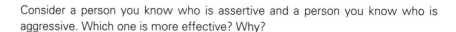

Consider a person you know who is assertive and a person you know who is aggressive. Which one is more effective? Why?

LO 4.6 Communicating in Special Circumstances

If you make an effort to develop good interpersonal skills, most patients will not be difficult to communicate with. You will, however, encounter patients in special circumstances, when they may be anxious or angry. These situations sometimes inhibit communication. Patients from different cultures may pose challenges to communication. Others may have some type of impairment or disability that makes communication difficult. Similarly, young patients, parents with children who are ill or injured, and patients with terminal illnesses may present communication difficulties. Learning about the special needs of these patients and polishing your own communication skills will help you become an effective communicator in any number of situations.

The Anxious Patient

It is common for patients to be anxious in a doctor's office or other health-care setting. This reaction is commonly known as the "white-coat syndrome." There can be many reasons for anxiety. A patient can become anxious because she is ill and does not know what is wrong with her—she may fear the worst. A patient may have recently been diagnosed with an illness that he knows nothing about, which may necessitate a severe lifestyle change. Fear of bad news or fear that some procedure is going to be painful can create anxiety. Anxiety can interfere with the communication process. For example, because of anxiety a patient may not listen well or pay attention to what you are saying.

Some patients—particularly children—may be unable to verbalize their feelings of fear and anxiety. Watch for signs of anxiety. They may include a tense appearance, increased blood pressure and rates of breathing and pulse, sweaty palms, reported problems with sleep or appetite, irritability, and agitation. Procedure 4–1 will help you communicate with patients who are anxious.

The Angry Patient

In a medical setting, anger may occur for many reasons. Anger may be a mask for fear about an illness or the outcome of surgery. Anger may come from a patient's feeling of being treated unfairly or without compassion. Anger may stem from a patient's resentment about being ill or injured. Anger may be a reaction to frustration, rejection, disappointment, feelings of loss of control or self-esteem, or an invasion of privacy.

As a medical assistant, you will encounter angry patients. Do not to take expressions of anger personally; you may just be the unlucky target. The goal with angry patients is to help them refocus emotional energy toward solving the problem. When possible, direct an angry person to a more private area and away from other patients. Study the following steps in communicating with an angry patient:

1. Learn to recognize anger and its causes. Anger is easy to recognize in most people, but it can be subtle in others. Patients who speak in a tense tone, are stubborn, or appear to ignore your attempts at communication may be angry.

2. Remain calm and continue to demonstrate genuineness and respect. Communicate that you respect and care about the patient's feelings.

3. Focus on the patient's physical and medical needs.

4. Maintain adequate personal space. Place yourself on the same level as the patient. If the patient is standing, encourage him to sit down. Maintain an open posture to show that you are receptive to listening. Maintain eye contact, but avoid staring at the patient, which can make the person angrier.

5. Avoid the feeling that you need to defend yourself or to give reasons why the patient should not be angry. Instead, listen attentively and with an open mind to what the patient is saying. Most patients' anger will lessen if they know someone is really listening to them and showing an interest in their emotions and needs.

6. Encourage patients to be specific in describing the cause of their anger, their thoughts about it, and their feelings. Be empathic and acknowledge the patient's feelings and perceptions. Follow through with any promises you might make concerning correction of a problem, but avoid totally agreeing or disagreeing with the patient. State what you can and cannot do for the patient.

7. Present your point of view calmly and firmly to help the patient better understand the situation. If patients are receptive to your viewpoint, their perspective may change for the better.

8. Avoid a breakdown in communication. Allow the patient to voice anger. Trying to outtalk the patient or overexplain will only annoy and irritate him. You might also suggest that the patient spend a few moments alone to gather his thoughts or to cool off before continuing any type of communication.

9. If you feel threatened by a patient's anger or if it looks as if the patient's anger may become violent, leave the room and seek assistance from one of the physicians or other members of the office staff. Document any threats in the patient's chart.

Patients of Other Cultures

Our beliefs, attitudes, values, use of language, and views of the world are unique to us, but they are also shaped by our cultural background. In any health-care setting, you will most likely have contact with patients of diverse cultures and ethnic groups. Each culture and ethnic group has its own behaviors, traditions, and values. Rather than viewing these differences as barriers to communication, strive to understand and be tolerant of them.

As a medical professional, it is important to understand the cultural differences of the patients who come to your medical office for care. Many medical facilities are located in heavily populated ethnic areas, and it is important that the medical staff understand the differences among patient cultures. A medical assistant who is employed in a medical facility in which the majority of its patients are Latino should learn as much as possible about the specific Latin culture in her area in order to provide good customer service. It is also important to understand the difference between stereotyping and generalizing. *Stereotyping* is making a negative statement about the specific traits of a group that is applied unfairly to an entire population. *Generalizing* is making a statement about common trends within a group, but it is understood that further investigation is needed to determine if the trend applies to an individual.

Remember that the beliefs of other cultures are neither superior nor inferior to your own. They are simply different. Never allow yourself to make value judgments or to stereotype a patient, a culture, or an ethnic group. Each patient is an individual in her own right.

Language Barriers   Patients who cannot speak or understand English may have difficulty expressing their needs or feelings effectively. Although family

Cultural Issues

Today's medical practices experience cultural diversity among their patients. One office reported 50 different languages spoken. This text cannot cover the numerous differences but can offer workable suggestions.

Patients' cultural backgrounds have a great effect on their attitudes toward health and illness. Many cultures often have beliefs about the causes of illness, what symptoms mean, and what to expect from health-care professionals that are different from those of modern medicine. Understanding some of these perceptions, behaviors, and expectations will help you communicate more effectively with patients of different cultures. If you are aware that a patient from another culture has an appointment, use credible Internet and other resources to gather information regarding social customs, diet and food preparation, beliefs regarding health, traditional dress, and recent events. This knowledge will help you understand the culture and better help the patient have a positive and effective experience. Review Chapter 5, Patient Education, for assistance determining the credibility of an Internet site.

Beliefs About Causes of Illness

Some cultures believe that illnesses are caused by hot or cold forces in the body. Others believe that having bad feelings toward others can create ill health. Because of such beliefs, it may be difficult to obtain an accurate history of patients' medical problems. It may also be difficult for some patients to realize the importance of taking medication to treat certain illnesses. In this case, you may have to be very persuasive and firm when giving the patient instructions. It may be helpful or necessary to involve other family members.

How Symptoms Are Presented and What They Mean

Perceiving and reporting symptoms may differ. In some cultures, individuals may express pain very emotionally because their culture may feel that suppressing pain is harmful. In contrast, people from other cultures may not admit that they are in pain, thinking that acknowledging pain is a sign of weakness. People of all cultures may be more likely to report physical symptoms of illness than they are to report psychological symptoms. Be aware of nonverbal indications of pain or other symptoms.

Treatment Expectations

Patients from other cultures may be totally unaccustomed to some of the practices of modern medicine. Many consult other types of healers before seeing a doctor. They are likely to have different expectations of treatment from each and may be wary of those that are unfamiliar.

This is especially true of some of the medical procedures and interventions considered to be state-of-the-art, such as laser surgery.

Avoid generalizations and cultural stereotyping, because there can be a variation of attitudes within ethnic groups. Treat each patient as an individual to ensure quality care.

members accompanying patients are often used as interpreters, federal policies require health-care providers who receive federal funds (i.e., Medicare) to provide interpretive services to their patients with limited English. Some nongovernmental agencies also require the use of interpreters. The interpreter should be certified and medically trained, especially if the patient is having surgery or needs to sign a consent form. An increasing number of medical practices require staff to pass an interpreter certification exam prior to translating with patients. Children should never be used to interpret. Translation services are also available through Skype-type modalities and via telephone carriers.

If your medical office has a large number of non-English speakers, it is a good idea to have forms translated and available for use. Another great idea is to also have non-English videos available that educate the patient about different procedures or illnesses. Procedure 4–2 will help you communicate with a non-English speaker when using an interpreter.

Patients with Reading Problems You will find on occasion that some of your patients are functionally illiterate. They may try to hide this by saying, "I didn't bring my glasses with me" or "this is too much to read right now." Be polite and go over the information with them and ask if they have any questions. Send the information home and have them further discuss it with a family

member before requesting that they sign forms such as consent forms or before having surgery.

There are several vendors that will publish your patient education materials at a specific readability level (see www.wordswork.com). It is recommended that patient education brochures not exceed fourth- to eighth-grade reading levels. Some state Medicaid programs specify that the reading level must be no higher than third grade. If patients with higher reading levels want to know more about a specific topic, make sure your office has additional reading materials on hand.

Another tool for providing services to patients with reading problems is to have videos on hand concerning medical topics and procedures.

The Patient with a Visual Impairment

When communicating with a patient who has a visual impairment, be aware of what you say and how you say it. Since people with visual impairments cannot usually rely on nonverbal clues, your tone of voice, inflection, and speech volume take on greater importance.

Following are some suggestions for communicating with a patient who has a visual impairment.

- Use large-print materials whenever possible.
- Make sure there is adequate lighting in all patient areas.
- Use a normal speaking voice.
- Talk directly and honestly. Explain instructions thoroughly.
- Don't talk down to the patient; preserve the patient's dignity.
- Provide Braille patient-education materials which may be found from specific vendors and the National Federation for the Blind (NFB). Some local libraries have the capability of transforming select materials into Braille.

The Patient with a Hearing Impairment

Hearing loss can range from mild to severe. How you communicate depends on the degree of impairment and on whether the patient has effective use of a hearing aid.

Following are some tips to help you communicate effectively with a hearing-impaired patient.

- Find a quiet area to talk, and try to minimize background noise.
- Position yourself close to and facing the patient. The patient will rely on visual clues such as the movement of your lips and mouth, your facial expression, and your body language (Figure 4–6).
- Speak slowly, so the patient can follow what you are saying.
- Remember that elderly patients lose the ability to hear high-pitched sounds first. Try speaking in lower tones.
- Speak in a clear, firm voice, but do not shout, especially if the patient wears a hearing aid.
- To verify understanding, ask questions that will encourage the patient to repeat what you said.
- Whenever possible, use written materials to reinforce verbal information.

figure 4–6

When communicating with a patient who has a hearing impairment, position yourself close to the patient and use gestures and effective body language.

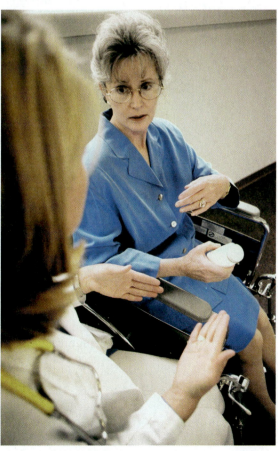

figure 4-7

The majority of older patients are very capable.

The Patient Who Is Mentally or Emotionally Disturbed

There may be times when you will need to communicate with patients who are mentally or emotionally disturbed. When dealing with this type of patient, you need to determine what level of communication the patient can understand. Keep these suggestions in mind to improve communication.

- It is important to remain calm if the patient becomes agitated or confused.
- Avoid raising your voice or appearing impatient.
- If you do not understand what the patient said, ask him to repeat what he said.

The Elderly Patient

Older patients are vastly different in their capabilities. Do not stereotype all elderly patients as frail or confused. Most are not, and each patient deserves to be treated according to her own individual abilities (Figure 4-7).

Always treat elderly patients with respect. Regardless of their physical or mental state, elderly patients are adults. Do not talk down to them. Use the title "Mrs." or "Mr." to address older people unless they ask you to call them by their first name. Procedure 4-4 will assist you in obtaining information from the elderly patient.

Denial or Confusion   Some elderly patients deny that they are ill. For example, in a survey of elderly people, the majority of whom had at least one chronic condition, 85% reported that they were in good or excellent health (Bradley and Edinberg, 1990). Patients' perception of how they feel may be quite different from their actual state of health.

The reverse situation can also occur. Elderly patients may overreact to a problem and consider themselves sicker than they really are. They may become dependent, passive, or anxious. Elderly patients may also over- or underestimate their ability to perform certain tasks or to deal with certain limitations.

Elderly patients may be confused if they have some impairment in memory, judgment, or other mental abilities. Signs of confusion can occur with Alzheimer's disease, senility, depression, head injury, or misuse of medications or alcohol. Elderly patients may or may not be aware of their condition. They may have difficulty understanding instructions.

The Importance of Touch   Because they often live alone, many elderly patients experience a lack of physical touch. Using touch—offering to hold a patient's hand or placing an arm around his shoulder—communicates that you care about the patient's well-being.

Terminally Ill Patients

Terminally ill patients are often under extreme stress and can be a challenge to treat. It is important that health-care professionals respect the rights of terminal patients and treat them with dignity. It is also important that you communicate with the family and offer support and empathy as their loved one accepts her condition. You should also provide information on **hospice,** which is an area of medicine that works with terminally ill patients and their families. Hospice workers often go to the home of the terminally ill. The role of the medical assistant may be to inquire if the patient has advance directives such as a living will which will be discussed in Chapter 6, Law and Ethics in the Medical Office.

hospice
A system of caring for terminally ill patients and their families in preparation for death.

Elisabeth Kübler-Ross, a world-renowned authority in the areas of death and dying, developed a model of behavior that terminal patients will experience on learning of their condition. This model is called the stages of dying or stages of grief and is widely used in work with terminally ill patients.

The five stages usually progress in the following order:

1. Denial. Patients are in direct denial or periods of disbelief. This defense is generally temporary.

2. Anger. Patients may suddenly realize what is really happening and respond with anger. They may display temper tantrums and fits of rage.

3. Bargaining. Patients attempt to make deals with physicians, clergy, and family members. Patients may become more cooperative and congenial.

4. Depression. The patient will begin to show signs of depression, such as withdrawal, lethargy, and sobbing. The patient's body is beginning to deteriorate, and the patient may experience more pain and realize that relationships with family and friends will soon be gone.

5. Acceptance. Patients accept the fact that they are dying. They will begin arrangements for when they expire, making funeral or burial requests. The patient's family needs the most support at this stage.

Even though these stages have been generalized to dying, many experts have applied them to the grieving process as well. Sudden death, such as from an unexpected heart attack, is often more difficult for families to accept since they have not had the opportunity to advance through the five stages.

The Young Patient

A doctor's office can be a frightening place for children. They often associate the doctor's office with getting a shot or being sick. Sometimes parents have misled their children about what to expect from a visit to the doctor. When dealing with children, it is better to recognize and accept their fear and anxiety than to dismiss these emotions. When children realize that you take their feelings seriously, they are more apt to be receptive to your requests and suggestions.

Explain any procedure, no matter how basic (such as testing a reflex with a reflex hammer), in very simple terms. Let the child examine the instrument.

Other suggestions include using praise ("You were very brave") and always being truthful. Do not tell children that a procedure will not hurt if it will, or you will lose their trust.

As children get older, you can use more detailed descriptions when explaining procedures. Remember that after the age of 7 or 8, children can tell if they are being talked down to or treated like babies. Encourage them to participate actively in their care, and direct any questions or instructions to them, when appropriate. You should also respect the adolescent's request not to have a parent present during private conversations. Parents are naturally concerned about their children and are likely to be worried or anxious when a child is ill. Children often react to a situation based on how they see their parents react. Reassuring parents and keeping them calm can also help children relax.

Patients' Families and Friends

Family members or friends sometimes accompany a patient to the office. These individuals can provide important emotional support to the patient. However, always ask patients if they want the family member or friend to accompany them to the examination room. Do not just assume their preference. Acknowledge family members and friends, and communicate with them as you do with patients. They should be kept informed of the patient's progress, whenever possible, to avoid unnecessary anxiety on their part. You must always protect

patient confidentiality. Chapter 6 will discuss the issue of patient confidentiality in depth. Too often, health-care workers think that it is acceptable to discuss patient cases in detail with family members without the consent of the patient.

CHECKPOINT
LO 4.6

What are some of the challenges you may anticipate in communicating with a sight-impaired patient?

LO 4.7 Communicating with Coworkers

The quality of the communication you have with coworkers greatly influences the development of a positive or negative work climate and a team approach to patient care. In turn, the workplace atmosphere ultimately affects your communication with patients.

Positive Communication with Coworkers

In your interactions with coworkers, use the same skills and qualities that you use to communicate with patients. Have respect and empathy; be caring, thoughtful, and genuine; and use active listening skills. These skills will help you develop **rapport,** which is a harmonious, positive relationship, with your coworkers (Figure 4–8).

Following are some rules for communication in the medical office.

rapport
A harmonious, positive relationship.

- Use proper channels of communication. For example, if you are having problems getting along with a coworker, try first to work it out with her. Do not go over her head and complain to her supervisor. Your coworker may not have realized the effect of her behavior and may wish to correct it without involving her supervisor. If you go to the supervisor right away, working relationships can become even more strained.

- Have the proper attitude. You can avoid conflict and resolve most problems if you maintain a positive attitude. A friendly approach is much more effective than a hostile approach. Remember that many problems are simply the result of misinformation or lack of communication.

figure 4–8

Rapport with coworkers is easy to build when you are open, friendly, and thoughtful.

As an example of good communication with coworkers, consider this exchange between Mai Lee, a medical assistant, and Margot, a coworker in a pediatric practice. Note the way Mai Lee demonstrates assertiveness.

Mai Lee: I know you spent a lot of time choosing the new toys for the reception area. I love the wooden safari animal puzzles.

Margot: Thanks. I think the children really enjoy themselves now.

Mai Lee: I wanted to mention to you, though, that I'm concerned about the cash register with coins. Anything that's smaller than a golf ball is a choking hazard to infants and toddlers.

Margot: I don't think the little ones pay much attention to the cash register. It's mostly for older kids.

Mai Lee: Yes, but I'm still afraid that a baby could put one of those pieces in his mouth. What if we replaced the coins with fake paper money?

Margot: I see your point. Sounds like a good idea to me.

Mai Lee started with a statement that acknowledged the coworker's situation and feelings. Then she stated her own opinion. When her coworker disagreed, she repeated her concern, describing what might happen if the situation remained unchanged. Then she made a constructive suggestion for solving the problem without hurting the coworker's feelings. As you interact with coworkers, be sensitive to the timing of your conversations, the manner in which you present your ideas and thoughts, and your coworkers' feelings.

Communicating with Management

Positive or negative communication can affect the quality of your relationships with your supervisor or manager. For example, problems arise when communication about job responsibilities is unclear or when you feel that your supervisor does not trust or respect you, or vice versa.

Consider these suggestions when communicating with your direct supervisor:

- Keep your supervisor informed. If the office copier is not working properly, talk to your supervisor. If several patients express the same types of complaint about the telephone system make sure the right people are told. If you reach a patient the doctor has asked you to call, tell the doctor.

- Ask questions. If you are unsure about an administrative task, for example, do not hesitate to ask your supervisor. It is better to ask before acting than to make a mistake. It is also better to ask than to impact patient care because you carried out a task incorrectly. Asking your supervisor or manager a question means that you respect him or her professionally.

- Minimize interruptions. For example, before launching into a discussion, make sure your supervisor has time to talk. Opening with "Can I interrupt you for a moment, or should I come back?" or "Do you have a minute to talk?" goes a long way toward establishing good communication. It is also better to go to your supervisor when you have several questions to ask rather than to interrupt her repeatedly.

- Show initiative. Any manager or supervisor will greatly appreciate this quality. For example, if you think you can come up with a more efficient way to get the office newsletter written and distributed, write out a plan and show it to your supervisor. He or she is likely to welcome any ideas that improve office efficiency or patient satisfaction.

- Plan an appropriate time for communication. If you have something important to discuss, schedule a time to do so. For example, if you want to talk with the office manager about renewing the lease on a piece of office equipment, tell him you would like to discuss that topic and ask him to let you know a time that is convenient.

Dealing with Conflict

Conflict, or friction, in the workplace can result from opposition of opinions or ideas or even from a difference in personalities. Conflict can arise when the lines of communication break down or when a misunderstanding occurs. Conflict can also result from prejudices or preconceived notions about people or from lack of mutual respect or trust between a staff member and management. Whatever the cause, conflict is counterproductive to the efficiency of an office.

conflict
An opposition of opinions or ideas.

Following these suggestions can help prevent conflict in the office and improve communication among coworkers.

- Do not "feed into" other people's negative attitudes. For example, if a coworker is criticizing one of the doctors, change the subject or walk away.

- Try your best at all times to be personable and supportive of coworkers. For example, everyone has bad days. If a coworker is having a bad day, offer to pitch in and help or to run out and get her lunch if she is too busy to go out.

- Refrain from passing judgment on others or stereotyping them (women are bad at math, men don't know how to communicate, and so on). Coworkers should show respect for one another and try to be tolerant and nonjudgmental.

- Do not gossip. You are there to work. Act professionally at all times.

- Do not jump to conclusions. For example, if you get a memo about a change in your schedule that disturbs you, bring your concern to your supervisor. She may be able to be flexible on certain points. You do not know until you ask.

boundaries

A physical or psychological space that indicates the limit of appropriate versus inappropriate behavior.

Set Boundaries in the Health-Care Environment   As a medical assistant, your professional behavior is extremely important. In many instances, when dealing with patients, physicians, and other staff members, you must set **boundaries,** whether physical or psychological. This will limit undesirable behavior.

If a patient, physician, or staff member is acting inappropriately toward you, you must take immediate action. Do not let the situation fester. You must act assertively and diplomatically. Let the aggressor know that his or her actions or language is inappropriate, and that you are not obligated in any way to accept such behavior.

If none of these actions assist with stopping the unacceptable behavior, report it to your immediate supervisor. If the aggressor is your immediate supervisor, follow the office policy and procedure (make sure you read your policy and procedure in detail before this type of situation arises).

**CHECKPOINT
LO 4.7**

Your coworker is on a performance improvement plan for arriving late. She knows she will be late the next day and asks you to clock her in. How do you respond?

LO 4.8 Managing Stress

Stress can be a barrier to communication. For example, if you are feeling very pressured at work, you might snap at a coworker or patient, or you might forget to give the physician an important message.

Professionals in the health-care field may experience high levels of stress in their daily work environment. Stress can result from a feeling of being under pressure, or it can be a reaction to anger, frustration, or a change in your routine. Stress can increase your blood pressure, speed up your breathing and heart rate, and cause muscle tension. To minimize stress—for the sake of your health as well as for good communication in the office—it is helpful to understand some basic information about this condition.

Stress—Good or Bad?

A certain amount of stress is normal. A little bit of stress—the kind that makes you feel excited or challenged by the task at hand—can motivate you to get things done and push you toward a higher level of productivity. Ongoing stress, however, can be overwhelming and affect you physically. For example, it can lower your resistance to colds and increase your risk for developing heart

disease, diabetes, high blood pressure, ulcers, allergies, asthma, colitis, and cancer. It can also increase your risk for certain autoimmune diseases, which cause the body's immune system to attack normal tissue.

Reducing Stress

Some stress at work is inevitable. An important goal is to learn how to manage or reduce stress. Take into account your strengths and limitations, and be realistic about how much you can handle at work and in your life outside work. Pushing yourself a certain amount can be motivating. Pushing yourself too much is dangerous. Table 4–3 lists tips for reducing stress.

Preventing Burnout

Burnout is the end result of prolonged periods of stress without relief. Burnout is an energy-depleting condition that will affect your health and career. Certain personality types are more prone to burnout than others. If you are a highly driven, perfectionist-type person, you will be more susceptible to burnout. Experts often refer to such a person as a characteristic Type A personality. A more relaxed, calm, laid-back individual is considered a Type B person. Type B personalities are less prone to burnout but still have the potential to suffer from it, especially if they work in health care.

burnout
The end result of prolonged periods of stress without relief; an energy-depleting condition that can affect one's health and career.

- Maintain a healthy balance in your life among work, family, and leisure activities.
- Exercise regularly.
- Eat balanced, nutritious meals and healthful snacks.
- Avoid foods high in caffeine, salt, sugar, and fat.
- Get enough sleep.
- Allow time for yourself, and plan time to relax.
- Rely on the support that family, friends, and coworkers have to offer. Don't be afraid to share your feelings.
- Try to be realistic about what you can and cannot do. Do not be afraid to admit that you cannot take on another responsibility.
- Try to set realistic goals for yourself. Remember that there are always choices, even when there appear to be none.
- Be organized. Good planning can help you manage your workload.
- Redirect excess energy constructively—clean your closet, work in the garden, do volunteer work, have friends over for dinner, exercise.
- Change some of the things you have control over. Keep yourself focused. Finish one project before starting another.
- Identify sources of conflict, and try to resolve them.
- Learn and use relaxation techniques, such as deep breathing, meditation, or imagining yourself in a quiet, peaceful place. Choose what works for you.
- Maintain a healthy sense of humor. Laughter can help relieve stress.
- Try not to overreact. Ask yourself if a situation is really worth getting upset or worried about.
- The only person you can change is yourself. Take full responsibility and do not blame others for your dissatisfaction and stress.
- Seek help from social or professional support groups, if necessary.

table 4–3

Tips for Reducing Stress

According to some experts on stress, there are five stages that lead to burnout (Miller and Smith). The road to burnout follows this path:

1. **The Honeymoon Phase.** During the honeymoon phase, your job is wonderful. You have boundless energy and enthusiasm, and all things seem possible. You love the job and the job loves you. You believe it will satisfy all your needs and desires and solve all your problems. You are delighted with your job, your coworkers, and the organization.

2. **The Awakening Phase.** The honeymoon wanes and the awakening stage starts with the realization that your initial expectations were unrealistic. The job isn't working out the way you thought it would. It doesn't satisfy all your needs, your coworkers and the organization are less than perfect, and rewards and recognition are scarce.

   As disillusionment and disappointment grow, you become confused. Something is wrong, but you can't quite put your finger on it. Typically, you work harder to make your dreams come true. But working harder doesn't change anything and you become increasingly tired, bored, and frustrated. You question your competence and ability, and start losing your self-confidence.

3. **The Brownout Phase.** As brownout begins, your early enthusiasm and energy give way to chronic fatigue and irritability. Your eating and sleeping patterns change, and you indulge in escapist behaviors such as partying, overeating, recreational drugs, alcoholism, and binge shopping. You become indecisive and your productivity drops. Your work deteriorates. Coworkers and managers may comment on it.

   Unless interrupted, brownout slides into later stages. You become increasingly frustrated and angry and project the blame for your difficulties onto others. You are cynical, detached, and openly critical of the organization, superiors, and coworkers. You are beset with depression, anxiety, and physical illness.

4. **The Full-Scale Burnout Phase.** Unless you wake up and interrupt the process or someone intervenes, brownout drifts remorselessly into full-scale burnout. Despair is the dominant feature of this final stage. It may take several months to get to this phase, but in most cases it takes three to four years. You experience an overwhelming sense of failure and a devastating loss of self-esteem and self-confidence. You become depressed and feel lonely and empty.

   Life seems pointless, and there is a paralyzing, "what's the use" pessimism about the future. You talk about "just quitting and getting away." You are exhausted physically and mentally. Physical and mental breakdowns are likely. Suicide, stroke, or heart attack is not unusual as you complete the final stage of what all started with such high hopes, energy, optimism, and enthusiasm.

5. **The Phoenix Phenomenon.** You can arise from the ashes of burnout (like a phoenix), but it takes time.

   First, you need to rest and relax. Don't take work home. If you're like many people, the work won't get done and you'll only feel guilty for being "lazy."

   Second, be realistic in your job expectations as well as your aspirations and goals. Whoever you're talking to about your feelings can help you, but be careful. Your readjusted aspirations and goals must be yours and not those of someone else. Trying to be and do what someone else wants you to be or do is a surefire recipe for continued frustration and burnout.

   Third, create balance in your life. Invest more of yourself in family and other personal relationships, social activities, and hobbies. Spread yourself out so that your job doesn't have such an overpowering influence on your self-esteem and self-confidence.

Procedure 4–1 Communicating with the Anxious Patient

GOAL To use communication and interpersonal skills to calm an anxious patient

MATERIALS None

METHOD

1. Identify signs of anxiety in the patient.

2. Acknowledge the patient's anxiety. (Ignoring a patient's anxiety often makes it worse.)

3. Identify possible sources of anxiety, such as fear of a procedure or test result, along with supportive resources available to the patient, such as family members and friends. Understanding the source of anxiety in a patient and identifying the supportive resources available can help you communicate with the patient more effectively.

4. Do what you can to alleviate the patient's physical discomfort. For example, find a calm, quiet place for the patient to wait, a comfortable chair, a drink of water, or access to the bathroom (Figure 4–9).

5. Allow ample personal space for conversation. Note: You would normally allow a 1½- to 4-inch foot distance between yourself and the patient. Adjust this space as necessary.

6. Create a climate of warmth, acceptance, and trust.

   a. Recognize and control your own anxiety. Your air of calm can decrease the patient's anxiety.

   b. Provide reassurance by demonstrating genuine care, respect, and empathy.

   c. Act confidently and dependably, maintaining truthfulness and confidentiality at all times.

7. Using open-ended questions and other appropriate communication skills, have the patient describe the experience that is causing anxiety, her thoughts about it, and her feelings. Proceeding in this order allows the patient to describe what is causing the anxiety and to clarify her thoughts and feelings about it.

   a. Maintain an open posture.

   b. Maintain eye contact, if culturally appropriate.

   c. Use active listening skills.

   d. Listen without interrupting.

8. Do not belittle the patient's thoughts and feelings. This can cause a breakdown in communication, increase anxiety, and make the patient feel isolated.

9. Be empathic to the patient's concerns.

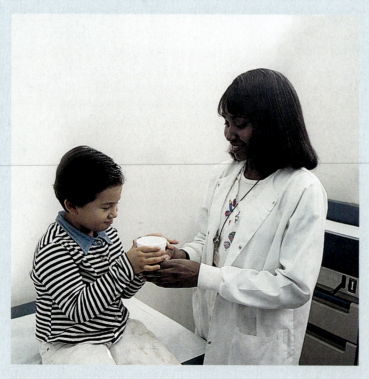

figure 4–9

You can calm children's anxiety by spending time talking with them, playing a game, reading a story, or letting them hold tools or materials.

10. Help the patient recognize and cope with the anxiety.

    a. Provide information to the patient. Patients are often fearful of the unknown. Helping them understand their disease or the procedure they are about to undergo will help decrease their anxiety.

    b. Suggest coping behaviors, such as deep breathing or other relaxation exercises.

11. Notify the doctor of the patient's concerns. The physician must be aware of all aspects of the patient's health, including anxiety, to allow for optimal patient care. Part of your job as a medical assistant is to act as a liaison between the patient and the physician.

Procedure 4–2   Obtaining Information from the Patient with a Hearing Aid

GOAL   To learn techniques to enhance communication with the patient with a hearing aid

MATERIALS   Dependent on materials required for the task such as specific forms, pen, or computer; include a writing tablet which may be necessary for communication.

METHOD

1. Approach the patient from the front in order to be seen and confirm the name.

2. Introduce yourself to the patient and give your title.

3. Escort the patient to a quiet area with little or no background noise.

4. Face the patient; speak in a normal clear tone and ask if he or she is able to hear you.

5. If the patient is having difficulty hearing you, speak slower and louder; avoid using a high pitch since this sometimes increases the problem.

6. Determine if the patient uses other tools for communication such as a computer, writing tablet, or other device, and access one if appropriate.

7. Explain to the patient verbally or in writing what you will be doing and why. Advise the patient to ask questions if he or she cannot hear or does not understand. It is important for you to get accurate information.

8. Show any forms that you will be using and have the patient verify what you write.

9. Use other visual aids that may be appropriate.

10. When the task is completed, ask if there are questions. If not, thank the patient for his or her time and ask if there is anything further you can do for them.

11. Document in the patient's medical record in the appropriate area, such as the billing information, that the patient was wearing a hearing aid, answered appropriately, reviewed the material, and acknowledged understanding.

Procedure 4-3 Obtaining Information from the Geriatric Patient

GOAL To obtain accurate information from the geriatric patient while demonstrating respect and caring

MATERIALS Appropriate form, pen, or computer for direct input

METHOD
1. Introduce yourself and provide your title.
2. Identify and greet the patient using Mr., Mrs., or Miss unless the patient asks to be called by first name; do not use terms such as "honey" or "sweetie."
3. Provide a private quiet setting with good lighting and a comfortable chair if possible.
4. Explain the types of questions you will be asking at the beginning of the interview and how the information will be used.
5. Follow the form you are using related to the needed information; determine if you need to speak slower or louder or repeat the information by observing the patient's ease at answering the questions and other nonverbal and verbal cues.
6. Keep the patient focused but, if possible, do not interrupt.
7. Explain medical terms in understandable language and frequently ask if the patient has questions.
8. Repeat the information back to the patient to ensure accuracy.
9. Assure the patient that you will return his or her insurance cards or other documents quickly if it is necessary to make copies.
10. Provide copies of documents in an envelope with a brief description of what they are, for example, consent for treatment or right to privacy information.
11. Thank the patient for his or her time; explain what will happen next and ask if there is anything else you can do.

Procedure 4-4 Communicating with the Assistance of an Interpreter

GOAL To demonstrate techniques to effectively communicate with a non-English speaking patient through an interpreter

MATERIALS Pen, forms, or computer and appropriate pictures and other visual aids if available

METHOD
1. Identify the patient by name and ask if you pronounced it correctly. Be sure to smile, even if you are feeling slightly awkward or unsure of yourself.

2. Introduce yourself with your title to the patient and the interpreter.

3. Ask the interpreter to spell his or her full name and provide you with identification such as his agency's identification or a business card. Retain his business card to file in the patient's medical record. If he or she does not have a business card, obtain contact information which will also be filed in the patient's medical record.

4. Do not take it personally if the patient appears abrupt or even rude; this behavior may be considered appropriate in the patient's culture. For example, in some cultures, male patients may not deal with a female staff member and that should be respected if possible. Ascertain from the interpreter if there is a problem.

5. Inquire of the interpreter if the patient speaks or understands any English and if there are any communication or other customs that you should know. For example, traditional Navajo people consider it rude to have direct eye contact.

6. Provide a quiet comfortable area.

7. Speak directly to the patient and speak slowly if the patient has any understanding of English.

8. If forms are to be completed, instruct the interpreter to translate with appropriate intervals and give opportunities for the patient to ask questions to ensure understanding. For example, if providing general consent for treatment, permission to send information and receive payment directly from the insurance company and privacy decisions, have one area translated at a time. Instruct the interpreter to ask if there are questions at each portion.

9. If the patient and interpreter are discussing an issue in depth or appear to be leaving you out of the conversation, ask the translator what is being said.

10. Provide the same information, services, and courtesies that you would to a native English speaker. If possible, provide written information in the patient's native language.

11. Document what you would ordinarily document; note on all forms that "translation was done by" and include the name, credential, and agency of the interpreter, as well as the date and time.

Case Study

PROFESSIONAL READINESS

Communications
Giving and receiving accurate information

Mary is 23 years old and has been a medical assistant for six months. She is currently working in a walk-in clinic in a large urban city. She has interviewed three patients this morning. One patient is a homeless, transient male who appears to have some type of mental incapacity; the second is a teenage girl who suspects she might be pregnant; and the third is a well-dressed professional male who complains of a sore throat.

Thinking Critically

1. How will Mary adapt her communication style to communicate with each patient?

2. What types of communication roadblocks might she encounter with each one?

3. What types of communication techniques will she use for each patient?

practice APPLICATIONS

1. With a partner or group, take turns using body language to indicate a variety of emotions and see if the others can correctly guess what message you are sending.

2. A patient asks you if the person he saw go into the treatment area is Carla Shafer who is his neighbor. How do you respond without violating HIPAA?

exam READINESS

There may be more than one correct answer. Circle the best answer.

1. [LO4.1] The main elements in the communication circle include

a. a message (verbal and nonverbal), a source, and a receiver.
b. a message and a receiver.
c. a receiver, feedback, a sender, and a source.
d. a source, feedback, and a receiver (verbal and nonverbal).
e. a message, a receiver, and a response.

2. [LO4.7] Good relationships with coworkers would not include

a. professionalism.
b. stress.
c. cooperation.
d. gossip.
e. integrity.

3. [LO4.3] Which is an example of negative communication?

a. Speaking sharply to the patient
b. Listening carefully
c. Being friendly and warm
d. Looking directly at the patient
e. Keeping quiet when appropriate

4. [LO4.6] One suggestion for communicating with visually impaired patients is to

a. speak very loudly so they can hear.
b. use large-print materials whenever possible.
c. make patients accept you as a health-care provider.
d. deny that they are visually impaired to make them feel better.
e. direct information to a family member or caregiver.

5. [LO4.8] To avoid burnout, the administrative medical assistant should

a. be realistic about his or her expectations and have balance in his or her life.
b. avoid stress by spending more time on what he or she likes.

c. discuss problems with patients and anyone who will listen.
d. become aggressive and stand up for himself/herself.
e. come into work later and leave earlier.

6. [LO4.2] The lowest level of Maslow's hierarchy is

a. psychological.
b. astrological.
c. biological.
d. physiological.
e. anatomical.

7. [LO4.1] An example of nonverbal communication is a

a. memo.
b. handshake.
c. text message.
d. telephone call.
e. lecture.

8. [LO4.6] The ability to identify with someone else's feelings is called

a. sympathy.
b. feedback.
c. empathy.
d. respect.
e. assertiveness.

9. [LO4.4] Encouraging a patient to stay on topic is referred to as

a. mirroring.
b. focusing.
c. summarizing.
d. reflecting.
e. clarifying.

10. [LO4.3] Poor communication could lead to all the following except

a. patient satisfaction.
b. errors in billing.
c. inefficient care.
d. malpractice.
e. anxiety.

learning outcome

LO 4.1 The communication circle involves a message being sent, a source, and a receiver that responds.

LO 4.2 Understand human relations and the correlation with professional relationships. Consider the life cycle and other factors when working within these interactions.

LO 4.3 Communication that promotes comfort and well-being is considered positive communication. Negative communication can be a turn-off. Medical assistants may not be aware of some of the signs of negative communication they display. Lack of eye contact with patients, except in specific cultures, or speaking sharply to a patient is considered negative communication. To assist in avoiding this type of communication, ask yourself, "Does this make me feel good?" or "Do I feel welcome?"

LO 4.4 Communication and other interpersonal skills can be strengthened by learning methods to improve listening, utilize feedback, ask questions, and incorporate other strategies. Become more involved in the communication process by offering feedback.

LO 4.5 Assertive medical professionals trust their instincts. They respect their self-worth, while still making the patient feel comfortable and important. Aggressive medical professionals try to impose their positions through manipulation techniques.

LO 4.6 Learning about the special needs of patients and polishing your communication skills will help you become an effective communicator. This will assist you with handling diversity in the workplace, handling anxious and annoyed patients, as well as dealing with others who may have language barriers.

LO 4.7 The quality of communication you have with your coworkers and your supervisor greatly influences the development of a positive or negative work climate. Use proper channels of communication. Be open-minded. Keep supervisors informed of office problems as they arise and show initiative in your work habits.

LO 4.8 Stress can be good or bad. However, it is how we handle stress that makes the difference. Stress can be reduced by exercising regularly, eating properly, and learning relaxation techniques.

medical assisting COMPETENCIES

CAAHEP

I. A (1) Apply critical thinking skills in performing patient assessment and care

I. A (2) Use language/verbal skills that enable patients' understanding

I. A (3) Demonstrate respect for diversity in approaching patients and families

IV. C (1) Identify styles and types of verbal communication

IV. C (2) Identify nonverbal communication

IV. C (3) Recognize communication barriers

IV. C (4) Identify techniques for overcoming communication barriers

IV. C (5) Recognize elements of oral communication using a sender-receiver process

IV. C (7) Identify resources and adaptations that are required based on individual needs, i.e., culture and environment, developmental life stage, language, and physical threats to communication

IV. C (13) Identify the role of self boundaries in the health care environment

IV. C (15) Discuss the role of assertiveness in effective professional communication

IV. C (16) Differentiate between adaptive and non-adaptive coping mechanisms

IV. P (5) Instruct patients according to their needs to promote health maintenance and disease prevention

IV. P (11) Respond to nonverbal communication

IV. P (13) Advocate on behalf of patients

IV. A (1) Demonstrate empathy in communicating with patients, family, and staff

IV. A (2) Apply active listening skills

IV. A (3) Use appropriate body language and other nonverbal skills in communicating with patients, family, and staff

IV. A (4) Demonstrate awareness of the territorial boundaries of the person with whom communicating

IV. A (5) Demonstrate sensitivity appropriate to the message being delivered

IV. A (6) Demonstrate awareness of how an individual's personal appearance affects anticipated responses

IV. A (7) Demonstrate recognition of the patient's level of understanding in communications

IV. A (8) Analyze communications in providing appropriate responses/feedback

IV. A (9) Recognize and protect personal boundaries in communicating with others

IV. A (10) Demonstrate respect for individual diversity, incorporating awareness of one's own biases

in areas including gender, race, religion, age and economic status

VII. A (2) Demonstrate sensitivity in communicating with both providers and patients

VII. A (3) Communicate in language the patient can understand regarding managed care and insurance plans

IX. C (2) Explore issue of confidentiality as it applies to the medical assistant

IX. C (3) Describe the implications of HIPAA for the medical assistant in various medical settings

X. C (3) Discuss the role of cultural, social, and ethnic diversity in ethical performance of medical assisting practice

X. A (3) Demonstrate awareness of diversity in providing patient care

XI. A (1) Recognize the effects of stress on all persons involved in emergency situations

XI. A (2) Demonstrate self-awareness in responding to emergency situations

ABHES

1. General Orientation
  d. Have knowledge of the general responsibilities of the medical assistant

5. Psychology of Human Relations
  a. Define and understand abnormal behavior patterns
  b. Identify and respond appropriately when working/caring for patients with special needs
  c. Use empathy with treating terminally ill patients
  d. Identify common stages that terminally ill patients go through and list organizations/support groups that can assist patients and family members of patients struggling with terminal illness
  e. Advocate on behalf of family/patients, having ability to deal and communicate with family
  f. Identify and discuss developmental stages of life
  g. Analyze the effect of hereditary, cultural, and environmental influences

8. Medical Office Business Procedures Management
  aa. Are attentive, listen, and learn
  bb. Are impartial and show empathy when dealing with patients

  cc. Communicate on the recipient's level of comprehension
  dd. Serve as liaison between physician and others
  ii. Recognize and respond to verbal and nonverbal communication
  kk. Adapt to individualized needs

9. Medical Office Clinical Procedures
  p. Advise patients of office policies and procedures
  q. Instruct patients with special needs

11. Career Development
  b. Demonstrate professionalism by:
    (2) Exhibiting a positive attitude and a sense of responsibility
    (3) Maintaining confidentiality at all times
    (4) Being cognizant of ethical boundaries
    (5) Exhibiting initiative
    (6) Adapting to change
    (7) Expressing a responsible attitude
    (8) Being courteous and diplomatic
    (9) Conducting work within scope of education, training, and ability

5 Patient Education

Learning Outcomes

After completing Chapter 5, you will be able to:

5.1 Identify the benefits of patient education and the medical assistant's role in providing education.

5.2 Describe factors that affect learning and teaching.

5.3 Implement teaching techniques.

5.4 Identify and select reliable patient education materials used in the medical office.

5.5 Explain how patient education can be used to promote good health habits.

5.6 Describe the types of information that should be included in the patient information packet.

5.7 Describe the benefits and special considerations of patient education prior to surgery.

Key Terms

consumer education
factual teaching
modeling
participatory teaching
philosophy
return demonstration
screening
sensory teaching

Preparation for Certification

RMA (AMT) Exam
- General reception of patients and visitors
- Oral and written communication

CMAS (AMT) Exam
- Reception
- Professionalism
- Patient information and community resources

CMA (AAMA) Exam
- Adapting communication according to an individual's needs
- Patient advocate
- Patient information booklet

Introduction ● ● ●

Health education should be a lifelong pursuit for all of us. The ultimate goal of all medical professionals is to encourage and teach healthy habits and behaviors to all patients. People first have to understand what is good for them, and then they have to make a decision to follow that advice. In patient education, the medical assistant shares health information and encourages patients to make good health decisions.

In this chapter you will learn about patient education. Understanding your role and scope of practice related to patient education is necessary. Then you will develop skills in recognizing and overcoming road blocks to education. You will become more comfortable with teaching and demonstrating procedures to others. Most importantly, you will begin to recognize the incredible responsibility of the medical assistant to correctly lead others to their highest level of health.

LO 5.1 The Educated Patient

Patient education is an essential process in the medical office. It encourages patients to take an active role in their medical care. It results in better compliance with treatment programs. When patients are suffering from illness, disease, or injury, education can often help them regain their health and independence more quickly. Simply put, patient education helps patients stay healthy. Educated patients are more likely to comply with instructions if they understand the why behind the instructions. Also, educated patients are more likely to be satisfied clients of the practice.

Patients benefit from education and the medical office benefits as well. Preoperative instruction to surgical patients, for example, lessens the chance that procedures will have to be rescheduled because surgical guidelines were not followed. Educated patients will also be less likely to call the office with questions. Thus, the office staff will have to spend less time on the telephone.

Patient education takes many forms and includes a variety of techniques. It can be as simple as answering a question that comes up during a routine visit. Patient education may involve printed materials or patient participation. No matter what type of patient education is used, the goal is the same—to help patients help themselves attain better health.

As an administrative medical assistant, you play a role in the process of patient education, primarily because of your constant interaction with patients in the office. The amount and type of education you provide will be decided by your place of employment and scope of practice. As an administrative medical assistant, even if you are not providing the education, you should be aware of the patient's ability to understand and educational needs. In addition, being a role model by practicing good health behaviors is important.

● ● ● ─────────────────────────────────

What three problems or complications can be prevented if adequate patient education is performed?

CHECKPOINT
LO 5.1

LO 5.2 Learning and Teaching

In order to provide patient education it is necessary to understand the process of learning. Learning is the acquiring of new knowledge, behaviors, or skills, which are also known as the *domains of learning*. Knowledge, the cognitive domain, includes the theoretical or practical understanding of a subject and the ability to recall it. Behavior, the affective domain, is how one approaches learning. It includes feelings, values, appreciation, enthusiasms, motivations, and

attitudes. Skills, the psychomotor domain, include physical movement, coordination, and use of motor skills to complete a task.

To better understand these domains, let's use the example of a patient who just found out he is diabetic. In order for him to be able to manage his diabetes and have the best outcome for his health, he will need to learn through all three of the domains.

1. Cognitive (Knowledge): The patient will need to understand and recall the basic information about diabetes, including the effects of diet, exercise, and treatments. The information can come in many formats as discussed later in this chapter. This information must be available to the person who is doing the teaching or the patient would need to find the information himself.

2. Affective (Behaviors): The patient must have the desire or be motivated to make a change in order to improve his health. Once he appreciates the need, is motivated, and has a positive attitude, he will then be able to make the change. This is part of the learning process. If he does not have the desire to learn about diabetes or is not motivated to improve his health, he will not make any change. Being aware of a patient's level of motivation and encouraging the patient are important parts of the teaching process.

3. Psychomotor (Skills): Once the patient has the basic knowledge and correct behavior, he will be able to learn and perform the skills necessary to improve his condition and keep his diabetes under control. This may include eating better foods, increasing exercise, and taking any medications that might be prescribed. These are all skills that are done as part of learning process.

For learning to occur, all three domains of learning must be considered during the teaching process. The patient must be provided the information, he must be motivated and have a desire to learn the information, and then he must perform the skills or "do" what is necessary to improve his condition.

CHECKPOINT
LO 5.2

What three factors are parts of the learning process? How does each factor affect the learning process?

LO 5.3 Teaching Techniques

Patient education can take many forms. Any instructions—verbal, written, or demonstrative—that you give to patients are a type of patient education. When providing education, three types of teaching can occur: **factual, sensory,** and **participatory.** These three types of teaching correspond to the three domains of learning.

1. Factual = Knowledge (cognitive domain)
2. Sensory = Behaviors (affective domain)
3. Participatory = Skills (psychomotor domain)

The combination of these teaching methods gives the patient an overall understanding because it encourages learning through all three of the domains of learning.

Factual Teaching

Factual teaching informs the patient of details of the information that is being taught. For example, when preparing a patient for surgery, you should tell the patient what will happen during the surgery, when it will happen, and why

factual teaching
A method of teaching that provides the patient with details of the information that is being taught.

sensory teaching
A method of teaching that provides patients with a description of the physical sensations they may have as part of the learning or the procedure involved.

participatory teaching
A method of teaching that includes demonstrations of techniques that may be necessary to show that something has been learned.

the procedure is necessary. Factual information provided to a patient before surgery can also include restrictions on diet or activity that may be necessary both before and after surgery. Factual information is usually supported with written materials so the patient can refer to the information as needed at a later date.

Sensory Teaching

Sensory teaching provides patients with a description of the physical sensations they may have as part of the learning or the procedure involved. This learning relates to how the person is affected, that is, the affective domain. For example, prior to surgery you might need to explain how much pain or what other sensations such as numbness or tingling the patient may feel. All five senses may be involved: feeling, seeing, hearing, tasting, and smelling.

Participatory Teaching

Participatory teaching includes demonstrations of techniques that may be necessary to show that something has been learned. For example, as part of preoperative teaching, aspects of postoperative care include cleaning the wound, changing the dressing, and applying ice packs. A new diabetic might need to be taught how to check his blood sugar. During this phase of teaching, you need to first describe the technique to the patient and then demonstrate it. The patient should then repeat the demonstration for you. This practice is called **return demonstration.** If any aspects of the technique are unclear to the patient, you should demonstrate the technique again. The patient should be capable of performing the procedure properly. This process of teaching a new skill by having the patient observe and imitate is called **modeling.**

return demonstration
Participatory teaching method in which the technique is first described to the patient and then demonstrated to the patient; the patient is then asked to repeat the demonstration.

modeling
The process of teaching the patient a new skill by having the patient observe and imitate it.

Verifying Patient Understanding

The key to the success of any educational process is verifying that patients have actually understood the information. A good way to check for understanding is to have patients explain in their own words what they have learned (this is a form of feedback). In addition, have them engage in return demonstrations.

Cultural and Educational Barriers

Some practices serve patients who cannot read well or who do not speak or understand English. It may be necessary to create educational materials written in very simple terms that present information through pictures and charts. The information may also need to be translated into one or more languages. Patients must understand the office's policies and procedures as well as any other educational information provided.

One-on-one explanations may be required for these patients. However, printed materials should still be taken home. Family members or friends may be able to read the materials for them, reinforcing what they learned in the office. When demonstrating a procedure to patients, keep in mind any physical limitations they may have and adjust the procedure accordingly. Make sure patients understand the instructions by asking them to perform the procedure for you.

It is important to match the learning materials to the patient's needs and to her level of understanding. Consider the patient's cultural background, age, medical condition, emotional state, learning style, educational background, disabilities, religious background, and readiness to learn when providing new materials. Review the section Communicating in Special Circumstances on page 76 in Chapter 4 and Practice Readiness, Respecting Patients' Cultural Beliefs on page 98. Keep in mind that patients can refuse treatment and information. If this occurs, notify the doctor and document the event in the patient's chart.

Respecting Patients' Cultural Beliefs

Patients come from many diverse cultures and often have different beliefs about the causes and treatments of illness. These differences may affect their treatment expectations, as well as their willingness to follow medical directions. When talking with patients, it is important to understand and respect their cultural beliefs. Patients may not be willing to accept instructions or consent to treatment based on their cultural background. Consider these simple steps when giving instructions to patients of diverse cultures:

1. Speak slowly and clearly.
2. Request or provide a translator as needed.
3. Ask for and look for feedback from the patient, indicating that she understands and intends to follow the patient instructions.
4. Ask the patient if there is any reason that she will not be able to follow the instructions.
5. Address any concerns indicated by the patient, notifying the doctor if the concerns will mean that patient is not likely to follow instructions.
6. Provide educational resources in the patient's primary language, if available.

CHECKPOINT
LO 5.3

A patient needs to lose weight to improve his overall health. What and how will you teach the patient using factual, sensory, and participatory teaching?

LO 5.4 Patient Education Materials

Most formal types of patient education involve some printed information. They may also include visual materials, such as videotapes, DVDs, and Internet sites. Patient education materials inform patients and enable and encourage them to become involved in their own medical care.

Printed Materials

Printed educational materials come in a variety of formats. They can be as simple as a single sheet of paper, or they can be several sheets that are folded or stapled together to form a booklet.

Brochures, Booklets, and Fact Sheets Many medical offices have materials available that explain procedures performed in the medical office or give information about specific diseases and medical conditions. For example, women who have had a cesarean section delivery may be given a fact sheet describing simple exercises they can do in bed to help regain strength in the abdominal muscles. Many educational aids are prepared by pharmaceutical companies and are provided free of charge to medical offices. Others may be written by the physician or members of the office staff. You may be asked to help prepare some of these materials.

Electronic health record systems provide the ability to create or import informational materials for patients. SpringCharts™ is one example of an electronic health record system that allows you to generate the information sheet and then save it as an RTF (rich text format) document on the computer (Figures 5–1 and 5–2). On the Internet you can also find patient information sheets that you import directly into SpringCharts™. Using electronic health records allows you to save multiple information sheets and access and modify them quickly and easily.

figure 5–1

A patient information sheet, such as this one, can be quickly and easily developed using an electronic health record system such as SpringCharts™.

figure 5–2

When using electronic health records you can import or create your own patient instruction sheets.

Anytime written materials of any kind are given to a patient, it must be noted in the patient's chart. Be sure to document exactly which brochure or leaflet was distributed. Creating and documenting patient receipt of pertinent information when using electronic health records is done quickly and easily. See Procedure 5–1, Creating Electronic Patient Instructions, at the end of this chapter.

Educational Newsletters   A popular patient education tool is the medical office newsletter. Newsletters contain timely, practical health-care tips. Regular newsletters can also offer updates on office policies, information about new diagnostic tests or equipment, and news about the office staff. Newsletters are often written by the doctor or office staff. Some publishing companies and medical groups also offer newsletters that can be customized to a particular practice, using the Internet or software programs such as Microsoft Publisher.

Community-Assistance Directory   Patients often require the assistance of health-related organizations within the community. For example, an elderly patient may need the services of a visiting nurse or a meals-on-wheels food program. Other patients may need the services of a day-care center, speech therapist, or weight clinic.

There are many community resources available in your local area that provide needed services to patients. The medical facility often works with outside resources such as laboratories, home health-care agencies, and social service agencies. It is beneficial to the patient if the medical assistant is familiar with services that could assist with his or her care. Good customer service is founded on providing or researching services that can assist in the goal of patient health and well-being.

The first step in developing a community resource library is to gather a listing of local agencies. You will need the correct name, address, Web address, phone number, contact person, and directions for submitting a referral for each resource listed. It may take some research on your part to locate and organize this information. The Internet and phone directory can be useful tools. Contact the community resource and request information such as brochures,

newsletters, and referral applications. Type up an inventory sheet or Excel spreadsheet of your resources and make sure that all appropriate departments have a copy. A filing drawer can be used to organize and maintain the informational material regarding each resource. A written community resource directory prepared by the office that is accessible to staff and patients is a valuable aid for referring patients to appropriate agencies. See Procedure 5–2, Identifying Community Resources, at the end of this chapter.

Visual Materials

Many patients are better able to comprehend complicated medical information when it is presented in a visual format. When using visual educational materials, it is usually best to provide corresponding written materials that patients can keep for reference.

DVDs or Videotapes   DVDs and videotapes are often used to educate patients about a variety of topics and to instruct them in self-care techniques. The use of DVDs or videotapes is especially effective when teaching about complex subjects and procedures. Examples of helpful DVDs used in patient education include those on breast self-examination, dressing change, and infant care.

Seminars and Classes   Many physicians conduct or arrange educational seminars or classes for their patients. For example, an obstetrician might offer classes in childbirth preparation for patients and their partners. Other seminars and classes may be conducted depending upon the type of medical practice (see Figure 5–3).

Libraries and Patient Resource Rooms   Most public libraries have an assortment of books, magazines, and electronic databases pertaining to health and medical topics. Many hospitals provide patient resource rooms, which include a variety of educational materials—such as books, brochures, and videotapes—for public use. A medical librarian is a health-care team member and, if available, a good contact to assist you with obtaining and providing patient education materials.

figure 5–3

Seminars and classes may be conducted as part of patient education.

Alzheimer's Disease Education and Referral Center
P.O. Box 8250
Silver Spring, MD 20907-8250
www.alzheimers.org

American Academy of Pediatrics
141 Northwest Point Boulevard
Elk Grove Village, IL 60007-1098
www.aap.org

American Cancer Society
19 West 56th Street
New York, NY 10019
www.cancer.org

American Diabetes Association
ATTN: National Call Center
1701 North Beauregard Street
Alexandria, VA 22311
www.diabetes.org

American Dietetic Association
120 South Riverside Plaza
Suite 2000
Chicago, IL 60606-6995
www.eatright.org

American Heart Association
National Center
7272 Greenville Avenue
Dallas, TX 75231
www.americanheart.org

Arthritis Foundation
P.O. Box 7669
Atlanta, GA 30357-0669
www.arthritis.org

Asthma and Allergy Foundation of America
1233 20th Street, NW
Suite 402
Washington, DC 20036
www.aafa.org

Centers for Disease Control and Prevention Department of Health and Human Services
1600 Clifton Road
Atlanta, GA 30333
www.cdc.gov

National AIDS Hotline
995 Market Street #200
San Francisco, CA 94103
www.sfaf.org

National Cancer Institute
NCI Public Inquiries Office
6116 Executive Boulevard
Room 3036A
Bethesda, MD 20892-8322
www.cancer.gov

National Clearinghouse for Alcohol and Drug Information
P.O. Box 2345
Rockville, MD 20847-2345
www.ncadi.samhsa.gov

National Health Information Center
P.O. Box 1133
Washington, DC 20013-1133
www.health.gov/nhic

National Kidney Foundation
30 East 33rd Street
New York, NY 10016
www.kidney.org

National Organization for Rare Disorders
55 Kenosia Avenue
P.O. Box 1968
Danbury, CT 06813-1968
www.rarediseases.org

President's Council on Physical Fitness and Sports Department W, 200 Independence Avenue, SW
Room 738-H
Washington, D.C. 20201-0004
www.fitness.gov

table 5–1

Patient Resource Organizations

Associations   Thousands of health organizations and associations can be contacted for information about preventive health care and virtually every known disease or disorder. The names, addresses, telephone numbers, and Web sites of these organizations are provided in several directories, which are available online or at most libraries. Table 5–1 provides a sample list of patient resource organizations. Search the Internet to obtain the latest contact information for each organization.

Online Health Information   The Internet is another widely used source of medical information. It will be helpful to suggest specific, reputable Web sites for patients to research. Web site addresses should be checked for credibility before using them or referring your patients to them. See Procedure 5–3, Locating Credible Patient Education Information on the Internet. You may need to obtain assistance and approval from the physician, a medical librarian, or other medical staff members. Developing a list of reputable sites to suggest to patients as part of patient education is a must.

Once you are comfortable with types of learning and teaching as well as the educational materials available, you should be ready to start patient education. Begin by creating a patient education plan. This plan includes identifying the education needs of the patient, creating an outline, collecting resources for teaching, carrying out the teaching, and then evaluating the effectiveness. Keep in mind that education is an ongoing process. However, the patient education plan gives you a place to start. See Procedure 5–4, Developing a Patient Education Plan, at the end of this chapter.

● ● ●

You have been assigned to teach a patient about hypertension. What are three types of patient education materials you could use? Why would you choose these three?

CHECKPOINT
LO 5.4

x

Working with the Health-Care Team

MEDICAL LIBRARIAN

Duties and Skills

Medical librarians' primary concern is research—helping other medical professionals such as doctors, nurses, and therapists to find books, articles, and Web sites that will help them provide better patient care. Medical librarians also help health consumers and other nonprofessionals find the answers to medical questions.

Medical librarians are able to not only find information but also to evaluate and organize it. Librarians choose most of the books and journals that reside in their libraries; they make sure the items are located in places where they can easily be found. They evaluate and purchase the computer systems that assist in organizing that material. Often, they help to design those computer systems.

Medical librarians are also teachers. They instruct those who come into the library on the use of the library itself; that is, on how to use the Internet and computer products that are located in the library. They teach library users on a one-to-one basis or in a classroom setting.

Educational Requirements

A medical librarian is a skilled professional who has a master's degree in library and information sciences.

Workplace Settings

Medical librarians work in many different settings: hospitals, colleges, drug and insurance companies, and public libraries.

The Medical Librarian as a Team Member

The medical librarian may interface with the medical practice and the medical assistant in several ways. For example, physicians or other licensed practitioners may want updated information about a disease or disorder regarding a patient they are treating. The medical librarian can provide timely, credible information to assist the practitioner with care. A medical librarian may also research specific patient care questions quickly and easily. He or she may help the medical assistant and other health-care practitioners research information for patient education and provide materials from a variety of resources including print, visual, or Internet.

For more information, visit the Web site of the following organization, which is available on the Online Learning Center at www.mhhe.com/houseradminmedassist

The Medical Library Association

LO 5.5 Promoting Health and Wellness Through Education

Maintaining or improving your health is the best way to protect yourself against disease and illness. It also part of being a good role model in your position as an administrative medical assistant. **Consumer education**—education that is geared, both in content and language, toward the average person—has helped Americans become more aware of the importance of good health. As a result, many people are beginning to take greater responsibility for their own health and well-being.

There are many ways to achieve good health. You can develop healthy habits, take steps to protect yourself from injury, and take preventive measures to decrease the risk of disease or illness. Patient education in the medical office should help patients achieve these goals.

consumer education
The process by which the average person learns to make informed decisions about goods and services, including health care.

Healthy Habits

Patient education can be used to promote good health habits by teaching patients the importance of

- Good nutrition, including limiting fat intake and eating an adequate amount of fruits, vegetables, and fiber
- Regular exercise
- Adequate rest (7 to 8 hours of sleep a night)
- Avoiding smoking and drug use
- Limiting alcohol consumption
- Safe-sex practices

- A balanced lifestyle of work and leisure activities (moderation)
- Safety practices

Whenever possible, these guidelines should be recommended to patients of all ages. Good health should be a top priority in life. Although it is best to incorporate healthy behavior before illness develops, remind patients that it is never too late to work toward improving their health.

Protection from Injury

Many accidents happen because people fail to see potential risks and do not develop plans of action. Following safety measures at home, at work, at play, and while traveling can help prevent injury. A discussion of ways to avoid accidents and injury should be part of the educational process. Table 5–2 lists tips for preventing injury at home and at work.

Another essential aspect of educating patients about injury prevention is teaching them about the proper use of medications. A prescription includes specific instructions for taking the medication. Emphasize to the patient that these instructions must be followed exactly. In addition, the patient must not change the dosage or mix medications of any kind without first checking with the physician. Patients who do not adhere to these rules run the risk of potentially dangerous side effects. Tell patients to report to the physician any unusual reactions

table 5–2

Tips for Preventing Injury

AT HOME

- Install smoke detectors, carbon monoxide detectors, and fire extinguishers.
- Keep all medicines, chemicals, and household cleaning solutions out of reach of children. Purchase products in childproof containers. Lock or attach childproof latches to all cabinets, medicine chests, and drawers that contain poisonous items.
- Keep chemicals in their original containers, and store them out of children's reach.
- Install adequate lighting in rooms and hallways.
- Install railings on stairs.
- Use nonskid backing on rugs to help prevent falls, or remove rugs altogether.
- In the bathroom use nonskid mats or strips that stick to the tub floor.
- Stay with young children when they are in the bathroom.
- Don't rely on bath seats or rings as a safety device for babies and children.
- Set the water temperature on the water heater at 120°F.
- Practice good kitchen safety: Store knives and kitchen tools properly. Unplug small appliances when not in use. Wipe up spills immediately.
- Shorten long electrical cords and speaker wires, or secure them with electrical tape. Avoid plugging too many electrical appliances into the same outlet.
- Never use appliances in the bathtub or near a sink filled with water.
- Exercise caution when using electrical appliances. Use outlet covers when outlets are not in use.
- To reach high places, use proper equipment, such as stepladders, not chairs.
- Use child safety gates at the top of stairwells.
- When cooking, take care to turn all handles of pots and pans inward, toward the cooking surface, to avoid spills and burns.

AT WORK

- Use appropriate safety equipment and protective gear, as required.
- Lift heavy objects properly: Bend at the knees, not at the waist. As you straighten your legs, bring the object close to your body quickly. That way, strong leg muscles do the lifting, not weaker back muscles.
- Never attempt to move furniture on your own. Request that a member of the office building maintenance staff be engaged to do so.
- Use surge protectors on computer and other electronic equipment to prevent overloading outlets.
- Make sure hallways, entrance areas, work areas, offices, and parking lots are well lit.
- If your job involves desk work, practice proper posture when sitting. Do not sit for long periods of time. Get up and stretch, or walk down the hall and back.

experienced when taking medications. Patients must also be cautioned to never share their medications with anyone else, no matter how tempting it may be to "help" a family member or friend.

When providing a patient with a new prescription, always ask the patient if he has told the doctor about all the medications he is already taking, including herbs, vitamins, and over-the-counter (OTC) medications. If the patient tells you that he has not, immediately inform the physician before the patient leaves the office. Some medications taken together or with certain foods can interfere with how well the drug works or cause side effects or adverse reactions. The physician needs to know about all drugs as well as herbal preparations and OTC medications that the patient is taking.

Preventive Measures

Preventive health care is an area in which patient education plays a vital role. Patients need to know that they can decrease their chances of getting certain illnesses and diseases by taking preventive measures and avoiding certain behaviors. Preventive techniques can be described on three levels: *health-promoting behaviors, screening,* and *rehabilitation.*

Health-Promoting Behaviors   The first level of disease and illness prevention involves adopting the health-promoting behaviors described in the section titled Healthy Habits. This primary level of prevention also includes educating patients about the symptoms and warning signs of disease.

screening
A diagnostic test performed on a person who is typically free of symptoms.

Screening   The second level of disease prevention is screening. **Screening** involves the diagnostic testing of a patient who is typically free of symptoms. Screening allows early diagnosis and treatment of certain diseases. Examples of screening tests include colonoscopy, mammography, and Pap smears for women and prostate examinations for men.

Annual screening is important to health maintenance. Although the requirements may differ according to the age and condition of the patient, annual screenings usually include: routine blood work, urinalysis, chest x-ray, EKG or ECG (electrocardiogram) and a physical examination (PE).

Rehabilitation   The third level of disease prevention involves the rehabilitation and management of an existing illness. At this level the disease process remains stable, but the body will probably not heal any further. The objective is to maintain functionality and avoid further disability. Examples of this level of prevention include stroke rehabilitation programs, cardiac rehabilitation, and pain management for conditions such as arthritis.

CHECKPOINT
LO 5.5

Why is it important for a patient educator to be a good role model?

LO 5.6 The Patient Information Packet

When patients come to the medical practice, they need to learn not only about health and medical issues but also about the medical office itself. The patient information packet explains the medical practice and its policies. Unlike most other patient education materials, the patient information packet deals mainly with administrative matters rather than with medical issues.

The patient information packet may be as simple as a one-page brochure or pamphlet. It may be a multipage brochure or a folder with multiple-page inserts. In some practices, the patient information packet is available online or through the EHR system for review or printing.

Benefits of the Information Packet

The patient information packet is a simple, effective, and inexpensive way to improve the relationship between the office and the patients. It provides important information about the practice and the office staff. This information helps patients feel more comfortable with the qualifications of the health-care professionals involved in their care. The packet may help clarify the roles that each office staff member has in patient care.

The information packet also informs patients of office policies and procedures. Patients will learn the doctor's office hours, how to schedule appointments, the office's payment policies, and other administrative details. This information helps limit misunderstandings about these procedures.

The patient information packet also benefits the office staff. It is both an excellent marketing tool and an aid to running the office more smoothly. Providing patients with a prepared information packet saves staff time by answering a number of potential patient inquiries. The information packet is also a good way to acquaint new office staff members with office policies.

Contents of the Information Packet

Regardless of what material the information packet contains, it must be written in clear language so that patients are able to read and understand it. All materials should be written at a sixth-grade reading level to accommodate the reading level of most patients. Information should not be presented in a technical medical style. Because you may be responsible for developing portions of the policy packet, you should be familiar with the contents of a typical packet.

Introduction to the Office   A brief introduction serves to welcome the patient to the office. It may be helpful to summarize the office's philosophy of patient care. The office's **philosophy** means the system of values and principles the office has adopted in its everyday practices.

philosophy
The system of values and principles an office has adopted in its everyday practice.

Physician's Qualifications   The packet commonly contains information about the physician's professional qualifications and training. It includes details about education, internship, and residency. It may list credentials such as board certification or board eligibility in a certain medical specialty. It may also list the physician's membership in professional societies. The information packet for a group practice may contain a paragraph or a page for each physician.

Description of the Practice   This should include a brief description of the practice, particularly if it is a specialty practice. Explaining the types of examinations or procedures that are commonly performed in the office as well as a list of any special services the office provides, such as physical examinations for employment, workers' compensation cases, or other occupational services would be helpful. Be sure to make medical terms and specialties clear by avoiding the use of initials. Spell out everything the first time the reference is made and place the appropriate initials in parentheses.

Introduction to the Office Staff   Many patients are not familiar with the qualifications and duties of the various members of the office staff. It is a good idea, therefore, to identify the staff positions according to their responsibilities and duties. Patients need to understand that some duties commonly thought to be a nurse's responsibilities may also be performed by a medical assistant. It may be helpful to include the professional credentials and licenses of key staff members.

Office Hours   This section should list the exact days and hours the office is open, including holidays. In addition, patients need to know what to do if an emergency occurs outside regular office hours. Tell the patient what number to

call first (for example, the answering service, 911, or the hospital emergency room) and what to do next. Include the telephone number and address of the emergency room at the hospital with which the doctor is affiliated. Assure patients that the doctor or a physician partner can be reached at all times through the answering service. Some practices have multiple offices, and the physicians rotate from office to office on a regular schedule. List all office addresses and phone numbers along with directions to all office sites.

Appointment Scheduling This section of the packet should explain the procedure for scheduling and canceling appointments. You might suggest that patients can benefit by scheduling routine checkups and visits as far in advance as possible. Also note if certain times of the day are reserved for sudden or unexpected office visits.

In this section encourage patients to be on time for appointments. Explain the problems that result from late or broken appointments. If the office charges a fee for breaking an appointment without advance notice, mention it here. Be careful to address these sensitive areas with a positive, nonthreatening tone. The office's written material should simply state the office policies and the problems that can result when functioning outside the policies.

Telephone Policy Providing the office's telephone policies in the information packet can help reduce the number of unnecessary calls to the office and thus save time for the office staff. Explain which procedures can be handled over the telephone and which cannot. Explain procedures such as calling in for prescription renewals or laboratory test results. If the physician returns patients' calls at a certain time of day, mention that policy in this section. Some practices bill patients for telephone calls in which medical advice is given but not for follow-up calls. For example, if a parent of a child who was vomiting uncontrollably called the physician to get immediate medical advice, the call might be billed. If the physician called to inform a patient of test results, however, the call would not be billed. It is important that patients know about these policies, particularly because many insurance plans do not cover charges for medical advice given over the phone, so the patient will be responsible for these charges.

Some offices (particularly pediatric offices) schedule a certain time of the day for patients (or parents and guardians) to call the physician for answers to their questions. This type of policy benefits both the office and the patients. The patients (or parents) have the assurance that they can speak with the physician about their concerns, and the office is spared interruptions during other times of the day.

Payment Policies Inform patients of the office's policies regarding payment and billing. State whether payment is expected at the time of a visit or whether the patient can be billed. List accepted forms of payment (for example, cash, personal checks, and credit cards). It is not common practice to mention specific fees in an information packet.

Insurance Policies List the major insurance carriers accepted by your office or state that *most major insurance plans are accepted.* Advise patients to bring proof of insurance coverage and a picture ID if this is their first visit to the office. A copy of this ID should be made and inserted in the patient's medical chart. State whether the office submits insurance claim forms directly to the insurance company or whether the patient has this responsibility. If the office or a billing service bills the insurance carrier, also include information regarding whether claims are submitted manually, using paper claims, or electronically. Generally, there is no charge for submission of the first insurance claim form; but if the office charges for submission of secondary insurance forms, this should be stated. Outline the practice's policy for handling Medicare coverage, including whether or not the office accepts assignment on Medicare claims. If

the office does not submit insurance claims directly, explain that the staff will help patients fill out insurance forms when necessary, and providing the appropriate paperwork (usually a superbill) containing dates of service, and procedure and diagnosis codes for attachment to the claim form.

Patient Confidentiality Statement The information packet must include a copy of the office privacy policy. Complete information regarding the privacy policy and HIPAA regulations can be found in Chapter 6, Law and Ethics in the Medical Office. An important first step of HIPAA compliance is informing the patient of his or her rights. These rights are communicated through the Notice of Privacy Practices (NPP), which must adhere to certain specifications as found on page 149 of Chapter 6.

The information packet must also state that no information from patient files will be released without a signed authorization from the patient. Each patient who receives a copy of the privacy notice must sign a document stating that he received the privacy notice and had the opportunity to have his questions about the notice answered. This document should remain in the patient's medical file.

Other Information The patient information packet may include the practice's policy on referrals. It may provide information about access to available community health resources or agencies. It may also include special instructions for common office procedures (for example, whether the patient needs to fast before a procedure or to avoid certain foods).

Distributing the Information Packet

For the information packet to be effective, you must make sure that new patients receive and read it. One way is to hand the packet to new patients at the time of their first office visit and briefly review the contents with them (Figure 5–4). Explain that they can find answers to many questions in the packet. Encourage patients to take the packet home, read the information, and keep it handy for future reference.

When new patients make an appointment, many offices send them a copy of the information packet if there is enough time before the appointment to get it to them by regular mail. (It is a nice gesture to include a detailed map or written directions to the office for new patients who are not familiar with the area.) In some cases, the patient is referred to the practice's Web site to review the patient information packet, complete patient registration forms, as well as obtain directions. Patients can review the packet and the consent for treatment form before coming to the office (Figure 5–5). Additional copies of the packet should be placed in an accessible area in the office so that patients can take them home.

figure 5–4

Give patients the patient information packet on their first visit to the office, or mail it prior to their first appointment.

● ● ●

Why is a patient information packet important?

CHECKPOINT
LO 5.6

LO 5.7 Patient Education Prior to Surgery

When a patient undergoes a surgical procedure, patient education is vital to a successful outcome. Although exact instructions vary according to the

Consent for Treatment
Dr. Matthew H. Rodriguez and Associates, Total Care Clinic, Inc.

I voluntarily give my permission to the health-care providers of Dr. Matthew H. Rodriguez and such assistants and other health-care providers as they may deem necessary to provide medical services to me. I understand by signing this form, I am authorizing them to treat me for as long as I seek care from Dr. Matthew H. Rodriguez, or until I withdraw my consent in writing.

____

Signature of Patient or Guardian **Date**

____

Printed Name of Patient or Guardian **Relationship to Patient**

Statement of Financial Responsibility/Assignment of Benefits
Dr. Matthew H. Rodriguez and Associates, Total Care Clinic, Inc.

I acknowledge that I am legally responsible for all charges in connection with the medical care and treatment provided by Dr. Matthew H. Rodriguez and Associates. I assign and authorize payments to Dr. Matthew H. Rodriguez I understand my insurance carrier may not approve or reimburse my medical services in full due to usual and customary rates, benefit exclusions, coverage limits, lack of authorization, or medical necessity. I understand I am responsible for fees not paid in full, copayments, and policy deductibles and co-insurance except where my liability is limited by contract or State or Federal law.

____

Signature of Patient or Guardian **Date**

____

Printed Name of Patient or Guardian **Relationship to Patient**

A duplicate or faxed copy of this form is considered the same as the original document.

figure 5–5
Sample patient consent for treatment form.

procedure, their purpose is to prepare the patient for the procedure and to aid the patient during the recovery period.

Providing Patient Education

Patients must receive information from the physician about the need for surgery and its nature. Educating and preparing patients for surgery may be your responsibility. You should provide support and explanations to patients. You must verify that they understand any information they may have been given by other members of the health-care team. Preoperative instruction may include discussion of postoperative care issues, such as temporary dietary restrictions or surgical wound care.

Determining whether patients have all the information they need before surgery, from both an educational and a legal standpoint is essential. All patients who are undergoing a surgical procedure must first sign an informed consent form. This legal document provides specific information about the surgical procedure, including its purpose, the possible risks, and the expected outcome. The informed consent form, along with documentation of all preoperative instruction, must be put in the patient's chart. (See Figure 5–6.)

figure 5–6

Sample patient surgical consent form.

Patient Surgical Consent Form

Your surgeon for this procedure is: _____

I hereby authorize and request the surgeon, along with any assistants he/she feels are necessary, to perform upon me the following operation(s):

_____

I understand that the nature and purpose of the above mentioned procedure(s) is/are to:

_____

_____

I also authorize the surgeon to do any therapeutic procedure or investigation that in his/her judgment may be advisable for my well-being.

The nature of the planned operation has been thoroughly explained to me by my surgeon and I have decided to proceed with this form of therapy over other alternative methods. The risks, benefits, and alternatives, including doing nothing, have been explained to me. I understand that the practice of medicine and surgery is not an exact science and I acknowledge that no guarantees have been made about the results of the operation or procedure planned. Furthermore, the risks and complications inherent in the operation have been explained to me and I accept these.

I further give permission to have such anesthetics administered to me as the surgeon or the anesthetist deems necessary or advisable.

Pictures may be taken of the treatment site for record purposes. I understand that these photographs/videos will be the property of the attending physician.

☐ I DO agree to allow these pictures to be used for publication or teaching purposes.

☐ I DO NOT agree to allow these pictures to be used for publication or teaching purposes.

If I agree, I understand that my name and identity will be kept confidential and protected.

I agree to keep the office of the surgeon informed of my post-operative progress and I agree to cooperate with instructions given for my post-operative care.

Patient or Legal Guardian (Signature) _____

Patient or Legal Guardian (Please Print) _____

Surgeon as Witness (Signature) _____

Surgeon as Witness (Please Print) _____

Date _____ _____ _____
           Year   Month   Day

_____

I hereby acknowledge receiving a copy of the post-operative instructions which have been reviewed with me. I understand the advice and restrictions given and agree to abide by them. I will notify my doctor immediately if any unusual bleeding, respiratory problems, or acute pain occurs after my discharge from this surgical facility.

Patient (Signature) _____   Witness (Signature) _____

Patient (Please Print) _____   Witness (Please Print) _____

Date _____ _____ _____
       Year   Month   Day

Preoperative Education

Preoperative education increases patients' overall satisfaction with their care. It helps reduce patient anxiety and fear, use of pain medication, complications following surgery, and recovery time. Letting the patient know what to expect during the surgery and afterward allows the patient to emotionally and educationally prepare for all aspects of the surgical procedure.

Using effective teaching techniques are essential to ensure patient understanding. Make sure the patient has a patient instruction sheet and can repeat the expectations back to you.

It may be difficult for a patient to visualize exactly what will take place in some surgical procedures. For example, think of arthroscopy of the knee. When told that the doctor will insert a viewing instrument into the knee, patients probably have no idea of the size of this scope. As a result, they may be particularly fearful of the procedure. A model, diagram, or photo is useful to show exactly what will happen and ease patients' fears.

Helping Relieve Patient Anxiety

When you provide preoperative education, be aware that the fear and anxiety of patients who are about to undergo a surgical procedure can adversely affect the learning process. Consequently, allow extra time for repetition and reinforcement of material.

Always consider your choice of words carefully, stressing the positive rather than the negative whenever possible. Involving family members in the educational process is often beneficial, particularly if the patient is especially apprehensive about the surgery. Provide patients with contact information in case they have additional questions after they leave. Remember to present your instructions and explanations in straightforward language that they can understand. Remember to be reassuring, but to not "promise" a specific result for which the physician may be held liable if the expected result is not the actual result. Remember to verify that they understand everything. This will also help to reduce their anxiety level. Procedure 5–5 will guide you through the process of Outpatient Surgery Teaching.

CHECKPOINT
LO 5.7

A 25-year-old female is scheduled for a biopsy on a breast lump. You are implementing the patient teaching and she says, "I am so scared. Do you think I could have cancer?" How do you respond?

Procedure 5–1 Creating Electronic Patient Instructions

GOAL   To create and administer patient instructions electronically

MATERIALS   An electronic health records software program (such as SpringCharts™) that includes a patient instructions feature

METHOD
1. Search the EHR to find the button or icon to create Patient Instructions. (Check the Help button or review the training manual.)
2. Determine if you will need to write your own or select from a previously created list of patient instructions. Select the correct button to proceed. (See Figure 5–1 on page 99 for an example using SpringCharts™ EHR.)

3. Create new instructions by either of the following methods:

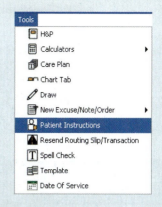

   a. Type your patient instructions directly in the open window or a word processing program. This will depend on the EHR you are using. SpringCharts™. (See Figure 5–2 on page 99 for an example of the open window taken from SpringCharts™.)

   b. Open the Web browser and navigate to a credible Internet site for patient instruction. (Review Procedure 5–3 before selecting this option.) If available on the site, select the "printer friendly" version. Highlight the information you want to use from the Web site, place your cursor at the beginning of the text, and with your left mouse button depressed, drag the cursor to the end of the instruction page. Right-click on any highlighted area and choose copy. Click in the patient instruction window or in the word processing program and, using the key pad, press [Ctrl] + [V] keys. Close the Web page and return to the EHR.

figure 5–7

Select the "Patient Instructions" link on the drop-down menu.

4. Import instructions by opening a previously created document saved as an .RTF or other word processing file type. Import the document according to the manufacturer's instructions.

5. Use existing instructions by selecting them from a list within EHR or a file folder on your computer. Check the specific directions for the EHR program you are using. See Figure 5–7 for an example of how to enter the existing Patient Instructions from SpringCharts™.

6. Record in the EHR that patient instructions were provided. In most programs this will occur when you generate the instructions and becomes a permanent record in the patient's chart. See Figure 5–8 for an example charting entry using SpringCharts™.

figure 5–8

As seen here, once patient instructions have been given to the patient it should be documented.

Procedure 5–2 Identifying Community Resources

GOAL To create a list of useful community resources for patient referrals

MATERIALS Computer with Internet access, phone directory, printer

METHOD

1. Determine the needs of your medical office and formulate a list of community resources. The specific needs of your patients will help you formulate your list. Being able to assist patients with finding outside assistance when necessary is the goal.

2. Use the Internet to research the names, addresses, Web addresses, and phone numbers of local resources such as state and federal agencies, home health-care agencies, long-term nursing facilities, mental health agencies, and local charities. Use the phone directory to assist in locating local agencies such as Meals on Wheels; Alcoholics Anonymous; shelters for abused individuals; hospice care; Easter Seals; Women, Infants, and Children (WIC); and support groups for grief, obesity, and various diseases.

3. Contact each resource and request information such as business cards and brochures. Some agencies may send a representative to meet with you regarding their services. If patients can access information easily, they are more likely to avail themselves of the services available to them.

4. Compile a list of community resources with the proper name, address, phone number, e-mail address, and contact name. Include any information that may be helpful to the office.

5. Update and add to the information often because outdated information will only frustrate you and your patients, creating even more anxiety.

6. Post the information in a location where it is readily available.

Procedure 5-3 Locating Credible Patient Education Information on the Internet

GOAL   To determine the credibility of patient education information on the Internet

MATERIALS   Computer with Internet access

METHOD

1. Open your Internet browser and locate a search engine. Search engines vary in the way they search so you may want to use more than one search engine for different results.

2. Search the topic. Be specific to the topic. For example, if you want to know about the proper diet for high cholesterol, you should type, "high cholesterol diet." For different or more medical sites, try using different terms; instead of high cholesterol try "hyperlipidemia."

3. Select a site from the list of results and evaluate the source.

    a. Click the "about us" link to find out who developed the site. Sites should have an active link available to contact the Webmaster and verify the source.

    b. Sites developed by professional organizations, educational institutions, or a branch of the federal government are generally better than those developed by an individual or a commercial company.

4. Review the "about us" page to determine the quality of the information.

    a. Review the mission statement or other detailed information about the developer.

    b. Look for information about the writers or authors of the site. Make sure they are medical professionals.

5. Check the content of the site.

    a. Avoid sites that have sensational writing or make claims that are too good to be true.

    b. Make sure the language of the information is at a level that you can understand. Avoid sites with lots of technical jargon for patient instruction.

6. Make sure the information is current by checking the copyright or by checking with the contact information on the site. Medical information changes frequently so check the date and avoid information over five years old.

7. Avoid Web sites with bias. For example, if the site is written by a pharmaceutical company, the site will only present information about the medication manufactured by that company. There may be alternative medications. Sites written by individuals are interesting but will be biased as well.

8. Protect your privacy. If the sites require you to register, review their Privacy Policy. They may be able to share your or your patient's information with other companies.

9. Once you have evaluated the site and decide to use it you may want to have your supervisor or licensed practitioner review the information you will be providing to the patient.

Procedure 5–4 Developing a Patient Education Plan

GOAL To create and implement a patient teaching plan

MATERIALS Pen, paper, various educational aids (such as instructional pamphlets and brochures), and/or visual aids (such as posters, videotapes, or DVDs)

METHOD
1. Identify the patient's educational needs in order to provide instruction at the patient's point of need. Consider the following:
   a. The patient's current knowledge
   b. Any misconceptions the patient may have
   c. Any obstacles to learning (loss of hearing or vision, limitations of mobility, language barriers, and so on)
   d. The patient's willingness and readiness to learn (motivation)
   e. How the patient will use the information
2. Develop and outline a plan using the various educational aids available and that addresses all the patient's needs. Include the following areas in the outline:
   a. What you want to accomplish (your goal)
   b. How you plan to accomplish it
   c. How you will determine if the teaching was successful
3. Write the plan. Try to make the information interesting for the patient.
4. Before carrying out the plan, share it with the physician to get approval and suggestions for improvement.
5. Perform the instruction. Be sure to use more than one teaching method. For instance, if written material is being given, be sure to explain or demonstrate the material instead of simply telling the patient to read the educational materials.
6. Document the teaching in the patient's chart for continuity of care and as to maintain a legal record.
7. Evaluate the effectiveness of your teaching session. Ask yourself:
   a. Did you cover all the topics in your plan?
   b. Was the information well received by the patient?
   c. Did the patient appear to learn?
   d. How would you rate your performance?
8. Revise your plan as necessary to make it even more effective. To be an effective teacher you must evaluate the methods you use.

Procedure 5-5 **Outpatient Surgery Teaching**

GOAL To inform a preoperative patient of the necessary guidelines to follow prior to surgery

MATERIALS Patient chart, surgical guidelines

METHOD
1. Review the patient's chart to determine the type of surgery to be performed and then ask the patient what procedure is being performed. This confirms the patient's knowledge of the procedure.
2. Tell the patient that you will be providing both verbal and written instructions that should be followed prior to surgery.
3. Inform the patient about policies regarding makeup, jewelry, contact lenses, wigs, dentures, and so on.
4. Tell the patient to leave money and valuables at home.
5. If applicable, suggest appropriate clothing for the patient to wear for postoperative ease and comfort.
6. Explain the need for someone to drive the patient home following an outpatient surgical procedure. Driving after even simple surgery can be very dangerous. Surgery can be canceled if a patient does not identify a responsible driver before surgery occurs.
7. Tell the patient the correct time to arrive at the office surgery center or the hospital for the procedure.
8. Inform the patient of dietary restrictions. Be sure to use specific, clear instructions about what may or may not be ingested and at what time the patient must abstain from eating or drinking. Also explain these points:
   a. The reasons for the dietary restrictions
   b. The possible consequences of not following the dietary restrictions
   c. Surgery can be canceled if the patient has not followed dietary instructions
9. Ask patients who smoke to refrain from or reduce cigarette smoking during at least the 8 hours prior to the procedure. Explain to the patient that reducing smoking improves the level of oxygen in the blood during surgery.
10. Suggest that the patient shower or bathe the morning of the procedure or the evening before.
11. Instruct the patient about medications to take or avoid before surgery. Surgery can be canceled if the patient has not followed medication instructions.
12. If necessary, clarify any information about which the patient is unclear.
13. Provide written surgical guidelines, and suggest that the patient call the office if additional questions arise. Patients may not understand or remember verbal instructions. Written instructions can be taken home and reviewed again.
14. Document the instructions in the patient's chart for continuity of care and as a legal record.

Case Study

PROFESSIONAL READINESS

Self-Confidence
Appears sure of own ability

Thinking Critically

1. How could Arely's lack of self-confidence affect the patient's response to her teaching?
2. What are special considerations when developing a teaching plan for this patient?
3. How will Arely ensure the patient understands?

practice APPLICATIONS

1. Write the section of a patient information brochure that describes the general roles of the medical office staff. Exchange your writing sample with that of another student, and critique each other's work.

2. Create patient educational brochures and health newsletters for a clinic or medical facility. Select topics of special interest to you and ensure the information is easy to read and understand.

exam READINESS

1. **[LO5.6]** A benefit of the patient information packet is that it
   a. promotes better compliance with treatment programs
   b. helps patients feel more comfortable with the qualifications of the health-care professionals who are caring for them
   c. can answer a treatment question that may come up during an office visit
   d. encourages patients to help themselves achieve better health
   e. ensures patient compliance

2. **[LO5.3]** Which of the following types of teaching gives patients a description of the physical sensations they may have during the procedure?
   a. Factual
   b. Sensory

   c. Participatory
   d. Modeling
   e. Media

3. **[LO5.4]** Which of the following is the most difficult way to create electronic patient instructions?
   a. Type the instructions directly into the open window
   b. Import the instructions from the Internet
   c. Use previously created instructions
   d. Print the instructions directly from the Internet
   e. Use preprinted instructions

4. **[LO5.1]** Which of the following is least likely a benefit of patient education?
   a. Patients are less likely to call the office
   b. Patients take a more active role in their medical care

c. Office staff are not interrupted as often by patient phone calls

d. Patients will not need as much medication

e. Patients are more likely to understand instructions

5. **[LO5.2]** Which of the following is an example of a psychomotor learning domain?

a. The patient is willing to read the brochure

b. The patient performs his own blood glucose test

c. The medical assistant tells the patient how she is going to feel during a procedure

d. The medical assistant provides the patient with a patient information package

e. The patient searches the Internet for information about his condition

6. **[LO5.4]** When checking an Internet site for credibility, which of the following is probably not necessary?

a. Use caution if the site uses a sensational writing style

b. Look for the author of the information you plan to use

c. Check the date of the document you plan to use

d. Click links on the site to make sure they are not broken and are kept up to date

e. Ensure the site is listed on at least two search engines

7. **[LO5.6]** Which of the following would least likely be in the patient information packet?

a. Office policies and hours

b. Patient instruction sheet regarding common tests done at the practice

c. Patient instruction sheet about healthy living

d. List of the physicians with their qualifications

e. Patient confidentiality statement

8. **[LO5.7]** What visual tool is especially helpful when performing preoperative education?

a. Anatomical model

b. Printed information sheet

c. Line drawing

d. Class or seminar

e. Sensory teaching

9. **[LO5.5]** Which of the following is a healthy habit that should be part of patient teaching?

a. Adequate rest (4 to 5 hours of sleep a night)

b. Limiting fruits, vegetables, and fiber

c. The use of cigarettes in moderation

d. Balancing lifestyle of work and leisure activities (moderation)

e. Exercise about 15 minutes per day

10. **[LO5.5]** Which of the following is a warning sign of cancer?

a. Nagging bleeding and discharge

b. Obvious change in swallowing

c. Thickening or lump in breast or elsewhere

d. A sore that heals rapidly

e. Daily bowel movements

learning outcome   SUMMARY

LO 5.1 Patients benefit from patient education because they will be less likely to call the office with questions, and therefore the office staff can spend less time on the telephone. Educated patients take a more active role in their medical care.

LO 5.2 Learning occurs in three domains: knowledge, behaviors, and skills. The patient must be able to recall the information, have the right attitude and be motivated to learn, and then implement the skills needed to demonstrate that the knowledge is retained.

LO 5.3 Depending on patient need and level of understanding, teaching methods and formats are adjusted for the best possible result. Knowing your patient and his needs and abilities, as well as the goal of the instruction, will allow for the best possible

education plan. Always assess your instruction at its completion and revise the plan as needed.

LO 5.4 The types of patient education materials that are in medical offices are brochures, booklets, fact sheets, newsletters, DVDs, Internet-based sites, and community-assistance directories. Using already completed print or electronic patient instruction sheets, ensuring that Internet sources are credible, and obtaining assistance from other health-care team members are all methods of ensuring reliability of educational materials.

LO 5.5 Patient education promotes good health by teaching patients the importance of developing healthy habits such as eating properly and exercising regularly.

LO 5.6 The contents of the patient's information packet should include an introduction to the medical office, the physician's qualifications, a description of the practice, an introduction to the staff, office hours, appointment scheduling, telephone policies, payment and insurance policies, a confidentiality statement, and other pertinent information.

LO 5.7 Educating patients prior to surgery is vital to a successful outcome and involves instructing them on proper procedures before surgery and also having the patient sign a surgical consent.

medical assisting COMPETENCIES

CAAHEP

IV. C (7) Identify resources and adaptations that are required based on individual needs, i.e., culture and environment, developmental life stage, language, and physical threats to communication

IV. C (14) Recognize the role of patient advocacy in the practice of medical assisting

IV. P (9) Document patient education

IV. P (12) Develop and maintain a current list of community resources related to patients' health-care needs

ABHES

2. Anatomy and Physiology
   a. Comprehend and explain to the patient the importance of diet and nutrition; effectively convey and educate patients regarding the proper diet and nutrition guidelines; identify categories of patients who require special diets or diet modifications

8. Medical Office Business Procedures Management
   e. Locate resources and information for patients and employers
   cc. Communicate on the recipient's level of comprehension
   dd. Serve as liaison between physician and others
   hh. Receive, organize, prioritize, and transmit information expediently
   ii. Recognize and respond to verbal and nonverbal communication
   kk. Adapt to individualized needs

9. Medical Office Clinical Procedures
   p. Advise patients of policies and procedures
   q. Instruct patients with special needs
   r. Teach patients methods of health promotion and disease prevention

11. Career Development
   b. Demonstrate professionalism by:
      (1) Exhibiting dependability, punctuality, and a positive work ethic
      (2) Exhibiting a positive attitude and a sense of responsibility
      (3) Maintaining confidentiality at all times
      (4) Being cognizant of ethical boundaries
      (5) Exhibiting initiative
      (8) Being courteous and diplomatic
      (9) Conducting work within scope of education, training, and ability

The Medical Office

When we do the best we can, we never know what miracle is produced in our life or the life of another.

Helen Keller

Preparation for Success

Interviewer: Jaci, you work as an administrative medical assistant for a busy gastroenterology office. I understand that you had quite a bit of excitement during your first week on the job.

Jaci: Yes, we do endoscopic procedures and I was checking in a patient when I noticed he looked apprehensive and pale. At first I thought it was because he could not eat because of the procedure he was having.

Interviewer: You were observant. What happened next?

Jaci: He seemed uncomfortable and I asked him if he felt okay. He said he was having a little chest pain. I remembered the class that talked about patients that should not be asked to wait in the reception area and should have immediate attention. I called the clinical area. They brought him back and put him on a cardiac monitor. Then the excitement started.

Interviewer: Tell us what happened next.

Jaci: The patient was having a heart attack and the doctor told me to call 911. I did and when the paramedics arrived, I brought them to the treatment area. Afterward, I was asked to document my observations and actions. They said I probably saved the patient's life.

Interviewer: Wow, that must have been a great feeling.

Jaci: Yes, it was and when I stopped shaking, I was very glad I had paid attention in class that day!

Interviewer: Jaci, you are now a team leader at the gastroenterology office. What advice do you have for students studying to be administrative medical assistants?

Jaci: Go to class every day, pay attention, and do your assignments. You never know when you will need the information you are studying and how important it may be. Even keying correct information into a patient's record could be significant.

unit **2**

6 Law and Ethics in the Medical Office

Learning Outcomes

After completing Chapter 6, you will be able to:

6.1 Explain the difference between laws and ethics.

6.2 List the responsibilities of the patient and physician in a patient-physician contract.

6.3 Define the four Ds of negligence required to prove malpractice and explain the four Cs of malpractice prevention.

6.4 Explain the importance of medical record documentation, including items that require documentation.

6.5 Summarize the HCQIA and the Federal False Claims Act.

6.6 Explain Occupational Safety and Health Administration (OSHA) requirements for a medical office.

6.7 Explain the impact that Health Insurance Portability and Accountability Act (HIPAA) regulations have in the medical office.

6.8 List six ways to protect patient confidentiality.

6.9 Explain the importance of ethics in the medical office.

6.10 Point out the differences among the practice management models.

Key Terms

abandonment
agent
arbitration
assault
authorization
battery
bioethics
breach of contract
civil law
consent
contract
controlled substances
corporation
credentialing
crime
criminal law
defamation
disclosure
doctrine of informed consent
doctrine of professional discretion
durable power of attorney
electronic transaction record
ethics
expressed contract
felony
fraud
group practice
implied consent
implied contract

informed consent
law
law of agency
liable
libel
malpractice claim
minors
misdemeanor
moral values
negligence
Notice of Privacy Practices (NPP)
partnership
Privacy Rule
protected health information (PHI)
qui tam
res ipsa loquitur
respondeat superior
risk management
Security Rule
slander
sole proprietorship
subpoena
subpoena duces tecum
subpoena ad testificandum
tort
treatment, payment, and operations (TPO)
uniform donor card
use
void

Preparation for Certification

RMA (AMT) Exam
- Medical ethics
- Compliance with OSHA guidelines and regulation of office safety
- Principles of medical ethics

CMAS (AMT) Exam
- Professionalism
- Legal and ethical considerations
- Confidentiality

CMA (AAMA) Exam
- Displaying professional attitude
- Legislation
- Maintaining confidentiality
- Working as a team member to achieve goals

Introduction ● ● ●

Medical law plays an important role in medical facility procedures and the way we care for patients. We live in a litigious society where patients, relatives, and others are inclined to sue health-care practitioners, health-care facilities, manufacturers of medical equipment and products, and others when medical outcomes are not acceptable. It is important for a medical professional to understand medical law, ethics, and the Health Insurance Portability and Accountability Act (HIPAA) of 1996.

A knowledge of medical law and ethics can help you gain perspective in the following three areas:

1. *The rights, responsibilities, and concerns of health-care consumers.* Health-care professionals need to be concerned about how law and ethics impact their respective professions and they must also understand how legal and ethical issues affect patients. As medical technology advances and the use of computers increases, patients know more about their options and rights as well as more about the responsibilities of health-care practitioners. Patients have come to expect favorable outcomes from medical treatment, and when these expectations are not met, lawsuits may result.

2. *The legal and ethical issues facing society, patients, and health-care professionals as the world changes.* Every day new technologies emerge with solutions to biological and medical issues. These solutions often involve social issues, and we are faced with decisions, for example, regarding reproductive rights, fetal stem cell research, and confidentiality with sensitive medical records.

3. *The impact of rising costs on the laws and ethics of health-care delivery.* Rising costs, both of health-care insurance and of medical treatment in general, can lead to questions concerning access to health-care services and the allocation of medical treatment. For example, should everyone, regardless of age or lifestyle, have the same access to scarce medical commodities such as transplant organs or very expensive drugs.

In today's society, medical treatment and decisions surrounding health care have become complex. It is therefore important to be knowledgeable about and aware of the ethical issues and the laws that govern patient care. As a member of the health-care team, always keep in mind that any health or financial information you obtain regarding a patient (past or present) is protected. It may be shared only with the patient's express permission, except in a few very specific instances that will be discussed in this chapter.

LO 6.1 The Difference between Law and Ethics

In order to understand medical law and ethics, it is helpful to understand the difference between law and ethics. A **law** is defined as a rule of conduct or action prescribed or formally recognized as binding or enforced by a controlling authority, such as local, state, and federal governments. **Ethics** is considered a standard of behavior and a concept of right and wrong beyond what the legal consideration is in any given situation. **Moral values** serve as a basis for ethical conduct. Moral values are formed through the influence of the family, culture, and society. Ethics will be discussed in further detail later in the chapter.

Classifications of Law

There are two types of law that pertain to health-care practitioners: criminal law and civil law.

law
A rule of conduct or action prescribed or formally recognized as binding or enforced by a controlling authority, such as local, state, and federal governments.

ethics
A standard of behavior and a concept of right and wrong beyond what the legal consideration is in any given situation.

moral values
Serve as a basis for ethical conduct. Moral values are formed through the influence of the family, culture, and society.

crime
Any offense committed or omitted in violation of a public law.

criminal law
Law involving crimes against the state.

felony
A crime such as abuse, fraud, and practicing medicine without a license. These crimes are punishable by imprisonment in a state or federal prison for more than one year or, in some cases, by death.

misdemeanor
Crime that is less serious than a felony, such as attempted robbery. Misdemeanors are punishable by fines or by imprisonment in a facility other than a prison for 1 year or less.

civil law
Involves crimes against the person. Lawsuits come under the heading of civil law.

tort
A civil wrong committed against a person or property that causes physical injury or damage to someone's property or that deprives someone of his or her personal liberty and freedom.

assault
The open threat of bodily harm to another, or acting in such a way as to put another in the "reasonable apprehension of bodily harm."

battery
Any action that causes bodily harm to another person.

defamation
Damaging a person's reputation by making public statements that are both false and malicious.

slander
Speaking damaging words intended to negatively influence others against an individual in a manner that jeopardizes his or her reputation or means of livelihood.

libel
Publishing in print damaging words, pictures, or signed statements that will injure the reputation of another.

fraud
Deceitful practices in depriving or attempting to deprive another of his or her rights, usually for the gain of another.

Criminal Law   A **crime** is any offense committed or omitted in violation of a public law. **Criminal law** involves crimes against the state. When a state or federal law is violated, the government brings criminal charges against the alleged offender, for example, *Ohio v. John Doe.* Criminal laws prohibit such crimes as murder, arson, rape, and burglary. A criminal act may be classified as a felony or misdemeanor. A **felony** is a crime punishable by death or by imprisonment in a state or federal prison for more than 1 year. Some examples of a felony include abuse (child, elder, or domestic violence), manslaughter, fraud, attempted murder, and practicing medicine without a license.

   Misdemeanors are less serious crimes than felonies. They are punishable by fines or by imprisonment in a facility other than a prison for 1 year or less. Some examples of misdemeanors are thefts under a certain dollar amount, attempted burglary, and disturbing the peace.

Civil Law   **Civil law** involves crimes against the person. Under civil law, a person can sue another person, a business, or the government. Court judgments in civil cases often require the payment of a sum of money to the injured party. Civil law includes a general category of law known as torts. A **tort** is broadly defined as a civil wrong committed against a person or property that causes physical injury or damage to someone's property or that deprives someone of his or her personal liberty and freedom. Torts may be intentional (willful) or unintentional (accidental).

Intentional Torts   When one person intentionally harms another, the law allows the injured party to seek a remedy in a civil suit. The injured party can be financially compensated for any harm done by the person guilty of committing the tort. If the conduct is judged to be malicious, punitive damages may also be awarded. Examples of intentional torts include the following:

- Assault. **Assault** is the open threat of bodily harm to another, or acting in such a way as to put another in the "ireasonable apprehension of bodily harm". In the medical office, if a patient were to feel threatened in any way, assault could be charged.

- Battery. **Battery** is an action that causes bodily harm to another. It is broadly defined as any bodily contact made without permission. In health-care delivery, battery may be charged for any unauthorized touching of a patient, including such actions as suturing a wound, administering an injection, or performing a physical examination.

- Defamation of character. Damaging a person's reputation by making public statements that are both false and malicious is considered **defamation** of character. Defamation of character can take the form of slander and libel. **Slander** is speaking damaging words intended to negatively influence others against an individual in a manner that jeopardizes his or her reputation or means of livelihood. If a patient hears members of the staff speaking about him in an unprofessional manner, or talking about his diagnosis with staff members without a "need to know," it could be considered slanderous. **Libel** is publishing in print damaging words, pictures, or signed statements that will injure the reputation of another.

- False imprisonment. False imprisonment is the intentional, unlawful restraint or confinement of one person by another. Preventing a patient from leaving the facility might be seen as false imprisonment.

- Fraud. **Fraud** consists of deceitful practices in depriving or attempting to deprive another of his or her rights, usually for the gain of another. Health-care practitioners might be accused of fraud for promising patients "miracle cures" or for accepting fees from patients while using mystical or spiritual powers to heal.

- Invasion of privacy. Invasion of privacy is the interference with a person's right to be left alone. Entering an exam room without knocking can be considered an invasion of privacy. The improper use of or a breach of confidentiality of medical records may be seen as an invasion of privacy.

Unintentional Torts The most common torts within the health-care delivery system are those committed unintentionally. Unintentional torts are acts that are not intended to cause harm but are committed unreasonably or with a disregard for the consequences. In legal terms, such acts constitute negligence. **Negligence** is charged when a health-care practitioner fails to exercise ordinary care and the patient is injured. Medical negligence is more commonly known as malpractice, which will be discussed in more detail later in this chapter.

Contracts

A **contract** is a voluntary agreement between two parties in which specific promises are made for a consideration. The elements of a contract are important to health-care practitioners because health-care delivery takes place under various types of contracts. To be legally binding, four elements must be present in a contract:

1. Agreement—One party makes an offer and another party accepts it. Certain conditions pertain to the offer:

   - It can relate to the present or the future.
   - It must be communicated.
   - It must be made in good faith and not under duress or as a joke.
   - It must be clear enough to be understood by both parties.
   - It must define what both parties will do if the offer is accepted.

   For example, a physician offers a service to the public by obtaining a license to practice medicine and opening a business. Patients accept the physician's offer by scheduling appointments, submitting to physical examinations, and allowing the physician to prescribe or perform medical treatment. The contract is complete when the physician's fee is paid.

2. Consideration—Something of value is bargained for as part of the agreement. The physician's consideration is providing service; the patient's consideration is payment of the physician's fee.

3. Legal subject matter—Contracts are not valid and enforceable in court unless they are for legal services or purposes. For example, a contract entered into by a patient to pay for the services of a physician in private practice would be **void** (not legally enforceable) if the physician was not licensed to practice medicine. **Breach of contract** may be charged if either party fails to comply with the terms of a legally valid contract.

4. Contractual capacity—Parties who enter into the agreement must be capable of fully understanding all its terms and conditions. For example, a mentally incompetent individual or a person under the influence of drugs or alcohol cannot enter into a contract.

Types of Contracts The two main types of contracts are expressed contracts and implied contracts. An **expressed contract** is clearly stated in written or spoken words. A payment contract is an example of an expressed contract. **Implied contracts** are those in which the conduct of the parties, rather than expressed words, indicates acceptance and creates the contract. A patient who rolls up a sleeve and offers an arm for an injection is creating an implied contract.

negligence
Charge when a health-care practitioner fails to exercise ordinary care and the patient is injured.

contract
A voluntary agreement between two parties in which specific promises are made for a consideration.

void
Contract or situation that is not legally enforceable.

breach of contract
Charge if either party in a contract fails to comply with the terms of a legally valid contract.

expressed contract
A contract clearly stated in written or spoken words.

implied contract
Contracts in which the conduct of the parties, rather than expressed words, indicates acceptance and creates the contract.

Legal Elements of a Contract   A contract is a legal agreement between two or more people to perform an act in exchange for payment. To be binding, the contract must include these main elements:

- An agreement between two or more competent people to do something legal
- Names and addresses of the people involved
- Consideration (whatever is given in exchange, such as money, work, or property)
- Starting and ending dates, as well as date(s) the contract was signed
- Signatures of the individuals involved in the contract

Employment Contract   Some medical practices use employment contracts for their employees. This type of contract would include these elements:

- A description of your duties and your employer's duties
- Plans for handling major changes in job responsibilities
- Salary, bonuses, and other forms of compensation
- Benefits, such as vacation time, sick days, life insurance, and participation in pension plans
- Grievance procedures
- Exceptional situations under which the contract may be terminated by either you or your employer
- Termination procedures and compensation
- Special provisions, such as job sharing, medical examinations, or liability coverage

If you are offered an employment contract, study it closely. Consider any local laws that may apply. It is wise to have a lawyer or business adviser review the contract prior to signing it.

CHECKPOINT
LO 6.1

Is it possible for a medical procedure to be legal yet be considered unethical by some members of our society? Explain your answer.

LO 6.2 The Patient-Physician Contract

A physician has the right, after forming a contract or agreeing to accept a patient under his or her care, to make reasonable limitations on the contractual relationship. The physician is under no legal obligations to treat patients who may wish to exceed those limitations. Under the patient-physician contract, both parties have certain rights and responsibilities.

Physician Rights and Responsibilities

A physician has the right to:

- Set up a practice within the boundaries of his or her license to practice medicine
- Set up an office where he or she chooses and to establish office hours
- Specialize
- Decide which services he or she will provide and how those services will be provided

While practicing within the context of an implied contract with the patient, the physician is not bound to:

- Treat every patient with medical care. A physician is free to use his or her discretion to form contracts within his or her practice, with one exception: If a physician is providing care to patients in a hospital emergency room or free clinic, then the physician must treat every patient who comes for treatment.
- Restore the patient to his or her original state of health
- Make a correct diagnosis in every case
- Guarantee the successful result of any treatment or operation. In fact, guarantees of "cures" may constitute fraud on the part of the physician.

Under an implied contract with the patient, the physician has the obligation or responsibility to:

- Use due care, skill, judgment, and diligence in treating patients that peers in the same specialty use
- Stay informed of the best methods of diagnosis and treatment
- Perform to the best of his or her ability, whether or not he or she is to receive a fee
- Furnish complete information and instructions to the patient about diagnoses, options, methods of treatment, and fees for services

Liability All competent adults are liable or legally responsible for their actions, in both their personal lives and their professional careers. It is important as an administrative medical assistant to know and understand your scope of practice within the state you are working. As health-care providers, medical assistants have general liability in the duties they perform, as well as the facility in which they work. By understanding the standard of care and the duty of care, medical assistants can function ethically and legally within their job scope. Medical assistants are held to the "reasonable person standard," which means to carry out your professional and interpersonal relationships without causing harm.

Patient Rights and Responsibilities

Patients have the right to choose a physician, although some managed care plans may limit choices. Patients also have the right to terminate a physician's services if they wish. Most states have adopted a version of the American Hospital Association's *Patient Care Partnership* (formerly called the Patient's Bill of Rights). The Patient Care Partnership is a list of standards that patients can expect in health care. The Joint Commission requires hospitals to post a copy of these standards and most managed care organizations also require contracted physicians to post a copy of them as well. Figure 6–1 is an example of a typical patient care partnership list for a medical office. The brochure given to the patient would go into each point in more detail.

Patient Responsibilities Patients are also part of the medical team involved in their treatment. Patients have the responsibility under an implied contract to:

- Follow any instructions given by the physician and cooperate as much as possible
- Give all relevant information to the physician in order to reach a correct diagnosis. If a patient fails to inform a physician of any medical conditions he or she may have and an incorrect diagnosis is made, the physician is not liable.
- Follow the physician's orders for treatment
- Pay the fees charged for services provided

TOTAL CARE CLINIC, PC

Patient Care Partnership
Understanding Expectations, Rights, and Responsibilities

Welcome to our medical practice. As our patient you have the right to certain expectations, including:

1. High-quality medical care

2. A clean and safe environment for your medical care

3. Informed involvement in your medical care

4. Protection of your privacy

5. Assistance obtaining referrals and appointments with outside providers

6. Help with billing and claim issues

You will receive a brochure outlining the details of these rights for your records. If you have any questions, comments, or suggestions regarding the information within the brochure or regarding your care with us, please let us know. We are always interested in improving your patient care experience with us.

figure 6-1

Example of a patient care partnership.

consent
The patient has given either expressed or implied permission for tests, physical exam, treatment, etc.

implied consent
Permission for treatment, physical exam, and so on, is understood through the patient's actions (such as making an appointment, rolling up the sleeve for venipuncture, etc.), rather than by written permission.

informed consent
The patient's right to receive all information relative to his or her condition and to make a decision regarding treatment based on that knowledge.

doctrine of informed consent
The legal basis for informed consent (or denial of treatment); usually outlined in a state's medical practice acts.

Consent **Consent** means that the patient has given permission, either expressed or implied, for the physician to examine him or her, to perform tests that aid in diagnoses, or to treat for a medical condition. When the patient makes an appointment to be examined by a physician, the patient has given **implied consent** to the examination and any diagnostic testing procedures needed for treatment.

Informed Consent **Informed consent** involves the patient's right to receive all information relative to his or her condition and to make a decision regarding treatment based upon that knowledge. The **doctrine of informed consent** is the legal basis for informed consent (or denial of treatment) and is usually outlined in a state's medical practice acts. Informed consent implies that the patient understands:

- Proposed treatment modes
- Why the treatment was necessary
- The risks involved in the proposed treatment
- Available alternative modes of treatment
- The risks of alternative treatments
- The risks involved if treatment is refused

Adult patients who are of sound mind are usually able to give informed consent. In the case of emancipated minors, courts have ruled that they understand as a competent adult would, and therefore are able to make decisions on their own. Mature minors are defined differently by each state but, in general, are minors who, depending on their medical condition, are considered capable of making their own medical decisions and do not require a guardian's consent for certain procedures such as contraception, STD treatment, and drug or alcohol addictions. It is wise to keep in mind that although mature minors may consent to treatment, they may not legally be allowed to enter into a financial contract for payment. The physician or business manager should make decisions regarding payment issues surrounding treatment of mature minors. Figure 6–2 gives state-by-state guidelines defining mature minors and what procedures and treatments they may consent to.

Those patients who cannot give informed consent include the following:

- **Minors** or persons under the age of majority, which excludes married minors

- The mentally incompetent

- Those who speak a foreign language—interpreters may be necessary

minors
Persons under the age of majority.

Informed consent is a vital part of the practice of medicine today. Physicians are often sued for negligence because of the failure to adequately inform patients of adverse surgical complications, drug reactions, and alternative treatment modes.

Terminating the Patient-Physician Contract

Ending the Patient-Physician Relationship A physician may wish to terminate care of a patient. Terminating care is sometimes called withdrawing from a case and must be undertaken carefully to avoid charges of abandonment. The following are some typical reasons a physician may choose to withdraw from a case:

- The patient refuses to follow the physician's instructions.

- The patient's family members complain incessantly to or about the physician.

- A personality conflict develops between the physician and patient that cannot be reasonably resolved.

- The patient habitually does not pay for or fails to make satisfactory arrangements to pay for medical services. A physician may stop treatment of such a patient and end the physician-patient relationship only if adequate notice is given to the patient.

- The patient fails to keep scheduled appointments. To protect the physician from charges of abandonment, all missed and cancelled appointments should be noted in the patient's chart.

A physician who terminates care of a patient must do so in a formal, legal manner, following these four steps.

1. Write a letter to the patient, expressing the reason for withdrawing from the case and recommending that the patient seek medical care from another physician as soon as possible. Thirty days is the usual norm for finding another physician. Figure 6–3 shows an example of a letter of termination.

2. Send the letter by certified mail with a return receipt requested. This will provide evidence that the patient received the notification by providing a signature on the return receipt.

3. Place a copy of the letter (and the return receipt, when received) in the patient's medical record.

4. Summarize in the patient record the physician's reason for terminating care and the actions taken to inform the patient.

figure 6-2

Minors' access to health care in the United States.

STATE	GENERAL MEDICAL HEALTH[b]	MENTAL HEALTH	SUBSTANCE ABUSE[c]	COMMUNICABLE DISEASES[d]	CONTRACEPTIVES	PRENATAL CARE
Alabama	✓ (3), (8)	✓	✓	✓ (1), (7)		✓
Alaska	✓ (9)			✓	✓	✓
Arizona			✓ (1)	✓	✓	
Arkansas	✓ (15)			✓ (7), (13)	✓	✓ (12), (13)
California		✓ (1), (7)	✓ (1), (7)	✓ (1)	✓	✓ (12)
Colorado		✓ (4), (7)	✓	✓	✓ (11), (19)	
Connecticut		✓	✓	✓		
Delaware	✓ (10)		✓ (1)	✓ (1), (7), (13)	✓ (1), (7)	✓ (1), (7), (12), (13)
District of Columbia		✓	✓	✓	✓	✓
Florida		✓ (2)	✓	✓	✓ (11), (17)	✓ (13)
Georgia			✓ (7)	✓ (7), (13)	✓	✓ (12)
Hawaii			✓ (7)	✓ (3), (7), (14)	✓ (3), (7), (14)	✓ (3), (7), (12), (14)
Idaho	✓		✓	✓ (3)	✓	
Illinois	✓ (11), (13)	✓ (1), (7)	✓ (1), (7)	✓ (1), (7)	✓ (9), (18)	✓ (13), (18)
Indiana			✓	✓		
Iowa			✓	✓ (20)		
Kansas	✓ (13), (21)		✓	✓ (7)	✓ (15)	✓ (13), (22)
Kentucky	✓ (7), (10)	✓ (5), (7)	✓ (7)	✓ (7)	✓ (7)	✓ (7), (12)
Louisiana	✓ (7), (13)		✓ (7)	✓ (7)		
Maine			✓ (7)	✓ (7)	✓ (10), (17)	
Maryland	✓ (7), (10)	✓ (5), (7)	✓ (7)	✓ (7)	✓ (7)	✓ (7)
Massachusetts	✓ (11)	✓ (5)	✓ (1), (23)	✓	✓	✓ (12)
Michigan		✓ (3)	✓ (7)	✓ (7)	✓ (27)	✓ (7)
Minnesota	✓ (7), (10)	✓	✓ (7)	✓ (7)	✓ (7)	✓ (7)
Mississippi			✓ (4), (7)	✓	✓ (10), (19)	✓ (13)
Missouri	✓ (10), (13)		✓ (7), (13)	✓ (7), (13)		✓ (7), (12), (13)
Montana	✓ (7), (11), (13)	✓ (5)	✓ (7), (13)	✓ (7), (13)	✓ (7)	✓ (7), (13)
Nebraska			✓	✓		

figure 6-2 (Continued)

STATE	GENERAL MEDICAL HEALTH[b]	MENTAL HEALTH	SUBSTANCE ABUSE[c]	COMMUNICABLE DISEASES[d]	CONTRACEPTIVES	PRENATAL CARE
Nevada	✓ (10), (15), (17)		✓	✓		
New Hampshire	✓ (15)		✓ (1)	✓ (3)		
New Jersey	✓ (11)		✓ (7)	✓ (7), (13)		✓ (7), (13)
New Mexico		✓		✓	✓	✓ (24)
New York	✓ (11)	✓ (7)	✓ (7)	✓	✓	✓
North Carolina	✓ (21)	✓	✓	✓	✓	✓ (12)
North Dakota			✓ (3)	✓ (3)		
Ohio		✓ (3)	✓	✓		
Oklahoma	✓ (7), (11)		✓ (7)	✓ (7)	✓ (7), (25)	✓ (7), (12)
Oregon	✓ (4), (7), (13)	✓ (3), (7)	✓ (3), (7)	✓ (13)	✓ (7)	
Pennsylvania	✓ (8)		✓ (7)	✓		✓
Rhode Island			✓	✓		
South Carolina	✓ (5), (26)	✓ (26)	✓ (26)	✓ (26)	✓ (26)	✓ (26)
South Dakota	✓ (21)		✓	✓		
Tennessee		✓ (5)	✓ (7)	✓	✓	✓
Texas		✓	✓ (7)	✓ (7), (13)	✓	✓ (7), (12), (13)
Utah				✓	✓ (7), (16)	✓
Vermont			✓ (1)	✓ (1)		
Virginia	✓ (21)	✓	✓	✓	✓	✓
Washington		✓ (2)	✓ (2)	✓ (3), (13)	✓	✓
West Virginia			✓	✓		
Wisconsin			✓ (1)	✓		
Wyoming				✓	✓	
N=	25	23	46	51	33	31
%	49%	45%	90%	100%	65%	60%

Exclusions and Limitations Key
(1) The minor must be at least 12 years old.
(2) The minor must be at least 13 years old.
(3) The minor must be at least 14 years old.
(4) The minor must be at least 15 years old.
(5) The minor must be at least 16 years old.
(6) The minor must be at least 17 years old.
(7) The heath-care provider may notify parents.

(Continued)

figure 6-2 *(Concluded)*

(8) The minor must be a high school graduate, married, pregnant, or a parent.

(9) Minor may consent if a parent.

(10) Minor may consent if a parent or if married.

(11) Minor may consent if a parent, married, or pregnant.

(12) Excludes abortive services.

(13) Includes surgical care.

(14) Excludes surgical care.

(15) Minor must be able to understand the nature and consequences of medical or surgical treatment proposed.

(16) Utah Code Ann. § 76-7-325 (LEXIS L. Publg. 2001), "Notice to parent or guardian of minor requesting contraceptive — Definition of contraceptives — Penalty for violation," stating "(1) Any person before providing contraceptives to a minor shall notify, whenever possible, the minor's parents or guardian of the service requested to be provided to such minor. Contraceptives shall be defined as appliances (including but not limited to intrauterine devices), drugs, or medicinal preparations intended or having special utility for prevention of conception. (2) Any person in violation of this section shall be guilty of a class C misdemeanor," was ruled unconstitutional by Planned Parenthood Ass'n v. Matheson, 582 F. Supp. 1001, 1983 U.S. Dist. LEXIS 10330 (D. Utah 1983) with respect to its failure to "provide a procedure whereby a mature minor or a minor who can demonstrate that his or her best interests are contrary to parental notification can obtain contraceptives confidentially." However, the court also noted that it "does not intend to imply by this decision that a law which provided a means for minors to demonstrate maturity or best interests contrary to parental involvement would be constitutional. All that the court has decided is that due to the failure to provide such a process, H.B. 343 goes beyond the constitutionally permissible point of regulating the right of minors to make independent decisions concerning whether to bear or to beget children."

(17) If minor is a parent, or provider believes minor will suffer probable health hazard if services withheld.

(18) If minor is a parent, or is referred by a doctor, clergy, or Planned Parenthood clinic.

(19) If minor is a parent, or is referred by a doctor, clergy, family planning clinic, school of higher education, or state agency.

(20) Parental notification required for positive outcome on HIV test.

(21) If parent or guardian is not "immediately available."

(22) If parent is not "available."

(23) Requires diagnosis of two health care providers, and excludes methadone treatment.

(24) Limited to pregnancy testing and diagnosis.

(25) Females can consent if they have ever been pregnant.

(26) Minors of any age when health care provider believes services are necessary; minors at least (16) years old may consent to all health services excluding operations.

(27) Under Mich. Comp. Laws § 400.14b (LEXIS L. Publg. 2001), "Family planning services; notice; referrals; furnishing drugs and appliances," minors may obtain contraceptive services (See Doe v Irwin 441 F.Supp. 1247 (W.D.Mich. 1977), rev'd on other grounds, 615 F.2d 1162 (6th Cir. Mich. 1980), cert denied, 449 U.S. 829 (1980) (the existence, if any, of a fundamental civil right among minors to obtain prescriptive contraceptives does not need to exist to total exclusion of any rights of the minor child's parents) Doe v Irwin 615 F.2d 1162 (6th Cir. Mich. 1980), cert denied, 449 U.S. 829 (1980) (a state-run clinic that distributed contraceptive devices and medication to unemancipated children without the knowledge and the consent of their parents did not infringe parents' constitutional right to care, custody, and nurture of their children).

(a) The age of majority in the 50 states and the District of Columbia is 18, with the exception of Alabama and Nevada, in which it is 19; Pennsylvania, in which it is 21; and Mississippi, in which it is 21, aside from consent for general health care, for which the age of majority is 18.

(b) The Alan Guttmacher Institute did not define the term "general medical health care." However, Minn. Stat. § 144.341 (LEXIS L. Publg. 2001), "Living apart from parents and managing financial affairs, consent for self," provides that "Notwithstanding any other provision of law, any minor who is living separate and apart from parents or legal guardian, whether with or without the consent of a parent or guardian and regardless of the duration of such separate residence, and who is managing personal financial affairs, regardless of the source or extent of the minor's income, may give effective consent to personal medical, dental, mental and other health services, and the consent of no other person is required," while Ala. Code § 22-8-4 (LEXIS L. Publg. 2001), "Minors; consent for self," provides that "Any minor who is 14 years of age or older, or has graduated from high school, or is married, or having been married is divorced or is pregnant may give effective consent to any legally authorized medical, dental, health or mental health services for himself or herself, and the consent of no other person shall be necessary." Thus, this term suggests that statutes indicated provide broad language covering medical, dental, mental, and possibly other, health services.

(c) Statutes typically encompass the broad terms "alcohol" and "drugs."

(d) Includes HIV testing and treatment, with the restriction of testing only in California, New Mexico, and Ohio.

Standard of Care

You are expected to fulfill the standards of the medical assisting profession for applying legal concepts to practice. According to the AAMA, medical assistants should uphold legal concepts in the following ways:

- Maintain confidentiality
- Practice within the scope of training and capabilities
- Prepare and maintain medical records
- Document accurately
- Use appropriate guidelines when releasing information

LETTER OF WITHDRAWAL FROM CARE

December 12, 2012

Jack Smallwood
PO Box 3457C
Funton, XY 12345-6789

Dear Mr. Smallwood:

This is to inform you of our intent to discontinue providing medical care to you due to the habitual and continued noncompliance in your treatment plan. Our records indicate that you have missed several appointments and have not complied with ordered testing. This discontinuance will go into effect 30 days from the date of this letter in order to allow you sufficient time to locate another physician. We will be happy to forward your medical records to the physician of your choice. There is 24-hour medical care available to you at the hospital.

If you need assistance in locating a new physician, please contact your insurance carrier or the Tennessee Medical Society at 1-800-666-9898.

Sincerely,

Matthew Rodriguez, MD

Matthew Rodriguez, MD (Internal Med)

- Follow legal guidelines and maintain awareness of health-care legislation and regulations
- Maintain and dispose of regulated substances in compliance with government guidelines
- Follow established risk-management and safety procedures
- Meet the requirements for professional credentialing

Often, state laws dictate what medical assistants may or may not do. For instance, in some states it is illegal for medical assistants to draw blood. No states consider it legal for medical assistants to diagnose a condition, prescribe a treatment, or let a patient believe that a medical assistant is a nurse. In addition to what is stated by law, you and the physician must establish the procedures that are appropriate for you to perform (known as scope of practice).

Closing a Medical Practice

Distressful economic circumstances may cause a medical practice to terminate and close its services to its patients. If this becomes necessary, make sure the medical staff and all physicians

- Comply with all HIPAA laws for maintaining confidentiality.
- Write letters to all patients, giving them knowledge that your practice will be closing (Figure 6–4).
- Give patients an option of choosing another physician, or make referrals. If the patient chooses another physician to take over his care, get written consent for his charts to be transferred to that physician properly.

figure 6–3

Physicians are required to inform patients in writing if they wish to withdraw from a case.

TOTAL CARE CLINIC, PC

342 East Park Blvd
Funton, XY   12345-6789
Tel: 521-234-0001
Fax: 521-234-0002
www.totalcareclinic.org

May 23, 201X

Ms. Gisele Monagon
234 Cutter Lane
Monson, MA 01057

Dear Ms. Monagon:

I find it necessary to inform you that our medical practice will be closing on July 15, 201X. My medical practice will be purchased by The Vaughn Group, 2345 Williamsburg Ct., Springfield, MA 01118

If you wish to use this group of medical practitioners, please sign the enclosed authorization release form so that your files can be sent to them promptly.

If you choose not to use this group of physicians, you may send me a letter with your signature, authorizing the release of your files to the physician of your choice.

It has been a pleasure serving you.

Sincerely,

Alexis N. Wyman, MD

Alexis N. Wyman, MD
mng
Enclosure: Authorization Form

figure 6-4

Sample letter informing patient of practice closure.

- Keep all files in a secured location for the maximum amount of time files should be saved if contact with patients cannot be made. You will have to choose a vendor that stores files. Make sure you choose a reputable vendor.
- Shred files if necessary; make sure you choose reputable vendors.
- Are up-to-date on any HIPAA laws that will affect the practice.

CHECKPOINT
LO 6.2

What are the six components necessary for consent to be considered "informed"?

LO 6.3 Preventing Malpractice Claims

Malpractice litigation not only adds to the cost of health care, it takes a psychological toll on both patients and health-care practitioners. Both sides would probably agree that prevention is preferable to litigation. Health-care practitioners

who use reasonable care in preventing professional liability claims are least likely to be faced with defending themselves against malpractice claims.

Risk management is the act or practice of controlling risk. This process includes identifying and tracking risk areas, developing risk improvement plans as part of risk handling, monitoring risks, and performing risk assessments to determine how risks have changed. Proper documentation, patient satisfaction, appropriate behavior, proper medical procedures, and safeguards against exposure assist with decreasing the risk of malpractice lawsuits brought against the medical facility physicians and their staff.

Medical Negligence

Malpractice claims are lawsuits by patients against physicians for errors in diagnosis or treatment. Medical negligence cases are those in which a person believes that a medical professional did not perform an essential action or performed an improper one, thus harming the patient.

Following are some examples of malpractice:

- Postoperative complications. For example, a patient starts to show signs of internal bleeding in the recovery room. The incision is reopened, and it is discovered that the surgeon did not complete closure (cauterization) of all the severed capillaries at the operation site.

- *Res ipsa loquitur.* This Latin term, which means "the thing speaks for itself," refers to a case in which the doctor's fault is completely obvious. For example, a case in which a surgeon accidentally leaves a surgical instrument inside the patient.

Following are examples of medical negligence:

- Abandonment. A health-care professional who stops care without providing an equally qualified substitute can be charged with **abandonment.** For example, a labor and delivery nurse is helping a woman in labor. The nurse's shift ends, but all the other nurses are busy and her replacement is late for work. Leaving the woman would constitute abandonment.

- Delayed treatment. A patient shows symptoms of some illness or disorder, but the doctor decides, for whatever reason, to delay treatment. If the patient later learns of the doctor's decision to wait, the patient may believe he has a negligence case.

Medical negligence cases are sometimes classified using the following three legal terms.

1. *Malfeasance* refers to an unlawful act or misconduct.
2. *Misfeasance* refers to a lawful act that is done incorrectly.
3. *Nonfeasance* refers to failure to perform an act that is one's required duty or that is required by law.

The Four Ds of Negligence The American Medical Association (AMA) lists the following four Ds of negligence:

1. Duty. Patients must show that a physician-patient relationship existed in which the physician owed the patient a duty.
2. Derelict. Patients must show that the physician failed to comply with the standards of the profession. For example, a gynecologist has routinely taken Pap smears of a patient and then, for whatever reason, does not do so. If the patient then shows evidence of cervical cancer, the physician could be said to have been derelict.
3. Direct cause. Patients must show that any damages were a direct cause of a physician's breach of duty. For example, if a patient fell on the sidewalk

risk management
The act or practice of controlling risk. This process includes identifying and tracking risk areas, developing risk improvement plans as part of risk handling, monitoring risks, and performing risk assessments to determine how risks have changed.

malpractice claim
Lawsuit by a patient against a physician for errors in diagnosis or treatment.

res ipsa loquitur
Latin term meaning "the thing speaks for itself"; refers to a case in which the doctor's fault is completely obvious.

abandonment
Charge when a health-care professional stops patient care without providing an equally qualified substitute.

and damaged her cast, she could not prove that the cast was damaged because it was incorrectly or poorly applied by her physician. It would be clear that the damage to the cast resulted from the fall. If, however, the patient's leg healed incorrectly because of the way the cast had been applied, she might have a case.

4. Damages. Patients must prove that they suffered injury.

To go forward with a malpractice suit, a patient must be prepared to prove all four Ds of negligence.

Malpractice and Civil Law Malpractice (medical negligence) lawsuits are part of civil law coming under the heading of torts. A tort is defined as the breach of an obligation that causes harm or injury and may intentional or unintentional. A breach of contract is the failure of one of the parties to adhere to the terms of the contract.

In the case of medical care contracts, which are often implied contracts, either the provider or the patient may breach the contract. The provider may breach the contract by not maintaining patient confidentiality or by not providing adequate medical care (negligence). The patient may breach the contract by not showing for appointments or by not following the physician's plan of care.

Settling Malpractice Suits Malpractice suits often require a trial in a court of law. Sometimes, however, they are settled through arbitration. **Arbitration** is a process in which the opposing sides choose a person or persons outside the court system, often with special knowledge in the field, to hear and decide the dispute. (Your local or state medical society has information about your state's policy on arbitration.) If injury, failure to provide reasonable care, or abandonment of the patient is proved to have occurred, the doctor must pay damages (a financial award) to the injured party.

If the doctor you work with becomes involved in a lawsuit, you should be familiar with subpoenas. A **subpoena** is a written court order addressed to a specific person, requiring that person's presence in court on a specific date at a specific time. If you were directly involved in the patient case or have knowledge of the events that precipitated the lawsuit, you might be subpoenaed to provide testimony under penalty, known as *subpoena testificandum.* Another important term to know is *subpoena duces tecum,* which is a court order to produce specific, requested documents required at a certain place and time to enter into court records. If you are in charge of patient records at the practice, you will be required to locate, assemble, photocopy, and arrange for delivery of the requested records or be charged with contempt of court if you do not comply.

Law of Agency According to the **law of agency,** an employee is considered to be acting as a doctor's **agent** (on the doctor's behalf) while performing professional tasks. The Latin term *respondeat superior,* or "let the master answer," is sometimes used to refer to this relationship. For example, the employee's word is as binding as if it were the doctor's (so you should never, for example, promise a patient a cure). Therefore, the doctor is responsible, or **liable,** for the negligence of employees. A negligent employee, however, may also be sued directly because individuals are legally responsible for their own actions. Therefore, a patient can sue both the doctor and the involved employee for negligence. The employer, or the employer's insurance company, can also sue the employee. Most likely, in a case of negligence, the doctor would be sued (because you as an employee are acting on the doctor's behalf), and you are usually covered by the doctor's malpractice insurance. Some medical assistants (usually clinical MAs) choose to obtain malpractice insurance. Obtaining personal malpractice insurance is a professional decision that depends on the type of work or facility

arbitration
The process in which the opposing sides choose a person or persons outside the court system, often with special knowledge in the field, to hear and decide the dispute.

subpoena
A written court order addressed to a specific person requiring that person's presence in court on a specific date at a specific time.

subpoena testificandum
Subpoena which requires the person to provide testimony in court under penalty.

subpoena duces tecum
A court order to produce specific, requested documents required at a certain place and time to enter into court records.

law of agency
Law that states that an employee is considered to act as the agent of the employer.

agent
One who acts on the behalf of another, such as an employee acting on behalf of the employer.

respondeat superior
"Let the Master Answer"–the employer is responsible for the employee's actions or inaction.

liable
One person being responsible for another's actions.

in which you are employed. The American Association of Medical Assistants offers medical assisting malpractice insurance through various insurance companies at reduced rates.

Courtroom Conduct   Most health-care practitioners will never have to appear in court. If you should be asked to appear, the following suggestions may prove helpful:

- Attend court proceedings as required. Failure to appear in court could result in either charges of contempt of court or the case being forfeited.
- Do not be late for scheduled hearings.
- Bring required documents to court and present them only when requested to do so.
- Before testifying, refresh your memory concerning all the facts observed about the matter in question, such as dates, times, words spoken, and circumstances.
- Speak slowly, clearly, and professionally. Do not use medical terms. Do not lose your temper or attempt to be humorous.
- Answer all questions in a straightforward manner, even if the answers appear to help the opposing side.
- Answer only the question asked, no more and no less.
- Appear well-groomed, and dress in clean, conservative clothing.

Professional Liability Coverage   Professional liability coverage, also known as malpractice insurance, is specialty coverage. It protects the physician and staff against financial losses from lawsuits filed against them by their clients or others. It protects the physician if she is found to be negligent in her actions, and it protects the physician and her staff if it is determined that the staff are negligent in their actions as well but the protection comes at an extremely high cost to the practice. Society in general and patients in particular have extremely high expectations of physicians and of the medical community. Malpractice lawsuits have become quite commonplace, with lawyers even advertising their assistance if a patient is unhappy with the medical care received.

Malpractice insurance can be one of the most expensive accounts payable in the office. Depending on the type of specialty and the area of the country the physician practices in, costs for an internist can be as low as $5000 per year in Minnesota (which has some of the lowest malpractice rates in the country) to a high of $56,000 (in 2009) in Florida, which has some of the highest rates in the country. Depending on the specialty and the location of the practice, specialists can expect to pay anywhere from $4000 to $142,000 per year for coverage.

Reasons Patients Sue

The following reasons were researched by interviewing families and patients who have sued health-care practitioners:

1. Unrealistic expectations. With the advancements in medical technology today, patients often expect perfection in medical outcomes. They may feel betrayed by the health-care system when a medical outcome is not what was expected.
2. Poor rapport and poor communication. Patients usually do not sue health-care practitioners that they like and trust. Health-care providers who do not return telephone calls or are otherwise unavailable to a patient's family members may be perceived as arrogant, cold, or uncaring. When such perceptions exist, patients and family members are more likely to sue if something goes wrong.

3. Greed and our litigious society. Financial gain is seldom the reason for medical malpractice, but in some cases it may be an influencing factor. Malpractice attorneys sometimes make it very easy for patients to retain their services, such as contingency arrangements.

4. Poor quality of care. Poor quality means that a patient is truly not receiving quality care. Poor quality in "perception" means that the patient believes he or she is not receiving quality care, even if it is not true. Either situation can lead to a malpractice lawsuit.

Statute of Limitations   Statutes of limitations are laws that set the deadline or maximum period of time within which a lawsuit or claim may be filed. The most common length of time is 2 years. The deadlines may vary depending on the circumstances and the type of case or claim. The periods of time also vary from state to state and depending on whether they are filed in federal or state court. The lawsuit or claim is barred if not filed before the statutory deadline. Under certain circumstances, a statute of limitations will be extended beyond its deadline. The following are examples for a civil claim for professional malpractice:

- *Medical:* 1 to 4 years from the act or occurrence of injury, or 6 months to 3 years from discovery; certain circumstances will extend the statute, including if the party is a minor, when a foreign object is involved, or in cases of fraud

- *Legal:* 1 to 3 years from date of discovery, or a maximum of 2 to 5 years from the date of the wrongful act

Four Cs of Medical Malpractice Prevention

1. *Caring.* As a health-care professional, caring about your patients and colleagues is your most important asset. Showing patients that you care about them may result in an improvement in their medical condition and, if you are sincere, decreases the likelihood that patients will feel the need to sue if treatment has unsatisfactory results or adverse events occur.

2. *Communication.* If you communicate in a professional manner and clearly ask for confirmation that you have been understood, you will earn respect and trust with your patients and other members of the allied health team.

3. *Competence.* Be competent in your skills and job knowledge by maintaining and updating your knowledge and skills frequently through continuing education.

4. *Charting.* Documentation is proof of competence. Make sure that all current reports and consultations have been reviewed by the physician and are evident in the chart. Chart every conversation or interaction you have with a patient.

How Effective Communication Can Help Prevent Lawsuits   Patients who see the medical office as a friendly place are generally less likely to sue. Physicians, medical assistants, and other medical office staff who have pleasant personalities and are competent in their jobs will have less risk of being sued. Medical assistants can help by:

- Developing good listening skills and nonverbal communication techniques so that patients feel the time spent with them is not rushed

- Setting aside a certain time during the day for returning patients' phone calls

- Checking to be sure that all patients or their authorized representatives sign informed consent forms before they undergo medical or surgical procedures

- Avoiding statements that could be construed as an admission of fault on the part of the physician or other medical staff
- Using tact, good judgment, and professional ability in handling patients
- Making every effort to reach an understanding about fees with the patient before treatment so that billing does not become a point of contention

CHECKPOINT
LO 6.3

Researchers give four reasons for patients suing their physician. Pick three of them and explain how you, as an administrative medical assistant, can help your physician avoid lawsuits of this nature.

LO 6.4 Administrative Duties and the Law

Many of a medical assistant's administrative duties are related to legal requirements and fall under the heading of risk management. When correct policies and procedures are followed, the risk of lawsuits decreases, but if a lawsuit is brought against the physician, these same policies and procedures will be the best defense. Keep in mind that everything you do and do not do, reflects not only on you, but also on the physician and the practice. Always follow office policies and procedures and follow your "best practices" at all times to do your part to avoid lawsuits.

Paperwork for insurance billing, patient consent forms for surgical procedures, and correspondence (such as a physician's letter of withdrawal from a case) must be handled correctly to meet legal standards. Documentation of appropriate and accurate entries in a patient's medical record not only provides proof of continuity of care, but is legally important should the physician ever require the record for a legal case involving the patient. You may also maintain the physician's appointment book. The appointment book is also considered a legal document, especially for tracking missed or canceled appointments.

You may also be responsible for handling certain state reporting requirements. Items that must be reported include births; certain communicable diseases such as acquired immunodeficiency syndrome (AIDS) and STDs; drug abuse; suspected child abuse or abuse of the elderly; injuries caused by violence, such as knife and gunshot wounds; and deaths. Reports are sent to various state departments, depending on the content of the report. For example, suspected child and elder abuse cases are reported to the state department of social services. Addressing these state requirements is called the physician's public duty.

Phone calls must be handled with an awareness of legal issues. For example, if the physician asks you to contact a patient by phone and you call the patient at work, you should not identify yourself or the physician by name to someone else without the patient's permission. You can say, for example, "Please tell Mrs. Arnot that her doctor's office is calling." If you do not take this precaution, the physician can be sued for invasion of privacy. You must abide by similar guidelines if you are responsible for making follow-up calls to a patient after a procedure or office visit and when leaving messages on answering machines or on voicemail where the message may be picked up by someone other than the person you are attempting to reach.

Documentation

Patient records are often used as evidence in professional medical liability cases, and improper documentation can contribute to or cause a case to be lost. Physicians should keep records that clearly show what treatment was performed and when it was done. It is important that physicians be able to demonstrate that nothing was neglected and that the care given fully met the standards demanded by law. One cliché to remember is "If it is not written down, then it was not

done." (Conversely, if it is written down, it is assumed that it was done.) Pay attention to spelling in charts and keep a medical dictionary handy if you are not sure of a spelling. Today's health-care environment requires complete documentation of actions taken and actions not taken. Medical staff members should pay particular attention to the following situations.

Referrals Make sure the patient understands whether the referring physician's staff will make the appointment and notify the patient, or whether the patient must call to set up the appointment. Document in the chart that the patient was referred and the time and date of the appointment, and follow up with the specialist to verify that the appointment was kept. If a paper referral is necessary, make sure a hard copy is placed in the patient's chart. Note whether reports of the consultation were received in your office, and document any further care of the patient from the referring physician.

Missed Appointments At the end of the day, a designated person in the medical office should gather all patient charts of those who missed or canceled appointments without rescheduling. Charts should be dated, stamped, and documented "No Call/No Show or" "Canceled/Not Rescheduled." The appointment book is also considered a legal document; make sure that all missed appointments are documented in the appointment book or in the computer. The treating physician should review these records and note whether follow-up is indicated.

Dismissals To avoid charges of abandonment, the physician must formally withdraw from a case. Be sure that a letter of withdrawal or dismissal has been filed in the patient's records. All mailing confirmations should be filed in the record, such as the return receipt from certified mail.

All Other Patient Contact Patient records should include reports of all tests, procedures, and medications prescribed, including prescription refills. Make sure all necessary informed consent papers have been signed and filed in the chart. Make entries into the chart of all telephone conversations with the patient. Correct documentation requires the initials or signature of the person making the notation on the patient's chart as well as the date and time.

Medical Record Correction Errors made when making an entry in a medical record or errors discovered later can be corrected, but corrections must be made in a certain manner so that if the medical records are ever used in a medical malpractice lawsuit, it will not appear that they were falsified. When deleting information, never black it out, never use correction fluid to cover it up, and never in any other way erase or obliterate the original wording. Draw a line through the original information so that it is still legible. Write or type in the correct information above or below the original line or in the margin. The chapter on health records (Chapter 15) describes the proper procedure for correcting chart errors.

Ownership of the Patient Record Patients' medical records are considered the property of the owners of the facility where they were created. A physician in a private practice owns his or her charts or records, while records in a hospital or clinic belong to the facility. Although the facility in which the records were created owns the records, the patient owns the information they contain. Upon signing a release, patients may usually obtain access to or copies of their medical records depending upon state law. Under HIPAA, patients who ask to see or copy their medical records must be accommodated with few exceptions, such as in mental health records where the physician decides if it may be harmful to the patient to see the record. The physician is protected under the **doctrine of professional discretion.**

doctrine of professional discretion
Under HIPAA, a patient's right to see or copy his or her medical record is protected. The doctrine of professional discretion protects the physician if he or she feels it will be harmful for a patient to access the medical record.

Retention and Storage of the Patient Record   As a protection against legal litigation, records should be kept until the applicable statute of limitations period has elapsed, which is generally 7 years. In some cases, the medical records for minor patients must be kept for a specified length of time after they reach legal age. Some states have enacted statutes for the retention of medical records. Because the Federal False Claim Act requires that financial records be kept for 10 years and medical records are often required to back up financial records, many legal experts suggest that medical records should also be kept for a minimum of 10 years. Most physicians retain records indefinitely to provide evidence in medical professional liability suits or for tax purposes. The medical record may provide the patient's medical history for future medical treatment. The chapter on Medical Records Management (Chapter 14) will go into more detail on this subject.

Credentialing

Credentialing is the term used by various organizations, including insurance carriers to ensure that health-care providers are appropriately qualified to provide services and meet all the necessary requirements to do so. The qualifications are determined and approved by unbiased physician peer review groups. Specific criteria vary according to the physician or provider specialty and the provider's scope of practice. Physicians are broken into two types according to medical licensure—MD or DO—and then further broken down according to specialty.

credentialing
The process of establishing qualifications for organizations or licensed professionals.

As an administrative medical assistant, you may be responsible for credentialing any new providers who come into the practice. In general, insurance companies require their doctors to hold and maintain the proper credentials. In order for a physician to participate with an insurance carrier like Medicare, he must have the necessary physician credentials and go through the Medicare credentialing process or he will not be allowed to bill Medicare for services provided to Medicare beneficiaries.

Medicare has three forms for credentialing:

1. 855B is used to establish or change a practice group number.

2. 855I is used to establish or reestablish a physician's individual number.

   In addition to completing this 29-page application, the physician must also provide his or her medical school diploma; individual NPI (national provider identifier); current license number, any board certifications for specialties; work history for at least 5 years; statement of any limitations; history of loss of licensure or felony convictions; history of loss or limitations of privileges; or disciplinary actions and outside verification of information provided.

3. 855R is used to link individual provider numbers to group practice numbers.

These forms are not complicated, but they are time consuming. More information about Medicare's credentialing process may be found on the CMS Web site at www.cms.gov/manuals/downloads/mc86c06.pdf. Once the Medicare credential is received, many other insurance plans will follow suit with credentialing or linking so the provider can also bill them for services provided. If a separate credentialing process is required, it is generally much less complicated than that required by Medicare.

Controlled Substances and the Law

It is important to know the right dosages and potential complications of all drugs, as well as prescription refill rules, in order to understand and interpret the directions of the physician in a legally responsible manner. This is particularly true of

controlled substances
Drugs or drug products categorized as potentially dangerous and addictive.

the drugs known as **controlled substances.** Controlled substances are drugs or drug products categorized as potentially dangerous and addictive.

The Controlled Substances Act (CSA) of 1970 maintains that facilities have close control of these types of drugs. They list them in five categories in descending order of potential for addiction. Medical assistants often have to discard outdated medicines that are in this category. Your medical facility should have enacted policies and procedures for storage and removal of controlled substances. Chapter 16 discusses the Controlled Substances Act, including the schedule of these substances, in more detail.

Legal Documents and the Patient

You need to be aware of several legal documents that are typically completed by a patient prior to major surgery or hospitalization: the advance medical directive durable power of attorney and the uniform donor card. Traditionally, these documents were completed outside the medical office or in the hospital. The current trend, however, is for medical practice personnel, including medical assistants, to assist patients in developing these important documents. Contact your state's Public Health Department Web site for additional information.

advance medical directive
A legal document addressed to the patient's family and health-care providers stating what type of treatment the patient wishes or does not wish to receive if she becomes terminally ill, unconscious, or permanently comatose.

Advance Medical Directive   An **advance medical directive** is a legal document addressed to the patient's family and health-care providers stating what type of treatment the patient wishes or does not wish to receive if she becomes terminally ill, unconscious, or permanently comatose (sometimes referred to as being in a persistent vegetative state). For example, an advance directive typically states whether a patient wishes to be put on life-sustaining equipment should she become permanently comatose. Some directives contain DNR (do not resuscitate) orders. These orders mean the patient does not wish medical personnel to try to resuscitate her should the heart stop beating. Advance medical directives are a means of helping families of terminally ill patients deal with the inevitable outcome of the illness and may help limit unnecessary medical costs.

The directive is signed when the patient is mentally and physically competent to do so. It must also be signed by two witnesses. Medical practices can help patients develop an advance medical directive, sometimes in conjunction with organizations that make available preprinted living will forms. The Partnership for Caring (based in Washington, D.C.) is one such organization.

Durable Power of Attorney

durable power of attorney
The part of the advance directive in which the patient names someone who will make decisions regarding medical care on his or her behalf if he or she is unable to do so.

Patients who have an advance medical directive are asked to name, in the second document called a **durable power of attorney** (also known as a health-care proxy), someone who will make decisions regarding medical care on their behalf if they are unable to do so. It is important that the person named in the durable power of attorney knows the patient's wishes ahead of time, so in the event they are required to make medical decisions, they are able to be confident they are carrying out the patient's wishes.

uniform donor card
A legal document which states that, upon death, a person wishes to make an anatomical gift such as organs or skin.

The Uniform Donor Card   In 1968 the Uniform Anatomical Gift Act was passed, setting forth guidelines for all states to follow in complying with a person's wish to make a gift of one or more organs (or the whole body) upon death. An anatomical gift is typically designated for medical research, organ transplants, or placement in a tissue bank. The **uniform donor card** is a legal document that states one's wish to make such a gift. People often carry the uniform donor card in their wallets. Many medical practices offer the service of helping their patients obtain and complete a uniform donor card. In some states the Department of Motor Vehicles makes the process simple by asking you if you would like to be an organ donor at the time you renew your driver's license

with a card being issued to you at that time and a notation made on the driver's license that you are an organ donor. The patient's family should be aware of his wish to be an organ donor so that the wishes are carried out upon his death.

● ● ● ●

Explain the ownership of the patient medical record.

LO 6.5 Federal Legislation Affecting Health Care

Congress has passed legislation intended to improve the quality of health care in the United States, to reduce fraud, and to ensure that patients will not be discriminated against by insurance providers. The most significant health-care laws passed in recent years are the Health Care Quality Improvement Act of 1986, the Federal False Claims Act, and the Health Insurance Portability and Accountability Act (HIPAA) of 1996. The Occupational Safety and Health Administration (OSHA) regulations, which are vitally important to the practice of health care, are reviewed and often updated by the administration.

Health Care Quality Improvement Act of 1986

The Health Care Quality Improvement Act of 1986 (HCQIA) is a federal statute passed to improve the quality of medical care nationwide. Congress created HCQIA because they found that there was an increasing occurrence of medical malpractice and a need to improve the quality of medical care. The act requires professional peer review in certain cases, limits damages to professional reviewers, and protects from liability those who provide information to professional review bodies. One of the most important provisions of the HCQIA was the establishment of the National Practitioner Data Bank. The use of the National Practitioner Data Bank was intended to improve the quality of medical care nationwide by encouraging effective professional peer review of physicians. Information that must be reported to the National Practitioner Data Bank includes medical malpractice payments, adverse licensure actions, adverse clinical privilege actions, and adverse professional membership actions. This data bank is a resource to assist state licensing boards, hospitals, and other health-care entities in investigating qualifications of physicians and other health-care practitioners.

Federal False Claims Act

The Federal False Claims Act is a law that allows individuals to bring civil actions on the behalf of the U.S. government for false claims made to the federal government, under a provision of the law call *qui tam* (from Latin meaning to bring an action for the king and for one's self). The law was enacted because of the rising cost of health care, fraud, and abuse within the health-care industry. As a result, laws have been passed to control three types of illegal conduct:

qui tam
From Latin, meaning to bring an action for the king and for oneself, allows individuals to bring civil actions on behalf of the U.S. government for false medical claims.

1. False billing claims. Fraudulently billing for services not performed is prohibited.

2. Kickbacks. Giving financial incentives to a health-care provider for referring patients or for recommending services or products is prohibited under the federal Anti-Kickback Law and by state laws.

3. Self-referrals. Referring patients to any service or facility where the health-care provider has financial interests is prohibited by the Federal Ethics in Patient Referral Act and other federal and state laws.

Violations of laws against health-care fraud and abuse can result in imprisonment and fines, a loss of professional license, a loss of health-care facility

staff privileges, and exclusion from participating in federal health-care programs such as Medicare and Medicaid.

CHECKPOINT
LO 6.5

What is the purpose of the Federal False Claims Act?

LO 6.6 OSHA Regulations

The Occupational Safety and Health Administration (OSHA), a division of the U.S. Department of Labor, has created federal laws to protect health-care workers from health hazards on the job. Medical personnel may accidentally contract a dangerous or even fatal disease by coming into contact with a virus a patient is carrying. Medical assistants may also be exposed to toxic substances in the office. OSHA regulations describe the precautions a medical office must take with clothing, housekeeping, record keeping, and training to minimize the risk of disease or injury. The chapter on Asepsis for the Administrative Areas (Chapter 9) discusses OSHA in more detail.

Some of the most important OSHA regulations are those for controlling workers' exposure to infectious disease. These regulations are set forth in the OSHA Bloodborne Pathogens Protection Standard of 1991. A pathogen is any microorganism that causes disease. Microorganisms are microscopic living bodies such as viruses or bacteria that may be present in a patient's blood or other body fluids (saliva or semen).

Of particular concern to medical workers are the human immunodeficiency virus (HIV), which causes AIDS, and the hepatitis B virus (HBV). AIDS damages the body's immune system and thus its ability to fight disease. AIDS is almost always fatal. HBV is a highly contagious disease that is potentially fatal. It causes inflammation of the liver and may cause liver failure. Every year, about 8,700 health-care workers become HBV-infected at work, and about 200 die from the disease.

OSHA requires that medical professionals in medical practices follow what are called "standard precautions." They were developed by the Centers for Disease Control and Prevention (CDC) to prevent medical professionals from exposing themselves and others to blood-borne pathogens. Exposure can occur, for example, through skin that has been broken from a needle puncture or other wound and through mucous membranes, such as those in the nose and throat. If these areas come into contact with a patient's (or coworker's) blood or body fluids, a virus could be transferred from one person to another. Chapter 9 covers the role of the CDC and standard precautions in more detail including your role as an administrative medical assistant in protecting yourself and others who enter your office.

CHECKPOINT
LO 6.6

What is the purpose of standard precautions?

LO 6.7 HIPAA

Today, health care is considered one of the largest industries in the United States according to the U.S. Department of Labor, providing 14.3 million jobs for wage and salaried employees in 2008. It is estimated that between 2008 and 2018, health care will generate 3.2 million new jobs; more than any other industry—largely due to the rapid increase in the elderly population.

On August 21, 1996, the U.S. Congress passed the Health Insurance Portability and Accountability Act (HIPAA). The primary goals of the act are to improve the portability and continuity of health-care coverage in group and individual markets; to combat waste, fraud, and abuse in health-care insurance and health-care delivery; to promote the use of medical savings accounts; to improve access to long-term care services and coverage; and to simplify the administration of health insurance.

The purposes of the act are to:

- Improve the efficiency and effectiveness of health-care delivery by creating a national framework for health privacy protection that builds on efforts by states, health systems, and individual organizations and individuals

- Protect and enhance the rights of patients by providing them access to their health information and controlling the inappropriate use or disclosure of that information

- Improve the quality of health care by restoring trust in the health-care system among consumers, health-care professionals, and the multitude of organizations and individuals committed to the delivery of care

HIPAA is divided into two main sections of law: Title I, which addresses health-care portability, and Title II, which covers the prevention of health-care fraud and abuse, administrative simplification, and medical liability reform. Although in this text we will discuss Titles I and II in detail, you should also be aware of three other titles included in HIPAA regulations: Title III—Tax-related health provisions governing medical savings accounts, Title IV—Application and enforcement of group health insurance requirements, and Title V—Revenue offset governing tax deductions for employers providing company-owned life insurance premiums.

Title I: Health-Care Portability

The issue of portability deals with protecting health-care coverage for employees who change jobs, allowing them to carry their existing plans with them to new jobs. HIPAA provides the following protections for employees and their families:

- Increases workers' ability to get health-care coverage when starting a new job

- Reduces workers' probability of losing existing health-care coverage

- Helps workers maintain continuous health-care coverage when changing jobs

- Helps workers purchase health insurance on their own if they lose coverage under an employer's group plan and have no other health-care coverage available

The specific protections of this title include the following:

- Limits the use of exclusions for preexisting conditions

- Prohibits group plans from discriminating by denying coverage or charging extra for coverage based on an individual's or a family member's past or present poor health

- Guarantees certain small employers, as well as certain individuals who lose job-related coverage, the right to purchase health insurance

- Guarantees, in most cases, that employers or individuals who purchase health insurance can renew the coverage regardless of any health conditions of individuals covered under the insurance policy

Title II: Prevention of Health-Care Fraud and Abuse, Administrative Simplification, and Medical Liability Reform

HIPAA Privacy Rule The HIPAA Standards for Privacy of Individually Identifiable Health Information provide the first comprehensive federal protection for the privacy of health information. The **Privacy Rule** is designed to provide strong privacy protections that do not interfere with patient access to health care or the quality of health-care delivery. This act creates, for the first time, national standards to protect individuals' medical records and other personal health information. The privacy rule is intended to:

- Give patients more control over their health information
- Set boundaries on the use and release of health-care records
- Establish appropriate safeguards that health-care providers and others must achieve to protect the privacy of health information
- Hold violators accountable, with civil and criminal penalties that can be imposed if they violate patients' privacy rights
- Strike a balance when public responsibility supports disclosure of some forms of data—for example, to protect public health

Before the HIPAA Privacy Rule, the personal information that moves across hospitals and doctors' offices, insurers or third-party payers, and state lines fell under a patchwork of federal and state laws. This information could be distributed—without either notice or authorization—for reasons that had nothing to do with a patient's medical treatment or health-care reimbursement. For example, unless otherwise forbidden by state or local law, without the Privacy Rule, patient information held by a health plan could, without the patient's permission, be passed on to a lender who could then deny the patient's application for a home mortgage or a credit card or could be given to an employer who could use it in personnel decisions.

Individually identifiable health information includes:

- Name
- Address
- Phone numbers
- Fax number
- Dates (birth, death, admission, discharge, etc.)
- Social Security number
- E-mail address
- Medical record numbers
- Health plan beneficiary numbers
- Account numbers
- Certificate or license numbers
- Vehicle identifiers and serial numbers, including license plate numbers
- Device identifiers and serial numbers
- Web Universal Resource Locators (URLs)
- Internet Protocol (IP) address numbers

The core of the HIPAA Privacy Rule is the protection, use, and disclosure of **protected health information (PHI).** Protected health information means individually identifiable health information that is transmitted or maintained by electronic or other media, such as computer storage devices. The Privacy Rule protects all PHI held or transmitted by a covered entity, which includes

health-care providers, health plans, and health-care clearinghouses. Other covered entities include employers, life insurers, schools or universities, and public health authorities. Protected health information can come in any form or media, such as electronic, paper, or oral, including verbal communications among staff members, patients, and other providers. *Use* and *disclosure* are the two fundamental concepts in the HIPAA Privacy Rule. It is important to understand the differences between these terms.

Use   **Use** refers to performing any of the following actions to individually identifiable health information by employees or other members of an organization's workforce:

use
Information is used when it moves within an organization.

- Sharing
- Employing
- Applying
- Utilizing
- Examining
- Analyzing

Information is used when it moves within an organization.

Disclosure   **Disclosure** occurs when the entity holding the information performs any of the following actions so that the information is outside the entity:

disclosure
Information is disclosed when it is transmitted between or among organizations.

- Releasing
- Transferring
- Providing access to
- Divulging in any manner

Information is disclosed when it is transmitted between or among organizations.

Under HIPAA, *use* limits the sharing of information within a covered entity, whereas *disclosure* restricts the sharing of information outside the entity holding the information.

The Privacy Rule covers the following PHI:

- The past, present, or future physical or mental health or condition of an individual
- Health care that is provided to an individual
- Billing or payments made for health care provided

Information that is not individually identifiable or unable to be tied to the identity of a particular patient is not subject to the Privacy Rule.

Managing and Storing Patient Information   Medical facilities have undergone many changes to the way they manage and store patient information. The Privacy Rule compliance was enforced in April of 2003. Many facilities contracted consultants that specialized in HIPAA and became certified in HIPAA compliance. See Figure 6–5 for an example of a HIPAA Privacy Notice. For the health-care provider, the Privacy Rule requires activities such as:

- Notifying patients of their privacy rights and how their information is used
- Adopting and implementing privacy procedures for its practice, hospital, or plan
- Training employees so that they understand the privacy procedures
- Designating an individual to be responsible for seeing that the privacy procedures are adopted and followed

figure 6–5

Notice of Privacy Practices.

TOTAL CARE CLINIC, PC

Notice of Privacy Practices

I understand that *Total Care Clinic* creates and maintains medical records describing my health history, symptoms, examinations, test results, diagnoses, treatments, and plans for my future care and/or treatment. I further understand that this information may be used for any of the following:

1. Plan and document my care and treatment
2. Communicate with health professionals involved in my care and treatment
3. Verify insurance coverage for planned procedures and/or treatments for the applicable diagnoses
4. Application of any medical or surgical procedures and diagnoses (codes) to my medical insurance claim forms as application for payment of services rendered
5. Assessment of quality of care and utilization review of the health care professionals providing my care

Additionally, it has been explained to me that:

1. A complete description of the use and disclosure of this information is included in a *Notice of Information of Privacy Practices* which has been provided to me
2. I have had a right to review this information prior to signing this consent
3. _____ has the right to change this notice and their practices
4. Any revision of this notice will be mailed to me at the address I provided to them prior to its implementation
5. I may object to the use of my health information for specific purposes
6. I may request restrictions as to the manner my information may be used or disclosed in order to carry out treatment, payment, or health information
7. I understand that it is not required that my requested restrictions be honored
8. I may revoke this consent in writing, except for those disclosures which may have taken place prior to the receipt of my revocation

At the time of the document signing, I request the following restrictions to disclosure or use of my health information: _____

_____

_____

_____   _____
Printed Name of Patient or Legal Guardian   Signature of Parent or Legal Guardian

_____   _____
Printed Name of Witness/Title   Signature of Witness/Title

Date: _____

- Securing patient records containing individually identifiable health information so that they are not readily available to those who do not need them

Under HIPAA, patients have an increased awareness of their health information privacy rights, which includes the following:

- The right to access, copy, and inspect their health-care information
- The right to request an amendment to their health-care information
- The right to obtain an accounting of certain disclosures of their health-care information
- The right to alternate means of receiving communications from providers
- The right to complain about alleged violations of the regulations and the provider's own information policies (Figure 6–6)

figure 6–6

Privacy Violation Complaint form.

TOTAL CARE CLINIC, PC

Privacy Violation Complaint Form

As per our Privacy Policies and Procedures, we are providing this form for individuals who feel they have a complaint regarding how their protected health information was handled by our office. You have the right to make a complaint and we may take no retaliatory actions against you because of it. We will respond to this complaint within 30 days of its receipt.

Patient Name: _____

Address: _____

DOB: _____   Date of Complaint: _____

Phone: H _____ Cell _____ Work _____

Best time to reach you: _____

Reason for the complaint (Please be as specific as possible, attaching additional documentation as necessary): _____
_____
_____
_____
_____

_____   _____
            Signature   Date

- -

Office Use Only
Received by: _____   Date_____
Follow-up Started on (date): _____

HIPAA allows for sharing of PHI
without specific consent if it is for
the reasons of treatment, payment,
or normal business operations such
as quality improvement.

Sharing Patient Information When sharing patient information, HIPAA will allow the provider to use health-care information for **treatment, payment, and operations (TPO).**

- Treatment. Providers are allowed to share information in order to provide care to patients
- Payment. Providers are allowed to share information in order to receive payment for the treatment provided
- Operations. Providers are allowed to share information to conduct normal business activities, such as quality improvement

If the use of patient information does not fall under TPO, then written authorization must be obtained before sharing information with anyone. Figure 6–7 is an example of an Authorization to Release Health Information form.

figure 6–7

Authorization to Release Health
Information form.

TOTAL CARE CLINIC, PC

Authorization to Release Health Information

I, _____ residing at

_____ and DOB

of _____ give permission to (name of practice) _____

_____ to release to _____

_____ of Total Care Clinic the following information:

_____

_____

_____

Reason for the request:

_____

_____

_____

Signature of Patient or Legal Guardian _____

Printed Name of Patient or Legal Guardian _____

If Guardian, relationship to Patient _____

This authorization will expire on: _____

YOU MAY REFUSE TO SIGN THIS AUTHORIZATION. You may revoke this authorization at any time by notifying Total Care Clinic in writing. Revocation will have no effect on actions taken prior to receipt of any revocation. Any disclosure of information carries the potential for unauthorized redisclosure and the information may not be protected by federal confidentiality rules.

Patient information may be disclosed without authorization to the following parties or in the following situations:

- Medical researchers
- Emergencies
- Funeral directors/coroners
- Disaster relief services
- Law enforcement
- Correctional institutions
- Abuse and neglect
- Organ and tissue donation centers
- Work-related conditions that may affect employee health
- Judicial/administrative proceedings at the patient's request or as directed by a subpoena or court order

When using or disclosing PHI, a provider must make reasonable efforts to limit the use or disclosure to the minimum amount of PHI necessary to accomplish the intended purpose. Providing only the minimum necessary information means taking reasonable safeguards to protect an individual's health information from incidental disclosure. State laws may impose more stringent requirements regarding the protection of patient information. Healthcare providers and staff should only have access to information they need to fulfill their assigned duties. The minimum necessary standard does not apply to disclosures, including oral disclosures, among health-care providers for treatment purposes. For example, a physician is not required to apply the minimum necessary standard when discussing a patient's medical chart information with a specialist at another hospital.

Patient Notification   Since the effective date of the HIPAA Privacy Rule, medical facilities have made major changes in how they inform patients of their HIPAA compliance. You may have noticed, as a patient yourself, the forms and information packets that are now provided by your health-care providers. The first step in informing patients of HIPAA compliance is the communication of patient rights. These rights are communicated through a document called **Notice of Privacy Practices (NPP).** A notice must:

- Be written in plain, simple language
- Include a header that reads: "This notice describes how medical information about you may be used and disclosed and how you can get access to this information. Please review carefully."
- Describe the covered entity's uses and disclosures of PHI
- Describe an individual's rights under the Privacy Rule
- Describe the covered entity's duties
- Describe how to register complaints concerning suspected privacy violations
- Specify a point of contact
- Specify an effective date
- State that the entity reserves to right to change its privacy practices

The second step in patient notification is to implement a document that explains the policy of the medical facility on obtaining **authorization** for the use and disclosure of patient information for purposes other than TPO. The authorization form must be written in plain language. Some of the core elements of an authorization form include:

- Specific and meaningful descriptions of the authorized information
- Persons authorized to use or disclose protected health information

- Purpose of the requested information
- Statement of the patient's right to revoke the authorization
- Signature and date of the patient

Procedure 6–3 at the end of the chapter outlines the steps to be taken to obtain an authorization to release PHI.

Security Measures   Health-care facilities can undertake a number of measures in order to help reduce a breach of confidentiality, including for information that is either stored or delivered electronically (that is, stored in computers or computer networks, or delivered via computer networks or the Internet).

HIPAA Security Rule   In February 2003, the final regulations were issued regarding the administrative, physical, and technical safeguards to protect the confidentiality, integrity, and availability of health information covered by HIPAA. The **Security Rule** specifies how patient information is protected on computer networks, the Internet, disks, and other storage media and extranets. The rapidly increasing use of computers in health-care today has created new dangers for breaches of confidentiality. The Security Rule mandates that:

- A security officer must be assigned the responsibility for the medical facility's security
- All staff, including management, receives security awareness training
- Medical facilities must implement audit controls to record and examine staff who have logged into information systems that contain PHI
- Organizations limit physical access to medical facilities that contain electronic PHI
- Organizations must conduct risk analyses to determine information security risks and vulnerabilities
- Organizations must establish policies and procedures that allow access to electronic PHI on a need-to-know basis

Computers are not the only concern regarding security of the workplace. The facility layout can propose a possible violation if not designed correctly. All facilities must take measures to reduce the identity of patient information. Some examples of facility design that can help reduce a breach of confidentiality include the security of patient charts, the reception area, the clinical station, and faxes sent and received.

Chart Security   When paper health records are used, patient charts and the information contained within them can be kept confidential by following these rules:

- Charts that contain a patient's name or other identifiers cannot be in view at the front reception area or nurse's station. Some offices have placed charts in plain jackets to prevent information from being seen.
- Charts must be stored out of the view of a public area so that they cannot be seen by unauthorized individuals.
- Charts should be placed on the filing shelves without the patient name showing.
- Charts should be locked when not in use. Many facilities have purchased filing equipment that can be locked and unlocked without limiting the availability of patient information.
- Every staff member who uses patient information must be logged and a confidentiality statement signed. Signatures of staff should be on file with the office.

Security Rule

Specifies how patient information is protected on computer networks, the Internet, disks, and other storage media and extranets.

Reception Area Security   To be compliant with security rules, the following steps should be taken to secure the reception area:

- Log off or lock your computer or terminal, shutting off the monitor when leaving your terminal or computer.
- The computer must be placed in an area where patients and unauthorized personnel cannot see the screen.
- Many facilities are purchasing flat screen monitors to prevent visibility of the screen.
- The sign-in sheet must be monitored and not left out in patient view. The names of patients must be blacked out so the next patient cannot read the names. It is best to put another system in place and to eliminate the sign-in sheet.
- Many offices are reviewing the reception area with regard to phone conversations. Some offices are creating call centers away from the patient reception area.

Patient Care Area Security   All health-care personnel should follow these guidelines to protect PHI in patient care areas:

- Log off or lock computer terminals turning off the monitor when leaving the computer station.
- When placing charts in exam room racks or in shelves, the name of the patient or other identifiers must be concealed from other patients.
- HIPAA does not have a regulation about calling patients' names in the reception area, but to increase privacy in your facility, you may suggest identifying patients by their surname or first name only.
- When discussing a patient with another staff member or with the physician, make sure your voice is lowered and that all doors to the exam rooms are closed. Avoid discussing patient conditions in heavy traffic areas.
- When discussing a condition with a patient, make sure that you are in a private room or area where no one can hear you.
- Avoid discussing patients in lunchrooms, hallways, or any place in a medical facility where someone can overhear you.

Fax Security   A lot of information is exchanged over the fax machine in a medical office. The fax machine is a vital link among physicians, hospitals, insurance companies, and other medical staff members. Private health information can be exchanged via faxes sent to covered entities. Here are some recommendations to help safeguard information exchanged via fax machines:

- Fax cover page. State clearly on the fax cover sheet that confidential and protected health information is included. Further state that the information included is to be protected and must not be shared or disclosed without the appropriate authorizations from the patient.
- Location of the fax machine. Keep the fax machine in an area that is not accessible by individuals who are not authorized to view PHI.
- Faxes with protected health information. Faxes that your office receives with PHI must be stored promptly in a protected, secure area.
- Fax number. Always confirm the accuracy of fax numbers to minimize the possibility of faxes being sent to the wrong person. Call people to tell them the fax is being sent.
- Confirmation. Program the fax machine to print a confirmation for all faxes sent, and staple the confirmation sheet to each document sent.
- Training. Train all staff members to understand the importance of safeguarding PHI sent or received via fax.

readiness

HIPAA and Electronic Health Records

Paper records have many shortcomings; only one person may use a chart at any one time, physicians have different ways of completing documentation, and information gets misfiled within the chart making it difficult to find quickly. They also are "left lying around" the office in areas where unauthorized personnel may have access to them.

Electronic health records eliminate most of these obstacles. Because they are electronic, information may easily be shared among multiple caregivers at the same time; most record formats are set up so that each type of information requires storage in a particular preset area; additionally, there is specific documentation that must be completed or the record cannot be saved—this is very important for continuity of care and for billing purposes. Most importantly regarding confidentiality, only medical personnel with specific clearances (associated with each person's individual password) may access and/or update the information. The one item that must be remembered by everyone with access to electronic health records is that you should *never* leave your computer station with a patient's medical record open so that others can access the information. If you must leave your station, either exit the medical record and log out or, if using a computer that only you have access to, lock the computer and shut off the screen so that no one else can "accidentally" see what you are working on.

Copier Security Medical assistants should follow these guidelines to protect PHI at the copier:

- Do not leave confidential documents anywhere on or near the copier where others can read the information.
- Do not discard copies in a trash container—shred them.
- If a paper jam occurs, be sure to remove from the copier the copy or partial copy that caused the jam.

Printer Security To maintain the confidentiality of printed materials, follow these guidelines:

- Do not print confidential material on a printer shared by other departments or in an area where others can read the material.
- Do not leave the printer unattended while printing confidential material.

- Before leaving the printing area, make sure all computer disks, CDs, DVDs, or "jump drives" containing confidential information and all printed material have been collected.
- Be certain that the print job is sent to the correct printer location.
- Do not discard printouts in a trash container—shred them.

Violations and Penalties Every staff member is responsible for adhering to HIPAA privacy and security regulations to ensure that PHI is secure and confidential. Anyone who uses or shares patient information is ethically obligated to comply with HIPAA. If PHI is abused or confidentiality is breached, the medical facility can incur substantial penalties or even the incarceration of staff. Violations of HIPAA law can result in both civil and criminal penalties.

Civil Penalties Civil penalties for HIPAA privacy violations can be up to $100 for each offense, with an annual cap of $25,000 for repeated violations of the same requirement.

Criminal Penalties Criminal penalties for the knowing, wrongful misuse of individually identifiable health information can result in the following penalties:

- For the knowing misuse of individually identifiable health information: up to $50,000 and/or one year in prison.
- For misuse under false pretenses: up to $100,000 and/or 5 years in prison.
- For offenses to sell for profit or malicious harm: up to $250,000 and/or 10 years in prison.

Administrative Simplification The main key to the set of rules established for HIPAA administrative simplification is standardizing patient information throughout the health-care system with a set of transaction standards and

code sets. The codes and formats used for the exchange of medical data are referred to as **electronic transaction records.** Regulated transaction information is given a transaction set identifier. For example, a health-care professional claim would be given an identifier of ASC X12N 837. This is a standard transaction code given to any facility that submits a health-care claim to an insurance company.

Standardized code sets are used for encoding data elements. The following books are used for the standardized code sets for all health-care facilities:

- *ICD-9-CM,* Volumes 1 and 2. This book is used to identify diseases and conditions.
- *CPT 4.* This book is used to identify physician services or procedures.
- *HCPCS.* This book is used to identify health-related services and procedures, such as pharmaceuticals or hearing and vision services that are not included in the CPT manual.

Frequently Asked Questions About HIPAA

1. May one physician's office send a patient's medical records to another physician's office without the patient's consent?

Yes, if the physician is caring for the patient.

2. Does the HIPAA Privacy Rule prohibit or discourage doctor/patient e-mails?

Health-care practitioners can continue to correspond with patients via e-mail, but appropriate electronic safeguards must be in place.

3. May a patient be listed in a hospital's directory without the patient's consent, and may the directory be shared with the public?

The HIPAA Privacy Rule allows hospitals to continue providing directory information to the public unless the patient has specifically chosen not to be included. Hospital directories can include the patient's name, location in the facility, and general condition.

4. May a patient's family member pick up prescriptions for the patient?

The Privacy Rule allows family members to pick up prescriptions, medical supplies, x-rays, or other similar forms of protected health information.

5. Is a hospital allowed to share patient information with the patient's family without the patient's expressed consent?

HIPAA provides that a health-care provider may "disclose to a family member, other relative, or a close personal friend of the individual, or any other person identified by the individual" medical information directly relevant to such a person's involvement with the patient's care or payment related to the patient's care.

6. Can patients sue health-care providers who do not comply with the HIPAA Privacy Rule?

The HIPAA Privacy Rule does not give patients the express right to sue. The patient can file a written complaint with the secretary of Health and Human Services (HHS) through the Office for Civil Rights. The HHS secretary then decides whether or not to investigate the complaint.

7. If a patient refuses to sign an acknowledgment stating that he or she received the health-care provider's notice of privacy practices, must the health-care provider refuse to provide services?

The Privacy Rule gives the patient a "right of notice" of privacy practices for protecting identifiable health information. It requires that providers make a "good faith effort" to have patients acknowledge receipt of the notice, but

the law does not give health-care practitioners the right to refuse treatment to people who do not sign the acknowledgment.

CHECKPOINT
LO 6.7

In pulling a completed encounter form to complete a health insurance claim form, you realize the patient is your significant other's mother. Can you pull her chart to gather more information about the reason for her medical care?

LO 6.8 Confidentiality Issues and Mandatory Disclosure

Related to law, ethics, and quality care is the issue of when the medical assistant can disclose information and when it must be kept confidential. The incidents that doctors are legally required to report to the state were outlined earlier in the chapter. A doctor can be charged with criminal action for not following state and federal laws.

Ethics and professional judgment are always important. Consider the question of whether to contact the partners of a patient who has a sexually transmitted disease (STD) and whether to keep the patient's name from those people. The law says that the physician must instruct patients on how to notify possibly affected third parties and give them referrals to get the proper assistance. If the patient refuses to inform involved outside parties, then the doctor's office may offer to notify current and former partners. The Practice Readiness section addresses this issue.

In general, the patient's ethical right to confidentiality and privacy is protected by law. Only the patient can waive the right to confidentiality. A physician cannot publicize a patient case in journal articles or invite other health professionals to observe a case without the patient's written consent. Most states also prohibit a doctor from testifying in court about a patient without the patient's approval. When a patient sues a physician, however, the patient automatically gives up the right to confidentiality.

Following are six principles for preventing improper release of information from the medical office.

1. When in doubt about whether to release information, it is better not to release it.

2. It is the patient's, not the doctor's, right to keep patient information confidential. If the patient wants to disclose the information, it is unethical for the physician not to do so.

3. All patients should be treated with the same degree of confidentiality, whatever the health-care professional's personal opinion of the patient might be.

4. You should be aware of all applicable laws and of the regulations of agencies such as public health departments.

5. When it is necessary to break confidentiality and when there is a conflict between ethics and confidentiality, discuss it with the patient. If the law does not dictate what to do in the situation, the attending physician should make the judgment based on the urgency of the situation and any danger that might be posed to the patient or others.

6. Get written approval from the patient before releasing information. For common situations, the patient should sign a standard release-of-records form.

The AMA has several standard forms for authorization of disclosure and includes disclosure clauses in many other forms. For example, the consent-to-surgery form includes a clause about consenting to picture taking and

Working with the Health-Care Team

THE COMPLIANCE OFFICER

Duties and Skills

The compliance officer, also known as the compliance specialist, works with the office compliance program to ensure that the laws and rules of the medical industry are followed by all members of the office staff. All aspects of the medical office from patient referrals to billing, coding, and documentation are coming under increasing scrutiny because of the focus federal and state regulators have placed on health care. The duties of the compliance officer are many and varied but may include:

- Reviewing and updating the office policies and procedures manual
- Creating and maintaining appropriate coding and billing policies including audit procedures
- Creating, conducting, and managing compliance education program for all staff
- Conducting or ensuring that compliance risk assessments are conducted
- Monitoring government sanction lists for excluded individuals/entities when considering potential employees or business associates
- Publicizing the reporting system for all providers, staff, vendors, and business associates
- Developing compliance audit plan; monitoring audits and audit results
- Recommending disciplinary and remedial action for noncompliance

Individuals interested in compliance generally are detail-oriented with strong, clear values regarding legal, regulatory, and ethical issues. Because of the teaching component inherent in this position, interest in and ability to share knowledge is a plus. The compliance officer frequently works with human resources, potential and new employees, administrators, and regulators, requiring excellent communication and interpersonal skills. Excellent audit, investigatory, and report-writing skills are also necessary.

Educational Requirements

Because compliance is a "newer" career opportunity there are different approaches to becoming a compliance specialist. Many office managers (administrative medical assistants) "assumed" the role as the need arose; attending conferences, seminars, and educational programs to gain expertise in this area. Several universities have certificate programs available that are accredited by the Health Care Compliance Association (HCCA) and that prepare the student to take his or her certification exam at the completion of the program. Those with "life experience" may also be eligible to sit for the certification exam, the passing of which results in the credential of CHC (Certified in Healthcare Compliance). The universities offering the certificate program are listed here:

- Quinnipiac University in Connecticut
- George Washington University in Washington, DC
- Florida Gulf Coast University in Florida
- Hamline University in Minnesota

Workplace Settings

Opportunities for employment as a compliance officer or specialist exist in almost any location where health care is delivered. Examples include hospitals, medical clinics, billing offices, physician practices and HMOs, nursing homes, insurance carriers, and government agencies.

The Compliance Officer as a Team Member

As the person in charge of office and procedure compliance, almost everyone in the medical office will be interacting with the compliance officer at some time. As an administrative medical assistant with access to both the patient medical and financial records, compliance will be an everyday concern. During orientation, you will first meet the compliance officer to go over the basics of compliance regulations affecting your position, as well as receive updates from the compliance officer as regulations change or an audit reveals the need for further training regarding policies or procedures. Additionally, should you ever have questions regarding a policy or procedure that may have compliance implications you should be in touch with your compliance officer for clarification on procedures.

For more information, visit the Web site of the following organization, which is available on the Online Learning Center at www.mhhe.com/houseradminmedassist

Healthcare Compliance Association

---

observation during the surgery. When using a standard form, cross out anything that does not apply in that particular situation. Medical practices often develop their own customized forms.

Why is a patient's right to confidentiality waived if he sues the physician?

CHECKPOINT
LO 6.8

Notifying Those at Risk for Sexually Transmitted Disease

Few things are more difficult for a patient with an STD than telling current and former partners about the diagnosis. In fact, some patients elect not to do so. When patients refuse to alert their partners, the medical office can offer to make those contacts. Often that responsibility lies with the medical assistant.

You are most likely to encounter such a situation if you are a medical assistant working in a family practice, an obstetrics/gynecology practice, or a clinic. Becoming familiar with all facets of the situation—from ensuring patient confidentiality to handling potentially difficult confrontations—will help you best serve the patient.

The first step is to get the appropriate information from the patient who has contracted the STD. Because the patient may be sensitive about revealing former and current partners, help him feel more comfortable. First, spend some time talking about the STD. How much does the patient know about it? Educate him about implications, including the probable short- and long-term effects of the disease. Explain how the STD is transmitted. Alert the patient as to precautions to take so he will not continue to transmit the disease to others. Help the patient understand why it is important for people who may have contracted the disease from him to be told they may have it.

Then, offer to contact the patient's former and current partners. Fully explain each step in the notification process, assuring the patient that his name will not be revealed under any circumstances. Answer any questions and address any concerns about the notification process. If the patient is still reluctant to provide information, give him some time to think about it away from the office, and follow up periodically with a phone call.

Once the patient agrees to reveal names, write down the names and other information, and preferably phone numbers. To make sure you have correct information, read it back to the patient, spelling each person's name in turn and reciting the phone number or address. Write down the phonetic pronunciations of any difficult names. Tell the patient when you will make the notifications.

You now are ready to contact these individuals. Professionals who work with STD patients recommend guidelines for contacting current and former partners to alert them about potential exposure to an STD. Note that these guidelines are applicable only to STDs other than AIDS.

Determine how you will contact each individual: in writing, in person, or by phone.

1. If you use U.S. mail, mark the outside of the addressed envelope "Personal." On a note inside, simply ask the person to call you at the medical office. Do not put the topic of the call in writing.

2. If you make the contact in person, ask where you can talk privately. Even if the person appears to be alone, others may still be able to overhear the conversation.

3. If you use the phone, identify yourself and your office, and ask for the specific individual. Do not reveal the nature of your call to anyone but that person. If pressed, tell the person who answers the phone that you are calling regarding a personal matter.

Once on the phone or alone with the person, confirm that you are talking to the correct person. Mention that you wish to talk about a highly personal matter, and ask if it is a good time to continue the discussion. If not, arrange for a more appropriate time.

Inform the individual that she has come in contact with someone who has an STD. Recommend that the person visit a doctor's office or clinic to be tested for the disease.

Be prepared for a variety of reactions, from surprise to anger. Respond calmly and coolly. Expect to respond to questions and statements such as:

- Who gave you my name?
- Do I have the disease?
- Am I really at risk? I haven't had intercourse recently (or) I've only had intercourse with my spouse.
- I feel fine. I just went to my doctor recently.

Let the person know that you cannot reveal the name of the partner because the information is strictly confidential. Assure the person that you will not reveal her name to anyone either.

Explain that exposure to the disease does not mean a person has contracted it. Encourage the person to get tested to know for sure.

Tell the person that she is still at risk, even if she hasn't had intercourse recently or has had it only with a spouse. Let the person know that someone with whom she came in close contact at some point has contracted the disease.

Even if the person says, "I feel fine," she may still have the disease. Again, stress the importance of getting tested.

Provide your name and phone number for contact about further questions. Recommend local offices and clinics for testing, and provide phone numbers. If the person will come to your office, offer to make the appointment.

Finally, document the results of your call. Log in the original patient's file the date that you completed notification. Include any pertinent details about the notification. Alert the patient when all people on the list have been notified.

LO 6.9 Ethics

Medical ethics is a vital part of medical practice and following an ethical code is an important part of your job. Ethics deals with general principles of right and wrong, as opposed to requirements of law. A professional is expected to act in ways that reflect society's ideas of right and wrong, even if such behavior is not enforced by law. Often, however, the law is based on ethical considerations.

Bioethics: Social Issues

Bioethics deals with issues that arise related to medical advances. For many people bioethical issues are particularly sensitive and highly personal issues. This may be true for you on a personal level as well. Remember that as an administrative medical assistant, you must remain non judgmental at all times regarding patient health care dilemmas and decisions. Here are three examples of bioethical issues.

bioethics
Ethical issues that arise related to medical advances.

1. A treatment for Parkinson's disease was developed that uses fetal tissue. Some women, upon learning about this treatment, might get pregnant just to have an abortion and sell the fetal tissue. Is this ethical?

2. If a couple cannot have a baby because of a medical condition of the mother, using a surrogate mother is an option some couples choose. The surrogate mother is artificially inseminated with the sperm of the husband and carries the baby to term. The couple then raises the child. Ethically speaking, who is the real mother, the woman who bears the child or the woman who raises the child? If the surrogate mother wants to keep the baby after it is born, does she have a right to do so?

3. When a liver transplant is needed by both a famous patient who has had a history of alcohol abuse and a woman who is a recipient of public assistance, what criteria are considered when determining who receives the organ? Who makes the decision? Ethically, treating physicians should not make the decision of allocating limited medical resources. Decisions regarding the allocation of limited medical resources should consider only the likelihood of benefit, the urgency of need, and the amount of resources required for successful treatment. Nonmedical criteria such as ability to pay, age, social worth, perceived obstacles to treatment, patient's contribution to illness, or the past use of resources should not be considered.

Practicing appropriate professional ethics has a positive impact on your reputation and the success of your employer's business. Many medical organizations, therefore, have created guidelines for the acceptable and preferred manners and behaviors, or etiquette, of administrative medical assistants and physicians.

The principles of medical ethics have developed over time. The Hippocratic oath, in which medical students pledge to practice medicine ethically, was developed in ancient Greece (see http://wikipedia.org/wiki/ Hippocratic_Oath). It is still used today and is one of the original bases of modern medical ethics. Hippocrates, the 4th century BC Greek physician commonly called the "father of medicine," is traditionally considered the author of this oath, but its authorship is actually unknown.

Among the promises of the Hippocratic oath are to use the form of treatment believed to be best for the patient, to refrain from harmful actions, and to keep a patient's private information confidential.

The AMA defines ethical behavior for doctors in *Code of Medical Ethics: Current Opinions with Annotations* (Chicago: American Medical Association, 1996). Medical assistants as well as doctors need to be aware of these principles.

AAMA Code of Ethics

The Code of Ethics of the AAMA shall set forth principles of ethical and moral conduct as they relate to the medical profession and the particular practice of medical assisting. Members of the AAMA dedicated to the conscientious pursuit of their profession, and thus desiring to merit the high regard of the entire medical profession and the respect of the general public which they serve, do pledge themselves to strive always to:

A. Render service with full respect for the dignity of humanity

B. Respect confidential information obtained through employment unless legally authorized or required by responsible performance of duty to divulge such information

C. Uphold the honor and high principles of the profession and accept its disciplines

D. Seek to continually improve the knowledge and skills of medical assistants for the benefit of patients and professional colleagues

E. Participate in additional service activities aimed toward improving the health and wellbeing of the community

The following is the AMT Standards of Practice.

AMT
American Medical Technologists
Certifying Excellence in Allied Health

AMT Standards of Practice

AMT seeks to encourage, establish, and maintain the highest standards, traditions and principles of the practices which constitute the profession of the Registry. Members of the AMT Registry must recognize their responsibilities, not only to their patients, but also to society, to other health care professionals, and to themselves. The following standards of practice are principles adopted by the AMT Board of Directors, which define the essence of honorable and ethical behavior for a health care professional:

1. While engaged in the Arts and Sciences, which constitute the practice of their profession, AMT professionals shall be dedicated to the provision of competent service.

2. The AMT professional shall place the welfare of the patient above all else.

3. The AMT professional understands the importance of thoroughness in the performance of duty, compassion with patients, and the importance of the tasks, which may be performed.

4. The AMT professional shall always seek to respect the rights of patients and of health care providers, and shall safeguard patient confidences.

5. The AMT professional will strive to increase his/her technical knowledge, shall continue to study, and apply scientific advanced in his/her specialty.

6. The AMT professional shall respect the law and will pledge to avoid dishonest, unethical or illegal practices.

7. The AMT professional understands that he/she is not to make or offer a diagnosis or interpretation unless he/she is a duly licensed physician/dentist or unless asked by the attending physician/dentist.

8. The AMT professional shall protect and value the judgment of the attending physician or dentist, providing this does not conflict with the behavior necessary to carry out Standard Number 2 above.

9. The AMT professional recognizes that any personal wrongdoing is his/her responsibility. It is also the professional health care provider's obligation to report to the proper authorities any knowledge of professional abuse.

10. The AMT professional pledges personal honor and integrity to cooperate in the advancement and expansion, by every lawful means, of American Medical Technologists.

American Medical Technologists
10700 W. Higgins Road, Suite 150
Rosemont, Illinois 60018
Phone: (847) 823-5169 – Fax: (847) 823-0458
Email: mail@amt1.com – www.amt1.com

A physician shall be dedicated to providing competent medical service with compassion and respect for human dignity.

This concept means that medical professionals will respect all aspects of the patient as a person, including intellect and emotions. The doctor must decide what treatment would result in the best, most dignified quality of life for the patient, and the doctor must respect a patient's choice to forgo treatment.

A physician shall deal honestly with patients and colleagues and strive to expose those physicians deficient in character or competence or who engage in fraud or deception.

Medical professionals, including medical assistants, should respect colleagues, but they must also respect and protect the profession and public welfare enough to report colleagues who are breaking the law, acting unethically, or unable to perform competently. Dilemmas may arise where one suspects, but is not able to prove, for instance, that a coworker has a substance abuse problem or another problem that is affecting performance. Ignoring such a situation in medical practice could cost someone's life as well as lead to lawsuits.

In terms of billing, a doctor should bill only for direct services, not for indirect ones, such as referrals. The doctor also should not bill for services that do not really pertain to the practice of medicine, such as dispensing drugs.

It is also unethical for the doctor to influence the patient about where to fill prescriptions or obtain other medical services when the doctor has a personal financial interest in any of the choices.

A physician shall respect the law and also recognize a responsibility to seek changes in requirements that are contrary to the patient's best interests.

Several legal or employer requirements have come under scrutiny as being contrary to a patient's best interests. Among them are discharging patients from the hospital after a certain time limit for certain procedures, which may be too soon for many patients. Insurance company payment policies have sometimes been criticized as unfair. So have health maintenance organization (HMO) financial policies that may conflict with a doctor's preference in treatment.

A physician shall respect the rights of patients, of colleagues, and of other health professionals and shall safeguard patient confidences within the constraints of law.

A physician shall continue to study; apply and advance scientific knowledge; make relevant information available to patients, colleagues, and the public; obtain consultation; and use the talents of other health professionals when indicated.

Keeping up with the latest advancements in medicine is crucial for providing high-quality, ethical care. Most states require doctors to accumulate "continuing education units" to maintain a license to practice. These units are earned by means of educational activities such as courses and scientific meetings. As discussed in Chapter 1, medical assistants who are certified by the AAMA, RMA, or CMAS have similar requirements by the sponsoring certification board to earn CEUs to maintain their credentialed status.

A physician shall, in the provision of appropriate patient care, except in emergencies, be free to choose whom to serve, with whom to associate, and the environment in which to provide medical services.

Ethically, doctors can set their hours, decide what kind of medicine to practice and where, decide whom to accept as a patient, and take time off as long as a qualified substitute performs their duties. Doctors may decline to accept new patients because of a full workload. In an emergency, however, a doctor may be ethically obligated to care for a patient, even if the patient is not of the doctor's

choosing. The doctor should not abandon that patient until another physician is available.

A physician shall recognize a responsibility to participate in activities contributing to an improved community. This ethical obligation holds true for the allied health professions as well.

In addition to knowing the physician's codes of ethics, medical assistants should follow the Code of Ethics for their certifying body, be it the AAMA or the AMT. (see the Practice Readiness box for the AAMA's Code of Ethics and the AMT's Standards of Practice on page 158).

CHECKPOINT
LO 6.9

What quality is repeatedly stressed when talking about health care and ethical issues, both toward the patient and medical colleagues?

LO 6.10 Legal Medical Practice Models

There are five basic types of medical practice:

- Sole proprietorship
- Partnership
- Group practice
- Professional corporation
- Clinics

Laws governing the various types of practice vary, but medical office personnel should be aware of the laws that apply to their employers' practice management models.

Sole Proprietorship

This type of practice is often referred to as a "solo practice." In this type of practice, a physician practicing alone assumes all the benefits for and liabilities of the business. **Sole proprietorship** practice management is no longer a popular option as a result of the increased expenses and decreased insurance reimbursements. Therefore, more physicians are joining group practices or professional corporations.

sole proprietorship
A physician practicing alone assumes all the benefits for and liabilities of the business.

Partnership

When two or more physicians decide to practice together, they may form a **partnership,** based on a legal contract that specifies the rights, obligations, and responsibilities of each partner. Advantages of partnerships include sharing the workload, expenses, profits, and assets. A disadvantage is that each partner has equal liability for acts of misconduct, losses, and deficits of the practice, unless specified as a contingency in the contract.

partnership
Two or more physicians decide to practice together, based on a legal contract that specifies the rights, obligations, and responsibilities of each partner.

Group Practice

Group practice is a medical practice model in which three or more licensed physicians share the collective income, expenses, facilities, equipment, records, and personnel for the practice. Physicians in group practice may be engaged in the same specialty, calling themselves, for example, Associates in Cardiology, or they can be several physicians offering similar specialties, such as ob/gyn and pediatrics.

group practice
A medical practice model in which three or more licensed physicians share the collective income, expenses, facilities, equipment, records, and personnel for the practice.

Professional Corporations

A **corporation** is a body formed and authorized by state law to act as a single entity. Physicians who form corporations are shareholders and employees of the

corporation
A body formed and authorized by state law to act as a single entity.

organization. There are financial and tax advantages to forming a corporation and the fringe benefits for employees may be greater than in a sole proprietorship or partnership.

In forming a corporation, the incorporators and owners have limited liability in case lawsuits are filed. Sometimes medical practices are "managed" by forprofit corporations that are either formed by outside business interests or subsidiary corporations organized by hospitals. Physicians are hired as salaried employees with bonus options. The management corporation provides the facility, office personnel, employee benefits, human resource services, and operating expenses.

Clinics

Patients can be admitted to clinics for special circumstances and research. Clinics are hard to distinguish from large medical facilities.

Clinics are broad in their range of specialties and subspecialties. They often have sophisticated medical equipment and renowned medical practitioners. Clinics may be housed inside of a hospital or may be free-standing. Urgent care centers, also known as walk-in clinics, exist so that patients will have the option of being seen without an appointment.

In-store clinics are becoming more prevalent. They are housed in large major chain stores, and sometimes in chain pharmacies. They offer smaller medical services such as vaccinations, flu shots, and eye exams. These types of clinics are quickly emerging.

Employment Law

Many administrative medical assistants find themselves promoted into supervisory and managerial positions. Knowledge of employment and labor laws such as those involving civil rights, sexual harassment, employment of the disabled, fair labor laws, and family medical leave are important to all employees, but particularly so for those who oversee other employees. Labor and employment laws are covered in detail in the practice management chapter (Chapter 22).

Why would it be legally advantageous for a physician partnership to incorporate?

CHECKPOINT
LO 6.10

Procedure **6–1** **Obtaining Signature for Receipt of Privacy Practices**

GOAL To follow HIPAA guidelines and obtain the patient's signature that he or she has received and understands the office privacy policies

MATERIALS Preprinted receipt of privacy practices information form (see Figure 6–5), pens, copy machine

METHOD 1. Explain to the patient the office privacy policy regarding protected health information.

2. Ask the patient to read the policy carefully and feel free to ask any questions he or she may have regarding the policy. Answer any questions that may arise.

3. When the patient's questions have been answered, witness the patient (or guardian) sign and print his or her name. Note any restrictions that may be placed on the document.

4. Print your name and sign the document as witness, including your title.

5. Date the document when all signatures have been completed

6. Make a copy of the document to file in the patient medical record and give the original to the patient.

Procedure 6-2 Completing a Privacy Violation Complaint Form

GOAL To assist the patient in completing a Privacy Violation Complaint form if she feels her PHI has been compromised

MATERIALS Privacy Violation Complaint Form (see Figure 6–6), pens, private room to complete form, copy machine

METHOD

1. Explain to the patient that all formal complaints must be made in writing.

2. Ask the patient if she feels assistance will be needed completing the form. If not, patient may complete the form on her own. Answer any questions she may have regarding completion of the form.

3. When the patient completes the form, read it carefully, making sure it is complete, legible, and the information regarding the breach of privacy clear.

4. If the patient requires that any copies be made for documentation backing the claim, make the copies, returning any originals to the patient.

5. Make sure the patient signs and dates the complaint.

6. As the person receiving the complaint, sign the document as indicated and date it.

7. Explain to the patient that the office will respond to the complaint within 30 days of today's receipt.

8. Make a copy of the document for the patient and keep the original for the office files.

Procedure 6-3 Obtaining Authorization to Release Health Information

GOAL To follow HIPAA guidelines when obtaining patient's protected health information without violating confidentiality regulations

MATERIALS Preprinted Authorization to Release Health Information form (see Figure 6–7), pens, copy machine

METHOD

1. Explain to the patient the need for the requested medical information.

2. Obtain the name and address of the practice to which the authorization is to be mailed.

3. Fill in the patient's name, address, and DOB as required.

4. Enter the physician's or practitioner's name from your practice who is requesting the PHI.

5. Enter the information that is being requested.

6. Complete the reason for request area explaining why the patient is requesting the information be sent to your office.

7. Enter an expiration date for the authorization, giving a reasonable amount of time for the request to be fulfilled.

8. Prior to signing the release, go over the information contained within the release with the patient, answering any questions that may arise. Be sure the patient understands the request may be withdrawn (in writing) at any time.

9. Witness the patient (or guardian) signature and dating; if necessary be sure the guardian relationship area is completed.

10. Sign and date the document as witness, including your title.

11. Make a copy of the document to file in the patient medical record and, if requested, give a copy to the patient as well.

12. Make a notation in the medical record of the document signing and note the date the authorization is mailed.

Case Study

Bill, a former paramedic, is currently working at Orthopedics Incorporated (OI). Mr. Fuller is a salesman for an orthopedic supply company that does business with OI. Bill recognizes him from an automobile accident to which his ambulance unit responded. He recalls that Mr. Fuller was charged with driving under the influence (DUI). During lunch Bill shares this information with the staff. A cousin of Mr. Fuller also works at OI and tells him about the lunchtime conversation. A few weeks later, OI cancels the contract with Mr. Fuller's company. Mr. Fuller is convinced that it is a result of Bill's informing Orthopedic Incorporated of his DUI. Mr. Fuller sues the orthopedic practice for slander jeopardizing his livelihood. The physicians and others at OI are also questioning Bill's integrity since confidentiality has always been a core value in health care. Under HIPAA, confidentiality is not only a core value, but a mandate.

PROFESSIONAL READINESS

Integrity
Sound and honest decision making within acceptable codes of values

Thinking Critically

1. Since Mr. Fuller was not a patient of OI, did Bill violate HIPAA?

2. Is OI responsible for Bill's actions under *respondeat superior*?

3. What do you think Bill and the other OI staff members learned from this situation?

practice APPLICATIONS

When completing these activities, search the Internet for your choice of topics.

1. Research a controversial topic from the following list:
   - Euthanasia
   - Surrogacy
   - Abortion
   - Fetal stem cell research
   - Cloning
   - Emergency contraceptive (morning-after pill)

Write a three-page report that presents both the pro side and the con side of the issue. Write a closing paragraph that gives your personal opinion and views and how you have been conditioned in that belief, for example, social, cultural, and religious beliefs.

2. Choose teams of four people, and stage debates on the controversial topics listed in question 1. Research your topics thoroughly and present arguments on both sides. Your purpose is to state facts and persuade your audience to your beliefs.
   Rules for the debate:
   - Participants must be courteous and professional
   - Presentations must be factual
   - Opening arguments are 4 minutes for each side
   - Each side presents, and then for 3 minutes each side is allowed to counter any fact
   - Closing arguments are 5 minutes for each side

Have the class vote on which side was more persuasive.

exam READINESS

1. **[LO6.1]** A standard of conduct that is generally accepted as a moral guide for moral values for behavior is
   a. civil law.
   b. professional medical ethics.
   c. medical etiquette.
   d. classification of law.
   e. mores

2. **[LO6.1]** The two types of law that pertain to health-care professionals are
   a. contract law and agency law.
   b. civil law and criminal law.
   c. civil law and medical law.
   d. litigation and malpractice.
   e. contract law and medical negligence.

3. **[LO6.6]** The main federal legislations that affect health care are
   a. OSHA regulations and HIPAA.
   b. the Healthcare Quality Improvement Act of 1986 and the Federal False Claims Act.
   c. HIPAA and Mandatory Disclosures.
   d. ADEA of 1987 and the Fair Labor Standards Act.
   e. Civil Rights Act and HIPAA.

4. **[LO6.4]** The Controlled Substances Act (CSA) of 1970 maintains that medical facilities keep drugs under close control, and they list them in _____ categories.
   a. two
   b. five
   c. ten
   d. seven
   e. three

5. **[LO6.2]** Informed consent requires that the patient understand
   a. the proposed treatment modes.
   b. the risks of alternative treatment.
   c. the risks involved in the proposed treatment.
   d. the alternative treatment modes.
   e. all of the above

6. **[LO6.7]** All of the following items EXCEPT _____ are considered protected health information.
   a. date of birth
   b. insurance ID number
   c. medical record number
   d. city or town of birth
   e. e-mail address

7. **[LO6.7]** What does the acronym TPO stand for?
   a. Therapy, payment, and operations
   b. Treatment, payment, and operations
   c. Treatment, procedures, and operations
   d. Treatment, payment, and options
   e. Therapy, payment, and options

8. **[LO6.8]** Which of the following is the correct definition for HIPAA?
   a. Health Insurance Practicality and Accountability Act
   b. Health Insurer Portability and Accountability Act
   c. Health Injury Procedures and Accident Act
   d. Health Insurance Practice and Accountability Act
   e. Health Insurance Portability and Accountability Act

9. **[LO6.3]** Which of the following items would *not* require documentation in the patient's medical chart?
   a. Missed appointments
   b. Canceled appointments
   c. Patient call to confirm an appointment
   d. Medical record corrections
   e. Prescription refills

10. **[LO6.3]** Which one of the following documents outlines the patient's wishes to the physician and family in the event he is unable to communicate them?
   a. Living will
   b. Advance directive
   c. Consent for treatment
   d. Durable power of attorney
   e. Health-care proxy

learning outcome SUMMARY

LO 6.1 A law is a rule or conduct or action prescribed or formally recognized as binding or enforced by local, state, or federal government. Ethics are standards of behavior or concepts of right or wrong beyond what the legal consideration is in any given situation.

LO 6.2 Physician responsibilities in a patient-physician contract include using due care, skill, judgment, and diligence in treating the patient; staying informed of current diagnosis and treatment; performing to the best of ability; providing complete information and instructions to the patient.

Patient responsibilities in a patient-physician contract include following instructions given by the provider and cooperating as much as possible; giving relevant information to provider; following physician instructions for treatment; paying fees for services provided.

LO 6.3 The four Ds of malpractice are duty—it must be proven that a patient-physician relationship exists; derelict—it must be proven that the physician failed to comply with standards of the profession; direct cause—it must be proven that any damages were directly caused by the physician's breach of duty; damages—it must be proven that the patient suffered an injury.

LO 6.4 In addition to providing information for continuity of care, the patient record is often used as

evidence in malpractice cases. Items to be included in the record include referrals, missed appointments, dismissals, all patient contact, and medical record corrections.

LO 6.5 HCQIA is the federal statute passed in 1986 to improve the quality of medical care in the United States. It requires peer review limits to damages in professional reviews and protects those who provide information to review bodies. It also established the National Practitioner Data Bank. The Federal False Claims Act was in response to increased health-care costs. Laws were enacted to control false billing claims, kickbacks, and self-referrals.

LO 6.6 OSHA requires protective clothing if exposure might occur, decontamination of exposed surfaces, appropriate disposal of sharps, reporting and care of exposure incidents, post-exposure procedures, handling of potentially infectious laundry, minimum requirements for workplace safety, training on OSHA's hazardous substances regulations for employees who might be exposed, and government regulations regarding documentation.

LO 6.7 The impact of HIPAA regulations include improved efficiency and effectiveness of health-care delivery; protection and enhancement of the rights of patients by providing access to their protected health

information and controlling inappropriate use or disclosure of information; improving quality of health care by restoring trust in the health-care system.

LO 6.8 Six principles for protecting patient confidentiality: (1)When in doubt about releasing information, do not. (2)It is the patient's right to release information, not the physicians. (3)Treat all patients with the same degree of confidentiality. (4)Be aware of all applicable laws and regulations regarding PHI release. (5)When there is a conflict between confidentiality and ethics, talk with the patient; ultimately, the physician may need to make the decision. (6)Get written permission from the patient before releasing confidential information.

LO 6.9 Ethics reflect the general principles of right and wrong. A professional, particularly a medical professional, is expected to follow especially high ethical standards.

LO 6.10 There are five basic types of practice management models: (1) sole proprietorship (one physician); (2) partnership (two or more physicians); (3) group practice (three or more physicians); (4) professional Corporation (a body formed and authorized by state law to act as a single entity; physicians are stakeholders and employees of the organization); and (5) clinics.

medical assisting COMPETENCIES

CAAHEP

IX. C (1) Discuss legal scope of practice for medical assistants

IX. C (2) Explore issue of confidentiality as it applies to the medical assistant

IX. C (3) Describe the implications of HIPAA for the medical assistant in various medical settings

IX. C (4) Summarize the Patient Bill of Rights

IX. C (5) Discuss licensure and certification as it applies to health-care providers

IX. C (6) Describe liability, professional, personal injury, and third party insurance

IX. C (7) Compare and contrast physician and medical assistant roles in terms of standard of care

IX. C (8) Compare criminal and civil law as it applies to the practicing medical assistant

IX C (9) Provide an example of tort law as it would apply to a medical assistant

IX. C (10) Explain how the following impact the medical assistant's practice and give examples
   a. Negligence
   b. Malpractice
   c. Statute of Limitations
   d. Good Samaritan Act(s)
   e. Uniform Anatomical Gift Act
   f. Living will/Advanced directives
   g. Medical durable power of attorney

IX. C (11) Identify how the Americans with Disabilities Act (ADA) applies to the medical assisting profession

IX. C (12) List and discuss legal and illegal interview questions

IX. C (13) Discuss all levels of governmental legislation and regulation as they apply to medical assisting practice, including FDA and DEA regulations

IX. C (14) Describe the process to follow if an error is made in patient care

IX. P (1) Respond to issues of confidentiality

IX. P (2) Perform within scope of practice

IX. P (3) Apply HIPAA rules in regard to privacy/release of information

IX. P (4) Practice within the standard of care for a medical assistant

IX. P (5) Incorporate the Patient's Bill of Rights into personal practices and medical office policies and procedures

IX. P (6) Complete an incident report

IX. P (8) Apply local, state, and federal health care legislation and regulation appropriate to the medical assisting practice setting

IX. A (1) Demonstrate sensitivity to patient rights

IX. A (2) Demonstrate awareness of the consequences of not working within the legal scope of practice

IX. A (3) Recognize the importance of local, state, and federal legislation and regulations in the practice setting

X. C (1) Differentiate between legal, ethical, and moral issues affecting health care

X. C (2) Compare personal, professional, and organizational ethics

X. C (4) Identify where to report illegal and/or unsafe activities and behaviors that affect health, safety, and welfare of others

X. C (5) Identify the effect personal ethics may have on professional performance

X. P (1) Report illegal and/or unsafe activities and behaviors that affect health, safety, and welfare of others to proper authorities

X. P (2) Develop a plan for separation of personal and professional ethics

X. A (1) Apply ethical behaviors, including honesty/integrity in performance of medical assisting practice

X. A (2) Examine the impact personal ethics and morals may have on the individual's practice

X. A (3) Demonstrate awareness of diversity in providing patient care

ABHES

4. Medical Law and Ethics
  a. Document accurately
  b. Institute federal and state guidelines when releasing medical records or information
  c. Follow established policies when initiating or terminating medical treatment
  d. Understand the importance of maintaining liability coverage once employed in the industry
  e. Perform risk management procedures
  f. Comply with federal, state, and local health laws and regulations

7

From Appointment to Payment

Learning Outcomes

After completing Chapter 7, you should be able to:

7.1 Explain the patient's entry into the medical practice.

7.2 Describe the functions that take place in the clinical areas of the medical practice.

7.3 List the steps for patient discharge.

7.4 Discuss the medical office functions following the patient's discharge.

Key Terms

assignment of benefits
daily log
encounter form
reception
sign-in
superbill
third-party payers

Preparation for Certification

RMA (AMT)
- Patient relations
- Employ appropriate interpersonal skills
- Reception
- Computer applications

CMAS (AMT)
- Legal and ethical considerations
- Professionalism
- Medical office computer applications
- Communication
- Safety
- Physical plant

CMA (AAMA)
- Professionalism
- Working as a team member to achieve goals
- Professional communication and behavior
- Receiving, organizing, and transmitting information
- Maintaining confidentiality
- Computer applications

Introduction ● ● ●

Health care is perhaps the most complex industry in the United States. A major reason is the person receiving the service is usually not the one directly paying for the service. The majority of patients are covered by a form of insurance through employers, government agencies, or private policies. These insurers are called **third-party payers.** As a result, the medical office has multifaceted functions and departments to accommodate both patient care and the complicated administrative responsibilities. Medical office staff must work as a team to ensure coordination of the processes. In addition to direct patient care, the processes include appointment scheduling, medical records management, insurance coding and billing, payment receipt, facility maintenance, and personnel management or human resources. While this textbook covers each area in depth, the administrative medical assisting student often experiences difficulty in understanding how the pieces fit together or integrate. To assist you, this chapter provides an overview of what happens from the time the patient calls for an appointment to the time payment is received. While offices differ depending on size, specialty, and ancillary services, you will follow Frank Ortiz, a fictitious patient, through a generic medical appointment (Figure 7–1).

third-party payer
The entity that pays for a service received from one party but provided by another party.

LO 7.1 Entry into the Medical Practice

Frank Ortiz is a 54-year-old male of Hispanic descent. He teaches mathematics at the local middle school and his school district covers his health insurance plan. Mr. Ortiz recently moved to a new locale. He is making an appointment with a new physician, Matthew Rodriguez, M.D., for treatment of his hypertension. The patient calls the Total Care Clinic to schedule an appointment. The administrative medical assistant, Kalisha Roberts, determines that the practice accepts the school district's insurance plan and makes the appointment. The office policy is to either mail the registration material or encourage the patient to access it through the practice's Web site. Mr. Ortiz elects to download the registration forms from the Web site, complete them, and bring them at the time of his appointment. Refer to Procedure 7–1, Registering the New Patient, located at the end of the chapter. Mr. Ortiz informs the staff member that he obtained his current medical record from his former physician.

When Mr. Ortiz arrives for his scheduled appointment, he **signs in** at the **reception** desk using a digital pad type device. This alerts staff that he has arrived. When it is his turn, the administrative medical assistant reviews Mr. Ortiz's completed forms and keys the information into the practice's electronic health record (EHR) (Figure 7–2). The patient signs the form to allow release of information to insurance companies, the **assignment of benefits,** and to acknowledge financial responsibility (Figure 7–3). He also signs the form to indicate that he was informed of the office's privacy practices as required

sign-in
The process in which an arriving patient lists his or her name and other information on a form in the registration area; also refers to the registration area.

reception
The area where patients enter the office, inform the staff of their presence by "signing in," receive a greeting, and await to be seen.

assignment of benefits
Written consent from the patient allowing the insurance company to directly pay the practitioner.

figure 7–1

Follow Frank Ortiz as he becomes a new patient.

Scheduling the appointment   Completing registration forms   Signing in

figure 7-2

Example of Patient Registration Form and required information.

TOTAL CARE CLINIC, PC

Patient Registration Form

Date: _____

Last name: _____ First name: _____ MI: _____

Address: _____ Birth date: ____/____/____

City/St/Zip: _____ SSN: _____

Marital status: (please circle) Single   Married   Divorced   Widowed   **Pt. language:** _____

Home phone: _____ Cell phone: _____ E-mail: _____

Referred by: _____ Patient's employer: _____

Employer's address: _____ City/St/Zip: _____

Primary insurance: _____ Phone: _____

Group name: _____ Group #: _____ ID #: _____

Subscriber's name: _____ Subscriber's birth date: ____/____/____

Secondary insurance: _____ Phone: _____

Group name: _____ Group #: _____ ID #: _____

Subscriber's name: _____ Subscriber's birth date: ____/____/____

Relative emergency contact: _____ Relationship: _____

Address: _____ Phone: _____

I have reviewed the above information and, to the best of my knowledge, it is correct.

Printed name of patient or legal representative: _____

Signature of patient or legal representative: _____

figure 7-3

Authorization for Release of Information, Assignment of Benefits, and Financial Responsibility Information form.

TOTAL CARE CLINIC, PC

342 East Park Blvd
Funton, XY 12345-6789
Tel: 521-234-0001
Fax: 521-234-0002
www.totalcareclinic.org

Instruction to Office Staff: Scan in as "Release" with date

PATIENT NAME: _____

Date of Birth: _____

Today's Date: _____

AUTHORIZATION TO RELEASE INFORMATION

I hereby authorize the Total Care Clinic (TCC) to release any medical information necessary to process insurance claims relating to the medical care rendered by the physicians and staff of TCC.

Signature:_____   Date: _____

ASSIGNMENT OF BENEFITS

I authorize payment of medical benefits to the Total Care Clinic for any medical care rendered to myself or to my dependents.

Signature:_____   Date: _____

FINANCIAL RESPONSIBILITY

I understand that payment of the portion of the bill that is my responsibility is due on the date service is rendered (any copay, unsatisfied deductible, no-show, less than 24-hour cancellation and co-insurance; if a cash pay patient, the full amount of the bill). I also understand that any service not covered by my insurance is my responsibility subject to the terms of any contract between the insurance plan and the Total Care Clinic.

Signature:_____   Date: _____

by HIPAA. Kalisha scans the forms along with the patient's insurance card and a photo identification, his driver's license. Per the office policy, his hand-carried medical record is copied and a folder made with the medical record number assigned by the EHR system. The medical record is used throughout the appointment and billing processes.

CHECKPOINT
LO 7.1

Why do you think the medical assistant determines if the office accepts Mr. Ortiz's insurance before making the appointment?

LO 7.2 The Clinical Areas

Mr. Ortiz signed in and became registered. The medical assistant created his medical record and electronically informed the clinical medical assistant, Brendan Conroy, that the patient is ready to be seen. Throughout the appointment, staff communication within the functional areas is imperative. The communication is electronic, hard copy, and verbal. Brendan goes to reception and calls Mr. Ortiz by name. When he responds, the medical assistant introduces himself and verifies the patient's identification, usually by birthday. The patient proceeds to the screening area where Brendan obtains vital signs, height, and weight and portions of the patient's medical history and medications are reviewed, including known allergies. The patient then goes to the treatment area and receives an examination gown and privacy to change. Dr. Rodriguez reviews the medical records brought by the patient and the patient's health history form. He examines the patient and, since Mr. Ortiz has a history of hypertension, or high blood pressure, the physician orders blood tests and an electrocardiogram (ECG). Brendan completes the ECG and draws blood for the tests. He places the specimens in a special box for collection by the reference laboratory. He also documents each process in the medical record. Dr. Rodriguez reviews the ECG, discusses the results, recommends that Mr. Ortiz consult with a cardiologist, and renews his current hypertension prescription directly through the electronic health record. The patient's insurance company requires a prior authorization for a cardiologist consultation. A **superbill** or **encounter form** is electronically initiated by the physician. This form is the method for listing the procedures and the charges for the office visit, the ECG, and the blood draw (Figure 7-4).

superbill (encounter form)
Form used to list services and charges for the patient's visit.

CHECKPOINT
LO 7.2

With your knowledge to this point in your medical assisting education, explain the importance of the medical record.

LO 7.3 Patient Discharge

Mr. Ortiz completed the clinical portion of his office visit and prepares for discharge. Brendan escorts him to the checkout area. He instructs Omalara, the administrative medical assistant at the discharge desk that the patient needs a cardiology consult requiring authorization from the insurance company. Since the office is on an electronic system, the administrative medical assistant directly enters the charges via computer. Omalara instructs Mr. Ortiz that the office will bill his insurance company and notify him when the office receives the prior authorization for his consult. She also validates his parking card since this facility has a restricted parking garage. Mr. Ortiz takes his reminder card and leaves (Figure 7-5).

HIPAA compliance is mandatory from the moment Mr. Ortiz calls the office to schedule his appointment to the end of his office visit. HIPAA compliance

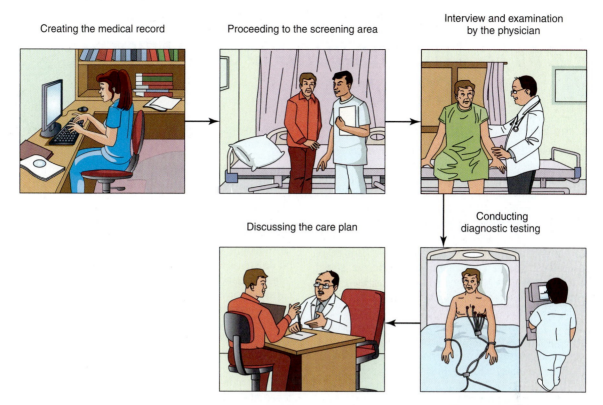

Creating the medical record

Proceeding to the screening area

Interview and examination by the physician

Conducting diagnostic testing

Discussing the care plan

figure 7–4

Mr. Ortiz proceeds to the clinical areas.

is also mandatory as the staff conducts other functions that follow the office visit. In addition, the staff should exhibit professional behaviors at all times. This includes a smile and kind word to the patient upon discharge. The little things, such as reminding the patient about validating his parking card if that is suitable, creates a positive experience for the patient and a more pleasant work environment for the staff.

● ● ●

Give examples of how staff members exhibited professional behaviors.

CHECKPOINT
LO 7.3

LO 7.4 Staff Functions Following Patient Discharge

Although Mr. Ortiz was discharged, that is not the end of the staff's functions. The charges from the encounter form are entered into the **daily log** or daily journal that accounts for the total charges and payments of the day. Chapter 21,

daily log
The sheet that records and calculates the total charges and payments received by the patient for the day.

figure 7–5

Discharging Mr. Ortiz.

Discharge

Scheduling follow-up appointment

Friendly farewells

Working with the Health-Care Team

THE MEDICAL LABORATORY TECHNICIAN

Duties and Skills

A common role of the administrative medical assistant is obtaining the patient's laboratory test results. The person that the medical assistant often interacts with is the medical laboratory technician (MLT), also referred to as the clinical laboratory technician (CLT). The MLT performs tests on blood, other body fluids, and cells to assist with the diagnosis and treatment of conditions and diseases. He or she prepares specimens; operates centrifuges, analyzers, and other sophisticated laboratory equipment; and performs select manual tests. In some instances the MLT will also draw blood from the patient for testing. The MLT also ensures the test results are properly reported by following the protocol of his or her organization. The technician may be responsible for reporting the test results directly to the physician's office. The position requires a person who pays attention to detail and has the ability to apply critical thinking skills.

Educational Requirements

The medical laboratory technician or clinical laboratory technician is a high school graduate with an MLT or CLT certificate or degree from a community college, post secondary school, or university. Some states require a license or registration and most employers require or prefer applicants with certifications from a recognized professional association, such as the American Medical Technologists (AMT) or the National Accrediting Agency for Clinical Laboratory Sciences (NAACLS).

Workplace Settings

Most medical laboratory technicians work in hospitals and diagnostic laboratories called reference laboratories. Some MLTs are also found in physicians' offices. However, the guidelines of the Clinical Laboratory Improvement Amendments of 1988 (CLIA '88) limit the tests performed in the medical office setting.

The Medical Laboratory Technician as a Team Member

The majority of medical offices order laboratory tests. The most common are a variety of blood tests that aid the physician in determining the correct diagnosis and monitoring the patient's progress. The specimen for these tests may be drawn at the medical office by a staff member or at a reference laboratory drawing site. The administrative medical assistant would send the patient or the specimen to the appropriate place. The MLT may be the person who draws the blood sample at the site and then processes simple tests. The administrative medical assistant follows up on the test results that are reported to the physician's office via computer, fax, or telephone. The administrative medical assistant is frequently acquainted with the lab tech through these encounters. It is not unusual for the office to call the MLT inquiring about instructions to give patients such as fasting requirements prior to a specific test. Office personnel and laboratory personnel also communicate regarding test results with critical values that must be reported to the physician immediately and tests that must be performed immediately. Good communication between the administrative medical assistant and the medical laboratory technician is an asset to good patient care.

For more information, visit the Web sites of the following organizations, which are available on the Online Learning Center at www.mhhe.com/houseradminmedassist

American Medical Technologists (AMT)

National Accrediting Agency for Clinical Laboratory Sciences (NAACLS)

Financial Practices, discusses this procedure, along with the other financial work that takes place.

Simultaneously, the entries into the day's accounting system are made and the encounter form information goes electronically to the area of the medical office that performs the coding of the procedures and the diagnoses. The medical record documentation validates the selected codes. Chapter 18, ICD-9-CM Coding, Chapter 19, ICD-10-CM Coding, and Chapter 20, CPT and HCPCS Coding, explain the complex processes. Coding is required to submit a claim to the insurance company for payment. If all goes well, the office receives the billed amount from the insurance company in 30 to 45 days (Figure 7–6). If the insurance company does not pay in full, the office sends the patient a statement requesting the balance.

Potential HIPAA Violations

As you learn the flow of the office processes, you should be creating an awareness of the many areas for potential HIPAA violations. Begin to develop good habits by putting violation prevention into practice. Simple actions include shredding all documents before discarding; using protective screens on computers and logging off computers when not in use; and avoiding leaving any forms or materials with patients' names in the open. Be cautious concerning telephone conversations that may be overheard by nonauthorized individuals. Other areas of common abuse are discussing patients and other confidential information in elevators, break rooms, and the local breakfast/lunch establishment. Two mnemonics may help you remember and become more conscious of patient privacy: "Zip the Lip" which means to be careful who is close by when discussing patients, and "Zone the Phone" which refers to using the telephone in private areas where conversations cannot be heard. Your employer is subject to heavy fines for a HIPAA violation and you would seriously jeopardize your job.

Other Patient-Related Responsibilities

You just followed Frank Ortiz through a routine office visit and learned the basic flow of a generic medical practice. As you continue to study administrative medical assisting, you will discover that many more administrative responsibilities are associated with the role and are covered in this textbook. Some of them include:

- Verifying insurance coverage
- Obtaining prior authorization
- Arranging referrals
- Scheduling inpatient and outpatient procedures
- Managing the physician's schedule
- Following up with patients
- Managing medical records
- Calling in prescriptions
- Ensuring diagnostic testing is completed and results obtained
- Screening and managing telephone calls
- Attempting to collect delinquent payments

figure 7–6

Next steps following a patient's discharge.

Entering charges   Coding and billing   Payment received

EHR readiness

Multiple Accesses to the Medical Record

The medical record or health record is used during every step of patient-related functions. The hard copy version must be hand carried from one location to another and may be used by only one person at a time. Sometimes staff will copy portions of the paper record to allow simultaneous completion of more than one task. The copying is time-consuming and the records and copies require extensive storage space. The potential for losing or misplacing the documents is very real. In contrast, the electronic health record is available to all authorized staff simultaneously and it does not require transport from one physical area to another. For example, the administrative medical assistant, the clinical medical assistant, the physician, and the coder may input into their necessary sections at the same time. This multiple access capability increases efficiency, decreases lost health records, and eliminates the need for large storage areas. The federal government is recommending that all health-care facilities adopt the EHR by 2014. New administrative medical assistants who begin their careers using an electronic health record will not experience the angst associated with a lost health record unless it is an old chart. These records must continue to be maintained and stored, which is discussed in detail in other chapters. For several years, office staff will have the challenge of incorporating patient information from the manual system into the electronic system.

By the end of your medical assisting program, you should have a working familiarity with all of these areas and others (Figure 7–7).

Non-Patient-Related Responsibilities

The medical office is a business. All businesses, whether they are medical or industrial, have specific requirements for personnel management (the staff), business management (licenses, insurance, etc.), and facilities management (the building and its systems). You now have an overview of the functions of the medical practice. As you proceed through your administrative medical assisting program, keep in mind how the pieces fit together and how each role and task impact others. This

figure 7–7

Overview of the medical office and its functions.

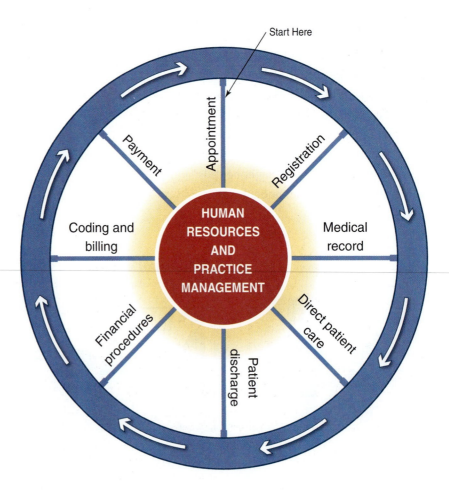

awareness helps to make you an invaluable administrative medical assistant and an important team member.

● ● ●
Describe the functions after the patient is discharged.

CHECKPOINT
LO 7.4

Procedure 7−1 Registering a New Patient

GOAL To accurately register the patient by obtaining all the necessary information for treatment

MATERIALS Registration form (you may use Figure 7–2), Authorization for Release of Information, Assignment of Benefits, and Financial Responsibility Information form (you may use Figure 7–3), pen or computer, copy machine or scanner

METHOD
1. Greet the patient and instruct him to sign in; this may be done manually or digitally, depending on the office technology.
2. Provide the patient with a registration form to complete or interview the patient and input the information directly into the computer.
3. Ensure all areas are addressed.
4. Obtain the patient's or legal representative's signature on the Authorization for Release of Information, Assignment of Benefits, and Financial Responsibility Information form. (Please note that procedures related to privacy practices are in Chapter 6, Law and Ethics in the Medical Office.)
5. Provide the patient with a copy.
6. Answer any questions and obtain the patient's or legal representative's signature.
7. Copy or scan the patient's or insured party's insurance card and a photo identification such as a driver's license.
8. Thank the patient and instruct him or her to have a seat until the clinical medical assistant calls the patient's name.

Case Study

Omalara has been with the Total Care Clinic for two weeks. She is responsible for obtaining the cardiology consultation for Mr. Ortiz as soon as possible. Omalara submits the request to the insurance company. In 24 hours, she receives a fax back that the diagnosis code does not correspond to a referral to a cardiologist. After reviewing the encounter form, she discovers an error. She finds the correct diagnosis in the medical record and assigns the correct code that she, again, submits to the insurance company. The next day, the insurance company faxes a refusal, stating that medical necessity was not demonstrated. Once again, Omalara reviews the medical record and finds a note from Dr. Rodriguez regarding an abnormal electrocardiogram. In the meantime, Mr. Ortiz is anxious

PROFESSIONAL READINESS

Acceptance of Criticism
Willing to consider suggestions and observations

and calling about the approval of his referral. Omalara is frustrated and goes to her supervisor who counsels her on having all the correct and necessary information on the first submission. The new employee agrees that she must be more organized and pay closer attention to detail. The supervisor notes the positive manner in which the new employee deals with the criticism.

Thinking Critically

1. Is the supervisor justified in counseling Omalara?
2. Do you think this experience will help Omalara become better at her job?
3. Is Omalara's job important? Explain your answer.

practice APPLICATIONS

1. Create an imaginary patient and follow him or her through an office visit as you followed Frank Ortiz. Briefly write each step. You may use a specialty medical practice.

2. Review Procedure 7–1, Registering the Patient. Visit one or more medical practices. Explain to them that you are an administrative medical assisting student and ask them for copies of the forms they use for registering their patients. Share the forms you obtain with your instructor and classmates as examples of various designs and uses.

exam READINESS

There may be more than one correct answer. Circle the best answer.

1. **[LO7.1]** Copying the patient's insurance card is part of the
   a. appointment scheduling.
   b. registration process.
   c. patient screening.
   d. encounter form.
   e. coding and billing.

2. **[LO7.2]** The acronym for the federal act that deals with privacy in the medical office is
   a. HIPPO.
   b. HIPPA.
   c. HIPAA.
   d. HIIPA.
   e. HIIPO.

3. **[LO7.3]** The form listing the patient's charges is referred to as the
   a. remittance form.
   b. claim form.
   c. registration form.
   d. encounter form.
   e. reminder card.

4. **[LO7.3]** An example of demonstrating a professional behavior would be to
   a. greet the patient as soon as he or she arrives.
   b. submit the claim.
   c. complete the charges.
   d. schedule the patient for a follow up appointment.
   e. record the patient's charges.

5. **[INTRO]** When an insurance company pays for the medical expenses of a patient, this is referred to as a
   a. direct payment.
   b. superbill.
   c. claim.
   d. third-party biller.
   e. third-party payer.

6. **[LO7.3]** Another term for the superbill is the

   a. daily log.

   b. encounter form.

   c. third-party payer.

   d. third-party biller.

   e. claim.

7. **[LO7.4]** All the charges and payments for the day are entered into the

   a. daily log.

   b. encounter form.

   c. registration form.

   d. superbill.

   e. claim.

8. **[LO7.2]** The clinical medical assistant uses the medical record to

   a. register the patient.

   b. bill the insurance company.

   c. enter the charges.

   d. schedule a follow up appointment.

   e. document the diagnostic procedures.

9. **[LO7.2]** When the patient is brought to the screening area

   a. the insurance is verified.

   b. the vital signs are taken.

   c. the consents are signed.

   d. the charges are entered.

   e. a follow up appointment is scheduled.

10. **[LO7.4]** In addition to patient related functions, the medical office has a person or department that is responsible for

   a. pharmacy.

   b. laboratory.

   c. scheduling appointments.

   d. human resources.

   e. registration.

learning outcome SUMMARY

LO 7.1 The processes of the medical office begin with the patient making an appointment. When the patient arrives for the appointment, he or she is requested to sign in. Registration forms are completed and a medical record initiated.

LO 7.2 The registration process is followed by the clinical portion of the visit which includes obtaining vital signs, reviewing the previous medical record, and addressing the reason for the appointment.

LO 7.3 After the clinical portion of the appointment, the patient is directed to the discharge area where

the charges are addressed. A follow-up appointment may be scheduled at that time. HIPAA compliance and professional behaviors should be are maintained throughout the visit.

LO 7.4 Following the patient's discharge, coding and billing of the patient's visit take place. Timely payment should occur. In addition to the functions related to the patient, the medical office, as a business, is responsible for human resource procedures and management of the practice.

medical assisting COMPETENCIES

CAAHEP

IV. C (9) Discuss applications of electronic technologies in effective communication

IV. P (2) Report relevant information to others succinctly and accurately

IV. P (4) Explain general office policies

V. P (6) Use office hardware and software to maintain office systems

V. P (7) Use Internet to access information related to the medical office

VII. P (1) Apply both managed care policies and procedures

IX. C (2) Explore issue of confidentiality as it applies to the medical assistant

IX. C (3) Describe the implications of HIPAA for the medical assistant in various medical settings

XI. C (2) Identify safety techniques that can be used to prevent accidents and maintain a safe work environment

XI. P (11) Use proper body mechanics

ABHES

1. General Orientation

b. Compare and contrast the allied health professions and understand the relation to medical assisting

d. Have knowledge of the general responsibilities of the medical assistant

4. Medical Law and Ethics

a. Document accurately

c. Follow established policies when initiating or terminating medical treatment

7. Basic Keyboarding/Computer Concepts

a. Perform basic keyboarding skills

b. Identify and properly utilize office machines, computerized systems, and medical software

8. Medical Office Business Procedures/ Management

a. Perform basic clerical functions

b. Prepare and maintain medical records

d. Apply concepts for office procedures

dd. Serve as liaison between physician and others

hh. Receive, organize, prioritize, and transmit information expediently

ll. Apply electronic technology

11. Career Development

b. Demonstrate professionalism by:

(1) Exhibiting dependability, punctuality, and a positive work ethic

(2) Exhibiting a positive attitude and a sense of responsibility

(3) Maintaining confidentiality at all times

(4) Being cognizant of ethical boundaries

(5) Exhibiting initiative

(6) Adapting to change

(7) Expressing a responsible attitude

(8) Being courteous and diplomatic

(9) Conducting work within scope of education, training, and ability

8 The Medical Office Environment

Learning Outcomes

After completing Chapter 8, you will be able to:

8.1 Describe the basic considerations for the design of the medical office reception area.

8.2 Explain the Americans with Disabilities Act (ADA).

8.3 Discuss the staff functions of the reception area.

8.4 Describe the purpose of the Red Flags Rule.

8.5 Identify the general supplies maintained in the medical office and describe the inventory process.

8.6 Explain the rationale for creating and maintaining a structured process for opening and closing the office.

8.7 Understand ergonomics and body mechanics.

Key Terms

Americans with Disabilities Act (ADA)
body mechanics
copayment
durable item
ergonomics
expendable item
inventory
invoice
medical identity theft
Occupational Safety and Health Administration (OSHA)
packing slip
petty cash
reception
receptionist
Red Flags Rule
requisition
sign-in

Preparation for Certification

RMA (AMT)
- Human relations
- Patient education
- Medical receptionist/secretarial/clerical

CMAS (AMT)
- Medical office computer applications
- Business organization management
- Safety
- Supplies and equipment
- Physical plant
- Risk management and quality assurance

CMA (AAMA)
- Professionalism
- Communication
- Equipment
- Computer concepts
- Maintaining the office environment

Introduction ● ● ●

The purpose of the medical office or clinic is to deliver appropriate care to those in need. The environment, created by the design and furnishings of the facility, is key to delivering this care and influences the patient's overall experience. Reception is the point of entry. It sets the stage for a successful interaction between the patient and the entire medical staff. This chapter discusses the considerations for the design and other factors for this area including patient educational materials. The type of practice and the special needs of the patient population are major influences. This chapter also addresses the Americans with Disabilities Act and the Red Flags Rule along with the role of reception staff. Ensuring correct and adequate supplies is another feature that creates an efficient office environment. The chapter also addresses ergonomics and body mechanics.

LO 8.1 The Design of the Medical Office Reception Area

The terms for identifying areas in the medical office are divided into two broad functional categories:

1. Clinical areas or back office where direct patient care takes place.
2. Administrative areas or front office where business and other nonclinical functions take place.

reception
The area where patients enter the office, inform the staff of their presence by "signing in," receive a greeting, and await to be seen.

Reception is an administrative area and is sometimes referred to as the front desk. The word *reception* literally means the place or event where one is greeted. In the medical office, **reception** is the area where the patient enters the practice, informs the staff of his or her presence by "signing in," receives a greeting, and waits to be seen. Avoid using the term *waiting room* since waiting is only one function and the term does not have a positive association. The practice manager is usually responsible for the design of the office. Awareness of the aspects that affect the design is valuable knowledge for the administrative medical assistant. The primary consideration in the design is the type of practice. The furnishings, colors, and patient flow patterns of a pediatric office would not be the same as an internal medicine office.

Size and Schedule

After identifying the type of practice, size is the next factor. Knowledge of the number of practitioners and the number of patients anticipated daily is important. Knowing when they plan to utilize the space is equally important. For example, a surgeon may have office hours on Mondays, Wednesdays, and Fridays and perform surgeries on Tuesdays and Thursdays. Alternatively, the surgeon may perform surgeries in the morning and see patients in the afternoon. His or her partner may do surgeries on the opposite days and times. This allows better utilization of space and relative ease in planning for the reception size. Other offices may have staggered hours where one physician will see patients between 7:00 A.M. and 3:00 P.M., and another physician in the practice will see patients from 11:00 A.M. to 7:00 P.M. This is challenging since more space is needed during the four overlap hours than the remainder of the day. Dealing with overlapping office hours and other time and space issues are often part of the administrative medical assistant's role.

Utilization of Space

Utilization of space differs by type of practice. For example, an orthopedic office or geriatric office where a significant number of patients will need room for wheelchairs and walkers requires more open space for mobility and devices than does a cardiologist's office. Often the assumption is that pediatric offices need a

smaller reception area since the patients are smaller. This is an incorrect assumption for a few reasons. First, a caregiver always accompanies the pediatric patient. Second, children require play space. Third, pediatric offices normally have separate "well child" and "sick child" areas in an attempt to avoid cross-contamination from sick to well patients.

Overcrowding in a reception area is undesirable for patient comfort and for the potential of disease transmission, which is discussed in Chapter 9, Asepsis for Administrative Areas. The reception area, which allows the patient to sit, is usually separated from the functional areas of the practice by a high counter and a sliding window. These areas should be HIPAA-compliant so the patient at the counter cannot overhear staff talking to or about other patients and cannot view an opened computer screen.

figure 8–1

Reception areas often reflect popular decorator colors.

Color

Color plays a significant role in the medical environment. Studies demonstrate that the use of color affects the moods of people. For example:

- Red increases heart rate and blood pressure.
- Blue causes the body to produce calming chemicals.
- Green is easy on the eyes and relaxing.
- Light browns are warm and inviting.
- Black and dark browns are associated with power and depression.
- White is related to cleanliness and purity.

Traditionally, the pediatric office incorporates primary colors. However, the use of red should be limited. Obstetric offices are often decorated in pastels; geriatric offices often use soft colors in beige tones. Other offices tend to use popular decorator color palettes such as earth tones and gemstones (Figure 8–1). Colors may also reflect the cultural preferences of the dominant patient population. Consider the effect of color when choosing scrubs or other attire.

Furnishings

Chairs should be comfortable but have a straight back to allow the patient to get up easily, especially in obstetric, geriatric, and orthopedic offices. Many attractive stain-resistant cloth fabrics are available for medical use. All furnishings should be dust-free and clutter-free. The following are additional considerations that the administrative medical assistant may have an influence in selecting:

- Artificial plants and floral arrangements are preferred due to allergies, poisons, and the potential for microbes associated with living plants; plants should be kept dust-free.
- Lighting should be adequate for reading and completing forms and provide a pleasant atmosphere; softer lights are preferred in geriatric offices since glare is a problem for this age group. Pediatric offices tend to have brighter lighting.
- Aquariums are popular and soothing but require upkeep; some offices have virtual aquariums.
- Music, the same as color, should not increase the heart rate or blood pressure; the recommendation for all practices is soft music.
- Refreshment centers (coffee, tea) are not wise for pediatric practices due to the danger of hot water, or for practices where many patients are fasting in preparation for procedures.

figure 8-2

Wall racks conserve space but are not always convenient for the patient.

- Toys and toy pieces should be easily and frequently disinfected and larger than would fit into a small child's mouth. Balls or other throwing toys are dangerous in the medical environment.

Educational/Entertainment Materials

Educational and entertainment materials appropriate to the type of practice are more likely to be read by patients if the materials are placed on tables close to the seating. While wall and countertop racks are appropriate and conserve space, keep some materials on tables for easier access by the elderly and disabled (Figure 8-2). Magazines, newspapers, and other reading material may also be present. The publications should be relatively current and reflect the interests and languages of the populations served. Materials should be neatly arranged, tasteful, and not torn or dirty. Avoid tabloids. Some large-print editions should be available for elderly and other sight-impaired patients.

Service Animals

A service animal may accompany patients with special needs (Figure 8-3). The dog is the most common service animal, but cats, monkeys, and even miniature ponies are in use. Service animals wear a special vest that identifies them and they should have a certification. These are not pets and they should not be distracted while "on duty." Service animals are well-behaved and calm unless their charge appears to be threatened.

CHECKPOINT
LO 8.1

The medical office where you work is redecorating. The practice manager asks for your suggestions. Provide your input on the reception area for the following practice types.

- Family practice.
- Obstetrics and gynecology.
- Gerontology.
- Ophthalmology.
- Pediatrics.

Americans with Disabilities Act (ADA)
Passed in 1990, this federal act is sometimes referred to as the civil rights act for the disabled since it forbids discrimination based on physical or mental handicaps.

figure 8-3

Service animals are not pets and should not be disturbed while "on duty."

LO 8.2 Americans with Disabilities Act

Passed in 1990, the **Americans with Disabilities Act (ADA)** is sometimes referred to as the civil rights act for the disabled since it forbids discrimination based on physical or mental handicaps. The intent is to provide equal access and reasonable accommodation in employment, facilities, sports, education, and more. The two sections involving medical practices are employment, discussed in Chapter 22, Practice Management, and facilities. The following are required and reasonable facility accommodations:

- Handicapped parking (Figure 8-4).
- Wheelchair ramps.
- Wheelchair accessible doors, halls, and bathrooms.
- Handrails in halls and bathrooms.
- Handicapped bathrooms including toilets, sinks, and room for a wheelchair to turn.
- Braille elevator floor indicators.
- Large-print patient forms.
- Devices to communicate with the hearing impaired as discussed in Chapter 11, Telecommunications in the Health-Care Setting.

LO 8.3 Staff Reception Functions

The person who works in the reception area, sometimes called the *front desk,* is the **receptionist.** The main function of the receptionist is to greet people, register them, direct them, and answer the phone as addressed in Chapter 11, Telecommunications in the Health-Care Setting. These tasks and other tasks that follow require organization and communication. Just as the space and furnishings of the office create an environment, the receptionist with his or her attitude and communication skills also creates an environment. This staff member, who is frequently an administrative medical assistant, should immediately acknowledge and greet the arriving patient with a smile and pleasant voice. If the receptionist is on the phone, looking up at the patient with a smile and head nod is appropriate. A gesture to indicate where to register helps expedite the process and makes the patient feel that the staff is attentive.

receptionist
The employee who greets people, checks them in, directs them, and answers the phone.

Patient Registration and HIPAA

Patient registration is often referred to as patient check-in or **sign-in.** The reason is that the patient is required to write his or her name, or sign in, upon arrival to notify staff that they are there. Two commonly used forms of check-in or sign-in are used: the paper version and the digital or electronic version. Both may include the time of arrival, time of appointment, and the name of the practitioner. Under HIPAA, this information is considered private and confidential. Maintaining this confidentiality is the role of the receptionist. With the paper version, to ensure privacy, you should:

sign-in
The process in which an arriving patient lists his or her name and other information on a form in the registration area; also refers to the registration area.

- Cross out the name with a heavy black marker.
- Cover the name with a special opaque tape.
- Provide individual sign-in sheets on a pad or other method.

With the electronic version, you should:

- Provide a digital pad (similar to electronic debit or charge).
- Use the computer in the reception area for patients to input information.

Once the patient has signed in, the receptionist will provide him or her with appropriate forms. Returning patients may receive a copy of their information to update. Some offices will interview the patient, line by line, and input directly into the system. This method is usually more time-consuming than having the patient provide hard copy and then inputting directly from the form. New patients receive a complete packet that includes:

- Demographic/insurance coverage form.
- Authorizations for release of information to insurance carriers, assignment of benefits, and financial responsibility.

figure 8–4

Providing handicapped parking is a requirement of the Americans with Disabilities Act.

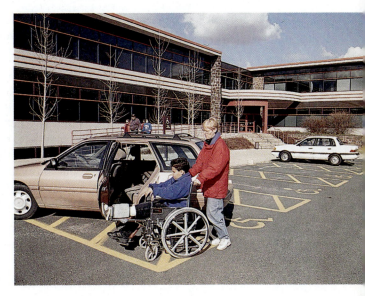

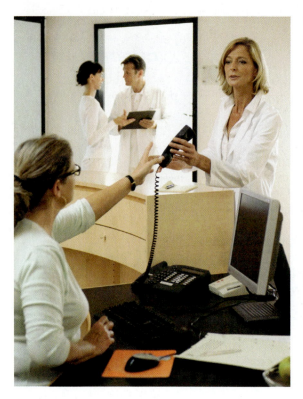

figure 8–5

Good communication between the reception area and the clinical area increases efficiency.

copayment
A set amount of money determined by the patient's insurance company, which must be paid by the patient at every visit.

- Notice of privacy practices.
- Health history.
- Information regarding the payment and other policies of the practice.

The forms must be completed and signed. The patient's or insured party's insurance card and a picture identifier such as a driver's license are copied or scanned. From this information, the medical assistant initiates a medical record or health record. The record may be a total electronic health record or a combination of electronic business information and a hard copy health or medical record. The components of the medical record are covered in Chapter 15, The Health Record. When the material is complete, the appropriate clinical staff member is notified that the patient is ready Figure 8–5).

Payments

Another reception responsibility is collecting the patient's **copayment,** which is done prior to the visit. The patient's insurance card usually gives the amount. The medical assistant provides a receipt. Usual payment methods are cash, check, debit, and charge card. Third-party checks are never accepted and the check should be written for the exact amount. Cash and checks are kept in a cash drawer that is locked when the reception desk is unmanned. In smaller offices, the patient will return to the reception area after the visit and may make a payment, which is discussed in depth in Chapter 21, Financial Practices. In smaller offices, follow-up appointments are also scheduled here. The receptionist should extend a pleasant farewell to all exiting patients.

Observation and Updates

Another function of the receptionist is to be observant. Some patients should not sit in the main reception area. These include patients who are

- Having chest pain (adults).
- Experiencing shortness of breath.
- Bleeding.
- Feeling faint (syncope), dizzy, light-headed.
- Vomiting.
- Experiencing an undiagnosed or contagious rash.

Immediately notify a member of the clinical staff who will determine where to place the patient. If concerned about the condition of any patient who appears to be seriously ill, do not hesitate to ask the advice of the clinical staff.

The administrative medical assistant should address spills, trash, and any potential hazards such as frayed cords, broken furniture, or tears in rugs as quickly as possible. If the reception area becomes overcrowded, "traffic control" is required. Ensure chairs are not occupied with personal items and determine if there is room in treatment areas. Keeping patients updated if appointments are running late is another function. If the wait time is significant, give the patient the option of rescheduling. Have respect for the patient's time.

CHECKPOINT
LO 8.3

List potential violations of HIPAA that could occur in the reception area.

LO 8.4 The Red Flags Rule

Identity theft is an increasing problem. **Medical identity theft** is using another person's name or insurance to seek health care. This form of identity theft results in millions of dollars in uncompensated care. It also creates the potential risk of a person receiving incorrect treatment if treatment is based on another person's medical record. On August 1, 2009, the Federal Trade Commission enacted the **Red Flags Rule.** This law requires certain businesses, including most medical offices and other health-care facilities, to develop written programs to detect the warning signs, or red flags, of identity theft. The law applies to and defines two categories that determine if a business must comply. Both pertain to the majority of medical practices:

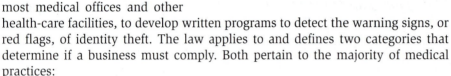

1. Creditors—entities that regularly defer payment for goods or services or arrange the extension of credit. An example of extending credit is billing patients after the service is rendered, including fees that are billed after insurance payments are received.

2. Covered account—a consumer (patient) account that allows multiple payments or transactions. Most patient records fall in this category.

Not adhering to the law may result in financial penalties. The more important issue is protection of the patients and the practice from the consequences of identity theft.

Red Flags

The red flags include

- Suspicious documents.
  - Altered or forged appearance.
  - Photo or description inconsistent with the patient's appearance.
  - Inconsistent information provided such as date of birth, chronic medical condition.
- Suspicious personal identifying information from other sources such as a Social Security number different from what you have on file.
- Suspicious activities such as mail being returned repeatedly but patient continuing to keep appointments and maintain that address on file (this emphasizes the importance of verifying patient information at every visit); inconsistency with physical exam and past medical treatment.
- Notifications of identity theft from patients or staff.

The Identity Theft Prevention Program

In many instances, HIPAA and medical identity theft go hand in hand. The person in the practice with the dual responsibility is generally the privacy or

medical identity theft
A person seeks health-care using another person's name or insurance.

Red Flags Rule
August 1, 2009, law requiring certain businesses, including most medical offices and other health-care facilities, to develop written programs to detect the warning signs, or red flags, of identity theft.

compliance officer. A three-pronged approach for the medical office's prevention program is recommended:

1. Prevention—implementing sound electronic and other security systems and HIPAA compliance
2. Detection—training of staff and electronic "red flagging" such as automatically identifying on the screen a difference in date of birth
3. Mitigation—ensuring medical records of the perpetrator and the authentic patient are not commingled; knowing reporting mechanisms

CHECKPOINT
LO 8.4

Give examples of five red flags that might alert you to medical identity theft.

LO 8.5 Supplies and the Inventory Process

Having the proper supplies to function is part of creating an efficient office environment. Think of your own home when you run out of groceries, cleaning supplies, paper for your copier, shampoo, and other hygiene items. Would you describe it as frustration, irritation, chaos, disorganization, annoyance, helplessness, paralysis? None of these feelings and conditions creates a positive environment; rather, they hinder performance. In the medical practice, it could also endanger patients. Precise processes ensure the correct supplies in the correct amounts at the correct times are available. The word *supply* refers to an **expendable item,** which is an item that is used then replaced, such as prescription pads. **Durable items** refer to pieces of equipment that are used indefinitely such as computers. Table 8–1, Typical Supplies in a Medical Office, contains a list of expendable items.

Supply Categories and Responsibility

Supplies fall into three broad categories:

1. Administrative—for business office use such as stationery, forms, copy paper, toner, and paperclips.
2. Clinical—for direct patient care such as syringes, alcohol swabs, and tongue depressors.
3. General—for staff and patient use such as soap, paper towels, and facial and toilet tissue.

The responsibility for managing supplies is dependent on the size of the practice. Generally, one medical assistant is responsible for the administrative and general supplies and another medical assistant for the clinical supplies.

Inventory and Storage

Ordering too much of an item results in the practice expending more money than necessary and risks supplies becoming outdated before use. Overordering is only prudent when the office receives significant discounts for large quantities. Under ordering risks staff not having the supplies they need to perform at a quality level. Office staff use two mechanisms to ensure optimum amounts of supplies.

The first method is establishing a supply list and optimal levels. Determine each item needed and the amount of that item used over an established period of time such as a month. **Inventory** is the list of the items on hand and is usually a computerized form with a line for each item that contains the following:

- Name of the item.
- Recommended supply level.

expendable item
An object that is used and then must be replaced.

durable item
A piece of equipment that is used indefinitely.

inventory
A list of supplies currently on hand.

ADMINISTRATIVE SUPPLIES	CLINICAL SUPPLIES	GENERAL SUPPLIES
Appointment books, daybooks (still used in noncomputerized offices) Back-to-school/back-to-work slips Clipboards Computer supplies Copy and facsimile (fax) machine paper File folders, coding tabs HIPAA forms (Notice of Privacy Practices, authorization forms, disclosure logs, request to inspect and copy medical record forms, request for amendment forms, acknowledgment of request for amendment forms) History and physical examination sheet cards Insurance forms: disability, HMO and other third-party payers, life insurance examinations, Veterans Administration, workers' compensation Insurance manuals Local welfare department forms Patient education materials Pens, pencils, erasers Prescription pads Rubber bands, paper clips Registration forms Social Security forms Stamps Stationery: appointment cards, bookkeeping supplies (ledgers, statement, billing forms), letterhead, second sheets, envelopes, business cards, prescription pads, notebooks, notepads, telephone memo pads	Alcohol swabs Applicators Bandaging materials: adhesive tape, gauze pads, gauze sponges, elastic bandages, adhesive bandages, roller bandages (gauze and elastic) Cloth or paper gowns and drapes Cotton, cotton swabs Culture tubes 50% dextrose solution Disposable sheaths for thermometers Disposable tips for otoscopes Gloves: sterile, examination Hemoccult test kits Iodine or Betadine pads Lancets Lubricating jelly Microscopic slides and Fixative Needles, syringes Nitroglycerin tablets Safety pins Silver nitrate sticks Sutures removal kits Sutures Table covers (examination) Tongue depressors Topical skin freeze Urinalysis test sticks Urine containers Injectable medications as appropriate to the type of practice Other medicines, chemicals, solutions, ointments, lotions, and disinfectants, as needed	Liquid hypoallergenic soap Paper cups Paper towels Tampons and sanitary pads Tissues: facial, toilet

table 8–1

Typical Supplies in a Medical Office

- Current supply level.
- Ordering unit, for example a box.
- Cost per unit.
- Quantity of units last ordered.
- Date items last received.
- Vendor.
- Date of inventory.
- Name or initials of the person conducting the inventory.

Using the form, the responsible person counts the number of each item in all the office areas where it is stored and places the total number on the correct line. An organized supply storage system facilitates a correct inventory. Supplies are usually kept in cabinets and drawers in the areas where they are used and the excess maintained in a general storage area. Lists of the items may be on the inside of the storage cabinet doors and the item names adhered to shelves or divided containers. Some facilities place a card in the supply containers to indicate the level is low and it is time to reorder. The most current items are stored in the back of the shelf or container and the oldest items stored in the front to ensure they do not outdate prior to use (Figure 8–6). Select items have an

figure 8–6

Ensuring items are stored in the proper place increases efficiency and prevents overordering.

Working with the Health-Care Team

OCCUPATIONAL SAFETY AND HEALTH ADMINISTRATION (OSHA) SAFETY OFFICER

Duties and Skills

As you progress through your educational journey, you will continue to learn about OSHA guidelines and the impact on the medical office. Each medical practice has a person designated as the OSHA safety officer. The practice may designate an employee such as the practice manager or laboratory supervisor as the safety officer, employ a person dedicated to this position, or contract with an individual or organization to carry out the duties. The position oversees the occupational health and safety applications of the medical office. It incorporates development and ongoing implementation and evaluation of policies and procedures that maintain OSHA compliance. These include

- Assessing safety practices with analysis of potential hazards and periodic inspections.
- Training staff.
- Ensuring access to proper equipment and materials such as personal protective equipment and MSDS.
- Responding to events that jeopardize safety.
- Facilitating corrective action.
- Recordkeeping of the program, data, and incidents.
- Reporting required information such as incidents and follow up reports.

Educational Requirements

To become a professional OSHA safety officer usually requires a bachelor's degree in safety management or a related field. Other qualifications may include obtaining

certification as an Associate Safety Professional (ASP) or Certified Safety Specialist (CSP).

Workplace Settings

The OSHA safety officer may work in any health-care or business setting that involves compliance with the **Occupational Safety and Health Administration (OSHA)**. The person may also work for a firm that provides safety consulting for medical offices or liaison functions between OSHA and the facility.

The OSHA Safety Officer as a Team Member

Each new employee receives training that involves safety and health precautions and the availability of specific immunizations. The expectation of the administrative medical assistant is to comply with the policies and procedures intended to protect him or her and other staff members and patients. To report violations immediately to the OSHA safety officer is another expectation and responsibility of all staff. If an OSHA auditor appears in the reception area, the administrative medical assistant asks for identification and immediately notifies the safety officer. Should this occur, stay calm and demonstrate professional behaviors. The safety officer facilitates the audit or investigation.

For more information, visit the Web site of the following organization, which is available on the Online Learning Center at www.mhhe.com/houseradminmedassist

Occupational Safety and Health Administration (OSHA)

Occupational Safety and Health Administration (OSHA)
The agency of the federal government responsible for safety in the workplace.

requisition
Order form.

packing slip
List of items and quantity of each shipped.

invoice
Bill for supplies or services.

expiration date. Remove these items from all areas prior to or at that date. Some vendors will issue credit for expired items. Refer to Procedure 8–1, Establishing and Conducting a Supply Inventory, located at the end of the chapter.

Ordering and Receiving

The inventory indicates which supplies require reordering. Complete a **requisition** (Figure 8–7) or order form for the vendor from whom the supplies are purchased. Dependent on the vendor and the office policy, this process may be done online, through the mail, or via fax or phone. A record of what was ordered is maintained electronically or on hard copy. When the items arrive, a **packing slip** (Figure 8–8) is contained in the order. Compare the packing slip with the materials received and the requisition to ensure accuracy. An **invoice** (Figure 8–9), which is the bill, will be included with the shipped items or sent separately. Check the requisition, packing slip, and invoice against the supplies ordered and the supplies received (Figure 8–10). Provide the invoice to the

REQUISITION

Funton Business Supplies
1021 North 1st Street
Funton, XY 12345-6789
Tel: 521-454-5211
Fax: 521-4544-5212

SHIP TO: Total Care Clinic, PC
342 E. Park Blvd
Funton, XY 12345-6789
Accountant #: 0060812 MD
Date ordered: 08/05/XX

Item #	Description	Unit Quantity	Price per unit	Total
65245	Toner	2	$65.00	$130.00
78769	Paper	3 boxes	$36.00	$108.00
Subtotal				$238.00
Tax				$10.10
Shipping				waived
Total				$248.10

appropriate department or person for payment. Refer to Procedure 8–2, Receiving Supplies.

Petty Cash

In some instances, it may become necessary to purchase a small amount of an item such as copy paper until the ordered supplies arrive. In other instances, something may arrive with postage due. The office maintains a set amount of cash in a drawer or container separate from the cash drawer for incidental expenses. This is called **petty cash.** One person is usually responsible for overseeing this fund.

The following are guidelines for managing the petty cash:

- Use petty cash only for unplanned or incidental items, usually under $50.
- Maintain a designated amount (usually $50 to $100) in the drawer.

figure 8–7

Example of a requisition to order supplies.

petty cash
A set amount of cash kept for incidental office expenses.

figure 8–8

Example of a packing slip.

PACKING SLIP

Funton Business Supplies
1021 North 1st Street
Funton, XY 12345-6789
Tel: 521-454-5211
Fax: 521-4544-5212

Date ordered: 08/05/XX
Date shipped: 08/06/XX
Order #: 0056211

SHIP TO: Total Care Clinic, PC
342 E. Park Blvd
Funton, XY 12345-6789
Accountant #: 0060812 MD

Item #	Description	Unit Quantity	Price per unit	Total
65245	Toner	2	$65.00	Backorder to ship 08/15/XX
78769	Paper	3 boxes	$36.00	$108.00
Subtotal				$108.00
Tax				$3.60
Shipping				waived
Total				$111.60

INVOICE

Funton Business Supplies	Date ordered: 08/05/XX	SHIP TO: Total Care Clinic, PC
1021 North 1st Street	Date shipped: 08/06/XX	342 E. Park Blvd
Funton, XY 12345-6789	Order #: 0056211	Funton, XY 12345-6789
Tel: 521-454-5211	Remit in full within 30 days	Accountant #: 0060812 MD
Fax: 521-454-5212	to avoid late charge	

Item #	Description	Unit Quantity	Price per unit	Total
78769	Paper	3 boxes	$36.00	$108.00
Subtotal				$108.00
Tax				$3.60
Shipping				waived
Total				$111.60

figure 8–9

Example of an invoice.

figure 8–10

When supplies are received, they should be checked for accuracy using the packing slip and requisition.

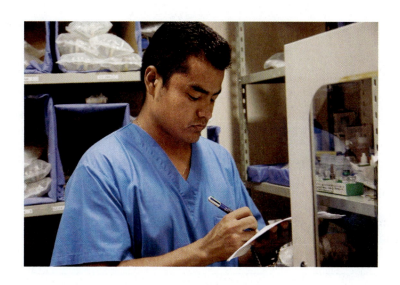

- Avoid using petty cash to "make change" for patients.
- Adhere to established policies assuring accurate daily accounting. Refer to Procedure 8–3, Managing the Petty Cash Fund.
- Lock the drawer when authorized staff is not in the area.

CHECKPOINT
LO 8.5

Explain the importance of establishing an accurate supply list and inventory process.

LO 8.6 Opening and Closing the Office

You are learning that efficiency in the medical office is a result of good organization and adhering to practices. It includes establishing set procedures for opening and closing the facility. This is generally the responsibility of the staff member in the reception area. Following a set routine and using specially designed check sheets ensures no process is overlooked. Some offices perform specific tasks when opening the office, such as restocking supplies, and other offices perform

these tasks at closing. Table 8–2, Daily Checklist for Opening the Office, and Table 8–3, Daily Checklist for Closing the Office, include typical duties.

Beginning the Day

The person opening the office arrives approximately 30 minutes prior to the scheduled time for office operations to begin. Safety is a consideration. Be aware of the activity outside the office door such as persons in the parking area, elevators, or hallways. If you feel uncomfortable, notify the facility's security or await the arrival of another staff member. Laboratory specimens, such as blood, obtained by staff for delivery to reference laboratories are often placed in a special container on the

table 8–2

Daily Checklist for Opening the Office

DAILY CHECKLIST: OPENING FACILITY (INITIAL WHEN COMPLETED) DATE: FROM _____ TO _____	M	T	W	TH	F	M	T	W	TH	F
1. Security system disarmed										
2. Messages/answering services retrieved										
3. Messages routed and ready for callback										
4. Fax machine checked										
5. Appointment book and insurance rosters checked										
6. Charts pulled and paperwork attached										
7. Equipment working properly										
8. Rooms supplied and ready										
9. Refrigerator temperature checked										
10. Emergency supplies including O2 checked										
11. Reception area in order and patient education material available										
12. Lab specimens from day before were picked up										

DAILY CHECKLIST: CLOSING FACILITY (INITIAL WHEN COMPLETED) DATE: FROM _____ TO _____											
	M	T	W	TH	F	M	T	W	TH	F	F
1. Computers are logged out and off											
2. Contaminated supplies/equipment are properly disposed											
3. Areas are restocked											
4. Patient's charts are pulled or reviewed for next day and any test results, etc., are available											
5. Laboratory specimens are in pick-up receptacle											
6. All equipment (i.e., coffee pot, EKG machine) is turned off											
7. Reception area is organized											
8. Calls are forwarded to voicemail/answering machine											
9. Medical records are secured											
10. All doors and windows are locked											
11. Security system is armed											

table 8–3

Daily Checklist for Closing the Office

figure 8–11

Arming the security system is usually the final task when closing the office.

office door or in the vicinity. Upon arrival in the morning, ensure the specimens were picked up from the previous day. Do not completely turn your back while unlocking the door. Once inside, deactivate the security system.

The first priority is accessing the answering service or answering machine to determine if any staff member may have called in with an emergency; patients have canceled appointments; patients need a same-day appointment; or hospitals reported patients seen during the night. Convey this vital information to the correct staff member as soon as possible. The fax machine is usually the next priority; turning it on if it is not kept on at night; reviewing newly arrived faxes; distributing them to the appropriate personnel; and ensuring the paper trays are full. Another task may be to turn on coffee makers for staff and patients. Some offices divide the responsibility for the administrative areas and the clinical areas (review Table 8–2).

Ending the Day

Ending the day efficiently is as important as beginning the day efficiently. It completes the day's responsibilities and sets the stage for the next day. The person closing the office that has extended or split hours may not be the same person who opened the office. Cooperation and good communication are essential between both staff members. Turn off equipment, such as the coffeemaker and the fax machine, if that is the office policy. This ensures that confidential information is not in view. Notify the answering service that the office is closing or turn on the answering machine. Ensure laboratory specimens are placed in the proper container for delivery. Activate the security system (Figure 8–11). Be alert when exiting the building (review Table 8–3). Refer to Procedure 8–4, Opening and Closing the Office.

CHECKPOINT
LO 8.6

Discuss safety considerations when opening and closing the medical office.

LO 8.7 Ergonomics and Body Mechanics

The many work functions of the medical office environment require many physical functions. Examples are using the computer; carrying and unpacking boxes; filling copy machine trays; and helping patients with impairments. The associated movements are performing repetitive motion, lifting, bending, stooping, and sitting. To prevent injury or an unwanted condition, the administrative medical assistant should become familiar with ergonomics and body mechanics.

Ergonomics is the science of adjusting the work environment to the human body. Simply stated it means making furniture and equipment in the work area comfortable and efficient—especially for your posture. The number one area is the computer station. Common injuries or conditions involve the forearm, wrist, hand, and back. Table 8–4 contains ergonomic excerpts from an OSHA computer station checklist to use in prevention.

While ergonomics involves design and fit of furniture for function, **body mechanics** is proper body movement to prevent injury and enhance physical

ergonomics
The science of adjusting the work environment to the human body.

body mechanics
Proper body movement to prevent injury and enhance physical capabilities.

table 8–4

OSHA Computer Station Tips

1. **Head** and **neck** to be upright, or in-line with the torso (not bent down/back).

2. **Head, neck,** and **trunk to** face forward (not twisted).

3. **Trunk** to be perpendicular to floor (may lean back into backrest but not forward).

4. **Shoulders** and **upper arms** to be in-line with the torso, generally about perpendicular to the floor and relaxed (not elevated or stretched forward).

5. **Upper arms** and **elbows** to be close to the body (not extended outward)

6. **Forearms, wrists,** and **hands** to be straight and in-line (forearm at about 90 degrees to the upper arm).

7. **Wrists** and **hands** to be straight (not bent up/down or sideways toward the little finger).

8. **Thighs** to be parallel to the floor and the **lower legs** to be perpendicular to floor (thighs may be slightly elevated above knees).

9. **Feet** rest flat on the floor or are supported by a stable footrest.

10. **Backrest** provides support for your lower back (lumbar area).

11. **Seat width** and **depth** accommodate the specific user (seat pan not too big/small).

12. **Seat front** does not press against the back of your knees and lower legs (seat pan not too long).

13. **Seat** has cushioning and is rounded with a "waterfall" front (no sharp edge).

14. **Armrests,** if used, support both forearms while you perform computer tasks and they do not interfere with movement.

15. **Keyboard/input device platform(s)** is stable and large enough to hold a keyboard and an input device.

16. **Input device** (mouse or trackball) is located right next to your keyboard so it can be operated without reaching.

17. **Input device** is easy to activate and the shape/size fits your hand (not too big/small).

18. **Wrists** and **hands** do not rest on sharp or hard edges.

19. **Top** of the screen is at or below eye level so you can read it without bending your head or neck down/back.

20. **User with bifocals/trifocals** can read the screen without bending the head or neck backward.

21. **Monitor distance** allows you to read the screen without leaning your head, neck or trunk forward/backward.

22. **Monitor position** is directly in front of you so you don't have to twist your head or neck.

(Continued)

table 8–4 (Concluded)

23.	**Glare** (for example, from windows, lights) is not reflected on your screen which can cause you to assume an awkward posture to clearly see information on your screen.
24.	**Thighs** have sufficient clearance space between the top of the thighs and your computer table/keyboard platform (thighs are not trapped).
25.	**Legs** and **feet** have sufficient clearance space under the work surface so you are able to get close enough to the keyboard/input device.
26.	**Telephone** can be used with your head upright (not bent) and your shoulders relaxed (not elevated) if you do computer tasks at the same time.
27.	Workstation and equipment have sufficient adjustability so you are in a safe working posture and can make occasional changes in posture while performing computer tasks.

Source: www.osha.gov/SLT/etools/computerworkstations/checklist.html.

capabilities. Lifting while using improper body mechanics is a major cause of back injuries. Some tips for proper lifting include:

- Avoid lifting anything more than half your weight
- Bend your knees not your waist and keep your back straight
- Avoid twisting your back; pivot your feet
- Keep object close to your body
- Tighten your stomach muscles

The ideal medical office environment is an efficient, safe, and caring place for patients, visitors, and staff.

CHECKPOINT
LO 8.7

Explain the difference between ergonomics and body mechanics.

Procedure 8–1 Establishing and Conducting a Supply Inventory

SUGGESTION If a simulated medical office or laboratory supplies are not available to practice performing an inventory, schools reported having fun with this procedure by placing Scrabble® tiles (or other creative items) sorted by letter in containers. Each letter represents a supply item. The letters in the actual game are not in equal amounts. This facilitates conducting the inventory.

GOAL To ensure the correct supplies are on hand and to determine which supplies require reordering

MATERIALS Vendor catalogs, pen and pencil, or computer with Internet access

METHOD 1. Create an inventory form with supply levels using Table 8–1; you may choose to create an electronic spreadsheet version or a paper version.

2. Research appropriate vendors for each item and include a vendor for each item on your inventory form (it may be the same vendor).

3. Use the vendor catalogs to determine costs and how quantities are supplied.

4. Count the number of items on hand and record on the inventory form.

5. Compare the number of each item on hand to the established supply level and determine if reorder is necessary.

Procedure 8–2 Receiving Supplies

GOAL
To follow an organized process when receiving supplies to ensure the order is complete and the charges correspond with those quoted during the requisition process

MATERIALS
Requisition or order form packing slip, invoice (you may use Figures 8–7, 8–8, and 8–9), pen, real or virtual supplies

METHOD
When the order arrives, it is generally the role of the medical assistant to verify that all the items shipped correspond with the items ordered.

1. Compare the items that arrived with the packing slip.

2. Compare the packing slip with the original requisition to ensure the proper items in the proper amounts were received.

3. Determine if an invoice was also included in the package or if the packing slip has a notation that it also functions as an invoice (bill).

4. If items are back ordered, you may be charged at this time. Make a notation on the invoice that the items were charged but not received.

5. File the invoice for payment or transport to the person responsible for payment.

6. Indicate on the inventory form the date and quantity of the items received or back ordered.

Procedure 8–3 Managing the Petty Cash Fund

GOAL
To provide the availability of petty cash for incidental expenses and a system to ensure accountability

MATERIALS
Pen, paper, receipts, money, cash box or cash drawer

METHOD
Petty cash is used for unexpected expenses (usually under $50), kept in a separate drawer or area from the cash drawer that holds patient payments. The responsibility for petty cash often belongs to the medical assistant. When a staff member requires petty cash, the following procedure ensures accountability.

1. Establish a predetermined amount to be kept in petty cash (usually $50 to $100).

2. Complete a voucher for the person requesting the cash, which includes the date, person's name, amount, and the expense, such as Band-aids. A slip of paper or pad may be used as a voucher. The person receiving the cash should sign the voucher.

3. Dispense the money and place the voucher in the petty cash container.

4. Attach the voucher to the receipt when the item is purchased. If change is returned, the amount is noted on the voucher and deducted from the initial amount dispersed.

5. Count the money in the petty cash container daily at the close of business. The remaining cash and the receipts should equal the predetermined amount. Often a log or sheet is signed or initialed to indicate the cash balanced on that day. If the amount and receipts do not correspond, this issue should be reported to the physician or practice manager.

6. Request additional cash as the remaining level decreases. The drawer should never have a higher or lower total than the sum of the cash on hand and the receipts indicating what was purchased.

7. Keep the petty cash container locked and secure.

Procedure 8–4 Opening and Closing the Office

GOAL To ensure readiness to receive and care for patients in an efficient, organized, and safe manner

MATERIALS Forms for opening and closing the office (use Tables 8–2 and 8–3), pen, telephone, pad of paper

METHOD
1. Using Table 8–2, Daily Checklist for Opening the Office, simulate the functions for opening the office.
   a. Begin with disarming the security system.
   b. Telephone the answering service, write any messages on the pad, and notify appropriate person.
   c. Conduct each task on the form and initial as you complete it.
2. Using Table 8–3, Daily Checklist for Closing the Office, simulate the functions for closing the office.
   a. Begin with logging out and turning off the computers.
   b. Use the telephone to notify the answering service that the office is closing.
   c. Conduct each task on the form and initial as you complete it.

Case Study

PROFESSIONAL READINESS

Organization
Independent tasks are planned and completed properly and orderly in a given time

Taking inventory and ordering supplies is Martha's responsibility. She must send the order by the end of the day to have the materials delivered in a timely manner. While doing this job, Martha is distracted because she is thinking about the concert at the arena that she is attending in the evening. Consequently, the inventory and order are incorrect. In addition, she forgets that the medical practice is holding an immunization event for the public next week, which will require many more syringes, gloves, vaccines, and other items. Two days later, Martha realizes her errors.

Thinking Critically

1. What are the potential problems for the medical practice resulting from Martha's lack of organization and concentration?
2. What should Martha do when she realizes what has happened?
3. What can Martha do to avoid this type of incident in the future?

practice APPLICATIONS

1. Develop a one-page questionnaire for patients to determine if the reception area meets their needs. Be sure to include questions that relate to special needs patients.

2. Your practice manager asked for your assistance in researching the Red Flags Rule to develop the required program. Go to ftc.gov/redflagsrule or other appropriate Internet sites and list the information that you think is useful for the program.

exam READINESS

There may be more than one correct answer. Circle the best answer.

1. **[LO8.3]** A potential for a HIPAA violation in the reception area is
   a. a frayed electrical cord.
   b. soiled furniture.
   c. patients' names on the sign-in sheet.
   d. an enclosed counter.
   e. requesting patients to complete forms.

2. **[LO8.1]** When designing a medical office, the first consideration should be the
   a. color.
   b. furnishings.
   c. patient education material.
   d. type of practice.
   e. music.

3. **[LO8.2]** One of the major intents of the Americans with Disabilities Act is to provide the handicapped with equal
   a. education.
   b. sports facilities.
   c. transportation.
   d. representation.
   e. access to facilities.

4. **[LO8.2]** A violation of the American with Disabilities Act might be not permitting
   a. smoking.
   b. service animals.
   c. charge cards.
   d. pharmacy refills.
   e. coffee or tea.

5. **[LO8.5]** When managing office supplies, the goal is to achieve
   a. efficiency.
   b. neatness.
   c. resourcefulness.
   d. independence.
   e. purchasing at the lowest price.

6. **[LO8.5]** Expendable items are those that are
   a. thrown away.
   b. used and restocked.
   c. used indefinitely.
   d. restored and reused.
   e. used only in clinical areas.

7. **[LO8.5]** The term *inventory* refers to
   a. ordering supplies.
   b. counting supplies.
   c. purchasing supplies.
   d. using supplies.
   e. storing supplies.

8. **[LO8.3]** When a physician is running very late, the receptionist should
   a. inform the patients they will be seen soon.
   b. offer refreshments while waiting.
   c. cancel appointments.
   d. provide patients with the option to reschedule.
   e. avoid eye contact with waiting patients.

9. **[LO8.7]** When lifting an object, bending at your knees and not at your waist is an example of proper:
   a. ergonomics.
   b. environment.
   c. body mechanics.
   d. ADA accommodations.
   e. OSHA requirements.

10. **[LO8.4]** The federal law that involves medical identity theft is
   a. Red Flags Rule.
   b. HIPAA.
   c. Rule of Nines.
   d. NEIN.
   e. ADA.

learning outcome SUMMARY

LO 8.1 The type and size of the practice as well as the space requirements of the patients are the first considerations when designing a reception area. Other factors include color, lighting, furnishings, music, and educational materials.

LO 8.2 The Americans with Disabilities Act (ADA) was passed in 1990. It is a federal act sometimes referred to as the civil rights act for the disabled since it forbids discrimination based on physical or mental handicaps.

LO 8.3 The functions of the receptionist include patient registration; copayment collection; observation for seriously ill patients; need for traffic control and potential hazards; and communication with patients regarding appointments running late.

LO 8.4 The Federal Trade Commission enacted the Red Flags Rule on August 1, 2009, requiring most medical offices to have a program to detect, prevent, and mitigate medical identity theft.

LO 8.5 Maintaining the proper amount of supplies is important for overall efficiency. This is ensured through an accurate inventory process, which requires counting all supplies on hand and ordering what is needed based on established levels and times.

LO 8.6 Maintaining a structured process for opening and closing the office ensures the necessary tasks by priority are always performed. The results are an efficient and prepared medical office.

LO 8.7 Ergonomics is the science of adjusting the work environment to the human body. Body mechanics is proper body movement to prevent injury and enhance physical capabilities.

medical assisting COMPETENCIES

CAAHEP

I. P (6) Perform patient screening using established protocols

I. P. (11) Perform quality control measures

IV. C (7) Identify resources and adaptations that are required based on individual needs, i.e., culture and environment, developmental life stage, language, and physical threats to communication

IV. P (2) Report relevant information to others succinctly and accurately

IV. P (4) Explain general office policies

V. C (11) Discuss principles using the Electronic Medical Record (EMR)

V. P (3) Organize a patient's medical record

V. P (10) Perform an office inventory

IX. C (2) Explore issue of confidentiality as it applies to the medical assistant

IX. C (3) Describe the implications of HIPAA for the medical assistant in various medical settings

IX. C (11) Identify how the Americans with Disabilities Act (ADA) applies to the medical assisting profession

IX. P (7) Document accurately in the patient record

IX. A (3) Recognize the importance of local, state, and federal legislation and regulations in the practice setting

XI. C (10) Identify principles of body mechanics and ergonomics

ABHES

1. General Orientation
   d. Have knowledge of the general responsibilities of the medical assistant

4. Medical Law and Ethics
   a. Document accurately
   f. Comply with federal, state, and local health laws and regulations

5. Psychology of Human Relations
   b. Identify and respond appropriately when working/caring for patients with special needs

8. Medical Office Business Procedures
   a. Perform basic clerical functions
   d. Apply concepts for office procedures
   l. Establish and maintain a petty cash fund
   x. Maintain medical facility

   z. Maintain inventory, equipment and supplies
   hh. Receive, organize, prioritize, and transmit information expediently
   kk. Adapt to individualized needs

9. Medical Office Clinical Procedures
   a. Obtain chief complaint, recording patient history

10. Medical Laboratory Procedures
   a. Practice quality control

11. Career Development
   b. Demonstrate professionalism by:
      (8) Being courteous and diplomatic
      (9) Conducting work within the scope of education, training, and ability

9 Asepsis for Administrative Areas

Learning Outcomes

After completing Chapter 9, you will be able to:

9.1 Identify and explain the cycle of infection.

9.2 Recognize the importance of asepsis in the medical office.

9.3 Discuss the roles of the CDC and OSHA.

9.4 Demonstrate proper hand washing.

9.5 Identify aseptic practices for administrative areas.

9.6 Describe opportunities and materials for patient education related to asepsis.

Key Terms

alcohol hand disinfectant (AHD)
asepsis
carrier
cycle of infection
epidemiology
fomite
health-care acquired infections (HAI)
immunocompromised
infection control
microbe
pandemic
pathogen
personal protective equipment (PPE)
reservoir host
standard precautions
subclinical case
susceptible host

Preparation for Certification

RMA (AMT) Exam
- Asepsis
- Medical terminology
- Patient education

CMAS (AMT) Exam
- Medical terminology
- Basic clinical medical office assisting
- Asepsis in the medical office
- Patient information and community resources

CMA (AAMA) Exam
- Principles of infection control
- Principles of asepsis
- Standard precautions
- Educate the patient in disease prevention
- Identify community resources for disease prevention

Introduction ● ● ●

Patients present to medical offices for many reasons. Some are for infectious illnesses such as tuberculosis. These diseases may be transmitted to other patients, visitors, and staff members. Staff members then become at risk for taking home pathogens to their families. The 2009 H1N1 influenza **pandemic** brought heightened awareness to the importance of the first point of contact in the medical office—the reception area. Knowledge of asepsis and appropriate application in this location has the potential for stopping or spreading infectious diseases to all persons within the facility.

This chapter addresses general aseptic techniques and infection control with an emphasis on the administrative areas. It describes causes and transmission of infectious diseases and how to prevent their spread. The roles of the Centers for Disease Control and Prevention (CDC) and the Occupational Safety and Health Administration (OSHA) are also discussed. In addition, the chapter provides tips for educating patients and family members on how to protect themselves from transmission of infectious diseases.

LO 9.1 The Cycle of Infection

Pathogens are disease-causing organisms that come in many sizes. Most are too small to see with the naked eye such as viruses and bacteria. These are called pathogenic **microbes.** The nonmedical person refers to them as germs. Some pathogens are clearly seen by the naked eye such as helminths, which are wormlike animals. These are not common in this country; examples are tapeworms and roundworms. The manner in which pathogens spread is called the **cycle of infection** which is sometimes referred to as the chain of infection. There are five steps in the cycle of infection (Figure 9–1).

Reservoir Host

The infection cycle begins when the pathogen finds a place to live and multiply. This "home" is called the **reservoir host** and may be an insect, animal, or human whose body is capable of sustaining the growth of the organism. Generally, the host exhibits symptoms of the infection or the disease caused by the pathogen but this does not always occur. Sometimes a human host may have a **subclinical case** of an infection which means that the symptoms are so slight that they may go unnoticed. A human **carrier** is a person who is a reservoir host and does not exhibit any symptoms yet unknowingly or knowingly spreads the disease to others. Perhaps the most infamous carrier was "Typhoid Mary," who appeared to be a healthy young woman but spread typhoid fever in the early 1900s through her employment as a cook. Mary carried the pathogen, although she was not ill. Typhoid is an infectious disease spread through water and food. As you follow the four remaining steps of the cycle of infection you will understand how this happened.

Means of Exit

The next step in the cycle is the means of exit, which is the route the pathogen takes to leave the reservoir host. Common exits are

pandemic
Widespread disease or outbreak that affects populations throughout the world.

pathogen
A disease-causing organism.

microbes
Living organisms too small to see with the naked eye.

cycle of infection
Also known as the chain of infection, the manner in which pathogens are spread.

reservoir host
An insect, animal, or human which has been invaded by a pathogen and is capable of sustaining its growth.

subclinical case
The symptoms of a disease that are so slight that they may go unnoticed.

carrier
A person who is a reservoir host and does not exhibit symptoms, yet spreads the disease to others.

figure 9–1
Cycle of infection.

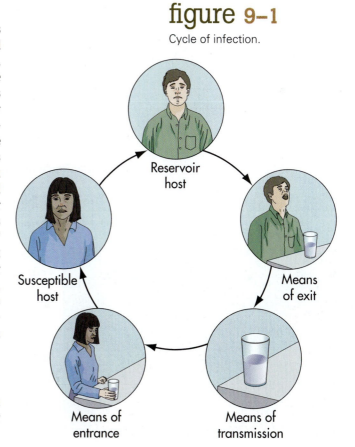

Reservoir host

Means of exit

Means of transmission

Means of entrance

Susceptible host

MEANS OF TRANSMISSION	EXAMPLES	COMMON DISEASES
Airborne	Dust and soil particles Droplets—sneezing, coughing, respirations	Influenza, varicella (chickenpox), measles, tuberculosis, RSV
Bloodborne: Direct or Indirect Blood	Blood transfusions, puncture wounds, broken skin or mucous membranes	Hepatitis B, Hepatitis C, HIV/AIDS,
Pregnancy and Childbirth	Placenta	Rubella (German measles), HIV, Hepatitis B
	Birth canal	Syphilis, gonorrhea, Chlamydia *pneumoniae*
Foodborne	Contaminated foods and liquids and fomites such as soda cans	*Escherichia coli* and *Salmonella* food poisoning, typhoid
Vectorborne (vector is a living organism that carries disease from one infected organism to another)	Fleas, flies, mosquitoes, ticks (Figure 9-2)	Plague, West Nile virus, malaria, Rocky Mountain spotted fever
Touch: Direct or Indirect	Hands, mouth, eyes, sexual organs	Conjunctivitis, herpes, Methicillin-resistant staphylococcus aureus (MRSA)

table 9–1

Transmission of Pathogens

- Through the nose, mouth, eyes, ears, rectum, vagina, penis, and urethra.
- In feces, urine, or vomit.
- In semen, vaginal fluid, or other reproductive tract discharges.
- In blood or drainage from open wounds.

Means of Transmission

After the pathogen exits the body of the reservoir host, it must find another host through transmission or travel (Table 9–1). Two general means of transmission are direct and indirect.

1. Direct transmission: The pathogen is transferred through contact with the infected person or the infected discharge of that person.
2. Indirect transmission: The pathogen exists outside the reservoir host and is capable of survival until it has an opportunity to take up residence in a new host; examples are drinking glasses, doorknobs, and shopping carts. These inanimate objects that transmit diseases are called **fomites.**

fomites
Inanimate objects that transmit diseases.

figure 9–2

Malaria-carrying mosquito.

Means of Entrance

After the pathogen exits the reservoir host and travels to a new host, it must find a means of entrance. The means of entrance are similar to the means of exit, such as the nose, mouth, eyes, ears, rectum, vagina, penis, urethra, and broken skin. For example, when a child with *haemophilus influenza* type b (Hib) sneezes, the sneeze is airborne and another child breathes in the minute droplets from that sneeze (direct transmission). The influenza pathogen has now traveled from the child with Hib to another child. Using the same example, a child with *haemophilus influenza* type b (Hib) sneezes on a toy in the medical office reception area. Another child plays with that toy and puts it in his mouth or plays with the toy then puts his hands in his mouth (indirect transmission). The influenza pathogen has

traveled from the child with Hib to the toy to the next child who plays with that toy. In this case the toy is a fomite. Figure 9–3 illustrates another common fomite.

Susceptible Host

Why is it that two people can be exposed to the same pathogen and one will get the disease and the other will not? In order to actually contract the disease or infection, the person must be a **susceptible host,** which means the individual has little or no immunity to that specific organism. Susceptibility is determined by a variety of factors including the following:

- Age
- Previous exposure to the organism
- Genetic predisposition
- Nutritional status
- Co-morbidities (other disease processes such as diabetes)
- Stress level
- Hygiene habits
- General health

All susceptible hosts are considered **immunocompromised** or immunodeficient, which means their immune system does not have the ability to effectively fight off that infectious disease. Contacting an infectious disease is especially dangerous for patients who are severely immunocompromised from AIDS, chemotherapy, or other debilitating illnesses.

The Cycle in Action

Returning to the example of Typhoid Mary, she was the reservoir host and provided a "home" for the *bacillus typhosis* which causes typhoid fever and is a foodborne pathogen. The bacterium is excreted through the gastrointestinal system. It probably entered the food Mary was preparing through improper hand washing after her bowel movements or tasting the ingredients as she cooked, then placing the utensil back into the main dish. The families ingested the bacteria with the food. Those who were susceptible to the pathogen became ill and some died. Unless broken, the cycle of infection continues.

EHR readiness

Outbreak Control

Due to an initial shortage of vaccine during the 2009 H1N1 influenza outbreak, medical offices had to identify the patients who were considered to be in high-risk categories for the disease. The risk factors were associated with certain ages and illnesses or conditions. These patients were targeted to receive the first available immunizations. Practices with electronic health record systems input the criteria, and the systems performed a relatively rapid search. Some systems also generated a notification to the patients. These practices were able to order the appropriate doses of the early vaccine and their patients were ready when it arrived. Offices on a manual system spent many labor-intensive hours attempting to identify all their high-risk patients. In some cases this resulted in significant staff overtime and increased costs. More important, the situation had the potential for delay in immunizing high-need patients and risking possible exposure to the disease.

susceptible host
An individual who has little or no immunity to that specific organism.

immunocompromised
Also known as immunodeficient, it is the inability to effectively fight off an infectious disease.

figure 9–3

The escalator as a fomite.

Is it possible for foodborne pathogens to spread in the medical office? Why or why not?

CHECKPOINT
LO 9.1

LO 9.2 The Importance of Asepsis

asepsis
Utilizing techniques to prevent the spread of or reduce or eliminate pathogens.

In the health-care setting, **asepsis** is important to

- Protect the patient and the public
- Protect health-care workers
- Prevent infectious diseases from starting
- Prevent infectious diseases from spreading

The principles of asepsis are designed to break the cycle of infection or stop it from starting. In the health-care setting, the means of transmission and means of entrance are probably the two areas of major concentration. Techniques and mechanisms are specific for each step of the cycle and should be used routinely. These practices are determined by organizations within the government (Figure 9–4).

CHECKPOINT
LO 9.2

Why is asepsis important for all areas of the medical office?

LO 9.3 The Roles of the Centers for Disease Control and Prevention (CDC) and the Occupational Safety and Health Administration (OSHA)

epidemiology
The study of the transmission and control of diseases.

health-care acquired infections (HAI)
Diseases that are a result of exposure in a health-care setting.

standard precautions
Techniques for health-care personnel to minimize the risk of catching or spreading an infection.

Two federal governmental agencies are primarily responsible for the guidelines and regulations that affect the prevention and spread of infection in the medical office. They are the Centers for Disease Control and Prevention (CDC) and the Occupational Safety and Health Administration (OSHA). These agencies may be assisted by state and local health departments.

Centers for Disease Control and Prevention (CDC)

The role of the CDC is to study the transmission and control of diseases. This branch of medical science is called **epidemiology** and it serves as the foundation for determining effective interventions for the public's health in combating illnesses and promoting preventive medicine. Diseases that spread in the health-care setting are called **health-care acquired infections (HAI),** formerly called nosocomial infections. After researching the epidemiology of these diseases, the CDC makes recommendations for the treatment and prevention and, if needed, outbreak control. Toward this end, the agency recommends the guidelines known as **standard precautions** which are techniques for health-care personnel to minimize the risk of catching or spreading an infection. These precautions are an expansion of the "universal precautions" which dealt with bloodborne pathogens. Standard precautions deal with all body fluids. The CDC also provides education through Web sites, videos, posters, and other media.

figure 9–4

Asepsis begins in the reception area.

Occupational Safety and Health Administration (OSHA)

While the CDC recommends guidelines based on epidemiology, OSHA creates and enforces the

Working with the Health-Care Team

PUBLIC HEALTH NURSE (PHN)

Duties and Skills

Public health nurses generally work for governmental agencies such as local health departments and other community organizations. Some of their duties include monitoring health trends and identifying health risks specific to a community; carrying out local, state, and federal priorities to improve access to health services for special populations; designing and implementing disease prevention activities such as immunizations, screenings, surveillance and follow-up; and providing education on nutrition, child care, and other health issues.

Educational Requirements

Public health nurses must earn an associates or bachelors degree in nursing and pass the registered nursing national licensing exam called the NCLEX-RN. Since community health is usually part of the nursing degree, some organizations will hire RNs and provide additional on-the-job training. Dependent on the organization and the job, a master's degree in public health may be required.

Workplace Settings

Public health nurses may work for governmental agencies, nonprofit organizations, community health centers, and other organizations with the mission of improving health at the community level.

The Public Health Nurse as a Team Member

The public health nurse may interface with the medical practice and the administrative medical assistant in several ways. For example, the administrative medical assistant, as part of his or her office role, may report a patient with a communicable disease to the PHN who will work with office staff to identify other exposed individuals and provide prophylaxis and prevent further spread. The PHN also provides education and training to medical offices on new disease preventable vaccines and other community interventions. Monitoring patient compliance with long-term drug regimes such as those required for treatment of tuberculosis and providing other resources to staff and patients including home visits are included in the scope of public health nursing. Offices that specialize in infectious diseases work closely with the public health nurse on a regular basis.

For more information, visit the Web site of the following organization, which is available on the Online Learning Center at www.mhhe.com/houseradminmedassist

The American Public Health Association

---

regulations associated with **infection control** and other workplace safety issues. Violation of these regulations may result in heavy fines or even closure of the practice. For administrative areas these regulations include:

- Occupational Exposure to Bloodborne Pathogens Standard
  - All employers must provide training
  - Safety manuals must be available
  - **Personal protective equipment (PPE)** must be available and supplied as appropriate
  - Hepatitis B vaccinations must be available if appropriate
  - An exposure control plan must be implemented
- Hazardous Communication Standard
  - Hazardous materials must be labeled by the manufacturer (these may include disinfectants used for cleaning equipment)
  - Material Safety Data Sheets (MSDS) must be supplied
  - Employee "right to know" information must be available

infection control
Stopping the spread of or reducing or eliminating pathogens through use of aseptic techniques.

personal protective equipment (PPE)
Disposable gloves, masks, eye shields, and gowns worn to protect health-care personnel from contamination with blood and body fluids.

If you were researching information on standard precaution guidelines for use with patients and visitors, would you most likely find "patient friendly" tips on the CDC or OSHA Web sites? Why or why not?

CHECKPOINT
LO 9.3

figure 9–5

Hand washing with soap and water.

alcohol hand disinfectant (AHD)
Gels, foams, and liquid rubs that are used when running water is not readily available.

LO 9.4 Hand Washing

The number one practice for controlling the spread of infections is to wash hands frequently (Figure 9–5). In the medical practice, four types of hand washing techniques may be utilized:

- General hand washing: Appropriate for administrative areas
- Medical aseptic hand washing: Appropriate for direct patient care staff
- Sterile or surgical aseptic hand washing: Appropriate for procedures requiring sterility such as surgeries
- Use of **alcohol hand disinfectant (AHD),** such as gels, foams, and liquid rubs: Appropriate when running water is not readily available.

The guidelines for general hand washing (Procedure 9–1) and the use of AHDs (Procedure 9–2) are described at the end of the chapter. When working in the medical office all staff should wash hands frequently.

In administrative areas, it is recommended that you wash hands:

- When arriving at the medical office
- After sneezing, coughing, or using a tissue or handkerchief
- After touching ears, eyes, nose, mouth, or hair
- After handling money or mail
- After routine cleaning of equipment or work surfaces
- After contact with soiled material or clothing
- After handling laboratory specimens
- After removing disposable or utility gloves
- After contact with infected or unsanitary areas of the body
- Before and after eating or handling food
- After using the restroom
- Before leaving the medical office

Antimicrobial soaps are only recommended for hand washing when dealing directly with body fluids. In other circumstances, non-antimicrobial soaps are suggested, since frequent use of antimicrobial soap may contribute to the development of antibiotic-resistant pathogens. It is important to follow the correct procedure when washing to reduce the amount of pathogens on your hands. The procedure also prevents recontamination by not directly touching areas such as the water faucet, which may act as a fomite. Sinks are not always readily available, so in those instances the work area should have an ample supply of an alcohol-based hand sanitizer. Many offices place a pump-type AHD dispenser at the point of entrance or the check-in window for patients and visitors.

**CHECKPOINT
LO 9.4**

Why is it important to wash your hands when you arrive and when you leave the medical office?

LO 9.5 Other Aseptic Practices for Administrative Areas

The following is a consolidation of the CDC precautions that apply to the administrative areas of the medical office and should be utilized for contact with all persons, including other staff members:

- Post signs requesting staff and visitors to cover mouth and nose with tissue when coughing and sneezing or to cough or sneeze into the sleeve; this is sometimes referred to as the "flu salute" (Figure 9–6).
- Request coughing persons to wear a mask.
- Attempt to maintain a distance of at least three feet from potentially infected persons (including patients with coughs and undiagnosed rashes).
- Ideally, place coughing patients or patients with undiagnosed rashes in an isolated waiting area or directly into an individual treatment area.
- Immediately dispose of used tissues into plastic-lined receptacles.
- Avoid touching surfaces in close proximity to potentially infected persons.
- Avoid touching your face, mouth, nose, and eyes.
- Wear gloves when contact with blood or other potentially infectious materials is a probability, such as working with a patient with a laceration or accepting a laboratory specimen that was collected at home (Procedure 9–3, Removing Contaminated Gloves).
- Wear disposable gloves or reusable utility gloves for cleaning the environment or equipment with the appropriate EPA-registered disinfectant for the pathogens most likely to contaminate the area.
- Establish policies and procedures for cleaning any toys present in the facility:
  - Select toys that can be easily cleaned and disinfected.
  - Do not permit use of stuffed furry toys if they will be shared.
  - Clean and disinfect large stationary toys (e.g., climbing equipment) at least weekly and whenever visibly soiled.
  - If toys are likely to be mouthed, rinse with water after disinfection or wash in a dishwasher.
  - When a toy requires cleaning and disinfection, do so immediately or store in a designated labeled container separate from toys ready for use.
  - Select furniture and window coverings that are easily cleaned and disinfected.
- Avoid contact with patient's clothing or other fabrics that touch the patient.
- Stay home when you are ill.
- Follow recommendations for communicable disease immunizations including the seasonal influenza vaccines
  - Employees have the right to refuse the immunization but generally are required to sign a waiver indicating that it was offered and declined.
  - The policy in some offices is that employees who have not received the influenza immunization must wear a mask during the flu season or outbreaks.

figure 9–6

Cover your cough.

Source: http://cdc.gov/flu/protect/covercough.htm.

Would you recommend to a medical office that a supply of gloves and masks be kept in administrative areas? Why or why not?

CHECKPOINT
LO 9.5

Asepsis in Use

The administrative medical assistant serves as a role model for patients. It is not appropriate to cough or sneeze without covering one's mouth with a tissue or coughing or sneezing into one's sleeve and then attempt to instruct patients to perform these practices. Alcohol-based hand sanitizer should be readily available in the administrative areas, and the administrative medical assistant should consistently use it between transactions involving different patients. Food and beverages are to be limited to staff lounges, and work and reception areas are always to be kept clean. The administrative medical assistant should routinely observe for general untidiness, soiled furniture, odors, or other unpleasant hygiene issues throughout the office. Dust on plants, both real and artificial, is often missed. Checking restrooms within the facility on an assigned schedule for cleanliness and adequate supplies is a common and important practice. Frequently, a log is maintained requiring the time and signature of the responsible party to ensure this is occurring. A mechanism should also be in place for emergency clean-ups. If high standards of cleanliness are not observed in the physician's office, it is unlikely that patients will have confidence in the care or the instructions provided by the staff. Noncompliant staff results in noncompliant patients. Not only is this type of carelessness a potential reservoir for pathogens, but it is a potential risk for safety issues. As a patient, what type of medical office environment would you prefer?

LO 9.6 Patient Education

As previously noted, the cycle of infection is also called the chain of infection. One break in the chain can nullify all other efforts to promote disease prevention. Staff members should be trained to assure good aseptic practices are maintained. It is also important for medical assistants working in the administrative areas, as well as the clinical areas, to look for opportunities to educate patients on the applications involved with preventing the spread of pathogens. An opening may be as easy as offering hand sanitizer to a patient who has just sneezed, or creating and distributing simple guidelines for hand washing. Videos for reception areas, pamphlets, and Internet sites are excellent sources of information. These and other materials are available from governmental agencies such as the CDC, insurance companies, nonprofit organizations, libraries, and commercial vendors. All educational materials should be reviewed and approved by the physician or practice manager. Asepsis is everyone's business and a team effort. When should you use it? ALWAYS!!

CHECKPOINT
LO 9.6

Consider the different areas of patient education related to asepsis that would most likely differ in a pediatric office versus an internal medicine office.

Procedure 9–1 General Hand Washing

GOAL To use a general hand washing technique, reducing pathogens on the hand surfaces and preventing recontamination in the process

MATERIALS Sink with running water, soap as determined appropriate by the facility, paper towels, plastic-lined trash receptacle

NOTE: General hand washing, not aseptic hand washing, is recommended for administrative areas; non-antimicrobial soap may be the facility's preference for reasons discussed earlier in this chapter.

METHOD

1. Turn on water faucet and wet hands using warm water.
2. Apply soap.
3. Lather well.
4. Rub your hands vigorously for at least 20 seconds, scrubbing all surfaces, including the backs of your hands, wrists, between your fingers, and your fingernails.
5. Rinse well.
6. Dry your hands with a disposable towel or air dryer.
7. Use a disposable towel to turn off the faucet without touching your hands to any of its surfaces.
8. Place the towel in the trash receptacle without touching your hands to any of its surfaces.

Procedure 9–2 Hand Cleansing with Alcohol Hand Disinfectant (AHD)

GOAL To use a hand-cleansing substance to reduce pathogens on the hand surfaces and prevent recontamination when soap and water is not readily available

MATERIAL 60–95% alcohol-based foam, gel, or liquid rub

METHOD

1. Pump the AHD onto the palm of the hand.
2. Rub the hands together vigorously ensuring the alcohol comes in contact with all surfaces, including backs of hands, between fingers, and fingernails.
3. Continue to rub the solution until it is evaporated and the hands are dry (10–15 seconds). **Do not** wave hands to hasten drying.
4. **Do not** use an AHD hand-cleansing procedure in the following circumstances:
   - When hands are visibly dirty
   - When hands are contaminated with proteinaceous material
   - Before or after eating
   - After toilet activities

Procedure 9–3 Removing Contaminated Gloves

GOAL To remove gloves contaminated with blood or body fluids, dirt, disinfectants, or other materials while avoiding the transfer of the substance to your hands or other areas

MATERIALS Contaminated gloves, plastic-lined trash receptacle (if gross amounts of blood or body fluids are present on the gloves, a biohazard trash receptacle should be used)

METHOD

1. Grasp the palm of the glove of your nondominant hand with your gloved dominant hand without touching bare skin.
2. Remove the glove, turning it inside out.
3. Continue to hold the glove in your dominant hand.
4. Slide the nongloved thumb into the inside of the glove of the dominant hand without touching the outside of the glove.
5. Continue to use the thumb to pull the glove over the fingers, removing the glove inside out and over the first glove which is now inside the second glove with no outside areas exposed.
6. Toss the gloves into the appropriate trash container.
7. Wash your hands.

Case Study

Jack, a medical assistant, loves to work on motorcycles during his time off. Consequently, his hands are sometimes stained with dark grease-like material. Mrs. Kim, a long-time patient of the practice, confides in Amy, the administrative medical assistant at the front desk, that she would prefer not to have Jack involved in her care because she does not feel he is clean. She is afraid she may "catch something" from him. Jack's lack of professionalism in his appearance and possible break in asepsis reflects not only on him, but on the practice.

Thinking Critically

1. Is it possible for Mrs. Kim to "catch something" from Jack's stained hands?
2. Are there precautions that Jack could use?
3. How should Amy respond to Mrs. Brown?

practice APPLICATIONS

1. Create a poster for your office describing the cycle of infection. You might choose a specific disease to illustrate the cycle.

2. With another student, role-play a scenario involving two staff members. One has a cold and is not using aseptic principles. The other staff member is afraid of catching the cold and bringing it home to her infant. What does the second staff member say and do to prevent this from happening?

exam READINESS

There may be more than one correct answer. Circle the best answer.

1. **[LO9.1]** A disease-causing organism is called a
   a. microbe.
   b. bug.
   c. pathogen.
   d. fomite.
   e. carrier.

2. **[LO9.1]** An example of a bloodborne pathogen is
   a. hepatitis A
   b. hepatitis B.
   c. chicken pox.
   d. typhoid fever.
   e. influenza.

3. **[LO9.1]** All of the following are airborne pathogens EXCEPT
   a. tuberculosis.
   b. influenza.
   c. common cold.
   d. measles.
   e. hepatitis A.

4. **[LO9.1]** A fomite that may be found in the medical office is
   a. water.
   b. bacteria.
   c. hand sanitizer.
   d. telephone.
   e. disinfectant.

5. **[LO9.3]** The governmental agency that may fine a medical practice for violation of its regulations dealing with standard precautions is
   a. OSHA.
   b. CDC.
   c. HIPAA.
   d. CMS.
   e. ADA.

6. **[LO9.3]** The governmental agency that studies communicable diseases and recommends guidelines such as the use of standard precautions is
   a. OSHA.
   b. CDC.
   c. HIPAA.
   d. CMS.
   e. ADA.

7. **[LO9.4]** The number one practice for preventing the spread of disease in the medical office is to
   a. provide masks for coughing patients.
   b. promote the "flu salute."
   c. wash hands frequently.
   d. eliminate furry toy animals.
   e. stay home when you are ill.

8. **[LO9.2]** Asepsis is important in all areas of the medical office since many patients may be
   a. carriers.
   b. fomites.
   c. uninsured.
   d. immunized.
   e. immunocompromised.

9. **[LO9.1]** All of the following are steps in the cycle of infection EXCEPT
   a. means of asepsis.
   b. means of exit.
   c. means of transmission.
   d. means of entry.
   e. susceptible host.

10. **[LO9.4]** A good aseptic practice when arriving at the medical office is to
    a. pick up messages.
    b. wash hands.
    c. check for open appointments.
    d. wipe off computer screens.
    e. refill pamphlet holders.

learning outcome SUMMARY

LO 9.1 The medical assistant is responsible for understanding the five steps in the cycle of infection.

LO 9.2 Sound aseptic practices break the cycle of infection and prevent disease transmission in the medical office.

LO 9.3 The CDC, through epidemiological studies, recommends guidelines for standard precautions to prevent infection. OSHA monitors compliance with these standards and other safety requirements in the workplace.

LO 9.4 Proper hand washing is the number one means of asepsis. The general hand washing technique is recommended for administrative areas.

LO 9.5 In addition to hand washing, other aseptic practices include but are not limited to:

- Maintaining general cleanliness in the environment
- Isolating patients with undiagnosed rashes or coughs and requiring them to wear a mask
- Establishing policies and procedures for cleaning toys and office furnishings
- Using gloves and other PPE as appropriate
- Staying home when you are ill

LO 9.6 The medical assistant also plays a vital role in educating other staff and patients in methods to prevent or stop the spread of infectious diseases. Information and materials are available through multiple sources.

medical assisting COMPETENCIES

CAAHEP

III. C (1) Describe the infection cycle, including the infectious agent, reservoir, susceptible host, means of transmission, portals of entry, and portals of exit

III. C (2) Define asepsis

III. C (3) Discuss infection control procedures

III. C (4) Identify personal safety precautions as established by the Occupational Safety and Health Administration (OSHA)

III. C (7) Match types and uses of personal protective equipment (PPE)

III. C (11) Describe Standard Precautions, including:
    a. Transmission-based precautions

    b. Purpose
    c. Activities regulated

III. C (13) Identify the role of the Center for Disease Control (CDC) regulations in health-care settings

III. P (1) Participate in training on Standard Precautions

III. P (2) Practice Standard Precautions

III. P (4) Perform hand washing

IV. P (4) Explain general office policies

XI. C (1) Describe personal protective equipment

ABHES

1. General Orientation
    b. Compare and contrast the allied health professions and understand their relation to medical assisting
    d. Have knowledge of the general responsibilities of the medical assistant

9. Medical Office Clinical Procedures
    b. Apply principles of aseptic techniques and infection control
    i. Use standard precautions
    p. Advise patients of office policies and procedures

Administrative
Practices

Preparation for Success

Interviewer: Hi, Marissa. The director of your medical assisting program reported that you received an interesting award at your graduation ceremony. Would you tell us about it?

Marisa: Oh, that was funny! It was called the *Super Woman* Award. I was pregnant with my second baby when I decided to become an administrative medical assistant. I was going to have a cesarean section. The doctor knew I was in school and scheduled the surgery for Friday on a holiday weekend. Everything went well and with my doctor's consent, I was back in class on Wednesday. My instructors and classmates were great about making sure I got the class notes and assignments, driving me to school, and even taking me to my class on the second floor in a wheelchair. At graduation, they surprised me with the *Super Woman* Award and my husband gave me a big bouquet from my two daughters who were also there. I cried.

Interviewer: You are a super woman to begin school with one baby at home and another on the way. You also had a job. Why did you decide to go back to school at that time?

Marissa: Ever since I was little, I was told that I wasn't very smart and would never get a good job. I was afraid it was true. After high school I could only get a job in a fast food restaurant. When I was pregnant, again, I knew that I needed a better job and I also needed to be an example for my children. How could I expect them to amount to anything if I couldn't do it? So I talked to a counselor through the Workforce Investment Act that arranged for payment of my tuition and books.

Interviewer: Marissa, you are now the supervisor of the appointment scheduling area for a community health center. You were also nominated for a statewide award, *Excellence in Medical Assisting,* because of your idea to coordinate well-baby checkups and the Women, Infants and Children (WIC) nutrition program visits for your patients. You worked hard and you should be proud of your accomplishments. What a great example for your daughters!

Marissa: Thank you. Yes, I am proud and now my husband has gone back to school, too.

Interviewer: Do you have any advice for others who are currently in school?

Marissa: Education is so important. It is hard, but you can do it. Don't let anyone tell you that you can't or that you are not smart enough. Don't ever tell your kids that either. You are their example and the most important thing in their lives. When you work in health care you should be a good example for everyone because a lot of people will look up to you.

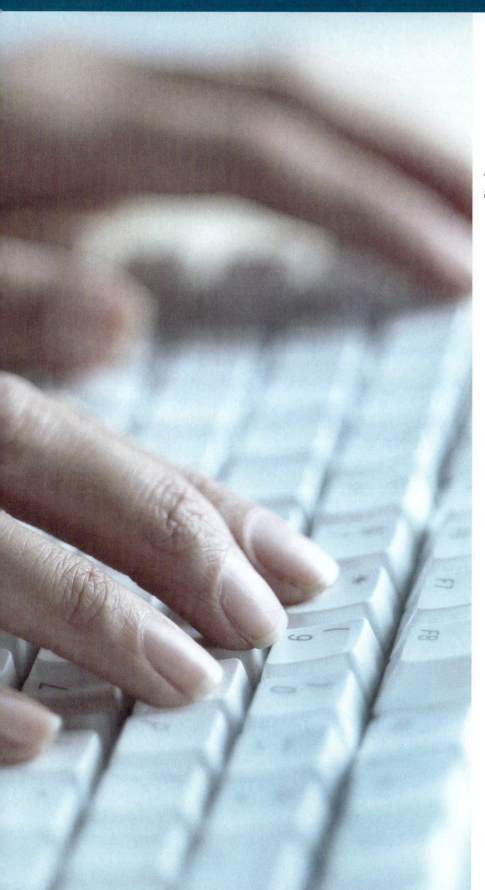

All the strength you need to
achieve anything is within you.

Sara Henderson

unit 3

10 Administrative Technologies

Learning Outcomes

After completing Chapter 10, you will be able to:

10.1 Identify common types of computers.

10.2 Describe computer hardware components and explain the functions of each.

10.3 Explain the difference between the two categories of computer software.

10.4 Describe the types of computer software commonly used in the medical office.

10.5 Explain how to select computer equipment for the medical office.

10.6 Explain security measures for computerized medical records, including HIPAA compliance.

10.7 Describe the basic care and maintenance required of computer equipment.

10.8 Distinguish advances in computer technology and explain their importance to the medical office.

10.9 Identify and briefly explain the purpose of the different types of office communication equipment.

10.10 Explain how administrative equipment can streamline everyday administrative tasks.

10.11 Outline the process to be used when purchasing office equipment.

10.12 Explain how to maintain office equipment for optimum performance.

Key Terms

abuse	microfilm
antivirus software	modem
CD-ROM	motherboard
central processing unit (CPU)	mouse
	multimedia
cover sheet	multitasking
covered entity	network
cursor	optical character recognition (OCR)
database	
disclaimer	random-access memory (RAM)
disk cleanup	
disk defragmentation	read-only memory (ROM)
dot matrix printer	
digital subscriber line (DSL)	scanner
	screen saver
electronic mail (e-mail)	service contract
electronic media	software
firewalls	tablet PC
hard copy	touch pad
hardware	touch screen
icon	tower case
ink-jet printer	trackball
interactive pager	troubleshooting
Internet	tutorial
LAN	voice mail
laser printer	VPN
lease	WAN
maintenance contract	warranty
microfiche	zip drive

Preparation for Certification

RMA (AMT) Exam	CMAS (AMT) Exam	CMA (AAMA) Exam

• Medical office computer application
• Supply and equipment management
	• Fundamentals of computing
	• Medical office computer applications
	• Supplies and equipment
		• Computer components
		• Computer applications
		• Equipment operation
		  • Maintenance and repair
		  • Equipment and supply inventory

Introduction ● ● ●

The practice of medicine has grown to be increasingly complex:

- Never before has so much medical information been available for the physician.
- Never before has the practice of billing and collecting for medical services rendered and also the scheduling and coordinating of services among multiple providers been so complicated.
- Never before have there been so many choices for administrative office equipment, including the "super computer," needed to assist with all aspects of a busy practice. We live in the age of information. The need for devices to organize correlate, store, and disseminate all this information has never been greater.

Although the computer is thought to be the integral tool of the medical office, other equipment such as telephone systems, cell phones, beepers, pagers, answering machines, and fax machines create the office communication system. Calculators and check writers are used in tandem with the office accounting software to streamline patient and insurance billing, banking, and payroll management. Maintenance of confidentiality when information is no longer needed is the job of the office paper shredder. The piece of equipment which is probably most taken for granted is the office photocopier, but can you imagine creating duplicate documents without it?

This chapter discusses in detail the computer skills required to efficiently run a medical office, as well as the administrative skills necessary to select, use, and maintain the various types of office equipment required in today's medical office.

LO 10.1 Types of Computers Used in the Medical Office

Computers have revolutionized the way we live and work. Tasks are completed more easily because computers process information accurately and quickly. Medical records do not take up vast amounts of space and get "lost in a pile"; they are stored within the computer hard drive or server and can be accessed by multiple providers at the same time.

As an administrative medical assistant, you need to understand not only the fundamentals of computers, but also the different types of software available for the medical office and how to use them. This knowledge will enable you to perform many office tasks with ease. It will also allow you to solve or avoid common computer problems, making you an even more valuable asset to the office.

Four basic types of computers are used today: supercomputers, mainframe computers, minicomputers, and personal computers. Each type of computer is suitable for a certain type of work in a particular kind of workplace.

Supercomputers

Supercomputers are the biggest, fastest, and most complex computers in use. They are primarily used in research medicine, including genetic coding and DNA and cancer research.

Mainframe Computers

Often used by government facilities and large institutions, including universities and hospitals, mainframes can process and store huge quantities of information. Large governmental service programs such as Medicare and Medicaid use mainframe computers.

Minicomputers

Minicomputers are smaller than mainframes but larger than personal computers and traditionally have been used in network settings. A **network** is a system that links several computers together. In this environment a minicomputer typically functions as a server, which is the centralized storage location for shared information. However, personal computers are becoming as powerful as minicomputers and may eventually replace them.

Personal Computers

Also called microcomputers, personal computers are found in homes, offices, and schools. They are ideal for these settings because they are small, self-contained units. To suit user needs, personal computers are available in three different types: desktop, notebook, and subnotebook.

Desktop The most common type of personal computer, a desktop model fits easily on a desk or other flat surface. The system unit of most desktop models is housed in a **tower case**, which is often placed on the floor next to the desk—to allow more surface area at the workstation (Figure 10–1). Both large and small medical offices commonly use desktop computers. Information is displayed on a monitor screen which is often a flat LCD (liquid crystal diode) monitor that resembles a framed picture. Older monitors often resemble a bulkier television screen, but most are being replaced with LCD screens which provide better privacy because they can't be seen from the side. They also generate less heat.

Laptop and Notebook A laptop computer is small—about the size of a magazine—and weighs only a few pounds. Laptops operate either on battery power or on an AC adapter. Advances in technology have made laptops smaller, more powerful, and less expensive, making then increasingly popular. Their portability makes them especially convenient for students, for those who travel, and for anyone who desires fast and easy access to the Internet. Notebook computers offer the same services as conventional laptops but are smaller in size.

Subnotebook Subnotebooks are smaller than laptops but larger than handheld computers, with screens that are 14 inches or less. Another new type of subnotebook is the **tablet PC**, a laptop or a slate-shaped mobile computer equipped with a touch screen or graphics table technology. This allows users to operate the computer with a stylus or a digital pen instead of a keyboard or mouse.

Personal Digital Assistant (PDA) PDAs, sometimes called palmtops, are common in medical offices and other health-care facilities. Doctors often use them to look up medications and other reference information (Figure 10–2). They may also enter data that is transferred into a patient's chart.

Cell Phones and the Internet Cell phones are now most often used personally and not professionally, but for research purposes the capabilities of cell phones have increased exponentially in the last several years and will continue to expand. Phones such as BlackBerry® and Apple's iPhone allow users to access the Internet and perform multiple applications in addition to simply making phone calls and sending text messages. Many "techies" believe that cell

network
A system that links several computers together.

tower case
A vertical housing for the system unit of a personal computer.

tablet PC
A laptop or slate-shaped mobile computer, equipped with a touch screen or graphics tablet to operate the computer with a digital pen or fingertip instead of a keyboard or mouse.

figure 10–1

Offices can free up much-needed desktop space by using computers in tower cases, which can be kept on the floor.

phones are the "computers of the future." Although convenient, be sure that you only use your personal cell phone for approved purposes and at approved times while at the office. Many offices now have written policies and procedures regarding personal cell phone use. Be sure you know and follow your office policy regarding personal cell phone usage.

● ● ● ●

Cell phones and PDAs are being used more and more in a professional capacity. How might this create confidentiality issues for medical professionals?

CHECKPOINT
LO 10.1

LO 10.2 Computer Hardware Components

Computer components are divided into hardware and software. **Hardware** comprises the physical components of a computer system, including the monitor, keyboard, and printer. **Software** is a program or set of instructions that tells the computer what to do. Software includes both the operating system and applications that run on the operating system.

The computer's hardware serves four main functions: inputting data, processing data, storing data, and outputting data. Various hardware components are needed to perform each of these functions. Traditionally, in order to work, hardware devices had to be connected by a cable, such as a USB or serial cable. Today, many offices are going "wireless." Utilizing new technology instead of the traditional copper cables, peripheral devices such as keyboards, the mouse, and printers can now be attached to the computer hard drive using wireless technology that allows them to communicate with one another using air as the conductor. You can literally be using a computer in your office but print the document down the hall on the printer containing the office letterhead.

Input Devices For a computer to handle information, such as patient records, the data must first be entered, or input. Several types of input devices may be used to enter data into the computer. Keyboards, pointing devices, modems, and scanners are input devices. After being entered into the computer, information can be displayed on the monitor, processed, or stored.

Keyboard The keyboard is the most common input device. The main part of a keyboard resembles a typewriter. Most keyboards have several additional keys, however. A typical keyboard contains the following:

- Standard typewriter keys to enter letters, numbers, symbols, and punctuation marks
- Separate numerical keypad for entering numbers faster and more easily
- Arrow keys to move the **cursor,** a blinking line or cube on the computer screen showing where the next character that is keyed will appear
- Function keys to perform such tasks as saving and printing files

When you use the keyboard, it is important to position your hands properly to avoid injury. The Practice Readiness section provides tips for preventing and coping with carpal tunnel syndrome, a

hardware
The physical components of a computer system, including the monitor, keyboard, and printer.

software
A program or set of instructions that tells a computer what to do.

cursor
A blinking line or cube on a computer screen that shows where the next character that is keyed will appear.

figure 10–2

A handheld computer or PDA like this one can be used as a handy reference to look up medications or perform calculations in the medical office. Handheld computers are also used as part of a sophisticated computer network for the physician to enter and receive patient data.

mouse
A pointing device that can be added to a computer that directs activity on the computer screen by positioning a pointer or cursor on the screen. It can be directly attached to the computer or can be wireless.

trackball
A pointing device with a ball that is rolled to position a pointer or cursor on a computer screen. It can be directly attached to the computer or can be wireless.

touch pad
A type of pointing device common to laptop and notebook computers that directs activity on the computer screen by positioning a pointer or cursor on the screen. It is a small, flat device or surface that is highly sensitive to the touch.

touch screen
A type of computer monitor that acts as an intake device, receiving information through the touch of a pen, wand, or hand directly to the screen.

modem
A device used to transfer information from one computer to another through telephone lines.

figure 10–3

Using a mouse, you can point and click to access a variety of functions.

condition resulting from repetitive motion such as continual use of a keyboard while inputting data.

Pointing Device   Most software programs need not only a keyboard but also a pointing device to enter information into the computer. When you move the pointing device, an arrow appears. You can point and click the arrow on various buttons that appear on the screen. The four common types of pointing devices are the mouse, the trackball, the touch pad, and the touch screen.

1. A **mouse,** the most common pointing device, has several buttons on top for the "point and click" feature and a track wheel that allows you to move rapidly through a document. Older mouse versions have a rolling ball on the bottom that rolls over a smooth service such as a mouse pad. A newer laser mouse detects movement through a laser and does not have a ball. As you move the mouse across a flat surface or mouse pad, you cause a light-sensing device on the bottom to move. This controls an arrow on the screen that points at the desired button or object on the screen. Then, as shown in Figure 10–3, you push one of the buttons on the mouse to access a function, such as opening a file.

2. A **trackball** is similar to a mouse except that the rolling ball is on the top of the device instead of on the bottom. Rather than pushing a trackball across a pad, you roll the ball with your fingers while the trackball remains stationary.

3. A **touch pad** is a form of pointing device common on laptop and notebook computers. It is a small, flat device that is highly sensitive to the touch. To move the arrow on the screen, you simply slide your finger across the touch pad. To click on an item, you push a button similar to that on a mouse or trackball, or you tap your finger on the touch pad.

4. A **touch screen** is a monitor screen that is illuminated at the touch of a pen, wand, or finger. When an object is touched on the screen, the touch itself acts as a pointing device and conveys information to the computer. Touch screens are increasingly being used in clinical and hospital settings.

Modem   The term **modem** is a shortened form of the words *modulator-demodulator.* A modem is used to transfer information from one computer to another over telephone lines. Because modems allow information to be transferred both to and from a computer, they are considered input/output devices. The speed at which a modem transfers data is called the bit rate. Modems may be internal, external, or wireless and are essential for any medical office that needs to transfer files electronically, as when submitting insurance claim forms.

A cable modem is a modem that operates over cable television lines to provide fast Internet access. **DSL (digital subscriber line)** modems operate over telephone lines but use a different frequency than a telephone frequency. This type of modem allows computer Internet access and telephone use at the same time.

An advanced type of modem is a fax modem. This device allows the computer to send and receive files much as a fax machine does. To use a fax modem, the information to be sent must be in a computer. Handwritten notes cannot be sent by fax modem unless they are first scanned into the computer.

Carpal Tunnel Syndrome

As the number of computers used in the home and workplace has escalated in recent years, the number of cases of carpal tunnel syndrome has also risen dramatically. Carpal tunnel syndrome is a hand disorder that is often associated with computer use. The term for this condition comes from the name for a canal (the carpal tunnel) located in the wrist. Several tendons pass through this tunnel, allowing the hand to open and close.

Carpal tunnel syndrome results from repetitive motion, such as keyboarding, for hours at a time. This motion may cause swelling to develop around the tendons and carpal tunnel. The swelling compresses the nerve. The people most likely to develop carpal tunnel syndrome are workers whose jobs require them to perform repetitive hand and finger motions.

Symptoms

The symptoms associated with carpal tunnel syndrome include the following:

- Tingling or burning in the hands or fingers
- Weakness or numbness in the hands or fingers
- Hands that go to sleep frequently
- Difficulty opening or closing the hands
- Pain that stems from the wrist and travels up the arm

Tips for Prevention

If you use a keyboard for extended periods, you should practice proper techniques to prevent carpal tunnel syndrome (Figure 10–4).

- While seated, hold your arms relaxed at your sides, and check to make sure that your keyboard is positioned slightly higher than your elbows. As you input, keep your elbows at your sides, and relax your shoulders (see Figure 10–4).
- Use only your fingers to press keys, and do not use more pressure than necessary. Use a wrist rest, and keep your wrists relaxed and straight.
- When you need to strike difficult-to-reach keys, move your whole hand rather than stretching your fingers. When you need to press two keys at the same time, such as "Control" and "F1," use two hands.

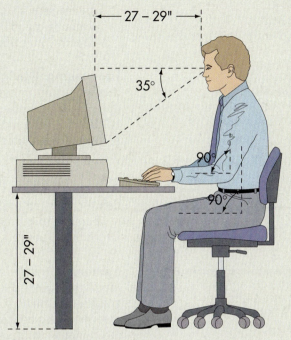

figure 10–4

Maintaining proper posture and hand positions helps to avoid strain or injury of the back, eyes, neck, or wrist when keyboarding.

- Try to break up long periods of keyboard work with other tasks that do not require computer use.

Tips for Relieving Symptoms

If you have symptoms of carpal tunnel syndrome, try these suggestions for relief.

- Elevate your arms.
- Wear a splint on the hand and forearm.
- Discuss your symptoms with a physician, who may prescribe medication.

DSL (digital subscriber line)
A type of modem that operates over telephone lines by using a different frequency than a telephone uses, allowing a computer to access the Internet at the same time that a telephone is being used.

scanner
An optical device that converts printed matter into a format that can be read by the computer and inputs the converted information.

Scanner A **scanner** is a device used to input printed matter and convert it into a format that can be read by the computer. Scanners are useful in the medical office because patient reports from another doctor, a hospital, or another outside source can be easily entered into the computer. Scanners are also making it possible to move into a paperless (EHR) system. Three types of scanners are available:

1. Handheld scanners are generally the least expensive but are more difficult to use and produce lower-quality results than the other two types.

2. A single-sheet scanner feeds one sheet of paper through at a time and looks similar to a single-sheet printer.

3. A flatbed scanner is the most expensive type of scanner but is the easiest to use and produces the highest-quality input. It works much like a small photocopier: the paper lies flat and still on a glass surface while the machine scans it. Today many photocopiers are configured with a scanning capability and can transmit the images of scanned documents directly into computers.

Processing Devices   There are two major processing components inside the system unit, or computer cabinet. The **motherboard** is the main circuit board that controls the other components in the system. The **central processing unit (CPU),** or microprocessor, is the primary computer chip responsible for interpreting and executing programs. Because it interprets instructions from software programs, the CPU is the most important part of the computer hardware.

Storage Devices   One of the main tasks of a computer is to store information for later retrieval. The computer uses memory to store information either temporarily or permanently. Several types of drives are used for permanent information storage.

Memory   Computers use two types of memory to store data: **random-access memory (RAM)** and read-only memory (ROM). RAM is temporary, or programmable, memory. While you are working on a software program, the computer is accessing RAM. In general, the more RAM that is available, the faster the computer will perform. As software programs become more sophisticated, they require more RAM.

Read-only memory (ROM) is permanent memory. The computer can read it, but you cannot make changes to it. The purpose of ROM is to provide the basic operating instructions the computer needs to function.

Hard Disk Drive   The hard disk drive is where information is stored permanently for later retrieval. Software programs and important data are usually stored on the hard disk for quick and easy access. The amount of hard disk space needed to store software programs is increasing rapidly. The more software programs you want to store, the larger the hard disk you will need.

CD, DVD, and CD-ROM   CD-ROM stands for "compact disc—read-only memory." The main advantage of a CD-ROM over a diskette is its ability to store large amounts of data. CD-ROMs can be used to back up information from the hard drive. The very latest computers also read and write to DVDs which allows for even more storage capacity.

CD-ROM drives have become standard equipment on most personal computers. Although many software packages are available on both CD-ROM and diskettes, some large programs are available only on CD-ROM. These programs include multimedia applications such as medical encyclopedias. **Multimedia** refers to software that uses more than one medium—such as graphics, sound, and text—to convey information (Figure 10–5).

Many computers have a CD and/or DVD burner or recorder, which allows information to be taken from one CD (or any other source) and "burned" to a CD or DVD. If your computer contains a CD or DVD burner, you can create CDs or DVDs of office information for patient use or for storage off-site. This is especially convenient for patients requiring information for a consultant. The records, x-rays, MRI/CT scans, and so on, can be burned to a CD for the patient to take with her, and the consultant can see not only the interpretation of the test, but the test itself on his own computer.

motherboard
The main circuit board of a computer that controls the other components in the system.

central processing unit (CPU)
The central processing unit, or microprocessor, is the primary computer chip responsible for interpreting and executing programs.

random-access memory (RAM)
The temporary or programmable memory in a computer.

read-only memory (ROM)
The permanent memory of a computer, which can be read by the computer but not changed. It provides the computer with the basic operating instructions it needs to function.

CD-ROM
A compact disc that contains software programs; an abbreviation for "compact disc–read-only memory."

multimedia
More than one medium such as graphics, sound, and text, used to convey information.

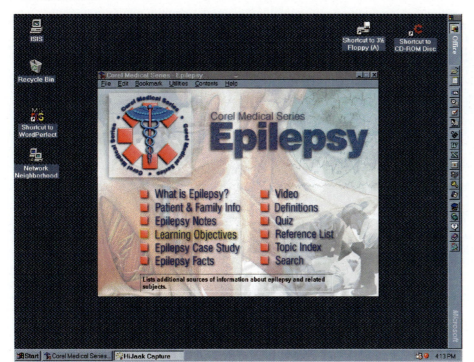

figure 10–5

A CD-ROM provides features, such as video and sound, that are not possible in a standard printed book.

Tape Drive This storage device is used to back up (make a copy of) the files on the hard disk. The information is copied onto magnetic tapes that resemble audiotapes. If the hard drive malfunctions, you will have a copy of the information on these tapes.

With most tape drives, the entire contents of the hard disk can be stored on one or two tapes. Store these tapes at night in a fireproof container.

Jump Drive A jump drive is an externally attached drive that is small enough to be carried on a key chain, yet holds 16 gigabytes (GB) or more of data. (Gigabytes are a measurement of memory space.) It also may be called a flash drive, a pen drive, a key drive, a memory key, a flash key, or simply a USB drive. It provides easy portability for large bodies of data. It may be used for backup operations in a medical practice when stored off-premise.

Zip Drive A **zip drive** is a high-capacity floppy disk drive developed by Iomega®. Zip disks are slightly larger and about twice as thick as a conventional floppy disk. Zip disks can hold up to 750 MB (megabytes) of data. They are durable and relatively inexpensive. They may be used for backing up hard disks and transporting large files.

zip drive

A high-capacity floppy disk drive developed by Iomega®. Zip disks are slightly larger and about twice as thick as a conventional floppy disk. Zip drives can hold 100–750 MB of data. They are durable and relatively inexpensive. They may be used for backing up hard disks and transporting large files.

Output Devices Output devices are used to display information after it has been processed. A monitor and a printer are two output devices needed in the medical office.

Monitor A standard computer monitor looks like a television screen or may be an LCD flat screen. It displays the information that is currently active, such as a word processing document, an Internet link, or e-mail. Monitors are available in a variety of sizes.

Color monitors vary in the number of colors they can display and in the resolution (crispness) of the images, which is measured in dot pitch. The lower the dot pitch, the higher the resolution. A monitor with a 0.26 dot pitch displays sharper images than a monitor with a 0.39 dot pitch. Using a high-resolution monitor can help you avoid eye strain.

figure 10–6

An "all-in-one" printer can send and receive faxes, print, and copy. Some models like this one can be networked to more than one computer in the medical office.

hard copy
A readable, paper copy or printout of information.

laser printer
A high-resolution printer that uses a technology similar to that of a photocopier. It is the fastest type of computer printer and produces the highest-quality output.

ink-jet printer
A nonimpact printer that forms characters by using a series of dots created by tiny drops of ink.

dot matrix printer
An impact printer that creates characters by placing a series of tiny dots next to one another.

Printer A printer is required to produce a **hard copy,** or printout of information. Printer resolution is noted in terms of dots per inch (dpi). The higher the dpi, the better the print quality. Printer output varies, depending on the type of printer and the model. The three most commonly used printers are dot matrix, ink-jet, and laser.

1. **Laser printers** are high-resolution printers that use a technology similar to that of photocopiers. Laser printers are the fastest and produce the highest-quality output. Laser printers are more expensive than dot matrix or ink-jet printers.

2. **Ink-jet printers** form characters using a series of dots. They are nonimpact printers in which the dots are created by tiny drops of ink. Many ink-jet printers are capable of printing in both black and color. Because of their high-quality output and affordable prices, ink-jet printers are popular for home and small-office use.

3. At one time, **dot matrix printers** were commonly used in medical offices. However, they are rarely used today except in instances where lab reports or other types of reports are used.

Because each type of printer has advantages and disadvantages, some medical offices may have more than one type. For example, a medical office may have a dot matrix printer for creating multipage insurance forms and a laser printer for creating documents whose quality resembles that of typeset documents.

A current trend in printers is the "all-in-one" model (Figure 10–6), which functions not only as an ink-jet printer but also as a fax machine, scanner, and photocopier. This type of machine may be convenient for a small medical office that requires each of these functions but does not have space for four separate devices. In addition, purchasing an all-in-one unit is usually more economical than purchasing the machines separately.

CHECKPOINT LO 10.2

What is the function of an operating system?

LO 10.3 Computer Software Components

The hardware of a computer is the structure or "home" for the information that may be contained within it. But like a house without furniture or appliances, you cannot accomplish tasks with a computer without appropriate software. Software is a program or set of instructions that tells the computer what to do. There are two types of computer software and both are equally important; the operating system and software applications that run on the operating system. The operating system controls the computer's operation. Application software allows you to perform specific tasks, such as scheduling appointments.

Operating System When you turn on a computer, the operating system starts working, providing instructions that the computer needs to function. Examples of operating system software include Microsoft Windows XP, Windows Vista, Windows 7, and Linux. Most computers come pre-installed with Windows XP, Windows Vista, or Windows 7.

Operating system software is sometimes referred to as the platform for the system. Most medical practices use IBM-compatible personal computers, which are most suitable for businesses that use computers primarily to manipulate words. Apple computers are used by businesses such as advertising agencies or design firms that are extensively involved in graphics, visual images, or desktop publishing.

Windows This operating system employs a graphical user interface (GUI). With a GUI, menu choices are identified by **icons,** or graphic symbols (Figure 10–7). For example, the "Lock Computer" command is identified by a button with a tiny illustration of a padlock on it. To lock the computer, move the pointing device until the arrow is on the padlock icon and then click the button.

Windows operating systems are easy to learn because you do not have to remember commands, you simply need to recognize the icon to know what command will be performed if the icon is clicked with the mouse. If you don't remember what task will be performed by an icon, you can place your mouse over the icon and its task description will be revealed for a short time. Another benefit of Windows is that it is a **multitasking** system—users can run two or more software programs simultaneously. You could, for example, enter patient information into a **database,** which is a collection of records created and stored on the computer, while a word processing program is running in the background. Using the minimize button in the top right corner of the window allows the program to pull the window into the task bar at the bottom of the screen and allows the program to continue to run while you work in another application open on the monitor screen. To open the previous application onto the screen, simply click on the program or document in the task bar.

Windows XP Windows XP is the operating system used by most medical offices utilizing IBM and IBM-compatible computers.

Windows Vista, the program that followed XP, included built-in accessibility settings and programs that are great for persons with visual or hearing loss and problems using their arms or hands. Those with reasoning and cognitive issues also found improvements in the following areas:

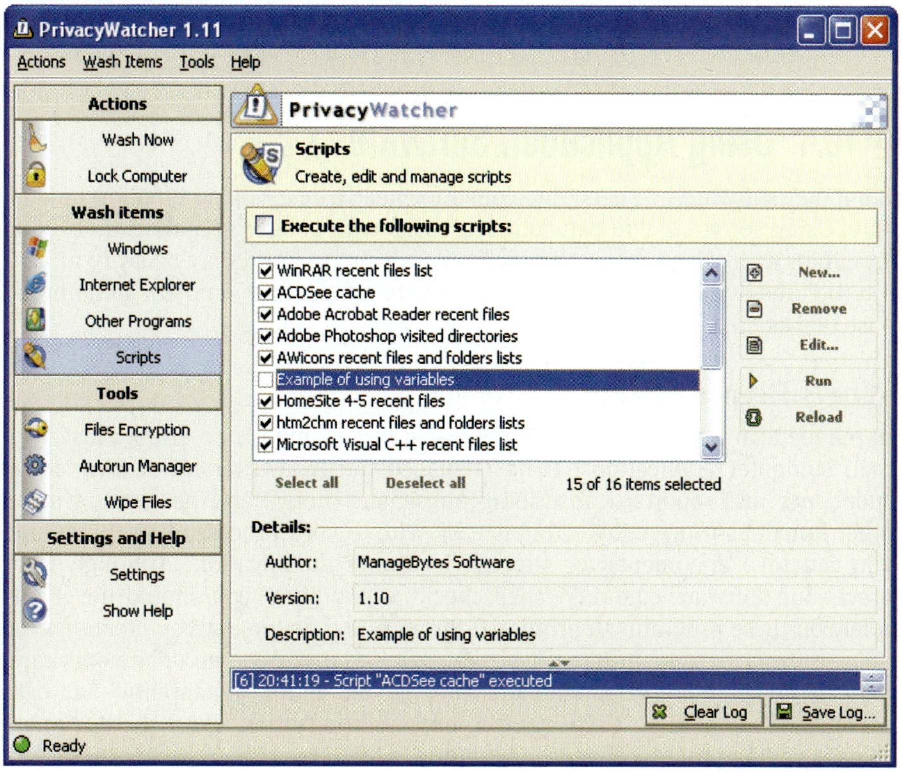

icon
A pictorial image on a computer screen; a graphic symbol that identifies a menu choice.

multitasking
Running two or more computer software programs simultaneously.

database
A collection of records created and stored on a computer.

figure 10–7

Computer screen showing the GUI (graphical user interface) symbols or icons such as the lock in the upper left column to show the user how to lock the computer.

- Settings and tools that make it easier to see, hear, and use the computer.
- Improved magnification capabilities.
- Improved text-to-speech capabilities.
- Speech recognition that lets the user interact with the computer by voice.

Windows Vista, however, did not become popular in office settings, and XP remained the operating system of choice. Windows 7 is the newest OS from Microsoft and, although its popularity in personal computers is growing, it remains to be seen whether it will replace XP in the business and/or medical office setting.

Applications   Most of the software sold in stores is application software. An example of application software is Microsoft® Office. Microsoft® Office includes word processing software (Word), presentation software (PowerPoint), spreadsheets (Excel), database management (Access), and desktop publishing (Publisher). Medical Manager®, Medware®, Medasis, and MediSoft™ are practice management applications. These software packages are specifically designed to meet the needs of a medical practice. Standard computer practice management software packages can be purchased. In addition, custom-made computer practice management software can be designed to meet the needs of a particular practice. Word processing, database, and accounting software are just a few examples of the wide variety of applications available.

optical character recognition (OCR)

The process or technology of reading data in printed form by a device that scans and identifies characters.

Optical Character Recognition   **Optical character recognition** or **OCR** software enables the conversion of images to text so they can be treated like any other type of word processing document. An OCR system includes an optical scanner for reading text and state-of-the-art software for analyzing images. An OCR system enables an article or patient file to be fed into an optical scanner, where it is transferred into an electronic computer file. It is then possible to manipulate and edit the file using a word processor.

CHECKPOINT
LO 10.3

What makes GUI programs more user-friendly than traditional operating systems?

LO 10.4 Using Application Software

Computer software has been developed for nearly every office function imaginable. Using software, you can complete tasks with greater speed, accuracy, and ease than with a manual system. Learning a new program may be scary at first, but the time it takes will allow you to be very efficient in completing computer-based tasks.

Word Processing

In the medical office, as in any office, word processing is one of the most common computer applications. It has replaced the typewriter for writing correspondence and reports, transcribing physicians' notes, and performing many other functions. Correcting errors is easy with a word processing program, and you can save documents for later retrieval and modification. Although word processing software contains "spell check" capabilities, you should never rely solely on these programs to proofread for you. Any document you create for the office reflects on you and the physician. Edit and proofread all documents carefully for spelling and grammatical errors, as well as for "readability" and ease of understanding. If possible, have someone else also proofread the document prior to sending it.

Time is also saved because instead of typing multiple documents, templates may be created and modified for individual patients, or mail merge may be used to simply insert the correct patient information within the document for a selection of patients chosen automatically with a few clicks of the mouse.

Procedure 10–1 at the end of the chapter outlines the method used to create a document using word processing software.

Database Management

A database is a collection of records created and stored on a computer. In a medical office, databases are used to store patient records such as billing information, medical chart data, and insurance company facts. These records can be sorted and retrieved in many ways and for a variety of purposes. You may be asked to find, add to, or modify information in a database. For example, you might use a database to determine all the patients covered by a particular insurance plan.

Accounting and Billing

Accounting and billing software is extremely useful in the medical office. It enables you to perform many tasks, including tracking patients' accounts, creating billing statements, submitting insurance claims, preparing financial reports, and maintaining tax records. (You will learn more about billing and accounting functions in Chapters 17 and 21.)

Appointment Scheduling

Instead of writing in an appointment book, you can use software to schedule appointments. Some scheduling packages allow you to enter patient preferences, such as day of the week and time, and then to list available appointments based on that information. If the office system is on a network, scheduling software is particularly valuable because more than one user can access the appointment schedule at a time.

Electronic Transactions

Using a computer equipped with a modem and communications software, you can perform several types of electronic transactions. This technology enables you to send and receive information instantaneously rather than waiting the days or weeks required for regular mail. Common electronic transactions include sending insurance claims and researching and communicating with insurance carriers, businesses, and other offices, including sending medical records in seconds.

Sending Insurance Claims Today, except in the smallest of medical offices, insurance claims are submitted electronically directly or via a clearinghouse from the medical office to an insurance company. This procedure enables claims to be processed quickly and efficiently. (Chapter 17 discusses health insurance billing procedures.)

Communicating The ability to communicate and share information with others is important in many medical offices. This communication may take place through electronic mail, online services, and the Internet. The upcoming Practice Readiness section gives valuable ideas for saving time online.

Another increasingly popular communication tool, particularly for larger offices, is the office Web site. Medical Web sites can generate more new patients than paper advertising. Additionally, within the Web site, doctors can include patient education material, newsletters, and other patient-related information Often there is a link available so that patients can e-mail the medical office personnel to ask questions and find out other pertinent nonprotected health

information. Your assistance in creating and updating the Web site may also be required.

electronic mail (e-mail)
Any transmissions that are physically moved from one location to another through the use of magnetic tape, disk, compact disc media, or any other form of digital or electronic technology.

Electronic Mail   Commonly known as e-mail, **electronic mail** is a method of sending and receiving messages almost instantly through a digital network. Through e-mail, it is possible to communicate with others in your own office, across town, or on the other side of the world. Unlike regular mail, e-mail operates in real time.

As the use of e-mail has increased, e-mail etiquette rules designed especially for Internet use have become important. E-mail etiquette has become increasingly important and is established when a practice creates a written e-mail policy spelling out the "dos" and "don'ts" concerning the use of the company's e-mail system. The implementation of e-mail etiquette rules can be monitored by using e-mail management software and response tools. Professional organizations such as the American Medical Informatics Association and Health E-mail (a nonprofit physician outreach program) have established policies relating to e-mail. Larger offices with Information Systems departments audit e-mail and Internet site usage. It is important to remember that while using the office computer system, no Internet site you access, nor e-mail you send is private; it belongs to the office and they have the right to monitor and even limit the access you have to the computer system.

Managing E-mail   E-mail management can be helpful in a medical office. Here are several management tools that you can use:

- Regularly check your office e-mail and empty any unwanted e-mails.
- If there is e-mail that you cannot identify, do not open it. All computers, especially computers in the office setting, should have up-to-date antivirus software running; however, you should always be very cautious of unsolicited e-mails.
- Set up subfolders for e-mails that have to be kept for an indefinite period of time.
- Set time limits for deleting or retaining messages.
- Save all e-mail responses that contain protected health information (PHI). See the Practice Readiness feature regarding PHI and e-mail.

Online Services   These services, known as servers, provide a means for health-care professionals to communicate with one another. Most online services contain forums that offer information and discussion groups focusing on a wide range of medical topics. Health-care workers can learn about the latest medical research and technology or exchange ideas with others in their field. In addition, some online services provide access to medical databases such as MEDLINE®, created by the National Library of Medicine. Users can search MEDLINE® for records and abstracts from thousands of medical journals from around the world.

Internet
A global network of computers.

Internet   The **Internet** is a global network of computers. Through the Internet, you can communicate with millions of computer users around the world. E-health or medical information and products are easy to access worldwide through the use of the Internet. Many large medical facilities, universities, and other organizations—such as the National Institutes of Health (NIH) and the Centers for Disease Control and Prevention (CDC)—provide medical resources, databases, and other information on the Internet. Users can visit Internet sites to find multimedia textbooks, presentations, and links to other related sites on the Internet. Table 10–1 describes some popular medical resources available on the Internet.

Protected Health Information and E-Mail

HIPAA law requires that all transactions containing protected health information be protected. Consider the following guidelines when sending e-mail within a medical practice:

1. Do not send e-mail containing protected health information without specific written authorization from the patient.

2. Always check the patient's medical record and the computer system for any special instructions for contacting the patient through e-mail. Follow all

patient requests. When in doubt, do not send an e-mail. Check with the office manager or supervisor.

3. Maintain virus protection to guard your computer system against viruses, which commonly infect a computer system through e-mail.

Search engines are specialized Web sites that search other Web sites for information. The user connects with the search engine and indicates a topic of interest. Typically, a box is provided for the topic and then the user selects a box marked "Go." The search engine electronically searches for the information requested and lists many different Web site link options for the user. Examples of popular search engines include Google™ and Yahoo!®. Remember, that although these sites are frequently used for both personal and professional reasons, you should not be on any site for personal purposes while you are at the office.

Research

The advent of CD-ROM and DVD-ROM technology has revolutionized the world of research and education. Not only can an immense amount of information

table 10–1

Medical Resources on the Internet

ORGANIZATION	WEB ADDRESS	DESCRIPTION
American Medical Association	www.ama-assn.org	News announcements and press releases; articles from *JAMA* and other AMA journals; links to other medicine-related Internet sites
eMedicineHealth	www.emedicinehealth.com	Health resource center where you can learn about health issues and the latest treatments available
MedlinePlus®	http://medlineplus.gov	A service of the U.S. National Library of Medicine and NIH; site includes current health news, medical encyclopedia, and directories for doctors, dentists, and hospitals
National Institutes of Health	www.nih.gov	Medical news and current events; press releases; biomedical information about health issues; scientific resources; links to Internet sites of related government agencies
National Library of Medicine	www.nlm.nih.gov	Internet site for world's largest biomedical library; research and development activities; connections to online medical information services
New England Journal of Medicine	http://content.nejm.org	Articles and abstracts; archives of past issues
Virtual Hospital	http://radiology.uiowa.edu	Information on a variety of health issues, medical resources, tutorials, and multimedia textbooks
WebMD Health®	www.webmd.com	Trustworthy, credible, and timely health information written by experts in medicine, journalism, and health communications

Working Efficiently Online

In the computerized medical office, there is a modem or a T1 or T3 telecommunications line for sending e-mail and transferring files electronically. The modem or "T-line" may also be used to access various online services and the Internet, a global network of computers. If your office is not yet computerized, there are likely plans to become computerized in the future. You may even be asked to help choose an online service or Internet provider for the office.

These services, known as *Internet service providers (ISPs)*, allow access to a network of servers that provides a means for health-care professionals to communicate with one another.

Choosing an Online Service

Compare several services for the following features:

- The speed and accessibility of services. A cable modem or DSL through the phone line has faster speeds for communicating information than a regular phone line service. Plus these services are always on and do not interfere with the telephone service at the facility.

- Free trial membership. Many services offer a free 1-month membership to try out the service. The trial periods enable office staff members to test several services to determine which one best suits their needs.

- Local access telephone number. Make sure the service provides an access number within the local dialing area of the office. If it does not, the office will be charged long-distance telephone rates each time someone goes online. These fees are separate from the online service's rates and can add up quickly.

- Extra fees. Although access to most of the information found in online services is included in the membership fee, some providers charge extra for premium or extended services. If you want to read or print out the full text of an article in a medical journal, for example, some providers charge an additional fee. Make sure you consider these extra fees when comparing costs of online services.

- Availability of health-care information. Some online services provide discussion groups (commonly known as chat rooms) and resources that would be useful to the medical office. Other services may not offer as much relevant information. By comparing several services, you can determine which service best meets the needs of the practice.

Sending and Receiving E-Mail

When using e-mail, follow these guidelines to manage your online time efficiently.

- Use computerized address books. As part of the e-mail system, most services provide an online address book in which you can store frequently used e-mail addresses. Instead of wasting time searching for an e-mail address in a standard card file, you simply click on the person's name in the address book and the mail is automatically sent to that person. You can also use the address book to send the same e-mail message to several people at once. If one message is being sent to several people, you can BCC (blind carbon copy) the other recipients. By using BCC, you are protecting the privacy of other recipients' e-mail addresses.

To use BCC effectively, insert your own e-mail address in the TO box. In the BCC box, enter the e-mail addresses of the people you wish to receive the e-mail. Each recipient will see only your name and e-mail address and no one else's, thus protecting the privacy of each person's e-mail address. In some cases, a group of people within an office or organization need to be updated. In this case, the privacy of BCC is not necessary and you may instead use the "Reply to All" feature as a shortcut. You can also create a group name such as "Medicare Billers" that contains the names and e-mail addresses of these billers in your office. When an e-mail needs to go to all of them, instead of inserting each address separately (and possibly skipping someone), you would choose only "Medicare Billers" and all the addresses would be inserted automatically.

- After sending an e-mail, watch for any alert that the message did not go through. If an alert appears, check the address again and resend the e-mail.

Doing Research

Although a great deal of valuable information can be found through online services and the Internet, searching for this information can be time-consuming. The following tips are provided to make the most of your online time.

- Use the "Favorites" feature. Keep a list of favorite places, or sites that you visit frequently.

- Refine your searches. Searching for *arthritis,* for example, might produce hundreds of references that you would have to read through to determine their relevance. Narrowing your search to *juvenile rheumatoid arthritis,* on the other hand, would produce fewer references but would provide more exact matches.

- Download files. *Download* means to transfer a file to the hard disk. Instead of reading through information while you are online, download the files and later retrieve them or print them to read later.

be contained on one compact disc, but CD-ROMs and DVDs usually provide additional information in the form of videos and sound (see Figure 10–5). A CD-ROM encyclopedia, for example, might also provide spoken pronunciations of medical terms. This type of software may help patients—especially children—understand the human body as well as various medical conditions.

Software Training

Software programs may seem quite complex. Most people need a period of training before they feel comfortable using the application. Several methods of training—some from outside sources and some provided by the software manufacturer—are available.

Classes   Many computer vendors offer training classes for the software packages they sell. In addition, community colleges and high schools sometimes offer adult education classes for a variety of applications, including word processing and communications. These classes may be offered for the beginner, intermediate, or advanced levels.

Tutorials   Many software packages come with a **tutorial,** which is a small program designed to give users an overall picture of the product and its functions. The tutorial usually provides a step-by-step walk-through and exercises in which you can try out your newly acquired knowledge.

tutorial
A small program included in a software package designed to give users an overall picture of the product and its functions.

Documentation   Nearly all software manufacturers provide some type of documentation with their programs. Documentation is usually in the form of written instruction manuals or online help that is accessed from within the program.

Manuals   Some manuals provide detailed information on software operation and may include an index and sections on troubleshooting and commonly asked questions. Other manuals may simply give installation instructions and brief information on program basics. This type of manual may refer users to the software's online help.

Online Help   In most software applications, users access the online help screen by clicking on a "Help" button or by pressing a certain function key, such as "F1." The online help usually provides a "Contents" section in which you can browse for topics. An index, in which you can search for key words, is also provided.

Technical Support   A software company's technical support service is designed to assist you with problems that go beyond the scope of the user's guide or manual. A call to technical support is important when you encounter a problem that cannot be solved by simple problem-solving techniques. By calling a toll-free number, you can access a knowledgeable team who will listen to the description of the problem and suggest solutions over the phone.
Before calling technical support:

- Check the system for errors to the best of your ability.
- Check your manual for answers. Ask your supervisor for assistance.
- Have the software registration number available.
- Be prepared to follow the instructions of the technical support personnel.
- Allow uninterrupted time to spend on the phone with the technical support person.
- Plan to call from a location that gives ready access to the computer with the problem.

Technical support is also helpful when you are upgrading software. Some software companies automatically notify their customers of available upgrades. The technical support service is always a good source of information regarding the latest products and their applications.

CHECKPOINT

LO 10.4

Which software application do you feel will be the most helpful in the medical office? Explain your answer.

LO 10.5 Selecting and Upgrading Computer Equipment

Most medical offices are computerized. If the decision is made to upgrade the system, you may be a part of the decision-making process in selecting equipment. As an administrative medical assistant who will be using the system, you may be asked for your input in selecting software, adding a network, or choosing a vendor.

The first step for helping in the selection process is to learn as much as you can about hardware and software. You can get information by taking an introductory computer class at an adult school or community college; by reading computer magazines or books; or by talking to coworkers and other medical officer personnel who use computers.

Upgrading the Office System

Computer hardware is changing and improving at such a rapid pace that a system seems to become outdated almost as soon as it is purchased. In addition, more advanced software is introduced every day, and this software requires more advanced hardware to run. Consequently, an office system purchased only a year or two ago may need to be upgraded. Sometimes an upgrade simply requires replacement or addition of certain components. For instance, a laser printer can take the place of an ink-jet printer, or a CD-ROM drive can be updated to include a CD burner. In other cases, such a solution is not possible or cost-effective, so an entirely new system must be purchased.

Selecting Software

After a decision is made regarding the type of software needed, such as medical billing and accounting program, a specific product must be chosen. To make an informed decision, you may read software reviews in computer magazines or trade publications. Most offices find it most helpful to speak with other offices in the area and find out what packages they are using; get a "reference" on available packages prior to purchase. Remember that when purchasing or upgrading both hardware and software, ensure the two you choose are compatible and will be able to grow with your practice and its expanding needs.

Adding a Network

There are several advantages to adding a network to the computer system in a medical office. A computer network enables users to share software programs and files and allows more than one person to work on the same patient's information at one time. While you are working on a patient's insurance claim, for example, another administrative medical assistant might be inputting billing information. Some medical offices are virtually paperless. They use a highly sophisticated network with a notebook or desktop computer in every examination room. Doctors input information into patients' computerized charts. If a doctor is in her office and a patient is waiting, a staff member at the front desk sends an e-mail message to the doctor's desktop computer, and a beep sounds as an alert. Networks also allow large medical facilities to communicate with employees via

e-mail. For instance, an internal memo about changes in office policies may be sent by e-mail to all employees.

Virtual Private Networks

When a group of two or more computer systems are linked together, it is known as a network system. Local-area networks are called **LAN**s. The computers in this system are geographically close together (for example, in the same building). Wide-area networks are known as **WAN**s. The computers in this network are farther apart and are connected by telephone lines. Virtual private networks, known as **VPN**s, are used to connect two or more computer systems. They are also constructed using public telephone lines. They use the Internet as the medium for transporting data. VPNs use encryption and other security methods to ensure that only authorized users can access the network. This type of network makes it possible for physicians to access patient records in a secure manner from a variety of locations.

Choosing a Vendor

When purchasing computer equipment, you should look for a reputable vendor who not only offers a reasonable price but, most important, also provides training, service, and technical support. A first step might be to check with personnel in other medical offices that use a computer system. Find out which dealer they use and if they are satisfied with the system, salespeople, and support. You can also ask dealers for names of references—medical offices that have purchased systems from them. It is a good idea to get cost estimates from at least three vendors, and it is preferable to buy all hardware components from the same vendor.

Choosing an EHR Software

There are multiple advantages to electronic medical records: They don't get "lost in an office," are not misfiled, and are easily readable, and information is always located in the same area regardless of who filed it. This sounds simple and perfect, right? Not so fast.

There are many types of medical record software packages out there and most are not compatible with each other. Large practices may have specially created packages that work perfectly for them, but they don't "communicate" with practices outside of their network. Programs for an internist many not have all of the options required for a specialty practice such as neurology or cardiology. Those in the practice choosing the package must also be constantly aware of the need for exceptional privacy and security safeguards to meet HIPAA safety and security requirements.

When choosing EHR software, talk to other practices with electronic records, preferably practices of the same or similar specialties and size as yours. What do they like about their system? What do they dislike? Talk to the software vendors. Tell them *exactly* what you are looking for in software capabilities and make sure your needs are met. Do you need the ability to "tweak" a program and do you have the ability to do so, or is it simply a template where you "fill in the blanks"? Is it compatible with the electronic billing program you have in place? Never make such an important decision for a practice quickly or without a lot of research, keeping in mind where the practice wants to be in 5 or 10 years and whether this software will allow for the type of growth projected.

LAN
Abbreviation for local area network.

WAN
Abbreviation for wide-area networks.

VPN
Abbreviation for virtual private networks, which are used to connect two or more computer systems.

● ● ● ●

Choosing and updating a computer system is a huge undertaking. Why is it important to anticipate how the practice is going to grow and change when making a decision on a new computer hardware or software purchase or upgrade?

CHECKPOINT
LO 10.5

LO 10.6 Security in the Computerized Office

Although security measures are important in any office, they are especially important in a computerized medical office. Great care must be taken to safeguard confidential files, make backup copies on a regular basis, and prevent system contamination. HIPAA law requires that privacy and security procedures

Confidentiality and the Medical Office Computer

The use of computers is widespread within the typical medical practice. Though the computer is valuable for many administrative functions, it also can be a risk in terms of patient privacy and HIPAA compliance. You must follow special safeguards for computers in order to protect the patient's privacy.

1. Computers are typically placed in or near the patient reception area. Keep the computer screen positioned so that it is not visible to unauthorized personnel or patients. Screensavers can be used to minimize the amount of time any information is visible on the screen.

2. Always log off the computer whenever you are leaving the area. If the computer is specifically for your use (such as in your office), you may instead lock the computer in your absence as only you have the password to unlock it.

3. All computers should automatically log the user off after a period of no activity. The computer should require that all users must reenter their password to regain access after an idle period.

4. Always keep your computer username and password confidential. Change your password often, using a variety of numbers, symbols, and both lower- and uppercase letters.

5. The office should utilize practice management software, which can track users and follow their activity within a computer system. If your practice does not have this type of software package, suggest that it be purchased.

6. Formal policies should be developed for every practice regarding the transfer and acceptance of outside protected health information. When using any computer system, always follow practice policy to assure that protected health information is being transferred in a secure and compliant manner.

---

are in place to prevent the misuse of protected health information. These procedures also must ensure confidentiality.

Safeguarding Confidential Files

electronic media
Any information stored on a computer storage device.

Much of the information collected in a medical office is confidential. Just as with paper records, confidential information stored as **electronic media** on the computer is covered by HIPAA privacy laws and should be accessible only to authorized personnel. Two common ways to provide security in a computerized office are to employ passwords and to install an activity-monitoring system.

Passwords   In many hospitals and physicians' offices, each employee who is allowed access to computerized patient files is given a password. The employee must enter the password into the computer when using the files. Access codes or passwords only allow the user into approved areas according to the individual's job description. If you are given a password, do not divulge it to anyone. If an employee leaves or is fired, the user account should be deleted. When you choose a password, do not use common ones such as your birthday.

Activity-Monitoring Systems   In conjunction with passwords, most health-care facilities use a computer system that monitors user activity. Whenever someone accesses computer records, the system automatically keeps track of the user's name and the files that have been viewed or modified. In this way, problems or security breaches can be traced back to specific employees. This is also important if a patient requests an audit trail of who has accessed her medical record, as she is allowed to do through HIPAA.

Preventing System Contamination

Another important security issue in the computerized medical office is computer viruses. Computer viruses are programs written specifically to contaminate the hard disk by damaging or destroying data.

Viruses can be passed from computer to computer through shared diskettes that have been infected. Computer viruses can also be spread through infected files retrieved from online services, the Internet, e-mails, and electronic bulletin boards. Several software programs are available to detect and correct computer viruses. Most are fairly inexpensive but provide an invaluable service.

Antivirus Software and Firewalls Chances are there are hundreds of security vulnerabilities awaiting your computer's system. You need to be concerned about everything on your computer from the operating system to the software applications. **Antivirus software** provides protection for your computer. It scans your system for viruses automatically and manually. If it finds a virus, it either destroys it automatically or alerts the user to respond by "cleaning" the file, thus destroying it. Antivirus software responds to spammers (persons that abuse e-mails by sending them in mass without permission). Many times spammers send malicious e-mails and files. If you do not know who sent you the e-mail, it is best not to open the file. Once a virus software is chosen, it is important to remember to obtain the periodic updates that will respond to new threats as they arise.

Firewalls (barriers to keep destructive forces away from your computer) are another security protection. Firewalls are helpful in putting a stop to offensive Internet sites and potential computer hackers (a person that can get inside of a computer—legally or illegally—and do anything) who are trying to gain access to your computer.

antivirus software
Provides protection for the computer. It scans the system for viruses automatically and manually. If it finds a virus, it either destroys it automatically or alerts the user to respond by "cleaning" the file, thus destroying it.

firewall
A system that protects a computer network from unauthorized access by users on its own network or another network such as the Internet.

● ● ●

Why is it important that you not share your password with anyone?

CHECKPOINT
LO 10.6

LO 10.7 Computer System Care and Maintenance

Like a car, a computer needs routine care and maintenance to stay in sound condition. The computer user's manual outlines the steps required. Also, a good general rule is not to eat or drink near the computer. Crumbs and spilled liquids can damage the system components and storage devices.

Disk Cleanup and Disk Defragmentation

Disk cleanup is a computer maintenance utility designed to free up space on your computer by getting rid of un-necessary files that are on your hard drive. It compresses old files, deletes temporary Internet files, and sends some files to the recycle bin. Microsoft Windows already has this capability included in its package.

Disk defragmentation physically organizes the contents of your hard disk drive to store pieces of each file closely. This also frees up space on your computer as well. Fragmentation occurs when the operating system cannot or will not allocate contiguous (adjacent) space to store a complete file as a unit.

disk cleanup
A computer maintenance utility designed to free up disk space on a computer user's hard drive.

disk defragmentation
A computer program designed to increase access speed by rearranging files stored on a disk to occupy contiguous storage locations, a technique commonly known as defragmenting.

System Unit

The system unit should be placed in a well-ventilated location, with nothing blocking the fan in the back of the cabinet. To keep the system's delicate circuitry from being damaged by an electrical power surge, you should use a power strip with a surge protector. You plug the computer into the power strip and then plug the power strip into the electrical outlet.

Monitor

A **screen saver** automatically changes the monitor display after short intervals of inactivity to protect the monitor screen (and remove potentially "private"

screen saver
A program that automatically changes the monitor display at short intervals or constantly shows moving images to prevent burn-in of images on the computer screen.

information from view). All Windows® operating systems come equipped with screen savers. A wide variety of screen savers are also available as separate software packages. Adding a screen cover to a monitor will protect the monitor.

To protect their screens, many monitors "power down" after a certain period of inactivity. If no one uses the computer for 30 minutes, for example, the monitor screen goes blank. To resume using the computer after the screen saver has been activated or the monitor has powered down, simply touch any key or move the mouse.

Printer

Maintenance of a printer generally consists of replacing the ink cartridge, or toner cartridge. When the cartridge needs to be changed, the ink on your print-outs becomes very light and colors become faded. Replacement is usually a simple process, described in the printer manual.

Information Storage Devices

Jump drives, CD-ROMs, DVDs, diskettes, jump drives, and magnetic tapes are highly sensitive devices. Even a small scratch may cause permanent damage or make it impossible to retrieve data. To avoid problems, handle and store disks and tapes properly.

Jump Drives Jump drives are connected to the computer through a USB port (Figure 10–8). This port should be protected when the drive is not attached to the computer, so be certain to put the cap back on the drive when you are transporting the drive to another location.

CD-ROMs and DVDs Figure 10–9 shows the proper way to handle a CD or DVD. When you pick it up, touch only the edges or the edge and the hole in the center. CDs and DVDs should be stored in the clear plastic case in which they are packaged, sometimes called a jewel case. If a CD or DVD becomes dusty or smudged with fingerprints, clean it by rubbing it gently with a soft cloth. Always rub from the center to the outside. *Never* rub in a circular motion.

Magnetic Tapes Magnetic tapes should be treated much the same as you would treat audiotapes. They should be stored in a relatively cool, dry place, away from magnetic fields.

Computer Disaster Recovery Plan

When any business is dependent on computer technology for daily functioning, a computer disaster recovery plan for the business must be in place (Figure 10–10, p. 240). A recovery plan offers a possible solution if the primary computer system should fail or "crash," making all information on the hard drive unavailable.

In a medical practice, it is important to discuss the computer disaster recovery plan with the staff so that everyone knows the part they will play if the computer system fails. As devices, systems, and networks become more complex, there are simply more things that can go wrong. As a result, computer disaster recovery plans have become more important and more sophisticated.

figure 10–8

A jump drive is a small portable storage device that attaches to the USB port and can store and move 16 gigabytes or more of electronic data.

A computer disaster recovery plan will vary from practice to practice. However, all plans should include these elements:

1. **Minimizing damage to equipment.** Automatic warnings are built into computer systems to indicate when a fatal error has occurred. Warnings also provide direction to help prevent loss of information and minimize damage to the computer equipment.

2. **Retrieving information.** A backup computer system should copy all of the information in the primary computer system every day. If the main system fails, this backup system will allow all the information to be retrieved and not permanently lost.

   This backup system can either be automated or manual. An example of an automated system is a second computer, networked to the first, to which information is regularly backed up in the event the primary computer system fails. With this type of backup, the operation of the office can continue while the primary system is repaired or replaced. If the practice does not have a second computer system available for backup, a daily backup may be done to tape drives. These drives are then stored away from the office in a fireproof, waterproof storage area where they would be available to restore the office information in case of a computer crash or hard drive failure. An example of a manual backup system, which is less useful, is a handwritten list of patients and the procedures performed each day. This type of system, of course, would not be practical if patient medical records are stored on the computer.

3. **Protecting protected health information.** Even during an office emergency, such as a computer failure, health-care professionals are still required to carefully guard the privacy of the patient records. If an electronic or manual backup system is implemented, safeguards to protect patient information must still be observed.

Disaster recovery planning can be purchased as a software application or a service, or it can be developed within an organization.

figure 10–9
When handling a CD-ROM, be careful not to touch the flat surface of the disc.

● ● ●

There are multiple storage devices available for today's computer. Why would it be important to utilize one of these alternate devices in addition to the hard drive contained within the computer?

CHECKPOINT
LO 10.7

LO 10.8 Medicine and Computers of Tomorrow

Computers are evolving at such a rapid pace that it is virtually impossible to predict the changes that will take place even in the next few years. Some important new technologies, however, have already been introduced in the medical office and will be improved in the near future. Telemedicine, Electronic Health Records, and speech recognition technology are only three examples of new computer technologies. Undoubtedly, more will be explored and developed every year.

figure 10–10

It is important to back up computer files and store them properly.

Telemedicine

Telemedicine refers to the use of telecommunications to transmit video images of patient information. These images are already used to provide medical support to physicians caring for patients in rural areas. The use of telemedicine and advancements in computer technology allow medical practices to quickly access vast amounts of current medical information.

Electronic Health Records

Some of the latest buzz in health care is the evolution of the electronic medical record—medical records stored in electronic format within a computer system. Many offices are embracing this technology. The next step, a dream of many health-care professionals, is the electronic health record. The idea behind electronic health records is to make patients' medical records, regardless of where they are stored, accessible to any health-care provider in the United States and possibly someday, even throughout the world. We will be discussing EHR in more detail in Chapter 15.

Speech Recognition Technology

Speech recognition technology enables the computer to comprehend and interpret spoken words through the use of a specialty software program. The user simply speaks into a microphone instead of inputting information with a keyboard or a scanner. Because every human voice is different, however, and the English language is vast and complex, this technology is difficult to perfect. As speech recognition technology becomes more advanced, more accurate, and less expensive, it will most likely gain widespread acceptance. It has a great deal of potential, including the ability to virtually eliminate the need for administrative medical assistants and transcriptionists to transcribe physicians' notes. There are a variety of speech recognition software applications available for use.

CHECKPOINT
LO 10.8

Video conferencing and computers with cameras are commonplace today. How might these advances, combined with telemedicine, change health care in the future?

LO 10.9 Office Communication Equipment

As the administrative medical assistant, you will not be using x-ray machines, blood pressure monitors, and stethoscopes, but you will be using business communication equipment, including telephones, facsimile machines, computers, and photocopiers on a daily basis. Part of your responsibilities as the administrative medical assistant is maintaining and operating the medical office's communication and administrative equipment.

Today's technology allows almost instantaneous communication of information throughout the world. This instant communication can be critical for the fast-paced medical profession, where information often translates to the need for immediate treatment, sometimes in life-threatening situations. Communicating effectively within a medical office can be as vital as providing the correct treatment to patients—and often ensures that they receive such treatment (Figure 10–11).

Telephone Systems and Call Handling

The telephone is one of the most important pieces of communication equipment in a medical practice. Not only is it the primary instrument patients use to communicate with the office, but it is also the primary means of communication with other doctors, hospitals, laboratories, and other businesses important to the practice.

Multiple Lines   Most medical offices have a telephone system that includes several telephones and telephone lines. The key telephone system with multiple buttons is a traditional choice in medical practices. This system has multiple lines for incoming or outgoing calls, an intercom line, and a button for putting a call on hold. The larger a practice becomes, the greater will be the demand on the phone system. Larger practices may need complex communications systems to handle all their needs.

A traditional setup in busy practices was to use a switchboard, a device that receives all calls, which the receptionist then routes to the appropriate telephone extensions.

A common alternative to the switchboard and receptionist is an automated voice response unit. This unit will automatically answer all calls. A recorded voice offers the caller various options for routing of the call. Once the caller selects an option, the system automatically routes the call to another detailed menu or to the designated department. The use of automated voice response units can provide greater flexibility for the medical staff, as well as enhanced service to the patient. However, the use of more than three menu levels may be frustrating to callers.

Advances in technology and the advent of the Internet is dramatically changing voice communications. Technologies such as Voice over Internet Protocol (VoIP), also known as Internet Voice, allow the integration of voice and data communication through the computer and Internet service. This means that medical practices have the option of using the computer for Internet access and telephone conversations.

Voice Mail   An automated menu is often used in conjunction with **voice mail,** which is a form of an answering machine. If the office is closed or the person the patient is calling is on the phone or away from her desk, the call is answered by voice mail, and the caller can leave a message. The advantage of a voice-mail system is that the caller never receives a busy signal. Another advantage to voice mail is that it is a more secure system, in that each person on a voice mail system has a unique password to retrieve only her messages.

Patient Courtesy Phone   Some offices have a patient courtesy phone, which provides an outside local phone line strictly for the use of patients. Traditionally this phone was used by patients to call for transportation or to contact their work or family as needed. The increasing availability of cell phones has decreased the need for these courtesy phones.

Cellular (Cell) Phones—Personal and Business Use   The use of cell phones has become widespread. Today, physicians, medical practice employees, and patients may all be carrying their own personal cell phones into the medical office. With all that technology available at the touch of a button, it is

figure 10–11

Most medical offices today rely on many up-to-date pieces of communication equipment.

voice mail

An advanced digital form of an answering machine that allows a caller to leave a message if the phone line or person requested is busy.

important to address cell phone etiquette. Generally, it is appropriate to turn off all personal cell phones inside a physician's office. The patient should be shown this consideration by the physician and staff, and the physician and staff deserve the same consideration from the patient. Many medical facilities post signs near their doors to ask the public to turn off all cell phones before entering. Cell phone calls from outside the practice are usually an interruption to the communication among the physician, the staff, and the patient. More importantly, the use of personal cell phones can interfere with other electronic equipment that may be functioning inside the medical practice.

However, cell phones do play an important part in the business functioning of the medical office. Physicians may use a cell phone to respond quickly to a message from staff or a hospital. Office staff may use personal cell phones in the case of emergency, when traditional phone systems fail. Some medical practices will even issue a cell phone to key employees who conduct business for the practice outside the office. In addition, patients may use their cell phones to call for a taxi after a doctor's appointment. If your medical office allows staff and patients to use cell phones, make sure that it is clearly noted in which areas cell phone use is permitted and for employees, when use of personal cell phones is permitted. In most offices personal cell phone usage is only permitted during break times. At other times the phones are to be turned off or left in vibrate mode.

Leaving a Message on an Answering Machine or Fax Machine On occasion, it is also important to leave a message on a patient's answering machine or to send a message to a patient's fax machine. It is now required by HIPAA law that you use these pieces of equipment correctly and confidentially. The goal in calling a patient's home is to speak directly to the patient or to leave a message with enough information to get the patient to call back. It is unlawful to disclose confidential patient information to anyone but the patient. The law requires that you guard the patient's private medical information to avoid charges of **abuse** which is defined as a practice or behavior that is not indicative of sound medical or fiscal practice. HIPAA requires that you *never* leave any information if unsure of the phone number dialed. You cannot ensure that only the intended patient will receive any message left on an answering machine or sent to a fax machine. To guard the patient's privacy, *state only the following information:*

- The name of the individual for whom the message is intended
- The date and time of the call
- The name of your office or practice
- Your name as the contact person in the office
- The phone number of your office or practice
- The hours the office is open for a return call
- A request for a return call

A word of caution: leave the name of the practice only if it does not reveal the purpose of the call. For instance, you would not state, "Please call Tiffany Heath from the STD Clinic." An example of an appropriate substitute would be, "Please call Tiffany Heath from Dr. Greene's office at 413-788-0001, Monday through Friday between 8 AM and 5 PM."

Alternatively, when patients sign the Office Privacy Agreement, a release may be added inquiring if messages may be left on an answering machine, voice mail, or e-mail and if there are any restrictions to that permission. A second release may also be added asking if there is anyone at the home number to whom the office may speak and the relationship of that person to the patient. Each release should be signed and dated by the patient. Be especially careful

abuse
A practice or behavior that is not indicative of, or in line with, sound medical or fiscal practices.

of the hasty and indiscriminate use of fax machines. HIPAA law states that the best format for the use of fax machines involves the use of a locked mailbox at the receiver's end of the transmission. Further information regarding this topic can be accessed on the HIPAA Web site, www.hipaa.org. Most in home users, however, will not have this feature. It is always best to simply fax a request containing only the same information that was recommended for answering machines.

Answering Machine   Many offices use a telephone answering machine or voice mail system to answer calls after office hours, on weekends and holidays, and when the office is closed for any reason. A typical recorded message announces that the office is closed and states when it will reopen. The message must always indicate how the caller can reach the doctor or the covering physician in an emergency.

An answering machine may be programmed simply to play a taped message from the office, or it may also record messages from callers. If callers can leave messages, you have a responsibility to check the answering machine to retrieve them at the start of each day and after the lunch break. See Chapter 11 for more information regarding using the office answering machine.

Answering Service   Instead of, or in addition to, an answering machine, many medical offices use an answering service. Unlike answering machines, answering services provide people to answer the telephone. They take messages and communicate them to the physician on call. The doctor on call is responsible for handling emergencies that may occur when the office is closed, such as at night or on weekends or holidays. Upon receiving a message from the answering service, the doctor calls the patient.

Chapter 11 will give you further information regarding interactions with the office answering service.

Some answering services specialize in medical practices. These medical specialty services will ask the medical practice to give specific directives for the triage of calls. Always ask any service for references before signing a contract for service.

Pagers (Beepers)

Physicians often need to be reached when they are out of the office, so many carry pagers. Pagers or beepers are small electronic devices that give a signal to indicate that someone is trying to reach the physician. Today, this is considered an outdated technology, but it is still used in some areas.

Technology of Paging   Each paging device is assigned a telephone number. When someone calls that number, the pager picks up the signal and beeps, buzzes, or vibrates to indicate that a call has been made. Most pagers have a window that displays the caller's telephone number so that the person who has been paged can return the call promptly. Certain models display a short message. Some pagers store telephone numbers so that the receiver can return several calls without having to write down the numbers.

Paging a Physician   Most messages can wait until the physician calls in, or returns, to the office but if the physician is required immediately, then paging is an efficient way to contact the physician. The paging process is as simple as making a telephone call.

1. A list of pager numbers for each physician in the practice should be kept in a prominent place in the office, such as by the main switchboard. Look up the telephone number for the pager of the physician you need to contact.
2. Dial the telephone number for the pager.

Routing Calls Through an Automated Menu

An automated menu system answers calls for you and separates requests into categories so that you can deal with them efficiently. You may already be familiar with automated menus, which are widely used by many large businesses. Someone who calls an automated system hears a recorded message identifying the business. The message gives the caller a list of options from which to choose to identify the purpose of the call. The caller selects an option by pressing the corresponding button on her push-button telephone. If she does not have a push-button telephone, her call is automatically routed so that she can talk to a person or leave a voice-mail message. For example, the voice response may say, "Press or say 1 for appointments. Press or say 2 for prescription renewals. Press or say 3 for referrals."

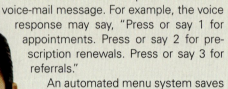

An automated menu system saves time and effort in a medical office because no one has to answer calls as they come in but can instead reserve a block of time in which to listen and respond to messages. This system allows you to complete other work without interruption. Though this practice is efficient, this is a policy that needs to be approved by the office manager and physicians within the practice before it is implemented. Some medical offices maintain a philosophy that places the importance of a patient's call above all other office tasks. Always ask the supervisor in charge of the office how you should use the automated system.

To set up an automated system, you need to plan specific categories from which patients can choose. Categories may include but are not limited to (1) making and changing appointments, (2) asking billing questions, (3) asking medical questions of the doctors or nurses, (4) reporting patient emergencies, and (5) receiving calls from another doctor's office.

When the caller presses the code for a patient emergency, the call rings in the office because it needs to be answered immediately. You or other staff members can respond to calls in the other categories in a timely fashion. Questions for doctors or nurses can be routed immediately to the appropriate voice mail, bypassing the front office lines.

Automated menu systems can be set up by telephone vendors listed in the Yellow Pages. When choosing an automated telephone system, be careful that callers do not become lost in the process. It is a good idea to set up a system that allows callers to return easily to the main menu and contain an option to request a live operator. Be sure to build in an option for rotary dial telephones as well. Following up on messages promptly also will help callers feel comfortable with your voice-mail system, so you should check for messages at least once every hour.

3. You will hear the telephone ringing and the call picked up. Listen for a high-pitched tone, which signals the connection between the telephone and the pager.

4. To operate most pagers, you need to dial the telephone number you wish the physician to call, followed by the pound sign (#), located below the number 9 on a push-button telephone. (Some pager services have an operator and work much like an answering service. Give the operator a message, and the operator will contact the physician.)

5. Listen for a beep or a series of beeps signaling that the page has been transmitted. Then hang up the phone. The physician will call the number at his earliest convenience.

Interactive Pagers (I-Pagers)

interactive pager
A pager designed for two-way communication. The pager screen displays a printed message and allows the receiver to respond by way of a mini keyboard.

Interactive pagers (I-pagers) are designed for two-way communication. The individual carrying the pager is paged in much the same way as the traditional pager. The pager can be set on "Audio" or "Vibrate" to alert the carrier that a message is coming in. However, the interactive pager screen displays a printed message and allows the physician to respond by way of a mini keyboard.

The physician can respond to the printed page by typing a return message (done by typing with the thumbs) responding back in real time to the office. The operator of the office computer and the physician enter into a conversation

much like e-mail or an Internet chat room. Many problems can be handled quickly and efficiently in this manner. Additionally, because the I-pager can function silently, the physician can communicate with her office while in a meeting without disturbing others.

Each interactive pager has its own wireless Internet address. The user types in the receiving party's e-mail address and creates a message on a monitor screen. The interactive pager will give the sender the status of his message by indicating on the screen when the message has been sent, received, or read.

I-pagers can communicate with other I-pagers as well. I-pagers also have broadcast capability, meaning the sender can send to more than one receiver at a time. For this reason, practices with multiple physicians may find them very helpful.

Interactive pagers can also send messages to traditional telephones. The message is typed into the pager, and the system "calls" the telephone number. When answered, an electronic-type voice reads the message to the individual who has answered.

Facsimile (Fax) Machines

Critical documents, such as laboratory reports or patient records, often need to be sent immediately to locations outside the office. Documents can be sent by means of a facsimile machine, or fax machine. A fax machine scans each page, translates it into electronic impulses, and transmits those impulses over the telephone line. When they are received by another fax machine, they are converted into an exact copy of the original document.

A fax machine in a medical office should have its own telephone line. A separate line ensures that transmission of incoming and outgoing faxes will not be interrupted and that the machine will not tie up a needed telephone line when sending or receiving information. The fax machine should be located in an area with limited traffic and should not be placed in areas where patients or visitors have access. Faxes frequently contain PHI and documents being sent and received should only be accessible by those with a "medical need to know."

Benefits of Faxing   A fax machine can send an exact copy of a document within minutes. The cost for sending a fax is the same as for making a telephone call to that location. For a short document, this is usually less expensive than an overnight mail service.

When faxing documents such as ultrasounds and other types of documents that are heat-sensitive, it is appropriate to copy them on separate sheets of paper and then fax the copies to the appropriate persons, as these documents can be easily destroyed by the use of a fax machine.

Many fax machines have a copier function and can be used as an extra copy machine. This function may only be useful, however, if the machine uses plain paper. The telephone for the fax may also be used as an extra extension for outgoing calls, if needed. Procedure 10–2 at the end of the chapter details the correct steps for using a facsimile (fax) machine.

Thermal Paper versus Plain Paper   Older fax machines print on rolls of specially treated paper called electrothermal, or thermal, paper, which reacts to heat and electricity. Because thermal paper tends to fade over time, documents received on thermal paper should be photocopied. Most models of fax machines use plain copy paper today, so copying faxes is no longer necessary. Information is transferred to the plain paper by either a carbon ribbon or a laser beam.

To maintain confidentiality, a fax should always be sent with a cover sheet. The minimum information on the cover sheet should include the name, telephone and fax numbers of the sender and receiver, date of transmission

TOTAL CARE CLINIC, PC

542 East Park Blvd
Funton, XY 12345-6789
Tel: 521-234-0001   Fax: 421-234-0002
www.totalcareclinic.org

Matthew Rodriguez, MD   Ravi Patel, MD   John Fredricks, MD

Sara Kacharski, DO   Linda F. Wiley, PA-C

FACSIMILE COVER SHEET

Date: _____

To: _____   From: _____

Fax #: _____   Fax #: _____

# of pages (including this cover sheet): _____

Message: _____
_____
_____
_____
_____

The information contained in this transmission is privileged and confidential, intended only for the use of the individual or entity named above. If the reader of this message is not the intended recipient, you are hereby notified that any dissemination, distribution, or copying of this communication is strictly prohibited. If you have received this transmission in error, do not read. Please immediately respond to the sender that you have received this communication in error and then destroy or delete it. Thank you.

figure 10–12

Every document that is sent by fax transmission should include a cover sheet, which provides details about the transmission. A disclaimer should be included on the cover sheet.

and number of pages (including the cover sheet). The cover sheet should also include a disclaimer regarding denial of legal liability on the part of the sender. Figure 10–12 displays an example of a cover sheet. Be sure to follow the manufacturer's directions for use of your particular fax and dial the number carefully to avoid misdialing. Most faxes will print a confirmation message; keep this with the fax as proof of sending. If your office policy includes calling to confirm receipt of fax, be sure to document the name of the person confirming receipt.

Receiving a Fax   Faxes can be received 24 hours a day if the fax machine is turned on and has an adequate supply of paper (Figure 10–13). Newer-model fax machines have memories and can store and receive documents. If the fax machine is not already sending or receiving a fax, the fax telephone rings, or the

machine buzzes briefly, signaling the start of a transmission. The transmission begins shortly thereafter, with the machine printing out the document as it is sent. When completed, the sending fax machine may print a transmission report for the sender that includes the number of pages, the date and time, and the fax number receiving the fax.

Typewriters

Typewriters are used very little in today's medical practice. They may still be used to complete medical forms brought in by patients or sent from an insurance company. These forms can be completed more clearly when the information is typed instead of handwritten but again, most offices use a computer to complete insurance claim forms instead of manually completing them with a typewriter.

Models and Features   Although typewriter models differ in features, all use a standard keyboard. Most typewriters have replaceable cartridge ribbons for printing and a second correction ribbon for corrections.

   Offices utilizing typewriters choose one of two types, electric or electronic. Electronic typewriters can store limited amounts of information for further use, but electric typewriters cannot. Both electric and electronic typewriters provide a selection of features, including, but not limited to, automatic carriage return, automatic centering, self-correction, and changeable typefaces or fonts. Today, most medical practices use computers with word processing software and scanners to create and manipulate word documents.

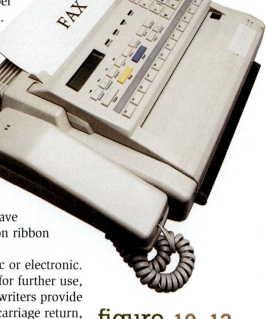

figure 10–13
Receiving a fax.

CHECKPOINT
LO 10.9

● ● ●

Many elderly patients become nervous and hang up when confronted with automated answering programs. How can the office automated answering system be more "user friendly" for these patients?

LO 10.10 Equipment for Administrative Tasks

Using automated administrative equipment enables you to perform a task more easily and quickly than doing it manually. For example, it is much quicker to add a long line of figures with a calculator than it is to do so by hand. Many of the administrative tasks in a medical practice utilize automated equipment allowing you to use your time more efficiently and accomplish more tasks in a shorter period of time.

Photocopiers

A photocopier, also called a copier or copy machine, instantly reproduces office correspondence, forms, bills, patient records, and other documents (Figure 10–14). Photocopiers have virtually made carbon paper extinct in medical offices.

   A photocopier takes a picture of the document it is to reproduce and prints it on plain paper using a heat process. Photocopiers use either liquid or dry toner (ink) and plain paper. Various kinds of paper can be used in the machine, including office stationery and colored paper. Most photocopiers accept different sizes of paper, from the standard 8½- by 11-inch paper to 8½- by 14-inch legal paper and even larger.

   Photocopiers come in many models, from desktop machines for limited use to industrial models for continual heavy use. Because copy machines vary in features and speed, always follow the manufacturer's instructions for use carefully. All styles of machines are available through purchase or lease. Procedure

figure 10-14

You may need to print out hard copies of documents to send to patients, vendors, insurance companies, or other doctors' offices.

10–3 at the end of this chapter describes the correct method for using a photocopier machine. When you have completed your copying task, always remember to remove the original from the copier and take all copies with you. It is also proper office etiquette to select the "clear" button when you are done so that any special features you may have chosen will not affect the task of the next person to use the copier.

If the copier jams, do your best to clear the jam using the Help feature. If you cannot clear the jam, get assistance. Never leave a jammed copier for a coworker to discover later in the day.

Special Features   Copiers offer a wide range of special features. They may collate (assemble sets of multiple pages in order) and staple pages, punch holes, enlarge or reduce images, and produce double-sided copies. Some also can adjust contrast and even track the cost of a job via a specific code input into the machine. Some photocopiers produce both black-and-white or color copies. Some copiers can make transparencies (text and images printed on clear acetate), which physicians often use for presentations. Many of today's copiers are multifunctional. In addition to making paper copies, they have scanning and facsimile capabilities. This allows an office to purchase one piece of equipment and receive the functionality of three separate pieces of equipment.

Most copiers today also have a Help function that displays directions in plain English to fix a paper jam or deal with other routine copier problems. Some copiers are even programmed to indicate that service is needed.

Adding Machines and Calculators

For handling tasks such as patient billing, bank deposits, and payroll, many medical practices depend on adding machines and calculators. There are two basic differences between adding machines and calculators. Adding machines typically require electricity and produce a tape of printed calculations. Calculators are often battery operated and although they have memory to store figures, they produce no paper tape.

Routine Calculations   Both adding machines and calculators are sufficient for most routine office calculations. In addition to basic addition, subtraction, multiplication, and division, many of today's models also calculate percentages and store data.

Checking Your Work   Because it is easy to hit an incorrect key or to key in a number twice when using an adding machine or a calculator, always double-check your work for accuracy.

If the machine produces a paper tape, check the numbers on the tape against the numbers you are adding. The paper tape is especially useful when adding a long series of numbers. Without a printed record, you must perform the same calculations again to make sure the total is correct.

Folding and Inserting Machines

Letter-folding equipment can help minimize the amount of time staff spends preparing large volumes of outgoing mail. Letter folders are also used for creating folded brochures. A medical practice may use folding and inserting machines

for a variety of items, including invoices, news-letters, checks, statements, letters, and flyers.

Lower-end folding equipment requires letters to be fed manually. The speed of this machine is limited to the speed an individual can feed in letters, which is typically about 200 pieces per hour. An automatic feeder is required for faster folding. Letter-folding machines can make many different types of folds, including standard business letter folds (c-fold), accordion folds (z-fold), single folds, right-angle folds, and brochure folds (Figure 10–15). Most machines can fold more than one sheet of paper together, but do not allow stapled pages to be fed and folded.

Many special features are available that may help the processing of mail and brochures. Batch counters and stackers help to prevent a letter-folding machine from folding more sheets than desired. A jogger helps align stacks of paper and dissipates static electricity. Some machines are better designed for certain types of paper, such as glossy or carbonless paper. Inserters are used to insert a folded document into an envelope.

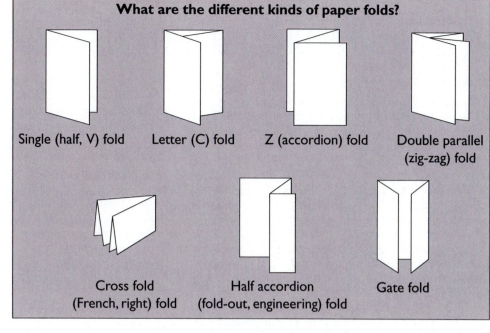

What are the different kinds of paper folds?

Single (half, V) fold   Letter (C) fold   Z (accordion) fold   Double parallel (zig-zag) fold

Cross fold (French, right) fold   Half accordion (fold-out, engineering) fold   Gate fold

figure 10–15

Folding machines can make many different kinds of paper folds.

figure 10–16

The postage meter is a convenient and cost-effective way to apply postage to office correspondence and packages.

Postage Meters

Every medical office uses the U.S. Postal Service. Patient bills, routine correspondence, purchase orders, and payments are just some of the items typically sent by mail. (See Chapter 13 for additional information on creating and mailing correspondence.)

Although some medical offices use stamps, most use a postage meter. A postage meter is a machine that applies postage to an envelope or package, eliminating the need for postage stamps (Figure 10–16). There are often two parts to a postage meter: the meter, which belongs to the post office, and the mailing machine, which the practice can own. The meter actually applies the postage, and the mailing machine (if available) seals the envelope.

Benefits of Using a Postage Meter There are several advantages to using a postage meter. It saves frequent trips to the post office. It also saves money for the office by providing the exact amount of postage needed for each item. Because an office cannot keep every denomination of stamp on hand, you may exceed the minimum required postage when you need to use a combination of stamps.

MEDICAL TRANSCRIPTIONIST

Duties and Skills

A medical transcriptionist creates written medical records for patients based on the physician's dictation or notes (Figure 10–17). Traditionally this was done on a typewriter, but most transcriptionists today utilize a word processing program or template on a computer. To create notes or other documents for the patient record, the transcriptionist listens to an audiocassette or tape bank, located at the hospital or clinic where the physician practices, containing information dictated by the physician. Typical information to be transcribed includes patient history and physical, admission and hospital notes, patient visit notes, physical exams, and so on. While listening to the dictation, the transcriptionist can slow down, speed up, or stop and start the information she is listening to as she types.

The medical transcriptionist must have excellent typing skills and a good command of medical terminology to use and spell the terms accurately. She may need to edit the physician's notes to follow standard English grammar and usage. Sometimes she must also reorganize the physician's comments to create an understandable and easy-to-follow medical record; however, she must never change the meaning of what is being said. After she finishes transcribing the record, she proofreads it carefully.

Educational Requirements

Medical transcriptionists may complete a training program at a 4-year college or university, community college, vocational institute, or adult education center. They receive instruction in medical terminology, anatomy and physiology, pharmaceuticals, laboratory procedures, and medical treatments. Some transcriptionists concentrate on a particular specialty, such as pathology, and acquire specialized training in that area. Medical transcriptionists can become certified if they meet the qualifying standards of the American Association for Medical Transcription.

Workplace Settings

Transcriptionists may work in a variety of settings including physician offices or medical groups, hospital medical records departments, nursing homes, clinics, insurance companies, or a variety of clinic settings. Additionally, transcriptionists may work for medical transcription companies, or be self-employed. With more and more home offices, telecommuting opportunities for medical transcriptionists are increasing and many now work out of their homes.

The Medical Transcriptionist as a Team Member

Depending on where the medical transcriptionist for your office is located, you may see and interact with her on a daily basis or very seldom. If she is in your office, you will work with her daily in completing medical records, possibly answering her questions to verify information contained within the dictation. If she is located off-site, you may seldom see her, with most of your interactions being over the phone. Whichever is the case, she is an integral part of the office health-care team, getting medical records completed in a timely, easily readable and understandable format.

For more information, visit the Web site of the following organization, which is available on the Online Learning Center at: www.mhhe.com/houseradminmedassist.

American Association for Medical Transcription

Many types of postage meters are available, from basic models for a small office to advanced models for large businesses. The latest machines include automatic date setting (important as the date must be current when applying the postage), memory to program a large mailing, and display alerts for low postage (the meter will not work if the postage amount in your account drops too low) or the need for ribbon replacement. Some models can apply postage to parcels without the use of labels or tape. Procedure 10–4 at the end of this chapter describes how to use a postage meter.

Prepaying for Postage   To use a postage meter, you must prepay the postage. You can take your meter to the post office to add postage, or you can use a postage meter service. A service maintains the postal account for you. Although the money in each account is the property of the U.S. Postal Service, the provider manages the account and adds postage to the meter. Postage can also be added to the meter by telephone or by modem, with data sent directly to the meter over the telephone line. The process takes only a few minutes, and the call is often toll-free. Before postage can be added, however, money must be deposited into an account. Keeping the postage account current ensures that all mail is sent on a timely basis. This task may be one of your responsibilities.

On any meter, you can check the amount of postage used and the amount remaining with the touch of a button. On some models, the meter must have $10 or more for the machine to apply postage to an envelope or package.

Postal Scales

Besides the postage meter, a medical practice also needs a postal scale. Postal scales are a good investment because they show both the weight and the amount of postage required. Some postage meters include an electronic scale. If you need a postal scale but one is not available, you can use any scale that weighs in ounces. When using a simple scale, you can then translate the weight into the correct postage by using a current postal rate chart, available from the U.S. Postal Service which cuts down on mail being returned for inadequate postage.

Posting Mail

Before you begin posting mail, make sure the envelope or package is complete, with all materials included. After applying the proper postage, place the postmarked envelope or package in the area of your office designated for mail pickup.

Dictation-Transcription Equipment

Physicians usually do not type their own correspondence, patient records, or other documents. Administrative medical assistants, although not professional medical transcriptionists, may be asked to transcribe recorded words into written text. Using dictation-transcription equipment is the most efficient way to complete this task. *Dictation* is another word for speaking; *transcription* is another word for writing. Together they mean to transform spoken words into written form.

Dictation-transcription equipment has greatly advanced. There are now "starter kits" that are generally for smaller medical offices, as well as more advanced digital dictation and transcription kits. SpeechMikes are great for the physicians. They are lightweight and when the physician speaks, the sounds are more audible to the transcriber. The standard functions of transcription equipment include controls for starting, stopping, reversing and fast-forwarding, volume, tone and speed control, headphones, and a counter.

Larger medical facilities may provide call-in transcription services for the physician. This type of service makes it easy to link to external databases. Doctors can dictate from remote locations and the information can be uploaded to the computer so that the medical assistant can transcribe it.

Voice recognition software is available to provide help to the physician when he or she wants to set up dictation via the computer. There are specialized programs that are provided for medical specialties.

Dictating   Quite often, the physician's handwriting can be confusing. Dictation is a wonderful tool that can keep the physician out of legal trouble caused by an illegible medical record.

figure 10–17

One of the responsibilities of a medical assistant may be to use dictation-transcription equipment.

1. Indicate the date and the type of document being dictated and provide explicit instructions about the document. For example, it is helpful to indicate that the document is a letter and that it is to be produced on office stationery and mailed to a patient.

2. Spell out all names and addresses as well as any unfamiliar terms.

3. Indicate punctuation by saying, for example, "comma" or "begin new paragraph."

4. Speak clearly and slowly. If possible, do not eat or drink when dictating nor dictate while in a noisy environment.

Procedure 10–5 at the end of the chapter outlines the steps to operate a dictation-transcription machine. Whenever you are transcribing, always remember to spell check and proofread the document carefully prior to giving it to the physician for signature. All documents in the office reflect your professionalism and that of the physician and office. Chapter 15 describes the medical transcription process in greater detail.

Check Writers

Medical practice personnel need to write checks to pay for equipment, supplies, and payroll. This common office procedure can be automated by using a check writer, which is a machine that imprints checks. Procedure 10–6 at the end of this chapter details the correct steps for operating a check-writing machine. The safety advantage of using such a machine is that the name of the payee (the person receiving the check) and the amount of the check, once imprinted, cannot be altered. There are numerous check-writing software packages that can assist you, such as QuickBooks, Checksoft, and VersaCheck. After the check is printed, double-check the information on the check for accuracy and submit it to the physician or other authorized person for signature. Without this signature, the check is not a valid negotiable document. You will learn more about banking procedures in Chapter 21.

Voiding a Check   If the information on an imprinted check is incorrect, it cannot be changed. Therefore, you must issue a new check and void the previous one. To void the check, write "VOID" in clear letters across it, or use a VOID stamp with red ink. Then file the check with the office bank records so that the practice's money manager is aware that it has been voided.

Paper Shredders

Paper shredders are quite common in medical practices. A paper shredder, such as the one shown in Figure 10–18, is often used when confidential documents, such as patient records, need to be destroyed. Paper shredders cut documents into tiny pieces to make them unreadable.

The most common type of shredder cuts paper into ribbonlike strips, which differ in width, depending on the model. Other shredders cut the paper in two directions, forming small pieces. Some paper shredders offer additional options, such as an electronic eye that automatically starts the machine when paper is inserted and stops when it is done. Other features available are paper jam detection, automatic reverse, and automatic shutdown when the machine gets too hot.

figure 10–18

As a medical assistant, you may be asked to use a paper shredder to destroy confidential documents that are no longer needed by the practice.

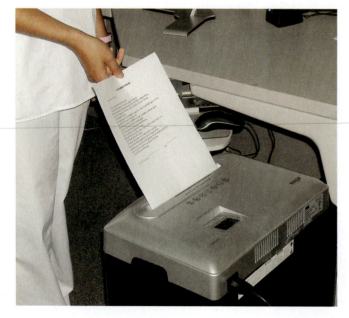

How to Shred Materials A paper shredder is ready to use when it is turned on. To shred a document, insert it into the feed tray at the top of the shredder. The machine feeds the paper through hundreds of knifelike cutters, instantaneously shredding the paper. A basket attached beneath the shredder catches the bits of paper. Different models can accommodate different amounts of paper through the cutters. Shredder baskets must be emptied periodically to allow room for additional shredded paper. Some shredders signal when the basket is full. It is very important not to wear loose-fitting clothing while operating a shredder to avoid accident and personal injury. If a shredder jams, turn it off and unplug it before attempting to remove the jam.

When to Shred Materials Because of the confidential nature of many documents in a medical office, a shredder must be used when destroying any unwanted documents containing PHI. Because of the inability to put shredded documents back together, every office will have a policy regarding when documents are to be shredded. If you are unsure whether or not to shred a document, check with the office manager prior to shredding. Many larger offices utilize external shredding companies for this task. Be sure to use a reputable vendor if your office decides on this option because as the **covered entity** under HIPAA your office is responsible for whoever has access to any PHI from your office.

Microfilm and Microfiche Readers

Microfilm is a roll of film imprinted with information and stored on a reel. Film also can be stored in cartridges to protect the film from being touched. **Microfiche** is film imprinted with information and stored in rectangular sheets. See Figures 10–19 and 10–20.

Although considered to be old technology, the use of microfilm and microfiche is still in use in some medical practices today. Even if your office does not store records on microfilm or microfiche, you may still have a reader because back issues of medical journals and other publications are often available only in these formats.

covered entity
Any organization that transmits health information in an electronic form that is related in any way with a HIPAA-covered entity.

microfilm
A roll of film stored on a reel and imprinted with information on a reduced scale to minimize storage space requirements.

microfiche
Microfilm in rectangular sheets.

figure 10–19

Storing information on microfilm helps reduce the amount of storage space needed by the practice.

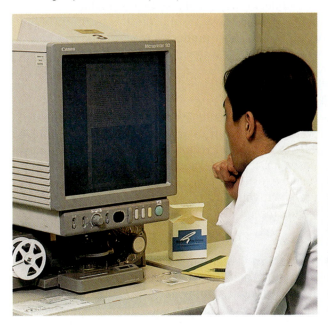

figure 10–20

Special equipment must be used to read text that has been converted to microfiche.

CHECKPOINT
LO 10.10

Explain steps to take when using copier and fax machines to avoid breach of patient confidentiality.

LO 10.11 Purchasing Office Equipment

As a medical assistant, you may be involved in making purchasing decisions for office equipment. For example, the physician or office manager may ask you to investigate whether the practice needs a certain piece of equipment, such as a new photocopier or microfiche reader. To make a sound decision about whether the office will benefit from such a purchase, you will need to conduct thorough research.

Evaluating Office Needs

Research is the first step in evaluating the equipment needs of the medical office. Take note of the equipment the office has available and its performance and shortcomings.

What advantages does a new piece of equipment offer over the current one? Compare the benefits offered by the new product to the capability of the currently used equipment. Many medical magazines review medical office equipment periodically and are good resources to consult in making your purchasing decisions. Go online to shop and compare products, features, and prices. Discuss with the office manager the budget for the equipment under consideration. Consider calling a supplier for more detailed information.

Contacting Suppliers   Put together a list of the features you would like in your new equipment. Then contact suppliers who sell models that offer those features. You can call or e-mail the manufacturer directly to find out the name of a local vendor. Many manufacturers prepare brochures giving information about their products. Request that this information be sent to you.

Go online or look in the Yellow Pages for office supply stores and other companies that sell office equipment. Obtain product and pricing information on each model. For certain equipment, such as photocopiers, a sales representative will come to your office to demonstrate and discuss the product.

Evaluating Warranty Options   Most products come with a warranty. A **warranty** is a contract that guarantees free service and replacement of parts for a certain period, usually 1 year. Warranties are valid only for specified service and repairs. They usually do not cover accidents, vandalism, acts of God (such as damage caused by floods or earthquakes), or mistreatment of the machine. In most cases, warranty repairs must be made at an authorized service center.

If you want more coverage than the warranty allows, consider buying an extended warranty. Extended warranties increase the amount of time that equipment is covered. For expensive pieces of equipment or parts, the additional cost of an extended warranty may be justified.

After you purchase a product, you must fill out the warranty card and mail it to the manufacturer. File the receipt in a safe place in the office where it can easily be retrieved.

Preparing a Recommendation   After you have obtained all the information, you are ready to evaluate it. To compare and contrast the different models, construct a chart. Place the product model names in columns across the top. Down the left side, list factors that will influence the purchase decision: cost, warranty options (including the length of the warranty and the price of an

warranty

A contract that specifies free service and replacement of parts for a piece of equipment during a specified period of time, often a year.

extended warranty), special features, and delivery time. Then fill in the information. This chart will provide an easy-to-use summary of your research.

Finally, analyze the list, and choose the product that will best meet the needs of the office. Meet with the physician or office manager to discuss your recommendation.

Leasing versus Buying Equipment

Once the product has been selected, there is one more decision to make: whether to lease or to buy the item. When buying a product, the purchaser becomes the owner of the product. Owners are free to do with the product anything they choose, which may include selling it to someone else.

For most large pieces of office equipment, such as photocopiers, there is also an option to **lease** the equipment. Leasing, or renting, usually involves an initial charge and a monthly fee. On average, the initial charge is equal to about two monthly payments. The ownership of a leased piece of equipment is retained by the leasing company.

lease
To rent an item or piece of equipment.

Lease Agreement   A lease is for a specified time, after which time the equipment is returned to the seller (Figure 10–21). Some leases allow purchase of the equipment at the end of the rental period for an additional payment. The details of the purchase option are covered in the lease agreement.

Advantages of Leasing   When you lease a product, your office does not own it, but you have several advantages.

1. Leasing allows purchasers to keep more of their money. The initial cost of obtaining the machine is a fraction of the full cost of purchasing it. Therefore, the remainder of the money can earn interest in the bank or be used for other expenses. Leasing is advantageous when you do not have

figure 10–21

Read lease agreements carefully.

Metropolitan Office Systems				Lease Agreement			
Customer (Location)				**Customer (Billing address, if different)**			
Total Care Clinic, PC							
Full Legal Name (Please Print)				Full Legal Name (Please Print)			
342 East Park Blvd							
Address				Address			
Funton	XY	12345-6789					
City	County	State	Zip	City	County	State	Zip
Billing Contact				Phone			
Dealer:							

Quantity	Description: Make, Model, and Serial Number	Quantity	Description: Make, Model, and Serial Number
1	FT 6655 Copier AA3365430358		
1	Sorter A337502010902		
1	Document Feeder A338506		
1	RT 314 Large-capacity Tray		

Minimum Lease Term:	Payment Due:	Amount of Monthly Payment With Sales, Use, and Property Tax:	Advance Payment of $965.56 (Tax Included) by Check #	Documentation Fee
60 Months	__X__ Monthly ___ Quarterly ___ Annually ___ Other: $455.46	$482.78	___ First Month's Rent __X__ First and Last ___ Security Deposit (Without Tax) ___ Other	$ —0—

enough money to buy the equipment but need the services it provides. In addition, leasing allows businesses to update equipment every few years at the end of each lease period. Updating may not be as affordable if you buy equipment.

2. Often the company that leases the product is also responsible for servicing it.

3. In most cases, businesses are able to take lease payments as a tax deduction each year.

Leasing is not always the best solution. It is important to weigh the advantages of leasing against the advantages of buying equipment for your medical practice.

Negotiating Whether you decide to lease or buy equipment, always ask whether there is room for negotiation regarding the price. Many discounts are never extended simply because the customer did not ask. Although some equipment prices are non-negotiable, terms can sometimes be negotiated on more expensive pieces of equipment. Companies that lease office equipment are often flexible in determining the monthly payment. Equipment companies may accept smaller payments in the beginning of the rental or purchase agreement period, and require larger payments near the end.

In a competitive market, some suppliers may match their competitors' prices. When purchasing several pieces of equipment at the same time, a supplier may be able to offer some savings on the total cost of the purchase or provide some service, such as delivery, free of charge.

CHECKPOINT
LO 10.11

What are three advantages of leasing office equipment?

LO 10.12 Maintaining Office Equipment

Office equipment must be regularly maintained to provide high-quality service. Daily or weekly maintenance, such as cleaning the glass on the photocopier or replacing toner, can be performed by the office staff. However, more extensive maintenance should be done by the equipment supplier. Consult the equipment manual for details about the care of each piece of equipment.

Equipment Manuals

The best source of information about maintaining a piece of equipment is the manual that comes with it. This booklet gives basic information about the equipment, including how to set it up, how it works, special features, and problems you may encounter. The information in an equipment manual is extremely valuable. If the manual is lost, call the manufacturer to obtain another one. Equipment manuals should be stored where they can be retrieved easily. Some large pieces of office equipment provide racks or slots on the side of the equipment for storage of the manual.

maintenance contract
A contract that specifies when a piece of equipment will be cleaned, checked for worn parts, and repaired.

service contract
A contract that covers services for equipment that are not included in a standard maintenance contract.

Maintenance and Service Contracts

Equipment suppliers provide standard maintenance contracts when office equipment is purchased. A **maintenance contract** specifies when the equipment will be cleaned, checked for worn parts, and repaired. A standard maintenance contract may include regular checkups as well as emergency repairs.

Some suppliers offer a **service contract,** which covers services that are not included under the standard maintenance agreement. A service contract

Equipment Manual Tips

It is helpful to write the following information on the inside front cover of the equipment manual upon initial setup. If there is a problem with the equipment that requires a maintenance call, this valuable information will be quick and easy to retrieve.

1. The date of purchase or lease

2. The serial number of the equipment

3. The phone number of the company contracted to repair the equipment

may cover emergency repairs not covered under standard maintenance. In some cases, service contracts are combined with maintenance contracts in one document.

It is important to keep track of all maintenance performed on your equipment. Many offices keep a maintenance log, where staff members record the date and purpose of each service call. This log is helpful in identifying whether equipment should be replaced because of the need for frequent servicing.

Troubleshooting

When a piece of equipment stops functioning properly, what is the correct course of action? **Troubleshooting** the problem often allows you to resolve the problem yourself and avoid the cost of a service call, which may or may not be covered by the service contract.

troubleshooting
Trying to determine and correct a problem without having to call a service supplier.

The first step in troubleshooting is to eliminate possible simple causes of a problem. For example, if the equipment is powered by electricity, make sure that it is plugged into a functioning outlet and that it is turned on. Are all doors and other openings in their correct positions? Are all machine connections firmly in place?

If you cannot discover a simple cause for the problem, it is time to test the machine to determine what it is failing to do. In the case of a malfunctioning photocopier, for example, try making a copy and note the response. Write down any error messages the machine provides.

Next, consult the equipment manual. Many manuals devote a section to troubleshooting. If you cannot find the solution after reading the manual, call the manufacturer or the place of purchase for additional assistance over the phone. Be prepared to explain the steps you have already taken toward resolving the problem. If these steps do not result in a resolution of the problem, it is now time for a service call.

Backup Systems

Occasionally, more than one piece of equipment can be affected by a single problem. For example, if the electricity goes off, all electrical equipment will go out at once. To avoid losing important information and records, it is important to have backup systems in place for all equipment, not just the computer system.

Telephones   The use of cell phones in addition to traditional phones offers a backup to communication in the event that phone service is interrupted. Cell phones are also helpful during emergency weather conditions.

Electricity   An emergency generator may supply emergency power for lighting in key hallways and exam rooms. Interior rooms and halls can quickly become very dark and hazardous when the electricity is unexpectedly cut off.

Battery Power   Battery power backup is a key component of security and warning system backups. Audio warning signals sound when it is time to replace the batteries in smoke and security detectors. All batteries should routinely be replaced every six months.

Fire Extinguishers   Fire extinguishers need to be serviced or replaced once a year to ensure maximum performance. The office may choose to contract with a local company to provide this annual maintenance evaluation.

Equipment Inventory

Each piece of equipment is an asset of a business. It is part of the business's net worth and should be listed on the medical practice's balance sheet. Therefore, taking inventory of office equipment provides relevant information for the practice's money manager. It may also indicate whether old equipment is due for replacement.

There are many different ways to take an office equipment inventory. Figure 10–22 shows one example. Many offices use a master inventory sheet to survey all equipment at a glance. The master sheet usually includes such general information as equipment name and purchase price, and the quantity of each type of equipment.

Many offices also keep more detailed information about each individual piece of equipment in a master equipment binder. Often this binder consists of the master inventory sheet in the front with the more detailed sheets about each piece of equipment after it. Detailed information may include the following:

figure 10–22

An equipment inventory sheet includes equipment names and the quantity of each type of equipment.

- Name of the equipment, including the brand name
- Brief description of the equipment
- Model number and registration number
- Date of purchase
- Place of purchase, including contact information
- Estimated life of the product
- Product warranty
- Maintenance and service contracts

EQUIPMENT INVENTORY

ITEM	PURCHASE DATE	PURCHASE PRICE
1. Office oak desk	07/25/10	$295.00
2. Office rolling desk chair	02/19/10	$119.00
3. Office 4-drawer file cabinet	12/21/11	$150.00
4. Office 2-drawer file cabinet	08/05/11	$100.00
5. HYtech Pentium 100 computer	03/10/12	$1150.00
6. HYtech 14-inch monitor	03/10/12	$200.00

All equipment inventories should be updated periodically, particularly when any equipment is replaced. Inventory software packages are becoming more effective in managing your equipment and supplies. Make sure you choose an inventory software package that best fits your needs.

● ● ●

Why is it an asset to the medical practice to be able to troubleshoot equipment issues?

CHECKPOINT
LO 10.12

Procedure 10–1

Creating a Document using Word Processing Software

GOAL   To use a word processing program to create a document

MATERIALS   Computer equipped with a word processing program, printer, document to be created, 8½- by 11-inch paper

METHOD

1. Turn on the computer. Select the word processing program.

2. Use the keyboard to begin entering text into a new document.

3. To edit text, press the arrow keys to move the cursor to the position at which you want to insert or delete characters, and enter the text. Either type directly or use the "Insert" mode to type over and replace existing text.

4. To delete text, position the cursor to the left of the characters to be deleted and press the "Delete" key. Alternatively, place the cursor to the right of the characters to be deleted and press the "Backspace" key (the left-pointing arrow usually found at the top right corner of the keyboard).

5. If you need to move an entire block of text, you must begin by highlighting it. In most Windows-based programs, you first click the mouse at the beginning of the text to be highlighted. Then you hold down the left mouse button, drag the mouse to the end of the block of text, and release your finger from the mouse. The text should now be highlighted. Right click the mouse and choose the button or command for cutting text. Then move the cursor to the place where you want to insert the text, right click the mouse again, and select the button or command for retrieving or pasting text.

6. As you input the document, it is important to save your work every 15 minutes or so. Some programs do this automatically. If yours does not, use the "Save" command or button to save the file. Be sure to save the file again when you have completed the letter.

7. Carefully proofread the document and use the spell checker, correcting any errors in spelling, grammar, or formatting.

8. Print the document using the "Print" command or button.

Procedure 10-2 Using a Facsimile (Fax) Machine

GOAL To correctly prepare and send a fax document, while following all HIPAA guidelines to guard patient confidentiality

MATERIALS Fax machine, fax line, cover sheet with statement of disclaimer, area code and phone number of fax recipient, document to be faxed, telephone line, and telephone

METHOD

cover sheet
A form sent with faxed information providing details about the transmission and disclaimer regarding to faxes received in error.

disclaimer
A statement that denies legal liability or that refutes the authenticity of a claim.

1. Prepare a **cover sheet,** which provides information about the transmission. Cover sheets can vary in appearance but usually include the name, telephone number, and fax number of the sender and the receiver; the number of pages being transmitted; and the date of the transmission. Preprinted cover sheets can be used.

2. All cover sheets must carry a statement of disclaimer to guard the privacy of the patient. A **disclaimer** is a statement of denial of legal liability. A disclaimer should be included on the cover sheet and may read something like the following:

   This fax contains confidential or proprietary information that may be legally privileged. It is intended only for the named recipient(s). If an addressing or transmission error has misdirected the fax, please notify the author by replying to this message. If you are not the named recipient, you are not authorized to use, disclose, distribute, copy, print, or rely on this fax and should immediately shred it.

3. Place all pages of the document, including the cover sheet, either facedown or faceup in the fax machine's sending tray, depending on the directions stamped on the sending tray.

4. If the documents are placed facedown, write the area code and fax number on the back of the last page.

5. Dial the telephone number of the receiving fax machine, using either the telephone attached to the fax machine or the numbers on the fax keyboard. Include the area code for long-distance calls.

6. When using a fax telephone, listen for a high-pitched tone. Then press the "Send" or "Start" button, and hang up the telephone. This step completes the call circuit in older-model fax machines. Your fax is now being sent. Newer fax machines do not require this step.

7. If you use the fax keyboard, press the "Send" or "Start" button after dialing the telephone number. This button will start the call.

8. Watch for the fax machine to make a connection. Often a green light appears as the document feeds through the machine.

9. If the fax machine is not able to make a connection, as when the receiving fax line is busy, it may have a feature that automatically redials the number every few minutes for a specified number of attempts.

10. When a fax has been successfully sent, most fax machines print a confirmation message. When a fax has not been sent, the machine either prints an error message or indicates on the screen that the transmission was unsuccessful.

11. Attach the confirmation or error message to the documents faxed. File appropriately.

12. If required by office policy, the sender should call the recipient to confirm the fax was received.

Procedure 10–3 Using a Photocopier Machine

GOAL To produce copies of documents

MATERIALS Copier machine, copy paper, documents to be copied

METHOD
1. Make sure the machine is turned on and warmed up. It will display a signal when it is ready for copying.
2. Assemble and prepare your materials, removing paper clips, staples, and self-adhesive flags.
3. Place the document to be copied in the automatic feeder tray as directed, or upside down directly on the glass. The feeder tray can accommodate many pages; you may place only one page at a time on the glass. Automatic feeding is a faster process, and you should use it when you wish to collate or staple packets. Page-by-page copying is best if you need to copy a single sheet or to enlarge or reduce the image. To use any special features, such as making double-sided copies or stapling the copies, press a designated button on the machine.
4. Set the machine for the desired paper size.
5. Key in the number of copies you want to make, and press the "Start" button. The copies are made automatically.
6. Press the "Clear" or "Reset" button when your job is finished.
7. If the copier becomes jammed, follow the directions on the machine to locate the problem (for example, there may be multiple pieces of paper stuck inside the printer), and dislodge the jammed paper. Most copy machines will show a diagram of the printer and the location of the problem.

Procedure 10–4 Using a Postage Meter

GOAL To correctly apply postage to an envelope or package for mailing, according to U.S. Postal Service guidelines

MATERIALS Postage meter, addressed envelope or package, postal scale

METHOD
1. Check that there is postage available in the postage meter.
2. Verify the day's date.
3. Check that the postage meter is plugged in and switched on before you proceed
4. Locate the area where the meter registers the date. Many machines have a lid that can be flipped up, with rows of numbers underneath. Months are represented numerically, with the number "1" indicating the month of January, "2" indicating February, and so on. Check that the date is correct. If it is incorrect, change the numbers to the correct date.
5. Make sure that all materials have been included in the envelope or package. Weigh the envelope or package on a postal scale. Standard business envelopes weighing up to 1 oz require the minimum postage (the equivalent of one first-class stamp). Oversize envelopes and packages

require additional postage. A postal scale will indicate the amount of postage required.

6. Key in the postage amount on the meter, and press the button that enters the amount. For amounts over $1, press the "$" sign or the "Enter" button twice.

7. Check that the amount you typed is the correct amount. Envelopes and packages with too little postage will be returned by the U.S. Postal Service. Sending an envelope or package with too much postage is wasteful to the practice.

8. While applying postage to an envelope, hold it flat and right side up (so that you can read the address). Seal the envelope (unless the meter seals it for you). Locate the plate or area where the envelope slides through. This feature is usually near the bottom of the meter. Place the envelope on the left side, and give it a gentle push toward the right. Some models hold the envelope in a stationary position. (If the meter seals the envelope for you, it is especially important that you insert it correctly to allow for sealing.)The meter will grab the envelope and pull it through quickly.

9. For packages, create a postage label to affix to the package. Follow the same procedure for a label as for an envelope. Affix the postmarked label on the package in the upper-right corner.

10. Check that the printed postmark has the correct date and amount and that everything written or stamped on the envelope or package is legible.

Procedure 10–5 Using a Dictation-Transcription Machine

GOAL To correctly use a dictation transcription-machine to convert verbal communication into the written word

MATERIALS Dictation-transcription machine, audiocassette or magnetic tape or disk with the recorded dictation, word processor or computer, and printer

METHOD
1. Assemble all the necessary equipment.

2. Select a transcription tape, cassette, or disk for dictation. Select any transcriptions marked "Urgent" first. If there are none, select the oldest-dated transcription first.

3. Turn on all equipment and adjust it according to personal preference.

4. Prepare the format and style for the selected letter or form.

5. Insert the tape or cassette and rewind.

6. While listening to the transcription tape, cassette, or disk, key in the text.

7. Adjust the speed and volume controls as needed.

8. Proofread and spell-check final document, making any corrections.

9. Print the document for approval and signature.

10. Turn off all equipment. Place the transcription tape, cassette, or disk in the proper storage area.

Procedure 10–6 Using a Check-Writing Machine

GOAL To produce a check using a check-writing machine

MATERIALS Check-writing machine, blank checks, office checkbook or accounting system

METHOD
1. Assemble all equipment.
2. Turn on the check-writing machine.
3. Place a blank check or a sheet of blank checks into the machine.
4. Key in the date, the payee's name, and the payment amount. The check-writing machine imprints the check with this information, perforating it with the payee's name. The perforations are actual little holes in the paper, which prevent anyone from changing the name on the check.
5. Turn off the check-writing machine.
6. A doctor or another authorized person then signs the check.
7. To complete the process, record the check in the office checkbook or accounting system.

Case Study

The new computer system arrives today. Everyone is excited about the changes ahead, but not everyone is certain this is going to be a positive experience.

Krystina, the administrative medical assistant in the front office, can't wait to get started. She knows the new software program is going to streamline her duties by allowing her to enter charges, collect and post copayments, bill insurance claims, and make patient appointments with a few keystrokes or click of a mouse. Krystina is realistic and knows that learning the new system will take some time and work on her part, but she has great faith in the software support team for the new system. She volunteered to be a member of the implementation team choosing the new system and spoke with other offices in the area that used the same software package and support team.

Alicia, the clinical medical assistant is not so sure. She finds change scary and feels that if this new system does everything they say it will, it will be complicated to learn. She is on the run all day with patients now. How is she expected to learn a new system and still keep up with her other duties? After all, for a while, they are going to have to do "double" the work—keep up the manual system and get the new computerized system up and running. What if she makes a horrible mistake and loses data or gets behind in her work because she does not understand the system? Why do things have to change?

PROFESSIONAL READINESS

Growth
Continual striving to improve and learn new material

Thinking Critically

1. Are you more like Krystina or Alicia? What history do you have with new technology that makes you feel the way you do?
2. What advantages of electronic systems are making so many practices realize that conversion is becoming a necessity and not a luxury?
3. Why is it important for an office to continue to use the manual system at the same time that it converts to a computerized system?

1. Using online vendors, cable services, the telephone book and other references, research ISPs (Internet service providers) in your area. Based on services provided, cost, speed, and so on, which ISP would you recommend for a small medical office in your area?

2. Your office is moving soon, and you have been asked to assist in the design of a new automated answering system for the practice. What features would you include in the new system?

1. **[LO10.1]** Which of the following computer types is most commonly found in a medical office?

   a. Supercomputers
   b. Mainframe computers
   c. Personal computers
   d. PDAs
   e. Notebooks

2. **[LO10.2]** All of the following are hardware components of a computer system *except* the

   a. CPU.
   b. modem.
   c. keyboard.
   d. mouse.
   e. printer.

3. **[LO10.4]** Which of the following software packages will assist you in tracking and reporting patient information?

   a. Word Processing
   b. Database management
   c. Billing and accounting
   d. Electronic transfer
   e. Appointment scheduling

4. **[LO10.6]** Which of the following procedures demonstrates HIPAA compliant security measures for the office computer?

   a. Use of passwords
   b. Logging off when leaving computer
   c. Sharing passwords only with trusted coworkers
   d. All of the above
   e. a, b, and c only

5. **[LO10.5]** When a group of two or more computer systems are linked together, it is known as a network system. When this occurs within a building it is known as a LAN which stands for

   a. lateral area network.
   b. legal area network.
   c. logical area network.
   d. local area network.
   e. low-band area network.

6. **[LO10.9]** A fax cover sheet should include which of the following information?

   a. Name/address/phone of sender
   b. Name/address/phone of receiver
   c. Date/fax number/number of pages/disclaimer
   d. b and c only
   e. a, b, and c

7. **[LO10.11]** Diagnosing and attempting to fix an equipment issue prior to calling for service is known as

   a. using a tutorial.
   b. diagnostics.
   c. defragmentation.
   d. troubleshooting.
   e. multitasking.

8. **[LO10.3]** Which of the following is a common operating system for many medical office computers?

   a. Windows XP
   b. Microsoft Office
   c. Encoder Pro
   d. Medisoft
   e. OCR Software

9. **[LO10.7]** Which of the following is not a portable storage device for the computer?

   a. CD-ROM
   b. C drive (hard drive)
   c. Diskette
   d. Jump drive
   e. All of the above are portable drives

10. **[LO10.10]** Which of the following pieces of office equipment will be helpful when preparing to mail the monthly patient billing statements?

    a. An answering machine
    b. Dictation-transcription equipment
    c. Postage meter
    d. Mail merge software
    e. Copy machine

LO 10.1 The supercomputer is the fastest and largest computer and is used for research in medicine and other complex uses. The mainframe computer is normally used by organizations such as government services (Medicaid and Medicare). They process huge quantities of information. Minicomputers are smaller than mainframes but are larger than personal computers. Personal computers are also called microcomputers. They are available as desktops, notebooks, and subnotebooks.

LO 10.2 Hardware comprises the physical components of a computer system, which includes the monitor, keyboard, CPU, and printer.

LO 10.3 Software is a set of instructions, or a program, that tells the computer what to do. The two types of software programs are operating systems and application software.

LO 10.4 There are various kinds of computer software for the medical office. Word processing is the most common application. Medical offices also use software for database management, accounting and billing, scheduling, electronic claims transfer and research.

LO 10.5 The first step in selecting computer equipment for the medical office is to learn as much as you can about hardware and software. Find a reputable vendor that has reasonable costs and make sure you choose software that meets the medical office's needs and the system requirements of the computer.

LO 10.6 Security measures are extremely important in the medical office. Law requires that privacy and security procedures are in place to prevent the misuse of health information.

LO 10.7 A computer needs routine care and maintenance to stay in good condition. The system should be in a well-ventilated area. Use a power surge protector. Your computer monitor's power setting can be set to meet the needs of the health-care facility. Replace printer cartridges as needed. Information storage devices are very sensitive, so be sure to safeguard them.

LO 10.8 Computers are evolving rapidly. New medical technology such as telemedicine and speech recognition is here now and nationwide electronic health records are coming. Your office computer system should be as up-to-date as possible so that you and the office computer system can take advantage of the advances in the medical and technological fields.

LO 10.9 Telephone systems are the primary communication tools in a medical office and include automated answering systems, cell phones, pagers, and interactive pagers. Answering machines and answering services allow messages to be left for medical office staff. Fax machines are used to send documents via electronic transmission.

LO 10.10 Administrative equipment found in the medical office may include any or all of the following: fax machines for transmitting information, photocopiers to make duplicates of documents, postage meters for preparing and applying postage, paper shredders to destroy documents containing PHI, dictation-transcription machines to create readable documents, scanners to create electronic documents, and all-in-one types of equipment (printer, fax, copier) to decrease the amount of equipment required to run an efficient medical office.

LO 10.11 When purchasing office equipment, you must first evaluate the equipment needs of the office and evaluate existing equipment. Next, research options for equipment online and check with area dealers. Create a list of "pros and cons" and prepare a recommendation. After deciding whether the office should purchase or lease major equipment, negotiate for the best price.

LO 10.12 If there is a maintenance and/or service contract, be sure to make appointments for routine maintenance per the contract. Daily care such as wiping glass surfaces and following the manufacturer's recommendations for use and care will keep repair needs to a minimum. Troubleshoot malfunctions by looking for simple causes for malfunction such as unplugged electrical equipment and checking the troubleshooting guide in the equipment manual. This will reduce the need for potentially costly service calls.

medical assisting COMPETENCIES

CAAHEP

IV. C (9) Discuss applications of electronic technology in effective communication

V. C. (14) Discuss the importance of routine maintenance of office equipment

V. P (6) Use office hardware and software to maintain office systems

V. P (9) Perform routine maintenance of office equipment with documentation

ABHES

7. Basic Computer Keyboarding/Computer Concepts

  a. Perform basic keyboarding skills

  b. Identify and properly utilize office machines, computerized systems and medical software

8. Medical Office Business Procedures Management

  a. Perform basic clerical functions

  d. Apply concepts for office procedures

  y. Perform routine maintenance of administrative and clinical equipment

  jj. Perform fundamental writing skills including correct grammar, spelling, and formatting techniques when writing prescriptions, documenting medical records, etc.

  ll. Apply electronic technology

Telecommunications in the Health-Care Setting

Learning Outcomes

After completing Chapter 11, you will be able to:

11.1 Explain the importance of communication skills when using telecommunication devices.

11.2 List and explain the four components of proper telephone etiquette.

11.3 Explain how to properly manage incoming telephone calls.

11.4 Give at least three examples of types of calls an administrative medical assistant might handle versus those the physician would handle.

11.5 List the components that must be included in a complete telephone message.

11.6 Define telephone triage and explain its importance in the medical office.

11.7 Describe the procedure for retrieving calls from an office answering service.

11.8 Outline the preparation required prior to making an outgoing phone call, and the skills used in making the phone call.

11.9 Describe the uses for the other types of telecommunication equipment used in the medical office.

Key Terms

enunciation
etiquette
pitch
pronunciation

telecommunication
    device for the deaf
    (TDD)
telephone triage

Preparation for Certification

RMA (AMT) Exam
- Professional development

CMAS (AMT) Exam
- Communication

CMA (AAMA) Exam
- Incoming calls management criteria
- Monitoring special calls

Introduction ● ● ●

In this chapter, you will learn the key terms and procedures associated with telecommunications in today's medical office. You will demonstrate effective handling of various types of incoming and outgoing calls using proper telephone etiquette, consisting of pronunciation, enunciation, tone, and courtesy.

Most offices have policies and procedures for routing calls coming into the office. You will learn to differentiate the types of calls that you may handle as the administrative medical assistant as well as the calls that should be directed to the clinical medical personnel or the physician. Included in this process is the ability to properly and effectively triage calls so that emergencies are handled correctly. Of equal importance, you will also learn how to take a complete telephone message and how to handle difficult telephone calls, including those from angry patients with complaints and callers who will not identify themselves.

Finally, in addition to using the telephone correctly, you will learn how other communication devices are used in the medical office, including TDDs, fax machines, e-mail, cell phones, and pagers.

LO 11.1 Communicating Effectively with the Telephone

The telephone is an important tool for promoting the positive, professional image of a medical practice. When you answer the telephone, you may be the first contact a person has with the practice. The impression you leave can be either positive or negative. Your job is to ensure that it is positive because first impressions are very often lasting impressions.

Good telephone management leaves callers with a positive impression of you, the physician, and the practice. Poor telephone management can result in bad feelings, misunderstandings, and an unfavorable impression. The telephone image you present should convey the message that the staff is caring, attentive, and helpful. Showing concern for a patient's welfare is a quality that patients rate highly when evaluating health-care professionals. In addition, you must sound professional and knowledgeable when handling telephone calls. Learning and using effective telephone management skills will help keep patients informed and ensure their satisfaction with the medical practice.

Communication Skills

The telephone is a communication and public relations tool that is essential to the operation of the medical office. Good communication skills are important in telephone management—they help to project a positive image and to satisfy the needs and expectations of the patient. Individuals who engage in good and effective communication employ the following communication skills:

- Using tact and sensitivity
- Showing empathy
- Giving respect
- Being genuine
- Displaying openness and friendliness
- Refraining from passing judgment or stereotyping others
- Being supportive
- Asking for clarification and feedback
- Paraphrasing to ensure an understanding of what others are saying
- Being receptive to patients' needs
- Knowing when to speak and when to listen
- Exhibiting a willingness to consider other viewpoints and concerns

As an administrative medical assistant, you can also apply the five Cs of communication to use the telephone effectively:

- Completeness—The message must contain all necessary information.
- Clarity—The message must be legible and free from ambiguity.
- Conciseness—The message must be brief and direct.
- Courtesy—The message must be respectful and considerate of others.
- Cohesiveness—The message must be organized and logical.

CHECKPOINT
LO 11.1

Answering the office phone with, "Dr. Frederick's office, can you hold please?" and immediately putting the caller on hold, without waiting for an answer, is not uncommon today. Why is this inappropriate for a physician's office?

LO 11.2 Using Proper Telephone Etiquette

Using proper telephone **etiquette** means handling all calls politely and professionally using good manners. Confidence in your role of providing quality patient care includes the ability to not only communicate effectively in person, but also on the telephone. Your professionalism and caring attitude must come through the phone to the caller. Following the guidelines listed here will help ensure that this occurs.

etiquette
Good manners.

Your Telephone Voice

Customer service is critical when using the telephone because it is only your voice representing the medical office. It must present your message effectively and professionally. Because you cannot rely on body language or facial expressions to help you communicate over the telephone, it is important to make the most of your telephone voice. Use the following tips to make your voice pleasant and effective.

pitch
The varying highs and lows of your voice.

pronunciation
Saying words correctly.

- Speak directly into the receiver. Otherwise, your voice will be difficult to understand.
- Smile. The smile in your voice will convey your friendliness and willingness to help (Figure 11-1).
- Visualize the caller, and speak directly to that person.
- Convey a friendly and respectful interest in the caller.
- You should sound helpful and alert.
- Use language that is nontechnical and easy to understand. Never use slang.
- Speak at a natural pace, not too quickly or too slowly.
- Use a normal conversational tone.
- Try to vary your pitch while you are talking. **Pitch** is the high or low level of your speech. Varying the pitch of your voice allows you to emphasize words and makes your voice more pleasant to listen to.
- Make the caller feel important.

figure 11-1

Smiling comes through on the phone; patients feel you want to help them.

Pronunciation Proper **pronunciation** (saying words correctly) is one of the most important telephone skills. If you are unsure of the correct pronunciation of

the name of the person on the phone, ask them to repeat it for you. This demonstrates respect for the person and shows him that he has your undivided attention. When clarifying the spelling of a name, verify letters that sound alike by repeating the letter and include a word that begins with that letter. Examples include D as in dog, V as in Victor, M as in Mary, N as in Nancy, and B as in balloon.

enunciation
Clear and distinct speech.

Enunciation Enunciation (clear and distinct speaking) is the opposite of mumbling. Good enunciation helps the person you are speaking to understand you, which is especially important when you are trying to convey medical information.

Speaking clearly over the telephone is very important because the speaker cannot be seen. Correct interpretation of the message is determined by hearing the words precisely. Activities such as chewing gum, eating, or propping the phone between the ear and shoulder hinder proper enunciation. Many offices today provide the administrative medical assistant and/or the receptionist with a wireless headset. These hands-free devices allow you to use your hands freely while on the phone, eliminating the need to hold the phone between your ear and shoulder. See Figure 11–2.

Tone Because you are not face-to-face with the caller, the most important measurements of good telephone communication are voice quality and tone. Always speak with a positive and respectful tone.

Making a Good Impression

In a sense your telephone duties include public relations skills. How you handle telephone calls will have an impact on the public image of the medical practice.

figure 11–2

Administrative medical assistant using a hands-free headset.

Exhibiting Courtesy Using common courtesy is a characteristic of professional office personnel. Courtesy is expressed by projecting an attitude of helpfulness. Always use the person's name during the conversation, and apologize for any errors or delays. When ending the conversation, be sure to ask the caller if there is anything else you can do for him and thank him before hanging up.

Giving Undivided Attention Do not try to answer the telephone while continuing to carry out another task. Before answering the phone, complete any conversations occurring in the office or excuse yourself while you answer the phone. Once you make sure that the call is not for an emergency, ask the caller if you may either put him on hold for a moment or call him back shortly. Detailed instructions relating to putting calls on hold follow below. By interrupting the patient in the office briefly and giving the caller the option as to how he would like his call handled, both patients receive the undivided attention they deserve.

Putting a Call on Hold Although you should try not to put a caller on hold, there will be times when it is unavoidable. Calls may come in on another line, or a situation in the office may prevent you from devoting your full attention to the caller. Sometimes you may have to check a file or ask someone else in the office a question on behalf of the caller. Before putting a call on hold, however, always let the caller state the reason for the call. This step is essential so that you

The Wireless Headset

The wireless headset, also called a hands-free headset, is becoming more and more popular in all offices, including the medical office. It allows the user to speak on the phone, while using her hands to schedule an appointment, look up information on the computer, or locate the physician for an emergency phone call. Because the headset eliminates the need to hold the handset between the ear and shoulder while attempting to multitask it reduces office-related neck, back, and shoulder pain.

One word of caution when using these headsets in the medical office—always keep HIPAA and patient confidentiality in mind if you must walk about the office while on the line with a patient. Anything you say will be heard by anyone within listening range. Although tempting, do not walk around the office while on the phone with a patient unless an emergency demands that you do so.

do not inadvertently put an emergency call on hold. Never answer the phone, "Dr. Appel's office, please hold," and immediately put the call on hold. You must ask permission to put the caller on hold and wait for the response.

The medical office may have a standard procedure for placing a call on hold. Typically, you will ask the caller the purpose of the call, state why you need to place the call on hold, and explain how long you expect the wait to be. Ask the caller if she would like to hold or if she would prefer you to return her call. If she requests a return call, ask her if there is a time that is better for the return call. If she decides to wait on hold and if you cannot end the task at hand quickly, return to the caller every 2 to 3 minutes asking her if she wishes to remain on hold. An excessive wait on hold makes people feel they have been "forgotten" or are "unimportant"; checking in with them and giving options minimizes these negative thoughts and feelings.

If you know you can return to the line shortly, you can put the caller on hold, then attend to the problem. If you need to answer a second call, get the second caller's name and telephone number, and put that call on hold until you have completed the first call. You can then return to the second call.

Handling Difficult Situations   At times it will be impossible to give your undivided attention to a caller because of a pressing issue or emergency in the office. If the call itself is not an emergency one, it is best to ask if you can call back. Explain that you are currently handling an urgent matter, and offer to return the call in a few minutes. Most people will appreciate your honesty. Obtain the caller's name and phone number, taking the time to repeat both to avoid errors. Return the call in a reasonable amount of time, and be sure to apologize for the inconvenience.

Remembering Patients' Names   When patients are recognized by name, they are more likely to have positive feelings about the practice. Using a caller's name during a conversation makes the caller feel important. If you do not recognize a patient's name, it is better to ask, "Has it been some time since you've been in the office?" rather than to ask if the patient has been to the practice before.

Checking for Understanding   When communicating by telephone, you do not have visual signals to convey the caller's feelings and level of understanding of the information you are discussing. If a call is long or complicated, summarize what was said to be sure that both you and the caller understand the information. Ask if the caller has any questions about what you have discussed. If a situation requires a lengthy conversation, it might be best to have the patient come into the office.

Communicating Feelings Whenever information is conveyed over the telephone, feelings are also communicated. When dealing with a caller who is nervous, upset, or angry, try to show empathy (an understanding of the other person's feelings). Communicating with empathy helps the caller feel more positive about the conversation and the medical office.

Ending the Conversation It is not useful to let a conversation run on if you can effectively complete the call sooner. Before hanging up, however, take a few seconds to complete the call so that the caller feels properly cared for and satisfied. You can complete the call by summarizing the important points of the conversation and thanking the caller. Then let the caller hang up first.

Occasionally you will encounter the patient who simply will not hang up. Often these patients are simply lonely and your friendliness and helpfulness eases their loneliness. In this case, you may find that you must politely but firmly explain that another patient (or the physician) needs your assistance and you must complete the call. When you put the receiver down, never slam it—even if the caller has already hung up. Remember that all your actions reflect the professional image of the medical practice. Patients in the reception area may see and hear you when you are talking on the telephone.

CHECKPOINT
LO 11.2

Why is it important that callers receive your undivided attention?

LO 11.3 Managing Incoming Calls

Telephone calls must always be answered promptly, (preferably before the third ring) either by a telephone answering system or by an administrative medical assistant/receptionist answering the phone. Both methods of managing incoming calls are discussed in this chapter. Guidelines are usually addressed in the office policies and procedures manual. If you are in an office where the medical assistant answers the phone, general guidelines state you should greet callers with the office name, followed by your name. This may feel awkward at first, but as a medical professional, it is important that callers always know to whom they are speaking.

No matter how hurried you are, you should be courteous, calm, and pleasant on the telephone. Even though you may answer the phone dozens of times a day, never slur your greeting. Remember to speak (enunciate) clearly. If the caller responds to your greeting by asking if they have reached the correct office or "what did you say your name is?" you are speaking too quickly. If the caller does not give a name, ask for it. Many calls result in pulling the patient's file, so it is important to obtain the correct name and date of birth of the patient. If the caller refuses to give his name, stating it is a personal matter for the physician, follow the office policies and procedures manual to handle this situation. Many physicians refuse to take calls unless they know who called and the reason for the call. If the caller still refuses to give his name, you might suggest he write the physician a letter, marking the envelope as personal and confidential.

A variety of telecommunication systems and devices such as multi-line phones, telecommunication devices for the deaf, and automated answering systems assist in handling incoming calls.

Multiline Phones Most offices today have multiline phones. Although convenient, multiple lines can also be distracting as often another line will ring while you are already assisting a caller. Politely ask the current caller if you may put her on hold briefly. Answer the second call and ask this caller if you may either put him on hold or take his number and return the call. If requested,

place the second caller on hold and return to the first call. Complete the first call. If the first call becomes more time consuming than planned, check in with the second caller again, giving the option of having his call returned instead of remaining on hold. If possible, ask a coworker to take the second call while you complete the first call. Never leave a caller on hold for more than a minute or two without checking back with him as to whether he wishes to remain or hold, leave a message in a voice mailbox (if available), or have his call returned later in the day.

Telecommunication Devices for the Deaf   If your office has a significant number of patients with hearing impairments, it may be equipped with a **telecommunication device for the deaf,** known as a TDD (formerly known as a TTY—teletypewriter). A TDD is a specially designed telephone that looks very much like a laptop with a cradle for the telephone receiver (Figure 11–3). To call the office, the patient places the telephone receiver in the cradle and instead of speaking, types her message using the TDD keyboard. If the office has a TDD, the message will be received in type format (similar to e-mail) on the TDD screen.

   If the office does not have TDD equipment, the message may still be received through the use of a telecommunications relay service (TRS). When a patient utilizes a TRS, a specialty relay operator will receive the patient's written message through TDD equipment and then read the message to you when you answer the office phone. When a relay operator is used, the operator will identify herself as a relay operator for the patient utilizing the service. She will read the typed information from the patient. When the message is completed she will say "go ahead" as your signal that it is your turn to reply. You will reply to the patient via the operator with spoken word, which she will then enter into the TDD device so that the patient can read your reply. You will also use the key terms "*go ahead*" when your message is completed.

   TDD devices are becoming more common in the United States and throughout the world. Keep in mind that keying information takes longer than speaking and be patient with the process. As with text messaging, there are certain abbreviations commonly used with a TDD. Table 11–1 lists some of them for your reference. Procedure 11–1 at the end of the chapter outlines the procedure for using a TDD.

telecommunication device for the deaf (TDD)
Formerly known as a TTY; a specially designed telephone that looks very much like a laptop with a cradle for the telephone receiver.

figure 11–3
Telecommunication device for the deaf.

table 11–1

Common Abbreviations for TDD

ga = go ahead	
sk = stop keying	
sksk = call complete	
q = question	
bec = because	
u = you	
ur = your	
pls = please	
nbr = number	
tmw = tomorrow	
am = morning	
pm = night	

Automated Answering Systems   Many medical offices now utilize automated answering systems to initially answer calls, directing callers to push specific numbered buttons on their touch-tone phones to reach the person or department they are looking for. Although this frees the front office staff from every phone call, do recognize that many patients get frustrated with these automated systems and simply "push a button" to get a live person. Should that occur, you must remain pleasant, courteous, and helpful while directing the patient's call appropriately. Returning patient phone calls relating to messages they leave on these automated answering systems is covered later in this chapter.

Guidelines for Effective Telephone Communication

The following guidelines will help you use the telephone effectively and professionally:

- If answering the phone, do so promptly by the second or third ring. Hold the telephone to your ear, or use a headset to hold the ear piece securely against your ear. Do not cradle the telephone with your shoulder; doing so can cause muscle strain and may cause your voice to sound muffled to the person on the other end of the phone.

- Hold the mouthpiece about an inch away from your mouth and leave one hand free to write with.

- If answering the phone, greet the caller first with the name of the medical office and then with your name. If accepting a call routed by an automated answering system, always identify yourself by name.

- Identify the caller and if your phone does not have caller ID, obtain the phone number she is calling from so you can call her back immediately if the call is unexpectedly disconnected. Demonstrate your willingness to assist the caller by asking, "Mrs. Hernandez, how may I help you?"

- Be courteous, calm, polite (say please and thank you), and pleasant no matter how hurried you are.

- Identify the nature of the call and devote your full attention to the caller. Repeat information as needed to clarify information you are given.

- If the caller must be put on hold, politely ask the caller if you may put them on hold briefly and then return to the call as quickly as possible.
- At the end of the call, say goodbye and use the caller's name, remembering to let the caller be the first to hang up the phone.

Following HIPAA Guidelines

As you learned in Chapter 6, the Health Insurance Portability and Accountability Act (HIPAA) was originally created in 1996 and has additions as recently as April 2006. This act is concerned with the privacy and confidentiality of patient information, including information communicated via the telephone.

In compliance with HIPAA guidelines, all medical providers have standards or written policies that require the following to be in a secure area where no one can see or overhear:

- Medical records
- Clerical forms
- Financial forms and reports
- Computer monitors
- Conversations
- Verbal reports

All employees must comply with the guidelines to safeguard patient information, including when talking on the telephone with a patient. Always be aware of who is within hearing distance of any conversation you are having with or about a patient, as well as the volume of your voice when on the phone.

Health-care providers are allowed to disclose patient information for the purpose of treatment, payment, and health-care operations (known as TPO). Any use of this information outside of these reasons would require a written authorization from the patient. Exceptions include emergency situations or information that is required by governmental agencies for compliance. Follow the guidelines in your office policy and procedures manual for disclosing patient information.

Screening Calls

Part of the responsibility of answering the telephone involves screening calls before you transfer them. Even if an answering system is used you may find you have to screen calls that are directed to you. When dealing with incoming calls, you will encounter a variety of questions and requests from numerous people. Many incoming calls are from patients but you will also receive calls from other people, including attorneys, other physicians, pharmaceutical sales representatives, and other salespeople. You will follow the office's policies and procedures manual for screening calls, but the procedure will remain basically the same whether the calls come directly to you as you answer the phone or if they are directed to you by a telephone answering system. The Practice Readiness section (p. 278) gives some guidelines for screening calls. Procedure 11–2 at the end of this chapter provides you the opportunity to demonstrate how to properly screen and, if necessary, route incoming phone calls.

Routing Calls

In general, there are three types of incoming calls to a medical office: calls dealing mainly with administrative issues, emergency calls that require immediate action by a physician, and calls relating to clinical issues that require the attention of the doctor, nurse, nurse practitioner, physician assistant, or clinical medical assistant.

Calls Handled by the Administrative Medical Assistant The most common calls to a medical office involve administrative and clinical issues. As the administrative medical assistant, you will be able to handle many of these calls yourself. They will concern the following matters:

- Appointments (scheduling, rescheduling, canceling)
- Questions concerning office policies, fees, and hours
- Billing inquiries
- Insurance questions
- Other administrative questions
- X-ray and laboratory reports
- Reports from hospitals regarding a patient's progress
- Reports from patients concerning their progress
- Requests for referrals to other doctors
- Requests for prescription renewals, where prior approval for refills is noted in the chart. If approval for the renewal is not noted in the patient's chart, prior to the renewal you should take the phone call, discuss it with the physician, chart it, and have the physician sign off on the chart. After this is completed, you may call in the prescription renewal to the patient's pharmacy.
- Complaints from patients about administrative matters

Depending on the practice, the office manager or someone in the billing department may handle some administrative calls. If there is a clinical medical assistant or nurse in the practice, they may be the ones to handle the calls regarding lab/x-ray reports, hospital reports, patient progress reports, and prescription refills. The calls you handle may include scheduling appointments, receiving or requesting reports or information, insurance and billing questions, and general inquiries, such as those concerning office hours.

Calls Requiring the Physician's Attention Certain calls will require the physician's personal attention. These include the following:

- Emergency calls
- Calls from other doctors
- Patient requests to discuss test results, particularly abnormal results
- Reports from patients concerning unsatisfactory progress
- Requests for prescription renewals (unless previously authorized on the patient's chart)
- Personal calls

Occasionally the patient may prefer to discuss symptoms only with the doctor. These requests should be honored. Depending on the doctor's preference and availability, you may call the doctor to the telephone to handle calls of this nature as they are received. Otherwise, the calls will be returned when the doctor has time available. As most doctors have a set time, such as a half hour in the late morning or at the end of the day, for returning nonemergency patient calls, you may tell the patient to expect a phone call from the physician at this set time. If the physician does not have a set time for returning phone calls, do not make a commitment as to the time of the return phone call.

Many practices have a nurse practitioner or physician assistant (or both) on staff and they frequently can take calls traditionally reserved for the physician in the past. For example, a nurse practitioner may be able to order a renewal of a regular prescription, provide advice for the care of a sprain, or answer well-baby questions or questions about the side effects of a drug.

understanding of his concerns and possible frustration that an answer does not appear to be "a simple process." No matter what your office policy is, if a patient is dissatisfied, document all appropriate comments and relay the information to the physician or office manager. If a bill has not been paid, ask if there are special circumstances affecting the patient's ability to pay. Always give this information to the physician or office manager.

Requests for Laboratory or Radiology Reports If a patient calls the office requesting test results, pull the patient's chart to see if the report has been received. If it has not, suggest that the patient call back in a day or two. Some offices will call the laboratory or radiology office for the results.

In some offices you may be authorized to give laboratory results by telephone if they are normal, or negative, so the patient does not have to wait for a call back from the physician or for the results to be mailed. Make a note on the patient's chart if you provide any information about test results. If a test result is abnormal, the physician will need to speak with the patient. In such a case tell the patient that the office has received the results and that the physician will call as soon as possible. Then place the patient's chart and the telephone message on the physician's desk.

Questions About Medications One of the most common types of calls from patients involves questions about medication. A patient may ask about using a current prescription or may want to renew an existing prescription.

Prescription Renewals Calls for prescription renewals occur frequently and may come from the patient's pharmacy or from the patient. A pharmacist usually calls to check before dispensing refills if more than a year has passed since the original prescription was written. If the physician has indicated on the patient's chart that renewals are approved, you may authorize the pharmacy to renew a prescription. In any other case, only the physician, PA, or Nurse Practitioner may authorize renewals. If the physician authorizes a renewal, you may be asked to telephone it in to the patient's pharmacy. All renewals must be documented in the patient's medical record, with the date and the name of the person authorizing the renewal and the initials of the person (if different from the person prescribing the medication).

Old Prescriptions Patients may call to ask if they can use a medication that was prescribed for a previous condition. In these instances, recommend that the patient come in for an appointment. Explain why the medication should not be used: it may be old and no longer effective, the current problem may not be the same as the one for which the medication was prescribed, so, the medication

EHR readiness

Billing Inquiries

Patients often call the office with questions about their bills. In a paper-based office, these questions often mean obtaining both the patient's medical record and the separate financial record in order to compare charges incurred and the procedures performed.

Electronic health records simplify the process. Although the medical staff will likely have restricted access to only the patient medical record, the billing, coding, and administrative personnel quite often have access to both the health and billing records so they can compare charges to the documentation in the medical record. Depending on the software program, the user opens either two sessions or two windows within the health record program; one for the medical information and the other for the billing information. The administrative medical assistant may then "toggle" between the two screens, easily comparing information in real time, while speaking with the patient (or insurance company) on the phone.

With the EHR, there is no more time spent searching for paper records; simply open a screen (or two) and obtain the information without ever having to put the patient on hold. Corrections, if necessary, can also be made immediately and if the patient requests, a copy of the correction may be sent to the patient via e-mail for his or her confirmation. This is another time and money saver, as the patient will not have to wait to receive a new bill in the mail nor will the office spend the time and money producing a new paper bill with the necessary postage for mailing.

Working with the Health-Care Team

CERTIFIED PHARMACY TECHNICIAN (CPhT)

Duties and Skills

After receiving the written prescriptions or telephone requests for prescription refills, Certified Pharmacy Technicians (CPhT) verify that the information on the prescription is complete and accurate. In local pharmacies, it is the technician who will call the insurance company to verify benefits and obtain any patient copay or co-insurance requirements. The technician then retrieves, counts, pours, weighs, measures, and if necessary, mixes the medication for the prescription (or script). The prescription label is then prepared and a container for the medication is selected. The label is affixed to the container and the technician prices the medication and files the script. Technicians are also responsible for establishing and maintaining patient profiles in the pharmacy computer and preparation of insurance claim submissions.

In retail pharmacies, technicians may also be responsible for taking inventory of prescription and over-the-counter (OTC) medications as well as assisting in equipment maintenance and managing the pharmacy cash register. Technicians employed in hospital settings are responsible for many of the same duties, although their orders generally come from the patient electronic (or paper) health record. All pharmacy technicians are supervised by the pharmacist under whom they work.

Educational Requirements

Currently, there are no state or federal regulations governing pharmacy technician training programs, but most employers favor technicians who have completed a certificate or associate's degree program from a community or technical college. Pharmacy technicians must be proficient in basic subjects such as math, spelling, and reading. A strong background in chemistry and health education courses including medical terminology, A&P, and pharmaceutical calculations/measurements and drug interactions/poisonings is recommended. Because so many pharmacy duties revolve around a computer today, strong data entry skills are also a plus, as are strong communication and customer service skills. Pharm techs can have no prior record of drug or substance abuse. Voluntary certification is available in each state and once obtained, 20 hours of continuing education is required every two years to maintain certification.

Workplace Settings

Certified pharmacy technicians work in local retail pharmacies, hospitals, and wholesale and online pharmaceutical centers.

For more information visit the Web sites of the following organizations, which are available on the Online Learning Center at www.mhhe.com/houseradminmedassist

Pharmacy Technician Certification Board
American Society of Health-System Pharmacists

---

may not be helpful for the current problem, and using the medication may mask the current condition's symptoms and make a diagnosis difficult.

If the patient does not want to make an appointment, relay the information to the physician, as she will probably want to speak with the patient.

Reports on Symptoms   Sometimes patients call the office about symptoms they wish to discuss with the physician. Here are tips for handling such calls.

- Listen attentively to the patient.
- If the patient is in real distress, try to schedule an appointment that day or as soon as possible. If the physician does not have an opening but the PA or NP does, ask the patient if they would like to see one of them in place of the physician.
- Write down all the patient's symptoms completely, accurately, and immediately. In many instances the physician may be able to suggest simple emergency relief measures that you can relay to the patient. These measures may make the patient comfortable until the time of the appointment.

Progress Reports   Physicians often ask patients to call the office to let them know how a prescribed treatment is working. If a patient has a satisfactory

progress report to make to the doctor, it is not necessary that the patient speak to the physician. It is important that you relay the information to the doctor and log the call in the patient's medical record immediately. You may also be responsible for making routine follow-up calls to patients to verify that they are following treatment instructions.

Requests for Advice Although a patient may ask you for your medical opinion, do not give medical advice of any kind. Explain that you are not trained to make a diagnosis or licensed to prescribe medication. Stress that the patient must see or speak with the physician. If the patient cannot come into the office, assure her that the physician will return the call or that you will call back after discussing the problem with the physician. Occasionally a patient wants to speak only with the physician, not other staff members. You must honor this request.

In some cases the physician may feel that a patient's symptoms warrant immediate attention and will insist on seeing the patient before prescribing any treatment. If the patient refuses to come to the office, note the reason on the chart. Stress to the patient that the physician feels the patient should be seen. Suggest to the patient that should symptoms become worse when the office is not open, he or she should go to a nearby urgent care center or emergency department. For legal reasons, as discussed in Chapter 6, it is important to document such conversations completely in the patient's chart, including the refusal of treatment. It is always appropriate and professional to offer to take a message to have the physician return the call.

Complaints Even when an office provides the highest quality care, complaints still occur. When a patient calls with a complaint, such as a billing error, it is important to listen carefully, without interrupting. Take careful notes of all the details, and read them back to the caller to ensure that you have written them down correctly. Let the caller know the person to whose attention you will bring the complaint and, if possible, when to expect a response.

Always apologize to the caller for any inconvenience the problem may have caused, even if the problem occurred through no fault of the office. Make sure the proper person receives the information about the complaint.

Sometimes a patient who calls with a complaint is angry. Responding to this type of call can be difficult and uncomfortable. You should always stay calm and try to pacify the caller. Follow these guidelines when dealing with an angry caller.

- Listen carefully and acknowledge the patient's anger. By understanding the problem, you will be better able to work toward a solution.
- Remain calm and speak gently and kindly. Do not act superior or talk down to the patient. Do not interrupt the patient. Do not return the anger or blame.
- Let the patient know that you will do your best to correct the problem. This message will convey that you care.
- Take careful notes, and be sure to document the call.
- Do not become defensive.
- Never make promises you cannot keep.
- Follow up promptly on the problem.
- Any time a staff member has a difficult time with a patient, it is important to inform the physician, even when the situation is resolved. Always inform the physician immediately if an angry patient threatens legal action against the office.

Other Calls

Besides calls from patients, a medical office receives many other types of calls. For example, family members and friends of patients may call the physician

at the office. Remember that a patient's information is confidential. HIPAA requires medical providers to obtain authorization from the patient before any information can be disclosed. This is usually in the form of a written authorization, signed by the patient, and indicates what type of information may be given out and to whom.

The use of the office telephone is never appropriate for personal calls for the physician or any other medical staff. The physician will let you know how to handle these calls when they are for him. In addition, personal cell phone use should also be limited to essential calls only as defined in your office manual which will include when and how cell phones may or may not be used in the office.

The following are guidelines for managing calls from attorneys, other physicians, and salespeople and for participating in a conference call.

Attorneys Refer to the procedures listed in your practice's office policy manual regarding how to handle calls from attorneys. Follow the office guidelines closely, and ask the physician or office manager how to proceed if you receive a call that does not fall within the guidelines. Remember, never release any patient information to an outside caller unless the physician has asked you to do so and you have express, written permission from the patient to release the information.

Other Physicians Patients at your practice may be referred to surgeons, specialists, and other physicians for consultations. Other physicians may also refer patients to your practice for consultations. Consequently, you may receive calls from those physicians' offices. Route those calls to the physician if the caller requests that you do so. Always remember to ask if the call is about a medical emergency. Also keep in mind that you may not give out any patient information—even to another physician—unless you have a written, signed release from the patient. The exception to this rule is information requested by physicians to whom you have referred the patient for care. Because of the referral, there is a contract involved for continuity of care. You may release medical information specific to the care that the physician has been asked to provide.

Salespeople As the administrative medical assistant, you will probably be the contact for salespeople, unless the office policy manual states that another staff member should handle this duty. When a salesperson calls requesting an appointment to talk about a new product or equipment, ask her to send you information about the product or equipment and explain that if the physician or staff are interested, you will call her to set up an appointment at a later date. Pharmaceutical sales representatives may want to meet with the physician. Forward such requests to the physician, asking that the physician let you know if he would like you to schedule the appointment. Many physicians see pharmaceutical sales representatives on certain days at certain times and often limit the number of representatives they will see in one day. Make sure you know your office policy.

Conference Calls Periodically, physicians may need to have a conference call with several individuals. Most newer telephone equipment can provide this type of service. The physician, nurse, and administrative medical assistant may need to talk with the insurance company's representative at the same time. Telephone conferencing is an ideal setup in this case.

Additionally, there are services that provide "call-in conferencing." The host will provide a number and the time for you or your physician to call in as a participant. All of the participants are given a code and are asked to identify themselves as they call into the system. The service will ask for an e-mail

address to confirm the information, time, date, and pass codes that will be given to each individual. Search the Internet for more information on free conference calling.

CHECKPOINT
LO 11.4

How would you fill in the two blanks in the following statement? No matter what emotion the patient displays while I am on the phone with him, I must remain _____ and _____ at all times.

LO 11.5 Taking Messages

Always have paper and a pen near the telephone so that you are prepared to write down messages (Figure 11–5). Proper documentation protects the physician if the caller takes legal action. A record of telephone calls should also be included in a patient's file or electronic health record as part of a complete medical history. Because of their importance as part of the patient's legal health record, messages should never be taken on pieces of "scrap paper" which are easily misplaced or accidentally discarded.

Documenting Calls

Documenting telephone calls is essential in a medical office, and several options are available to assist the administrative medical assistant with taking a complete message every time. You can use telephone message pads, a manual telephone log book, or an electronic (computerized) telephone log. Again, remember that many calls (for example, those concerning clinical problems or referrals) and the actions or decisions they lead to need to be documented in patients' charts. Every entry into a patient's chart is considered a legal document; therefore, the information must be accurate and legible. As discussed in Chapter 6, accurate documentation helps guard against lawsuits.

Telephone Message Pads   You can use preprinted telephone message pads, which often come in brightly colored paper, to record the following information:

- Date and time of the call
- Name of the person for whom you took the message
- Caller's name, or the patient's name if different from the caller
- Caller's telephone number (always include the area code and extension, if any)
- A description or an action to be taken, including comments such as "Urgent," "Please call back," "Wants to see you," "Will call back," or "Returned your call"
- The complete message, such as "Dr. Stephenson wants to reschedule the committee meeting."
- Name or initials of the person taking the call

Figure 11–6 shows an example of a completed preprinted telephone message.

The Manual Telephone Log   Some medical offices use spiral-bound, perforated message books with carbonless forms to record messages (Figure 11–7). The top copy, or original, of each message is given to the appropriate person, and a copy is kept in the

figure 11–5

Use one hand or a telephone rest to hold the telephone so that the hand you write with is free to take messages.

TELEPHONE MESSAGE

For: *Linda Wiley*

_____

Patient calling as requested with update. She is feeling much better after

3 days on Abx. Temperature is back to normal. No more sore throat; body aches

and pains are less.

_____

_____

_____

Name of Caller: *Micha Ward*

Name of Patient (if not caller): _____

Date/Time Called: *4/12/2012 @ 11:15 a.m.*

Message Taken by: *Kalisha Roberts*

figure 11–6

Example of a completed telephone message with all items completed.

book for future reference in the event that the original is misplaced or accidentally destroyed.

The Electronic Telephone Log   Some medical offices use an electronic or computer-based system to record messages. The message is keyed in as it is received, creating an automatic backup copy for the office record. A copy of the message can be stored in an electronic record, printed out, or e-mailed as needed.

Tips for Ensuring Accurate Messages   The following suggestions will help you provide accurate documentation for incoming messages:

- Always have a pen and paper on hand.
- Jot down notes as the information is given.
- Verify information, especially the spelling of patient or caller names and the correct spelling of medications.
- Patient DOB (date of birth) if pulling the chart is necessary, in case there are two patients with the same name.
- Verify the correct callback number.
- When taking a phone message for the physician, never make a commitment on behalf of the physician by saying, "I'll have the physician call you." An appropriate response would be, "I will give your message to the physician."

Maintaining Patient Confidentiality

When you are on the phone with a patient discussing confidential information, be aware of the people around you and the volume of your voice when verifying such information. If necessary, move to a private office for such conversations so that patient confidentiality will not be inadvertently breached. When leaving patient messages for the physician containing confidential information, insert the message in a folder marked "Confidential" so it cannot be readily seen by others. Confidential fax information should be handled in the same manner.

CHECKPOINT
LO 11.5

Why is the technique of taking accurate and concise messages so important in a medical practice?

LO 11.6 Telephone Triage

telephone triage
Deciding the nature of a phone call, the proper routing of the call, and the action to take regarding each call.

As more and more practices include physician assistants and nurse practitioners, many physicians delegate much of the routine clinical decision making to these staff members. In these instances, **telephone triage** is used as a process of deciding to whom phone calls should be routed and what necessary action to take. The word *triage* refers to the screening and sorting of emergency incidents. Performing telephone triage correctly is an important skill in the medical office. As the administrative medical assistant in the office, you should learn as much as possible about triage techniques.

Learning the Triage Process

Proper training of office staff is vital in providing safe, sound, and cost-effective medical care over the telephone. An increasing number of medical practices are preparing guidelines for the administrative staff to follow when patients call the office with specific medical problems or questions.

Guidelines are often written for common questions, such as how to deal with sniffles and fevers during cold and flu season or how to make a child with chickenpox more comfortable. As the administrative medical assistant, you must realize, however, that your primary responsibility is to determine whether a caller needs additional medical care or the advice of a licensed medical professional. Remember, you are not licensed to give out medical advice and should not do so. Always keep in mind your scope of practice and never give the impression that you have the training to give out medical advice.

Office guidelines outline the specific information the telephone staff must obtain from the patient. In general, this information is the same type as that obtained during an office visit. It should include the patient's age, symptoms, when the problem began, any remedies attempted, and the patient's level of anxiety about the problem.

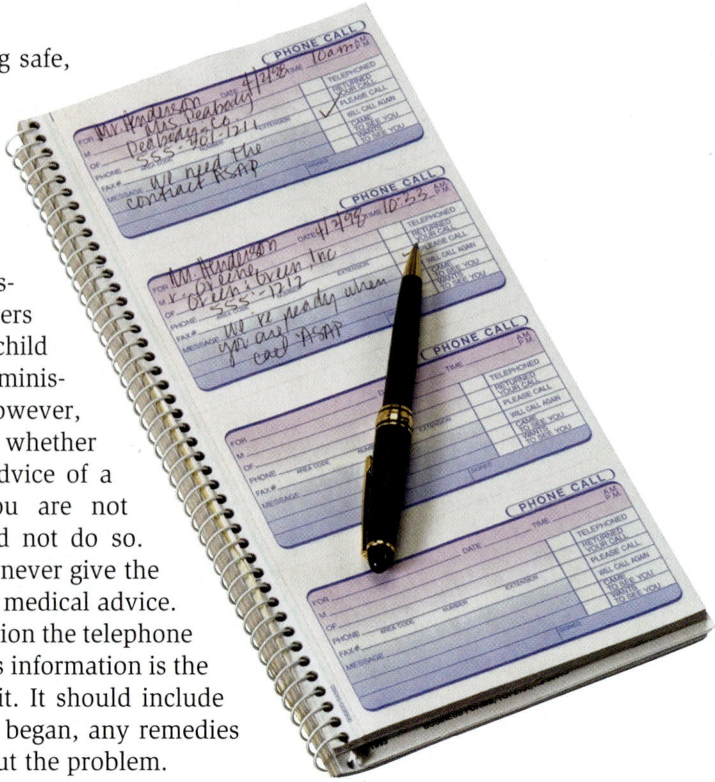

Emergencies Emergency calls must be immediately routed to the physician if he is in the office. Emergency situations include serious or life-threatening medical conditions, such as severe bleeding, a reaction to a drug, injuries, poisoning, suicide attempts, loss of consciousness, severe burns, or whatever your medical office deems an emergency. As always, it will be your duty to remain calm during real or potential emergency situations. The person(s) on the phone may be very upset and it is up to you to keep them calm so they can be of the most help to the patient. It is particularly important in emergency situations that you obtain the patient's name, location, the phone number where the call is coming from, and the name of the person making the call if it is not the patient. This is vital because if the call is interrupted, you will still be able to call for assistance for the patient. Table 11–2 lists symptoms and conditions that require immediate help.

If someone calls the office on behalf of a patient who is experiencing any of these symptoms or conditions, you may instruct the caller to dial 911 to request an ambulance. You will learn more about handling actual emergency situations in Chapter 23.

Automated Telephone Triage An increasing number of practice are installing an automated system for telephone triaging. Administrative medical assistants often spend a great deal of time on the telephone calling patients to remind them of appointments, or missed appointments and leaving other types of messages. More detailed information regarding automated telephone answering systems can be found in Chapter 10.

Categorizing Patient Problems and Providing Patient Education

After the patient information is obtained, the guidelines help the staff categorize the problem according to severity. The telephone staff then decides if the problem can be handled safely with advice over the telephone, whether the patient

figure 11–7

When using a telephone message pad or telephone log, be sure to fill out the form completely and accurately.

table 11-2

Symptoms and Conditions That Require Immediate Medical Help

- Unconsciousness
- Lack of breathing or difficulty breathing
- Severe bleeding
- Pressure or pain in the abdomen that will not go away
- Severe vomiting or bloody stools
- Poisoning
- Injuries to the head, neck, or back
- Choking
- Drowning
- Electrical shock
- Snakebites
- Vehicle collisions
- Allergic reactions to foods or insect stings
- Chemicals or foreign objects in the eye
- Fires, severe burns, or injuries from explosions
- Human bites or any deep animal bites
- Heart attack. Symptoms include chest pain or pressure; pain radiating from the chest to the arm, shoulder, neck, jaw, back, or stomach; nausea or vomiting; sweating; weakness; shortness of breath; pale or gray skin color.
- Stroke. Symptoms include seizures, severe headache, slurred speech, and sudden inability or difficulty in moving a body part or one side of the body.
- Broken bones. Symptoms include being unable to move or put weight on the injured body part. The injured part is very painful or looks misshapen.
- Shock. Symptoms include paleness; feeling faint and sweaty; weak, rapid pulse; cold, moist skin; confusion or drowsiness.
- Heatstroke (sunstroke). Symptoms include confusion or loss of consciousness; flushed skin that is hot and may be moist or dry; strong, rapid pulse.
- Hypothermia (a drop in body temperature during prolonged exposure to cold). Symptoms include becoming increasingly clumsy, unreasonable, irritable, confused, and sleepy; slurred speech; slipping into a coma with slow, weak breathing and heartbeat.

needs to come into the office, or if the problem requires immediate attention at an emergency room.

If a problem is deemed appropriate for telephone management, the guidelines may include recommendations for nonprescription treatment that may relieve symptoms and anxiety. This information falls under the category of patient education. Advise the caller that recommendations are based on the symptoms and are not a diagnosis. Remember that only the doctor PA or NP is authorized to make a diagnosis and prescribe medication. Ask the caller to repeat any instructions you give, and tell the patient to call back within a specified time if symptoms worsen. Be sure to document in the medical record the critical elements of the conversation that relate to the patient's health status. If the patient has any questions regarding the recommended written guidelines, you should refer the patient to the appropriate clinical personnel or the physician. As the administrative medical assistant, under no circumstances should you attempt to give out medical advice.

Taking Action

Clinical triage involves determining the extent of medical emergencies and deciding on the appropriate action. If a caller is having chest pains, you would be performing a type of triage by instructing him to go to the emergency room immediately, preferably by ambulance. Telephone triage is also used in handling common minor medical problems and questions by directing the patient's call to the correct medical personnel. Whatever the nature of the problem, the situation must be dealt with appropriately to protect the health and safety of the patient. Once the patient has been triaged and a plan of action taken, don't forget to fully document the episode in the patient's chart. If the patient was sent to the Emergency Department or other facility, you will also need to notify the

physician as soon as possible regarding this development. You will be learning much more about triage and preparing for emergencies in Chapter 23.

● ● ●

What is telephone triage?

CHECKPOINT
LO 11.6

LO 11.7 Telephone Answering Systems

An office telephone system can range from a single telephone line to a complex multiline system. Most medical offices use one or more of the following pieces of equipment and services to provide efficient management of telephone calls: an automated voice mail system, an answering machine, and/or an answering service. Chapter 10 describes these systems in more detail. One of your responsibilities may be to retrieve messages from the practice's answering service. It is a good idea to call the answering service at a set time (or multiple times, if the service is employed during office hours) each day. In doing so, you ensure that messages are not missed. When calling the service to retrieve messages, as when receiving any information, verify the information for correctness and completeness before ending the call. Procedure 11–3, located at the end of this chapter, describes how to do so.

● ● ●

Why is it advisable to call the answering service at a specific time (or times) during the day?

CHECKPOINT
LO 11.7

LO 11.8 Placing Outgoing Calls

You will often be required to place outgoing calls on behalf of the medical office. You may need to return calls, obtain information, provide patient education, or arrange patient consultations with other physicians. Occasionally, you may be asked to assist with long-distance calls. It is important to determine the time zone and the time of day in the location you are calling before you place a call. Time zones can be determined by checking the front of the phone book, going online, or speaking with a telephone operator. For information on time zones, go to www.time.gov.

Locating Telephone Numbers

Before you can place an outgoing call, of course, you must have the correct telephone number. If you are calling a patient, the telephone number should be in the patient's chart. To find other telephone numbers, you may need to consult a telephone directory, Internet phone directory such as www.anywho.com/ (by AT&T), or the company Web site or call for directory assistance.

The medical office should have at least one telephone directory, or telephone book, for the local calling area and perhaps additional directories for surrounding areas. Use these books to locate telephone numbers for outside calls. The office may also have a card file, a list, or an electronic record of commonly used telephone numbers, or these numbers may be listed in the office policies and procedures manual.

If you need to find a long-distance telephone number, many offices use the directory assistance service. You can reach this service by dialing 1-[area code]-555-1212. You also can search the Internet for free "411" services. Use directory assistance only when you have exhausted other options, however, because most long-distance carriers charge a fee each time you use the service. If you are required to call out of the country, you will need to use an international dialing

code. These codes, as well as area codes and long distance numbers, can be located through the Internet as well as through directory assistance.

Area Codes   There are numerous area codes for calling within the U.S. calling area. You can search the Internet to find any area code that you desire. Here are two websites that are helpful for finding information on area codes:www. nanpa.com and www.lincmad.com/areacodemap.html.

Applying Your Telephone Skills

You can apply the telephone skills you use for answering incoming calls when placing outgoing calls. Here are additional tips for handling outgoing calls.

- Plan before you call. Have all the information you need in front of you before you dial the telephone number. Plan what you will say, and decide what questions to ask so that you will not have to call back for additional information.
- Double-check the telephone number. Before placing a call, always confirm the number. If in doubt, look it up in the telephone directory. If you do dial a wrong number, be sure to apologize for the mistake.
- Allow enough time, at least a minute or about eight rings, for someone to answer the telephone. When calling patients who are elderly or physically disabled, allow additional time.
- Identify yourself. After reaching the person to whom you placed the call, give your name and state that you are calling on behalf of the doctor or practice.
- Ask if you have called at a convenient time and whether the person has time to talk with you. If it is not a good time, ask when you should call back.
- Be ready to speak as soon as the person you called answers the telephone. Do not waste the person's time while you collect your thoughts.
- If you are calling to give information, ask if the person has a pencil and piece of paper available. Do not begin with dates, times, or instructions until the person is ready to write down the information.

Arranging Conference Calls

It may be necessary for you to schedule conference calls with patients, hospital personnel or other doctors to discuss tests or surgical results. When dealing with several people, suggest several time slots in case someone is not available at a particular time. Also keep in mind the various time zones in the country. Make sure that all the conference-call participants are given the proper time in their time zone to expect the call. As stated previously in this chapter, the office phone system will likely have an option allowing you to set up a conference call. If it does not, there are services available that will allow you to do so. Two such services are, www.freeconference.com and www.freeconferencecalling.com.

**CHECKPOINT
LO 11.8**

What should you do prior to placing an outgoing call?

LO 11.9 Other Telecommunication Devices

Pagers, Cell Phones, and E-Mail

A pager, sometimes called a beeper, is a simple personal telecommunication device for short messages. There are two main types of pagers. The first one

is a one-way numeric pager, which can only receive a message consisting of a few digits, typically a phone number that the user is then expected to call. The second type is a two-way pager that has the ability to send and receive e-mail messages and numeric pages.

Another telecommunication device that is beneficial for the medical practice and the physician is the cell phone. A cell phone is a long-range, electronic device used for mobile voice or data communication over a network of specialized base stations known as cell sites containing the antennas and electronic communication equipment necessary for a cell network. Cell phones are so common, it is not unusual for many members of the medical staff, as well as physicians and patients, to have them. Pagers and cell phones are discussed in detail in Chapter 10.

Another popular "personal" communication method combining telecommunications procedures and the written word, used extensively in business, and finding its way into medical offices is e-mail. Many patients, particularly younger patients, find that e-mail is a great way to stay in touch with the members of their health-care team. More and more offices also have Web sites offering the public information about their services as well as a "patient area" accessed via a password. Patients may choose the provider they wish to communicate with and send the provider a "confidential" e-mail to which the provider can respond. If the office utilizes an EHR program such as SpringCharts, all e-mail is screened by the e-mail administrator who forwards the message to the provider/ user. The added bonus of such a program is that if the patient's e-mail address is in the program's database, the e-mail will automatically be attached to the patient's medical chart. Figure 11–8 shows an example of an incoming e-mail message utilizing the SpringCharts program.

One word of caution; e-mail, like cell phone communication, is not considered a secure delivery system. Before sending e-mail to patients, you must have specific written permission from them allowing the sharing of information (with the allowed types of information specified) via e-mail. Figure 11–9 shows an example of such a consent. Sensitive patient information is best shared in person and not via e-mail. Also remember that e-mail is considered written communication and so all e-mail should be sent with the same care and professionalism given to any other written communication. More information on e-mail is found in Chapters 10 and 13.

Procedure 11–4 found at the end of this chapter outlines the way to compose a professional e-mail message.

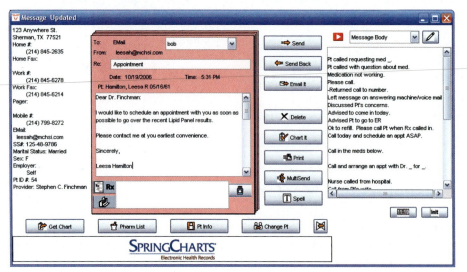

figure 11–8

Incoming e-mail as new message.

TOTAL CARE CLINIC, PC

342 East Park Blvd
Funton, XY   12345-6789
Tel: 521-234-0001
Fax: 521-234-0002
www.totalcareclinic.org

Consent to Use E-Mail Communication

As with all information regarding our patients, we will use reasonable measures to protect the security and confidentiality of e-mail messages sent or received by our office. We, however, cannot guarantee the confidentiality or security of communications shared via e-mail and we will not be held liable for any disclosures of confidential information not caused by professional misconduct on the part of our office. In order for us to honor your request to utilize e-mail, we require written consent agreeing to the following conditions:

1. All e-mail messages to or from the patient regarding diagnosis or treatment will become a permanent part of the patient health record. As part of the health record, authorized office personnel such as billing and coding staff will have access to the information contained within the e-mail message.

2. We will not forward e-mail messages or the information contained within them to any third parties, including insurance carriers, without the patient's prior written consent, unless otherwise authorized or required by law.

3. We cannot guarantee that e-mail messages will be received or read within any particular time frame. For this reason, e-mail is not to be used for any type of medical emergency nor for transmitting any type of time-sensitive information.

4. It is the patient's responsibility to schedule and keep any medically necessary appointments or follow-up appointments.

I have read and understand the above outlined risks associated with e-mail communication between Total Care Clinic and me. I agree to abide by the conditions and instructions outlined above, as well as to any other instructions or limitations Total Care Clinic may impose regarding communication via e-mail. All of my questions were answered and I understand I may withdraw this consent in writing at any time.

_____   _____
              Patient Signature   Date

_____   _____
              Patient Name   Patient E-Mail Address

figure 11–9

E-mail consent form.

Facsimile (Fax) Machines

Facsimile machines, or fax machines, are commonly used in physicians' offices. A fax is sent over telephone lines from one fax modem to another. Fax machines may be used to send referrals, reports, insurance approvals, or medication refill approvals. Per HIPAA guidelines, a patient's confidentiality must be protected

by placing the fax machine in a secure location that only authorized personnel can access. You may refer back to Chapter 10 for more detailed information regarding fax machines and their use.

Why is it important to review the telecommunications invoice carefully each month?

CHECKPOINT
LO 11.9

Procedure 11–1 Using a Telecommunication Device for the Deaf

GOAL   To properly communicate with the hearing-impaired patient using a TDD

MATERIALS   Telephone, TDD (if available), patient chart for documentation, pen

METHOD

Answering a Call with a TDD

1. Answer the phone as usual. If you hear a rapid clicking sound, you know you have a TDD call. You may hear no sound at all; do not hang up, it may still be a TDD call.
2. If you know (or believe) this is a TDD call, place your phone receiver on the TDD as directed.
3. Type your normal office greeting: "Total Care Clinic, Brendan Conroy. How may I help you?"
4. When you complete your message type "GA" which stands for "Go Ahead." This tells the patient you have completed your message and it is his turn to respond.
5. Give the patient time to type his response. When you see "GA" at the end of his message, it is your turn to respond.
6. When the patient receives all of the information required, he will type "Bye, SK" which stands for Good-Bye, Stop Keying.
7. If you agree the call is completed, you may also reply "Bye, SK". This will give the patient the opportunity to be the one to end the call.
8. When you receive a response of SKSK (Stop Keying, Stop Keying) the conversation is complete and you may hang up and turn off the TDD.

Making a Call with a TDD

1. Turn on the TDD.
2. Dial the patient's phone number on your standard telephone and listen for the phone to ring.
3. When you hear the TDD sound, place the phone receiver on the TDD as directed.
4. After the patient types a greeting and "GA" appears on the TDD display, identify yourself and proceed with the conversation.
5. Remember to type "GA" when you complete your message so that the patient knows it is his turn to respond.
6. Even though you were the one to initiate the call, you should still allow the patient to make the decision that the call is completed by keying "SKSK".

Procedure 11–2 — Performing Telephone Screening and Call Routing

GOAL To properly screen incoming telephone calls

MATERIALS Telephone, telephone pad, pen or pencil, appointment book or computerized scheduling software (computer)

METHOD

1. Make sure all of the materials are within reach of the telephone equipment.

2. Answer the telephone promptly within two to three rings.

3. Identify the medical office and identify yourself. Make sure you know office procedure for answering the phone in your facility even if a telephone answering system is employed to route calls to you. For example: "Total Care Clinic, this is Denise Bagwell, how may I help you?"

4. If the caller does not identify himself, ask him to do so and the number he is calling from, writing down this information. Find out the reason for the call. Is it an emergency (Refer to Table 11–1), if so follow office policy If it should be transferred to a specific department or person, do so. If you can handle the call, take care of the query. Listen carefully to what the caller has to say, listening for tone and feeling. If this is a call that needs to be transferred to someone, tell the caller to whom and to what number you will be transferring the call.

5. If you need to take a message, make sure you repeat the information that is given to you, especially the name of the person and his phone number.

6. If you have to transfer a caller, ask permission to place him on hold. Make sure you write down the caller's name and phone number in case the call is dropped. Never place a caller on hold longer than 30 seconds. Come back to the caller and let him know that you are still waiting for the other individual to answer. If the other staff member does not answer promptly or the staff member is on another line, ask the caller if he would like to call back, be transferred to the staff member's voice mail (if available), or would like to leave a message.

7. If the caller describes a symptom that is in need of immediate care, ask questions to assess the information (ask for his name and telephone number). If it is indeed an emergency call and the physician, PA or nurse is in the office, transfer the call immediately. If the doctor, PA or nurse is not in the building, do not let the caller hang up. Have another staff member dial 911 immediately with the name and address of the patient and his symptoms, while you stay on the phone with the patient keeping him calm and aware that help is on the way.

Procedure 11–3 — Retrieving Messages from an Answering Service

GOAL To follow standard procedures for retrieving messages from an answering service

MATERIALS Telephone message pad, manual telephone log, or electronic telephone log

METHOD

1. Set a regular schedule for calling the answering service to retrieve messages.
2. Call at the regularly scheduled time(s) to see if there are any messages.
3. Identify yourself and state that you are calling to obtain messages for the practice.
4. For each message, write down all pertinent information on the telephone message pad or telephone log, or key it into the electronic telephone log. Be sure to include the caller's name and telephone number, time of call, message or description of the problem, and action taken, if any.
5. Repeat the information, confirming that you have the correct spelling of all names.
6. When you have retrieved all messages, route them according to the office policy.

Procedure 11–4   Compose a Professional E-Mail Message

GOAL   To compose a professional e-mail message

MATERIALS   Computer with e-mail (Internet) capabilities; e-mail message requiring response

METHOD

1. Check the patient's medical record verifying that a "Consent to Use E-mail" form for communication with the office has been signed.
2. Use a classic easy-to-read font such as Times New Roman at 12 point (14 point is also acceptable). Keeping a professional appearance in mind, use black ink only.
3. If responding to a patient e-mail, open the e-mail and choose "Reply." If composing a new message, choose "New" to open a new e-mail document and carefully enter the patient's e-mail address.
4. Add the e-mail address to the office address book for easy reference for later e-mails.
5. If answering a patient e-mail, you may keep the subject line from the original message. If you are writing a new e-mail, enter a descriptive subject line.
6. Insert a salutation, using the patient's surname as you would with an ordinary letter.
7. Compose the body of the message, aligning the information with the left margin.
8. Double space at the end of the message and insert your name. Include a signature line with the practice information if available.
9. Spell-check and proofread the message carefully for any errors.
10. Click "Send" and wait for the message informing you the message has been sent.
11. If the message is returned as undeliverable, verify the e-mail address was entered correctly. If necessary, correct the address and attempt delivery again.
12. If the message is returned a second time as undeliverable, contact the patient by phone or by another alternate method to be sure he or she received the required information.

Case Study

Judgment

Ability to come to an appropriate conclusion and act accordingly

Meg is new to Dr. Garcia's practice. It is her responsibility to open the office in the morning, and one of her first duties is to retrieve messages from the answering machine. This is a new procedure for her as Dr. Halford, her previous employer, used an answering service. In fact, all of the telecommunications technology between the two offices is different. Dr. Garcia uses a combination cell phone/personal digital assistant (PDA) and Dr. Halford uses a pager. Dr. Garcia's office uses a standard fax machine and Dr. Halford's office has faxing capability through the use of electronic health records (EHR). Meg has been considering the variety of modalities used to communicate with patients and wonders how a practice decides what technology best serves their needs. She realizes that good judgment is necessary for many aspects of the medical practice, including efficient running of the practice.

Thinking Critically

1. What factors might go into the choice of an answering machine versus an answering service?
2. Could a fax sent to the wrong location impact the care of a patient?
3. Besides patients, with what other categories of people do medical practices communicate and how might the technology differ?

practice APPLICATIONS

1. Compose an e-mail responding to patient Marcus James's request for information regarding the "Living with Diabetes" classes being offered by the office PA, Linda Wiley, on Wednesday evenings.

2. With a partner, practice playing the part of both the patient and the administrative medical assistant in the following scenarios:

   a. Caller insists on speaking with the physician but will not give his name nor the reason for the call.

   b. Patient's wife calls the office, angry about his bill. She states they have met their deductible and does not understand why their part of the medical expenses are so high. (You note that their coinsurance amount is 30% after deductible has been met.)

   c. The schedule for today is packed and Dr. Rodriguez will be out of the office tomorrow. Mrs. Maxim calls with what sounds like a cold, insisting she needs to be seen immediately.

1. **[LO11.1]** Which is NOT one of the five Cs of communication to use the telephone effectively?
   a. Compassion
   b. Clarity
   c. Conciseness
   d. Cohesiveness
   e. Courtesy

2. **[LO11.4]** Calls from which of the following will require a doctor's immediate attention?
   a. Bill collector
   b. An old close friend
   c. Calls from other doctors
   d. A pharmaceutical salesman
   e. Calls from a patient's progress report

3. **[LO11.1]** What does HIPAA stand for?
   a. Health Issues Portability and Accountability Act
   b. Health Insurance Practice and Accountability Act
   c. Health Incompetent Practice and Accountability Act
   d. Health Insurance Portability and Accountability Act
   e. Health Insurers Portability and Accountability Act

4. **[LO11.4]** Which of the following calls would the administrative medical assistant routinely handle?
   a. Returning patient calls for positive test results
   b. Advising a new mother about her infant's 102 temperature
   c. Unsatisfactory patient progress reports
   d. Patient complaints
   e. Requests for appointment rescheduling

5. **[LO11.2]** Proper pronunciation refers to
   a. the tone of your voice.
   b. clear and distinct speaking.
   c. saying words correctly.
   d. speaking slowly.

6. **[LO11.6]** Which of the following outlines the telephone triage process?
   a. Sort, screen, categorize, and take action
   b. Screen, sort, categorize, and take action
   c. Categorize, screen, sort, and take action
   d. Screen, categorize, sort, and take action
   e. Sort, categorize, screen, and take action

7. **[LO11.5]** Which is NOT a component of a complete telephone message?
   a. Name of the caller
   b. Patient name if not the caller
   c. Date and time of call
   d. Who the call is for and concise message
   e. All components are necessary

8. **[LO11.7]** When should you call the office answering service to pick up messages?
   a. First thing in the morning
   b. At set intervals during the day
   c. Both a and b
   d. At the end of the day
   e. Both a and d

9. **[LO11.8]** What pieces of information should you be aware of prior to placing an outgoing call?
   a. Correct area code and phone number
   b. Possible time zone differences
   c. Reason for call
   d. Documentation needed to place the call
   e. All of the above

10. **[LO11.9]** When using alternate telecommunication devices, which of the following is the most important consideration?
    a. Ease of use
    b. Using a cover sheet
    c. Protection of patient information
    d. All of the above
    e. None of the above

learning outcome SUMMARY

LO 11.1 Excellent communication skills are necessary when using the telephone and other telecommunication devices such as cell phones, e-mail, and faxes because you do not have the advantage of visual clues to tell you whether the recipient truly understands the message you are sending. Additionally, the person answering the phone often provides a patient's initial impression of the office and its staff.

LO 11.2 The four components of telephone etiquette are voice, pronunciation, enunciation, and tone.

LO 11.3 Managing incoming calls requires that you remain calm and professional at all times, utilizing excellent telephone screening, triage, and routing techniques to keep the office running smoothly and the patients feeling cared about and well taken care of.

LO 11.4 Examples of the types of calls the administrative medical assistant might receive include appointment requests; basic administrative questions; billing inquiries; insurance questions; x-ray and laboratory reports; patient progress reports from patients or hospitals; referral requests; and prescription renewals. Calls for the physician might include emergency calls; calls from other doctors; patient requests to discuss abnormal test results; unsatisfactory patient progress reports; new prescription requests; and personal calls.

LO 11.5 Components that must be included in a telephone message include the intended recipient of the message; the caller and the reason for the call; the date and time of the call; the action to be taken; and the name of the person who took the message.

LO 11.6 Telephone triage is the process of screening, sorting, routing, and determining the degree of emergency surrounding the telephone call so it is handled in the appropriate manner.

LO 11.7 Calls should be retrieved from the answering service at set times to ensure that no calls are missed. When you call the service, identify yourself and the office you are calling from and ask for any messages. Take any message information down carefully, reading it back to the person reading you the information to make sure it is received correctly. Route the messages to the appropriate office personnel.

LO 11.8 Prior to placing an outgoing call, be sure to have all necessary information in front of you, including the name of the person to be reached and the correct phone number. Dial the number carefully, identifying yourself when the phone is answered, asking for the person you need to reach. As always use the five Cs of communication to complete the exchange.

LO 11.9 Other telecommunications devices used in the medical office include cell phones, pagers, facsimile machines, e-mail, and possibly TDD equipment for hearing-impaired patients.

medical assisting COMPETENCIES

CAAHEP

Psychomotor Skills

Concepts of Effective Communication

IV. C (9) Discuss applications of electronic technology in effective communication

IV. P (7) Demonstrate telephone techniques

IV. A (1) Demonstrate empathy in communicating with patients, family, and staff

IV. A (8) Analyze communications in providing appropriate responses/feedback

V. P (7) Use Internet to access information related to the medical office

VII. A (2) Demonstrate sensitivity in communicating with both providers and patients

ABHES

8. Medical Office Business Procedures Management

ee. Use proper telephone techniques
hh. Receive, organize, prioritize, and transmit information expediently
ii. Recognize and respond to verbal and nonverbal communication.

11. Career Development

b. Demonstrate professionalism by:
(2) Exhibiting a positive attitude and a sense of responsibility
(3) Maintaining confidentiality at all times
(8) Being courteous and diplomatic
(9) Conducting work within scope of education, training, and ability

Schedule Management

Learning Outcomes

After completing Chapter 12, you will be able to:

12.1 Describe how the appointment book is key to the continuity of patient care.

12.2 Identify how to properly apply a matrix to an appointment book.

12.3 Describe different types of appointment scheduling systems.

12.4 Identify ways to arrange and organize appointments for patients.

12.5 Model how to handle special scheduling situations.

12.6 Explain how to schedule appointments that are outside the medical office.

12.7 Implement ways to keep an accurate and efficient physician schedule.

Key Terms

advance scheduling
agenda
cluster scheduling
double-booking system
itinerary
locum tenens
matrix
minutes
modified-wave
 scheduling
no-show
open-hours
 scheduling
overbooking
time-specified
 scheduling
underbooking
walk-in
wave scheduling

Preparation for Certification

RMA (AMT) Exam
- Appointment scheduling systems

CMAS (AMT) Exam
- Appointment management and scheduling
- Address cancellations and missed appointments
- Prepare information for referrals and pre-authorizations

CMA (AAMA) Exam
- Utilizing appointment schedules/types
- Appointment guidelines
- Appointment protocol

Introduction ● ● ●

As an administrative medical assistant, you will need to know all aspects of how to create and utilize an appointment book and/or electronic scheduler. In this chapter you will learn how to identify the different types of scheduling systems, how each is used, and which type of practice each system would work best in. You will also learn how to handle many types of scheduling situations within the medical office, including patient appointments, emergencies, pharmaceutical representatives, and the scheduling of outside appointments with other medical facilities. Legal aspects of the appointment book are discussed and proper documentation is stressed. Additional topics include appointment cards, reminder mailings, reminder calls, and recall notices for patients.

LO 12.1 The Appointment Book

Time is of great value for everyone involved, both physician and patient. Scheduling appointments in an organized fashion shows respect for everyone's time and creates an efficient patient flow. If the schedule is changed for any reason, the administrative medical assistant must update the appointment book or scheduler and make sure that everyone involved is aware of the change. A well-managed appointment book, regardless of whether it is an actual book or is in an electronic format within a computer system, is key to patient continuity of care and presents the office in a positive, professional manner, ultimately keeping all parties involved on task and on time.

The office is dependent upon physician preferences and habits, the facilities available, and the patient need. Although most patients understand that they may have to wait in the reception area before they are seen by the physician, few patients are willing to wait more than 20 minutes. Offices that routinely have long waiting times can end up with dissatisfied patients which can lead to other problems. You may find that some patients will get creative in an attempt to avoid waiting. They may deliberately arrive after their scheduled appointment time to avoid waiting or come in earlier in hopes of being seen before their scheduled appointment time. Still others may avoid the schedule entirely and walk in expecting to be seen. All of these behaviors, if accommodated, can throw the office schedule off track. Other patients may become resentful and decide to seek medical care with a competing practice.

Even in a well-run office, however, unexpected events can disrupt the schedule. Some patients may require the physician to spend more time with them than was originally scheduled and patients who are ill will need to be added to the schedule, sometimes with little or no notice. Still others will forget appointments or arrive later than scheduled. For these reasons, making an office schedule flow smoothly can be a challenge. A schedule that "plans for the unexpected" combined with excellent communication between the physician, staff, and patients will allow a medical practice to run smoothly despite these obstacles.

● ● ●

CHECKPOINT
LO 12.1

What patient behaviors can be avoided by abiding by each patient's scheduled appointment time?

matrix
The basic format of an appointment book, established by blocking off times on the schedule during which the doctor is not available to see patients.

LO 12.2 Applying the Matrix

Before you begin scheduling appointments, you need to prepare the appointment book or electronic scheduler. The first step is to establish the **matrix,** or basic outline of times the physician is and is not available to see patients.

To create the matrix, block off times within the schedule during which the doctor is not available to see patients. In a paper format, drawing an "X" through the unavailable time slots with a brief explanation is standard practice to avoid errors. The type of appointment book used—whether it uses 10- or 15-minute units—will determine how many "blocks" are crossed out for each designation. Electronic schedulers often use colors to designate the reason the provider is out; they may also place an "X" in the time frames selected. For example, the schedule will show when the doctor is away for the following reasons:

- Hospital rounds
- Surgery/procedures
- Lunch
- Vacation days
- Holidays
- Personal appointments for the physician
- Scheduled meetings (for example, pharmaceutical, medical supply company, or in-service meetings)

The day's schedule is then built around the established matrix. Should the physician or office manager direct that a meeting has been canceled and patients should be seen during a time that had been blocked out, the "X" should be removed and patients scheduled as usual. Some offices prefer the "X" remain and the initials of the person approving the new schedule be added to the appointment time frame. The same is true for an electronic format; the time frame is unblocked and patients are then scheduled as usual. See Figure 12–1 for an example of a matrix for a multi-physician office. For a single-physician schedule with appointments in 15-minute increments, see Figure 12–2 on page 301. Procedure 12–1 provides the opportunity to practice completing an appointment matrix using an appointment book and Procedure 12–2 outlines the procedure when using an electronic scheduler. Both procedures can be found at the end of this chapter.

Obtaining Patient Information

When the matrix has been established, you can begin scheduling appointments. Some practices enter the information into both traditional paper appointment books and computerized systems. Then, if the computer fails to work for some reason, the office has the book for reference. Some doctors who have been in practice for many years are used to the appointment book method and do not want to give it up for a computer system. Other offices are completely computerized. Per your office policy, you should obtain the following patient information in order to efficiently book a patient appointment:

- Patient's full name. Obtain the correct spelling of the patient's name.
- Daytime telephone numbers. Repeat phone numbers to ensure accuracy.
- Purpose of the visit. Use a brief description and utilize approved abbreviations when possible without disclosing the patient's diagnosis or violating HIPAA. Do not create your own abbreviations as this can lead to errors or misunderstandings regarding the reason for the patient appointment.

Commonly Used Abbreviations

If you are the person who maintains the appointment book, you will find that certain procedures and conditions occur frequently. Usage of the abbreviation will depend on the office specialty. Only approved universal medical

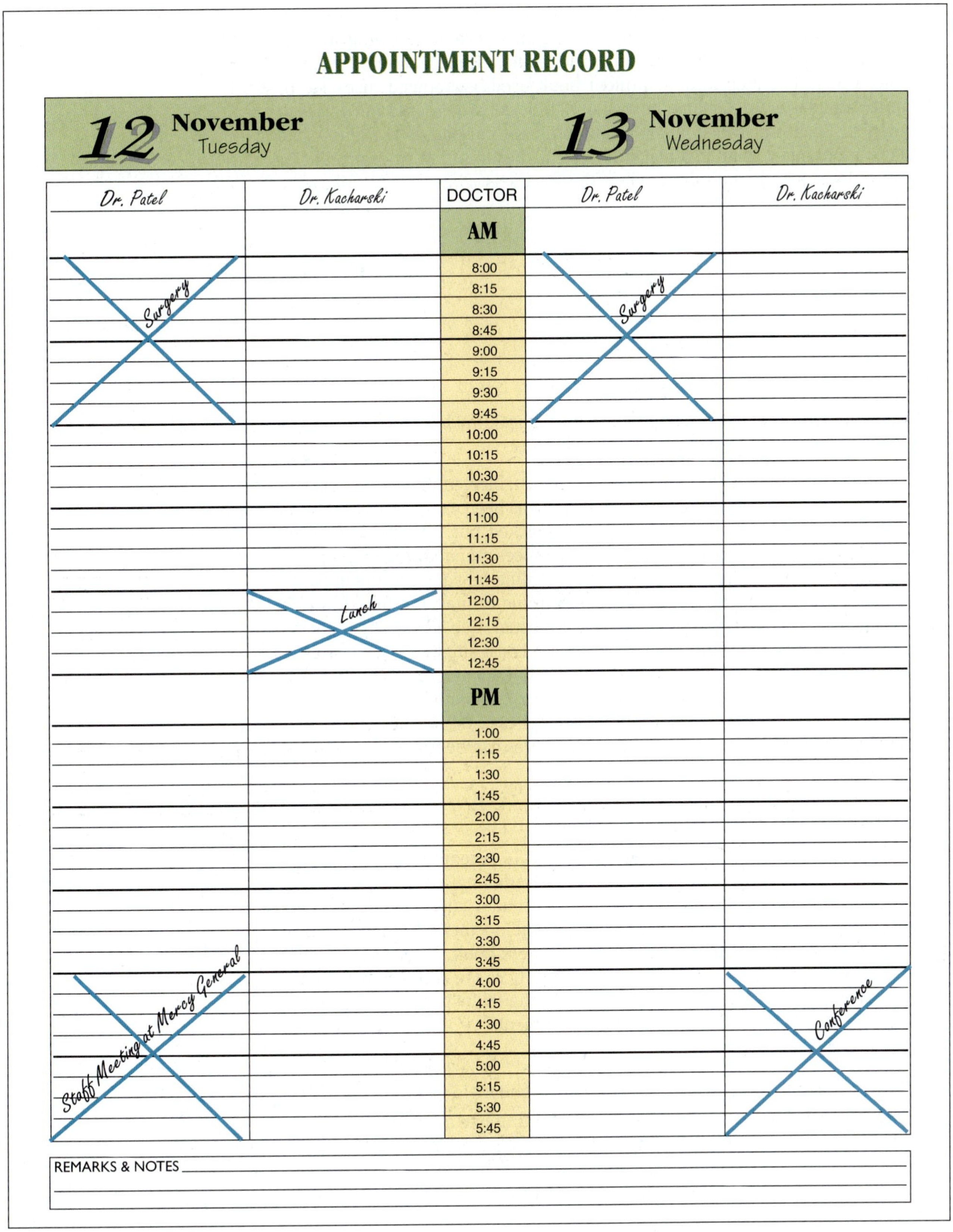

APPOINTMENT RECORD

		DOCTOR		
12 November Tuesday			**13** November Wednesday	
Dr. Patel	Dr. Kacharski	DOCTOR	Dr. Patel	Dr. Kacharski
		AM		
Surgery		8:00	Surgery	
		8:15		
		8:30		
		8:45		
		9:00		
		9:15		
		9:30		
		9:45		
		10:00		
		10:15		
		10:30		
		10:45		
		11:00		
		11:15		
		11:30		
		11:45		
	Lunch	12:00		
		12:15		
		12:30		
		12:45		
		PM		
		1:00		
		1:15		
		1:30		
		1:45		
		2:00		
		2:15		
		2:30		
		2:45		
		3:00		
		3:15		
		3:30		
		3:45		
Staff Meeting at Mercy General		4:00		Conference
		4:15		
		4:30		
		4:45		
		5:00		
		5:15		
		5:30		
		5:45		

REMARKS & NOTES _____

figure 12–1

It is important to establish a matrix in the appointment book so that appointments are not scheduled for times when the physician is not available to see patients.

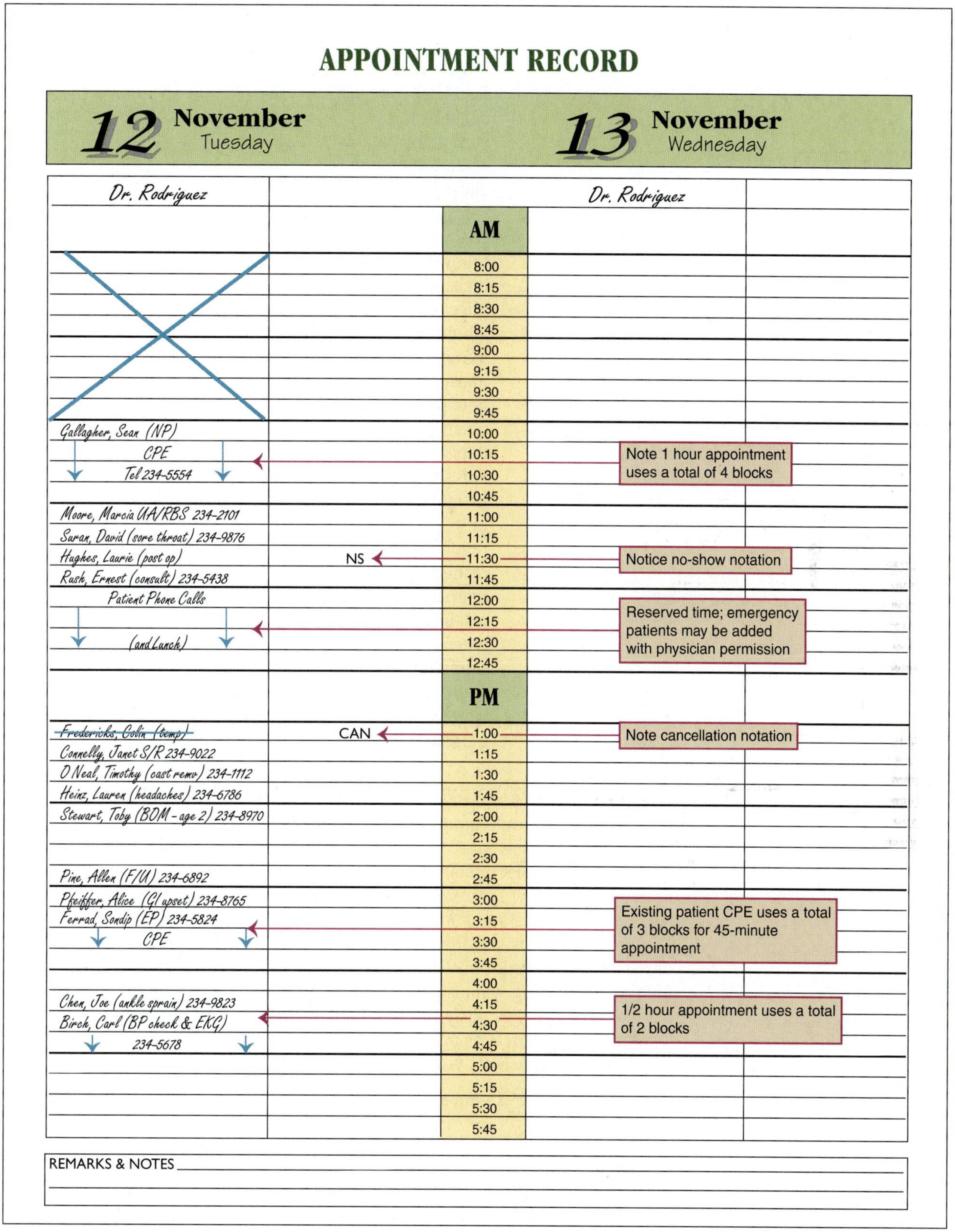

APPOINTMENT RECORD

12 November — Tuesday | 13 November — Wednesday

Dr. Rodriguez | **Dr. Rodriguez**

Tuesday Nov 12		AM	Wednesday Nov 13
		8:00	
		8:15	
		8:30	
		8:45	
		9:00	
		9:15	
		9:30	
		9:45	
Gallagher, Sean (NP)		10:00	
CPE		10:15	Note 1 hour appointment uses a total of 4 blocks
Tel 234-5554		10:30	
		10:45	
Moore, Marcia UA/RBS 234-2101		11:00	
Swan, David (sore throat) 234-9876		11:15	
Hughes, Laurie (post op)	NS	11:30	Notice no-show notation
Rush, Ernest (consult) 234-5438		11:45	
Patient Phone Calls		12:00	
		12:15	Reserved time; emergency patients may be added with physician permission
(and Lunch)		12:30	
		12:45	
		PM	
Fredericks, Colin (temp)	CAN	1:00	Note cancellation notation
Connelly, Janet S/R 234-9022		1:15	
O'Neal, Timothy (cast remv) 234-1112		1:30	
Heinz, Lauren (headaches) 234-6786		1:45	
Stewart, Toby (BOM - age 2) 234-8970		2:00	
		2:15	
		2:30	
Pine, Allen (F/U) 234-6892		2:45	
Pfeiffer, Alice (GI upset) 234-8765		3:00	
Ferrad, Sondip (EP) 234-5824		3:15	Existing patient CPE uses a total of 3 blocks for 45-minute appointment
CPE		3:30	
		3:45	
		4:00	
Chen, Joe (ankle sprain) 234-9823		4:15	
Birch, Carl (BP check & EKG)		4:30	1/2 hour appointment uses a total of 2 blocks
234-5678		4:45	
		5:00	
		5:15	
		5:30	
		5:45	

REMARKS & NOTES _____

figure 12–2

Time-specified appointment scheduling is commonly used in the medical office. This example demonstrates the use of a 15-minute appointment block schedule for a single physician.

abbreviations should be used. To save space and time when entering information, use these abbreviations:

BP	blood pressure check
FBS	fasting blood sugar
can/cx	cancellation
c/o	complains of
cons	consultation
CP	chest pain
CPE	complete physical examination
ECG/EKG	electrocardiogram
FU or f/u	follow-up appointment
I & D	incision and drainage
inj	injection
lab	laboratory studies
minor surg.	minor surgery
N & V	nausea and vomiting
NP	new patient
NS	no-show patient
P & P	Pap smear (Papanicolaou smear) and pelvic examination
Pap	Pap smear
pt	patient
PT	physical therapy
RBS	random blood sugar
re	recheck
ref	referral
RS	reschedule
Rx	prescription
sig	sigmoidoscopy
S/R	suture removal
surg	surgery
US	ultrasound

Determining Standard Procedure Times

If you are to schedule appointments efficiently, you must have an estimate of how long visits will take. Working with the physician or physicians in your practice, create a list of standard procedure times. Also indicate on the list how much time to allow for tests that are commonly performed in the practice. This list, kept beside the appointment book or programmed into the electronic scheduling system, helps you identify which openings are appropriate for the procedure or test involved. This list is intended as a guide only, as each patient visit is unique. This listing will also assist you in choosing an appropriate appointment book or scheduler, as most are based on 10-, 15-, or 30-minute increments. The lengths and types of tests and procedures will depend on the practice policy and procedure manual. Following are typical lengths of common procedures:

Complete physical examination	30–60 minutes
New patient visit	30–45 minutes or more
Follow-up office visit	5–10 minutes
Emergency office visit	15–20 minutes
Prenatal examination	15 minutes
Pap smear and pelvic examination	15–30 minutes
Minor in-office surgery, such as a mole removal	30 minutes
Suture removal	10–20 minutes

A Legal Record

The appointment book is considered a legal record. Some experts advise holding on to old appointment books for at least three years. Because the appointment

book could be used as evidence in legal proceedings, entries must be clear and easy to read. Many offices, if still using the paper method, will use pencils to record the initial entry although management consultants suggest that because the appointment book is a legal document, the schedule should be written in blue ink (although many offices still prefer black ink). Never erase a name or use correction fluid to blot the name out. Instead, draw a single line through the name and beside it write in the reason such as "NS" or "can". You may also write the date, time of the new appointment if known, with "RS" and the new date, and reason (if known) why the appointment was missed or canceled, then initial the entry. This information should also be documented in the patient's chart.

Some offices permit the use of pencil to allow for changes or corrections if necessary. If pencil is used, at the end of each day you should write directly over the penciled entries in ink to create a permanent document. Remember too that when a patient skips or changes her appointment, documentation should also be made in the medical record.

● ● ●

Why is it important to use universally approved medical abbreviations when recording in an appointment book?

CHECKPOINT
LO 12.2

LO 12.3 Appointment Scheduling Systems

There are several possible appointment scheduling systems. The method chosen usually depends on the type of practice and physician preferences. No matter which method your office uses, it should be regularly reviewed to see whether it is meeting its goals: a smooth flow of patients and minimal waiting time.

Open-Hours Scheduling

In the **open-hours scheduling** system, patients arrive at their own convenience with the understanding that they will be seen on a first-come, first-served basis. The only thing that may alter this is an emergency. Depending on how many other patients are ahead of them, they may have a considerable wait. The open-hours system eliminates the problems caused by broken appointments because there are no assigned timed appointments, but it increases the possibility of inefficient downtime for the physician and office staff. In addition to possible long wait times, the medical assistant cannot retrieve patients' charts before they arrive.

Most private practices have replaced this system with scheduled appointments. Open-hours systems are still used by rural practices, emergency rooms, and urgent care centers. An open-hours system still requires the use of an appointment book or electronic scheduling system to record patients as they come into the office. You still also must establish a matrix so that you will know when a doctor is out of the office or unavailable.

open-hours scheduling
Patients arrive at their own convenience with the understanding that they will be seen on a first-come, first-served basis unless there is an emergency.

Time-Specified Scheduling

Time-specified scheduling (also called stream scheduling) assumes a steady stream of patients all day long at regular, specified intervals. Once the matrix has been applied and physician availability has been established, it can be determined how many slots or blocks should be used for each appointment type. Most appointment books and schedulers are set up in 10- or 15-minute intervals. Figure 12–1 provides an example of a matrix for a multi-physician office and Figure 12–2 demonstrates a completed appointment page for a single-physician office. Most minor medical problems, such as sore throats, earaches, or blood pressure follow-ups, usually require only 10- to 15-minute appointment slots. More time may be required for appointments such as physical exams, which usually require 60 minutes, or new patient visits, which usually require

time-specified scheduling
Assumes a steady stream of patients all day long at regular, specified intervals; also called stream scheduling.

30 minutes (Figure 12–1). When a visit requires more time, you simply assign the patient additional back-to-back slots. Using arrows or parentheses on both sides of the appointment entry will allow the scheduler to easily see the length of existing appointments and the remaining open time slots. Refer to Procedure 12–2 at the end of this chapter.

Wave Scheduling

Wave scheduling works effectively in larger medical facilities that have enough departments and personnel to provide services to several patients at the same time. This method of scheduling is based on the reality that some patients will arrive late and that others will require more or less time than expected with the physician. Wave scheduling has the flexibility to allow for appointments that require more time than anticipated or for patients who miss appointments. The goal is to begin and end each hour with the overall office schedule on track. You determine the number of patients to be seen each hour by dividing the hour by the length of the average visit. If the average is 15 minutes, for example, you schedule four patients for each hour. An example of wave scheduling would be:

10:00 A.M.	Patient A	555-5683	Sore throat
10:00 A.M.	Patient B	555-7322	Low back pain
10:00 A.M.	Patient C	555-4673	FU B/P
10:00 A.M.	Patient D	555-2854	B12 inj

You ask all four to arrive at the beginning of the hour and have the physician see them in the order of their actual arrival. The main problem with wave scheduling is that patients may realize they have appointments at the same time as other patients. The result may be confusion and possibly annoyance or anger.

Modified-Wave Scheduling

The wave system can be modified in several ways. With **modified-wave scheduling,** as shown in Figure 12–3, patients might be scheduled in 15-minute increments. Another option is to schedule four patients to arrive at planned intervals during the first half hour, leaving the second half hour unscheduled. Appointments that are anticipated to require more time should be scheduled at the beginning of the hour. Appointments that are expected to be less time-consuming should be scheduled in 10- to 20-minute time slots. This method allows time for catching up before the next hour begins.

Double-Booking

With a **double-booking system,** two or more patients are purposely scheduled for the same appointment slot. Unlike the wave or modified-wave system, however, the double-booking system assumes that both patients will actually be seen within the scheduled period. If the types of visits are usually short (5 minutes, for example), it is reasonable to book two patients for one 15-minute opening. If both patients require the entire 15 minutes, however, the office falls behind schedule.

This type of system is especially useful when one patient does not necessarily need to see the physician. This may occur when a patient can be managed by another member of the allied health-care team such as a nurse practitioner or physician assistant for an immunization or blood pressure check. Double-booking systems work most effectively in practices in which more than one patient can be attended to at a time.

Double-booking can be helpful if a patient calls with a problem and needs to be seen that day but no appointments are available. You could double-book this

APPOINTMENT RECORD

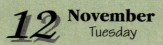

12 November — Tuesday

Dr. Hilbert

		AM		
Auerbach, Conrad	Sinclair, Monica	8:00		
FU	FU	8:15		
		8:30	Purdy, Marianne	Ganzalez, Hector
		8:45	INJ	INJ
Molini, Francesca	Jacobson, Eloise	9:00		
BP	LAB	9:15		
		9:30	Baffer	Sherbert, Philip
		9:45		LAB
Willis, Nina	Smith, Marshall	10:00		
	FU	10:15		
		10:30	Chandler, Larry	MacDonald, Liam
		10:45	GI	GI
Baffer	Ward, Sylvia	11:00		
	UTI	11:15		
		11:30	Campbell, Joel	Ramoson, Katrina
		11:45	FU	PMS
		12:00		
		12:15		
		12:30		
		12:45		
		PM		
Gibble, Cora	Bunsen, Elmer	1:00		
ECG	SOB	1:15		
		1:30	Moskowitz, Matthew	Cheng, Amy
		1:45	ECG	BP
Silberstein, Sidney	Burns, Laura	2:00		
SOB	ECG	2:15		
		2:30	Baffer	Osborne, Jonathan
		2:45		BP
Warren, Mary	Harris, Noel	3:00		
CP	CP	3:15		
		3:30	McDermott, Elizabeth	Corbin, Allicia
		3:45	FU	FU
Baffer	Warner, Steve	4:00		
	RE	4:15		
		4:30	Thompson, Will	Stein, Merle
		4:45	CPE	CPE
Cabrisi, Claudia	Velone, Tina	5:00		
US	US	5:15		
		5:30	Tucker, Bob	Kapoor, Fatima
		5:45	CONS	CONS

REMARKS & NOTES _____

figure 12–3

Modified-wave scheduling allows more flexibility than wave scheduling.

patient with an already scheduled patient. In such cases you should explain that the caller might have to wait a bit before being seen by the doctor.

Cluster Scheduling

Cluster scheduling groups similar appointments together on a specific day or for a specific block of time during the day or week (also called categorization scheduling). Cluster scheduling is often used for appointments such as blood sugar screenings, school physicals, and the like; for instance, Wednesdays after 3 P.M. might be set aside for school physicals as it would be a more convenient time for parents. Cluster schedules are also helpful in offices where specialized equipment or services (such as physical therapy or ultrasound) are available only at certain times.

Advance Scheduling

In some specialties patients might be booked weeks or months in advance, as for annual gynecologic examinations. In such practices **advance scheduling** is used. It is still advisable to leave a few slots open each day, however, for patients who call with unexpected or unusual problems.

Combination Scheduling

Some practices combine two or more scheduling methods. For example, they might use cluster scheduling for new patients and double-booking for quick follow-ups such as sore throats, hypertension, or a new medication.

Computerized Scheduling

Computerized scheduling systems are becoming more common in medical offices because they have several advantages over handwritten systems (Figure 12–4). As more practices become compliant with electronic health record regulations, the advantages seem to outweigh the disadvantages. Some of the advantages of computerized scheduling include:

1. It enables locking out selected areas for designated purposes, such as last-minute or emergency visits.

2. It allows information to be accessed from multiple areas within the office.

figure 12–4

Many medical offices use computerized scheduling instead of or in addition to a traditional appointment book.

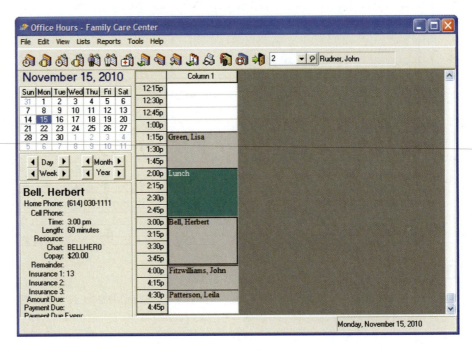

3. It helps staff to identify problem patients for cancellations, no-shows, and late arrivals.

4. It provides a "search" for upcoming appointments to ensure proper follow-up care is given.

5. It provides reports on overall scheduling practices.

6. It adds color coding as a visual aid to identify areas designated for certain types of appointments.

7. It allows for searches for requested day or time availability.

Online Scheduling

Online scheduling is relatively new and not recommended for all office types. The patients schedule themselves or request an appointment via the computer and Internet. Many offices have not implemented this system because of cost and security; however, new security measures have been put in place to ensure protection of patient data online. Putting an online scheduler in your medical office takes time and requires training of the medical staff. If staffing levels are low, online scheduling may not be cost-effective.

Before you adopt an e-scheduler, assess your needs, survey patients for access to the Web, and find out about privacy issues. One of the frontrunners in e-scheduling is www.compassscheduling.com.

CHECKPOINT
LO 12.3

1. Describe the different types of appointment scheduling systems.
2. What are the advantages of a computerized scheduling system?

LO 12.4 Organizing and Arranging Appointments

As you determine patient needs and office availability when arranging appointments, you should keep in mind that you are representing the office. How you interact with patients will have either a positive or negative impact depending on your actions and choices. Being polite and courteous while maintaining a professional manner is key. Try to be as accommodating as possible to the patient but at the same time uphold the policies and protocols of the office.

As discussed earlier in the chapter, patient status and chief complaint must be clearly identified prior to scheduling any appointment, as this will dictate the length of time the physician will spend with the patient.

New Patients

Patients who have never been seen in the practice or have not been seen by the practice in three or more years are considered to be new patients. Appointments for new patients are most often arranged over the telephone. Be sure to obtain all the necessary information, including the correct spelling of the person's name, home address, daytime telephone number, and date of birth. It is helpful to obtain insurance information as well as the full name of the guarantor or responsible party (if not the patient) and his or her relationship to the patient at the time of new patient scheduling so that insurance verification can be made before the patient comes into the office.

When arranging the appointment, keep in mind that the matrix will dictate availability of some types of appointments. When scheduling an appointment for a new patient, make sure to allow enough time for filling out forms. Have the new patient arrive 15 to 30 minutes early to do this. Information about the office may be mailed out prior to the first appointment, including a patient information brochure, medical history forms, and a patient registration form if time allows. The patient should be instructed to complete the forms and bring

the completed forms with him for the first appointment. Upon arrival, the new patient should also be given the HIPAA guidelines for your office while his or her chart is being prepared for the visit. Receipt of the signed HIPAA guidelines from the patient is now a requirement for all patients. Refer to Procedure 12–3 at the end of this chapter on how to determine patient status.

Established Patients

It is always good practice to ask patients returning to the reception area if they need to schedule another appointment. It may be helpful to routinely schedule return appointments at the same time and/or day that the patient has had previously. Getting them to make the appointment then will save you from having to do so by telephone later on. Procedure 12–3 at the end of the chapter outlines the procedure utilized in making patient appointments.

Appointment Confirmations and Reminders

Some patients may have trouble remembering their next appointment, especially if they arrange it far in advance. To help patients keep track of their appointments, you can use several types of appointment reminders.

Appointment Cards In many offices the medical assistant fills out and hands the patient an appointment reminder card upon checkout, like the one shown in Figure 12–5. Figure 12–6 consists of a superbill with the return appointment information area noted at the bottom of the superbill. To reduce the chance of error, enter the appointment in the appointment book or scheduler first, then fill out the card. Otherwise, when the patient takes the appointment card, you have to rely on your memory when entering the appointment in the book and in a busy office this often can lead to errors. Refer to Procedure 12–4 at the end of the chapter for the steps in completing an appointment card.

Encounter Forms/Superbills As the patient leaves the office, he or she may be given paperwork to return to the front desk. This form, commonly known as the superbill or encounter form, lists items services performed, diagnoses, health insurance, and demographic information regarding the patient, as well as account balance. This can also serve as a receipt if payments are made and as an appointment reminder for the next appointment to be scheduled. See Figure 12–6.

Reminder Mailings When making a follow-up appointment in person, you can ask the patient to address to himself a postcard on which you have written the next appointment's date and time. This postcard serves as a backup in case the patient loses the original appointment reminder card. Place the postcard in the tickler file under the day when it should be sent (usually a week or two before the appointment). Reminder mailings can also be sent to patients who make appointments over the telephone. In this case, of course, you must address the postcard for the tickler file yourself. Although reminder mailings are useful when appointments are made many months in advance or for geriatric patients, they can become costly for the practice and should be limited when possible.

Reminder Calls Depending on office policy and available time, you might also call patients 1 or 2 days before their appointments to confirm the scheduled time. This technique can be especially helpful for patients with a history of late arrivals or for **no-shows** (patients who do not call to cancel and do

no-show
Patients who do not call to cancel and do not come to the appointment.

figure 12–5
Before patients leave the office, be sure to give them an appointment card if they are scheduled to return to the office.

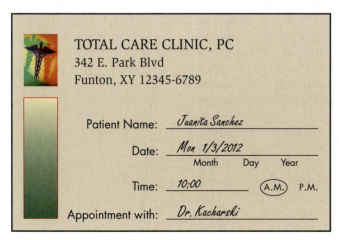

TOTAL CARE CLINIC, PC
342 E. Park Blvd
Funton, XY 12345-6789

Patient Name: _Juanita Sanchez_

Date: _Mon 1/3/2012_
　　　　Month　Day　Year

Time: _10:00_　(A.M.)　P.M.

Appointment with: _Dr. Kacharski_

TOTAL CARE CLINIC, PC
342 E. Park Blvd
Funton, XY 12345-6789

Phone: 521-234-0001   Fax: 521-234-0002   www.totalcareclinic.org

☐ PRIVATE   ☐ BLUECROSS   ☐ IND.   ☐ MEDICARE   ☐ MEDI-CAL   ☐ HMO   ☐ PPO

PATIENT'S LAST NAME	FIRST	ACCOUNT #	BIRTHDATE / /	SEX ☐ MALE ☐ FEMALE	TODAY'S DATE / /
INSURANCE COMPANY	SUBSCRIBER		PLAN #	SUB. #	GROUP

ASSIGNMENT: I hereby assign my insurance benefits to be paid directly to the undersigned physician. I am financially responsible for non-covered services.
SIGNED: (Patient, or Parent, if Minor)   DATE: /   /

RELEASE: I hereby authorize the physician to release to my insurance carrers any information required to process this claim.
SIGNED: (Patient, or Parent, if Minor)   DATE: /   /

✔	DESCRIPTION	M/Care	CPT/Mod	DxRe	FEE	✔	DESCRIPTION	M/Care	CPT/Mod	DxRe	FEE	✔	DESCRIPTION	M/Care	CPT/Mod	DxRe	FEE
	OFFICE CARE						PROCEDURES						INJECTIONS/IMMUNIZATIONS				
	NEW PATIENT						Tread Mill (In Office)		93015				Tetanus		90718		
	Brief		99201				24 Hour Holter		93224				Hypertet	J1670	90782		
	Limited		99202				If Medicare (Set up Fec)		93225				Pneumococcal		90732		
	Intermediate		99203				Physician Interpret		93227				Influenza		90724		
	Extended		99204				EKG w/Interpretation		93000				TB Skin Test (PPD)		86585		
	Comprehensive		99205				EKG (Medicare)		93005				Antigen Injection-Single		95115		
							Sigmoidoscopy		45300				Multiple		95117		
	ESTABLISHED PATIENT						Sigmoidoscopy, Flexible		45330				B12 Injection	J3420	90782		
	Minimal		99211				Sigmoidos. , Flex. w/Bx.		45331				Injection, IM		90782		
	Brief		99212				Spirometry, FEV/FVC		94010				Compazine	J0780	90782		
	Limited		99213				Spirometry, Post-Dilator		94060				Demerol	J2175	90782		
	Intermediate		99214										Vistaril	J3410	90782		
	Extended		99215										Susphrine	J0170	90782		
	Comprehensive		99215				LABORATORY						Decadron	J0890	90782		
							Blood Draw Fee		36415				Estradiol	J1000	90782		
	CONSULTATION-OFFICE						Urinalysis, Chemical		81005				Testosterone	J1080	90782		
	Focused		99241				Throat Culture		87081				Lidocaine	J2000	90782		
	Expanded		99242				Occult Blood		82270				Solumedrol	J2920	90782		
	Detailed		99243				Pap Handling Charge		99000				Solucortef	J1720	90782		
	Comprehensive 1		99244				Pap Life Guard		88150-90				Hydeltra	J1690	90782		
	Comprehensive 2		99245				Gram Stain		87205				Pen Procaine	J2510	90788		
	Dr.						Hanging Drop		87210								
	Case Management		98900				Urine Drug Screen		99000				INJECTIONS - JOINT/BURSA				
													Small Joints		20600		
	Post-op Exam		99024										Intermediate		20605		
							SUPPLIES						Large Joints		20610		
													Trigger Point		20550		
													MISCELLANEOUS				

	DIAGNOSIS:	ICD-9										
	Abdominal Pain	789.0		Gout	274.0		C.V.A. - Acute	436.		Electrolyte Dis.	276.9	Herpes Simplex 054.9

DIAGNOSIS: ICD-9
- Abdominal Pain 789.0
- Abscess (Site) 682.9
- Adverse Drug Rx 995.2
- Alcohol Detox 291.8
- Alcoholism 303.90
- Allergic Rhinitis 477
- Allergy 995.3
- Alzheimer's Dis. 290.1
- Anemia 285.9
- Anemia - Pernicious 281.0
- Angina 413.9
- Anxiety Synd. 300.00
- Appendicitis 541
- Arterioscl. H.D. 414.0
- Arthritis, Osteo. 715.90
- Rheumatoid 714.0
- Lupus 710.0

- Gout 274.0
- Asthma 493.90
- Asthmatic Bronchitis 493.90
- Atrial Fib. 427.31
- Atrial Tachi. 427.0
- Bowel Obstruct. 560.9
- Breast Mass 611.72
- Bronchitis 490
- Bursitis 727.3
- Cancer, Breast (Site) 174.9
- Metastatic (Site) 199.1
- Cancer, Rectal 154.1
- Colon 153.9
- Lung (Site) 162.9
- Skin (Site) 173.9
- Card. Arrhythmia (Type) 427.9
- Cardiomyopathy 425.4
- Cellulitis (Site) 682.9

- C.V.A. - Acute 436.
- Cere. Vas. Accid. (Old) 438
- Cerumen 380.4
- Chestwall Pain 786.59
- Cholecystitis 575.0
- Cholelithiasis 574.00
- COPD 492.8
- Cirrhosis 571.5
- Cong. Heart Fail. 428.9
- Conjunctivitis 372.30
- Contusion (Site) 924.9
- Costochondritis 733.99
- Depression 311.
- Dermatitis 692.9
- Diabetes Mellitus 250.00
- Diabetic Ketosis 250.1
- Diverticulitis 562.11
- Diverticulosis 562.10

- Electrolyte Dis. 276.9
- Fatigue 780.7
- Fibrocys. Br. Dis 610.1
- Fracture (Site) 829.0
- Open/Close
- Fungal Infect. (Site) 110.8
- Gastric Ulcer 531.90
- Gastritis 535.0
- Gastroenteritis 558.9
- G.I. Bleeding 578.9
- Glomerulonephritis 583.9
- Headache 784.0
- Headache, Tension 307.81
- Migraine (Type) 346.9
- Hemorrhoids 455.6
- Hernia, Hiatal 553.3
- Inguinal 550.9
- Hepatitis 573.3

- Herpes Simplex 054.9
- Herpes Zoster 053.9
- Hydrocele 603.9
- Hyperlipidemia 272.4
- Hypertension 401.9
- Hyperthyroidism 242.9
- Hypothyroidism 244.9
- Labyrinthitis 386.30
- Lipoma (Site) 214.9
- Lymphoma 202.8
- Mit. Valve Prolapse 424.0
- Myocard. Infarction (Area) 410.9
- M.I., Old 412
- Myositis 729.1
- Nausea/Vomiting 787.0
- Neuralgia 729.2
- Nevus (Site) 216.9
- Obesity 278.0

DIAGNOSIS: (IF NOT CHECKED ABOVE)

SERVICES PERFORMED AT: ☐ Office   ☐ E.R.   ☐ CLAIM CONTAINS NO ORDERED REFERRING SERVICE   REFERRING PHYSICIAN & I.D. NUMBER
☐   ☐

RETURN APPOINTMENT INFORMATION: 5 - 10 - 15 - 20 - 30 - 40 - 60 [DAYS] [WKS.] [MOS.] [PRN]	NEXT APPOINTMENT M - T - W - TH - F - S DATE / / TIME:	ACCEPT ASSIGNMENT? AM ☐ YES PM ☐ NO	DOCTOR'S SIGNATURE

INSTRUCTIONS TO PATIENT FOR FILING INSURANCE CLAIMS:		
1. Complete upper portion of this form, sign and date. 2. Attach this form to your own insurance company's form for direct reimbursement. **MEDICARE PATIENTS - DO NOT SEND THIS TO MEDICARE. WE WILL SUBMIT THE CLAIM FOR YOU.**	☐ CASH ☐ CHECK # ☐ VISA ☐ MC ☐ CO-PAY	TOTAL TODAY'S FEE OLD BALANCE TOTAL DUE AMOUNT REC'D. TODAY

INSUR-A-BILL ® BIBBERO SYSTEMS, INC. • PETALUMA, CA • UP. SUPER. © 6/94 (BIBB/STOCK)

figure 12-6

An example of an encounter form with an area for return appointment at the bottom.

not come to the appointment). Writing patients' phone numbers next to their names in the appointment book makes it convenient for you to make appointment reminder calls. Procedure 12–5 at the end of the chapter outlines the steps in making appointment reminder calls. Many offices who utilize electronic phone systems, also utilize the system to make reminder calls for them, freeing the office staff from this task. Be aware of patients who do not wish to be contacted by phone or to have messages left. Having the patient fill out a verbal contact agreement at their first visit can limit HIPAA violations. Figure 12–7

figure 12-7

HIPAA verbal agreement form.

TOTAL CARE CLINIC, PC

342 E. Park Blvd
Funton, XY 12345-6789
Tel: (521)-234-0001
Fax: (521)-234-0002
www.totalcareclinic.org

MRN:
NAME:
DOB:
DATE:

VERBAL RELEASE OF INFORMATION

Total Care Clinic is allowed to give verbal information or updates about your condition to you, your Power of Attorney for Healthcare/Legal Representative as listed in your medical record.

If you wish others, such as relatives or friends WHO ASK about your condition, to have the right to be verbally informed about your condition when they ask, please list the names of those individuals on the lines provided below.

I _____ am authorizing the release of verbal medical information regarding my treatment, care, and updates on my condition to the following individuals.

NAME: _____   RELATIONSHIP: _____

NAME: _____   RELATIONSHIP: _____

NAME: _____   RELATIONSHIP: _____

NAME: _____   RELATIONSHIP: _____

- I understand the Total Care Clinic will continue to rely on the information on this form when communicating with family members or others involved in my care unless I request changes.

- I understand that I may revoke this verbal agreement authorization at any time.

- I understand that if I choose to revoke this authorization, I MUST do so in writing and present my written revocation to the Privacy Officer at Total Care Clinic. The revocation will NOT apply to information that has already been disclosed prior to the receipt of the written revocation for which we will have 30 days to comply with your request.

_____   _____

SIGNATURE OF PATIENT OR GUARDIAN   DATE

provides an example of a HIPAA-compliant verbal agreement form. If patients agree that messages may be left on voice mail or answering machines, this information should be added to the verbal agreement form.

Recall Notices   Some offices book appointments no more than a few weeks in advance, or may not have the next year's schedule available when a patient is ready to book a return appointment. In either case, if your office has such a policy, you need a way to make sure patients do not forget to call for appointments that are 6 months—or even a year—away from their last appointments.

Suppose, for example, that the physician tells a patient she should have an annual breast examination. How can you help her remember to call to schedule one at the appropriate time? One way is to use a system of recall notices. In a tickler file enter the patient's name under the month when she should call the office. When the time arrives, send a form letter reminding her that she will soon be due for a breast examination and asking her to call for an appointment.

E-mail Notifications   With more practices trying to accommodate all patient groups, a newer approach to appointment scheduling is through the use of e-mail. Patients sign up and are assigned passwords by the office. The patient may request an appointment as long as it is not needed immediately. When a scheduled appointment is approaching, an automatically generated notification goes out to the patient's e-mail address. This is not suitable for all patients or all types of appointments. Some appointment types will still need to be handled by the office staff either by phone or in person.

What are the ways that you can remind a patient of an upcoming appointment?

CHECKPOINT
LO 12.4

LO 12.5 Special Scheduling Situations

In most cases scheduling is routine; however, critical thinking, creativity, and flexibility are necessary for scheduling some special cases. These special situations often involve patients, but they may also involve physicians.

Patient Scheduling Situations

On some days all patients will keep their appointments and arrive on time. On many other days, however, patients may walk in without appointments, arrive late for scheduled appointments, or miss appointments entirely. Being able to anticipate needs and being prepared for these possibilities allows you to handle them more efficiently, keeping the office schedule running smoothly.

Emergencies   Your training as an administrative medical assistant will help you recognize the signs of an emergency. In some instances you will refer the caller to the nearest hospital emergency room or instruct the caller to call emergency medical services (EMS) for an ambulance. The procedure you will follow will be dependent on office policies and procedures. In other instances you will ask the caller to come to the office right away so you can "work" them into the schedule. It is vital that doctors see emergency patients before patients who are already in the waiting area or on the schedule. It is best to explain to waiting patients that there has been an emergency (without giving details). This announcement helps them understand and accept the delay and also gives them an opportunity to reschedule their appointments if they are unable to wait.

Referrals   Sometimes other doctors refer their patients to the practice for second opinions or special consultations. A patient seeking a second opinion before

Scheduling Emergency Appointments

As a multiskilled medical assistant, you will be well-prepared to tell the difference between acute conditions that are emergencies and those that are not. Guidelines on types of emergencies to be seen in the office and types to be referred elsewhere will vary. If you have any doubt, kindly interrupt the physician to ask for instructions.

Even with allotted times built into the daily schedule, emergencies are still disruptive to most practices. Your ability to stay calm, respond quickly, and remain flexible will be of great comfort to the emergency patient and to others in the waiting area. Read the following story to see how an emergency situation can be handled skillfully.

The Situation

It is 4:15 P.M. in a busy family practice. The telephone rings. The caller is the father of a 10-year-old boy. Maria, the medical assistant, can hear the panic in his voice. His son Kyle has injured his knee while playing football with friends. Kyle cannot straighten the knee, and it is quite swollen.

Maria consults the physician, who suspects torn cartilage. The physician tells Maria to have the father wrap ice in a towel, apply it to Kyle's knee, and bring him in immediately. Maria relays this advice to the father and asks him how soon he can get to the office.

"It will take about 25 minutes," he replies.

The office schedule includes a time opening at 4:30, but based on the father's estimate, Kyle cannot possibly arrive until 4:40. Maria notes that Mrs. Griffin, a good-natured retiree, is scheduled to come in for her weekly blood pressure check at 4:45 P.M. Hers is the last scheduled appointment of the day.

The Solution

Mrs. Griffin lives about 5 minutes from the office. Maria calls her home and explains that there has been an emergency. She offers Mrs. Griffin three choices: she can come in at 4:30 and be seen then; she can arrive at the usual time and expect to wait; or she can be rescheduled for tomorrow due to an opening in the schedule.

"No problem," Mrs. Griffin says cheerfully. "I'll come right over."

Mrs. Griffin arrives at 4:35. At 4:40, Kyle hobbles in, supported by his father. Maria greets them and offers Kyle a chair on which to prop his foot.

Mrs. Griffin's blood pressure check is complete at 4:45. Kyle waits only 5 minutes before he is seen.

Thanks to Maria's quick thinking, the office stays on schedule—essentially by switching one appointment for another and accommodating both with minimal interruptions.

---

deciding on surgery, often at the request of his or her insurance carrier, should be fit into the schedule as soon as possible. Other referred patients should also be seen sooner rather than later, as a matter of professional courtesy to the referring doctor as well as good business practice.

Many office manuals maintain a listing of preferred physicians and facilities that they would like their patients to see and use. This list should contain the doctor or facility names, specialty, address, and their phone numbers. When arranging a referral, try to give the patient two referral names to choose from, along with the referral phone numbers and addresses. When choosing the referral names of either physicians or facilities, be sure that the facility accepts the patient's insurance and all of the paperwork required by the insurance company has been completed. All referrals should be documented in the patient's medical record. Some insurance carriers require a specific referral form be filled out, some require the use of a point of service (POS) device where the office enters the information into the insurance company database, and others require a phone request where the office speaks to a customer service representative or enters specific information into an automated voice response telephone system.

Fasting Patients Some procedures and tests require patients to fast or refrain from eating or drinking anything beginning the night before. Scheduling these patients as early in the day as possible shows consideration for their needs. When scheduling appointments that require the patient to fast, be sure to inform the patient of the need to fast and when fasting should start, including the fact that the test may not be completed if the patient does not fast.

Patients with Diabetes

Like fasting patients, patients with diabetes can use extra consideration when you schedule their appointments. In general, patients who take insulin must eat meals and snacks at regular times. This routine keeps their blood sugar from dropping too low—a condition that can result in confused thinking or even loss of consciousness. Therefore, you might want to avoid scheduling patients with diabetes for slots in late morning. If the schedule is running late by the time these patients arrive, they will be waiting in your reception area at a time when they really need to eat.

EHR readiness

Referrals from the Managed Care Company

As more medical offices become computerized, insurance companies are doing the same. Previously, when a patient needed a referral to another physician or service, the referring office had to contact the insurance company by phone or complete a paper referral. More and more insurance companies today are allowing the physicians to resource their databases and software to determine eligibility, authorizations, and in-network services. This frees up representatives from both offices to work with the more complicated cases. It also makes the referral process more efficient as approvals are usually submitted and approved within a matter of minutes online.

Repeat Visits   Some patients need regular appointments, such as for prenatal checkups or physical therapy. If possible, schedule these appointments for the same day and time each week. Establishing a routine helps patients remember their appointments and simplifies the office schedule.

Late Arrivals   If the practice has patients who are routinely late and gentle reminders to be on time have not helped, you might try booking them toward the end of the day. Even if a patient arrives late for a late-afternoon appointment, the doctor has already seen most of the day's patients and the late patient will not disrupt the schedule. Document late arrivals or missed appointments in the patient's chart. With documentation, patients who are habitually late can be called to discuss the reasons for their lateness. The goal of the discussion should be to find a solution so that patients can make their appointments on time and the schedule will run smoothly.

Walk-Ins   From time to time, a patient may arrive without an appointment and still expect to see the doctor. These people are called **walk-ins.** Office policies on how to handle walk-ins will vary. If the person is experiencing an emergency, handle the situation as you would handle any emergency. Otherwise, you might politely explain that the doctor is fully booked for the day and offer to schedule an appointment in the usual manner. If, by chance, the doctor is available and willing to see the walk-in, you should still ask the person to call to schedule appointments in the future. If your physician's office has a policy of no walk-ins, post a sign in the patient check-in area stating that patients are seen by appointment only.

walk-in
A patient who arrives at the office without an appointment and expects to see the physician.

Cancellations   When patients call to cancel appointments, try to reschedule the appointment while they are on the telephone. If patients say they will call later to reschedule, note this information in the appointment book and thank them for the notice.

You should also write "canceled" in the appointment book, drawing a single line through the patient's name. To avoid confusion, cancel the first appointment *before* entering the patient's rescheduled appointment. Remember that the appointment book is a legal record. If you forget to cross out the name at the time of the first appointment, it may later seem that the doctor saw the patient twice. It is also important to note the cancellation in the patient's medical record. This notation can protect the practice from possible legal action. For

example, a patient whose incision became infected could not blame the doctor if the patient canceled a scheduled appointment for a dressing change.

You may be able to fill slots created by cancellations by calling patients who have appointments scheduled for later in the day or week. Some patients may be willing to come in earlier than planned. When you make appointments, you can ask patients if they would be interested in coming in earlier if openings occur. Placing the names of interested patients in a tickler file or on a cancellation list can save time later.

Missed and Wrong-Day Appointments It is important for legal reasons to document a no-show in the appointment book and patient medical record. Always inform the physician of any missed appointments in case the patient's condition requires a follow-up. The physician may want you to call the patient with a polite reminder that the patient has missed an appointment and needs to reschedule. There may have been a misunderstanding about the time, or the patient may simply have forgotten the appointment. Some offices, especially ones that use computerized scheduling systems, send out form letters when patients miss appointments. If failure to keep the appointment could endanger the patient's health, mention this possibility to the patient, or ask the physician to tell the patient over the telephone and at his or her next visit. Some physicians limit the number of times that a patient can miss or not show up for appointments, as this can lead to liability issues for the physician. Again, always document any missed or canceled appointment in the patient medical record.

Periodically, physicians charge for missed appointments, especially if patients habitually miss their appointments. These missed appointment charges are for missed business opportunities and not for services rendered. If your office implements this policy, make sure that you let patients know in advance before you start charging them for missed appointments. Some offices opt for a notation on the appointment cards that states patients will be charged for appointments that are cancelled with less than 24 hours notice.

Sometimes a patient may show up on the wrong day for her appointment. If the patient lives in the local area, rescheduling makes sense. But if the patient made special transportation arrangements or traveled from a long distance, it is good business practice to try to work the patient into the schedule for that day. If the patient provides an appointment card verifying the appointment for that day, but she is not on the schedule, the office is obligated to honor the appointment if the physician is in the office. When in doubt about the best course of action, consult with the doctor or office manager.

Physician Scheduling Situations

Not all scheduling problems result from patients. Sometimes physicians disrupt the office schedule as well. They may be called away on an emergency, may be delayed at the hospital, or may simply arrive late.

Some physicians may occasionally be late for appointments, while others are frequently late, either when arriving in the morning or when returning from lunch or a scheduled meeting. If this situation occurs in your office, you might approach it in several ways.

At a staff meeting you could mention that the morning or afternoon schedule often seems to get off to a late start. Then you might ask if anyone has suggestions for improving this situation. The physician may recognize that she is the cause of the problem and decide to resolve it.

If the physician does not take responsibility for the problem, however, you may need to adjust the office schedule to handle the situation. Suppose, for example, that the first patient appointment slot is at 8:30 A.M., but the physician usually does not arrive until 8:35 A.M. You could simply avoid scheduling

patients between 8:30 and 8:45 A.M. If a physician is often 15 minutes late returning from lunch or from meetings, you might leave open the first appointment slot after the scheduled arrival time in an attempt to avoid long wait times for patients; keeping satisfied clients.

CHECKPOINT
LO 12.5

Describe how to handle the special scheduling situations in which fasting patients must be scheduled.

LO 12.6 Scheduling Outside Appointments

You may be responsible for arranging patient appointments outside the medical office. These appointments may include:

- Consultations with or referrals to other physicians
- Laboratory work
- Radiology (x-ray, CT scans, MRI)
- Other diagnostic tests (EKG, stress testing)
- Hospital stays
- Inpatient and outpatient surgeries

Always verify the patient's type of insurance before choosing which facility or physician the referral will be sent to. Today, a patient's insurance coverage may dictate where a procedure may be performed as well as the physician who may be allowed to provided the service. A prior approval or referral from the insurance carrier may also be required. As the administrative medical assistant, you will often be the person responsible for knowing not only the preferred physicians and facilities of the physician, but also the physicians and facilities allowed by specific insurance carriers. Obtaining referrals and prior authorizations will also often be your responsibility. (Refer to Chapter 17 for more information on this topic.)

Once a facility and provider has been agreed upon by the physician, patient, and insurance carrier, document any referrals or prior authorization numbers (again, refer to Chapter 17). Assuming the procedure is elective, ask the patient if there is a preferred date and time. If the request fits into the provider and facility schedule, try to accommodate them, as this small gesture allows the patient to have some small control of the situation.

Before calling the surgery center, laboratory, or in- or outpatient department required for the procedure, be sure that you have the patient's medical record, the exact name of the procedure to be performed, the approximate amount of time required (if your physician is performing the service), diagnosis, the patient's insurance information, date of birth, phone number, and home address. Give this information to the scheduler, keeping in mind the patient's preferred time frame if it can be accommodated. Once an appointment time has been agreed upon, ask the scheduler for any patient instructions, carefully documenting them to relay to the patient. If paperwork will be sent to the patient from the facility, be sure the patient also understands this.

When arrangements have been made, inform the patient orally and also provide him with written instructions, asking about and answering any questions the patient may have. Be sure they understand any pre-procedure instructions. Be sure the patient understands that if the instructions are not followed perfectly, the procedure may need to be rescheduled or repeated. Remember to note in the patient's chart the date and time of the procedure as well as instructions provided to the patient. Procedure 12–6 outlines the procedure for booking an outpatient surgical appointment It is found at the end of this chapter.

Duties and Skills

When a patient is in acute distress and the treatment provided in the office is not adequate, a direct hospital admission may be required. The health-care professional employed by the hospital to assist with this process is the hospital admissions clerk, also known as the unit secretary or unit clerk. The physician's administrative medical assistant will call the admissions clerk with the diagnosis, medications the patient is on, diagnostic and therapeutic treatments ordered for the admission, and the approximate duration of the stay in the hospital, all of which should be in the physician's admitting orders. Once provided with this information, the hospital admissions clerk will determine bed availability and provide you with the hospital floor and bed number assigned to your patient. In some cases, the patient will be allowed to go directly to the floor, but depending on hospital rules, the patient may need to be admitted through the emergency department. The admissions clerk will provide you with the necessary instructions for each patient admission.

The hospital admissions clerk is responsible for all clerical duties surrounding patient admission and discharge and has a clear understanding of hospital regulations and legal guidelines ensuring patient confidentiality and continuity of patient care from admission to discharge (and beyond).

Educational Requirements

The admissions clerk must have a high school diploma or equivalent. Most employers also require an associate's degree or certificate from a medical secretarial, medical administrative, or medical assisting program because of the medical terminology, computer software, and medicolegal classes contained within such programs. Strong communication skills, both oral and written, are mandatory with this position, as is the ability to multi-task and work effectively both independently and as a multi-skilled team member.

Workplace Settings

Most hospital admission clerks are employed in acute care hospitals, but they may also be found in emergency departments, ambulatory surgery centers, and long-term care centers.

The Hospital Admissions Clerk as a Team Member

The hospital admissions clerk works with almost every member of the health-care team—physicians, nurses, PAs, social workers, physician office staff, and all hospital personnel as well as patients and family members. As an administrative medical assistant, you will speak with a hospital admissions clerk or unit clerk whenever a patient is to be a direct admission to the hospital or when a patient is in the hospital and you must obtain information for the physician from the hospital unit, as more often than not, the unit clerk will be the one answering the phone and either directly answering your inquiries or directing your call to the person who can assist you.

For more information, visit the following Web sites, which are available on the Online Learning Center at www.mhhe.com/houseradminmedassist

www.ehow.com/about_5065915_job-description-admissions-clerk.html

http://careers.stateuniversity.com/pages/439/Ward-Clerk.html

www.allalliedhealthschools.com

CHECKPOINT
LO 12.6

When would it not be acceptable to allow patients to schedule their own virtual appointments?

LO 12.7 Maintaining the Physician's Schedule

The schedules of busy physicians are not limited to office visits with patients. Physicians also need to attend professional meetings, travel to conferences, present speeches to colleagues, complete paperwork, and perform other duties. Your job is to help physicians make the most efficient use of their time.

One way is to avoid overbooking appointments with patients. **Overbooking** (scheduling more patients than can reasonably be seen in the time allowed) creates stress for the physician and the staff, and makes it difficult to maintain a timely schedule.

overbooking
Scheduling appointments for more patients than can reasonably be seen in the time allowed.

The opposite problem, **underbooking**—leaving large, unused gaps in the schedule—does not make the best use of the physician's time. Of course, you have no control over patients who cancel or do not show for appointments but as mentioned previously, there are ways to decrease this, such as calling patients to remind them of their appointments a day or two ahead of the scheduled appointment. If you cannot reschedule another patient for the empty slot, the physician can use the time to catch up on telephone calls to patients or to attend to other matters.

At times you will have to cancel appointments because the physician has been delayed or called away by an emergency. Apologize to waiting patients on behalf of the physician, and offer them a choice. Explain that they can wait in the office (give an estimated waiting time), leave to run errands and return later, or reschedule their appointments for another day. Documentation should be noted in the patient's chart that because of an emergency in the office, the appointment had to be rescheduled by the office so the patient is not held at fault for the cancellation. Be sure to write the date of the rescheduled appointment in the chart as well. Always make sure patients who need immediate attention are seen by another physician if available; staying within office policies.

Reserving an Operating Room

If the doctor in your office plans to perform surgery at a hospital, you will need to call the operating room scheduler to reserve the facility. Give the preferred dates and times, the type of surgery, and the length of time the doctor will need the operating room. After the day and time are set, provide the scheduler with all relevant patient information. Relay any requests from the doctor, such as the blood type and units of blood that may be needed. It may also be your responsibility to make arrangements for surgical assistants, an anesthetist, and a hospital bed for the patient following surgery. Make sure that all health insurance requirements such as referrals and prior authorizations are met and copies of forms and authorization numbers are filed appropriately. As when scheduling outpatient procedures, be sure the patient receives all necessary oral and written instructions and information regarding pre- and post-surgical care and that all questions are answered. Procedure 12–7 found at the end of the chapter outlines the steps for booking an inpatient surgical appointment.

Visits Outside the Office

Some physicians provide care outside of the office—in patient homes, in nursing homes, or during rounds within the hospital when their patients have been admitted.

House Calls   Physicians may want to check on home-bound or nonambulatory patients as part of their follow-up care. Although not as common as it once was, house calls are a valuable service that physicians can provide to patients who can no longer easily make it to the doctor's office for their appointments. Many insurance companies allow for the physician to bill for these services with restrictions that vary depending on the plan. Supplies required for visits will vary depending on the type and location of the visit, but general supplies that should be kept in a medical bag include the following:

- Blood pressure cuff
- Stethoscope
- Specimen containers
- Otoscope
- Ophthalmoscope
- Prescription pad

underbooking
Leaving large, unused gaps in the doctor's schedule; this approach does not make the best use of the doctor's time.

- Pen light
- Thermometer
- Gloves, face shield

Hospital Rounds   Historically, physicians typically visited their own patients when they became hospitalized. More and more physicians and hospitals are turning this responsibility over to a physician/specialist known as a hospitalist. A hospitalist is a physician who does not hold office hours and does not maintain a practice, but only sees patients while they are hospitalized. If your office utilizes this service, the hospitalist will report back to your office on the patient's progress and findings.

Nursing Home Visits   Some physicians will check on their patients even when they are receiving around-the-clock care from a skilled nursing facility. Some physicians have seen their patients for years and will stay involved because of the long-standing relationship or because the patient may be returning home and will need follow-up care.

"Mouse Calls"   With all of the new technology available to them, physicians are learning new ways to communicate with their patients. In their daily schedule, time is often allotted for physicians to return phone calls, which today can also include "mouse" calls—physicians answering e-mail inquiries from their patients. These can also be "virtual visits" covered by some insurance plans.

Scheduling Pharmaceutical Sales Representatives

Drug manufacturers often send pharmaceutical sales representatives into medical offices with printed information about new drugs as well as free samples that can be given to patients. This is an added benefit for your patients but can be time consuming as the representatives will want to market their products. The representatives are required to obtain signatures from the physicians in order to leave the samples behind, and for this reason, some doctors do not want to meet with pharmaceutical representatives. Other doctors are willing to spend a few minutes if time permits and if the products are likely to be useful to their patients. Some doctors set aside certain times or days during the week when they will meet with pharmaceutical representatives. Others prefer that the representative leave a business card with the products represented, and if the physician is interested, he will call and arrange for an appointment at a mutually agreeable time. When a pharmaceutical representative who is unknown to you comes into the office, ask for a business card and check with the physician or business manager before scheduling an appointment (Figure 12–8).

figure 12–8

If pharmaceutical representatives come into the office without an appointment, you can ask them to leave a business card.

itinerary
A detailed travel plan listing dates and times for specific transportation arrangements and events, the location of meetings and lodgings, and phone numbers.

Making Travel Arrangements

You may be responsible for arranging transportation and lodging when physicians attend meetings, speaking engagements, and other events out of town. You may be responsible for contacting the airlines, car rental agencies, hotels, or other services yourself or you may use an online service such as Orbitz or work through a travel agent. No matter which method is used to make travel arrangements, always request confirmation documents of travel and room reservations.

Before the day of departure, obtain an itinerary from the travel agent or online service, or create one yourself. An **itinerary** is a detailed travel plan,

listing dates and times of flights and events, locations of meetings and lodgings, and telephone numbers. Give several copies to the physician, and keep one for the office (Figure 12–9).

You may also be responsible for scheduling and confirming professional coverage of the practice during the physician's absence. In larger practices and more urban area, often physicians in the same or nearby practice will provide coverage while the physician is away. This coverage may be important for legal reasons, most importantly so the physician cannot be charged with "abandoning" his patients. If a local physician is not readily available, a **locum tenens,** or substitute physician, may be hired to see patients while the regular physician is away. (*Locum tenens* is Latin for "one occupying the place of another.") You may have more than one locum tenens on call, depending on the practice. In

locum tenens
A substitute physician hired to see patients while the regular physician is away from the office.

figure 12–9

An example travel itinerary.

Dr. Matthew Rodriguez
Travel Itinerary

TOTAL CARE CLINIC, PC

342 E. Park Blvd
Funton, XY 12345-6789
Phone: 521-234-0001   Fax: 521-234-0002
www.totalcareclinic.org

Client Information

Traveler's Name	Matthew Rodriguez, M.D.
Address	560 Williamsburg Ct., Atlanta, GA
Telephone Number	404-279-0098
Fax Number	404-279-0099
E-Mail Address	
Travel Dates	May 5 – 9, 201X

Departure Flight

Date	May 5, 201X
Airline	United International
Flight Number	567
From	Atlanta
Departure Time	6:45 am
Departure Terminal/Gate	56C
To	Los Angeles, CA
Arrival Time	9:45 am Pacific time
Length of Flight	5 hours
Class	First Class
Seat Number	12a
Status	confirmed

Monday – May 5, 201X

• Morning:

8:00 – 8:45	Physician Recruiter
9:00 – 10:00	Formal interview with Team, facilitated by Recruiter
10:00 – 11:00	Medical Director
11:00 – 12:00	Tour of UCLA including department with Area Manager

• Afternoon:

12:30 – 1:30	Lunch with physician(s) from another department with similar interests
2:00 – 3:00	One (1) hour with Department Chair and/or Physician Area Manager
4:00 – 6:00	One-on-one interviews with department or other physicians
	Informal time in interviewing department, as appropriate

• Evening:

7:00 – until	Dinner* ** (or private dinner on their own)

some areas special firms provide these services and other temporary medical and nursing assistance. Before hiring locum tenens physicians, you may want to contact some of the major insurance carriers providing health insurance coverage for your patients to find out their credentialing and claim requirements so that the services provided by the locum tenens physicians will be considered covered services.

Planning Meetings

You may help the doctor set up meetings for professional societies or committees. To do so, you will need to know how many people are expected to attend, how long the meeting will last, and the purpose of the meeting. In addition, ask the doctor if a meal is to be served.

Some groups always meet at the same location. If there is no established meeting place, you must choose and reserve one. Select a location with an adequately sized meeting room, sufficient parking, and, if needed, food services. Be sure also to arrange for necessary audiovisual (AV) equipment, such as a microphone, podium, or projector. Many conference centers and hotels have an on-site catering manager or conference manager to assist you with these arrangements. When the facility has been booked, mail an invitation to all those expected to attend the meeting. On the invitation, provide the topic, names of the speakers, date, time, place, and admission costs or fees associated with the event if applicable.

With direction from the physician, you may also be responsible for creating the meeting's agenda. An **agenda** is a list of topics to be discussed or presented at a meeting in order of presentation, and may or may not include approximate time frames for each topic to be discussed. After the meeting, you may also be asked to prepare the **minutes,** or the report of what was discussed and decided at the meeting.

Scheduling Time with the Physician

You and the physician should meet on a scheduled basis to discuss any irregularities or changes in the day-to-day workings of the office. These meetings may be held between you and the physician alone or include the office manager. If items are not pressing or "private," many discussions may be included in regularly scheduled office meetings. Examples of recurring deadlines include those for state medical license renewal, Drug Enforcement Agency (DEA) registrations, and documentation of the physician's continuing medical education (CME) requirements. Table 12–1 lists items that are often part of a physician's recurring schedule.

agenda
The list of topics discussed or presented at a meeting in order of presentation.

minutes
A report of what happened and what was discussed and decided at a meeting.

table 12–1

Common Items on a Physician's Schedule

Payments, Dues, and Fees
- Association dues
- Health insurance premium
- Payment for laundry service
- Liability insurance premium
- Life insurance premium
- Office rent
- Property insurance premium
- Paychecks for staff
- Payment for janitorial services
- Payment for leased equipment
- Taxes

table 12-1 (Concluded)

> — Quarterly federal tax payments
> — Quarterly state tax payments
> — Annual federal and state tax filing deadline
>
> **Time Commitments**
> - Committee meetings
> - Conventions
>
> **Renewals and Accreditations**
> - Facility accreditation
>   — State requirements
>   — Certificate of necessity
>   — Laboratory registration
>   — Federal requirements
>   — Ambulatory surgical centers
>   — Physician office laboratory
> - Medical license renewal
> - Narcotics license renewal
> - Drug Enforcement Agency registrations
> - CME accreditations

What is the purpose of an agenda when planning a meeting?

CHECKPOINT
LO 12.7

Procedure 12-1   Creating an Appointment Matrix

GOAL   To create an appointment matrix to indicate the days and the hours the physician is not scheduling patients

MATERIALS   Appointment book, pencil or pen, physician schedule of meetings, conferences, vacations and other times of unavailability, including staff meetings and hours when patients are not seen

METHOD
1. Using the physician schedule of availability as the base for the matrix, confer with the physician or office manager to ensure that no additional schedule changes are planned.
2. Indicate within each area the reason why the time is being closed to appointments, such as lunch, hospital rounds, AAMA meeting, etc.
3. If the office utilizes cluster scheduling for certain appointments such as physical exams, blood sugar testing, etc., these time frames must also be set apart. Following office policy, such as using brackets, note the appropriate appointment type to be scheduled during this time frame.

Procedure 12-2 Creating an Appointment Matrix for an Electronic Scheduling System

GOAL Using an electronic scheduling system, indicate the days and times when the office is not scheduling appointments

MATERIALS Electronic scheduling program, physician schedule of meetings, conferences, vacations, and other times of unavailability, including staff meetings and hours when patients are not seen

METHOD

1. Using the physician schedule of availability as the base for the matrix, confer with the physician or office manager to ensure that no additional schedule changes are planned.

2. Open the office appointment scheduler per the program format.

3. Block the dates and times when the general office or physician will not be available for patient appointments using the physician and office schedules as guides.

4. Choose the appropriate option if the time frame is repeatedly unavailable.

5. Enter a reason that the time is not available for future reference. The office program may use color coding to assist with this process.

6. If cluster scheduling is used for the office, most schedulers allow you to specify what types of appointments may be entered; again, color coding may be used by the scheduler to outline specific types of appointments.

7. Many programs will allow you to specify time frames necessary for different types of appointments and these may be set up now also. For instance, physical exams for new patients may require 45 minutes, and visits for BP typical sick visits are set up for 15 minutes. If the program allows, set up these matrixes now also.

Procedure 12-3 Scheduling Appointments

GOAL Utilizing the previously created matrix, book patient appointments applying the correct amount of time for each appointment

MATERIALS Appointment book and pen or electronic scheduler, template outlining time frames for patient appointment types

METHOD

1. Establish the type of appointment required by the patient, particularly if this is a new patient or a returning patient.

2. If necessary, consult the template for the amount of time required for the patient appointment. Keep in mind the time reason for the appointment when scheduling (i.e., is the patient required to be fasting) as that will affect the time frame for the appointment.

3. When possible, schedule appointments earlier in the day first and then move to later time frames. Do ask the patient if he/she has a preferred time frame in mind and, if at all possible, accommodate the request.

4. When using an appointment book, enter the patient name, phone number, and reason for the appointment in the appropriate space, blocking out additional blocks of time if necessary to accommodate a longer appointment time.

5. If an electronic scheduler is used, use the search option to find the next available appointment for the time frame required for the appointment. Enter the patient name, phone number, and reason for the appointment.

6. Repeat the appointment information to the patient giving any necessary instructions to the patient regarding preparation for the appointment, such as early arrival for blood tests, completion of paperwork, etc. Also, this is a good time to remind patients about any copayments that will be due at the time of the appointment.

Procedure 12–4 Completing a Patient Appointment Card

GOAL To accurately complete a patient appointment card for the patient's next appointment

MATERIALS Appointment book or electronic scheduler, pen, appointment card

METHOD
1. After entering the patient's appointment in the appointment book or electronic scheduler, repeat the appointment date and time to the patient to verify accuracy.

2. Complete the patient appointment card entering the appointment date and time on the card. If the practice has multiple providers, there may also be a place for the appropriate physician name to be entered and you should do so.

3. Repeat appointment information to patient one more time when giving the card to him/her again verifying the information.

Procedure 12–5 Making Appointment Confirmation Calls

GOAL To decrease the number of "no-show" patients by making appointment confirmation calls 24–48 hours prior to the scheduled appointment

MATERIALS Office appointment book, electronic scheduler or listing of patients scheduled to be seen tomorrow or the next day with their home phone numbers

METHOD
1. Starting with the first appointment of the day, call the first patient listed.

2. If the phone is answered, ask for the patient. If you reach the patient, give your name and the name of the practice and state that you are confirming the patient's appointment for the applicable date and time.

3. Remind the patient about any special instructions regarding the appointment such as fasting, bringing in medical record or registration information and copayments due.

4. If the patient is not available, leave your name and phone number asking that the patient return your call.

5. If a voice mail or answering machine system is reached, follow the practice confidentiality rules unless you have permission from the patient to leave explicit information on voice mail.

6. Thank the patient for his/her time, stating you will see them at the stated date and time.

7. Allow the patient to hang up first, so if there are questions, you may answer them.

Procedure 12-6 Scheduling Outpatient Surgical Appointments

GOAL To schedule an outpatient surgical procedure

MATERIALS Patient medical record, scheduling form, calendar, telephone, pen

METHOD

1. From the physician and patient medical record, obtain detailed information regarding the name of procedure to be performed, the amount of the time the outpatient surgical suite will be needed and the reason (diagnosis) for the procedure.

2. Place a call to the appropriate surgery center or outpatient surgical unit at the requested facility. Have the name of the surgeon, assistant, or PA (if they will be used) available, as well as the patient and physician's preferred dates for the procedure available.

3. When the appointment scheduler answers the phone, identify yourself, the practice, and the procedure you need to schedule, as well as the preferred date for the procedure.

4. When a date for the procedure is agreed upon by the patient, give the scheduler the patient's name, address, phone number, DOB, gender, and insurance information including the prior authorization number if needed. Also give the patient's diagnosis as required for medical necessity.

5. Inquire as to any pre-procedure testing that may need to be done as well as any patient preparation required prior to the procedure, including patient arrival time.

6. Confirm the appointment date and time prior to hanging up. If necessary, book any pre-procedure testing for the patient and document these appointments in the patient instructions and appropriate office form(s) such as the surgical check off sheet and/or within the patient's medical record.

7. Provide the patient with written instructions from the physician as well as all information obtained while booking the appointment. The patient should also be informed that he should arrange for someone to drive him to and from this appointment.

8. Go over the written dates and instructions with the patient, asking the patient if there are any questions, answering them if possible and if not, asking a clinical member of the team to do so.

9. Give a copy of instructions and information to the patient and keep a copy in the patient record. Remind the patient to feel free to call the office at any time with any questions or concerns.

Procedure 12-7 Scheduling Inpatient Surgical Appointments

GOAL To schedule an inpatient surgical procedure

MATERIALS Patient medical record, scheduling form, calendar, telephone, pen

METHOD

1. From the physician and patient medical record, obtain detailed information regarding the name of procedure to be performed, the amount of the time the operating room will be needed and the reason (diagnosis) for the procedure.

2. Place a call to the appropriate surgical unit at the requested hospital. Have the name of the surgeon, assistant or PA (if they will be used) available, as well as the patient and physician's preferred dates for the procedure available.

3. When the appointment scheduler answers the phone, identify yourself, the practice and the procedure you need to schedule, as well as the preferred date for the procedure.

4. When a date for the procedure is agreed upon by the patient, give the scheduler the patient's name, address, phone number, DOB, gender and insurance information including the prior authorization number if needed. Also give the patient's diagnosis as required for medical necessity.

5. Inquire as to any pre-procedure testing that may need to be done as well as any patient preparation required prior to the procedure, including patient arrival time.

6. Confirm the appointment date and time prior to hanging up. If necessary, book any pre-procedure testing for the patient and documenting these appointments in the patient instructions and appropriate office form(s) such as the surgical check off sheet and/or within the patient's medical record.

7. Provide the patient with written instructions from the physician as well as all information obtained while booking the appointment. The patient should also be informed that they should arrange for someone to drive them to and from this appointment.

8. Go over the written dates and instructions with the patient, asking the patient if there are any questions, answering them if possible and if not, asking a clinical member of the team to do so.

9. Give a copy of instructions and information to the patient and keep a copy in the patient record. Remind the patient to feel free to call the office at any time with any questions or concerns.

Case Study

Ms. Comstock is always late for office visits with Dr. Patel. Jesse, who is responsible for scheduling appointments, decided to tell Ms. Comstock that her appointment was 30 minutes earlier than it actually was. She thought that this would ensure the patient arrived by the time of her real appointment. Ms. Comstock surprised everyone and arrived at the earlier time she was given. When she had to wait she was angry and loudly stated to everyone in the reception area that this was the reason she was never on time. She complained to Dr. Patel who was confused since he prided himself on being efficient and was not aware of what Jesse had done. Although Jesse had good intentions, the outcome was disastrous because she did not communicate accurate, honest information.

Thinking Critically

1. What would you communicate to patients who are habitually late?

2. Is there ever a circumstance that justifies giving patients inaccurate information?

3. Is there anything Jesse could do regarding the unfortunate situation with Ms. Comstock? Explain.

1. Dr. Thompson, the only physician in your office, is out of town at a medical meeting. She is due back tomorrow morning. At 4:00 P.M., Dr. Thompson calls to say that a blizzard has closed the airport and she will be forced to stay away for another day. You look at tomorrow's schedule. She has a full patient load. What should you do?

2. Using a blank appointment schedule page and the suggested schedule time frames shown on page 302 in the text, schedule the following patients as they requested. (Note: appointments must be made in the order in which they appear.)

Jayne Moore New Pt (60 min) early A.M.

Morris Wyman FU (15 min) late afternoon

Nicole James prenatal (15 min) after 4 P.M.

Nevaeh Cordiano GYN exam (30 min) noontime

Mark James mole remov (30 min) 1–2 P.M.

MariLou Whalen FU (15 min) 1–2 P.M.

Kathryn Stark NP (60 min) 3 P.M. or later

Gerald Ward NP (60 min) early A.M.

exam READINESS

1. **[LO12.1]** What is the correct abbreviation for injection?
   a. I & J
   b. inj
   c. injc
   d. Injtn
   e. Injc

2. **[LO12.3]** Which type of scheduling is also called *stream scheduling*?
   a. Time-specified
   b. Wave
   c. Open-hour
   d. Cluster
   e. Modified wave

3. **[LO12.3]** _____ scheduling groups similar appointments together on a certain day of the week or for certain times of day which may be helpful with equipment and staffing.
   a. Time-specified
   b. Wave
   c. Open-hour
   d. Cluster
   e. Modified wave

4. **[LO12.4]** No-show in regards to appointment scheduling means
   a. the patient has passed away
   b. the patient is no longer coming to the office
   c. the patient does not call or show up for his scheduled appointment
   d. the patient comes to his appointment but then leaves before seeing the doctor
   e. the patient shows up early for his appointment

5. **[LO12.5]** What is the best approach to handling the cancellation of an appointment by the patient?
   a. Send the patient a letter pointing out she canceled a necessary appointment
   b. Attempt to schedule another patient in the canceled slot later
   c. Schedule other activities in those canceled slots
   d. Encourage the physician to take time off
   e. Remind the patient of the importance of follow-up care and schedule her another appointment at that time

6. **[LO12.2]** When should you apply the matrix to your appointment book?
   a. On the first day of the new year
   b. When you first get them, if possible
   c. When scheduling appointments
   d. After appointments have been made
   e. At the beginning of every quarter

7. **[LO12.6]** When scheduling an appointment for the radiology department for an abdominal CAT scan, what should the administrative medical assistant do?
   a. Book appointments while the patient is in the office
   b. Call the patient later with the appointment time and date
   c. Schedule the appointment for the next available time
   d. Give written instructions on any preparations along with the date and time of the appointment
   e. Mail the patient the information

8. **[LO12.6]** Why should the insurance company be contacted prior to scheduling an appointment outside of the office?

a. To pay for services
b. As a courtesy of the office
c. Because it is doctor-ordered
d. To give them the confirmation number
e. To get authorization and determine if the service is covered

9. **[LO12.7]** When scheduling certain types of appointments, why is it a good idea to use a flow sheet?

a. To give to referring physician
b. So that all parties involved have the necessary information

c. Because the doctor will order you to
d. To give to surgeon
e. Because it's an insurance company requirement

10. **[LO12.7]** When planning a meeting for your office, you may need to also put together an agenda. What does an agenda tell the attendees?

a. Dates and times of meetings
b. Lists of topics discussed
c. List of members
d. List of topics to not be discussed
e. Report of what was discussed and decided on at the meeting

learning outcome SUMMARY

LO 12.1 The appointment book and its matrix, when used properly, allow the office staff to respect both the physician's and patients' time by keeping an efficiently and timely flow of patients throughout the day.

LO 12.2 To create a matrix, either in an appointment book or an electronic scheduler, you must know the usual schedule of physician availability to see patients as well as the times the physician (or practice) will not be open to see patients. The latter times should be X'd out with a short reason given as to why the time is unavailable. Follow the instructions for the electronic scheduler to block out the appropriate time frames.

LO 12.3 The most commonly used types of scheduling systems are open-hour, time-specified, wave, modified wave, double booking, and cluster scheduling.

LO 12.4 When organizing and arranging appointments for patients, always maintain a positive, professional image as a representative of the office. The patient's status as a new or established patient should be considered as well as patient preference whenever possible. The goal is to accommodate the patient as much as possible, while maintaining an efficient office schedule. Appointments should be confirmed through appointment cards, phone calls, and mailing recall notices.

LO 12.5 Handling special scheduling situations requires critical thinking skills and creativity. These types of scheduling situations can arise by the physician running late or a patient requiring an

emergency appointment. Special scheduling situations may also include a patient who does not show, arrives late, or arrives on the wrong day. Documentation of such appointment issues should be recorded in the patient's medical record for legal purposes.

LO 12.6 Outside appointments may also need to be made to laboratories, radiology services, surgeries, hospital stays, or for other diagnostic tests. You will require the patient's demographic and health insurance information along with the procedure or service to be performed and the reason for the service. Preferred dates and times should also be noted. If referrals or prior authorizations are required, you may also be required to obtain these so that the procedure/service is eligible for payment by the patient's insurance plan.

LO 12.7 As an administrative medical assistant, part of your duties include accuracy of the office schedule. It should be an efficient way to identify and maintain the doctor's schedule and ensure an even flow of patients throughout the day. Errors or overbooking may require you to rearrange appointments as necessary and to accommodate emergency appointments with minimal interruptions to the already established schedule. If the schedule is consistently overbooked or patient wait time becomes consistently too long, it will be your responsibility to find the cause(s) and corrections for the issues and present these to the physician or office manager.

medical assisting COMPETENCIES

CAAHEP

IV. C (9) Discuss applications of electronic technology in effective communication

V. C (1) Discuss pros and cons of various types of appointment management systems

V. C (2) Describe scheduling guidelines

V. C (3) Recognize office policies and protocols for handling appointments

V. C (4) Identify critical information required for scheduling patient admissions and/or procedures

V. C (13) Identify time management principles

V. P (1) Manage appointment schedule, using established priorities

V. P (2) Schedule patient admissions and/or procedures

V. A (2) Implement time management principles to maintain effective office function

ABHES

8. Medical Office Business Procedures/ Management
  c. Schedule and manage appointments
  f. Schedule inpatient and outpatient admissions

11. Career Development
  b. Demonstrate professionalism by:
    (3) Maintaining confidentiality at all times

(4) Being cognizant of ethical boundaries
(8) Being courteous and diplomatic
(9) Conducting work within scope of education, training, and ability

13 Written Communications

Learning Outcomes

After completing Chapter 13, you will be able to:

13.1 Identify the supplies necessary for creating and mailing professional-looking correspondence.

13.2 Identify the components of effective writing.

13.3 Describe the parts of the business letter and the different letter and punctuation styles.

13.4 List the heading components of an interoffice memorandum.

13.5 Explain the tasks involved in editing and proofreading.

13.6 Explain the process of preparing outgoing mail.

13.7 List common mailing equipment and supplies, giving the purpose of each.

13.8 Differentiate between the services provided by the United States Postal Service (USPS) and other delivery services.

13.9 Describe the steps required to properly process incoming mail.

Key Terms

- annotate
- body
- clarity
- complimentary closing
- concise
- courtesy title
- dateline
- editing
- enclosure
- full-block letter style
- identification line
- inside address
- key
- letterhead
- modified-block letter style
- notations
- optical character recognition (OCR)
- proofreading
- salutation
- signature block
- simplified letter style
- subject line
- template

Preparation for Certification

RMA (AMT) Exam
- Principles of medical ethics

CMAS (AMT) Exam
- Professionalism
- Business organization management

CMA (AAMA) Exam
- Screening and processing mail

Introduction ● ● ●

As with every profession, excellent communication skills are important for the medical profession in general and for the administrative medical assistant in particular. Written correspondence from health care professionals to patients, colleagues, and others demonstrate the office staff's ability to communicate effectively and professionally. The reputation of the entire medical practice is judged by its written communication. One carelessly prepared document will reflect negatively not only the staff member who wrote the document, but also affect the reputation of every member of the practice, including the physicians. All will be viewed as being careless, unprofessional, and possibly incompetent. Conversely, when letters and correspondence are neat, concise, and well organized, the physicians and staff members are perceived as organized, intelligent, and competent.

In this chapter, you will learn how to write effectively and develop skills to compose effective, polished documents, including the all-important business letter. You will learn and use different styles and formats of business writing and practice how to manage all forms of correspondence commonly used and received in the ambulatory care setting. By learning how to create, send, and receive letters and other types of correspondence, you will ensure positive, effective communication between your office and others. Well-written, neatly prepared documents are one of the most important means of communicating a professional image for the medical office (Figure 13–1).

letterhead
Formal business stationery on which the practice name and address are printed.

figure 13–1
The correspondence that goes out of and comes into a medical office is vital to a well-run practice.

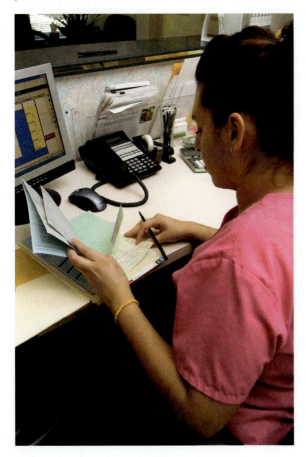

LO 13.1 Choosing Correspondence Supplies

The first step in preparing professional-looking correspondence is choosing the right supplies. Many offices already have most of these supplies on hand. However, you may be responsible for choosing and ordering such supplies. You may need to make decisions about letterhead paper, envelopes, labels, invoices, and statements.

Letterhead Paper

Letterhead refers to the formal business stationery on which the practice name and address are printed. Although the format and designs for letterhead vary widely, in addition to the practice name, the following information is usually included within the letterhead: address, phone and fax numbers, Web site address (if available), and the associates in the practice. Letterhead is used for correspondence with patients, colleagues, and vendors. Letterhead is used only for the first page of a letter. If a letter is more than one page, all additional pages of the letter are printed on a plain paper (the same color and bond as the letterhead).

Letterhead paper can be cotton fiber bond (sometimes called rag bond) or sulfite bond. Cotton fiber bond is usually more expensive than other types of paper. Cotton bond contains a watermark, which is an impression or pattern that can be seen when the paper is held up to the light. A watermark indicates that the paper is of high quality. The most popular cotton bond used for letterhead is 25% cotton because it is economical, but higher grades may be used.

The two most common sizes of letterhead paper are standard and legal. Standard or letter size paper is $8^1/_2 \times 11$ inches. Legal size is $8^1/_2 \times 14$ inches. Most general

business correspondence is produced on standard size paper. Legal size paper, as the name indicates, is used for legal documents, especially very lengthy documents.

A formal invitation or announcement may be engraved or embossed. Embossing involves a process where the letters are pressed into the paper. The letters are often set in black, gold, or silver. Invitations to the opening of a new practice location or to meet new practice associates may be produced using engraved or embossed paper.

Envelopes

Envelopes are used for correspondence, invoices, and statements. The envelopes for correspondence should be of matching bond and color as the letterhead and are preprinted with the office name and address, usually in the upper left corner of the envelope. Most offices also have the office name, address, and phone number printed on their invoices and statements, although these are typically produced on a lower bond paper than is the letterhead.

Familiarize yourself with the several types of envelopes used in the medical office.

- The most common envelope size used for correspondence is the No. 10 envelope (also called business size). It measures 4⅛ by 9½ inches.
- Envelopes used for invoices and statements can range from No. 6 (3⅝ by 6½ inches to No. 10. These envelopes commonly have a transparent window that allows the recipient's address on the invoice or statement to show through, saving time and reducing the potential for errors involved in retyping the address.
- Smaller payment-return envelopes—preaddressed to the practice office— are often included along with a bill, for the patient's convenience.
- Tan kraft envelopes, also called clasp envelopes, are available in many sizes and are used to send large or bulky documents.
- Padded envelopes are used to send documents or materials, such as slides, that may be damaged in the normal course of mail handling.
- The stock and quality of the envelope should always match the stationery. An office typically has two grades of envelopes with a return address. One, a less expensive stock and paper quality with a block format return address printed in black, is used for day-to-day office needs. The second, a more expensive stock and paper quality with a block format return address printed in black or other dark color, is used for professional correspondence, such as letters from consultants to primary care physicians regarding patient care.
- Data mailers are produced by a computer and are used by larger businesses and hospitals for batch mailings for items such as paychecks, appointment reminders, and some invoices. The envelopes are opened by tearing off perforated sides, peeling the envelope apart, or by a pull tab.

Labels

Address labels, printed from a computerized mailing list, can greatly speed the process of addressing envelopes for bulk mailings. For example, you may have to send a notice of a change in office hours or a quarterly office newsletter to a large number of patients in a practice. Using preprinted labels will greatly reduce the time required to address each item.

You may choose to set up a system for frequently used labels. Many practices write referrals and other business letters to the same addresses again and again. For fast and easy access, it is helpful to print out labels a full page at a time of the same address. Pages of labels can then be stored in alphabetized folders near the transcription desk. Excel databases can also be set up to print

template
Standard preset formats within many software programs.

labels and to insert names and addresses in standardized **templates**. Additionally, the mail merge feature of many word processing software packages allows you to create labels for all patients in the practice or even for certain "subsets" of patients, such as those with diabetes, who would be interested in a new diabetes teaching program being held in your office.

Invoices and Statements

There are several different types of invoices and statements in use today. They include:

- Preprinted invoices (used to send an original bill)
- Preprinted statements (used to send a reminder when an account is 30 or more days past due)
- Computer-generated invoices and statements
- Superbills (discussed in Chapter 17)

**CHECKPOINT
LO 13.1**

What informational items are usually included in letterhead?

LO 13.2 Effective Writing

concise
To be direct and to the point.

To create effective, professional correspondence that reflects well on the practice, be sure that you use an appropriate style, clear and **concise** language, and the active voice. All forms of communication must be written in such a way as to convey information clearly. Most medical practices use internal memos and many types of external forms of communication, including all types of business letters. Increasingly, medical offices are using e-mail to communicate not only with colleagues, but also (with the appropriate consent) with patients. Although considered a "less formal" form of communication, when e-mail comes from an office, it faces the same scrutiny as other written communication and must be written and proofread with the same care as a document that is mailed. Following are some general tips to help you write more effectively.

- Before you write, know to whom you are writing. Is the letter to a physician, a patient, a vendor, or fellow staff members? Decide if the tone should be formal or more relaxed.
- Know the purpose of the letter before you begin, and make sure your letter accurately conveys that purpose. Making notes concerning topics you want to cover in the letter, before you begin writing, will be helpful with this step.
- Be concise. Use short sentences. Be brief. Be specific.
- Do not use unnecessary words. Use the simplest way to say what you mean.

clarity
To be clear in meaning.

- Show **clarity** in your writing; state your message so that it can be understood easily.
- Use the active voice whenever possible. Voice shows whether the subject of a sentence is acting or is being acted upon. Here is an example of the active voice:

  "Dr. Huang is seeing 18 patients today."

  Here is an example of the same sentence, written in the passive voice:

  "Eighteen patients will be seen by Dr. Huang today."

  Note that the active voice is more direct and livelier to read.

- Use the passive voice, however, to soften the impact of negative news:

  "Your account will be turned over to a collection agency if we do not receive payment promptly."

  It would sound harsher to say:

  "We will turn your account over to a collection agency if we do not receive payment promptly."

- Always be polite and courteous.
- Always check spelling and the accuracy of dates, medical terminology used, and monetary figures.
- Always check your grammar. Do not use slang.
- Avoid leaving "widows and orphans" or dangling words and phrases. These are words and short phrases at the end or beginning of paragraphs that are left to sit alone at the top or bottom of a page or column or separated from the rest of the thought. To avoid this, if you start a paragraph at the end of a page and only a sentence or part of a sentence remains on the bottom of the page with the rest of the sentence or paragraph appearing on the next page, move the information at the bottom of the page on to the next page.
- Once the letter (or document) is completed, re-read the letter carefully, as if you were seeing it for the first time. Does it make sense? Are all concepts clear? If you are unsure, ask a coworker to read the letter and get her input. Make any changes necessary and read it again.
- If at all possible, hold the letter until the next day (or at least wait an hour or two) and re-read it again making sure all items are present and clearly presented. You are then ready to send your letter, confident in its message and presentation.

● ● ●

What is clarity?

CHECKPOINT
LO 13.2

LO 13.3 The Business Letter

A business letter is a form of communication—much like holding a conversation in person. The recipient will form an impression of the physician and the office based on the letter. Therefore, all letters must be clear and well written and must politely and professionally convey the appropriate information.

The purpose of most letters is to explain, clarify, or give instructions or other information. Correspondence includes letters of referral; appointment reminders or cancellations; patient reports for insurance companies; instructions for examinations or laboratory tests; answers to insurance or billing questions; and cover letters or form letters to order supplies or equipment. You may transcribe a dictated letter for the physician or be asked to compose a letter based on specific information. Regardless of how the letter comes about, the guidelines for writing correspondence remain the same.

Commonly used paragraphs and even entire letter formats are saved as templates and used repeatedly in some practices. It is handy to save these bodies of text in the computer for quick and easy repeated access. With very few keystrokes, the material can be selected and displayed quickly. The document is then edited for minor changes such as name and address updates prior to being sent. Be very careful when using templates and be sure to change all necessary information. You don't want to change the name and address from Dr. Sanchez's information to Dr. Mallard's information, but then forget to change the salutation so that the letter to Dr. Mallard contains the salutation "Dear Dr. Sanchez."

Document Templates

Medical offices create and produce multiple documents and correspondence on a daily basis. The computerized medical office has an advantage over its noncomputerized counterparts via its word processing software package which allows the office to create templates or outlines of documents that are used repeatedly. Using templates allows the administrative medical assistant to quickly create new documents with just a few keystrokes instead of retyping an entire document. The use of mail merge software makes creating multiples of the document to many people even easier.

Offices with EHR programs can take this concept several steps further. Using the template capability of the EHR program allows not only the ease of creating these documents quickly and accurately, but also the convenience of sending them to the patient via e-mail, as long as the office has written permission from the patient to do so. A copy of the document is then saved directly to the medical record with just a couple of mouse clicks. Copies no longer need to be made and then hand-filed in the medical record, and instead of waiting for conventional mail service delivery, the patient receives the document almost immediately.

It is also helpful to use the cut, paste, and copy features in word processing software to quickly piece together a correspondence that uses sentences or paragraphs from other documents. Large and small bodies of text can easily be moved or copied from document to document, saving time for the administrative medical assistant.

Parts of a Business Letter

Figure 13–2 illustrates the parts of a typical business letter. Details about format may vary from office to office.

Letterhead   The letterhead is the preprinted portion of formal business stationery.

dateline
The date the letter was written.

Dateline   The **dateline** consists of the month, day, and year. It should begin about three lines below the preprinted letterhead on approximately line 15. The month should always be spelled out, and there should be a comma after the day.

inside address
The name and address of the person to whom the letter is addressed.

Inside Address   The **inside address** contains all the necessary information for correct delivery of the letter. The inside address spells out the name and address of the person to whom the letter is being sent. In general, you should:

key
The act of inputting or entering information into a computer.

- **Key,** or type, the inside address on the left margin, two to four spaces down from the date. It should be two, three, or four lines in length.
- Include a **courtesy title** (Dr., Mr., Mrs., and so on) and the intended receiver's full name.
- Include the intended receiver's title on the same line with the name, separated by a comma, or on the line below it. Note: If Dr. is used as a courtesy title, do not use M.D. after the name. For example, either of these forms is acceptable: Dr. Dawn Greene or Dawn Greene, M.D. This form is not acceptable: Dr. Dawn Greene, M.D. Generally the M.D. format (Dawn Greene, M.D.) is used for the inside address and the Dr. format (Dr. Dawn Greene) is used for the salutation.

courtesy title
A person's formal title: Mr., Mrs., Dr., etc.

- Include the company name, if applicable.
- Use numerals for the street address, except the single numbers one through nine, which should be spelled out—for example, Two Markham Place.
- Spell out numerical names of streets (and buildings) if they are numbers less than, for example, 1252 Eighth Avenue.
- If the delivery address is short, it is best to spell out the words *Street, Drive,* and so on. If abbreviations are used, it is best to refer to the United States Postal Service (USPS) listing of acceptable address abbreviations at www.usps.com/ncsc/lookups/usps_abbreviations.html.
- Include the full city name; do not abbreviate.

Letterhead

TOTAL CARE CLINIC, PC

342 East Park Blvd
Futon, XY 12345-6789
Tel: 521-234-0001   Fax: 521-234-0002
www.totalcareclinic.org

Dateline (about line 15)

November 14, 2012

CERTIFIED MAIL

Inside address

Mr. Hunter Boyd
4080 Magnolia Point Drive
Jacksonville, FL 32223

Salutation

Dear Mr. Boyd:

Reference or Subject line

RE: RESCHEDULING OF APPOINTMENT

Body

We are writing to inform you that it is necessary to reschedule the appointment
for your annual physical. Dr. Rodriguez will not be available to see patients on
December 5, 2012. Please call our office at your earliest convenience to arrange
a new appointment date and time.

Your health and well-being is of great concern to us and we apologize for any
inconvenience this may cause. We look forward to hearing from you and thank
you for allowing us to provide your health care needs.

Complimentary closing

Sincerely,

Signature block

Darlene M. Elliott
Office Manager

Identification line

DE/kr

Notations

Enc: Appointment calendar

c: Kalisha Roberts, CMA (AAMA) Scheduling Coordinator

- Use the two-letter state abbreviation recommended by the U.S. Postal Service. If you are unsure of the proper abbreviation for a particular state, they can be found the previously mentioned Web site.
- Leave one space between the state and the zip code; include the zip + 4 code, if known. If a zip code is unknown, visit the USPS zip code finder at http://zip4.usps.com/zip4/welcome.jsp.

figure 13-2

Knowing the parts of a typical business letter enables medical assistants to create written communications that reflect well on the office.

Attention Line   An attention line is used only when a letter is addressed to a company but sent to the attention of a particular individual. If you do not know the name of the individual, call the company directly to inquire the name of the appropriate contact person. A colon between the word *Attention* and the person's name is optional.

salutation
The greeting of a letter.

Salutation   When addressing a person by name, use a **salutation,** a written greeting such as "Dear," followed by Dr., Mr., Mrs., or Ms., and the person's last name. The salutation should be keyed at the left margin on the second line below the inside address. A colon should follow. When you do not know the name of the specific person to receive the letter, it is becoming common practice to use the business title or department in the salutation, as in "Dear Sir:" "Dear Laboratory Director:" or "Dear Claims Representative:" This also avoids confusion if you do not know the gender of a person with a name such as Pat or Chris.

subject line
Sometimes used in a letter to bring the reader's attention immediately to the purpose of the letter.

Subject or Reference Line   A **subject line,** also known as a reference line (RE:), is sometimes used to bring the subject of the letter to the reader's attention. The subject line is not required. However, if it is used, it should be keyed on the second line below the salutation. The subject line is generally flush with the left margin, but may be indented five spaces, or centered on the page. The subject line should be limited to two to three words and should be keyed in all capital letters to capture the attention of the reader.

body
The main portion of the letter.

Body   The **body** of the letter begins two lines below the salutation or subject line. The text is single-spaced with double-spacing between paragraphs.

If the body contains a list, set the list apart from the rest of the text. Leave an extra line of space above and below the list. For each item in the list, indent five to ten spaces from each margin. Single-space within items, but leave an extra line between items. A bulleted list has a small, solid, round circle before each item and in a numbered list, each item is preceded by a number in consecutive order.

complimentary closing
The formal close of the letter such as *Sincerely* or *Very truly yours.*

Complimentary Closing   The **complimentary closing** is placed two lines below the last line of the body. Capitalize only the first word of the closing. "Sincerely" is a common closing. "Very truly yours" and "Best regards" are also acceptable closings in business correspondence. A comma is placed after the complimentary closing.

signature block
The writer's name and title, following the complimentary closing, leaving space for the writer's signature.

Signature Block   The **signature block** contains the writer's name on the first line and the writer's business title on the second line. The block is aligned with the complimentary closing and typed three to four lines below it, to allow space for the signature. If the writer has a large, sprawling signature, it is acceptable to insert 5–6 lines to allow adequate space for the signature.

identification line
The initials of the person dictating or writing the letter as well as the initials of the typist with a colon or forward slash separating the two.

Identification Line   The letter writer's initials (in capital letters) followed by a colon or forward slash and the typist's initials (in lower case type) are sometimes included at the bottom of the letter. These initials are called the **identification line.** This line is typed flush left, two lines below the signature block. If the writer and typist are the same person, the identification line is often omitted.

notations
Information at the end a letter including enclosures and carbon copy notations.

enclosure
Letter notation signaling the receiver that there are documents included with the letter.

Notations   **Notations** include information such as the number of **enclosures** (make sure to specify what is enclosed) that are included with the letter and the names of other people who will be receiving copies of the letter (sometimes noted as c:). If there are enclosures, a notation should appear flush left, one or two lines below the identification line (or one or two lines below the signature

block, if no identification line is present). You may abbreviate the word *Enclosure* by typing "Enc," or "Encs" (with or without punctuation, depending on the style of the letter you are writing). The copy notation, "c," appears after the enclosure notation and includes one or more names or initials.

Punctuation Styles

Two different styles of punctuation are used in business correspondence: open punctuation and mixed punctuation. Remember to use one punctuation style consistently throughout a letter.

Open Punctuation   This style uses no punctuation after the following items when they appear in a letter:

- The salutation
- The complimentary closing

Figure 13–3 demonstrates open punctuation.

Mixed Punctuation   This style includes the following punctuation marks used in specific instances:

figure 13–3

Example of a block letter style which demonstrates an open punctuation format.

TOTAL CARE CLINIC, PC

342 East Park Blvd
Funton, XY 12345-6789
Tel: 521-234-0001   Fax: 521-234-0002
www.totalcareclinic.org

April 19, 2012

Mr. Shawn Collins
234 Deerfield Drive
Daytona, FL 32114

Dear Mr. Collins

Congratulations! Your lab results have come back and overall your screenings are great. However, we are a bit concerned about your cholesterol screening result, which is 225. We like to see our patients with levels under 200. Please call our office to schedule another screening six months from today.

In the meantime, please check our Web site (www.totalcareclinic.org) to find ways that you can lower your cholesterol. If you have any questions or concerns prior to your appointment in six months, please do not hesitate to contact me at any time.

Sincerely

Ravi Patel, MD

Ravi Patel, M.D.

RP:kr

All the lines are on the left margin

- A colon after *Attention* in the attention line
- A colon after the salutation
- A comma after the complimentary closing
- A colon after the enclosure notation
- A colon after the copy notation

Figure 13–4 shows the use of mixed punctuation.

Letter Format

Follow these general formatting guidelines for all letters.

- The margin is the space around the edges of a form or letter that is left blank. The standard setting for margins in business correspondence is one inch (left and right margins) for 8½-inch-wide paper.
- Center the letter on the page according to the length of the letter. For shorter letters, you can use wider margins and start the address farther

figure 13–4

Example of a modified-block letter style with reference line and mixed punctuation.

TOTAL CARE CLINIC, PC

342 East Park Blvd
Funton, XY 12345-6789
Tel: 521-234-0001   Fax: 521-234-0002
www.totalcareclinic.org

April 19, 2012

Mr. Shawn Collins
234 Deerfield Drive
Daytona, FL 32114

Dear Mr. Collins:

RE: LAB RESULTS

Congratulations! Your lab results have come back and overall your screenings are great. However, we are a bit concerned about your cholesterol result, which is 225. We like to see our patients with levels under 200. Please call our office to schedule another screening six months from today.

In the meantime, please check our Web site (www.totalcareclinic.org) to find ways that you can lower your cholesterol. If you have any questions or concerns prior to your appointment in six months, please do not hesitate to contact me at any time.

Sincerely,

Ravi Patel, MD

Ravi Patel, M.D.

RP:kr

The dateline, complimentary closing, and signature block begin at the center of the page or slightly to the right

down the page. For longer letters, use standard margins but start higher up on the page.

- Single-space the body of the letter. Double-space between paragraphs or parts of the letter.
- Use short sentences (no more than 20 words on average).
- Include at least two to three sentences in each paragraph.
- Divide long paragraphs—more than 10 lines of type—into shorter ones.

For multipage letters, use letterhead for the first page and matching plain bond paper for the subsequent pages. (When you order letterhead, be sure to order plain paper of the same texture and color as the letterhead for subsequent sheets.) Using a 1-inch margin at the top, include a heading with the addressee, date, and page number on all pages following the first one. Resume typing or printing the text about three lines below the heading.

Letter Styles

Different letter styles are used for different purposes. Your office is likely to have a preferred style in place. The four most common letter styles are full-block, modified-block, modified-block with indented paragraphs, and simplified.

Full-Block Style   The **full-block letter style,** also called block letter style, is typed with all lines flush left. Figure 13–3 shows an example of the block letter style (with open punctuation). This style may include a subject line two lines below the salutation. Block letter style is quick and easy to type because there are no indented paragraphs to slow the typist. Block style is one of the most common formats used in the medical office.

full-block letter style
Letter format where all information within the letter begins at the left margin.

Modified-Block Style   The **modified-block letter style** is similar to full block but differs in that the dateline, complimentary closing, and signature block, are aligned and begin at the center of the page or slightly to the right of center. (See Figure 13–4 which also demonstrates the mixed punctuation style). This type of letter has a traditional, balanced appearance.

modified-block letter style
Similar to block style, except that the dateline, complimentary close, and signature block all begin at or slightly to the right of center.

Modified-Block Style with Indented Paragraphs   This style is identical to the modified-block style except that the paragraphs are indented one-half inch from the right margin. (Figure 13–5).

Simplified Style   The **simplified letter style** is a modification of the full-block style. Figure 13–6 shows an example of the simplified letter style. The salutation is omitted, eliminating the need for a courtesy title. A subject line in all-capital letters is placed between the address and the body of the letter. The subject line summarizes the main point of the letter but does not actually use the word *subject*. All text is typed flush left. The complimentary closing is omitted, and the sender's name and title are typed in capital letters in a single line at the end of the letter. Note that this letter style always uses open punctuation, so it is both easy to read and quick to type. In most situations in a medical office, however, the simplified letter style is considered too informal for widespread use. For more information on letter styles and formats, visit www.englishplus.com.

simplified letter style
Block letter style with elimination of the salutation and courtesy title, with a subject line placed between the address and body of the letter (in all caps). Complimentary close is omitted and the writer's name is again typed in all caps.

E-Letters to Patients   As more and more offices use e-mail to communicate with patients and others outside of the office, it becomes necessary to have formats and templates for these "E-letters" just as are available for conventional paper letters.

For offices that do not yet have access to EHR technology, there are two choices; use the e-mail window to compose the document or create a letter

TOTAL CARE CLINIC, PC

342 East Park Blvd
Funton, XY 12345-6789
Tel: 521-234-0001   Fax: 521-234-0002
www.totalcareclinic.org

April 19, 2012

Mr. Shawn Collins
234 Deerfield Drive
Daytona, FL 32114

Dear Mr. Collins:

   Congratulations! Your lab results have come back and overall your screenings are great. However, we are a bit concerned about your cholesterol result, which is 225. We like to see our patients with levels under 200. Please call our office to schedule another screening six months from today.

   In the meantime, please check our Web site (www.totalcareclinic.org) to find ways that you can lower your cholesterol. If you have any questions or concerns prior to your appointment in six months, please do not hesitate to contact me at any time.

Sincerely,

Ravi Patel, MD

Ravi Patel, M.D.

RP:kr

Paragraphs are indented (otherwise the same as modified block style)

figure 13–5

An example of the modified-block letter style with indented paragraphs and mixed punctuation.

using the same formats used for a traditional letter and then attach this document to a short e-mail message.

When using the e-mail window to compose a message to the patient, use a variation of the simplified letter format (see Figure 13–6). The date should be included, but the inside address and subject line may both be omitted; the mailing address is not necessary and the e-mail will contain a subject line. Even though e-mail is being used, do keep the information contained within the document professional in tone and, as with any communication, use spell-check and proofread the document carefully prior to hitting the "send" icon. Some office e-mail programs allow for a signature; if your program does, insert the writer's signature at the end of the e-mail. If a signature is not possible, type the writer's name at the end of the communication. Because letterhead is not being used, you should also include the office phone number within the e-mail in case the recipient wishes to call the office.

If your office procedure states that an actual letter must be created and sent by e-mail, type a traditional letter using your word processing software. Create a short introductory e-mail message to the patient explaining that a document containing important information is attached. Be sure to remember to attach the document to the e-mail prior to hitting the "send" icon.

Offices that have EHR technology such as SpringCharts will have access to letter templates within the EHR program (Figures 13–7 and 13–8). These

TOTAL CARE CLINIC, PC

342 East Park Blvd
Funton, XY 12345-6789
Tel: 521-234-0001   Fax: 521-234-0002
www.totalcareclinic.org

April 19, 2012

Mr. Shawn Collins
234 Deerfield Drive
Daytona, FL 32114

LAB RESULTS

Congratulations! Your lab results have come back and overall your screenings are great. However, we are a bit concerned about your cholesterol result, which is 225. We like to see our patients with levels under 200. Please call our office to schedule another screening six months from today.

In the meantime, please check our Web site (www.totalcareclinic.org) to find ways that you can lower your cholesterol. If you have any questions or concerns prior to your appointment in six months, please do not hesitate to contact me at any time.

Ravi Patel, MD

RAVI PATEL, M.D.
RP:kr

> **A subject line is added and the salutation, courtesy title, and complimentary closing are omitted**

> **The sender's name and title are typed in all capital letters**

templates are used in the same way that word processing templates are used. Select the New Letter Template and a blank letter screen will appear. You then can fill in the blanks with the information you would like the patient to have. Once the letter is completed, you will have the option to save it as a new template. The next time you select the template option, you can choose this letter as your base information, so that repetitive information does not require re-keying. Procedure 13–2 outlines how to use the SpringCharts EHR Program to create an e-mail letter.

figure 13–6

The simplified letter style is considered by some to be the most readable style for correspondence.

● ● ●

Which letter format and punctuation style do you feel is most appropriate for the medical office? Why?

CHECKPOINT
LO 13.3

LO 13.4 Interoffice Memorandums (Memos)

Interoffice memorandums (memos) are periodically used by medical offices, clinics, and hospitals to disseminate written information quickly throughout the facility, when a less formal form of communication is appropriate. In general, there are three types of memos: informative, which provide necessary information; directive, which generally contain brief instructions for the recipients; and administrative, which usually relate to policies and procedures. Most word

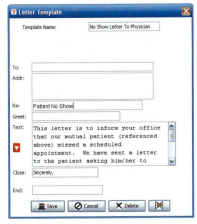

figure 13-7

New letter template window.

processing software has templates that can be used to format an interoffice memo but memos can also be easily created without the use of templates. See Figure 13–9 for memorandum example.

In general, memos are printed on plain paper with the word "Memo" or "Memorandum" printed at the top of the page. If a template is used, the following headings will appear automatically at the left margin, and the administrative medical assistant simply enters the appropriate information to the right of the colon: TO:, FROM:, DATE:, and SUBJECT or RE:. Some memo formats also include a heading of CC: which often contains a notation that a copy should be filed for future reference. If a template is not available, the same headings can be created with a word processing program. They should be keyed using all capital letters and many offices also use a bold font for these headings. Double spacing should be used between the headings.

To insert the necessary information after each heading, the tab key should be used to place the information neatly to the right of the colon. Be sure to tab over far enough that there is a space between the colon of the longest heading term and information being inserted. Figure 13–9 provides a guide to how a completed heading should appear.

The body of a memo, like that of a letter, is single-spaced with double spacing between paragraphs. You will use the office procedure guide to decide whether a block or indented paragraph format will be used. There is no signature block with a memo, as the writer's name appears in the heading at the "FROM:" block. Dependent on office policy, you may double space after the final period and insert the writers initials (capitalized) followed by a forward slash or colon and then your initials as the typist in lower case, but many offices omit this item.

If a memo continues onto a second page, insert a heading one inch from the top of the second page consisting of name of the addressee, date, and page number. Triple space and then continue with the body of the memo. Memos are usually delivered via interoffice mail but they may also be delivered via the office e-mail system. If this method is employed, the date and name of the sender will appear within the e-mail and the subject will appear in the e-mail subject line, so may be omitted. However, if the writer wishes or feels that the

figure 13-8

New letter window.

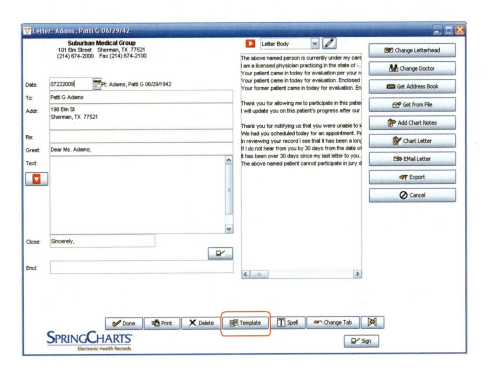

INTEROFFICE MEMO

TO: Darlene M. Elliott, Kalisha Roberts, CMA

FROM: John Fredericks, M.D.

DATE: February 24, 2012

SUBJECT: The Copier, Fax, and Confidentiality

CC: File

It has come to my attention that a patient's lab test result was left on the glass of the copy machine. Although I am sure this was not purposeful, we must always keep HIPAA regulations regarding patient confidentiality in mind when going about our day-to-day duties.

Please be sure that all staff members understand that it is of utmost importance that all staff members make patient confidentiality a top priority. Since implementing EHR, I am afraid we are losing sight of the fact that paper records are still required by other offices and many of our patients. Because of this, our greatest weakness regarding HIPAA and our patient records appears to be the use of the copy and fax machines. Please remind all staff members to carefully check the area around the copy and fax machines after use. HIPAA law states that the information within a patient chart is protected health information and should only be seen by members of our staff and other business associates on a "business need-to-know basis."

JF/kr

figure 13–9

Example of an interoffice memo.

recipients will be printing the memo for their records, the usual format may be used.

What are the three types of interoffice memorandums?

CHECKPOINT
LO 13.4

LO 13.5 Editing and Proofreading

Editing and proofreading take place after you create the first draft of a letter. **Editing** involves checking a document for factual accuracy, logical flow, conciseness, clarity, and tone. **Proofreading** involves checking a document for grammatical, spelling, and formatting errors. When possible, ask another person to proofread your work as well. *Never* skip over the very important steps of editing and proofreading! Spell-check alone is not enough. It will not catch correctly spelled words used in the incorrect manner.

editing
Checking a document for factual accuracy, logical flow, conciseness, clarity, and tone.

proofreading
Checking a document for grammatical, spelling, and formatting errors.

Tools for Editing and Proofreading

Reference books can help you prepare letters that appear professional. Keep the following tools available.

Dictionary An up-to-date dictionary gives you more than definitions of words. A dictionary tells you how to spell, divide, and pronounce a word and

what part of speech it is, such as a noun or adjective. A dictionary can be accessed on the Internet or in book form.

Medical Dictionary   It is nearly impossible for even the most experienced health-care professional to be familiar with every medical term and its correct spelling. A medical dictionary will serve as a handy reference for terms with which you are unfamiliar or about which you would like more information. Like a regular dictionary, a medical dictionary can also be accessed on the Internet or in book form. However, a medical dictionary in book form may not have the most updated terms. Like other medical reference books, a medical dictionary needs to be replaced periodically.

Becoming familiar with some of the prefixes, suffixes and word roots commonly used in medical terms can help you understand the meanings of many words. Appendix I at the back of the book lists some common medical word parts.

Thesaurus   A thesaurus provides synonyms or similar words to a word you are using. It helps you avoid repetition in your writing and helps you find a word for an idea you have in mind. A thesaurus can be found in word processing programs, in print, and online.

Physicians' Desk Reference (PDR)   The *PDR* is a dictionary of medications. Published yearly, it provides up-to-date information on both prescription and nonprescription drugs. Consult the *PDR* for the correct spelling of a particular drug or for other information about its usage, side effects, contraindications, and so on. The easiest way to locate the correct spelling of a drug will be to use Section 2, The Brand- and Generic-Name Index (the pink section) of the *PDR*. Procedure 13–4 at the end of this chapter outlines the procedure for using the *PDR*, particularly as a spelling reference guide.

English Grammar and Usage Manuals   These manuals answer questions concerning grammar and word usage. They usually contain sections on punctuation, capitalization, and other details of written communication.

Word Processing Spelling Checkers   Most word processing programs used in medical offices have built-in spelling checkers. There are also programs designed specifically to check spelling in medical documents. These spelling checkers include most common medical terms that would not be found in a regular software program.

Spelling checkers pick up many spelling errors and often give suggestions for correct spellings. If you indicate the choice you meant to input, the program automatically replaces the misspelled word. These programs may not detect all spelling errors, however. They should not be relied on as the only means of checking a document. For example, spelling checkers cannot tell you that you used the wrong word if you type the word *form* instead of *from* because *form* is also a correctly spelled word.

You may be able to add words that are not currently recognized by the spelling checker in your computer. Use this feature to add medical terms. A word of caution is important here! Before you add the word to the computer's dictionary, be sure to look up the exact spelling in a medical dictionary. The computer will recognize only the spelling you add. If you place the *wrong* spelling in the computer, your spelling checker will not correct it.

When you type e-mails, take special care to use correct grammar and punctuation. Spelling checkers are available in most e-mail programs and should be used at the completion of the e-mail. The e-mail spelling checker does not automatically point out mistakes as you type.

Some software packages offer grammar-checking and style-checking features. These programs can identify certain problems, but the person using them still needs to know basic rules of grammar and style to correct errors.

Editing

The editing process ensures that a document is accurate, clear, and complete; free of grammatical errors; organized logically; and written in an appropriate style. It is a good idea to leave some time between the writing and editing stages so that you can look at the document in a fresh light. As you edit, you must examine language usage, content, and style.

Language Usage   Learn basic grammar rules. When in doubt, refer to a grammar handbook or reference manual. Make sure all sentences are complete. Continually ask yourself, "Is this the best way to convey what I want to say? Do my word choices reflect the overall tone of the document?" For example, in a business letter, you would avoid choosing phrases that are too casual such as, "Thanks a million" or "Take it easy." These expressions are inappropriate for a business letter.

Content   A business letter should contain all the necessary information the writer intends to convey. If you are editing someone else's letter and something appears to be missing, check with the writer. She or he may have omitted information by mistake.

The content of a letter should follow a logical thought pattern. Create a clean, concise letter by:

- Stating the purpose of the letter in the first sentence
- Discussing one topic at a time
- Changing paragraphs when you change topics
- Listing events in chronological order
- Sticking to the subject
- Selecting words carefully
- Reading over what you have written before printing

Style   Use a writing style that is appropriate to the reader. A letter written to a patient is likely to require a different style than one written to a physician.

Proofreading

Proofreading means thoroughly checking a document for errors. After editing a document, put it aside for a short time before proofreading it. Ideally, have a coworker proofread your work. Someone else will often notice errors that you may miss. There are three types of errors that can occur when preparing a document: formatting, data, and mechanical.

Formatting Errors   These errors involve the positioning of the various parts of a letter. They may include errors in indenting, line length, or line spacing. To avoid these errors, take the following two steps:

1. Scan the letter to make sure that the indentions are consistent, that the spacing is correct, and that the text is centered from left to right and top to bottom.
2. Follow the office style consistently. Do not indent some paragraphs and not others or use a modified block format for the date and a block format for the closing.

Data Errors   Data errors involve mistyping monetary figures, such as a balance on a patient statement. Verify the accuracy of all figures by checking them twice or by having another coworker check them.

Mechanical Errors Mechanical errors are errors in spelling, punctuation, spacing between words, and division of words. Make sure that your word processing spell-checker has medical terminology included; otherwise, medical terms may be overlooked. Mechanical errors also include reversing words or characters, typing them twice, or omitting them altogether. Here are some tips to help you avoid mechanical errors.

- Learn basic spelling, punctuation, and word division rules. When in doubt, be sure to check a manual on English usage. Table 13–1 presents some basic rules of writing. Table 13–2 lists some of the most commonly misspelled medical terms and other words.

table 13–1

Basic Rules of Writing

Word Division	Divide: • According to pronunciation • Compound words between the two words from which they derive • Hyphenated compound words at the hyphen • After a prefix • Before a suffix • Between two consonants that appear between vowels • Before *-ing* unless the last consonant is doubled; in that case, divide before the second consonant Do not divide: • Such suffixes as *-sion, -tial,* and *-gion* • A word so that only one letter is left on a line
Capitalization	Capitalize: • All proper names • All titles, positions, or indications of family relation when preceding a proper name or in place of a proper noun (not when used alone or with possessive pronouns or articles) • Days of the week, months, and holidays • Names of organizations and membership designations • Racial, religious, and political designations • Adjectives, nouns, and verbs that are derived from proper nouns (including currently copyrighted trade names) • Specific addresses and geographic locations • Sums of money written in legal or business documents • Titles, headings of books, magazines, and newspapers

Plurals	• Add *s* or *es* to most singular nouns (plural forms of most medical terms do not follow this rule)
	• With medical terms ending in *is,* change the *i* to *e*
	    metastasis/metastases
	    epiphysis/epiphyses
	• With terms ending in *um,* change the *um* to *a:*
	    diverticulum/diverticula
	    atrium/atria
	• With terms ending in *us,* change the *us* to *i:*
	    calculus/calculi
	    bronchus/bronchi
	    (Two exceptions to this are virus/viruses and sinus/sinuses.)
	• With terms ending in *a,* keep the *a* and add *e:*
	    vertebra/vertebrae

Possessives	To show ownership or relation to another noun: • For singular nouns, add an apostrophe and an *s* • For plural nouns that do not end in an *s,* add an apostrophe and an *s* • For plural nouns that end in an *s,* just add an apostrophe
Numbers	Use numerals: • In general writing, when the number is 11 or greater • With abbreviations and symbols • When discussing laboratory results or statistics • When referring to specific sums of money • When using a series of numbers in a sentence Tips: • Use commas when numerals have more than three digits • Do not use commas when referring to account numbers, page numbers, or policy numbers • Use a hyphen with numerals to indicate a range

- Type any handling instructions (such as PERSONAL or CONFIDENTIAL) three lines below the return address. This information should also be outside the area that OCR can read.

- Letters going to foreign countries should have the name of the country on the last line of the address block in all-capital letters.

- Some letters may be appropriate for interoffice or company mail systems. These letters are usually placed in a large envelope with multiple address lines. The envelope can be reused many times by crossing out the previous name and address and using the next line. Place interoffice mail in a specially designated area or basket for pickup. Be sure not to mix it with outgoing mail.

Folding and Inserting Mail

Letters and invoices must be folded neatly before they are inserted into the envelopes. The proper way to fold a letter depends on the type of envelope into which the letter will fit.

- With a small envelope, fold the letter in thirds. Fold the bottom third up, then the top third down over the bottom third and insert it.

- With a regular business-size envelope, fold the letter in thirds. Fold the bottom third up first, then the top third down, and insert the letter (Figure 13–12).

- With a window envelope, use an accordion fold. Fold the bottom third up. Then, fold the top third back so that the address appears in the window and insert the enclosure.

Before folding the letter, double-check that it has been signed, that all enclosures are included, and that the address on the letter matches the one on the envelope. Any enclosures that are not attached to the letter should be placed

figure 13–12

It is important to fold a business letter correctly.

How to Fold a Standard Letter

A business letter is folded twice into horizontal thirds and placed into an envelope. This ensures a little privacy for the contents of the letter. The letter is also easy to unfold after opening the envelope. The following diagram shows how a letter is normally folded. This type of fold is used regardless of letter style.

If the letter needs to have the address face out an envelope window, make the second fold in the same location but opposite direction. The letter will then be folded in a Z shape and the address can be positioned to face out the window of the envelope.

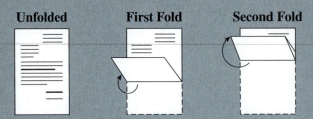

Unfolded   First Fold   Second Fold

Make a second horizontal crease one third from the top of the letter where the bottom of the letter had been folded to. Tuck the bottom into this crease and fold the top over it. The letter will be folded into thirds. It will fit any standard envelope.

If you are folding the letter so the address faces out the envelope window, fold the letter toward the back instead of the front. The letter address will appear through the envelope window, but it will still be folded in thirds.

inside the folds so that they will be removed from the envelope along with the letter. (See Chapter 10 for information about folding and inserting machines.)

CHECKPOINT
LO 13.6

Write out the following address using correct placement so that the delivery will be to the office address, not the P.O. box.

P.O. Box 213; The Law Offices of Ward and Whalen, PC; Blackstone, XY 00001; 305 Main Street

LO 13.7 Mailing Equipment and Supplies

The proper equipment and supplies will help you handle the mail efficiently and cost-effectively. In addition to letterhead, blank stationery for multipage letters, and envelopes, you will need some standard supplies. The USPS provides forms, labels, and packaging for items that need special attention, such as airmail, Priority Mail, Express Mail, certified mail, and registered mail. Private delivery companies, such as United Parcel Service (UPS), DHL International, and Federal Express (FedEx), also provide shipping supplies to their customers.

Airmail Supplies

In the past, any piece of mail that was transported by air was designated as airmail. Today nearly all first-class mail outside a local area is routinely sent by air. However, airmail services are still available for some packages and for most mail going to foreign countries.

If you are sending an item by airmail, attach special airmail stickers, available from the post office, on all sides. (The word *AIRMAIL* can also be neatly written on all sides.) Special airmail envelopes for letters can be purchased from the USPS.

Envelopes for Overnight Delivery Services

For correspondence or packages that must be delivered by the next day, a number of overnight delivery services are available through the USPS and private companies. Most companies require the use of their own envelopes and mailing materials. Make sure you keep adequate supplies on hand.

Postal Rates, Scales, and Meters

Postal rates and regulations change periodically, and every medical office should have a copy of the latest guidelines. These guidelines are available from the USPS. Chapter 10 describes postal scales and meters and their use in the medical office.

CHECKPOINT
LO 13.7

Why are proper mailing supplies and equipment important to a medical practice?

LO 13.8 Delivery Options

Most mail delivery from the medical office is delivered by the United Postal Services, but there are other methods also available. In this section, we will discuss these options.

The USPS offers a variety of domestic and international delivery services for letters and packages. The USPS Web site at www.usps.com/all/shippingandmailing/welcome.htm provides users with specific information about all the services

provided by the post office. As a result of a comprehensive USPS Transformation Plan in 2002, many new services were added to the post office. As a result, the post office became much better able to compete with other mail and package delivery services. The following sections include brief descriptions of USPS mail services you are likely to use in the health-care setting.

Regular Mail Service

Regular mail delivery includes several classes of mail as well as other designations such as Priority Mail and Express Mail. The class or designation determines how quickly a piece of mail is delivered.

First-Class Mail Most correspondence generated in a medical office—letters, postcards, and invoices—is sent by first-class mail. Items must weigh 11 ounces or less to be considered first-class. (An item over 11 ounces that requires quick delivery must be sent by Priority Mail, which is discussed later in the chapter.) The cost of mailing a first-class item is based on its weight. The standard rate is for items 1 ounce or less that are not larger than 6⅛ inches high, 11½ inches wide, and ¼ inch thick. Additional postage is required for items that are heavier or larger. Postage for postcards is less than the letter rate. First-class mail is forwarded at no additional cost.

Second- and Third-Class Mail Newspapers and periodicals are delivered by second-class mail. It is a class seldom used by medical offices. Third-class mail, also known as media mail or book rate, is available only for authorized mailers and is not available for medical offices.

Parcel Post This type of mail was formerly called fourth-class mail. It is used for items that weigh at least one pound but not more than 70 pounds and that do not require speedy delivery. Rates are based on weight and distance. There is a special fourth-class rate for mailing books, manuscripts, and some types of medical information.

Bound Printed Matter Formerly called special fourth-class mail, this is a rate applied to promotional advertising, directories, and other types of advertisements. No personal correspondence is allowed. Bulk rates are available for a minimum of 300 pieces.

Priority Mail Priority class is useful for heavier items that require quicker delivery than is available for fourth-class mail. Any first-class item that weighs between 11 ounces and 70 pounds requires Priority Mail service. Although the rate for Priority Mail varies with the weight of the item and the distance it must travel, the USPS offers a flat rate for all material that can fit into its special Priority Mail envelope. The USPS guarantees delivery of Priority Mail items in 2 to 3 days.

Express Mail Express Mail is the quickest USPS service. Different types are available, including next-day and second-day delivery. Express Mail deliveries are made 365 days a year. Rates vary, depending on the weight and the specific service. A special flat-rate envelope is also available. Items sent by Express Mail are automatically insured against loss or damage. You can drop off packages at the post office or arrange for pickup service.

Special Postal Services

The USPS offers a variety of special mail delivery services in addition to the regular classes of mail. These services usually require an additional fee above and beyond the cost of postage.

Online Postage

Postage can now be purchased online by using software that has been approved by the USPS. By using this software, customers are able to purchase products via the Internet. Pitney Bowes has software called ShipStream™; however, you may search the Internet for other USPS-approved software. USPS.com also sells postage online as well as other shipping and mailing supplies.

Certified Mail Certified mail offers a guarantee that the item has been received. The item is marked as certified mail and requires the postal carrier to obtain a signature on delivery (Figure 13–13). The signature card is then returned to the sender. The card should be added to the patient's file. This documentation is evidence that the document was not only mailed but also received. The receiver's name is clearly printed along with the signature. The certified mail signature card becomes a legal document, which may be important in court.

Return Receipt Requested You may request a return receipt (for a small additional fee) to obtain proof that an item was delivered. The receipt indicates who received the item and when. This type of mail service is very important when a medical practice requires proof that a letter was received. When returned to the office, the return receipt should be carefully added to the patient's record. It may become an important legal document and may be required at a later date in a court of law.

Registered Mail Use registered mail to send items that are valuable, irreplaceable, or otherwise important. Registered mail provides the sender with evidence of mailing and delivery. It also provides the security that an item is being tracked as it is transported through the postal system. Because of this tracking process, delivery may be slightly delayed.

To register a piece of mail, take it to the post office and indicate the full value of the item. Both first-class mail and Priority Mail can be registered.

Delivery Confirmation Delivery confirmation is a service that tracks your mail with a tracking number by the delivery date and signature. There is an added fee involved.

International Mail

The USPS offers both surface (via ship) and airmail service to most foreign countries. Information on rates and fees is available from the post office.

There are various types of international mail, which are similar to the domestic classes. The USPS also provides international Express Mail and Priority Mail services, along with special mail delivery services such as registered mail, certified mail, and special delivery.

Tracking Mail

If a piece of registered or certified mail does not reach its destination by the expected time, you can ask the post office to track it (Figure 13–14). You will need to present your original receipt for the item. You can also track mail through the USPS Web site (www.USPS.com) by entering the label or receipt number received from the post office at the time the item was mailed. Tracking is also available for Express and Priority Mail items.

United Parcel Service

United Parcel Service (UPS) delivers packages and provides overnight letter and express services. You can either drop off packages at a UPS location or have them picked up at your office. Fees vary with the services provided, such as ground or air. Packages are automatically insured against theft or damage.

Back side of signature card

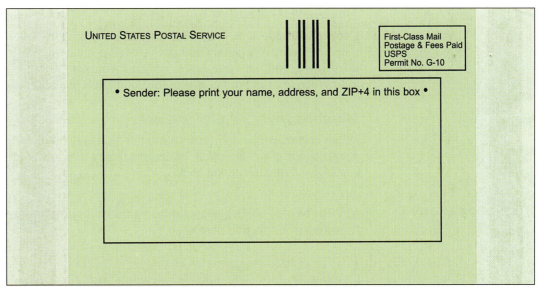

UNITED STATES POSTAL SERVICE

First-Class Mail
Postage & Fees Paid
USPS
Permit No. G-10

• Sender: Please print your name, address, and ZIP+4 in this box •

Front side of signature card

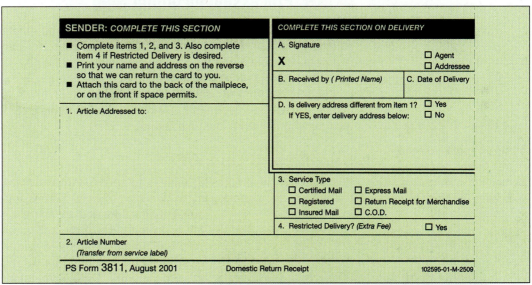

SENDER: *COMPLETE THIS SECTION*

- Complete items 1, 2, and 3. Also complete item 4 if Restricted Delivery is desired.
- Print your name and address on the reverse so that we can return the card to you.
- Attach this card to the back of the mailpiece, or on the front if space permits.

1. Article Addressed to:

COMPLETE THIS SECTION ON DELIVERY

A. Signature

X
☐ Agent
☐ Addressee

B. Received by (*Printed Name*)

C. Date of Delivery

D. Is delivery address different from item 1? ☐ Yes
If YES, enter delivery address below: ☐ No

3. Service Type
☐ Certified Mail ☐ Express Mail
☐ Registered ☐ Return Receipt for Merchandise
☐ Insured Mail ☐ C.O.D.

4. Restricted Delivery? *(Extra Fee)* ☐ Yes

2. Article Number
(Transfer from service label)

PS Form 3811, August 2001   Domestic Return Receipt   102595-01-M-2509

Certified mail receipt

U.S. Postal Service
CERTIFIED MAIL RECEIPT
(Domestic Mail Only; No Insurance Coverage Provided)

O F F I C I A L   U S E

Postage $

Certified Fee

Return Receipt Fee
(Endorsement Required)

Restricted Delivery Fee
(Endorsement Required)

Total Postage & Fees $

Postmark
Here

Sent To

Street, Apt. No.;
or PO Box No.

City, State, ZIP+ 4

PS Form 3800, January 2001   See Reverse for Instructions

PLACE STICKER AT TOP OF ENVELOPE TO THE RIGHT
OF THE RETURN ADDRESS. FOLD AT DOTTED LINE

CERTIFIED MAIL

7001 1140 0000 7637 2652

figure 13–13

Certified mail offers a guarantee that the item has been received. The item is marked as certified mail and requires the postal carrier to obtain a signature on delivery. Registered mail provides the sender with evidence of mailing and delivery.

Express Delivery Services

Companies such as Federal Express and DHL provide several types of quick delivery services for letters and packages. Rates vary according to weight, time of delivery, and, in some cases, whether you have the package picked up at your office or drop it off at one of the company's local branches or drop boxes.

Messengers or Couriers

When items must be delivered within the local area on the same day, local messenger services are an option. Many messenger companies are listed in the Yellow Pages of the telephone book.

CHECKPOINT
LO 13.8

What type of USPS mailing service would be used to verify that the patient received the physician's letter?

LO 13.9 Processing Incoming Mail

Mail is an important connection between the office and other professionals and patients. Often an office has an established procedure for handling the mail. It is best to set aside a specific time of the day to process all the incoming mail at once rather than trying to do a little bit at a time.

Although it sounds simple, processing mail involves more than merely opening envelopes. In general, it involves the following steps: sorting, opening, recording, annotating, and distributing.

Sorting and Opening

The first step in processing mail is to sort it. Always place any personal or confidential mail aside. Unless you have special permission never open personal mail addressed to another person. Carefully lay it on the desk of the addressee, unopened. Sort remaining mail according to priority. Always sort all mail in an uncluttered area to avoid mixing it with other paperwork. Follow a regular sorting procedure each time so that you do not miss any steps. When opening mail, tapping the envelope on the desk will ensure that the contents are at the bottom of the envelope and will not inadvertently be torn by the letter opener. Using a letter opener helps avoid paper cuts. All incoming correspondence should be stamped with a date stamp to note the date the item was received which could be important if there is ever a legal dispute regarding when information was received. Procedure 13–5 found at the end of the chapter outlines suggested steps for managing incoming mail. The Practice Readiness section on the next page discusses how to recognize urgent incoming mail.

Recording

Keep a log of each day's mail. This daily record lists the mail received and indicates follow-up correspondence and the date it is completed. This method helps in tracing items and keeping track of correspondence.

figure 13–14

Tracking an item is a service that post offices perform when important items are delayed or do not reach their destinations.

How to Spot Urgent Incoming Mail

How can you tell if a piece of incoming mail is urgent? First-class mail marked "Urgent" tells you that it requires immediate attention. Here are some other signals to look for (Figure 13–15).

figure 13-15
Urgent materials receive top priority upon arrival at an office.

Overnight Mail
Any package that has been sent by an overnight carrier or by USPS Express Mail should be considered urgent and should be opened immediately.

Certified Mail
Certified mail requires your signature on delivery. The sender used certified mail to be sure that the item would be sent to the proper person.

Registered Mail
Items sent by registered mail typically are valuable, irreplaceable, or otherwise important. Registered mail provides the sender with evidence of mailing and delivery.

Special Delivery
An item sent by special delivery is likely to be delivered sometime before the normal mail delivery—possibly even on a Sunday or holiday. The sender requested special delivery to ensure that the item would be delivered promptly after it was received at the addressee's post office.

Annotating

Because you will be reading much of the incoming mail, you may also be encouraged to annotate it. To **annotate** means to underline or highlight key points of the letter or to write reminders, comments, or suggested actions in the margins or on self-adhesive notes. An example of annotating is including "please sign here" next to where a signature should be. Annotating may involve pulling a patient's chart or any previous related correspondence from a file and attaching it to the letter.

annotate
Underlining, highlighting, or commenting in documents or letters to draw attention to certain portions of the document.

Distributing

Sort letters into separate batches for distribution. These batches might include correspondence that requires the physician's attention, payments to be directed to the person in charge of billing and accounts receivable, and correspondence that requires your attention. Each batch should be presented to the appropriate person in a file folder or interoffice envelope and arranged with the highest-priority items on top. You may be given specific instructions on how to distribute magazines, newspapers, and advertising circulars.

Handling Drug and Product Samples

Many physicians receive a number of drug and product samples in the mail. Handling procedures vary from office to office. Samples of nonprescription products, such as hand creams or cough drops, may be placed in the patient treatment area for patient distribution as directed by the physician.

Follow office policy regarding receipt of any new prescription drug samples. All drug samples should be stored in a locked cabinet sorted and labeled by category. Samples should be given to patients only under the direction of licensed personnel (M.D., P.A., N.P.). If samples are given to a patient, document the information in the patient's health record.

CHECKPOINT
LO 13.9

What is the purpose of annotating incoming correspondence?

Procedure 13–1 Creating a Letter

GOAL To follow standard procedure for constructing a business letter

MATERIALS Word processor or personal computer, letterhead paper, dictionaries or other sources

METHOD

1. Format the letter according to the office's standard procedure. Use the same punctuation and style throughout. Refer to Figures 13–2 through 13–6 for spacing and formatting suggestions.

2. Start the dateline three lines below the last line of the printed letterhead. (Note: Depending on the length of the letter, it is acceptable to start between two and six lines below the letterhead.)

3. Two lines below the dateline, type in any special mailing instructions (such as REGISTERED MAIL, CERTIFIED MAIL, and so on).

4. Three lines below any special instructions, begin the inside address.

   Type the addressee's courtesy title (Mr., Mrs., Ms.) and full name on the first line. If a professional title is given (M.D., RN, Ph.D.), type this title after the addressee's name instead of using a courtesy title.

5. Type the addressee's business title, if applicable, on the second line.

   Type the company name on the third line. Type the street address on the fourth line, including the apartment or suite number.

   Type the city, state, and zip code on the fifth line. Use the standard two-letter abbreviation for the state, followed by one space and the zip code.

6. Two lines below the inside address, type the salutation, using the appropriate courtesy title (Mr., Mrs., Ms., Dr.) prior to typing the addressee's last name.

7. Two lines below the salutation, type the subject line, if applicable.

8. Two lines below the subject line, begin the body of the letter. Single-space between lines. Double-space between paragraphs.

9. Two lines below the body of the letter, type the complimentary closing.

10. Leave three blank lines (return four times), and begin the signature block. (Enough space must be left to allow for the signature.)Type the sender's name on the first line. Type the sender's title on the second line.

11. Two lines below the sender's title, type the identification line. Type the sender's initials in all capitals and your initials in lowercase letters, separating the two sets of initials with a colon or a forward slash.

12. One or two lines below the identification line, type the enclosure notation, if applicable.

13. Two lines below the enclosure notation, type the copy notation, if applicable.

14. Edit the letter.

15. Proofread and spell-check the letter.

Procedure 13-2 Sending an Electronic Patient Letter

GOAL To create and send an electronic letter to a patient

MATERIALS Information necessary to create required letter; EHR software program containing letter templates such as SpringCharts

METHOD

1. Access the *New* menu in the *Practice View* screen. Choose *New Template > New Letter Template*. In the *Re* window, key the subject line for the letter, such as *Welcome to Total Care Clinic, PC.*

2. In the *Text* box, you will key the body of the letter. Begin the letter with an introductory welcoming statement, such as "Thank you for choosing Total Care Clinic for your health-care needs. We look forward to working with you."

   Enter pertinent information that will be needed by a new patient such as the address, phone, fax, and Web site information for the practice. Including the names of the practitioners at Total Care Clinic and their usual office hours is also a good idea. Also include the paraprofessional personnel and their titles.

3. When you complete the letter, give this new template a name, for example, *Welcome Patient Letter* and click the "Save" button.

4. Open the new patient's chart. Click on the *New* menu and select *Welcome Patient Letter.* Note that because you are in the patient chart, the letter is already addressed to the patient and that the default greeting and closure are also present. Click the "Template" button at the bottom of the screen and highlight (select) *Welcome Patient Letter.*

5. Add a signature to the bottom of the letter by clicking on the "Sign" icon at the bottom of the window. Choose the correct provider to enter his/her name to the closing of the letter.

6. You can now choose to print the letter to send it via USPS mail or choose the e-mail option if you have written permission from the patient to do so.

7. Click the "Done" button and save the letter under the *Letters* category; saving the letter under "Welcome Patient Letter."

Procedure 13-3 Writing a Memo

GOAL To follow standard procedures to write a memo for interoffice use

MATERIALS Word processor or personal computer, plain paper, dictionaries, and other source texts such as *PDR* or policies and procedures manuals as required

METHOD

1. Gather all necessary documents to create the memo.

2. Decide whether the memo will be created "free-hand" or through the use of a template.

3. If using a template, fill in the headings as listed with appropriate information. If the memo is being created free-hand, use the headings, DATE:, TO:, FROM:, and SUBJECT: and then complete the resulting blanks with the appropriate information.

4. Double or triple space after the memo headings or, if using a template, move to the body area of the memo and begin typing the information to be included in the memo.

5. Single space the information within the memo and double space between paragraphs. Use either the block or indented paragraph format, depending on office policy.

6. At the end of the memo, if required by office policy, double space after the last line of the memo and insert reference initials.

7. Spell-check and proofread the document carefully, correcting errors as necessary.

Procedure 13–4 Using the *PDR* as a Spelling Reference

GOAL To use the *PDR* as a spelling reference

MATERIALS Document, such as a letter to a patient or physician, including one or more references to specific medications; *PDR;* pen or word processing software package

METHOD

1. After completing the document, use spell-check.

2. Note any terms, including medication names not recognized by the spell-checker.

3. Open the *PDR* to Section 2 (pink section), Brand- and Generic-Name Index.

4. The index is in alphabetic order. Locate the alphabetic area where the drug in question is located.

5. When the medication name is located, note the spelling carefully and correct it within your document.

6. If there are several medications listed that appear to be "possibilities" for the medication you are checking, it may be necessary to check with the physician so that you do not mistakenly list an incorrect drug.

7. If the office word processing software contains a medical dictionary spell-checker, you may wish to carefully enter this new medical term into the dictionary for future reference.

8. Carefully double-check the spelling of all other medications in the document, correcting spelling as necessary.

9. Proofread and edit the rest of the document prior to sending it to the intended recipient.

Procedure 13-5   Managing Mail

GOAL   To follow a standard procedure for sorting, opening, and processing incoming office mail

MATERIALS   Letter opener, date and time stamp (manual or automatic), stapler, paper clips, adhesive notes

METHOD

1. Check the address on each letter or package to be sure that it has been delivered to the correct location.

2. Sort the mail into piles according to priority and type of mail. Your system may include the following:

   - Top priority. This pile will contain any items that were sent by overnight mail delivery in addition to items sent by registered mail, certified mail, or special delivery. (Faxes and e-mail messages are also top priority.)

   - Second priority. This pile will include personal or confidential mail.

   - Third priority. This pile will contain all firstclass mail, airmail, and Priority Mail items. These items should be divided into payments received, insurance forms, reports, and other correspondence.

   - Fourth priority. This pile will consist of packages.

   - Fifth priority. This pile will contain magazines and newspapers.

   - Sixth priority. This last pile will include advertisements and catalogs.

3. Set aside all letters labeled "Personal" or "Confidential." Unless you have permission to open these letters, only the addressee should open them.

4. Arrange all the envelopes with the flaps facing up and away from you.

5. Tap the lower edge of the envelope to shift the contents to the bottom. This step helps to prevent cutting any of the contents when you open the envelope.

6. Open all the envelopes.

7. Remove and unfold the contents, making sure that nothing remains in the envelope.

8. Review each document, and check the sender's name and address.

   - If the letter has no return address, save the envelope, or cut the address off the envelope, and tape it to the letter.

   - Check to see if the address matches the one on the envelope. If there is a difference, staple the envelope to the letter, and make a note to verify the correct address with the sender.

9. Compare the enclosure notation on the letter with the actual enclosures to make sure that all items are included. Make a note to contact the sender if anything is missing.

10. Clip together each letter and its enclosures.

11. Check the date of the letter. If there is a significant delay between the date of the letter and the postmark, keep the envelope.

12. If all contents appear to be in order, you can discard the envelope.

13. Review all bills and statements.

- Make sure the amount enclosed is the same as the amount listed on the statement.
- Make a note of any discrepancies.

14. Stamp each piece of correspondence with the date (and sometimes the time) to record its receipt. If possible, stamp each item in the same location—such as the upper-right corner.

Case Study

PROFESSIONAL READINESS

Quality of Work
Striving for excellence in performing work

Melody works for Dr. Gianini, a general surgeon. One of Melody's responsibilities is to send surgery and pathology results to patients and their primary care physicians (PCPs). A template letter is used, but knowledge of medical terminology is an absolute necessity. She is preparing a letter to Mr. Kurzich informing him that his recent biopsy revealed a carcinoid, which is a benign condition. She mistakenly uses the term carcinoma, which is a malignant condition. Melody is in a hurry and does not proofread the letter before she sends it. When the letter is received, the term *carcinoma* distresses both the patient and the PCP. They immediately contact Dr. Gianini. This error had the potential for dire consequences.

Thinking Critically

1. What other measures besides proofreading can be taken to ensure the quality of any written communication?
2. Could this error jeopardize Melody's job?
3. If the office had a medical terminology spell-check, would the error have been caught?

practice APPLICATIONS

1. A young patient of Dr. Fredericks, Rodney Sills, has broken his wrist and Dr. Fredericks says that Rodney will be unable to participate in gym class for 10 weeks. Create a letter notifying Rodney's gym instructor of the situation.

2. Using proper letter formatting technique and the basic rules of writing reviewed in this chapter, correct the following letter:

September 18th, 2012

Mountainside Hospital
Samuel Adams, Educational Coordinator
1 Mountainside Lane
San Francisco, California, 94112

Dear mr. Adams:
I am writing in response to your letter of the 10th. I am very interested in presenting a talk at your Health Fare in February. I am available to speak on either the 20th or the 21st.

If there is any flexibility in scheduling, I would prefer to present my talk in the afternoon. Also, please let me know how long I should prepare to speak. I am including a copy of an article I recently wrote on the same subject for the local paper.

I am looking forward to hearing from you.

Sincerly,
Enclosure
Sara Kacharski, DO

1. **[LO13.3]** The _____ is the space around the edges of a form or letter that is left blank.
   a. formatting
   b. heading
   c. letterhead
   d. margin
   e. tabs

2. **[LO13.3]** The complimentary closing is placed how many lines below the last line of the body?
   a. 2
   b. 6
   c. 4
   d. 3
   e. 5

3. **[LO13.8]** What type of mail is required for sending items that are valuable, irreplaceable, or otherwise important?
   a. Certified
   b. Special delivery
   c. Registered
   d. Return receipt requested
   e. First-class

4. **[LO13.5]** Which of the following is spelled correctly?
   a. professor
   b. proffessur
   c. profesur
   d. profesor
   e. proffesor

5. **[LO13.1]** Choose the supplies necessary to create professional correspondence.
   a. Letterhead
   b. Envelopes
   c. Reference materials
   d. a and b only
   e. a, b, and c

6. **[LO13.2]** Which of the following terms is NOT used to describe effective writing?
   a. Concise
   b. Complete
   c. Clear
   d. Style
   e. Voice

7. **[LO13.4]** Which of the following describes the types of memos used in a medical office?
   a. Informative
   b. Directive
   c. Administrative
   d. Medical
   e. All of the above

8. **[LO13.6]** Preparing an envelope correctly allows for the use of OCR by the USPS. What does OCR stand for?
   a. Optical Character Recognition
   b. Official Character Release
   c. Optional Character Reader
   d. Optional Capitalization Reader
   e. Optical Character Reader

9. **[LO13.7]** Which mail delivery system allows for handwritten instructions on the item to be delivered?
   a. Airmail
   b. Registered
   c. Certified
   d. Return Receipt Requested
   e. Special Delivery

10. **[LO13.9]** Which step in processing incoming mail involves highlighting or making notes on the correspondence prior to giving it to the addressee?
    a. Sorting
    b. Opening
    c. Recording
    d. Annotating
    e. Distributing

learning outcome SUMMARY

LO 13.1 Choose the right supplies for professional-looking office correspondence. Letterhead should be formal with the practice name, address, and phone number printed on the sheet. Envelopes, labels, charge sheets, and invoices are generally ordered together and are also preprinted with the practice name and address. Some office software programs contain the option of printing your own labels for use with bulk mailings such as the office newsletter.

LO 13.2 To create effective, professional correspondence, use an appropriate style, clear and concise language, and active voice.

LO 13.3 The parts of the business letter are the dateline, the subject line, the attention line, the body of the letter, the complimentary close, the signature block, the identification line, and notations. Letter styles include full-block style, modified-block style, modified block with indented paragraphs, and simplified style. The two different styles of punctuation used in correspondence are open punctuation and mixed punctuation. Be consistent in your choices throughout the document.

LO 13.4 The components of a memo heading include *Date, To, From, RE* (or *Subject*), and *cc* if necessary.

LO 13.5 Editing means checking a document for factual accuracy, logical flow, conciseness, clarity, and tone. Proofreading is checking a document for grammatical, spelling, and formatting errors. Tools such as a medical dictionary, thesaurus, *PDR*, and English grammar manuals are helpful in these processes.

LO 13.6 Preparation for mailing includes having the letter signed, preparing the envelope, and folding and inserting the letter into the envelope. It will then be ready for postage to be calculated and affixed.

LO 13.7 Mailing equipment and supplies include the postage scale, meter, and postage rate chart and any of the following depending on office need: airmail supplies, overnight delivery envelopes, certified and registered mail supplies and stickers, as well as any supplies for any private delivery services used by the office.

LO 13.8 The United States Postal Service (USPS) has increased and updated its services for letters and packages so that it now has the ability to compete with private services such as FedEx, DHL, and UPS. The services provided by the USPS and the private services are now virtually the same.

LO 13.9 The process of handling incoming mail includes properly sorting, opening, recording, annotating, and distributing the mail.

medical assisting COMPETENCIES

CAAHEP

IV. C (8) Recognize elements of fundamental writing skills

IV. C (12) Organize technical information and summaries

IV. P (10) Compose professional/business letters

ABHES

7. Basic Keyboarding/Computer Concepts
   a. Perform basic keyboarding skills including:
   (1) Locating the keys on a keyboard
   (2) Typing medical correspondence and basic reports
   b. Identify and properly utilize office machines, computerized systems, and medical software such as:
   (1) Efficiently maintain and understand different types of medical correspondence and medical reports
   (2) Apply computer application skills using a variety of different electronic programs

including both practice management software and EMR software

8. Medical Office Business Procedures/ Management
   a. Perform basic clerical duties
   d. Apply concepts for office procedures
   ii. Recognize and respond to verbal and nonverbal communication
   jj. Perform fundamental writing skills including correct grammar, spelling, and formatting techniques when writing prescriptions, documenting medical records, etc.

11. Career Development

b. Demonstrate professionalism by:

(1) Exhibiting dependability, punctuality, and a positive work ethic

(2) Exhibiting a positive attitude and a sense of responsibility

(3) Maintaining confidentiality at all times

(7) Expressing a responsible attitude

(8) Being courteous and diplomatic

(9) Conducting work within scope of education, training, and ability

Medical

Records

The past cannot be changed. The future is yet in your power.

Mary Pickford

Preparation for Success

Interviewer: Ruben, you and I met a few years ago when you were studying to be an administrative medical assistant. As I recall, the road was a little rocky.

Ruben: That's a good way of putting it! I was on a soccer team and we practiced and played in the evening and on weekends. My teammates always seemed to talk me into going out afterward. I got behind on my coursework and was coming to class late.

Interviewer: How did that change?

Ruben: The school evaluated us using a professional attributes form similar to what you showed me in this textbook. I was not doing well and was told that if I was late one more time I could be kicked out of the program. I knew they meant it and I had six months left. It came down to going out with my buddies or getting kicked out of school. I decided that six months was not that long and I really wanted a good career.

Interviewer: What you did next must have been tough.

Ruben: Yes, I knew if I stayed on the same soccer team, my habits would not change because the other players would always give me a hard time about not going out. I switched teams. Right after practice or a game, I'd go home, study, and get to sleep so I could get up on time the next day.

Interviewer: Not only did you finish the program but you were hired at a medical office where you were a part of the implementation team for a state-of-the-art electronic health record.

Ruben: Yes, and as other new staff started, I trained them on the system. A couple of years later I was offered a position by the EHR vendor to help train for implementations in other medical practices. Since I know the job of the administrative medical assistant, I was good at making the training relevant and real world. It's also exciting for me to see how offices differ and to share tips from one practice to another. The practices are always looking for ways to be more efficient and appreciate the information.

Interviewer: Ruben, what advice do you have for students studying to be administrative medical assistants?

Ruben: My advice is simple and I learned that it not only applies to school but to my life. Hang around with people who are supportive of you and your goals, people who do not try to hold you back. I don't think the others are really friends. True friends help you and are not just interested in having a good time or taking your time.

Interviewer: It appears that you found some good friends to support you. You have a successful career and your soccer team is playing for the city championship tonight. Good luck.

unit 4

14 Medical Records Management

Learning Outcomes

After completing Chapter 14, you will be able to:

14.1 Describe the purposes of the medical record.

14.2 Explain the six elements of medical records management.

14.3 Describe the various types and other components of filing systems.

14.4 Demonstrate knowledge of electronic and paper-based medical records maintenance and the associated HIPAA requirements.

14.5 Explain the proper retention and destruction of the medical record.

Key Terms

active file
alphabetical order
alphabetic filing system
closed file
compactible file
file guide
inactive file
indexing rules
lateral file
middle digit
numeric filing system

out guide
records management
  system
retention schedule
sequential order
tab
terminal digit
tickler file
unit
vertical file

Preparation for Certification

RMA (AMT) Exam
- Medical records management
- Protect, store, and retain medical records according to HIPAA regulations

CMAS (AMT) Exam
- Legal and ethical considerations
- Medical records systems
- Medical records procedures
- Confidentiality
- Procedures

CMA (AAMA) Exam
- Maintaining confidentiality
- Filing guidelines
- Needs, purposes, and terminology of filing systems

Introduction ● ● ●

You are learning that a major function of the administrative medical assistant is working with the medical record. It is also called the health record or chart. The management of these individual files is vital to the care of each patient and to the smooth operation of the medical office. Understanding the purposes of the medical record will help in understanding the processes for medical records management.

This chapter discusses the multifaceted areas of medical records as a system or medical records management, the HIPAA implications, and the proposed changes from the federal government. These changes involve the electronic health record (EHR) or electronic medical record (EMR) to which you were introduced in earlier chapters.

LO 14.1 The Purposes of the Medical Record

Understanding the purposes or uses of the medical record helps to understand its importance. The purposes of the medical record are to

- Direct continuity of care by "telling the patient's story." The record should contain medical and family histories; diagnostic and monitoring tests; diagnoses; physicians' names; and basically who did what, the results, the plan, and how the patient is doing. This provides knowledge to all of the patient's physicians to hopefully avoid errors and duplication.

- Provide legal protection to the patient and the physician by documenting what has been done or not done. Whenever care is questioned through a legal entity, the medical record is always requested. The record is reviewed to determine indications of negligence or other issues. Refer to Chapter 6, Law and Ethics in the Medical Office.

- Act as a tool for monitoring quality of care by indicating if appropriate standards were followed. Accrediting and governmental agencies, insurance companies, and internal quality care entities would, for example, review the medical records for all the two-year-old patients in the practice to determine if immunizations were up to date per the recommendations.

- Supply information for use in education and research. For example, medical assisting and other health-care students would review the medical record to determine treatment of an asthmatic, or a study might be done to determine the outcome of a patient on a specific medication.

The patient's consent for release of information and HIPAA requirements are followed as appropriate. This topic is discussed further in the next section of this chapter.

● ● ●

State the purposes of the medical record.

CHECKPOINT
LO 14.1

LO 14.2 The Six Elements of Medical Records Management

The **records management system** refers to the following six elements.

1. Creating or assembling the medical record
2. Filing the medical record

records management system
An established process for creating, filing, maintaining, and destroying files.

3. Maintaining/protecting the medical record

4. Releasing the medical record

5. Retaining the medical record

6. Destroying the medical record

Traditionally, medical records were in a hard-copy folder-type form (Figure 14–1). As part of the Health Information Technology for Economic and Clinical Health Act (HITECH ACT) the federal government is proposing that all medical records convert to an electronic health record with a target date of 2014. Government reimbursement or payment may differ for those health-care providers who have the EHR and those who do not have the EHR. There is no question that electronic health records will be in common use.

As the EHR replaces the hard-copy medical record, the methods for completing the required elements listed above are dramatically changing. It is predicted that over the next few years the medical assistant will be working simultaneously with the following three systems:

1. Diminishing hard-copy records

2. Transitional combinations of hard-copy and electronic medical records

3. The total electronic medical record

Chapter 15, The Health Record, covers the individual health record.

CHECKPOINT
LO 14.2

Briefly describe the six elements of medical records management.

LO **14.3** Filing the Medical Record

Filing generally refers to placing records, or files, in a specific location where they are housed. Filing cabinets are one option and may contain a series of pull-out drawers in which files are hung. The disadvantage of some filing cabinets is that access is limited to one person at a time because the drawer setup provides limited maneuvering room. In addition, cabinets require more floor space than filing shelves. About twice the depth of the file drawer is needed to allow it to fully open.

vertical file
A filing system that usually contains a metal frame or bar in hanging file folders.

lateral file
A horizontal filing cabinet with shelves where files are arranged with sides facing out.

A **vertical file** features pullout drawers that usually contain a metal frame or bar equipped to handle letter-size or legal-size documents. Hanging file folders are hung on this frame, with identifying names facing out. Vertical files may have two, three, four, or six drawers.

Horizontal filing cabinets, called **lateral files,** often feature doors that flip up and pullout drawers. Files are arranged with sides facing out. Lateral files require more wall space but do not extend as far into the room as vertical file drawers.

Compactible Files

compactible files
Files kept on rolling shelves that slide along permanent tracks in the floor and are stored close together or stacked when not in use.

Large medical practices conserve space by using **compactible files** kept on rolling shelves that slide along permanent tracks in the floor. When not in use, these files can be stored close together—even one on top of another—to save space. When needed, they can be rolled out into an open area so that the staff can easily use them. Compactible files can be moved manually or automatically with the touch of a button.

Regardless of which type of filing equipment your office uses, files should be clearly labeled on the outside of the drawer so that you do not have to open doors or drawers to know the contents. Labeling allows you to go directly to the appropriate place when retrieving a file. The label lists the range of files the drawer or shelf contains.

Security Measures

All filing equipment must be secured to protect the confidentiality of medical records. *Never* place patient records in an unsecured filing system.

Most filing cabinets come with a lock and key. To protect filing shelves in a separate room, you can lock the file room. Security of the keys to that room then becomes an important issue. The number of staff members who have keys to that room should be limited. Because the files remain open during the day, it is important to make sure they are not placed in areas where unauthorized people can obtain access to them. Posting a sign on the file room door stating "Authorized Personnel Only" helps ensure that files remain secure. To ensure office security after hours, some practices install alarm systems.

Keys and locks bring a measure of security only when they are *used.* Many office staff become lazy and routinely overlook locking file rooms and cabinets. Security survey teams will always ask to see the keys to any locked door or cabinet and ask the staff to demonstrate that they work. Within a medical office, conducting regular security drills at the same time that fire drills are held will aid staff in staying sharp and aware of security risks.

File Folders

The most basic filing supply is the file folder, often referred to as a manila folder. File folders come in two sizes: letter size, which is 8½ by 11 inches, and legal size, which is 8½ by 14 inches. The folder should have a metal clasp to securely hold all the record's documents. Figure 14–2 shows the various types of filing supplies used in the medical office.

An important feature of file folders is the **tab,** the tapered rectangular or rounded extension at the top or side of the folder. The tabs on file folders are labeled to identify the individual patient's folder. Printing labels from templates that are available at any office supply store is an option.

File Guides

To identify a group of file folders in a file drawer, you may use **file guides,** which are heavy cardboard or plastic inserts. These guides contain the beginning number or numbers of the group of files contained in that section up to the next file guide.

Out Guides

Another filing supply is an **out guide.** An out guide is a marker made of stiff material. It is used as a placeholder when a file has been removed from the filing system. Some out guides include pockets that can hold the name of the file that belongs in that place or the name of the individual who took the file, and its due date for return. On another type of out guide, you can write the information on the out guide and cross it out when the file is returned. Out guides can be used for both shelf and cabinet filing.

Manual filing systems in large practices often have an electronic medical records "checkout" system, similar to a library with bar codes.

Filing Methods

A filing system is a method by which files are organized. Any of a variety of filing systems may be used, but every system places patient records in some sort

figure 14–1

Medical records filed on shelves are being replaced by those filed electronically.

tab
A tapered rectangular or rounded extension at the top of a file folder.

file guide
A heavy cardboard or plastic insert used to identify a group of file folders in a file drawer or shelf.

out guide
A marker made of stiff material and used as a placeholder when a file is taken out of a filing system.

figure 14-2

The typical supplies needed for the paper-based chart are not needed for the EHR.

sequential order
One after another in a predictable pattern or sequence.

alphabetical order
A filing system in which the files are arranged in alphabetical order, with the patient's last name first, followed by the first name and middle initial.

indexing rules
Rules used as guidelines for the sequencing of files based on standard business practice.

unit
A part of an individual's name or title used in filing.

numeric filing system
A filing system that organizes files by numbers assigned to a name instead of by the name.

figure 14-3

Due to HIPAA, very few offices continue to use alphabetic filing on medical records' labels.

of **sequential order**—one after another in a pattern, or sequence, that can be predicted. It is important to find out which filing system your office is using and to follow it exactly. Any deviation can result in lost or misplaced records. Never make any changes in the filing system without first consulting the doctors and other staff members in the practice.

A very common filing system for maintaining patient files in sequential order is the alphabetic system. It is simple and easy to use.

Alphabetic To comply with confidentiality standards, patient names are no longer placed on the outside of patient medical records. Other files used in the medical office, such as tickler files, are kept in **alphabetical order** (last name, first name, middle initial), as shown in Figure 14–3. Tickler files contain the patient's last name first, followed by the first, or given, name and the middle initial with an associated identifying number that is assigned to the actual medical record.

There are specific rules to follow when filing personal names alphabetically (Table 14–1). These rules are called **indexing rules** (Table 14–2). Indexing rules are rules used as guidelines for the sequencing of files based on current business practice. They define a consistent method for the ordering of filed materials. The Association of Records, Managers, and Administrators monitors and updates these suggested methods periodically. Individual medical practices may choose to deviate from some of these accepted practices. However, indexing rules are generally the norm followed by most medical practices.

Indexing rules define each separate part of a person's name or title as a **unit.** Indexing rules then describe the order to display and manage each unit in an alphabetized system. See Table 14–2.

Numeric A **numeric filing system** organizes files by numbers instead of by names. In this system each patient name is assigned a number. New patients are assigned the next unused number in sequence. Then, instead of being filed by name, the files are arranged in numeric order—1, 2, 3, 4, and so on. The resulting files may be sequential by the order in which patients have come to the practice or randomly assigned by a computerized system.

Only the numbers are indicated on the files.

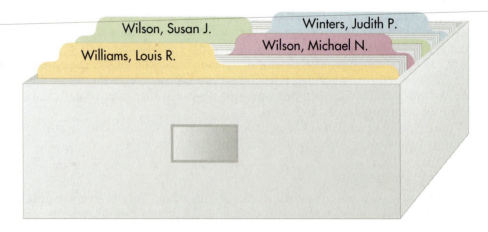

table 14–1

Rules for Alphabetic Filing of Personal Names

In alphabetizing, treat each part of a patient's name as a separate unit, and look at the units in this order: last name, first name, middle initial, and any subsequent names or initials. Disregard punctuation.

NAME	UNIT 1	UNIT 2	UNIT 3	UNIT 4
Stephen Jacobson	JACOBSON	STEPHEN		
Stephen Brent Jacobson	JACOBSON	STEPHEN	BRENT	
B.T. Jacoby	JACOBY	B	T	
C. Bruce Hay Jacoby	JACOBY	C	BRUCE	HAY
D. Jones	JONES	D		
David Jones	JONES	DAVID		
Kwong Kow Ng	NG	KWONG	KOW	
Philip K. Ng	NG	PHILIP	K	

Treat a prefix, such as the O' in O'Hara, as part of the name, not as a separate unit. Ignore variations in spacing, punctuation, and capitalization. Treat prefixes—such as De La, Mac, Saint, and St.—exactly as they are spelled.

NAME	UNIT 1	UNIT 2	UNIT 3	UNIT 4
A. Serafino Delacruz	DELACRUZ	A	SERAFINO	
Victor P. De La Cruz	DELACRUZ	VICTOR	P	
Irene J. MacKay	MACKAY	IRENE	J	
Walter G. Mac Kay	MACKAY	WALTER	G	
Kyle N. Saint Clair	SAINTCLAIR	KYLE	N	
Peter St. Clair	STCLAIR	PETER		

Treat hyphenated names as a single unit. Disregard the hyphen.

NAME	UNIT 1	UNIT 2	UNIT 3	UNIT 4
Victor Puentes-Ruiz	PUENTESRUIZ	VICTOR		
Jean-Marie Vigneau	VIGNEAU	JEANMARIE		

A title, such as Dr. or Major, or a seniority term, such as Jr. or Sr., should be treated as the last filing unit, to distinguish names that are otherwise identical.

NAME	UNIT 1	UNIT 2	UNIT 3	UNIT 4
Dr. George B. Diaz	DIAZ	GEORGE	B	DR
Major George B. Diaz	DIAZ	GEORGE	B	MAJOR
James R. Foster Jr.	FOSTER	JAMES	R	JR
James R. Foster Sr.	FOSTER	JAMES	R	SR

Source: Adapted from William A. Sabin, *The Gregg Reference Manual*, 10th ed. (Columbus, OH: Glencoe/McGraw-Hill, 2005)

table 14–2

Indexing Rules

RULE 1: INDIVIDUAL NAMES

The (last name) is the first indexing unit, the (first name) is the second unit, and the (middle name) is the third unit. If an initial is used instead of a name, the single initial is viewed as the entire unit.

NAME	UNIT 1	UNIT 2	UNIT 3	UNIT 4
D. Jones	Jones	D.		
David	Jones			
David R. James Jones	Jones	David	R.	James

RULE 2: BUSINESS NAMES

As written (on letterhead); each word is a unit. If "The" is used as the first word, it is considered the last unit.

NAME	UNIT 1	UNIT 2	UNIT 3	UNIT 4
Jones Hearing Supplies	Jones	Hearing	Supplies	
The Jones Hearing Supplies	Jones	Hearing	Supplies	The

RULE 3: HYPHENATION AND ABBREVIATIONS

All hyphenated names are considered to be one unit (i.e., Terry-Jones, Sheila); an abbreviated name is combined to form the unit. An abbreviated name such as Wm. for William is filed as Wm without the use of a period.

NAME	UNIT 1	UNIT 2	UNIT 3	
Terry-Jones, Sheila	Terryjones	Sheila		
St. Mary, William	Stmary	William		
St. Mary, Wm.	Stmary	Wm		

RULE 4: TITLES AND SENIORITY TERMS

Titles are normally disregarded unless they are used to distinguish between two patients with the same name. If there are patients with the same name and a title precedes the name, use as a fourth unit. Seniority terms such as Jr. or Sr. may be indexed as a last unit. It is important to remember that if a male child has exactly the same name as his father, he is considered Jr. He is a "III" if his father and his grandfather have the same name. If II or III is used as a seniority title, the basic rule states that numbers come before letters, so David Jones III would be filed before David Jones Jr.

NAME	UNIT 1	UNIT 2	UNIT 3	UNIT 4
David Jones Jr.	Jones	David	Jr.	
David Jones Sr.	Jones	David	Sr.	
David C. Jones	Jones	David	C.	
Rev. David C. Jones	Jones	David	C.	Rev.

RULE 5: PREFIXES

If the last name has as a prefix such as Mc, Van, or de, the prefix is part of the last name. It starts the first indexing unit. The prefixes Mc and Mac are usually filed in regular order.

NAME	UNIT 1	UNIT 2	UNIT 3	
Elias De Longino	Delongino	Elias		
Drew MacDreamy	MacDreamy	Drew		
Drew McDreamy	McDreamy	Drew		
Elias D. van Collins	vanCollins	Elias	D.	

table 14–2 (Concluded)

RULE 6: NAMES OF MARRIED WOMEN

A woman may retain her maiden name as her last name instead of taking her husband's surname, or she may use both names and hyphenate them (see hyphenation). She will always keep her first and middle name as part of her original name. A married woman's name may take several forms.

NAME	UNIT 1	UNIT 2	UNIT 3	
Mrs. Gisele M. Monagan-Jones	Monagan Jones	Gisele	M.	
Mrs. David (Cindy M.) Jones	Jones	Cindy	M.	
Mrs. Gisele Marie Jones	Jones	Gisele	Marie	

RULE 7: IDENTICAL NAMES

If two names are identical, make sure you index them first under their names; The birthday is generally the next unit for the individual and the address beginning with the city for a business.

The numeric system can be expanded to indicate the location of files. For example, if the last three numbers represent the patient's number, the number 113306 may represent the file of the 306th patient, which can be found in the eleventh filing cabinet in the third drawer.

A numeric system must include a master list or **tickler file,** which is a reminder list, of patients' names and corresponding numbers. Refer to Procedure 14–1: Using a Tickler File, for an additional use of a tickler list for the medical office.

To find a patient's file number using a computer system, a staff member might input a password or access code, and then type in the first three letters of the patient's last name. If the patient's last name was Mulligan, for example, the staff member would type in Mul. The computer would then show all patients whose last names begin with Mul. The staff member would scroll the names, find the patient, highlight the patient name, and hit the "Enter" key. The computer would then give the number of the patient's chart.

Terminal digit filing is often used in conjunction with a general numerical system and allows for an endless number of files with minimal amount of searching to obtain the correct files. Numbers are assigned in small groups of two or three numbers, similar to a social security number, and are read from right to left. Filing is done numerically, starting with the lowest number and moving to the highest, according to the last group of numbers. For example, the number 78 32 57 would be read in three sections, from right to left, 57 32 78.

Middle digit filing is similar to terminal digit filing. Middle digit filing uses the middle group of numbers as the primary index. Table 14–3 provides examples.

Numeric, terminal digit, and middle digit filing can all be used in combination with color coding to add even more information to the filing system.

Color Coding Color coding is used when there is a need to distinguish files within a filing system.

An example of a color-coding system might be based on a combination of patient factors. The records of patients under the age of 18 might be color-coded

tickler file
A reminder file for keeping track of time-sensitive obligations.

terminal digit
Groups of two to three numbers used as patient identifiers in a filing system and read left to right.

middle digit
A small group of two to three numbers in the middle of a patient number that is used as an identifying unit in a filing system.

MEDICAL RECORD #	FILING METHOD	PRIMARY #	SECONDARY #	FINAL #
78 32 57	Terminal Digit	57	32	78
78 32 57	Middle Digit	32	78	57

table 14–3

Examples of terminal and middle digit filing

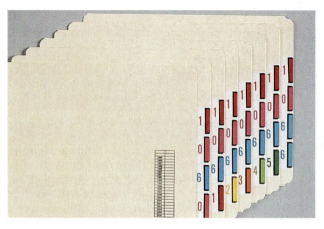

figure 14–4

Color coding can make it easier to find a misfiled record.

blue. The records of patients who are insulin-dependent might be color-coded green. The records of patients who are hemophiliacs might be coded with a half-red/half-white sticker. In an emergency situation, as when a patient with diabetes passes out while in the office, the color coding could give staff quick and vital information at a glance. Another common use of color coding is to identify the patients of each physician in a multi-physician practice.

The codes should be prominently posted on a legend in the file room so that all staff members are aware of them. Remember to update color-coded files consistently, coding new ones and revising older ones as a patient's status changes.

Color can be used in a similar way with numeric systems. The numerals 1 to 9 may each be assigned a distinct color, as shown in Figure 14–4. Then, numerals 1, 21, 31, 41, and 51, for example, would share the same color in the ones place of their numeric designation.

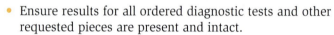

CHECKPOINT
LO 14.3

Discuss the reasons associated with HIPAA why many medical practices no longer file health records using an alphabetic system.

figure 14–5

In some practices, patient records are pulled for the patients scheduled on the next day.

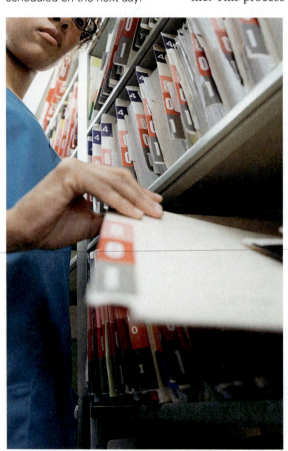

LO 14.4 Maintaining and Protecting the Medical Record

The next step in medical records management is maintaining and protecting the file. This process involves the following steps:

- Ensure results for all ordered diagnostic tests and other requested pieces are present and intact.
- Securely place all diagnostic tests results, correspondence, and other forms in the correct area of the correct patient's record with the appropriate patient identifier on each side of each page.
- Check for neatness when filing forms into the record.
- Place new blank pages as needed, such as progress notes, in the record with the patient identifier on the front and back of each page. This is a safety measure when copying charts and when health-care staff write on charts.
- File or reshelve records correctly and as soon as possible after use. This is office dependent and may be done at various times during the day or at the end of the day. Check for correct placement before and after reshelving (Figure 14–5).
- Ensure all records are accounted for and locate missing records by first checking for misfiling and the physician's desk. Any missing file should be reported immediately to the physician or practice manager after standard efforts to locate the chart have been attempted.
- Ensure strict confidentiality and security of the medical record.

HIPAA and the Health Record

The health record is confidential information that should be secured at all times. The following are standard measures for protecting the material contained in medical records:

- Lock all areas containing medical records when unattended.
- Forbid unauthorized individuals access to the record or any portion of the information.
- Use computer screens that prevent unauthorized persons from seeing opened information.
- Shut down computers when not in use and attended (especially in treatment areas).
- Never share your computer password or other passwords.
- Avoid leaving medical records where they may be seen, such as on counter tops.
- Ensure the prescribed firewalls are in place for electronic transmittal of patient information.

Release of Medical Record Information

Release medical records only if a valid release of information form has been signed (refer to Procedure 6–3, Obtaining Authorization to Release Health Information) or if satisfaction of conditions as described in Chapter 6, Law and Ethics in the Medical Office, are met. The patient's insurance company does not have a right to information unless a consent is signed. This authorization is usually obtained with the general consents when the patient registers. (Refer to Procedure 7–1, Registering the New Patient.) The patient's attorney or anyone claiming to be an attorney does not have a right to patient information without the signed consent for release of information. Never release the original medical record, release a copy. Often the patient or attorney is charged a fee to cover the costs of duplication.

CHECKPOINT
LO 14.4

When organizing a new hard-copy medical record, why do you think it is important to place the patient's name and an additional identifier on both sides of each form?

LO 14.5 Retaining and Storing the Medical Record

Medical records must be retained for 7 years; however, the Federal False Claims Act requires financial records be kept for 10 years. Because financial records and insurance claims must be backed up by the medical record, the American Health Information Management Association (AHIMA) and many legal experts are suggesting that medical records also be kept for 10 years instead of the legally required 7 years. Files of children must be kept for 7 to 10 years after the

Care of Medical Records

When you begin your externship, one of the first areas in your orientation is usually medical records. Be sure you understand the practice's medical record system and the protocol for paper-based charts since not all practices will scan into the EHR and patients will continue to present with paper information. You may be asked to retrieve and refile paper charts or documents along with other related duties. If you are not clear with any function or system, be sure to ask. You do not want to be responsible for a lost medical record or diagnostic test result. Also, if you see forms and other documents that are not securely fastened in the chart, take the initiative to adhere them properly and in the correct order. It is frustrating and distressing to look for information, such as a diagnostic test result, and not locate it due to mis-filing in an incorrect section of the record.

---

active file
The file for an active patient, or one has been seen by a member of the practice within two years.

inactive file
A file of a patient not seen by the medical practice in a given time period, usually two years.

closed file
A file for a patient who has died, moved away, or for some other reason is no longer treated by the medical practice.

child reaches the age of majority which is state dependent. In some states it is 18 years of age and in other states it is 21 years of age.

Active versus Inactive Files

At any given time, there are files that you use frequently and files that you use infrequently or not at all. Files that you use frequently are called **active files.** Files that you use infrequently are called **inactive files.** The general rule is that an active patient is one who has been seen by a member of the practice within two years and an inactive patient is one who has not been seen by a member of the practice within two years.

There is a third category of files, called closed files. **Closed files** are files of patients who have died, have moved away, or for some other reason no longer consult the office. Although closed files could be moved immediately to storage, they are usually treated in the same manner as inactive files. That is, they are kept in the office for a certain length of time to make sure that there are no requests for the information in the file.

Retention of Other Information

Legal requirements also exist for retaining other types of medical practice information:

- The National Childhood Vaccine Injury Act of 1986, requires permanent retention of all immunization records.
- The Labor Standards Act states that doctors must keep employee health records for 3 years.
- The statute of limitations—the law stating the time period during which lawsuits may be filed—varies by state for civil suits. The most common length of time is 2 years. If a case involves a child or someone mentally incompetent, the statute of limitations extends the deadline. Regardless of the statute of limitations, it is always advisable for doctors to seek legal advice before destroying any records.
- The Internal Revenue Service usually requires doctors to keep financial records for up to 10 years. Doctors are required to keep medical records of minors previously under their care for 2 to 7 years after the child reaches legal age, depending on the state. Some doctors keep these records indefinitely.

- The American Medical Association, the American Hospital Association, and other groups generally suggest that doctors keep patient medical and financial records for up to 10 years after a patient's final visit or contact.

For the most updated and complete list of required record retention periods according to HIPAA law, go to the HIPAA advisory Web site (www.hhs.gov/ocr/hipaa). At this Web site you will also find a number of other federal record-keeping laws that have specific record-keeping requirements.

This guide is updated annually. State and local retention requirements can be obtained from offices with which you regularly conduct business, such as insurance companies, state and local agencies, and medical associations. If you do business in more than one state, follow the schedule that requires the longest retention time for materials. Also, if your state's retention requirements are more stringent than HIPAA laws, follow your state's requirements.

When counting years in a **retention schedule**, remember not to count the year in which the document was produced but to begin counting with the following year. This way, documents produced near the end of a calendar year will be tracked more efficiently.

retention schedule
A timeframe that details how long to keep different types of patient records in the office after they have become inactive or closed and how long the records should be stored.

Storage Options

Due to the extensive time period required by law and standards for retaining medical records, most storage is currently done off site by commercial entities, usually at significant expense to the medical practice (Figure 14–6). Off-site storage may take up to two weeks for retrieval and a charge is involved which is usually passed on to the patient. The same rules for security and confidentiality apply. Therefore, medical practices should only select credible off-site storage. The files must be readily retrievable even when stored. Options include:

- Microfiche, microfilm, and cartridges, which are no longer in popular use but currently store many files.
- Scanning and storage on computers or discs, which is very labor-intensive and does not accommodate older forms of medical imaging and other procedures.
- Hard-copy medical records stored in boxes designed for this purpose:
  - Boxes must be labeled to indicate the files contained.
  - Records are marked with a bar code indicating the storage area which is quickly identified via computer.
- Electronic health records, whereby files are already on computer and easily stored on hard drives (internal and external), DVD, CD, or flash drive. Software programs are designed to accommodate this storage method which is usually the easiest and least expensive.

Prior to sending hard-copy medical records to storage, each file is conditioned. This term refers to preparing the record for retention by securing all loose documents, checking for completeness, and ensuring the correct filing order of the contents.

figure 14–6

Commercial records centers manage stored documents for medical practices. Select a reputable company.

Storage Safety

No matter where you store files, you must consider the issue of safety as well as security. Paper,

Working with the Health-Care Team
REGISTERED HEALTH INFORMATION TECHNICIAN

Duties and Skills

Sometimes called a medical record technician or a medical chart specialist, a Registered Health Information Technician (RHIT) manages patient records for a physician, or group of physicians, or hospital. The RHIT is responsible for ensuring that all medical information is accurate and complete. In a hospital, a RHIT deals strictly with health information and has no patient contact. In a medical office, however, the RHIT may have additional clerical duties such as answering the telephone.

The Registered Health Information Technician checks all patient charts for completeness and accuracy. The RHIT makes sure that all necessary forms related to the patient's care are included, properly filled out, and signed.

Educational Requirements

Most Registered Health Information Technicians have completed a two-year associate degree program at a private or community college. Course work includes biology, anatomy and physiology, medical terminology, data processing, coding, and statistics. The certification for RHIT is administered by the American Health Information Management Association (AHIMA).

Workplace Settings

The majority of RHITs work in medical record departments of hospitals. Others work in nursing homes, group practices, and health maintenance organizations (HMOs). A few RHITs work in federal or state government offices, public health departments, health and property insurance companies, or accounting and law firms. Some RHITs are self-employed and work as consultants.

Working with the RHIT as a Team Member

Almost every staff member in the medical practice uses the medical record. The RHIT interacts with all and provides a function that maintains the office efficiency. This role is key during accreditation visits and internal and external audits.

For more information, visit the Web site of the following organization, which is available on the Online Learning Center at www.mhhe.com/houseradminmedassist

American Health Information Management Association (formerly the American Medical Record Association)

computer, and film files are easily damaged and destroyed by fire, water, and extreme temperatures. Old, brittle paper files are particularly susceptible. Therefore, it is wise to evaluate the storage site and to take some basic precautions.

- Choose a site with moderate temperatures year-round and adequate ventilation.
- Select storage containers that can withstand intense heat and are waterproof. When possible, use boxes that are designated as fireproof and waterproof. Cardboard boxes, although often used for storage, are not as strong or durable. If cardboard storage boxes are used, they need to be placed on shelving well off the floor to avoid water damage.
- Choose a site equipped with a smoke alarm, sprinkler system, and fire extinguishers.
- Select a site that is away from flood hazards. One way to find out if a site is susceptible to flooding is to inquire whether the facility has flood insurance, a requirement for sites at risk.
- Choose a site that is kept locked, is regularly patrolled, or has an alarm system, to prevent theft or vandalism.

Taking the time to thoroughly research storage options ultimately saves time and effort as you manage stored files.

Medical Record Destruction

When records may finally be eliminated, they cannot simply be thrown away. Even old records hold confidential information about patients. Therefore, they must be completely destroyed by shredding or burning in commercial furnaces for this purpose. Be careful not to destroy records prematurely because they cannot be re-created. It is vital that you retain a list of records that have been destroyed.

The final phase of medical record management is to destroy the medical record after the prescribed retention time. This destruction must be done in a nature that prohibits identification of a patient or the contents of the medical record. The hard-copy medical record may be thoroughly shredded and or burned. This includes materials on microfiche and standard x-ray film. The integrity of the facility that stores the medical record must include thorough destruction.

The electronic health record is destroyed in a more rapid and environmentally friendly manner. The record is removed from the computer system in a format referred to as a "military delete" which "scrubs" the information from the system using very specific software. Records stored on CDs and DVDs are destroyed using shredder-like mechanisms that grind the discs. Protection of the medical record is a serious responsibility from the time it is created to the time of its destruction.

● ● ●

Why do you think the length of time to retain medical records for children differs from the length of time to retain medical records for adults?

CHECKPOINT
LO 14.5

Procedure 14–1   Creating an Office Tickler File

GOAL   To create a comprehensive office tickler file designed for year-round use

MATERIALS   12 manila file folders, 12 file labels, pen and paper or computer

METHOD

1. Write or type 12 file labels, 1 for each month of the year. Abbreviations are acceptable. Do *not* include the current calendar year, just the month.

2. Affix one label to the tab of each file folder.

3. Arrange the folders so that the current month is first. Months should follow in chronological order.

4. Write or type a list of upcoming responsibilities and activities. Next to each activity, indicate the date by which the activity should be completed. Leave a column after this date to indicate when the activity has been completed. Use a separate sheet of paper for each month and place one in the front of each of the 12 folders.

5. In place of folders and files, an Excel-type spreadsheet may be used listing each month with the corresponding activities.

6. File the folders, with the current month first, continuing to add documents, such as certificate renewals, to the appropriate month.

7. Review the tickler file weekly on the same day, preferably Monday.

8. Complete the activities as scheduled recording date and name or initials of person completing the task. If tasks are not completed on time, place a note with the reason. Report the delay to your supervisor or physician and document in the file.

9. At the end of the month, place the folder at the back of the file. If there are notes remaining in that month's folder, that are not completed, report to the supervisor or physician. If instructed, add to the next month's activities.

10. Continue to add new notes and activities to the appropriate month's file.

Case Study

Foday is responsible for the maintenance of medical records in a multi-specialty practice. He is very thorough and observant. Following a mass influenza immunization event, he is busily inputting information from the immunization forms into the patients' permanent medical records. Foday notices that the doses and lot numbers for the vaccine are the same on the pediatric and adult forms. He knows the vaccine for children and adults is different and should have different lot numbers. It may be an error in documentation or the incorrect dose or vaccine may have been given. Foday knows this is serious. The team had worked very hard during the event. It is late and everyone is tired. In addition, Katy, the practice manager, was complaining of a headache and looked ill. He is afraid of being unpopular if he calls the situation to her attention. Foday is also afraid there could be serious consequences for the patients and decides to report his discovery to Katy. He displayed integrity in his decision.

Thinking Critically

1. What are other reasons that a member of the health-care team may be afraid to report troublesome findings in a medical record?

2. If a member of the health-care team finds or suspects errors in a medical record, does he or she have an obligation to report it?

3. What are the elements involved in maintaining medical records?

practice APPLICATIONS

1. Arrange these 10 patient names in order as they would appear in an alphabetic filing system.
Jordan, Larry W.
Everett James
Angie Jones
John B. James
Florence Glenn Jones
Stafford, Samantha L.
A. James Ingersol
Stafford, G. E.
Sarah Coats
Curtis W. Weaver

2. Using your class list, develop a numeric filing system and a master list that matches each number to a specific person. Then set up an alphabetic filing system based on students' last names. Discuss with your classmates which system is most useful in an educational setting and why.

1. **[LO14.5]** According to the National Childhood Vaccine Injury Act of 1986, doctors must keep all immunization records on file in the office for
   a. 5 years.
   b. 7 years.
   c. permanently.
   d. 3 years.
   e. 10 years.

2. **[LO14.3]** Closed files are files that are of
   a. patients who have moved.
   b. patients who have died.
   c. patients who are no longer seen there.
   d. patients who are not returning.
   e. All of the above.

3. **[LO14.3]** The medical record filing system using small groups of two or three numbers, read from right to left is called
   a. numerical.
   b. alphabetical.
   c. terminal digit.
   d. color coding.
   e. indexing.

4. **[LO14.1]** All of the following are purposes of the medical record EXCEPT
   a. continuity of care.
   b. research.
   c. education.
   d. HIPAA compliance.
   e. documentation for legal purposes.

5. **[LO14.2]** Of the six elements of medical record management, the first step is:
   a. filing.
   b. assembling.
   c. retaining.
   d. maintaining.
   e. securing.

6. **[LO14.4]** A violation of HIPAA concerning a medical record would be to
   a. release a medical record to the patient's insurance company without consent.
   b. release a medical record to an attorney with the patient's consent.
   c. release the medical record to the medical assistant for the patient's appointment.
   d. omit placing the diagnostic test results in the medical record.
   e. omit filing the medical record in the correct area of the storage shelf.

7. **[LO14.3]** Which of the following is a true statement concerning alphabetical filing?
   a. Frank Smith, Jr. is filed before Frank Smith, Sr.
   b. Frank Smith, Sr. is filed before Frank Smith, Jr.
   c. Frank Smith III is filed after Frank Smith, Jr.
   d. Frank is the first unit in Frank Smith, Sr.
   e. Sr. is the second unit in Frank Smith, Sr.

8. **[LO14.3]** When filing alphabetically, which of the following patient names would come first?
   a. Williams, William
   b. Williams, William A.
   c. William, William
   d. Williams, Bill
   e. William, Bill

9. **[LO14.1]** If a medical student performing an internship in a physician's office reviewed the medical records of all asthmatic patients seen within that day, the purpose would probably be
   a. quality of care.
   b. education.
   c. continuity of care.
   d. legal documentation.
   e. confidentiality.

10. **[LO14.2]** The amount of time to store a patient's record falls under which of the following elements of medical records management?
    a. Filing.
    b. Assembling.
    c. Maintaining.
    d. Retaining.
    e. Securing.

learning outcome SUMMARY

LO 14.1 The purposes of the medical record are continuity of care; legal protection for the patient and physician; indicators for quality care; and tools for education and research.

LO 14.2 The six elements of medical records management are:

1. Creating or assembling the medical record
2. Filing the medical record
3. Maintaining/protecting the medical record
4. Releasing the medical record
5. Retaining the medical record
6. Destroying the medical record

LO 14.3 Filing the medical record involves understanding the alphabetic, numeric, and color coding systems.

LO 14.4 Medical records maintenance has to do with protecting the integrity and physical safety of the medical record, ensuring that all the required documents are included and securely fastened. The files must be housed in an area away from danger. It also involves the HIPAA privacy requirements. In addition to strict confidentiality and measures to guarantee privacy, the prescribed method for the release of medical records must be followed.

LO 14.5 The amount of time medical records must be retained is governed by federal and local requirements and standards. The general consensus is that retention of the adult medical record is between 7 and 10 years. For children, the records are retained for a given amount of time after the child reaches the age of majority which is state-specific. Immunization records must be kept permanently. When the period of time for retention elapses, the destruction of the record must be complete to continue to ensure that information is not inadvertently discovered.

medical assisting COMPETENCIES

CAAHEP

V. C (5) Identify systems for organizing medical records

V. C (6) Describe various types of content maintained in a patient's medical record

V. C (7) Discuss pros and cons of various filing methods

V. C (8) Identify both equipment and supplies needed for filing medical records

V. C (9) Describe indexing rules

V. C (10) Discuss filing procedures

V. C (11) Discuss principles of using Electronic Medical Records (EMR)

V. C (12) Identify types of records common to the healthcare setting

V. P (3) Organize a patient's medical record

V. P (4) File medical records

V. P (5) Execute data management using electronic healthcare records such as the EMR

V. P (8) Maintain organization by filing

V. A (1) Consider staff needs and limitations in establishment of a filing system

IX. C (2) Explore issue of confidentiality as it applies to the medical assistant

IX. C (3) Describe the implications of HIPAA for the medical assistant in various medical settings

ABHES

1. General Orientation

d. Have knowledge of the general responsibilities of the medical assistant

4. Medical Law and Ethics

b. Institute federal and state guidelines when releasing medical records or information

6. Pharmacology

e. Comply with federal, state, and local health laws and regulations

7. Basic Keyboarding/Computer Concepts

a. Perform basic keyboarding skills
b. Identify and properly utilize office machines, computerizes systems and medical software such as:

(2) Apply computer application skills using a variety of different electronic programs including both practice management software and EMR software

8. Medical Office Procedures Management

b. Prepare and maintain medical records
d. Apply concepts for office procedures
ll. Apply electronic technology

11. Career Development

b. Demonstrate professionalism by:
(3) Maintaining confidentiality at all times
(4) Being cognizant of ethical boundaries
(9) Conducting work within scope of education, training, and ability

15 The Health Record

Learning Outcomes

After completing Chapter 15, you will be able to:

15.1 Explain the importance of accurate patient medical records.

15.2 Explain the differences between SOMR and POMR records, and define SOAP and CHEDDAR.

15.3 List the documents commonly used in the medical record.

15.4 Explain the purpose of the initial patient interview including the name of the document completed in that interview that becomes the basis for the patient's medical record.

15.5 List and describe the components of the six Cs of medical charting.

15.6 Compare the paper medical record to the electronic health record.

15.7 Explain and demonstrate the process used to correct errors in the medical record.

15.8 Outline the procedure used to correctly and legally release patient medical information.

Key Terms

audit	noncompliant
CHEDDAR	objective
documentation	patient record/chart
electronic health records (EHR)	POMR
	sign
electronic medical records (EMR)	SOAP
	SOMR
individual identifiable health information (IIHI)	subjective
	symptom
	transcription
informed consent form	transfer

Preparation for Certification

RMA (AMT) Exam
- Protect, store, and retain medical records according to HIPAA regulations
- Release of protected health information adhering to HIPAA regulations
- Charting guidelines and regulations

CMAS (AMT) Exam
- Procedures

CMA (AAMA) Exam
- Patient interviewing techniques
- Legislation
- Medical records (paper/ electronic)

386

Introduction • • •

The administrative medical assistant plays a major role in creating, documenting, and maintaining patient records. These records act as a chronological history of the evaluation and treatment given to the patient. Patient medical records are critical to patient continuity of care. Without accurate and complete patient records, medical care could easily be compromised.

Patient medical records have many parts or sections that describe these facets of every patient:

- Personal information or data
- Physical and mental condition
- Medical, family, and social histories
- Medical care
- Medical future if the patient is referred to other physicians

In this chapter you will learn how to carefully manage the patient medical record, using both the traditional paper format, as well as the electronic health record format. You will understand that if the medical care is not documented, in a legal sense, the medical care did not occur at all.

LO 15.1 Importance of Patient Records

In Chapter 14 we discussed the importance of choosing and maintaining an appropriate filing system for paper medical records so that records are easily and efficiently located at all times. Once the record is located, one of the most important duties of an administrative medical assistant is initiating and maintaining accurate and thorough patient records. **Patient records,** also known as **charts,** contain important information about a patient's medical history, present condition, and treatment plans. Patient records also serve as communication tools as well as legal documents. They also play a role in patient and staff education and may be used for quality control and research. The medical record in either paper or electronic format is initiated by the administrative medical assistant or another staff member and is consistently updated whenever the patient has contact with the office. The medical facility owns the physical record in either its paper or electronic format, but the patient owns the information contained within that record as it is his information.

patient record/chart
Documentation of important information about a patient's medical history and present condition serving as both a communication tool and legal record.

The patient chart, whether paper or electronic, provides physicians and other medical care providers with all the important information, observations, and opinions that have been recorded about a patient. The health-care professional can read the complete patient medical history and information about treatment and outcomes. The information in the record can also be sent to other physicians or health-care specialists if the patient needs further treatment, changes physicians, or moves to a new location. The information recorded provides a "map" or plan to follow for the continuity of patient care. The medical record also serves as supporting documentation for billing and coding purposes, and as a legal document that is admissible in a court of law. The overarching guidelines and standards apply to both hard copy and the EHR. Medical records include the following general information about the patient:

- Address and phone number
- Occupation
- Patient medical history
- Past, family, and social histories
- Current complaint or condition

- Health-care needs
- Medical treatment plan or services received
- Medical imaging and laboratory reports
- Response to care

Paper patient records are usually assembled for new patients well before their actual use. It is the administrative medical assistant's responsibility to make sure there are adequate patient records prepared to meet the needs of the practice.

Legal Guidelines for Patient Records

Patient records are important for legal reasons. As a general rule, if information is not documented, no one can prove that an event or procedure took place. Medical records are used in lawsuits and malpractice cases to support a patient's claim of malpractice against a doctor and to support the doctor in defense against such a claim. As you learned in Chapter 6, medical records must be kept for 7 years and pediatric records for 7 years past the age of majority. Because financial records must be kept for 10 years and medical records must back any billing records, many legal experts suggest that medical records should also be kept for 10 years instead of the legally required 7.

All medical care, evaluation, and instruction given to the patient by the physician must be documented. Every chart entry must be clear, accurate, legible, and dated. HIPAA guidelines suggest using blue ink in medical records as it is more difficult to match, making changes in records easy to see. But most offices continue to use black ink as it copies better. The patient chart is a legal document. Always consider how the patient record would present if it was called into a court of law for review.

noncompliant

A medical term used to describe a patient who does not follow the medical advice he or she is given.

Additionally, it is very important to document when a patient is **noncompliant.** *Noncompliant* is a medical term used to describe a patient who does not follow the medical advice he or she is given. After a clear record has been made of the directions given to a patient for optimum health, it is essential to record the level of patient compliance. For example, after you have instructed a patient, you may write in her chart that "Patient stated she understood all directions. Written instruction given to patient." If it is determined that a patient did *not* follow the medical advice, it is then essential to chart this as well. The physician may wish to withdraw from the care of a patient because of the patient's noncompliance. Without a proper and accurate documentation of the patient's noncompliance, the physician may not be able to withdraw care without becoming legally liable for abandoning the patient. Additionally, documented noncompliance can be used in the physician's defense in a malpractice suit if it can be proven that, due to patient noncompliance, the physician was not solely responsible for inadequate medical care or result.

Standards for Records

Records that are complete, accurate, and well-documented can be convincing evidence that a doctor provided appropriate care. On the other hand, altered, incomplete, inaccurate, or illegible records may imply that a doctor's entire medical practice is below standard.

It is important to understand that the physicians in a practice are not the only people who chart medical records within that practice. If an employee of the practice charts inappropriately or inaccurately in a patient's chart, the physician is held legally responsible for that action. All records, both medical and financial, are the responsibility of the physician. As the administrative medical assistant, you are responsible to the patient and the physician for any administrative procedures you perform and the accurate recording of those procedures.

Additional Uses of Patient Records

Each patient record serves as an ongoing reference about that individual's medical care. It is also a valuable resource for patient education, quality of patient care, and research.

Patient Education A patient's record can be used to educate the patient about medical conditions and treatment plans. The physician can point out how test results have changed or how the patient's general health has improved or worsened. The physician can also emphasize the importance of following treatment instructions. As the administrative medical assistant, you may use some of this information to educate the patient about his condition and its management. The record may also be used to educate the health-care staff about unusual medical conditions, patient progress, or results of treatment plans.

Quality of Care The patient record may also be used to evaluate the quality of patient care provided by a physician or facility. Auditing groups, such as peer-review organizations or The Joint Commission (TJC), may review select patient charts to monitor whether the care provided and the fees charged meet accepted standards. Records also provide statistics for health-care analysis and future health-care plans and policy decisions.

Research Some patient records may also play an important role in medical research. For example, a medical research team may be testing a new hypertension drug with volunteers who fit certain medical criteria perhaps men between the ages of 45 and 54 who have high blood pressure. Carefully kept medical records are valuable sources of data about patient responses, behavior, symptoms, side effects, and outcomes (Figure 15–1).

Information in charts may spur researchers to begin a study. For example, the records may show that 80% of all patients taking a particular heart medication experience the symptom of dizziness. Researchers can investigate why this reaction might be happening.

figure 15–1

Medical researchers may rely on data gathered from patient records.

● ● ●

Why is it important to document noncompliant patient behavior in the medical record?

CHECKPOINT
LO 15.1

LO 15.2 Types of Medical Records

You should be familiar with the different approaches to storing information within the patient medical record. The most common methods are conventional/source-oriented and problem-oriented medical records.

Conventional, or Source-Oriented, Records

In the conventional, or source-oriented medical record **(SOMR)** patient information is arranged according to who supplied the data—the patient, doctor, specialist, laboratory or x-ray department, or other source. The medical form may have a space for patient remarks, followed by a section for the doctor's comments.

Used with paper medical records, the SOMR often uses colored tabs to separate the different categories of information that are placed in the chart in reverse

SOMR
Source-oriented medical record.

chronological order. This means that the most recent information or test result is placed on top of the previously filed information within the appropriate category. Although this method is still popular in offices that use paper records, because it is easy to maintain, there is a disadvantage to this system. Because information is placed in groups, it is difficult to quickly get an overall picture of the patient's treatment or illness course for a particular date because the information is often found in several different locations.

Problem-Oriented Medical Records

One way to overcome the disadvantages of the SOMR method is to use the problem-oriented medical record (**POMR**) system of for medical records. This approach, developed by Lawrence L. Weed, MD, makes it easier for the physician to keep track of a patient's progress. The information in a POMR includes the database; problem list; educational, diagnostic, and treatment plans; and progress notes.

POMR
Problem-oriented medical record.

Database The database includes a record of the patient's history; information from the patient's initial interview (for example, "Patient unemployed—second time in past 12 months"); all findings and results from physical examinations (such as "Pulse 105 bpm, BP 210/80"); and the results of any tests, x-rays, and other procedures.

Problem List Each problem (condition of diagnosis) a patient has is listed separately, given its own number, and dated. The problem is then identified by its number throughout the record. Work-related, social, or family problems that may be affecting the patient's health are also often listed. For instance, the problem list for example, the patient who is unemployed might include "Severe stomach pain, worse at night and after eating."

You can alert the doctor to the fact that the patient has lost two jobs within 1 year. Such radical life changes can often provoke strong physical reactions. In this patient's case the elevated blood pressure may be related to the job losses, and stress may be causing the stomach pain.

When you document problems, be careful to distinguish between patient signs and symptoms. **Signs** are objective, or external, factors—such as blood pressure, rashes, or swelling—that can be seen or felt by the doctor or measured by an instrument. **Symptoms** are subjective, or internal, conditions felt by the patient, such as pain, headache, or nausea. Together, signs and symptoms help clarify a patient's problem.

sign
Objective or external factor such as elevated BP, rash, or swelling that can be seen or felt by the physician or measured by an instrument.

symptom
Subjective or internal condition felt by the patient (such as a headache) that generally cannot be seen or felt by the physician or measured by instruments.

Educational, Diagnostic, and Treatment Plan Each problem should have a detailed educational, diagnostic, and treatment summary in the record. The summary contains diagnostic workups, treatment plans, and instructions for the patient. Here is an example.

Problem 2, Stomach Pain, 2/2/XX [date]

- *Upper GI exam negative, CBC normal.*
- *Prescribed over-the-counter antacid, 2 tablets by mouth t.i.d. after each meal.*
- *Set up appointment for patient with Dr. R. Neil at stress-management clinic (Broughten Professional Center) for Monday, February 4, 20XX at 4:30 p.m.*
- *Patient's anxiety is high. Recheck in 1 week.*

Progress Notes Progress notes are entered for each problem listed in the initial record. The documentation always includes—in chronological order—the patient's condition, complaints, problems, treatment, and responses to care. Here is an example.

Problem 2, Stomach Pain, 2/9/XX. Patient enrolled in stress-reduction class. Reports stomach pain has diminished— "I can eat without pain; only a little discomfort at night." Vital signs improved: pulse 85 bpm, BP 115/70, respiration 20. Reduced antacid to one tablet by mouth two times daily after meals. Anxiety much reduced. Recheck anxiety level in 2 weeks.

SOAP Documentation

Many medical records, such as the POMR format, emphasize the **SOAP** approach to documentation, which provides an orderly series of steps for dealing with any medical case. SOAP documentation lists the patient's symptoms, objective findings by exam or testing, the diagnosis, and the suggested treatment. Information is documented in the record in the following order.

SOAP
Subjective, objective, assessment, and plan.

1. S: **Subjective** data comes from the patient; the patient describes his or her signs and symptoms and supplies any other opinions or comments. A good way to remember subjective information is that it comes "from the subject", but there is no way to touch, smell, taste see, or hear what they are telling you.

subjective
Data from the patient describing history of symptoms; usually in his or her own words.

2. O: **Objective** data comes from the physician and other staff members and includes examinations and test results such as BP readings, cholesterol level elevated at 250 and right rest is swollen and red. Objective findings are those that can be seen, felt, heard, smelled or heard; they are measurable.

objective
Data from the physician examination and from test results.

3. A: *Assessment* is the diagnosis or impression of a patient's problem.

4. P: *Plan* of action includes treatment options, chosen treatment, medications, tests, consultations, patient education, and follow-up.

Whether you keep conventional or POMR charts, you can include these steps for each problem. Figure 15–2 shows an example of SOAP notes. If you abbreviate any term when charting (entering data into the records), use only approved medical abbreviations. For example, use "5 g" instead of "5 grams." Several resources, including those published by TJC and the American Medical Association, list approved medical abbreviations for measurements, instructions

figure 15–2

The SOAP approach to documentation is one way to organize information in a patient record.

OUTLINE FORMAT PROGRESS NOTES

Patient Name: Hansen (LAST) Christopher (FIRST) M. (MIDDLE) Date of Birth 3 / 1 / 65 Chart # H234

Prob. No. or Letter	DATE	S Subjective	O Objective	A Assess	P Plans	Page 1
	6/16/12	S: Patient complaining of pain in lower right quadrant. Has been running fever of between 100.5° F and 101.3° F since Sunday morning. Has queasy feeling in stomach and has been unable to eat since yesterday morning.				
		O: BP 125/75. Temperature 101.2° F. Abdominal exam revealed rebound tenderness and distension in lower right quadrant.				
		A: Appendicitis				
		P: 1. Admit to hospital 2. Appendectomy				

Linda F. Wiley, PA-C

Start each Progress Note (Subjective, Objective, Assessment, and Plans) at the appropriate shaded column to create an outline form. Write through the intervening columns to the right margin of the page.

© 1976 Bibbero Systems, Inc., Petaluma, CA   **PROGRESS NOTES**   TO REORDER CALL TOLL FREE: (800)BIBBERO (800 242-2376) FORM # 26-7215-01

for taking medication, and other topics. Keep these references readily available in the office.

CHEDDAR Format

CHEDDAR
Chief complaint, history, examination, details of problems and complaints, drugs and dosages, assessment, and return.

The **CHEDDAR** format of medical records documentation takes the SOAP format a step further. CHEDDAR stands for

C: *C*hief complaint, presenting problems, subjective statements

H: *H*istory; social and physical history of presenting problem as well as contributing information

E: *E*xamination, including extent of body systems examined

D: *D*etails of problem and complaints

D: *D*rugs and dosage—for example, a list of current medications used with dosage and frequency

A: *A*ssessment of the diagnostic process and the impression (diagnosis) made by the physician

R: *R*eturn visit information or referral, if applicable

Refer to Figure 15–5 for an example of a progress note utilizing the CHEDDAR format.

CHECKPOINT
LO 15.2

What does SOAP stand for?

LO 15.3 Contents of Patient Charts

You will create a medical record for each new patient who comes to the office. Although each office has its own forms or screen completion requirements for electronic health records and medical chart or health record format, in general, all records must contain certain standard information which is outlined here.

Standard Chart Information

Standard chart information covers a spectrum of different, carefully detailed notes and facts about a patient, from his medical history to the doctor's diagnosis and comments on follow-up care. You must have not only an understanding of what each part means but also its importance in each patient's continuity of care.

Patient Registration Form Initial patient information includes the registration form and the patient medical history form (discussed below). Both forms are completed by the patient prior to, or collected at the beginning of, the first patient visit. In today's electronic age, many offices now offer new patients the option of completing the registration information on line instead of doing so by hand which can be a real convenience both for the patient and office, particularly if electronic health records are used in the office. The patient registration form should list the date of the patient's current visit, the patient's age, DOB (date of birth), address, Social Security number, medical insurance information, occupation and employer, marital status, number of children, and the name and telephone number(s) of the person to contact in an emergency.

The completed registration form (with front and back copies of the patient's insurance card) is the base document for each patient's financial record. Patient financial and medical records are separated into two distinct records which are filed separately from one another. The medical record is kept in the medical record or HIM (health information management) department, and the financial

chart is kept in the patient accounting or billing department. In smaller offices the separation may be as simple as neighboring filing cabinets. In larger practices, they may be housed in different buildings. In offices with electronic records (EHR), this separation is accomplished by the use of distinctly different screens which are only accessible by those with passwords or access codes. Only users with a business "need to know" can access information contained within the screens of each of these distinctly different record types. Figure 15–3 is an example of a patient registration form.

Patient Medical History   The medical history form, the second part of the registration process, includes the patient's past medical history (including illnesses, surgeries, known allergies, and current medications), family medical history, and social and occupational history (including diet, exercise, smoking, and use of alcohol or drugs). Usually, the history form ends with a section for the patient to describe the condition or complaint that is the reason for her visit. Medicare and managed care plans now require that the patient's complaint be entered into the medical record. Known as the chief complaint, this information should be recorded in the patient's own words if at all possible. The patient medical history form is used as the foundation for the patient's medical record in both electronic and paper formats. In traditional paper formats, it is usually found on the left side of the chart. In electronic formats, it is either the first document scanned into the record or is the basis for the EHR, being the initial document used to begin the health record.

Physical Examination Results   Sometimes a form is used to record the results of a general physical examination. Figure 15–4 shows a combination medical history and physical examination form. If a form is not used, the physician often dictates or writes the physical exam results using a "head to toe" approach to documentation.

Results of Laboratory and Other Tests   Test results include findings from tests performed in the office and those received from other physicians, hospitals, independent laboratories or other outside sources. Some offices use a laboratory summary sheet to help the doctor detect and track significant changes more easily.

Test results received from sources outside the practice are best organized in sections within this part of the medical chart. Each section is determined by the type of the information. For example, all x-ray reports may be grouped together in one section, cardiography (heart studies) in another area, laboratory results in yet another, and so on. Each section should be arranged in reverse chronological order, with the latest report on the top.

Records from Other Physicians or Hospitals   Incoming records from other sources must be entered into the patient's chart. A copy of the patient's written request authorizing release of the records from the other sources must also be included. Many offices also group these types of records together as well, so that consults are together and hospital reports such as admission reports, operative reports, and discharge summaries are kept together; again, in reverse chronological order.

If electronic health records are used in both offices, the medical records may be transmitted between the offices electronically. If your office uses electronic health records, but the office sending the records is using a paper record format, your office will likely scan these records into the computer for inclusion in the patient's electronic health record.

Physician's Diagnosis and Treatment Plan   The physician's diagnosis and the treatment plan, which may consist of treatment options, the final

figure 15–3

The patient registration form is most often the first document used in initiating a patient financial record.

TOTAL CARE CLINIC, PC

342 East Park Blvd
Funton, XY   12345-6789
521-234-0001   Fax: 521-234-0002

Patient Registration
Patient Information

Name: _____ Today's Date: _____

Address: _____

City: _____ State: _____ Zip Code: _____

Telephone (Home): _____ (Work): _____ (Cell): _____

Birthdate: _____ Age: _____ Sex: M   F   No. of Children _____ Marital Status: M S W D

Social Security Number: _____ Employer: _____ Occupation: _____

Primary Physician: _____

Referred by: _____

Person to Contact in Emergency: _____

Emergency Telephone: _____

Special Needs: _____

Responsible Party

Party Responsible for Payment: Self   Spouse   Parent   Other

Name (If Other Than Self): _____

Address: _____

City: _____ State: _____ Zip Code: _____

Primary Insurance

Primary Medical Insurance: _____

Insured party: Self   Spouse   Parent   Other

ID#/Social Security No.: _____ Group/Plan No.: _____

Name (If Other Than Self): _____

Address: _____

City: _____ State: _____ Zip Code: _____

Secondary Insurance

Secondary Medical Insurance: _____

Insured party: Self   Spouse   Parent   Other

ID#/Social Security No.: _____ Group/Plan No.: _____

Name (If Other Than Self): _____

Address: _____

City: _____ State: _____ Zip Code: _____

figure 15–4

In some doctors' offices, the medical history form and the physical examination form are combined. Whether combined or separate, the medical history form is the basis for all patient medical records (electronic or paper).

Total Care Clinic, PC
Medical History

Name _____ Age _____ Sex _____ S M W D

Address _____ Phone _____ Date _____

Occupation _____ Ref. by _____

Chief Complaint _____

Present Illness _____

_____

_____

_____

History —Military _____

—Social _____

—Family _____

—Marital _____

—Menstrual _____ Menarche _____ Para. _____ LMP _____

—Illness Measles Pert. Var. Pneu. Pleur. Typh. Mal. Rh. Fev. Sc. Fev. Diphth. Other

—Surgery _____

—Allergies _____

—Current Medications _____

Physical Examination

Temp. _____ Pulse _____ Resp. _____ BP _____ Ht. _____ Wt. _____

General Appearance _____ Skin _____ Mucous Membrane _____

Eyes: _____ Vision _____ Pupil _____ Fundus _____

Ears: _____

Nose: _____

Throat: _____ Pharynx _____ Tonsils _____

Chest: _____ Breasts _____

Heart: _____

Lungs: _____

Abdomen: _____

Genitalia: _____

Rectum: _____

Pelvic: _____

Extremities: _____ Pulses: _____

Lymph Nodes: _____ Neck _____ Axilla _____ Inguinal _____ Abdominal _____

Neurological: _____

Diagnosis: _____

_____

Treatment: _____

_____

Laboratory Findings: _____

Date _____ Blood _____

_____

Date _____ Urine _____

_____

treatment list, instructions to the patient, and any medications prescribed must be clearly documented in the patient medical record. The doctor may also put specific comments or impressions on record. All of this information is recorded for every patient visit and contact, including phone calls. This is vitally important, because as discussed before, legally, if it is not written down, it did not happen. (Figure 15–5).

Operative Reports, Follow-Up Visits, and Telephone Calls Continuation of the record lasts as long as the patient is under the doctor's care. You should record and date all procedures, surgeries, follow-up care, and additional notes the doctor makes regarding the patient's case. You can use continuation forms to add more pages. In addition, record all phone calls to and from the patient, either within the patient's chart notes or in a separate log of telephone calls. Be sure that the patient's name and/or medical record number is included on all pages of information. One of the conveniences of the electronic health record is that of the "never-ending page," as the information is simply continued on the next screen. If messages or notes are handwritten, many offices will then scan them into a predetermined area of the medical record.

figure 15–5

An example of progress notes using CHEDDAR format.

DATE	PROGRESS NOTES
11/11/12 10:30 am	

C Patient states, " I have had a fever and a sore throat for the past two days"

H Patient was healthy and well until two days ago when she noted the onset of fever and sore throat.

Past history includes strep pharyngitis

E Vital signs: T 101.1 P 96 R 24 BP 124/76 Weight: 155 Height: 5_7_

General: patient seems alert. HEENT: sclera clear. Pharynx red with pus pockets noted.

Heart: regular w/o murmur

Lungs: clear to auscultation and percussion. Abdomen: negative for tenderness.

D Other than sore throat and fever with noted temperature elevation, patient has no other complaints.

D Patient takes no daily medication except for a multi-vit. She is given an Rx for Amoxicillin 250 mg

1 tab q8h for 10 days

A Strep Pharyngitis

R Schedule follow-up appointment for three weeks from today for repeat throat culture

Matthew Rodriguez, MD – Attending Physician

Brendan Conroy, RMA (AMT)   Date: November 11, 2012

Form OMB-1243

Informed Consent Forms **Informed consent forms,** such as the one shown in Figure 15–6, verify that a patient understands the treatment offered and the possible outcomes or side effects of the treatment. Consent forms should also specify what the outcome might be if the patient receives no treatment. They also describe alternative treatments and possible risks. The patient signs the consent form but may withdraw consent at any time.

Hospital Discharge Summary Forms The discharge summary form generally includes information that summarizes the reason the patient entered the hospital; tests, procedures, or surgeries performed in the hospital; medications administered in the hospital; and the disposition, or outcome, of the case. Elements of the form may include the following:

- Date of admission
- Brief history
- Date of discharge
- Admitting diagnosis
- Surgeries and procedures or hospital course (course of action taken in the hospital)
- Complications
- Discharge disposition, including where the patient was discharged to (home, nursing home, etc), as well as patient instructions for follow-up care.
- Physician's signature

informed consent form
Document signed by the patient to verify that the patient understands the treatment offered and the possible outcomes or side effects of the treatment.

figure 15–6

Patients are asked to sign informed consent forms to confirm that they understand the treatment offered.

 TOTAL CARE CLINIC, PC

342 East Park Blvd
Funton, XY 12345-6789
521-234-0001 Fax: 521-234-0002

CONSENT TO OPERATION, ADMINISTRATION OF ANESTHETICS,
AND RENDERING OF OTHER MEDICAL SERVICE

Patient: _____ Age: _____
Date: _____ Time: _____

1. I AUTHORIZE AND DIRECT _____ , with the associates
   and assistants of his/her choice, to perform upon myself the following operation
   _____
   _____
   _____

   If any unforeseen conditions arise in the course of the operation or in the postoperative period, calling in their judgment for other operations or procedures, I further request and authorize them to do whatever is deemed advisable for my health and well-being.

2. The positive and negative aspects of autologous blood transfusions (receiving my own blood donated prior to surgery), designated blood transfusions (donated in advance by family/friends for my use), or homologous blood transfusions (from general donor population) have been explained to me. I understand autologous and designated transfusions can be accommodated only for nonemergency surgery.

6. I certify that I understand the above consent to operation and that the explanations referred to have been made.

_____   _____
Witness (of signature only)   Signature

Guidelines for Protecting Information within the Medical Record

HIPAA law states that all patients have rights regarding their health information, which is known as Protected Health Information (PHI). A patient's PHI is stored in the patient's medical chart. Federal law protects the individual's rights to know about how her or his PHI is used and disclosed.

The term use means the employment, application, utilization, sharing, examination or analysis of **individual identifiable health information (IIHI).** For example, when an administrative medical assistant keys in a patient's health insurance number to determine the status of payment from the insurance company, the patient's PHI is being used. The term disclosure means the release or transfer in any way of patient IIHI beyond the confines of the health-care practice to which the information was given. For example, when an administrative medical assistant gives patient information to another medical office to which the patient is being referred, PHI is being disclosed.

Patients have the following rights under HIPAA law:

1. *The right to notice of privacy practices.* Because it is unlikely that your patients will be reading federal laws, the law states it is your responsibility to give them a copy of the laws that protect them concerning their PHI. Patients must receive a written notice of privacy practices on their first visit to a health-care provider. They should sign a form stating they have received this information. This signed form must be carefully filed in the patients' medical record.

2. *The right to limit or request restriction on their PHI and its use and disclosure.* This means that patients can limit how your office uses their medical information, and how much of that information is shared. For example, a patient with a history of sexually transmitted disease may not wish to have that information released to the orthopedic physician who is setting his broken arm. It is not necessary. In general, only the minimal amount of patient information should be released to meet the current needs of the patient. This is called the "Need to Know" general rule.

3. *The right to confidential communications.* This means that patients can request to receive PHI in a manner other

than during a medical appointment. For example, your patients may request that you call them at a variety of different numbers, including home, work, or cell phone number. The patient does not have to explain the request. The law says you must make a reasonable effort to communicate with the patient in a confidential manner as the patient requests.

4. *The right to inspect and obtain a copy of their PHI.* This means that patients have a right to request and receive a copy of their own medical records. There are a few exceptions to this rule; however, in general, the medical assistant receives and processes all patient requests for medical records. It is important to always follow the protocols established in your office for medical record copying. It is considered an acceptable practice to act on a request within 30 days of the request, and to charge a reasonable fee to cover the expense for copying supplies and labor.

5. *The right to request an amendment to their PHI.* Health-care providers have the right to require that a request to amend a record be made in writing. The request may be denied if the health-care provider receiving the request is not the original recorder of the PHI, or if the PHI is believed to be accurate and complete. All requests for amendment and response must be carefully documented and filed in the medical chart.

6. *The right to know if their PHI has been disclosed and why.* Providers are required to keep a written record of every disclosure made of a patient's PHI. You must also keep a written record of any request by the patient for this information and the response of the health-care provider. This information is usually filed in the patient's medical record. When making a disclosure of information, always record the date of the disclosure, the name and address of the person receiving the PHI, a brief summary of the information released, and the purpose of the disclosure.

Please refer to Chapter 6 for detailed information on HIPAA including forms and documents used to outline office privacy practices, release of PHI, and complaint forms used if a patient believes his or her privacy rights have been violated.

individual identifiable health information (IIHI)
Information such as patient SSN or insurance policy number that easily reveals patient identity.

Correspondence with or About the Patient All written correspondence from the patient or from any other doctors, laboratories, health-care facilities, or independent health-care agencies must be kept in the patient's chart. Each piece of correspondence should be marked or stamped with the date the doctor's office received the document.

Information Received by Fax

Some information—such as laboratory results, physician comments, or correspondence—may be received by fax transmission. With more and more offices using computer programs, faxed records are being replaced by electronic files or even by e-mailed pdf files. However the information is received, it should always be filed appropriately in the medical record, either as hard copy in the paper medical record or in the electronic record using the method preferred by office receiving the information. If a fax copy is followed up by a paper copy in the mail, be sure to shred the faxed copy after filing the new copy in the record.

Dating and Initialing

You must be careful not only to date everything you put into the patient chart but also to initial the entry. This system makes it easy to tell which items the assistant enters into the chart and which items others enter. In many practices the physician initials reports before they are filed to prove that he saw them.

● ● ●

Name the financial and the medical forms found in the medical record.

CHECKPOINT
LO 15.3

LO 15.4 Initiating and Maintaining Patient Records

Besides the receptionist, you will often be the first health-care professional that new patients talk with when they visit the physician's office. During or before this first contact, as you initiate the patient record, you will record the information the new patient gives to you. Recording information in the medical record is called **documentation**. Complete, thorough documentation ensures that the doctor will have detailed notes about each contact with the patient and about the treatment plan, patient response (progress), and treatment outcomes.

documentation
Recording information in the medical record.

Initial Interview

Depending on the office policies and on your experience level, as the office administrative medical assistant you may complete any or all of the following tasks related to the initial interview. Familiarize yourself with each task.

Completing Medical History Forms Making sure that the medical history form—the base document in the medical chart—is completed fully is an important aspect of initiating the medical chart. Type the patient's name and other identifying information on the first page, as well as on subsequent pages of any forms. If the patient is transferring her care to your practice, you may be asked to obtain a release of medical information so that the patient's previous medical records may be incorporated into her new chart.

The process for offices using electronic records may be very similar, with the patient completing the same forms either on paper, which are then scanned into the program, or submitting them via e-mail and the information is added to the new record. In either case, most EHR programs have an icon or short cut for entering new patient information, which will then bring the user to the correct menu screen for entering patient information. Figure 15–7 shows the new patient screen for the SpringCharts® Electronic Health Records program.

In some offices, the administrative assistant or other member of the staff interviews the patient based on the medical history form and completes the

figure 15-7

New patient setup window for SpringCharts® Electronic Health Records Software.

New Patient

First Name*:	Joshua	Home Phone:	(214) 512-4589
MI:	R	Home Fax:	
Last Name*:	Hill	Work Phone:	(214) 513-4589
Date of Birth*:	05/22/1987	Work Fax:	
Address:	215 Wommack Blvd.	Pager:	
City:	Colorado Springs	Mobile Phone:	(214) 225-8719
State:	CO	EMail:	downunder@yahoo.com
Zip:	80934	SS#:	048-56-1248
Sex:	⦿ Male ◯ Female	PMS ID:	
Marital Status:	Single	Provider:	Stephen C. Finchman, M. D.
Employer:	Student	Patient ID:	
* Required			

Save   Cancel   Copy Patient

form based on the patient's answers. Others have the patient complete the form himself but go over it carefully, making sure no blanks are left. Some doctors prefer to ask patients questions themselves. Others believe that people sometimes talk more freely with an assistant than they do with the doctor, but the doctor will usually confirm the information on the form when he first interviews the patient.

Documenting Patient Statements You will record any signs, symptoms, or other information the patient wishes to share. It is important that you document this information in the patient's own words, not your interpretation of the words. Record this data in specific detail. For example, if the patient drinks alcohol, you should record the number of drinks per week, the type of liquor consumed, and whether the drinking has affected the patient's behavior and health. Chart this information by writing "Patient states that . . ." and then, whenever possible, complete the sentence with the exact words the patient used.

figure 15-8

Conduct interviews with patients in a private or semiprivate room to make them feel more comfortable.

Conduct any interviews in a private room or in a semiprivate office away from the reception area, as shown in Figure 15–8, to protect patient confidentiality. Patients should never be required to speak of their medical conditions, problems, or histories in areas of the office where others might possibly hear the conversation. Your opinion of the patient, such as "the patient seems mentally unstable," is your own and should not be discussed or documented (as fact) in the medical record.

Documenting Test Results Insert in the medical record copies of any test results, x-ray reports, or other diagnostic results that the patient has brought with him. If part of office policy you may also record this information on a separate test summary sheet in the chart.

Examination Preparation and Vital Signs
Depending on office policy, the administrative medical

assistant may prepare patients for their examinations. If this is the case, you will record vital signs, medication the patient is currently taking, and any responses to treatment. Before you leave a patient, ask, "Is there anything else you would like the doctor to know?" The patient may be more comfortable sharing further information with you than with the doctor, but be sure to document what the patient tells you and share it with the physician.

Follow-Up

After you record the initial interview and background information, the doctor decides what entries will be made regarding examinations, diagnosis, treatment options and plans, and comments or observations about each case. You will then maintain the patient medical record by performing some or all of the following duties:

- Transcribing notes the doctor dictates about the patient's progress, follow-up visits, procedures, current status, and other necessary information
  - Note that transcription by the administrative medical assistant does not occur in all practices.
- Posting laboratory results, other test results, or results of examinations in the paper or electronic medical record or on the summary sheet
- Recording telephone calls from the patient and, if requested, summaries of calls that the doctor or other office staff members make to the patient. (Figure 15–9) Usually calls to the patient are documented, signed and dated by the physician or staff member who makes the call.
  - Telephone calls can be an important part of good follow-up care. Calls must be dated, and the content of the conversations must be documented and initialed by the person recording the contents of the call. If you are recording the contents of the call but are not the person who spoke to the patient, be sure to include the appropriate staff person's name within the documentation. Even if the doctor did not reach the patient, the call should be recorded and dated. State whether the doctor got an answer, left a message on an answering machine or with a person, and so on. It will be equally important to document when or if the patient returns the call and the results of the call at that time.
- Recording medical instructions or discharge instructions the doctor gives
  - At the doctor's request, you may counsel or educate the patient regarding the treatment regimen or home-care procedures the patient must follow. This information must be entered into the record, dated, and initialed. Some offices have software that produces general instructions for the patient which can be customized to fit the individual. Others may make photocopies of patient instructions which are initialed by the patient after the instructions are given, as proof the instructions were given and understood by the patient. The original is given to the patient and the copy is filed in the medical record.

Procedure 15–1, found at the end of the chapter, outlines the steps in preparing a paper patient medical record/chart. Procedure 15–2, also at the end of the chapter, outlines the same procedure using an EHR system.

figure 15–9

All telephone conversations to and from the patient must be logged in the patient record.

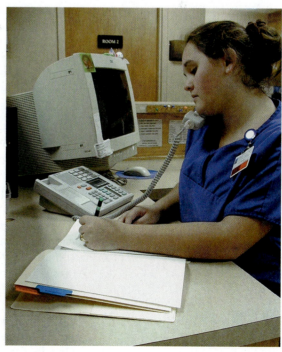

LO 15.5 Accuracy, Appearance, and Timeliness of Records

You must ensure that the medical records are complete. As legal documents, they must be written neatly and legibly (typewritten notes are preferable if the office uses paper records), contain up-to-date information, and present an accurate, professional record of a patient's case.

The Six Cs of Charting

To maintain accurate patient records, always keep these six Cs in mind when filling out and maintaining patient records: *Client's* (patient's) words, *Clarity, Completeness, Conciseness, Chronological* order, and *Confidentiality.*

1. **Client's words.** Be careful to record the patient's exact words rather than your interpretation of them. For instance, if a client says, "My right knee feels like it's thick or full of fluid," write that down. Do not rephrase the sentence to say, "Client says he's got fluid on the knee." Often the patient's exact words, no matter how odd they may sound, provide important clues for the physician in making a diagnosis.

2. **Clarity.** Use precise descriptions and accepted medical terminology when describing a patient's condition. For instance, "Patient got out of bed and walked 20 feet without shortness of breath" is much clearer than "Patient got out of bed and felt fine."

3. **Completeness.** Fill out completely all the forms used in the patient record. Provide complete information that is readily understandable to others whenever you make any notation in the patient chart.

4. **Conciseness.** While striving for clarity, also be concise, or brief and to the point. Abbreviations and specific medical terminology can often save time and space when recording information. For instance, you can write "Patient got OOB and walked 20 ft w/o SOB." OOB and SOB are standard abbreviations for "out of bed" and "shortness of breath," respectively. Every member of the office staff should use the same abbreviations to avoid misunderstandings. Table 15–1 lists some common medical abbreviations.

5. **Chronological order.** All entries in patient records must be dated to show the order in which they are made. This factor is critical, not only for documenting patient care but also in case there is a legal question about the type and date of medical services.

6. **Confidentiality.** All the information in patient records, including forms, is confidential. To protect the patient's privacy only the patient, attending physicians, and the medical staff (who need the record to tend to the patient and/or to make entries into the record) are allowed to see the contents of the medical record without the patient's written consent. Never discuss the information within a patient's record, forward information to another office, fax information, or show the record (or any content of the record) to anyone but the physician unless you have the patient's written permission to do so. Confidentiality includes protecting the computer from the view of others. (Review Chapter 6 and the Practice Readiness section from this chapter regarding these legal guidelines.)

ABBREVIATION	MEANING	ABBREVIATION	MEANING
AIDS	acquired immunodeficiency syndrome	inj.	injection
a.m.a.	against medical advice	IV	intravenous
b.i.d./BID	twice a day	MI	myocardial infarction
BP	blood pressure	MM	mucous membrane
bpm	beats per minute	NPO	nothing by mouth
CBC	complete blood count	NYD	not yet diagnosed
C.C.	chief complaint	OOB	out of bed
CNS	central nervous system	OPD	outpatient department
CPE	complete physical examination	OR	operating room
CV	cardiovascular	PH	past history
D & C	dilation and curettage	PRN	as needed
Dx	diagnosis	PT	physical therapy
ECG/EKG	electrocardiogram	Pt	patient
ED/ER	emergency department/emergency room	q.i.d./QID	four times a day
FH	family history	ROS/SR	review of systems/systems review
Fl/fl	fluid	s.c./subq.	subcutaneously
F/U	follow up	SOB	shortness of breath
GBS	gallbladder series	S/R	suture removal
GI	gastrointestinal	stat	immediately
GU	genitourinary	t.i.d./TID	three times a day
GYN	gynecology	TPR	temperature, pulse, respiration
HEENT	head, ears, eyes, nose, throat	UCHD	usual childhood diseases
HIV	human immunodeficiency virus	VS	vital signs
I & D	incision and drainage	WNL	within normal limits
ICU	intensive care unit		

table 15–1

Common Medical Abbreviations

Neatness and Legibility

One of the advantages of the EHR is that legibility is not an issue but some form of paper informational sources will remain. A medical record is useless if the doctor or others requiring access to the patient's medical information have difficulty reading it. The administrative medical assistant should be sure that every word and number in the record is clear and legible. These tips will help keep charts neat and easy to read.

- Use a good-quality pen that will not smudge or smear.
- HIPAA requires that original documents be maintained in the patient's hard-copy medical record and all original entries in the EHR. Blue ink is suggested for charting because it will copy as black, making the original and copy look different, which can reduce the possibility of error. Blue ink is also more difficult to match, making any additions to the medical record easy to spot. Most medical offices with paper records, however, use black ink instead of blue because of the consistency of its appearance.

- Use highlighting pens to call attention to specific items such as allergies. Be aware, however, that unless the office has a color copier, most colored ink will photocopy as black or gray. Highlighting-pen marks may not be visible on a photocopy. The electronic medical record usually has a method of automatically emphasizing vital information such as color or flashing which must also be considered when sending a hard copy version.

- Make sure all handwriting is legible. Take time to write names, numbers, and abbreviations clearly. If at all possible, information and chart notes should be typed. Again, this is not an issue with the EHR.

- Make any corrections to the chart by following your office's policies and procedures for corrections. Basic instructions are covered later in the chapter and you will practice these techniques following the outline given in Procedure 15–3 at the end of this chapter.

Timeliness

Medical records should always be kept up to date and readily available when the doctor or other health-care professional needs to see them. Follow these guidelines to ensure that the most recent information on a patient can be located easily when it is needed.

- Record all findings from exams and tests as soon as they are available.

- If a test result, finding, or communication is not entered into the record when it occurs or when it is received by the office, record both the original date of receipt and the date of the actual documentation into the record.

- To document telephone calls, record the date and time of the call, who initiated it, the information discussed, and any conclusions or results. Depending on office policy, the telephone call may be entered directly into the record or a notation made referring the doctor to a separate telephone log located within the paper or electronic record.

- Establish a procedure for retrieving a file quickly in case of emergency. Should the patient be in a serious accident, for example, the emergency doctor will need the patient's medical history immediately. The EHR provides a major advantage in this situation.

Accuracy

The physician must be able to trust the accuracy of the information in the medical records. Make it a priority to check the accuracy of all data you enter in a chart either manually or electronically. To ensure accurate data, follow these guidelines.

- Never guess at or assume knowledge of names, procedures, medications, findings, or any other information about which there may be a question. Always check all the information carefully. Make the extra effort to ask questions of the patient, physician, or senior staff member and to verify information.

- Double-check the accuracy of findings and instructions recorded in the chart. Verify that all numbers are recorded accurately and any patient instructions, including those for medications, are clear and complete.

- Be sure the most up-to-date information has been entered into the chart so that the physician has an accurate picture of the patient's current condition.

Professional Attitude and Tone

Part of timely, accurate records is maintaining a professional tone in your writing when recording information. Record information from the patient using his own words. Also record the doctor's observations and comments as well as

any laboratory or test results if that is part of your job. Never record personal or subjective comments, judgments, opinions, or speculations about a patient's words, problems, or test results. Attention may be called to a particular problem or observation, by attaching a note to the chart but do not make such comments part of the patient's permanent medical record.

Medical Transcription

Your knowledge of abbreviations, medical terminology, and medical coding will be invaluable when transcribing a doctor's notes or dictation (either recorded or direct). **Transcription** means transforming spoken notes into accurate written form. These written notes are then entered into the paper patient record. As is the case with information in medical charts, all dictated materials are confidential and should be regarded as potential legal documents. They are part of the patient's continuing medical history, and the documents transcribed often include findings, treatment stages, prognoses, and final outcomes. As with all medical record documentation, all transcription should be dated, signed by the dictator, and initialed by the transcriptionist.

transcription
Transforming spoken notes into accurate written form.

Strive to make transcribed material accurate and complete. Excellent grammar, correct spelling, and an accurate use of medical abbreviations and terminology are important in maintaining patient records. When dealing with abbreviations, if there is any doubt as to the meaning or use of an abbreviation, the standard rule of thumb in health care is "when in doubt, spell it out." Use the medical dictionary and the medical computer spelling check to verify the spelling or meaning of words. Ask the physician only if you cannot find something in a reference source. Always proofread transcribed material carefully. If dictated material appears to contain an error, type the material as dictated, using a "call out" or sticky note to draw the physicians attention to the potential error, so it may be corrected prior to being inserted into the medical record. Above-average typing or word processing accuracy and speed are also important. (See Chapter 10, Procedure 10–5, Using a Dictation-Transcription Machine.)

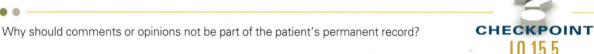

Why should comments or opinions not be part of the patient's permanent record?

CHECKPOINT
LO 15.5

LO 15.6 Electronic Health Records versus Paper Health Records

Electronic health records (EHR), or **electronic medical records (EMR),** are becoming increasingly essential to the quality of health care and the improvement of patient safety. More and more offices across the country are adopting this technology. The federal government is encouraging all health-care entities to make the switch by 2014.

Listed are some of the advantages and disadvantages of EHRs and EMRs:

electronic health records (EHR)
Medical records kept in an electronic format, which <u>are</u> available to providers outside of the medical office that has ownership.

electronic medical records (EMR)
Medical records kept in an electronic format, which <u>are generally not</u> available to providers outside of the medical office that has ownership.

Disadvantages

- costly
- retraining needed for entire staff
- may need to hire an IT staff member
- downtime of system

Advantages

- overall, more efficient and less labor-intensive medical records management

- fewer lost medical records
- decreased repeated or duplicated medical tests
- reduced transcription costs
- readability/legibility of charts resulting in increased patient safety
- more access to charts after hours
- easier to access patient education materials
- improved billing
- more efficient transfer of records
- decreased physical space and cost for storage

Overall, the benefits outweigh the disadvantages. If your practice is in the process of converting to an EHR, experts recommend that the system be endorsed by the Certification Commission for Health Information Technology (CCHIT), the recognized United States certifying body.

Electronic Medical Records

Extensive information, including practice guidelines and the best practices for EHR problems can be found on the American Health Information Management Association (AHIMA) Web site, www.ahima.org, and go to the e-HIM Practice Guidelines.

Additional Advantages of Computerizing Records

In a setting in which several terminals in a network are connected to a main computer, computerizing medical records presents several advantages. A physician can call up the record on his or her own or another computer monitor whenever the record is needed, review or update the file, and save it to the central computer again.

Computerized records can also be used in teleconferences, where people in different locations can look at the same record on their individual computer screens at the same time. Records can also be sent by modem to the physician's home computer so that the physician will have a patient's records on hand for calls after hours. Computer access to patient records is also helpful for health-care providers with satellite offices in different cities or different parts of a city.

Review the Practice Readiness box for more information about electronic health records.

Another advantage of electronic medical records is the ability to "tickle" an account to, alert staff members about patients who are due for yearly checkups or who require follow-up care. Some facilities, including physician offices, have begun to use electronically scanned images of patients' thumbprints and license photos to keep track of records and identify patients prior to providing care as another security measure ensuring that each patient receives the correct treatment. Both systems save time, helps maintain the security of patient records, ensures compliance with correct patient/correct treatment and avoids some forms of identity theft and fraud.

Security Concerns

When medical records are kept electronically, it is essential that the facility have policies in place to ensure security and confidentiality of records. In addition, electronic

figure 15–10

Computerized medical records, laptop computers, and the Internet provide physicians with easy access no matter where they are.

Working with Electronic Health Records

Electronic health records (EHRs) are essentially a computer-based or a digital recording of patient information. They are also called computer records, electronic medical records (EMRs), electronic charts, and computer health records. Paper records can be lost and information is not consistent. In addition, handwriting is often illegible. EHRs provide a multitude of advantages, including the following:

- Access. Electronic records can be accessed by health-care providers at various locations, including the laboratory, pharmacy, and even the medical records department.

- Availability. Information is immediately available, so health-care providers do not have to wait for the paper document to get written and sent. The data are entered and then immediately viewed at any electronic record location.

- Security. Electronic records provide security through special passwords for each individual entering the records. Passwords can be set to open access to only the parts necessary for the type of health-care provider.

- Safety. Sophisticated programs help prevent patient identification errors by including a picture of each patient as part of the patient record.

- Extra Features. Electronic software programs can alert the health-care provider to abnormal results to tests or the need for routine tests to be performed. More sophisticated programs can document health

trends, provide voice recognition, and convert notes to complete sentences.

As a medical assistant working with electronic records, you should keep the following in mind:

- Become familiar with the software and hardware used at your facility. Make sure you are not focused on the computer when you are with the patient. Becoming comfortable with the system you are using will help you to focus on the patient. If necessary, take notes and enter them in the computer when the patient is not present until you become comfortable.

- Retrieve the patient record carefully just as you would a paper record. Make sure you have identified the patient with at least two identifiers such as the name, date of birth, and/or medical record number.

- Keep your password information secure. Change the password on a regular basis or as directed by the health-care facility.

- Secure the computer that maintains the electronic records and keep a backup of electronic files.

- Check your entries carefully before hitting the enter button. An EHR is a legal document just like a paper chart.

---

files must be backed up on a regular basis to avoid accidental loss of data. Whether you are documenting by hand or electronically, accuracy is always important. Careful key entry is essential to maintain accurate electronic files.

Protecting the confidentiality of patient records in computer files is the greatest concern of electronic health records. Just as paper health-care records must be kept secure, so should the electronic health-care records be secure. Review Chapter 10 for more information about maintaining computer confidentiality when using the computer and other electronic devices.

 Explain the advantages and disadvantages of the electronic health record.

CHECKPOINT
LO 15.6

LO 15.7 Correcting and Updating Patient Records

In legal terms, medical records are regarded as having been created in "due course." All information in the record should be entered at the time of patient contact or visit and not days, weeks, or months later. Information corrected or added some time after a patient's visit or other contact can be regarded as "convenient" and may damage a doctor's position in a lawsuit. Untimely submissions can also jeopardize patient care.

Using Care with Corrections

If changes to the medical record are not done correctly, the record can become a legal problem for the physician and the practice. A physician may be able to more easily explain poor or incomplete documentation than to explain a chart where the original documentation appears to have been altered. Always be extremely careful to follow the appropriate procedures for correcting patient records.

Mistakes in medical records are not uncommon. The best defense is to correct the mistake immediately or as soon as possible after the original entry was made. To correct any mistake in a medical record, carefully draw a single line through the error, making sure that the original entry is still legible. Write or type the corrected information above or below the original entry or even in the margin, as close as possible to the original entry. If there is not enough room near the error to make the full correction, make a notation near the error as to where in the chart the correction may be found. When making the correction, note the date and reason for the correction and initial the completed correction. If at all possible, have another staff member witness the correction and also initial it as witness. Procedure 15–3 at the end of the chapter outlines the steps to correct the paper patient record and Procedure 15–5 shows how to make an addition or correction in the EHR.

Updating Patient Records

All additions to a patient's record—test results, observations, diagnoses, procedures—should be done so there could be no interpretation of deception on the physician's part. In a note accompanying the material, the physician should explain why the information is being added to the record. The material may simply be the physician's recollections or observations regarding a patient visit that occurred in the past. Each item added to the record must be dated and initialed. The electronic record usually does dates and times automatically and credits the person whose password is used. This reinforces the standard of never allowing anyone else to use your password. As the administrative medical assistant, you may be asked to act as a third party witness to the addition these additions to paper records. In the case of electronic records, once a note is written and approved, there is often the option for the writer to sign and then lock the record so further additions cannot be made. Should the provider decide later that something was omitted or requires an update, they will add an addendum to the record instead of adding the information directly to the previous entry. Figure 15–11A represents the screen the provider would use to lock and sign a record using the SpringCharts EHR system and 15–11B is a representation of the window explaining that the record is not editable and asking the user an addendum is desired. Figure 15–12 shows a record with the completed addendum.

Most hospitals clinics and larger medical practices have detailed guidelines for late entries and corrections to patient charts. You must follow these guidelines carefully to avoid potential legal problems (See Procedure 15–4 at the end of this chapter for a list of steps for adding information to paper patient record.) The process will be similar for electronic records; Procedure 15–5 at the end of this chapter outlines these steps.

**CHECKPOINT
LO 15.7**

Why is it important that any correction to the medical record does not cover up or mask the original documentation?

LO 15.8 Release of Records

All physical medical records, including x-rays, test results, and medical notes created by the physician, are considered the property of the practice. However, the information contained within the physical record belongs to the patient and

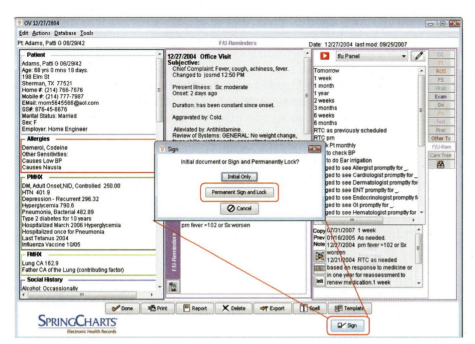

figure 15-11A

Office visit notes can be permanently locked.

figure 15-11B

Adding an addendum to a locked office visit note.

is regarded as confidential. Even though the practice owns the records, no one can see the information within them or obtain information from them without the patient's written consent. However, the law may require the physician to release them, as in the case of a patient with a contagious disease or when the records are subpoenaed by a court. Under no circumstances should you release patient information to insurance companies over the telephone. This information should be released in writing after the patient has signed a written release statement. Under HIPAA, release of information over the telephone may be problematic.

Additionally, any request to release medical records should be approved by the physician.

Procedures for Releasing Records

Physicians often receive requests from lawyers, other physicians, insurance companies, government agencies, and the patient himself for copies of a patient's records. Follow these steps for releasing medical information.

1. Obtain a signed and newly dated release from the patient authorizing the **transfer** of specific information—that is, giving information to another party outside the physician's office. *Verbal consent in person or over the telephone is not considered a valid release.* The release form should be filed in the patient's record. Refer to Chapter 6 for detailed information on releasing patient information and Procedure 6-3 for an outline for obtaining an authorization to release health information form.

2. Make photocopies of the original material. Copy and send only those portions of the record covered by the release and usually only records originating from your facility. Unless the patient specifically requests that you do so, you should not release records that were obtained from other sources, such as consultations or tests done in a hospital. Do not send original

transfer

With patient consent, giving PHI to another party outside the treating physician's office.

figure 15-12

Office visit note addendum.

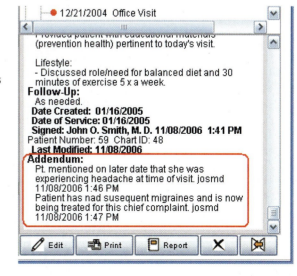

documents. If for any reason you cannot make copies, send the originals (if being sent by U.S. Postal Service or other mail delivery system, be sure to send the documents requesting signature and return receipt, so that you have documentation of the documents having been received) and tell the recipient that they must be returned. Follow up with the recipient until the originals have been returned and are placed in the patient's files. Often, the recipient is also asked to sign a statement of responsibility for the original records until they are returned to the office. Document in the chart who has possession of the original document, the date the recipient received the originals, and the date they are returned.

3. Call the recipient to confirm that all materials were received. Avoid faxing confidential records unless they can be sent to a secure, password-protected fax machine so that only the intended recipient can obtain the information. Otherwise, there is no way to know who will see documents sent by fax.

Special Cases

It may not always be immediately clear who has the right to sign a release-of-records form. When a couple divorces, for example, both parents are still considered legal guardians of their children, and either one can sign a release form authorizing transfer of medical records. If a patient dies, the patient's next of kin or legally authorized representative, such as the executor of the estate, may see the records or authorize their release to a third party. When you are in doubt regarding who is authorized to sign, always ask your supervisor before releasing confidential medical records.

Confidentiality

When children reach age 18, most states consider them adults with the right to privacy. No one, not even their parents, may see their medical records without the children's written consent. Some states extend this right to privacy to emancipated minors who are under the age of 18 and living on their own or are married, a parent, or in the armed services. This is particularly the case with minors seeking care for STDs, pregnancy, birth control, and drug or alcohol counseling. In these instances, the minor is considered a "mature minor" and her treatment cannot be discussed with her parents without her permission, even though the parents may still be held responsible for payment of such treatment through insurance or self-payment unless the patient pays for treatment at the time of service.

The main legal and ethical principle to keep in mind is that you must protect each patient's right to privacy at all times. Refer to Chapter 6 for more detailed information regarding patient confidentiality and the laws regarding release of information.

Auditing Medical Records

audit
To examine and review a group of patients' records for completeness and coding correctness.

The auditing of medical records is a great quality assurance tool. To **audit** a record means to examine and review a random group of patient records for completeness and accuracy. There are two types of audits: internal and external. The administrative medical assistant, and generally the medical office manager, and others that handle medical records for a medical office should periodically perform an audit. The frequency of these internal audits vary, larger practices may audit a small number of random charts monthly, where smaller offices may only do so every quarter or every six months. Many physicians' offices are now hiring compliance specialists to do internal auditing of their charts.

Internal Audits Internal audits can be done by the medical staff. Records are chosen randomly. Audits should be done before billing is submitted

Working with the Health-Care Team

MEDICAL CHART AUDITOR

Duties and Skills

Medical chart auditors are medical and coding specialists who, because of current government regulations clamping down on fraudulent billing practices, are in high demand by insurance carriers, government agencies (such as CMS), and proactive private practices who wish to be sure they are following all regulations. Many medical chart auditors are experienced medical coding specialists who have amassed knowledge in medical necessity, coding and compliance regulations, auditing and abstracting ability, and quality assurance and risk analysis. Excellent communication skills are also extremely helpful, particularly for auditors in the private sector as they explain to practices where and why improvement is needed in the office medical chart documentation.

Educational Requirements

Both the AAPC (American Academy of Professional Coders) and AAMAS (American Association of Medical Audit Specialists) offer certification for medical auditing specialists. The AAPC requires a high school diploma or equivalent, and AAMAS requires a minimum of 60 college semester units or evidence of being a licensed medical professional with proof of courses in accounting, finance, mathematics, or statistics. Each also state that the applicant must be a member in good standing of the organization by which certification is being sought and only experienced coders with auditing experience should attempt the exam. The AAPC suggests a minimum of two years of coding and auditing experience prior to taking the examination. Areas covered in both certification exams include compliance and regulatory guidance, coding concepts, scope and statistical sampling, medical record auditing skills including RAC (Medicare Recovery Audit Contractors) audits and abstracting ability, quality assurance and risk analysis, communication skills, and medical record analysis.

Workplace Settings

As the demands for certified medical auditors increase, so do the settings where employment may be found. Current employment possibilities include insurance companies and managed care organizations, hospitals and large medical facilities, government agencies such as CMS, auditing contracting firms, and self-employment.

The Medical Chart Auditor as a Team Member

Medical chart auditors may be in the office as a consultant at the request of the practice as a proactive measure to be sure that medical records meet current documentation guidelines for billing and coding or they may be present because of an outside audit requested by an insurance plan or government agency such as Medicare or Medicaid. Regardless of the reason why the auditor is present, she will be requesting random medical charts to compare the documentation within the medical record to the codes and information that was billed out to the insurance carrier. Prompt response to auditor requests is always required, as is a professional attitude and behavior toward her befitting the audit procedure.

If the audit is an internal one, pay close attention to the report at the end of the audit, as the information contained within that report may assist the practice in avoiding an external audit, or at least be sure that the medical records will defend them in the event of an external audit in the future. In this case, the auditor is there to assist the practice in avoiding problems in the documentation and coding procedures. If the audit is an external one, also pay attention to the findings because if the records do not back up the findings, large fines (or possibly worse) may be the result and improved documentation must be the ultimate result to avoid such fines in the future.

For more information, visit the Web sites listed below, which are available on the Online Learning Center at www.mhhe.com/houseradminmedassist.

American Association of Medical Audit Specialists

The American Academy of Professional Coders

(*prospective*) and after billing is submitted (*retrospective*). The audit schedule should be determined by the medical office. Some offices prefer biannual audits, while others prefer quarterly audits. A sample chart review form created by Ronald Bradshaw MD, CPA, can be found at www.aafp.org/fpm/20000400/chartreviewform.pdf. Additionally, see Figure 15–13 for a sample of a medical record audit form.

External Audits External audits are done by government entities such as the TJC, managed care organizations, and private insurance carriers. Over the past few years, government audits, particularly for Medicare and Medicaid providers, have increased in order to recover possible over-payments. External auditors may want to investigate the medical records further by interviewing

figure 15–13

An example of medical record audit form.

Medical Record Audit

Select 10 active patient charts with at least 3–5 prior visits: the most recent visit should have taken place within the past 6–12 months. If information should be present and is not, place a 0 in the box for that chart. If information is present, rate the quality of the information with 3 = Superior, 2 = Satisfactory, and 1 = Unacceptable. Use "NA" to score items that do not apply to a given chart (e.g., patient has no allergies).

Chart number	1	2	3	4	5	6	7	8	9	10
Pages have patient ID										
Contains biographical and/or personal data										
Person providing care identified on each chart entry										
Entries are dated										
Entries are legible										
Problem list is complete										
Allergies and adverse drug reactions are prominent										
Absence of allergies and reactions prominent										
Appropriate past medical HX										
Smoking, alcohol, or substance abuse HX documented										
Pertinent HX and physical										
Lab and other tests ordered as appropriate										
Working diagnoses are consistent with findings										
Plans of action/treatment are consistent with diagnosis(es)										
Problems from previous visits addressed										
Evidence of appropriate use of consultants										
Evidence of continuity and coordination of care between primary and specialty physicians										
Consultant summaries, lab, and imaging study results reflect primary care physician review										
Completed immunization record										
Prescriptions and refills noted										
Med sheet used and appropriately located										
Chronology maintained										
Informed consent noted for all procedures and appropriate prescriptions										
Patients are adequately informed (i.e., there is documentation of patient education, follow-up instructions)										

the staff, patient, and all physicians who participated in the care of the patient. If there is anything that is fraudulent in the billing that is discovered, the physician may have to refund monies or could be penalized.

● ● ●

What is the difference between an internal and external audit?

CHECKPOINT
LO 15.8

Procedure 15–1 Initiating a Paper-based Patient Medical Record/Chart

GOAL To assemble new paper-based patient medical record/chart

MATERIALS File folder, labels as appropriate (alphabet, numbers, dates, insurance, allergies, etc.), forms (patient information, advance directives, physician progress notes, referrals, laboratory forms), hole punch

METHOD
1. Carefully create a chart label according to practice policy. This label may include the patient's last name followed by the first name, or it may be a medical record number for those offices that utilize numeric or alphanumeric filing.
2. Place the chart label on the right edge of the folder, extending the label the length of the tab on the folder.
3. Place the date label on the top edge of the folder, updating the date according to the practice's policy. (The date is usually updated annually, provided the patient has come into the office within the last year.)
4. Place an allergy label on the outer edge of the chart (per office policy) noting any patient allergies, or NKA if no allergies are given. If the office uses insurance labels documenting Medicare, Medicaid, HMO or PPO. This may also be placed on the chart edge.
5. Punch holes in the appropriate forms (patient medical history, physical exam, blank chart note and any records that may have arrived from referring or previous physicians) for placement within the patient's medical record/chart. Each paper form must also include patient identifying information on each sheet; both front and back.
6. Place all the forms in appropriate sections of the patient's medical record/chart.

Procedure 15–2 Creating a New Patient Record using an EHR Program

GOAL To create a new patient record in an EHR program

MATERIALS Initial patient forms (patient information, advance directives, physician progress notes, referrals, laboratory orders)

METHOD

1. Open the New Patient Window of the EHR software as directed by the software vendor.

2. Enter the patient's full name as directed, being careful to enter the name in the correct order (some software programs require first name, middle name, last name while others start with the last name).

3. If the patient has a family member who also comes to the office, you may be able to use a short cut to copy the patient's address from the existing patient; otherwise, enter the patient's demographic information of address and phone number. Be sure to fill in each screen completely and accurately before moving on to the next screen.

4. Follow the software directions for completing each screen including the patient's insurance, guarantor, and employer information.

5. Depending on the office policy, you may also enter the patient's medical history information. Open the medical history screen of the software program and carefully key in the information required for each screen.

6. Carefully inspect all information for accuracy and save the new patient record as directed by the software program instructions.

7. Depending on the office policy, information from a hard copy medical record may be scanned into the EHR or a manual file created to maintain it.

Procedure 15–3 Correcting Paper Medical Records

GOAL   To follow standard procedures for correcting a paper medical record

MATERIALS   Patient file, other pertinent documents that contain the information to be used in making corrections (for example, transcribed notes, telephone notes, physician's comments, correspondence), good ballpoint pen

METHOD

1. Corrections and additions should be made so that the original information remains readable; so that there can be no suggestion of intent to conceal information. Draw a single line through the information to be replaced.

2. Write or type in the correct information above or below the original line or in the margin. The location in the chart for the new information should be clear. If a separate sheet of paper or another document is required for the correction or addition, clearly note in the record "See attached document A" or similar wording to indicate where the corrected information can be found.

3. Place a note near the correction or addition stating why it was made (for example, "error, wrong date; error, interrupted by phone call.") Make sure you initial and date the correction. This indication can be a brief note in the margin or an attachment to the record. Do not make any changes or additions in a record without noting the reason for them.

4. Enter the date and time, and initial the correction or addition.

5. If possible, have another staff member or the physician witness and initial the correction to the record when you make it.

Procedure 15-4 Entering Information in a Paper Medical Records

GOAL To document continuity of care by creating a complete, accurate, timely record of the medical care provided at your facility

MATERIALS Patient file, other pertinent documents (test results, x-rays, telephone notes, correspondence), blue ballpoint pen, notebook, keyboard, transcribing equipment

METHOD

1. Verify that you have the correct chart for the documents to be filed. Carefully check the patient's name, DOB, and medical record number (if available) as verification.

2. Transcribe dictated doctor's notes as soon as possible, and enter them into the patient record. If notes are handwritten, be sure they are filed in the correct location within the medical record.

3. Spell out the names of disorders, diseases, medications, and other terms the first time you enter them into the patient record, followed by the appropriate abbreviation (for example: "congestive heart failure [CHF]"). Thereafter, you may use the abbreviation alone.

4. Enter only what the doctor has dictated. Do *not* add your own comments, observations, or evaluations. Use self-adhesive flags or other means to call the doctor's attention to something you have noticed that may be helpful to the patient's case. Date and initial each entry.

5. Follow office procedure to record routine or special laboratory, x-ray, or other test results. They may be posted in a particular section of the file or on a separate test summary form. If you use the summary form, make a note in the file that the results were received and recorded. Place the original report in the patient's file if required to do so by office policy. Date and initial each entry. File all correspondence and hospital records in the appropriate area of each chart, using reverse chronological order so that the most recent record is on top. Be sure that each document is initialed or stamped by the physician as having been seen, prior to filing it within the patient's chart.

6. Make a note in the record of all telephone calls to and from the patient. Date and initial the entries. These entries also may include the doctor's comments, observations, changes in the patient's medication, new instructions to the patient, and so on. If calls are recorded in a separate telephone log, note in the patient's record the time and date of the call and refer to the log. It is particularly important to record such calls when the patient resists or refuses treatment, skips appointments, or has not made follow-up appointments.

7. Make notations in the medical record of any immunizations and vaccines that have been given to the patient. Notations should be posted in the patient's immunization record inside the medical chart. Input them into your state's public health database as well. Immunization records are kept indefinitely.

8. Read over the entries for omissions or mistakes. Ask the doctor to answer any questions you have.

9. Make sure that you have dated and initialed each entry.

10. Be sure that all documents are included in the file and within the appropriate location so they may be located easily when needed.

11. Replace the patient's file in the filing system as soon as possible.

Procedure 15-5 Making an Addition (Addendum) to the Electronic Health Record

GOAL To follow standard procedures for correcting or making an addendum to an electronic health record

MATERIALS Access to the patient's electronic health record, other pertinent documents that contain the information to be used in making corrections (for example, handwritten notes, telephone notes, physician's comments, correspondence, lab results)

METHOD
1. Open the patient record requiring the correction or addendum.
2. Click the *Edit* button as directed by the software program.
3. When the pop-up window appears stating the record is *not editable* (signed and locked), but asking if an addendum is desired, choose *Yes*.
4. The program will now automatically date, time stamp the entry with the current date and time, as well as initial stamp the entry with the user's initials when the *Save* button is chosen once the entry is written.

Case Study

PROFESSIONAL READINESS

Persistence
Ability to continue the course of action in spite of difficulty

The day Dr. Wilson's office "went live" with the new electronic health records (EHR) was a day to remember. Since everyone was unfamiliar with the new system, it slowed the work processes considerably and the tension was palpable. Also, the interfaces for ordering laboratory tests and prescriptions were not active, so consequently, the staff was performing some functions using the EHR and some functions manually. The medical records for the scheduled patients were scanned into the EHR but emergency patient records were not available electronically. Alicia, who is responsible for registering patients, remained calm and focused. Although the patients were sent a letter regarding the change, Alicia took the time to explain what was happening and jokingly requested that the "patient be patient" which helped relieve the tension on this unique day. She was able to work around each challenge as it arose. She obtained hard-copy records as needed for unscheduled patients and when the office closed she ensured the records were input into the new system. When it came time for Alicia's annual performance evaluation, Katy, the practice manager, praised her for her persistence on that day. This is one of the professional attributes that contributed to Alicia's raise related to her performance evaluation.

Thinking Critically

1. What might have happened on a follow-up visit if Alicia did not ensure information for patients seen on the "go live" date was input into the EHR?
2. What are some of the advantages the EHR has over the hard-copy medical record?
3. What are some of the concerns regarding the EHR?

APPLICATIONS

1. Role-play in groups of three students. One student should play the patient, one the administrative medical assistant, and one the observer. Role-play a scenario in which the patient requests to have her medical records released to another physician. The administrative medical assistant should explain to the patient the process for the release of her medical records.

   The observer should not speak but should observe and take notes on the scenario as acted out by the other two students. The observer should compare the scenario to the steps provided in the text for the release of records. Note what is done well and what needs improvement.

   Each student should rotate through all three roles.

2. Photocopy the blank combination medical history and physical examination form shown in Figure 15–4. Fill out the form by using the following patient information:

   For medical history section: Date: 2/14/12; the patient is Heather R. MacEntee, age 35, living at 344 Westwind Lane, Apartment 28, Round Tree, IL 60012; telephone (708) 333-5555. She is a real estate broker, married, with a 6-year-old child. Her father died at age 55; her mother is 62 and has congestive heart disease. She has no siblings. The family has a history of heart disease and diabetes. The patient had chickenpox and mumps at age 7 and surgery for an ovarian cyst at 22. She has an allergy to ragweed but is not taking any medications at present.

   For physical examination section: Ms. MacEntee weighs 142 lb, is 5 ft 10 in tall, and her temperature and respiration are normal. Her pulse is 74, her blood pressure is 110/75, and her chest sounds are normal. Her chief complaint is discomfort in the area of the gallbladder. She has intense pain after eating. Blood tests are normal. The doctor's initial impression is suspected gallstones, and an ultrasound scan of the gallbladder is ordered. Treatment plan depends on the scan results.

exam READINESS

1. [LO15.3] A patient's illness and reason for visit to the physician would be found in the
   a. patient's medical history.
   b. records from other health-care providers.
   c. patient registration form.
   d. informed consent form.
   e. physical examination.

2. [LO15.3] The first document(s) found in a patient medical record is the
   a. patient registration form.
   b. doctor's diagnosis and treatment plan.
   c. patient medical history.
   d. records from other physicians or hospitals.
   e. patient physical examination.

3. [LO15.1] All of the following are uses for medical records EXCEPT
   a. research.
   b. quality of care.
   c. patient education.
   d. All of the above.
   e. b and c only.

4. [LO15.2] POMR stands for
   a. Patient-Oriented Medical Record.
   b. Problem-Obvious Medical Record.
   c. Problem-Oriented Medicine Record.
   d. Patient-Oriented Medicine Record.
   e. Problem-Oriented Medical Record.

5. [LO15.5] Documenting a patient's walk down a hall as "fine" violates which "C" of charting?
   a. Completeness
   b. Clarity
   c. Conciseness
   d. Chronological order
   e. Client's words

6. [LO15.4] Why is it important to ensure that the medical history form is filled out completely and accurately?
   a. It cuts down on the questions the physician must ask.
   b. Less testing will need to be done to understand the patient's complaint.

c. It is an ice-breaker for difficult discussions between the patient and physician.

d. It is the basis for the rest of the patient medical record.

e. All of the above.

7. **[LO15.5]** Why is blue ink preferred (by HIPAA recommendations) for medical record documentation?

a. It photocopies in the original color.

b. It is easy to duplicate exactly when amending information.

c. It is easy to differentiate between the original and a copy.

d. It is a legal requirement.

e. It is usually readily available.

8. **[LO15.7]** Which of the following is necessary when correcting or making additions to paper medical records?

a. Draw a single line through the error.

b. Make the correction as close as possible to the original entry.

c. Note the reason for the correction and sign and date the correction.

d. A witness should also initial the entry.

e. a–c are required; d is advisable.

9. **[LO15.6]** Which of the following disadvantages of the EHR may affect smaller medical practices?

a. Cost

b. Fear of technology

c. Possible need for an IT specialist

d. Training requirements

e. All of the above

10. **[LO15.6]** Which of the following is not an advantage of EHR?

a. Multiple providers may access one record at the same time.

b. Records are easily accessed.

c. There are multiple software vendors for EHR with varying requirements.

d. Records are secured through passwords and access codes.

e. Information is available in real-time.

learning outcome SUMMARY

LO 15.1 Medical records are legal documents that give a complete, concise, chronological history of a patient's medical history, treatment plan, and treatment outcome. Additionally, they act as a communication tool between care providers. Regardless of the type of record, the patient chart provides physicians and other medical care providers with all the important information, observations, and opinions that have been recorded about a patient.

LO 15.2 SOMR stands for source-oriented medical records. All items within the patient medical record are filed according to the location from which they originated. POMR stands for problem-oriented medical records. Items filed in these medical records are filed under the problem (number) to which they relate. SOAP format of documentation is used with POMR records and stands for subjective, objective, assessment, and plan. CHEDDAR format of documentation takes the SOAP format to the next level and stands for chief complaint, history, exam, detailed problem/complaint, drugs and dosages, assessment, and return information (if applicable).

LO 15.3 Documents commonly found in the paper medical record include patient registration; medical history and physical examination forms;

laboratory, x-ray, and other results; records from other physicians, hospitals, and other providers; physician diagnosis and treatment plans; operative and other hospital reports; and consent forms for any information that has been released to or received from other providers.

LO 15.4 The initial interview provides the base information for a new patient coming to the medical practice. It introduces the practice to the patient and the patient to the practice. Prior to, or during, the initial interview, the patient will complete the medical history form which is the basis of the patient medical record.

LO 15.5 The 6 Cs of medical charting are: client's words, clarity, completeness, conciseness, chronological order, and confidentiality.

LO 15.6 The federal government recommends that all health records become electronic by 2014. The electronic health record has many advantages over the paper health record such as simultaneous access from more than one site and low risk for record loss. A dual system of paper and electronic records will continue for several years since conversion will not occur for all existing records.

LO 15.7 The proper way to make corrections in a medical record is to draw a single line through the error so that the original entry is still legible. Make the correction as close as possible to the original entry, noting the reason for the correction; date and initial the correction.

LO 15.8 In order to release any medical record, express written permission from the patient must be received. Unless it is impossible to do so, copies should be made and the originals should remain in the office. If originals must be released, verification that the records have been received and by whom should be noted in the chart. Follow-up should take place until the original records are returned to the office.

medical assisting COMPETENCIES

CAAHEP

IV. C (6) Differentiate between subjective and objective information

IV. P (1) Use reflection, restatement, and clarification techniques to obtain a patient history

IV. P (2) Use reflection, restatement and clarification techniques to obtain a patient history

IV. P (3) Use medical terminology, pronouncing medical terms correctly, to communicate information, patient history, data and observations

IV. P (8) Document patient care

IV. P (9) Document patient education

IV. A (8) Analyze communications in providing appropriate responses/feedback

V. C (5) Identify systems for organizing medical records

V. C (6) Describe various types of content maintained in a patient's medical record

V. C (11) Discuss principles of using electronic medical records (EMR)

V. C (12) Identify types of records common to the healthcare setting

V. P (3) Organize a patient's medical record

V. P (5) Execute data management using electronic health-care records such as the EMR

VII. A (2) Demonstrate sensitivity in communicating with both providers and patients

IX. C (14) Describe the process to follow if an error is made in patient care

IX. P (3) Apply HIPAA rules in regard to privacy/release of information

IX. P (7) Document accurately in the patient record

ABHES

4. Medical Law and Ethics
  b. Institute federal and state guidelines when releasing medical records or information

7. Basic Keyboarding/Computer Concepts
  a. Typing medical correspondence and basic reports
  b. Identify and properly utilize office machines, computerized systems and medical software such as:
    (1) Efficiently maintain and understand different types of medical correspondence and medical reports
    (2) Apply computer application skills using variety of different electronic programs including both practice management software and EMR software

8. Medical Office Business Procedures Management
  a. Prepare and maintain medical records
  d. Apply concepts for office procedures
  gg. Use pertinent medical terminology
  ii. Recognize and respond to verbal and nonverbal communication
  ll. Apply electronic technology

11. Career Development
  Demonstrate professionalism by:
    (1) Exhibiting dependability, punctuality, and a positive work ethic
    (2) Exhibiting a positive attitude and a sense of responsibility
    (3) Maintaining confidentiality at all times
    (9) Conducting work within scope of education, training, and ability

Learning Outcomes

After completing Chapter 16, you will be able to:

16.1 Differentiate between prescription and over-the-counter (OTC) drugs and their chemical, generic, or trade names.

16.2 Identify the major drug categories and sources for drug information.

16.3 Describe how to register or renew a physician with the Drug Enforcement Administration (DEA) for permission to administer, dispense, and prescribe controlled drugs.

16.4 Interpret a prescription and carry out the procedure for managing prescription renewals.

16.5 Manage laboratory and diagnostic tests, consultations, and other patient records and reports.

Key Terms

authorized prescriber (AP)
controlled substance
consultation
e-prescribing
Food and Drug Administration (FDA)
generic name
Medicare Improvements for Patients and Providers Act of 2008 (MIPPA)

over-the-counter (OTC) drugs
prescription
requisition
Surescripts
trade name

Preparation for Certification

RMA (AMT) Exam
- Medical terminology associated with pharmacology
- Commonly used drugs and their categories
- Classes of drug schedules and legal prescriptions requirements for each
- Drug Enforcement Agency regulations for ordering, dispensing, storage of, and documentation of medication use
- Drug reference books (*PDR, Pharmacopeia, Facts and Comparisons, Nurses Handbook*)

CMAS (AMT) Exam
- Pharmacology
- Prescriptions
- Documentation/reporting

CMA (AAMA) Exam
- Basic pharmacological concepts and terminology

Introduction •••

Working as an administrative medical assistant, you will be involved with the patient's medical record, including medications and prescriptions, on an ongoing basis. Whether the medical record is electronic or paper, it is necessary to understand the information it includes, when it is used, its purpose, and what recording and reporting must be completed. This chapter focuses on information and skills related to prescriptions, medical tests, and other reports.

LO 16.1 Medications

Most patients will be taking some type of medication. These may include prescription or nonprescription medications. Nonprescription medications are more commonly called **over-the-counter (OTC) drugs.** An OTC drug is one that the FDA has approved for use without the supervision of an authorized prescriber. The consumer must follow the manufacturer's directions to use the drug safely. The number of prescription drugs that have been granted OTC status is increasing. Although OTC drugs are safe when used as directed on the package, patient education contributes significantly to their safe use. A **prescription** drug is one that can be used only by order of an **authorized prescriber (AP)** such as a physician, nurse practitioner, or physician's assistant. It is dispensed by a licensed health-care professional, such as a pharmacist, physician, podiatrist, or licensed midwife. Some prescription drugs are dispensed as OTC medications at much lower strengths.

When a new patient comes to a health-care facility, a record of his or her current medications including prescription and OTC drugs must be completed. This record becomes part of the patient's chart (Figure 16–1). In an electronic health records system such as Spring Charts, entering and editing of the patient's current routine medications and over-the-counter (OTC) meds is done electronically (Figure 16–2).

Drug Names

In order to communicate information about medications, you must first know a little about how drugs are named. One drug may have several different names,

over-the-counter (OTC) drugs
Drugs that can be bought without a prescription.

prescription
A physician's written order for medication.

authorized prescriber (AP)
A health-care professional who is legally allowed to order prescription medications; includes physicians, nurse practitioners, and physician assistants.

figure 16–1

A list of current medications, both prescription and OTC, must be kept on the patient's chart.

| Name | Jennifer Haddix | | DOB | 12/05/84 | | Date | 08/28/12 |

ALLERGIES: Bee Stings, Penicillin   Note

Review of Systems

Systems	NL	Note	Systems	NL	Note
Constitutional			Musculoskeletal		
Eyes			Skin/breasts		
ENT/mouth			Neurologic		
Cardiovascular			Psychiatric		
Respiratory			Endocrine		
GI			Hem/lymph		
GU			Allergy/immun		
Current Medicines			Date	Current Diagnosis	

H: 5'7"   W: 140   T: 97.8   P: 88   R: 20

B/P Sitting 122/78   or Standing _____   Supine _____

Last Tetanus 06/12/09

L.M.P. 08/20/12

O2 Sat: 98%   Pain Scale: 6/10

Social Habits Yes No
Tobacco ___ ⌄
Alcohol ⌄ occ
Rec. Drugs ___ ⌄

Current Medicines:
ClaritinD prN
MVI T̄qd
Ortho Novum 7/7/7 T̄qd

CC: Ⓛ Shoulder pain X 3 days due to fall.
"Sharp pain that hurts when I move"

HPI:

figure 16-2

Electronic charts allow you to enter, modify, and update the medications a patient is taking.

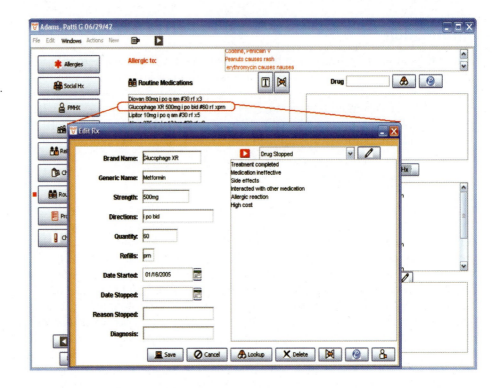

generic name
A drug's official name.

trade name
A drug's brand or proprietary name.

including the drug's official name (also known as the **generic name),** international nonproprietary name, chemical name, and **trade name** (brand or proprietary name). To demonstrate, the trade-name prescription antibacterial drug Keflex® or Biocef is also identified by the following names:

- Cephalexin *(generic name)*
- Cefalexin *(international nonproprietary name)*
- 7-(D-amino-phenylacentomido)-3-methyl-3-cephem-4-carboxylic acid, monohydrate *(chemical name)*

Generic and trade names are used most frequently. In general, think of the generic name of a drug as a simple form of its chemical name. For each new drug marketed by a drug manufacturer, the United States Adopted Names (USAN) Council selects a generic name. This name is nonproprietary; that is, it does not belong to any one drug manufacturer. A generic name is also considered a drug's official name, which is listed in the *United States Pharmacopeia/National Formulary.*

A drug's trade name is selected by its manufacturer. It is protected by copyright and is the property of the drug manufacturer. When a new drug enters the market, its manufacturer has a patent on that drug, which means that no other manufacturer can make or sell the drug for 17 years. When the patent runs out, any manufacturer can sell the drug under the generic name or a different trade name. The original manufacturer, however, is the only one allowed to use the drug's original trade name. For example, the antibiotic cephalexin has two trade names, Keflex® and Biocef. These names are owned by different manufacturers. Generic drugs are usually less expensive and prescribed frequently.

A physician or other authorized prescriber (AP) may prescribe a drug by its generic or trade name. Many states allow pharmacists to substitute a generic drug for a trade-name drug unless the AP specifies otherwise. In fact, most health insurance prescription plans now require the substitution of generic drugs for trade-name drugs (unless otherwise specified by a physician). Frequently, they also require the pharmacy to charge a higher copay amount for trade-name drugs than for generic drugs. Some prescription plans now offer a mail-in

pharmacy through which a patient can obtain generic drugs with a reduced copayment or without any copayment. In addition, many retail pharmacies are providing low-cost prescription medications of selected generic medications.

Explain why an administrative medical assistant might need to know the generic and trade names of medications.

**CHECKPOINT
LO 16.1**

LO 16.2 Drug Categories and Information

Administrative medical assistants must have basic knowledge of drug categories to record drug information. Drugs are categorized by their action on the body, general therapeutic effect, or the body system affected. Table 16–1 lists a variety of drug categories, their actions, and example medications.

table 16–1

Selected Drug Categories

DRUG CATEGORY	ACTION OF DRUG	EXAMPLES* GENERIC NAME (TRADE NAME)
Analgesic	Relieves mild to severe pain	Acetaminophen (Tylenol®)* Acetylsalicylic acid, or Aspirin Morphine sulfate (MS Contin®)* Oxycodone HCl (Percocet)*
Anesthetic	Prevents sensation of pain (generally, locally, or topically)	Lidocaine HCl (Xylocaine®, Lidoderm®)* Tetracaine HCl (Pontocaine)
Antacid/Antiulcer	Neutralizes stomach acid	Calcium carbonate (Tums®) Esomeprazole (Nexium®) Lansoprazole (Prevacid®) Pantoprazole sodium (Protonix®)*
Anthelmintic	Kills, paralyzes, or inhibits the growth of parasitic worms	Mebendazole (Vermox®) Pyrantel pamoate (Combantrin®, Antiminth®)
Antiarrhythmic	Normalizes heartbeat in cases of certain cardiac arrhythmias	Disopyramide phosphate (Norpace®) Propafenone hydrochloride (Rythmol®) Propranolol HCl (Inderal®)*
Antiasthmatic	Treats or prevents asthma attacks	Montelukast (Singulair®)* Fluticasone propionate/salmeterol (Advair diskus®)* Albuterol (ProAir HFA®)*
Antibiotics (antibacterial)	Kills bacterial microorganisms or inhibits their growth	Amoxicillin (Amoxil®)* Azithromycin (Zithromax®)* Cefprozil (Cefzil®)* Ciprofloxacin (Cipro®)* Clarithromycin (Biaxin® XL)* Levofloxacin (Levaquin®)*
Anticholinergic	Blocks parasympathetic nerve impulses	Atropine sulfate (Isopto® Atropine) Diclomine HCl (Bentyl®) Ipratropium (Atrovent®)
Anticoagulant	Prevents blood from clotting	Enoxaparin sodium (Lovenox®) Heparin sodium (Hep-Lock) Warfarin sodium (Coumadin®)*
Anticonvulsant	Relieves or controls seizures (convulsions)	Clonazepam (Klonopin®)* Divalproex (Depakote®)* Phenobarbital sodium* (Luminol® Sodium)* Phenytoin (Dilantin®)*
Antidepressant (four types)		
Tricyclic	Relieves depression	Amitriptyline HCl (Elavil)* Doxepin HCl (Sinequan)*
Monoamine oxidase inhibitor (MAOI)		Phenelzine sulfate (Nardil®) Tranylcypromine sulfate (Parnate®)
Selective serotonin reuptake inhibitor (SSRIs)		Escitalopram (Lexapro®)* Fluoxetine HCl (Prozac®)* Paroxetine (Paxil®)* Sertraline HCl (Zoloft®)*
Serotonin-norepinephrine reuptake inhibitor (SNRI)		Venlafaxine hydrochloride (Effexor XR®)* Duloxetine hydrochloride (Cymbalta®)*

(Continued)

table 16–1 (Continued)

Antidiabetic	Treats diabetes by reducing glucose	Metformin (Glucophage®)* Glipizide (Glucotrol®)* Glyburide (Micronase®)* Pioglitazone hydrochloride (Actos®)
Antidiarrheal	Relieves diarrhea	Bismuth subsalicylate (Pepto-Bismol®) Kaolin and pectin mixtures (Kaopectate®) Loperamide HCl (Imodium®)
Antiemetic	Prevents or relieves nausea and vomiting	Prochlorperazine (Compazine®) Promethazine (Phenergan®)* Trimethobenzamide HCl (Tigan)
Antifungal	Kills or inhibits growth of fungi	Amphotericin B (Fungizone®) Fluconazole (Diflucan®)* Nystatin (Mycostatin®)* Terbinafine (Lamisil®)*
Antihistamine	Counteracts effects of histamine and relieves allergic symptoms	Cetirizine HCl (Zyrtec®)* Diphenhydramine HCl (Benadryl®) Fexofenadine (Allegra®)* Desloratadine (Clarinex®)*
Antihypertensive	Reduces blood pressure	Amlodipine (Norvasc®)* Diltiazem hydrochloride (Cartia XL®) Quinapril (Prinivil®)* Metoprolol succinate (Toprol XL®)* Valsartan (Diovan®)*
Anti-inflammatory (two types)	Reduces inflammation	
Nonsteroidal (NSAIDs)		Naproxen (Aleve) Colchicine* Ibuprofen (Motrin®, Advil®)* Celcoxib (Celebrex®)*
Steroids		Dexamethasone (Decadron®) Methylprednisolone (Medrol®)* Prednisone (Deltasone)* Triamcinoline (Kenalog®)
Antilipidemic	Lowers blood lipids such as triglyeride	Gemfibrozil Atorvastatin (Lipitor®)* Fenofibrate (TriCor)* Ezetimibe/simvastatin (Vytorin®)* Exetimibe (Zetia®)* Rosuvastatin (Crestor®)*
Antineoplastic	Poisons cancerous cells	Bleomycin sulfate (Blenoxane®) Dactinomycin (Cosmegen®) Paclitaxel (Taxol®) Tamoxifen citrate (Nolvadex®)*
Antipsychotic	Controls psychotic symptoms	Chlorpromazine HCl (Thorazine®) Clozapine (Clozaril®) Haloperidol (Haldol®) Risperidone (Risperdal®) Thioridazine HCl (Mellaril®)
Antipyretic	Reduces fever	Acetaminophen (Tylenol®) Acetylsalicylic acid, or aspirin
Antiseptic	Inhibits growth of microorganisms	Isopropyl alcohol, 70% Povidone-iodine (Betadine) Chlorhexidine gluconate (PerioChip)
Antitussive	Inhibits cough reflex	Codine Dextromethorphan hydrobromide (component of Robitussin® DM)
Bronchodilator	Dilates bronchi (airways in the lungs)	Albuterol (Proventil®)* Epinephrine (Epinephrine Mist) Salmeterol (Severent)
Cathartic (laxative)	Induces defecation, alleviates constipation	Bisacodyl (Dulcolax®) Casanthranol (Peri-Colace) Magnesium hydroxide (Milk of Magnesia®)
Contraceptive	Reduces risk of pregnancy	Ethinyl estradiol and norgestimate (Ortho Tri-Cyclen®)* Norethindrone and ethinyl estradiol (Ortho-Evra®)* Norgestrel (Ovrette)
Decongestant	Relieves nasal swelling and congestion	Oxymetazoline HCl (Afrin) Phenylephrine HCl (Neo-Synephrine®) Pseudoephedrine HCl (Sudafed®)

table 16-1 *(Concluded)*

Diuretic	Increases urine output, reduces blood pressure and cardiac output	Bumetanide (Bumex®) Furosemide (Lasix®)* Hydrochlorothiazide (Hydrodiuril®)* Mannitol
Expectorant	Liquefies mucus in bronchi; allows expectoration of sputum, mucus, and phlegm	Guaifenesin (component of Robitussin®)
Hemostatic	Controls or stops bleeding by promoting coagulation	Aminocaproic acid (Amicar) Phytonadione or vitamin K_1 (Mephyton®) Thrombin (Thrombogen)
Hormone replacement	Replaces or resolves hormone deficiency	Insulin (Humulin)* for pancreatic deficiency Levothyroxine sodium (Synthroid®)* for thyroid deficiency Conjugated estrogens (Premarin Tabs®)*
Hypnotic (sleep-inducing) or sedative	Induces sleep or relaxation (depending on drug potency and dosage)	Chloral hydrate (Noctec®) Ethchlorvynol (Placidyl) Secobarbital sodium (Seconal® Sodium) Zolpidem (Ambien®)*
Muscle relaxant	Relaxes skeletal muscles	Carisoprodol (Rela or Soma®) Cyclobenzaprine HCl (Flexeril)*
Mydriatic	Constricts vessels of eye or nasal passage, raises blood pressure, dilates pupil of eye in ophthalmic preparations	Atropine sulfate (Allergan) for ophthalmic use Phenylephrine HCl (Alcon Efrin) for ophthalmic use or (Neo-Synephrine® HCl) for nasal use
Stimulant (central nervous system)	Increases activity of brain and other organs, decreases appetite	Amphetamine sulfate (Benzadrine) Caffeine (No-Doz); also component of many analgesic formulations and coffee
Vasoconstrictor	Constricts blood vessels, increases blood pressure	Dopamine HCl (Intropin) Norepinephrine bitartrate (Levophed)
Vasodilator	Dilates blood vessels, decreases blood pressure	Enalopril (Vasotec®) Lisinopril (Prinivil®)* Nitroglycerin (Nitrostat®)* , NitroQuick®)

*Indicates commonly prescribed drug.

Source: *Physicians' Desk Reference* (*PDR*), 2009.

Resources for Drug Information

It is important to keep several up-to-date sources of drug information available when detailed information about a specific drug is needed. Sources for drug information are available in print or electronic format.

Print Resources   Common print resources include the *Physicians' Desk Reference, Drug Evaluations,* and the *United States Pharmacopeia/National Formulary.*

Physicians' Desk Reference (*PDR*) publishes annually, along with supplements twice a year. The company also publishes separate editions for generic, nonprescription, and ophthalmologic drugs as well as a guide to drug interactions, adverse effects, and indications. It is also available electronically.

The *PDR* presents information provided by pharmaceutical companies about more than 2500 prescription drugs. The *PDR* has the following sections:

- Section 1—Manufacturer's index (color-coded white), which includes the pharmaceutical company's name, address, emergency telephone number, and available products
- Section 2—Brand- and generic-name index (color-coded pink)

Using Your Knowledge of Medications

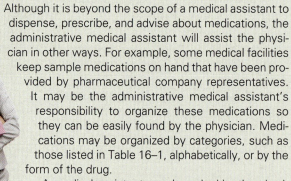

Although it is beyond the scope of a medical assistant to dispense, prescribe, and advise about medications, the administrative medical assistant will assist the physician in other ways. For example, some medical facilities keep sample medications on hand that have been provided by pharmaceutical company representatives. It may be the administrative medical assistant's responsibility to organize these medications so they can be easily found by the physician. Medications may be organized by categories, such as those listed in Table 16–1, alphabetically, or by the form of the drug.

A medical assistant may be asked by the physician to provide medication instructions to the patient in written format or to review instructions with a patient. Although these instructions do not replace information that must be provided by the physician and pharmacist, the medical assistant may be asked questions about these instructions. Instructions will be vital to helping the patient improve medically and also increasing the probability of patient safety and compliance.

When a patient takes a medication incorrectly, serious problems can occur, including hospitalization. Make sure the patient can repeat the medication instructions. Be alert for medications that look alike and sound alike such as Celebrex® for arthritis and Celexa® for depression. Always check a reliable source for drug information for spelling as well as have the patient bring the medications to the appointment to ensure accuracy.

- Section 3—Product category index (color-coded blue)
- Section 4—Product identification guide with full-color photos of more than 2400 actual medications
- Section 5—Product information
- Section 6—Diagnostic product information

The information is provided for the *PDR* by the manufacturer and is either the drug package insert or closely resembles it. The package insert for each drug describes the drug, its purpose and effects (clinical pharmacology), indications, contraindications (conditions under which the drug should not be administered), warnings, precautions, adverse reactions, drug abuse and dependence, overdosage, dosage and administration, and how the drug is supplied (for example, tablets in different doses, or liquid). See Figure 16–3.

United States Pharmacopeia/National Formulary (*USP/NF*) is the official source of drug standards in the United States and is published about every five years. As the official public standards-setting authority for all prescription medications, OTC drugs, dietary supplements, and other health-care products, by law, every product sold under a name listed in the *USP/NF* must meet the strict standards of the *USP*. The *USP/NF* describes each product approved by the federal government and lists its standards for purity, composition, and strength as well as its uses, dosages, and storage. The *NF* portion of the book provides the chemical formulas of the drugs.

Electronic Resources Electronic resources are delivered in a variety of methods including CD, DVD, Internet, personal digital assistant (PDA) devices, smart phones, and electronic health records. As mentioned earlier, the *PDR* is available online through the Internet site www.PDR.net. This site allows authorized prescribers as well as those in training access to medication information when they register. It includes FDA-approved product labeling, multidrug interaction checker, daily updates, *PDR* e-books, patient educations, MEDLINE, and Stedman's Medical Dictionary. Also available is a consumer and patient site called PDRhealth (Figure 16–4).

Epocrates is an electronic program that can be loaded on to a PDA or smart phone. This electronic resource includes more than 3,300 brand and generic

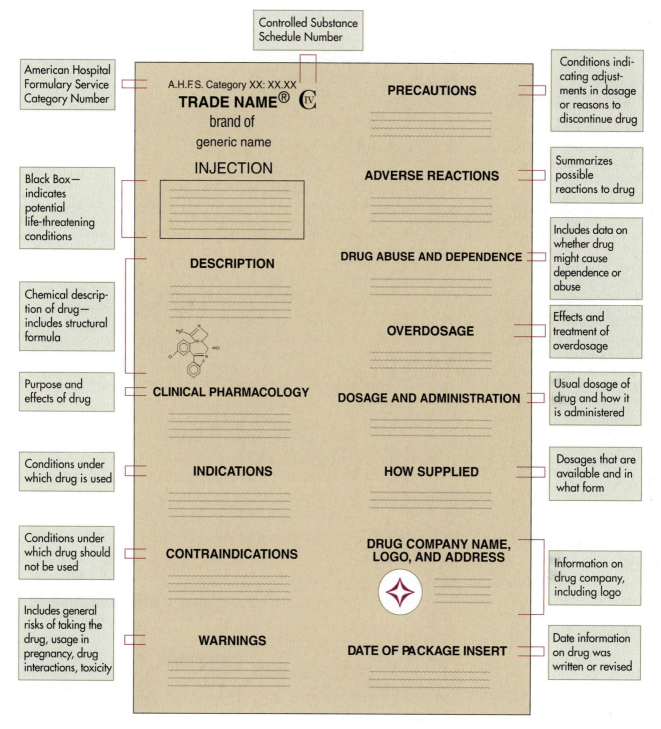

Controlled Substance Schedule Number

American Hospital Formulary Service Category Number

A.H.F.S. Category XX: XX.XX
TRADE NAME® Ⓒ IV
brand of
generic name
INJECTION

Black Box— indicates potential life-threatening conditions

Chemical description of drug— includes structural formula

Purpose and effects of drug

Conditions under which drug is used

Conditions under which drug should not be used

Includes general risks of taking the drug, usage in pregnancy, drug interactions, toxicity

DESCRIPTION

CLINICAL PHARMACOLOGY

INDICATIONS

CONTRAINDICATIONS

WARNINGS

PRECAUTIONS

ADVERSE REACTIONS

DRUG ABUSE AND DEPENDENCE

OVERDOSAGE

DOSAGE AND ADMINISTRATION

HOW SUPPLIED

DRUG COMPANY NAME, LOGO, AND ADDRESS

DATE OF PACKAGE INSERT

Conditions indicating adjustments in dosage or reasons to discontinue drug

Summarizes possible reactions to drug

Includes data on whether drug might cause dependence or abuse

Effects and treatment of overdosage

Usual dosage of drug and how it is administered

Dosages that are available and in what form

Information on drug company, including logo

Date information on drug was written or revised

figure 16–3

A package insert provides detailed information about the drug. This information is also found in the *PDR* and other drug references.

drugs, alternative medicines, a drug-drug interaction checker, an IV compatibility checker, health insurance Medicare Part D formularies, and an infectious disease treatment guide. A direct link is available to the Epocrates Web site to check on drug interactions and formulary references when entering medications into electronic health records such as SpringCharts®. Refer to Procedure 16–1 on page 443).

● ● ●

Why is it easy for a patient to be confused about her medications and how can you help the patient?

CHECKPOINT
LO 16.2

Working with the Health-Care Team

PHARMACEUTICAL REPRESENTATIVE

Duties and Skills

Pharmaceutical sales representatives typically work for drug manufacturers. Their objective is to market and sell medications. Their major duties include distributing information and medication samples to physicians and other authorized prescribers. In addition to the daily physician visits, reps may be required to attend sales meetings, conference calls, or training sessions with the management team. Drug reps may also do lunchtime presentations at physicians' offices, supplying lunch for the office staff and discussing the drug's indications, side effects, features, and benefits.

Educational Requirements

Pharmaceutical representatives typically have a bachelor's degree in a health-care field or business, and some training in health care. Before they can begin working for a company, they will receive intensive training and education about the company's products.

Workplace Settings

Pharmaceutical representatives may work out of a home-based office with a company car. They will visit the company they work for as well as health-care practices and pharmacies in a selected area, known as a territory.

The Pharmaceutical Representative as a Team Member

The pharmaceutical representative may schedule an appointment to visit the authorized prescriber. They may leave medication samples and literature. The pharmaceutical representative may need to sign in when he or she arrives. The policy varies depending upon your facility. In some cases the representative may be allowed in the drug storage area to inventory and provide more samples. In other facilities he or she may not be allowed to visit but rather just drop off pamphlets. In many facilities the representative provides vouchers for drug samples to be given to patients by the physician. It is important to know that according to the anti-kickback law, physicians may not exchange referrals for medication in exchange for payment.

For more information, visit the Web site of the following organization, which is available on the Online Learning Center at www.mhhe.com/houseradminmedassist.

National Association of Pharmaceutical Representatives

figure 16–4

PDRhealth, found at www.PDRhealth.com, is a consumer and patient Web site with up-to-date drug and patient information.

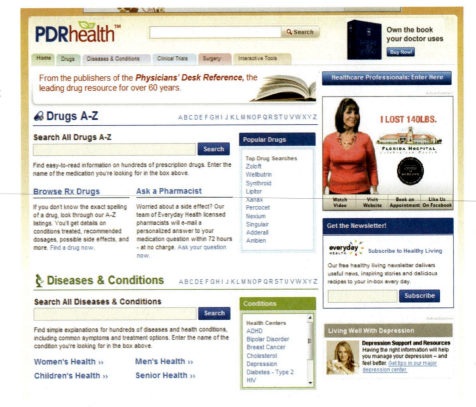

LO 16.3 Medication Laws and Controlled Substances

Federal laws related to medications were enacted as early as 1906. These laws are designed to minimize the abuse and improve the safety of drugs. They affect the handling, distribution, safety, and control of medications. In order to assist the physician in complying with these laws you will need to have a basic understanding of them.

Ensuring Drug Safety

Prior to the Pure Food and Drug Act of 1906, salesmen would travel from community to community selling products to the townspeople. These sales representatives would make promises about their products to the customer without any scientific or medical backing. One product might be used to cure a headache, reduce a fever, kill an infection, settle a stomachache, heal a scar, or make a woman fertile. These products may have been compounded in the back of a home or outdoors. The water may have been secured from a local stream or lake, and the quantities of the ingredients would vary in each batch. Often, the traveling salesmen would cross state lines to sell his products. The Pure Food and Drug Act required that drugs marketed in interstate commerce meet their professed minimal standards of strength, purity, and quality.

As a continuation of the Pure Food and Drug Act of 1906, the Food, Drug and Cosmetic Act of 1938 was enacted. Prior to 1938, the **Food and Drug Administration (FDA)** did not exist as we know of it today. Because of this act, the FDA was created. The FDA initiated a process that all new drug products must follow in order to be approved. This process included the performance of clinical studies, and required that drug manufacturers submit a New Drug Application (NDA) to the FDA before the drug entity would be approved. Any product on the market prior to 1938 did not need these requirements unless petitioned by the FDA. Vitamins and nutritional supplements are not required to undergo this process due to the Dietary Supplement Health and Education Act of 1994. The FDA ensures that drugs are pure, labeled accurately and completely, and do not mislead potential users.

The Durham-Humphrey Amendment of 1952 amended the Food, Drug and Cosmetic Act of 1938. It separated medications into legend (prescription) drugs and nonlegend (OTC) drugs. The Durham-Humphrey Amendment prevents a prescription from being refilled unless it was indicated on the original prescription or authorized from the prescriber. This amendment allows a prescriber to send the prescription to the patient's pharmacy of choice.

Food and Drug Administration (FDA)
An organization of the government that sets standards for all new drugs to be approved and sold.

Controlled Substances

A **controlled substance** is a drug or drug product that is categorized as potentially dangerous and addictive. The greater the potential for addiction and abuse, the more severe the limitations on prescribing it. Use of these controlled drugs is strictly regulated by federal laws. States, municipalities, and institutions must adhere to these laws but may also impose their own regulations.

The Comprehensive Drug Abuse Prevention and Control Act, also known as the Controlled Substances Act (CSA) of 1970, is the federal law that created the Drug Enforcement Administration (DEA) and strengthened drug enforcement authority. The CSA designates five schedules, according to degree of potential for a substance to be abused or used for a nontherapeutic effect. The five schedules and examples of substances in each are outlined in Table 16–2. Sometimes the DEA reclassifies drugs. For example, a Schedule III drug may eventually be found to be less addictive than originally determined and therefore reclassified as a Schedule IV drug.

controlled substance
A drug or drug product that is categorized as potentially dangerous and addictive and is strictly regulated by federal laws.

Controlled Substance Labeling The Controlled Substances Act also set up a labeling system to identify controlled substances. An example of this label

SCHEDULE	DESCRIPTION	PRESCRIPTION AND LEGAL CONSIDERATIONS	EXAMPLES
I	High abuse (no accepted medical use)	No prescriptions written	GHB, Heroin, LSD, Mescaline
II	High abuse (accepted medical use; abuse may lead to dependence)	• Must be written by DEA licensed physician and include DEA number • Multiple and/or special forms may be required • Must be filled in 7 days and cannot be refilled • Must be stored under lock and key • Dispensing records are kept for two years	Opioids—morphine (MS-Contin), meperidine (Demerol), fentanyl, barbiturates—secobarbital, amphetamines—methylphenidate (Ritalin®)
III	Lower abuse than Schedule I and II drugs (accepted medical use; abuse may lead to moderate dependence)	• Five refills are allowed in 6 months • Handwritten by physician • Can only be telephoned by physician	Anabolic steroids, hydrocodone/codeine (Vicodin®, Tylenol 3®), barbiturate—talbutal, paregoric
IV	Lower abuse than Schedule III drugs (accepted medical use; abuse may lead to limited dependence)	• Five refills are allowed in 6 months • Must be signed by physician • Refills may be authorized over the phone	Benzodiazepines—alprazolam (Xanax®), chloridiazepoxide (Librium®), diazepam (Valium®), zolpidem (Ambien®), pentazocine (Talwin®)
V	Lower abuse than Schedule IV drugs (accepted medical use; very limited physical dependence)	• Inventory records must be kept on these drugs • Five refills are allowed in 6 months • Must be signed by physician • Can only be telephoned by a physician or, in some states, a physician's representative	Antitussive and antidiarrheals that combine small amounts of opioids including (Lomotil®), (Kaolin), and (Robitussin A-C®)

Source: U.S. Department of Justice Drug Enforcement Administration Office of Diversion Control, www.deadiversion.usdoj.gov.

table 16-2

Schedule of Controlled Substances

figure 16-5

This symbol indicates that the drug is a Schedule II Controlled substance.

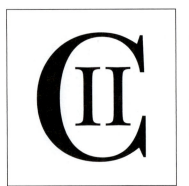

is shown in Figure 16–5. The large C means that the drug is a controlled substance, and the Roman numeral inside the C corresponds to the DEA schedule to which the drug belongs.

Doctor Registration   Under the CSA, doctors who administer, dispense, or prescribe any controlled substance must register with the DEA and must have a current state license to practice medicine and, if required, a state controlled substance license. They must also comply with all aspects of the CSA. According to the Controlled Substances Act, doctors may issue prescriptions for controlled drugs only in the schedules for which they are registered with the DEA. To register the doctor with the DEA, submit DEA Form 224 (Figure 16–6), called the Application for Registration under Controlled Substances Act of 1970. This form is available online. A fee must accompany the form when sent to the DEA.

Registration must be renewed every three years with DEA Form 224a. The renewal is done by mail or through the Internet through a log-in process. Doctors who administer or dispense drugs at more than one office must register at each location. Each registration is assigned a unique number, which indicates to suppliers and pharmacies that the doctor is properly authorized. Form 224 can be printed from the U.S. Department of Justice Web site. Renewal application (Form 224a) can be completed through registration at this site.

Ordering Drugs that Are Controlled Substances   If Schedule II drugs are needed for the practice, they must be ordered by using the U.S. Official Order Forms—Schedules I & II (DEA Form 222), which you can obtain from the DEA through the mail or Internet (Figure 16–7). One copy of the form goes to

figure 16–6

DEA Form 224 is used to register the physician with the Drug Enforcement Agency. It is usually completed online through the U.S. Department of Justice Drug Enforcement Administration Office of Diversion Control at www.deadiversion.usdoj.gov

Form-224	APPLICATION FOR REGISTRATION Under the Controlled Substances Act	APPROVED OMB NO 1117-0014 FORM DEA-224 (10-06) Previous editions are obsolete

INSTRUCTIONS

Save time—apply on-line at www.deadiversion.usdoj.gov

1. To apply by mail complete this application. Keep a copy for your records.
2. Print clearly, using black or blue ink, or use a typewriter.
3. Mail this form to the address provided in Section 7 or use enclosed envelope.
4. Include the correct payment amount. FEE IS NON-REFUNDABLE.
5. If you have any questions call 800-882-9539 prior to submitting your application.

IMPORTANT: DO NOT SEND THIS APPLICATION AND APPLY ON-LINE.

DEA OFFICIAL USE:

Do you have other DEA registration numbers?
☐ NO   ☐ YES

MAIL-TO ADDRESS   Please print mailing address changes to the right of the address in this box.

FEE FOR THREE (3) YEARS IS $551
FEE IS NON-REFUNDABLE

SECTION 1   APPLICANT IDENTIFICATION   ☐ Individual Registration   ☐ Business Registration

Name 1   (Last Name of individual -OR- Business or Facility Name)

Name 2   (First Name and Middle Name of individual -OR- Continuation of business name)

Street Address Line 1 (if applying for fee exemption, this must be address of the fee exempt institution)

Address Line 2

City   State   Zip Code

Business Phone Number   Point of Contact

Business Fax Number   Email Address

DEBT COLLECTION INFORMATION

Mandatory pursuant to Debt Collection Improvements Act

Social Security Number (*if registration is for individual*)

Provide **SSN** or **TIN**.
See additional information note #3 on page 4.

Tax Identification Number (*if registration is for business*)

FOR Practitioner or MLP ONLY:

Professional Degree: *select from list only*

Professional School:

Year of Graduation:

National Provider Identification:

Date of Birth (*MM-DD-YYYY*):

SECTION 2
BUSINESS ACTIVITY

Check one business activity box only

☐ Central Fill Pharmacy
☐ Retail Pharmacy
☐ Nursing Home
☐ Automated Dispensing System

☐ Practitioner
(DDS, DMD, DO, DPM, DVM, MD or PHD)
☐ Practitioner Military
(DDS, DMD, DO, DPM, DVM, MD or PHD)
☐ Mid-level Practitioner (MLP)
(DOM, HMD, MP, ND, NP, OD, PA, or RPH)
☐ Euthanasia Technician

☐ Ambulance Service
☐ Animal Shelter
☐ Hospital/Clinic
☐ Teaching Institution

FOR Automated Dispensing System (ADS) ONLY:

DEA Registration # of Retail Pharmacy for this ADS

An ADS is automatically fee-exempt.
Skip Section 6 and Section 7 on page 2.
You must attach a notarized affidavit.

SECTION 3
DRUG SCHEDULES

Check all that apply

☐ Schedule II Narcotic
☐ Schedule II Non-Narcotic

☐ Schedule III Narcotic
☐ Schedule III Non-Narcotic

☐ Schedule IV
☐ Schedule V

(Continued)

figure 16-6 *(Concluded)*

SECTION 4

STATE LICENSE(S)

Be sure to include both state license numbers if applicable

You MUST be currently authorized to prescribe, distribute, dispense, conduct research, or otherwise handle the controlled substances in the schedules for which you are applying under the laws of the **state** or jurisdiction in which you are operating or propose to operate.

State License Number (required)

Expiration Date (required)   /   /
MM - DD - YYYY

What state was this license issued in? _____

State Controlled Substance License Number (if required)

Expiration Date   /   /
MM - DD - YYYY

What state was this license issued in? _____

SECTION 5

LIABILITY

IMPORTANT

All questions in this section must be answered.

1. Has the applicant ever been **convicted of a crime** in connection with controlled substance(s) under state or federal law, or is any such action pending?   YES ☐ NO ☐

   Date(s) of incident MM-DD-YYYY: ☐☐ – ☐☐ – ☐☐☐☐

2. Has the applicant ever surrendered (for cause) or had a **federal** controlled substance registration revoked, suspended, restricted, or denied, or is any such action pending?   YES ☐ NO ☐

   Date(s) of incident MM-DD-YYYY: ☐☐ – ☐☐ – ☐☐☐☐

3. Has the applicant ever surrendered (for cause) or had a **state** professional license or controlled substance registration revoked, suspended, denied, restricted, or placed on probation, or is any such action pending?   YES ☐ NO ☐

   Date(s) of incident MM-DD-YYYY: ☐☐ – ☐☐ – ☐☐☐☐

4. If the applicant is a **corporation** (other than a corporation whose stock is owned and traded by the public), association, partnership, or pharmacy, has any officer, partner, stockholder, or proprietor been **convicted of a crime** in connection with controlled substance(s) under state or federal law, or ever surrendered, for cause, or had a **federal** controlled substance registration revoked, suspended, restricted, denied, or ever had a **state** professional license or controlled substance registration revoked, suspended, denied, restricted or placed on probation, or is any such action pending?   YES ☐ NO ☐

   Date(s) of incident MM-DD-YYYY: ☐☐ – ☐☐ – ☐☐☐☐   *Note: If question 4 does not apply to you, be sure to mark 'NO'. It will slow down processing of your application if you leave it blank.*

EXPLANATION OF "YES" ANSWERS

Applicants who have answered "YES" to any of the four questions above **must provide a statement to explain each "YES" answer.**

Use this space or attach a separate sheet and return with application

Liability question # _____

Location(s) of incident: _____

Nature of incident:

Disposition of incident:

SECTION 6 EXEMPTION FROM APPLICATION FEE

☐ Check this box if the applicant is a federal, state, or local government official or institution. Does not apply to contractor-operated institutions.

Business or Facility Name of Fee Exempt Institution. **Be sure to enter the address of this exempt institution in Section 1.**

The undersigned hereby certifies that the applicant named hereon is a federal, state or local government official or institution, and is exempt from payment of the application fee.

FEE EXEMPT CERTIFIER

Provide the name and phone number of the certifying official

Signature of certifying official (other than applicant)   Date

Print or type name and title of certifying official   Telephone No. (required for verification)

SECTION 7

METHOD OF PAYMENT

Check one form of payment only

Sign if paying by credit card

☐ Check   Make check payable to: **Drug Enforcement Administration**
See page 4 of instructions for important information.

☐ American Express   ☐ Discover   ☐ Master Card   ☐ Visa

Credit Card Number   Expiration Date

Signature of Card Holder

Printed Name of Card Holder

Mail this form with payment to:

U.S. Department of Justice
Drug Enforcement Administration
P.O. Box 28083
Washington, DC 20038-8083

FEE IS NON-REFUNDABLE

SECTION 8

APPLICANTS SIGNATURE

Sign in ink

I certify that the foregoing information furnished on this application is true and correct.

Signature of applicant (sign in ink)   Date

Print or type name and title of applicant

WARNING: Section 843(a)(4)(A) of Title 21, United States Code states that any person who knowingly or intentionally furnishes false or fraudulent information in this application is subject to imprisonment for not more than four years, a fine of not more than $30,000.00 or both.

---

the DEA for overall surveillance of drug distribution. In most states this form can be used to obtain Schedule II drugs from the normal drug supplier. When Schedule II drugs are ordered from an out-of-state company, some states require the doctor to send a copy of the purchase agreement (not the DEA Form 222) to

DEA Form-222 (Oct. 1992)

U.S. OFFICIAL ORDER FORMS - SCHEDULES I & II
Drug Enforcement Administration
SUPPLIER'S Copy 1

See Reverse of PURCHASER'S Copy for Instructions

No order form may be issued for Schedule I and II substances unless a completed application form has been received. (21 CFR 1305.04).

OMB APPROVAL No. 1117-0010

To: (Name of Supplier)

Street Address

Address

City ___ State

Date (MM-DD-YYYY) ___ Suppliers DEA Registration No.

To Be Filled in By PURCHASER

Line No.	No. of Packages	Size of Package	Name of Item
1			
2			
3			
4			
5			
6			
7			
8			
9			
10			

To Be Filled in By SUPPLIER

National Drug Code	Packages Shipped	Date Shipped

◄ LAST LINE COMPLETED   *(MUST BE 10 OR LESS)*

Signature of PURCHASER or Attorney or Agent

Date Issued ___

Schedules

Registered As a

No. of This Order Form

DEA Registration No.

Name and Address of Registrant

figure 16–7

DEA Form 222 is used to order Schedule II drugs. This renewal can be completed online.

the state attorney general's office within 24 hours of placing the order. Schedules III through V drugs require less complicated ordering. They require only the doctor's DEA registration number.

Drug Security Always store drugs that are controlled substances in a locked cabinet or safe. If required by state law, use double locks for opioids. The doctor or other licensed practitioner, such as a nurse, should keep the key(s) at all times. If controlled drugs are stolen from the doctor's office, call the regional DEA office at once. Also notify the state bureau of narcotic enforcement and

the local police. File all reports required by the DEA and other agencies as a follow-up.

Record Keeping   A doctor who administers or dispenses (as opposed to prescribing) controlled drugs to patients must maintain two types of records: dispensing records and inventory records. Note that these requirements don't apply to doctors who only prescribe drugs but who do not administer or dispense controlled drugs.

Dispensing Records   The dispensing record for Schedule II drugs must be kept separate from the patient's regular medical record. Each time a drug is administered or dispensed, the doctor must note the date, the patient's name and address, the drug, and the quantity dispensed. The dispensing record for Schedules III through V drugs must include the same information. The record for these drugs may be kept in the patient's medical record unless the doctor charges for the drugs dispensed. All dispensing records must be kept for two years and are subject to inspection by the DEA.

Inventory Records   A doctor who regularly dispenses controlled drugs must also keep inventory records of all stock on hand. This regulation applies to all scheduled drugs. To take an inventory, count the amount of each drug on hand. Compare this amount with the amount of the drug ordered and the amount dispensed to patients. The controlled drug inventory must be repeated every two years. You must include copies of invoices from drug suppliers in the inventory record. All inventories and records of Schedule II drugs must be kept separate from other records. Inventories and records of other controlled drugs must be separate or easily retrievable from ordinary business and professional records. All records on controlled drugs must be retained for two years and made available for inspection and copying by DEA officials if requested.

Disposing of Drugs   If the doctor asks you to dispose of any outdated, non-controlled drugs, you will most likely use the disposal company that takes your biohazardous waste. The DEA does not allow businesses to flush any medications, and medications should not be placed in the trash. If the doctor needs to dispose of controlled drugs, such as expired samples, obtain DEA Form 41 (Figure 16–8), called Registrants Inventory of Drugs Surrendered, which is available from the nearest DEA office or on the Internet. Complete the form in quadruplicate, have the doctor sign it, and call the DEA to obtain instructions for disposal of the drugs. If you must ship the drugs, use registered mail. After the drugs have been destroyed, the DEA will issue the doctor a receipt, which you should keep in a safe place.

If doctors terminate their medical practice, they must return their DEA registration certificate and any unused copies of DEA Form 222 to the nearest DEA office. To prevent unauthorized use, write the word *VOID* across the front of these forms. Regional DEA offices will tell doctors how to dispose of any remaining controlled drugs. Refer to Procedure 16–2, Assist the Authorized Prescriber in Complying with the Controlled Substances Act of 1970, on page 443 at the end of this chapter.

CHECKPOINT
LO 16.3

What forms are completed as part of helping a physician comply with the Controlled Substances Act of 1970?

LO 16.4 Prescriptions

Any drug that is not available over the counter requires a prescription. As an administrative medical assistant, you should be able to interpret a prescription in order to discuss it with the authorized prescriber, patient, or pharmacist.

U.S. Department of Justice/Drug Enforcement Administration
REGISTRANTS INVENTORY OF DRUGS SURRENDERED

PACKAGE NO.

The following schedule is an inventory of controlled substances which is hereby surrendered to you for proper disposition.

FROM: *(Include Name, Street, City, State and ZIP Code in space provided below.)*

Signature of applicant or authorized agent

Registrant's DEA Number

Registrant's Telephone Number

NOTE: CERTIFIED MAIL (Return Receipt Requested) IS REQUIRED FOR SHIPMENTS OF DRUGS VIA U.S. POSTAL SERVICE. See instructions on reverse (page 2) of form.

NAME OF DRUG OR PREPARATION Registrants will fill in Columns 1, 2, 3, and 4 ONLY.	Number of Containers	CONTENTS (Number of grams, tablets, ounces or other units per container)	Controlled Substance Content, (Each Unit)	FOR DEA USE ONLY		
				DISPOSITION	QUANTITY	
					GMS.	MGS.
1	*2*	*3*	*4*	*5*	*6*	*7*
1						
2						
3						
4						
5						
6						
23						
24						

The controlled substances surrendered in accordance with Title 21 of the Code of Federal Regulations, Section 1307.21, have been received in _____ packages purporting to contain the drugs listed on this inventory and have been: **(1) Forwarded tape-sealed without opening; (2) Destroyed as indicated and the remainder forwarded tape-sealed after verifying contents; (3) Forwarded tape-sealed after verifying contents.

DATE _____   DESTROYED BY: _____

**Strike out lines not applicable.   WITNESSED BY: _____

INSTRUCTIONS

1. List the name of the drug in column 1, the number of containers in column 2, the size of each container in column 3, and in column 4 the controlled substance content of each unit described in column 3; e.g., morphine sulfate tabs., 3 pkgs., 100 tabs., 1/4 gr. (16 mg.) or morphine sulfate tabs., 1 pkg., 83 tabs., 1/2 gr. (32 mg.), etc.
2. All packages included on a single line should be identical in name, content and controlled substance strength.
3. Prepare this form in quadruplicate. Mail two (2) copies of this form to the Special Agent in Charge, under separate cover. Enclose one additional copy in the shipment with the drugs. Retain one copy for your records. One copy will be returned to you as a receipt. No further receipt will be furnished to you unless specifically requested. Any further inquiries concerning these drugs should be addressed to the DEA District Office which serves your area.
4. There is no provision for payment for drugs surrendered. This is merely a service rendered to registrants enabling them to clear their stocks and records of unwanted items.
5. Drugs should be shipped tape-sealed via prepaid express or certified mail (**return receipt requested**) to Special Agent in Charge, Drug Enforcement Administration, of the DEA District Office which serves your area.

PRIVACY ACT INFORMATION

AUTHORITY: Section 307 of the Controlled Substances Act of 1970 (PL 91-513).
PURPOSE: To document the surrender of controlled substances which have been forwarded by registrants to DEA for disposal.
ROUTINE USES: This form is required by Federal Regulations for the surrender of unwanted Controlled Substances. Disclosures of information from this system are made to the following categories of users for the purposes stated.
   A. Other Federal law enforcement and regulatory agencies for law enforcement and regulatory purposes.
   B. State and local law enforcement and regulatory agencies for law enforcement and regulatory purposes.
EFFECT: Failure to document the surrender of unwanted Controlled Substances may result in prosecution for violation of the Controlled Substances Act.

Under the Paperwork Reduction Act, a person is not required to respond to a collection of information unless it displays a currently valid OMB control number. Public reporting burden for this collection of information is estimated to average 30 minutes per response, including the time for reviewing instructions, searching existing data sources, gathering and maintaining the data needed, and completing and reviewing the collection of information. Send comments regarding this burden estimate or any other aspect of this collection of information, including suggestions for reducing this burden, to the Drug Enforcement Administration, FOI and Records Management Section, Washington, D.C. 20537; and to the Office of Management and Budget, Paperwork Reduction Project no. 1117-0007, Washington, D.C. 20503.

You must become familiar with the doctor's style of writing or the electronic prescription process at your facility. In addition, you may be responsible for managing a prescription renewal.

figure 16–8

DEA Form 41 is used to report disposal of controlled drugs.

Interpreting a Prescription

Prescriptions for new or renewed medications are completed or approved by the physician. A prescription has specific parts that must be present before

it can be filled or renewed (Figure 16–9). The basic components of a prescription are:

1. *Prescriber information:* Name, address, telephone number, and other information identifying the prescriber.
2. *Patient information:* Date, the patient's full name, date of birth, and address and other information to identify the patient.
3. *Medication prescribed:* Includes generic or brand name, strength, and quantity. This is sometimes called the inscription and is found after the Rx.
4. *Subscription:* Instructions to the pharmacist dispensing the medication. This may include generic substitution and refill authorization.
5. *Signa:* Also known as the transcription; refers to patient instructions. These instructions generally follow the abbreviation Sig, which means *mark.*
6. *Signature:* Prescriber's signature for handwritten prescriptions. The prescriber's signature must be in ink but it cannot be a stamped signature. A digital signature is used if it is secure, otherwise the prescription will need to be printed or otherwise authorized.
7. *DEA number:* This is required for prescriptions of Schedules II, III, IV, and V medications only.

Many terms and abbreviations are used in prescriptions. See Table 16–3 for examples. Abbreviations for drug names should not be used because there are similar abbreviations for multiple drugs. Certain abbreviations should not be used because they tend to cause errors. See Appendix III on page 727. A medical assistant must be able to interpret a prescription with accuracy. Refer to Procedure 16–3, Interpret a Prescription, located on page 444.

figure 16–9

A prescription must include all the parts.

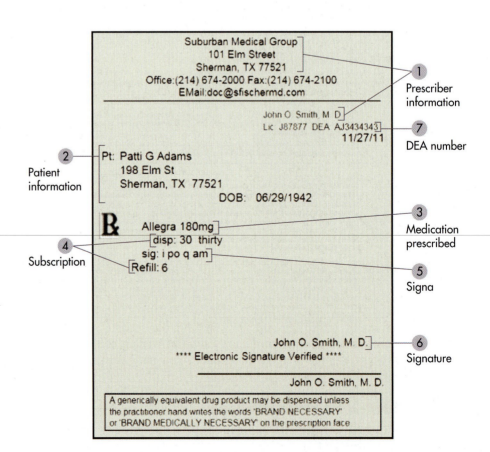

table 16–3

Abbreviations Used in Prescriptions

ABBREVIATION	MEANING	ABBREVIATION	MEANING
a	Before	min	Minute, minimum
aa	Of each	mL	Milliliters
ac	Before meals	mm	Millimeters
AM	Morning	neb	Nebulizer
amp	Ampule	noct	Night
apl	Applicatorful	NPO	Nothing by mouth
aq	Water	nr	No refills
bid	Twice daily	oz	Ounce
c̄	With	pc	After meals
cap	Capsule	per	By means of; through
cd	Cycle day (menstrual cycle)	PM	Evening or nighttime
cmpd	Compound	po, PO	By mouth
cr	Cream	PR, pr	Rectally
d	Daily or day	q	Every
DAW	Dispense as written (no generic)	qam	Every morning
disp	Dispense	q4h	Every 4 hours
ds	Double strength	qid	Four times daily
dx	Diagnosis	qs	Sufficient amount
elix	Elixir	r, rec	Rectally
eq	Equivalent	rept	Repeat
g, gm	Gram	rf	Refill(s)
gen	Generic	s	Without
gr	Grain (60 to 65 mg)	subcut	Subcutaneously
gtt	Drop(s)	stat	Immediately
h, hr	Hour	sup	Suppository
H_2O	Water	susp	Suspension
IM	Intramuscularly	sx	Symptoms
inj	Inject, injection	syr	Syrup
IV	Intravenously	tab	Tablet(s)
kg	Kilogram	tsp	Teaspoon
L	Liter	tbsp	Tablespoon
liq	Liquid	tx	Treatment
lot	Lotion	ud, utd	As directed
MDI	Metered dose inhaler	ung	Ointment
mEq	Milliequivalent	vag	Vaginally, into vagina
mg	Milligram(s)	YO	Years old

Prescription Security

With the advent of electronically printed prescriptions and e-prescribing, prescription blanks are becoming a thing of the past. They are usually preprinted with the doctor's name, address, telephone number, state license number, and DEA registration number. Most blanks also provide space for writing the patient's name and address, the date, and other information. To prevent unauthorized use of prescription blanks, never leave them unattended.

If something about any type of prescription arouses suspicion, the pharmacist who receives it may call the doctor's office to verify it. You should be able to check the patient's records and tell the pharmacist whether the doctor wrote a prescription for that patient. If the prescription is a forgery, notify the doctor and, if she gives you authorization, notify the DEA.

The doctor should not use a prescription to obtain drugs for office stock. When the office needs drugs (other than Schedule II drugs), they should be obtained from a pharmacy with an order form. When the drugs are delivered, you should receive an invoice from the pharmacist.

Managing a Prescription Renewal

e-prescribing
When prescription medication orders are entered electronically and transmitted directly to a pharmacy to be filled.

Prescriptions may be typed or handwritten on a prescription blank. They may also be entered electronically and printed, or entered electronically and transmitted directly to a pharmacy. When the information is entered electronically and transmitted directly this is known as **e-prescribing.** With e-prescribing, the medication information is received at the pharmacy and the actual prescription is never in the hands of the patient.

If requested by the doctor, you may telephone a new or renewal prescription to the patient's pharmacy. You may not, however, telephone a prescription for a Schedule II drug. In an emergency situation, when a patient needs a drug immediately and no alternative is available, the doctor may telephone a prescription for a Schedule II drug. The amount must be limited to the period of emergency, and a written prescription must be sent to the pharmacist within 72 hours. The pharmacist must notify the DEA if a written or electronic prescription does not arrive within the specified time. Requests for telephone prescription renewals occur on a daily basis from patients. You may be asked to call these refills into the pharmacy. The renewal requests may be called into the receptionist or left on a designated phone mail system. It is the medical assistant's responsibility to handle the prescription renewals/refills in an appropriate manner. Refer to Procedure 16–4, Manage a Prescription Refill, on page 444.

CHECKPOINT
LO 16.4

Explain how e-prescribing improves prescription security.

LO 16.5 Managing Medical Reports

consultation
When a health-care professional evaluates a patient (consults) at the request of another health care professional.

In the paper or electronic chart, certain items must be ordered or recorded, tracked, and maintained for easy access and review. For example, the report from a **consultation** or referral of another physician, a post-operative surgical report, or diagnostic and laboratory test results must be recorded when ordered and make their way back to the patient's chart when complete. To help keep track of pending tests, reports, and their results, a log is maintained for tests, referrals, and procedures ordered and performed outside of the facility. This may be handwritten or part of your electronic health records data.

If the office is transitioning to EHR, then there may be electronic as well as paper files. This type of hybrid environment requires that the paper files become accessible electronically. This is usually done through scanning of paper documents. Once the paper file is electronic, it will need to be added, inserted, or attached to the electronic record. How this is done depends upon the EHR program you are using. In the hybrid environment, an accurate log prevents the loss of important results that are provided in paper format.

Reports and Referrals

A consultation is a type of medical report that becomes part of the patient's chart. It is a permanent, legal document regarding the results of an examination and recommended treatment for a patient. The results may be in the form of a letter or report. A consultation report occurs when a patient is referred to another practitioner. Referrals may be made to another physician, such as a surgeon, a physical therapist, a nutritionist, or other licensed practitioners.

When a referral is made, make sure the patient understands whether the referring physician's staff will make the appointment and notify the patient, or whether the patient must call to set up the appointment. Document in the chart that the patient was referred and the time and date of the appointment, and follow up with the specialist to verify that the appointment was scheduled and kept. If a paper referral is necessary, make sure an extra copy is placed in the patient's chart. (Figure 16–10) Make sure the referring physician knows when the report has been returned and is placed on the chart.

Tests

When a laboratory test is ordered you may be required to complete some type of requisition form (Figure 16–11). A **requisition** is simply an order for a test or procedure. The form must be completed properly. Missing information can lead to improper testing or lost results. If a specimen is collected, the completed form should be included with the specimen collected or sent with the patient to the laboratory.

The following information is typically included as part of a requisition or order for diagnostic or laboratory tests:

- Patient's full name, sex, date of birth, and address
- Patient's insurance information
- Physician's name, address, and phone number
- Test

EHR readiness

E-Prescribing

On July 15, 2008, the **Medicare Improvements for Patients and Providers Act of 2008 (MIPPA)** was enacted by Congress and became law. MIPPA provides positive incentives for practitioners who use e-prescribing in 2009 through 2013. Electronic prescribing is intended to bring greater safety to patients by providing for automatic drug and allergy interaction checking and the elimination of medication errors due to poor handwriting. E-prescribing is also designed to bring a greater efficiency to the prescribing process for providers. It will dramatically decrease communication from pharmacies requesting clarification of prescriptions.

Surescripts is the national clearinghouse for e-prescribing. The company electronically connects physicians, pharmacists, and payers nationwide enabling them to exchange health information and prescribe without paper. Surescripts collaborates with national EHR vendors, pharmacies, and health plans to support physicians using EHR software. With this network in place, health-care providers can electronically access prescription information from pharmacies, health plans, and other providers to see the patient's total prescription history from all sources. Through e-prescribing, EHRs are providing meaningful improvements in cost, quality, and patient safety. For example, when a medication is taken off the market, a record of all patients who have been prescribed this medication can be queried electronically and the physicians and patients notified of the change.

Medicare Improvements for Patients and Providers Act of 2008 (MIPPA)
Law enacted in 2008 that among other things provides positive incentives for physicians to use e-prescribing.

Surescripts
The national clearinghouse for e-prescribing. This company electronically connects physicians, pharmacists, and payers nationwide enabling them to exchange health information and prescribe without paper. Surescripts collaborates with national EHR vendors, pharmacies, and health plans to support physicians using EHR software.

requisition
A formal request from a staff member or doctor for the purchase of equipment or supplies.

REQUEST FOR SERVICES

Facility: _____

Provider: _____

Address: _____

_____

Phone: _____ Fax: _____

PATIENT INFORMATION

Patient name _____ TCC# _____

Date of Birth _____ Home Phone _____ Alt Phone _____

REASON FOR REQUEST

Reason for request / Specific question(s) to be answered:

1. _____

2. _____

History / Symptoms / Specific question(s) to be answered: _____

_____

_____

_____

☐ Check here if additional clinical information is included with this request.

SERVICES REQUESTED

☐ Abnormal Weight Gain
☐ Adolescent Medicine/Teen Health Center
☐ Aerodigestive
☐ Allergy Clinic
☐ Audology (Hearing)
☐ Behavioral Medcine & Clinical Psychology
☐ Brachial Plexus Clinic
☐ Breast Feeding Clinic
☐ Cardiology
☐ Cardiothoracic Surgery
☐ Cerebral Palsy Center
☐ Chronic Pain Management
☐ Colorectal Surgery
☐ Comprehensive Weight Management Center
☐ Craniofacial Center
☐ Dentistry
☐ Dermatology

☐ Developmental & Behavioral Pediatrics
☐ Diabetes
☐ Diagnostic Clinic
☐ Endocrinology
☐ ENT (Otolaryngology)
☐ Feeding Team
☐ Fetal Surgery
☐ Gastroenterology-GI
☐ Gynecology
☐ Healthworks
☐ Hemangioma & Vascular Malformation Team
☐ Hematology-Oncology
☐ Human Genetics
☐ Hypertension / Cholesterol Clinic
☐ Infectious Diseases-ID
☐ International Adoption Center-IAC
☐ Nephrology

☐ Neurology
☐ Neurosurgery
☐ Nutrition'
☐ Ophthalmology / Eye Clinic
☐ Orthopaedics
☐ Physical Medicine & Rehabilitation
☐ Plastic Surgery
☐ Psychiatry
☐ Pulmonary Medicine
☐ Rheumatology
☐ Safe & Healthy Children Center
☐ Sleep Center
☐ Sports Medicine
☐ Surgery (General & Thoracic Surgery)
☐ Urology
☐ Other_____

REQUESTING PRACTITIONER / GROUP

TOTAL CARE CLINIC, PC
342 East Park Blvd.
Futon, XY 12345-6789
www.totalcareclinic.org

Physician Name _____

Tel: 521-234-0001
Fax: 521-234-0002

figure 16–10

Example referral form.

- Preliminary diagnosis
- Additional clinical information (fasting, medications, time of specimen collection, etc.)

If a specimen accompanies the form it should include the source of the specimen and the date and time the specimen was collected. If the requisition is

Account Information

TCC Account Number		
Patient Account Number		
Address - Street		
City	State	ZIP Code

Ship to: Total Care Laboratories
1400 West Park Blvd.
Funton, XY 12345-6789

TCC Internal Use

Place Barcode Label Here

Patient Information

Patient Name (Print Clearly)-Last	First	Middle Initial	Gender ☐ Male ☐ Female	Birth Date (mm/dd/yyyy)	Age
Patient Number	Sample or Hospital Number		Collection Date (mm/dd/yyyy)		Collection Time ☐ AM ☐ PM
Referring Physician (Print Clearly)-Last	First	Middle Initial	Phone or Fax (Area Code and Number)		

Call Back information - Complete ONLY if CALL BACK is required

Phone of Fax for Call Back - Select One ☐ Phone ☐ Fax - number given must be from a fax machine that complies with applicable HIPAA regulations	Phone or Fax (Area Code and Number)

Test(s) Requested

Test Number	Test Name
Source/ Specimen Type	If Urine TV-

figure 16-11

A requisition form is used when tests are ordered to be performed at another facility.

---

for a diagnostic test such as an ECG or mammogram, it should include special instructions for the patient.

Once a laboratory test is complete, the results in the form of a laboratory report will need to be added to the patient chart. A laboratory report will identify the tests completed, the normal values and the patient's result (Figure 16-12). If the patient's result is outside of the normal value, this information is flagged so that the physician is notified and the patient can be contacted if necessary. Laboratory imaging and other medical tests can be easily ordered and processed with electronic health records such as SpringCharts. Refer to Procedure 16-5, Electronically Order and Track Medical Test Results.

When reports from diagnostic tests are received from another facility, they need to be included in the patient's chart. Again, the physician ordering the tests must be notified that the results have been received. With electronic health records, when the results come from another facility with a compatible electronic interface, they can be imported into the record. If the results are paper or from an incompatible electronic interface, they may need to be converted to a compatible file type or scanned and added to the patient's chart.

If all facilities were connected electronically, how would it make it easier to order and track laboratory and diagnostic tests?

CHECKPOINT
LO 16.5

figure 16-12

Report of laboratory results.

Morris A. Turner, MD

TCP LAB

Total Care Laboratories
1400 West Park Blvd.
Funton, XY 12345-6789

C.L.I.A. #21-1862

WELLS, KARLA	09/12/12	09/12/12	09/13/12
Patient Name	Date Drawn	Date Received	Date of Report

F 43
Sex Age

Linda F. Wiley, PA-C
342 East Park Blvd.
Funton, XY 12345-6789

23341
ID Number

67294
Account Number

166241809
Patient ID/Soc. Sec. Number

897211
Specimen Number

TEST NAME	RESULT ABNORMAL	RESULT NORMAL	UNITS	REFERENCE RANGE
CHEM-SCREEN PANEL				
GLUCOSE		76.0	MG/DL	65.0–115
SODIUM		139.0	MMOL/L	134–143
POTASSIUM		4.00	MMOL/L	3.60–5.10
CHLORIDE		107.0	MMOL/L	96.0–107
BUN		17.0	MG/DL	6.00–19.0
BUN/CREATININE RATIO		14.2		
URIC ACID		4.30	MG/DL	2.20–6.20
PHOSPHATE		2.40	MG/DL	2.40–4.50
CALCIUM		9.50	MG/DL	8.60–10.0
MAGNESIUM		1.75	MEG/L	1.40–2.00
CHOLESTEROL	237.0		MG/DL	130–200
CHOL. PERCENTILE	90.0		PERCENTILE	1.00–75.0
HDL CHOLESTEROL	41.0		MG/DL	48.0–89.0
CHOL./HDL RATIO		5.80		
LDL CHOL., CALCULATED	175.0		MG/DL	65.5–130
TRIGLYCERIDES		104.0	MG/DL	00.0–200
TOTAL PROTEIN		6.60	GM/DL	6.40–8.00
ALBUMIN		4.10	GM/DL	3.70–4.80
GLOBULIN		2.50	GM/DL	2.20–3.60
ALB/GLOB RATIO		1.64		1.10–2.10
TOTAL BILIRUBIN		0.80	MG/DL	0.20–1.30
DIRECT BILIRUBIN		0.15	MG/DL	0.00–0.20
ALK. PHOSPHATASE		44.0	UNITS/L	25.0–125
G-GLUTAMYL TRANSPEP.		8.00	UNITS/L	1.00–63.0
AST (SGOT)		21.0	IU/L	1.00–40.0
ALT (SGPT)		14.0	IU/L	1.00–50.0
LD		134.0	IU/L	90.0–250
IRON		130.0	MCG/DL	35.0–180

Procedure 16–1   Record Medications in a Patient's Chart

GOAL To create and/or maintain a current list of medications in the patient's chart

MATERIALS Medication list and electronic health record such as SpringCharts

METHOD
1. Obtain a list of current medications the patient is taking from the patient or from the written or electronic chart.
2. Verify the spelling of each medication before adding it to the printed health record. This can be done while entering into the electronic health record through an electronic resource.
3. Identify the amount the patient takes of each medication, for example "1 tablet."
4. Include how often and/or when the patient takes the medication, for example, "daily" or "3 times a day with meals."
5. Enter the patient electronic chart and select the medication link.
6. Perform a search for the desired medication and select. Most programs have a database or a direct link to a medication site such as Epocrates to check on drug interactions and formulary references.
7. Enter new medications and edit any existing medications according to the directions for the EHR program you are using.
8. Check and verify all medication entries before exiting the program.

Procedure 16–2   Assist the Authorized Prescriber in Complying with the Controlled Substances Act of 1970

GOAL To comply with the Controlled Substances Act of 1970

MATERIALS Access to DEA forms 224, 224a, 222, and 41 and ability to complete them with either pen or Internet access.

METHOD
1. Use DEA Form 224 (shown in Figure 16–6) to register the physician with the Drug Enforcement Administration. Be sure to register each office location at which the physician administers or dispenses drugs covered under Schedules II through V.
2. Renew all registrations every three years using DEA Form 224a.
   a. Calculate a period of three years from the date of the original registration or the most recent renewal. Note that date as the expiration date of the physician's DEA registration.
   b. Subtract 45 days from the expiration date and mark this date on the calendar or create a reminder in your electronic calendar program.
   c. Before the expiration deadline, complete the DEA form and have the physician sign it. Prepare or request a check for the fee.
   d. For paper forms, submit the original and one copy of the completed form with the appropriate fee to the DEA so that it will arrive before the deadline. Keep one copy for the office records.
   e. Applicants are encouraged to use the online forms system for electronic renewal. Search the Internet for DEA Form 224A. Note: The DEA form

Web site is for renewals only and Internet renewals should not be done if you have already sent a paper application or renewal. Update and complete the areas of the form including Personal Information, Activity, State License(s), Background Information, Payment, and Confirmation. You will be able to print copies of the form once completed.

3. Order Schedule II drugs using DEA Form 222, shown in Figure 16–7, as instructed by the physician. (Stocks of these drugs should be kept to a minimum.) Accurate instruction from the physician is necessary to ensure safety.

4. Include the physician's DEA registration number on every prescription for a drug in Schedules II through V or the prescriptions will not be accepted by the pharmacy.

5. Complete an inventory of all drugs in Schedules II through V every two years (as permitted in your state; this task may be reserved to other health-care professionals).

6. Store all drugs in Schedules II through V in a secure, locked safe or cabinet (as permitted in your state) to prevent theft.

7. Keep accurate dispensing and inventory records for at least two years.

8. Dispose of expired or unused drugs according to the DEA regulations. Always complete DEA Form 41 (shown in Figure 16–8) when disposing of controlled drugs.

Procedure 16–3 Interpret a Prescription

GOAL To read and accurately interpret a prescription

MATERIALS Prescription, Abbreviations Used in Prescriptions Table 16–3, method of recording (pen or electronic)

METHOD
1. Verify the prescriber information. This is especially important in a multi-physician practice or electronic health record.

2. Ensure patient information is accurate including correct spelling of name, date of birth, and address. For written prescriptions, check legibility.

3. Confirm the date of the prescription.

4. Check the medication name and double-check spelling.

5. Verify that instructions to the pharmacist are complete and include refill authorization and generic substitution.

6. Translate the instructions to the patient using Table 16–3.

7. Make sure that the prescription is signed in ink for handwritten prescriptions and digitally for electronic prescriptions.

Procedure 16–4 Manage a Prescription Refill

GOAL To ensure a complete and accurate prescription is received by the patient

MATERIALS Telephone, appropriate phone numbers, message pad or prescription refill request form, pen, and patient chart with prescription order

METHOD

1. Take the message from the call or the message system. For the prescription to be complete, you must obtain the patient's name, date of birth, phone number, pharmacy name and/or phone number, medication, and dosage.

2. Follow your facility policy regarding prescription renewals. Typically, the prescription is usually called into the pharmacy the day it is requested. An example policy may be posted at the facility and may state "Nonemergency prescription refill requests must be made during regular business hours. Please allow 24 hours for processing."

3. Communicate the policy to the patient. You should know the policy and let the patient know the policy and the time when the refills will be reviewed. For example, you might state, "Dr. Alexander will review the prescription between patients and it will be telephoned within one hour to the pharmacy. I will call you back if there is a problem."

4. Obtain the patient's chart or reference the electronic chart to verify you have the correct patient and that the patient is currently taking the medication. Check the patient's list of medications, which are usually part of the chart.

5. Give the prescription refill request and the chart to the physician or prescriber. Do not give a prescription refill request to the physician without the chart or chart access information. Wait for an authorization from the physician before you proceed.

6. Once the physician authorizes the prescription, prepare to call the pharmacy with the renewal information. Be certain to have the physician order, the patient's chart, and the refill request in front of you when you make the call. The request should include the name of the drug, the drug dosage, the frequency and mode of administration, the number of refills authorized, and the name and phone number of the pharmacy.

7. Telephone the pharmacy. Since only an identified representative from a medical practice can authorize a refill, you must identify yourself by name, the practice name, and the doctor's name.

8. State the purpose of the call. (Example: "I am calling to authorize a prescription refill for a patient.")

9. Identify the patient. Include the patient's name, date of birth, address, and phone number. It is essential that the correct drug be prescribed for the correct patient according to doctor's order.

10. Identify the drug including the strength of the drug (spelling the name when necessary), the dosage, the frequency and mode of administration, and any other special instructions or changes for administration (such as "take at bedtime").

11. State the number of refills authorized.

12. If leaving a message on a pharmacy voicemail system set up for physicians, state your name, the name of the doctor you represent, and your phone number before you hang up. If the pharmacist has any questions, he must be able to reach the physician.

13. Document the prescription renewal in the chart after the medication has been called into the pharmacy. Include the date, the time, the name of pharmacy, the person taking your call, the medication, dose, amount, directions, and number of refills. Sign your first initial, last name, and title.

An example of charting follows:

5/03/xx Rx telephoned to Beth Stone at Funton Pharmacy: Zyrtec 10 mg, one tablet daily at bedtime, #30, 6 refills.

. . . . *K. Buckwalter, RMA (AMT)*

Electronically Order and Track Medical Test Results

GOAL To order and track medical tests electronically

MATERIALS Electronic patient chart, such as SpringCharts, and the medical test ordered

METHOD

1. Access the patient's electronic chart. In SpringCharts the electronic chart can be accessed from many different places. For example, in the Practice View screen it can be accessed by clicking on the patient's name in the Scheduler, the patient's name in the Patient Tracker, or by selecting a ToDo or Message associated with a patient.

2. Access the test menu within the electronic chart. In SpringCharts, use the *Actions* menu (Figure 16–13). In SpringCharts, the term *tests* includes lab tests, imaging tests, and medical tests.

3. Search and then select the test to be ordered. Double-check that you have the right test before making your final selection. In SpringCharts, use the *Order Test* window (Figure 16–14). In EHR, actions can be completed by selecting different items. You should be familiar with the EHR you are using.

4. When results are received, locate and store the results in the *tests* area of the EHR. For SpringCharts, once the test is ordered it is stored in the *Pending Tests* area.

5. Enter the results in the patient chart and notify the physician. For SpringCharts when data is entered manually into the *Pending Tests,* it is sent to the *Completed Tests* area of the program for the physician's viewing. Once the tests have been viewed by the physician, they are permanently filed in the patient's chart.

figure 16–13

Actions menu.

figure 16–14

Order test window.

Case Study

Sam works in a busy oncology office. His responsibilities include reviewing diagnostic reports, ensuring they are seen by the physician, and filing them in the patient's medical record. The office "went live" with EHR two weeks ago. Overall, it has made Sam's job more efficient since he can see the lab tests that are pending and an icon appears when results are electronically sent. These results will automatically copy to the patient's record after they are reviewed. This alleviates the cumbersome process of manually keeping track of lab tests, looking for results, and pulling medical records to file them. The manual system had a high potential for test results "falling through the cracks." In an oncology

practice, missing abnormal findings could be life threatening. However, not all of the laboratories used by this office have an electronic interface. Sam's familiarity with both the electronic and manual systems and his understanding of the importance of the laboratory reports sparked an idea. He worked with the EHR vendor to create a screen similar to a spreadsheet for nonelectronic lab results, allowing Sam to input pending tests and track the flow. While it was more labor-intensive than the interface and required him to scan the actual results into the patient's medical record, it was more efficient than the totally manual system. Sam's ability to understand and put his knowledge into practice resulted in an effective approach to a problem.

Thinking Critically

1. Do you think Sam is an asset to this practice and why?
2. Did the idea require more understanding of his responsibilities or more technical expertise?
3. What other types of reports might require a dual electronic and manual system?

practice APPLICATIONS

1. Interpret the prescription in Figure 16–9 by identifying the following components and translating the prescription: Prescriber Information, Patient Information, Medication Prescribed, Subscription, Signa, Signature, and DEA number.

2. Practice ordering consultations, laboratory and other diagnostics tests using sample forms (Figures 16–10, 16–11, and 16–12) or an electronic health record system.

exam READINESS

There may be more than one correct answer. Circle the best answer.

1. **[LO16.1]** Which of the following is a trade name for a medication?

    a. Aspirin
    b. Acetylsalicylic acid
    c. Bayer
    d. Acetaminophen
    e. Amoxicillin

2. **[LO16.1]** An example of an OTC medication is

    a. Glucophage.
    b. Lasix.
    c. Coumadin.

    d. Darvocet.
    e. Prevacid.

3. **[LO16.2]** Prozac is categorized as an

    a. NSAID anti-inflammatory.
    b. SNRI antidepressant.
    c. Antilipidemic.
    d. SSRI antidepressant.
    e. antipsychotic.

4. **[LO16.2]** Which of the following drug resources has a consumer option?

    a. *PDR*
    b. *USP/NF*
    c. Epocrates
    d. DEA 222
    e. Mayo Clinic

5. [LO16.3] Which form is used to renew a physician's DEA registration?

    a. DEA 41
    b. DEA 41a
    c. DEA 224a
    d. DEA 222
    e. DEA 224

6. [LO16.3] Which of the following controlled substances would be kept in a locked location?

    a. Schedule I
    b. Schedule II
    c. Schedule III
    d. Schedule V
    e. b, c, and d

7. [LO16.4] The Sig line of a prescription reads: "ī tab po qd". What does it mean?

    a. Take one tablet by mouth twice a day.
    b. The order is not accurate and cannot be used.
    c. Take 1 tablet by mouth daily.
    d. Take ½ tablet daily.
    e. Take daily one tablet.

8. [LO16.4] All of the following need to be documented when a prescription refill is called in to a pharmacy EXCEPT

    a. the person taking the call.
    b. your signature and title.
    c. medication dose amount and directions.
    d. patient's name and phone number
    e. date, time, and name of pharmacy.

9. [LO16.5] A consultation is

    a. the result of a blood test.
    b. the result of an X-ray.
    c. the result of an examination.
    d. a method of examination.
    e. a way of tracking pending tests.

10. [LO16.5] The appointment for a referral is made by the

    a. pharmaceutical representative.
    b. physician.
    c. medical assistant.
    d. patient.
    e. c and d.

learning outcome SUMMARY

LO 16.1 Drugs have two important names to recognize, the generic or "official name" and the trade name given by the company that manufactures the drug. OTC drugs can be bought without a prescription. Prescription drugs must be authorized by a physician or other authorized prescriber.

LO 16.2 Many categories of drugs are available for patient treatment. These categories are outlined in Table 16–1. Resources for drug information include electronic and print versions of *PDR*, *USP/NF*, and Epocrates.

LO 16.3 All physicians must be registered with the Drug Enforcement Administration and follow the legal requirements of the Controlled Substances Act of 1970 to administer, dispense, and prescribe controlled

drugs. The medical assistant must follow these legal requirements when registering the physician.

LO 16.4 A prescription must be complete to be filled. The medical assistant must be able to interpret a prescription in order to manage new and refilled medications. Telephone refills may be done for all medications except schedule II and III drugs.

LO 16.5 Referrals are ordered and consultation reports must be filed on the chart when received. Medical tests including laboratory tests, diagnostic tests, and x-rays are ordered through specific forms or the EHR. The results must be returned to the patient chart and the physician notified.

medical assisting COMPETENCIES

CAAHEP

I. C (11) Identify the classifications of medications, including desired effects, side effects, and adverse reactions

II. A (2) Distinguish between normal and abnormal test results

IV. P (7) Demonstrate telephone techniques

IX. C (13) Discuss all levels of governmental legislation and regulation as they apply to medical assisting practice, including FDA and DEA regulations

ABHES

3. Medical Terminology
  d. Recognize and identify acceptable medical abbreviations

4. Medical Law and Ethics
  b. Institute federal and state guidelines when releasing medical records or information
  f. Comply with federal, state, and local health laws and regulations

6. Pharmacology
  b. Properly utilize *PDR*, drug handbook, and other drug references to identify a drug's classification, usual dosage, usual side effects, and contraindications
  c. Identify and define common abbreviations that are accepted in prescription writing

  d. Understand legal aspects of writing prescriptions, including federal and state laws
  e. Comply with federal, state, and local health laws and regulations

8. Medical Office Business Procedures Management
  jj. Perform fundamental writing skills including correct grammar, spelling, and formatting techniques when writing prescriptions, documenting medical records, etc.

9. Medical Office Clinical Procedures
  f. Screen and follow up patient test results
  g. Maintain medication and immunization records
  o. Perform:
    (3) Telephone and in-person screening

Financial

Practices

Volunteers aren't paid, not because they are worthless, but because they are priceless.

Sherry Anderson

Preparation for Success

Interviewer: Heather, we have been relating stories from graduates of administrative medical assisting programs. You are not a graduate but currently a student. Tell us why you are studying this field.

Heather: When I was in high school we had to do a project that involved volunteering in the community. My best friend volunteered in an ambulatory care clinic at the hospital close to where I lived. I knew I did not want to do anything of a clinical nature; she said there were non-clinical parts, too. I signed up so we could go together.

Interviewer: In what part of the clinic did you volunteer?

Heather: I started in the pediatric reception area greeting patients and taking patients to the lab and other places. I got to know the people who worked in the clinic and they would tell me about their jobs. Learning about medical records, appointment scheduling, coding, and dealing with patient accounts was so interesting to me. They helped me with my project. I did a comparison of costs and charges for patients with three different kinds of payment plans: Medicaid, sliding fee scale, and a commercial health insurance including where the patients could go for care with the different plans. It helped me understand our health system and gave me an appreciation for the administrative side of health care. My high school teacher gave me an "A."

Interviewer: But the "A" was not the only good thing that came out of the project.

Heather: No, I realized how important community service is. My volunteer job helped make the patients' clinic visits easier and more pleasant. The staff said I made their jobs easier, too, and they could be more efficient. What I thought was a small thing made a difference for bunches of people. I continued to volunteer after the project was done and decided I wanted to become an administrative medical assistant. Then I received a junior volunteer scholarship from the healthcare organization. It is helping to pay for my schooling and a job is waiting when I finish.

Interviewer: You also spread your spirit of community service to your class.

Heather: I have great classmates and they wanted to get involved, even those that had kids and jobs. The clinics were changing to an electronic health record. They had thousands of records that needed scanning. I had an idea. Our school has a contract for externships with the health-care system. Our instructor arranged for us to scan outside of our class hours and receive extra credit. We are learning a ton from this project and making the medical record conversion go a lot faster.

Interviewer: Do you have any advice you would like to give other students who, like you, are studying to become administrative medical assistants?

Heather: I learned that finding time to give something to the community should be a part of lives. Not only because I got a scholarship and a job but because it is the right thing to do. You are rewarded in so many ways besides money when you help others.

Interviewer: Great thoughts! Thank you, Heather, and best wishes to you as you complete your educational program.

17 Insurance and Billing

Learning Outcomes

After completing Chapter 17, you will be able to:

17.1 Define the key insurance terminology.

17.2 Explain the differences among fee-for-service plans, HMOs, and PPOs.

17.3 Outline the key requirements for coverage by the Medicare and Medicaid programs.

17.4 Explain the formula for RBRVS and define allowed charge, contracted fee, and capitation.

17.5 List the components of the claims process.

17.6 Produce a clean CMS-1500 health insurance claim form.

17.7 Define accounts receivable and accounts payable, and give the common payment methods accepted in medical practices today.

17.8 List the different types of documents used as statements to bill patients.

17.9 Outline the differences among open book, written contract, and single entry accounts, and explain the purpose of creating an accounts receivable aging.

17.10 Explain the purposes of the following credit and collections acts: ECOA, FCRA, and FDCPA.

17.11 List the required components of a Truth in Lending statement.

17.12 Define the two common types of problem collection accounts in the medical office.

Key Terms

accounts payable
accounts receivable
age analysis
allowed charge
balance billing
benefits
birthday rule
capitation
Centers for Medicare and Medicaid Services (CMS)
CHAMPVA
charge slip
class action lawsuit
clearinghouse
coinsurance
coordination of benefits
credit
credit balance
credit bureau
cycle billing
damages
deductible
disability insurance
disclosure statement
elective procedure
electronic data interchange (EDI)
encounter form (superbill)
exclusion
explanation of benefits (EOB)
fee-for-service

fee schedule
formulary
health maintenance organization (HMO)
liability insurance
lifetime maximum benefit
Medicaid
Medicare
Medicare Advantage plans
Medigap
open-book account
Original Medicare Plan
overpayment
palliative care
participating physicians
preauthorization
precertification
preferred provider organization (PPO)
premium
punitive damages
referral
remittance advice (RA)
resource-based relative value scale (RBRVS)
skips
third-party payer
TRICARE
written-contract account
X12 837 Health Care Claim

Preparation for Certification

RMA (AMT) Exam
- Patient billing procedures
- Medical finance terminology
- Financial applications of medical insurance
- Claim forms

CMAS (AMT) Exam
- Insurance processing

CMA (AAMA) Exam
- Processing claims
- Applying managed care policies and procedures
- Fee schedules

Introduction ● ● ●

As an administrative medical assistant, it is very likely that you will be taking on many administrative duties that involve patient financial accounts. This may include health insurance billing (also known as third-party billing) and patient billing. When insurance billing is done correctly, you will receive an explanation of benefits from the insurance carrier explaining what they paid on the claim and what the patient now owes the practice; resulting in a need to now bill the patient.

The purpose of this chapter is to give you the necessary understanding of insurance billing terminology and billing procedures that are required to properly complete the health insurance claim form, to read and understand the insurance carrier's explanation of benefits (EOB), and to initiate successful patient billing and collection methods.

LO 17.1 Basic Insurance Terminology

The first step in understanding insurance is learning some basic terminology. Medical insurance, also known as health insurance, is a written contract in the form of a policy between a policyholder and a health plan (insurance carrier). The policyholder may also be called the insured, the member, or the subscriber.

Under the insurance policy, the policyholder pays a **premium,** which is the charge for keeping the insurance policy in effect. In exchange, the health plan provides **benefits**—payments for medical services—for a specified time period. The policy may cover dependents of the policyholder, such as a spouse or children. The contract may specify a **lifetime maximum benefit,** which is a total sum that the health plan will pay out over the patient's life.

As you learned in Chapter 6, there is an implied contract between the patient who is considered the *first party* and the physician who is the *second party*. In order to fulfill part of his obligation in this contract, the patient is legally responsible for paying the physician for these services. Often, to assist with this responsibility, the patient has a second contract with an insurance plan that becomes the *third party* (payer) in this contract. As the third party, the health plan agrees to pay for at least part of the cost of the medical services.

Depending on the type of health plan, the policyholder may pay a **deductible**—a fixed dollar amount that must be paid or "met" once a year, in addition to the premium, before the third-party payer begins to cover medical expenses. The patient may also have to pay **coinsurance,** a fixed percentage of covered charges after the deductible is met. The coinsurance rate represents the health plan's percentage of the charge followed by the insured's percentage, such as 80-20, which means the insurance carrier would pay 80% of allowed charges and the patient would be responsible for the remaining 20%. If the patient belongs to a managed care health plan, such as a health maintenance organization (HMO), instead of paying co-insurance, the patient is responsible for a per visit copayment; a small fixed fee that is collected at the time of the visit. The health plan then pays an agreed-upon contracted payment for the charges with any balance being adjusted off by the service provider per its *preferred provider* contract with the health plan.

Some expenses, such as routine eye examinations or dental care, may not be covered under the insured's contract. These uncovered expenses are called **exclusions**. Many insurance plans offer prescription drug benefits, but be aware that such benefits often require the use of drugs that are listed on the plan's **formulary**, a list of approved brands. If a prescription for a nonformulary medication is written, often the physician will be contacted by the pharmacy or health plan case manager, asking if a substitution of a drug on the formulary

premium
The basic annual cost of health care insurance.

benefits
Payment for medical services.

lifetime maximum benefit
The total sum that a health plan will pay out over the patient's lifetime.

deductible
A fixed dollar amount that must be paid (yearly) by the insured before additional expenses are covered by the insurer.

coinsurance
A fixed percentage of covered charges paid by the insured person after a deductible has been met.

exclusion
An expense that is not covered by a particular insurance policy, such as an eye exam or dental care.

formulary
An insurance plan's list of approved prescription medications.

can be made. If not, the patient may be responsible for a large portion, if not all of, the entire cost of the prescription.

Many procedures and surgeries done today are "planned" procedures; that is, done at the convenience of the physician or surgeon and the patient. This type of procedure is known as an **elective procedure**. Many of these procedures are covered by third-party payers but only if certain rules prior to performance of these procedures are followed. **Precertification**, also called **preauthorization**, describes the process of the provider contacting the insurance plan to see if the proposed procedure is a covered service under the patient's insurance plan. Specific information for the particular patient's case is also given to the insurance carrier. If the insurance plan agrees that the patient requires the procedure, in other words, it is medically necessary, they will issue a prior authorization number approving the need for the service or procedure. The prior authorization does not, however, mean they agree to pay for the service. This requires the next step of predetermination, where the insurance plan informs the physician the maximum amount they will pay for the procedure to be performed.

CHECKPOINT
LO 17.1

Why is a thorough knowledge of insurance terminology necessary for an administrative medical assistant?

LO 17.2 Private Health Plans

All insurance companies have their own rules about benefits and procedures. Many companies also have their own manuals, printed or online, that you must keep handy in the office for reference. Most insurance plans also have Web sites and toll free numbers available for providers to answer questions. Don't be afraid to use these tools. Be aware, however, that it is not uncommon to call two or three people with the same question and receive two or three different answers. If the first answer you receive does not sound correct, hang up and call back. You will more than likely get a different representative. Ask your question again. If you get the same answer the second time, it is more likely to be correct. Always get the name and extension number of the representative you speak with and document the call. Many companies also give you a call reference number in case a similar issue arises later. Keep all of this information with the patient's financial or insurance record for further reference.

In the United States the majority of individuals with insurance are covered by group policies, usually through their employers. Some people (often the self-employed) have individual plans. Many are covered under a government plan (Medicare, Medicaid, TRICARE), which will be discussed later. Still others—over 47 million Americans (according to the U.S. Census bureau figures for 2007)—have had no health-care insurance. The federal government through the Obama administration has changed that. On March 23, 2010, President Barack Obama signed into law a massive health-care overhaul bill. The core of this new law, which will take several years to fully phase in (2014 is the goal), is the extension of insurance coverage to the 32 million Americans who now lack health-care coverage. Also included in the law is a ban on the ability of private insurance carriers to impose lifetime limits on coverage, denial of coverage for pre-existing conditions, and policy cancellations when an insured person becomes ill. Parents will also be allowed to keep their children covered under the family policy until age 26.

Traditionally, every insurance plan issued each of their providers an identification number, similar to the policy number given to each subscriber. Since the advent of HIPAA, although individual insurers may still issue individual ID numbers, every physician and provider who submits a claim to an insurance

carrier must now use a specific provider number, known as a National Provider Identifier (NPI), from the Centers for Medicare and Medicaid Services (CMS).

During the transition period, while providers obtained their NPIs, certain non-NPI numbers and two-character identifiers (Table 17–1) were allowed. Now that all providers have an NPI, these non-NPI numbers and their identifiers are used only for certain payers who still require them.

Fee-for-Service and Managed Care Plans

There are two major types of health plans: traditional fee-for-service plans and managed care plans. **Fee-for-service** plans, the oldest and most expensive type, repay policyholders for costs of health care due to illnesses and accidents. The policy lists the medical services that are covered. The amount charged for services is controlled by the physician who provides them, although the amount paid for each service is controlled by the insurance carrier.

Managed care organizations (MCOs) control both the financing and the delivery of health care to policyholders. They enroll policyholders, and they also enroll physicians and other providers, to provide services for their members at reduced rates. In this way they control both the providers their members may see and the fees that the providers may charge the MCO and charge the patients in the form of copayments. Many people who are insured through their employers are covered by some form of a managed care plan.

Physicians who enroll with managed care plans are called **participating physicians**. They have contracts with the MCOs that stipulate not only the physician fees, but also the credentials they must have and their responsibilities to the patients and to the MCO itself. Most MCOs also publish their participating physicians' names in booklets and on their Web site so that policyholders can easily choose a participating provider from the list.

Managed care plans pay their participating physicians in one of two ways—either by contracted fees or a fixed prepayment called **capitation**. In most plans, the primary care physician, or PCP, is reimbursed using the capitation method, which involves payment of a fixed amount per patient who signs up with a

fee-for-service
Formerly a major type of health plan. It repays policyholders for the costs of health care due to illness and injuries.

participating physicians
Physicians who enroll in managed care plans. They have contracts with MCOs that stipulate their fees.

capitation
A payment structure in which a health maintenance organization prepays an annual set fee per patient to a physician.

table 17–1

National Uniform Claim Committee (NUCC) Non-NPI Qualifiers

These qualifiers are for use in CMS-1500 (and X12 837). These identifiers may be used in the following fields: 17a, 19, 24I, 32a, and 32b.

QUALIFIER	DESCRIPTION
0B	State License Number
1B	Blue Shield Provider Number
1C	Medicare Provider Number
1D	Medicaid Provider Number
1G	Provider UPIN Number
1H	CHAMPVA Identification Number
E1	Employer's Identification Number
G2	Provider Commercial Number
LU	Location Number
N5	Provider Plan Network Identification Number
SY	Social Security Number (this may not be used for Medicare)
X5	State Industrial Accident Provider Number
ZZ	Provider Taxonomy

particular PCP. The physician is paid for each patient enrolled in her practice, regardless of whether she sees that patient multiple times during the month or not at all. In addition to these capitated payments, the PCP will be paid additional contracted fees for certain other services they provide for the patient such as labs and immunizations. In most managed care plans, specialists are paid in a negotiated fee-for-service manner. These fees are usually less than those paid by private fee-for-service plans, but more than those paid by the government health plans. Providers and insurance carriers negotiate these contracts and fee schedules on a periodic basis.

As shown in Figure 17–1, more than half of all health plans are **preferred provider organizations (PPOs)**. A PPO is a managed care plan that establishes a network of providers to perform services for plan members. In exchange for the PPO sending them patients, the physicians agree to charge discounted fees. In most PPOs, plan members may also choose to receive care from doctors or providers outside the network, but if they do so, they are responsible for paying a higher percentage of the charges for these visits and may also be subject to a deductible that they would not be responsible for if they saw in-network providers.

Another common type of managed care system, covering 20% of those with private health-care insurance, is a **health maintenance organization (HMO)**. Physicians with HMO contracts are often paid a capitated rate, or they may be employees of the organization who are paid salaries. Patients who enroll in an HMO pay premiums and usually also pay a copayment, often $10 to $20, at the time of the office visit. No other fees are required for any covered service that a member needs. In HMOs, patients must usually choose from a specific group of health-care providers for care. If they seek services from a provider who is not in the health plan, the HMO does not pay for the care. Patients also pay for excluded services.

Blue Cross and Blue Shield

Many people think that Blue Cross and Blue Shield (BCBS) is one large corporation. Rather, it is a nationwide federation of nonprofit and for-profit service organizations that provide prepaid health-care services to BCBS subscribers.

preferred provider organization (PPO)

A managed care plan that establishes a network of providers to perform services for plan members.

health maintenance organization (HMO)

A health-care organization that provides specific services to individuals and their dependents who are enrolled in the plan. Physicians who enroll with an HMO agree to provide certain services in exchange for a prepaid fee or capitation payment.

figure 17–1

Distribution of health plan enrollment for covered workers by plan type, 1988–2009.

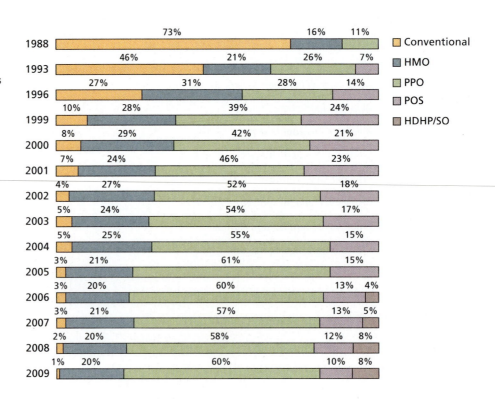

Each local organization operates under its own state laws, and specific plans for BCBS can vary greatly.

In addition to health insurance, there are two other special types of insurance available to cover medical expenses. They are liability insurance and disability insurance. **Liability insurance** covers injuries that are caused by the insured or that occurred on the insured's property. If an individual (or company) has home, business, automobile, or health liability insurance, the injured person can claim benefits under the insured's policy. To obtain specific details about coverage of the individual policy, you would need to contact the liability insurance company.

Disability insurance may be offered to employees (at employee expense), provided by an employer for its employees, or purchased privately by self-employed individuals. Disability insurance is activated when the insured is injured or disabled for non-work-related reasons. Disability insurance is not health insurance and does not cover medical expenses. When an insured person cannot work, and can provide the insurance with documentation as to the medical reason he or she cannot work, the insurance company pays the insured a prearranged monthly amount to assist with the insured's normal daily expenses. There are two types of disability policies. Short-term policies offer coverage for shorter periods of time, usually 7 (consecutive) days to 6 months, and long-term disability policies may last for 1 year or more depending on policy stipulations.

liability insurance
A type of insurance that covers injuries caused by the insured or injuries that occurred on the insured's property.

disability insurance
Insurance that provides a monthly, prearranged payment to an individual who cannot work as a result or an injury, illness, or disability.

Why do you believe that managed care programs are so much more popular today than the more traditional fee-for-service plan?

CHECKPOINT
LO 17.2

LO 17.3 Government Plans

Government plans are generally designed to offer health care to retirees, low-income and disadvantaged individuals, and active or retired military personnel and their families. Some of these plans still maintain many of the features of managed care plans.

Medicare

The largest federal program providing health care is **Medicare**, which provides health insurance for citizens aged 65 and older. Patients under the age of 65 may also be eligible. They include those who are dependent widows aged 50 to 65, the disabled, and the blind, as well as workers of any age who have chronic kidney disease requiring dialysis or end-stage renal disease (ESRD) requiring transplant. Kidney donors are also eligible for Medicare. The Medicare program is managed by the **Centers for Medicare and Medicaid Services (CMS)**. There are two Web sites available to obtain more information regarding Medicare: www.medicare.gov (supplies patients and beneficiaries with information) and www.cms.gov includes provider and claims information for both Medicare and Medicaid.

Part A Medicare is divided into two main parts. Part A is the hospital benefit, which is billed by hospitals (or other health-care facilities). Medicare Part A is financed through contributions collected from the Federal Insurance Contributions Act (FICA) tax on income earned by workers and the self-employed. Currently the FICA tax for workers is 6.2% and 12.4% for the self-employed up to a wage maximum of $94,200. You will learn more about FICA tax deductions in Chapter 21. It pays most of the costs for the following individuals:

Medicare
A national health insurance program for Americans aged 65 and older, as well as some patients under age 65 who meet specific criteria.

Centers for Medicare and Medicaid Services (CMS)
A congressional agency designed to handle Medicare and Medicaid insurance claims. It was formerly known as the Health Care Financing Administration.

- Patients who are admitted as inpatients for up to the 90-day benefit period. A benefit period begins the day a patient is admitted to the hospital and ends when that patient has not been hospitalized or placed in a skilled nursing facility for a period of 60 continuous days after discharge.

The 90-day benefit period is divided into two parts. The initial benefit period is 60 days where after the patient pays a deductible, hospital coverage is at 100%. After the first 60 days the patient enters into a 30-day period called coinsurance days. During this 30-day period, the patient must pay an additional per-day payment or co-insurance. If the hospital stay extends beyond the 30 coinsurance days, the patient may use up to 60 lifetime reserve days, which also include a per-day charge. It is important to note these 60 lifetime reserve days are not renewable. Once they are used up during the patient's lifetime, they are no longer available. If the patient is admitted to the hospital again for longer than 90 days, after the reserve days are exhausted, the patient will be responsible for all charges after the 90th day.

- A patient who has been admitted to a skilled nursing facility (SNF) after inpatient hospitalization. Coverage is for no more than 100 days in each benefit period, which is usually 1 calendar year.

- A patient who is receiving medical care at home.

- A patient receiving hospice care either at home or in a hospice facility. Terminally ill patients with a prognosis (prediction) of 6 months or less to live are eligible for hospice care. Hospice programs provide **palliative care** including pain relief and support for terminal patients and their family members.

- A patient who requires psychiatric treatment. Currently Medicare covers only 190 days of psychiatric hospitalization in a patient's lifetime.

- A patient who requires respite care. In certain clearly and narrowly defined circumstances, Medicare provides for a respite, or short break, for the person who cares for a terminally ill patient at home. The terminally ill patient is moved to a care facility for the respite.

Anyone who receives Social Security benefits is automatically enrolled in Part A and does not have to pay a premium. Individuals aged 65 or older who are not eligible for Social Security benefits may enroll in Part A, but they must pay premiums for the coverage.

Part B Part B covers a portion (usually 80%) of the allowed charges for a wide range of outpatient procedures and supplies. For example, it covers physician services, outpatient hospital services, diagnostic tests, clinical laboratory services, and outpatient physical and speech therapy as long as these services are considered medically necessary. Individuals entitled to Part A benefits automatically qualify for Part B benefits. In addition, U.S. citizens and permanent residents over the age of 65 are also eligible. Part B is a voluntary program; eligible persons may or may not take part in it. However, those desiring Part B must enroll because coverage is not automatic. The Medicare beneficiary has a 6 month time frame to apply, beginning 3 months prior to his 65th birthday until 3 months after it. If the deadline is missed, the beneficiary must wait until open enrollment, which is from January 1–March 31 of each year. If the Medicare B enrollment takes place more than 12 months after the initial enrollment period, there is a permanent 10% increase in the premium for each year the beneficiary was eligible to enroll, but did not. Unlike Part A, Part B coverage is not premium-free. Starting in 2007, the Medicare Part B premium is based on the beneficiary's income. The cost ranges between $0 and $211.90 per month, and the premium usually increases annually.

Each Medicare enrollee receives a health insurance card. This card lists the beneficiary's name, sex, effective dates for Part A and Part B coverage, and Medicare number. The Medicare number is assigned by CMS and usually consists of the Social Security number followed by an alpha or alphanumeric suffix. See Table 17–2 for an explanation of Medicare A and B premium, deductible, and benefit differences.

palliative care
Care that provides comfort only; care is not meant to be curative in nature. Hospice services are palliative in nature.

table 17–2

Comparison of Medicare A and B Premiums, Deductible, and Benefits

MEDICARE PLAN	PREMIUM	DEDUCTIBLE	BENEFIT PERIOD	PATIENT COINSURANCE
Medicare A	None	Yes/per admission		
Hospitalization			Days 1–60 Days 61–90 Days 91–150 (includes 60 lifetime reserve days) After 150 Days	$0—Medicare pays 100% $283/day $566/day 100%—No Medicare benefit
Skilled Nursing Facility (Patient must have been hospitalized at least 3 days and be admitted to approved SNF within 30 days of hospital discharge)			Days 1–20 Days 21–100 After 100 days	$0—Medicare pays 100% $141.50/day 100%—No Medicare benefit
Home Health Care (Includes P/T home nursing and aide services, durable medical equipment and supplies)			Unlimited as long as MCR criteria are met and services are *medically necessary*	$0 for home health service 20% of allowed charges for DME
Hospice Services Palliative care for the terminally ill and family members			Patient elects hospice care and physician certifies need for hospice care	$0 except for outpatient medication and inpatient hospital care
Blood				First 3 pints per year
Medicare B Outpatient Medical	Yes	Yes/per year	January 1–December 31	20% of approved charges
Outpatient Mental Health				50% of approved charges
Outpatient Laboratory				$0 of approved charges
Home Health Care (Includes P/T home health nursing and aides, PT/OT/ST DME supplies and services)				$0 for home care 20% for DME
Blood				First 3 pints and 20% of approved charges
Ambulatory Surgery				20% of predetermined charge after deductible

Medicare Part C and Part D Medicare Part C was introduced in 1997 and provides several choices for individuals in the types of plans they utilize. They are called Medicare Advantage plans and include PPOs, HMOs, private fee-for-service (PFFS) plans, special needs plans, and Medicare medical savings account plans (MSA). The MSA plan started in 2007.

The Medicare Part D prescription drug plan was passed by the legislature in 2003 and coverage began January 1, 2006. All Medicare beneficiaries can enroll in a prescription drug plan through the Medicare Prescription Drug plan, Medicare Advantage, or other Medicare plans, as well as through employers and unions. Figure 17–2 is the Medicare Part D Coverage Determination Request Form.

Medicare Plan Options Medicare beneficiaries can choose from among a number of insurance plan options including fee-for-service and Medicare Advantage plans consisting of different types of managed care plans.

Fee-for-Service: The Original Medicare Plan The Medicare fee-for-service plan, referred to by Medicare as the **Original Medicare Plan**, allows the beneficiary to choose any licensed physician certified by Medicare. Each time the beneficiary receives outpatient services, a fee is billable. Part of this fee is generally paid by Medicare and part is due from the beneficiary. Once the patient meets the annual deductible, if the patient sees a participating provider, Medicare pays 80% of approved charges directly to the provider and the patient is responsible for the remaining 20% as well as any disallowed charges. Providers who accept the Medicare allowed charge as payment in full are known as those who "accept assignment." These providers cannot charge the patient more than the Medicare-allowed charge, no matter what the original fee may have been. A Medicare beneficiary may choose a provider who does not participate in the Medicare program and who does not accept assignment. In that case, the provider does not have to accept the Medicare allowable as payment in full and may charge the patient up to the "limiting charge" as described by Medicare. The limiting charge is usually defined as 115% of the nonparticipating allowable fee. This arrangement usually results in an increased out-of-pocket expense for the patient.

To help with the responsibility of the 20% coinsurance, individuals enrolled in the Original Medicare B Plan often buy additional insurance called a **Medigap** plan. These plans frequently reimburse the patient's Part B deductible and pick up the 20% of the Medicare allowed charge. If Medicare does not pay a claim, Medigap is not required to pay the claim either. Although private insurance carriers offer Medigap plans, coverage and standards are regulated by federal and state law. In exchange for Medigap coverage, the policyholder pays a monthly premium. A number of different options labeled A through J are available. Monthly premiums vary widely across the different plan levels as well as within a single plan level, depending on the insurance company selected. While coverage varies from policy to policy, a set of core benefits is common to all Medigap plans, including the Part B coinsurance amount (usually 20% of approved charges) and the deductible. Prior to 2009, insurance carriers in each state bid for the Medicare A and B contracts to process Medicare claims. These carriers were known as fiscal carriers for Part A and fiscal intermediaries for Part B. The Medicare Prescription Drug, Improvement and Modernization Act of 2003 (MMA) changed this process. In an effort to streamline the process and make it more competitive and performance-based, CMS changed how claims are processed through Medicare contracting reform. At the forefront of these changes is the creation of Medicare Administrative Contractor (MAC) Jurisdictions for claims processing. Table 17–3 outlines 15 jurisdictions for MCR medical claims and the states contained within each jurisdiction. DME claims are separated from medical claims and are submitted to MACS set up specifically for DME.

Original Medicare Plan
The Medicare fee-for-service plan that allows the beneficiary to choose any licensed physician certified by Medicare.

Medigap
Private insurance that Medicare beneficiaries can purchase to reduce the gaps in Medicare coverage; the amount they would have to pay from their own pockets after receiving Medicare benefits.

Medicare Advantage plans
PPOs, HMOs, private fee-for-service plans, and Medicare medical savings accounts that provide Medicare beneficiaries with plan coverage choices in addition to the traditional Medicare plan.

Plan Name _____

Phone # _____

Fax # _____

Medicare Part D Coverage Determination Request Form

This form cannot be used to request:

➤ Medicare non-covered drugs, including barbiturates, benzodiazepines, fertility drugs, drugs prescribed for weight loss, weight gain or hair growth, over-the-counter drugs, or prescription vitamins (except prenatal vitamins and fluoride preparations).

➤ **Biotech or other specialty drugs for which drug-specific forms are required. [See <Part D plan website.>] OR [See links to plan websites at http://www.cms.hhs.gov/PrescriptionDrugCovGenIn/04_Formulary.asp]**

Patient Information		Prescriber Information	
Patient Name:		Prescriber Name:	
Member ID#:		NPI# (if available):	
Address:		Address:	
City:	State:	City:	State:
Home Phone:	Zip:	Office Phone #: Office Fax #:	Zip:
Sex (circle): M F DOB:		Contact Person:	

Diagnosis and Medical Information

Medication:	Strength and Route of Administration:	Frequency:
☐ New Prescription OR Date Therapy Initiated:	Expected Length of Therapy:	Qty:
Height/Weight: Drug Allergies:	Diagnosis:	
Prescriber's Signature:		Date:

Rationale for Exception Request or Prior Authorization
FORM CANNOT BE PROCESSED WITHOUT REQUIRED EXPLANATION

☐ Alternate drug(s) contraindicated or previously tried, but with adverse outcome (eg, toxicity, allergy, or therapeutic failure)

➔ Specify below: (1) Drug(s) contraindicated or tried; (2) adverse outcome for each; (3) if therapeutic failure, length of therapy on each drug(s);

☐ Complex patient with one or more chronic conditions (including, for example, psychiatric condition, diabetes) is stable on current drug(s); high risk of significant adverse clinical outcome with medication change

➔ Specify below: Anticipated significant adverse clinical outcome

☐ Medical need for different dosage form and/or higher dosage

➔ Specify below: (1) Dosage form(s) and/or dosage(s) tried; (2) explain medical reason

☐ Request for formulary tier exception

➔ Specify below: (1) Formulary or preferred drugs contraindicated or tried and failed, or tried and not as effective as requested drug; (2) if therapeutic failure, length of therapy on each drug and adverse outcome; (3) if not as effective, length of therapy on each drug and outcome

☐ Other:_____ ➔ Explain below

REQUIRED EXPLANATION:_____

_____

_____

_____

Request for Expedited Review

☐ REQUEST FOR EXPEDITED REVIEW [24 HOURS]

➔ BY CHECKING THIS BOX AND SIGNING ABOVE, I CERTIFY THAT APPLYING THE 72 HOUR STANDARD REVIEW TIME FRAME MAY SERIOUSLY JEOPARDIZE THE LIFE OR HEALTH OF THE MEMBER OR THE MEMBER'S ABILITY TO REGAIN MAXIMUM FUNCTION

Information on this form is protected health information and subject to all privacy and security regulations under HIPAA.

Medicare Advantage Plans   Medicare also offers a group of plans called the **Medicare Advantage plans**. Beneficiaries can choose to enroll in one of three major types of plans instead of the Original Medicare Plan:

1. Medicare Managed Care Plans
2. Medicare Preferred Provider Organization Plans (PPO)
3. Medicare Private Fee-for-Service Plans

figure 17–2

Medicare Part D Coverage Determination Request Form.

A/B MAC JURISDICTIONS JURISDICTION NUMBER	STATES INCLUDED IN JURISDICTION
1	American Samoa, California, Guam, Hawaii, Nevada, and Northern Mariana Islands
2	Alaska, Idaho, Oregon, and Washington
3	Arizona, Montana, North Dakota, South Dakota, Utah, and Wyoming
4	Colorado, New Mexico, Oklahoma, and Texas
5	Iowa, Kansas, Missouri, and Nebraska
6	Illinois, Minnesota, and Wisconsin
7	Arkansas, Louisiana, and Mississippi
8	Indiana and Michigan
9	Florida, Puerto Rico, and U.S. Virgin Islands
10	Alabama, Georgia, and Tennessee
11	North Carolina, South Carolina, Virginia and West Virginia
12	Delaware, District of Columbia, Maryland, New Jersey, and Pennsylvania
13	Connecticut and New York
14	Maine, Massachusetts, New Hampshire, Rhode Island, and Vermont
15	Kentucky and Ohio

Source: www.cms.hhs.gov/MedicareContractingReform/Downloads/MACJurisdictionFactSheet.pdf.

table 17-3

Medicare MAC Jurisdictions for Medical Claims

referral

An authorization from a medical practice for a patient to have specialized services performed by another practice; often required for insurance purposes.

Medicare Managed Care Plans charge a monthly premium and a small copayment for each office visit, but not a deductible. Like private payer managed care plans, Medicare managed care plans often require patients to select a primary care physician (PCP) who oversees and manages the patient's medical care through **referrals**. Usually patients are also required to use a specific network of physicians, hospitals, and facilities. Some plans allow members the option of receiving services from providers outside the network but the member's portion of the charges will be higher. Medicare MCOs offer coverage for services not reimbursed in the Original Medicare Plan, such as physical examinations and immunizations.

In the *Medicare Preferred Provider Organization Plan (PPO)*, patients pay less when they use doctors within a network, but they may choose to go outside the network for additional costs, such as a higher copayment or higher coinsurance. Patients do not need a PCP, and referrals are not required.

Under a *Medicare Private Fee-for-Service Plan,* patients receive services from the provider they choose, as long as Medicare has approved the provider or facility. The plan is operated by a private insurance company that contracts with Medicare to provide services to beneficiaries. The plan sets its own rates for services, and physicians are allowed to bill patients the amount of the charge not covered by the plan. A copayment may or may not be required.

Recovery Audit Contractor (RAC) Program In 2008, CMS announced aggressive new steps to find and prevent waste, fraud, and abuse in Medicare. CMS is working closely with beneficiaries and providers, consolidating its fraud detection efforts, strengthening its oversight of medical equipment suppliers and home health agencies, and launching the national recovery audit contractor (RAC) program.

CMS took the next steps in the agency's comprehensive efforts to identify improper Medicare payments and fight fraud, waste, and abuse in the Medicare

program by awarding contracts to four permanent RACs, each of which audit one-fourth of the country, designed to guard the Medicare Trust Fund.

The goal of the recovery audit program is to identify improper payments made on claims of health-care services provided to Medicare beneficiaries. Improper payments may be overpayments or underpayments. Overpayments can occur when health-care providers submit claims that do not meet Medicare's coding or medical necessity policies. Underpayments can occur when health-care providers submit claims for a simple procedure, but the medical record reveals that a more complicated procedure was actually performed. Health-care providers that might be reviewed include hospitals, physician practices, nursing homes, home health agencies, durable medical equipment suppliers, and any other provider or supplier that bills Medicare Parts A and B. For further information, go to www.cms.hhs.gov/RAC/.

Medicaid

Medicaid, also run by CMS, is a health-benefit program designed for low-income, blind, or disabled patients; needy families; foster children; and children born with birth defects. Medicaid is a health cost assistance program, not an insurance program. The federal government provides funds to all 50 states to administer Medicaid (covering specified mandated services), and states add their own funds (for optional services in addition to the federally funded services). Every state has a program to assist with medical expenses for citizens who meet its qualifications. Such programs may have different names and slightly different rules, but they provide basically the same assistance. This assistance includes:

Medicaid
A federally funded health cost assistance program for low-income, blind, and disabled patients; families receiving aid to dependent children; foster children; and children with birth defects.

- Physician services
- Emergency services
- Laboratory services and x-rays
- Skilled nursing facility (SNF) care
- Early diagnostic screening and treatment for minors (those aged 21 and younger)
- Vaccines for children

Accepting Assignment   A physician who agrees to treat Medicaid patients also agrees to accept the established Medicaid payment for covered services. This agreement is called accepting assignment. It means that the physician will accept the amount of money that Medicaid will pay as payment in full for the Medicaid-covered service. If the physician's fee is higher than the Medicaid payment, the patient cannot be billed for the difference. The physician can bill the patient for services that Medicaid does not cover, however. It is important to note that, as a federally funded assistance program, Medicaid is known as the *payer of last resort*. This means that if a patient is covered by both a private insurance plan and Medicaid, the private plan must be billed before Medicaid. It is considered fraud to knowingly bill Medicaid if another insurance company provides medical coverage for a patient.

Medi/Medi   Older or disabled patients who have Medicare and who cannot pay the difference between the bill and the Medicare payment may qualify for Medicare and Medicaid. This type of coverage is known as Medi/Medi. In such cases, Medicare is the primary payer, and Medicaid is the secondary payer. The patient with Medi/Medi is never billed for a balance unless the service provided is a non-covered service, or Medicare/Medicaid states that the patient may be billed.

State Guidelines   Medicaid benefits can vary greatly from state to state. Eligibility for Medicaid is based on how much income the patient reported for

the previous month. It is important to understand the Medicaid guidelines in your state so that your office's Medicaid reimbursement is prompt and trouble-free. Here are some suggestions:

- Do not submit a claim to Medicaid without verification of Medicaid membership and benefit eligibility. Doing so may constitute fraud. You should contact Medicaid to verify eligibility every time the patient is seen in the office.

- Ensure that the physician signs all claims, unless claims are submitted electronically, in which case the physician's signature is kept on file. Send the completed and signed claims to the state's Medicaid-approved contractor (which pays on behalf of the state) or to the state department that administers Medicaid (for example, the state department of social services or public health). Check with your state Medicaid office if you are unsure where to send the claim.

- Unless the patient has a medical emergency, Medicaid often requires authorization before services are performed. Authorization must be obtained from the state Medicaid office in advance. If the patient is seen on an emergency basis, it may also be required that the Medicaid office be notified of the emergency treatment.

- Check the time limit on claim submissions. It can be as short as 2 months or as long as 1 year. Verify deadlines with your local Medicaid office.

- Meet the deadlines. If a Medicaid claim is submitted after the time limit, the claim may be rejected. If a claim deadline is missed, it is considered provider error and the patient cannot be billed for the services.

- Treat Medicaid patients with the same professionalism and courtesy that you extend to other patients. Simply because a patient qualifies for Medicaid assistance does not mean that the patient is in any way inferior to those with private insurance.

TRICARE

A program that provides health-care benefits for dependents of military personnel and military retirees.

figure 17–3

TRICARE covers health-care services for family members of military personnel and military retirees at facilities such as the military base hospital pictured here.

TRICARE and CHAMPVA

The U.S. government provides health-care benefits to families of current military personnel, retired military personnel, and veterans through the TRICARE and CHAMPVA programs. Unless you work in a military-related facility, you will probably see TRICARE and CHAMPVA patients only for emergency services or for nonemergency care that a military base cannot provide.

TRICARE Run by the Defense Department, **TRICARE** (formerly known as CHAMPUS or Civilian Health and Medical Program for Uniformed Services) is not a health insurance plan. Rather, it is a health-care benefit for families of uniformed personnel and retirees from the uniformed services, including the Army, Navy, Marines, Air Force, Coast Guard, Public Health Service, and National Oceanic and Atmospheric Administration (Figure 17–3). TRICARE offers families three choices of health-care benefits:

1. TRICARE Prime, a health maintenance organization
2. TRICARE Extra, a managed care network of health-care providers that families can use on a case-by-case basis without a required enrollment
3. TRICARE Standard, a fee-for-service plan

Another program, TRICARE for Life, is aimed at Medicare-eligible military retirees and

Medicare-eligible family members. TRICARE for Life offers the opportunity to receive health care at a military treatment facility to individuals aged 65 and older who are eligible for both Medicare and TRICARE.

In the past, individuals became ineligible for TRICARE once they reached age 65, and they were required to enroll in Medicare to obtain any health-care coverage. Beneficiaries could still seek treatment at military treatment facilities, but only if space was available. Under TRICARE for Life, enrollees in TRICARE who are aged 65 and older can continue to obtain medical services at military hospitals and clinics as they did before they turned 65. TRICARE for Life acts as a secondary payer to Medicare; Medicare pays first, and the remaining out-of-pocket expenses are paid by TRICARE.

CHAMPVA CHAMPVA (Civilian Health and Medical Program of the Veterans Administration) covers the expenses of the families (dependent spouses and children) of veterans with total, permanent, service-connected disabilities. It also covers surviving spouses and dependent children of veterans who died in the line of duty or as a result of service-connected disabilities.

TRICARE and CHAMPVA Eligibility You must verify TRICARE eligibility. All TRICARE patients should have a valid identification card. To receive TRICARE benefits, eligible individuals must be enrolled in the Defense Enrollment Eligibility Reporting System (DEERS), a computer database.

Eligibility for CHAMPVA is determined by the nearest Veterans Affairs medical center. Contact this center if any questions arise. Patients can choose the doctor they wish after CHAMPVA eligibility is confirmed.

Under TRICARE and CHAMPVA, participating doctors have the option of deciding whether to accept patients on a case-by-case basis. Make sure you know the policy of the doctor or doctors in your office on this issue.

CHAMPVA (Civilian Health and Medical Program of the Veterans Administration)
A type of insurance that covers the expenses of dependents of veterans with total, permanent, service-connected disabilities. It also covers the surviving dependents of veterans who die in the line of duty or as a result of service-connected disabilities.

State Children's Health Insurance Plan

In 2009, the State Children's Health Insurance Plan (SCHIP) was reauthorized. The plan was originally enacted in 1997. The plan allows states to provide health coverage to uninsured children in families whose incomes are too high to qualify for Medicaid but too low to afford private insurance. States have raised eligibility levels to provide coverage to more families. Check your state's requirements for this plan through its Web site.

Workers' Compensation

Workers' compensation insurance covers employmentrelated accidents or diseases. Federal law requires employers to purchase and maintain a certain minimum amount of workers' compensation insurance for their employees. Workers' compensation laws vary from state to state. In most states, workers' compensation includes these benefits:

- Basic medical treatment.
- A weekly amount paid to the patient for a temporary disability. This amount compensates workers for loss of job income until they can return to work.
- A weekly or monthly sum paid to the patient for a permanent disability.
- Death benefits.
- Rehabilitation costs to restore an employee's ability to work again.

Not all medical practices accept workers' compensation cases. Every procedure or treatment that is deemed necessary must be approved in order for payment to be made. Prior to treating a patient who states her care is related to a work-related illness or injury, call the employer to verify this information.

When contacting the employer, speak to the office manager or human resources department. Be sure to get the name and extension of the person who verifies information for you. Give the verifier the patient's name and ask if the treatment is to be covered by workers' compensation. If the answer is yes, be sure to get the date of the original injury or illness and a brief description of the event causing the illness or injury. Ask the verifier if a workers' compensation case has been opened by the employer with the insurance carrier and obtain the case number. If a case has not been opened, ask them to report the incident. Until this report, known as the Employer's First Report of Illness or Injury, is received from the employer, the insurance carrier will not open a case, which means you will not be paid. Obtain the name, address, and phone number of the insurance carrier and carefully document this information. After completing the call to the employer and receiving permission to treat the patient, call the insurance carrier and verify that the employer has an active workers' compensation policy with them.

Records management of workers' compensation varies by state. If you see a patient privately and then she comes to you for a work-related illness or injury, be sure to keep the medical and financial records of the private care and the care related to the workers' compensation case separate. Because the employer and the insurer have contracted with the physician to provide care, they have the right to see any and all treatment and applicable financial records related to the workers' compensation claim without patient consent. It is up to the office to maintain the patient's confidentiality related to any care provided to her that is not related to the workers' compensation claim and keeping separate files makes it easier to do so.

Procedure 17–1, found at the end of the chapter, outlines the steps for verifying a patient's workers' compensation coverage.

CHECKPOINT
LO 17.3

What is the difference between Medicare and Medicaid?

LO 17.4 Fee Schedules and Charges

Physicians establish a list of their usual fees for the procedures and services they frequently perform. The usual fees are those that they charge to most of their patients most of the time under typical conditions. These fees are listed on the office **fee schedule**. Figure 17–4 shows a sample of an office fee schedule.

Medicare Payment System: RBRVS

fee schedule
A list of common services and procedures (performed by a physician) and the charges of each.

Third-party payers set the fees they are willing to pay providers, and often these fees are less than the physician's fee schedule. Most payers base their fees on the amounts that Medicare allows because the Medicare method of fee setting takes into account important factors other than only the usual fees.

resource-based relative value scale (RBRVS)
The payment system used by Medicare. It establishes the relative value units for services, replacing the provider consensus on usual fees.

The payment system used by Medicare is called the **resource-based relative value scale (RBRVS)**. The RBRVS establishes the relative value units for services, replacing providers' consensus on fees (the "usual" or historical charges) with amounts based on resources (what each service really costs to provide).

There are three parts to an RBRVS fee, which uses the formula is RVU × GAF × CF. Listed below is an explanation for each part of this formula:

1. The nationally uniform relative value unit (RVU). The relative value of a procedure is based on three cost elements: the physician's work, the practice cost (overhead), and the cost of malpractice insurance. For example, the relative value unit for a simple office visit, such as

TOTAL CARE CLINIC, PC

Multi-Specialty Fee Schedule

SERVICES RENDERED	CPT	FEE	SERVICES RENDERED	CPT	FEE
Initial OV	99204	$100.00	EKG with Interp	93000	$80.00
Follow-up Visit	99214	$65.00	24-Hour Holter Monitor	93224	$300.00
LCMDM Consultation	99241	$120.00	Sigmoidoscopy	45330	$350.00
HCMDM Consultation	99245	$180.00	Spirometry	94010	$35.00
Hospital Admission	99223	$150.00	Throat Culture	87081	$25.00
Hospital Consultation	99253	$150.00	Flu Immunization	90724	$25.00
ER Visit	99284	$75.00–$150.00	Pneumococcal Immunization	90732	$25.00
Hospital Visit	99232	$55.00	Allergy Injection, Single	95115	$25.00
Urinalysis w/ Micro	81000	$25.00	Allergy Injection, Multiple	95117	$60.00
Culture	87086	$45.00	Hemoccult x 3	82270	$30.00
CBC	85025	$60.00	Tetanus Injection	90718	$20.00
Venipuncture	36415	$35.00	Screening Mammography	77057	$250.00

figure 17-4

The fee schedule shows the charges for services provided by the practice.

to administer a flu shot, is much lower than the relative value for a complicated encounter such as planning the treatment of uncontrolled diabetes in a patient.

2. A geographic adjustment factor (GAF). A geographic adjustment factor is used to adjust each relative value to reflect a geographical area's relative costs, such as office rents.

3. A nationally uniform conversion factor (CF). A uniform conversion factor is a dollar amount used to multiply the relative values to produce a payment amount. It is used by Medicare to make adjustments according to changes in the cost-of-living index.

When RBRVS fees are used, providers receive considerably lower payments than when usual fees are used. Each part of the RBRVS—the relative values, the geographic adjustment, and the conversion factor—is updated each year by CMS. Each year's Medicare fee schedule (MFS) is published by CMS in the *Federal Register* at www.cms.hhs.gov/FeeScheduleGenInfo/.

Payment Methods

Most third-party payers use one of three methods for reimbursing physicians:

1. Allowed charges
2. Contracted fee schedule
3. Capitation

Allowed Charges Many payers set an **allowed charge** for each procedure or service. This amount is the most the payer will pay any provider for that

allowed charge
The amount that is the most the payer will pay any provider for each procedure or service. The payer's payment is based on this allowed charge.

work. The term *allowed charge* has many equivalent terms, including *maximum allowable fee, maximum charge, allowed amount, allowed fee,* or *allowable charge.*

The physician's usual charge is often greater than a plan's allowed charge. If the physician participates in the plan, only the allowed charge will be the basis for the payment by the payer. The plan's rules govern whether the provider is permitted to bill a patient for the part of a usual charge that the payer does not cover. Billing a patient for the difference between a higher usual fee and a lower allowed charge is called **balance billing**. Under most contracts, participating providers may not bill the patient for the difference. Instead, the provider must write off the difference, meaning that the difference between the fee charged and the allowed charge is subtracted from the patient's bill and never collected. The common term for this write-off is *adjustment.*

For example, Medicare-participating providers may not collect an amount greater than the Medicare-allowed charge from the Medicare fee schedule. The Original Medicare Plan is responsible for paying 80% of this allowed charge (after patients have met their annual deductible). Patients are responsible for the other 20%.

Here is an example of a Medicare billing. A Medicare-participating provider reports a usual charge of $200 for a service, and the Medicare-allowed charge is $84. The provider must write off the difference between the two charges. The patient is responsible for 20% of the allowed charge, not of the provider's usual charge:

Provider's usual fee:	$200.00
Medicare-allowed charge:	$84.00
Medicare pays 80%	$67.20
Patient pays 20%	$16.80

The total that the provider can collect is $84. The provider must write off the difference between the usual fee and the allowed charge, or $116.00 in this example. It is important to remember that in this example, it is assumed that the patient has paid her deductible for the year.

Contracted Fee Schedule Some payers, particularly PPOs, establish fixed fee schedules with their participating physicians. The terms of the plan determine what percentage of the charges, if any, the patient owes and what percentage the payer covers. Participating providers can typically bill patients their usual charges for procedures and services that are not covered by the plan.

Capitation The fixed prepayment for each plan member in capitation contracts is determined by the managed care plan that initiates contracts with providers. The plan's contract with the provider lists the services and procedures that are covered by the cap rate. For example, a typical contract with a primary care provider might include the following services:

- Preventive care, including well-child care, adult physical exams, gynecological exams, eye exams, and hearing exams
- Counseling and telephone calls
- Office visits
- Medical care, including medical care services such as therapeutic injections and immunizations, allergy immunotherapy, electrocardiograms, and pulmonary function tests
- The local treatment of first-degree burns, the application of dressings, suture removal, the excision of small skin lesions, the removal of foreign bodies or cerumen from the external ear

balance billing
Billing the patient for the difference between a higher usual fee and the lower allowed charge.

These services are covered in the per-member charge for each plan member who selects the PCP. Noncovered services can be billed to patients using the physician's usual rate. Plans often require the provider to notify the patient in advance that a service is not covered and to state the fee for which the patient will be responsible. As stated earlier, it would be a good idea to have the patient sign a waiver of liability in this case, a notification in writing that he will be responsible for the noncovered charges.

Calculating Patient Charges

The patients of medical practices have a variety of health plans, so they have different financial responsibilities. In addition to premiums, patients may be obligated to pay deductibles, copayments, coinsurance, excluded and over-limit services, and balance billing (only if allowed by the insurance contract between the provider and the insurance plan).

All payers require patients to pay for excluded (noncovered) services. Physicians generally can charge their usual fees for these services. Likewise, in managed care plans that set limits on the annual (or other period) usage of covered services, patients are responsible for usage beyond the allowed number. For example, if one preventive physical examination is permitted annually, additional preventive examinations are paid for by the patient.

Communications with Patients About Charges

When patients have office visits with a physician who participates in the plan under which they have coverage, such as a Medicare-participating (PAR) provider, they generally sign an assignment of benefits statement. When this occurs, the provider agrees to prepare health-care claims for patients, to receive payments directly from the payers, and to accept a payer's allowed charge. Patients are billed for charges that payers deny or do not pay. When patients have encounters with nonparticipating (nonPAR) providers, the procedure is usually different. To avoid the difficulty of collecting payments at a later date from a patient, practices may require that the patient either (1) assigns benefits or (2) pays in full at the time of services.

Patients often call the office regarding statements they receive from the practice. For example, suppose a patient receives a bill for $100 from your practice. She calls to say that she has paid her deductible for the year, so her insurance company should have paid 80% of the charges. You call the patient's insurance company and learn that her deductible increased to $200 this year and she still has to pay $100 to meet her deductible. If she pays the $100 bill in full, her deductible will then be met. You now can call the patient to explain these facts to her.

To estimate patients' responsibility for charges, you should check with the payer to find out:

- The patient's deductible amount and whether it has been paid in full, the covered benefits, and coinsurance or other patient financial obligations
- The payer's allowed charges for the services that the provider anticipates providing

If the patient's request comes after the appointment, the superbill can be used to tell the payer what procedures are going to be reported on the patient's claim to determine the likely payer reimbursement.

Patients should always be reminded of their financial obligations under their plans, including claim denials, according to practice procedures. The practice's financial policy regarding payment for services is usually either displayed on the wall of the reception area or included in a new patient information packet. The policy should explain what is required of the patient and when payment is due. For example, the policy may state the following:

- For unassigned claims: Payment for the physician's services is expected at the time of your appointment, unless you have made other arrangements with our practice manager.
- For assigned claims: After your insurance claim is processed by your insurance company, you will be billed for any amount that is your responsibility. You are responsible for any part of the charges that are denied or not paid by the carrier. All patient accounts are due within 30 days of the date of the statement.
- For managed care members: Copayments must be paid prior to seeing the practitioner.

It is also a good practice to notify patients in advance of the probable cost of procedures that are not going to be covered by their plan. For example, many private plans as well as Medicare do not pay services such as chiropractic care and some preventative services. Patients should be asked to sign a document known as a waiver of liability, which should specify why the service will not be covered and the cost of the procedure.

The Advance Beneficiary Notice of Noncoverage (ABN) is a notice given to beneficiaries in the Original Medicare Plan to convey that Medicare is not likely to provide coverage in a specific case. "Notifiers" include physicians, providers (including institutional providers like outpatient hospitals), practitioners, and suppliers paid under Part B (including independent laboratories), as well as hospice providers and religious nonmedical health care institutions (RNHCIs) paid exclusively under Part A. As of March 1, 2009, the ABN-G (general) and ABN-L(laboratory) were invalid; and notifiers began using the revised Advance Beneficiary Notice of Non-coverage (CMS-R-131). See Figure 17–5.

The ABN must be verbally reviewed with the beneficiary or his or her representative, and any questions raised during that review must be answered before it is signed. The ABN must be delivered far enough in advance that the beneficiary or representative has time to consider the options and make an informed choice. Employees or subcontractors of the notifier may deliver the ABN. ABNs are never required in emergency or urgent care situations. Once all blanks are completed and the form is signed, a copy is given to the beneficiary or representative. In all cases, the notifier must retain the original notice on file.

CHECKPOINT
LO 17.4

Explain why it is good for the practice to have the patient sign an assignment of benefits form.

LO 17.5 The Claims Process: An Overview

From the time the patient enters a physician's office until the time the insurer pays the practice for that office visit and associated services, several steps are carried out. In brief, the physician's office performs the following services:

- Obtains patient information
- Delivers services to the patient and determines the diagnosis and fee
- Records charges and codes, records payment from the patient, and prepares health-care claims
- Reviews the insurer's processing of the claim, remittance advice, and payment

Most administrative medical assistants use a medical billing program to support administrative tasks such as:

- Gathering and recording patient information
- Verifying patients' insurance coverage

figure 17–5

Advance Beneficiary Notice of Noncoverage.

Source: Centers for Medicare and Medicaid Services.

(A) **Notifier(s):**

(B) **Patient Name:** _____ *(C)* **Identification Number:** _____

ADVANCE BENEFICIARY NOTICE OF NONCOVERAGE (ABN)

NOTE: If Medicare doesn't pay for *(D)*_____ below, you may have to pay.

Medicare does not pay for everything, even some care that you or your health care provider have good reason to think you need. We expect Medicare may not pay for the *(D)*_____ below.

*(D)*_____	*(E)* Reason Medicare May Not Pay:	*(F)* Estimated Cost:

WHAT YOU NEED TO DO NOW:

- Read this notice, so you can make an informed decision about your care.
- Ask us any questions that you may have after you finish reading.
- Choose an option below about whether to receive the *(D)*_____ listed above.
    Note: If you choose Option 1 or 2, we may help you to use any other insurance that you might have, but Medicare cannot require us to do this.

(G) OPTIONS: Check only one box. We cannot choose a box for you.

❏ **OPTION 1.** I want the *(D)*_____ listed above. You may ask to be paid now, but I also want Medicare billed for an official decision on payment, which is sent to me on a Medicare Summary Notice (MSN). I understand that if Medicare doesn't pay, I am responsible for payment, but **I can appeal to Medicare** by following the directions on the MSN. If Medicare does pay, you will refund any payments I made to you, less co-pays or deductibles.

❏ **OPTION 2.** I want the *(D)*_____ listed above, but do not bill Medicare. You may ask to be paid now as I am responsible for payment. **I cannot appeal if Medicare is not billed.**

❏ **OPTION 3.** I don't want the *(D)*_____ listed above. I understand with this choice I am **not** responsible for payment, and **I cannot appeal to see if Medicare would pay.**

(H) Additional Information:

This notice gives our opinion, not an official Medicare decision. If you have other questions on this notice or Medicare billing, call **1-800-MEDICARE** (1-800-633-4227/**TTY**: 1-877-486-2048).

Signing below means that you have received and understand this notice. You also receive a copy.

(I) **Signature:**	*(J)* **Date:**

According to the Paperwork Reduction Act of 1995, no persons are required to respond to a collection of information unless it displays a valid OMB control number. The valid OMB control number for this information collection is 0938-0566. The time required to complete this information collection is estimated to average 7 minutes per response, including the time to review instructions, search existing data resources, gather the data needed, and complete and review the information collection. If you have comments concerning the accuracy of the time estimate or suggestions for improving this form, please write to: CMS, 7500 Security Boulevard, Attn: PRA Reports Clearance Officer, Baltimore, Maryland 21244-1850.

Form CMS-R-131 (03/08)   Form Approved OMB No. 0938-0566

- Recording procedures and services performed
- Records applicable diagnosis and codes for each procedure performed
- Filing insurance claims and billing patients
- Reviewing and recording payments

Billing programs streamline the important process of creating and following up on health-care claims sent to payers and bills sent to patients. For example, a large medical practice with a group of providers and thousands of patients may receive a phone call from a patient who wants to know the amount owed on an account. With a billing program, the medical assistant can key the first few letters of the patient's last name and the patient's account data will appear on the screen. The outstanding balance can then be communicated to the patient. Billing programs are also used to exchange health information about the practice's patients with health plans. Using **electronic data interchange (EDI)**, similar to the technology behind ATMs, information is sent quickly and securely.

electronic data interchange (EDI)
Transmitting electronic medical insurance claims from providers to payers using the necessary information systems.

Obtaining Patient Information

You will need certain information to be able to complete insurance claims and bill correctly for the patients of the medical practice where you work. This information is usually completed on a patient registration form, as shown in Chapter 15.

Basic Facts   When the patient first arrives, obtain or verify the following personal information:

- Name of patient (be sure to get the correct spelling of the patient's legal name)
- Current home address
- Current home telephone number
- Date of birth (month, day, and the four digits of the year)
- Social Security number
- Next of kin or person to contact in case of an emergency

Obtain the following insurance information:

- Current employer (may be more than one)
- Employer address and telephone number
- Insurance carrier and effective date of coverage
- Insurance group plan number
- Insurance identification number
- Name of subscriber or insured

Depending on state law, obtain the following release signatures:

- Patient's signature on a form authorizing release of information to the insurance carrier
- Patient's signature on a form for assignment of benefits

Eligibility for Services   After the patient completes the registration form, verify the personal and insurance information given, copy or scan the front and back of the patient's insurance card, and obtain the release signatures for inclusion in the patient's financial record. Without the signed authorization to release information, you do not have legal permission to give the insurance carrier information regarding the patient's diagnosis and treatment. The assignment of benefits signature is important because without it, the insurance carrier may send the payment for services to the patient instead of to the office.

Also verify the effective date of insurance coverage because services performed before this date will not be covered by the insurance carrier. To reduce possible payment problems, inform the patient before a service is performed if there is a possibility it may not be covered. Many offices now have a patient sign a waiver of liability form, giving the reason it is believed that a procedure will not be covered. By signing the form, the patient agrees to accept responsibility for payment should the insurer not pay for the service. The office should retain the original waiver of liability in the patient's financial record and also give a copy to the patient for his records.

Obtaining Prior Authorization   As stated earlier in the chapter, patients often need prior authorization in order for the physician to receive payment for many elective procedures. In today's office, prior authorization can often be initiated over the phone or on the insurance carrier Web site. When calling the insurance company, have the patient's insurance group number and ID number available, as well as the name, address, phone number, and date of birth for identification purposes. If the patient is not the subscriber (insured), you should have the subscriber's name and birth date available as well as the relationship between the patient and the subscriber. You will also need the name and CPT code of the planned procedure, as well as the diagnosis and ICD-9 code as the reason for the procedure to document medical necessity.

If you call the insurance carrier, ask for or choose the option for the prior authorization department. You will likely be speaking to a nurse case manager who will take down the information regarding the planned procedure. She may give authorization over the phone and if so, carefully write down the authorization number and place it in the patient's chart for further reference. The authorization itself will be mailed to the office, usually with a disclaimer that prior authorization is not a guarantee of payment, simply agreement that with the information given, it appears that there is medical necessity for the planned procedure. Should the insurance plan Web site give you the ability to obtain prior authorization on the Web site, you will complete the authorization form as directed inserting the above information as required. The authorization will be given either immediately or within 24 hours and an authorization sent to the office via secure e-mail. Keep this authorization in the patient's record as proof of receipt. As always, note the authorization number for insertion in block 23 of the CMS-1500 claim form when submitting the procedure for payment. Procedure 17–2 at the end of this chapter outlines the steps for obtaining prior authorization.

Coordination of Benefits   Coordination of benefits refers to legal clauses in insurance policies that prevent duplication of payment. These clauses restrict payment by insurance companies to no more than 100% of the cost of covered benefits. In many families, husband and wife are both wage earners. They and their children are frequently eligible for health insurance benefits through both employers' plans. In such cases the two insurance companies coordinate their payments to pay up to 100% of a procedure's cost. A payment of 100% includes the policyholder's deductible and co-insurance or copayment. The *primary,* plan is the policy that pays benefits first. The *secondary,* or supplemental, plan then pays the deductible and co-insurance or copayment. A policyholder's primary plan is always his employer group health plan. If both a husband and wife have insurance through their employers, the husband's plan is his primary plan and the wife's insurance plan is her primary plan. To determine the primary plan for dependents, in many states, the **birthday rule** is followed. It states that the insurance policy of the policyholder whose birthday comes first in the calendar year is the primary payer for all dependents.

For example, if a husband's birthday is July 14 and his wife's birthday is June 11, following the birthday rule, the wife's insurance plan is the primary

coordination of benefits
A legal principle that limits payments by insurance companies to 100% of the covered expenses.

birthday rule
A rule that states that the insurance policy of a policyholder whose birthday comes first in the year is the primary payer for all dependents.

payer for their children and the husband's is the secondary payer. If a husband and wife were born on the same day, the policy that has been in effect the longest is the primary payer.

The birthday rule is applied in most states in which dependents are covered by two or more medical plans. Not all states are covered by the birthday rule, so be sure to check with your state's insurance commission whenever you are in doubt. Table 17–4 describes widely used coverage guidelines.

Delivering Services to the Patient

To ensure accuracy in claims processing, any services delivered to the patient in the office by the physician or other members of the health-care team must be entered into the patient record. Referrals to outside physicians or specialists must also be entered into the record but of course, there is no charge involved in making a referral.

Physician's Services   The physician who examines the patient notes the patient's symptoms in the medical record. The physician also notes a diagnosis and treatment plan (including prescribed medications) and specifies if and when the patient should return for a follow-up visit. After completing the visit with the patient, the physician writes the diagnosis, treatment, and sometimes the fee on an **encounter form (superbill)** (Figure 17–6) or **charge slip** (Figure 17–7) and instructs the patient to give you the superbill or charge slip before leaving. If the patient has a per visit copayment, it is usually collected at the time the patient is leaving the office.

Medical Coding   Today, the superbill used by most offices are preprinted with the most common procedures and procedure codes. If the charges are not preprinted, there is a space next to each procedure so that the current charge may be inserted. If the patient has a procedure that is not listed on the superbill, a blank space at the bottom is completed with the procedure name, procedure code, and charge. Even though the procedures and their codes are preprinted on the superbill, it is critical to verify that the procedure checked off on the form was actually completed by comparing the superbill to the medical

encounter form (superbill)
A form that can be used as the original record of services performed for a patient and the charges for those services. The form can also be used as a charge slip and invoice, and can be submitted with insurance claims.

charge slip
The original record of services performed for a patient and the charges for those services.

table 17–4

Guidelines for Determining Primary Coverage

- If the patient has only one policy, it is primary.

- If the patient has coverage under two plans, the plan covering the employee for the longest period of time is primary. However, if an active employee has a plan with the present employer and is still covered by a former employer's plan as a retiree or a laid-off employee, the current employer's plan is primary.

- If the patient is also covered as a dependent under another insurance policy, the patient's plan is primary.

- If an employed patient has coverage under the employer's plan and additional coverage under a governmentsponsored plan, the employer's plan is primary. An example of this is a patient enrolled in a PPO through employment who is also on Medicare.

- If a retired patient is covered by the plan of the spouse's employer and the spouse is still employed, the spouse's plan is primary, even if the retired person has Medicare.

- If the patient is a dependent child covered by both parents' plans and the parents are not separated or divorced (or have joint custody of the child), the primary plan is determined by which parent has the first birth date in the calendar year (the birthday rule).

- If two or more plans cover the dependent children of separated or divorced parents who do not have joint custody of their children, the children's primary plan is determined in this order:

  1. The plan of the custodial parent
  2. The plan of the spouse of the custodial parent (if the parent has remarried)
  3. The plan of the parent without custody

figure 17-6

An encounter form (superbill) can also be used as a charge slip and invoice, and can be submitted with insurance claims.

Total Care Clinic, PC
342 East Park Blvd
Funton, XY 12345-6789

☐ PRIVATE ☐ BLUECROSS ☐ IND. ☐ MEDICARE ☐ MEDICAID ☐ HMO ☐ PPO

PATIENT'S LAST NAME	FIRST	ACCOUNT #	BIRTHDATE / /	SEX ☐ MALE ☐ FEMALE	TODAY'S DATE / /
INSURANCE COMPANY		SUBSCRIBER	PLAN #	SUB. #	GROUP

ASSIGNMENT: I hereby assign my insurance benefits to be paid directly to the undersigned physician. I am financially responsible for non-covered services.
SIGNED: (Patient, or Parent, if Minor)   DATE: / /

RELEASE: I hereby authorize the physician to release to my insurance carrers any information required to process this claim.
SIGNED: (Patient, or Parent, if Minor)   DATE: / /

✔ DESCRIPTION	M/Care	CPT/Mod	DxRe	FEE
OFFICE CARE				
NEW PATIENT				
Brief		99201		
Limited		99202		
Intermediate		99203		
Extended		99204		
Comprehensive		99205		
ESTABLISHED PATIENT				
Minimal		99211		
Brief		99212		
Limited		99213		
Intermediate		99214		
Extended		99215		
Comprehensive		99215		
CONSULTATION-OFFICE				
Focused		99241		
Expanded		99242		
Detailed		99243		
Comprehensive 1		99244		
Comprehensive 2		99245		
MCR Pts - use E/M codes				
Case Management		98900		
Post-op Exam		99024		

✔ DESCRIPTION	M/Care	CPT/Mod	DxRe	FEE
PROCEDURES				
Tread Mill (In Office)		93015		
24 Hour Holter		93224		
If Medicare (Set up Fee)		93225		
Physician Interpret		93227		
EKG w/Interpretation		93000		
EKG (tracing only)		93005		
Sigmoidoscopy		45300		
Sigmoidoscopy, Flexible		45330		
Sigmoidos. , Flex. w/Bx.		45331		
Spirometry, FEV/FVC		94010		
Spirometry, Post-Dilator		94060		
LABORATORY				
Blood Draw Fee		36415		
Urinalysis, Chemical		81000		
Throat Culture		87081		
Occult Blood		82270		
Pap Handling Charge		99000		
Pap Life Guard		88150-90		
Gram Stain		87205		
Hanging Drop		87210		
Urine Drug Screen		80100		
SUPPLIES				

✔ DESCRIPTION	M/Care	CPT/Mod	DxRe	FEE
INJECTIONS/IMMUNIZATIONS				
Tetanus/Diphtheria		90718		
MMR		90707		
Pneumococcal		90732		
Influenza		90656		
TB Skin Test (PPD)		86580		
Antigen Injection-Single		95115		
Multiple		95117		
B12 Injection	J3420	90782		
Injection, IM		90782		
Compazine	J0780	90782		
Demerol	J2175	90782		
Vistaril	J3410	90782		
Susphrine	J0170	90782		
Decadron	J0890	90782		
Estradiol	J1000	90782		
Testosterone	J1080	90782		
Lidocaine	J2000	90782		
Solumedrol	J2920	90782		
Solucortef	J1720	90782		
Hydeltra	J1690	90782		
INJECTIONS - JOINT/BURSA				
Small Joints		20600		
Intermediate		20605		
Large Joints		20610		
Trigger Point		20552		
MISCELLANEOUS				

DIAGNOSIS:

	ICD-9			
Abdominal Pain	789.0	Gout	274.0	C.V.A. - Acute	436.	Electrolyte Dis.	276.9	Herpes Simplex	054.9

	ICD-9		ICD-9		ICD-9		ICD-9		ICD-9
Abdominal Pain	789.0	Gout	274.0	C.V.A. - Acute	436.	Electrolyte Dis.	276.9	Herpes Simplex	054.9
Abscess (Site)	682.9	Asthma	493.90	Cere. Vas. Accid. (Old)	438	Fatigue	780.7	Herpes Zoster	053.9
Adverse Drug Rx	995.2	Asthmatic Bronchitis	493.90	Cerumen	380.4	Fibrocys. Br. Dis	610.1	Hydrocele	603.9
Alcohol Detox	291.8	Atrial Fib.	427.31	Chestwall Pain	786.59	Fracture (Site)	829.0	Hyperlipidemia	272.4
Alcoholism	303.90	Atrial Tachi.	427.0	Cholecystitis	575.0	Open/Close		Hypertension	401.9
Allergic Rhinitis	477	Bowel Obstruct.	560.9	Cholelithiasis	574.00	Fungal Infect. (Site)	110.8	Hyperthyroidism	242.9
Allergy	995.3	Breast Mass	611.72	COPD	492.8	Gastric Ulcer	531.90	Hypothyroidism	244.9
Alzheimer's Dis.	290.1	Bronchitis	490	Cirrhosis	571.5	Gastritis	535.0	Labyrinthitis	386.30
Anemia	285.9	Bursitis	727.3	Cong. Heart Fail.	428.9	Gastroenteritis	558.9	Lipoma (Site)	214.9
Anemia - Pernicious	281.0	Cancer, Breast (Site)	174.9	Conjunctivitis	372.30	G.I. Bleeding	578.9	Lymphoma	202.8
Angina	413.9	Metastatic (Site)	199.1	Contusion (Site)	924.9	Glomerulonephritis	583.9	Mit. Valve Prolapse	424.0
Anxiety Synd.	300.00	Colon	153.9	Costochondritis	733.99	Headache	784.0	Myocard. Infarction (Area)	410.9
Appendicitis	541	Cancer, Rectal	154.1	Depression	311.	Headache, Tension	307.81	M.I., Old	412
Arteriosci. H.D.	414.0	Lung (Site)	162.9	Dermatitis	692.9	Migraine (Type)	346.9	Myositis	729.1
Arthritis, Osteo.	715.90	Skin (Site)	173.9	Diabetes Mellitus	250.00	Hemorrhoids	455.6	Nausea/Vomiting	787.0
Rheumatoid	714.0	Card. Arrhythmia (Type)	427.9	Diabetic Ketosis	250.1	Hernia, Hiatal	553.3	Neuralgia	729.2
Lupus	710.0	Cardiomyopathy	425.4	Diverticulitis	562.11	Inguinal	550.9	Nevus (Site)	216.9
		Cellulitis (Site)	682.9	Diverticulosis	562.10	Hepatitis	573.3	Obesity	278.0

DIAGNOSIS: (IF NOT CHECKED ABOVE)

SERVICES PERFORMED AT: ☐ Office ☐ E.R. ☐ CLAIM CONTAINS NO ORDERED REFERRING SERVICE
☐ Rodriguez Patel ☐ Fredericks Kacharski ☐ Wiley

REFERRING PHYSICIAN & I.D. NUMBER

RETURN APPOINTMENT INFORMATION: 5 - 10 - 15 - 20 - 30 - 40 - 60 [DAYS] [WKS.] [MOS.] [PRN]	NEXT APPOINTMENT M - T - W - TH - F - S DATE / / TIME: AM PM	ACCEPT ASSIGNMENT? ☐ YES ☐ NO	DOCTOR'S SIGNATURE

INSTRUCTIONS TO PATIENT FOR FILING INSURANCE CLAIMS:

1. Complete upper portion of this form, sign and date.
2. Attach this form to your own insurance company's form for direct reimbursement.

MEDICARE PATIENTS - DO NOT SEND THIS TO MEDICARE.
WE WILL SUBMIT THE CLAIM FOR YOU.

☐ CASH
☐ CHECK #____
☐ VISA
☐ MC
☐ CO-PAY

TOTAL TODAY'S FEE	
OLD BALANCE	
TOTAL DUE	
AMOUNT REC'D. TODAY	

INSUR-A-BILL ® BIBBERO SYSTEMS, INC. • PETALUMA, CA • UP. SUPER. © 6/94 (BIBB/STOCK)

DATE	DESCRIPTION–CODE	CHARGE	PAYMENT	CURRENT BALANCE

521-234-0001   Tax ID No. 11-0004004

TOTAL CARE CLINIC, PC
243 East Park Blvd
Funton, XY 12345-6789

99205	Office Visit, New Patient	36425	Venipuncture	59025	NST
99215	Office Visit, Established Patient	57454	Colposcopy with Biopsy	54150	Circumcision
99213	Office Visit, Established, Brief	57511	Cryosurgery	58300	IUD Insertion
88155	Pap	58100	Endometrial Biopsy	57170	Diaphragm Fitting
84703	Urine Pregnancy Test	56600	Vulva Biopsy		

NAME _____ DX _____   No. 0005807

figure 17–7

A charge slip shows the services performed for a patient and the charges for those services.

record. This step ensures that the patient is not inadvertently charged for a procedure that did not take place. If your office uses a charge slip instead of a superbill, you will need to translate the procedures listed on the charge slip into charge codes for the insurance carrier. This topic is covered in depth in Chapter 18.

Referrals and Authorizations for Other Services You may be asked to secure authorization from the insurance company for additional procedures. If so, contact the insurance company to explain the reason for the procedure(s) and obtain an authorization number from the insurance carrier. Enter this authorization number in the billing program for inclusion on claims related to this procedure.

Frequently you will be asked to arrange an appointment for required services, particularly if the physician believes they are urgently needed. For example, a physician may send a patient to a specialist's office for evaluation or x-ray on the same day the patient visits your office. If the patient is a member of a managed care program, prior to making the required appointment, you will need to verify with the insurance plan that the specialist requested is allowed by the insurance company. If so, a referral may also be needed. Depending on the insurance plan and your office capabilities, this referral may be completed in writing or via the insurance plan's Web site.

Preparing the Health-Care Claim

Everyone who receives services from a doctor in the practice where you work is responsible for paying the practice for those services. When the patient brings you the superbill from the doctor, you may perform one or more of the following procedures, depending on the policy of your practice:

- Prepare and transmit a health-care claim on behalf of the patient directly to the insurance company.

- Accept payment from the patient for the full amount. The patient will submit a claim to the insurance carrier for reimbursement.

- Accept an insurance copayment.

Filing the Insurance Claim   If you are going to transmit the claim directly to the payer, you will prepare an insurance claim, often electronically. The billing program will create a log of transmitted claims, or if paper claims are filed a register such as the one shown in Figure 17–8 may be maintained.

Time Limits   Claims must be filed in a timely manner. Time limits for filing claims vary from company to company. For example, some insurers will not pay a claim unless it is filed within 8 weeks of the date of service, others will allow up to a year for claim submission.

As of January 1, 2010, The Patient Protection and Affordable Care Act, changed the Medicare timely filing limit. Medicare providers have up to one year after the date of service to file a Medicare claim. Previous regulations had allowed claims to be submitted by December 31 of the year after the date of service.

Medicaid states that claims must be filed no later than 1 year from the date of service. The time frame for refiling rejected claims varies by state. In Indiana (which allows one year from the date of rejection for resubmission of claims), for example, if you filed a claim for a service performed on January 2, 2009, and the claim was rejected on May 31, 2009, you would have until May 31, 2010, to refile the claim. Other states may allow only 60ñ90 days for refiling a claim, so it is important to know your individual state rules and regulations.

Even if an insurance plan allows up to a year to file a claim, it is poor business practice to wait so long. In the typical medical practice, claims are transmitted within a few business days after the date of service. Many large practices file claims every day or twice a week.

Insurer's Processing and Payment

Your transmitted claim for payment will undergo a number of reviews by the insurer. Currently, much of the review process occurs electronically.

Review for Medical Necessity   The insurance carrier reviews each claim to determine whether the diagnosis and accompanying treatment are compatible and whether the treatment is medically necessary, as explained in Chapters 18–20.

Review for Allowable Benefits   The claims department also compares the fees the doctor charges with the benefits provided by the patient's health insurance policy. This review determines the amount of deductible and/or coinsurance the patient owes. The amount the patient owes the practice is known as subscriber liability.

figure 17–8

After submitting a claim to an insurer, track each claim in an insurance claim register, such as the one pictured here.

Patient Name	Insurance Company	Claim Filing		Insurance Response Pd, Denied, Rejct, Suspd, Info Req	Date Resubmitted	Payment		Patient Balance	Date Patient Billed
		Date	Amount	Date		Date	Amount		

Payment and Remittance Advice   After reviewing the claim, the insurer pays a benefit, either to the subscriber (patient) or to the practice, depending on whether an assignment of benefits was signed and on the policy of the insurance carrier. With the payment, the insurer sends a **remittance advice (RA)**, formerly called an **explanation of benefits (EOB)**. If the payment is made electronically, the RA will also be received electronically. In this case the RA is known as an electronic remittance advice (ERA) or electronic explanation of benefits (EEOB). A patient who receives the payment receives an RA summary containing only his information and the practice receives a practice RA that typically contains information for multiple patients at one time. Each insurance plan has its own EOB (RA) format and you will learn those of your office's most popular payers. Because many patients may be included on each EOB (RA), you may find it easiest to use a ruler to read each line of a paper RA and check off each line as you credit each patient's account. If a secondary insurance carrier requires a copy of a patient's primary insurance EOB, remember to black out any information on the EOB that does not pertain to the patient information required by the insurance carrier, to protect the information of the other patients on the EOB. The RA or the EOB explains the medical claim. For each service submitted to an insurer, the RA or EOB form gives the following information:

- Name of the insured and identification number
- Name of the beneficiary
- Claim number
- Date, place, and type of service (coded)
- Amount billed by the practice
- Amount allowed (according to the subscriber's policy)
- Amount of subscriber liability (coinsurance, copayment, deductible, or noncovered services)
- Amount paid and included in the current payment
- A notation of any services not covered and an explanation of why they were not covered (for example, many insurance plans do not cover a woman's annual gynecologic examination and only a certain dollar amount of well-baby visits for infants)

Reviewing the Insurer's RA and Payment

Verify all information on the RA, line by line, using your records for each patient represented on the RA. In a large practice, you will frequently receive payment and an RA for multiple patients at one time. An example of a Medicare RA, which is called a Medicare Remittance Advice, is shown in Figure 17–9.

If all numbers on the RA agree with your records, you can make the appropriate entries in the insurance follow-up log for claims paid. In a small practice, the insurance follow-up log is used to track filed claims, using such information as patient name, date the claim was filed, services the claim reflects, notations about the results of the claim, and any balance due from the patient. Larger practices tend to track claims in the computer billing program in a file called, for example, "Unpaid Claims." If all the numbers do not agree, you will need to trace the claim with the insurance company.

When a claim is rejected or denied, the RA states the reason. You will need to review the claim, examining all procedural and diagnosis codes for accuracy and comparing the claim with the patient's insurance information. You will probably need to contact the insurance company by telephone to find out how to resolve the claim problem.

CHECKPOINT
LO 17.5

Explain how to decide coverage priority for dependent children of divorced parents who both have insurance coverage.

figure 17-9

The insurer sends the remittance advice form to the medical practice.

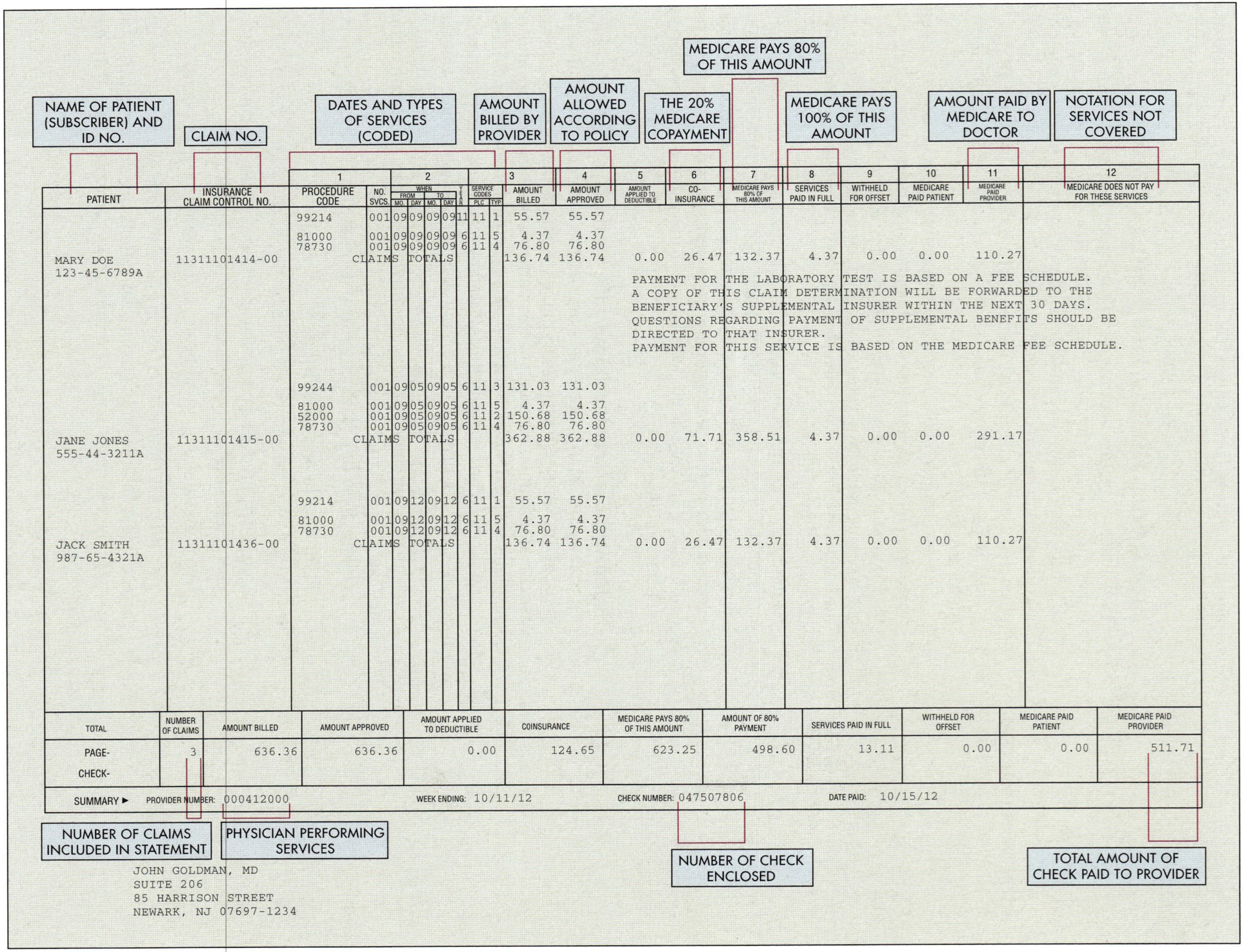

NAME OF PATIENT (SUBSCRIBER) AND ID NO.

CLAIM NO.

DATES AND TYPES OF SERVICES (CODED)

AMOUNT BILLED BY PROVIDER

AMOUNT ALLOWED ACCORDING TO POLICY

THE 20% MEDICARE COPAYMENT

MEDICARE PAYS 80% OF THIS AMOUNT

MEDICARE PAYS 100% OF THIS AMOUNT

AMOUNT PAID BY MEDICARE TO DOCTOR

NOTATION FOR SERVICES NOT COVERED

PATIENT	INSURANCE CLAIM CONTROL NO.	PROCEDURE CODE 1	NO. SVCS.	WHEN 2 FROM MO DAY	TO MO DAY	SERVICE CODES PLC TYP	3 AMOUNT BILLED	4 AMOUNT APPROVED	5 AMOUNT APPLIED TO DEDUCTIBLE	6 CO-INSURANCE	7 MEDICARE PAYS 80% OF THIS AMOUNT	8 SERVICES PAID IN FULL	9 WITHHELD FOR OFFSET	10 MEDICARE PAID PATIENT	11 MEDICARE PAID PROVIDER	12 MEDICARE DOES NOT PAY FOR THESE SERVICES
MARY DOE 123-45-6789A	11311101414-00	99214	001	0909	0909	11 11 1	55.57	55.57								
		81000	001	0909	0909	611 5	4.37	4.37				4.37				
		78730	001	0909	0909	611 4	76.80	76.80								
		CLAIMS TOTALS					136.74	136.74	0.00	26.47	132.37	4.37	0.00	0.00	110.27	
JANE JONES 555-44-3211A	11311101415-00	99244	001	0905	0905	611 3	131.03	131.03								
		81000	001	0905	0905	611 5	4.37	4.37								
		52000	001	0905	0905	611 2	150.68	150.68								
		78730	001	0905	0905	611 4	76.80	76.80								
		CLAIMS TOTALS					362.88	362.88	0.00	71.71	358.51	4.37	0.00	0.00	291.17	
JACK SMITH 987-65-4321A	11311101436-00	99214	001	0912	0912	611 1	55.57	55.57								
		81000	001	0912	0912	611 5	4.37	4.37								
		78730	001	0912	0912	611 4	76.80	76.80								
		CLAIMS TOTALS					136.74	136.74	0.00	26.47	132.37	4.37	0.00	0.00	110.27	

PAYMENT FOR THE LABORATORY TEST IS BASED ON A FEE SCHEDULE. A COPY OF THIS CLAIM DETERMINATION WILL BE FORWARDED TO THE BENEFICIARY'S SUPPLEMENTAL INSURER WITHIN THE NEXT 30 DAYS. QUESTIONS REGARDING PAYMENT OF SUPPLEMENTAL BENEFITS SHOULD BE DIRECTED TO THAT INSURER. PAYMENT FOR THIS SERVICE IS BASED ON THE MEDICARE FEE SCHEDULE.

PHYSICIAN PERFORMING SERVICES

NUMBER OF CLAIMS INCLUDED IN STATEMENT

NUMBER OF CHECK ENCLOSED

TOTAL AMOUNT OF CHECK PAID TO PROVIDER

TOTAL	NUMBER OF CLAIMS	AMOUNT BILLED	AMOUNT APPROVED	AMOUNT APPLIED TO DEDUCTIBLE	COINSURANCE	MEDICARE PAYS 80% OF THIS AMOUNT	AMOUNT OF 80% PAYMENT	SERVICES PAID IN FULL	WITHHELD FOR OFFSET	MEDICARE PAID PATIENT	MEDICARE PAID PROVIDER
PAGE-	3	636.36	636.36	0.00	124.65	623.25	498.60	13.11	0.00	0.00	511.71
CHECK-											

SUMMARY ▶ PROVIDER NUMBER: 000412000

WEEK ENDING: 10/11/12

CHECK NUMBER: 047507806

DATE PAID: 10/15/12

JOHN GOLDMAN, MD
SUITE 206
85 HARRISON STREET
NEWARK, NJ 07697-1234

LO 17.6 Preparing and Transmitting Health-Care Claims

Health-care claims are a critical communication between medical offices and payers on behalf of patients. Processing claims is a major task in most offices, and the numbers can be huge. For example, a 40-physician group practice with 55,000 patients served annually typically processes 1000 claims daily!

Electronic Claims and Paper Claims

Two types of claims are in use: (1) the predominant HIPAA electronic claim transaction and (2) the older CMS-1500 paper form. The electronic claim transaction is the HIPAA Health-Care Claim or Equivalent Encounter Information; it is commonly referred to as the "HIPAA claim" or simply the "837P (P for physician claim)". Its official name is **X12 837 Health Care Claim**. The paper format is the "universal claim" known as the CMS-1500 claim form (formerly, the HCFA-1500).

As of October 2003, Medicare mandated the X12 837 transaction for all Medicare claims except those from very small practices. Third-party payers may continue to accept paper transactions. Practices that elect to use paper claims must have two versions of their medical billing software: one to capture the necessary data elements for HIPAA-compliant electronic Medicare claims and another version to generate CMS-1500 claims. Also, under HIPAA regulations, only medical offices that do not handle any other HIPAA-related transactions may still use paper claims. More and more payers are accepting electronic claims. As the process becomes more streamlined and cost efficient, even smaller offices are beginning to submit electronic claims, which in general are paid in a week or two instead of the usual 6-8 weeks for paper claim reimbursement.

Preparing Electronic Claims The information entered on claims is called data elements. Many elements, such as the patient's personal and insurance information, are entered in the billing program before or at the time of the patient appointment, based on the patient registration form and on communications with payers. After the patient's appointment is concluded, the claim is completed when the administrative medical assistant keys the billing transactions—the services, charges, and payments—as detailed on the superbill (encounter form) into the billing claims software program. The administrative medical assistant then instructs the software program to prepare claims for editing ("scrubbing") and transmission.

Follow these tips when entering data in medical billing programs:

- Enter data in all capital letters
- Do not use prefixes for people's names, such as Mr., Ms., or Dr.
- Unless required by a particular insurance carrier, do not use special characters such as hyphens, commas, or apostrophes
- Use only valid data in all fields; avoid words such as "same"

The X12 837 transaction requires many data elements, and all must be correct. Most billing programs or claim transmission programs automatically reformat data such as dates into the correct formats. These data elements are reported in five major sections:

1. Provider
2. Subscriber (the insured or policyholder)
3. Patient (who may be the subscriber or another person) and payer
4. Claim details
5. Services

X12 837 Health Care Claim

An electronic claim transaction that is the HIPAA Health Care Claim or Equivalent Encounter Information.

Not all data elements are required. Some are considered situational and are required only when a certain condition applies. When it does apply, then that data element also becomes required. For example, if a claim involves pregnancy, the date of the last menstrual period is required. If the claim does not involve pregnancy, that date should not be reported.

Before the HIPAA mandate for standard transactions, some payers required additional records, such as their own information sheet, when providers billed them. Some payers also used their own coding systems. The HIPAA Electronic Health Care Transactions and Code Sets (TCS) mandate means that all health plans are required to accept the standard claim submitted electronically.

Other standard transactions also support the claim process, such as advising the office of claim status, payment, and other key information. These transactions standards apply to the treatment, payment, and operations (TPO) information that is exchanged between medical offices and health plans. Each electronic transaction has both a title and a number. Each number begins with X12, which is the number of the EDI format, followed by a unique number that stands for the transaction. Here are some examples of titles and numbers that medical assistants may encounter while processing X12 837 health-care claims:

Number	Title
X12 276/277	Claim status inquiry and response
X12 270/271	Eligibility inquiry and response
X12 278	Referral authorization inquiry and response
X12 835	Payment and remittance advice
X12 820	Health plan premium payments
X12 834	Enrollment in and withdrawal from a health plan

Preparing Paper Claims   The process for preparing paper claims is similar to the X12 837 claim. Usually, the medical billing program is updated with information about the patient's office visit. Then the program is instructed to print the data on a CMS-1500 paper form, shown in Figure 17–10. This claim may be mailed or faxed to a third-party payer.

Because of the HIPAA mandate, the paper claim is not as widely used as previously; however, the information it contains is essentially very similar to the X12 837. The CMS-1500 contains 33 form locators, which are numbered blocks. Blocks 1–13 refer to the patient information and the patient and guarantor insurance coverage information. Blocks 14–33 contain information about the provider and the transaction information, including the patient's diagnoses, procedures, and charges.

The following instructions provide step-by-step guidance in completing a CMS-1500 paper form, which you can practice with Procedure 17-4, Completing the CMS-1500 Claim Form, found at the end of this chapter. Figure 17–11 is an example of a completed Medicare claim, which includes a secondary payer.

HIPAA laws are just as important when working with patient financial information as they are when working patient PHI in the medical record. Remember to keep access to patient medical and financial records confidential at all times, including the information contained within a paper or electronic health or claim file (information on electronic claim filing is discussed later in this chapter). Refer back to Chapter 6 for more detailed information on HIPAA and PHI.

Completing the CMS-1500 Form   Here is how to complete blocks 1–13, the patient and insured's information:

Block 1   Place an X in the appropriate insurance box.

   Note: Each box is slightly to the left of the insurance plan it represents.

1. MEDICARE	MEDICAID	TRICARE CHAMPUS	CHAMPVA	GROUP HEALTH PLAN	FECA BLK LUNG	OTHER
☐ (Medicare #)	☐ (Medicaid #)	☐ (Sponsor's SSN)	☐ (Member ID#)	☐ (SSN or ID)	☐ (SSN)	☐ (ID)

figure 17–10

The CMS-1500 is a paper health insurance claim form.

1500

HEALTH INSURANCE CLAIM FORM

APPROVED BY NATIONAL UNIFORM CLAIM COMMITTEE 08/05

PICA | PICA

CARRIER

1. MEDICARE (Medicare #) | MEDICAID (Medicaid #) | TRICARE CHAMPUS (Sponsor's SSN) | CHAMPVA (Member ID#) | GROUP HEALTH PLAN (SSN or ID) | FECA BLK LUNG (SSN) | OTHER (ID)

1a. INSURED'S I.D. NUMBER (For Program in Item 1)

2. PATIENT'S NAME (Last Name, First Name, Middle Initial)

3. PATIENT'S BIRTH DATE MM DD YY SEX M F

4. INSURED'S NAME (Last Name, First Name, Middle Initial)

5. PATIENT'S ADDRESS (No., Street)

6. PATIENT RELATIONSHIP TO INSURED Self Spouse Child Other

7. INSURED'S ADDRESS (No., Street)

CITY STATE

8. PATIENT STATUS Single Married Other

CITY STATE

ZIP CODE TELEPHONE (Include Area Code) ( )

Employed Full-Time Student Part-Time Student

ZIP CODE TELEPHONE (Include Area Code) ( )

9. OTHER INSURED'S NAME (Last Name, First Name, Middle Initial)

10. IS PATIENT'S CONDITION RELATED TO:

11. INSURED'S POLICY GROUP OR FECA NUMBER

a. OTHER INSURED'S POLICY OR GROUP NUMBER

a. EMPLOYMENT? (Current or Previous) YES NO

a. INSURED'S DATE OF BIRTH MM DD YY SEX M F

b. OTHER INSURED'S DATE OF BIRTH MM DD YY SEX M F

b. AUTO ACCIDENT? YES NO PLACE (State)

b. EMPLOYER'S NAME OR SCHOOL NAME

c. EMPLOYER'S NAME OR SCHOOL NAME

c. OTHER ACCIDENT? YES NO

c. INSURANCE PLAN NAME OR PROGRAM NAME

d. INSURANCE PLAN NAME OR PROGRAM NAME

10d. RESERVED FOR LOCAL USE

d. IS THERE ANOTHER HEALTH BENEFIT PLAN? YES NO *If yes*, return to and complete item 9 a-d.

READ BACK OF FORM BEFORE COMPLETING & SIGNING THIS FORM.

12. PATIENT'S OR AUTHORIZED PERSON'S SIGNATURE I authorize the release of any medical or other information necessary to process this claim. I also request payment of government benefits either to myself or to the party who accepts assignment below.

SIGNED ______ DATE ______

13. INSURED'S OR AUTHORIZED PERSON'S SIGNATURE I authorize payment of medical benefits to the undersigned physician or supplier for services described below.

SIGNED ______

PATIENT AND INSURED INFORMATION

14. DATE OF CURRENT: MM DD YY ◀ ILLNESS (First symptom) OR INJURY (Accident) OR PREGNANCY(LMP)

15. IF PATIENT HAS HAD SAME OR SIMILAR ILLNESS. GIVE FIRST DATE MM DD YY

16. DATES PATIENT UNABLE TO WORK IN CURRENT OCCUPATION FROM MM DD YY TO MM DD YY

17. NAME OF REFERRING PROVIDER OR OTHER SOURCE

17a.

17b. NPI

18. HOSPITALIZATION DATES RELATED TO CURRENT SERVICES FROM MM DD YY TO MM DD YY

19. RESERVED FOR LOCAL USE

20. OUTSIDE LAB? YES NO $ CHARGES

21. DIAGNOSIS OR NATURE OF ILLNESS OR INJURY (Relate Items 1, 2, 3 or 4 to Item 24E by Line)

1. ___ . ___

2. ___ . ___

3. ___ . ___

4. ___ . ___

22. MEDICAID RESUBMISSION CODE ORIGINAL REF. NO.

23. PRIOR AUTHORIZATION NUMBER

24. A. DATE(S) OF SERVICE From MM DD YY To MM DD YY	B. PLACE OF SERVICE	C. EMG	D. PROCEDURES, SERVICES, OR SUPPLIES (Explain Unusual Circumstances) CPT/HCPCS MODIFIER	E. DIAGNOSIS POINTER	F. $ CHARGES	G. DAYS OR UNITS	H. EPSDT Family Plan	I. ID. QUAL.	J. RENDERING PROVIDER ID. #
1								NPI	
2								NPI	
3								NPI	
4								NPI	
5								NPI	
6								NPI	

PHYSICIAN OR SUPPLIER INFORMATION

25. FEDERAL TAX I.D. NUMBER SSN EIN

26. PATIENT'S ACCOUNT NO.

27. ACCEPT ASSIGNMENT? (For govt. claims, see back) YES NO

28. TOTAL CHARGE $

29. AMOUNT PAID $

30. BALANCE DUE $

31. SIGNATURE OF PHYSICIAN OR SUPPLIER INCLUDING DEGREES OR CREDENTIALS (I certify that the statements on the reverse apply to this bill and are made a part thereof.)

SIGNED DATE

32. SERVICE FACILITY LOCATION INFORMATION

a. NPI b.

33. BILLING PROVIDER INFO & PH # ( )

a. NPI b.

NUCC Instruction Manual available at: www.nucc.org

APPROVED OMB-0938-0999 FORM CMS-1500 (08/05)

figure 17-11

Completed CMS-1500 claim form for a Medicare patient with secondary insurance coverage.

Block 1a   Insert the insured's ID number exactly as it appears on the insurance card.

1a. INSURED'S I.D. NUMBER	(For Program in Item 1)

Block 2   Enter the patient's name in this order: last, first, middle initial (if used).

2. PATIENT'S NAME (Last Name, First Name, Middle Initial)

Block 3   Enter patient's birth date in the 8-digit format: XX/XX/XXXX. Place an X in the box representing the patient's sex.

3. PATIENT'S BIRTH DATE MM ｜ DD ｜ YY	SEX M ☐ F ☐

Block 4   Enter insured's name in this order: last, first, middle initial (if used). If the insured is the patient, enter SAME; if Medicare, leave blank; if TRICARE, enter the Sponsor's name.

4. INSURED'S NAME (Last Name, First Name, Middle Initial)

Block 5   Enter the patient's street address, city, state, zip code, and phone number.

5. PATIENT'S ADDRESS (No., Street)

Block 6   Enter an X for the patient's relationship to the insured. If patient is insured, use Self; if Medicare, leave blank; if TRICARE, enter patient's relationship to the Sponsor.

6. PATIENT RELATIONSHIP TO INSURED
Self ☐ Spouse ☐ Child ☐ Other ☐

Block 7   Enter the insured's street address, city, state, zip code, and phone number.

7. INSURED'S ADDRESS (No., Street)

Block 8   Use an X to note the patient's marital status as single, married, or other. Note whether the patient is employed or a F/T or P/T student.

8. PATIENT STATUS
Single ☐   Married ☐   Other ☐
Employed ☐   Full-Time Student ☐   Part-Time Student ☐

Block 9a–d   *Note: Block 9 is used for the secondary insurance information and block 11 is used for the primary insurance information. You may find it easier to complete blocks 11 and 10 first, and then come back to block 9.*

9   If the patient has a *secondary* policy, enter the name (last, first, middle initial) of the insured for this *secondary* policy.

9a   Enter the *secondary* policy's group number or individual policy ID number. For a Medigap plan, enter the word "Medigap" before the ID number.

9b   Enter the date of birth of the insured for the *secondary* policy using the 8-digit format (XX/XX/XXXX) and mark the box for the insured's sex with an X.

9c Enter the employer or school name of the insured for this *secondary* plan. If this is a Medigap plan, enter the plan address here.

9d Enter the name of this *secondary* insurance plan. If this is a Medigap plan, enter the 9-digit PAYERID assigned by CMS.

9. OTHER INSURED'S NAME (Last Name, First Name, Middle Initial)
a. OTHER INSURED'S POLICY OR GROUP NUMBER

Block 10a–c   Place an X in the correct Yes or No box in each area to indicate whether the patient's condition is related to employment, auto accident, or other accident. If auto accident is answered Yes, insert the two-letter abbreviation for the state in which the accident occurred. (*Note: If any of these questions are answered yes, a workers' compensation, automobile, or other liability insurer may be responsible for the charges.*)

10. IS PATIENT'S CONDITION RELATED TO:
a. EMPLOYMENT? (Current or Previous)
☐ YES ☐ NO
b. AUTO ACCIDENT?   PLACE (State)
☐ YES ☐ NO └___┘
c. OTHER ACCIDENT?
☐ YES ☐ NO

Block 10d   If the secondary payer is Medicaid, some states require insertion of the abbreviation *MCD* followed by the Medicaid number here instead of in block 9. Check your state's regulations. For other payers if attachments are required with the claim, insert the word *ATTACHMENT* here.

10d. RESERVED FOR LOCAL USE

Block 11a–d   *Block 11 is used for the* primary *insurance information. Many administrative assistants and billers find it easiest to complete block 11 before completing blocks 9 and 10.*

11 Enter the group number for the primary insurance plan. If Medicare is the primary payer, enter the word NONE here and leave 11a–d blank. (The word NONE tells Medicare that it is the primary payer. Without its presence, Medicare assumes it is the secondary payer.)

11a For primary payers other than Medicare, enter the insured's date of birth (XX/XX/XXXX) and sex.

11b Enter the primary insured's employer or school name (if this information is completed, Medicare is NOT the primary payer).

11c Enter the insurance plan name.

11d Place an X in the appropriate box indicating if there is a secondary payer or not. If Yes is chosen, then blocks 9a–d will be completed; if No is chosen, blocks 9a–d will be left blank.

```
11. INSURED'S POLICY GROUP OR FECA NUMBER

a. INSURED'S DATE OF BIRTH                           SEX
        MM    DD      YY
                                          M  [ ]        F  [ ]

b. EMPLOYER'S NAME OR SCHOOL NAME

c. INSURANCE PLAN NAME OR PROGRAM NAME

d. IS THERE ANOTHER HEALTH BENEFIT PLAN?
      [ ] YES      [ ] NO      If yes, return to and complete item 9 a-d.
```

Block 12   The patient or authorized representative signs here, giving the provider permission to release his/her medical information to the insurance carrier.

Block 13   The patient or authorized representative signs here, authorizing the insurance carrier to send payment directly to the provider.

```
                  READ BACK OF FORM BEFORE COMPLETING & SIGNING THIS FORM.        13. INSURED'S OR AUTHORIZED PERSON'S SIGNATURE I authorize
12. PATIENT'S OR AUTHORIZED PERSON'S SIGNATURE I authorize the release of any medical or other information necessary   payment of medical benefits to the undersigned physician or supplier for
to process this claim. I also request payment of government benefits either to myself or to the party who accepts assignment   services described below.
below.

SIGNED_____ DATE_____        SIGNED_____
```

Here's how to complete blocks 14–33, the provider's information:

Block 14   Enter the date of the current illness, injury, or pregnancy using the 8-digit format.

```
14. DATE OF CURRENT:      ◀ ILLNESS (First symptom) OR
      MM    DD     YY        INJURY (Accident) OR
                             PREGNANCY(LMP)
```

Block 15   Enter the date the patient was first seen for the illness or injury using the 8-digit format; for Medicare, leave this block blank.

```
15. IF PATIENT HAS HAD SAME OR SIMILAR ILLNESS.
      GIVE FIRST DATE   MM    DD     YY
```

Block 16   Enter the dates the patient is or was unable to work using the 8-digit format (this information could signal a workers' compensation case if work-related).

```
16. DATES PATIENT UNABLE TO WORK IN CURRENT OCCUPATION
            MM    DD     YY              MM    DD     YY
     FROM                        TO
```

Block 17   Enter the name of the referring physician, laboratory, or other source. Some payers will require the treating physician's name here, if there was no referring physician. Check the individual insurer's guidelines.

Block 17a–b   Some insurers require provider identifiers other than the NPI.

17a If required, enter the approved two-digit qualifier from Table 17–1 with the provider identifier next to it; otherwise leave blank.

17b Enter the referring provider NPI number.

```
17. NAME OF REFERRING PROVIDER OR OTHER SOURCE   17a.
                                                 17b. NPI
```

Block 18   If applicable, enter the dates the patient was hospitalized during this claim.

```
18. HOSPITALIZATION DATES RELATED TO CURRENT SERVICES
            MM    DD     YY              MM    DD     YY
     FROM                        TO
```

Block 19   Block 19 is used for varying information depending on insurance carrier; check carrier instructions as to information requested

here. If non-NPI identifiers are requested, be sure to use the appropriate qualifier from Table 17–1. Leave blank if no information is required.

```
19. RESERVED FOR LOCAL USE
```

Block 20   If the office is billing for services provided by an outside laboratory, place an X in the Yes box and enter the amount being billed for the lab and enter the laboratory name, address, and NPI in block 32. If only labs performed in your office are being billed, enter an X in the No box.

```
20. OUTSIDE LAB?            $ CHARGES
       [ ] YES    [ ] NO |
```

Block 21   Enter the multi-digit ICD-9-CM codes indicating the patient diagnoses. (You will learn more about diagnosis coding in Chapter 18). Enter the codes in spaces 1–4 in descending order of importance. Do NOT use decimal points when inserting the diagnosis codes.

```
21. DIAGNOSIS OR NATURE OF ILLNESS OR INJURY (Relate Items 1, 2, 3 or 4 to Item 24E by Line)

1. L____ . _____         3. L____ . _____

2. L____ . _____         4. L____ . _____
```

Block 22   For Medicaid claims, enter the Medicaid resubmission code and original reference number if applicable; for all other payers, leave blank.

```
22. MEDICAID RESUBMISSION
    CODE              ORIGINAL REF. NO.
```

Block 23   If required, enter the prior authorization number received by the payer for the procedure performed (if prior authorization is required and not received, or if authorization is received, but the number is not present on the claim, the claim will be denied).

```
23. PRIOR AUTHORIZATION NUMBER
```

Blocks 24a–j   The six service lines here are used to enter the services provided to the patient. They are divided horizontally between shaded and nonshaded areas to accommodate NPI and non-NPI identifiers if required. The NPI is inserted in the nonshaded areas and the non-NPI information is inserted in the shaded areas. Follow individual payer requirements for use of these shaded areas.

24a Enter the dates of service using the 8-digit format. If the service is provided on one date, enter the same date twice.

24b Enter the two-digit place of service code from Table 17–5. Keep a listing nearby for handy reference.

24c EMG stands for emergency services. If the insurer requires this information, and the service was provided on an emergency basis, enter a Y for yes. If service was not provided on an emergency basis or if the insurer does not require the information, leave blank. For Medicare, leave blank.

24d Enter the appropriate CPT or HCPCS code with modifier, one per line, to represent each service provided. (You will learn more about CPT and HCPCS coding in Chapter 20.)

table 17–5

Place of Service Codes for CMS-1500 Form

CODE	PLACE OF SERVICE
11	Office
12	Home
21	Inpatient hospitalization
22	Outpatient hospitalization
23	Emergency room—hospital
23	Ambulatory surgical center
25	Birthing center
36	Military hospital or clinic
31	Skilled nursing facility
32	Nursing facility
33	Custodial care facility

24e Enter the reference number 1,2,3,4 from block 21 to represent the diagnosis code that is associated with each procedure or service performed. This identifies the medical necessity for the service provided.

24f Enter the fee charged for each service provided.

24g Enter the days or units for each service provided. For instance, if the patient had three 15-minute (15 minutes = 1 unit) physical therapy treatments, enter 3. Even if the unit is one, the number 1 must be entered.

24h EPSDT stands for Early, Periodic, Screening, Diagnosis, and Treatment. It is for Medicaid programs. If the procedure is related to EPSDT for a Medicaid patient, enter Y; otherwise leave blank.

24i If a non-NPI identifier is required by the payer, enter its qualifier (Table 17–1) in the shaded area. If it is not required, leave blank.

24j If a non-NPI qualifier was entered in the shaded area, enter the appropriate non-NPI identifier in the shaded area. If it is not required, leave the shaded area blank. Enter the provider's NPI number in the nonshaded area.

Block 25   Enter the provider's Tax ID number. Place an X in the box identifying it as SSN (Social Security Number) or EIN (Employer Identification Number).

Block 26	Enter the patient's account number (if used by your office).

```
26. PATIENT'S ACCOUNT NO.
```

Block 27	Place an X in the Yes box to indicate the provider is accepting assignment on the claim (the check will be issued directly to the provider). Place an X in the No box to indicate the provider is not accepting assignment on the claim (the check will be issued to the patient).

```
27. ACCEPT ASSIGNMENT?
(For govt. claims, see back)
☐ YES   ☐ NO
```

Block 28	Enter the total charges for the claim by totaling charges from column 24f in lines 1–6.
Block 29	Enter any amount paid by a primary payer. If this is a primary claim, leave blank. For Medicare claims, leave blank.
Block 30	Subtract block 29 from 28. Enter the difference in block 30 as the amount due. For Medicare claims, leave blank.

```
28. TOTAL CHARGE    29. AMOUNT PAID    30. BALANCE DUE
$                   $                  $
```

Block 31	The physician or provider should sign and date the form here.

```
31. SIGNATURE OF PHYSICIAN OR SUPPLIER
INCLUDING DEGREES OR CREDENTIALS
(I certify that the statements on the reverse
apply to this bill and are made a part thereof.)


SIGNED              DATE
```

Block 32	Enter the name and address of the facility providing the services

32a Enter the servicing provider's NPI.

32b If required by the insurer, enter the servicing provider's appropriate two-digit qualifier followed by the non-NPI identifier required.

```
32. SERVICE FACILITY LOCATION INFORMATION




a.    NPI         b.
```

Block 33	Enter the name, address, and phone number of the billing provider (this often repeats the information from block 32, with the addition of the phone number).

33a Enter the billing provider's NPI.

33b If required by the insurer, enter the billing provider's appropriate two-digit qualifier, followed by the non-NPI identifier required.

```
33. BILLING PROVIDER INFO & PH #  (    )




a.    NPI         b.
```

Although the basic information required to complete the CMS-1500 claim is the same for every provider and for every insurance plan, you will find that the instructions for completing the claim form may vary among insurance carriers. Be sure to follow the individual carrier's instructions carefully to obtain a clean claim with every submission. Procedure 17-4 will give you an outline to follow in completing the CMS-1500 claim.

Transmission of Electronic Claims

Practices handle the transmission of electronic claims—which may be called electronic media claims, or EMC—in a variety of ways. Some practices transmit claims themselves; others hire outside vendors to handle this task for them.

Claims are prepared for transmission after all required data elements have been posted to the medical billing software program. The data elements that are transmitted are not seen physically, as they would be on a paper form. Instead, these elements are in a computer file.

Three major methods are used to transmit claims electronically: direct transmission to the payer, clearinghouse use, and direct data entry.

Transmitting Claims Directly   In the direct transmission approach, medical offices and payers exchange transactions directly. To do this, providers and payers need the necessary information systems, including a translator and communications technology, to conduct electronic data interchange (EDI).

clearinghouse
A group that takes nonstandard medical billing software formats and translates them into the standard EDI format.

Using a Clearinghouse   Many offices whose medical billing software vendors do not have translation software must use a **clearinghouse** in order to send and receive data in the correct EDI format. Clearinghouses can take in nonstandard formats and translate them into the standard format. To ensure that the standard format is compliant, the clearinghouse must receive all the required data elements from the physician. Clearinghouses are prohibited from creating or modifying data content.

Medical offices may use a clearinghouse to transmit all their claims, or they may use a combination of direct transmission and a clearinghouse. For example, they may send claims directly to Medicare, Medicaid, and a few other major commercial payers, and use a clearinghouse to send claims to other payers.

Using Direct Data Entry   Online direct data entry (DDE) is offered by some payers. It uses an Internet-based service into which employees key the standard data elements. Although the data elements must meet the HIPAA standards requirements regarding content, they do not have to be formatted for EDI. Instead, they are loaded directly in the health plans' computer.

Generating Clean Claims

table 17-6

Common Errors When Filing Claims

Although health-care claims require many data elements and are complex, often simple errors prevent you from generating "clean" claims—that is, those accepted for processing by the payer. Claims should be carefully checked

- Missing or incomplete service facility name, address, and identification for services rendered outside the office or home; this includes invalid zip codes or state abbreviations
- Missing Medicare assignment indicator or benefits assignment indicator
- Missing part of the name or the identifier of the referring provider
- Missing or invalid subscriber's birth date
- Missing information about secondary insurance plans, such as the spouse's payer
- Missing payer name and/or payer identifier, required for both primary and secondary payers

before transmission or printing. Be alert for common errors (see Table 17–6). Prior to submitting any insurance claim, make sure you have access to the insurance carrier's most recent claim submission manual. Following the instructions in that manual carefully will result in the most clean claims. It also provides you with back-up if you submit a claim as instructed and still have an issue with claim acceptance by the carrier.

If you receive a paper query from an insurance carrier or electronic notification of claim rejection for any reason (including those shown in Table 17–6), provide the missing or corrected information in the manner required - sometimes this is as simple as answering a question within a letter - or if required, submit a new claim with corrected information. For instance, if any facility information is missing, insert the missing information and submit a corrected claim. If a provider number is missing, obtain the correct provider number from the referring or treating physician's office and submit a corrected claim with the appropriate ID number. Do note that most errors are errors of omission and if claims are checked carefully prior to submission, most errors can be caught prior to submission, resulting in clean claims the first time and less "re-work" on the back end.

Many offices use a specialized software program called a "claim scrubber" to check

Electronic Claims Transmission

Although hospitals and large practices have been using the X12 837 health-care claims for quite some time now, many smaller offices are still using paper claims for much if not all of their claims submission. Even many larger practices that have been utilizing electronic claims processing have been hesitant about choosing an electronic health records software. When they do so, they will find that health claims filing will become more efficient. Many EHR software programs not only make keeping medical records easier (at least once everyone becomes used to the program), they can also make coding those records much simpler.

EHR programs often include computer-assisted coding programs which assign codes in a variety of ways. For those who utilize EHR templates to produce medical records, the codes can be chosen by looking for key words in the medical record that are included in the medical record template. Other programs actually analyze the words, phrases, or sentences used within the record to obtain the correct code. No matter which method is used, a professional coder will review and verify the codes chosen. If the coder wishes to access the information within the health record, this is easily accomplished via the EHR program; no more reading through pages of handwritten documentation. Coding through EHR also reduces the chance of mistakenly coding a procedure that was ordered but did not take place, simply because the provider only documents the service provided, and so the program will also only code the services provided. Now that the record is coded, the EHR program will move the process to the next step of producing the health-care claim, which is also done electronically. This process is also greatly streamlined as the claim information is added to the patient record at the time of service. There is no need to repeatedly hand write, type, or produce a computer-generated claim. The electronic claim template contains the instructions on placement of the information within the electronic claim and the information is pulled from the patient record automatically with a few simple keystrokes by the medical biller to queue the claim for processing. At the time of transmission, all queued "clean" claims are transmitted with a few simple computer commands either directly to the payer or to the office clearinghouse as the intermediary and then on to the payer. Because claims are sent electronically, the office will immediately be notified by the payer or clearinghouse of any rejected or errored claims and the reason for the rejection. The account can then quickly be corrected as required and sent back to the payer in hours or even minutes instead of the days and weeks required for manual paper claims. (Refer to Chapter 15 for more in-depth coverage of EHR.)

claims before they are released and to allow errors to be fixed. Clearinghouses also apply software checks to claims they receive and transmit back reports of errors or missing information to the sender.

Claims Security

Electronic data about patients are stored on a computer system. Most medical offices use computer networks in which personal computers are connected to a local area network (LAN), so users can exchange and share information and hardware. The LAN is linked to remote networks such as the Internet by a router that determines the best route for data to travel across the network. Packets of data traveling between the LAN and the Internet—such as electronic claims—must usually pass through a firewall, a security device that examines

Data Elements for HIPAA Electronic Claims

The X12 837 health-care claim requires many of the same data elements as a paper claim, but some elements require understanding new terms. Here are tips for locating these types of information.

Reporting Provider Information

The *billing provider* is the entity that is transmitting the claim to the payer. Medical offices often use a billing service or a clearinghouse to serve as the billing provider and transmit their claims. When this is done, the outside organization is the billing provider, and the practice is the *pay-to provider* that receives the payment from the insurance carrier. If an office sends claims directly to the payer, it is the billing provider and there is no additional pay-to provider to report.

Another term associated with claim preparation is *rendering provider*. A rendering provider is the physician who, as a member of the practice, treats the patient.

Reporting Taxonomy Information

A *taxonomy code* is a 10-digit number representing a physician's medical specialty. Physicians select the taxonomy code that most closely matches their education, license, or certification. The code is reported on claims because payment for some services is impacted by the particular specialty of the doctor performing them and by payers' contracts. For example, nuclear medicine is usually a higher paid specialty than internal medicine. An internist who also has a specialty in nuclear medicine would report the nuclear medicine taxonomy code when billing for that service and use the internal medicine taxonomy code when reporting internal medicine claims.

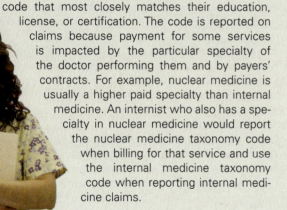

Reporting HIPAA National Identifiers

HIPAA *national identifiers* are established for:

- Employers
- Health-care providers
- Health plans
- Patients

Identifiers are numbers of predetermined length and structure, such as a person's Social Security number. As the HIPAA rules establishing these identifiers are passed, the correct data elements must be reported on the claim. For example, the employer identifier has been adopted; it is the Employer Identification Number (EIN) issued by the Internal Revenue Service.

Until the identifiers for the three other entities are adopted, these rules are in effect:

- For health care providers, report the tax identification number or Social Security number
- For health plans, report the appropriate code; here are some common codes

Code	Definition
09	Self-pay
12	Preferred provider organization (PPO)
15	Indemnity insurance
BL	Blue Cross/Blue Shield
CH	TRICARE
CI	Commercial insurance company
HM	Health maintenance organization
MB	Medicare Part B
MC	Medicaid
WC	Workers' compensation health claim

- For patients, report the policyholder's health plan identification number

information (for example, e-mails) that enter and leave a network, determining whether to forward them to their destination.

The HIPAA rules set standards for protecting individually identifiable health information when it is maintained or transmitted electronically. Medical offices must protect the confidentiality, integrity, and availability of this information. A number of security measures are used:

- Access control, passwords, and log files to keep intruders out
- Backups (saved copies of files) to replace items after damage to the computer
- Security policies to handle violations that do occur

Administrative medical assistants participate in the protection of patients' health information. One way is to select a good password for your computer. Never give out your password, nor allow anyone to use a computer terminal

where you are logged in. Before you walk away from a computer, be sure you log out. Doing so will require that anyone else needing to use the computer logs in, using her or his own password. Here are tips for selecting a good password:

- Always use a combination of letters and numbers that are not real words and also not an obvious number string such as 123456 or a birth date.
- Do not use a user ID (log-on or sign-on) as a password. Even if it has both numbers and letters, it is not secret.
- Select a mixture of both uppercase and lowercase letters if the system can distinguish between them, and, if possible, include special characters such as @, $, or &.
- Use a minimum of six to eight alphanumeric characters. The optimal minimum number varies by system, but most security experts recommend a length of at least six to eight characters.
- Change passwords periodically, but not too often.

Forcing frequent changes can actually make security worse because users are more likely to keep passwords written down.

Why is it important that insurance claims, paper and electronic, be submitted correctly on the first submission?

CHECKPOINT
LO 17.6

LO 17.7 Patient Payments in the Office

Once the claims are filed and the insurance pays its portion of the patient's charges, the patient will be held accountable for his portion of the fees. In any business, basic accounting involves managing accounts receivable and accounts payable. **Accounts receivable (A/R)** is the term for income, or money, owed to the business. **Accounts payable (A/P)** is the term for money owed by the business. In a medical practice, accounts receivable represents the money patients (and insurance companies) owe in return for medical services. Accounts payable describes the money the medical practice must pay out to run the practice. You will learn more about accounts payable in Chapter 18. Billing and collections are vitally important tasks because they convert the practice's accounts receivable into income, or cash flow, from which the accounts payable can be paid. Unless billing and collections are carried out effectively, a practice might have plenty of money due in accounts receivable but not enough cash on hand to pay its accounts payable, including staff salaries!

There are methods of improving billing and collection procedures to increase income for the practice. You will need to know about standard payment, billing, and collection procedures as well as credit arrangements and common problems in collecting payment. As stated earlier, when patients belonging to MCOs have copayments, most practices prefer to collect the small copayment at each office visit. Immediate payment not only brings income into the practice faster, but it saves the cost of preparing and mailing statements (patient bill) and collection of past-due accounts. Many offices post a small sign at the reception desk that states, for example, "Payment is requested when services are rendered unless other arrangements are made in advance." As the administrative medical assistant, you are responsible for collecting these payments. If the patient cannot pay all or part of the charges at the time of the visit, it may be your responsibility to bill for the physician's services.

accounts receivable
Income or money owed to a business; the practice's income.

accounts payable
Money owed by a business; the practice's expenses.

Accepting Patient Payment

When the patient comes to you at the completion of his visit with the superbill, you enter the charges for the services provided (if they are not preprinted on the form)

and ask for payment. There are several effective yet diplomatic ways to request payment. Two examples are, "For today's visit, the total charge is $50. How would you like to pay?" and "The charge for your laboratory work today is $80. Would you like to pay for that now?" The first example is the preferred method because in the second example, asking the patient if he would like to pay for the service now leaves him open to say, "No, bill me," which will slow your cash flow and cost the practice the expense of sending an invoice. Most practices accept several forms of patient payment, including cash, check, and debit and credit cards.

Cash If the patient chooses to pay in cash, count the money carefully to be sure you have received the proper amount. Next, record the payment on the patient's ledger card or, with a computerized system, credit the patient's account as per system instructions and give the patient a receipt. (Patient ledger cards are explained in Chapter 21.)

Once the money is posted to the account, a computerized billing program will give you the option of printing a receipt which you can give to the patient. A superbill (see Figure 17–6), a carbonless form consisting of 2–3 copies, automatically creates a receipt, as one of the copies is given to the patient. If your office does not use either of these methods, prepare a cash receipt manually, as shown in Figure 17–12. Be sure that whatever method is used, the office also retains a copy of the receipt. Then place the money in the cash drawer or cash box.

Check If your office accepts checks, always ask for proof of identity if you do not know the person writing the check to avoid the accidental acceptance of fraudulent checks. The check should be completed fully and correctly. Many offices have a stamp with the office name on it for patient convenience and to assure the practice name is spelled correctly. Unless the patient has made previous arrangements, the check should be made out for the full amount owed. Verify that the check is dated for the current date and signed when accepting it. Endorse it immediately and place it with other checks for the day's deposit. If a check is returned for nonsufficient funds (NSF), notify the patient immediately requesting payment in full by another method. Many offices will subsequently insist that the patient be seen on a cash only basis, unless the patient can produce a valid credit card (assuming the office takes credit cards). The office is also allowed to charge the patient an additional fee for the expense of processing the NSF check. You will learn more about this in Chapter 21.

figure 17–12

After writing a receipt for cash, record the payment on the patient's ledger card.

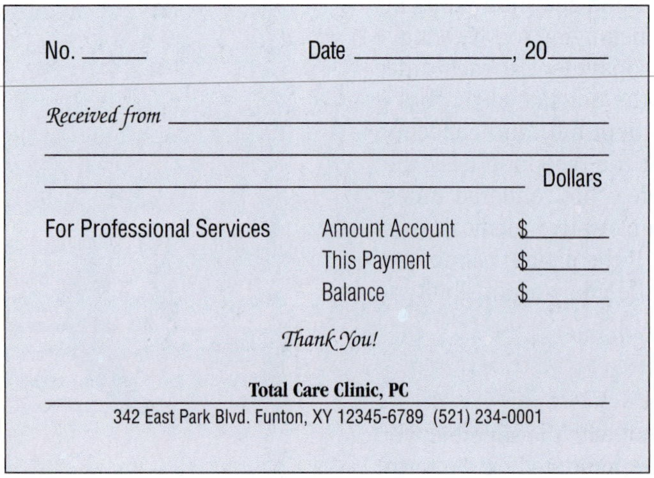

No. _____	Date _____ , 20 _____

Received from _____
_____
_____ Dollars

For Professional Services | Amount Account | $ _____
| This Payment | $ _____
| Balance | $ _____

Thank You!

Total Care Clinic, PC
342 East Park Blvd. Funton, XY 12345-6789 (521) 234-0001

Debit Card Many patients now use debit cards instead of paying by cash or check. A debit card looks like a credit card but immediately transfers the funds from the patient's account to the practice account. The advantage to the practice is that if there are insufficient funds in the account, the transaction will be refused and other arrangements can be made immediately. Debit cards, like credit cards, are read through electronic readers (Figure 17–13) and the patient inputs a PIN (personal identification number) verifying his or her wish that funds be transferred.

Credit Card Many doctors' offices accept credit cards, such as Visa or MasterCard. This payment method offers advantages for both the practice and the patient. For the practice, it provides prompt payment from the credit card company, thus increasing cash flow. It also reduces the amount of time and money spent on preparing and mailing invoices, thus decreasing expenses. For the patient, it is convenient and allows a large bill to be paid in several smaller amounts, usually once a month.

Credit cards have one major disadvantage for the practice—cost. The credit card company deducts a percentage of each transaction for its collection service, usually between 1% and 5%. If a patient charges $100 in services on a credit card, for example, the practice receives only $95 to $99. The credit card company keeps the difference. A disadvantage for patients is the accrued interest charges on unpaid balances.

If the practice accepts credit card payments, the American Medical Association (AMA) suggests several guidelines.

- Do not set higher fees for patients who pay by credit card.
- Do not encourage patients to use credit cards for payment.
- Do not advertise outside the office that the practice accepts credit cards.

figure 17–13

Using a device like this one, you can swipe the patient's credit or debit card through the machine and obtain instant authorization from the credit card company or financial institution (for debit cards).

If a patient chooses to pay by credit card, process the transaction carefully to ensure that the credit card company charges the patient correctly. Check the expiration date on the front of the credit card. If the card has expired, it cannot be used for payment. Swipe the card through an electronic reader or record it through the use of a credit card machine that mechanically records the information on the card. To operate a credit card machine, place the credit card in the machine and place a credit card voucher on top of it. Slide the imprint arm firmly to the right and back across the machine. Remove the voucher from the machine. Write in the date and circle the type of credit card, such as Visa or MasterCard, after it is removed from the machine. Return the credit card to the patient.

Next, obtain the authorization code from the credit card company. Some offices have devices that read the magnetic strip on the credit card and automatically transmit the information to the credit card company by telephone line (Figure 17–13). If your office has such a device, type in the amount to be charged on its keypad. Then, the credit card company issues an authorization code, which appears on the device's screen.

If your office does not have such a device, call the credit card company for the authorization code. Give the operator the patient's credit card number and the amount of the payment. The operator then gives you the authorization code.

Write the authorization code in the box marked "Authorization" on the credit card voucher. Initial the voucher in the appropriate box. Then, fill in the services provided and the amount of the charges. Enter the total charges in the box marked "Total."

Give the receipt to the patient to sign. Compare the patient's signature on the receipt with the signature on the back of the credit card (they should, of course, be identical). Keep one copy of the receipt for the office. Give the other copy and the credit card to the patient.

Using the Pegboard System for Posting Payments

While not often used, some physicians' offices still use the pegboard system to post payments and generate receipts for patients. If your office uses the pegboard system, you may use the pegboard to record the payment on the ledger card and receipt simultaneously. You handle this task in basically the same way, whether the patient pays immediately or later, in response to a statement. (See Chapter 21 for more information about pegboard systems.)

Responsibility for Minors As discussed in Chapter 6, when a child's parents are married, either parent may consent to treatment for the minor child. Both parents are responsible for payment for the minor's treatment. If you must send them a bill, it should be addressed to both parents to ensure payment. Emancipated minors are the exception to this process. If you have been shown legal proof of emancipation, any bills will be addressed to the emancipated minor; because of the emancipation process, the minor is legally responsible for her bills.

Divorce or separation may create confusion as to which parent may legally consent to treatment and who is responsible for payment. The legal and financial arrangements of a divorced couple are private. Unless you have legal documentation stating otherwise (and if you receive such documentation, make a copy and put it in the patient's financial record), you should assume that the parent bringing the patient to the office has consent ability and payment responsibility. It is not up to the office to be put in the middle of a financial dispute between divorced parents. Unless you have documentation otherwise, it should be made clear to the parents, that payment is due at the time of the visit, regardless of which parent brings the child to the office.

Responsibility for Elderly Patients and Patients with Disabilities
Sometimes elderly patients or patients with disabilities are brought in for medical care. The administrative medical assistant may be asked to send the bill to another party such as an adult child. Because of HIPAA confidentiality laws, do not send a patient's bill to another without first obtaining written consent to do so from the patient and the person accepting responsibility for payment. If the patient is incompetent, request proof of legal guardianship prior to sending a bill.

Refunding and Overpayment Periodically, the insurance payments and patient payments exceed the allowed charges. This is called an **overpayment** and results in a **credit balance**, meaning the office now owes the patient money which will need to be refunded. You will learn about the process of reversing a credit balance and issuing a refund in Chapter 21.

Professional Courtesy Although much less common than in years past, a doctor may treat some patients free of charge or for just the amount covered by the patient's insurance. This practice is known as professional courtesy. These patients often include other doctors and their families, the practice's staff members and their families, other health-care professionals, and clergy members. If the patient is part of a managed care organization or has Medicare, the provider must collect any copayment or deductible as part of the contracted agreement with the insurance carrier. It is considered fraud to consistently not collect copayments or deductibles if the collection of such payments is stipulated in the provider-insurer contract.

Follow the office policy regarding provision of professional courtesy. If you are unsure, check with the physician or office manager.

overpayment
Payment made that is more than the amount billed; results in a credit balance.

credit balance
A negative balance on an account that occurs when more money than is owed is paid to the practice.

CHECKPOINT
LO 17.7

What payment methods are commonly accepted in medical offices?

LO 17.8 Standard Billing Procedures

In today's practice, most offices receive payments from insurance carriers and then find they must bill the patient for any balance due. As the administrative medical assistant, part of your duties may include preparing these patient billing

statements. You may also have to manage related billing responsibilities, such as establishing and maintaining billing cycles.

Preparing Statements

As an administrative medical assistant, part of your job may be to prepare statements to mail to patients who do not pay when services are rendered or who make only a partial payment. Figure 17–14 shows a statement with an itemized list of services. You can obtain most of the information for the statement from the patient ledger card or from the patient's computerized account. Regardless of the format used, all statements should include the following information:

- Practice name, address, and telephone number (usually preprinted on the statement, or prepared by the computer program)

figure 17–14

The statement shows an itemized list of services and charges, organized by date, for the current month.

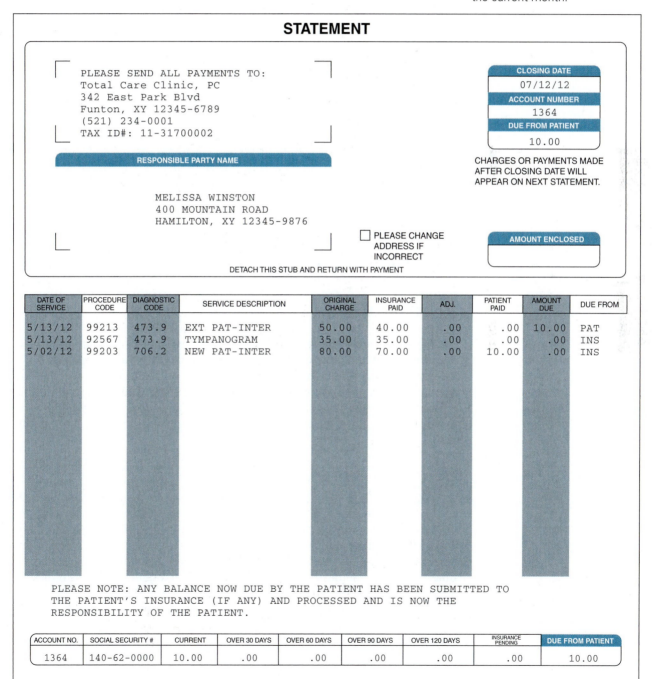

STATEMENT

PLEASE SEND ALL PAYMENTS TO:
Total Care Clinic, PC
342 East Park Blvd
Funton, XY 12345-6789
(521) 234-0001
TAX ID#: 11-31700002

CLOSING DATE
07/12/12
ACCOUNT NUMBER
1364
DUE FROM PATIENT
10.00

CHARGES OR PAYMENTS MADE AFTER CLOSING DATE WILL APPEAR ON NEXT STATEMENT.

RESPONSIBLE PARTY NAME

MELISSA WINSTON
400 MOUNTAIN ROAD
HAMILTON, XY 12345-9876

☐ PLEASE CHANGE ADDRESS IF INCORRECT

AMOUNT ENCLOSED

DETACH THIS STUB AND RETURN WITH PAYMENT

DATE OF SERVICE	PROCEDURE CODE	DIAGNOSTIC CODE	SERVICE DESCRIPTION	ORIGINAL CHARGE	INSURANCE PAID	ADJ.	PATIENT PAID	AMOUNT DUE	DUE FROM
5/13/12	99213	473.9	EXT PAT-INTER	50.00	40.00	.00	.00	10.00	PAT
5/13/12	92567	473.9	TYMPANOGRAM	35.00	35.00	.00	.00	.00	INS
5/02/12	99203	706.2	NEW PAT-INTER	80.00	70.00	.00	10.00	.00	INS

PLEASE NOTE: ANY BALANCE NOW DUE BY THE PATIENT HAS BEEN SUBMITTED TO THE PATIENT'S INSURANCE (IF ANY) AND PROCESSED AND IS NOW THE RESPONSIBILITY OF THE PATIENT.

ACCOUNT NO.	SOCIAL SECURITY #	CURRENT	OVER 30 DAYS	OVER 60 DAYS	OVER 90 DAYS	OVER 120 DAYS	INSURANCE PENDING	DUE FROM PATIENT
1364	140-62-0000	10.00	.00	.00	.00	.00	.00	10.00

- Patient's name and address.
- Guarantor's name (if different from the patient)
- Balance (if any) from the previous month(s)
- Itemized list of services and charges, by date, for the current month
- Payments from the patient or insurer during the month
- Total balance due

Whatever invoicing procedure you use, enclose a self addressed envelope with the statement to encourage prompt payment. Some offices have found that using a lightly colored return envelope, such as pale yellow, actually encourages faster payment because the color stands out against the usual white envelopes, jogging the patient's memory to "pay that one."

Using Codes on the Statement   Write the name of each procedure on the itemized list, or use abbreviations for common procedures, such as OV for office visit. If you use abbreviations, be sure that an explanation of the abbreviations appears with the statement, usually at the bottom. Using an itemized list of services provided on statements is standard practice in most physicians' offices as it decreases the number of patient calls asking, "What is this bill for?" After completing the statement, fold it in thirds, and mail it in a typewritten or window business envelope.

Using the Patient's Ledger Card as a Statement   A common alternative to typing the statement, especially in smaller, noncomputerized offices, is to photocopy the patient's ledger card and fold the photocopy so that the patient's address shows through the window in a window envelope. If your practice uses ledger cards for this purpose, be sure there are no stray marks or comments on the card and that the copy is clean and easy to read.

Computer Generated Statements   In computerized offices, you may print out a statement for each patient account that has a balance due. Follow the instructions in the software procedure manual. You can then fold the printouts and mail them in window envelopes.

Using an Independent Billing Service   Large practices may have both their insurance and patient billing procedures handled by an independent billing service. In addition to billing the insurance plan, the billing service may rapidly copy ledger cards or produce computer-generated statements from the office computer for patients with balances due. The statements are then mailed to patients, usually with an envelope for sending payment directly to the provider's office.

Using the Superbill

As stated earlier in the chapter, many practices use the superbill (encounter form), which lists the charges and procedure codes (CPT) for services rendered on that day, including appropriate diagnoses and codes (ICD-9). As a carbonless form, when the charges and any payments are entered on the superbill, an automatic receipt and first statement is generated all at the same time, saving time and money. Some offices even give the patient a return envelope if there is a balance on the account to encourage prompt payment. Procedure 17–5 located at the end of the chapter will give you practice billing with a superbill.

Managing Billing Cycles

Smaller practices send out their statements monthly, usually at the end of the month.

Larger practices tend to spread the billing process out over the month in a process known as **cycle billing**. In cycle billing the accounts are split in groups and statement mailing dates are staggered.

For example, you may bill on the fifth of the month for patients whose last names begin with A through D. Then, on the tenth of the month, you may bill patients whose names begin with E through H, and so on. Using cycle billing not only staggers the work load throughout the month, it also tends to spread out the payments coming into the office, giving the office a more even cash flow.

cycle billing
A system that sends statements to groups of patients every few days, spreading out the work of billing all patients over the period of a month, while billing each patient only once.

What two types of codes are commonly found on the patient superbill (encounter form)?

LO 17.9 Standard Collection Procedures

Although most patients pay statement within the standard 30-day period, some do not. When a patient does not pay his bill during the standard period, you need to take steps to collect the payment. For example, you may need to call or write the patient to determine the reason for nonpayment or to set up a payment arrangement.

Whether you use telephone calls, notes, or letters, there are laws, such as statutes of limitations, and professional standards to guide your efforts to collect overdue payments from patients.

State Statute of Limitations

The **statute of limitations** is a state law that sets a time limit on when a collection suit on a past-due account can legally be filed. The time limit varies with the type of account and the state in which the debt was incurred.

statute of limitations
A state law that sets a time limit on when a collection suit on a past-due account can legally be filed.

Open-Book Account An **open-book account** is one that is open to charges made occasionally as needed. Most of a physician's long-standing patients have this type of account. An open-book account uses the last date of payment or charge for each illness as the starting date for determining the time limit on that specific debt.

open-book account
An account that is open to charges made occasionally as needed.

Written-Contract Account A **written-contract account** is one in which the physician and patient sign an agreement stating that the patient will pay the bill in more than four installments. Some states allow longer time limits for these accounts than for open-book accounts. Written-contract accounts are regulated by the Truth in Lending Act, discussed later in this chapter.

written contract account
An agreement between a service provider and the receiver of services stating exactly what service will be provided and the fee that is agreed upon for that service.

Single-Entry Account A **single-entry account** is an account with only one charge. For example, someone vacationing in your area might come in for treatment of a cold. This person's account would list only one office visit. If the vacationer did not become a regular patient, the account would be considered a single-entry account. Some states impose shorter time limits on single-entry accounts than on open-book accounts.

single-entry account
An account that has only one charge, usually for a small amount, for a patient who does not come in regularly.

Using Collection Techniques

Individual practices have their own ways of approaching the task of collection. Most begin the process with telephone calls, letters, or statements.

Initial Telephone Calls or Letters When calling a patient (or sending a letter) about collections, be friendly and sympathetic. Call the patient at home

unless you have specific permission to call him at work. The first phone call to the patient should occur if payment has not been received after 30–45 days. Because the patient received a receipt or superbill at the time of the visit, any statement mailed after that is essentially the second notice of payment due. The first mailed statement usually contains a message that is friendly in tone such as, "Your prompt payment is appreciated." When you call, assume that the patient forgot to pay or was temporarily unable to pay. You should ask the patient for the full amount due but have a minimum amount you would accept in mind. If the patient states that he cannot afford full payment, ask him what amount he feels could be sent and if the amount is acceptable, obtain a date you can expect to receive the payment. If you do not receive the payment within 24 hours of the stated date, another statement may be sent. The message on this statement will be more urgent in tone because the patient did not respond to your phone call and the tone of any subsequent communication will be still more urgent.

Follow-Up Statements and Collection Letters   Once an account is 60 days past due, it is advisable to send an initial letter of inquiry. Usually this letter still has a friendly, "we want to help" tone, giving the patient options to take care of his obligation, but makes it clear that the patient must take some sort of action. Figure 17–15 shows an example of such a letter.

If an account is 90 days past due, your collection letter can contain stronger wording. For example, it might say, "Please let us know when you plan to pay the $250 past-due balance. We have sent you three monthly reminders. If you cannot pay in full now, please contact us at (number) to make payment arrangements. We want to be understanding but need your cooperation."

If an account is 120 days or more past due, you can send a final letter. It might state, "Every courtesy has been extended to you in arranging for payment of your long overdue account. Unless we hear from you by (date), the account will be given to (name of collection agency) for collection." Be sure to note the cutoff date on the patient's ledger card. By law, you cannot threaten to send an account to a collection agency unless it will actually be sent on that cutoff date. Therefore, you must be sure you are ready to do so before you send such a letter. This collection letter should be mailed by certified mail with return receipt so you have proof that the letter was sent and that the intended recipient received the letter.

If the patient does not respond with payment prior to the date stated in the letter, the physician will have no choice but to turn the account over to the office collection agency. We will discuss collection agencies later in the chapter.

Preparing an Age Analysis

age analysis

The process of clarifying and reviewing past due accounts by age from the first date of billing.

Age analysis is the process of classifying and reviewing past-due accounts by age from the first date of billing. A monthly age analysis, such as that shown in Figure 17–16, helps you keep on top of past-due accounts and determine which ones need follow-up.

Computer billing programs will prepare an age analysis for you, but you can also prepare one by hand if your office is not computerized. Offices that uses ledger cards to track patient accounts often have a procedure to track how long since the last payment has been received. For instance color coded tags may be placed on the cards; yellow denoting 30 days past due, green 60 days past due, red 90 days past due and black for 120 days past due. By pulling the ledger cards by color grouping, an age analysis can be completed easily either on graph paper or by using a spreadsheet. Include the patient's name, balance due, date of charges, date of most recent payment and how long each part of the

TOTAL CARE CLINIC, PC

342 East Park, Blvd
Funton, XY 12345-6789
Telephone: 521-234-0001

Matthew Rodriguez, MD
Ravi Patel, MD
John Fredericks, MD
Sara Kacharski, DO
Linda F. Wiley, PA-C

May 5, 2012

Mr. J. J. Andrews
1414 First Avenue
Funton, XY 12345-6789

Dear Mr. Andrews:

It has been brought to my attention that your account in the amount of $240.00 is past due.

Normally at this time the account would be placed with a collection agency. However, we would prefer to hear from you regarding your preference in this matter.

( )   Payment in full is enclosed.

( )   Payment will be made in _____ days.

( )   I would like to make regular weekly/monthly payments of $ _____ until this account is paid in full. My first payment is enclosed.

( )   I would prefer that you assign this account to a collection agency for enforcement of collection. (Failure to return this letter within 30 days will result in this action.)

( )   I don't believe I owe this amount for the following reason(s):

Signed: _____

Please indicate your preference and return this letter within 30 days. Please do not hesitate to call if you have any questions regarding this matter.

Sincerely,

Darlene M. Elliott
Office Manager

figure 17–15

Standard collection letters are available for you to fill in the details.

balance has been "waiting" on the A/R. It may also be helpful to insert a column at the end for action the office has taken in attempting to collect this debt. Procedure 17–6 at the end of the chapter outlines this process.

Define *statute of limitations* as relating to collecting a debt.

CHECKPOINT
LO 17.9

ACCOUNTS RECEIVABLE–AGE ANALYSIS

Date: October 1, 2012

Patient	Balance	Date of Charges	Most Recent Payment	30 days	60 days	90 days	120 days	Remarks
Black, K.	120.00	5/24	5/24			75.00	45.00	3rd Notice
Brown, R.	65.00	8/30	8/30	65.00				
Green, C.	340.00	8/25						Medicare filed
Jones, T.	500.00	6/1	6/30		125.00	125.00	250.00	3rd Notice
Perry, S.	150.00	7/28	7/28	75.00	75.00			1st Notice
Smith, J.	375.00	6/15	7/1			375.00		2nd Notice
White, L.	200.00	6/24	7/5	20.00	30.00	150.00		2nd Notice

figure 17–16

An age analysis organizes past-due accounts by age.

LO 17.10 Laws That Govern Credit and Collections

Federal and state laws govern debt collection. Table 17–7 outlines the penalties for violating laws that regulate credit and debt.

Fair Debt Collection Practices Act of 1977 This act (also called Public Law 95-109) governs the methods that can be used to collect unpaid debts. Its goal is to eliminate abusive, deceptive, or unfair debt collection practices, such as threatening to take action that is illegal or that is not actually planned. It is this law that states if you threaten to turn an account over to a collection agency if a payment is not made by the 15th of the month, that you must actually do so. Following are guidelines for sending letters and making calls requesting payment from patients. For further information, visit www.ftc.gov/bcp/edu/pubs/consumer/credit/cre27.pdf.

- Do not call the patient before 8 A.M. or after 9 P.M. Calling outside those hours can be considered harassment.
- Do not make threats or use profane language. For example, do not state that an account will be given to a collection agency in 7 days if it will not be.
- Do not discuss the patient's debt with anyone except the person responsible for payment. If the patient is represented by a lawyer, discuss

LAW	REQUIREMENTS	PENALTIES FOR BREAKING LAW
Equal Credit Opportunity Act (ECOA) www.ftc.gov/bcp/edu/pubs/consumer/credit/cre15.shtm	• Creditors may not discriminate against applicants on the basis of sex, marital status, race, national origin, religion, or age. • Creditors may not discriminate because an applicant receives public assistance income or has exercised rights under the Consumer Credit Protection Act.	• If an applicant sues the practice for violating the ECOA, the practice may have to pay **damages** (money paid as compensation), penalties, lawyers' fees, and court costs. • If an applicant joins a class action lawsuit against the practice, the practice may have to pay damages of up to $500,000 or 1% of the practice's net worth, whichever is less. (A **class action lawsuit** is a lawsuit in which one or more people sue a company that wronged all of them the same way.) • If the Federal Trade Commission (FTC) receives many complaints from applicants stating that the practice violated the ECOA, the FTC may investigate and take action against the practice.
Fair Credit Reporting Act (FCRA) www.ftc.gov/os/statutes/fcra.htm	• This act requires credit bureaus to supply correct and complete information to businesses to use in evaluating a person's application for credit, insurance, or a job.	• If one applicant sues the practice in federal court for violating the FCRA, the practice may have to pay damages, **punitive damages** (money paid as punishment for intentionally breaking the law), court costs, and lawyers' fees. • If the FTC receives many complaints from applicants stating that the practice violated the FCRA, the FTC may investigate and take action against the practice.
Fair Debt Collection Practices Act (FDCPA) www.ftc.gov/bcp/edu/pubs/consumer/credit/cre27.pdf	• This act requires debt collectors to treat debtors fairly. It also prohibits certain collection tactics, such as harassment, false statements, threats, and unfair practices.	• If one debtor sues the practice in a state or federal court for violation of the FDCPA, the practice may have to pay damages, court costs, and lawyers' fees. • If the debtor joins a class action suit against the practice, the practice may have to pay damages of up to $500,000 or 1% of the practice's net worth, whichever is less. • If the FTC receives many complaints from debtors stating that the practice violated the FCRA, the FTC may investigate and take action against the practice.
Truth in Lending Act (TLA) www.occ.treas.gov/handbook/til.pdf	• This act requires creditors to provide applicants with accurate and complete credit costs and terms, clearly and obviously.	• If one applicant sues the practice in a federal court for violation of the TLA, the practice may have to pay damages, court costs, and lawyers' fees. • If the FTC receives many complaints from applicants stating that the practice violated the TLA, the FTC may investigate and take action against the practice.

table 17-7

Laws That Govern Credit and Collections

class action lawsuit
A lawsuit in which one or more people sue a company or other legal entity that allegedly wronged all of them in the same way.

damages
Money paid as compensation for violating legal rights.

punitive damages
Money paid as punishment for intentionally breaking the law.

the problem only with the lawyer, unless the lawyer gives you permission to talk to the patient.

• Do not use any form of deception or violence to collect a debt. For example, do not pose as a government employee or other authority figure to try to force a debtor to pay.

Telephone Consumer Protection Act (TCPA) of 1991 This act protects telephone subscribers from unwanted telephone solicitations, commonly known as telemarketing. The act prohibits autodialed calls to emergency service providers, cellular and paging numbers, and patients' hospital rooms. It prohibits prerecorded calls to homes without prior permission of the resident, and it prohibits unsolicited advertising via fax machine.

These regulations do not apply to people who have an established business relationship with the telemarketing firm or people who have previously given the telemarketing firm permission to call. The law also does not apply to telemarketing calls placed by tax-exempt nonprofit organizations, such as charities.

Although most provisions of this federal law do not apply to medical practices, you should be aware of the law. One way to avoid an unknowing violation of this law is to limit your calls to patients to the hours between 8 A.M.

Choosing a Collection Agency

If a patient does not respond to your final collection letter or has twice broken a promise to pay, the practice may choose to seek the help of a collection agency. This step should be taken carefully, however. Some collection agencies use illegal and unethical tactics to obtain payment. For example, some collectors have made repeated, profane phone calls to frighten debtors. Others have threatened debtors with prison for nonpayment. A good collection agency reflects the humanitarian and ethical standards of the medical profession.

To help select an effective—and ethical—collection agency, ask for a referral from the doctor's colleagues, fellow specialists, or hospital associates. You may also contact the following organizations:

American Collectors Association International
ACA International
P.O. Box 390106
Minneapolis, MN 55439
(952) 926–6547
www.acainternational.org

After obtaining a referral, contact the agency and request samples of its letters, reminder notices, and other print material for debtors. Be sure this material is courteous and reflects the way you would handle the collection. Also, be sure the agency uses a persuasive approach rather than simply suing debtors. Ask if the agency reports cases that deserve special consideration to the doctor's office.

Determine what methods the agency uses for out-of-town accounts. For example, it may use out-of-town services to help with those collections. Ask the agency about its collection percentage and fees for large, small, and out-of-town accounts. Be sure the percentages and fees are appropriate for the collection amounts.

After selecting a collection agency, supply all pertinent data to the agency, such as the patient's name, address, and full amount of the debt. Mark the patient's ledger card so that you do not call or write to the patient about the debt. If the patient contacts the office about the account, refer the patient to the collection agency.

If you receive any payments from the debtor, alert the collection agency immediately. (The agency takes a portion of any payments it collects.) Also, contact the agency if you learn anything new about the patient's address or employer.

and 9 P.M. (some states, however, have exceptions for the TCPA provisions). Do not use an automated dialing device for calls to patients; always place the calls yourself. For more information on this act visit the American Teleservices Association Web site: www.ataconnect.org/public/consumers/teleconsumer protection.php.

Observing Professional Guidelines for Finance Charges and Late Charges

According to the AMA, it is appropriate to assess finance charges or late charges on past-due accounts if the patient is notified in advance. Advance notice may be given by posting a sign at the reception desk, giving the patient a pamphlet describing the practice's billing practices, or including a note on the invoice.

The physician must adhere to federal and state guidelines that govern these charges. The physician should also use compassion and discretion when assigning charges, especially in hardship cases. Because of the nature of medical care, many offices choose not to assess finance or late charges to patient accounts.

Using Outside Collection Agencies

If your collection efforts do not result in payment, the practice may wish to select a collection agency to manage the account. Because collection agencies keep a percentage of any funds they collect for their clients (usually between 40% and 60% of the collected amount), the office staff should use all reasonable methods to collect un-paid balances prior to sending an account to collection. Because of the humanitarian and ethical standards of the medical profession, physicians must be careful to avoid collection agencies that use harsh or harassing

collection practices. The Practice Readiness section gives information about selecting an outside collection agency.

When giving a patient's account to an agency, supply the following information about the patient:

- Full name and last known address
- Occupation and business address
- Name of spouse, if any
- Total debt
- Date of last payment or charge on the account
- Description of actions you took to collect the debt
- Responses to collection attempts

Once an account has been turned over to the collection agency, all communication between the patient and the office concerning her debt must cease. All inquiries must be referred to the collection agency. If a payment is received after the account has been turned over, follow the procedure outlined in the agreement with the agency—some agencies allow the office to deposit the check and send them their percentage, and others ask you to return the check to the patient with the request that the patient call the agency.

Because the debt is now the responsibility of the collection agency, it is important to note all accounts that have been turned over to them. For computerized accounts, a comment may be made to the account or the patient's name and account number may be "color coded," denoting collection proceedings have begun. As stated earlier in the chapter, for practices that use ledger cards, the color-coded tabs used for aging may also be used to denote collection proceedings (often black tabs are used for this purpose).

Lastly, it should always be the practice's decision (and not the collection agency) whether to pursue legal action in court regarding an account or to adjust the debt off the books. All collection agencies should make a monthly report to the office documenting the activity on the accounts they are working. Give the collection agency a set amount of time to collect the debt, such as 60–90 days. After that time, the practice should decide how to best deal with the account.

Insuring Accounts Receivable

To protect the practice from lost income because of nonpayment, the practice may buy accounts receivable insurance. One type of accounts receivable policy pays when a large number of patients do not pay and the physician must absorb the lost income. It protects the practice's cash flow and helps ensure that the practice will have sufficient income to cover expected expenses.

Why must medical practices be particularly careful when choosing a collection agency?

CHECKPOINT
LO 17.10

LO 17.11 Credit Arrangements

Sometimes a doctor agrees to extend credit to a patient who is unable to pay immediately. This situation is not uncommon when a patient's medical bills are high. By extending **credit**, the doctor gives the patient time to pay for services, which are provided on trust. If the doctor knows the patient well, she may offer credit without checking the patient's credit history. However, to avoid charges of discrimination under the Equal Credit Opportunity Act (ECOA), you will normally perform a credit check prior to extending credit.

credit
An extension of time to pay for services, which are provided on trust.

Following Laws Governing Extension of Credit

When you help the doctor decide whether to grant credit to a patient, you must comply with certain laws governing extension of credit.

Equal Credit Opportunity Act   The Equal Credit Opportunity Act states that credit arrangements may not be denied based on a patient's sex, race, religion, national origin, marital status, or age. Credit also cannot be denied because the patient receives public assistance or has exercised rights under the Consumer Credit Protection Act, such as disputing a credit card bill or a credit bureau report.

Under ECOA, the patient has a right to know the specific reason that credit was denied. Some reasons might include having too little income or not being employed for a certain period of time. Vague reasons about not meeting minimum standards or not receiving enough points on a credit-scoring system are not acceptable. In order to comply with ECOA, a credit check is required on any patient the practice is considering for extension of credit.

Performing a Credit Check   To perform a credit check, be sure you have the patient's most current information. You will need the patient's address, telephone number, and Social Security number as well as the name, address, and telephone number of the patient's employer. With this information you can verify employment and generate a credit bureau report.

Employment Verification   Explain to the patient that you will be calling his employer to verify employment. Many employers have someone designated to handle such calls. The patient may be able to give you that name before you call the place of employment. After calling, record the updated information on the patient's registration card, along with any credit references obtained from the patient.

credit bureau

A company that provides information about the creditworthiness of a person seeking credit.

Credit Bureau Report   A **credit bureau** is a company that provides information about the creditworthiness of a person seeking credit. If a patient's credit history is in question, you may request a report from a credit bureau. A sample credit report is shown in Figure 17–17. A credit bureau collects information about an individual's payment history on credit cards, student loans, and similar accounts. The three leading national credit bureaus are TRW Inc., Equifax Inc., and Trans Union Credit Information Company. The practice may decide not to extend credit, based on the credit report. If so, the Fair Credit Reporting Act states that you must inform the patient in writing that credit was denied based on the credit report. You must also provide the name and address of the credit bureau; however, you do not need to discuss the information obtained from the report. The patient may contest the credit report and have any inaccurate information corrected. Once the information has been corrected, the provider may then decide to extend credit to the patient.

Extending Credit   If the doctor decides to extend credit, several possible arrangements can be made. Two common arrangements are the unilateral agreement and the mutual agreement.

Unilateral Agreement   If the patient offers to pay the debt over a period of months, and the physician agrees, the patient will be billed every month for the full amount owed and should make whatever payment is possible each month. This type of arrangement is considered a unilateral agreement and is not regulated by the Truth in Lending Act.

Mutual Agreement   Another option is the mutual, or bilateral, agreement between physician (practice) and patient. They might agree that the patient

To the Consumer:
This is a copy of your current credit file. It is being furnished to you based on the information you have provided in accordance with the "Fair Credit Reporting Act." Please use the file number shown on this report on all correspondence. Refer to the reverse side for explanations of codes and abbreviations used in this disclosure.

File No.		
Date 1/8/12		
Amount Received $15.00	**Payment Type**	
Credit Card No.		**Exp. Date**

In File Since	10/94

Consumer Name and Address	SSN	Date Rptd.
	Spouse Name SSN	
	Tel.	
	Date Rptd.	

Former Address

Present Employer and Address	Position Income	Empl. Date	Date Verif.

Former Employer and Address

Spouse's Employer and Address

Subscriber Name	Subscriber Code	Date Opened	High Credit	Date Verif.	Present Status		Payment Pattern 1–12 Months 13–24 Months	Type Account & MOP
					Balance Owed	Amount Past Due		
Account Number		Terms	Credit Limit	Dated Closed	Maximum Delinquency Date Amount MOP		Historical Status No. of Months 25–39 40–59 60+	
Collateral				Remarks	Type Loan			
MIDLANTIC	B382D021	4/92 MIN10	$850	11/98A	$325	$0	111111111111 X11111111111 12 0 0 0	R01
LINCOLN SAV B	B814M006	6/88 360M34	$30.5K	10/94A	$16K	$0	1111X11X1111 111X11111X1X 29 0 0 0	M01
BANK AMER	B196P017	11/89 10M	$5000	10/96A	$1136	$0	111111111111 11111111111X 48 0 0 0	R01
MACY D	D787D008	1/84 MIN20	$475 $1000	11/97A	$0	$0*	111XXXXXXXXX 1111111111XX 48 0 0 0	R01
			CREDIT LINE CLOSED BY CUSTOMER					
UJ BK MC	33DB0002	7/91 MIN20	$3000	3/96A	$310	$0	111111111111 111X111111XX 47 0 0 0	R01

figure 17–17

Credit reports are generated by credit bureaus.

will be billed for the full amount owed each month and will pay a minimum amount each month. If the physician does not assess finance charges, and if the total number of payments is four or fewer, this type of agreement is also not covered by the Truth in Lending Act. However if the physician and patient make a bilateral agreement that includes more than four payments, or if the practice assesses finance charges, the agreement is subject to the requirements of the Truth in Lending Act.

Truth in Lending Act

The Truth in Lending Act comes under Regulation Z of the Consumer Credit Protection Act. This act covers credit agreements that involve more than four payments. It requires the practice and patient to discuss, sign, and retain copies of a **disclosure statement** (frequently called a federal Truth in Lending statement), which is a written description of the agreed terms of payment (Figure 17–18). According to the Truth in Lending Act, a disclosure statement must meet the following two requirements:

1. The agreement must be discussed with the patient when the terms are first determined. The practice and the patient must agree on the payment terms.

2. Both the physician (or his representative) and the patient must sign the document to indicate mutual agreement on the written terms.

disclosure statement
A written description of agreed terms of payment; also called a federal Truth in Lending statement.

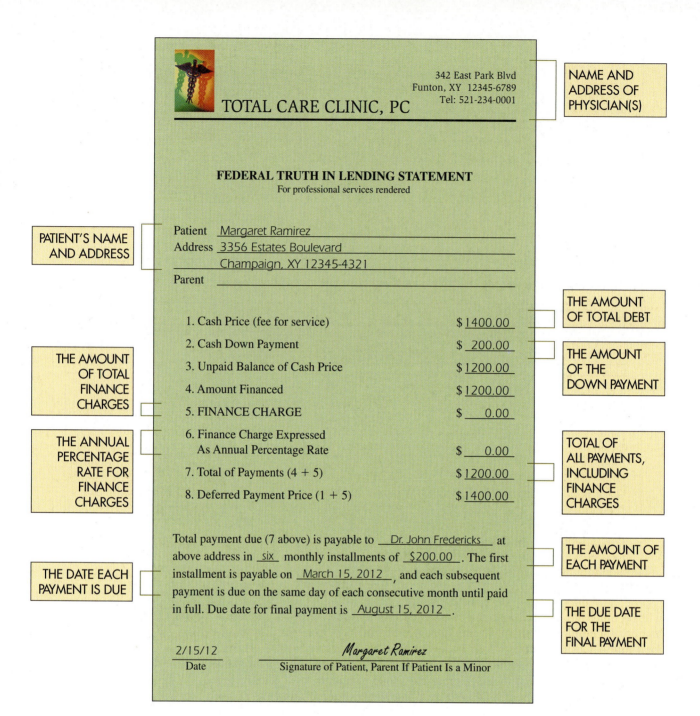

figure 17–18

The federal Truth in Lending Act mandates that a written disclosure statement be completed and signed by the physician and patient.

Further, a disclosure statement must include the following six pieces of information:

1. The amount of total debt (the amount for which the patient is receiving credit).
2. The amount of the down payment.
3. The amount of each payment (which may be weekly or monthly or for another period) and the date it is due. (Frequently the total number of payments to be made after the down payment is also included.)
4. The due date for the final payment and the amount of the final payment if different from the other payment amounts.

5. The interest rate, if interest is to be paid, expressed as an annual percentage.
6. The total finance charges, if any. (If interest is charged, the total amount of interest accrued during the course of the debt will be entered here.)

The practice and the patient should each keep a copy of the signed disclosure agreement. Under the Truth in Lending Act, the patient is billed only for

figure 17–19

Patient letter outlining the agreed-upon Truth in Lending statement, including the payment dates and the amount of each payment.

TOTAL CARE CLINIC, PC

342 East Park Blvd
Funton, XY   12345-6789
Tel: 521-234-0001
Fax: 521-234-0002
www.totalcareclinic.org

February 15, 2012

Margaret Ramirez
3356 Estates Boulevard
Champaign, XY 12345-4321

RE: Monthly Payment Agreement

Dear Ms. Ramirez:

As outlined in the Truth and Lending Statement signed in our office today, for your convenience we have outlined below your monthly payment schedule.

Amount Financed: $1200.00

Monthly Payments: $200.00

Date of Payment	Current Balance
3/15/2012	$1000.00
4/15/2012	$ 800.00
5/15/2012	$ 600.00
6/15/2012	$ 400.00
7/15/2012	$ 200.00
8/15/2012	$ 0.00

If for any reason, you cannot make the agreed-upon monthly payment as outlined above, please call me immediately so a new arrangement may be made.

As always, we thank you for choosing Total Care Clinic, PC for your health care needs.

Sincerely,

Darlene M. Elliott

Darlene M. Elliott
Office Manager

DE/kr

the monthly amount agreed upon and not the total amount of the debt. To avoid mailing a monthly statement, some offices create a master document given to the patient at the time of the agreement signing, which outlines each month's due date and the amount due, with a running total of the new balance once the payment is made. Figure 17–19 is an example of such a document.

CHECKPOINT
LO 17.11

Under ECOA, for what reasons may credit not be denied?

LO 17.12 Common Collection Problems

There are two common collection problems that medical practices encounter. The first is patients who cannot pay—also called hardship cases—and the second is patients who have moved without leaving a forwarding address and have not received an invoice.

Hardship Cases

A physician may decide to treat some patients without charge—or at a deep discount—simply because they cannot pay. These patients may be poor, uninsured, under-insured, or elderly and on a limited income. They may be patients who have suffered a severe financial loss or family tragedy. Medical ethics require physicians to provide care to individuals who need it, regardless of their ability to pay. Nevertheless, free treatment for hardship cases is at the physician's discretion.

Keep in mind as stated earlier, that under the Equal Credit Opportunity Act (ECOA), if a patient is given free or reduced-fee treatment based on her inability to pay and another patient under similar circumstances is treated, she must also be extended the same financial consideration or a charge of discrimination may be levied against the physician. Some providers treat such patients for urgent problems and then refer the patients to federally funded clinics that are allowed to provide free or reduced-fee services related to their government funding.

Patient Relocation and Address Change

Sometimes an invoice remains unpaid because the patient has moved without leaving a forwarding address and has not received the invoice. These patients are known as **skips**. Obviously, you will have a problem if you are trying to reach such a patient about a billing statement.

Remember not to discuss a debt with anyone except the person responsible for the charges. When you make a telephone call for collection, however, you may ask a third party for the patient's new address. If the third party states the new address is not known, do not call again unless there is reason to believe that the third party has learned of the person's address since the first inquiry. You may ask the post office for a forwarding address, but if the patient cannot be located, the patient may be labeled a skip. It is acceptable to refer the patient to the office collection agency. Be sure to keep the returned statement and envelope stamped by the post office as "addressee unknown" or "no forwarding address" to prove a reasonable attempt to collect the debt.

skips
People who move and leave no forwarding information in the hopes that they will not be found.

CHECKPOINT
LO 17.12

When would a patient be described as a skip?

BILLING AND INSURANCE SPECIALIST

● ● ●

Duties and Skills

A billing and insurance specialist is responsible for verifying patient insurance coverage and for processing insurance claims and obtaining fees for procedures and services performed, from both patients and insurance companies.

Educational Requirements

Insurance and Billing specialists may receive their training through accredited programs, continuing education courses, workshops, and seminars, as well as through on-the- job training. A high school diploma or its equivalent is required to be eligible for this training. After completing the training, Billing Specialists may receive certification through the American Medical Billing Association (AMBA) and through the American Medical Technologists (AMT).

Workplace Settings

Billing and insurance specialists work in many health-care settings, including hospitals, nursing homes, billing companies and physicians' practices. Some are employed by insurance companies.

The Billing and Insurance Specialist as a Team Member

The billing and coding specialist will work with all members of the medical staff, working particularly closely with the practice medical coders (Chapters 18–20) to be sure that the superbills or encounter forms are coded correctly. She will verify with the coders (or clinical staff if coders are not employed by the office) that the matching (or code linkage) of the procedure and diagnosis codes document the medical necessity for each procedure or service performed. Without verification of this important information, the claims she submits to the insurance carriers will be denied or review requested, holding up payment or resulting in a lower payment than the provider is entitled to receive.

She will bill Medicare or Medicaid, and/or other private insurance companies, including workers compensation and liability carriers. If the insurance company has questions about a claim it may request copies of the patient's medical records to verify that a particular procedure was medically necessary, and she will reproduce the necessary documents and send them to the carrier in a timely fashion.

The coding, billing, and insurance specialist also assists patients with the claims process. She will explain their benefits to them so that they understand the deductible and copayment or coinsurance requirements. If referrals or prior authorization is required for a procedure, she will also explain the process to the patient and explain why the patient may be required to see specific providers depending on the insurance carrier specifications.

The billing and insurance specialist also processes responses from the insurance companies, including the explanation of benefits (EOB), also known as the remittance advice (RA). She checks the EOB against the claim form to make sure that the insurance company addressed all procedures that were performed. Sometimes a balance remains because the insurance company did not pay the total amount due on all procedures. In those cases the billing and insurance specialist sends a bill to the patient or responsible party, or adjusts balances as required by contracted agreement. She may discover an error in the EOB. In such instances she looks for the source of the error and then contacts the insurance company to so the error may be corrected.

For more information, visit the Web sites of the following organizations, which are available on the Online Learning Center at www.mhhe.com/houseradminmedassist

American Medical Technologists (AMT)

American Medical Billing Association (AMBA)

Procedure 17-1   Verifying Workers' Compensation Coverage

GOAL   To verify workers' compensation coverage before accepting a patient

MATERIALS   Telephone, paper, pencil

METHOD   1. Call the patient's employer and verify that the accident or illness occurred on the employer's premises or at an employment-related work site.

2. Obtain the employer's approval to provide treatment. Be sure to write down the name and title of the person giving approval, as well as his phone number.

3. Ask the employer for the name of its workers' compensation insurance company. (Employers are required by law to carry such insurance. It is a good policy to notify your state labor department about any employer you encounter that does not have workers' compensation insurance, although you are not required to do so.)

   You may wish to remind the employer to report any workplace accidents or injuries that result in a workers' compensation claim to the state labor department within 24 hours of the incident.

4. Contact the insurance company and verify that the employer does indeed have a policy with the company and that the policy is in good standing.

5. Obtain a claim number for the case from the insurance company. This claim number is used on all bills and paperwork.

6. At the time the patient starts treatment, create a patient record. If the patient is already one of the practice's regular patients, create separate medical and financial records for the workers' compensation case.

Procedure 17–2 Submitting a Request for Prior Authorization

GOAL   To submit a request for prior authorization

MATERIALS   Patient medical chart with planned procedure and CPT code, diagnosis and ICD-9 code for proof of medical necessity, patient financial record or the following information: patient name, address, DOB, subscriber name and relationship to patient if not the same, insurance policy group, and ID numbers

METHOD
1. Place a call to the insurance carrier or access the Web site if available.

2. When you reach the nurse manager for the patient's policy, explain that you would like to obtain prior authorization for the requested procedure. She will ask a series of questions regarding the patient, procedure, and diagnosis. Answer these questions using the assembled materials from the patient's medical and financial records.

3. If obtaining authorization via the insurance carrier Web site, access the Web site utilizing your user ID and password. Enter the prior authorization area of the Web site and enter the required information using the assembled materials from the patient's medical and financial records.

4. When prior authorization is obtained, carefully record the authorization number and the name and extension number of the person issuing the authorization (if obtained over the phone). If the authorization is obtained via a Web site, print out the authorization documentation.

5. Place the authorization number and/or documentation in the patient medical and financial record for further reference as it will be required when submitting the patient's health insurance claim.

Procedure 17–3   Tracking Insurance Claims Submissions

GOAL   To create a spreadsheet to track insurance claims submission

MATERIALS   CMS-1500 claims prepared for submission or record of CMS-1500 claims submitted electronically; spreadsheet or grid for handwritten record with pen; or computer with software program such as MS Excel, allowing for creation of a spreadsheet

METHOD
1. Using Figure 17–8 as a guide, create columns with the following (or similar) headings: Patient Name (and/or account number); Insurance Company; Date of Submission and Amount of the Claim; Insurance Response and Date of Response; Date of Resubmission; Date of Payment; Payment Amount; Patient Balance; and Date of Patient Billing.
2. Using the list of claims being submitted, complete the blanks for patient name, insurance company, date of submission, and amount of the claim.
3. When the RA (EOB) is received, complete the date and response columns, including whether the claim is paid, rejected, denied, or a request was made for more information.
4. If resubmission is required, enter the date of resubmission.
5. If payment is received, enter the date of receipt and the amount of the payment.
6. Record patient balance (if any) and the date the patient is billed.

Procedure 17–4   Completing the CMS-1500 Claim Form

GOAL   To complete the CMS-1500 claim form correctly

MATERIALS   Patient record, CMS-1500 form, typewriter or computer, patient ledger card or charge slip

METHOD

Note: The numbers below correspond to the numbered fields on the CMS-1500.

Patient Information Section

1. Place an *X* in the appropriate insurance box.
1a. Enter the insured's insurance identification number as it appears on the insurance card.
2. Enter the patient's name in this order: last name, first name, middle initial (if any).
3. Enter the patient's birth date using an 8-digit format. Indicate the sex of the patient: male or female.
4. If the insured and the patient are the same person, enter SAME. If not, enter the policyholder's name.
5. Enter the patient's mailing address, city, state, and zip code.

6. Enter the patient's relationship to the insured. If they are the same, mark SELF.

7. Enter the insured's mailing address, city, state, zip code, and telephone number. If this address is the same as the patient's, enter SAME. For Medicare, leave blank.

8. Indicate the patient's marital, employment, and student status by placing an *X* in the boxes.

9. Enter the last name, first name, and middle initial of any other insured person whose policy might cover the patient. If the claim is for Medicare and the patient has a Medigap policy, enter the patient's name again.

9a. Enter the policy or group number for the other insured person.

9b. Enter the date of birth and sex of the other insured person (field 9).

9c. Enter the other insured's employer or school name.

9d. Enter the other insured's insurance plan or program name. If the plan is Medigap and CMS has assigned it a nine-digit number called PAYERID, enter that number here.

10. Place *X*s in the appropriate YES or NO boxes in a, b, and c to indicate whether the patient's place of employment, an auto accident, or other type of accident precipitated the patient's condition. If an auto accident is responsible, for PLACE, enter the two-letter state postal abbreviation for the location of the accident.

11. Enter the insured's policy group number. For Medicare claims, fill out this section only if there is other insurance primary to Medicare; otherwise, enter NONE and leave fields 11a–d blank.

11a. Enter the insured's date of birth and sex as in field 3, if the insured is not the patient.

11b. Enter the employer's name or school name here. This information will determine if Medicare is the primary payer.

11c. Enter the insurance plan or program name.

11d. Place an *X* to indicate YES or NO related to another health benefit plan.

12. The patient or an authorized representative signs and dates the form here. If a representative signs, have the representative indicate the relationship to the patient. If signatures are on file this may noted by inserting "Signature on File" or for some payers, the abbreviation "SOF" is also acceptable.

13. Have the insured (the patient or another individual) sign here. If signatures are on file this may noted by inserting "Signature on File" or for some payers, the abbreviation "SOF" is also acceptable.

Physician Information Section

14. Enter the date of the current illness, injury, or pregnancy, using eight digits.

15. Enter date patient was first seen for illness or injury. Leave it blank for Medicare.

16. Enter the dates the patient is or was unable to work. This information could signal a workers' compensation claim.

17. Enter the name of the referring physician, clinical laboratory, or other referring source.

17a. Depending on insurance carrier instructions, enter an approved 2-digit qualifier (refer to Table 17–1) in the small space and the appropriate referring provider identifier next to it. If the carrier requires only the NPI, leave this box blank.

17b. Enter the referring provider NPI number.

18. If the patient was hospitalized during this encounter, enter the dates here.

19. Use your payer's current instructions for this field. In many cases, it may be left blank.

20. Place an *X* in the YES box if a laboratory test was performed outside the physician's office, and enter the test price if you are billing for these tests. Place an *X* in the NO box if the test was done in the office of the physician who is billing the insurance company.

21. Enter the ICD-9-CM code number for each diagnosis or nature of injury (see Chapter 18). Enter up to four codes in order of importance.

22. Enter the Medicaid resubmission code and original reference number if applicable.

23. Enter the prior authorization number if required by the payer.

24. The six service lines in block 24 are divided horizontally to accommodate NPI and other proprietary identifiers per insurance carrier instructions. Otherwise, use the nonshaded areas.

24a. Enter the date of each service, procedure, or supply provided. Add the number of days for each, and enter them, in chronological order, in field 24G.

24b. Enter the two-digit place-of-service code (see Table 17–6).

24c. EMG stands for *emergency care*. Check with insurer to see if this information is needed. If it is required and emergency care was provided, enter *Y*; if it is not required or care was not on an emergency basis, leave this field blank.

24d. Enter the CPT/HCPCS codes with modifiers for the procedures, services, or supplies provided (see Chapter 20).

24e. Enter the diagnosis code (or its reference number—1, 2, 3, or 4— depending on carrier regulations) that applies to that procedure, as listed in field 21.

24f. Enter the dollar amount of fee charged.

24g. Enter the days or units on which the service was performed.

24h. This field is Medicaid-specific for early periodic screening diagnosis and treatment programs.

24i. If required by the insurance carrier, enter the appropriate non-NPI indentifier here. If not required, leave this area blank.

24j. If a non-NPI number is required by the carrier, enter the PIN identified in 24I in the shaded area. Use the nonshaded area below this to enter the provider's NPI in 24I.

25. Enter the physician's or care provider's federal tax identification number or Social Security number.

26. Enter the patient's account number assigned by your office, if applicable.

27. Place an *X* in the YES box to indicate that the physician will accept Medicare or TRICARE assignment of benefits.

28. Enter the total charge for the service.

29. Enter the amount already paid by any primary insurance company or the patient, if it pertains to his deductible.

30. Enter the balance due your office. For primary Medicare claims, leave blank.

31. Have the physician or service supplier sign and date the form here. In most cases, because claims are filed electronically, the signature is on file and the typed name of the provider is acceptable in this block.

32. Enter the name and address of the organization or individual who performed the services. If performed in the patient's home, leave this field blank.

   a. In field 32a, enter the NPI for the service facility.

   b. Use field 32b if required by the insurance carrier. In this case, enter the appropriate two-digit qualifier immediately followed by the identification number being used. Do not place any spaces or punctuation between the qualifier and the identification number.

33. List the billing physician's or supplier's name, address, zip code, and phone number.

   a. In field 33a, enter the NPI of the billing provider.

   b. If required by the insurance carrier, enter the non-NPI qualifier in field 33b, immediately followed by the identification number being used. Do not place any spaces or punctuation between the qualifier and the identification number.

Procedure 17–5 Completing the Encounter Form (Superbill)

GOAL To complete an encounter form or superbill accurately (make sure the doctor's name and address appear on the form)

MATERIALS Superbill, patient ledger card, patient information sheet, fee schedule, insurance code list, pen

METHOD

1. From the patient ledger card and information sheet, fill in the patient data, such as name, sex, date of birth, and insurance information.

2. Fill in the place and date of service.

3. Attach the superbill to the patient's medical record, and give them both to the doctor.

4. Accept the completed superbill from the patient after the patient sees the doctor. Make sure that the doctor has indicated the diagnosis and the procedures performed. Also make sure that an appropriate diagnosis is listed for each procedure.

5. If the doctor has not already recorded the charges, refer to the fee schedule for procedures that are marked. Then fill in the charges next to those procedures.

6. In the appropriate blanks, list the total charges for the visit and the previous balance (if any).

7. Calculate the subtotal.

8. Fill in the amount and type of payment (cash, check, money order, or credit card) made by the patient during this visit.

9. Calculate and enter the new balance.

10. Have the patient sign the authorization-and-release section of the superbill.

11. Keep a copy of the superbill for the practice records. Give the original to the patient along with one copy to file with the insurer.

Procedure 17–6 Preparing an Age Analysis

GOAL To create and examine an age analysis

MATERIALS Computer, patient accounts, ledger cards (if being done by hand), accounts receivable aging record analysis form (optional), policy and procedure manual, pen

METHOD

1. Using the reporting section of your billing computer program, create an age analysis report for patients and insurance companies. This also can be done manually by pulling patient ledger cards, noting balances due and dates of last payments. Use Figure 17–16 as a guide to create a spreadsheet for your findings.

2. Review the accounting report. Check the report—highlight for proposed actions for each account according to your office policy.

3. Mark the accounts that are under 31 days as NO ACTION TO BE TAKEN AT THIS TIME.

4. Bills that are unpaid at more than 31 days should be marked as "Contact or follow up with insurance company."

5. Accounts that are 31–60 days old should be marked according to your office policy. An initial phone call may be made inquiring as to payment arrangements.

6. Accounts that are 61–90 days old should be marked according to your office policy. Make notations such as "Account Past Due." A follow-up phone call and/or more insistent statement message letter for payment may be in order.

7. Accounts that are 91–120 days old should be marked according to your office policy. A last phone call to attempt discussing the account and more insistent collection statement/letter should be sent.

8. For accounts older than 120 days, make sure you review previous collection attempts. At this point, after discussion with the physician, a letter stating the account will be turned over to the collection agency will take place with a specific date listed in the letter. This letter should be mailed by certified, return receipt mail.

9. Record all actions that have been taken beside each account.

10. Finally, write follow-up letters to patients and document any agreements that you and the patient have discussed via telephone. Be sure to keep a copy of any correspondence mailed to the patient in the financial record.

Case Study

Dora works in the insurance and billing section of Dr. Goldberg's office. When a patient is having a problem with a bill or insurance, Dora is the "go-to" person. She not only understands the subjects, she also has the ability to explain them using a clear, pleasant approach. Patients understand her and usually respond in a positive manner. Coworkers call her the "EOB queen" because she can decipher an explanation of benefits for anyone to comprehend. Dora has empathy for the layperson attempting to navigate the complicated health-care payment

PROFESSIONAL READINESS

Communications
Ability to give and receive clear, accurate information

system. She also uses her excellent communication skills to work with patients to develop reasonable payment options, with coders to correctly code claims, and with insurance companies to review decisions.

Thinking Critically

1. Do you think Dora enjoys her job? Why or why not?

2. What might result if staff in the billing and coding sections do not work well together?

3. Are you able to decipher an EOB?

practice APPLICATIONS

1. You need to calculate how much a patient needs to pay. He is a member of a preferred provider organization (PPO) that has a contract that allows all members a 25% discount. The patient's total bill for services rendered today is $300.00. The patient has a copayment of 20%. The patient states that he can only pay $50.00 today. Does the patient have enough to cover the amount due today?

2. Using the guidelines described in this chapter, write a collection letter to a fictional patient. The patient owes the doctor $125, and the account is 60 days past due. Share your letter with a classmate to analyze how well you complied with federal collection guidelines.

exam READINESS

1. [LO17.3] The first national health insurance for Americans age 65 and older is

a. Medicaid.
b. Medicare.
c. disability insurance.
d. liability insurance.
e. workers' compensation.

2. [LO17.4] The authorization for an insurance carrier to pay the physician or practice directly is the

a. copayment.
b. provider of medical services.
c. assignment of benefits.
d. health insurance provider.
e. authorization to release information.

3. [LO17.1] A fixed dollar amount the subscriber must pay or "meet" each year before the insurer begins to cover expenses is the

a. copayment.
b. deductible.

c. premium.
d. coinsurance.
e. lifetime maximum.

4. [LO17.2] Most specialists are paid by MCOs using which of the following methods?

a. Fee-for-service
b. Capitation
c. Copayment
d. Coinsurance
e. Negotiated per-service fees

5. [LO17.6] Why is it important that each procedure on the CMS-1500 be matched with a diagnosis code?

a. It proves the procedure was performed.
b. It keeps the coder employed.
c. It increases the reimbursement amount.
d. It proves medical necessity for the procedure.
e. It truly does not matter.

6. **[LO17.7]** Which of the following is a diplomatic way to ask a patient for payment?

   a. "I need $50 for today's visit."
   b. "For today's visit, the total charge is $50. How would you like to pay?"
   c. "That will be $50. What is your check number?"
   d. "Your charge for today's visit is $50. We take cash, check, credit, and debit cards."
   e. Any of the above is acceptable.

7. **[LO17.8]** Which of the following information should be included on a patient statement?

   a. The patient's income
   b. The balance from the previous month and an itemized list of charges
   c. The patient's credit card information
   d. The patient's occupation and place of employment
   e. b, c, and d

8. **[LO17.9]** Which of the following account types is most common in the medical office?

   a. Written contract accounts
   b. Single-entry accounts

   c. Accounts involving Truth in Lending statements
   d. Skip Accounts
   e. Open book accounts

9. **[LO17.10]** Which of the following laws govern credit policies in medical practices?

   a. ECOA
   b. FCRA
   c. FDCPA
   d. TLA
   e. a, b, and d

10. **[LO17.11]** Which of the following is NOT one of the three leading credit bureaus in the United. States?

    a. Equifax
    b. TRW
    c. TransUnion
    d. All of the above are leading credit bureaus
    e. Only a and c are leading credit bureaus

learning outcome SUMMARY

LO 17.1 The following are key terms used by insurance companies, knowledgeable administrative medical assistants, medical billers, and coders: premium, benefit, lifetime maximum, deductible, coinsurance, copayment, exclusions, formulary, elective procedure, precertification, preauthorization, liability insurance, and disability insurance.

LO 17.2 Fee-for-service plans are traditional plans where after a yearly deductible is met, the insurance plan pays for a percentage of the charges and the patient is responsible for the other percentage (often 80% insurance plan and 20% patient). HMOs are prepaid plans that pay the providers either by capitation or by contracted fee-for-service with patients choosing a PCP, seeing preferred providers, and paying a fixed per visit copay. A PPO is a managed care plan that establishes a network of providers to perform services for plan members. Members may seek care out-of-network, but their costs will be higher.

LO 17.3 Medicare provides health insurance for citizens aged 65 and older as well as for certain disabled workers, disabled widows of workers, and patients with long-term disability related to chronic kidney disease

on dialysis and end-stage renal disease requiring transplant. Medicaid is a health benefit plan for low-income, blind, or disabled patients; needy families; foster children; and children born with birth defects.

LO 17.4 RBRVS stands for resource-based relative value scale. Its formula is RVU x GAF x CF. An allowed charge is the maximum dollar amount an insurance carrier will base its reimbursement on—it is also the maximum amount a participating provider is allowed to collect. A contracted fee is a negotiated fee between the MCO and the provider.

LO 17.5 The claims process includes: obtaining patient information; delivering services to the patient and determining the diagnosis and fee; recording charges and codes, documenting payment from the patient, and preparing the health-care claims; and reviewing the insurer's processing of the claim, remittance advice, and payment.

LO 17.6 Using the step-by-step instructions within the chapter and Procedure 17–2, and given a completed encounter form (superbill) with all necessary information, the student should produce a legible, clean, and acceptable CMS-1500 claim form.

LO 17.7 Accounts Receivable refers to the money that is owed to the practice (able to be received). Accounts Payable refers to the money that the practice owes other vendors (able to be paid). Common payment methods accepted by medical practices include cash, check, and debit and credit cards.

LO 17.8 Common statement documents include the use of superbills, typed or computer-produced itemized statements, and copies of ledger cards.

LO 17.9 An open-book account is the account type most commonly found in a medical practice, consisting of periodic charges and payments added on an as needed basis as patients are seen in the practice. A written-contract account is used when the physician and patient sign a contract for a specific service or procedure. A single-entry account is one used for patients when it is expected they will be seen only once, such as for a relative visiting the area on vacation. An age analysis is the process of classifying and reviewing past-due accounts by age from the first date of billing. It helps you keep on top of past-due accounts and determine which ones need follow-up.

LO 17.10 ECOA is the Equal Credit Opportunity Act. It prohibits discrimination based on sex, marital status, race, national origin, religion, or age. Applicants also cannot be discriminated against for receiving public assistance income or exercising their rights under the Consumer Credit Protection Act. The Fair Credit Reporting Act (FCRA) requires credit bureaus supply correct and complete information to businesses to use in evaluating a person's application for credit, insurance, or a job. The Fair Debt Collections Practices Act or FDCPA requires debt collectors to treat debtors fairly and prohibits certain collection tactics, including harassment, false statements, threats, and unfair practices.

LO 17.11 The Truth in Lending statement must include the following elements: the amount of total debt, the amount of the down payment, the amount of each payment and the date due, the due date for the final payment, the interest rate, (if any) expressed as an annual percentage rate, and the total finance charges (if any).

LO 17.12 The two most common types of collection problems in the medical office are hardship cases, who simply cannot afford to pay their debt, and accounts known as skips, where the debtor moved and left no valid forwarding information so it is not possible to bill the patient.

medical assisting COMPETENCIES

CAAHEP

VI. C (9) Explain both billing and payment options

VI. C (13) Discuss types of adjustments that may be made to a patient's account

VII. C (1) Identify types of insurance plans

VII. C (2) Identify models of managed care

VII. C (3) Discuss workers' compensation as it applies to patients

VII. C (4) Describe procedures for implementing both managed care and insurance plans

VII. C (6) Discuss referral process for patients in a managed care program

VII. C (7) Describe how guidelines are used in processing an insurance claim

VII. C (8) Compare processes for filing insurance claims both manually and electronically

VII. C (9) Describe guidelines for third-party claims

VII. C (10) Discuss types of physician fee schedules

VII. C (11) Describe the concept of RBRVS

VII. C (12) Define diagnosis-related groups (DRGs)

VII. P (2) Apply third party guidelines

VII. P (3) Complete insurance claim forms

VII. P (4) Obtain precertification, including documentation

VII. P (5) Obtain preauthorization, including documentation

VII. P (6) Verify eligibility for managed care services

VII. A (1) Demonstrate assertive communication with managed care and/or insurance providers

VII. A (2) Demonstrate sensitivity in communicating with both providers and patients

VII. A (3) Communicate in language the patient can understand regarding managed care and insurance plans

IX.C (6) Describe liability, professional, personal injury, and third-party insurance

ABHES

8. Medical Office Business Procedures Management
   i. Perform billing and collections procedures
   k. Perform accounts receivable procedures
   r. Apply third-party guidelines

   s. Obtain managed care referrals and precertifications
   u. Prepare and submit insurance claims
   v. Use physician's fee schedule
   ll. Apply electronic technology

18 ICD-9-CM

Coding

Key Terms

Alphabetic Index
chief complaint (CC)
conventions
cross-reference
diagnosis (Dx)
diagnosis code
E code
International
  Classification of
  Diseases, Ninth
  Revision, Clinical
  Modification
  (ICD-9-CM)

primary diagnosis
principal diagnosis
secondary diagnosis
Tabular List
V code

Preparation for Certification

RMA (AMT) Exam
- ICD-9 coding applications
- Medical insurance terminology

CMAS (AMT) Exam
- Coding

CMA (AAMA) Exam
- Applying managed care policies and procedures
- Relationship between procedure and diagnosis codes

Introduction ● ● ●

Patients who come to the medical office have a variety of reasons for seeking medical care. Each of those reasons results in at least one diagnosis. The word diagnosis, when split into its component word parts, literally means "the condition of complete knowledge" (osis–condition, dia–complete, gnos–knowledge). When submitting claims to insurance carriers to receive reimbursement for the care the patient receives, this knowledge must be converted into numeric and alpha numeric codes known as ICD-9-CM which stands for International Classification of Diseases, Ninth Revision, Clinical Modification.

With the passage of the Medicare Catastrophic Coverage Act of 1988, diagnosis coding using ICD-9-CM became mandatory for Medicare claims and shortly thereafter, for Medicaid and commercial insurance carriers. Just as you learn medical terminology to communicate with all members of the health-care team, as an administrative medical assistant, it is equally important to learn the *language* of coding—both ICD-9 in this chapter and CPT and HCPCS procedure coding in Chapter 20, as well as receive an introduction to the ICD-10 diagnosis coding program to be introduced in 2013, found in Chapter 19. Because insurance carriers pay claims, based not on the medical record but on the codes assigned to describe the information within the medical record, it is vitally important that you have an understanding of what the codes mean and how to choose the correct code based on the information found on the encounter forms and within the patient medical record.

LO 18.1 The Reason for ICD-9-CM

Patients present physicians with a description of their medical problem, called their **chief complaint (CC)** in the documentation of their visits. To diagnose a patient's condition, the physician follows a complex process of decision making based on the patient's statements, an examination, and the physician's evaluation of this information. The physician establishes a **diagnosis (Dx)** that describes the primary condition for which a patient is receiving care. Additional conditions or symptoms that affect the patient's management are called coexisting conditions. These conditions may be related or totally unrelated to the primary condition, but if they currently affect the patient's condition or treatment, they must also be noted in the chart, coded, and reported to the insurance carrier. The diagnoses listed on a health-care claim form should prove medical necessity for the treatment provided.

The diagnosis is communicated to the third-party payer through a **diagnosis code** on the health-care claim. The diagnosis codes used in the United States are found in the **International Classification of Diseases, Ninth Revision, Clinical Modification,** commonly referred to as the **ICD-9-CM** or simply ICD-9. Also available on CD-ROM, this code set is based on a system maintained by the World Health Organization (WHO) of the United Nations.

The use of the ICD-9 codes in the health-care industry is mandated by the Health Insurance Portability and Accountability Act (HIPAA) for reporting patients' diseases, conditions, or their signs and symptoms if no actual diagnosis has been assigned. The codes are updated every year and new ICD-9 manuals are available prior to October 1, which is when the new diagnosis codes are to be used on claims. The edition of diagnosis code being used is based on the date of service, not on the date the claim is submitted. For instance when completing claims on October 1, 2011, you will use 2011 ICD-9 codes on a claim for services provided on September 30, 2011. However, for a claim reporting services provided on October 1, 2011, the new 2012 ICD-9 codes would be used. As of this writing, the plan is that on October 1, 2013, ICD-9 will be replaced by a new coding system known as ICD-10. You will be introduced to this system

chief complaint
The patient's primary reason for seeking care.

diagnosis (Dx)
The physician's determination of the primary condition for which a patient is seeking care.

diagnosis code
The alphanumeric designation used to communicate the diagnosis to the third-party payer on the health-care claim form.

International Classification of Diseases, Ninth Revision, Clinical Modification (ICD-9-CM)
Code set based on a system maintained by the World Health Organization. The use of ICD-9 codes is mandated by HIPAA for reporting patient diseases, conditions, and signs and symptoms.

in Chapter 19. Medical offices should always have the current year's reference book and should update office forms and computer programs containing diagnosis codes; using outdated codes will result in denied claims.

ICD-9-CM was originally created for the classification of patient morbidity (sickness) and mortality (death) statistics and to provide access for medical research, education, and administration. Today, however, ICD-9 codes are increasingly important and they are used for the following reasons:

- Facilitation of payment for medical services
- Evaluation of utilization patterns (patient use of health-care facilities)
- Study of health-care costs
- Research regarding quality of health care
- Prediction of health-care trends
- Planning for future health-care needs

Keep in mind as you learn coding that just as whatever you document in a patient's health record becomes part of their permanent record, so does any code you assign to the patient for receipt by the insurance carrier. It may also be part of statistical reporting for communicable diseases, pregnancies, cancer diagnosis, and so on; so it is of paramount importance that you understand the information you are coding and the descriptions of the codes you are assigning.

CHECKPOINT
LO 18.1

What does ICD-9-CM stand for?

LO 18.2 Format and Conventions of ICD-9

The ICD-9-CM used in medical offices has two parts, the Tabular List, known as Volume 1, and the Alphabetic Index, known as Volume 2, which is actually found at the beginning of the manual. Hospitals use an edition that includes Volume 3, which is a tabular and alphabetic listing of procedures performed primarily in hospitals.

Tabular List
One of two ways that diagnoses are listed in the ICD-9-CM. In the Tabular List, the diagnosis codes are listed in numeric order with additional instructions regarding the use of the code for each diagnosis.

Diseases and Injuries: Tabular List, Volume 1 The **Tabular List** has 17 chapters of disease descriptions and codes, as well a chapter for services provided for patients who seek care but are not considered ill (such as those with a family history of a disease, or those who are seen for an annual physical to prevent illness), known as V codes, and a chapter for causes of illnesses and injuries, known as E codes. We will discuss these in detail later in the chapter. ICD-9 also includes five appendixes. Table 18–1 outlines the list of chapters in the Tabular List.

Alphabetic Index
One of two ways diagnoses are listed in the ICD-9-CM. They appear in alphabetic order with their corresponding diagnosis code(s).

Diseases and Injuries: Alphabetic Index, Volume 2 The **Alphabetic Index** provides the following:

- An index of the disease descriptions in the Tabular List
- An index in table format of drugs and chemicals that cause poisoning
- An index of external causes of injury, such as accidents and poisonings (the previously mentioned E codes).

Diagnoses are listed two ways in the ICD-9, as illustrated in Figure 18–1. In the Alphabetic Index, diagnoses appear in alphabetic order with at least the 3 digit *rubric* of their corresponding diagnosis codes. In Figure 18–1 for the diagnosis of Trichinosis, the rubric is noted as 124. In the Tabular List, the diagnosis codes are listed in numerical order with additional instructions that

Chapter	Categories
1 Infectious and Parasitic Diseases	001–139
2 Neoplasms	140–239
3 Endocrine, Nutritional, and Metabolic Diseases, and Immunity Disorders	240–279
4 Diseases of the Blood and Blood-Forming Organs	280–289
5 Mental Disorders	290–319
6 Diseases of the Central Nervous System and Sense Organs	320–389
7 Diseases of the Circulatory System	390–459
8 Diseases of the Respiratory System	460–519
9 Diseases of the Digestive System	520–579
10 Diseases of the Genitourinary System	580–629
11 Complications of Pregnancy, Childbirth, and the Puerperium	630–679
12 Diseases of the Skin and Subcutaneous Tissue	680–709
13 Diseases of the Musculoskeletal System and Connective Tissue	710–739
14 Congenital Anomalies	740–759
15 Certain Conditions Originating in the Perinatal Period	760–779
16 Symptoms, Signs, and Ill-Defined Conditions	780–799
17 Injury and Poisoning	800–999
SUPPLEMENTARY CLASSIFICATIONS	
V Codes—Supplementary Classification of Factors Influencing Health Status and Contact with Health Services	V01–V83
E Codes—Supplementary Classification of External Causes of Injury and Poisoning	E800–E999

table 18–1

Tabular List Organization

are necessary to choose the final diagnosis code. In Figure 18–1, code 124 is shown with the diagnosis of Trichinosis and shows the additional information that diagnoses of Trichinella spiralis and trichinellosis would also be coded with ICD-9 code 124. Both the Alphabetic Index and the Tabular List are used to find the right code. The Alphabetic Index is *never* used alone because it does not contain all the necessary information. After you locate a code in the index, look it up in the Tabular List. Notes in this list may suggest or require the use of additional codes, or indicate that conditions should be coded differently because of exclusion from a category.

Although the official order of the volumes puts the Tabular List before the Alphabetic Index, the correct use is to examine the Alphabetic Index when you are researching a term and then to verify your selection in the Tabular List. For this reason, commercial printers usually reverse the order, printing the Alphabetic Index at the front and the Tabular List behind it.

ICD-9-CM Conventions

A list of abbreviations, punctuation, symbols, typefaces, and instructional notes appears at the beginning of the ICD-9. These items, called **conventions,** provide guidelines for using the code set. Here are some important conventions:

conventions
A list of abbreviations, punctuation, symbols, typefaces, and instructional notes appearing in the beginning of ICD-9. The items provide guidelines for using the code set.

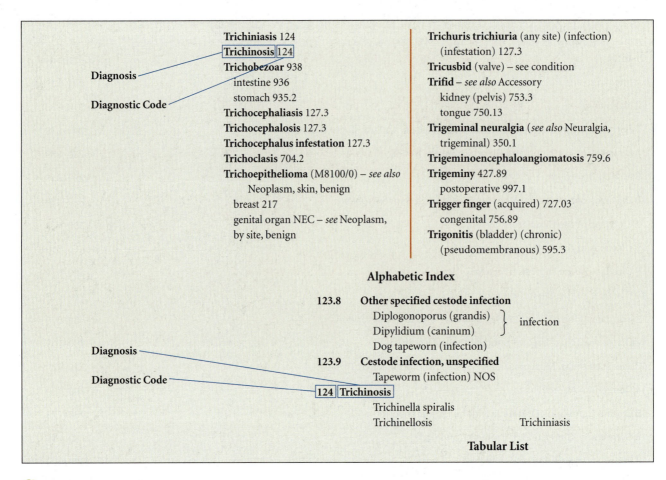

figure 18–1

ICD Alphabetic Index and Tabular List.

Source: International Classification of Diseases, Ninth Revision, Clinical Modification, 2010, Volumes 1, 2, and 3.

- NOS. This abbreviation means "not otherwise specified," or "unspecified." It is used when a condition cannot be described more specifically. In general, codes with NOS should be avoided unless no other option is available. The physician should be asked for more specific information to help select a more specific code, if possible. Most of the NOS codes end with the number 9.

  Example:

038.9	**Unspecified septicemia**
	Septicemia NOS

- NEC. This abbreviation means "not elsewhere classified." It is used when the ICD-9 does not provide a code specific enough for the patient's condition. Only use these codes when you are sure a more specific code does not exist. In general, the NEC codes end with the number 8.

  Example:

244.8	**Other specified acquired hypothyroidism**
	Secondary hypothyroidism NEC

- [ ] Brackets. These are used around synonyms, alternative wordings, or explanations.

  Example:

482.2	**Pneumonia due to Hemophilus influenzae [H. influenza]**

- *[ ]* Slanted brackets appear in the Alphabetic Index and indicate that two codes will be required to completely code the diagnosis. The code in the slanted bracket will be the secondary code.

  Example:

  > **Fleischer (-Kayser) ring** (corneal pigmentation)
  >   275.1 *[371.14]*

- *( )* Parentheses. These are used around descriptions in the Alphabetic Index that do not affect the code, that is, nonessential or supplementary terms.

  Example:

  > **Fleischer (-Kayser) ring** (corneal pigmentation)
  >   275.1 *[371.14]*

- *: Colon.* This is used in the Tabular List after an incomplete term that needs one of the terms that follows the colon to make it assignable to a given category.

  Example:

  > | 009.2 | **Infectious diarrhea** |
  > |---|---|
  > | | Diarrhea: |
  > | | dysenteric |
  > | | epidemic |

- *} Brace.* This encloses a series of terms, each of which is modified by the statement that appears to the right of the brace.

  Example:

  > | 308.0 | **Predominant disturbance of emotions** |
  > |---|---|
  > | | Anxiety |
  > | | Emotional crisis } as acute reaction to exceptional |
  > | | Panic state } [gross] stress |

- *Includes.* This note indicates that the entries following it further define the content of a preceding entry.

  Example:

  > | 249 | **Secondary diabetes mellitus** |
  > |---|---|
  > | | **INCLUDES** diabetes mellitus (due to)(in) (secondary(with): |
  > | | drug-induced or chemical induced infection |

- *Excludes.* These notes, which are boxed and italicized, indicate that an entry is not classified as part of the preceding code. The note may also give the correct location of the excluded condition to assist you in locating the correct code.

  Example:

  > | 246.2 | **Cyst of thyroid** |
  > |---|---|
  > | | **EXCLUDES** cystadenoma of thyroid (226) |

- *Use additional code.* This note indicates that an additional code should be used, if available. The additional code is always listed after the primary code.

  Example:

  > **599.6 Urinary obstruction**
  >   Use additional code to identify urinary incontinence
  >   (635.6, 788.30-788.39)

- *Code first underlying disease.* This instruction appears when the category is not to be used as the primary diagnosis. These codes may not be used as the first code; they must always be preceded by another code for the primary diagnosis.

Example:

| 362.0 | **Diabetic retinopathy** |
| | Code first diabetes (249.5, 250.5) |

- *Code, if applicable, any causal condition first.* This note means that the code may be used as a primary diagnosis if the underlying or "causal condition" is unknown or not applicable.

Example:

590.0	**Chronic pyelonephritis**
	Chronic pyelitis
	Chronic pyonephrosis
	Code, if applicable, any causal condition first

Two other conventions found in the Tabular List to be aware of are the use of bold and italicized type face. Boldface is used for all codes and titles in the Tabular List. Italicization is used for all exclusion notes and to identify codes that are not used to describe the primary diagnosis; they are only used as secondary diagnoses.

The Alphabetic Index includes two notations you should also be aware of:

- *Omit Code* is used to let you know that the medical term should not be coded as a diagnosis.

Example:

| **Metaplasia** |
| Cervix –omit code |

- *See Condition.* When found in the Alphabetic Index it is meant to refer you to a different "main term" for the condition. For instance, if you look up the term *Cervix* in the Alphabetic Index, you will be directed to *See condition.* Cervix is not a diagnosis, it is a location. Keep in mind that the diagnosis (and its main term) is "what is wrong with the patient." The location will be used as a subterm. If the patient has a diagnosis of cervical cancer, you would then look up neoplasm, cervix; neoplasm being the main condition

Example:

| **Cervix**—See Condition |

- *See* Also. If the diagnosis for the patient is cervical inflammation, the main term is inflammation. When you look up inflammation, cervix (subterm for the location of the inflammation), you are directed to 616.0, but you are also directed to *See also* "Cervicitis."

Example:

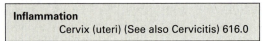

| **Inflammation** |
| Cervix (uteri) (See also Cervicitis) 616.0 |

The direction "See condition" is a directive; you must do so to locate the code. "See also" is a suggestion; you might find a better code for the diagnosis you are coding. In the case of "cervicitis" you will find multiple codes available depending on what is causing the cervicitis. Follow all directions in ICD-9.

It will make you a better coder and in many cases increase the reimbursement for the provider because you are giving the insurance carrier the most specific information available for the medical necessity for the services provided.

The Coding Guidelines section of the ICD-9 manual is the most important and most overlooked area of the manual. Broken out by section, the guidelines give very specific instructions on how to code each of the 17 chapters of the ICD-9 manual as well as the best use of E codes and V codes. Read this area and highlight sections that give you trouble for easy access. You will be glad you did.

The Alphabetic Index

After reading the guidelines, the Alphabetic Index is your starting point. It contains all the medical terms necessary to locate codes in the Tabular List. For some conditions, it also has common terms that are not found in the Tabular List. The index is organized by the condition, not by the body part in which the condition occurs. To use the Alphabetic Index, think about what is wrong (the problem) and not where the problem occurred. For example, you would find the term *wrist fracture* by looking under *fracture* (the condition) and then, below it, *wrist* (the location), rather than by looking under *wrist* to find *fracture*. In fact, if you look up the word *wrist,* you will be told "See also condition," telling you to look up the problem with the wrist.

The assignment of the correct code begins with looking up the medical term that describes the patient's condition in the Alphabetic Index. The following example illustrates the index's format. Each main term is printed in boldface type and is followed by its code number. For example, if the diagnostic statement is "the patient presents with blindness," the main term *blindness* is located in the Alphabetic Index.

> **Blindness** (acquired) (congenital) (both eyes) 369.00
>> deafness V49.85
>> blast 921.3
>>> with nerve injury—see Injury, nerve, optic
>> Bright's—see Uremia
>> color (congenital) 368.59
>>> acquired 368.55
>>> blue 368.53
>>> green 368.52
>>> red 368.51
>>> total 368.54
>> concussion 950.9
>> cortical 377.75

Any other terms that are needed to select correct codes are printed and indented after the main term. These terms, called *subterms,* may show the cause or source of the disease, or describe a particular type or body site for the main term. In this shortened example, the main term *blindness* is followed by five additional terms, each indicating a different type—such as color blindness—for this medical condition. Additionally, when coding color blindness, note that each of its subterms, which denote the actual type of color blindness, has its own code. When cross-referencing with the Tabular List, you will note that the main code of 368 represents a visual disturbance. The fourth digit (after the decimal point) of 5 represents color vision deficiencies, and the fifth digit changes to indicate the type of color blindness.

Other helpful terms, in parentheses, known as *nonessential terms,* may also be shown. Nonessential terms are those that assist you in choosing the correct code, but it is not mandatory that they be present within the code description. In the example, any of the terms *acquired, congenital,* and/or *both eyes* may be in the diagnostic statement, such as "the patient presents with blindness acquired in childhood."

As previously stated in the conventions section, some entries use **cross-references.** If the cross-reference *see* appears after a main term, you *must* look up the term that follows the word *see* in the index. The **see** reference means that the main term where you first looked is not correct; another category must be used. In the previous example regarding color blindness, to code *Bright's,* you are instructed to *See* the term *Uremia* to locate the correct code.

The Tabular List

The diseases, conditions, and injuries in the Tabular List are organized into chapters according to the source or body system. The Tabular List also includes two kinds of supplementary codes, V codes and E codes, which will be discussed later in the chapter. Very simply, the Tabular List contains very specific information in numeric sequence, to back up, or expand on, the information found in the Alphabetic Index. When coding is done, the Alphabetic Index gives you the "starting point" to find the appropriate diagnosis code and the Tabular List gives you the "final destination"; the exact code, including any fourth or fifth digits required to give you the most specific, accurate diagnosis code available for the information you are given in the medical record.

Code Structure   ICD-9-CM diagnosis codes are made up of three, four, or five digits. The system uses three-digit categories known as rubrics, for diseases, injuries, and symptoms. Many of these categories are divided into four-digit codes known as subcategories. Some codes are further subdivided into five-digit codes that are known as subclassifications. For example:

> 415 Acute pulmonary heart disease *[three digits]*
>> 415.1 Pulmonary embolism and infarction *[four digits; more specific]*
>>> 415.11 Iatrogenic pulmonary embolism and infarction *[five digits; most specific]*

When listed in the ICD-9, four- and five-digit diagnosis codes must be reported on claims because they represent the most specific diagnosis documented in the patient medical record. When they are available, the use of fourth and fifth digits is not optional; it is known as coding to the highest level of specificity and payers require it. For example, the Centers for Medicare and Medicaid Services (CMS) rules state that a Medicare claim will be rejected when the most specific code available is not used. In the above example, it would be incorrect to use code 415 or 415.1 because code 415.11 is available and so, as the most specific code, it must be used. Always keep in mind that the minimum code contains 3 digits, but if a fourth digit is available, it must be used, and if a fifth digit is available, it also must be used. The fourth and fifth digits are preceded by a decimal point. When placing diagnosis codes on the CMS-1500 form, however, the decimals points are omitted. (Refer to Chapter 17).

V Codes and E Codes   As mentioned at the beginning of this chapter, there are two additional types of codes at the end of the chapters of the Tabular List:

1. **V codes** identify encounters for reasons other than illness or injury, such as annual checkups, immunizations, and normal childbirth. The

descriptions for V codes are found throughout the main portion of the Alphabetic Index. V codes can be used either as primary codes for an encounter or as additional codes. You should be aware that some insurance carriers, such as Medicare, do not cover V codes, so the charges associated with them may become the patient's responsibility.

2. **E codes** identify the external causes of injuries and poisoning. E (for external) codes are used for injuries resulting from various environmental events, such as transportation accidents, accidental poisoning by drugs or other substances, falls, and fires. Some beginning coders find it easy to remember that if a diagnosis makes you question "How did that happen?" at least one E code will be required to answer the question. An E code is never used alone as a diagnosis code. It always supplements the code that identifies the injury or condition itself. You might find it helpful to also think that in addition to "external," that the E also stands for "extra," so you will not be tempted to let an E code stand by itself. E codes are often used in collecting public health information. The alphabetic descriptions for E codes are found at the end of the Alphabetic Index in two sections. Section 2 is the alphabetic Table of Drugs and Chemicals, which is used to identify drugs and chemicals responsible for poisonings. Immediately following this, in Section 3, is the Alphabetic Index for all E codes.

E code

A type of ICD-9 code that identifies external causes of injuries and illnesses, such as accidents and poisonings.

Both V and E codes are alphanumeric; they contain letters followed by numbers. For example, the code for a complete physical examination of an adult is V70.0. The code for a fall from a ladder is E881.0. The same rule for specificity applies to E and V codes regarding fourth and fifth digits; that is, if a fourth or fifth digit is available, it must be utilized or the code will be rejected by the insurance carrier.

Appendixes of ICD-9-CM

The appendixes of the ICD-9 manual contain helpful research and technical information. Appendix A is the Morphology of Neoplasms. As you remember from your A&P and terminology classes, the term *morphology* means to change or develop. This table defines the development or changing nature of diagnosed neoplasms (new growths), most of which are malignant or cancerous. These codes, sometimes referred to as "M" codes, as they always begin with that letter, are not reported on insurance claim forms, are used with "O" codes developed by WHO (World Health Organization) for tracking of oncology diagnoses. Administrative medical assistants and other coders can assign M codes while coding diagnoses, but certified tumor registrars are responsible for assigning the M codes based on the M code assigned. M codes are noted in the Alphabetic Index in parentheses.

Example:

> **Paget's disease** (osteitis deformans) 731.0
> with infiltrating duct carcinoma of the breast
> (M8541/3) — See Neoplasm, breast, malignant

In the above example, in order to code Paget's disease with breast cancer, you would look up neoplasm, breast, malignant. The instructions also direct you to the morphology code of M8541/3. In looking at Appendix A, you will find that code M8541/3 reads "Paget's disease with infiltrating duct carcinoma of the breast." The M code itself defines the type of cancer and the digit after the forward slash (/) represents the morphology (behavior) of the neoplasm as listed below:

/0   Benign

/1   Uncertain whether benign or malignant. Borderline malignancy

/2	Carcinoma in situ
	Intraepithelia (within epithelial cells)
	Noninfiltrating (cancer that has not spread to other nearby areas)
	Noninvasive (cancer that has not spread outside of the original site)
/3	Malignant, primary site
/6	Malignant, metastatic (or secondary) site
/9	Malignant, uncertain whether primary or metastatic site

When coding malignant neoplasms, the primary site is the location where the cancer originated. The secondary or metastatic site(s) describes the area where the cancer or malignancy has spread.

Appendix B formerly contained the glossary of Mental Disorders. It was officially deleted on 10/1/04.

Appendix C is the Classification of Drugs by American Hospital Formulary Service Number and the ICD-9 Equivalent. These are equivalent codes between AHA Formulary and ICD-9. The Formulary number is in the left column, the description in the middle and the ICD-9 code in the right column.

Example:

AHFS	Description	ICD-9-CM
8:12.16	The Penicillins	960.0

Appendix D is the Classification of Industrial Accidents According to Agency. It lists the 3-digit categories for occupational hazards divided into the following subcategories:

1. Machines
2. Means of Transport and Lifting Equipment
3. Other Equipment
4. Materials, Substances and Radiations
5. Working Environment
6. Other Agencies, Not Elsewhere Classified
7. Agencies Not Classified for Lack of Sufficient Data

Again, these codes are not placed on insurance claims; instead they are used by state and federal agencies to summarize industrial accidents.

Appendix E consists of a listing of the Three Digit Categories used by ICD-9-CM, labeled for the chapter each represents. An example is shown here:

17. **INJURY AND POISONING**	
Fracture of skull (800-804)	
800	Fracture of vault of skull
801	Fracture of base of skull
802	Fracture of face bones
803	Other and unqualified skull fractures
804	Multiple fractures involving skull or face with other bones

CHECKPOINT
LO 18.2

Why is it important to understand the conventions used in the ICD-9-CM?

LO 18.3 Using ICD-9

You may think that if your office uses a superbill, you will not need to understand coding because the physician will simply check off the appropriate diagnosis (and procedure) to be inserted in the claim form. This is simply not true. Remember

from Chapter 15, that if it is not written down, it did not happen. Every diagnosis and procedure checked off on the encounter form must be verified in the medical record. With the limited room on an encounter form, it is very possible that the most specific diagnosis code available for the patient's condition is not listed on the encounter form. It will be the administrative medical assistant's responsibility to locate the "best code for the job". If the physician uses a SOAP note format (Chapter 15), you can locate the diagnosis in the assessment area. If a more "freehand" approach is used, a little detective work may be needed.

Example #1, from a Patient Medical Record:

CC: *Chest and epigastric pain; feels like a burning inside. Occasional reflux.*

Exam: *Abdomen soft, flat without tenderness. No bowel masses or organomegaly.*

Dx: *Peptic ulcer.*

The diagnosis is peptic ulcer.

Now, decide what the main term is for the condition or the diagnosis. For the diagnosis in the above scenario, the main term is *ulcer*. The word *peptic* (meaning stomach) describes the type of ulcer and is considered a subterm. Because there is an exact diagnosis, the pain and reflux will not be coded in outpatient facilities such as physician offices. Inpatient facilities such as hospitals have different rules and the symptoms would be coded.

Example #2:

The diagnosis is sebaceous cyst. Look under *cyst*, the condition, and not *sebaceous*, the descriptive subterm. Many entries in the Alphabetic Index are cross ( ) referenced, so if you look up a descriptive word, the ICD-9 will lead you to alternate words to assist you in finding the correct description. For example, *sebaceous* is followed by instructions in parentheses that say "(*see also* Cyst, sebaceous)." Be sure to follow all cross-reference instructions.

Once you find the description, locate the code given for that description; it is usually to the right of the description or just below it. Now go to Volume 1, the Tabular List, to verify the code. Be sure to read all instructions in this section because there are often more specific instructions in the Tabular List that will help you find the right code or affirm that you have the correct code.

Examples:

1. For the first diagnosis of peptic ulcer, the main 3-digit code for peptic ulcer is 533. The fourth digit, 9, indicates that the ulcer is not specified as acute or chronic and there is no mention of hemorrhage or perforation. The fifth digit, 0, is chosen as there is no mention of obstruction. The final code for the peptic ulcer is 533.90.

2. In the second scenario, the sebaceous cyst, the main code is 706, which denotes diseases of the sebaceous glands. The fourth digit, 2, indicates that the "disease" is a sebaceous cyst. In this example, there is no fifth digit, so the final code for a sebaceous cyst is 706.2.

In both of these cases, the level of specificity of each diagnosis was greatly increased by the addition of the fourth and fifth digits, underlining the importance of these "optional" additions to the main codes; they truly are not optional at all.

Lastly, don't forget to look for instructions such as *Code also* and *Code first underlying condition,* as well as *includes* and *excludes* notes that assist you in deciding on the correct code or codes.

Additional Guidelines for ICD-9 Coding

Now that you understand that you look up the main term and then the subterm in the Alphabetic Index, and then confirm the code in the Tabular List (a step that can never be skipped), let's look at some further guidelines that will make your coding more specific and efficient.

Acute versus Chronic Conditions   An acute (including subacute for coding purposes) condition is defined as one that is of sudden onset or a more long-standing (chronic) condition that has suddenly worsened. There are times, such as with bronchitis, where the patient has both the acute form (466.0) and the underlying chronic form (491.9). When this occurs and both codes must be reported, the acute code is always listed first, followed by the code for the chronic form of the condition.

Combination Codes   A combination code is one in which two diagnoses are included in one code. This may be a diagnosis with an associated secondary process (known as a manifestation) or a diagnosis with an associated complication. When a combination code is available, it must be used in place of the two single codes. An example of this is cholelithiasis (gallstones), code 574.20 with acute cholecystitis (gallbladder inflammation), code 575.0. However, because they are being diagnosed together, when you look up cholecystitis and look at the subterm "with" you will find a direction that should the cholecystitis be associated with calculus (stones) in the gallbladder—See Cholelithiasis. When you do so, you will note that cholelithiasis with cholecystitis, acute, is coded at 574.0 with a notation for a fifth digit. Just above this is a box indicating that fifth digit 0 is used if there is no mention of obstruction and 1 is used if there is obstruction. As we have no mention of obstruction in the description, the final code will be 574.00. See Figure 18–2.

Multiple Coding   There are many instances when one code does not fully describe the patient's diagnosis. This often occurs when a disease or condition is the result (manifestation) of another condition. Most complications of diabetes mellitus fall under this category. Diabetes, as the underlying condition, is coded first (250.xx), followed by the manifestation, for instance gangrene

figure 18–2

a. Alphabetic Index for cholecystitis directing you to cholelithiasis; b. Alphabetic Index showing final code for acute cholecystitis with cholelithiasis (√ indicates need for fifth digit); c. Tabular List for 574.00 verifying correct description of calculus of gallbladder with acute cholecystitis.

Source: International Classification of Diseases, Ninth Revision, Clinical Modification, 2010, Volumes 1, 2, and 3.

a.
Cholecystitis 575.1
  with
    calculus, stones in bile duct (common) (hepatic)-see Choledocholithasis
          gallbladder – see Cholelithiasis
  acute 575.0

b.
Cholelithaisis (impacted) (multiple) 574.2 √

Note – Use the following fifth-digit subclassification with category 574:
  0   without mention of obstruction
  1   with obstruction

  With cholecystitis 574.1√
      acute 574.0√

c.
√4ᵗʰ   574   **Cholelithiasis**

Note – Use the following fifth-digit subclassification with category 574:
  0   without mention of obstruction
  1   with obstruction
      √5ᵗʰ 574.0 **Calculus of gallbladder with acute cholecystitis**
        [0-1]   Biliary calculus   }
                 Calculus of cystic duct} with acute cholecystitis
                 Cholelithiasis   }

(785.4). Regardless of whether you look up gangrene, diabetic or diabetes, with gangrene, you will see the 250.7x code listed first with 785.4 for the gangrene in parentheses as the secondary code. Figure 18–3 outlines combination coding using the diagnosis of gangrene due to diabetes.

As the above case outlines, no matter how you look up the code in the Alphabetic Index or check it in the Tabular List, you are directed which code to use first. The only information you don't have is what digit to use in the fifth position for the diabetes code. At the beginning of the diabetes section of the Alphabetic Index (Figure 18–3a) as well as at the beginning of the Tabular List of

figure 18–3

a. Alphabetic Index for diabetes, gangrene;
b. Alphabetic Index for gangrene, diabetic;
c. Tabular List for code 250.7x.
d. Tabular List for 785.4.

Gangrene, gangrenous (anemia) (artery) (cellulitis (dermatitis) (dry) (infective) (moist) (pemphigus) (septic) (skin) (stasis) (ulcer) 785.4
with
arteriosclerosis (native artery) 440.24
bypass graft 440.30
autologous vein 440.31
nonautologous biological 440.32
diabetes (mellitus) 250.7 ✓ *[785.4]*
due to secondary diabetes
249.7 ✓ *[785.4]*
abdomen (wall) 785.4
adenitis 683
alveolar 526.5
angina 462
diphtheritic 032.0
anus 569.49
appendices epiploicae — *see* Gangrene, mesentery
appendix — *see* Appendicitis, acute
arteriosclerotic — *see* Arteriosclerosis, with, gangrene
auricle 785.4
Bacillus welchii (*see also* Gangrene, gas) 040.0
bile duct (*see also* Cholangitis) 576.8
bladder 595.89
bowel — *see* Gangrene, intestine
cecum — *see* Gangrene, intestine
Clostridium perfringens or welchii (*see also* Gangrene, gas) 040.0
colon — *see* Gangrene, intestine
connective tissue 785.4
cornea 371.40
corpora cavernosa (infective) 607.2
noninfective 607.89
cutaneous, spreading 785.4
decubital (*see also* Ulcer, pressure) 707.00 *[785.4]*
diabetic (any site) 250.7 ✓ *[785.4]*
due to secondary diabetes 249.7 ✓ *[785.4]*

(b)

Diabetes, diabetic (brittle) (congenital) (familial) (mellitus) (severe) (slight) (without complication) 250.0 ✓

> *Note — Use the following fifth-digit subclassification with category 250:*
>
> 0   *type II or unspecified type, not stated as uncontrolled*
>
> *Fifth-digit 0 is for use for type II patients, even if the patient requires insulin*
>
> 1   *type I [juvenile type], not stated as uncontrolled*
>
> 2   *type II or unspecified type, uncontrolled*
>
> *Fifth-digit 2 is for use for type II patients, even if the patient requires insulin*
>
> 3   *type I [juvenile type], uncontrolled*

with
coma (with ketoacidosis) 250.3 ✓
due to secondary diabetes 249.3 ✓
hyperosmolar (nonketotic) 250.2 ✓
due to secondary diabetes 249.2 ✓
complication NEC 250.9 ✓
due to secondary diabetes 249.9 ✓
specified NEC 250.8 ✓
due to secondary diabetes 249.8 ✓
gangrene 250.7 ✓ *[785.4]*
due to secondary diabetes
249.7 ✓ *[785.4]*

(a)

§ ✓5th **250.7** **Diabetes with peripheral circulatory disorders**
[0-3]   Use additional code to identify manifestation, as:
diabetic:
gangrene (785.4)
peripheral angiopathy (443.81)
DEF: Blood vessel damage or disease, usually in the feet, legs, or hands, as a complication of diabetes.
AHA: 1Q, '96, 10; 3Q, '94, 5; 2Q, '94, 17; 3Q, '91, 10, 12; 3Q '90, 15; **For code 250.70:** 1Q, '04, 14
E10.51 Type 1 DM w/diab periph angiopathy w/o gangrene | 1-10 |

(c)

785.4 Gangrene | CC |
Gangrene:
NOS
spreading cutaneous
Gangrenous cellulitis
Phagedena
Code first any associated underlying condition
| EXCLUDES | *gangrene of certain sites — see Alphabetic Index*
gangrene with atherosclerosis of the extremities (440.24)
gas gangrene (040.0)

DEF: Gangrene: necrosis of skin tissue due to bacterial infection, diabetes, embolus and vascular supply loss.
DEF: Gangrenous cellulitis: group A streptococcal infection; begins with severe cellulitis, spreads to superficial and deep fascia; produces gangrene of underlying tissues.
CC Excl: 338.0-338.4, 440.24, 780.91-780.99, 785.4, 799.81-799.89
AHA: 1Q, '04, 14; 3Q, '91, 12; 3Q, '90, 15; M-A, '86, 12
196 Gangrene not elsewhere classified | 1-10 |

(d)

✔4th   250 Diabetes mellitus

EXCLUDES   *gestational diabetes (648.8)*
hyperglycemia NOS (790.2)
neonatal diabetes mellitus (775.1)
nonclinical diabetes (790.29)
secondary diabetes (249.0–249.9)

The following fifth-digit subclassification is for use with category 250:
0 type II or unspecified type, not stated as uncontrolled
   Fifth digit 0 is for use for type II patients, even if the patient
   requires insulin
1 type I (juvenile type) not stated as uncontrolled
2 type II or unspecified type, uncontrolled
   Fifth-digit 2 is for use for type II patients even if the patient
   requires insulin
   Use additional code if applicable, for associated long-term
   (current) insulin use (V58.67)
3 type I (juvenile type) uncontrolled

DEF: *Diabetes mellitus: Inability to metabolize carbohydrates, proteins,
and fats due to insufficient secretion of insulin. Symptoms may be
unremarkable, with long-term complications, involving kidneys,
nerves, blood vessels and eyes.*

DEF: *Uncontrolled diabetes: A nonspecific term indicating that the
current treatment regimen does not keep the blood sugar level of a
patient within acceptable levels.*

AHA: *4Q,'04, 56;2Q,'04,17;2Q,'02,13; 2Q,'01,16; 2Q '98,15; 4Q,'97,32;
2Q,'97,14; 3Q,'96,5; 4Q,'93,19; 2Q,'92,5; 3Q,'91,3; 2Q,'90,22; N-D,
'85, 11*

TIP: *Use of insulin does not ensure type I DM; if patient is on routine
insulin, assign also V58.67 Long-term (current) use of insulin*

figure 18–4

Fifth-digit subclassifications for category 250 (diabetes mellitus).

Source: International Classification of Diseases, Ninth Revision, Clinical Modification, 2010, Volumes 1, 2, and 3.

principal diagnosis
The first diagnosis listed for inpatient claims as the *principal* reason found, after study, for the patient's hospitalization.

primary diagnosis
The first diagnosis listed for outpatient claims as the *primary* reason for the patient's visit.

diagnosis
The condition for which the patient is seeking care.

(250), you will find the box represented in Figure 18–4 to assist you.

Note that diabetes codes always require a fifth digit. Be sure not to inadvertently "drop" the fourth digit prior to adding the fifth digit. 250.3 is not juvenile diabetes uncontrolled; it is the rubric for diabetes with other coma and still requires one of the above numbers to complete the code.

Coding Unclear Diagnoses

Physicians frequently do not have an exact diagnosis documented. Terms such as *"probable," "suspected," "likely," "questionable," "possible,"* or *"rule out"* flag a diagnosis as being uncertain. Although inpatient coders can code as if the condition exists because of their payment method (Diagnosis-related group), outpatient records will be coded using the symptoms that lead the patient to seek care, until an absolute diagnosis is made.

Example:

> Diagnosis: Nonproductive cough, fever, rule out bronchitis
> Inpatient diagnosis: Bronchitis (490)
> Outpatient diagnosis: Cough (786.2) and Fever (780.60)

A similar situation occurs with "impending" or "threatened" conditions.

If the condition actually occurs, code it as a confirmed diagnosis. If it did not occur, check to see if a code exists for the threatened condition and if it exists, use it. If it does not exist, code the underlying conditions or symptoms as if the condition did not exist.

Example:

> #1
> Diagnosis: Hemorrhage in early pregnancy with threatened abortion
> CPT: **640 Hemorrhage in early pregnancy**
>   **640.0 Threatened abortion**

Use code 640.0 as it describes exactly the diagnosis given

Principal versus Primary Diagnosis

The **principal diagnosis** is sequenced first in inpatient coding and is defined by the Uniform Hospital Discharge Data Set (UHDDS) as "that condition established after study to be chiefly responsible for occasioning the admission of the patient to the hospital for care." Outpatient coding tends instead to use the term **primary diagnosis,** defining it as the main reason for the patient's visit. The **secondary** (or subsequent) **diagnoses** are other conditions that are also affecting the patient at the time of the visit and so are coded after the primary diagnosis.

Procedure 18–1 at the end of this chapter outlines the steps for locating an ICD-9-CM code.

CHECKPOINT
LO 18.3

Why is it important to code all current diagnoses on the patient?

LO 18.4 V Codes and E Codes

As stated earlier, V codes are defined by ICD-9-CM as *Supplementary Classification of Factors Influencing Health Status and Contact with Health Services.* This is a very long title for codes that describe patients who are not currently ill but come to the office for reasons including history of an illness (personal or family); preventative medicine (such as immunizations and physical exams); employment, school, and camp examinations; well-baby care; contraception; screenings; aftercare (such as post surgical care); carrier status; organ donor; testing for status; and so on.

Because the patient is basically "healthy," V codes are generally used in the outpatient setting. Examples of common V codes include the following:

- V04.81   Influenza *vaccination* (remember this is a diagnosis, not a procedure code)
- V58.11   (*Encounter* for) Chemotherapy treatment

    (The patient does have cancer, but the reason for the visit today is the chemotherapy administration. This will be followed by the appropriate code for the neoplasm being treated)
- V14.0   *History* (personal) of allergy to penicillin
- V30.00   Vaginal *delivery* of single, live-born newborn (status of the newborn child)

V codes are coded via the same Alphabetic Index as the other ICD-9 codes. For the above examples, the key terms are italicized. Their Tabular List for verification is located directly after the injury and poisoning codes (800-999). Procedure 18–2 outlines the procedure for using a V code.

The official title for E codes is *Supplementary Classification of External Causes of Injury and Poisoning.* As stated earlier, these are "extra" codes that tell the insurance company *how* an illness or injury came about. If you see a friend coming down the hall on crutches and he tells you he broke his ankle, your first question will logically be, "How did you do that?"—there is an E code for whatever explanation he gives you! E codes also include burns, poisonings, and other exposure incidences. Coding E codes can be complicated and we will just be introducing the concepts here. Both the Table of Drugs and Chemicals and the Alphabetic Index for E codes are found at the end of the main Alphabetic Index for ICD-9 codes. Some of the major categories of E codes include transport accidents; poisonings and adverse effects; accidental falls; accidents from fire and flames; accidents due to natural and environmental factors; late effects of accidents; assaults or self-injury; assaults or purposely inflicted injury and suicide; or self-inflected injury. We will discuss some specifics for E codes here.

General Use of E Codes

E codes are used with any diagnosis code from 001-V84.4, except for CMS (Medicare) which does not require E codes on their claim forms, although you can place them there without receiving a rejection or denial from them. In general, E codes are only used for the initial treatment for the acute illness or injury, and not for subsequent visits. The exception to this rule is treatment for acute fractures. In this case, use the E code for as long as acute treatment of the fracture is taking place. Use as many E codes as necessary to completely explain how the incident occurred. For instance, if a patient accidentally overdoses on a combination of alcohol and Valium, at least two E codes will be necessary to explain the overdose of both substances. Another example may relate to your friend with the broken ankle. It is possible that two E codes

may be applicable. If he was at work and fell from scaffolding while painting a house, two codes, would be necessary—fall from scaffolding (E881.1) and a place of occurrence code denoting that the accident took place at a private residence (E849.0). Place of occurrence codes are found under the key term of *Accident*. All accidents occurring while using machinery or any type of motorized vehicle (including boats, motorcycles, ATVs, heavy machinery, etc.) require an E code describing the vehicle involved in the accident. Many of these codes require a fifth digit that describes the person injured—driver (1); passenger (2); motorcyclist (3); passenger of motorcycle (4); rider of animal (5); pedal cyclist (6); pedestrian (7); other specified person (8); or unspecified person (9). As with all other diagnosis codes, if a fourth or fifth digit is available, it must be used, so watch for the notes in the Tabular List ($\sqrt{4}^{th}$ or $\sqrt{5}^{th}$) so you do not forget them and code incorrectly, resulting in possible claim rejection or denial.

Poisonings and Adverse Effects

The Table of Drugs and Chemicals is located directly after the Alphabetic Index. The table consists of a row for each drug name and then six columns with the following titles: Poisoning, Accident, Therapeutic Use, Suicide Attempt, Assault, and Undetermined. The poisoning column is for use when the medical record states "poisoning," "overdose," "wrong substance given or taken," or "intoxication." The poisoning codes (960–989) will be listed first. You then will stay in the same row but move to the column that describes how the poisoning occurred. Remember, if it is not in the medical record, it did not occur. You can only code what is described in the record. The following definitions will be helpful when deciding which column to use when choosing the E code:

- Accidental poisoning (E850–E869). This column is used for accidental overdose, wrong substance given or taken, drug taken by mistake, accidental drug usage, and accidents in drug usage in a medical facility.

- Therapeutic use (E930–E949). This column is used when the correct substance is properly administered in the correct dosage but caused a poisoning or other adverse effect.

- Suicide attempt (E950–E952). This column is used only when there is documentation of self-inflicted injury or poisoning.

- Assault (E961–E962). Documentation indicates that the injury or poisoning was inflicted by another person with the intent to injure or kill the patient.

- Undetermined (E980–E982). These codes are to be used when the intent of the poisoning or injury cannot be determined.

Examples:

#1		
	Diagnosis:	Hives (urticaria) due to newly diagnosed Penicillin allergy (taken as prescribed)
	ICD-9 Codes:	708.9 (allergic urticaria) and E930.0 (Penicillin therapeutic use)
		(There was no poisoning, so no code is used from the poisoning column)
#2		
	Diagnosis:	Vomiting due to intentional overdose of Valium
	ICD-9 Codes:	787.03 (vomiting), 969.4 (Valium poisoning), E950.3 (intentional OD = suicide attempt)

Burns

Coding burns typically requires three codes: the degree of the burn (if there are multiple burns, they are sequenced with the highest degree first); the extent (percentage of the body burned); and the E code for how the burn occurred. To code burns, first use the key term *Burn* and then find the *indented subterm* for the burn location and, finally, the subclassification for the extent of the burn (1st, 2nd, or 3rd degree). Locations with multiple burn degrees are coded to the highest extent of the burn. Once that code is completed, return to the key term *Burn* and subterm *Extent.* Using the *Rule of Nines* which is found in the Tabular List at the beginning of the 949 section, calculate the percentage of the body burned. Finally, locate the E code description from the Alphabetic Index for External Cause Codes and verify it in the Tabular List.

Example:

Diagnosis:	Patient presents with 1st and 2nd degree burns to right hand and wrist from boiling water
ICD-9 Codes:	944.20 (2nd degree burn hand and wrist), 948.10 (less than 10% of body surface burned and fifth digit 0 for less than 10% at 3rd degree) and E924.0 (burn by hot liquid)

Always remember that E codes are *never* the primary or first diagnosis listed. When used, they are listed after the primary (or secondary diagnosis) to which they relate. More than any other type of diagnosis code, E codes require practice to get perfect. Procedure 18–3 found at the end of the chapter outlines how to use E codes.

● ● ●

Give two types of visits that would require the use of a V code.

CHECKPOINT
LO 18.4

LO 18.5 A New Revision: The ICD-10-CM and ICD-10-PCS

When the United States modified ICD-9 to create ICD-9-CM more than 30 years ago, a third volume was added to capture (primarily hospital) procedure codes; what we know today as ICD-9 Volume 3. Now that we have again "outgrown" ICD-9 and ICD-10-CM looms around the corner in 2013, Volume 3 will become obsolete. Instead of appending a short volume of procedure codes to ICD-10-CM, a complete classification, ICD-10-PCS (procedural coding system), was developed. This procedural coding system is much more detailed and specific than the short number of procedure codes included in ICD-9-CM volume 3.

PCS is used only in the hospital inpatient setting by those reporting ICD-9-CM procedure codes. All other entities will continue to report CPT and HCPCS codes.

The ICD-10-CM system consists of more than 68,000 diagnosis codes, compared to approximately 13,000 ICD-9-CM diagnosis codes. ICD-10-PCS consists of 87,000 procedure codes. Both of these systems, by the using a combination of letters and number, have a much greater capacity for expansion and specificity than does ICD-9. You will be introduced to the ICD-10 coding system in Chapter 19.

● ● ●

What does PCS in ICD-10-PCS stand for?

CHECKPOINT
LO 18.5

EHR readiness

Patient Health Screenings

V codes are used to code services provided to patients who are not ill but are seeking health services, many times for procedures such as physicals and screening procedures such as cholesterol and blood sugar screenings, BP checks, colonoscopies, Pap smears, mammograms, and immunizations in order to keep themselves healthy or to find a disease in its early stages so it may be treated. In the world of paper medical records, the physician must "remember" the patient's family history or the patient must insist that procedures be done. It is more or less a "hit or miss" system.

The electronic health record can change that. EHR systems such as SpringCharts contain programs known as chart evaluations that allow the provider to define preventative health screening criteria for patients and then to assess the records for these screenings. Figure 18–5 is a screen from the program outlining the criteria for mammograms to be performed on female patients every 52 weeks after the age of 35. These health-care check-up recommendations are added to each patient's electronic health record.

An evaluation may then be done on the records to see if the patient is up-to-date with the recommendations (Figure 18–6). In the case shown in Figure 18–6, the patient's screen is incomplete. The provider can then make the listed recommendations and the provider then has the option of editing the screen with a patient response, such as, "Patient states unwilling to have procedure at this time. Check back in 6 months." In this way, a tracking mechanism is also employed. Because guidelines are just that, the system also has the ability to override guidelines, changing and updating them as the patient history of practice requires.

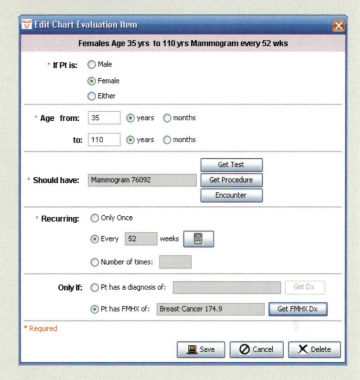

figure 18–5

Edit *Chart Evaluation* window.

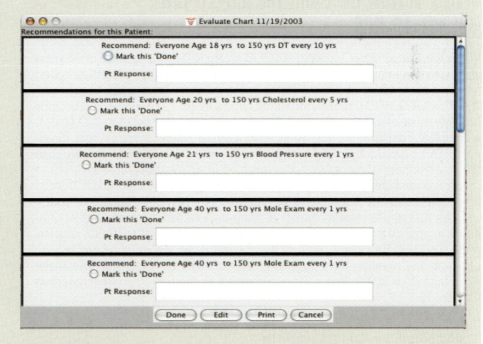

figure 18–6

Chart Evaluation window in patient's chart.

MEDICAL CODER, PHYSICIAN PRACTICE

Duties and Skills

Outpatient medical coders review patient medical records and assign diagnosis and procedure codes to accurately inform insurance carriers of the procedures and services provided to patients, including the reason or medical necessity for these services. All coders, including those working in medical offices, must stay abreast of coding updates and requirements on an ongoing basis. The position of medical coding specialist is growing in importance in physician practices. Accurate coding is a critical part of ensuring that claims follow the legal and ethical requirements of Medicare and other third-party payers as well as HIPAA regulations. Accurate coding also ensures optimum reimbursement for submitted claims. Without the expertise of medical coders, coding requirements for claims would often not be met and claims would be denied or sent for review instead of being paid promptly.

Educational Requirements

Traditionally, medical coders often were high school graduates who gained on-the-job experience in medical offices. Today, with the more complicated coding rules and regulations and legal implications for incorrect coding, many coders attain education through college HIM (Health Information Management) programs or through technical school or community college certificate or diploma programs. Once they complete an approved educational program, they are eligible to sit for a coding certification either through AHIMA or AAPC. AHIMA offers the certified coding associate (CCA) for those who recently completed an educational program or certified coding specialist-physician (CCS-P) for those with three or more years of experience. AAPC offers the certified professional coder-associate (CPC-A) or certified professional coder-physician (CPC-P). Both certifications are much in demand as physicians find that certified coders increase the funds coming into the practice and decrease the risk of coding noncompliance. Certification as a professional coder offers an excellent route to success as a medical coder in the medical practice setting. Some employers require certification for employment; many others state that certification must be earned after a certain amount of time in the position, such as 6 months. Once certification is achieved, it is maintained by achieving a mandatory number of approved continuing education units (CEUs) by attending conferences, teleconferences, and reading literature from AHIMA and AAPC and then completing quizzes found within the literature.

Workplace Settings

Medical coding specialists work in a number of health-care settings, including medical practices, hospitals, government agencies, and insurance companies. Coders who work in physician practices review patients medical records and assign diagnosis and procedure codes. They are knowledgeable about the coding rules and procedures for physicians' work, which are different from those for coding hospital services. More and more, as rules and regulations become more complicated, another aspect of the coder's position is that of teaching providers to document adequately and appropriately so that the codes chosen are absolutely backed up by the information found within the medical record.

The Medical Coder as Team Member

The medical coder frequently interacts with many members of the medical office, both by phone and in person, to resolve questions regarding dates of service, procedures, and/or services provided and to verify medical diagnoses. It is also not uncommon for medical coders to visit the medical office for the purposes of training the clinical staff regarding medical charting requirements necessary for accurate and compliant coding to take place. Coders are also often contacted by clinical personnel regarding the best way to document a procedure or service or even to assist a physician or other health-care provider in choosing the best code to use after providing a particular service or even in correctly coding a complicated diagnosis properly.

For more information, visit the Web sites of the following organizations, which are available on the Online Learning Center at www.mhhe.com/houseradminmedassist.

The American Health Information Management Association (AHIMA)

The American Association of Professional Coders (AAPC)

Procedure 18–1 Locating an ICD-9-CM Code

PROCEDURE GOAL To analyze diagnoses and locate the correct ICD code

MATERIALS Patient record, charge slip or superbill, ICD-9-CM manual

METHOD
1. Locate the patient's diagnosis.
   a. This information may be located on the superbill (encounter form) or elsewhere in the patient's chart. If it is on the superbill, verify documentation in the medical chart.
2. Find the diagnosis in the ICD-9's Alphabetic Index. Look for the condition first, then locate the indented subterms that make the condition more specific. Read all cross-references to check all the possibilities for a term, including its synonyms and any eponyms.
3. Locate the code from the Alphabetic Index in the ICD-9's Tabular List.
4. Read all information to find the code that corresponds to the patient's specific disease or condition.
   a. Study the list of codes and descriptions. Be sure to pick the most specific code available. Check for the symbol that shows that fourth (and) fifth digits may be required.
5. Carefully record the diagnosis code(s) on the insurance claim and proofread the numbers.
   a. Be sure that all necessary codes are given to completely describe each diagnosis. Check for instructions stating an additional code is needed. If more than one code is needed, be sure instructions are followed and the codes are listed in the correct order.

Procedure 18–2 Locating a V Code

GOAL To analyze the patient record (or encounter form) and decide whether a V code is an appropriate diagnosis code

MATERIALS Patient record, superbill or encounter form, ICD-9-CM manual

METHOD
1. Locate the patient's diagnosis.
   a. This information may be located on the superbill (encounter form) or elsewhere in the patient's chart.
   If it is on the superbill, verify documentation in the medical chart.
2. If the reason for the patient encounter relates to a physical exam, immunization, well-child visit, or other visit where there is no diagnosis or condition of illness found, a V code will be used to code the reason for the visit (diagnosis).
3. Find the diagnosis in the ICD-9's Alphabetic Index. Look for the condition first and then locate any indented subterms that make the condition more specific. Read all cross-references.

4. Locate the code from the Alphabetic Index in the V code area of the ICD-9's Tabular List.

5. Read all descriptive information to find the code that corresponds to the patient's specific reason for today's visit.

   a. Be sure to pick the most specific code available. Check for the symbol that shows that a fourth and (possibly) a fifth digit is required.

6. Carefully record the diagnosis code(s) on the insurance claim and proofread the numbers.

   a. Be sure that that no other codes are required to describe the patient's reason for the visit. Check for instructions stating an additional code is needed. If more than one code is needed, be sure instructions are followed and the codes are listed in the correct order.

Procedure 18-3 Locating an E Code

GOAL To analyze the patient record (or encounter form) and decide whether an E code is necessary to completely code the encounter

MATERIALS Patient record, superbill or encounter form, ICD-9-CM manual

METHOD 1. Locate the patient's diagnosis.

   a. This information may be located on the superbill (encounter form) or elsewhere in the patient's chart. If it is on the superbill, verify documentation in the medical chart.

2. If the patient's diagnosis begs the question, "How did that happen?" an E code is required to give the insurance carrier as much information as possible.

3. After coding the diagnosis of the condition requiring treatment, open the ICD-9 manual to the External cause Alphabetic Index or if necessary use the Table of Drugs and Chemicals. Find the appropriate description in the ICD-9's Alphabetic Index, looking for the condition first, and then locate any indented subterms that make the condition more specific. Read all cross-references.

4. Locate the code from the Alphabetic Index in the E code area of the ICD-9's Tabular List.

5. Read all descriptive information to find the code that corresponds to how the patient's current condition came about.

   a. Be sure to pick the most specific code available. Check for the symbol that shows that a fourth and (possibly) a fifth digit are required; many E codes require these.

6. Carefully record the diagnosis code(s) on the insurance claim and proofread the numbers.

   a. E codes are always secondary, so be sure that that the primary diagnosis code is listed first. Check for instructions stating an additional code (s) is needed. If more than one code is needed, be sure instructions are followed and the codes are listed in the correct order.

Case Study

The Metropolitan Health Center (MHC) operates a very large obstetrical department. The organization is contracted with Anchor Health Insurance. On a busy Tuesday, an auditor from Anchor arrives unannounced and requests access to the medical records of 20 specific patients covered by his company. After reviewing the records, the representative meets with the practice manager. In the past 45 days, Anchor received claims for these patients with the diagnosis of poisoning; psychostimulants (969.7x). As a quality assurance measure, the insurance company decided to investigate to determine if the psychostimulants were ordered through MHC, which would be contrary to the standard of care for obstetrical patients. The medical records review indicated that none of these patients had experienced a poisoning and all had had Cesarean sections.

Surprisingly, Anchor had not received a single claim involving the C-sections. After some investigation, the puzzled practice manager called in Bonnie from the coding department who immediately recognized the error as a possible code transposition when codes were updated in the abstracting coding system. She believes the correct code should be 669.7x. In addition to the resources involved on the part of both the insurance company and the practice in researching and correcting the error, there could have been serious ramifications for the physician and the patients because of the erroneous diagnosis of psychostimulant poisoning. This is an example of the importance of always striving for perfection in the workplace and staying focused.

Thinking Critically

1. What are some of the potential ramifications for the physicians and patients with the original erroneous diagnosis code of poisoning by psychostimulants?

2. Should the ICD-9 code 669.7x be routinely used for Cesarean sections?

3. Why is the insurance company interested in the quality of care for their patients?

practice APPLICATIONS

1. A. A female patient is taking a medication that is known to affect the lining of the endometrium. She received an endometrial biopsy and pelvic ultrasound to monitor changes. What type of ICD-9 code is used to describe the medical need for these services?

   B. A patient fell off a ladder while on the job, spraining his left ankle and fracturing the right femur. In addition to the main code, what type of ICD-9 code is used to report his diagnosis?

2. Underline the main term in each of the following diagnoses and then determine the correct ICD-9 codes.

   a. Cerebral atherosclerosis

   b. Spasmodic asthma with status asthmaticus

   c. Congenital night blindness

   d. Recurrent inguinal hernia with obstruction

   e. Incomplete bundle branch heart block

1. **[LO18.2]** The Alphabetic Index for ICD-9-CM is organized by

   a. the part of the body involved.
   b. symptoms the patient displays.
   c. codes found in the Tabular List.
   d. the condition.
   e. b and d.

2. **[LO18.2]** The Tabular List of ICD-9-CM is organized by

   a. the condition of the patient.
   b. the codes found in the Alphabetic Index.
   c. the symptoms of the patient.
   d. the part of the body involved.
   e. All of the above.

3. **[LO18.1]** Which of the following is the correct meaning for ICD-9-CM?

   a. International Coding of Diagnoses Ninth ed, Clinical Modification
   b. International Classification of Diagnoses, Ninth Revision, Clinical Modifiers
   c. Internal Classification of Diseases, Ninth Revision, Clinical Modification
   d. Internal Classification of Diagnoses, Ninth Revision, Clinical Modification
   e. International Classification of Diseases, Ninth Revision, Clinical Modification

4. **[LO18.3]** What is the first step in choosing an ICD-9 code?

   a. Locating Volume 1
   b. Locating Volume 2
   c. Locating the "what is wrong with the patient"
   d. Locating "where the problem is located"
   e. c and d

5. **[LO18.4]** Which of the following would require a V code?

   a. Physical exam with no findings
   b. Physical exam with findings
   c. A fall from a ladder

   d. Visual condition such as astigmatism
   e. All of the above

6. **[LO18.4]** Which of the following would require an E code?

   a. Physical exam with no findings
   b. Physical exam with findings
   c. A fall from a ladder
   d. Visual condition such as astigmatism
   e. None of the above

7. **[LO18.5]** When will ICD-10-CM and ICD-10-PCS be implemented?

   a. January 2012
   b. October 2012
   c. January 2013
   d. October 2013
   e. A date is not yet confirmed

8. **[LO18.3]** What is the correct ICD-9 code for noninsulin-dependent diabetes mellitus without complication?

   a. 250.00
   b. 250.01
   c. 250.0
   d. 250.1
   e. a and c

9. **[LO18.3]** What are the correct code(s) and sequence for a patient with hypertension in congestive heart failure (CHF)?

   a. 428.0, 402.91
   b. 402.91, 428.0
   c. 402.11, 428
   d. 402.90, 428.1
   e. 428.0, 402.90

10. **[LO18.3]** Which of the following is the correct format to code *Strep throat*?

    a. 462, 041.00
    b. 462, 041,02
    c. 462, 038
    d. 034.0
    e. 034.0, 462

learning outcome SUMMARY

LO 18.1 ICD-9-CM codes are used in the following ways: Facilitation of payment for medical services; evaluation of utilization patterns (patient use of health-care facilities); study of health-care costs; research regarding quality of health care; prediction of health-care trends; and planning for future health-care needs.

LO 18.2 The conventions used in ICD-9-CM include: NOS; NEC; brackets; slanted brackets; parentheses;

colon; brace; includes and excludes notes; instructions to *use additional code, code first underlying disease, and code, if applicable, any causal condition first.* Additionally, bold and italics are used in both the Alphabetic Index and Tabular List. Instructions to *omit code, see condition,* and *see also* are found exclusively in the Alphabetic Index.

LO 18.3 To choose an ICD-9 code, check the encounter form (superbill) and/or patient medical record for all applicable diagnoses. Find the key term in the Alphabetic Index and then search for any applicable subterms. Once the code has been located, verify its description in the Tabular List, again reading all applicable notations for other coding options and instructions. Document each code carefully using instructions as to code sequencing on the CMS-1500 claim form.

LO 18.4 V codes are defined as *Supplementary Classification of Factors Influencing Health Status and Contact with Health Services.* They are used for patients who, though not ill, are seeking health care. They are used for exams (V70.0), counseling (V61.10), donors (V59.01), and so on. E codes are defined as *Supplementary Classification of External Causes of Injury and Poisoning.* They are used to explain how an illness or injury came about. Examples of E codes include cyclist accident (E826.1), accidental poisoning by antibiotics (E856), and exposure to laser radiation (E926.4).

LO 18.5 ICD-10 and ICD-10-PCS have been created because more specificity regarding diagnosis and hospital procedures is necessary as we gain more knowledge of illnesses and injuries. As the procedures performed become more involved and complicated, more detail becomes necessary. ICD-10 is more "expandable" than ICD-9 and will be better able to meet these needs.

medical assisting COMPETENCIES

CAAHEP

VII. C (12) Define Diagnosis-Related Groups (DRGs)

VIII.C (1) Describe how to use the most current procedural coding system

VIII.C (3) Describe how to use the most current diagnostic coding classification system

VIII.P (2) Perform diagnostic coding

VIII.A (1) Work with the physician to achieve the maximum reimbursement

ABHES

8. Medical Office Business Procedures Management

   t. Perform diagnostic and procedural coding

19 ICD-10-CM Coding

Learning Outcomes

After completing Chapter 19, you will be able to:

19.1 Explain the basic differences between the ICD-9-CM and the ICD-10-CM.

19.2 Understand the ICD-10-CM general coding guidelines.

19.3 Describe unique coding applications for neoplasms, diabetes mellitus, fractures, R codes, poisonings, and Z codes.

19.4 List the five items that should be considered when planning for a smooth transition from ICD-9-CM to ICD-10-CM.

Key Terms

categories
chapters
etiology
ICD-10-CM
morbidity

mortality
subcategories
World Health
  Organization (WHO)

Preparation for Certification

RMA (AMT) Exam
- Identify and apply insurance-related terminology
- Identify and apply HIPAA mandated coding systems

CMAS (AMT) Exam
- Coding

CMA (AAMA) Exam
- Apply third-party and managed care policies, procedures and guidelines
- Perform procedural and diagnostic coding for reimbursement

Introduction • • •

This chapter introduces an overview of the International Classification of Diseases, Tenth Revision, Clinical Manifestations of the **ICD-10-CM,** due for implementation on October 1, 2013. This system increases the specificity of diagnostic codes, providing a more precise clinical picture of the patient and enhancing the diagnostic reporting and tracking of **morbidity** (illness) and **mortality** (death) statistics within the United States. The Centers for Medicare and Medicaid Services (CMS) initiated steps to introduce the ICD-10-CM in 2007. This chapter introduces the ICD-10, 2010 version, which is now being adopted. The CMS delayed implementation to allow health-care organizations time to reconfigure data transmissions and payment systems, design new claims and encounter forms, and facilitate training. This chapter also introduces a plan to assist in the new ICD-10 implementation.

LO 19.1 A Basic Comparison of the ICD-9-CM and the ICD-10-CM

The ICD was originally introduced in 1893 as the first International List of Causes of Death, requiring physicians to better track a patient's diagnosis and medical care (Figure 19–1). The copyright belongs to **World Health Organization (WHO).** The current edition, introduced in 1975, does not allow the addition of new, more precise diagnoses that developed over the years. There are approximately 14,200 codes in the ICD-9-CM, while the new ICD-10-CM contains over 68,000 codes. This allows greater specificity for diagnosis classifications and provides expansion for new codes.

The agencies responsible for overseeing all changes, revisions, or modifications for the ICD-10-CM are the U.S. Department of Health and Human Services, the Centers for Medicare and Medicaid Services (CMS), and the National Center for Health Statistics (NCHS). The NCHS works in conjunction with WHO to coordinate the official codes for the classification of diseases. At this time, many other countries in the world have adopted at least some version of ICD-10-CM. It should be noted that up to and immediately following full implementation in the United States revisions will most likely continue. This chapter is meant to be an introduction to the new ICD-10 format. The information contained within it is in no way the final version, which at this time has not been completed. In CMS and other documents, the abbreviation I-10 is also used. While the ICD-10-CM will be required for medical practices to report diagnoses, the Current Procedural Terminology (CPT) and Healthcare Common Procedural Coding Systems (HCPCS) will remain the reporting/claims mechanism for procedures and other charges.

As with the transition of the manual medical record to the electronic medical record, the transition period from the ICD-9 to ICD-10 presents challenges to the administrative medical assisting student and the medical offices. The student must learn both systems instead of only one system, as in the past. The medical offices must not only learn the new system but accommodate both systems during an overlap period. Table 19–1 shows basic comparisons of the two systems.

Alphabetic and Numeric Indexes

Both the 9th and 10th editions contain the Alphabetic (Alpha) Index of the diseases, conditions, and related terms. In both systems, the coder begins with the Alpha Index that may direct the coder to a

---

ICD-10-CM
International Classification of Diseases, Tenth Revision, Clinical Modification.

morbidity
Causes and severity of illnesses.

mortality
Causes of death.

World Health Organization (WHO)
A specialized agency of the United Nations (UN) that acts as a coordinating authority on international public health.

figure 19–1

Physicians began better record keeping in the late 1800s to accommodate the new classification system.

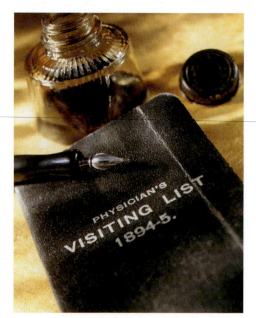

FEATURE	ICD-9-CM	ICD-10-CM
Number of codes	14,200	68,000
Format	3–5 characters. First character may be alpha or numeric; 2–5 are numeric	3–7 characters. First character alpha (uppercase); 2 and 3 are numeric; 4–7 may be alpha or numeric
Specificity	Limited	Expanded
Laterality	None	Has laterality
Decimal point	After 3rd character; not always used	Decimal must be used after the third character
Placeholder	0 as 4th digit is present when 5th digit required	"x" used as placeholder for a nonexistent digit when 6th or 7th digit is required for code specificity
Combination codes	Some	Expanded number of combination codes
External causes of morbidity and mortality including poisonings	E codes	Instead of a separate section, external causes are included as V01–Y98 codes
Factors influencing health status	V codes	Instead of a separate section, health status codes are included as Z00–Z99 codes

table 19–1

Basic Comparison of ICD-9-CM and ICD-10-CM

chapters
Divisions of ICD-10 named either for a body system or specific disease type.

categories
The 3-digit-code subdivisions of ICD-10.

subcategories
In the Alpha Index, subdivisions of the ICD-10 chapters containing a clinical description of the code range and the guidelines for coding; in the Tabular List, the codes consisting of four or five characters specifying the level of complexity of the diagnosis.

related term such as "pain." Once the term is identified in the Alpha Index, it directs the coder to the lists of appropriate codes in the Tabular (numeric) List. The I-10 Tabular List incorporates 21 **chapters** with the alphanumeric range for each as listed in Table 19–2. A **category** has 3 characters and a **subcategory** has 4–5 characters, the code may have up to 7 characters. The conventions become clearer as examples are provided later in the chapter.

Characters and Specificity

As demonstrated in Table 19–1, the ICD-9 contains over 14,200 codes while the ICD-10-CM contains over 68,000. The I-10 expansion results from beginning the code with an alpha character and increasing the number of characters from 3–5 (ICD-9) to 3–7 (ICD-10). Again, the intent of the I-10 is to provide a more precise clinical picture of the patient and enhanced trending analysis. Table 19–3 provides an example of the increased specificity of the new coding system using the diagnosis of breast cancer.

Note that in the example in Table 19–3:

- The ICD-9 code contains 4 numeric characters.
- The ICD-10 code contains 6 alphanumeric characters.
- The ICD-10 codes D05.01 and D05.11 are located in chapter or category 2 "Neoplasms" and accommodate laterality (unilateral—right or left—or bilateral).

Placeholders

The ICD-9 did not incorporate a placeholder for new codes. If a 5th digit was required, a 4th digit was present and had to be used before adding the "optional" 5th digit. The ICD-10 uses an "x" to hold a place for future expansion of the code's specificity. An example is illustrated in Table 19–4.

Chapter 19 "S" (injury) codes that require a 7th digit encounter determination as shown in Table 19–3:

- "A" designates an initial encounter
- "D" designates a subsequent encounter
- "Q" designates sequela

CHAPTER	DESCRIPTION	CODE RANGE
1	Certain infectious and parasitic diseases	A00–B99
2	Neoplasms	C00–D48
3	Diseases of the blood and blood-forming organs and certain disorders involving the immune mechanism	D50–D89
4	Endocrine, nutritional, and metabolic diseases	E00–E90
5	Mental and behavioral disorders	F01–F99
6	Diseases of the nervous system	G00–G99
7	Diseases of the eye and adnexa	H00–H59
8	Diseases of the ear and mastoid process	H60–H95
9	Diseases of the circulatory system	I00–I99
10	Diseases of the respiratory system	J00–J99
11	Diseases of the digestive system	K00–K93
12	Diseases of the skin and subcutaneous tissue	L00–L99
13	Diseases of the musculoskeletal system and connective tissue	M00–M99
14	Diseases of the genitourinary system	N00–N99
15	Pregnancy, childbirth, and the puerperium	O00–O99
16	Certain conditions originating in the perinatal period	P00–P96
17	Congenital malformations, deformations, and chromosomal abnormalities	Q00–Q99
18	Symptoms, signs, and abnormal clinical and laboratory findings; not elsewhere classified	R00–R99
19	Injury, poisoning, and certain other consequences of external causes	S00–T98
20	External causes of morbidity	V01–Y99
21	Factors influencing health status and contact with health services	Z00–Z99

table 19–2

Chapters and Descriptions

table 19–3

Example of ICD-10-CM Specificity versus ICD-9-CM

ICD-9 LIMITED	ICD-10 EXPANDED
Example: 233.0 Carcinoma in situ breast (cannot designate which breast)	Example #1: D05.01 Lobular carcinoma in situ of right breast or Example #2: D05.11 Intraductal carcinoma of right breast

table 19–4

Example of Placeholder

ICD-9-CM	ICD-10-CM
Myocardial infarction initial episode	Abrasion of scalp initial encounter
410 Myocardial infarction (5th digit required to designate episode)	S00 Superficial injury of the head (7th digit required to designate encounter)
410.01 (410 designates myocardial infarction, "0" designates the anterolateral wall (location of the MI) and, "1" designates initial episode of care)	S00.01xA (S00 superficial injury of the head, S00.01 designates abrasion of scalp, "x" designates placeholder, "A" designates initial encounter)

ICD-9-CM	ICD-10-CM
995.92 Severe sepsis and 785.52 Septic shock	R65.21 Severe sepsis with septic shock

table 19–5

Example of a Combined Code

Combination Codes

The ICD-9-CM accommodates only a relatively small number of combination codes, often requiring the use of multiple codes to completely code a condition, illness, or injury. The ICD-10-CM contains many more combination codes, greatly cutting down on the need for multiple codes for a single diagnosis. An example of a combined code appears in Table 19–5.

In some cases, multiple codes are also used with ICD-10 coding when appropriate. One example is coding for pregnancy and prenatal visits which is described later in the chapter on page 557.

CHECKPOINT
LO 19.1

State the number and type of characters for ICD-9-CM codes and the ICD-10-CM codes.

LO 19.2 ICD-10-CM Basic Coding Guidelines

Diagnostic coding cannot be performed without a coding manual or software program. This textbook is not intended to replace either of them. Just as with ICD-9, conventions are used in ICD-10 to assist the coder in finding and choosing the correct code. Many of the conventions found in ICD-9 are still used in ICD-10 and the basic guidelines remain the same. Although manuals and software are publisher specific and may include color coding and formatting assists, the conventions are universal. These coding guidelines and conventions have been adopted in accordance with HIPAA requirements and intended for use by any physician or midlevel health-care practitioner who may legally diagnose. The general steps "walk" you through the coding structure to locate the correct code. They may be compared to putting together the pieces of a puzzle. The guidelines for ICD coding are:

- Locate the term in the Alphabetic Index.
- Refer to the notes under the appropriate heading.
- Read and follow the terms in the parenthesis and brackets.
- Proceed to the Tabular List number(s) as directed by the Alphabetic Index.
- Follow instructional terms to direct you to the appropriate code.
- Use caution with chapter categories that have an alphabetical character that may be mistaken for a numerical character such as the letter "O" for Chapter 15, Pregnancy, Childbirth, and the Puerperium (may be mistaken for the number "0").
- Assign the appropriate code using the highest degree of specificity.
- Assign an additional appropriate code for other signs and symptoms that may not be routinely associated with the condition or disease process.

To follow these steps it is also necessary to understand the terms, abbreviations, and symbols found in Table 19–6.

The importance of the medical record is emphasized throughout this text. To accurately code a diagnosis, the coder must first obtain an accurate diagnostic description from the medical record. The ICD-10 requires more detailed physician documentation to attain the level of description required by the new

Preparing Your Office for ICD-10

Although October 1, 2013, seems to be a long time away, being prepared and adapting to change is essential in the medical practice and the changes coming with ICD-10 are no exception. Although it may be too early to delve deeply into learning ICD-10 codes themselves, as an aid in learning the new coding system, CMS has agreed to a partial code freeze, consisting of the following points:

- The last regular update to ICD-9 and ICD-10 codes sets will be made on October 1, 2011.
- As of October 1, 2012, there will be only limited code updates to ICD-9 and ICD-10 to capture new technologies and diseases.
  - On October 1, 2013, there will be only limited code updates to ICD-10 to capture new technologies and diagnoses. (There will be no ICD-9 updates as it will no longer be used for reporting.)
  - On October 1, 2014, regular updates to ICD-10 will begin.

In addition to the ICD-10 changes, administrative medical assistants and other medical professionals involved with billing, coding, and information systems should be keeping abreast of the changes and challenges coming out of WHO and CMS on an almost daily basis. Read and talk about the impending changes and keep your coworkers and administrators abreast of new information that you come across. Ask if you can be part of the implementation team and attend the many conferences and audio seminars and online informational programs available on preparing for ICD-10. Talk to your existing EHR and billing software vendors to find out if they are ready and what they are doing to help prepare your office. If you are told not to worry about it, then red flags should go up. Your vendors should be upfront with the information they have and how they are going to accommodate these updates. If they are not, it may be time to start talking to new vendors. The more information the medical practice seeks out and shares with all members of the facility, the easier these new applications will be to learn and understand when the changes become mandatory.

table 19–6

Common Conventions Found in ICD-10-CM

system. Like the ICD-9, NEVER code directly from the Alpha Index (Figure 19–2). All codes must be verified in the Tabular List to be sure descriptions are correct and all notes are followed. Always select the code that corresponds to the medical record documentation.

CONVENTION	MEANING	EXAMPLE
Code First/Use Additional Code	The underlying condition must be listed first and any manifestation caused by this condition is listed second. In the Alphabetic Index, the manifestation code is listed in brackets	F02 Dementia in other diseases classified elsewhere Code first underlying physiological condition, such as: Alzheimer's (G30.-)
NEC (Not elsewhere classifiable)	In the index, this means "other specified." When a specific code is not available, you are directed to an "other specified" code	Dislocation of foot, specified site NEC S93.33- (the dash means an additional digit will be given in the Tabular List to complete the code)
NOS (Not otherwise specified)	The provider has not given enough information to choose a more specific code	A04.9 Bacterial intestinal infection, unspecified
Code Also	Instruction that two codes may be required if enough information is provided, in order to completely code the scenario; but sequencing information is not given	J44 Other chronic obstructive pulmonary disease Code also type of asthma, if applicable (J45.-)
See and See Also	*See* follows a main term in the Alpha Index and instructs that another term should be investigated. *See also* is also in the Alpha Index and indicates that another term may be helpful in choosing the correct description	Amentia—See also Retardation, mental Dilatation cardiac (acute) (chronic) see also Hypertrophy
Default codes	Codes listed next to a main term. It represents the condition commonly associated with the main term or the unspecified code for that condition	K37 Appendicitis (If no other information about the patient's condition is given, this default code will be used)

table 19–6 *(Continued)*

CONVENTION	MEANING	EXAMPLE
Includes	Terms/conditions listed may be included with the diagnosis	J36 Peritonsillar abscess Includes: abscess of tonsil peritonsillar cellulitis quinsy
Excludes1	The code is excluded and should never be used at the same time as the code above the Exclude1 note. The two conditions cannot occur together	E11 Type 2 diabetes Excludes1: gestational diabetes (O24.4-) Type 1 diabetes (E10.-)
Excludes2	The condition is excluded as not part of the condition represented by the code, but if the patient actually has both conditions, both may be coded	J03 Acute tonsillitis Excludes2: chronic tonsillitis (J35.0)
[] Brackets	Brackets are used in the Alphabetic Index and indicate manifestation (secondary) codes	Disease, diseased Alzheimer's G30.9 [F02.80]
() Parentheses	Parentheses are used in both indices enclosing supplemental or "nonessential" information which will not affect the code selection	Discord (with) boss Z56.4 classmates Z55.4
: Colon	A colon is used after an incomplete term that requires one or more of the modifiers that follow it to allow the code to be assigned	J33 Nasal polyp Use additional code to identify: exposure to environmental tobacco smoke (Z77.22) exposure to tobacco smoke in the perinatal period (P96.81)
, Comma	Words following a comma are essential modifiers and must be present in the diagnosis in order to use the code	K40.0 Bilateral inguinal hernia, with obstruction, without gangrene

ICD-10-CM INDEX TO DISEASES and INJURIES

A

Aarskog's syndrome Q87.1
Abandonment - see Maltreatment, abandonment
Abasia (-astasia) (hysterical) F44.4
Abderhalden-Kaufmann-Lignac syndrome (cystinosis) E72.04
Abdomen, abdominal - see also condition
- acute R10.0
- angina K55.1
- muscle deficiency syndrome Q79.4
Abdominalgia - see Pain, abdominal
Abduction contracture, hip or other joint - see Contraction, joint
Aberrant (congenital) - see also Malposition, congenital
- adrenal gland Q89.1
- artery (peripheral) Q27.8
- - basilar NEC Q28.1
- - cerebral Q28.3
- - coronary Q24.5
- - digestive system Q27.8
- - eye Q15.8
- - lower limb Q27.8
- - precerebral Q28.1
- - pulmonary Q25.7
- - renal Q27.2
- - retina Q14.1
- - specified site NEC Q27.8
- - subclavian Q27.8
- - upper limb Q27.8
- - vertebral Q28.1
- breast Q83.8
- endocrine gland NEC Q89.2
- hepatic duct Q44.5

figure 19–2

First "page" of the ICD-10-CM Index.

CHECKPOINT
LO 19.2

When coding an ICD-10-CM would you initially look in the Tabular List or Alpha Index and why?

● ● ●

LO 19.3 Unique Coding Applications

The majority of ICD-10-CM codes follow the general guidelines. However, unique coding applications exist. These include but are not limited to neoplasms, diabetes mellitus, fractures, pregnancy, external causes of morbidity and mortality, R codes, poisonings, and expanded Z codes (formerly V codes).

Chapter 1: Certain Infectious and Parasitic Diseases (A00–B99)

In an outpatient setting, requesting a confirmatory serology or culture for HIV is not enough to code HIV positivity. Only the diagnostic statement such as "known HIV" or "positive HIV" is adequate from the provider. When no definitive diagnosis or manifestation of HIV is present and the patient has an inconclusive serology, code R75, inconclusive laboratory evidence of human immunodeficiency virus, should be assigned. Patients who have had a positive serology or culture and have developed an HIV-related illness, should be assigned code B20 on every encounter. Patients who are HIV positive but asymptomatic in status should be assigned code Z21. This code should be assigned for all patients with the diagnostic statement of positive HIV. When a patient presents with any signs or symptoms while being seen for HIV testing, code only the signs and symptoms. If counseling is provided during the same encounter, an additional counseling code out of Z71.7 may be reported.

Chapter 2: Neoplasms (C00–D48)

Chapter 2 of ICD-10-CM deals with neoplasms and is very similar to the ICD-9. To assign a proper code, documentation of the neoplasm must state whether it is benign, malignant, in-situ, or of uncertain behavior. These are presented in a table format listed by anatomic location such as an adenoma (a tumor of a gland). Once the site of the neoplasm is identified, any additional instructions for coding must be observed. An additional code, such as one identifying exposures to carcinogenic (cancer causing) substances that may be the underlying cause of the patient's cancer diagnosis, may be required. Two examples of carcinogens as underlying causes are exposure to tobacco smoke (Z77.22) or exposure to tobacco smoke in the perinatal period (P96.81).

The correct coding and sequencing of neoplasms is critical. As when coding in ICD-9, if the treatment is directed at the primary neoplasm, that code is used as the principal (or primary) diagnosis. If the neoplasm has metastasized and the patient's treatment is for the secondary site, then the secondary neoplasm would become the primary diagnosis. If chemotherapy, radiation therapy, or immunotherapy, although generally considered procedures not diagnoses, is the primary reason for medical care, it is coded first, followed by the code for the malignancy being treated.

Chapter 4: Endocrine, Nutritional, and Metabolic Diseases (E00–E90)

Chapter 4 contains the codes for diabetes mellitus. The documentation and the assignment of codes within this ICD-10 chapter are very similar to the ICD-9. Codes for diabetes mellitus are combination codes that include the type of diabetes:

Working with the Health-Care Team

CERTIFIED MEDICAL REIMBURSEMENT SPECIALIST (CMRS)

Duties and Skills

The Certified Medical Reimbursement Specialist (CMRS) is a skilled medical billing (and often medical coding) professional who is a certified "expert" in facilitating the claims paying process from "patient to payment." CMRS billers play a critical role in a health-care provider's daily business operations, whether he or she is employed by the medical facility or self-employed as a contractor to assist the practice with its accounts receivable processes.

Educational Requirements

Because certification in the medical billing field is not yet a requirement, the CMRS examination and its certification is voluntary. The minimal requirement to sit for the exam is a high school diploma and experience in the medical billing and coding process. To successfully pass the certification exam, the candidate must be knowledgeable in ICD-9 (and soon, ICD-10), CPT and HCPCS coding; medical terminology; insurance claims submission; billing and reimbursement; appeals and denials; fraud and abuse laws; HIPAA and OIG compliance; information systems; and Web technology. Most reimbursement specialists today either have years of on-the-job experience or have graduated from an accredited medical billing or coding program prior to sitting for the exam. Once the credential is achieved, 15 CEUs are required per year to maintain the credential.

Workplace Settings

The CMRS will be found anywhere medical billing, coding, and reimbursement techniques are required. As stated previously, the CMRS may be self-employed; work in a small or large practice, medical billing facility, hospital, or nursing home; work for an insurance carrier; or work as an independent contractor conducting audits and charge master reviews.

The Certified Reimbursement Specialist as a Team Member

The CMRS will work as a team member in the office, as a consultant, or possibly as your billing service. The CMRS may require time with the physician or practice manager to go over medical records, require more detailed documentation for coding purposes, or require copies of records to submit an appeal for a denial. As a reimbursement specialist, the practice's A/R is the CMRS's specialty and concern. She will work with you on a daily, weekly, or monthly basis to bring in the reimbursement the practice is entitled to for the services provided; both from the insurance carriers and from the patients themselves.

For more information, visit the Web site of the following organization which is available on the Online Learning Center at www.mhhe.com/houseradminmedassist.

American Medical Billing Association

- Type 1—insulin dependent diabetes (IDDM); sometimes referred to as juvenile diabetes
- Type 2—noninsulin dependent diabetes (NIDDM)

In addition to the type of diabetes, the body system affected by diabetes and the condition affecting the anatomical structure are included. When the type of diabetes is not documented in the medical record (and the physician cannot be queried), then the patient should be assigned a code for type 2 diabetes mellitus. The coding and sequencing rules for diabetes mellitus remain the same for ICD-10 as for ICD-9. As shown in Figure 19–3, any underlying condition must be sequenced first. If the diabetes causes a complication (such as retinopathy), code the diabetes first and code the retinopathy second. If documentation supports the patient's use of insulin, then assignment of code Z79.4 should be sequenced after the diabetes diagnosis is coded completely.

Chapter 5: Mental and Behavioral Disorders (F01–F99)

When patients experience pain, whether acute or chronic, it should be documented that the pain is exclusively psychological. Pain that is associated with

figure 19–3

Diabetes mellitus codes with underlying conditions.

etiology

Cause of disease or condition.

and is exclusively psychological should be assigned code F45.41: pain disorder with related psychological factors, followed by the appropriate code from the category G89.

Chapter 6: Diseases of the Nervous System (G00-G99)

The nervous system chapter in ICD-10 no longer includes the eye and ear; they have each been given individual chapters (7 and 8); otherwise, the coding from the nervous system has changed very little since ICD-9. As stated above, code G89 is used for pain diagnoses. This code may be used as a first listed diagnosis when the reason for the encounter is the treatment of the pain. If the patient is seen for a definitive diagnosis (such as cancer) and pain is also noted, then the definitive diagnosis should be listed first followed by the most specific pain code possible. If malignant neoplasm is the underlying cause of the pain, the appropriate pain code is G89.3.

Chapters 7 and 8 are new for ICD-10 and as of the writing of this chapter, specific instructions for coding the eye and adnexa (Chapter 7) and ear and mastoid process (Chapter 8) are not yet available.

Chapter 9: Diseases of the Circulatory System (I00-I99)

ICD-10, like ICD-9, uses the hypertension table in the Alpha Index and the rules for coding hypertension have not changed. Primary hypertension, also known as essential hypertension, is coded as I10. When hypertension is caused by an underlying condition (secondary hypertension), two codes are required—the first to identify the underlying **etiology** (cause) and the second to code the hypertension. A patient who has elevated blood pressure may not necessarily have a diagnosis of hypertension. This is known as transient hypertension, and the code R03.0 should be assigned.

Chapter 10: Diseases of the Respiratory System (J00-J99)

Coding within the respiratory system has also changed very little between ICD-9 and ICD-10. It should be noted, however, that positive laboratory documentation is not required in order to code either avian or H1N1 influenza as a diagnosis. When the physician's documentation states, "suspected or probable" avian influenza or H1N1 influenza, codes should be assigned as if the condition exists (J09.0 category). Documentation of any another type of influenza should be assigned codes from the J10 category. Figure 19–4 shows the difference in the Tabular List between Avian influenza codes and descriptions and those for Influenza due to other influenza virus. Note that manifestations of avian and H1N1 virus are included in the code descriptions.

Chapter 13: Diseases of the Musculoskeletal System and Connective Tissue (M00–99)

This chapter contains the categories for fractures which are coded quite differently in the ICD-10 than in ICD-9. Laterality for fractures is new and designated as follows:

- unilateral—4th digit "1"
- laterality designated by—5th digit:
  - 0—unspecified
  - 1—right
  - 2—left

Another major change in ICD-10 is addition of a 7th character designating the type of encounter for which the patient is being seen. Pathological fractures due to osteoporosis include this 7th character as shown in Figure 19–5 are the six capital letters used for this mandatory 7th character. For the purposes of these 7th character extensions, the term *initial* means an active fracture that is still healing, *subsequent* defines follow-up after the active fracture care and *sequela* refers to care after the injury has healed, but there are now different issues related to the initial injury that must be attended to. To better understand the coding concepts within this section, let's take a look at Figure 19–6 for a patient who has age-related osteoporosis with a current pathological fracture of the right shoulder. Based on the information in Figure 19–7, the code would be M80.011; however, because of the information we received on the necessary 7th characters (Figure 19–6), we know that if the patient had a subsequent visit for the fracture as a routine check up for a healing fracture, we would use the code M80.011D.

Chapter 14 Diseases of the Genitourinary System (N00-N99)

ICD-10 provides for four stages of chronic kidney disease (CKD). Code N18.1 is the beginning stage, N18.2 mild CKD, N18.3 moderate CKD, and N18.4 severe CDK. If end-stage renal disease (ESRD) is documented, use code N18.6. This code will be used alone, even if both chronic kidney disease and end-stage renal disease are documented. Keep in mind that kidney transplant (Z94.0–kidney transplant status) may not totally restore kidney function so both Z94.0 and a code for chronic kidney disease, if still present, may be coded.

Chapter 15: Pregnancy, Childbirth, and the Puerperium (O00–O99)

Similar to the ICD-9 that requires a 5th digit (the highest specificity for the system) when coding pregnancies, the ICD-10 often requires a 7th digit (the highest specificity for the system). With many codes, the 7th digit specifies the trimester of the pregnancy in which the condition occurs. Read these descriptions carefully. If the patient is in a different trimester than the one stated, you must look for a different code. With codes describing pregnancy conditions related to multiple gestation, the 7th digit specifies the number of fetuses in utero. Maternity

---

J09.098   Influenza due to identified avian influenza virus with other manifestations
Influenza due to identified avian influenza virus encephalopathy
Influenza due to identified avian influenza virus myocarditis
Influenza due to identified avian influenza virus otitis media

J09.1   Influenza due to identified novel H1N1 influenza virus
2009 H1N1 [swine] influenza virus
Novel 2009 influenza H1N1
Novel H1N1 influenza
Novel influenza A/H1N1
Swine flu

J09.11   Influenza due to identified novel H1N1 influenza virus with respiratory manifestations
Acute influenzal upper respiratory infection due to identified novel H1N1 influenza virus
Influenzal laryngitis due to due to identified novel H1N1 influenza virus
Influenzal pharyngitis due to due to identified novel H1N1 influenza virus
Influenzal pleural effusion due to due to identified novel H1N1 influenza virus
Code also any associated pneumonia (J12-J18)

(A)

J10   Influenza due to other influenza virus
Influenza due to unspecified influenza virus
Code first any associated lung abscess (J85.1)
Use additional code to identify the virus (B97.-)
Excludes2:Hemophilus influenzae [H. influenzae] infection NOS (A49.2)
Hemophilus influenzae [H. influenzae] laryngitis (J04.0)
Hemophilus influenzae [H. influenzae] meningitis (G00.0)
Influenza due to avian influenza virus (J09.0-)
Influenza due to novel H1N1 influenza virus (J09.1-)
Influenza due to swine flu (J09.1-)

J10.1   Influenza due to other influenza virus with respiratory manifestations
Acute influenzal upper respiratory infection due to other influenza virus
Influenza NOS
Influenzal laryngitis due to other influenza virus
Influenzal pharyngitis due to other influenza virus
Influenzal pleural effusion due to other influenza virus
Code also any associated pneumonia (J12-J18)

J10.8   Influenza due to other influenza virus with other manifestations
J10.81   Influenzal gastroenteritis
Excludes1: "intestinal flu" [viral gastroenteritis] (A08.-)
J10.89   Influenza due to other influenza virus with other manifestations
Influenzal encephalopathy
Influenzal myocarditis
Influenzal otitis media

(B)

figure 19–4

(A) Tabular List for influenza due to avian influenza virus and (B) Tabular List for influenza due to other influenza virus.

M80 Osteoporosis with current pathological fracture
Includes: osteoporosis with current fragility fracture
Note: fragility fracture is defined as a fracture sustained with trauma no more than
        a fall from a standing height or less that occurs under circumstances that
        would not cause a fracture in a normal healthy bone
Use additional code to identify major osseous defect, if applicable (M89.7-)
Excludes1: collapsed vertebra NOS (M48.5)
          pathological fracture NOS (M84.4)
          wedging of vertebra NOS (M48.5)
Excludes2: personal history of (healed) osteoporosis fracture (Z87.310)
The appropriate 7th character is to be added to each code from category M80:
          A   initial encounter for fracture
          D   subsequent encounter for fracture with routine healing
          G   subsequent encounter for fracture with delayed healing
          K   subsequent encounter for fracture with nonunion
          P   subsequent encounter for fracture with malunion
          S   sequela

figure 19–5

Codes and 7th characters for osteoporosis with pathological fracture.

Chapter 17: Congenital Malformations, Deformations, and Chromosomal Abnormalities (Q00–Q99)

Codes from this chapter are used exclusively in the medical record of a patient when the documentation specifically states that the diagnosis or condition is congenital or chromosomal in nature. Codes Q00–Q99 may be listed as either primary or secondary diagnoses, dependent on the instructions given within the coding instructions. Diseases and conditions found within this section include hydrocephalus, spina bifida, atrial septal defect, limb malformations and deformities, cleft lip/palate, Trisomy 21 (Down syndrome), and many others.

Chapter 18: Signs, Symptoms and Abnormal Clinical and Laboratory Findings (NEC) (R00–R99)

Chapter 18, Signs, Symptoms and Abnormal Clinical and Laboratory Findings (NEC), R00–R99, is primarily used to code for the following types of conditions:

- Cases which do not have a more specific diagnosis after all the findings are analyzed
- Transient signs and symptoms at the initial encounter with undetermined cause
- Provisional diagnosis in a patient not returning for further care
- Cases without a definitive diagnosis referred elsewhere
- Cases in which a definitive diagnosis could not be determined
- Additional information that represents a significant but currently asymptomatic medical problem (such as an asymptomatic HIV positive patient)

There are multiple combination codes available in this chapter. Watch for them and follow guidelines for their use. If a combination code is available, it must be used to avoid "unbundling" the code.

coding can be complicated, but thorough reading of the medical record documentation and understanding of the coding guidelines specific to this chapter will allow confidence in coding.

Chapter 19: Injury, Poisoning and Certain Other Consequences of External Causes, (S00–T98)

With the exception of the new 7th character extension used in ICD-10, coding from this chapter is very similar to coding with ICD-9. As in ICD-9, the table format for poisonings is also used in ICD-10. You will also note that because poisoning codes require very specific codes, that the "x" placeholder is often found in the 5th position and that the 7th digit of A (initial), D (subsequent), or S (sequelae) is again used to describe the type of encounter. An illustration for the substance "sufonazide" is in Table 19–7.

Note that the table does not give you the 7th digit options. A perfect example of why you must always verify codes in the Tabular List to obtain the entire

figure 19–6

Tabular List for Subclassification M80.01 Age-Related Osteoporosis with Current Pathological Fracture, Shoulder.

M80.01   Age-related osteoporosis with current pathological fracture, shoulder
   M80.011   Age-related osteoporosis with current pathological fracture, right shoulder
   M80.012   Age-related osteoporosis with current pathological fracture, left shoulder
   M80.019   Age-related osteoporosis with current pathological fracture, unspecified shoulder

correct code. If a 7th digit is required and is not in place, the insurance carrier will not accept the code.

Burns and Corrosions Burns are classified by three factors: depth of the burn (first-degree, second-degree, or third-degree), the extent (total body area—based on the rule of nines), and the agent (fire, thermal, or appliance). Burns that are caused by a corrosive material are coded the same as any burn with the additional code for the corrosive material being sequenced first.

As with poisonings, the appropriate extension (A, D, or S) must accompany codes listed within the burn categories. Burns that are non-healing and/or necrotic should be coded as an acute burn. Sequence burn codes so that the most severe burn (for instance, third-degree) is listed first with any other burns listed in decreasing order of severity.

Adverse Effects, Poisoning, Underdosing, and Toxic Effects Very little has changed from the ICD-9 to the ICD-10 when coding from this category, with the exception of codes T36–T65. These codes are combination codes for adverse effect and underdosing of specific substances. An example of an adverse effect combination code would be one in which a specific drug was administered properly but caused a problem (such as vomiting or respiratory failure) for the patient.

V10–V19	Pedal cyclist injured in transport accident
V20–V29	Motorcycle rider injured in transport accident
V30–V39	Occupant of three-wheeled motor vehicle injured in transport accident
V40–V49	Car occupant injured in transport accident
V50–V59	Occupant of pick-up truck or van injured in transport accident
V60–V69	Occupant of heavy transport vehicle injured in transport accident
V70–V79	Bus occupant injured in transport accident
V80–V89	Other land transport accidents
V90–V94	Water transport accidents
V95–V97	Air and space transport accidents
V98–V99	Other and unspecified transport accidents
W00–X58	Other external causes of accidental injury
W00–W19	Slipping, tripping, stumbling and falls
W20–W49	Exposure to inanimate mechanical forces
W50–W64	Exposure to animate mechanical forces
W65–W74	Accidental drowning and submersion
W85–W99	Exposure to electric current, radiation and extreme ambient air temperature and pressure
X00–X08	Exposure to smoke, fire and flames
X10–X19	Contact with heat and hot substances
X30–X39	Exposure to forces of nature
X52, X58	Accidental exposure to other specified factors
X71–X83	Intentional self-harm
X92–Y08	Assault
Y21–Y33	Event of undetermined intent
Y35–Y38	Legal intervention, operations of war, military operations, and terrorism
Y62–Y84	Complications of medical and surgical care
Y62–Y69	Misadventures to patients during surgical and medical care

figure 19–7

Tabular List of external cause code ranges.

Chapter 20: External Causes of Morbidity and Mortality (V01–Y99)

Codes within this chapter identify who, what, when, and where an accident or injury occurred. They are used for data in determining research and prevention strategies for injuries. These codes may be used as secondary codes to describe health conditions and are applicable for categories A00–T88.9 and Z00–Z99. Figure 19–7 shows some of the categories for these secondary codes, previously referred to as E codes in ICD-9. The use of these codes should completely identify the patient's cause of injury. An example would be a sprained ankle while playing football. The cause of the injury is a fall, the activity is football, and the location is the playground at the time of injury. When assigning multiple external cause codes, the code indicating the cause or intent, or medical misadventure, is reported before the code for the place, activity, or external status codes. When reporting multiple causes of injuries, codes for child and adult abuse take priority over all other external cause codes. Read the guidelines carefully.

Chapter 21: Factors Influencing Health Status and Contact with Health Services (Z00–Z99)

The unique ICD-9 V codes (used to code for health-care encounters other than injury or illness such as prenatal care or administration of immunizations) were

table 19–7

Excerpt from the ICD-10 Poisoning Table

SUBSTANCE	POISONING ACCIDENTAL	POISONING INTENTIONAL	POISONING ASSAULT	POISONING UNDETERMINED	ADVERSE EFFECT	UNDERDOSING
Sulfonazide	T37.1x1	T37.1x2	T37.1x3	T37.1x4	T37.1x5	T37.1x6

replaced by Chapter 21, Factors Influencing Health Status and Contact with Health Services, Z00–Z99 in ICD-10 (Figure 19–8). In addition to incorporating the traditional ICD-9 V codes, this category is greatly expanded to include, but is not limited to, the following reasons for health-care encounters:

- Chemo, radiation, and immunotherapy
- After care
- Administrative exams (such as sports physical)
- Family history if the patient may be at risk for like illness
- Personal history if the patient's habits or past illnesses or condition place him at risk

CHECKPOINT LO 19.3

Describe the two types of diabetes found when coding in Chapter 4.

LO 19.4 Transitioning from ICD-9 to ICD-10

Preparing for ICD-10-CM is a huge undertaking for every medical practice, but with adequate planning, it does not need to be extremely stressful. Some every day office items, such as the office encounter forms (superbills), will require updating regardless of whether they are preprinted or developed from the office EHR program. The CPT codes will remain the same. The office billing system will require recoding or replacing to reflect the ICD-10-CM. The increase from 3–5 characters to up to 7 characters necessitates more room (both on paper and on any electronic screen). The medical office may even need a new coding software vendor. These new codes are HIPAA compliant, but the security system will also require updating. The billing system will also require new processes. If paper claims are allowed (there is discussion they will not be), then these, too, will require updating. The existing electronic format for claims submission will not accommodate these new codes and so a new electronic claim form is under development.

A lot of work is to be done with these new ICD-10 codes, but slow and steady preparation of the staff and the processes they utilize will allow them to be ready and confident when October 1, 2013, arrives.

Strategies for Implementation

To make a smooth transition, consider the following:

- Needs of the practice
- Structure of a compliance team
- Necessary changes in policy and procedures
- Financial impact
- Information and security system upgrade
- Administrative and clinical staff training requirements

Identify the Needs of the Practice Identifying the specific needs within your practice is the first step toward implementing the new coding system. Develop a plan for addressing the major issues such as additional employees, resources available, impact on practice operating hours during the transition, and the amount of time it will take your practice to fully implement ICD-10. You should also identify

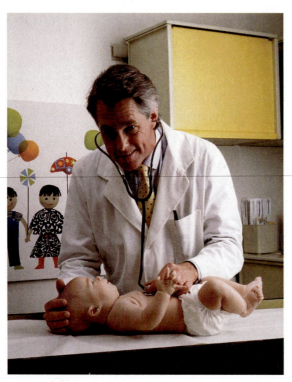

figure 19–8

Wellness-related codes are generally Z00–Z99.

the individual needs of personnel within the practice. Consideration should be given to the function of each employee and how this transition will affect him or her.

Structure a Compliance Team

The structure of your compliance team may seem like the easiest to accomplish, but this may not be so depending on the size of your office. There should be one person who is held responsible for coordinating and overseeing the timely completion of all assignments. Often, the overseer or lead for the ICD-10 implementation will be the office manager, who will be held responsible for assigning tasks and ensuring that each task is done on time. The office manager should create a time line of tasks for each department and identify the member of the compliance team responsible for completing each assigned task on time (Figure 19–9).

Changes in Policies and Procedures

Consideration of the practice policies and procedures will also have a large impact on your practice. Identify the changes that have to be made prior to and once ICD-10 is implemented. Determine whether there will be added job functions for your employees, and if so, who will be responsible. One of the major changes that will be required will be the responsibility of the physicians and midlevel providers in the practice. It will be up to them to ensure that documentation is clear and explicit enough to allow for accurate ICD-10 coding using the medical records. Training for this level of documentation will often be up to the compliance and coding team members, who may suggest that the providers attend seminars regarding the new level of documentation needed for ICD-10 to be effective.

Financial Impact

The financial impact on your office will be an important factor to consider when making the transition. Compare vendors who are offering mapping systems from the ICD-9 to the ICD-10. Is it easy to understand and what are the costs involved? How much training is required? Can this be accomplished without completely closing the practice? Another thing to consider is whether training is done on-site or if it is Web-based. Can your current vendor supply

EHR readiness

Understanding EHR Processes

Throughout this text, you learned the uses and various stages of implementation of the electronic health record. The very recent availability of the ICD-10-CM codes will require all medical practices, regardless of their current EHR systems, to reconfigure or replace any current EHR system currently in the office. The system must either provide screens with increased space for more thorough narrative type documentation or provide screens with drop down menus that accommodate the multiplied number of diagnostic options and requirements. The interface with the billing system is another issue along with HIPAA compliance and staff training, which will be discussed later in the chapter.

When the current administrative medical assisting student goes to his or her externship site, the office will most likely be in the midst of unprecedented change and stress. The motivated extern will ensure a clear overview and understanding of

- the general medical record and its uses
- the electronic medical record
- the ICD-9-CM and the ICD-10-CM coding conventions
- the type of documentation required
- HIPAA

This knowledge will not only enhance the externship experience but make you an asset to the medical office staff and management. The practice may be interested in hiring a new administrative medical assistant and this working knowledge could move you to the top of the list!

figure 19–9

A team approach for ICD-10 implementation.

your needs? Other things to consider are the amount of overtime your employees will need during the transition. To compare the potential financial impact, make a spreadsheet and keep track of the costs for each vendor, training costs, and potential loss of income during transition.

Information and Security Systems How up-to-date is your computer system? What type of information system are you using—an EMR, EHR, or another system? The largest amount of time will be spent updating the computers and software programs in your office. Check to make sure you have enough memory to hold all the new codes and other requirements for billing and claims transmission. Consider the storage of medical documentation—is it backed up offsite or by someone in the office? What is the financial cost to update your system compared to that of purchasing a new computer system? Are they HIPAA compliant?

Administrative and Clinical Training The training of personnel is imperative. Accurate, complete, and concise physician documentation will be paramount for accurate billing procedures. Start training your physician now. Request more specific documentation in diagnosis and procedures performed in the office. It will make it easier when you start to make the transition. Consider all employees for training needs. Some may learn faster than others. This will cost the practice time and money. Consider how much testing the new system will require. Give each department enough time to fully understand the new computer system and how to document, code, and process claims and reimbursements. Once your timeline for implementation is in place, stay on schedule.

CHECKPOINT
LO 19.4

What item will take the most time in transitioning to ICD-10?

Procedure 19–1 Coding from the ICD-10

GOAL To analyze diagnoses and locate the correct ICD-10 code

MATERIALS Patient record, charge slip or superbill, access to ICD-10-CM codes on the CMS Web site: www.cms.hhs.gov/ICD10/01_Overview.asp, or access to a draft copy of the 2010 ICD-10-CM manual

METHOD
1. Locate the patient's diagnosis. This information may be located on the superbill (encounter form) or elsewhere in the patient's chart. If it is on the superbill, verify documentation in the medical chart.
2. Find the diagnosis in the ICD-10 Alpha Index. Look for the condition first, then locate the indented subterms that make the condition more specific. Read all cross-references to check all the possibilities for a term, including its synonyms and any eponyms.
3. Following the directions in the Alpha Index, locate the code or code range from the Alpha Index in the ICD's Tabular List.

4. Read all information and instructions carefully to find the code that exactly corresponds to the patient's specific disease or condition.

    a. Study the list of codes and descriptions. Be sure to pick the most specific code available.

    b. Watch for instructions advising of the need for additional codes as well as instructions regarding coding sequence and need for 6th and 7th digits or placeholders.

5. Document the chosen codes carefully, remembering sequencing instructions.

Case Study

Miriam has been involved with coding in Dr. Celaya's office for 15 years. She is concerned that she will have difficulty with the new ICD-10 coding system after working with the ICD-9 system for so many years. Dr. Celaya is noticing the apprehension associated with the new system among the staff. She convenes a staff meeting and informs them that she is also nervous about the change, since the livelihood of the practice is closely tied to correct and efficient coding. Dr. Celaya compares it with the conversion to the electronic health record which recently occurred. She assures her staff that they were all initially hired because they have the ability and willingness to learn and adapt to new applications and technologies. The physician also explains that a transition plan will be developed and training on ICD-10 will be provided.

Dr. Celaya asks for volunteers to help develop and design the transition plan. Miriam volunteers since she is now encouraged that she can not only comprehend and use ICD-10 successfully, but also assist other members of the office with the changes.

Thinking Critically

1. What are some of the main differences between ICD-9 and ICD-10?

2. What challenges are there in learning the new system?

3. In addition to staff training, what are some of the other considerations for a medical practice in converting to ICD-10?

practice APPLICATIONS

1. You are in charge of getting the physicians in your practice "up to speed" on documentation requirements for ICD-10. You know there is going to be resistance. Be creative in explaining to them why this increased "work" of documentation is going to be helpful to the practice in the long run (think of the information you learned in your legal and medical records chapters when you complete this assignment).

1. **[LO19.1]** All of the following agencies are involved with the ICD-10 code revisions and processes, EXCEPT
   a. WHO.
   b. CMS.
   c. NCHS.
   d. NCIS.
   e. All of the above.

2. **[LO19.1]** Which ICD-10 chapter contains a code for schizophrenia?
   a. 1
   b. 5
   c. 10
   d. 22
   e. 20

3. **[LO19.2]** Which convention is new to ICD-10?
   a. NEC
   b. NOS
   c. Colon
   d. Brackets
   e. "x"

4. **[LO19.2]** In the Tabular List, what term describes codes consisting of 6 and 7 characters?
   a. Codes
   b. Subcategories
   c. Categories
   d. Chapters
   e. None of the above

5. **[LO19.3]** Which of the following scenarios would require both the diagnosis and signs and symptoms be coded?
   a. URI with headache, fever, and chills
   b. URI with urinary frequency and burning
   c. Acute MI with discovery of painless breast lump on exam
   d. All of the above
   e. b and c

6. **[LO19.3]** All of the codes below describe chronic instability of the knee. Which code is used if the condition is affecting only one knee?
   a. M23.52
   b. M23.51
   c. M23.50
   d. M23.5
   e. c or d may be used

7. **[LO19.4]** Which chapter uses the terms benign, malignant, in situ and uncertain behavior?
   a. 2
   b. 6
   c. 11
   d. 19
   e. 22

8. **[LO19.4]** Which code block (range) in ICD-10 describes what ICD-9 called V codes?
   a. R00–R99
   b. S00–T98
   c. V01–Y98
   d. Z00–Z99
   e. U00–U99

9. **[LO19.5]** Which member of the staff will NOT require at least some training in ICD-10?
   a. Physicians
   b. Administrative medical assistants
   c. Clinical medical assistants
   d. Office manager
   e. Everyone will require at least some training

10. **[LO19.5]** What aspect of ICD-10 preparation and transition is going to take the most time?
   a. Planning
   b. Updating computer systems and software
   c. Training
   d. Documentation
   e. Convincing the staff it will all be worth it

learning outcome SUMMARY

LO 19.1 The intent of the ICD-10-CM is to provide a more precise clinical picture of the patient and enhanced trending analysis. The number of codes increases from 15,000 in the ICD-9 to 120,000 in the ICD-10 and the characters from 3–5 numerical (with the exception of the E and V codes) to 3–7 alphanumeric. Both the 9th and 10th revisions contain the Alphabetic Index of the diseases, conditions, and related terms. The I-10 Tabular List incorporates 21 chapters with a corresponding range of codes. Many codes use an "X" as a placeholder for future expansion.

LO 19.2 As with the ICD-9-CM coding guidelines, the diagnosis or symptom is located first in the Alphabetic Index and all notes considered. The coder then moves to the Tabular List as instructed in the Alpha Index. After following terms, abbreviations and symbols, the appropriate code with the highest specificity supported by medical record documentation is selected.

LO 19.3 The majority of CM codes follow the general guidelines. However, unique coding applications exist. These include but are not limited to neoplasms, diabetes mellitus, fractures, R codes, poisonings, and new Z codes.

LO 19.4 Consider the following for a smooth transition from the ICD-9 to the ICD-10: needs of the practice; creation of a compliance team; changes in policies and procedures; financial impact; changes to and for information systems; and need for administrative and clinical training.

medical assisting COMPETENCIES

CAAHEP

VIII. C (3) Describe how to use the most current diagnostic coding classification system

VIII. P (2) Perform diagnostic coding

ABHES

8. Medical Office Business Procedures Management

t. Perform diagnostic and procedural coding

20 CPT and HCPCS Coding

Key Terms

add-on code
bundled codes
concurrent care
consultation
counseling
critical care
Current Procedural Terminology (CPT)
downcoding
E/M code
established patient

global period
HCPCS Level II codes
Healthcare Common Procedure Coding System (HCPCS)
modifier
new patient
panel
procedure code
unbundling
upcoding

Preparation for Certification

RMA (AMT) Exam	CMAS (AMT) Exam	CMA (AAMA) Exam
• CPT coding applications • HIPAA-mandated coding systems • Medical insurance terminology	• Coding	• Applying managed care policies and procedures • Relationship between procedure and diagnosis codes

Introduction ● ● ●

In Chapters 18 and 19 you were introduced to diagnosis coding, the reason why the patient sought health care. In this chapter, you are introduced to the language of procedural coding. You will learn how to translate the medical terms for the procedures and services provided to patients into code numbers selected from standardized procedural coding systems. These codes, when placed correctly on the health-care claims introduced in Chapter 17, explain to third-party payers the services that patients received from the provider.

After the concepts of procedure or CPT codes are explored, we discuss the "linking" of the diagnosis codes with the procedure codes to explain the medical necessity of each procedure or service performed. Finding the correct codes can require detective work! The reward is accurate procedure codes that when combined with accurate and appropriate diagnosis codes bring the maximum appropriate reimbursement to the physicians in your medical office.

LO 20.1 The CPT Manual

After an office or clinic visit, hospital or nursing home visit, inpatient or outpatient consultation, or even a house call, each procedure and service performed on or for a patient is reported on health-care claims using a **procedure code.** These codes represent medical procedures, such as surgery and diagnostic tests, and medical services, such as physical examinations to evaluate a patient's condition. Administrative medical assistants often choose procedure codes based on the information given to them by the physician on the encounter form, or from within the patient medical chart or electronic health record and use them to report physicians' services.

The most commonly used system of procedure codes is found in the *Current Procedural Terminology* or simply **CPT,** a reference manual published by the American Medical Association (AMA). CPT is the HIPAA required code set that translates descriptions for physicians and other provider health-care-related procedures into 5-digit codes.

Like ICD-9-CM, the CPT manual is updated yearly with the new codes being used for services provided beginning January 1 of each new year. In each new edition, newly developed procedures are added and old ones are revised or, if obsolete, deleted. These changes are also available in an electronic file for computerized medical offices. As with ICD-9, it is important to remember that the choice of which set of codes to use is based on the date of service not the date of the claim. If claims are submitted January 2, 2012, and the date of service was December 23, 2011, CPT codes from 2011 would be used; for services provided on January 2, 2012, the 2012 edition of the CPT codes would be used.

Medical offices should have the current year's CPT available for reference and keep forms up to date. Like ICD-9 codes, if current codes are not used, medical claims are often denied. Previous editions of each coding manual should be kept for at least several months after the new edition is released for use with claims for dates of service in the prior year, as well as for reference in case questions arise regarding previously submitted claims.

procedure code
Codes that represent medical procedures, such as surgery and diagnostic tests, and medical services, such as examination to evaluate a patient's condition.

Current Procedural Terminology (CPT)
A reference with the most commonly used system of procedure codes; the HIPAA- required code set for physician procedures.

Organization of the CPT Manual

CPT codes are organized into six main sections:

Section	Range of Codes
Evaluation and Management	99201–99499
Anesthesiology	00100–01999
	99100–99140
Surgery	10021–69990
Radiology	70010–79999
Pathology and Laboratory	80048–89356
Medicine (except for anesthesia)	90281–99199
	99500–99602

In looking at the section numbers above, you will note that except for the Evaluation and Management section, the sections are listed in numeric order by code range. Because Evaluation and Management (or E/M codes) are used so frequently, they are placed in the front of the manual for easy reference.

The Introduction to the CPT manual gives the user important general instructions for the use of CPT. In this section you will also find helpful information regarding common prefixes, suffixes, and word roots found within the manual. CPT is also full of helpful illustrations of the human body. A descriptive list of illustrations and the page number where each can be found is also in the Introduction. In addition, pay close attention to the guidelines found at the beginning of each new section. Each set of guidelines will give you important overall information for coding in each section. The sections of the CPT are divided into categories. These in turn are further divided into headings according to the type of test, service, or body system. Code number ranges included on a particular page are found in the upper-right corner. This helps to locate a code quickly after using the index. An example is shown in Figure 20–1.

Note that each page also gives you other important information:

- Section Name — The section is the name used by CPT to denote each chapter. In Figure 20–1 the section name is Surgery.

- Subsection Name — The subsection is the area within the section detailing the body system you are in. In Figure 20–1, the subsection is General. Note the next subsection for Surgery, which is Integumentary, starts part way down on the page.

- Subheading — The subheading describes the body area for the body system you are looking at. Figure 20–2 shows we are looking at the subheading of Skin, Subcutaneous, and Accessory Structures.

- Category — The category describes the procedure area. In Figure 20–2, we are in the Incision and Drainage (or I&D) category.

CHECKPOINT
LO 20.1

What information does the section category give the CPT user?

figure 20-1

Top of CPT manual page showing Edition, Section Name, Subsection Name, and Code Range.

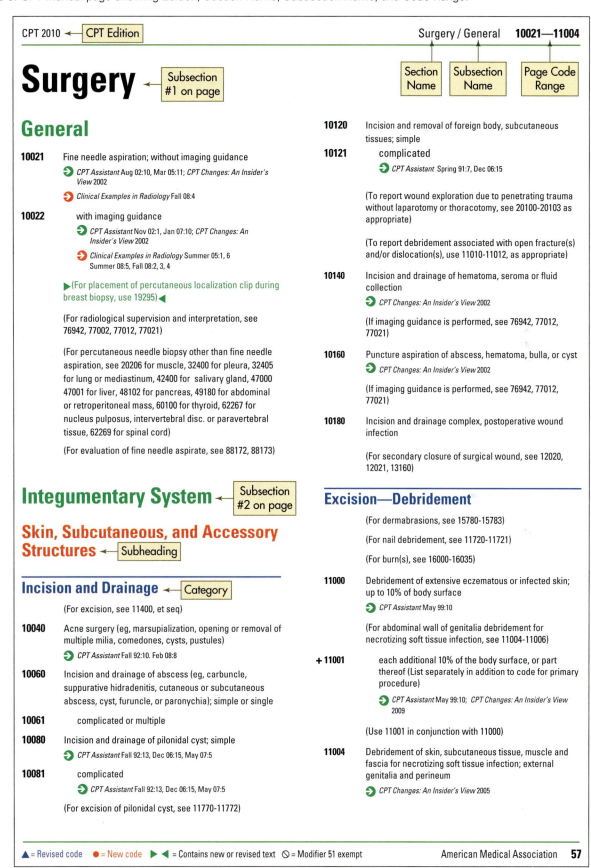

CPT 2010 ← CPT Edition

Surgery / General   **10021—11004**

Section Name | Subsection Name | Page Code Range

Surgery ← Subsection #1 on page

General

10021 Fine needle aspiration; without imaging guidance
  ⊙ *CPT Assistant* Aug 02:10, Mar 05:11; *CPT Changes: An Insider's View* 2002
  ⊙ *Clinical Examples in Radiology* Fall 08:4

10022 with imaging guidance
  ⊙ *CPT Assistant* Nov 02:1, Jan 07:10; *CPT Changes: An Insider's View* 2002
  ⊙ *Clinical Examples in Radiology* Summer 05:1, 6 Summer 08:5, Fall 08:2, 3, 4

▶(For placement of percutaneous localization clip during breast biopsy, use 19295)◀

(For radiological supervision and interpretation, see 76942, 77002, 77012, 77021)

(For percutaneous needle biopsy other than fine needle aspiration, see 20206 for muscle, 32400 for pleura, 32405 for lung or mediastinum, 42400 for salivary gland, 47000 47001 for liver, 48102 for pancreas, 49180 for abdominal or retroperitoneal mass, 60100 for thyroid, 62267 for nucleus pulposus, intervertebral disc. or paravertebral tissue, 62269 for spinal cord)

(For evaluation of fine needle aspirate, see 88172, 88173)

Integumentary System ← Subsection #2 on page

Skin, Subcutaneous, and Accessory Structures ← Subheading

Incision and Drainage ← Category

(For excision, see 11400, et seq)

10040 Acne surgery (eg, marsupialization, opening or removal of multiple milia, comedones, cysts, pustules)
  ⊙ *CPT Assistant* Fall 92:10. Feb 08:8

10060 Incision and drainage of abscess (eg, carbuncle, suppurative hidradenitis, cutaneous or subcutaneous abscess, cyst, furuncle, or paronychia); simple or single

10061 complicated or multiple

10080 Incision and drainage of pilonidal cyst; simple
  ⊙ *CPT Assistant* Fall 92:13, Dec 06:15, May 07:5

10081 complicated
  ⊙ *CPT Assistant* Fall 92:13, Dec 06:15, May 07:5

(For excision of pilonidal cyst, see 11770-11772)

10120 Incision and removal of foreign body, subcutaneous tissues; simple

10121 complicated
  ⊙ *CPT Assistant* Spring 91:7, Dec 06:15

(To report wound exploration due to penetrating trauma without laparotomy or thoracotomy, see 20100-20103 as appropriate)

(To report debridement associated with open fracture(s) and/or dislocation(s), use 11010-11012, as appropriate)

10140 Incision and drainage of hematoma, seroma or fluid collection
  ⊙ *CPT Changes: An Insider's View* 2002

(If imaging guidance is performed, see 76942, 77012, 77021)

10160 Puncture aspiration of abscess, hematoma, bulla, or cyst
  ⊙ *CPT Changes: An Insider's View* 2002

(If imaging guidance is performed, see 76942, 77012, 77021)

10180 Incision and drainage complex, postoperative wound infection

(For secondary closure of surgical wound, see 12020, 12021, 13160)

Excision—Debridement

(For dermabrasions, see 15780-15783)

(For nail debridement, see 11720-11721)

(For burn(s), see 16000-16035)

11000 Debridement of extensive eczematous or infected skin; up to 10% of body surface
  ⊙ *CPT Assistant* May 99:10

(For abdominal wall of genitalia debridement for necrotizing soft tissue infection, see 11004-11006)

+ 11001 each additional 10% of the body surface, or part thereof (List separately in addition to code for primary procedure)
  ⊙ *CPT Assistant* May 99:10; *CPT Changes: An Insider's View* 2009

(Use 11001 in conjunction with 11000)

11004 Debridement of skin, subcutaneous tissue, muscle and fascia for necrotizing soft tissue infection; external genitalia and perineum
  ⊙ *CPT Changes: An Insider's View* 2005

▲ = Revised code   ● = New code   ▶ ◀ = Contains new or revised text   ⊘ = Modifier 51 exempt   American Medical Association   **57**

figure 20-2

Subsection for Integumentary System.

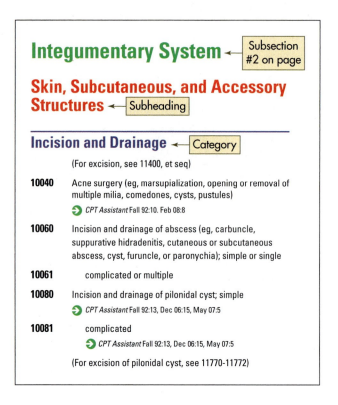

Integumentary System ← Subsection #2 on page

Skin, Subcutaneous, and Accessory Structures ← Subheading

Incision and Drainage ← Category

(For excision, see 11400, et seq)

10040   Acne surgery (eg, marsupialization, opening or removal of multiple milia, comedones, cysts, pustules)

    ➔ *CPT Assistant* Fall 92:10. Feb 08:8

10060   Incision and drainage of abscess (eg, carbuncle, suppurative hidradenitis, cutaneous or subcutaneous abscess, cyst, furuncle, or paronychia); simple or single

10061   complicated or multiple

10080   Incision and drainage of pilonidal cyst; simple

    ➔ *CPT Assistant* Fall 92:13, Dec 06:15, May 07:5

10081   complicated

    ➔ *CPT Assistant* Fall 92:13, Dec 06:15, May 07:5

(For excision of pilonidal cyst, see 11770-11772)

LO 20.2 General CPT Guidelines

As stated earlier, each section of CPT contains guidelines for that particular section. There are also general guidelines found at the beginning of the manual that are followed throughout. We will discuss these general guidelines here.

CPT Code Format

CPT codes are 5-digit numeric codes. Most codes are stand-alone codes with the complete description listed next to the appropriate code. The exception to this rule is the code description containing a semicolon, which is then followed by a code with an indented description. An indented description means that you refer back to the previous code description, reading the information prior to the semicolon and adding the indented code information after the colon to complete the description. Let's look at the following example:

Example:

25500	Closed treatment of radial shaft fracture; without manipulation
25505	with manipulation

To read the full description for code 25505, read code 25500 up to the semicolon and then substitute the description for 25505 after the semicolon. Following these instructions, the full description for 25505 is: *Closed treatment for radial shaft fracture; with manipulation.*

Add-On Codes

A plus sign (+) is used for **add-on codes.** These codes are used to describe procedures that are not done alone but done in addition to a "main" procedure. For example, in Figure 20–1 you will note that code 11001 has a plus sign in front of it with a description of *each additional 10% of body surface or part thereof (List separately in addition to code for primary procedure).* It is also an indented code, meaning it is related to the code immediately preceding it; in this case code 11000. The description for code 11000 is *Debridement of extensive eczematous or infected skin up to 10% of body surface.* In putting the two codes together you would be telling the insurance carrier that more than 10% of the body surface was debrided.

add-on code

A CPT code that indicates that this code is usually done in addition to a primary procedure (code) and is only reported in addition to the primary code.

Example #1: Debridement of 20% of body surface area.

Code 11000	(debridement of first 10% of body surface)
	And
Code 11001	(debridement of second 10% of body surface area or part thereof)

Example #2: Debridement of 25% of body surface area.

Code 11000	(debridement of first 10% of body surface)
	And
Code 11001	(debridement of second 10% of body surface area)
	And
Code 11001	(debridement for the next 5% as the description states "next 10% or part thereof")

Code 11000 (first 10%) and 11001 ×2 (2nd 10% and again for the next 5% as the description is "next 10% of part thereof")

Appendix D in the CPT manual contains a complete listing of all add-on codes.

As stated previously, also be alert for indented codes. For these codes you will read the description of the "parent code" up to the semicolon, and then replace the information following the semicolon with the information found in the indented code description. In Figure 20–1, codes 10022, 10061, 10081, and 10121 are all examples of indented codes. Add-on codes are never reported alone. They are always used with the primary code.

Symbols Used in CPT

The CPT manual uses instructional symbols to give repetitive information without adding multiple pages to the manual. Refer to Table 20–1 for examples of each symbol.

- **Blue triangle.** This symbol tells the user that the description of the code has been revised in some way from last year. You will note in Table 20–1 that codes 27327, has a blue triangle next to it. This tells you that the code description has changed in some way from the description contained in the 2009 CPT manual. This information could be important as the change could mean that the procedure performed by the physician may now require a different code. It could also mean something as simple as the placement of a comma or semicolon has changed.

- **Red dot.** The symbol denotes a new code for this edition of CPT. In Table 20–1, you will note that code 27337 is a new procedure code as of 2010 CPT.

table 20–1

Common CPT Symbols, Descriptions, and Examples

SYMBOL	MEANING	EXAMPLE
▲ (blue triangle)	Code description changed since last revision	**27327** Excision, tumor, soft tissue of thigh or knee area, subcutaneous; less than 3 cm
● (red circle)	New code since last revision	**27337** 3 cm or greater (indented code; includes description for code 27327 replacing information after semi colon)
#	Codes not in numeric sequence	**27337** 3 cm or greater **27328** Excision, soft tissue of thigh or knee area, subfascial (eg, intramuscular); less than 5 cm
▶◀ (green triangles)	Text between triangles new or revised	**27365** Radical resection of tumor, femur or knee ▶(for radical resection of tumor, soft tissue of thigh or knee area, see **27329, 27364**)◀
⊘	Multiple procedures performed or add-on code which does not require multiple procedure modifier of 51	= Modifier 51 Exempt ⊘ **20974** Electrical stimulation to aid bone healing; noninvasive (nonoperative)
(lightning diamond)	FDA approval pending	**90650** Human Papilloma virus (HPV) vaccine, types 16,18, bivalent, 3 does schedule, for intramuscular use
◉	Moderate (conscious) sedation included in the procedure	**44385** Endoscopic evaluation of small intestinal (abdominal or pelvic) pouch; diagnostic, with or without collection of specimen(s) by brushing or washing (separate procedure)

- **The # sign.** The # (pound) sign is a new symbol in 2010. It is used to note codes that are out of numeric sequence. Referring to Table 20–1, new (indented) code 27337 "works with" code 27327. It is followed by code 27328—causing it to be out of numeric order.

  Example:

27327	Excision, tumor, soft tissue of thigh or knee area, subcutaneous; less than 3 cm
27337	3 cm or greater
27328	Excision, tumor, soft tissue of thigh or knee area, subfascial (eg, intramuscular); less than 5 cm

This was done so that code numbers would not be "reshuffled" every year. If the pound sign were not used and codes were to remain in numeric order, for code 27327 to have an indented code, code 27328 would have to be used. Code 27328 had previously been assigned its description. To keep all codes in numeric order, all codes from 27328 with its new description and all other codes on this page would have to be assigned new descriptions. This is a lot of work and very confusing with constantly changing code descriptions on a yearly basis. You will note that each code is also found in red, in its "proper numeric place" with directions telling the coder in what code range to locate the out-of-sequenced code.

- **Triangles pointing toward each other.** Triangles pointing toward each other with text between them denote new or revised text information. Traditionally these arrows were green, but you will also see them used for the out-of-sequence coding information. Look at code 27365 in Table 20–1.

  Example:

27365	Radical resection of tumor, femur or knee
	▶(For radical resection of tumor, soft tissue of thigh or knee area see 27329, 27364)◀

  The instructions tell you where to look for the appropriate code, but the description is different from last year, because now we have the involvement of resequenced codes.

- **Circle with diagonal line.** This symbol is noted in Table 20–1 as "Modifier 51 Exempt." As you will learn shortly, modifier 51 is used when multiple procedures are performed in the same session. Modifier 51 exempt codes are those where the multiple procedure modifier does not apply. Appendix E of the CPT manual lists the modifier 51 except codes. Additionally, modifier 51 is never appended to a designated add-on code.

- **Lightning bolt.** The lightning bolt is used to denote vaccines that are pending FDA approval. Appendix K in the CPT manual lists the vaccines affected by this symbol. When the vaccines are approved, they will be listed on the AMA site at www.ama-assn.org/ama/pub/category/10902. html and then in subsequent editions of CPT.

- **Bull's-eye.** The bull's-eye symbol denotes moderate (conscious) sedation. This symbol means that it is understood that conscious sedation is necessary for the procedure performed and so is included in the procedure; it cannot be billed separately. Many of the endoscopy procedures include this symbol.

  Example:

44385	Endoscopic evaluation of small intestinal (abdominal or pelvic) pouch; diagnostic, with or without collection of specimen(s) by brushing or washing (separate procedure)

  Because this code includes sedation as part of the procedure, administered by the physician performing the procedure, there will be no separate charge for the anesthesia. Appendix G of the CPT manual lists all codes that include moderate (conscious) sedation.

Whenever you are coding, always watch carefully for these symbols. Their instructions are explicit and must be followed to ensure correct procedural coding.

Modifiers

One or more two-digit **modifiers** (up to three per procedure) may be assigned to the five-digit main code. Modifiers are written in column 24D on the CMS-1500 Claim Form (see Figure 17–10). The use of a modifier shows that one or more special circumstance applies to the service or procedure the physician performed. For example, in the surgery section, the modifier-62 indicates that two surgeons worked together, each performing part of a surgical procedure during an operation. Each physician will be paid part of the amount normally reimbursed for that procedure code. Appendix A of the CPT explains the proper use of each modifier. Some section guidelines also discuss the use of modifiers with the section's codes Table 20–2 gives a brief overview with examples of common CPT modifiers.

modifier
One or more two-digit alphanumeric codes assigned in addition to the five-digit CPT code to show that some special circumstance applies to the service or procedure performed by the physician.

table 20–2

Common CPT Modifiers

MODIFIER	DESCRIPTION	EXAMPLE
22	**Increased Procedural Services.** When the work required to complete the service is much more than usually required, modifier 22 may be added to the CPT code. Medical record documentation will be required. May not be attached to E/M code.	Because of extreme scarring and previous surgeries, lysis of adhesions (CPT 58740) requires almost twice the normal time frame. Code: 58740-22
23	**Unusual Anesthesia.** Once in a while, because of unusual situations, a procedure that normally does not require anesthesia or anesthetic will require general anesthesia.	Excision of subcutaneous tumor of neck because of patient age of 4, requires general anesthesia. Code 11424-23
24	**Unrelated E/M Service by the Same Physician during a Post-Operative Period.** The patient may require the services of the physician for treatment of an unrelated condition during a global surgical period.	The patient is one week post-op laparoscopic cholecystectomy. During post-op check, patient states asthma appears to be in exacerbation. Code 99024 for post-op visit. Code 99213-24 for E/M visit for asthma
25	**Significant, Separately Identifiable E/M Service By the Same Physician on the Same Day of the Procedure or Other Service.** While in the office for a specific procedure, the patient may require an E/M service above and beyond that normally provided during usual pre- and/or post-procedure period.	Patient comes in for a previously scheduled mole removal (11401). Prior to procedure physician notes BP is elevated. When procedure is completed, BP is still noted to be elevated. Physician makes adjustment to patient's anti-hypertensive medication and counsels diet adjustments. Code 11401 Code 99212-25
26	**Professional Component.** Some procedures (such as radiology) contain a combination of professional and technical components. If the physician provides only the professional component, modifier 26 is added.	Screening mammography, bilateral (CPT 77057). Hospital performs the mammogram, physician provides interpretation. Code 77057-26
TC	**Technical Component.** This is the HCPCS modifier that is the "reverse" of modifier 26. It designates the provision of the technical component only.	Screening mammography, bilateral (CPT 77057). Hospital performs the mammogram, physician provides interpretation. Hospital Code 77057-TC
32	**Mandated Services.** Service (such as a consult) is required by insurance carrier, governmental or regulatory agency.	Insurance carrier requires a second opinion prior to an elective surgical procedure. Physician performs consult regarding need for surgery. Code: 99242-32
47	**Anesthesia by Surgeon.** Surgeon provides and administers anesthesia other than local anesthesia. Modifier is appended to the surgical procedure.	Procedure performed is shoulder manipulation under regional anesthesia by orthopedic surgeon. Code: 23700-47
50	**Bilateral Procedure.** Modifier used if procedure is not defined as bilateral but procedure is performed on both sides of the body.	Procedure: Bilateral knee arthroscopy. Code: 29870-50
51	**Multiple Procedures.** When multiple procedures (other than E/M, PT, and Rehab or supply provision) are performed in the same session by the same provider, the first procedure is listed as usual, and subsequent procedures should include the addition of modifier 51.	Code 15877 Suction assisted lipectomy; trunk Code 15879-51 Suction assisted lipectomy; lower extremity
52	**Reduced Services.** Due to circumstances, service is reduced or eliminated by the physician.	Exploratory laparotomy for removal of malignant neoplasm, but cancer is widely metastasized so procedure is halted. Code: 49000-52
53	**Discontinued Procedure.** Similar to modifier 52, except in this case, the procedure is discontinued due to patient condition becoming endangered.	Patient is undergoing diagnostic colonoscopy when significant PVCs become evident and uncontrollable. Procedure is halted. Code: 45330-53
54	**Surgical Care Only.** Surgeon provides only the surgical care with other physician(s) providing pre- and post-op care.	Total abdominal hysterectomy with bilateral salpingo-oophorectomy (TAH-BSO) surgery only. Code: 58150-54

table 20–2 *(Continued)*

MODIFIER	DESCRIPTION	EXAMPLE
55	**Postoperative Management Only.** Physician provides postoperative care only.	Total abdominal hysterectomy with bilateral salpingo-oophorectomy (TAH-BSO) postoperative care only. Code: 58150-55
56	**Preoperative Management Only.** Physician provides preoperative care only.	Total abdominal hysterectomy with bilateral salpingo-oophorectomy (TAH-BSO) preoperative care only. Code: 58150-56
57	**Decision for Surgery.** During an E/M service, decision is made that surgery is required.	Patient in office for biopsy results. Decision is made that treatment option includes mastectomy. Code: 99214-57
58	**Staged or Related Procedure or Service by the Same Physician during the Postoperative Period.** Circumstances may include staged (planned) procedure, procedure being more extensive than originally thought, or therapy following original procedure.	Patient has breast biopsy which has a post-op period. During this period, mastectomy is decided on and performed. Code: 19302-58
59	**Distinct Procedural Service.** Used when the secondary procedure is identified as *different session, different procedure/surgery, different site or organ system. Separate incision/excision, separate lesion, separate injury or area of injury when injuries are extensive.* (Note that Medicare has edits that state certain procedures cannot be performed together regardless of use of 59 modifier.)	Medical records indicate that colonoscopy with polyp removal using snare (45385) and colonoscopy with hot biopsy forceps (45384) were done same session. Code: 45385 Code 45385-59
62	**Two Surgeons.** Modifier indicates that two surgeons performed procedure that normally is performed by one surgeon; each performing distinct aspects of the procedure.	Two surgeons work as team for spinal cord exploration and decompression. Code: 63075-62 Code: 63077-62
66	**Surgical Team.** As with modifier 62, this modifier is used when a team of surgeons is required for a complicated procedure.	Patient requires a heart-lung transplant. Team includes cardiac surgeon, thoracic surgeon, perfusionist, and anesthesiologist. Code: 33935-66
76	**Repeat Procedure or Service By Same Physician.** Procedure is performed and complication requires repeat or related service. Used to explain that this is not a duplicate service but is medically necessary.	Patient undergoes arteriovenous anastomosis (36821) but anastomosis does not hold and requires repeat procedure. Code: 36821-76
77	**Repeat Procedure by Another Physician.** As with modifier 76 a second procedure is required, but in this case, a different physician provides the service.	Patient undergoes arteriovenous anastomosis (36821) but anastomosis does not hold and requires repeat procedure; performing physician is not available. Code: 36821-77
78	**Unplanned return to the OR by the same Physician following Initial Procedure for Related Procedure during the Postoperative Period.** Complications related to the initial procedure are most often the reason for the return to surgery.	Patient undergoes implantation of central venous access device (36558) which clots off later in the day requiring declotting. Code: 36593-78
79	**Unrelated Procedure or Service By the Same Physician during the Postoperative Period.** Usually patient undergoes a primary procedure and for unrelated issue, requires a second surgery or procedure during the post-op period.	Patient undergoes laparoscopic cholecystectomy (47562). Two weeks later experiences acute appendicitis episode and undergoes emergency appendectomy. Code: 44970-79
80	**Assistant Surgeon.** Surgeon acts as assistant to primary surgeon (A physician assistant may function in this role).	Surgeon performs total knee replacement with assistant surgeon. Code: 27447-80

(Continued)

table 20–2 (Concluded)

MODIFIER	DESCRIPTION	EXAMPLE
81	**Minimum Assistant Surgeon.** This modifier is used only when minimal assistance during surgery is required.	Patient undergoing 4-vessel CABG. Second physician asked to assist only in stabilizing patient during procedure. Code: 33536-81 Code: 33518-81
82	**Assistant Surgeon (when qualified resident surgeon is not available).** This modifier is used only in teaching hospitals where resident surgeons are normally available.	Patient undergoing 4-vessel CABG. Second physician asked to assist only in stabilizing patient during procedure because the surgical resident is assisting with another procedure. Code: 33536-82 Code: 33518-82
90	**Reference (Outside) Laboratory.** Modifier is used when physician is billing for services provided by an outside laboratory. (Not allowed by Medicare.)	Provider office billed for comprehensive metabolic panel performed by "Allied Labs" and then reimbursed the lab. Code: 80053-90
91	**Repeat Clinical Diagnostic Laboratory Test.** This modifier is used when serial (multiple) labs are required on the same day to monitor the patient's condition.	After surgery, the patient appears to be in acute renal failure, requiring monitoring of kidney function. Code: 80069-91
92	**Alternative Laboratory Platform Testing.** Modifier 92 is used for disposable kit testing, such as HIV testing.	Patient is tested for HIV using disposable test at hospital bedside. Code: 86701-92
99	**Multiple Modifiers.** Used when more than three modifiers are applicable to CPT code being used and the payer only accepts one modifier per code.	Medical Insurance Inc accepts only one modifier per line, requiring modifier 99 be used and applicable modifiers be listed in block 19 of the CMS form. Procedure performed: Bilateral (50) mastectomy with assistant surgeon (80). Code: 19307-99

Note: You can see a complete listing of all the modifiers in the *Current Procedural Terminology* manual, Appendix A.

Source: American Medical Association, *Current Procedural Terminology,* 2011 Professional Edition, copyright 2011.

Category II Codes, Category III Codes, and Unlisted Procedure Codes

Category II codes are optional, supplemental tracking codes used to track healthcare performance measures, such as programs and counseling to avoid tobacco use. Category III codes are temporary CPT codes for emerging technology, services, and procedures. If available, these codes should be used instead of the *unlisted codes* found throughout the CPT manual.

When no code is available to completely describe a procedure, a code for an unlisted procedure is selected. Unlisted procedure codes are used for new services or procedures that have not yet been assigned codes in CPT. When these codes are used, which is rare, a procedure or service description (usually from the medical record) is sent with the submission of the claim. Some payers, including Medicare and Medicaid, prefer the use of HCPCS codes (when they are available) instead of the unlisted procedure codes used with CPT. Check with individual payers to understand each payer's preferences.

Coding Terminology

Before you begin coding, you must have a basic understanding of common terminology used throughout the CPT manual. Some of these terms are defined in the following paragraphs.

Bundled codes consist of any code that includes more than one procedure in its description. Read code descriptions carefully as it is unethical (and often considered fraudulent) to intentionally unbundle procedures into component codes when a bundled procedure code is available. For instance, all therapeutic procedures include diagnostic codes unless noted otherwise, so if a diagnostic knee arthroscopy (29870) is turned into a therapeutic arthroscopy (29871), only the therapeutic arthroscopy will be reported.

Concurrent care is described as similar care being provided by more than one physician. Concurrent care frequently occurs when a patient is hospitalized and multiple specialists are caring for the patient. The services provided may be similar but because of the differing specialties, the care is not considered to be duplication of services.

Critical care is provided to unstable, critically ill patients. Constant bedside attention is needed in order to code critical care, so the physician's documentation must be explicit regarding the time spent with the patient. The time need not be continuous, but the time is added together so that critical care codes chosen are based on the sum total of the critical care given during one particular date. Unlike emergency care codes, which can only be used when the patient's care is provided in an emergency department, the patient need not be in a critical care or intensive care bed in order for the codes to be used; but their condition must be critical in nature.

Consultations are at the request of other health-care providers. A service can only be considered a consultation if the 3R's are present—*request* (from another physician), *recording* (documentation) of findings and recommendations, and *report* to the referring physician. If the consulting physician takes over the care of the patient, then he is no longer considered a consulting physician, but a treating physician. Note that as of January 2010, Medicare no longer accepts consultation codes and comparable inpatient and outpatient E/M service codes are to be used instead.

Counseling is considered part of E/M (evaluation and management) services, but if a complete history and physical exam does not take place, counseling codes may be used. These codes may be used when discussing with the patient and family questions or concerns regarding one or more of the following: diagnostic results and recommendations, prognosis, risks and benefits of options, instructions for treatment and/or follow up, importance of compliance, risk factor reduction, and patient/family education.

Downcoding is the term used when the insurance carrier bases reimbursement on a code level lower than the one submitted by the provider. This can occur for several reasons:

- The coding system used by the insurer does not match that used by the provider. This can occur if the provider uses a HCPCS code that the insurer does not recognize. Always verify the code set accepted by the payer.

- If a workers' compensation carrier bases payment on a RVS (relative value system), the carrier may convert a CPT code to the lowest paying code within the system. Again, check with the payer as to the system in use.

- If a payer requests back up documentation (medical records) on a case and finds that the documentation does not "back up" the level of code used on the claim. This is by far the most common cause of downcoding in medical offices. Be sure your provider documentation backs up the level of code used.

Unbundling, as stated above in the bundling definition, is defined as breaking a bundled code into its component parts for higher reimbursement and is not allowed. Code 77055 is defined as mammography, unilateral. Without research, you might think that a bilateral mammography would be coded by adding modifier 50, but this is not the case. Code 77056 is an indented code

upcoding
Purposely choosing a code of a higher level than that of the service provided in order to achieve higher reimbursement.

with the description of mammography, bilateral, and must be used for a bilateral mammography.

Upcoding refers to coding a procedure or service at a higher level than that which was provided to receive a higher level of reimbursement. Other terms for this process are *code creep*, *overcoding*, and *overbilling*, and all are fraudulent practices when done knowingly.

CHECKPOINT
LO 20.2

What is the purpose of modifiers?

LO 20.3 Evaluation and Management Services

E/M codes
The codes used to describe the wide range of time, effort, skill, and locations used by physicians for different patients to diagnose conditions and plan treatments.

To diagnose conditions and plan treatments, physicians use a wide range of time, effort, and skill for different patients and circumstances. Evaluation and management codes (**E/M codes**) are often considered the most important of all CPT codes because they can be used by all physicians in any medical specialty. Table 20–3 gives the E/M breakdown by type with code range.

table 20–3

E/M Code Breakdown by Type Including Code Ranges

E/M TYPE	CODE RANGE
Office/Other Outpatient Services	New Pt 99201–99202 Est. Pt 99211–99215
Hospital Observation Services	99217–99220
Hospital Inpatient Services	99221–99239
Consultations	Outpt 99241–99245 InPt 99251–99255
Emergency Department Services	99281–99288
Critical Care Services	99291–99292
Nursing Facility Services	99304–99318
Domiciliary, Rest Home (Boarding Home), or Custodial Care Services	New Pt 99324–99328 Est. Pt 99334–99337
Domiciliary, Assisted Living Facility or Home Care Plan Oversight Services	99339–99340
Home Services	New Pt 99341–99345 Est. Pt 99347–99350
Prolonged Services	99354–99360
Case Management Services	99363–99368
Care Plan Oversight Services	99374–99380
Preventative Medicine Services (includes counseling services)	New Pt 99381–99387 Est. Pt 99391–99397
Non-Face-to-Face Physician Services	99441–99444
Special Evaluation and Management Services	99450–99456
Newborn Care Services	99460–99465
Inpatient Neonatal Intensive Care Services Pediatric and Neonatal Critical Care Services	99466–99480
Other Evaluation and Management Services	99499

Source: 2011 AMA CPT Manual.

Many E/M codes are divided based on the patient status of **new patient** versus **established patient.** This is simply because in many cases a physician will need to spend more time with a new patient, getting to know him and his history, than will be necessary with a patient who has been coming to the practice for several years and whose history is well-known. The general rule of thumb is that if a patient has been seen by a physician of the same specialty in the same practice within 3 years, she is an existing patient. If the patient has not been seen in the practice within the last 3 years, she is considered a new patient.

Figure 20–3 shows an example of a new versus established patient decision tree.

Key Factors in Determining Level of Service

The E/M section guidelines explain how to code different levels of these services. Three key factors documented in the patient's medical record help determine the level of service:

1. The extent of the patient history taken
2. The extent of the examination conducted
3. The complexity of the medical decision making

Let's look briefly at each of these key factors.

Patient History   The elements of a history include the chief complaint (CC); history of present illness (HPI); review of systems (ROS); and past, family, and/or social history (PFSH). When coding, the history is described using one of the following terms:

- Problem-focused—limited to the chief complaint and brief history of present problem
- Expanded problem-focused—includes the chief complaint, brief history of the current problem, and a "problem-pertinent" review of systems

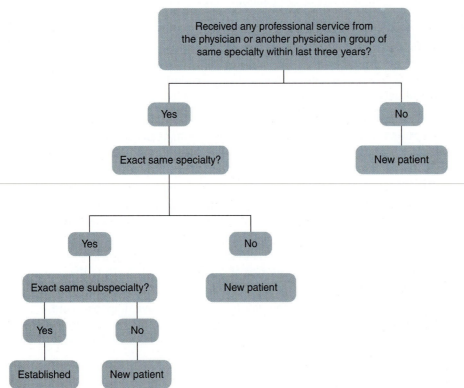

figure 20-3

Decision tree for new versus established patients.

- Detailed—still focuses on the chief complaint, but includes an extensive history of the current problem and extended review of systems and pertinent past, family, and/or social history
- Comprehensive—the most complex of the histories, all four components of CC, HPI, ROS, and PFSH are documented

Physical Exam The elements of the physical exam include the same terminology but relate to the level of examination performed. There are three elements to the physical exam. Constitutional exam includes any of the following: BP sitting or lying, pulse, respirations, temperature, height, weight, and general appearance. Body areas (BA) include head (including face), neck, chest (including breasts and axillae), abdomen, genitalia, groin and buttocks, back, and each extremity. Organ systems (OA) include ophthalmologic (eyes), otolaryngologic (ears, nose, throat, and mouth), cardiovascular, respiratory, GI (gastrointestinal), GU (genitourinary), musculoskeletal, integumentary (skin), neurologic, psychiatric, and hematologic/lymphatic/immunologic (blood, lymph, immunity). Physical exam terms include:

- Problem-focused—exam is limited to the body area or organ system directly related to the chief complaint. (1 BA or OS)
- Expanded problem-focused—limited exam of the affected body area or organ system as well as any other symptomatic or related BA or OS. (2–7 limited BA or OS)
- Detailed—includes an extended exam of the affected body area and any other related, symptomatic BA or OS. (2-7 extended BA or OS)
- Comprehensive—the most extensive exam, it includes either a complete single-specialty exam or a complete multisystem examination. (8+ BA or OS)

Medical Decision Making The most important key component in establishing an E/M code is the medical decision making (MDM) and it is probably the most difficult to document. It is based on the complexity of the decision making by the provider about the patient's care and diagnosis. The three elements that must be documented to establish MDM include the following: number of diagnoses or management options (minimal, limited, multiple, or extensive); amount or complexity of date to be reviewed (none or minimal, limited, moderate or extensive); and risk of complication or death if condition is untreated (minimal, low, moderate or high). Here we outline the complexity levels of medical decision making:

- Straightforward MDM—there are minimal diagnosis and management options with no or a minimal amount or complexity of data to be reviewed and minimal risk to the patient of complication or death if the condition is left untreated.
- Low-complexity MDM—there are a limited number of diagnoses and management options with a limited amount/complexity of data to be reviewed and low risk of complication or death if the patient is not treated.
- Moderate-complexity MDM—there are now multiple diagnoses and management options with a moderate amount and complexity of data to review. There is a moderate risk of complication or death to the patient if the condition is not treated.
- High-complexity MDM—the physician has extensive diagnoses and management options with an extensive amount and complexity of data for review. The patient is at high risk for complication and/or death if not treated.

Some administrative medical assistants and billers/coders like to utilize a grid similar to Table 20–4 to assist with the MDM decision-making process when assigning E/M codes.

Three Contributory Factors in Assigning Codes

In addition to these three key components, some E/M codes take three *contributory factors* into consideration when codes are assigned. The three contributory factors are listed here:

1. Counseling. Counseling is only considered as a component for E/M codes when counseling is the reason for the encounter and constitutes 50% or more of the total time of the visit.

2. Coordination of care. The time the physician uses to coordinate patient care with other health-care agencies such as home care or nursing home care.

3. Nature of the presenting problem. This is another term for the severity of the patient's chief complaint.

   - Minimal complaint is one that may not require the presence of a physician but service is provided under the physician supervision such as a BP reading or dressing change.

   - Self-limited complaint is a minor problem that will run a "known" course and is transient in nature. A problem with a good prognosis when the patient is compliant may also be considered self-limiting.

   - Low severity complaints are those with a low risk of morbidity and mortality (death) if there is no treatment. Full recovery is expected.

   - Moderate severity complaints have a moderate risk of morbidity and mortality if there is no treatment. Prognosis is uncertain and there is increased risk of impairment.

   - High severity complaints are those of high to extreme risk. Risk of death is moderate to high and a high risk of prolonged functional impairment.

Last, *time* is listed as a component to some codes after being incorporated in 1992 to assist with code choice. The times listed are considered averages and unless the code choice, such as with face-to-face contact codes, is based on time, time should not be considered a critical factor when choosing an E/M code. Appendix C of the CPT code manual lists clinical examples of each E/M code type to assist you in choosing appropriate E/M codes for your provider.

As noted in Table 20–2, the location of the service is also important because different E/M codes apply to services performed in a physician's office or other outpatient location, a hospital inpatient room, a hospital emergency department, a nursing facility, an extended-care facility, or a patient's home.

ELEMENTS	STRAIGHTFORWARD	LOW	MODERATE	HIGH
Number of diagnostic or management options	Minimal	Limited	Multiple	Extensive
Amount or complexity of data to be reviewed	Minimal/None	Limited	Moderate	Extensive
Risk of complication or death	Minimal	Low	Moderate	High

table 20–4

Medical Decision-Making Elements for E/M Codes

LO 20.4 Surgical Coding

Figure 20–4 illustrates an encounter form listing codes from the integumentary part of the surgical section. Many insurance carriers cover the surgical procedures found in CPT as part of a *surgical package.* Included in most surgical packages are the preoperative exam and testing, the surgical procedure itself, including local or regional anesthesia if used, and routine follow-up care for a set period of time. Payers assign a fee to each of these packaged codes that pays for all the services provided in this package. If other than local anesthesia is used, an anesthesia code would be used by the anesthesiologist billing for his services.

The period of time that is covered for follow-up care is called the **global period.** For example, the global period for repairing a tendon might be set

global period
The period of time after many procedures for follow-up care that is considered included in the payment for that procedure.

figure 20–4

Superbill with procedure codes and diagnosis code showing medical necessity for procedures performed.

TOTAL CARE CLINIC, PC

342 East Park Blvd
Funton, XY 12345-6789
Tel: 521-234-0001
Fax: 521-234-0002

PATIENT NAME	APPT. DATE/TIME	
Scott Yeager	10/14/12	11:00am

PATIENT NO.	DX
YEAGESCO	1. Major open wound. Infected 2. 3. 4.

Note the diagnosis code showing medical necessity for the procedure performed

DESCRIPTION	✓	CPT	FEE	DESCRIPTION	✓	CPT	FEE
EXAMINATION				PROCEDURES			
New Patient				Acne Surgery		10040	
Problem Focused		99201		I&D Cyst/Abscess		10060	
Expanded Problem Focused	✓	99202	50	I&D Multiple		10061	
Detailed		99203		I&D Remove Foreign Body	✓	10120	60
Comprehensive		99204		Debridement		11000	
Comprehensive/Complex		99205		Paring/Curett. (Benign)		11055	
Established Patient				Paring/Curett. (2-4)		11056	
Minimum		99211		Paring/Curett. (Over 4)		11057	
Problem Focused		99212		Excision Skin Tags (1-15)		11200	
Expanded Problem Focused		99213		Cyrosurgery		17340	
Detailed		99214		Skin Biopsy		11100	
Comprehensive/Complex		99215		Skin Biopsy (EA additional)		+11101	

First procedure performed → (Expanded Problem Focused)

Second procedure performed → (I&D Remove Foreign Body)

at 15 days. A global period for major surgery such as an appendectomy might be set at 100 days. During the global period, any care provided related to the surgical procedure is included in the surgical fee and cannot be billed separately; any attempt to do so is called *unbundling* and is considered fraud. As discussed earlier, if a patient is seen for an unrelated problem, the service or procedure may be billed separately using a modifier 24 for E/M services, or modifier 79 for an unrelated surgical procedure taking place in a global period. After the global period ends, additional services related to the initial surgery can be reported separately for payment.

As we learned in Chapter 17, to make the coding process more efficient, medical offices often list frequently used procedures and their applicable CPT codes on superbills or encounter forms. After seeing the patient, the physician checks off the appropriate procedures or services which the patient returns to the administrative medical assistant at the front desk, who inputs the information into the facility computer system, if the office is computerized. If the office uses a manual system, the administrative medical assistant will put the office copy of the completed superbill in a designated area so that it can be used to quickly and efficiently complete the CMS-1500 form for submission to the patient's insurance carrier. An example of a practice's superbill is shown in Figure 20–4. This sample superbill lists the E/M codes for new and established patient office visits as well as common procedures for the office. If superbills are used in the office, it is important to remember to update both the ICD-9 and CPT codes on the superbills and in any computer programs when the new codes are available each year (October for ICD-9 codes and January for CPT codes). Let's look at each subsection of the surgery chapter with a brief overview of coding guidelines for each area.

Integumentary System

Integumentary subheadings are: skin; subcutaneous and accessory structures; nails; pilonidal cyst; introduction; repair (closure); destruction; and breast. These are further subdivided by the procedures done within each subheading, such as I&D, excision, paring, biopsy benign and malignant lesions, and so on. Many codes in this section are based on size and location; choose carefully. Carefully read instructions regarding closure of any removed or repaired lesion. Simple closure is often included in the main code, so you will often only be coding closures if they are intermediate (layered) or complex (greater than layered). The instructions within the Integumentary section give great information as to how to choose the correct closure type. Read everything carefully and follow the instructions exactly.

Musculoskeletal System

The musculoskeletal subheadings begin with general and then start with the head and work their way down to the foot and toes. You will find this to be true for the rest of the CPT manual. Codes start from the top of the body and work their way down within each section and subsection. Casts and strappings as well as endoscopy and arthroscopy are also found in this chapter. Probably the most common codes from this section include the fracture codes. The following are a couple of straightforward rules:

- A fracture treatment is closed unless stated otherwise; that is, treatment occurs without opening the skin. Open treatment means that surgery occurred to repair the fracture. Percutaneous treatment (fixation) immobilizes the fracture with hardware (pins) inserted using x-ray guidance.
- Be careful with cast and strapping codes. Fracture repair assumes cast application and includes it. Cast application and removal for fractures

are only coded when the physician applying or removing the cast did not initially treat the patient's fracture.

- Last, any therapeutic procedure (such as arthroscopy) includes the diagnostic procedure, so if a diagnostic procedure becomes a therapeutic (surgical) procedure, in the end, only the therapeutic procedure will be coded.

Respiratory System

The most important item to remember when coding the respiratory system is to code to the furthest extent of the procedure. For instance many endoscopy procedures for the respiratory system begin with the nose and proceed further into the respiratory system. If the procedure results in a laryngoscopy, the scope passes through the trachea, so the code includes scoping of the trachea, which is not coded separately, as the description for code 31515 states *with or without laryngoscopy*. Be sure to also read information regarding the approach for the procedure. Many procedures can be done via a scope (scopy) or as an open procedure using an incision (tomy); these procedures are very different, so be cautious when coding similar procedures using different approaches. Be alert also for *incision* codes (cutting into-suffix tomy) versus *excision* (removal-suffix ectomy); and for the suffix *plasty* signifying a repair procedure such as rhinoplasty. You will find your terminology knowledge to be invaluable when coding.

Cardiovascular System

As you might expect, cardiology coding consists of some of the more complicated coding scenarios. Often, in order to completely code cardiovascular surgery, codes from the cardiovascular surgery section, medicine section (for nonsurgical services), and radiology section (for diagnostic or visualization assistance) will all be necessary. When coding bypass procedures, read instructions carefully. You must know not only whether veins or arteries (or both) are used in the bypass, but also the correct coding sequence; the right codes in the wrong order will also hold up a claim. Injection codes will be used for diagnostic and therapeutic procedures and you will also find embolectomy and thrombectomy codes in this section. Nonsurgical cardiography procedures include ECGs, Holter monitors, and exercise tests. The echocardiography area includes all cardiac ultrasound procedures as well as vascular doppler procedures for noncardiac vascular areas, such as the extremities. Read *everything* and make sure to code procedures completely, using as many codes as necessary.

Hemic/Lymphatic Systems and Mediastinum and Diaphragm

These two short subsections of the surgery section include procedures on the spleen, bone marrow, and lymph nodes as well as surgical procedure related to the mediastinum and diaphragm. Coding in these sections is very straightforward as long as you read carefully.

Digestive System

The most common procedures found in the upper digestive system are incisions and excisions followed by repairs. The lower digestive system (stomach, intestines, rectum) include these as well as endoscopies (and laparoscopies). As always, remember that therapeutic procedures include diagnostic procedures unless you are specifically instructed within the chapter that two codes may be used. You will also find procedures on the liver, pancreas, biliary tract, abdomen, and peritoneum in this chapter.

Urinary System

The most "intense" coding in the urinary system revolves around the kidneys and renal function and treatment, including services for renal transplantation. In addition to kidney procedures, you will find diagnostic (including urodynamics) and therapeutic procedures for the ureters, bladder, and urethra. Again, as with the respiratory and digestive system, many procedures may be done laparoscopically as well as through an open incision, so read notes and code descriptions carefully to be sure to choose the correct approach.

Male Genital System

Because of the many repair codes associated with it, the subheading Penis is the largest within the male genital section. Other procedure codes found throughout this chapter include excision, incision, biopsy, destruction (of lesions) including laser surgery (treatment for BPH and prostate cancer), and brachytherapy (radiotherapy). The two codes for intersex surgery (male to female and female to male) are also found in this section.

Female Genital System/Maternity and Delivery

Administrative medical assistants and coders either use this section extensively or almost never as the codes found here are used almost exclusively by OB/GYN providers. This chapter is set up from "the outside in" starting with the introitus moving to the ovaries within the pelvis, with a separate subsection devoted to labor and delivery. There are many definitions and specialized guidelines for this chapter that are too numerous to cover here, but if you find yourself coding for the specialty of OB/GYN, read the entire chapter carefully, taking notes and highlighting important information. Seeking the assistance of an experienced OB/GYN coder will be very helpful when you start out.

Endocrine System

Another short section, the endocrine system codes include those for procedures on the thyroid, parathyroid, thymus, adrenal glands, pancreas, and carotid body. Procedures include incisions, excisions, and laparoscopies.

Nervous System

Codes describing procedures on the brain, spinal cord, and peripheral nerves are all found in this section. Anatomic sites create the subheadings which are subdivided by the procedure performed. Because of the complicated nature of coding procedures related to this delicate system, there are multiple specialized guidelines found within this chapter. The approach again is an important consideration when coding surgery on the brain (anterior, middle, or posterior cranial fossa) as is the definitive procedure that describes the procedure done to the lesion and the reconstruction or repair necessary at the end of the surgery. Lumbar punctures, CSF shunt procedures for hydrocephalus treatment, and all treatments for spinal column and cord defects and peripheral nerve repair and destruction are found in this chapter.

Eye and Ocular Adnexa

This chapter covers everything for every day eye exams and removal of foreign body from the external eye to enucleation surgery to remove the contents of the eye socket. Many of the procedures found here are highly specialized and require careful reading of instructions and guidelines. The codes are divided by anterior and posterior segments, ocular adnexa, and conjunctiva (including the lacrimal system). Procedures include incisions, excisions, repairs, destruction, and reconstructions.

Auditory System

The auditory system section is divided by the external ear diagnostics and treatments, middle ear diagnostics and treatments and then the inner ear diagnostics and treatments, followed by temporal bone procedures. An operating microscope is necessary for many procedures and code descriptions must be read carefully to avoid unbundling as some procedures include this component and others allow a separate code for its use. Procedures include incisions (including "tubing" or tympanostomy), excisions, introductions, and repairs (tympanoplasty).

Radiology

The radiology section includes diagnostic radiology (imaging), diagnostic ultrasound, radiologic guidance, mammography, bone and joint procedures, radiation oncology, and nuclear medicine.

Many diagnostic radiology procedures use modifiers 26 (professional component) and TC (technical component); however, read descriptions carefully. When a code states, "radiologic supervision and interpretation" as with code 77031, the code is all-inclusive and modifiers cannot be used with that code. There are many instructions throughout this chapter leading you to correct code usage. Read all includes and excludes instructions carefully.

Laboratory Procedures

panel
Lab tests frequently ordered together that are organ- or disease-oriented.

Organ or disease-oriented **panels** listed in the pathology and laboratory section of the CPT include tests frequently ordered together. An electrolyte panel, for example, includes tests for carbon dioxide, chloride, potassium, and sodium. Each element of the panel has its own procedure code. However, when the tests are performed together, the code for the panel must be used rather than the separate procedure codes. To code a panel correctly, the physician must order each test listed within the panel and there must be a need for each of them. If a panel is appropriate but one or two laboratory tests are also ordered that are not included in the panel, code the panel and then the additional tests separately.

If each test in a panel or procedure in a surgical package is listed separately, it will cause unbundling of the panel or package. The review performed by the insurance carrier's claims department will rebundle the services under the appropriate code, which could delay payment. Remember that when unbundling is done intentionally or repeatedly to receive more payment than is correct, you and the practice can come under investigation for fraud.

Medicine and Immunizations

Injections and infusions of immune globulins, vaccines, toxoids, and other substances require two codes, one for giving the injection and one for the particular vaccine or toxoid that is given. An E/M code is not used along with the codes for immunization unless a significant evaluation and management service is also performed and documented appropriately by the doctor. Modifier 59 would be appended to the E/M code in this case indicating the need for both procedures.

CHECKPOINT
LO 20.4

What components are generally included in a surgical package?

LO 20.5 Using the CPT

Now that you have a basic understanding of the format of the CPT manual, its conventions, and its sections, including where to find section guidelines and instructions, it is time to actually use the CPT manual. Remember that when choosing E/M codes you must know whether the patient is a new or established patient as well as where the services took place. Use all of the information we have discussed as well as the chapter guidelines to assist you in locating the correct codes.

The next step is to find the procedures and services provided by the office. As with diagnosis codes, these may be found on the superbill, but remember to check the patient's chart to verify that documentation on the procedures and services exists within the medical chart (if it is not written down, it did not happen). When coding E/M codes, you may find it easiest to go directly to the E/M section in the front of the CPT manual to choose the correct code. For all other procedures, you will need to use the alphabetic listing of procedures found in the back of the CPT manual.

The number or number range in the index to the right of the description represents the coding possibilities for the description. If a hyphen is between two codes, this indicates a code range and each code in the range will need to be checked in the numeric index to choose the correct code. Code numbers with commas between them indicate that there is more than one location possibility. Again, all codes will have to be checked. In some cases, the patient's medical record may show an abbreviation, an *eponym* (a person or place for which a procedure is named), or a synonym. For example, the record might state "treated for bone infection." In CPT's index, the entry for "Infection, Bone," is followed by the instruction "See Osteomyelitis." The greater your knowledge of anatomy and physiology and terminology, the easier it will be for you to code.

Example 1: To find the code for "dressing change," first look alphabetically in the index for that procedure. Then find the procedure code in the body of the CPT to be sure the code accurately reflects the service performed. The procedure code 15852 explains the dressing change is for "other than burns" and "under anesthesia (other than local)." (A dressing change without anesthesia would be included in an E/M code.) Per the notes in CPT, a dressing for a burn is found in procedure codes 16010–16030.

Example 2: To code the excision of a vaginal cyst, you would first look under "Excision" (the main term). There is a listing for the subterm "Cyst" beneath "Excision," followed by a list of organs, regions, or structures involved. Note that each subterm is indented under the main term. Additionally, the subterms relating to cyst locations are indented even further under that subterm. This is a common occurrence in the CPT manual. Look for "Vagina" to find the code (57135). Another way to find the code is to look under "Vagina" as the main term and then find the listing for "Cyst Excision" as a subterm beneath it.

Once you decide on the appropriate CPT code(s), the next step is to check for any applicable modifiers. The use of modifiers can greatly enhance your reimbursement and can cut down on claim inquiries from the insurance carrier, but the ability to use modifiers correctly and proficiently will require practice. As discussed earlier, Appendix A of the CPT manual contains all CPT modifiers and many times the section guidelines also contain information regarding the use of modifiers within that section. This is not an optional step. Modifier use is required if there is one that is available for the situation.

Example: A bilateral breast reconstruction requires the modifier −50. Find the code for "breast reconstruction with free flap": 19364. To show the insurance carrier that the procedure was performed on both breasts, attach the −50: 19364-50. (Some insurers will require that you list the code once and then a second time with the modifier: 19364, 19364-50.) The insurance company will often pay the full charge for the first procedure and then pay the second procedure at 50%.

Once all procedures and services have been assigned a CPT code and modifier as needed, carefully enter the 5-digit code(s) and modifiers in block 24d of the CMS-1500 form (Chapter 17). Remember that the primary procedure, often the one that is most labor intensive or is the principal reason for the patient's encounter, is listed first and is often matched with the appropriate diagnosis code, often the primary diagnosis, to demonstrate medical necessity for the insurance carrier. After the principal procedure is listed, enter all other procedures provided to the patient during this date of service and match each with its appropriate diagnosis to verify its medical necessity as well.

Procedure 20-1 found at the end of this chapter outlines the correct steps for locating a CPT code.

CHECKPOINT
LO 20.5

Why must each procedure be attached to a diagnosis code?

LO 20.6 HCPCS

Healthcare Common Procedural Coding System (HCPCS)
A coding system developed by the Centers for Medicare and Medicaid Services that is used in coding services for Medicare (and some other payers') patients.

HCPCS Level II codes
Codes that cover many supplies such as sterile trays, drugs, DME; also referred to as national codes. They also cover services and procedures that may not be found in CPT.

The **Healthcare Common Procedure Coding System,** commonly referred to as **HCPCS,** was developed by the Centers for Medicare and Medicaid Services (CMS) for use in coding services for Medicare patients. Today, in addition to Medicare, some HCPCS codes are also accepted by Medicaid and private insurance programs. To avoid claim denials due to an invalid or unacceptable code, be sure to check with the insurance carrier to see if they accept HCPCS codes and, if so, which ones. The HCPCS (pronounced "hic-picks") coding system has two levels:

1. HCPCS Level I codes are more commonly known as CPT codes.

2. **HCPCS Level II codes,** issued by CMS, are called national codes and cover many supplies, such as sterile trays, drugs, injections, and DME (durable medical equipment). If CPT and HCPCS have identical descriptions, the HCPCS Level I (CPT) code should be used. However, if CPT has a generic description and HCPCS has a more specific description, HCPCS Level II should be used. Level II codes also cover services and procedures not included in the CPT. For instance CPT has one (generic) code to cover the supplies and materials used for in-office procedures (99070) whereas the HCPCS manual lists very specific codes for each item supplied.

The HCPCS codes for Level II have five characters, either numbers, letters, or a combination of both. At times there are also two-character modifiers, either two letters or a letter with a number. These modifiers are different from the CPT modifiers, but may be used with CPT codes as well as with Level II codes. For example, HCPCS modifiers may indicate social worker services or equipment rentals. Appendix 2 of the HCPCS manual gives a complete list of all HCPCS modifiers.

Examples of Level II codes are:

Code Number	Description
A0225-QN	Ambulance service, neonatal transport, base rate, emergency transport, one way, furnished directly by the provider of services

EHR readiness

Creating Customized Superbills

In the paper-based medical office, the superbill lists procedures and diagnoses most commonly used in the practice. If a new procedure is provided or if a patient has a new diagnosis, in order for the physician to relay that information, she must hand write the procedure performed or the diagnosis made in blank spaces left on the preprinted encounter form for this purpose. The staff must then read the handwriting, which sometimes in and of itself is no small feat, and then translate it into the appropriate code(s). The same is true when ICD-9 diagnosis codes change in October and CPT codes change in January. The encounter form (superbill) is no longer current, requiring the staff to cross out incorrect information and insert the corrected information by hand. Alternatively, the practice experiences the yearly expense of disposing of "old forms" and creating new ones with corrected information.

In the electronic medical office, the office administrator will often have the option of creating a customized superbill using the computer software program installed on the desktop computers (Figure 20–5). If a provider begins providing a new service or procedure, the administrator may enter the superbill template and, under the appropriate category heading, add the new procedure description and code which can then be added to any encounter form by the front office personnel or by the physician herself. When codes and/or descriptions change in October and January, this same editing will take place and new encounter forms will be created on site.

figure 20-5

Superbill setup window.

Procedures		Lab		Splint/Cast		Injections		Supplies	
36000	IV Catheter	36415	Venipuncture	29105	Splint Long Arm	90782	Therapeutic Injectio	45673	Surgical Tray
				29125	Splint Short Arm	90471	Immunization		
				29130	Splint Finger	90472	additional Immuniza		
				29505	Splint Long Leg	90788	Inj Antibiotic		
				29515	Splint Short Leg				

E0781	Ambulatory infusion pump
G0001	Routine venipuncture
G0104	Colorectal cancer screening; flexible sigmoidoscopy
Q0091	Screening Papanicolaou (Pap) smear; obtaining, preparing, and conveyance of cervical or vaginal smear to laboratory
V5299	Hearing service, miscellaneous

In medical offices where the HCPCS system is used, regulations issued by CMS are reviewed to determine the correct code and modifier for use on a particular payers' claims. Administrative medical assistants who code with the HCPCS manual, find that the steps for coding with it mimic those of CPT, except that the Alphabetic Index is found in the front of the manual with the alphanumeric index found toward the back of the manual.

The first step is to locate the description of the service, procedure or item in the Alphabetic Index. Once this is located, note the code(s) or code range given and move to that area of the alphanumeric index to verify the description. Choose the code description that exactly matches the service, procedure or item supplied as documented in the medical record. If you are coding medications that were supplied to the patient, you will find it easiest to locate the drug name in the Table of Drugs found in Appendix 1 of HCPCS. This table will list the unit, route of administration, and the appropriate "J" code. Even though only one code is given, do not skip the step of verifying the information in the alphanumeric index.

Once all CPT and HCPCS codes are located and verified, enter them in block 24d of the CMS-1500 form if your office is not computerized. Otherwise, enter the codes in the appropriate area of the office medical billing software so the information may be transmitted to the health insurance carrier electronically. Procedure 20–2 at the end of the chapter outlines the steps for locating a HCPCS code.

**CHECKPOINT
LO 20.6**

What does HCPCS stand for?

LO 20.7 Avoiding Fraud: Coding Compliance

Physicians have the ultimate responsibility for proper documentation and correct coding as well as for compliance with regulations, and many expect their administrative medical assistants to have working knowledge of this as well. Administrative medical assistants help ensure maximum appropriate reimbursement for reported services by submitting correct health-care claims. These claims, as well as the process used to create them, must comply with the rules imposed by federal and state law and with payer requirements.

Code Linkage

As we learned in Chapter 17, clean claims are those where each reported service is connected to a diagnosis that supports the procedure as necessary to investigate or treat the patient's condition. Insurance company representatives analyze this connection between the diagnostic and the procedural information, called code linkage, to evaluate the medical necessity of the reported charges (Refer to Figure 20–4 of superbill with procedure codes and diagnosis codes to prove medical necessity). Correct claims also comply with many other regulations from government agencies.

The possible consequences of inaccurate coding and incorrect billing include:

- Denied claims
- Delays in processing claims and receiving payments
- Reduced payments
- Fines and other sanctions
- Loss of hospital privileges
- Exclusion from payers' programs
- Prison sentences
- Loss of the physician's license to practice medicine

To avoid errors, the codes on health-care claims are checked against the medical documentation. A code review, also known as a coding audit, checks these key points:

- Are the codes appropriate to the patient's profile (age, gender, condition; new or established), and is each coded service billable?
- Is there a clear and correct link between each diagnosis and procedure?
- Have the payer's rules about the diagnosis and the procedure been followed?
- Does the documentation in the patient's medical record support the reported services?
- Do the reported services comply with all regulations?

Insurance Fraud

The majority involved in the delivery of health care are trustworthy persons devoted to patients' welfare. However, some people are not. For example, according to the Department of Health and Human Services (DHHS), in 1 year alone, the federal government recovered more than $1.3 billion in judgments, settlements, and other fees in health-care fraud cases. Fraud is an act of deception used to take advantage of another person or entity (Refer to Chapter 6). For example, it is fraudulent for people to misrepresent their credentials or to forge another person's signature on a check.

Claims fraud occurs when physicians or others falsely represent their services or charges to payers. For example, a provider may bill for services that were not performed (phantom billing), overcharge for services, or fail to provide complete services under a contract. A patient may exaggerate an injury to get a settlement from an insurance company or ask an administrative medical assistant to change the date a service was actually provided so that the service is covered by a health plan policy which is no longer active.

A number of coding and billing practices are fraudulent. Investigators reviewing physicians' billings look for patterns like these:

- Reporting services that were not performed.
  Example: A lab bills Medicare for a general health panel (CPT 80050), but fails to perform one of the tests in the panel.
- Reporting services at a higher level than was carried out.
  Example: After a visit for a flu shot, the provider bills the encounter as an evaluation and management service plus an injection
- Performing and billing for procedures that are not related to the patient's condition and therefore not medically necessary.
  Example: After reading an article about Lyme disease, a patient is worried about having worked in her garden over the summer and requests a Lyme disease diagnostic test. Although no symptoms or signs have been reported, the physician orders and bills for the Lyme disease test stating an exposure had occurred.
- Billing separately for services that are bundled in a single procedure code (unbundling).
  Example: When a physician orders a comprehensive metabolic panel (CPT 80053), the provider bills for the panel as well as for a quantitative glucose test, which is in the panel.
- Reporting the same service twice.

Note that HIPAA calls for penalties for giving remuneration to anyone eligible for benefits under federal health-care programs. The forgiveness or waiver of copayments may violate the policies of some payers; others may permit

ELECTRONIC CLAIMS PROFESSIONAL (ECP)

Duties and Skills

An electronic claims professional (ECP) acts as the link between small- and medium- sized physician practices or health-care facilities and major health insurers such as Medicare. After contracting with a physician practice or health-care facility, the ECP enters patient demographic and insurance billing information into the computer billing software and transmits it to the appropriate health insurance provider. Submitting electronic medical (health) insurance claims to an insurance carrier via an ECP ensures accurate submission resulting in prompt payment by the health insurance carrier.

Educational Requirements

Most ECPs are highly experienced claims professionals who have completed approved medical billing and coding programs and achieved certification in billing or coding or both. They are also knowledgeable in various computer software billing programs as well as the required HIPAA compliant data code and transmission sets to achieve prompt and correct reimbursement for health-care claims. Certification is voluntary through The National Association of Claims Assistance Professionals (NACAP).

Workplace Settings

The costs and technologic "know how" of electronic claims submission has made this valuable tool out-of-reach for many small- to medium-sized physician practices.

The electronic claims professional takes the burden of claim preparation and submission for the practice, allowing the practice to reduce staff training and overhead costs. By far, the biggest bonuses brought to the practice by the ECP include faster claims payment, reduced-error processing, and lower outstanding accounts receivable for the medical practice. The ECP provides the accountability and technological control the small- to medium-sized group practice needs in electronic claims handling.

The Electronic Claims Professional as a Team Member

If your practice uses an ECP, your interactions with him or her may come about in several ways. As an independent contractor, the ECP may come to your office to input information, do so from his or her office, or actually have the administrative medical assistant input the information and the ECP will act as a "scrubber," validating that the correct information is present for claims submission and then sending the electronic claim to the payer. No matter which method is used, it will be up to the physician's staff to make sure that the ECP has correct and verifiable information for claims submission.

For more information, visit the Web site of the following organization, which is available on the Online Learning Center at www.mhhe.com/houseradminmedassist

The Alliance of Claims Assistance Professionals (ACAP)

---

forgiveness or waiver if they are aware of the reasons for the forgiveness or waiver, such as the patient's inability to pay (be sure to have documentation of such inability to avoid charges of discrimination). Routine forgiveness or waiver of copayments or deductibles constitutes fraud when billing federal programs such as Medicare or TRICARE. The physician practice should ensure that its policies on copayments are consistent with applicable law and with the requirements of their agreements with payers.

Compliance Plans

To avoid the risk of fraud, medical offices have a compliance plan to uncover compliance problems and correct them. A compliance plan is a process for finding, correcting, and preventing illegal medical office practices. Its goals are to:

- Prevent fraud and abuse through a formal process to identify, investigate, fix, and prevent repeat violations relating to reimbursement for health-care services provided

- Ensure compliance with applicable federal, state, and local laws, including employment laws and environ-mental laws as well as antifraud laws

- Help defend physicians if they are investigated or prosecuted for fraud by showing the desire to behave compliantly and thus reduce any fines or criminal prosecution

When a compliance plan is in place, it demonstrates to payers such as Medicare that honest, ongoing attempts have been made to find and fix weak areas of compliance with regulations. The development of this written plan is led by a compliance officer and committee with the intention to (1) audit and monitor compliance with government regulations, especially in the area of coding and billing; (2) develop written policies and procedures that are consistent; (3) provide for ongoing staff training and communication; and (4) respond to and correct errors.

Although coding and billing compliance are the plan's major focus, it covers all areas of government regulation of medical practices, such as equal employment opportunity (EEO) regulations (for example, hiring and promotion policies) and OSHA regulations (for example, fire safety and handling of hazardous materials such as bloodborne pathogens). For further information, go to www.oig.hhs.gov/fraud/docs/complianceguidance/thirdparty.pdf.

● ● ●

What is the purpose of a compliance plan?

CHECKPOINT
LO 20.7

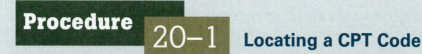

Procedure 20–1   Locating a CPT Code

GOAL   To locate correct CPT codes

MATERIALS   Patient record, superbill or charge slip, CPT manual

METHOD

1. Find the services listed on the superbill (if used) and in the patient's record.
   a. Check the patient's record to see which services were documented. For E/M procedures, note whether the patient is a new or established patient and then look for clues as to the location of the service, extent of history, examination, and medical decision making that were involved.

2. Look up the procedure code(s) in the Alphabetic Index of the CPT manual.
   a. Verify the code number in the numeric index, reading all notes and guidelines for that section.
   b. If a code range is noted, look up the range and choose the correct code from the range given. If the correct description is not found, start the process again. Use the same process if multiple codes are given, looking each one up in the numeric index until the correct code description is found.

3. Determine appropriate modifiers.
   a. Check section guidelines and Appendix A to choose a modifier if needed to explain a situation involving the procedure being coded, such as bilateral procedure, surgical team, or a discontinued procedure.

4. Carefully record the procedure code(s) on the health-care claim or if the office is computerized, enter the codes into the office billing system for placement on an electronic health claim form. Usually the primary procedure, the one that is the primary reason for the encounter or visit, is listed first.

5. Match each procedure with its corresponding diagnosis. The primary procedure is often (but not always) matched with the primary diagnosis.

GOAL   To locate the proper HCPCS code for a service or piece of equipment

MATERIALS   HCPCS manual, patient record, charge slip or superbill

METHOD

1. Locate the service, supplies, and equipment requiring a HCPCS code from the encounter form from the patient's record. If an encounter form is used, verify procedure completion in the medical record.

2. Use the index at the back of the manual to locate the section in which the category of codes is found.

3. Find the code or code range by seeking first the initial letter and then the four-digit number. They are arranged alphabetically and numerically. Make sure you read the description thoroughly and determine the correct code. Do not code from the index.

4. Make sure the code is valid for the type of insurance the patient carries.

5. Enter the correct code(s) on the superbill or encounter form (if necessary) and, if the office uses a computerized billing program, in the patient's computerized record so that it can be used for billing purposes. Otherwise, place the HCPCS code in block 24d of the 1500 claim form for submission to the insurance carrier. Match each HCPCS code with the appropriate diagnosis code to demonstrate medical necessity.

Case Study

PROFESSIONAL READINESS

Cooperation
Appropriately and willingly works with others in the best interest of the work

Julie assists with coding and submitting claims. She will be going on maternity leave shortly and is training Miguel to assist with these responsibilities while she is gone. Miguel usually works in the business area for the laboratory and is familiar with laboratory CPT codes and encounter forms. He likes his friends in the lab housed in the next building and is not sure he wants to take on this new role. Julie senses his reluctance. After working together for a few days, Julie tells Miguel how much she appreciates his willingness to help out while she is away. He confesses that he is not excited about being away from his "lab rats," which he jokingly calls his colleagues but states he will do his best. When Miguel comes into Julie's work station on the first day she is gone, he finds a picture of his "lab rats" sitting on the desk. Fortunately, both Julie and Miguel are team players and know the meaning of cooperation.

Thinking Critically

1. Do you think Julie's coworkers may have been anxious about having Miguel work in their area while she was gone?

2. If CPT and HCPCS codes are not submitted correctly or in a timely fashion, what are the potential consequences?

3. What is the difference between a CPT and an HCPCS code?

practice APPLICATIONS

1. Using Table 20–3, what is the code range for ED services? From the CPT manual, do you need to know whether the patient is a new or existing client in order to assign these codes?

2. Review Figure 20–1. What is the correct code for a complicated removal of a foreign body from subcutaneous tissues?

exam READINESS

1. **[LO20.3]** The ____ codes are considered to be the most important of the CPT codes.
   a. modifier
   b. E/M
   c. add-on
   d. unlisted procedure
   e. surgical

2. **[LO20.3]** For reporting purposes, CPT considers a patient "new" if he or she has not received professional services within the past ____ year(s).
   a. one
   b. two
   c. three
   d. four
   e. five

3. **[LO20.6]** The Healthcare Common Procedure Coding System (HCPCS) was developed for use in coding services for
   a. Blue Cross.
   b. HMOs.
   c. Medicare patients.
   d. Managed care organizations.
   e. Medicaid.

4. **[LO20.1]** All of the following are sections of the CPT manual EXCEPT
   a. anesthesiology.
   b. E/M.
   c. surgery.
   d. pathology and lab.
   e. integumentary.

5. **[LO20.2]** Which of the following CPT conventions indicates the code is new to the current edition?
   a. Triangle
   b. Plus sign
   c. Lightning bolt
   d. Red dot
   e. Bull's-eye

6. **[LO20.2]** Which of the following CPT conventions indicates the code description is revised?
   a. Blue triangle
   b. Plus sign
   c. Lightning bolt
   d. Red dot
   e. Bull's-eye

7. **[LO20.4]** Which of the following are components of a surgical package?
   a. Preoperative work-up
   b. Surgery itself
   c. Usual postoperative follow-up
   d. All of the above
   e. b and c only

8. **[LO20.5]** Which of the following is the correct code for vaginal hysterectomy (250 g) including removal of fallopian tubes and ovaries with appendectomy?
   a. 58290
   b. 58290, 44950
   c. 58260, 44955
   d. 58262, 44950
   e. 58262, 44955

9. **[LO20.6]** What is the correct HCPCS code for a walker with wheels?
   a. E0143
   b. E0141
   c. E0149
   d. E0148
   e. E0144

10. **[LO20.1]** Which modifier signifies that a procedure was "required"?
    a. 22
    b. 25
    c. 32
    d. 57
    e. 59

learning outcome

LO 20.1 The sections for the CPT manual are Evaluation and Management, Anesthesiology, Surgery, Radiology, Pathology and Laboratory, and Medicine with code ranges from 00100-99602.

LO 20.2 The CPT manual general guidelines include the following symbols, each of which represents important information about the code being described: blue triangle, red dot, # sign, triangles facing each other, circle with a diagonal through it, lightning bolt, bull's-eye, as well as add-on codes and modifiers. Always begin coding by looking up the description in the Alphabetic Index and verifying in the Tabular (numeric) List. Carefully read all guidelines and information surrounding the codes.

LO 20.3 The E/M code types include: office and other outpatient services, hospital observation, hospital inpatient, consultations, ED services, critical care, nursing facility, domiciliary and rest home services, domiciliary and assisted-living services, home care plan oversight, home services, prolonged services, case management, care plan oversight, preventative medicine, non-face-to-face physician services, special E/M, newborn care, neonatal ICU and critical care services, and other E/M services.

LO 20.4 Surgical Coding sections include: integumentary, musculoskeletal, respiratory, cardiovascular, digestive, urinary, male and female genital systems, endocrine, nervous, eye and ear, radiology, pathology and lab, and medicine.

LO 20.5 Student answers will vary depending upon the information (encounter forms or mock medical records) they are given to practice coding with the CPT manual. They should be able to select an accurate code for simple, straightforward coding scenarios.

LO 20.6 Student answers will vary depending upon the information (encounter forms or mock medical records) they are given to practice coding with the HCPCS manual. They should be able to select an accurate code for simple, straightforward coding scenarios.

LO 20.7 Code linkage demonstrates the medical necessity of services provided to the patient by accurately linking each procedure code to its appropriate diagnosis. All procedures, services, and diagnoses must be documented in the patient's medical record to be used on any health insurance claim form.

medical assisting COMPETENCIES

CAAHEP

VIII. C (1) Describe how to use the most current procedural coding system

VIII. C (2) Define upcoding and why it should be avoided

VIII. C (4) Describe how to use the most current HCPCS coding

VIII. P (1) Perform procedural coding

VIII. A (1) Work with the physician to achieve the maximum reimbursement

ABHES

8. Medical Office Business Procedures Management

   t. Perform diagnostic and procedural coding

21 | Financial Practices

Learning Outcomes

After completing Chapter 21, you will be able to:

21.1 Explain the importance of accuracy when updating bookkeeping records and outline the procedures to be used to maintain accurate records.

21.2 Describe the differences among the accounting systems.

21.3 Describe the proper way to accept, endorse, and deposit checks coming into a medical practice and explain the process of reconciling a bank statement.

21.4 List the three main types of accounts payable in the medical practice.

21.5 Explain the process of classifying themes in a disbursements journal and outline the steps in recording a payment (disbursement) in the journal.

21.6 Explain how to calculate an employee's gross earnings, deductions, and net earnings for a pay period.

21.7 List the tax forms commonly used in the medical office and explain the purpose of the office tax liability account.

Key Terms

ABA number	money order
bookkeeping	negotiable
cash flow statement	net earnings
cashier's check	patient ledger card
certified check	pay schedule
charge	payee
check	payer
counter check	pegboard system
dependent	power of attorney
endorse	quarterly return
Federal Insurance	reconciliation
Contributions Act	State Unemployment
(FICA)	Tax Act (SUTA)
Federal Unemployment	tax liability account
Tax Act (FUTA)	third-party check
gross earnings	tracking
journalizing	traveler's check
limited check	voucher check

Preparation for Certification

RMA (AMT) Exam
- Financial calculations and accounting procedures
- Employee payroll
- Office banking procedures
- Fundamental medical office accounting procedures

CMAS (AMT) Exam
- Fundamental financial management
- Patient accounts
- Payroll

CMA (AAMA) Exam
- Banking procedures (processing accounts receivable, preparing bank deposit)
- Accounts payable
- Bookkeeping principles

Introduction ● ● ●

As an administrative medical assistant, your responsibilities will often include financial practices for the office such as accounting, bookkeeping, and payroll. These responsibilities may include many duties typically handled by an office manager. This chapter describes the key areas of accounting and bookkeeping you may encounter.

LO 21.1 The Business Side of a Medical Practice

Traditionally, a medical practice is thought of as the place where services are provided to and for patients. For a medical practice to be successful, it must also be recognized as a business. In order to be successful, any business, including a medical practice, must be profitable, that is, its income must exceed its expenses. To determine if it is profitable, an office must accurately record all the daily financial transactions occurring within the practice. As an administrative medical assistant you may be asked to do **bookkeeping,** or the systematic recording of business transactions. These records must be accurate and up-to-date, as they will often be reviewed and used in reports by and for the practice manager and office accountants to track the financial health of the practice.

Bookkeeping and banking are two key administrative responsibilities of the administrative medical assistant. To perform these duties you must first understand basic accounting principles, systems, and applicable financial terms and develop financial management skills.

Importance of Accuracy

Because bookkeeping records form a chain of information, you must strive for 100% accuracy. Any undetected errors in a link will be carried throughout all the other links in the chain. Examples of undetected errors can include billing a patient twice for the same visit, omitting bank deposits, or making improper payments to suppliers. These actions can result in the eventual loss of patients who will seek a more efficient and professional-appearing office for their health-care needs, which causes a financial loss for the practice.

Establishing Procedures

A consistent procedure not only helps you remember important aspects of bookkeeping and banking but also helps ensure that your books are accurate. Here are some general suggestions for maintaining accuracy in bookkeeping and banking procedures for a medical practice.

- Be organized. Maintain the practice's bookkeeping and banking procedures in a logical and organized way.
- Be consistent. Always handle the same type of transactions in exactly the same way. For example, endorse all checks with the same information, regardless of who wrote them or when you will be depositing them.
- Use markers. Using check marks as you complete a task will help you avoid losing your place and ensure recording of all entries, thereby maintaining accuracy. For example, place a red check mark on each check stub as you reconcile the bank statement.
- Write clearly. Always use the same type and color pen. If more than one person performs bookkeeping and banking tasks, each person should initial her part of the procedure to identify her work. It is recommended that as few people as possible perform these tasks, however. You may use pencil for trial balances and worksheets, but you should use pen for bookkeeping entries.

bookkeeping
The systematic recording of business transactions.

- Check your work. Frequent inspections of your work will make errors easier to find and to correct. To correct errors, draw a straight line through the incorrect figure, and write the correct figure above it. Do not erase errors or delete them with correction fluid or tape. As with medical records, the office financial records are legal documents and every entry, even corrected ones, need to be legible at all times.

- Keep all columns of figures straight, so that decimal points align correctly.

Using set procedures will help you organize your work, help ensure accuracy, and make you a more valuable member of the practice staff.

● ● ●

How can inaccurate bookkeeping affect the medical practice financially?

CHECKPOINT
LO 21.1

LO 21.2 Patient Accounting Methods

Patient accounting methods within a medical practice may be computerized or manual. Computerized patient accounting is the most commonly used type of system. Three types of manual accounting systems may be used by medical practices that are not computerized: single-entry, double-entry, and **pegboard system** (also known as the write-it-once system). All accounting systems record income, **charges** (money owed to the practice), disbursements (money paid out by the practice), and other financial information. The choice of system is based on the size and complexity of the practice.

Electronic Bookkeeping

Physicians or office managers who choose to set up the practice's bookkeeping system on the computer enjoy several important benefits over traditional bookkeeping methods. With computerized bookkeeping:

- you save time.
- the computer performs repetitive tasks.
- the computer automatically performs mathematical calculations within the software.
- built-in tax tables are available that calculate tax liabilities for you.

Many bookkeeping software programs or practice management software programs are available on the market and perform the same tasks performed manually. Understanding these tasks is an essential part of managing books on a computer as well as with a manual system. The practice in which you work may already have a computerized bookkeeping program in place, which you should learn. It is also a good idea to stay current by reading computer software magazines. You may learn about a new software program you might recommend to the physician or office manager, or you may read about a new or more efficient way to use the practice's current software program.

Bookkeeping Systems

Traditionally there were two types of accounting systems: single-entry and double-entry. In the single-entry system, a transaction is listed "once" in the patient ledger, the daily log, and the checkbook. Although simple to use, this system is not self-balancing and errors may easily go undetected. In the double-entry system, all entries are listed twice, based on the accounting formula of Assets = Capital + Liabilities. Assets are anything owned by the company. Capital is the portion of the asset which is paid for and liabilities are monies owed by the practice. To better understand this process, consider the new ECG

pegboard system
A bookkeeping system that uses a lightweight board with pegs on which forms can be stacked, allowing each transaction to be entered and recorded on four different bookkeeping forms at once; also called the write-it-once system.

charge
A debit to an account.

machine purchased by the practice in the example shown below. The cost of the machine is $12,000 and the office made a downpayment of $5000.

Example:

$12,000 (Asset) = $5000 (capital) & $7000 (liability)

Every month, when a payment is made, the asset amount will remain the same, but the capital amount will increase and liability amount will decrease, but both sides of the equation will continue to balance.

Write-It-Once System Most medical offices use the **pegboard** (or "write-it-once") **system,** which contains a formula to check your work. The write-it-once system used the same bookkeeping forms as the single- and double-entry systems, but the day sheet daily log has prepunched holes on the right or left side of the log. There are similar holes in the shingled (layered) charge sheets that are placed in designated areas on top of the day sheet which has been placed on the pegboard. Each charge sheet is made with a no-carbon-required (NCR) paper, so when the patient ledger card is placed between the day sheet and charge sheet and an entry is made, it appears on all three documents at the same time—hence the term "write-it-once."

Each of these systems use similar forms and records to maintain the bookkeeping records. Each form is discussed in further detail below.

Bookkeeping Forms and Records

Daily Log The daily log is also known as a general ledger, day sheet, or daily journal depending on the practice. Regardless of the name used, it is a chronological list of the charges to patients, any payments made on the account, and any adjustments on the account (such as the difference between the charge billed to the insurance carrier and the "allowed charge" that the payment is based on). See Figure 21–1. In the daily log, you record the name of each patient

pegboard system

A bookkeeping system that uses a lightweight board with pegs on which forms can be stacked, allowing each transaction to be entered and recorded on four different bookkeeping forms at once; also called the write-it-once system.

figure 21–1

A daily log is used to record daily activity from the office such as charges, payments, and adjustments.

Dr. _____		Date _____				
Hour	**Patient**	**Service Provided**	**Charge**	**Payment**	**Adj**	**Balance**
1						
2						
3						
4						
5						
6						
7						
8						
9						
10						
11						
12						
13						
14						
15						
16						
				Totals		

seen that day. Across from the name, you record the service provided (using the proper codes), the fee charged, and the payment received (if any). This process is called **journalizing.** You then post (copy) the charges, adjustments, and payments from the daily log to patient ledger cards. Using a daily or monthly cash control sheet, you record checks and cash received as well as deposits made each day.

There are still a few physicians in individual practices who keep a daily log at their desks for entering information after they see each patient. In such cases, it may be helpful to write the name of each scheduled patient in the log to provide an appointment list. You may be responsible for this task.

In most offices, the administrative medical assistants maintain the daily log. You can obtain the information needed to post transactions from the charge slip (encounter form or superbill). (Note: A charge slip is the original record of all of the doctor's charges and services performed on that day. Some practices also use it as a receipt and an appointment reminder, hence the term superbill. Typically, a charge slip/receipt includes a duplicate [and sometimes a triplicate] copy underneath to use for bookkeeping purposes. Remember, you need to track charges *and* receipts for payment, regardless of whether the practice uses separate charge slips and receipts or a combination.) There may also be records of outside visits, such as to nursing homes or hospital emergency departments so additional copies of charge slips may be sent with the physician for his use when visiting these outside facilities as well.

Be sure to record any night calls or other unscheduled visits in the daily log. Simply check with the physician each morning to determine if a charge slip needs to be generated to record the proper fees. If the physician has not noted the charge amount on a charge slip/receipt or record of outside visits, remember that you may have to apply the appropriate fees according to the agreed upon fee schedule for your office.

Other payments may come into the office by mail from both insurance companies and patients. These payments must also be recorded in the daily log for proper tracking of accounts receivable. When payment is sent from an insurance company, it is usually in the form of a check (or electronic payment) and will have an explanation of benefits (EOB) that will display the amount paid on each patient's behalf. You must post the amount indicated to each individual patient account as well as record any adjustment that may be required per the contract the practice may have with the insurance company.

If extra columns are available, you can record additional financial information in the daily log. For example, in addition to showing the total amount charged to the patient, you can show a breakdown of that total into the amounts generated by different physicians in a group practice or by different functions of the office, such as laboratory or x-ray.

At the end of each day, total the charges and receipts in the daily log, and post these totals to the monthly summary of charges and receipts. To double-check your totals, perform the following as shown in Procedure 21–1 found at the end of this chapter:

- Ensure that the day's total cash and check receipts are the same as the day's total bank deposit.
- Ensure that the sum of the day's charges for each type of service is the same as the total of the day's charges.

Patient Ledger Cards   Another bookkeeping task is preparing a patient ledger card for each patient. The **patient ledger card** includes the patient's name, address, home and work telephone numbers, the name of the guarantor (the one who is responsible for payment of the charges if different from the patient), health insurance information, Social Security number, employer's name, and any special billing instructions. Figure 21–2 shows an example of a patient ledger card.

journalizing
Recording in the daily journal services provided, the fee charged, and any payment received.

patient ledger card
Individual patient financial record containing patient's name, address, telephone numbers, guarantor name, insurance information, and any special billing instructions.

figure 21-2

Patient ledger cards are used to show how much each patient owes.

TOTAL CARE CLINIC, PC
342 East Park Blvd
Funton, XY 12345-6789

Patient's Name   Jonathan Jackson

Home Phone   (612) 555-9921   **Work Phone** (612) 555-1000

Social Security No.   111-21-4114

Employer   Ashton School District

Insurance   National Insurance Co.

Policy #   123-4-56-788

Person Responsible for Charges (if Different from Patient)

JONATHAN JACKSON
123 Fourth Avenue
Funton, XY 12345-6789

Date	Reference	Description	Charge	Credits		Current Balance
				Payments	Adj.	
		Balance Forward ———→				$28 00
4/19/-	J128	OV, Stress test	$125 00	$20 00		$133 00
5/23/-	J236	Insurance payment		$92 00		$41 00

Please Pay Last Amount in This Column ▲

OV—Office Visit   C—Consultation   EX—Examination
X—X-ray   NC—No Charge   INS—Insurance
ROA—Received on Account   MA—Missed Appointment

You will use the patient ledger card to record charges incurred by the patient, payments received, adjustments made, and the resulting balance owed to the doctor as shown in Procedure 21–1. Because these cards document the financial transactions of the individual patient account, they are sometimes called *account cards*. In some practices, they are photocopied for use as monthly statements.

The information for the patient ledger cards comes from the daily log, superbill, or charge slip. It is best to complete all the cards at the end of each business day. If this is not possible, you may complete them as time permits during the next business day. To prevent double or omitted postings, put a small check mark next to each entry in the daily log after you post it to the proper ledger card (s). Take great care when posting, because errors posted on the patient's ledger card will be reflected on the patient billing statements. To ensure accuracy, add up the total charges and receipts from the ledger cards, and make sure the information matches the total charges and receipts in that day's daily log.

Accounts Receivable Every day, you must also update the accounts receivable record, which shows the total owed to the practice (the amount able to be received but not yet received). Total up the items on the accounts receivable record, and then total up the outstanding balances on the patient ledger cards. The two numbers should match. If they do not, recheck your work to find the cause of the discrepancy.

Accounts Payable Accounts payable are the amounts the practice owes to vendors (the amount able to be paid but not yet paid). If your responsibilities include accounts payable, keep careful records of equipment and supplies ordered, and compare orders received against the invoices. In the checkbook register, keep detailed and accurate records of accounts paid.

Record of Office Disbursements The record of office disbursements is a list of the amounts paid for such items as medical supplies, office rent, office utilities, employee wages, postage, and equipment over a certain period of time. It shows the **payee** (the person who will receive the payment), the date, the check number, the amount paid, and the type of expense. Figure 21–3 is an example of a disbursement record.

payee
The person to whom the check is written.

A checkbook register may be used to record office disbursements. As an alternative, a disbursement journal or the bottom section of the daily log may be used to record office disbursements. For income tax purposes, this record should include only office expenses. The doctor's personal expenses should not be listed here.

Summary of Charges, Receipts, and Disbursements Charges, receipts, and disbursements are usually summarized at the end of each month, quarter, or year depending on your office policies and procedures (Figure 21–4). The summary is used to compare the income and expenses of the current period with the income and expenses from any previous period.

By analyzing summaries, a physician (or practice) can see which functions of the practice are profitable, the total amount charged for services, the payments received for services, the total cost of running the office, and a breakdown of expenses into various categories. Based on this information, the practice can make vital business decisions. For example, after analyzing monthly summaries, it may decide to budget expenses differently, collect payments more promptly, cut unprofitable services, or expand profitable services.

Although an accountant may prepare these reports, an experienced administrative medical assistant can prepare them. If you are asked to prepare them, follow these guidelines.

figure 21-3

A record of office disbursements lists the amounts paid over a certain period of time.

Record of Office Disbursements
April 2012

DATE	PAYEE	CK. NO.	TOTAL AMOUNT	RENT	UTILITIES	POSTAGE	LAB./X-RAY	MEDICAL SUPPLIES	OFFICE SUPPLIES	WAGES	INSURANCE	TAXES	TRAVEL	MISC.
01	Philips' Med. Suppl.	1778	125.00					125.00						
01	Postage	1779	16.85			16.85								
02	Medi Path	1780	32.50				32.50							
02	Quik Service Co.	1781	82.40						82.40					
02	Philips' Med. Suppl.	1782	92.00					92.00						
02	Jean Medina	1783	77.06							77.06				
05	State Dept. of Rev.	1784	189.16									189.16		
06	General Insurance	1785	165.92								165.92			
07	Postage	(Cash)	5.19			5.19								
07	Micah Smith	(Cash)	15.00										15.00	
08	IRS	1786	419.41									419.41		
12	Quik Service Co.	1787	124.00						124.00					
13	City Laundry	1788	75.00											75.00
13	National Insurance	1789	189.00								189.00			
14	Broyer Assoc.	1790	1 500.00	1 500.00										
14	Postage	(Cash)	12.11			12.11								
15	City Gas Co.	1791	125.00		125.00									
19	Jean Medina	1792	85.92							85.92				
19	Postage	(Cash)	8.95			8.95								
21	Philips' Med. Suppl.	1793	85.00					85.00						
23	Medi Path	1794	67.90				67.90							
24	Micah Smith	(Cash)	10.00										10.00	
24	Elena Paxson	1795	126.00							126.00				
27	Postage	1796	17.32			17.32								
28	Johnson Assoc.	1797	123.45				123.45							
	Total		3770.14	1500.00	125.00	60.42	223.85	302.00	206.40	288.98	354.92	608.57	25.00	75.00

figure 21-4

Creating a summary of charges, receipts, and disbursements is a regular bookkeeping task, performed monthly, quarterly, or based on office policies and procedures.

Quarterly Summary of Charges, Receipts, and Disbursements, 2012

	MONTH	1 CHARGES	2 RECEIPTS	3 DISBURSE-MENTS	4 WAGES	5 RENT & UTILITIES	6 OFFICE EXPENSES	7 GENERAL MEDICAL	8 X-RAY/ LAB.	9 TAXES	10 PERSONAL	11 MISC.
1	Jan.	15400.00	14800.00	6218.14	3349.50	1625.00	129.86	93.45	241.86	589.02	100.00	89.45
2	Feb.	18255.00	18950.00	7050.40	3872.80	1683.08	235.00	118.72	266.00	611.20	186.60	77.00
3	Mar.	13850.00	13250.00	6530.14	3666.10	1702.85	43.85	243.11	187.02	577.00	88.11	22.10
4												
5	Subtotal	47505.00	47000.00	19798.68	10888.40	5010.93	408.71	455.28	694.88	1777.22	374.71	188.55
6												
7	Apr.											
8	May											
9	June											
10												
11	Subtotal											
12												
13	July											
14	Aug.											
15	Sept.											
16												
17	Subtotal											
18												
19	Oct.											
20	Nov.											
21	Dec.											
22												
23	Subtotal											
24												
25	Grand Total											
26												
27												
28												
29												
30												
31												
32												
33												
34												
35												
36												

Types of Disbursements

- Every business day, post the total charges and receipts from the daily log to the appropriate line and column of the monthly summary.
- Every business day, also post the disbursements from the record of office disbursements to the appropriate lines and columns of the monthly summary.
- At the end of the month, total the columns on the monthly summary.
- At the end of each quarter, post the charges, receipts, and disbursements for each of the previous 3 months to the quarterly summary. Then, total each column.
- At the end of the year, post the charges, receipts, and disbursements for each of the previous 12 months (or 4 quarters) to the annual summary. Then, total each column.

Remember that the total charges and total receipts in any summary should be almost the same. They may not be identical because some bills may not have been fully collected. Procedure 21–1 at the end of this chapter offers a plan for setting up a medical practice accounting system.

In-Office Patient Transactions

Many transactions take place within the office on a daily basis. Some examples include patients with appointments incurring charges and making payment, payments from patients and insurance carriers requiring payment posting and adjustments, and even the occasional "bounced check." In this section we will look at these transactions in more detail.

Starting the Business Day   Place a daily log sheet on the pegboard at the beginning of each day. Then, place the stack of charge slips/receipts on the pegs, aligning the top line of the first charge slip/receipt with the daily log top line. Because the charge slips/receipts are layered one over the other from top to bottom, alignment of the first will align all others. The charge slips/receipts are prenumbered. This numbering promotes good cash control and theoretically prevents embezzlement. Figure 21–5 shows the set up for the pegboard system.

figure 21–5

A correctly aligned ledger card and charge slip using the pegboard system.

Upon Patient Arrival As each patient comes into the office, place the patient's ledger card under the next available charge slip/receipt. Be sure to align the card's first blank line with the carbon strip on the charge slip/receipt. Write the date, the patient's name, and the patient's previous balance on the charge slip section. The information will automatically be recorded in the daily log and on the patient ledger card.

Attaching the Charge Slip/Receipt to the Patient Chart Next, remove the charge slip/receipt and attach it to the patient chart so it is ready for the doctor to check off both the services provided and the applicable diagnoses for the day's visit. After examining the patient, the doctor fills in the appropriate charges and diagnoses on the charge slip, indicates when the next appointment is needed, and gives the charge slip/receipt to the patient to return to the front desk on the way out.

Before the Patient Leaves The patient returns the completed charge slip/receipt, and you again place the ledger card between the charge slip/receipt and the daily log, checking to ensure that you align it properly. On the charge slip/receipt, write the charge slip/receipt number, date, procedure (or code), charges, payments, new balance, and the date and time of the next appointment (if any). As you write this information, it should be automatically transferred onto the ledger card and daily log. Finally, tear off the receipt, and give it to the patient. You can now return the patient ledger card to the file.

Payments After the Patient Visit If you receive payments sometime after the patient visit, either by mail or in person, record them on the patient ledger card and day sheet as you normally would. Record charges for doctor visits to hospitalized patients or other out-of-office visits in the same way. If required, you can use the pegboard system to record bank deposits and petty cash disbursements in the daily log, but you will need the appropriate disbursement journal and overlapping forms.

Returned Checks If a patient's check does not clear due to nonsufficient funds (NSF), you must adjust the account accordingly. NSF payments are first deducted from the office checking account. The patient's account is then updated with a negative payment (noted in parentheses in the payment column) for the amount of the check, adding that amount back to the patient balance. An office fee may also be charged for the inconvenience of dealing with the NSF check. Any fees your office charges for NSF must be clearly stated and in plain view for patients to see. In addition, if the bank imposes a fee on the office, these bank fees should also be passed to the patient to recoup the loss for the practice, and marked on the patient's ledger. Depending on office policy, the patient may now be seen on a *cash only* basis by the practice. Procedure 21–2 at the end of this chapter explains the procedure for posting an NSF payment.

Refunding an Overpayment Periodically, the insurance payments and patient payments exceed the allowed charges. This is called an overpayment. Sometimes this happens when patients feel they have not met their annual deductible, pay their balance, and then the insurance carrier also makes a payment on the patient's behalf. After posting the payments, the account balance will be a negative number, which is called a *credit balance*. When this happens, the medical office owes the patient money. In some medical offices, if this amount is small they leave it in place so that the next scheduled visit's new charges will be applied against this amount. Procedure 21–3 found at the end of this chapter outlines the procedure for processing a credit balance.

Sometimes, however, the administrative medical assistant will need to refund the overpayment amount to the patient. This refunded amount is notated

Working with the Health-Care Team

CLEARINGHOUSE CLAIMS REPRESENTATIVE

Duties and Skills

The clearinghouse claims representative acts as a "scrubber" to ensure clean claims, which allows prompt and correct payment of medical claims once they are received by the insurance carrier. Some of the duties of the claims representative include verifying patient coverage, investigating covered services, acting as a customer service representative for the medical offices represented by the clearinghouse, and submitting claims to the correct carriers via electronic claims processing while adhering to individual payer requirements.

Educational Requirements

High school diploma or equivalent with subsequent completion of a medical billing and coding program or equivalent work experience related to billing and coding; including basic computer software applications such as Word, Excel, and Access; understanding of MCOs, ICD-9, CPT, and HCPCS coding; and excellent understanding of both paper (CMS 1500 and UB04) claim requirements as well as electronic 837I and 837P requirements. Updated knowledge on procedures must be maintained through seminars, CEU programs, and in-facility training programs.

Workplace Setting

Common workplace settings for clearinghouse representatives include medical billing clearinghouses, large medical billing departments, and private billing companies.

The Clearinghouse Representative as a Team Member

Unless your office employs an in-house "scrubber," chances are most of your interactions with the clearinghouse representative will be either on the phone or via e-mail and WebEx sessions as the two of you problem-solve claim issues and medical insurance carriers' edits and requirements for clean claims. Clearinghouse representatives can be a great source of information regarding what the office can do to ensure timely, clean claims so in turn your payments will be timely and correct in reimbursement amount.

For more information, visit the Web sites of the following organizations, which are available on the Online Learning Center at www.mhhe.com/houseradminmedassist

Medicaljobs.com

Medical Group Management Association

---

in the patient's account, bringing the balance to zero. When this happens, the administrative medical assistant generates a letter explaining how the overpayment occurred with the check for the refund amount. Procedure 21–4 outlines the steps for processing refunds to patients and is found at the end of this chapter.

End of the Day   At the end of each day, total and check the calculations in all columns. If you find an error, correct it immediately by drawing a line through it and making a new entry on the next available writing line. Remember to make the correction on the patient ledger card also and to issue a new receipt to the patient. To balance a pegboard system or patient ledger card, after adding the figures in each column, use the following formula for the column totals:

Previous balance + Today's charges − (Payments + Adjustments)
    = New accounts receivable total

CHECKPOINT
LO 21.2

How does understanding the concepts of the write-it-once (pegboard) system assist with understanding a computerized bookkeeping system?

LO 21.3 Banking for the Medical Office

Your administrative responsibilities may also include handling the banking for the practice. Because a practice may use traditional (manual) or electronic (computerized) banking methods, you should be familiar with both. Regardless of

which method you use, remember to keep all banking materials secure because they represent the finances of the practice. For example, to prevent theft of checks, always put the checkbook in a securely locked place when it is not in use. Also, file deposit receipts promptly. If they are lost, you have no proof that a deposit was made. Lack of proof could cost the practice thousands of dollars. Because you will be responsible for office funds, it is important that protocols are in place and followed regarding to whom within the practice you also report suspected lost or stolen funds.

Banking Tasks

Banking tasks for the medical practice include:

- Writing checks
- Accepting checks
- Endorsing checks
- Making deposits
- Reconciling bank statements
  - Record keeping of accounts
  - Balancing accounts

To perform these tasks properly, you must be familiar with several terms and concepts related to banking.

Checks A **check** is a bank draft or order for payment (Figure 21–6). The person who writes the check is called the **payer.** By writing a check, the payer directs the bank to pay a sum of money on demand to the payee. In order to be considered **negotiable** (legally transferable from one person to another), a check must:

- Be written and signed by the payer or maker
- Include the amount of money to be paid, considered a promise to pay a specified sum
- Be made payable to the payee or bearer
- Be made payable on demand or on a specific date
- Include the name of the bank that is directed to make payment

Types of Checks and Other Negotiable Papers You may receive other negotiable paper in addition to standard personal and business checks.

- **Cashier's check**—a check issued from the bank's account and signed by a bank representative. It is usually purchased by individuals who do not have checking accounts or for use in purchases where large sums are required, such as some car or house down payments.
- **Certified check**—a payer's check written and signed by the payer and stamped "CERTIFIED" by the bank. This stamp means the bank has already drawn the money from the payer's account and set it aside to guarantee that the check will be paid when submitted. Many banks no longer use certified checks, instead issuing a cashier's check from the bank.
- **Voucher check**—a business check with a perforated stub attached for record keeping. Voucher checks come in various styles and usually are in a 3-ring binder.
- **Limited check**—a check valid for only 30–90 days and often used for payroll. Some accounts will also limit the amount of checks written as well as the valid time frames.

check
A bank draft or order for payment.

payer
The person who writes the check.

negotiable
Legally transferable from one person to another.

cashier's check
A check issued from the bank's account and signed by a bank representative. Funds are withdrawn from the requester's account at the time the check is written.

certified check
A personal check written and signed by the payer and stamped "CERTIFIED" by the bank, guaranteeing funds will be available.

voucher check
Business checks with perforated stubs attached for record keeping.

limited check
Checks that are stamped as being negotiable only for specific amounts or limited time frames.

- **Counter check**—a special bank-issued check that allows the depositor to withdraw funds from his account only. It states "PAY TO THE ORDER OF MYSELF ONLY." This may be used when the physician wants to draw off of the account in absence of his or her checkbook.

- **Traveler's check**—a check preprinted in established denominations of $10, $20, $50, and $100. These checks must be signed at the location where they were purchased. When using a traveler's check, it must be signed in the presence of the payee and the signatures must match.

- **Money order**—another kind of guaranteed payment. It must be purchased in cash and includes a small fee to the vendor.

Check Codes   The face (front) of every check contains two important items: the American Banking Association (ABA) number and the magnetic ink character recognition (MICR) code. The **ABA number** appears as a fraction, such as 60–117/310, on the upper edge of all printed checks. It identifies the geographic area and specific bank on which the check is drawn.

Found at the bottom of a check, the MICR code consists of numbers and characters printed in magnetic ink, which can be read by MICR equipment at the bank. This code enables checks to be read, sorted, and recorded by computer.

Types of Checking Accounts   A physician is likely to have three different types of checking accounts: a personal account, a business account for office expenses, and an interest-earning account. The interest-earning account will be used for paying special expenses, such as property taxes and insurance premiums. Most of your work will be with the business checking account. You may sometimes, however, make payments from, or transfer money to, the interest-earning account, as directed.

Parts of a Check   Checks that you may accept in your facility contain many important parts that should be inspected upon receipt to ensure prompt payment is received. They are encoded with Magnetic ink character recognition (MICR) codes so they are able to be read, sorted, and recorded by computers and MICR equipment at the banks. See Figure 21–6 for a labeled example.

- **Payer**—account holder's legal name that is usually preprinted with address and possibly other information such as phone numbers and e-mail addresses.

- **Date line**—date that is written in by the payer stating that the funds are available as of this date.

- **Check number**—indicates the number in a series.

- **ABA number**—preprinted numbers appearing as a fraction such as 55-12/345 identifying the geographic area and specific bank on which the check is drawn.

- **Payee**—the name written on the pay to the order of line to whom the payer wishes the funds to be paid.

- **Amount box**—box in which the numerical amount of check should be entered.

- **Amount line**—line where the dollar amount of the check is written out in words and the cents are usually put into a fraction over one hundred followed by a line to reduce the ability for someone to write in information. If there is a discrepancy between the amount box and line, the amount line is what is used to pay out the funds.

- **Bank information**—information that identifies the processing facility or the city and state of the account holder's branch bank that the funds are coming from and may list the logo, address, e-mail, or any other special branch information.

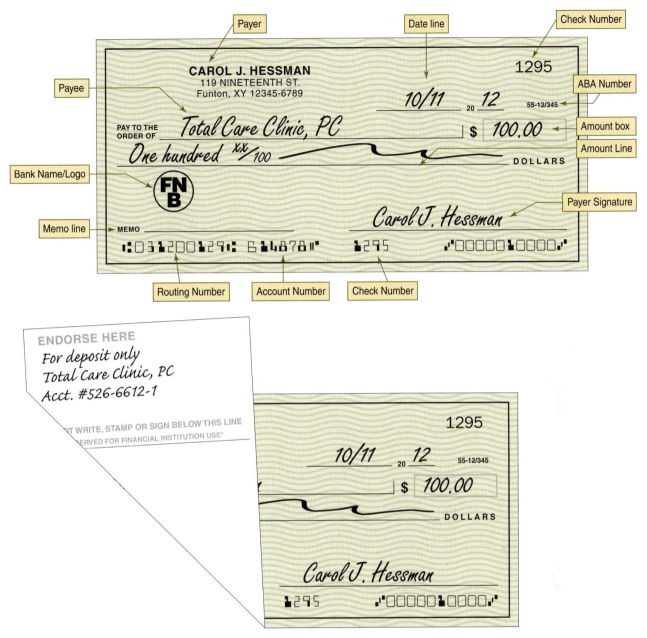

- **Memo line**—line that can be left blank but should be filled in to ensure the payment is credited to the correct account. This can be done by entering any account information, which is extremely helpful when the payer is someone other than the patient such as the spouse or parent.
- **Payer signature line**—line where the payer MUST sign the check in order for the funds to be legally drawn.
- **Routing number**—9-digit MICR numbers that route the check back to the issuing bank and should match the bank name and ABA fraction code number.
- **Account number**—part of the MICR numbers that indicate the payer's account within the bank.
- **Check number**—part of the MICR numbers that identify and refer back to the check number at the top right of the check.
- **MICR recording area**—space for bank use only to record the branch and amount of the check.

figure 21–6

Parts of a check with an example of a restrictive endorsement.

Accepting Checks Before accepting any check, review it carefully. First be sure the check has the correct date, amount, and signature and that no corrections have been made. Refer once more to Figure 21–6 which shows a correctly written and endorsed check. Do not accept a **third-party check** (one made out to the patient rather than to the practice) unless it is from a health insurance company. Also, do not accept a check marked "Payment in Full" unless it actually does pay the complete outstanding balance. You may accept a check signed by someone other than the payer if the person who signed the check has power of attorney. **Power of attorney** gives a person the legal right to handle financial matters for another person who is unable to do so. Frequently power of attorney is granted to a patient's spouse, son, or daughter.

Be sure to follow the policy of your practice when accepting a check. For example, if a patient is new or unfamiliar, office policy may require you to request patient identification and to compare the signature on the identification with the signature on the check. Policy may also require that you not accept a check for more than the amount due.

Endorsing Checks Once a check has been presented for payment and received by the office, it should be inspected and then immediately endorsed. The best type of endorsement to use is a restrictive endorsement, because it prevents the check from being cashed if it is lost or stolen because the only way the check can be redeemed is by deposit into the specified account.

Be sure to endorse the check in ink, using a pen or rubber stamp. Place the endorsement in the 1.5-inch area indicated on the back of the check. Most personal and business checks have a number of lines or a shaded area preprinted on the checks for this purpose. (Refer to Figure 21–6.) Leave the rest of the back of the check blank for the use of the bank.

Completing the Deposit Slip After endorsing the check, post the payment to the patient ledger card, and to the daily log or day sheet. Then put the check with others to be deposited. Even if your office does not make daily deposits, it is a good idea to have a deposit slip started and add each check to the deposit slip as you receive it, as shown in Figure 21–7. In this way, you will have a running list of checks to be deposited and can compare this to the day sheet at any time to verify the amount of the payments received by the office. The account number is printed on deposit slips in MICR numbers that match those on the checks. As mentioned, these numbers enable checks and deposit slips to be read, sorted, and recorded by computer.

Banks will accept a list of deposited items on something other than the bank-provided deposit slip if the bank's deposit slip is attached. For example, if you are depositing 50 checks, you may create a computer printout listing the payers' names, check numbers, amount of each check, and total. You can then attach the printout to a deposit slip with the total written on the deposit slip. Another method is to attach a calculator or adding machine tape listing the individual check amounts and a total.

Making the Deposit Plan to deposit checks and cash into the practice's bank account in person at the bank, as described in Procedure 21–5. Make sure you are aware of your surroundings when making deposits because of safety issues. Avoid sending cash through the mail, but if it is absolutely necessary to do so, use registered mail. Always obtain a deposit receipt from the bank.

Again, depending on practice size, the frequency of deposits may be limited to several days a week; however, it should be done as often as possible to reduce theft, loss, bounced checks, and inaccurate recordings.

figure 21-7

List each check on the deposit slip, including the check number and amount.

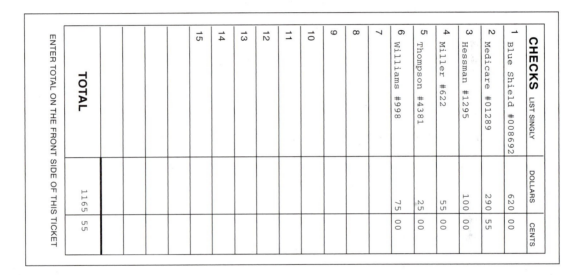

Reconciling Bank Statements Another banking task is reconciling the bank statement. **Reconciliation** involves comparing the office's financial records with the bank records to ensure that they are consistent and accurate. In most practices this task is performed once a month when the practice receives the monthly checking account statement from the bank. An example of a bank statement is shown in Figure 21–8 and an example of a reconciliation worksheet is shown in Figure 21–9. The process of reconciliation is explained in Procedure 21–6.

Electronic Banking

Compared with traditional banking methods, electronic banking has several advantages. Electronic banking can improve productivity, cash flow, and accuracy. The use of electronic banking can also speed up many banking tasks.

reconciliation

Comparing the office's financial records with the bank records to ensure that they are consistent and accurate.

figure 21-8

Each month you will receive a current bank statement, which you should reconcile with the previous statement and your checkbook register.

1st **First State Bank of Englewood**
CN 1
Funton, XY 12345-7890

PAGE 1

ACCOUNT NO.   518-833-3

STATEMENT PERIOD
07/19/12 TO 08/20/12

TOTAL CARE CLINIC, PC
342 EAST PARK BLVD.
FUNTON, XY 12345-6789

YOUR ACCOUNT SUMMARY

DEPOSIT ACCOUNTS	BALANCE
CHECKING ACCOUNT	2,088.08
SAVINGS ACCOUNT	10,602.54
TOTAL	12,690.62

CHECKING ACCOUNT

TOTAL CARE CLINIC, PC

SUMMARY OF ACCOUNT   518-833-3

BEGINNING BALANCE ON 07/18/12	3,055.24
DEPOSITS AND CREDITS	+3,819.02
CHECKS & WITHDRAWALS	−4,786.18
ENDING BALANCE ON 08/20/12	2,088.08

CHECKS PAID: 38

CHECK	AMOUNT	DATE PAID	REFERENCE#	CHECK	AMOUNT	DATE PAID	REFERENCE#
CHECK	450.00	07/19/12	81569110	2226	181.00	08/12/12	05105878
2202	146.23	07/31/12	29521570	2227	24.74	08/19/12	06120827
2203	122.03	07/29/12	29141271	2228	140.00	08/12/12	05022086
2210*	43.00	07/29/12	07046380	2229	148.71	08/16/12	27248941
2211	60.09	08/01/12	04597911	2230	53.16	08/13/12	27852752
2214*	123.59	07/24/12	29470425	2231	50.00	08/14/12	01018325
2215	47.70	07/19/12	12357289	2232	50.00	08/13/12	05080148
2216	9.00	07/22/12	05479786	2233	15.00	08/16/12	04709533
2217	30.00	07/26/12	29841864	2234	13.95	08/19/12	06008593
2218	19.00	07/30/12	04330539	2235	123.59	08/14/12	27050650
2219	12.00	07/24/12	04037820	2236	50.00	08/13/12	05099115
2220	35.93	07/24/12	04068844	2237	50.00	08/15/12	03014667
2221	10.00	08/12/12	05091269	2238	20.00	08/16/12	04675854
2222	23.48	07/24/12	29465653	2239	47.70	08/14/12	06172997
2223	242.43	07/26/12	29804419	2240	24.74	08/19/12	06120925
2224	150.00	07/30/12	29405827	2243*	400.00	08/14/12	29652307
2225	830.00	08/07/12	02242873	2344	400.00	08/14/12	29652306

figure 21-9

Reconciliation worksheet.

BANK RECONCILIATION

CLIENT NAME: _____ MONTH OF: _____

BANK: _____ ACCOUNT NO. : _____

GENERAL LEDGER		BALANCE PER BANK STATEMENT	
ACCOUNT BALANCE............................		AS OF:	
ADD DEBITS:		ADD DEPOSITS IN TRANSIT:	
....		....	
....		....	
....		....	
....		....	
....		....	
TOTAL DR.............	0.00		
TOTAL...............................	0.00	TOTAL IN TRANSIT	0.00
		TOTAL....................................	0.00
LESS CREDITS:			
Checks			
Auto Withdrawals			
Bank Fees			
		LESS CHECKS OUTSTANDING:	
		(SEE LIST BELOW)	
TOTAL CR.............	0.00	TOTAL.................	0.00
BANK BAL PER GENERAL LEDGER..	0.00	BANK BALANCE PER REC..................	0.00

CHECKS:

NUMBER	AMOUNT	NUMBER	NUMBER	NUMBER	AMOUNT
				TOTAL	0.00
TOTAL	0.00	TOTAL		GRAND TOTAL	0.00

If your medical office uses electronic banking, your basic tasks will be the same as in an office that uses traditional banking methods. How these tasks are performed, however, may be quite different. When you use electronic banking, you are still responsible for recording and depositing checks, just as if you were using traditional methods, but you will see these differences.

- Rather than your recording each check in a paper checkbook and determining the new balance, the computer software calculates the new balance for you.
- Rather than your reconciling the office bank statement on paper, the computer software does it automatically.
- Rather than putting the checkbook and banking forms in a securely locked place at the end of the day, you use a computer password for security.

Many medical office software programs are available today. Each one has a different interface, uses different menus, and prompts you for information in different ways. Certain general concepts apply to all. For specific information, consult the user's manual that comes with your practice's computer software. All software will allow you to perform the following tasks:

- Record deposits
- Pay bills
- Display the checkbook
- Balance the checkbook

Record Deposits   If you select "Record Deposits," a message on the computer screen prompts you to enter information about each check to be deposited that day. This information usually includes the check writer's name and the amount of the check. The check's ABA number may also be requested. After you enter this information, the computer gives you a chance to double-check it. If all the information is correct, you continue entering and checking the other deposits, one at a time. You can then select a command to print a deposit slip that contains the information you have just entered. To make the deposit, place the cash and checks in a deposit bag along with the computerized deposit slip and the bank's deposit slip.

Pay Bills   The bill-paying function allows you to log checks that you write into a computerized checkbook register. For each check you want to write, a message on the computer screen should prompt you for information, such as the payee and the amount of the check. The computer should also give you a chance to verify and correct this information before moving on to the next check or printing the actual checks.

Some software programs automatically assign the next available check number to each new check you enter. To double-check that the computer-assigned check numbers match those on the actual checks, print a list of the checks you have entered and compare it with the checks before mailing them.

Display the Checkbook   The checkbook display function allows you to review the electronic checkbook register. Although you cannot change information that appears in the register, you can print it out. Thus, you can be sure the checks have been recorded properly, and you can check your latest balance.

If you select "Display Checkbook" from the "Banking" menu, the computer displays a list of all checks that have been entered into the register. Information

Telephone Banking

Telephone banking is a form of electronic banking that enables you to access your bank's computer system by phone to obtain account information and perform simple banking tasks. To use telephone banking, you should have a push-button telephone, the telephone personal identification number (TPIN) assigned to your practice by the bank, and the telephone number that accesses the telephone banking system.

The telephone banking system prompts you for information. You use the push-button pad on the telephone to provide the information. For example, an automated voice may ask you to press 1 to inquire about deposits or 2 to inquire about withdrawals. Telephone banking is especially useful for the following banking tasks:

- Checking the current balance of an account
- Determining whether deposited funds are available
- Obtaining the date and amount of the last few deposits and the last few checks paid (usually the last three)

- Finding out if a specific check has been paid
- Transferring funds between accounts (if the practice has more than one account)
- Stopping payment on checks

Although this form of electronic banking is especially useful for some services, you cannot use it to manage all banking tasks. For example, you cannot use it to make deposits or reconcile a bank statement. However, it can be quite convenient for the day-to-day banking tasks just listed. If you have a hearing impairment and have a telecommunications device for the deaf (TDD) installed on the telephone, you can bank by phone.

---

includes check number, date, payee, and amount. Scrolling up and down reveals all the checks in the register. (Some banks also allow you to access this information by telephone. The Practice Readiness section gives more information about telephone banking.)

Balance Checkbook The "Balance Checkbook" option electronically reconciles the monthly bank statement. After you enter the appropriate date or dates, the computer screen displays all the checks and deposits that were logged into the register in the order they were posted. Figure 21–10 shows an example of account activity to allow you to balance the checkbook.

The next screen highlights each check or deposit that has not been seen on a previous bank statement. You are prompted to indicate whether that item appears on the current statement, usually using Y for yes and N for no. After the computer queries these items, it may ask you to enter any items that appear on the current bank statement but are not in the checkbook, such as service charges.

Finally, a message on the screen prompts you to enter the current account balance from the bank statement. Then, the computer reconciles the bank statement. It will alert you if the system balance does not agree with the balance on the bank statement. If the balance does not agree, recheck the information you entered for possible error. If your work is correct, and the balances still do not agree, call the bank to determine if a bank error has been made.

figure 21–10

Electronic banking will allow you to see the "Account Activity" on the screen.

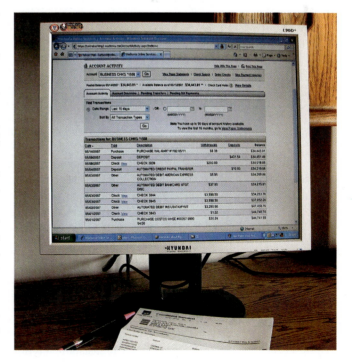

LO 21.4 Managing Accounts Payable

Accounts payable are the practice's expenses (money leaving the business), and accounts receivable reflect a practice's income (money coming into the business). This section focuses on accounts payable, including payroll. A basic accounting principle to bear in mind is that when a practice's income exceeds its expenses, it has a profit. When a practice's expenses exceed its income, it has a loss.

Because of this relationship between income and expenses, most practices try to reduce expenses by controlling accounts payable. As an administrative medical assistant, you play an important role in helping control accounts payable and maximize profits.

Accounts payable fall into three main groups:

1. Payments for supplies, equipment, and practice-related products and services

2. Payroll, which may be the largest of the accounts payable

3. Taxes owed to federal, state, and local agencies

A practice's accounting system usually consists of several elements. These elements include the daily log, patient ledger cards, the checkbook, the disbursements journal, the petty cash record, and the payroll register.

The daily log and patient ledger cards are used primarily for accounts receivable. The disbursements journal, petty cash record, and payroll register are used primarily in accounts payable. Procedure 21–7 tells you how to set up and use these accounting tools effectively.

LO 21.5 Managing Disbursements

A disbursement is any payment the physician's office makes for goods or services. One of the most common disbursements is payment for office supplies. Other disbursements include payments for equipment, dues, rent, taxes, salary, and utilities. No matter what type of disbursement you make on behalf of the practice, you must keep accurate records of the purchase and the payment.

Included in the office disbursement journal is the petty cash account used for small office expenses (such as stamps, return receipts, office lunches). The setup, use, and maintenance of the petty cash journal is discussed in detail in Chapter 8.

Managing Supplies

In many practices, one person is responsible for the ordering of supplies and equipment repairs. This person is often the office manager or the administrative medical assistant. Frequently, this person keeps a record of often-used supplies in a log or on a spreadsheet in the computer. As supplies become low, they are

then reordered. Guidelines for purchasing supplies are discussed in detail in Chapter 8 and information on equipment purchasing and maintenance is found in Chapter 10.

Writing Checks

Virtually all disbursements are made by check. Paying by check gives the practice complete, accurate records of all financial transactions.

Before writing a check, make sure the checking account balance is up-to-date and large enough to cover the check you want to write. Enter the date, check number, payee information, and reason for the payment on the check stub, and then subtract the amount of each check from the previous balance, enter the new balance, and carry that balance forward to the next stub. Do this step before writing the check so the payment entry is not accidentally omitted from the disbursement journal.

If you use a pegboard system, you will automatically record the date, check number, payee, and check amount on the check register as you write out the check. You must note the reason for payment and the new balance manually, however. Record that information in the appropriate spaces on the register.

If you make an error when completing a check, write VOID in ink across the front of the check in large letters so that it cannot be used again. Then file the voided check in numerical order with the returned checks.

After filling out the check properly, detach it from the checkbook and give it to the doctor to sign, along with the invoice to be paid. Mark the date, check number, and amount paid on the invoice. Make a copy of the invoice for your records. Keep these copies with supporting documents, such as order forms or packing slips, in a paid-invoice file. Then, mail the check and the original invoice to the payee in a neatly hand-addressed or typewritten envelope. If you use a window envelope, be sure the payee's address shows through the window.

Recording Disbursements

You may record disbursements in a check register, in a disbursements journal, or on the bottom section of the daily log.

If you use a disbursements journal, follow these steps to record disbursements.

1. When beginning a new journal page, give each column a heading to reflect the type of expense, such as utilities or rent.
2. For each check, fill in the date, payee's name, check number, and check amount in the appropriate columns.
3. Determine the expense category of the check.
4. Record the check amount in the column for that type of business expense.
5. If you must divide a check between two or more expense columns, record the total in the check amount column. Then record the amount that applies to each type of expense in the appropriate column. The total amount must equal the sum of the amounts listed between the columns.

Recording disbursements in columns for each type of expense allows you to total and track expenses by category. **Tracking** (watching for changes) is important because it helps control expenses. Before tracking, check your calculations by performing a trial balance.

tracking
Watching for changes in spending so as to help control expenses.

1. Total the check amount column.
2. Find the total for each expense column.
3. Add together all the expense column totals. The combined expense column total should match the total in the check amount column.

4. If the amounts do not match, recheck every entry until you find the error. When you find it, draw a line through it, and record the correct information neatly above it or to the side.

5. When the two amounts match (or balance), carry forward all column totals to the disbursements journal for the next month. Remember to prepare summaries and perform balances at the end of every month, quarter, and year.

Understanding Financial Summaries

The physician may periodically analyze the income and expenses of the practice. Financial summaries provide an easy-to-read report on the business transactions for a given period, such as a month or a year.

An accountant usually prepares financial summaries. Although you will probably not have to create these summaries, you may need to request them from the accountant or select them from an electronic software so a basic understanding of the information within them will be helpful.

Statement of Income and Expense   Also called a profit-and-loss statement, a statement of income and expense highlights the practice's profitability. It shows the physician the practice's total income and then lists and subtracts all expenses.

cash flow statement
A statement that shows the cash on hand at the beginning of a period, the income and disbursements made during that period, and the new amount of cash on hand at the end of the period.

Cash Flow Statement   A **cash flow statement** shows how much cash is available to cover expenses, to invest, or to take as profits. The cash flow statement begins with the cash on hand at the beginning of the period and shows the income and disbursements made during that period. It concludes with the new amount of cash on hand at the end of the period.

Trial Balance   The doctor may review trial balances periodically to ensure that the books balance. The combined expense column total should match the total in the check amount column. If the amounts do not match, recheck every entry until you find the error.

CHECKPOINT
LO 21.5

Why is tracking expenses important to a practice?

LO 21.6 Handling Payroll

You may be responsible for handling the office payroll (Table 21–1). If so, your duties may include:

- Obtaining tax identification numbers
- Creating employee payroll information sheets
- Calculating employees' earnings
- Subtracting taxes and other deductions
- Writing paychecks
- Creating employee earnings records
- Preparing a payroll register
- Submitting payroll taxes

Applying for Tax Identification Numbers

Every employer—whether a single physician or a corporate practice—must have an employer identification number (EIN). An EIN is required by law for federal

FREQUENCY	DUTIES
Upon assuming payroll responsibilities	• Apply for an employer identification number (EIN) with Form SS-4 if the physician does not already have an EIN.
Whenever a new employee is hired	• Have the employee complete an Employee's Withholding Allowance Certificate (Form W-4) and Employment Eligibility Verification (Form I-9). • Record the employee's name and Social Security number from the employee's Social Security card.
Every payday	• Withhold federal income tax as well as state and local income taxes (if any). • Withhold the employee's share of FICA taxes (for Social Security and Medicare). Record a matching amount for the employer's share. • Calculate how much the practice must pay for each employee's federal and state unemployment tax.
Monthly or biweekly (depending on your deposit schedule)	• Deposit withheld income taxes, withheld and employer Social Security taxes, and withheld and employer Medicare taxes.
Quarterly (by April 30, July 31, October 31, and January 31)	• File Employer's Quarterly Federal Tax Return (Form 941). With the return, pay any taxes that were not deposited earlier. • Deposit federal unemployment tax, if over $100.
At least once a year	• Have all employees update their W-4 forms.
On or before January 31	• Give employees their Wage and Tax Statements (Form W-2), which show total wages and various withheld taxes. • File Employer's Annual Federal Unemployment (FUTA) Tax Return (Form 940) with tax amount due.
On or before February 28	• File Transmittal of Wage and Tax Statements (Form W-3) along with the government's copies of the W-2 forms.

table 21-1
Payroll Duties

tax accounting purposes. An EIN is obtained by completing Form SS-4 (Application for Employer Identification Number) from www.federaltaxid.us and then submitting it to the Internal Revenue Service (IRS) which can be done at www.irs.gov. Some states also require employer tax reports, for which the practice must have a state identification number, obtained from the proper state agency.

Creating Employee Payroll Information Sheets

The practice must maintain up-to-date, accurate payroll information about each employee. You should prepare a payroll information sheet for each employee. Each sheet should have the following information:

- The employee's name, address, Social Security number, and marital status
- An indication that the employee has completed an Employment Eligibility Verification (Form I-9), verifying that the employee is a U.S. citizen, a legally admitted alien, or an alien authorized to work in the United States
- A new hire reporting form (NHR) must also be completed by the employer on the employee's behalf and submitted to the applicable state agency before the employee receives her first paycheck. Most often this form is collected along with the W-4 and I-9 forms. Each state has its own format but the information gathered is universal. Some states allow electronic submission, while others accept the information via mail. Figure 21–11 shows an example of an NHR form.
- The employee's pay schedule, number of dependents, payroll type, and voluntary deductions

Pay Schedule and Payroll Type On the payroll information sheet, list the employee's **pay schedule,** showing how often the employee is paid. Common pay schedules are weekly, biweekly, and monthly.

pay schedule
How often an employee is paid (weekly, biweekly, etc.).

figure 21-11

NHR Form.

Form NHR
New Hire and Independent
Contractor Reporting Form

Rev. 01/2010
Massachusetts
Department of
Revenue

TO ENSURE ACCURACY, PRINT (OR TYPE) NEATLY IN UPPER-CASE LETTERS AND NUMBERS, USING A DARK, BALLPOINT PEN.

Employee Information

FIRST NAME*   MI   LAST NAME*

SOCIAL SECURITY NUMBER*   DATE OF HIRE OR REINSTATEMENT*

ADDRESS*

CITY/TOWN*   STATE*   ZIP*   +4 (OPTIONAL)

IT'S THE LAW! - Massachusetts regulations require employers with 25 or more employees to report their new hires and independent contractors electronically.

For more information, go to **www.mass.gov/dor** and select the **For Businesses** tab located at the top of the page.

Employer Information

EMPLOYER IDENTIFICATION NUMBER*

CORPORATE NAME*

PAYROLL ADDRESS TO WHICH THE INCOME WITHHOLDING ORDER WILL BE SENT*

PAYROLL ADDRESS (Continued)

CITY/TOWN*   STATE*   ZIP*   +4 (OPTIONAL)

NOTE: All fields on this form with an * are mandatory fields. Please ensure all information entered is legible and accurate prior to submitting the form to DOR.

Helpful Hint: Once you have completed your employer information, you may copy this form to save time when reporting future new hires and independent contractors.

Send Completed Form NHR to:

Massachusetts Department of Revenue, PO Box 55141, Boston, MA 02205-5141 or, you may fax the completed form to 617-376-3262.

List the employee's payroll type—hourly wage, salary, or commission—on the payroll information sheet. An hourly wage is a set amount of money per hour of work. A salary is a set amount of money per pay period, regardless of the number of hours worked. A commission is a percentage of the amount an employee earns for the employer. Salespeople, for example, are often paid by commission.

Number of Dependents Record the number of **dependents** (people who depend on the employee for financial support that will be claimed by the employee). Dependents may include a spouse, children, and other family members.

You can find the number of dependents on the Employee's Withholding Allowance Certificate (Form W-4), which should have been completed when the employee was hired (Figure 21–12). Remember to keep the completed W-4 forms in the physician's personnel file, and update them annually.

dependent
Persons who depend on the employee for financial support.

Voluntary Deductions Voluntary deductions are those items not required by law to be deducted from the employee's paycheck. These may include additional federal withholding taxes, contributions to a 401(k) retirement plan, or payments to a company health insurance plan. Employees who want additional federal taxes taken out of their paycheck will indicate this deduction on their W-4 form.

Gross Earnings

Gross earnings refers to the total amount of income earned before deductions. Gross earnings must be calculated for each employee as a first step in the payroll process.

gross earnings
The total amount of income earned before deductions.

Calculating Gross Earnings For every payroll period, use data from the payroll information sheet to compute each employee's gross earnings. For an hourly employee, use this equation:

Hourly Wage × Hours Worked =Gross Earnings

An employee who earns $12.50 per hour and works 35 hours, for example, has gross earnings of $437.50 ($12.50 × 35 hours) per week.

For a salaried employee, use the salary amount as the gross earnings for the pay period, no matter how many hours the employee worked. An employee who earns a weekly salary of $500, for example, receives that amount whether she worked 30, 40, or 50 hours during that week.

Fair Labor Standards Act The Fair Labor Standards Act primarily affects employees who earn hourly wages. It limits the number of hours they may work, sets their minimum wage, and regulates their overtime pay. It also requires the employer to record the number of hours they work, usually on a time card or in a time book.

For hourly employees, this act mandates payment of:

- Time and a half (1½ times the normal hourly wage) for all hours worked beyond the normal 8 in a regular workday.

- Time and a half for all hours worked on the sixth consecutive day of the work week.

- Twice the normal wage (double time) for all hours worked on the seventh consecutive workday.

- Double time, plus normal holiday pay, for all hours worked on a company-approved holiday.

The Fair Labor Standards Act also requires overtime payments for part-time hourly employees for every hour worked beyond the normal 8 in a day or 40 in a week.

figure 21–12

An Employee's Withholding Allowance Certificate (W-4) should be completed upon hire and updated annually thereafter.

Form W-4 (2010)

Purpose. Complete Form W-4 so that your employer can withhold the correct federal income tax from your pay. Consider completing a new Form W-4 each year and when your personal or financial situation changes.

Exemption from withholding. If you are exempt, complete **only** lines 1, 2, 3, 4, and 7 and sign the form to validate it. Your exemption for 2010 expires February 16, 2011. See Pub. 505, Tax Withholding and Estimated Tax.

Note. You cannot claim exemption from withholding if (a) your income exceeds $950 and includes more than $300 of unearned income (for example, interest and dividends) and (b) another person can claim you as a dependent on his or her tax return.

Basic instructions. If you are not exempt, complete the **Personal Allowances Worksheet** below. The worksheets on page 2 further adjust your withholding allowances based on itemized deductions, certain credits, adjustments to income, or two-earners/multiple jobs situations.

Complete all worksheets that apply. However, you may claim fewer (or zero) allowances. For regular wages, withholding must be based on allowances you claimed and may not be a flat amount or percentage of wages.

Head of household. Generally, you may claim head of household filing status on your tax return only if you are unmarried and pay more than 50% of the costs of keeping up a home for yourself and your dependent(s) or other qualifying individuals. See Pub. 501, Exemptions, Standard Deduction, and Filing Information, for information.

Tax credits. You can take projected tax credits into account in figuring your allowable number of withholding allowances. Credits for child or dependent care expenses and the child tax credit may be claimed using the **Personal Allowances Worksheet** below. See Pub. 919, How Do I Adjust My Tax Withholding, for information on converting your other credits into withholding allowances.

Nonwage income. If you have a large amount of nonwage income, such as interest or dividends, consider making estimated tax

payments using Form 1040-ES, Estimated Tax for Individuals. Otherwise, you may owe additional tax. If you have pension or annuity income, see Pub. 919 to find out if you should adjust your withholding on Form W-4 or W-4P.

Two earners or multiple jobs. If you have a working spouse or more than one job, figure the total number of allowances you are entitled to claim on all jobs using worksheets from only one Form W-4. Your withholding usually will be most accurate when all allowances are claimed on the Form W-4 for the highest paying job and zero allowances are claimed on the others. See Pub. 919 for details.

Nonresident alien. If you are a nonresident alien, see Notice 1392, Supplemental Form W-4 Instructions for Nonresident Aliens, before completing this form.

Check your withholding. After your Form W-4 takes effect, use Pub. 919 to see how the amount you are having withheld compares to your projected total tax for 2010. See Pub. 919, especially if your earnings exceed $130,000 (Single) or $180,000 (Married).

Personal Allowances Worksheet (Keep for your records.)

A Enter "1" for **yourself** if no one else can claim you as a dependent . . . . **A** _____

B Enter "1" if:
- You are single and have only one job; or
- You are married, have only one job, and your spouse does not work; or
- Your wages from a second job or your spouse's wages (or the total of both) are $1,500 or less. } . . **B** _____

C Enter "1" for your **spouse**. But, you may choose to enter "-0-" if you are married and have either a working spouse or more than one job. (Entering "-0-" may help you avoid having too little tax withheld.) . . . . . . **C** _____

D Enter number of **dependents** (other than your spouse or yourself) you will claim on your tax return . . . . . **D** _____

E Enter "1" if you will file as **head of household** on your tax return (see conditions under **Head of household** above) . **E** _____

F Enter "1" if you have at least $1,800 of **child or dependent care expenses** for which you plan to claim a credit . . **F** _____
(**Note.** Do **not** include child support payments. See Pub. 503, Child and Dependent Care Expenses, for details.)

G **Child Tax Credit** (including additional child tax credit). See Pub. 972, Child Tax Credit, for more information.
- If your total income will be less than $61,000 ($90,000 if married), enter "2" for each eligible child; then **less** "1" if you have three or more eligible children.
- If your total income will be between $61,000 and $84,000 ($90,000 and $119,000 if married), enter "1" for each eligible child plus "1" **additional** if you have six or more eligible children. . . . . **G** _____

H Add lines A through G and enter total here. (**Note.** This may be different from the number of exemptions you claim on your tax return.) ▶ **H** _____

For accuracy, complete all worksheets that apply. {
- If you plan to **itemize or claim adjustments to income** and want to reduce your withholding, see the **Deductions and Adjustments Worksheet** on page 2.
- If you have **more than one job** or are **married and you and your spouse both work** and the combined earnings from all jobs exceed $18,000 ($32,000 if married), see the **Two-Earners/Multiple Jobs Worksheet** on page 2 to avoid having too little tax withheld.
- If **neither** of the above situations applies, **stop here** and enter the number from line H on line 5 of Form W-4 below.

- - - - - - - - - - - **Cut here and give Form W-4 to your employer. Keep the top part for your records.** - - - - - - - - - - -

Form W-4 — Employee's Withholding Allowance Certificate

Form **W-4**
Department of the Treasury
Internal Revenue Service

▶ **Whether you are entitled to claim a certain number of allowances or exemption from withholding is subject to review by the IRS. Your employer may be required to send a copy of this form to the IRS.**

OMB No. 1545-0074

2010

1	Type or print your first name and middle initial.	Last name	2	Your social security number

Home address (number and street or rural route)

3 ☐ Single ☐ Married ☐ Married, but withhold at higher Single rate.
Note. If married, but legally separated, or spouse is a nonresident alien, check the "Single" box.

City or town, state, and ZIP code

4 If your last name differs from that shown on your social security card, check here. You must call 1-800-772-1213 for a replacement card. ▶ ☐

5 Total number of allowances you are claiming (from line **H** above **or** from the applicable worksheet on page 2) **5** _____

6 Additional amount, if any, you want withheld from each paycheck . . . . **6** $ _____

7 I claim exemption from withholding for 2010, and I certify that I meet **both** of the following conditions for exemption.
- Last year I had a right to a refund of **all** federal income tax withheld because I had **no** tax liability **and**
- This year I expect a refund of **all** federal income tax withheld because I expect to have **no** tax liability.
If you meet both conditions, write "Exempt" here . . . . ▶ **7** _____

Under penalties of perjury, I declare that I have examined this certificate and to the best of my knowledge and belief, it is true, correct, and complete.

Employee's signature
(Form is not valid unless you sign it.) ▶

Date ▶

8 Employer's name and address (Employer: Complete lines 8 and 10 only if sending to the IRS.)	9 Office code (optional)	10 Employer identification number (EIN)

For Privacy Act and Paperwork Reduction Act Notice, see page 2.   Cat. No. 10220Q   Form **W-4** (2010)

Making Deductions

The law requires all employers to withhold money from employees' gross earnings to pay federal, state, and local (if any) income taxes and certain other taxes. In addition, employees may wish you to make certain voluntary deductions. For example, you might be asked to deduct an amount for child care, if the practice or hospital provides on-site child care. You might also deduct employee contributions to health insurance premiums.

You must deposit all employee deductions and employer payments into separate accounts, one for each deduction type. Monies from these **tax liability accounts** are used to pay taxes to appropriate government agencies.

tax liability account
Account where money is deposited and which is used to pay taxes to appropriate government agencies.

Income Taxes You must withhold enough money to cover the employee's federal income tax for the pay period. You can determine this amount by finding the employee's number of exemptions (from Form W-4) and referring to the tax tables in *Circular E, Employer's Tax Guide,* published by the IRS.

Consult the state and local tax tables for other income taxes.

FICA Taxes For FICA tax, withhold from the employee's check half of the tax owed for the pay period. Pay the other half from the practice's accounts. The amount of FICA tax that funds Social Security differs from the amount that funds Medicare. Report these two amounts separately. Check IRS *Circular E* for the latest FICA tax percentages and level of taxable earnings.

Unemployment Taxes Federal unemployment tax is not a deduction from the employees' paychecks but rather is based on their earnings and paid by the employer. The **Federal Unemployment Tax Act (FUTA)** requires employers to pay a percentage of each employee's income, up to a certain dollar amount. The percentage may be reduced if the employer also pays state unemployment taxes.

Federal Unemployment Tax Act (FUTA)
Requires employers to pay a percentage of each employee's income, up to a certain dollar amount, to cover unemployment compensation.

States calculate unemployment taxes differently. Some states tax employers and employees; others tax only employers. State unemployment tax usually varies with the employer's past employment record. Employers with few layoffs, such as physicians, have lower tax rates than those with many layoffs. To compute state unemployment tax, apply the assigned tax rate to each employee's earnings, up to a maximum for the calendar year. For details, consult your state unemployment insurance department.

Workers' Compensation Some states require employers to insure their employees against possible loss of income resulting from work-related injury, disability, or disease. Although state laws vary, they typically require doctors to carry this insurance with a state insurance fund or state-authorized private insurer. Usually, a medical practice's insurance agent will audit the payroll books annually and then issue a bill for the workers' compensation premium due.

Calculating Net Earnings

Add each employee's required and voluntary deductions together to determine the total deductions. Then, subtract the total deductions from the gross earnings to get the employee's **net earnings,** or take-home pay. Use the following equation:

net earnings
Take-home pay. Gross Earnings − Total Deductions = Net Earnings.

Gross Earnings − Total Deductions = Net Earnings

The exception to this rule may be contributions the employee makes to the employer retirement plan, if available. When sponsored by an employer, as with a 401(k) account, these deductions are often taken before taxes are calculated, reducing the employee's taxable income, which encourages the employee to take part in these plans.

Handling Payroll Through Electronic Banking

An electronic funds transfer system (EFTS) enables you to handle the practice's payroll without writing payroll checks manually. The physician must sign up for EFTS with the bank, and employees must supply their bank account numbers to the employer. Then, the bank electronically deposits employees' paychecks into their bank accounts, as directed.

Most employees like to have their paychecks deposited automatically. The money is available on the day of deposit, and no one has to worry about losing a paycheck, getting to the bank before it closes, or carrying a paycheck around. Also, employees still receive a check stub along with a notification of deposit, so they can track their earnings and deductions.

Contact your bank for more information and specific procedures for setting up EFTS and electronic payroll.

Preparing Paychecks

The way you prepare the practice's payroll will depend on the system the practice uses. In a small practice, you may write paychecks manually. In this case, write the check amount for the employee's net earnings, and deduct the check amount from the office checkbook. Payroll may also be handled through electronic banking; see the Practice Readiness section.

If the practice uses a payroll service, you may supply time cards or payroll data to the service by mail or electronically. The service calculates all the deductions, prepares paychecks, and mails them to the practice for distribution.

No matter how paychecks are prepared, they should include information about how the check amount was determined. This information usually appears on the check stub. It should match the information on the employee earnings records and payroll register. Procedure 21–8 at the end of the chapter explains the process for generating payroll.

Maintaining Employee Earnings Records

You need to keep an employee earnings record for each employee (Figure 21–13). When you create the record, list the employee's name, address, phone number, Social Security number, birth date, spouse's name, number of dependents, job title, employment starting date, pay rate, and voluntary deductions.

Then, for each pay period, record the employee's gross earnings, individual deductions, net earnings, and related information. Properly completed earnings records show each employee's earning history.

Maintaining a Payroll Register

A payroll register summarizes vital information about all employees and their earnings (Figure 21–14). At the end of each pay period, record each employee's earnings to date, hourly rate, hours worked, overtime hours, overtime earnings, and total gross earnings. Also, list the gross earnings subject to unemployment taxes and FICA, all required and voluntary deductions, net earnings, and the paycheck number. Refer to Procedure 21–8 at the end of this chapter for an example of how to prepare and complete a payroll register.

Handling Payroll Electronically

Manual payroll preparation and related tasks may take an hour per week for each employee. To save time and to provide the convenience for employees of having their paychecks automatically deposited, some practices handle payroll tasks electronically.

figure 21-13

Earnings records show the earning history of each employee at your practice.

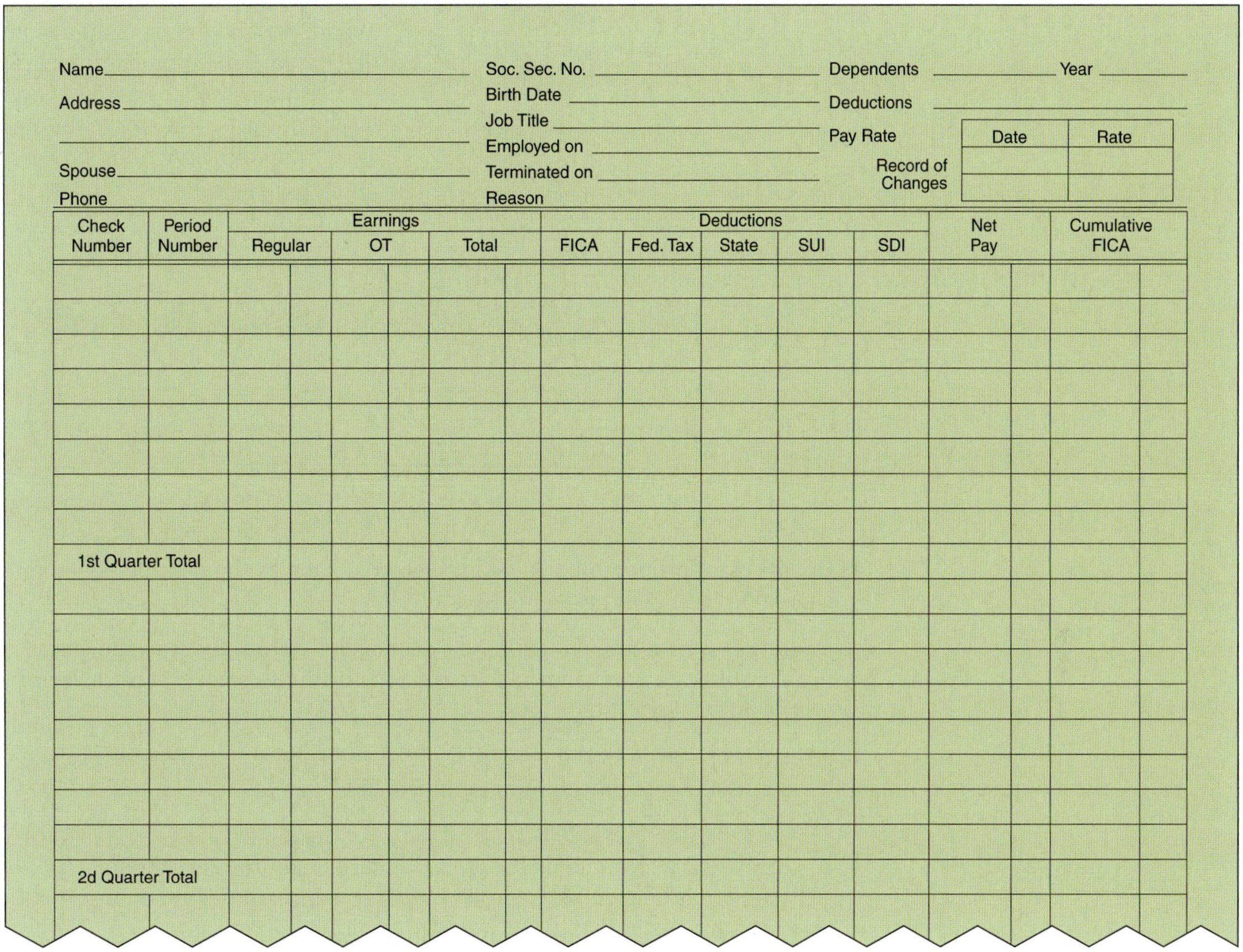

Name					Soc. Sec. No.				Dependents			Year		
Address					Birth Date				Deductions					
					Job Title				Pay Rate		Date		Rate	
					Employed on				Record of Changes					
Spouse					Terminated on									
Phone					Reason									

Check Number	Period Number	Earnings			Deductions					Net Pay	Cumulative FICA
		Regular	OT	Total	FICA	Fed. Tax	State	SUI	SDI		
1st Quarter Total											
2d Quarter Total											

figure 21-14

A payroll register is designed to summarize information about all employees and their earnings.

Pay Period 6/1–6/14

Emp. No.	Name	Earnings to date	Hrly. Rate	Reg. Hrs.	OT Hrs.	OT Earnings	TOTAL GROSS	Earnings Subject to Unemp.	Earnings Subject to FICA	Social Security (FICA)	Medicare	Federal W/H	State W/H	Health Ins.	Net Pay	Check No.
0010	Scott, B.	9,823.14	14.00	70.00			980.00	980.00	980.00	60.50	14.10	147.92	15.10	25.00	717.38	11747
0020	Wilson, J.	14,290.38	17.00	70.00	6.50	153.00	1343.00	1343.00	1343.00	83.26	19.47	160.45	15.85	67.50	996.47	11748
0030	Diaz, J.	2,750.26	5.50	46.25			254.37	254.37	254.37	15.77	3.68	38.20	3.75		192.97	11749
0040	Ling, W.	2,240.57	6.80	30.00			204.00	204.00	204.00	12.66	2.96	26.02	3.12		159.54	11750
0050	Harris, E.	2,600.98	10.00	23.50			235.00	235.00	235.00	14.57	3.41	33.52	3.36		180.14	11751

EHR readiness

Generating Payroll

Because computer software programs have increased the accuracy and ease of payroll calculations, even offices that continue to do other tasks manually have turned to computer programs or outside payroll vendors to complete this office function. Once the appropriate figures (such as the number of hours worked) or percentages (such as percentage of state or federal taxes) are inserted in their designated blocks, these programs automatically calculate the correct deduction. This greatly reduces the number of hours spent manually making and checking calculations and saves the office time and money as staff can now move on to other tasks that require manual intervention. The functions performed and the "extras" available with these payroll programs vary, but all have basic functions of calculating total regular and overtime hours worked, insurance deductions, voluntary deductions such as retirement and disability insurances (before and after taxes), and tax deductions, arriving at the net pay for each employee.

If you work in a relatively small practice, you may handle all payroll tasks in the office, using accounting or payroll software. If you work in a large practice, you may prepare payroll information on the computer and transmit it by modem to an outside payroll service for processing. Depending on which system and software the practice has, you may use the computer to:

- Create, update, and delete employee payroll information files
- Prepare employee paychecks, stubs, and W-2 forms
- Update and print employee earnings records
- Update all appropriate bookkeeping records, such as the payroll ledger and general ledger, with payroll data

To perform these payroll functions electronically, follow the specific instructions in the software manual or get instructions from the payroll service. Generally, you would follow these steps.

1. Select an option from the "Payroll" menu. Wait for the prompt and select the appropriate employee from employee list.
2. Creating a new employee file.
   a. Enter employee name, address, SSN, marital status, pay schedule, number of dependents, payroll type, and voluntary deductions.
   b. Print two copies—one for the employee and one for the personnel file.
3. Updating employee payroll information after a life change such as change in marital status, birth of a child, change of address, or voluntary change in deductions.
   a. Select "Update Employee File."
   b. Make required changes.
   c. Print the form for the employee signature after he confirms information is correct.
   d. Print two signed copies—one for the employee and one for the personnel file.
   e. Payroll information must be correct and current. It should be updated yearly for each employee.
4. Deleting an employee from payroll.
   a. Select "Terminate Employee."
   b. Print a copy of the file before deleting it as the employer is required to keep employee payroll records for four years.
5. Generating paychecks and paystubs.
   a. Select employee from the employee list.
   b. Choose the "Print Paycheck" option.
   c. Answer each prompt displayed (for example, hours worked).

d. From the payroll information entered previously, the program calculates the employee's net earnings, generates a paycheck, and prints a pay stub with the appropriate information.

6. Creating an employee earnings record.

   a. Select "Creating Employee Earnings Record."

   b. Follow the prompts to enter the required information.

   c. Depending on the software program used, this information may be updated automatically with each paycheck generated.

Select an option from the "Payroll" menu. Wait for the prompt, then select the appropriate employee from a list of employees.

● ● ●

What are the types of deductions that can be made voluntarily?

CHECKPOINT
LO 21.6

LO 21.7 Calculating and Filing Taxes

In many practices, administrative medical assistants set up tax liability accounts for money withheld from paychecks. These accounts are used to submit this money to appropriate agencies. Visit www.irs.gov for further information.

Setting Up Tax Liability Accounts

It is important to hold the money deducted from paychecks until it can be sent to the appropriate government agencies. Deductions from employees' paychecks for federal, state, and local income taxes and FICA taxes, as well as employer payments based on payroll, such as federal and state unemployment taxes, must be deposited until payment is due. For these accounts, choose a bank that is authorized by the IRS to accept federal tax deposits. If the practice makes other paycheck deductions, as for workers' compensation or a 401(k) plan, maintain accurate records for this money as well.

Each time you prepare paychecks, deposit the withheld money into the proper account as dictated by your particular practice. Record the deposited amounts as debits in the practice's checking account.

Understanding Federal Tax Deposit Schedules

You will probably deposit federal income taxes and FICA taxes (which together are known as employment taxes) on a quarterly, monthly, or biweekly (every-other-week) schedule. Every November IRS personnel decide which deposit schedule your office should use for the next year.

If the IRS does not notify you about this matter, determine your deposit schedule based on the total employment taxes your office reported on the previous year's Employer's Quarterly Federal Tax Returns (Form 941). For example, if your office reported $50,000 or less in employment taxes during the past year, you would make monthly employment tax deposits the present year. If your office reported more than $50,000 during the past year, you would make semi-monthly tax deposits.

There are exceptions to the monthly or semimonthly tax deposit schedules: the $500 rule and the $100,000 rule. The $500 rule applies to employers who owe less than $500 in employment taxes during a tax period (such as a quarter). These employers do not have to make a deposit for that period. The $100,000 rule applies to employers who owe $100,000 or more in employment taxes on any one day during a tax period. These employers must deposit the tax by the next banking day after the day that ceiling is reached.

Submitting Federal Income Taxes and FICA Taxes

Some businesses must submit federal income taxes and FICA taxes to the IRS by electronic funds transfer (EFT). The EFT program, known as TAXLINK, began in 1995. Since then, more taxpayers have been required to use it each year. If your practice is not required to use EFT but wishes to do so voluntarily, contact the IRS, Cash Management Site Office, to enroll.

If your practice does not use EFT, you must submit these employment taxes with a Federal Tax Deposit (FTD) Coupon (Form 8109) (see Figure 21–15). FTD Coupons are supplied by the IRS. They are printed with the physician's name, address, and EIN. They have boxes for filling in the type of tax and the tax period for which the deposit is being made.

To make the deposit, write a single check or money order for the total amount of federal income taxes and FICA taxes withheld during the tax period. Make the check payable to the bank where you make the deposit. This must be a Federal Reserve Bank or another bank authorized to make payments to the IRS. Also, complete the FTD Coupon. Then, mail or deliver the check and FTD Coupon to the bank. The bank will give you a deposit receipt.

If you work in a practice with a large payroll, you may need to make deposits every few days. In most practices, however, you will probably make deposits once a month. Then, every 3 months, a more complete accounting is required on a **quarterly return,** Form 941: Employer's Quarterly Federal Tax Return (Figure 21–16).

Submitting Federal Unemployment Tax Act (FUTA) and State Unemployment Tax Act (SUTA) Taxes

FUTA taxes provide money to workers who are unemployed. If the practice owes more than $100 in federal unemployment tax at the end of the quarter, deposit the tax amount with an FTD Coupon (Form 8109). At the end of the year, file an Employer's Annual Federal Unemployment (FUTA) Tax Return (Form 940) with any final taxes owed (Figure 21–17).

Generally, an employer must pay FUTA taxes if employees' wages total more than $1500 in any quarter (3-month period) and if those employees are not seasonal or household workers. The FUTA tax, which is 6.2%, is applied to the first $7000 of income for a year.

quarterly return

The Employer's Quarterly Federal Tax Return; a form submitted to the IRS every three months that summarizes the federal income and employment taxes withheld from employees' paychecks.

figure 21–15

Practices that do not use TAXLINK to submit taxes electronically must submit federal income and FICA taxes with a Federal Tax Deposit (FTD) Coupon (Form 8109).

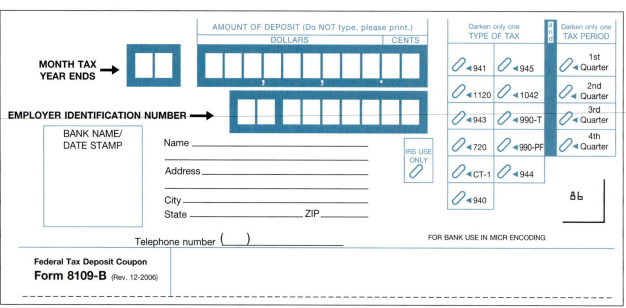

figure 21-16

Most practices make tax deposits monthly and then make a more complete accounting once every three months on the Employer's Quarterly Federal Tax Return (Form 941), the first page of which is shown here.

Form **941 for 2010:** Employer's **QUARTERLY** Federal Tax Return

(Rev. October 2010)

Department of the Treasury — Internal Revenue Service

951110

OMB No. 1545-0029

(EIN)
Employer identification number
☐☐ – ☐☐☐☐☐☐☐

Name *(not your trade name)*

Trade name *(if any)*

Address

Number Street Suite or room number

City State ZIP code

Report for this Quarter of 2010
(Check one.)

☐ **1:** January, February, March

☐ **2:** April, May, June

☐ **3:** July, August, September

☐ **4:** October, November, December

Read the separate instructions before you complete Form 941. Type or print within the boxes.

Part 1: Answer these questions for this quarter.

1 Number of employees who received wages, tips, or other compensation for the pay period including: *Mar. 12* (Quarter 1), *June 12* (Quarter 2), *Sept. 12* (Quarter 3), or *Dec. 12* (Quarter 4) **1**

2 Wages, tips, and other compensation **2**

3 Income tax withheld from wages, tips, and other compensation **3**

4 If no wages, tips, and other compensation are subject to social security or Medicare tax ☐ **Check and go to line 6e.**

	Column 1		Column 2
5a Taxable social security wages* .		× .124 =	
5b Taxable social security tips* . .		× .124 =	
5c Taxable Medicare wages & tips*		× .029 =	

Report wages/tips for this quarter, including those paid to qualified new employees, on lines 5a–5c. The social security tax exemption on wages/tips will be figured on lines 6c and 6d and will reduce the tax on line 6e.

5d Add *Column 2* line 5a, *Column 2* line 5b, and *Column 2* line 5c **5d**

6a Number of qualified employees *first* paid exempt wages/tips this quarter

6b Number of qualified employees paid exempt wages/tips this quarter

See instructions for definitions of qualified employee and exempt wages/tips.

6c Exempt wages/tips paid to qualified employees this quarter × .062 = **6d**

6e Total taxes before adjustments (line 3 + line 5d – line 6d = line 6e) **6e**

7a Current quarter's adjustment for fractions of cents **7a**

7b Current quarter's adjustment for sick pay **7b**

7c Current quarter's adjustments for tips and group-term life insurance **7c**

8 Total taxes after adjustments. Combine lines 6e through 7c **8**

9 Advance earned income credit (EIC) payments made to employees **9**

10 Total taxes after adjustment for advance EIC (line 8 – line 9 = line 10) **10**

11 Total deposits, including prior quarter overpayments **11**

12a COBRA premium assistance payments (see instructions) **12a**

12b Number of individuals provided COBRA premium assistance . .

12c Number of qualified employees paid exempt wages/tips March 19–31

Complete lines 12c, 12d, and 12e only for the 2nd quarter of 2010.

12d Exempt wages/tips paid to qualified employees March 19–31 × .062 = **12e**

13 Add lines 11, 12a, and 12e **13**

14 Balance due. If line 10 is more than line 13, enter the difference and see instructions . . . **14**

15 Overpayment. If line 13 is more than line 10, enter the difference Check one: ☐ Apply to next return. ☐ Send a refund.

▶ You MUST complete both pages of Form 941 and SIGN it.

Next ▶

For Privacy Act and Paperwork Reduction Act Notice, see the back of the Payment Voucher. Cat. No. 17001Z Form **941** (Rev. 10-2010)

figure 21-17

Tax dollars filed with FUTA tax returns (Form 940) provide income to workers who are temporarily unemployed.

Form **940 for 2010:** **Employer's Annual Federal Unemployment (FUTA) Tax Return**

850110

Department of the Treasury — Internal Revenue Service

OMB No. 1545-0028

(EIN)
Employer identification number

Name (not your trade name)

Trade name (if any)

Address

Number   Street   Suite or room number

City   State   ZIP code

Type of Return
(Check all that apply.)

☐ **a.** Amended

☐ **b.** Successor employer

☐ **c.** No payments to employees in 2010

☐ **d.** Final: Business closed or stopped paying wages

Read the separate instructions before you fill out this form. Please type or print within the boxes.

Part 1: Tell us about your return. If any line does NOT apply, leave it blank.

1 If you were required to pay your state unemployment tax in ...

    1a One state only, write the state abbreviation . . . . **1a** ☐☐

    - OR -

    1b More than one state (You are a multi-state employer) . . . . **1b** ☐ Check here. Fill out Schedule A.

2 If you paid wages in a state that is subject to CREDIT REDUCTION . . . . **2** ☐ Check here. Fill out Schedule A (Form 940), Part 2.

Part 2: Determine your FUTA tax before adjustments for 2010. If any line does NOT apply, leave it blank.

3 Total payments to all employees . . . . **3** ☐ .

4 Payments exempt from FUTA tax . . . . **4** ☐ .

    Check all that apply: **4a** ☐ Fringe benefits   **4c** ☐ Retirement/Pension   **4e** ☐ Other
                   4b ☐ Group-term life insurance **4d** ☐ Dependent care

5 Total of payments made to each employee in excess of $7,000 . . . . **5** ☐ .

6 Subtotal (line 4 + line 5 = line 6) . . . . **6** ☐ .

7 Total taxable FUTA wages (line 3 – line 6 = line 7) . . . . **7** ☐ .

8 FUTA tax before adjustments (line 7 × .008 = line 8) . . . . **8** ☐ .

Part 3: Determine your adjustments. If any line does NOT apply, leave it blank.

9 If ALL of the taxable FUTA wages you paid were excluded from state unemployment tax, **multiply line 7 by .054** (line 7 × .054 = line 9). Then go to line 12 . . . . **9** ☐ .

10 If SOME of the taxable FUTA wages you paid were excluded from state unemployment tax, **OR you paid ANY state unemployment tax late** (after the due date for filing Form 940), fill out the worksheet in the instructions. Enter the amount from line 7 of the worksheet . . . . . **10** ☐ .

11 If credit reduction applies, enter the amount from line 3 of Schedule A (Form 940) . . . . **11** ☐ .

Part 4: Determine your FUTA tax and balance due or overpayment for 2010. If any line does NOT apply, leave it blank.

12 Total FUTA tax after adjustments (lines 8 + 9 + 10 + 11 = line 12) . . . . **12** ☐ .

13 FUTA tax deposited for the year, including any overpayment applied from a prior year . **13** ☐ .

14 Balance due (If line 12 is more than line 13, enter the difference on line 14.)

    • If line 14 is more than $500, you must deposit your tax.
    • If line 14 is $500 or less, you may pay with this return. For more information on how to pay, see the separate instructions . . . . **14** ☐ .

15 Overpayment (If line 13 is more than line 12, enter the difference on line 15 and check a box below.) . . . . **15** ☐ .

Check one: ☐ Apply to next return.
           ☐ Send a refund.

▶ You **MUST** fill out both pages of this form and **SIGN** it.

Next ▶

For Privacy Act and Paperwork Reduction Act Notice, see the back of Form 940-V, Payment Voucher.

Cat. No. 11234O

Form **940** (2010)

Some states are also governed by a **State Unemployment Tax Act (SUTA)**. These taxes are filed along with FUTA taxes. Make sure you know the laws governing unemployment taxes in your state.

State Unemployment Tax Act (SUTA)
Taxes withheld by some states; these taxes are filed along with FUTA taxes.

Filing an Employer's Quarterly Federal Tax Return

Each quarter, file an Employer's Quarterly Federal Tax Return (Form 941) with the IRS (Figure 21–16). This tax return summarizes the federal income and FICA taxes (employment taxes) withheld from employees' paychecks.

As a general rule, you should file Form 941 at the nearest IRS office by the last day of the first month after the quarter ends. If the practice has deposited all taxes on time, you have an additional 10 days after the due date to file.

Handling State and Local Income Taxes

Send withheld state and local income taxes to the proper agencies, using their forms, procedures, and schedules. If required, prepare quarterly or other tax forms for your state or local agency. If you are unsure you can visit your state Web site or the IRS Web site at www.irs.gov.

Filing Wage and Tax Statements

After the end of each year, file a Wage and Tax Statement (Form W-2) with the appropriate federal, state, and local government agencies for each employee who had federal income and FICA taxes withheld during the previous year (Figure 21–18). Also, supply copies of Form W-2 to each employee.

Form W-2 shows the employee's total taxable income for the previous year. It also shows the exact amount of federal income taxes and FICA taxes

figure 21-18

A Wage and Tax Statement (Form W-2) records the total amount of taxes withheld during the previous year for each employee.

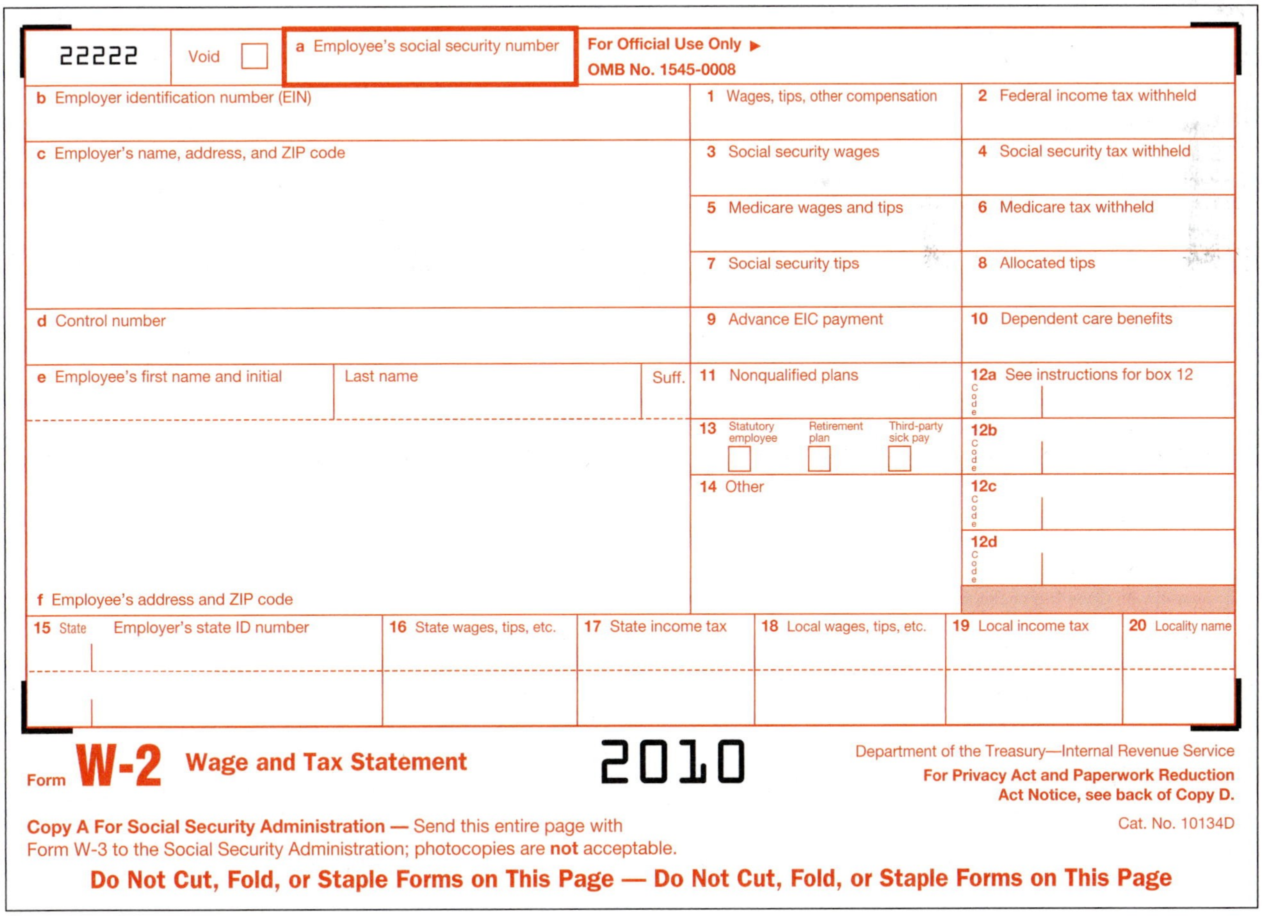

figure 21–19

Submit a Transmittal of Wage and Tax Statements (Form W-3) with the W-2 forms.

DO NOT STAPLE

a Control number 33333	**For Official Use Only ▶** OMB No. 1545-0008

b Kind of Payer	941 ☐ Military ☐ 943 ☐ 944 ☐ CT-1 ☐ Hshld. emp. ☐ Medicare govt. emp. ☐ **Third-party sick pay** ☐

1 Wages, tips, other compensation	**2** Federal income tax withheld
3 Social security wages	**4** Social security tax withheld
5 Medicare wages and tips	**6** Medicare tax withheld
7 Social security tips	**8** Allocated tips
9 Advance EIC payments	**10** Dependent care benefits
11 Nonqualified plans	**12a** Deferred compensation
13 For third-party sick pay use only	**12b** HIRE exempt wages and tips

c Total number of Forms W-2   **d** Establishment number

e Employer identification number (EIN)

f Employer's name

14 Income tax withheld by payer of third-party sick pay

g Employer's address and ZIP code

h Other EIN used this year

15 State Employer's state ID number	**16** State wages, tips, etc.	**17** State income tax
	18 Local wages, tips, etc.	**19** Local income tax

Contact person	Telephone number ( )	For Official Use Only
Email address	Fax number ( )	

Under penalties of perjury, I declare that I have examined this return and accompanying documents, and, to the best of my knowledge and belief, they are true, correct, and complete.

Signature ▶   Title ▶   Date ▶

Form **W-3 Transmittal of Wage and Tax Statements**   **2010**   Department of the Treasury Internal Revenue Service

Send this entire page with the entire Copy A page of Form(s) W-2 to the Social Security Administration.

Do not send any payment (cash, checks, money orders, etc.) with Forms W-2 and W-3.

Reminder

Separate instructions. See the 2010 Instructions for Forms W-2 and W-3 for information on completing this form.

Purpose of Form

A Form W-3 Transmittal is completed only when paper Copy A of Form(s) W-2, Wage and Tax Statement, are being filed. Do not file Form W-3 alone. Do not file Form W-3 for Form(s) W-2 that were submitted electronically to the Social Security Administration (see below). All paper forms **must** comply with IRS standards and be machine readable. Photocopies are **not** acceptable. Use a Form W-3 even if only one paper Form W-2 is being filed. Make sure both the Form W-3 and Form(s) W-2 show the correct tax year and Employer Identification Number (EIN). Make a copy of this form and keep it with Copy D (For Employer) of Form(s) W-2 for your records.

Electronic Filing

The Social Security Administration (SSA) strongly suggests employers report Form W-3 and W-2 Copy A electronically instead of on paper. SSA provides two free options on its Business Services Online (BSO) website:

• **W-2 Online.** Use fill-in forms to create, save, print, and submit up to 20 Forms W-2 to SSA.

• **File Upload.** Upload wage files to SSA that you have created using payroll or tax software that formats the files according to SSA's *Specifications for Filing Form W-2 Electronically (EFW2)*.

For more information, go to *www.socialsecurity.gov/employer* and select "First Time Filers" or "Returning Filers" under "BEFORE YOU FILE."

When To File

Mail any paper Forms W-2 under cover of this Form W-3 Transmittal by February 28, 2011. Electronic fill-in forms or uploads are filed through SSA's Business Services Online (BSO) Internet site and will be on time if submitted by March 31, 2011.

Where To File Paper Forms

Send this entire page with the entire Copy A page of Form(s) W-2 to:

Social Security Administration
Data Operations Center
Wilkes-Barre, PA 18769-0001

Note. If you use "Certified Mail" to file, change the ZIP code to "18769-0002." If you use an IRS-approved private delivery service, add "ATTN: W-2 Process, 1150 E. Mountain Dr." to the address and change the ZIP code to "18702-7997." See Publication 15 (Circular E), Employer's Tax Guide, for a list of IRS-approved private delivery services.

For Privacy Act and Paperwork Reduction Act Notice, see the back of Copy D of Form W-2.

Cat. No. 10159Y

(for Social Security and Medicare) withheld, along with the amounts of state and local taxes withheld (if any).

Along with the W-2 forms, submit Form W-3, a Transmittal of Wage and Tax Statements (Figure 21–19). This form lists the employer's name, address, and EIN and summarizes the amount of all employees' earnings and the federal income taxes and FICA taxes withheld.

What makes up what we know as employment taxes?

CHECKPOINT
LO 21.7

Procedure 21–1 Posting Charges, Payments, and Adjustments

GOAL To maintain a system that promotes accurate record keeping for the practice

MATERIALS Daily log sheets, patient ledger cards, and check register, or computerized bookkeeping system; summaries of charges, receipts, and disbursements

METHOD

1. Use a new log (day sheet) each day. For each patient seen that day, record the patient name, the relevant charges, and any payments received, calculating any necessary adjustments and new balances. If you're using a computerized system, enter the patient's name or account number, the relevant charges, and any payments received and adjustments made in the appropriate areas. The computer will calculate the new balances. The day sheets will also be used to do month-end reports and MUST be balanced before the next business day's transactions can be added to the system.

2. Create a ledger card for each new patient, and maintain a ledger card for all existing patients. The ledger card should include the patient's name, address, home and work telephone numbers, and insurance company. It should also contain the name of the guarantor (if different from the patient). Update the ledger card every time the patient incurs a charge or makes a payment. Be sure to adjust the account balance after every transaction. In a computerized system, a patient record is the same as a ledger card. This record must also be maintained and updated as this is the most up-to-date financial record for each patient's account.

3. Record all deposits accurately in the check register. File the deposit receipt—with a detailed listing of checks, cash, and money orders deposited—for later use in reconciling the bank statement. The deposit amount should match the amount of money collected by the practice for that day.

4. When paying bills for the practice, enter each check in the check register accurately, including the check number, date, payee, and amount before writing the check.

5. Prepare and/or print a summary of charges, receipts, and disbursements every month, quarter, or year, as directed. Be sure to double-check all entries and calculations from the monthly summary before posting them to the quarterly summary. Also, double-check the entries and calculations from the quarterly summary before posting them to the yearly summary.

Procedure 21-2 Posting a Nonsufficient Funds (NSF) Check

GOAL To post a nonsufficient funds (NSF) check to patient's account

MATERIALS Computer, returned check, patient ledger, calculator (optional), daily log sheet

METHOD

1. Locate the patient's account on the computer or pull the patient's ledger card for manual processes.
2. Use your medical facility's code for an NSF check (if used), and using today's date, create a new charge log for the patient. Using the code and the description *Check returned by bank* in the description column.
3. In the payment/adjustment column insert the amount of the NSF check in parenthesis as it was actually never received and the parentheses informs you to "do the opposite of usual"; in this case, add the payment to the balance instead of subtracting it.
4. Add the amount of the NSF check to the previous balance and insert that figure in the current balance column.
5. On the next line, also using today's date, add the description of *NSF Office Fee* with the office charge for NSF checks returned by the bank. Add this charge to the previous balance to obtain the new current balance.

DAILY LOG TOTAL CARE CLINIC, PC							
DATE	CODE	PATIENT	TODAY'S CHARGE	PAYMENT/ ADJUSTMENT	CURRENT BALANCE	PREVIOUS BALANCE	PROVIDER
3/22	Ashley Wilkins	Payment—Ck #102		15.00	0.00	15.00	WC
3/30	Ashley Wilkins	(NSF) Ck returned by Bank		(15.00)	15.00	0.00	WC
3/30	Ashley Wilkins	NSF Office Fee	35.00		50.00	15.00	WC

Procedure 21-3 Processing a Credit Balance

GOAL To process a credit balance

MATERIALS Daily log sheet or day sheet, checks, ledger card, computer, calculator, RA (Remittance Advice), or an Explanation of Benefits (EOB)

METHOD

1. Locate the patient's account in the computer or pull the patient's ledger card for paper-based systems.
2. Review the policy manual to make sure you are following the guidelines for posting credit balances.

3. Review the EOB and check to be sure that the payment is being credited to the correct patient account.

4. Post the payment to the patient's account by writing (or keying) the remittance amount in the paid column.

5. Subtract the payment amount from the previous balance and insert the new balance in the balance column. Check calculations carefully, particularly if it appears that an overpayment has been made.

6. Review the account thoroughly in case more insurance payments are expected on the patient's account.

7. Adjust the credit balance off the patient's account by issuing a refund (see Procedure 21–4).

Procedure 21–4 Processing Refunds to Patients

GOAL   To process refunds to patients

MATERIALS   Payment (check), ledger card, computer, calculator, Remittance Advice (RA) or an Explanation of Benefits (EOB)

METHOD
1. Calculate and determine the amount to be refunded (from Procedure 21–3).
2. Write a check to the patient for the amount to be refunded.
3. Ask the physician or business manager to sign the check so that it can be given or mailed to the patient.
4. Post the refund as a negative payment (credit) to the patient's ledger card or to the patient's account if a computerized system is being used. Using parentheses around the figure is a common way to record credits.
5. Make a copy of the check, retaining a copy in the patient's financial record. Give or mail the check to the patient. If the check is being mailed, be sure to verify the patient's address prior to mailing and utilize certified return receipt mail to be sure the patient receives the check.

Procedure 21–5 Making a Bank Deposit

GOAL   To prepare cash and checks for deposit and to deposit them properly into a bank account

MATERIALS   Bank deposit slip and items to be deposited, such as checks, cash, and money orders

METHOD
1. Divide the bills, coins, checks, and money orders into separate piles.
2. Sort the bills by denomination, from largest to smallest. Then, stack them, portrait side up, in the same direction. Total the amount of the bills, and write this amount on the deposit slip on the line marked "currency" or cash.

3. If you have enough coins to fill coin wrappers, put them in wrappers of the proper denomination. If not, count the coins, and put them in the deposit bag. Total the amount of coins, and write this amount on the deposit slip on the line marked "Coin."

4. Review all checks and money orders to be sure they are properly endorsed with a restrictive endorsement. List each check on the deposit slip, including the check number and amount.

5. List each money order on the deposit slip. Include the notation "money order" or "MO" and the name of the writer.

6. Calculate the total deposit (total of amounts or currency, coin, checks, and money orders). Write this amount on the deposit slip on the line marked "Total." If you do not use deposit slips that record a copy for the office, photocopy the deposit slip for your office records.

7. Record the total amount of the deposit in the office checkbook register.

8. If you plan to make the deposit in person, place the currency, coins, checks, and money orders in a deposit bag. If you cannot make the deposit in person, put the checks and money orders in a special bank-by-mail envelope, or put all deposit items in an envelope and send it by registered mail.

9. Make the deposit in person or by mail.

10. Obtain a deposit receipt from the bank. File it with the copy of the deposit slip in the office for later use when reconciling the bank statement.

Procedure 21–6 Reconciling a Bank Statement

GOAL To ensure that the bank record of deposits, payments, and withdrawals agrees with the practice's record of deposits, payments, and withdrawals

MATERIALS Previous bank statement, current bank statement, reconciliation worksheet (if not part of current bank statement), deposit receipts, red pencil, check stubs or checkbook register, returned checks

METHOD
1. Check the closing balance on the previous statement against the opening balance on the new statement. The balances should match. If they do not, call the bank.

2. Record the closing balance from the new statement on the reconciliation worksheet (Figure 21–9). This worksheet usually appears on the back of the bank statement.

3. Check each deposit receipt against the bank statement. Place a red check mark in the upper right corner of each receipt that is recorded on the statement. Total the amount of deposits that do *not* appear on the statement. Add this amount to the closing balance on the reconciliation worksheet.

4. Put the redeemed checks in numerical order. (Your bank may send you several sheets consisting of photocopies or scans of the checks instead of the actual checks.)

5. Compare each redeemed check with the bank statement, making sure that the amount on the check agrees with the amount on the statement. Place a red check mark in the upper-right corner of each redeemed check that is recorded on the statement. Also, place a check mark on the check stub or

check register entry. Any checks that were written but that do not appear on the statement and were not returned as redeemed are considered "outstanding" checks. You can find these easily on the check stubs or checkbook register because they have no red check mark.

6. List each outstanding check separately on the worksheet, including its check number and amount. Total the outstanding checks, and subtract this total from the bank statement balance.

7. If the statement shows that the checking account earned interest, add this amount to the checkbook balance.

8. If the statement lists such items as a service charge, check printing charge, or automatic payment, subtract them from the checkbook balance.

9. Compare the new checkbook balance with the new bank statement balance. They should match. If they do not, repeat the process, rechecking all calculations. Double-check the addition and subtraction in the checkbook register. Review the checkbook register to make sure you did not omit any items. Ensure that you carried the correct balance forward from one register page to the next. Double-check that you made the correct additions or subtractions for all interest earned and charges.

10. If your work is correct, and the balances still do not agree, call the bank to determine if a bank error has been made. Contact the bank promptly because the bank may have a time limit for corrections. The bank may consider the bank statement correct if you do not point out an error within a specified time. Check with your individual bank for their policy.

Procedure 21–7 Setting Up the Accounts Payable System

GOAL To set up an accounts payable system

MATERIALS Disbursements journal, petty cash record, payroll register, pen

METHOD **Setting Up the Disbursements Journal**

1. Write in column headings for the basic information about each check: date, payee's name, check number, and check amount.

2. Write in column headings for each type of business expense, such as rent and utilities.

3. Write in column headings (if space is available) for deposits and the account balance.

4. Record the data from completed checks under the appropriate column headings.

5. Be sure to subtract payments from the balance and add deposits to it.

Setting Up the Payroll Register

1. Write in column headings for check number, employee name, earnings to date, hourly rate, hours worked, regular earnings, overtime hours worked, and overtime earnings.

2. Write in column headings for total gross earnings for the pay period and gross taxable earnings.

3. Write in column headings for each deduction. These may include federal income tax, Federal Insurance Contributions Act (FICA) tax, state income tax, local income tax, and various voluntary deductions.

4. Write in a column heading for net earnings.

5. Each time you write payroll checks, record earning and deduction data under the appropriate column headings on the payroll register.

Procedure 21-8 Generating Payroll

GOAL To handle the practice's payroll as efficiently and accurately as possible for each pay period

MATERIALS Employees' time cards, employees' earnings records, payroll register, IRS tax tables, check register

METHOD

1. Calculate the total regular and overtime hours worked, based on the employee's time card. Enter those totals under the appropriate headings on the payroll register.

2. Check the pay rate on the employee earnings record. Then multiply the hours worked (including any paid vacation or paid holidays, if applicable) by the rates for regular time and overtime (time and a half or double time). This yields gross earnings.

3. Enter the gross earnings under the appropriate heading on the payroll register. Subtract any nontaxable benefits, such as health-care or retirement programs.

4. Using IRS tax tables and data on the employee earnings record, determine the amount of federal income tax to withhold based on the employee's marital status and number of exemptions. Also compute the amount of FICA tax to withhold for Social Security (6.2%) and Medicare (1.45%).

5. Following state and local procedures, determine the amount of state and local income taxes (if any) to withhold based on the employee's marital status and number of exemptions.

6. Calculate the employer's contributions to FUTA and to the state unemployment fund, if any. Post these amounts to the employer's account.

7. Enter any other required or voluntary deductions, such as health insurance or contributions to a 401(k) fund.

8. Subtract all deductions from the gross earnings to get the employee's net earnings.

9. Enter the total amount withheld from all employees for FICA under the headings for Social Security and Medicare. Remember that the employer must match these amounts. Enter other employer contributions, such as for federal and state unemployment taxes, under the appropriate headings.

10. Fill out the check stub, including the employee's name, date, pay period, gross earnings, all deductions, and net earnings. Make out the paycheck for the net earnings.

11. Deposit each deduction in a tax liability account.

Case Study

Taylor is involved with the financial aspects of the practice. She knows her job is very important since it is good financial management that keeps the office open and allows the office to provide quality patient care. As she is performing an age analysis on the accounts receivable, she notes that the number of records with outstanding balances older than 90 days is increasing. First, she ensures that all claims have been sent and all claims posted. She discovers that a growing number of patients are not covered by insurance. Taylor also suspects that some of these patients may be eligible for Medicaid. She brings this to the attention of Katy, the practice manager. Taylor also suggests to Katy that perhaps improved training for the registration team may result in determining Medicaid eligibility for more patients. Katy agrees with Taylor and appreciates having such a quality employee.

Thinking Critically

1. Did Taylor go beyond the call of duty to further investigate the cause of the nonpayments and recommend possible solutions?

2. Explain an age analysis.

3. Is it possible for a medical practice that provides outstanding patient care to go out of business?

practice APPLICATIONS

1. Record the following disbursements made on September 9, 2011, in a disbursements journal: Check no. 1234, payee—Tom Jones (electrician), check amount—$125; Check no. 1235, payee—Postmaster (postage), check amount—$32; Check no. 1236, payee—Gateway Property Management (rent), check amount—$900.

2. A medical assistant in a medical practice is hired to work 8 hours a day, 4 days a week at an hourly rate of $10.00/hour. Checks are issued every 2 weeks. Her total deductions each week equal 10% of her gross earnings. What are her gross earnings per week? What is her "take-home" pay in each check?

exam READINESS

1. [LO21.1] Checks with stubs attached are called
   a. counters.
   b. vouchers.
   c. limited.
   d. certified.
   e. traveler's.

2. [LO21.3] What type mark indicates a restrictive endorsement has been assigned to a check?
   a. Signature of office representative
   b. The words "For deposit only" with account number to where it is being deposited into
   c. Account number of payer

d. Bank name to which the deposit will be made
e. Both a and b

3. **[LO21.3]** A banking task can include

   a. writing, accepting, and endorsing checks.
   b. making personal withdrawals.
   c. reconciliation of bank statements.
   d. transferring funds from business to private accounts.
   e. Both a and c

4. **[LO21.1]** Which of the following is NOT a record used in accounting systems?

   a. Day sheet
   b. Patient ledger card
   c. Disbursements journal
   d. Payroll record
   e. I-9 Form

5. **[LO21.2]** Which accounting method is most often found in medical practices?

   a. Single-entry system
   b. Pegboard system
   c. Write-it-once system
   d. Both b & c
   e. Double-entry system

6. **[LO21.4]** Which of the following is the correct definition for accounts payable?

   a. Accounts that have been paid by the office
   b. Accounts that are awaiting payment by the office
   c. Accounts waiting to be paid by patients
   d. Accounts that have been paid by patients
   e. Both a and b are correct

7. **[LO21.3]** When an error is made completing a check, you should

   a. use correction fluid and write in the correct information.

b. write "VOID" across the back of the check.
c. draw a single line through the entry, write "corr," and add in the correct information with the date and your initials.
d. write "VOID" across the face of the check.
e. tear up the check and write a new one.

8. **[LO21.3]** An asterisk on a bank statement can indicate

   a. the wrong date of cashed check.
   b. a gap in check numbers that have cleared the account.
   c. a missing signature of payer.
   d. the wrong account number.
   e. nothing.

9. **[LO21.5]** Looking for changes in office expenses by watching the disbursements journal is known as

   a. tracking.
   b. recording.
   c. bookkeeping.
   d. journaling.
   e. disbursing.

10. **[LO21.2]** To verify that the patient accounts are balanced using the pegboard system, which of the following formulas may be used?

    a. Current balance + (payments + adjustments) = previous balance
    b. Previous balance + (payments + adjustments) = current balance
    c. Previous balance + charges − (payments + adjustments) = current balance
    d. Previous balance − charges + (payments + adjustments) = current balance
    e. Current balance = previous balance + (payments − adjustments) + charges

learning outcome SUMMARY

LO 21.1 Traditional bookkeeping systems in the medical office are also known as patient accounting methods. Many medical offices still use manual systems, although most use computerized systems. All bookkeeping systems record income (patient charges), disbursements, and other financial information.

LO 21.2 Bookkeeping types include single-entry, double-entry, and pegboard systems. Single-entry systems are simple to learn but errors are difficult to detect. Double-entry systems require trained personnel

to use but detect errors more quickly because they use a consistent accounting formula. Most medical office systems are based on the pegboard system which also contains a formula to check your work.

LO 21.3 Accepting and endorsing checks from patients and insurance companies require consistency and attentiveness. Endorse all checks with a restrictive endorsement as soon as they are received. Calculate deposits carefully and make deposits promptly, noting deposits in the disbursements journal and/or check

register. To reconcile a bank statement, compare the bank record of deposits, payments, and other withdrawals with the medical facility's records. Make appropriate adjustments, and when the reconciliation is completed, the practice balance and the bank balance should agree.

LO 21.4 Payments for supplies, equipment, and practice-related products and services, payroll, and taxes owed to local, state and federal agencies are the three main types of disbursements made in a medical practice.

LO 21.5 Disbursements are classified related to the reason the payment is being made. Accurate records must be kept so the practice can easily identify the items or services on which money is being spent. To replenish petty cash, write a check for cash for the amount that the fund is "short" of the approved amount to keep on hand. Cash the check at the bank asking for coin and small bills. Receipts for all money spent from the fund should be kept and balanced on a periodic basis.

LO 21.6 To calculate an employee's gross earnings, multiply the hours worked by the hourly rate. Using state, local, and federal tax guidelines, calculate the employee's tax deductions. Add to these any voluntary deductions and subtract the total deductions to obtain the employee's net earnings. Using the employee payroll record containing the employee's name, address, SSN, and number of exemptions, record the employee's gross earnings, deductions (including mandatory and voluntary deductions), and net paycheck.

LO 21.7 Tax forms used in a medical practice include, but are not limited to, W2, W3, and W4 forms, NHR forms, I-9s, quarterly federal tax forms, wage and tax statements, and FUTA and SUTA forms. The practice liability account is set up to hold the money deducted from employees' paychecks until the funds can be appropriately disbursed to the government agencies. There may be separate accounts for federal and state taxes as well as unemployment and retirement funds. Record the tax amounts deposited in the liability account as debits in the practice checking account.

medical assisting COMPETENCIES

CAAHEP

VI. C (1) Explain basic bookkeeping computations

VI. C (2) Differentiate between bookkeeping and accounting

VI. C (3) Describe banking procedures

VI. C (4) Discuss precautions for accepting checks

VI. C (5) Compare types of endorsement

VI. C (6) Differentiate between accounts payable and accounts receivable

VI. C (7) Compare manual and computerized bookkeeping systems used in ambulatory healthcare

VI. C (8) Describe common periodic financial reports

VI. C (9) Explain both billing and payment options

VI. C (10) Identify procedure for preparing patient accounts

VI. C (11) Discuss procedures for collecting outstanding accounts

VI. C (12) Describe the impact of both the Fair Debt Collection Act and the Federal Truth in Lending Act of 1986 as they apply to collections

VI. C (13) Discuss types of adjustments that may be made to a patient's account

VI. P (1) Prepare a bank deposit

VI. P (2) Perform accounts receivable procedures, including
   a. Post entries on a day sheet
   b. Perform billing procedures
   c. Perform collection procedures
   d. Post adjustments
   e. Process a credit balance
   f. Process refunds
   g. Post nonsufficient funds (NSF) checks
   h. Post collection agency payments

VI.P (2) Utilize computerized office billing systems

VI.A (1) Demonstrate sensitivity and professionalism in handling accounts receivable activities with clients

ABHES

8. Medical Office Business Procedures Management

g. Prepare and reconcile a bank statement and deposit record

h. Post entries on a day sheet

j. Perform accounts payable procedures

k. Perform accounts receivable procedures

m. Post adjustments

n. Process credit balance

o. Process refunds

p. Post non-sufficient funds (NSF)

q. Post collection agency payments

w. Use manual or computerized bookkeeping systems

ll. Apply electronic technology

Practice
Management

Every small positive change we make in ourselves repays us in confidence in the future.

Alice Walker

Preparation for Success

Interviewer: Emila, you grew up in Bosnia during a time of turmoil in that country and you have a very personal story to share.

Emila: During the combat in Bosnia, we often did not go to school due to safety. The times we did go, we would not want to be noticed or call attention to ourselves. As a result, we did not ask questions. Coming to this country, everyone thought I was quiet due to a language problem, but I knew English well. It was difficult for me to grasp that in this culture you are free to ask questions.

Interviewer: That must have been very difficult since you were studying to be an administrative medical assistant and the health systems of the two countries are very different. Were there times you did not understand what was being taught and wanted to ask the question "why"?

Emila: Yes, often and my grades were not that good which disappointed my parents. Then one of my instructors sat down with me and said that she knew from my entry assessment test that I comprehended English and she knew that I was working hard. She asked why I did not ask questions if I did not understand the material. I must have looked shocked because she asked if I was all right. When I explained the reason she said it was okay to ask questions and I agreed I would. It was hard for me to get the courage to change but I did and my grades improved. I graduated with a 3.5 grade average.

Interviewer: You finished your associate degree, became an administrative medical assistant, and then a medical office coordinator. What is your favorite part of the job?

Emila: My favorite part of the job is orienting new staff and encouraging them to ask questions if they do not understand. I also speak to classes at the allied health school in our town and tell students to never be afraid to ask questions. Not only is it okay, but it is their obligation to ensure they understand the material that is being taught. They will also be asking questions of patients, family members, insurance companies, other medical offices, laboratories, and coworkers. Asking thoughtful questions as a student is important and helps build confidence which is necessary to be effective in health care. This is a quality that our human resources specialist looks for in people that interview.

Interviewer: Emila, I'm sure you are an inspiration and an amazing mentor to the students and staff that work with you.

Emila: Thank you.

unit 6

22 Practice Management

Learning Outcomes

After completing Chapter 22, you will be able to:

22.1 Understand basic organizational designs of the medical office and the relationship of the physician and the medical assistant with the practice manager and direct supervisors.

22.2 Describe the general responsibilities of the practice manager.

22.3 Identify components of managing the facility and health and safety considerations.

22.4 Explain the purpose of risk management and quality assurance for the medical office.

22.5 Understand the basic human relations functions.

22.6 Explain employee benefits and labor relations.

Key Terms

agenda	mediation
budget	midlevel provider
chain of command	organizational chart
employee handbook	policies and procedures
exposure control plan	(P&Ps)
Form I-9	probationary period
grievance process	quality assurance (QA)
incident report	risk management (RM)
labor relations	sexual harassment
Material Safety Data	W-2 tax form
Sheets (MSDS)	W-4 tax form

Preparation for Certification

RMA (AMT)
- Medical ethics
- Human relations
- Medical receptionist/secretarial/clerical

CMAS (AMT)
- Legal and ethical considerations
- Professionalism
- Office communications
- Business organization management
- Payroll
- Human resources
- Safety
- Physical office plant
- Risk management and quality assurance

CMA (AAMA)
- Professionalism
- Communication
- Medicolegal guidelines and requirements
- Computer concepts
- Maintaining the office environment
- Office policies and procedures

Introduction ● ● ●

The previous chapters describe the myriad of complex systems, procedures, requirements, and roles in the present-day medical office. It is almost impossible for the physician to care for patients and manage the office as he or she may have done in the past (Figure 22–1). While the management of the health-care facility differs by ownership, size, and other variables, one person is generally in charge of overseeing the day-to-day operations. The title of this person has varying names such as *practice* or *office manager, executive,* or *director* or *health-care administrator.* This chapter discusses this person's position, responsibilities, and relationship with the physician and medical assistant. The terms "medical practice manager" and "office manager" represent the role. Risk management and the functions of human resources, also referred to as personnel services or people services, are also discussed.

LO 22.1 Organizational Design

Every medical office has an organizational design that may or may not be represented by a formal **organizational chart.** The design and chart show the supervisory structure and reporting relationships between different functions and positions. In other words, it shows who is responsible for whom and what. In most states, the medical assistant is required to be under the direct supervision of the physician, physician assistant, or nurse practitioner for direct patient care activities. However, the practice manager or that person's designee is usually responsible for interviewing, hiring, firing, evaluating, and ensuring training and credentialing, which are all considered administrative and not direct patient care functions.

> **organizational chart**
> A model showing the supervisory structure and reporting relationships between different functions and positions in an organization.

figure 22–1

With the complexities of today's medical practices, very few physicians can manage the office and conduct patient care as in the past.

Physician-Owned Medical Practice

Figure 22–2 represents a simplified organizational chart of a physician-owned practice. A physician-owned medical practice sometimes obtains the legal designation of a professional corporation (PC). The owner is usually an individual doctor or group of physicians. The placement of the boxes and lines shows that the physician carries the ultimate responsibility but designates it to the person below him who is the practice manager. The practice manager reports to the physician who also pays his or her salary. The manager is the physician's employee who oversees the daily operations and the administrative functions of the entire office and staff, including the medical assistants. The solid line from the physician to the medical assistant demonstrates that the physician also has direct responsibility for the medical assistants. As mentioned previously, this responsibility involves the direct patient care. Depending on the size of the practice, other supervisory personnel might report to the practice manager. Each supervisor would then have staff reporting directly to him or her. Additional supervisory staff titles include team leader or supervisor and supervisors or managers of various departments such as human resources, laboratory, and billing. In multispecialty organizations, supervisors may be designated by specialty such as pediatrics, internal medicine, and cardiology.

figure 22–2

Physician-owned medical practice organizational chart.

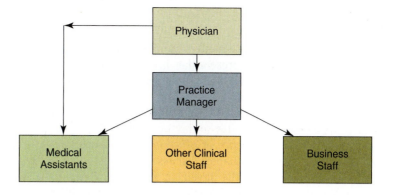

Company-Owned Medical Practice

Figure 22–3 represents a simplified organizational chart of a company-owned medical facility. The company may be nonprofit such as a community health center or for-profit such as Cigna HealthCare. The president or chief executive officer (CEO) has the ultimate responsibility. Again, the practice manager is in charge of the day-to-day operations with the exception of the direct patient care functions of the medical assistants and the physicians who are accountable to the medical director. The medical director is also in charge of the physician assistants and nurse practitioners. These positions are referred to as **midlevel providers.** The dotted lines between the practice manager and the medical director indicate they are equal in rank and collaborate with each other. The dotted line from the practice manager to the other physicians indicates collaboration. For example, the practice manager may ensure the physicians are properly credentialed. The medical director has the majority of the responsibilities for the physicians such as scheduling and evaluating. The president, practice manager, medical director, and other physicians and staff are employees of the company and paid by the company. A board of directors is ultimately responsible through the CEO but not involved in the daily operations of the company.

The Chain of Command

The phrase **chain of command** began in the military to demonstrate how each rank is accountable to those directly superior and how the authority passes from one link in the chain to the next, or from the top to the bottom. An example would be that a private is accountable to the sergeant who is accountable to the lieutenant and so on. The lieutenant would give an order

midlevel provider
A medical caregiver who is not a physician but is licensed to diagnose and treat patients, usually under the supervision of a licensed physician.

chain of command
Term first used in the military to describe how each rank is accountable to those directly superior and how the authority passes from one link in the chain to the next, or from the top to the bottom.

figure 22–3

Corporate-owned medical practice organizational chart.

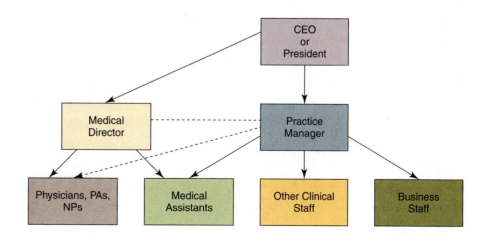

to the sergeant who gives it to the private. There are many steps at each level determining the equipment, training, and strategies needed to carry out the order or mission. The majority of today's businesses, including medical offices, operate using a chain of command. The organizational chart shows the chain from the top and includes your position. It is important to understand the chain of command in the facility where you work. Since medical assistants work closely with physicians, the tendency may be to go to the physician with requests such as asking for time off. It is not appropriate to ask the physician if this is the function of the practice manager or your supervisor. It is also not appropriate to go outside the chain of command with a complaint, even if the complaint is about your supervisor. You should first address the issue with your supervisor. If not resolved, then go to the next person in the chain of command. This person may be the practice manager. Most offices have policies and procedures to handle complaints. Should you seek other employment, that organization will contact your previous supervisor for references. No matter how friendly or informal the medical practice is, stay within the chain of command.

● ● ●

Explain the purpose of an organizational chart.

CHECKPOINT
LO 22.1

LO 22.2 Practice Management Responsibilities

The role of the practice manager includes providing avenues of communication for all constituents; ensuring that the legal, business, and health and safety requirements are in compliance; guaranteeing the adequacy of the technology and physical plant; providing for the practice's financial viability; and monitoring risk management and customer care and satisfaction. In some instances, the person may be in charge of multiple sites.

Communication

Chapter 4, Professional Communication, described general communication techniques and communication with patients, persons with special needs, and co-workers. The practice management position requires excellent verbal and written communication and interpersonal skills. Listed are some of the routine individuals and groups with whom the practice manager communicates on a regular basis:

- Staff
- Patients
- Physicians (within and in other practices)
- Hospitals
- Insurers
- Vendors
- Employers
- Contractors
- Governmental agencies
- Other regulatory and professional agencies
- Educational facilities
- Bankers
- Attorneys
- Community organizations

Communicating with each individual and group requires knowledge of the business or situation and, often, excellent problem-solving techniques. The role of the manager is also to ensure that all communication is appropriate, respectful, timely, and HIPAA compliant. Many offices have policies and procedures related to communication, especially electronic communication.

Working with the Health-Care Team

THE PHYSICIAN ASSISTANT

Duties and Skills

The physician assistant (PA) practices medicine under the laws of the specific state and the supervision of a physician. PAs provide diagnostic, therapeutic, and preventive health-care services, as designated by the supervising physician. Physician assistants take medical histories; order laboratory and medical imaging tests; examine, diagnose, treat, counsel, and follow up with patients. They also perform suturing, casting, and splinting for minor injuries, and some PAs assist in surgery. PAs also prescribe certain medications. In some cases, managerial duties may be performed such as purchasing and maintaining equipment and hiring and firing personnel. The physician assistant may also take call duty for the practice and share the responsibility for after-hours call duty with the physician.

Educational Requirements

Admission requirements for physician assistant programs vary. Generally, a degree is required and experience in health care. Most programs specify the minimum number of hours, for example 2,000, required in health care before an application to PA school is accepted. PAs must complete an accredited education program and pass a national and, in some cases, a state exam to obtain licensure.

Workplace Settings

The physician assistant generally works in the medical office but may work in surgery as first or second assistant and in hospital emergency departments. The PA may be the primary care provider in rural or inner-city clinics where a physician is present only one or two days a week. In these circumstances, the PA confers with the supervising physician as needed and as required by law. PAs may also make house calls and go to hospitals and nursing care facilities to see patients.

The Physician Assistant as a Team Member

The physician assistant is a midlevel provider who may supervise the medical assistant. Together the PA and medical assistant, following state law, function as the patient's caregiving team. The PA, in some instances, may assume some or all of the duties of the practice manager.

For more information, visit the Web site of the following organization, which is available on the Online Learning Center at www.mhhe.com/houseradminmedassist

American Academy of Physician Assistants

Staff Communication

The effective manager ensures convenient two-way, open, and consistent avenues of communication with the staff. The following modalities are often used:

agenda
A list of meeting topics and the order they will be addressed.

- Staff meetings—Staff meetings should be at a consistent time each month when patients are not seen. The time is blocked off in the appointment matrix. The location should allow privacy. An **agenda,** which is the list of meeting topics and the order they will be addressed, should be used (Figure 22–4). See Procedure 22–1, Preparing an Agenda, located at the end of this chapter. Formal minutes (the meeting record) may or may not be kept but at least meeting notes should be maintained by the practice manager that contain the date and time, who was present and absent, what was discussed, and who was responsible for any follow-up actions. These minutes may be needed for credentialing and licensing agencies or as proof of educational and informational topics addressed and as a tool for staff evaluations.

- E-mail—A large number of offices have email for each employee or group of employees. Electronic communication is rapid and convenient but should be read and edited carefully. Staff and management messages should maintain a professional tone and responses provided in a reasonable time. Attachments of new policies, and so on, make this method environmentally friendly and provide easy filing for information that may require retrieval.

- Newsletters—Larger practices may have a monthly or quarterly electronic or hard copy newsletter that may be the responsibility of the practice manager. The content usually provides information on what is going

figure 22-4

Sample staff meeting agenda.

Total Care Clinic: Staff Lounge
Staff Meeting Agenda
October 1, 20XX
12:00 to 1:30 p.m.

Lunch provided

Introductions	**Darlene Elliott**
Staff News	**All**
Quality Assurance Report	**Linda Wiley**
Policies and Procedures Update	**Darlene Elliott**
EHR Committee Report	**Ravi Patel**
Report from AHIMA Conference	**Kalisha Roberts**

Old Business:
- **Extending office hours**   **Mathew Rodriguez**
- **Upcoming flu shot clinic**   **Brendan Conroy**

New Business:
- **Holiday Party**   **Darlene Elliott**
- **Volunteers for Flu Preparedness**   **John Fredericks**
  Committee

Other

Adjournment

Next meeting November 3, 20XX, 12:00 to 1:30 p.m.

on in the practice, new policies and procedures or requirements, accomplishments and awards, internal and community events, and often highlights staff members or departments.

- Bulletin boards—Usually located in the staff lounge, these boards should not contain any confidential or sensitive information since janitorial staff and others outside of the practice may have access.

- Communication books—Notebooks or binders with new policies and procedures, events, and other information the manager wants to inform the staff about is kept in a central location. Employees may be required to initial each entry to ensure it was read. Communication books are kept and may be used during orientation of new staff or even in legal situations. Electronic communication of this information is replacing books.

- Open-door policy—This policy, maintained by many practice managers, gives staff the freedom to come talk any time the manager's office door is open. Staff should be respectful of the manager's time and, if the topic is involved and lengthy, schedule an appointment.

- Suggestion boxes—In some facilities, staff and sometimes patients are encouraged to place ideas in a box; they submit it with a name or anonymously. If the suggestion is implemented, some organizations provide a monetary or other award.

Legal and Business Functions

Another role of the practice manger is to ensure the organization is compliant and meets the legal requirements and the standard for medical and business practices. This responsibility involves many systems and processes. Some of the more common ones follow.

Policies and Procedures   Developing, maintaining, reviewing, and updating (usually, annually) policy and procedure manuals is one of the major methods used to meet standards. **Policies and procedures** are often referred to as the **P&Ps.** The policy is a statement of the intent, the commitment, or the goal. The procedure incorporates the correct manner for performing or carrying out the individual policy. It is the map for reaching the goal. An example is a policy that states that OSHA guidelines for bloodborne pathogens will be maintained by all staff at all times. The procedure(s) would describe the steps expected to maintain bloodborne pathogen guidelines. Facilities may have more than one P&P manual, such as one for human resources, one for safety, and one for clinical procedures. The office manager must stay current with new practices and standards of the community and the professional organizations. In addition, new laws and requirements of the governmental agencies such as OSHA and CMS must be monitored and incorporated. Reading the policy and procedure manuals is a portion of new employee orientation. The P&Ps are where an employee should look if he or she is unsure about a specific duty or task.

policies and procedures (P&Ps)
Policies are statements of intent, commitment, or goals; procedures prescribe the correct method for performing or carrying out the individual policy.

Licenses, Certifications, and Contracts   The medical practice includes many positions and facets that require federal, state, or local approval. The approvals may be in the form of a license, certification, or other credential or contract. Some are very expensive and complicated. Common ones are ensuring that

- Physicians and midlevel providers are properly licensed.
- Physician and midlevel provider DEA forms are up-to-date.
- Medical assistants, phlebotomists, coders, and other personnel are properly trained and certified or credentialed according to federal, state, and professional standards.
- Required licenses to operate the facility, such as local business licenses, are up-to-date.
- CMS and accrediting approvals are in place and up-to-date.
- Insurance requirements such as malpractice and liability contracts are up-to-date and reflect current values.
- Health insurance companies, laboratories, attorneys, and service contracts necessary to conduct business are in place (Figure 22–5).
- Required reporting to authorities such as communicable diseases is in compliance.

figure 22-5

Negotiating and signing contracts is a vital role of the practice manager.

Depending on the size of the health-care organization, the manager may have other employees involved in carrying out these duties. However, the manager has the ultimate responsibility to guarantee that these jobs are done and done properly.

Budget and Overall Finances   With the exception of large organizations that have a chief financial officer (CFO), the responsibility for the practice's finances is part of the manager's extensive role. A **budget** is created annually and reviewed at least monthly. The budget predicts the expenses and revenues related to operations over a given period of time. First, the manager must know the total expenses. Salaries are usually the biggest budget expense. The manager reviews the health-care insurance and governmental agencies' patient care contracts and other sources of income. Sometimes the manager must renegotiate the contract if costs have risen. If revenues are lower than expected and the costs are higher, the manager must make unpopular cuts in the budget.

budget
The predicted expenses and revenues to operate over a given period of time.

Financial responsibility is the role of every employee. Something as simple as taking pens home for your family to use may have an impact, if all employees did the same. Integrity is a professional behavior.

Scheduling and Travel   Ensuring that adequate staff are on duty at all times for the business to function properly is an additional aspect of the practice manager's role. Scheduling is a job that may be relegated to a supervisor or other person, depending on the size of the practice. It is monitored by the manager. Sometimes physicians and other staff, such as medical assistants, travel for educational purposes with expenses covered by the practice (Figure 22–6). Procedure 22–2 at the end of this chapter provides you with practice in completing a travel expense report. Planning to staff the office when personnel are gone may be necessary. If the physician is unavailable, the office may be closed during that time.

Other Business Functions   The contemporary medical office relies on technology for communication, appointment scheduling, coding, billing, diagnostic test ordering and reporting, prescription refills, and the electronic health record. These areas require highly specialized skills to install and maintain. The office manager evaluates and purchases the systems that fit the needs and budget of the practice, facilitates the installation and staff training, then oversees the ongoing operations through an in-house technical support person or through a service contract. Other managerial functions include ensuring mailing and shipping services, inventory and supply purchases, and appropriate market and public relation strategies which may include Web sites, brochures, and sponsorship of community events.

Why is financial responsibility in the medical office the role of all employees?

**CHECKPOINT
LO 22.2**

LO 22.3 The Facility and Health and Safety

The facility or physical plant is the building or buildings, offices, parking structures, furniture, and mechanical systems. To promote an efficient workplace the practice manager facilitates the following:

- Utilization of space (Figure 22–7)
- Payment of mortgage or rental, utilities, and so on

figure 22-6

Accounting for travel expenses is done using a travel expense form.

TOTAL CARE CLINIC, PC

342 East Park Blvd
Funton, XY 12345-6789
Tel: 521-234-0001
Fax: 521-234-0002

TRAVEL EXPENSE REPORT
(Travel with estimated expenses must be approved prior to the event)

Applicant's name: _____ Date: _____

Applicant's address: _____

Applicant's cell phone and home phone: _____

Name of activity and type (example: professional meeting, conference; attach Web or brochure information): _____

Purpose of travel: _____

Location of activity: _____

Dates: _____ Number of days: _____

Registration fee	$
Transportation: *indicate major mode of travel _____	$
Airport shuttle or parking	$
Taxi	$
Lodging (daily rate_____ ✕ _____number of days)	$
Meals ($30 per day ✕ _____ number of days)	$
Other (explain)	$
Total	$

Did you miss work days: ☐ NO   ☐ YES (If "YES" include dates and number of days)

Dates: _____ Number of days: _____

Signature: _____

*If using your own vehicle, mileage is reimbursed at the current rate. Check with your supervisor prior to travel.

This form must be submitted with receipts in 10 working days upon return. Noncompliance may result in denial of reimbursement or if funds were previously awarded, payroll deduction may occur to recover the amount.

For Management Use Only

☐ Not approved   ☐ Approved   Amount:_____

Name (print):_____ Date:_____

Signature:_____

- Selection and purchase or lease of capital equipment such as copy machines and telephone systems
- Establishment of contracts and oversight of janitorial, biohazardous waste disposal, and other services
- Required maintenance of elevators, heating, air conditioning, and other equipment; pavement of parking lot; and replacement of light bulbs
- Replacement of worn furniture, carpeting, and so on
- Compliance with ADA requirements
- Availability of adequate supplies and materials
- Emergency repairs such as unclogging drains
- Security
- Landscape maintenance
- Plans for future needs

Health and Safety Compliance

In addition to an efficient and ADA compliant facility, federal, state, and local regulations regarding a safe work environment must be followed. The practice manager ensures compliance by first developing or facilitating the development of policies and procedures which are then incorporated in a safety manual and **exposure control plan.** The exposure control plan describes personnel protective equipment and other safety engineering devices and processes. It also provides instructions of what an employee should do if an exposure occurs.

Next, staff must be educated and trained according to the manual and exposure control plan, and systems must be established to make them work, such as contracts in place with an approved waste management group for proper disposal of biohazardous waste.

Another component of the exposure control plan is the purchase of **Material Safety Data Sheets (MSDS)** which supply information on the potentially hazardous substances. The information sheets provide workers and emergency personnel with the procedures for handling or working with these substances if a spill or other accident occurs. Updates and additions are made frequently.

Influenza and hepatitis B vaccines are additional health and safety protocols. The manager maintains records of safeguards, inspections, and exposures as required. Some of these duties may be delegated to a safety officer or other personnel, but the manager has the overall responsibility. Health and safety also includes emergency preparedness plans as discussed in Chapter 23, Emergency Preparedness.

● ● ●

Why is the practice manager required to keep records of safeguards, inspections, and exposures?

figure 22–7
Determining how space is used is a practice management function.

exposure control plan
Describes personnel protective equipment and other safety engineering devices and processes; it provides instructions of what an employee should do if an exposure occurs.

Material Safety Data Sheets (MSDS)
Forms which address the potentially hazardous substances used and provide workers and emergency personnel with the procedures for handling or working with these substances if a spill or other accident occurs.

CHECKPOINT
LO 22.3

LO 22.4 Risk Management and Quality Assurance

Risk management (RM) comprises a plan and processes that continually identify, assess, correct, and monitor functions of the medical office. It should prevent negative outcomes and minimize exposure to risk and consequent

risk management (RM)
A plan and processes that continually assess, identify, correct, and monitor functions of the medical office to prevent negative outcomes and minimize exposure to risk.

Selecting a System

As a practice manager, selecting an EHR system is a serious decision. The first thing is to look for the certification of the system by the Certification Commission for Healthcare Information Technology (CCHIT) ensuring the system has the required standards and associated features, such as secure communication between providers and direct pharmacy communications. Listed are other common considerations for the practice manager:

• What are total costs including time for staff training?
• What are the technology requirements (computer specifications, additional computers, memory, etc.)?
• How much screen development must be done by the practice?
• How will hard copy medical records be incorporated?
• How does it interface with current scheduling, billing, and other systems?
• What is involved with installation?
• What is the company's experience with "go live" installations?
• How is staff training conducted and by whom?
• What is the cost of ongoing maintenance and upgrades?
• What are the backup and storage systems?

When you go to your externship site, inquire why the practice chose its EHR and how the decision was made. Often, a committee of management and staff evaluate the choices. If an EHR committee is meeting at your externship site, ask permission to attend.

quality assurance (QA)
Ensuring that the services meet or exceed the requirements and standards.

liability. Immediately recognizing and addressing potential problems is everyone's focus. Risk management also identifies opportunities for improvement. The procedures for opening and closing the office discussed in Chapter 8 are examples. **Quality assurance (QA)** is ensuring that the services meet or exceed the requirements and standards. Quality assurance also encompasses *utilization review* (UR), which is ensuring that the treatment plan and services are appropriate and cost effective. Determining medical necessity is usually required. These areas include almost every aspect of the practice manager's role and are a huge responsibility. The Joint Commission (TJC) and the National Committee on Quality Assurance (NCQA) review the office's RM and QA plans and outcomes during accreditation visits. They look for a problem-solving model that follows the issue to resolution. This is referred to as *closing the loop*. The following is an example of a typical five-step problem-solving model (Figure 22–8):

1. Identification
2. Assessment
3. Correction (design and implementation of an improvement plan)

figure 22–8
The problem-solving process.

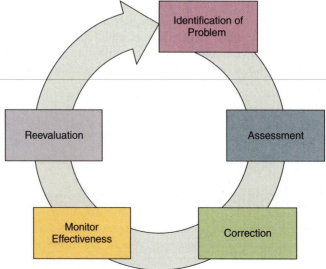

4. Monitoring to ensure effectiveness of the plan

5. Reevaluation

A simple example would be that Denise, the practice manager at the Total Care Clinic, notices the carpet in the reception area is torn. Patients and staff are placed at risk of falling (identification). She examines the tear and the entire carpet (assessment). Denise places tape over the tear and orders replacement carpeting (correction). The staff is made aware and asked to be observant for other tears and similar problems (monitor effectiveness). Denise will reevaluate the condition of the carpet at intervals to ensure it is not a risk for tripping and falling.

Incident Reports

An **incident report** (Figure 22–9), or occurrence report, is a special form required by a facility when an adverse outcome or event with risk of liability occurs. Refer to Procedure 22–3, Completing an Incident Report. A fall caused by the torn carpeting would have required an incident report.

The report contains only factual information. Opinions and assumptions are omitted. Incident reports are not placed in a patient's medical record and some institutions prefer that the actual incident report is not completed in the presence of the injured party. The standard practice is that no copies of an incident report are made and only the original is maintained in a dedicated risk management file. As part of risk management, the practice manager routinely monitors and trends incident reports. While risk management includes anyone who enters the medical office, quality assurance generally involves the patient and his or her care.

incident report (or occurrence report)
A special form required by a facility when an adverse outcome or event with risk of liability occurs.

● ● ●

Describe the elements in the five-step problem-solving model.

CHECKPOINT
LO 22. 4

LO 22.5 Basic Human Relations Functions

The role of the practice manager includes the human resources (HR) component of the medical office. This department or area of an organization is probably the only one that does not involve the patient. It may have its own coordinator or supervisor who may report to the practice manager. The functions directly concern employees such as hiring, training, benefits, and labor relations. Other names are human relations, personnel services, personnel department, or people services. This chapter uses the term *human resources* and follows Kalisha Roberts, CMA (AAMA), through the Total Care Clinic (TCC) hiring process.

The Hiring Process

Federal, state, and local governments regulate hiring practices. Violation could result in monetary and other penalties. Understanding and maintaining currency with these often complex laws is a major HR role. The Total Care Clinic's hiring practices comply with the following employment laws.

- Equal Employment Opportunity Commission (EEOC) prohibiting job discrimination for race, color, religion, sex, or national origin (Figure 22–10)

- Fair Labor Standards Act prohibiting child labor and providing a minimum wage and provisions for overtime

- Equal Pay Act prohibiting sex-based pay discrimination for men and women performing the same jobs

- Age Discrimination in Employment Act prohibiting job discrimination for people 40 years and older

figure 22–9

Incident report.

TOTAL CARE CLINIC, PC

342 E. Park Blvd
Funton, XY 12345-6789
Tel: 521-234-0001
Fax: 521-234-0002

Incident Report

(Only for Internal Use)

Date/time of incident: _____   Location: _____

Name of injured or at risk party: _____

Circle one: **Patient**   **Staff Member**   **Other (complete blank)** _____

Address of above party: _____

Phone numbers of above party: home _____ cell _____

Describe the incident (use back of sheet if additional space needed): _____

_____

_____

Describe action(s) taken and by whom: _____

_____

_____

_____

Name(s)/contact information of witnesses: _____

_____

_____

Name(s)/time of parties notified: _____

_____

Name of person completing report: _____   Date/time: _____

Report submitted to: _____   Date/time: _____

(Submit form to immediate supervisor of area where the incident occurred)

Employee Participation

Every employee has an opportunity for involvement with the operations of the practice. Add topics to the staff meeting agenda that are of importance or concern to you. Provide input at staff meetings. Volunteer for committees. Provide suggestions for improvement. Keep up with policies and procedures. Be alert for potential risk issues and contribute to the quality assurance effort. A healthy, happy work environment is one where everyone participates and takes responsibility. Patients and employees benefit.

- Americans with Disabilities Act (ADA) prohibiting discrimination against people with disabilities in employment, transportation, public accommodation, communications, and governmental activities
- Family Medical Leave Act (FMLA) allowing employees up to 12 job-protected weeks leave without pay for family or medical needs (Figure 22–10)

When the Total Care Clinic decided to hire an administrative medical assistant, a job description was written that consisted of the following:

- Name of organization
- Name of the position
- Employment grade
- Summary of position
- Job responsibilities
- Requirements and qualifications
- Title of the supervisor

One of the job description requirements was a CMA (AAMA) or a RMA (AMT) certification. The next step was to recruit qualified candidates. Kalisha Roberts was a CMA (AAMA) who applied for the position. Her application was one of those selected. She interviewed, her references were checked, and Kalisha was offered the job with an appropriate salary. HR maintains a personnel file for every employee and the Total Care clinic initiated a file for Kalisha.

figure 22–10

The EEOC prohibits job discrimination based on race, color, religion, sex, or national origin.

Welcome message	EEOC statement	Performance reviews and improvement plans
Organization's mission	Employment applications	Personal communications
ADA statements	Equipment and facility use	Personnel records
Attendance policies	Grievance process	Probationary period
Benefits	Holidays	Risk management and incident reports
Bereavement	Job Descriptions	Safety and security
Confidentiality and HIPAA	Jury duty	Schedules, accountability and requests for time off
Continuing education and tuition reimbursement	Leaves of Absence	Sexual harassment guidelines
Disability benefits	On the job injuries	Smoking policy
Disaster preparedness and emergency response	Orientation	Substance abuse
Dress code	OSHA	Subpoenas
Drug testing	Overtime	
Electronic communication and device use	Payroll periods	Wage increases and adjustments

table 22-1

Typical Employee Handbook Topics

employee handbook

A synopsis of an organization's policies, procedures, and expectations for all employees.

sexual harassment

Unwelcome verbal, visual, or physical conduct of a sexual nature that is severe or pervasive and affects working conditions or creates a hostile work environment.

Orientation and Staff Development

Human resources provides orientation for new employees and facilitates training and staff development for established employees. Orientation has three overarching sections: the organization; health and safety; and the employee's job. The United States Department of Labor (DOL) publishes and provides online copies of the Employment Law Guide that addresses many aspects of each of these sections. An **employee handbook** provides a synopsis of the HR policies and procedures. The employee handbooks and HR policies should address **sexual harassment.** It is a violation of federal and some state laws. The legal definition is *unwelcome verbal, visual, or physical conduct of a sexual nature that is severe or pervasive and affects working conditions or creates a hostile work environment.* Other topics in a typical employee handbook are found in Table 22-1.

The human resources area facilitates staff development and training. Kalisha, along with other staff members, was scheduled to attend training for the new electronic health record that the clinic is implementing. Other trainings may include new policies and procedures, cultural diversity and sensitivity, CPR certification, new equipment, and wellness topics such as stress management.

The medical practice may provide tuition reimbursement and expenses to attend conferences for continuing education units. All trainings and staff development activities are maintained in the employee's personnel file.

CHECKPOINT
LO 22.5

Describe the elements in a job description.

LO 22.6 Employee Benefits and Labor Relations

During orientation, Kalisha learned of her benefits including vacations and other time off, health insurance, disability insurance, and life insurance options. The new employee completed an Employment Eligibility Verification form (**Form I-9**), certifying United States citizenship, legal alien status, or legal authorization to work in this country. She also signed federal **W-4 tax form** stating the number of deductions the employee wishes to claim for income tax (Figure 22–11). This impacts the amount of money that will be withheld from her paycheck for federal taxes. As required by law, HR sends each employee a **W-2 tax form** by January 31 each year. The W-2 states how much gross income the organization paid the employee and the amount of taxes withheld. The employee uses the form to file his or her federal income tax. Payroll is a function shared by HR and the financial area of the office as described in Chapter 21, Financial Practices.

When Kalisha begins her employment she is on a 90-day **probationary period,** sometimes called a *trial period.* It allows the employee and organization an opportunity to decide if they are a "good fit." The organization may terminate Kalisha without cause during this time. The Total Care Clinic conducts employee performance reviews at the end of the probationary period and then annually. The performance review typically includes the responsibilities in the job description and a form of the professional behaviors discussed throughout this textbook. Salary increases are usually based on the review rating.

Labor Relations

Labor relations is a role of human resources and refers to issues between employees and management. Termination or firing is often a labor relations issue. Another labor relations matter is overseeing the **grievance process** if the employee feels he or she was unjustly treated. HR may also mediate or arrange **mediation** for differences between employees, groups of employees, or employees and management. The role of the mediator is to facilitate communication between the parties, assist them in focusing on the real issues of the disagreement in a nonadversarial manner, and attempt to reach conflict resolution.

The role of the practice manager is not easy but carries the opportunity for many personal and professional rewards. Seeing the organization provide good patient care in a safe, financially sound environment where staff are happy to come to work is an accomplishment of much pride and satisfaction. To create or sustain this environment, the manager, as all positions in health care, must stay current in the field by reading appropriate journals and books; attending seminars and courses; maintaining membership in his or her professional organizations; and networking with local, state, and national managers. When you experience your externship, think about the many jobs of the practice manager.

What form is the employer required to send the employee by January 31 each year?

figure 22–11

The new employee determines how many deductions to claim for income tax purposes.

Form I-9
Employment Eligibility Verification form, certifying the employee's United States citizenship, legal alien status, or legal authorization to work in this country.

W-4 tax form
Form stating the number of deductions the employee wishes to claim.

W-2 tax form
The employer states how much gross income the organization paid the employee for the year and the taxes withheld on this form.

probationary period
An allotted period of time when a new employee may be terminated without cause; a trial period.

grievance process
A specific, formal procedure to address employee dissatisfaction on a certain topic or event.

mediation
A process in which a third party assists in resolving a disagreement between two or more parties.

CHECKPOINT
LO 22.6

Procedure 22–1 — Preparing an Agenda

GOAL To facilitate a meeting's organization and focus by providing a list of meeting topics, the name of the person reporting, and the order in which each topic will be addressed

MATERIALS Paper and pen or computer, copy machine, minutes from last meeting

METHOD

1. Approximately one week before the meeting, email or post a memo to staff offering them an opportunity to add items to the agenda. This is referred to as a *Call for Agenda Items*.

2. Place the following on top of the form used to create the agenda:
   - Name of the practice
   - Site name, if the practice has more than one location
   - Title: *Staff Meeting Agenda*
   - Date and time the meeting is scheduled to begin and end

3. Many offices have standing topics which go on the agenda every month; examples are:
   - Introduction of new staff members
   - Approval of minutes if formal minutes are kept
   - Staff news (promotions, birthdays, weddings, births, etc.)
   - Quality assurance report
   - Policy and procedure updates
   - Committee reports
   - Report from individuals who may have attended a conference

4. Review the minutes from the previous meeting to determine any topics that required action with the person responsible. List these on the agenda under *Old Business*.

5. Add topics obtained from the *Call for Agenda Items* and any new topics the manager wishes to discuss. List these under *New Business*.

6. Add *Other* on the agenda to allow announcements or other brief information.

7. Place the date and time of the next meeting at the end of the agenda.

8. At least one week prior to the meeting, inform and verify persons on the agenda who will present a topic at the meeting.

9. Send agenda to staff members prior to the meeting.

10. Make copies available at the staff meeting.

Procedure 22–2 — Preparing a Travel Expense Report

Imagine that you attended the latest AAMA or AMT annual conference. Research the price of airfare from your locale to the city of the conference. Determine registration and other costs. Use these figures to perform the procedure.

GOAL To obtain reimbursement or account for preapproved travel funds; to provide documentation of expenses for the medical office

Travel expense form (Figure 22–6), pen, receipts, conference Web information, calculator

METHOD

1. Ensure your travel was prior approved.
2. Save receipts from the event.
3. Complete the personal identifying information on the form.
4. Insert the purpose of the travel, the location, dates, and number of days.
5. Place the amounts as labeled in the expense table.
6. Total the amounts.
7. Check the appropriate box to indicate if you missed work and the dates and amount of days.
8. Sign and date the form.
9. Attach receipts (generally, original receipts are submitted; keep copies for your own records).
10. Submit completed form and receipts.

Procedure 22–3 Completing an Incident Report

GOAL To provide documentation of an adverse occurrence or potential risk to facilitate investigation, correction, and aid in the avoidance of future occurrences.

MATERIALS A paper and pen, an incident report (Figure 22–9 may be used)

METHOD After initial first aid and other appropriate assistive steps are taken:

1. Interview the person to whom the incident occurred, gathering the required facts as needed for the incident report including contact information.
2. Interview witnesses, gathering the required facts as needed for the incident report including contact information.
3. Ensure information is complete.
4. Transfer the information to the incident report form.
5. Review the form for accuracy and clarity.
6. Submit the form to the appropriate supervisor.

Case Study

Jan is a heavy smoker and despite using breath mints, brushing her teeth frequently, washing her hands, smoking only outdoors, using a special shampoo, and other measures, she smells like a stale cigarette. She works in the reception area of an oncology office with many patients combating nausea from chemotherapy and radiation. The odor is offensive and increases the patients' discomfort. Personnel policy addresses professional dress and hygiene. Jan and the practice manager have discussed the odor issue in the past and it is not resolved. Today is Jan's annual evaluation and her raise depends on it. To Jan's surprise, she is not only denied a raise but she is given three months to be smoke-free or she will be terminated. The office policy does not state she has to

PROFESSIONAL READINESS

Appearance
Adheres to dress code
Practices good hygiene

stop smoking, but that she must be free of any trace of smoke during her duty hours. The practice offers to pay for Jan to attend a smoking cessation program if she chooses to stop. Jan will meet again with the practice manager in one month to discuss her progress.

Thinking Critically

1. Does the practice have the right to ask Jan to be free of smoke odor?
2. What factors do you think went into the personnel decision?
3. Is it important for employees to know the personnel policies and procedures of their workplace? Why or why not?

practice APPLICATIONS

1. Interview a practice manager from a local medical office on: *What Is It Like in the Day of a Practice Manager?*
2. Select an imaginary problem for the administrative area. For example, diagnostic test results are getting lost, resulting in patients having to repeat tests and delaying diagnoses. Using the five-step problem-solving model, what would you do? This may be a collaborative exercise with other class members.

exam READINESS

There may be more than one correct answer. Circle the best answer.

1. [LO22.1] The model that shows the chain of command is called the

   a. practice management.
   b. staff assignments.
   c. practice ownership.
   d. organizational chart.
   e. corporate plan.

2. [LO22.3] If a medical practice has a health and safety violation, the organization involved would be

   a. CDC.
   b. MSDS.
   c. CMS.
   d. P&P.
   e. OSHA.

3. [LO22.5] The hiring and firing role of the practice manager comes under the category of

   a. health and safety.
   b. communications.
   c. human resources.
   d. people positions.
   e. verification of credentials.

4. [LO22.2] The topics to be discussed at a staff meeting are included in the

   a. minutes.
   b. agenda.
   c. chain of command.
   d. in-service.
   e. policies and procedures.

5. [LO22.2] The topics discussed at a staff meeting are reported in the

   a. minutes.
   b. agenda.
   c. chain of command.
   d. in-service.
   e. itinerary.

6. [LO22.3] Management of the physical plant involves

   a. leasing the facility.
   b. selecting the EHR system.
   c. complying with CMS.
   d. managing payroll.
   e. mailing and shipping.

7. **[LO22.4]** Through which of the following is the manager most likely to discover a problem?

a. Policies and procedures
b. Organizational chart
c. Risk management
d. Physical plant
e. Human resources

8. **[LO22.6]** If an employee felt he or she was treated unjustly, what type of process might be initiated?

a. Termination
b. Evaluation
c. Grievance
d. Mediation
e. Improvement plan

9. **[LO22.6]** The form the employee signs indicating the number of deductions for federal income tax is called

a. HIPAA.
b. CMS.
c. MSDS.
d. W-2.
e. W-4.

10. **[LO22.4]** A study to determine the most beneficial and cost-effective antibiotic for the practice to use in treating otitis media is an example of

a. risk management.
b. infection control.
c. OSHA compliance.
d. utilization review.
e. mediation.

learning outcome SUMMARY

LO 22.1 The organizational chart shows the supervisory structure and reporting relationships between different functions and positions. It is important to know who your direct supervisor is and stay within the chain of command.

LO 22.2 The general responsibilities of the office manager are legal and business functions that include policies and procedures, licenses, credentials, contracts, budget and finances, scheduling, travel, and technology. Communication is an element that is incorporated in all of these functions.

LO 22.3 The medical practice facility involves the building, parking and other physical structures. Compliance with the many governmental health and safety requirements are ultimately the practice manager's responsibility.

LO 22.4 Risk management and quality assurance are additional roles of the practice manager that require everyone's participation and dedication. The problem-solving model is used to identify and resolve issues or potential issues that put staff or patients at risk for harm. The model is also used to improve patient care.

LO 22.5 The human resource role refers to how employees are managed by the business and deals with such elements as hiring, firing, payroll, benefits, and training and orientation.

LO 22.6 Benefits and labor relations are managed by human resources. Labor relations generally involve issues between employees and management.

medical assisting COMPETENCIES

CAAHEP

IV. P (4) Explain general office policies

IV. A (10) Demonstrate respect for individual diversity, incorporating awareness of one's own biases including gender, race, religion, age and economic status

V. C (12) Identify types of records common to the healthcare setting

V. P (8) Maintain organization by filing

VII. C (5) Discuss utilization review principles

IX. C (2) Explore issue of confidentiality as it applies to the medical assistant

IX. C (5) Discuss licensure and certification as it applies to the healthcare providers

IX. C (11) Identify how the Americans with Disabilities Act (ADA) applies to the medical assisting profession

IX. P (6) complete an incident report

IX. P (8) Apply local, state, and federal health legislation and regulation appropriate to the medical assisting practice setting

IX. A (3) Recognize the importance of local, state, and federal legislation and regulation in the practice setting

X. A (1) Apply ethical behaviors including honesty/integrity in the performance of medical assisting practice

XI. C (3) Describe the importance of Materials Data Safety Sheets (MSDS) in a healthcare setting

XI. C (9) Discuss requirements for responding to hazardous material disposal

XI. P (2) Evaluate the work environment to identify safe vs. unsafe working conditions

ABHES

1. General Orientation

b. Compare and contrast the allied health professions and understand their relation to medical assisting

c. Understand medical assistant credentialing requirements and the process to obtain the credential; comprehend the importance of credentialing

4. Medical Law and Ethics

e. Perform risk management processes.

f. Comply with federal, state, and local health laws and regulations.

8. Medical Office Business Procedures/ Management

d. Apply concepts for office procedures

10. Medical Laboratory Procedures

a. Practice quality control

11. Career Development

b. Demonstrate professionalism by:
  (2) Maintaining confidentiality at all times
  (9) Conducting work within scope of education, training, and ability

23 Emergency Preparedness

Learning Outcomes

After completing Chapter 23, you will be able to:

23.1 Explain the purpose of and how to contact the emergency medical services (EMS) system.

23.2 Identify equipment used and general guidelines to follow in emergencies.

23.3 Recognize and respond to patients who require immediate assistance.

23.4 Illustrate your role in responding to natural disasters and those caused by humans.

Key Terms

anaphylaxis
automated external
   defibrillator (AED)
bioterrorism
cardiopulmonary
   resuscitation (CPR)
crash cart

emergency medical
   services (EMS)
first aid
recovery position
triage
ventricular fibrillation
   (VF)

Preparation for Certification

RMA (AMT) Exam
- Identify and apply proper communication methods in patient instruction
- Develop, assemble, and maintain patient resource materials
- Emergencies and first-aid procedures
- Emergency crash cart supplies
- Legal responsibilities as a first responder

CMAS (AMT) Exam
- Medical office emergencies
- Safety

CMA (AAMA) Exam
- Emergencies
- Preplanned action
  - Policies and procedures
  - Legal implications and action documentation
  - Equipment
- Assessment and triage
- Emergency preparedness
- First aid

Introduction ● ● ●

Emergencies of all types can occur when you are working as an administrative medical assistant. Patients may come to your facility with an acute illness or an injury and you will need to respond appropriately. Additionally, you could experience a disaster—anything from a simple office fire to a bomb threat or bioterrorism. As an administrative medical assistant you must be prepared to determine the urgency with which a patient needs to be seen as well as handle patients with urgent needs and office emergencies. Remember to stay calm and think through each situation in order to respond appropriately and create the best outcome.

first aid

The immediate care given to someone who is injured or suddenly becomes ill, before complete medical care can be obtained.

emergency medical services (EMS)

A network of qualified emergency services personnel who use community resources and equipment to provide emergency care to victims of injury or sudden illness.

crash cart

A rolling cart of emergency supplies and equipment.

LO 23.1 Medical Emergencies

A medical emergency is any situation in which a person suddenly becomes ill or sustains an injury that requires immediate help by a health-care professional. For example, a patient in the waiting room may have chest pains that could indicate a heart attack is imminent. You may see emergencies that are not life-threatening, such as a coworker sustaining a minor injury on the job. You may also encounter emergencies outside the office. For example, a family member might cut a finger while using a kitchen knife, or a patron in a restaurant might choke on a piece of food.

The administrative medical assistant will be faced with determining the urgency at which a patient needs to be seen. He or she may have to administer basic emergency care to a patient until one of the clinical personnel is available to assist. The administrative medical assistant will frequently be needed to contact the emergency medical services (EMS) or document the patient care given during an emergency. In both of these cases the administrative assistant plays a vital role by freeing up all the clinical personnel to focus on care of the patient.

In or out of the office, a medical emergency may require you to perform first aid. **First aid** is the immediate care given to someone who is injured or suddenly becomes ill, before complete medical care can be obtained. Prompt and appropriate first aid can:

- Save a life
- Reduce pain
- Prevent further injury
- Reduce the risk of permanent disability
- Increase the chance of early recovery

figure 23-1

The crash cart will need to be restocked on a regular basis.

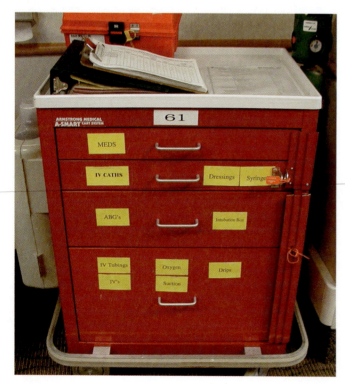

During an emergency, one of your most important allies will be the local **emergency medical services (EMS)** system. An EMS system is a network of qualified emergency services personnel who use community resources and equipment to provide emergency care to victims of injury or sudden illness.

Although the telephone number for the local EMS system is 911 in most parts of the country, a few areas may not have 911 service. Post the area's EMS system telephone number at every telephone and on the **crash cart** (the rolling cart of emergency supplies and equipment, Figure 23–1) or first-aid tray. The crash cart or first-aid tray will need checked and restocked on a regular basis. Follow the protocol at your facility if your are assigned this task and it is within your scope of practice.

Every office employee should have quick access to all emergency numbers. If the community has no EMS system, post the telephone number of the local ambulance or rescue squad. You should also post the telephone numbers of the nearest fire company, police station, poison control center, women's shelter, rape hotline, drug and alcohol center, and other emergency contacts.

When you call the EMS system for medical assistance and transport, speak clearly and calmly to the dispatcher. Be prepared to provide all the pertinent information. Do not hang up until the dispatcher gives you permission to do so. Follow Procedure 23–1 on page 684 when contacting the EMS.

● ● ● ───────────────────────

What information must be provided when contacting the EMS?

CHECKPOINT
LO 23.1

LO 23.2 Handling Emergencies

In addition to contacting EMS, a medical emergency requires you to take certain steps. First you must know how to locate the crash cart or tray containing basic drugs, supplies, and equipment for medical emergencies. Most crash carts also contain a first-aid kit with supplies for managing minor injuries and ailments. Table 23–1 lists the usual items in a first-aid kit. The actual contents of the crash cart or tray may vary slightly from practice to practice. Become familiar with the contents and location of the first-aid supplies and crash cart. You may be called upon to retrieve items from either of these locations when a emergency occurs. You should also be able to note the presence of serious conditions that threaten the patient's life. Then take action, within your scope of practice and guidelines of the facility where you are employed. Prior to an emergency you should find out from your supervisor or physician what you may or may not be expected to do.

table 23–1

Contents of a First-Aid Kit

- Absorbent cotton (sterile)
- Adhesive tape
- Airway or mouthpiece
- Analgesics, such as aspirin or acetaminophen
- Antiseptic solution or spray
- Antiseptic wipes
- Calamine lotion
- Chemical cold packs
- Diphenhydramine (Benadryl®)
- Disposable gloves
- Elastic bandages in various sizes
- Emergency blanket
- First-aid book or information card
- Glucose tablets or sugar source
- Personal protective equipment (PPE): gloves, mask and goggles or face shield, gown, shower cap, booties, pocket mask or mouth shield
- Plastic bags
- Premoistened towelettes or hand cleaner
- Scissors
- Splints in various sizes
- Sterile gauze pads in various sizes
- Sterile rolls of gauze
- Sterile saline solution
- Sunscreen
- Triangular bandage
- Tweezers
- Waterproof flashlight with extra batteries

Telephone Emergencies

triage
Assessment of the urgency and types of conditions patients present as well as their immediate medical needs.

Sometimes a patient or a patient's family member calls the medical office with an emergency. It may be your responsibility to **triage** the injuries by telephone. Triaging is the classification of injuries according to severity, urgency of treatment, and place for treatment.

To handle emergency calls, follow the practice's telephone triage protocols. For example, if a parent calls to say her daughter has broken her arm and the child's bone is visible, tell her to call the local EMS system for immediate care and transport to the hospital. If, however, a parent calls to say her son swallowed half a bottle of baby bath, tell her to remain calm and give her the telephone number of the poison control center. Depending on circumstances, you may offer to make the necessary telephone call yourself.

Adhere to the following general guidelines in any emergency situation.

- Stay calm
- Reassure the patient
- Act in a confident, organized manner

Personal Protection

Whenever you administer first aid and emergency treatment, try to reduce or eliminate the risk of exposing yourself and others to infection. Follow Standard Precautions and assume that all blood and body fluids are infected with bloodborne pathogens. To protect yourself and others, take the following basic precautions. Include personal protective equipment (PPE) in your first-aid kit at work and at home. As discussed in Chapter 9, standard PPE includes gloves, goggles and mask or face shield, gown, cap, and booties. A pocket mask or mouth shield provides personal protection when you perform rescue breathing (Figure 23–2). Plan to use specific PPE based on the condition of the patient. Table 23–2 provides examples of PPE to use in various emergency situations. When in doubt, wear more PPE than you may think is called for It is better to be safe than sorry.

Wear gloves if you expect hand contact with blood, body fluids, including emesis (vomit), mucous membranes, torn skin, or potentially contaminated articles or surfaces. In addition, if you have any cuts or lesions, wear PPE over the affected area.

Minimize splashing, splattering, or spraying of blood or other body fluids when performing first aid. If blood or other body fluids splash into your eyes, nose, or mouth, flush the area with water as soon as possible.

Wash your hands thoroughly with soap and water after removing the gloves. Also wash other skin surfaces that have come in contact with blood or

figure 23–2

A pocket mask or mouth shield provides protection when you perform rescue breathing.

EQUIPMENT	CONDITIONS FOR USE	SAMPLE EMERGENCIES REQUIRING EQUIPMENT
Gloves	Chance of contact with blood or other body secretion or excretion during emergency	Open wound, eye trauma
Goggles and mask or face shield and possible head cover	Chance of blood or other body secretion or excretion being splattered, coughed, or sprayed onto the mucus membranes of the eyes, mouth, or nose	Bleeding, vomiting, most emergency care for small children (because of squirming)
Gown and possible booties	Chance of contact with excessive bleeding or secretion and excretion	Childbirth, severe nosebleed
Pocket mask or mouth shield	Needed for CPR or rescue breathing	Heart attack, respiratory arrest

table 23-2

Personal Protective Equipment (PPE) for Emergencies

other body fluids. Do not touch your mouth, nose, or eyes, and do not eat or drink after providing emergency care until you have washed your hands thoroughly. If you have been exposed to blood or other body fluids, be sure to tell the doctor. You may need postexposure treatment.

Safety Signs, Symbols, and Labels

To maintain safety as well as be prepared for an emergency, recognizing safety signs, symbols, and labels is essential. These labels, signs, and symbols are required by the Occupational Safety and Health Administration (discussed in Chapter 8). Along with OSHA, three additional organizations are involved in safety sign standardization and compliance: the International Standards Organization (ISO), the National Fire Protection Association (NFPA), and the American National Standards Institute (ANSI). Safety signs and labels and emergency codes are an important part of any serious effort to reduce risk and promote safety. See Tables 23–3 and 23–4.

Evaluating the Patient

Assess the situation and surroundings to determine whether it is safe for you to assist. In many cases the administrative medical assistant will step aside and let the clinical personnel take charge of emergencies; however, you cannot always count on someone being available. So knowing the following basic steps will help prepare you for emergencies:

1. Put on personal protective equipment (PPE), such as gloves.

2. Form a general impression of the patient, including his level of responsiveness, level of distress, facial expressions, age, ability to talk, and skin color. How is he or she acting?

3. If the patient can communicate clearly, ask what happened. If not, ask someone who observed the accident or injury. Someone may have brought the patient into the office and can give you more information.

4. If the patient does not respond, tap on his shoulder and ask, "Are you OK?" If there is no response, proceed to check the ABCs (airway, breathing, and circulation). Problems with the airway, breathing, or the circulation are life-threatening and must be treated first. See section LO 23.3.

5. If the patient does respond, check from head to foot for bleeding, bruising, swelling, tenderness, or other deformities.

6. Document and/or report any problems to the clinical personnel such as the EMS or the physician.

7. Continue to assist as needed.

8. Remove your gloves and/or other PPE and wash your hands.

SIGN, SYMBOL, OR LABEL	TITLE	MEANING
	Biohazard	Indicates the actual or potential presence of a biohazard including equipment, containers, rooms, and materials that present a risk or potential risk. The biohazard symbol is black. The background is typically fluorescent orange, orange-red, or other contrasting color.
	Fire Safety	A fire extinguisher sign is placed at the location of the extinguisher. An exit sign like this one indicates the appropriate method of exit in case of a fire. Elevators and escalators are not typically in use during an emergency.
	First Aid and Automated External Defibrillator (AED)	The sign would indicate a first-aid kit and an automated external defibrillator is available for use. These are placed at the location of the equipment.
	Wash Your Hands	Hands should be washed frequently. This is a reminder. Usually placed in locations where contamination to hands can occur and available hand-washing equipment is nearby.
	Handicap	This symbol indicates the route a handicapped person should take. Consider this for patients who are unable to walk or need to avoid steps for any reason.
	General Safety Signs	Provide notices of general practice and rules relating to health, first aid, medical equipment, sanitation, housekeeping, and suggestions relative to general safety measures. For example, an eye wash station is used when chemicals, blood, or other foreign items get in the eye.

table 23–3

Signs, Symbols, and Labels

Patient Stress

In emergency situations, patients and family members are under a great deal of stress. Individuals react differently to emergency situations. Be alert for abnormal behavior or patients who cannot focus or follow directions. Your role during many emergency situations may be to keep victims and their families and

CODES	EMERGENCY CODE DEFINITIONS
FIRE	RED—Procedures staff should follow to protect patients, staff, visitors, themselves, and property from a confirmed or suspected fire.
MEDICAL EMERGENCY	BLUE—Facilitate the arrival of equipment and specialized personnel to the location of an adult medical emergency. Provide life support and emergency care.
INFANT/CHILD ABDUCTION	PINK—Activate response to protect infants and children from removal by unauthorized persons, and identify the physical descriptions and actions of someone attempting to kidnap an infant from the medical facility.
COMBATIVE ASSAULT PERSON	GRAY—Activate facility and staff response when staff members are confronted by an abusive/assaultive person.
BOMB THREAT	GREEN—Activate response to a bomb threat or the discovery of a suspicious package.
PERSON WITH WEAPONS OR HOSTAGE	SILVER—Activate facility and staff response to event in which staff members are confronted by persons brandishing a weapon or who have taken hostages in the medical facility.
HAZARDOUS MATERIAL SPILL	YELLOW—Identify unsafe exposure conditions, safely evacuate an area, and protect others from exposure due to a hazardous materials spill release. Perform procedures to be taken in response to a minor or major spill.
INTERNAL DISASTER	TRIAGE INTERNAL—Activate response to incidents that require or may require significant support from several departments in order to continue patient care.
EXTERNAL DISASTER	TRIAGE EXTERNAL—Activate response to external emergencies that require or may require significant support from several departments in order to continue patient care.
POWER BLACK OUT	CODE EDISON—Activate response to a rolling power failure.

table 23-4

Emergency Codes

friends calm. You can promote calmness by listening carefully and giving your full attention. Your first priority, at all times, is the victim's well-being. If he is very distraught, for example, hold his hand or pat him gently as appropriate. If one of his relatives is crying and causing him to become emotional, suggest that the relative do something to help—for example, fill out paperwork in another room. You may face special challenges when communicating with victims during emergencies. Victims may not speak your language, or they may have a visual or hearing impairment. In such instances, follow these guidelines:

- Use gestures throughout the process for non-English-speaking victims. Continue to speak, however, because they may be able to understand some English.

- Tell patients who have visual impairments what you are going to do before you do it, and maintain voice and touch contact while caring for them.

- Ask patients who have hearing impairments whether they can read lips. If they can, speak slowly to them and never turn away while you are speaking. If they cannot read lips, communicate by writing and using gestures. At all times try to remain face to face and keep direct physical contact.

Documentation

Document all office emergencies in the patient's chart. As an administrative medical assistant, you will typically be responsible for documenting emergencies while the clinical medical assistant, nurses, and physician perform the actual care. Be sure to include the assessment, treatment given, and the patient's response. If the patient was transported to another facility, record the location. Include the date and time with the documentation, as well as your signature and credentials.

CHECKPOINT
LO 23.2

Why should the emergency cart and/or first-aid tray be checked and stocked on a regular basis?

cardiopulmonary resuscitation (CPR)

A series of ventilations and compressions used on a person who has stopped breathing or whose heart has stopped beating.

LO 23.3 Patient Emergencies

First aid and **cardiopulmonary resuscitation (CPR)** training are a valuable asset to all individuals. When an injury takes place, whether it is to ourselves, a patient, or a fellow employee, knowing what to do and being able to react quickly can limit the severity of the injury or even prevent a death. So, no matter where you encounter an emergency, your knowledge and certifications should enable you to provide first aid for the patient until a physician or EMT arrives. Keep in mind, if you are providing emergency first aid outside of your work environment you may be covered by the *Good Samaritan* laws of your state. These laws are meant to protect the first-aid provider from legal action and encourage individuals to provide first aid.

The ability to recognize life-threatening emergencies and patients that need immediate assistance may be required of the administrative medical assistant. In this section we will discuss some emergencies an administrative medical assistant may encounter including: choking, falls, hemorrhaging, hyperventilation, nosebleed, vomiting, anaphylaxis, heart attack, respiratory arrest, and seizures.

Choking

Choking occurs when food or a foreign object blocks a person's trachea, or windpipe. The main symptom of a choking emergency is the inability to speak. A choking person who cannot talk may give the universal sign of choking—a hand up to the throat and a fearful look. If you see someone giving the universal sign, be prepared to act promptly.

Procedure 23–2 at the end of this chapter provides guidelines for assisting an adult or a child who is responsive and choking. The American Heart Association generally considers anyone between the ages of one and eight years old a child. Procedure 23–3 provides the guidelines for assisting an infant who is responsive and has a foreign body airway obstruction. An infant is defined by the American Heart Association as any child younger than the age of 1 year.

Falls

If a patient falls from a chair or an examining table and cannot get up, call for help. Do not move the patient until the physician or an EMT examines him. Instruct the patient not to move his head, neck, or back if injuries to those areas are suspected. If possible, have someone hold the patient's neck to stabilize it until the physician or EMT arrives. Move the patient only in a life-threatening situation, such as if the building is on fire. Arrange for transport to the hospital, and document the fall and injury in the patient's chart.

If the fall results in only a bump, ice may be applied and the patient observed for bruises and swelling. Give the patient time to collect himself. Be sure to notify the doctor, who should examine the patient. Then document the fall, the injury, and the treatment in the patient's chart.

Hemorrhaging

Hemorrhaging (heavy or uncontrollable bleeding) is generally the result of an injury. It may also be caused by an illness. Control external bleeding to prevent rapid blood loss and shock. Direct pressure and dressings should be applied. If blood soaks through, an additional dressing should be applied. Do not remove

the original dressing or bandage. The physician will evaluate the bleeding and determine the need for transport to an emergency care facility.

Hyperventilation

Some patients who are under a great deal of stress lack the skills to deal with the stress effectively. They may seem anxious, frazzled, and more emotional than average patients. Patients under stress may begin to hyperventilate, or breathe too rapidly and too deeply. Patients who are hyperventilating may also feel light-headed and as if they cannot get enough air. In addition, they may have chest pain and feel apprehensive. The hyperventilating patient may need to be moved to a quiet area.

Nosebleed

Treat a nosebleed by having the patient sit up with the head tilted forward to prevent blood from running down the back of the throat. Next, have the patient gently pinch the nostrils shut at the bottom for at least 5 minutes. An ice pack or cold compress may be applied to the nose and face.

Vomiting

Vomiting is a symptom common to many disorders, ranging from food poisoning to various infections. When severe, it can lead to dehydration and dangerous changes in electrolyte levels, especially in patients who are very young, very old, or diabetic or who also have diarrhea. Because these problems can be severe, notify the doctor and provide appropriate care. Procedure 23–4 at the end of this chapter describes how to provide emergency care for a patient who is vomiting.

Anaphylaxis

Anaphylaxis, or anaphylactic shock, is a severe, often life-threatening allergic reaction. The reaction can be immediate or delayed up to 2 hours. It happens to people who have become sensitized to certain substances. For example, it can result from eating a type of food, being stung by an insect, or taking a particular type of medication, such as penicillin.

The first sign of anaphylaxis usually comes from the patient's skin. It becomes itchy, turns red, feels hot, and develops hives. The face may also become puffy. The throat may swell so that the patient has trouble breathing and swallowing and feels as if he has a "lump in the throat." Other symptoms include pallor, perspiration, and a weak, rapid, irregular pulse. If you detect these symptoms or if the patient becomes restless, has a headache, or says that his throat feels as if it is closing up consider possible anaphylaxis. Notify the clinical personnel immediately if you suspect anaphylactic shock.

Some severely allergic patients carry an epinephrine autoinjector prescribed by a physician (See Figure 23–3). It should be used by the patient when signs of anaphylaxis appear. However if they need assistance, you should know the procedure for use. Follow these steps:

1. Remove the autoinjector from the packaging (box and/or plastic tube).
2. Pull back the gray cap.
3. Place the black tip of the injector on the outside of the upper thigh. (The injector can go through clothing.)

anaphylaxis
A severe allergic reaction with symptoms that include respiratory distress, difficulty in swallowing, pallor, and a drastic drop in blood pressure that can lead to circulatory collapse.

figure 23–3

Epinephrine autoinjectors come prepackaged, containing the correct amount of the drug for an adult or a child.

4. Press firmly into the thigh and hold for 10 seconds.

5. Remove the autoinjector and massage the injection site for a few minutes.

6. Call your physician or go to the emergency room of a nearby hospital.

This autoinjector is for emergency supportive therapy only. It is not a replacement or substitute for immediate medical or hospital care.

Heart Attack

Chest pain is the cardinal symptom of a heart attack. The patient may describe the pain as crushing, burning, heavy, aching, or like that of indigestion. The pain may radiate down the left arm or into the jaw, throat, or both shoulders. It may be accompanied by shortness of breath, sweating, nausea, and vomiting. The patient may be pale and have a feeling of doom. If you cannot easily detect pallor (paleness) because the patient has dark skin, check the patient's inner lip for paleness. Elderly patients may experience atypical symptoms of a heart attack, such as jaw pain, because responses to pain diminish during the aging process. The pain of a heart attack is not relieved by nitroglycerin.

If you think a patient is having a heart attack, notify the physician and/or EMS system immediately. Do not let the patient walk. Loosen tight clothing and have the patient sit up to aid breathing. Stay with the patient, observe the ABCs, and begin CPR if needed. See Procedure 23–5, Performing Cardiopulmonary Resuscitation, at the end of the chapter.

Ventricular fibrillation (VF) is an abnormal heart rhythm. It is the most common cause of cardiac arrest. An **automated external defibrillator (AED)** is a computerized defibrillator programmed to recognize VF and other lethal heart rhythms (Figure 23–4). These devices are found in many public places, including airports. Know where this emergency device is located in your facility in case you are asked to retrieve it during an emergency.

Respiratory Arrest

Respiratory arrest, or lack of breathing, is usually preceded by symptoms of respiratory distress. Symptoms you may note include difficulty breathing, sweating, and/or pale or bluish skin. If a patient shows these symptoms, notify the doctor right away. If the patient develops respiratory arrest, CPR will need to be performed and the EMS system contacted immediately. See Procedure 23–5 at the end of the chapter.

Seizures

A seizure, or convulsion, is a series of violent and involuntary contractions of the muscles.

If a seizure occurs in the waiting area call for help and then:

1. Remove objects that may cause injury.

2. Place the patient on the floor or the ground. If possible, position him on his side with his head turned to the side to help keep the airway open and unobstructed by the tongue. This position is especially important if the patient vomits, to prevent aspiration of vomitus into the lungs.

3. Loosen restrictive clothing, and never place anything in the patient's mouth.

4. Protect the patient from injury, but do not try to hold him still during convulsions.

ventricular fibrillation (VF)
An abnormal heart rhythm that is the most common cause of cardiac arrest.

Automated external defibrillator (AED)
A computerized defibrillator programmed to recognize lethal heart rhythms and deliver an electrical shock to restore a normal rhythm.

figure 23–4

An automated external defibrillator delivers an electric current to the heart to stop a chaotic rhythm such as ventricular fibrillation.

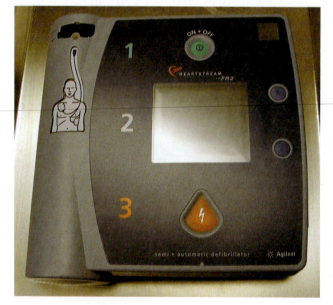

Working With the Health-Care Team

CPR INSTRUCTOR

To gain medical assistant credentials, you must fulfill the requirements of either the American Association of Medical Assistants (for a Certified Medical Assistant) or the American Medical Technologists (for a Registered Medical Assistant). After obtaining your medical assistant certification or registration, you may wish to acquire additional skills in specialty areas through course work or on-the-job training. Although this course work or training may not lead to an additional certification or degree, it will enable you to expand your role in the medical office and advance your career as the demand for skilled health professionals increases.

Duties and Skills

A CPR (cardiopulmonary resuscitation) instructor provides people with the knowledge and skills necessary to help save a person's life in an emergency. He teaches his students how to:

- Call for help.
- Help sustain life.
- Reduce pain.
- Minimize the consequences of injury or sudden illness until professional medical help arrives.

To teach a CPR class, an instructor must plan and coordinate the course in conjunction with a local American Red Cross unit or American Heart Association affiliate. He demonstrates the appropriate skills to his students and observes their technique. He then provides constructive feedback as they learn skills and make decisions regarding the appropriate action to take in an emergency.

The instructor is responsible for identifying participants who are having difficulty with the skills. He must develop effective strategies to help these students meet the course objectives. At the end of the course, the CPR instructor submits completed course records to the local American Red Cross chapter or American Heart Association affiliate.

Educational Requirements

CPR instructors teach classes in a variety of settings, including schools and universities, community rooms, camps, religious institutions, and medical clinics. Some employers, such as operators of swimming pools, camps, and daycare facilities, may require CPR instruction as a condition of employment.

Workplace Settings

To be certified as a CPR instructor by the Red Cross, you must complete two Red Cross courses. The first, the

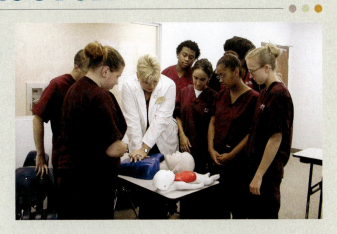

instructor candidate training course, provides instruction in teaching methods, evaluation, and reporting. After completing this course, you will be awarded an instructor candidate training certificate, which qualifies you to take the first aid and CPR instructor course. You must then pass a written test with a grade of 80% or better to gain certification. CPR instructors must teach one class every 2 years for recertification from the Red Cross.

The American Heart Association also provides training for CPR instructors. You must first pass the basic life support course for health-care providers, which teaches CPR skills. You then must take the instructor course, which covers teaching methods. After passing the instructor course, you must co-teach a CPR class with an experienced instructor, who will monitor your performance. You will then become an approved instructor. CPR instructors affiliated with the American Heart Association are required to teach a minimum of two classes a year. The association has no minimum age to become an instructor.

The CPR Instructor as a Team Member

Anyone you work with or you may be a CPR instructor. You can become certified no matter what your background as long as you are at least 17 years of age. Typically a CPR instructor is not a person's main profession. As an administrative medical assistant, the CPR instructor for a class administered by the National Safety Council, American Heart Association, or American Red Cross will be your point of contact to prepare for emergencies.

For more information, visit the Web sites of the following organizations, which are available on the Online Learning Center at www.mhhe.com/houseradminmedassist

American Heart Association National Center
American Red Cross National Safety Council

CHECKPOINT
LO 23.3

Why should the administrative medical assistant be prepared for an emergency situation?

LO 23.4 Office Emergencies and Disasters

Up until this point, we have discussed emergencies that can occur related to patients. In this section we will focus on emergencies and disasters related to the environment. For example, administrative medical assistants should be prepared to respond to fires and other natural or man-made disasters. In preparation for office emergencies and disasters, knowledge of first-aid and CPR training are recommended and will be an enormous help to your office and community. To be fully effective, you must also be familiar with standard protocols for responding to disasters. Table 23–5 shows ways that you can help in certain types of disasters. Participation in fire or other disaster drills will help to familiarize yourself with emergency procedures.

In any disaster, you may be asked to assist in performing triage. During triage, each injured victim is given a tag that classifies the person as emergent (needing immediate care), urgent (needing care within several hours), nonurgent (needing care when time is not critical), or dead. The triage process is outlined in Procedure 23–6 at the end of the chapter.

table 23–5

Assisting in a Disaster

TYPE OF DISASTER	ACTION TO TAKE
Weather disaster, such as a flood or hurricane	• Report to the community command post. • Have your credentials with you. • Receive an identifying tag or vest and assignment. • Accept only an assignment that is appropriate for your abilities. Expect to be part of a team. • Document what medical care each victim receives on each person's disaster tag.
Office fire	• Activate the alarm system. • Use a fire extinguisher if the fire is confined to a small container, such as a trash can. • Turn off oxygen. • Shut windows and doors. • Seal doors with wet cloths to prevent smoke from entering. • If evacuation is necessary, proceed quietly and calmly. Direct ambulatory patients and family members to the appropriate exit route. Assist patients who need help leaving the building.
Bioterrorist attack	• Be alert for rapidly increasing incidence of disease in a healthy population (clusters). • Take appropriate isolation precautions. • Use Standard Precautions when cleaning/decontaminating patient rooms and equipment. • Inform local health departments of suspected bioterrorism agent.
Chemical emergency	• Don appropriate PPE to avoid secondary contamination. • Identify the chemical if possible and report to the local authorities. • Determine if there is a protocol for the specific chemical, if known. • Assist with patient decontamination. • Monitor patient's ABCs and vital signs if indicated. • Document what medical care each victim receives. • Arrange for patient transport if possible.
Mass casualties	• Assess the situation for safety. • If there is an explosion, do not go toward the explosion. • Report to the community command post. • Triage victims as necessary. • Render first aid as required. • Document what medical care each victim receives.

Handling Fires and Electrical Emergencies

Fires and electrical emergencies are safety hazards anywhere, but more likely in a health-care facility when high-powered equipment, gas tanks, and flammable chemicals are housed. It is critical for an administrative assistant to know how to respond to a fire or electrical accident. You should:

- Familiarize yourself with the location of all fire extinguishers and fire blankets.
- Review the floor plan, noting the location of fire exits.
- Make sure you know how to operate the fire extinguishers.
- Participate in all office fire drills.
- Familiarize yourself with the location of circuit breakers and emergency power shutoffs.

Fire Prevention   Be aware of anything that might cause a fire. Keep your area clear of clutter such as boxes or empty storage containers. Such materials can feed, or even start, a fire. Be alert to the following potential hazards. If you cannot correct the situation yourself, report the hazard to your supervisor.

- Frayed electrical wires, overloaded outlets, and improperly grounded plugs. These present a danger of electric shock and fire. Contact a licensed electrician to remedy these problems.
- Materials that are extremely flammable, including alcohol and some disinfectants. Supplies such as paper table coverings also can ignite and spread flames quickly in the event of a fire. Check to make sure that all such items are stored and disposed of properly to minimize the fire danger. Flammable liquids should never be kept near a heat source. If you are not sure whether a chemical is flammable, read the manufacturer's label or Material Safety Data Sheet. These were discussed in Chapter 22.
- Smoking. Smoking should not be permitted anywhere in a medical facility. In addition to causing health problems, smoking is a fire hazard. "No Smoking" signs should be posted prominently throughout the office.
- Inoperative smoke detectors. Make sure that smoke detectors throughout the office are working properly. Replace batteries promptly. If smoke detectors are wired into the building's electrical system, report any malfunction to the building manager

The following safeguards reduce electrical hazards.

- Avoid using extension cords. If they must be used, be sure the circuit is not overloaded. Tape extension cords to the floor to avoid tripping.
- Repair or replace equipment that has a broken or frayed cord.
- Dry your hands before working with electrical devices, including just plugging them in.
- Do not position electrical devices near sinks, faucets, or other sources of water. Be sure electrical cords do not run through water.

Using Safety Equipment   The number of fire extinguishers in the office depends on the size and number of rooms in the office. Regardless of the total number of extinguishers, an all-purpose fire extinguisher should be located in or close to each exam room. Figure 23–5 shows how to operate a typical fire extinguisher. Have the fire extinguisher professionally serviced once a year to ensure its effectiveness. Each employee should learn how to use a fire extinguisher. OSHA recommends that employees know the "PASS" system:

- **P**ull the pin.
- **A**im at the base of the fire.

figure 23-5

To use a fire extinguisher: (1) hold it upright, (2) remove the safety pin, (3) push the top handle down, and (4) direct the hose at the base of the fire.

- **S**queeze the trigger.
- **S**weep side to side.

Posters with the "PASS" acronym are available from OSHA. You also can contact your local fire department for more information about fire safety training.

Planning an Evacuation Route   An evacuation route provides a safe way out of a building during an emergency. Learn the location of fire alarms, fire doors, and fire escapes in relation to the exam room. Use exit signs as a guide in unfamiliar areas of the building. Stage fire drills with your coworkers so that you can evacuate the facility and lead patients to safety. Plan what you will do if your route becomes blocked.

Evacuation and Shelter-in-Place Plans

Every office should have evacuation and shelter-in-place plans in the event of an emergency. "Shelter-in-place" refers to an interior room or rooms within your medical facility with few or no windows, and is a place to take refuge. Plans should include means of communication for employees during and after

the emergency. Maps of the facility with escape routes clearly marked should be posted. These plans should be in writing and there should be periodic practice drills. Employees should be trained in shelter-in-place procedures and their roles in implementing them. If a shelter-in-place option is a part of your emergency plan, be sure to implement a means of alerting your employees to shelter-in-place that is easy to distinguish from alerts used to signal an evacuation.

Bioterrorism

Bioterrorism is the intentional release of a biologic agent with the intent to harm individuals. The Centers for Disease Control and Prevention (CDC) defines a biologic agent as a weapon when it is easy to disseminate, has a high potential for mortality, can cause a public panic or social disruption, and requires public health preparedness. There are numerous biologic agents identified as weapons, including anthrax, tularemia, smallpox, plague, and botulism. The CDC maintains an Internet site with current information about identified biologic agents at www.bt.cdc.gov.

Physicians' offices will be on the front lines should a biologic agent be intentionally released. It will be up to physicians and their staff to sound the alarm to public officials that something may be amiss. Physicians and medical assistants should be vigilant about cases that present themselves as well as common trends in syndromes. Be on the lookout for unusual patterns in affected patients. Indications of a bioterrorist attack might include many patients having been in the same place at the same time or an unusual distribution for common illnesses, such as an increase in chicken-pox-like illness in adults that might be smallpox.

If you suspect that bioterrorism is responsible for an illness, report your suspicions to the physician. It is the responsibility of your facility to immediately contact the local public health department. The information about the patient should be recorded, and appropriate tests should be performed. The laboratory should be notified of the potential for bioterrorism. Additionally, consultations with specialists and discussions of all findings are necessary when bioterrorism is suspected. The following is a list of clues of a bioterroristic attack as defined by the American College of Physicians—American Society of Internal Medicine.

- Unusual temporal or geographic clustering of illness
- Unusual age distribution of common disease, such as an illness that appears to be chicken-pox in adults but is really smallpox
- A large epidemic with greater caseloads than expected, especially in a discrete population
- More severe disease than expected
- Unusual route of exposure
- A disease that is outside its normal transmission season or is impossible to transmit naturally in the absence of its normal vector
- Multiple simultaneous epidemics of different diseases
- A disease outbreak with health consequences to humans and animals
- Unusual strains or variants of organisms or antimicrobial resistance patterns

bioterrorism
The intentional release of a biologic agent with the intent to harm individuals.

What types of behavior are most effective in handling office emergencies and disaster situation?

CHECKPOINT
LO 23.4

Procedure 23-1 Contacting Emergency Medical Services System

GOAL To contact emergency medical services quickly and efficiently when an emergency occurs

MATERIALS Telephone

METHOD
1. Call 911 or the appropriate number. Emergency numbers should be posted by the telephone for quick access.
2. Relax and speak clearly and calmly to the dispatcher.
3. Be prepared to provide the following information:
   a. Your name, telephone number, and location
   b. Nature of the emergency
   c. Number of people in need of help; condition of the injured or ill patient(s)
   d. Summary of the first aid that has been given
   e. Directions on how to reach the location of the emergency
4. Ensure that the dispatcher has all needed information.
5. Do not hang up until the dispatcher gives you permission to do so.
6. Notify other personnel that the EMS services have been contacted and when they are expected to arrive.

Procedure 23-2 Foreign Body Airway Obstruction in a Responsive Adult or Child

GOAL To correctly relieve a foreign body from the airway of an adult or child

OSHA GUIDELINES This procedure does not involve exposure to blood, body fluids, or tissues

MATERIALS Choking adult or child patient
Caution: Never perform this procedure on someone who is not choking

METHOD
1. Ask, "Are you choking?" If the answer is "Yes," indicated by a nod of the head or some other sign, ask, "Can you speak?" If the answer is "No," tell the patient that you can help. A choking person cannot speak, cough, or breathe, and exhibits the universal sign of choking. If the patient is coughing, observe him closely to see if he clears the object. If he is not coughing or stops coughing, use abdominal thrusts.
2. Position yourself behind the patient. Place your fist against the abdomen just above the navel and below the xiphoid process.
3. Grasp your fist with your other hand, and provide quick inward and upward thrusts into the patient's abdomen (Figure 23-6). The thrust should be sufficient to move enough air from the lungs so that the object can be displaced from the airway.

Note: If a pregnant or obese person is choking, you will need to place your arms around the chest and perform thrusts over the center of the breastbone (Figure 23–7).

4. Continue the thrusts until the object is expelled or the patient becomes unresponsive.

5. If the patient becomes unresponsive, call EMS and position the patient on his back.

6. Use the head tilt–chin lift to open the patient's airway.

7. Look into the mouth. If you see the foreign body, remove it using your index finger. **Do not perform any blind finger sweeps on a child** (Figure 23–8).

8. Open the airway and look, listen, and feel for breathing. If the patient is not breathing, attempt a rescue breath. Observe the chest. If it does not rise with the breath, reposition the airway and administer another rescue breath. If the chest does not rise after the second attempt, assume that the airway is still blocked and begin CPR (Procedure 23–5).

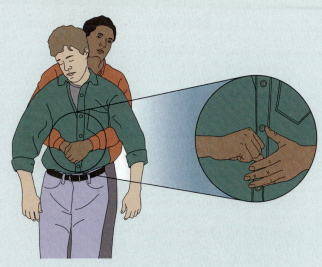

figure 23–6

Perform abdominal thrusts on a conscious choking victim.

figure 23–7

Use a chest thrust for a choking victim who is pregnant or obese.

figure 23–8

If you see the foreign body, use your index finger to remove it from the mouth. Do not perform a blind finger sweep on children or infants.

Procedure 23-3   Foreign Body Airway Obstruction in a Responsive Infant

GOAL   To correctly relieve a foreign body from the airway of an infant

OSHA GUIDELINES   This procedure does not involve exposure to blood, body fluids, or tissues

MATERIALS   Choking infant
Caution: Never perform this procedure on an infant who is not choking

METHOD

1. Assess the infant for signs of severe or complete airway obstruction, which include:

   a. Sudden onset of difficulty in breathing.

   b. Inability to speak, make sounds, or cry.

   c. A high-pitched, noisy, wheezing sound, or no sounds while inhaling.

   d. Weak, ineffective coughs.

   e. Blue lips or skin.

2. Hold the infant with his head down, supporting the body with your forearm. His legs should straddle your forearm and you should support his jaw and head with your hand and fingers. This is best done in a sitting or kneeling position (Figure 23–9).

3. Give up to five back blows with the heel of your free hand, as shown in Figure 23–9. Strike the infant's back forcefully between the shoulder blades. At any point, if the object is expelled, discontinue the back blows.

4. If the obstruction is not cleared, turn the infant over as a unit, supporting the head with your hands and the body between your forearms (Figure 23–10).

5. Keep the head lower than the chest and perform five chest thrusts. Place two fingers over the breastbone (sternum), above the xiphoid. Give five quick chest thrusts about ½ to 1 inch deep. Stop the compressions if the object is expelled.

6. Alternate five back blows and five chest thrusts until the object is expelled or until the infant becomes unconscious. If the infant becomes unconscious, call EMS or have someone do it for you.

7. Open the infant's mouth by grasping both the tongue and the lower jaw between the thumb and fingers, and pull up the lower jawbone. *If you see the object, remove it using your smallest finger.* **Do not use blind finger sweeps on an infant. A blind finger sweep may push the object deeper into the airway.**

8. Open the airway and attempt to provide rescue breaths. If the chest does not rise, reposition the airway (both head and chin) and try to provide another rescue breath.

9. If the rescue breaths are unsuccessful, begin CPR. Hold the infant, supporting her body with your forearm and her head with your hand and fingers. Deliver 30 chest compressions about ½ to 1 inch deep.

10. Open the infant's mouth and look for the foreign object. If you see an object, remove it with your smallest finger.

11. Open the airway and attempt to provide rescue breaths. If the chest does not rise, continue CPR until the doctor or EMS arrives.

figure 23–9

Use back blows for a choking infant.

figure 23–10

Keep the infant's head and neck supported.

Procedure 23–4   Caring for a Patient Who Is Vomiting

GOAL   To increase comfort and minimize complications, such as aspiration, for a patient who is vomiting

OSHA GUIDELINES

MATERIALS   Emesis basin, cool compress, cup of cool water, paper tissues or a towel, and (if ordered) intravenous fluids and electrolytes and an antinausea drug

METHOD
1. Wash your hands and put on exam gloves and other PPE.
2. Ask the patient when and how the vomiting started and how frequently it occurs. Find out whether she is nauseated or in pain.
3. Give the patient an emesis basin to collect vomit. Observe and document its amount, color, odor, and consistency. Particularly note blood, bile, undigested food, or feces in the vomit.
4. Place a cool compress on the patient's forehead to make her more comfortable. Offer water and paper tissues or a towel to clean her mouth.
5. Monitor for signs of dehydration, such as confusion, irritability, and flushed, dry skin. Also monitor for signs of electrolyte imbalances, such as leg cramps or an irregular pulse.
6. If requested, assist by laying out supplies and equipment for the physician to use in administering intravenous fluids and electrolytes. Administer an antinausea drug if prescribed.
7. Prepare the patient for diagnostic tests if instructed.
8. Remove the gloves and wash your hands.

Procedure 23–5   Performing Cardiopulmonary Resuscitation (CPR)

GOAL   To provide ventilation and blood circulation for a patient who shows none

OSHA GUIDELINES

MATERIALS   Mouth shield, or if not in the office, a piece of plastic with a hole for the mouth

METHOD

1. Assess the area for safety, put on gloves if available. Check responsiveness.
   - Tap shoulder.
   - Ask, "Are you OK?"

2. Call 911 or the local emergency number or have someone place the call for you according to these guidelines. For sudden collapse: call EMS first, get AED, start CPR, use AED. For drowning or other arrest due to lack of oxygen: perform 2 minutes of CPR first, call EMS, resume CPR/AED.

3. Place the heel of one hand on the patient's sternum between the nipples. Place your other hand over the first, interlacing your fingers (Figure 23–11).

4. Give 30 chest compressions at least 2 inches deep. You should compress the chest hard and fast (at least 100 compressions per minute) (Figure 23–12). Give compressions of sufficient depth and rate and allow chest recoil with minimal interruptions in compressions. Rapid chest compression increases the likelihood of blood reaching the brain and other vital tissues.

5. Open the patient's airway.
   - Tilt the patient's head back, using the head tilt–chin lift maneuver (Figure 23–13). For a trauma victim, use jaw thrust to open airway; only use the head tilt–chin lift if jaw thrust is not effective.

   Simply opening the airway may cause the patient to start breathing again.

6. Check for breathing.
   - If the patient is not breathing or has inadequate breathing, position the patient on his back and give two rescue breaths, each one second long. Each breath should cause the chest to rise. When giving rescue breaths, use one of three methods:

     a. Mouth-to-mouth or mouth-to-nose rescue breathing (Figures 23–14 and 23–15):
        - Place your mouth around the patient's mouth and pinch the nose, or close the patient's mouth and place your mouth around the patient's nose.
        - Deliver two slow breaths. Use a face shield.

     b. Mouth-to-mask device (Figure 23–16).

     c. Bag-mask ventilation (Figure 23–17). Ensure the adequate rise and fall of the patient's chest. If his chest does not rise, reposition the airway and try again. If on the second attempt the chest does not rise, your patient may have an airway obstruction. See Procedure 23–2.

7. Continue cycles of 30:2 until the patient begins to move, an AED is available, qualified help arrives, or you are too exhausted to continue.

8. If the patient starts moving, check for breathing. If the patient is breathing adequately, put him in the **recovery position** and monitor him until the doctor or EMS arrives.

figure 23–11

Place the heel of one hand on the patient's sternum between the nipples. Place your other hand over the first, interlacing your fingers.

figure 23–12

Align your shoulders directly over the victim's sternum, with your elbows locked.

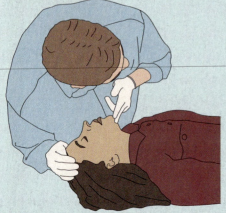

figure 23–13

Use the head tilt–chin lift maneuver to open an airway.

recovery position
The position a person is placed in after receiving first aid for choking or cardiopulmonary resuscitation.

figure 23–14

Perform mouth-to-mouth rescue breathing.

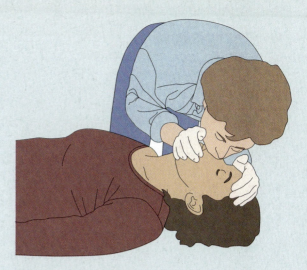

figure 23–15

Use mouth-to-nose breathing if mouth-to-mouth breathing is not possible.

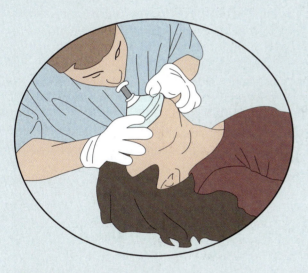

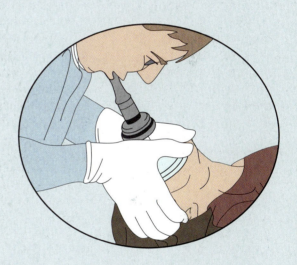

figure 23–16

The side or the head technique can be used when performing mouth-to-mask ventilations.

figure 23–17

When using the bag-mask ventilation, circle the top edges of the mask with your thumb and index finger and use your other three fingers to lift the jaw and open the airway.

Procedure 23-6 Assisting with Triage in a Disaster

GOAL To prioritize disaster victims

OSHA GUIDELINES

MATERIALS Disaster tag and pen

METHOD
1. Wash your hands and put on exam gloves and other PPE if available.
2. Tag victims by type of injury and need for care, classifying them as emergent, urgent, nonurgent, or dead. Sorting of the victims, completed by clinical personnel, allows for rapid treatment based on need.
3. Label the emergent patients no. 1, and send them to appropriate treatment stations immediately. Emergent patients, such as those who are in shock or who are hemorrhaging, need immediate care.
4. Label the urgent patients no. 2, and send them to basic first-aid stations. Urgent patients need care within the next several hours. Such patients may have lacerations that can be dressed quickly to stop the bleeding but can wait for suturing.
5. Label nonurgent patients no. 3, and send them to volunteers who will be empathic and provide refreshments. Nonurgent patients are those for whom timing of treatment is not critical, such as patients who have no physical injuries but who are emotionally upset.
6. Label patients who are dead no. 4. Ensure that the bodies are moved to an area where they will be safe until they can be identified and proper action can be taken.

Case Study

PROFESSIONAL READINESS

Judgment
Ability to come to an appropriate conclusion and act accordingly

Susan is responsible for ensuring that the office emergency equipment is always ready for use and following the OSHA guidelines pertaining to it. No emergencies have occurred in the two years that Susan has had this responsibility. She likes her job but this is the only aspect of it that she finds boring. Consequently, she takes shortcuts when it comes to OSHA compliance and checklists. To her surprise, the office receives an unannounced visit from OSHA. This governmental agency notes several deficiencies including the fire extinguishers. Susan has neglected to conduct and record a monthly visual inspection and an annual maintenance check as stated in the OSHA guidelines. The result is a heavy fine for the practice. Susan feels very guilty about her poor judgment and resulting carelessness. She is concerned she may lose her job.

Thinking Critically

1. In addition to the fine, what other consequences may have occurred as a result of Susan's poor judgment?

2. What is the proper way to use a fire extinguisher and the associated acronym?

3. Do you know the location of the closest fire extinguisher to your classroom?

practice APPLICATIONS

1. With two other students, role-play calling the EMS system. Have one student act as the EMS dispatcher and the other provide a description of an emergency situation and then a critique of your performance.

2. Determine the potential hazards/emergencies that could occur in your community. Create a report that includes the five most likely emergencies that could occur in your area and what your role as a medical assistant may be if the emergency occurs.

exam READINESS

There may be more than one correct answer. Circle the best answer.

1. **[LO23.3]** An AED is used to
   a. avoid a disaster.
   b. help a patient stay calm.
   c. clear a patient's airway.
   d. stop a cardiac arrest.
   e. prevent an infection.

2. **[LO23.1]** During an emergency, the administrative medical assistant will most likely
   a. wear a mask and face shield.
   b. document the care.
   c. call EMS.
   d. take care of the other patients.
   e. allow the clinical personnel to do all the work.

3. **[LO23.4]** Which of the following is part of the acronym PASS?
   a. Squeeze from side to side
   b. Sweep the trigger
   c. Aim at the base of the fire
   d. Aim at the top of the fire
   e. Push the pin

4. **[LO23.2]** The acronym ABC stands for
   a. air vent, blankets, continued care.
   b. allow, breathing, constantly.
   c. airway, breathing, cardiopulmonary resuscitation.

   d. airway, beating, circulation.
   e. airway, breathing, circulation.

5. **[LO23.1]** A mobile cart that contains emergency medical supplies is a/an
   a. AED.
   b. first-aid kit.
   c. crash cart.
   d. pocket mask.
   e. extinguisher.

6. **[LO23.2]** Which of the following is a general guideline to follow during an emergency?
   a. Wear a gown at all times.
   b. Stock the first-aid tray.
   c. Speak only to the physician and other personnel.
   d. Speak loud and fast.
   e. Stay calm.

7. **[LO23.3]** If a patient needs rescue breathing, what device would you use?
   a. Gown
   b. Goggles
   c. Crash cart
   d. AED
   e. Pocket mask

8. **[LO23.3]** Which of the following is correct?
   a. Choking can occur when the patient is speaking clearly.
   b. After a fall, move the patient onto an exam table so the physician can check for injuries.

c. Notify the clinical personnel if a patient becomes restless or says that his throat is closing up.

d. Use an AED when a patient stops breathing.

e. Hold a patient firmly during a seizure to prevent injury.

9. **[LO23.4]** Which of the following patients would be cared for first during triage?

a. Urgent patients no. 1

b. Nonurgent patients no. 3

c. Urgent patients no. 2

d. Emergent patients no. 2

e. Emergent patients no. 1

10. **[LO23.4]** A shelter-in-place is a/an

a. outside building used for refuge.

b. interior room with few or no windows in which to take refuge.

c. exterior room with few or no windows in which to take refuge.

d. evacuation route.

e. dangerous place in case of bioterrorism.

learning outcome SUMMARY

LO 23.1 An EMS system is a network of qualified emergency services personnel who use community resources and equipment to provide emergency care to victims of injury or sudden illness. When contacting EMS, remain calm and be prepared to provide clear and complete information about the event.

LO 23.2 The crash cart and first-aid kit should include all appropriate drugs, supplies, and equipment needed for emergencies.

LO 23.3 The administrative medical assistant may need to provide urgent or emergency care when clinical personnel are not available. Telephone and patient emergencies should be triaged. The administrative medical assistant will typically take an active role in documenting emergency patient care.

LO 23.4 An administrative medical assistant should be familiar with standard protocols for responding to fires and disasters, and know both the evacuation plan and the shelter-in-place plan.

medical assisting COMPETENCIES

CAAHEP

I. A (1) Apply critical thinking skills in performing patient assessment and care

III. C (12) Discuss the application of Standard Precautions with regard to:

a. All body fluids, secretions, and excretions

b. Blood

c. Non-intact skin

d. Mucous membranes

III. P (3) Select appropriate barrier/personal protective equipment (PPE) for potentially infections situations

XI. C (2) Identify safety techniques that can be used to prevent accidents and maintain a safe work environment

XI. C (4) Identify safety signs, symbols, and labels

XI. C (5) State principles and steps of professional/provider CPR

XI. C (6) Describe basic principles of first aid

XI. C (7) Describe fundamental principles for evacuation of a healthcare setting

XI. C (8) Discuss fire safely issues in a healthcare environment

XI. C (5) State principles and steps of professional/provider CPR

XI. C (11) Discuss critical elements of an emergency plan for response to a natural disaster or other emergency

XI. C (12) Identify emergency preparedness plans in your community

XI. C (13) Discuss potential role(s) of the medical assistant in emergency preparedness

XI. P (1) Comply with safety signs, symbols, and labels

XI. P (3) Develop a personal (patient and employee) safety plan

XI. P (4) Develop an environmental safety plan

XI. P (5) Demonstrate the proper use of the following equipment:

  b. Fire extinguishers

XI. P (6) Participate in a mock environmental exposure event with documentation of steps taken

XI. P (7) Explain an evacuation plan for a physician's office

XI. P (8) Demonstrate methods of fire prevention in the healthcare setting

XI. P (9) Maintain provider/professional level CPR certification

XI. P (10) Perform first aid procedures

XI. P (12) Maintain a current list of community resources for emergency preparedness

XI. A (1) Recognize the effects of stress on all persons involved in emergency situations

XI. A (2) Demonstrate self-awareness in responding to emergency situations

ABHES

8. Medical Office Business Procedures/ Management

  ee. Use proper telephone techniques

9. Medical Office Clinical Procedures

  e. Recognize emergencies and treatments and minor office surgical procedures

  o. Perform:

    (5) First aid and CPR

Workforce

Readiness

Things often happen when you least expect them.

A Spanish proverb

Chapter 24

The Externship and Employment Search

Preparation for Success

Interviewer: Chris, you were telling me that when you were preparing for your externship you were very unhappy about the site that was selected for you. Would you explain?

Chris: Before becoming an administrative medical assistant I worked in retail, selling skincare products. My reason for going into the program was to obtain a job in a plastic surgeon's office that carried skincare products. I thought I could sell a lot and make a lot of money. My attitude was that I only had to learn the ICD and CPT codes and other procedures that applied to a plastic surgery office. When it came time for my externship, the school placed me in a family practice office. I was mad and disappointed. My externship coordinator told me that I was getting a certificate in medical assisting not just in working for a plastic surgeon.

Interviewer: Tell us what happened next.

Chris: I decided, okay, just do what you have to do to get through this and then go find a job where you want. After the first week, I started to notice how interesting it was to meet all kinds of patients of all ages and to experience so many different parts of medical assisting. One day I was able to help a young single mother who had some confusion with her Medicaid. She was so happy and relieved that she cried. I realized that I genuinely helped her. Suddenly, it was no longer only about making money. It was about being in a job that I liked and that I could be good at. When I finished my externship I was offered and accepted a position at the family practice office.

Interviewer: Congratulations! That must have been a great feeling. What advice would you give to students going into their externships?

Chris: Go in with an open mind and a good attitude. You never know where it will lead you.

Interviewer: What is your current position?

Chris: The medical office was bought by a large health-care organization and I'm still there working as an administrative medical assistant and doing research coordination. My new title is Research Coordinator.

Interviewer: That sounds like another great way to help people. Good luck in your new position and thank you for the advice to students.

RÉSUMÉ

unit 7

24 The Externship and Employment Search

Introduction ● ● ●

A vital part of medical assisting training is the externship, practicum, or clinical. This opportunity allows you to hone the skills you learned, experience the "real world" of health care and integrate the roles of the health-care team members that you learned. In addition, the professional behaviors discussed throughout the text are incorporated. This chapter provides knowledge and guidelines for a successful externship. It also offers insight into what the sites desire when hiring a medical assistant, how to search and apply for a position, and how to complete a résumé, a cover letter, and a follow-up letter. You will form a strategic plan to secure a position in administrative medical assisting, and you will gain interviewing techniques needed to compete in today's health-care world.

LO 24.1 The Externship Process

Externships are experiential learning, provided by educational facilities that give students practical experiences in their field of study. Externships are a preparation for seeking regular employment. As opposed to interns, externs are not paid but usually receive educational credit. The process is a mandatory requirement for completion of a medical assisting program in educational institutions that are accredited by the Accrediting Bureau of Health Education Schools (ABHES) and the Commission on Accreditation of Allied Health Education Programs (CAAHEP). Medical assisting externships may be performed at physician offices, laboratories, urgent care centers, administrative billing offices, community health centers, and limited areas in hospitals such as outpatient clinics.

externship
Experiential learning through educational facilities giving students practical experiences in their field of study prior to seeking regular employment.

Externship Site Responsibilities

The educational institution partners with local medical facilities throughout the area. Externship sites are required to review and sign an **affiliation agreement** or contract (Figure 24–1). Typical site responsibilities include:

affiliation agreement
A contract between the school and externship site stating the responsibilities of both parties.

- Providing reasonable, safe, and meaningful educational experiences for the student to complete the required competencies

- Assigning qualified personnel to supervise in a manner that provides safe practice

- Validating the student's required competencies, professional behaviors, and hours

- Retaining complete responsibility for the care of the patients

- Conferring with the student and school externship coordinator concerning student performance and progress

- Notifying the externship coordinator immediately regarding any problems

- Providing a written evaluation of the student's clinical competencies, professional behaviors, and hours

figure 24–1

The school usually signs an affiliation agreement with the externship site.

preceptor

A teacher or mentor.

externship coordinator (practicum coordinator)

The representative of the school who generally ensures that affiliation agreements are in place and the responsibilities of all parties are met which includes scheduling, monitoring, problem solving, and facilitating students.

The person assigned to supervise and work with the student at the externship site is often referred to as a **preceptor.** The student may have more than one preceptor during a comprehensive externship.

Externship Coordinator Responsibilities

Each educational institution assigns an **externship coordinator,** or practicum coordinator, who is familiar with medical assisting and the medical community. The coordinator's responsibilities may include selecting and qualifying externship sites. Generally, the coordinator attempts to provide sites that will offer the most complete experience for the student. Other responsibilities of the coordinator include:

- Ensuring that the student is capable of performing the assigned duties involved in the externship

- Providing the required student documentation, such as immunization records which are often necessary, to the site

- Placing students at externship sites best suited to the individual

- Orienting the evaluator, preceptors, and other site staff to their roles and the requirements

- Monitoring student progress through meetings or reports at designated intervals

- Being available to provide direction to the site and the student for problems such as health and safety exposures (each school usually has an exposure plan) or other issues that may arise

- Reviewing documentation at the end of the externship to determine if the student successfully completed the competencies and required hours

- Providing a grade for the student

- Ensuring documentation is maintained according to school policy

Extern Responsibilities

The extern's or student's responsibilities include

- Concurring with the externship coordinator regarding the days and times of the externship

- Arriving on time, dressed appropriately and ready to work

- Wearing the official name badge designating identification as a medical assisting student

- Maintaining professional behaviors at all times

- Notifying the site contact person and the externship coordinator in the event of a delay prior to the scheduled start of duty

- Documenting and obtaining appropriate signatures for hours and competencies per the school documentation system and procedures

- Following all school and site policies and procedures

- Observing HIPAA compliance at all times (Figure 24–2)

- Contacting the coordinator immediately involving any questions, concerns, difficulties, or issues

- Participating in the required evaluations

MARICOPA COUNTY COMMUNITY COLLEGE DISTRICT
2411 West 14ᵗʰ Street, Tempe, AZ 85281-6942

MARICOPA
COMMUNITY
COLLEGES

PATIENT PRIVACY AND DATA SECURITY AGREEMENT
for MCCCD Allied Health and Nursing Programs Clinical Training

Name (Print) : _____ Check One: ☐ Student ☐ Staff ☐ Faculty

College: _____

The discussions, uses, and disclosures addressed by this agreement mean any written, verbal, or electronic communications.

I understand that I am never to discuss or review any information regarding a patient at a clinical site unless the discussion or review is part of my educational program. I understand that I am obligated to know and adhere to the privacy and data security policies and procedures of any clinical site to which I am assigned. I acknowledge that health records, accounting information, patient information, and conversations between or among healthcare professionals about patients are confidential under law and this agreement.

I understand that, while in the clinical setting, I may not disclose any information about a patient during the clinical portion of my assignment to anyone other than the site's designated health care professionals.

I understand that I may not remove any original health record from the clinical site. I further understand that I may not remove any copy, in part or in total, of the health record without prior written authorization of the clinical site. Additionally, I understand that, before I use or disclose patient information in a learning experience, classroom, case presentation, class assignment, or research, I must exclude as much of the following information as possible:

- Names of the patient or the patient's relatives, employers, or household members
- Geographical subdivisions smaller than a state
- Dates of birth, admission, discharge, and death
- Telephone numbers
- Fax numbers
- E-mail addresses
- Social security numbers
- Medical record numbers
- Health plan beneficiary numbers
- Account numbers

- Certificate/license numbers
- Vehicle identifiers
- Device identifiers
- Web locators (URLs)
- Internet protocol addresses
- Biometric identifiers
- Full face photographs
- Any other unique identifying number, characteristic, or code
- All ages over 89 years

Additionally, I acknowledge that any patient information may only be used or disclosed for health care training and educational purposes at MCCCD, and must otherwise remain confidential.

I understand that I must promptly report any violation of the clinical site's privacy policies and procedures, applicable law, or this confidentiality agreement, by me, or an MCCCD student or faculty member to the appropriate MCCCD program clinical coordinator or program director.

Finally, I understand that, if I violate the privacy policies and procedures of the clinical site, applicable law, or this agreement, I will be subject to disciplinary action.

By signing this agreement, I certify that I have read and understand its terms, and will comply with them.

Signed: _____

Date: _____

MC-PPDSA (10/22/08)   Page 1 of 1

figure 24–2

An example of a HIPAA confidentiality agreement for students, staff, and faculty.

Describe the responsibilities of the externship site, the externship coordinator, and the student.

CHECKPOINT
LO 24.1

LO 24.2 Externship Success

The intent of the externship is to verify that you are capable and workforce ready. This readiness incorporates three major areas:

1. Skills competency

2. Professional behavior

3. Fulfillment of the required hours

Each area is evaluated according to the educational institution's policies and procedures. The previous sections describe the externship process and responsibilities; in addition to the three major evaluation categories, 17 savvy,

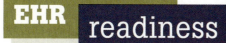

EHR readiness

Your Externship Site

Your externship site will be in one of the following phases related to the electronic health record:

- Introductory phase (beginning to think about it)
- Selection phase (investigation of available systems, costs; refer to the EHR feature in Chapter 22, Practice Management)
- Training/implementation phase (installation and education of staff to begin to use the selected system)
- Application phase (utilization of the system)

Do not miss an opportunity to gain hands-on experience no matter what the EHR phase of your externship site. Some schools provide an opportunity for students to come together for a post-externship debriefing. A discussion of the EHR phase at the site of each extern and the individual experiences could be very helpful in preparation for actual employment. If a group debriefing is not an option, share experiences among your colleagues. Familiarity with the EHR may be an interview question when you are applying for a medical assisting position.

sensible success tips are listed in Table 24–1 to guide you through a successful externship.

Research your externship site prior to starting. Many health-care organizations have Web sites and brochures. Know their mission, types of services, and other general information that will give you some familiarity with the site. It also demonstrates that you are proactive.

At the end of your externship, you should write a thank-you letter to the practice manager and your preceptor. Refer to Procedure 24–1, Writing Thank-you Notes. If a position is open at the externship site and the extern receives good evaluations, he or she will most likely be considered for the position. Participating in externships is labor-intensive for the health-care facilities. One of the

table 24–1

Guidelines for a Successful Externship

1. Review your manual prior to the start of your externship; know the expectations and skills you must complete.
2. Avoid scheduling personal appointments, vacations, or any time off during the externship.
3. Ensure you have reliable transportation and child-care arrangements including sick-child care (Figure 24–3).
4. If you are unsure or uncomfortable with a skill, attempt to improve it prior to proceeding to the site.
5. Arrive on time and ready to work (not with a doughnut and coffee in hand). Notify both your clinical site preceptor and the school externship coordinator if you are late or absent.
6. Make sure your cell phone is OFF at all times with the exception of lunch and breaks.
7. Ensure your appearance is clean and neat and meets the standards of the school and facility. Wear your designated name badge at all times.
8. Demonstrate your willingness to learn. DO NOT sit back and wait to be asked to participate.
9. Use your time wisely. If there are slow periods, perhaps there is medical literature or an interesting case study available or filing you can do.
10. Adhere to confidentiality and HIPAA requirements AT ALL TIMES. Do not discuss patients at home or in public places.
11. Stay within the scope of practice.
12. Call the externship coordinator in a timely manner if there are any questions, concerns, or problems.
13. Be appropriately assertive but not aggressive about completing the required skills; e.g., if appointment scheduling is done in another department, check with your preceptor about going to that department to perform the competency.
14. Keep up with the required documentation. Murphy's Law guarantees that the person you need to sign off on hours or procedures will be on an extensive leave if you wait.
15. Attitude is almost everything; demonstrate a responsible positive attitude at all times.
16. Avoid "office politics." DO NOT gossip or take sides in disagreements among staff, and do not ask about or discuss salaries with staff.
17. **Remember, you represent your school and yourself. The health-care community is a small world. Do not, in any way, act in an unprofessional manner. It may come back to haunt you when you least expect it (perhaps when you are applying for that ideal job). It may also influence the site's willingness to accept future externs from your school.**

reasons they take on the responsibility is to have an opportunity to observe the potential employee firsthand prior to hiring. Ask your site practice manager and physicians to write a letter of reference that you may use for future job searches.

The majority of students enjoy the externship experience and consider it the highlight of their medical assisting educational program. This practicum is also the gateway to your new career. Your hard work is paying off and you are getting closer to your goal.

● ● ●

Select three of the guidelines for a successful externship. Elaborate on possible consequences for neglecting them.

CHECKPOINT
LO 24.2

LO 24.3 Seeking Employment

After you complete your externship and obtain your certification, you are ready to seek employment as an administrative medical assistant. You can take advantage of a number of other resources in seeking employment within the field of administrative medical assisting. These resources include classified ads, Internet sites, employment services, and networking with classmates and others. See Figure 24–4. Most accredited schools have a career services department. Its primary focus is job placement after graduation. The department's counselors will assist you in writing your résumé, improving your interviewing skills, and learning about positions in your field. Many employers will contact a school's career services department to recruit medical personnel. It is important to work closely with the career services department in the beginning of your career to assist you in obtaining your first position. In staying in touch with them after you obtain your position, you may help a future medical assistant obtain his or her first position at the place of your employment.

Classified ads are placed by many prospective employers in area newspapers. The advertisement usually describes the duties and responsibilities of the position as well as the type of education and experience preferred.

Internet sites are good resources for potential positions. As with any other Internet search, use only credible sources, especially when providing personal information. Sites of newspapers, health-care organizations, professional organizations, and your school career center are generally safe. Recognized job search Web sites such as www.monster.com and www.jobing.com are also useful. Whether you apply online or in hard copy, follow the recommendations for completing an application, cover letter, and other protocols that are discussed in this chapter.

Employment services and temporary agencies provide assistance in locating a specific job. Both types of agencies have a variety of job openings on file. Agencies also place classified ads. You should call to make an appointment with an employment counselor. Agencies usually require you to fill out an application, take a basic health-care knowledge test, and provide a résumé. If the agency has positions that match

figure 24–3

Ensure you have reliable child care prior to your externship.

Externship Readiness

Using the Professional Behaviors rubric in Chapter 2 (refer to Figure 2–8), repeat your self-assessment. Compare the results to the first self-assessment you conducted at the beginning of your medical assisting training. Do you feel you demonstrated improvement?

Are there areas that need more work before you proceed to your externship? Some students believe that they "will be different" in the externship. This does not happen. Address poor habits now. Review Chapter 4, Professional Communication, and Chapter 6, Law and Ethics in the Medical Office, to ensure externship readiness.

your skills, it contacts the employer. If the service has no appropriate listings, it will place your résumé on file.

Employment services are an excellent way to gain experience and select a position. You are given an opportunity to try out the office or facility at little commitment on your part. Many permanent opportunities can result from a temporary job assignment. Ensure you know the terms of the agreement with the agency regarding accepting a position where you were placed. There may be a waiting period and associated costs.

networking
Making contacts with relatives, friends, and acquaintances who may have information about how to find a job in your field.

Contact with relatives, friends, and acquaintances that may have information about how to find a job in your field is referred to as **networking.** People in your network may be able to give you job leads or tell you about openings. Word-of-mouth referrals—finding job information by talking with other people—can be very helpful. Other people may be able to introduce you to others who work in, or know people who work in, your field. Networking is a valuable tool. It can advance your career even while you are employed. Joining a medical assisting organization and attending conferences are the easiest ways to network. Attend an organization's local chapter meetings, such as the AAMA and AMT county or state chapters, and talk with as many people as possible.

Classmates are often a good source of networking. It is important to build lasting friendships with classmates and keep in touch after graduation. Often they will know of positions as they gain employment. Networking begins in the classroom.

figure 24–4

Seeking employment.

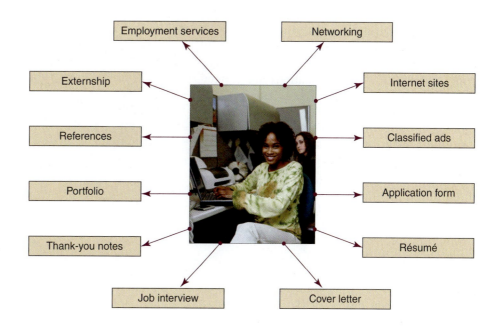

"Cold calling" is another employment search technique. The term is used when you visit a practice without an appointment, inquire about employment opportunities and leave a résumé. This technique is especially effective when a new medical office with multiple practices is constructed and they are in need of new employees. When "cold calling," dress as if you were going to an interview and follow the same strategies. Take several copies of your résumé. If a practice does not have a job opening, ask the staff if they know of other opportunities in the building or other sites. Also, suggest that the office keep your résumé on file if a future position becomes available.

References

A **reference** is a recommendation for employment from a person who is considered to have credibility and some expertise in determining if you are fit for the position. During your job search you will be asked to provide the names of people who will provide references. Ask your externship site practice manager and physicians for reference letters. Also, ask if you may include them on your reference list. Never include someone without their prior knowledge and permission. Three to five references are generally required. You will be asked to provide the name, position, contact information, and your relationship with that person. Sometimes you are asked for the length of time you have known the individual.

Excellent references include program faculty and other former teachers, health-care professionals that know you, former employers, and professional colleagues. Relatives are not acceptable references.

reference
A recommendation for employment from a facility or a preceptor.

The Job Application

Most organizations require you to submit a job application as the first step in applying for a position. The application form is obtained at the facility or online. It is an official document and represents you; it must be accurate. False or misleading information may be considered fraudulent and could lead to dismissal. The document, itself, is specific to that organization but the majority of applications contain the same information. Also, the information is generally the same as what is contained in your résumé. However, it is not acceptable to write "see résumé." The forms are very prescriptive with precise information required in exact areas with a limited amount of space. They are, generally, designed with computerized parameters to search for qualified candidates. Prepare your résumé first and use it as a guide for completing the application. Ensure employment, education, dates, and so forth are the same on the résumé and the application. When preparing your application, include the same terminology as the job posting. The computer parameters will include these key words for selecting applications.

Some applications are completed directly online. Most of the electronic versions do not contain a spell-checker! Whether completing the form electronically or by pen, ensure words are spelled correctly and the overall appearance is neat. Read and follow instructions carefully.

Submit the application as instructed which may be online, by e-mail or regular mail. Refer to Procedure 24–2, Completing a Job Application.

● ● ●

Now that you have reviewed the methods for seeking employment, decide which one(s) you will most likely use. Why did you choose these options?

CHECKPOINT
LO 24.3

LO 24.4 The Résumé and Cover Letter

The résumé and cover letter are vital parts of the employment process. They both provide potential employers with information about your educational and work history and other aspects of your background. The main purpose is to

make a good impression by demonstrating you have the required qualifications and secure an interview. A cover letter should always accompany a résumé.

Creating the Résumé

A résumé should:

- Contain only truthful information or it may be considered fraudulent and reason for termination.
- Include only one or two pages.
- Avoid half pages, using the suggestions in Figure 24–5 for added material.
- Use 8½ by 11-inch paper, 16 to 24 weight, in white or ivory with a matching envelope—no pastel or other colored paper.
- Provide information using the terms in the organization's job description; initial screening may be done by a computer that searches for these key words.
- Avoid using the word "I"; it is your résumé and, therefore, not necessary.
- Space lines and topics in an easy-to-read format.
- Ensure your name is in a footer on the second page, if résumé is more than one page.
- Review the finished product carefully for errors and overall appearance.

Résumé Components

While there are various types of résumés, the **targeted résumé** focuses on a specific job target. This style is most effective for graduates seeking a position in administrative medical assisting. The targeted résumé is used in this text. Refer to Procedure 24–3, Writing a Résumé. The recommended components follow.

Heading   Include your name, address, e-mail, and one telephone number. Potential employers do not have the time or inclination to call more than one number. Do not include other information in the heading.

Professional Objective   A professional objective is a brief, general statement that demonstrates a career goal. Ensure the objective is compatible with the job description. For example, do not state that your objective is to be a practice manager when you are applying for an administrative medical assistant position. Your long-range goal is not your current objective, which is to obtain the medical assistant position.

Language   Due to the diversity of patient populations, bilingual employees in many languages are in demand. If you are bilingual, addressing this skill early in your résumé catches the attention of the person who is screening. Being bilingual means one has the ability to speak, read, write, and translate in two languages fluently.

Education   In providing your educational history, list your degrees and certifications from a post secondary school in reverse chronological order with the most recent first. The most recent is probably your administrative medical assisting education. Include the completion date for the degree or certification, the degree or certificate earned, and the name and address of the institution.

Experience   Most medical assisting positions require experience. Use your externship(s) to demonstrate experience. Begin with the time period, your position, the site name, address, telephone number, and a brief description of duties. Use this area to document the qualifications and requirements of the job posting.

figure 24-5

Targeted résumé template with examples.

Name
Address
Phone
E-mail

Objective:

To work as an administrative medical assistant applying skills in patient relations, patient registration, billing and coding, financial practices, the electronic health records, and other areas while gaining increased responsibility.

Bilingual:

Speak, write, read, and translate _____ and English

Education:

March 2011	Administrative Medical Assisting Certification Funton College 1656 N. Main St. Funton, XY 12324
June 2008	Diploma Central High School 6539 S. Main St. Funton, XY 12324

> Put dates and school for any other college degrees and post-secondary school programs resulting in a certificate

Experience:

September 2010 to December 2010	Administrative Medical Assisting Externship Total Care Clinic 342 E. Park Blvd Funton, XY 12345 Tel: 521-234-0001

Appointment scheduling, registering patients, opening and closing the office, collecting copayments, obtaining diagnostic testing results, performing supply inventory and ordering, conducting follow-up phone calls, managing medical records, processing financial procedures, electronic health record experience (SpringCharts)

January 2011	Administrative Medical Assisting Externship Magnum Healthcare Systems 1600 Oak Ave. Funton, XY 12356 Tel: 521-234-1112

Insurance billing and coding, claims processing

June 2008 to September 2009	Sales Associate Tweens and Teens 4212 N. 16th Street Funton, XY 12341

Maintained excellent client relations; managed inventory, performed accounting procedures, trained and supervised new employees, opened and closed facility
Reason for leaving: To pursue further education

> Add other job experience as appropriate but no more than past 10 years.

Other Qualifications:

Proficient in Microsoft Word, Excel, and Publisher

> Include qualifications that you possess described in the position posting that are not found in other areas of your résumé

Additional Certifications:

Current Cardiopulmonary Resuscitation (CPR)

> Add other appropriate certifications

Professional Memberships and Awards:

2010 to present	American Association of Medical Assistants (AAMA)
2010 to present	American Medical Technologists (AMT)
2009, 2010	Funton College Honors Student

> If your résumé fits on one page that's okay—add line for "References upon request" at the end; if your résumé goes over to a second page and you need filler, add Strengths and Community Service if appropriate. Examples are listed here.

Strengths:

1   Excellent attendance
2   Good communication skills
3   Conscientious and self motivated

Community Service:

Fall 2007–present	Bethany Presbyterian Church 7702 North 35th Avenue Funton, XY 12366

> Example

Assisting with the annual health fair and providing preventive health information

References available upon request

> Check for typos and formatting before submitting!

Follow with other job experiences with the beginning and ending dates you were employed (listing the most recent first), the position title, and a brief description of your duties. Use skills describing your duties that would appropriately transfer to a health-care setting. For example, most jobs involve customer service which is reasonable to include. Refer to Table 24–2, Effective Résumé Terms, to assist you. Do not clutter your résumé with needless details or irrelevant jobs that you held for less than six months. Include your employment history for no more than 10 years. Unexplained gaps in employment that were not related to education or training are often considered suspicious. Be prepared to explain the gaps during your interview. If you were employed in different positions over a 10-year span, you should include a line at the end of this section stating "employment history prior to _____ available upon request." For example, if it is 2011, you would include employment from 2001, which is the date you would place in the blank. Include other skills and qualifications that are related to the job posting but are not previously covered. Computer and other relevant digital proficiency may be examples.

Additional Certifications   Your administrative medical assisting degree or certification is listed in the Education section. You are most likely CPR-certified and perhaps also certified in first aid. Add these credentials to this section with the beginning and ending date when you were certified and the certification. Do not add expired certifications.

Professional Memberships and Awards   List any professional memberships that are related to your career. Student memberships are available through the American Medical Technologists (AMT) and the American Association of Medical Assistants (AAMA). You can contact the AMT and request a copy of the student by-laws and directions on how to form a student membership in your school. The AAMA provides continuing education through their local chapters. They sponsor local meetings periodically throughout the year. Employers prefer medical professionals who are involved in their disciplines. It demonstrates a commitment and dedication to their chosen field. This is also the section to include awards that demonstrate achievement and workforce readiness.

Strengths   Remember, the résumé is limited to two pages. If you have space, list your strengths—excellent attendance, good communicator, team player, and self-motivated are desirable. Only list the strengths that you have. The organization

table 24–2

Effective Résumé Terms

administered	inspected
advised	introduced
analyzed	maintained
billed	managed
carried out	motivated
compiled	negotiated
completed	operated
conducted	ordered
contacted	organized
coordinated	oversaw
counseled	performed
designed	planned
developed	prepared
directed	presented
distributed	produced
established	reviewed
functioned as	supervised
implemented	taught
improved	trained

will check your references and expect to hear these same strengths. Ask yourself "What are my strengths that are observed by others?" This may be another opportunity to include key terms from the job posting.

Community Service If you have additional space, without creating a crowded appearance, cite your community service or volunteer work. Again, use key terms from the job posting if appropriate.

Closing The last line of the résumé should state "References available upon request."

The Cover Letter

The professional expectations of a job search include a cover letter to accompany your résumé. This piece of correspondence provides an explanation of why you are submitting your résumé and an additional opportunity to highlight your qualifications. A cover letter is also an introduction to your résumé. Cover letters are just as important as your résumé in your job search. An effective cover letter motivates the employer to review the résumé and interview the candidate. Many strong résumés are ignored due to a poorly written cover letter.

Your cover letter should be direct and to the point, no longer than one page, and typed on paper that matches your résumé. If possible, your cover letter should be addressed to a specific person in the organization. You can call the facility and ask to whom you should address the letter. If a name is not available, it is acceptable to address the letter to "Human Resources Manager" or "Practice Manager." Research the facility prior to writing the letter. This information can help you tailor your letter to show how your qualifications and interests directly relate to the needs of the medical facility. As with the résumé, make sure the description of your qualifications and interests reflects the words used by the company in the advertisement. Always be truthful about the information in the cover letter; employers often verify all facts. Check for errors in spelling, grammar, and punctuation. An example of a cover letter is shown in Figure 24–6.

Sending the Cover Letter and Résumé

When sending the cover letter and résumé, make sure you have the correct name, address, and zip code of the facility. This information should be typed on a matching envelope. Many software programs have an envelope template feature that allows you to print an envelope using the address in your cover letter. Do not hand-write envelopes; professional-looking mail is often opened first. Make sure that you attach sufficient postage.

When faxing, verify the fax number and person or department intended to receive it. Make sure your name is on all the faxed pages. If your fax machine provides a fax completion printout, save it to verify that the fax was delivered.

Some classified ads request that you send your information via e-mail. In order to accomplish this, you must first have an account with an Internet service provider (ISP). Do not use a casual name for your e-mail address; prospective employers will see your name in their in-box. Instead, choose an address that is conservative and professional. Most e-mail programs have an attachment feature that will allow you to send a Microsoft Word or other form of document via e-mail. The application, cover letter, and résumé are sent as attachments. Verify that your e-mail was sent by checking your sent items.

You may post your résumé and cover letter on the Internet by using a career/job search Internet site. Most Internet job sites have local employers posting positions daily. A job search Internet site will provide clear directions on how to post your résumé and cover letter. Some school career services departments

figure 24–6

The object of a cover letter is to convince the recipient to read your résumé.

**Your Street Address
City, State, Zip Code**

Date

**Name of person to whom you are writing
Title
Company or Organization
Street Address
City, State, Zip Code**

Dear Dr., Mr., Mrs., Miss, or Ms. _____:

<u>1st Paragraph:</u> Tell why you are writing. Name the position or general area of work that interests you. Mention how you learned about the job opening. State why you are interested in the job.

<u>2nd Paragraph:</u>Refer to the enclosed résumé and give some background information. Indicate why you should be considered as a candidate, focusing on how your skills can fulfill the needs of the company. Relate your experiences to their needs and mention results/achievements. Do not restate what is said on your résumé—you want to pull together all the information and tell how your background fits the position.

<u>3rd Paragraph</u>: Close by making a specific request for an interview. Say that you will follow up with a phone call to arrange a mutually convenient interview time. Offer to provide any additional information that may be needed. Thank the employer for his/her time and consideration.

Sincerely,

(your handwritten signature)

Type your name

Enclosure

host online job fairs and will assist you in posting your résumé. Many employers prefer electronic submission of the application and résumé through their own Web sites.

● ● ●

If you were a busy practice manager, why would you prefer to receive a targeted résumé from an administrative medical assisting job applicant?

CHECKPOINT
LO 24.4

LO 24.5 The Interview

If a candidate's application, résumé, and cover letter are found satisfactory, the next step is an invitation to interview. The general method to contact him or her is by telephone. Most potential employers will only call once. It is important to have voice mail or an answering machine in case you are not available. As with the e-mail address, ensure that your telephone message is professional and succinct.

Preparing a Portfolio

Prior to the interview, you should organize all your employment documentation into a portfolio. A **portfolio** is a collection of documents such as your résumé; cover letter; reference list or reference letters; awards for volunteer service in a health-related field; and student recognition certificates such as student of the year or month, perfect attendance, or academic honors. Include a copy of your transcript, diploma or degree, and medical assisting credentials such as your CMA (AAMA) or RMA (AMT). You can also include any other certifications you hold, such as a CPR card or phlebotomy certification.

Since you will most likely work with **vulnerable populations,** groups considered at risk for coercion and exploitation such as children, the elderly, and persons with special needs, some employers require a criminal background check. This check is usually done through fingerprinting. Some employers also request proof of immunizations, so include these records in your portfolio. Give your portfolio a professional presentation by printing your documents on a high-quality printer and organizing them in a nice binder or folder. A professional portfolio can help you obtain employment. If needed, look for a service that specializes in creating professional portfolios. Sometime during the employment hiring process, you will be asked for your social security card and a picture identification, generally your driver's license. Have these documents available but do not place them in your portfolio.

portfolio
A collection of an applicant's résumé, reference letters, and other documents of interest to a potential employer.

vulnerable populations
Groups considered at risk for coercion and exploitation; generally, children, elderly, and groups with special needs.

Potential Interview Questions

In order to prepare for your interview, you can anticipate any of the following questions:

- Tell me about yourself.
- What would your instructors and colleagues say are your strengths?
- What areas of your professional life do you think may need improvement?
- What are you doing to work on these areas?
- What qualifications do you have that make you a good candidate for this position?
- Do you prefer to complete a task by yourself or with others?
- Describe a difficult situation you encountered and what you did about it.
- What does diversity mean to you?
- Where do you see yourself five years from now? (Figure 24–7.)

Health-care administrator

Practice manager

Medical office supervisor

Medical assistant specialist

Administrative medical assistant

figure 24–7

You may want to position yourself to move up the career ladder.

- Will you be able to work overtime?
- Do you have the flexibility to work various shifts?
- What has been your major accomplishment to date?
- Why did you choose medical assisting as your career?
- Do you have any questions that you would like to ask?

It is helpful to be prepared with any questions that you may have for the interviewer about the position or the facility. Questions about salary and benefits are not appropriate in a first interview. An interviewer may ask you questions that you are not obligated to answer. These questions refer to age, race, sexual orientation, marital status, number of children, country of origin, pregnancy, holidays you observe, and chronic illnesses or disabilities. If the interviewer asks even one of these questions, you should reconsider whether you want to work for the organization.

Interview Planning and Strategies

Just as the résumé is important for opening the door to opportunity, the job interview itself is critical for allowing you to present yourself professionally and to clearly articulate why you are the best person for the job. As you learned in Chapter 4, Professional Communication, being successful in an administrative medical assisting career is centered on communication—both verbal and nonverbal. These communication skills will be assets during your job interviews.

Plan to begin the interview by greeting the interviewer with a smile. The interview is an opportunity to sell yourself to the employer. Offer your hand for a firm, confident handshake, and be alert to the interviewer's body language. The flow of conversation during an interview should be natural. Maintain eye contact, pay attention to the interviewer, and show interest. Ask intelligent questions that you have prepared before the interview. Remember, the interview is an opportunity for both the prospective employer and the prospective employee to gather information and make a good impression. In addition to reviewing the experience listed on your résumé, the interviewer will evaluate your personality and behavior. At the same time, you will be observing the office and learning more about the position. Try to be aware of the office's atmosphere, its equipment and supplies, and the attitudes of the staff. Does it seem like a pleasant, professional place to work? Ask yourself if you would be happy in that work environment. The following list provides additional strategies that will help you improve the interview process.

Practice Interviewing Rehearse the possible questions in the previous section and be prepared to answer them. Have a friend or family member interview you as you sit in front of a mirror and observe your body language.

Learn about the Company Be prepared; research the company or medical facility. What is the type of specialty? How many physicians are there?

Dress Appropriately In most situations, you will be safe if you wear clean, pressed, conservative business clothes in neutral colors. Do not wear current fashions or fad clothing to an interview. Pay special attention to grooming. Keep makeup light, and wear minimal jewelry. Cover body art. Make sure that your hair and nails are clean and styled conservatively. Simply carry a pen, your portfolio with extra copies of your résumé, and a small pad for taking notes.

Turn Off Cell Phone and Other Electronic Devices It is easy to forget that they are on. Place a note in your vehicle to remind yourself to turn them off before you go into the interview.

Be Punctual If you arrive late for the interview, a prospective employer may conclude that you will be late in arriving to work. Make certain you know the location and the time of the interview. Allow time for traffic, parking, and other preliminaries.

Be Professional Being too familiar in your manner can be a barrier to a professional interview. Never call anyone by his or her first name unless you are asked to. Know the interviewer's title and the pronunciation of his or her name. Do not sit down until the interviewer does.

Be Poised and Relaxed Avoid nervous habits such as tapping your pencil, playing with your hair, or covering your mouth with your hand. Watch language such as "you know," "ah," and "stuff like that." Use proper grammar and pronunciation as you talk with the interviewer—do not use slang. Do not smoke, chew gum, fidget, or bite your nails.

Relate Your Experience to the Job Use every question as an opportunity to show how your skills relate to the job. Use examples taken from school, previous jobs, your externship, volunteer work, leadership in student organizations, and personal experience to indicate that you have the personal qualities, aptitude, and skills needed for this job. Be thorough but succinct, respecting the interviewer's time.

Be Honest While it is important to be confident and stress your strengths, it is equally important to be honest. Dishonesty always catches up to you sooner or later. Someone will verify your background, so do not exaggerate your accomplishments, grade point average, or experience.

Focus on How You Can Benefit the Company Again, don't ask about benefits, salary, or vacations until you are offered the job. During a first interview, try to show how you can contribute to the organization. Do not appear to be too eager to move up through the company or suggest that you are more interested in gaining experience than in contributing to the company.

Close the Interview on a Positive Note Thank the interviewer for his or her time, shake hands, and state you are looking forward to hearing from him or her. Ask when he or she anticipates making a decision. Also ask if you will be notified even if you are not selected. This information is important to know since you may interview for more than one position. You may not want to accept the first offer if you are waiting to hear from other facilities. Also, you do not want to wait if someone else was already selected.

On the way out of the office, thank the staff members involved in the interview. Ask for a business card from anyone whom you think you might want to send a thank-you note. After leaving the interview, write down any additional information you want to remember. Every interview provides you with information about the medical assisting profession. Even if an interview does not result in a job, you will have met new people, developed a larger network of professional contacts, and gained valuable interviewing experience.

The Follow-Up Letter

Within 2 days after the interview, send a follow-up or thank-you letter to the person or persons from the organization who conducted your interview.

It should be brief, but express your appreciation for the opportunity to have met with the interviewer. Reaffirm your interest in the organization, and state your desire to remain a part of the selection process. By sending a thank-you letter, you display common business courtesy, which can make a difference in the employer's hiring decision. Even if you are not interested in continuing the interview and selection process, you should thank the employer for holding the interview. Procedure 24–1 explains how to write and send a thank-you letter.

Reasons for Not Being Hired

Employers in business were asked to list reasons for not hiring a job candidate. The 15 biggest complaints are the following:

1. Poor appearance and grooming; inappropriate dress
2. Acting like a know-it-all
3. Not communicating clearly; poor voice tone, diction, and grammar
4. Lack of planning for the interview—disorganized responses and no goals communicated
5. Lack of confidence or poise
6. No interest in or enthusiasm for the job
7. Arriving late for the interview
8. Exhibiting interest only in the highest salary offer
9. Poor school record, either in academics, attendance, or both
10. Unwillingness to begin in an entry-level position
11. Making excuses about an unfavorable record
12. No tact
13. No maturity
14. Unsatisfactory references
15. Being critical of past employers

Avoiding these pitfalls; submitting a correct and complete application, cover letter and résumé; thorough preparation for the interview; remembering the aspects of professional communication during the interview; and a properly written thank-you letter will greatly enhance the likelihood of obtaining the position. As you come to the end of this text, the authors would like to wish you the best in your new career and leave you with this thought:

Believe in the best,

think your best, study your best,

never be satisfied with less than your best;

try your best, and in the long run

things will turn out the best

Henry Ford

CHECKPOINT
LO 24.5

Review the possible interview questions provided in this section. Determine which question would be the most difficult for you and determine how you would answer it.

Procedure 24–1 Writing Thank-You Notes

OBJECTIVE To develop an appropriate, professional thank-you note after an interview or externship

MATERIALS Paper; pen; dictionary; thesaurus; computer; #10 business envelope

METHOD
1. Complete the letter within 2 days of the interview or completion of the externship. Begin by typing the date at the top of the letter.
2. Type the name of the person who interviewed you (or who was your mentor in the externship) if that is who you are thanking. Include credentials and title, such as Dr. or Director of Client Services. Include the complete address of the office or organization.
3. Start the letter with "Dear Dr., Mr., Mrs., Miss, or Ms."
4. In the first paragraph, thank the interviewer for his time and for granting the interview. Discuss some specific impressions, for example, "I found the interview and tour of the facilities an enjoyable experience. I would welcome the opportunity to work in such a state-of-the-art medical setting." If you are writing to thank your mentor for her time during your externship and for allowing you to perform your externship at her office, practice, or clinic, discuss the knowledge and experience you gained during the externship.
5. In the second paragraph, mention the aspects of the job or externship that you found most interesting or challenging. For a job interview thank-you note, state how your skills and qualifications will make you an asset to the staff. When preparing an externship thank-you letter, mention interest in any future positions.
6. In the last paragraph, thank the interviewer for considering you for the position. Ask to be contacted at his earliest convenience regarding his employment decision.
7. Close the letter with "Sincerely," and type your name. Leave enough space above your typewritten name to sign your name.
8. Type your return address in the upper-left corner of the #10 business envelope. Then type the interviewer's name and address in the envelope's center, apply the proper postage, and mail the letter. You can also e-mail your thank-you letter. Proper letter format and professional tone and appearance still apply. Send the thank-you letter as an attachment.

Procedure 24–2 Completing a Job Application

GOAL To complete an accurate and legible job application

MATERIALS Job application (paper or electronic), personal and reference information including dates and contact information or completed sample application (See Sample Application for Employment, Figure 24–8.)

figure 24–8

A sample application for employment requires specific personal information and references.

APPLICATION FOR EMPLOYMENT

PERSONAL INFORMATION

DATE OF APPLICATION: _____

Name: ....

Last   First   Middle

Address: ....

Street   (Apt)   City, State   Zip

Alternate Address: ....

Street   City, State   Zip

Contact Information: (   )   (   ) ....

Home Telephone   Mobile   E-mail

How did you learn about our facility?

POSITION SOUGHT: _____   **Available Start Date:** _____

Desired Pay Range: _____   **Are you currently employed?**_____

By Hour or Salary

EDUCATION

	Name and Location	Graduate?—Degree?	Major/Subjects of Study
High School			
College or University			
Specialized Training, Trade School, etc.			
Other Education			

Please list your areas of highest proficiency, special skills, or other items that may contribute to your abilities in performing the above-mentioned position.

....

....

....

figure 24–8 *(Concluded)*

PREVIOUS EXPERIENCE

Please list, beginning from most-recent [add pages if needed].

Dates Employed	Company Name	Location	Role/Title

Job notes, tasks performed, and reason for leaving:

....

Dates Employed	Company Name	Location	Role/Title

Job notes, tasks performed, and reason for leaving:

....

REFERENCES

Provide names and contact information.

Name: **Job Title or Relationship:**

Address:
          Street   (Apt)   City, State   Zip

Contact Information: (   )   (   )
                   Phone   Fax   E-mail

Name: **Job Title or Relationship:**

Address:
          Street   (Apt)   City, State   Zip

Contact Information: (   )   (   )
                   Phone   Fax   E-mail

Name: **Job Title or Relationship:**

Address:
          Street   (Apt)   City, State   Zip

Contact Information: (   )   (   )
                   Phone   Fax   E-mail

Applicant's Signature:_____   **Date:**_____

[For Office Use Only] Date: _____   Initials: _____   *Follow-Up:* _____

METHOD

1. Review the application form completely before beginning. Directions may be on the last page.

2. Complete the personal information carefully, following all directions.

   - For paper applications, look at the fine print. For example, some forms require the last name to be written first or may request that all information be printed. A black-ink pen should be used unless the directions state otherwise. Pens cannot be erased so go slow and be precise.

   - For electronic forms, read each direction before you begin to input the information. Be careful not to hit the Tab or Enter key until you have checked your entries in each space of the form.

3. Complete the rest of the application referring to your completed sample application or list of personal and reference information.

4. Complete all of the requested information. Do not leave any blanks. Finish the application once you have all the requested information. This may require you to cancel the process electronically or take the application home.

5. List your most recent employment first and be certain to include all education such as vocations training, certifications, or other courses you may have taken.

6. List any skills you have that are relevant to the position. Be specific.

7. When completing salary requirements, either include a range or insert "negotiable" or "flexible." These can be discussed in more detail once you are offered the job.

8. Include complete information about your references. References do not always have to be professional. If you have volunteered you can use members of the organizations that you have helped. You may want to ask teachers or your supervisor at your externship site. In all cases, ask for permission prior to using the person for a reference.

9. Review your application for completeness, accuracy, spelling, grammar, and legibility.

10. Sign and date your application and submit it to the appropriate person or send it electronically.

Procedure 24–3 Writing a Résumé

GOAL   To develop a résumé that defines your career objective and highlights your skills

MATERIALS   Paper; pen; dictionary; thesaurus; computer

METHOD

1. Type your full name, address (temporary and permanent, if you have both), telephone number with area code, and e-mail address.

2. List your general career objective. You may also choose to summarize your skills.

3. List the highest level of education or the most recently obtained degree first or certificate. Include the school name, degree earned, and date of graduation.

4. Summarize your work experience. List your most recent employment first. Describe your responsibilities, and list job titles, company names, and dates of employment. Summer employment, volunteer work, and student externships may also be included. Use short sentences with strong action words such as *directed, designed, developed,* and *organized.* For example, condense a responsibility into "Processed insurance and billing" or "Drafted correspondence as requested."

5. List any memberships and affiliations with professional organizations. List them alphabetically or by order of importance.

6. Do not list references on your résumé.

7. Do not list the salary you wish to receive in a medical assisting position. Salary requirements should not be discussed until a job offer is received.

8. Print your résumé on an 8½- by 11-inch sheet of high-quality white, off-white, or other light-colored bond paper. Carefully check your résumé for spelling, punctuation, and grammatical errors. Have someone else double-check your résumé whenever possible.

Case Study

The Allied Health Professions' School is known for its excellent externs and graduates. The externship sites appreciate that the school does not send them "problem" students. Consequently, many of the school's externs are hired upon completion. When the sites have employment opportunities, they frequently contact the school regarding graduates who may be seeking employment. The educational institution utilizes the Professional Behaviors rubric introduced in Chapter 2 (refer to Figure 2–8) to ensure professional readiness before the students begin externships. Charlie, one of the allied health students, receives high grades in most classes based on his academic performance and technical skills. He works independently; gets the job done under the allotted time; and his attendance is excellent. However, during his Professional Behaviors evaluation in the middle of his program, he was rated "questionable" in the elements of cooperation and communication. He does not like to participate in group exercises and has a manner that makes his team members feel inferior since he thinks he can get the job done better by himself. In class, he is intolerant of fellow students who ask questions and need clarification of material. Charlie is impatient when told he must give better explanations of the procedure to be performed with his "practice patients" who are his classmates. He and his instructor developed an improvement plan to address his questionable scores.

PROFESSIONAL READINESS

Cooperation
Appropriately and willingly works with others in the best interest of the work

Communication
Ability to give and receive clear, accurate information

Thinking Critically

1. Was an improvement plan justified for Charlie since he receives high grades?

2. How could you help Charlie if he became impatient with you as one of his "practice patients" prior to his externship?

3. Why is it important for all students of the institution to exhibit professional readiness at their externships?

1. Write your own goals and expectations of an externship.

2. Bring in classified ads from your local newspaper or the employment Web site. Review the job postings and discuss those appropriate for an administrative medical assistant. Select one and write a cover letter describing how your skills would benefit the organization.

There may be more than one correct answer. Circle the best answer.

1. **[LO24.2]** An issue that could lead to immediate dismissal from the externship is
   a. arriving late.
   b. performing a procedure excessively slow.
   c. waiting to document hours.
   d. violating HIPAA.
   e. avoiding gossip.

2. **[LO24.1]** The primary purpose of the externship is for the student to
   a. obtain a job.
   b. learn new skills.
   c. earn continuing education credits.
   d. hone skills in the actual health-care setting.
   e. practice professional behaviors.

3. **[LO24.2]** Staying within the extern's scope of practice means to
   a. practice professional behaviors.
   b. ensure hours of accountability are recorded.
   c. observe HIPAA.
   d. do whatever the extern's preceptor asks.
   e. do only what is legal and one was trained to do.

4. **[LO24.2]** The three major areas of externship evaluation are skills' competency, professional behaviors, and:
   a. hours of accountability.
   b. knowledge of office policies.
   c. friendliness.
   d. speed in performing skills.
   e. appearance.

5. **[LO24.3]** Networking
   a. involves making contacts with relatives, friends, and acquaintances that may have information about how to find a job in your field.
   b. is used by individuals who have job experience. It lists your most recent job first and ends with your first job.
   c. is an introduction to your résumé.
   d. is a recommendation for employment from the facility and the preceptor.
   e. is a collection of documents that portrays you skills and experience.

6. **[LO24.5]** Which of the following is least likely to be a question you will answer during an interview?
   a. How would your instructors describe you?
   b. How well do you work under pressure?
   c. Do you have any questions that you would like to ask?
   d. Why did you choose administrative medical assisting as your career?
   e. How will your marriage and family affect your employment?

7. **[LO24.5]** Why should you send a thank-you letter within two days of completing an interview or externship?
   a. To ensure you do not forget
   b. To ensure the interviewer or externship site will remember you
   c. To ask what the salary will be
   d. To ensure that your résumé is received
   e. To present yourself again as a candidate

8. **[LO24.3]** Falsifying information on a job application may be considered
   a. abuse.
   b. slander.
   c. fraud.
   d. libel.
   e. Okay.

9. **[LO24.4]** The main purpose of the résumé is to
   a. secure a job.
   b. provide personal information.
   c. list education and employment.
   d. obtain an interview.
   e. expand on your application information.

10. **[LO24.4]** The document that should always accompany a résumé is the:

   a. application.
   b. follow-up letter.
   c. list of references.
   d. cover letter.
   e. job posting.

11. **[LO24.5]** Which of the following is the *most likely* reason you are not hired?

   a. Interest and enthusiasm for the job
   b. Displaying maturity and curiosity for the job
   c. Acting like a know-it-all
   d. Willingness to begin in an entry-level position
   e. Careful planning for the interview

learning outcome SUMMARY

LO 24.1 The student should understand the responsibilities and expectations of the externship site, the externship coordinator, and the extern prior to beginning the externship experience.

LO 24.2 In addition to the three evaluation categories of skills competency, professional behaviors, and required hours, 17 tips or guidelines are provided that support student success in the externship and carry over into the workplace. The externship may lead to a permanent position.

LO 24.3 Career centers, classified advertisements, employment Web sites, networking, employment agencies, and "cold calling" may be helpful in searching for a position. Most organizations require potential candidates to complete a job application as the first step in pursuing employment.

LO 24.4 The résumé and cover letter provide potential employers with information about your educational and work history and other aspects of your background. They should demonstrate the required job qualifications and secure an interview. The targeted résumé is the most appropriate type for new administrative medical assistant graduates, since the components emphasize the candidate's qualifications for the position.

LO 24.5 Interview preparation includes creating a portfolio, anticipating and practicing potential questions, appropriate grooming and appearance, and knowledge of professional behaviors and courtesies. The interview should incorporate all aspects of professional communication—both verbal and nonverbal. It is important to follow up with a thank-you letter.

medical assisting COMPETENCIES

CAAHEP

IV. C (5) Recognize the elements of oral communication using a sender-receiver process

IV. C (8) Recognize elements of fundamental writing skills

IV. C (9) Discuss applications of electronic technology in effective communication

IV. A (6) Demonstrate awareness of how an individual's personal appearance affects anticipated responses

IV. A (9) Recognize and respect personal boundaries when communicating with others

IX. C (1) Discuss legal scope of practice for medical assistants

IX. C (2) Explore issue of confidentiality as it applies to the medical assistant

IX. C (3) Describe the implications of HIPAA for medical assistant in various medical settings

IX. P (2) Perform within the scope of practice

IX. P (3) Apply HIPAA rules in regard to privacy/release of information

IX. P (4) Practice within the standard of care for a medical assistant

X. C (5) Identify the effect personal ethics may have on professional performance

X. A (1) Apply ethical behaviors including honesty/integrity in performance of medical assisting practice

ABHES

1. **General Orientation**

   d. Have knowledge of the general responsibilities of the medical assistant

4. **Medical Law and Ethics**

   a. Document accurately

8. **Medical Office Business/Procedures Management**

   aa. Graduates are attentive, listen, and learn
   ff. Graduates interview effectively

11. **Career Development**

   a. Perform the essential requirements for employment such as résumé writing, effective interviewing, dressing professionally, and following up appropriately

b. Demonstrate professionalism by:
   (1) Exhibiting dependability, punctuality and a positive work ethic
   (2) Exhibiting a positive attitude and sense of responsibility
   (3) Maintaining confidentiality at all times
   (4) Being cognizant of ethical boundaries
   (5) Exhibiting initiative
   (6) Adapting to change
   (7) Expressing a responsible attitude
   (8) Being courteous and diplomatic
   (9) Conducting work within the scope of education, training and ability

Prefixes, Suffixes, and Word Roots in Commonly Used Medical Terms

PREFIXES

a-, **an**- without, not

ab- from, away

ad-, **-ad** to, toward

ambi-, **amphi**- both, on both sides, around

ante- before

antero- in front of

anti- against, opposing

auto- self

bi- twice, double

brachy- short

brady- slow

cata- down, lower, under

centi- hundred

chol-, **chole**-, **cholo**- gall

circum- around

co-, **com**-, **con**- together, with

contra- against

cryo- cold

de- down, from

deca- ten

deci- tenth

demi- half

dextro- to the right

di- double, twice

dia- through, apart, between

dipla-, **diplo**- double, twin

dis- apart, away from

dys- difficult, painful, bad, abnormal

e-, **ec**-, **ecto**- away, from, without, outside

em-, **en**- in, into, inside

endo- within, inside

ento- within, inner

epi- on, above

erythro- red

eu- good, true, normal

ex-, **exo**- outside of, beyond, without

extra- outside of, beyond, in addition

fore- before, in front of

gyn-, **gyno**-, **gyne**-, **gyneco**- woman, female

hemi- half

hetero- other, unlike

homeo, homo- same, like

hyper- above, over, increased, excessive

hypo- below, under, decreased

idio- personal, self-produced

im-, **in**-, **ir**- not

in- in, into

infra- beneath

inter- between, among

intra-, **intro**- into, within, during

juxta- near, nearby

leuco-, **leuko**- white

macro- large, long

mal- bad

mega-, **megalo**- large, great

melan-, **melano**- black

mes-, **meso**- middle

meta- beyond

micro- small

mono- single, one

multi- many

neo- new

non-, **not**- no

nuli- none

olig-, **oligo**- few, less than normal

ortho- straight

oxy- sharp, acid

pachy- thick

pan- all, every

par; para- alongside of, with; woman who has given birth

per- through, excessive

peri- around

pluri- more, several

poly- many, much

post- after, behind

pre-, **pro**- before, in front of

presby-, **presbyo**- old age

primi- first

pseudo- false

quadri- four

re- back, again

retro- backward, behind

semi- half

steno- contracted, narrow

stereo- firm, solid, three-dimensional

sub- under

super-, **supra**- above, upon, excess

sym-, **syn**- with, together

tachy- fast

tele- distant, far

tetra- four

trans- across

tri- three

ultra- beyond, excess

uni- one

SUFFIXES

-aesthesia sensation

-al characterized by

-algia pain

-ase enzyme

-asthenia weakness

-cele swelling, tumor

-centesis puncture, tapping

-cidal killing

-cide causing death

-cise cut

-cyst bladder, sac

-cyte, cell, cellular

-derm skin

-dynia- pain

-ectomy cutting out, surgical removal

-emesis vomiting

-emia blood

-esthesia sensation

-gene, -genic, -genetic, -genesis arising from, origin, formation

-gram recorded information

-graph instrument for recording

-graphy the process of recording

-gravida pregnant female

-ia condition

-iasis condition of

-ic, -ical pertaining to

-ism condition, process, theory

-itis inflammation of

-ium membrane

-ize to cause to be, to become, to treat by special method

-kinesis, -kinetic motion

-lepsis, -lepsy seizure, convulsion

-logy science of, study of

-lysis setting free, disintegration, decomposition

-malacia abnormal softening

-mania insanity, abnormal desire

-meter measure

-metry process of measuring

-odynia pain

-oid resembling

-ole small, little

-oma tumor

-opia vision

-opsy to view

-osis disease, condition of

-ostomy to make a mouth, opening

-otomy incision, surgical cutting

-ous having

-pathy disease, suffering

-penia too few, lack, decreased

-pexy surgical fixation

phagia, -phage eating, consuming, swallowing

-phobia fear, abnormal fear

-phylaxis protection

-plasia formation or development

-plastic molded

-plasty operation to reconstruct, surgical repair

-plegia paralysis

-pnea breathing

-rrhage, -rrhagia abnormal or excessive discharge, hemorrhage, flow

-rrhaphy suture of

-rrhea flow, discharge

-sclerosis hardening

-scopy examining

-sepsis poisoning, infection

-spasm cramp or twitching

-stasis stoppage

-stomy opening

-therapy treatment

-thermy heat

-tome cutting instrument

-tomy incision, section

-tripsy surgical crushing

-trophy nutrition, growth

-tropy turning, tendency

-uria urine

WORD ROOTS

adeno- gland, glandular

adipo- fat

aero- air

andr-, andro- man, male

angio- blood vessel

ano- anus

arterio- artery

arthro- joint

bili- bile

bio- life

blasto-, blast- developing stage, bud

bracheo- arm

broncho- bronchial (windpipe)

carcino- cancer

cardio- heart

cephal-, cephalo- head

cerebr-, cerebro- brain

cervico- neck

chondro- cartilage

chromo- color

colo- colon

colp-, colpo- vagina

coro- body

cost-, costo- rib

crani-, cranio- skull

cysto- bladder, bag

cyto- cell, cellular

dacry-, dacryo- tears, lacrimal apparatus

dactyl-, dactylo- finger, toe

dent-, denti-, dento- teeth

derma-, dermat-, dermato- skin

dorsi-, dorso- back

encephalo- brain

entero- intestine

esthesio- sensation

fibro- connective tissue

galact-, galacto- milk

gastr-, gastro- stomach

gingiv- gums

glosso- tongue

gluco-, glyco- sugar, sweet

haemo-, hemato-, hem-, hemo- blood

hepa-, hepar-, hepato- liver

herni- rupture

histo- tissue

hydra-, hydro- water

hyster-, hystero- uterus

ictero- jaundice

ileo- ileum

karyo- nucleus, nut

kera-, kerato- horn, hardness, cornea

lact- milk

laparo- abdomen

latero- side

linguo- tongue

lipo- fat

lith-, -lith stone

mast-, masto- breast

med-, medi- middle

meno- month

metro-, metra- uterus

my-, myo- muscle

myel-, myelo- marrow

narco- sleep

nas-, naso- nose

necro- dead

nephr-, nephro- kidney

neu-, neuro- nerve

niter-, nitro- nitrogen

nucleo- nucleus

oculo- eye

odont- tooth

omphalo- navel, umbilicus

onco- tumor

oo- ovum, egg

oophor- ovary

ophthalmo- eye

orchid- testicle

os- mouth, opening

oste-, osteo- bone

oto- ear

pedo- child

palpebro- eyelid

path-, patho- disease, suffering

pepso- digestion

phag-, phago- eating, consuming, swallowing

pharyng- throat, pharynx

phlebo- vein

pleuro- side, rib

pneumo- air, lungs

pod foot

procto- rectum

psych- the mind

pulmon-, pulmono- lung

pyelo- pelvis (renal)

pyo- pus

pyro- fever, heat

reni-, reno- kidney

rhino- nose

sacchar- sugar

sacro- sacrum

salpingo- tube, fallopian tube

sarco- flesh

sclero- hard, sclera

septi-, septico- poison, infection

stomato- mouth

teno-, tenoto- tendon

thermo- heat

thoraco- chest

thrombo- blood clot

thyro- thyroid gland

tricho- hair

urino-, uro- urine, urinary organs

utero- uterus, uterine

vaso- vessel

ventri-, ventro- abdomen

vesico- blister

xantho- yellow

Appendix II

Abbreviations and Symbols Commonly Used in Medical Notations

ABBREVIATIONS

a   before

aā, ĀĀ   of each

a.c.   before meals

ADD   attention deficit disorder

ADL   activities of daily living

ad lib   as desired

ADT   admission, discharge, transfer

AIDS   acquired immunodeficiency syndrome

a.m.a.   against medical advice

AMA   American Medical Association

amp.   ampule

amt   amount

aq., AQ   water; aqueous

ausc.   auscultation

ax   axis

Bib, bib   drink

b.i.d., bid, BID   twice a day

BM   bowel movement

BP, B/P   blood pressure

BPC   blood pressure check

BPH   benign prostatic hypertrophy

BSA   body surface area

c̄   with

Ca   calcium; cancer

cap, caps   capsules

CBC   complete blood (cell) count

C.C., CC   chief complaint

CDC   Centers for Disease Control and Prevention

CHF   congestive heart failure

chr   chronic

CNS   central nervous system

Comp, comp   compound

COPD   chronic obstructive pulmonary disease

CP   chest pain

CPE   complete physical examination

CPR   cardiopulmonary resuscitation

CSF   cerebrospinal fluid

CT   computed tomography

CV   cardiovascular

D&C   dilation and curettage

DEA   Drug Enforcement Administration

Dil, dil   dilute

DM   diabetes mellitus

DOB   date of birth

DTaP   diphtheria-tetanus-acellular pertussis

Dr.   doctor

DTs   delirium tremens

D/W   dextrose in water

Dx, dx   diagnosis

ECG, EKG   electrocardiogram

ED   emergency department

EEG   electroencephalogram

EENT   eyes, ears, nose, and throat

EP   established patient

ER   emergency room

ESR   erythrocyte sedimentation rate

FBS   fasting blood sugar

FDA   Food and Drug Administration

FH   family history

Fl, fl, fld   fluid

F/u   follow-up

Fx   fracture

GBS   gallbladder series

GI   gastrointestinal

Gm, gm   gram

gr   grain

gt, gtt   drop, drops

GTT   glucose tolerance test

GU   genitourinary

GYN   gynecology

HA   headache

HB, Hgb   hemoglobin

HEENT   head, ears, eyes, nose, throat

HIV   human immunodeficiency virus

HO   history of

h.s., hs, HS   hour of sleep/at bedtime

Hx   history

ICU   intensive care unit

I&D   incision and drainage

I&O   intake and output

IM   intramuscular

inf.   infusion; inferior

inj   injection

IT   inhalation therapy

IUD   intrauterine device

IV   intravenous

KUB   kidneys, ureters, bladder

L1, L2, etc.   lumbar vertebrae

lab   laboratory

lb   pound

liq   liquid

LLE   left lower extremity (left leg)

LLL   left lower lobe

LLQ   left lower quadrant

LMP   last menstrual period

LUE   left upper extremity (left arm)

LUQ   left upper quadrant

MI   myocardial infarction

mL   milliliter

MM   mucous membrane

MRI   magnetic resonance imaging

MS   multiple sclerosis

NB   newborn

NED   no evidence of disease

no. number

noc, noct night

npo, NPO nothing by mouth

NPT new patient

NS normal saline

NSAID nonsteroidal anti-inflammatory drug

NTP normal temperature and pressure

N&V nausea and vomiting

NYD not yet diagnosed

OB obstetrics

OC oral contraceptive

OD overdose

oint ointment

OOB out of bed

OPD outpatient department

OPS outpatient services

OR operating room

OTC over-the-counter

p- para-

$\bar{p}$ after

P&P Pap smear (Papanicolaou smear) and pelvic examination

PA posteroanterior

Pap Pap smear

Path pathology

p.c., pc after meals

PE physical examination

per by, with

PH past history

PID pelvic inflammatory disease

po by mouth

p/o postoperative

POMR problem-oriented medical record

PMFSH past medical, family, social history

PMS premenstrual syndrome

p.r.n., prn, PRN whenever necessary

Pt patient

PT physical therapy

PTA prior to admission

PVC premature ventricular contraction

pulv powder

q. every

q2, q2h every 2 hours

q.a.m., qam every morning

q.h., qh every hour

qhs every night, at bedtime

q.i.d., QID four times a day

qns, QNS quantity not sufficient

qs, QS quantity sufficient

RA rheumatoid arthritis; right atrium

RBC red blood cells; red blood (cell) count

RDA recommended dietary allowance, recommended daily allowance

REM rapid eye movement

RF rheumatoid factor

RLE right lower extremity (right leg)

RLL right lower lobe

RLQ right lower quadrant

R/O rule out

ROM range of motion

ROS/SR review of systems/systems review

RUE right upper extremity (right arm)

RUQ right upper quadrant

RV right ventricle

Rx prescription, take

$\bar{s}$ without

SAD seasonal affective disorder

SIDS sudden infant death syndrome

Sig directions

sig sigmoidoscopy

SOAP subjective, objective, assessment, plan

SOB shortness of breath

sol solution

S/R suture removal

ss, $\overline{ss}$ one-half (Latin *semis*)

Staph staphylococcus

stat, STAT immediately

STD sexually transmitted disease

Strep streptococcus

subling, SL sublingual

subq, SubQ subcutaneously

surg surgery

S/W saline in water

SX symptoms

T1, T2, etc. thoracic vertebrae

T & A tonsillectomy and adenoidectomy

tab tablet

TB tuberculosis

tbs., tbsp tablespoon

TIA transient ischemic attack

t.i.d., tid, TID three times a day

tinc, tinct, tr tincture

TMJ temporomandibular joint

top topically

TPR temperature, pulse, and respiration

TSH thyroid stimulating hormone

tsp teaspoon

Tx treatment

UA urinalysis

UCHD usual childhood diseases

UGI upper gastrointestinal

ung, ungt ointment

URI upper respiratory infection

US ultrasound

UTI urinary tract infection

VA visual acuity

VD venereal disease

Vf visual field

VS vital signs

WBC white blood cells; white blood (cell) count

WNL within normal limits

wt weight

y/o year old

SYMBOLS

Weights and Measures

pounds

° degrees

′ foot; minute

″ inch; second

μm micrometer

μ micron (former term for micrometer)

mμ millimicron; nanometer

mEq milliequivalent

mL milliliter

dL deciliter

mg% milligrams percent; milligrams per 100 mL

Mathematical Functions and Terms

number

+ plus; positive; acid reaction

− minus; negative; alkaline reaction

± plus or minus; either positive or negative; indefinite

× multiply; magnification; crossed with, hybrid

÷ , / divided by

= equal to

≈ approximately equal to

> greater than; from which is derived

< less than; derived from

≮ not less than

≯ not greater than

≤ equal to or less than

≥ equal to or greater than

≠ not equal to

√ square root

³√ cube root

∞ infinity

: ratio; "is to"

∴ therefore

% percent

π pi (3.14159)—the ratio of circumference of a circle to its diameter

Chemical Notations

Δ change; heat

⇌ reversible reaction

↑ increase

↓ decrease

Warnings

Ⓒ Schedule I controlled substance

Ⓒ Schedule II controlled substance

Ⓒ Schedule III controlled substance

Ⓒ Schedule IV controlled substance

Ⓒ Schedule V controlled substance

☠ poison

☢ radiation

☣ biohazard

Others

℞ prescription; take

□, ♂ male

○, ♀ female

† one

†† two

††† three

ISMP's List of Error-Prone Abbreviations, Symbols, and Dose Designations

The abbreviations, symbols, and dose designations found in this table have been reported to the Institute for Safe Medication Practices (ISMP) through the ISMP Medication Errors Reporting Program (MERP) as being frequently misinterpreted and involved in harmful medication errors. They should NEVER be used when communicating medical information. This includes internal communications, telephone/verbal prescriptions, computer-generated labels, labels for drug storage bins, medication administration records, as well as pharmacy and prescriber computer order entry screens. The Joint Commission has established a National Patient Safety Goal that specifies that certain abbreviations must appear on an accredited organization's "do-not-use" list; we have highlighted these items with a double asterisk (**). However, we hope that you will consider others beyond the minimum Joint Commission requirements. By using and promoting safe practices and by educating one another about hazards, we can better protect our patients.

ABBREVIATIONS	INTENDED MEANING	MISINTERPRETATION	CORRECTION
μg	Microgram	Mistaken as "mg"	Use "mcg"
AD, AS, AU	Right ear, left ear, each ear	Mistaken as OD, OS, OU (right eye, left eye, each eye)	Use "right ear," "left ear," or "each ear"
OD, OS, OU	Right eye, left eye, each eye	Mistaken as AD, AS, AU (right ear, left ear, each ear)	Use "right eye," "left eye," or "each eye"
BT	Bedtime	Mistaken as "BID" (twice daily)	Use "bedtime"
cc	Cubic centimeters	Mistaken as "u" (units)	Use "mL"
D/C	Discharge or discontinue	Premature discontinuation of medications if D/C (intended to mean "discharge") has been misinterpreted as "discontinued" when followed by a list of discharge medications	Use "discharge" and "discontinue"
IJ	Injection	Mistaken as "IV" or "intrajugular"	Use "injection"
IN	Intranasal	Mistaken as "IM" or "IV"	Use "intranasal" or "NAS"
HS hs	Half-strength At bedtime, hours of sleep	Mistaken as bedtime Mistaken as half-strength	Use "half-strength" or "bedtime"
IU**	International unit	Mistaken as IV (intravenous) or 10 (ten)	Use "units"
o.d. or OD	Once daily	Mistaken as "right eye" (OD-oculus dexter), leading to oral liquid medications administered in the eye	Use "daily"

(Continued)

ABBREVIATIONS	INTENDED MEANING	MISINTERPRETATION	CORRECTION
OJ	Orange juice	Mistaken as OD or OS (right or left eye); drugs meant to be diluted in orange juice may be given in the eye	Use "orange juice"
Per os	By mouth, orally	The "os" can be mistaken as "left eye" (OS-oculus sinister)	Use "PO," "by mouth," or "orally"
q.d. or QD**	Every day	Mistaken as q.i.d., especially if the period after the "q" or the tail of the "q" is misunderstood as an "i"	Use "daily"
qhs	Nightly at bedtime	Mistaken as "qhr" or every hour	Use "nightly"
qn	Nightly or at bedtime	Mistaken as "qh" (every hour)	Use "nightly" or "at bedtime"
q.o.d. or QOD**	Every other day	Mistaken as "q.d." (daily) or "q.i.d." (four times daily) if the "o" is poorly written	Use "every other day"
q1d	Daily	Mistaken as q.i.d. (four times daily)	Use "daily"
q6PM, etc.	Every evening at 6 PM	Mistaken as every 6 hours	Use "daily at 6 PM" or "6 PM daily"
SC, SQ, sub q	Subcutaneous	SC mistaken as SL (sublingual); SQ mistaken as "5 every;" the "q" in "sub q" has been mistaken as "every" (e.g., a heparin dose ordered "sub q 2 hours before surgery" misunderstood as every 2 hours before surgery)	Use "subcut" or "subcutaneously"
ss	Sliding scale (insulin) or ½ (apothecary)	Mistaken as "55"	Spell out "sliding scale;" use "one-half" or "½"
SSRI SSI	Sliding scale regular insulin Sliding scale insulin	Mistaken as selective-serotonin reuptake inhibitor Mistaken as Strong Solution of Iodine (Lugol's)	Spell out "sliding scale (insulin)"
i/d	One daily	Mistaken as "tid"	Use "1 daily"
TIW or tiw (also BIW or biw)	TIW: 3 times a week BIW: 2 times a week	TIW mistaken as "3 times a day" or "twice in a week" BIW mistaken ad "2 times a day"	Use "3 times weekly" Use "2 times weekly"
U or u**	Unit	Mistaken as the number 0 or 4, causing a 10-fold overdose or greater (e.g., 4U seen as "40" or 4u seen as "44"); mistaken as "cc" so dose given in volume instead of units (e.g., 4u seen as 4cc)	Use "unit"
UD	As directed ("ut dictum")	Mistaken as unit dose (e.g., diltiazem 125 mg IV infusion "UD" misinterpreted as meaning to give the entire infusion as a unit [bolus] dose)	Use "as directed"

DOSE DESIGNATIONS AND OTHER INFORMATION	INTENDED MEANING	MISINTERPRETATION	CORRECTION
Trailing zero after decimal point (e.g., 1.0 mg)**	1mg	Mistaken as 10 mg if the decimal point is not seen	Do not use trailing zeros for doses expressed in whole numbers
No leading zero before a decimal point (e.g., .5 mg)**	0.5 mg	Mistaken as 5 mg if the decimal point is not seen	Use zero before a decimal point when the dose is less than a whole unit
Drug name and dose run together (especially problematic for drug names that end in "l" such as Inderal 40 mg; Tegretol 300 mg)	Inderal 40 mg Tegretol 300 mg	Mistaken as Inderal 140 mg Mistaken as Tegretol 1300 mg	Place adequate space between the drug name, dose, and unit of measure
Numerical dose and unit of measure run together (e.g., 10 mg, 100 mL)	10 mg 100 mL	The "m" is sometimes mistaken as a zero or two zeros, risking a 10- to 100-fold overdose	Place adequate space between the dose and unit of measure
Abbreviations such as mg. or mL. with a period following the abbreviation	mg mL	The period is unnecessary and could be mistaken as the number 1 if written poorly	Use mg, mL, etc. without a terminal period
Large doses without properly placed commas (e.g., 100000 units; 1000000 units)	100,000 units 1,000,000 units	100000 has been mistaken as 10,000 or 1,000,000; 1000000 has been mistaken as 100,000	Use commas for dosing units at or above 1,000, or use words such as 100 "thousand" or 1 "million" to improve readability

DRUG NAME ABBREVIATIONS	INTENDED MEANING	MISINTERPRETATION	CORRECTION
ARA A	vidarabine	Mistaken as cytarabine (ARA C)	Use complete drug name
AZT	zidovudine (Retrovir)	Mistaken as azathioprine or aztreonam	Use complete drug name
CPZ	Compazine (prochlorperazine)	Mistaken as chlorpromazine	Use complete drug name
DPT	Demerol-Phenergan-Thorazine	Mistaken as diphtheria-pertussis-tetanus (vaccine)	Use complete drug name
DTO	Diluted tincture of opium, or deodorized tincture of opium (Paregoric)	Mistaken as tincture of opium	Use complete drug name
HCl	hydrochloric acid or hydrochloride	Mistaken as potassium chloride (The "H" is misinterpreted as "K")	Use complete drug name unless expressed as a salt of a drug
HCT	hydrocortisone	Mistaken as hydrochlorothiazide	Use complete drug name
HCTZ	hydrochlorothiazide	Mistaken as hydrocortisone (seen as HCT250 mg)	Use complete drug name
MgSO4**	magnesium sulfate	Mistaken as morphine sulfate	Use complete drug name
MS, MSO4**	morphine sulfate	Mistaken as magnesium sulfate	Use complete drug name
MTX	methotrexate	Mistaken as mitoxantrone	Use complete drug name

(Continued)

DRUG NAME ABBREVIATIONS	INTENDED MEANING	MISINTERPRETATION	CORRECTION
PCA	procainamide	Mistaken as patient controlled analgesia	Use complete drug name
PTU	propylthiouracil	Mistaken as mercaptopurine	Use complete drug name
T3	Tylenol with codeine No. 3	Mistaken as liothyronine	Use complete drug name
TAC	triamcinolone	Mistaken as tetracaine, Adrenalin, cocaine	Use complete drug name
TNK	TNKase	Mistaken as "TPA"	Use complete drug name
ZnSO4	zinc sulfate	Mistaken as morphine sulfate	Use complete drug name

STEMMED DRUG NAMES	INTENDED MEANING	MISINTERPRETATION	CORRECTION
"Nitro" drip	nitroglycerin infusion	Mistaken as sodium nitroprusside infusion	Use complete drug name
"Norflox"	norfloxacin	Mistaken as Norflex	Use complete drug name
"IV Vanc"	intravenous vancomycin	Mistaken as Invanz	Use complete drug name

SYMBOLS	INTENDED MEANING	MISINTERPRETATION	CORRECTION
ℨ	Dram	Symbol for dram mistaken as "3"	Use the metric system
♏	Minim	Symbol for minim mistaken as "mL"	
x3d	For three days	Mistaken as "3 doses"	Use "for three days"
> and <	Greater than and less than	Mistaken as opposite of intended; mistakenly use incorrect symbol; "< 10" mistaken as "40"	Use "greater than" or "less than"
/ (slash mark)	Separates two doses or indicates "per"	Mistaken as the number 1 (e.g., "25 units/10 units" misread as "25 units and 110" units)	Use "per" rather than a slash mark to separate doses
@	At	Mistaken as "2"	Use "at"
&	And	Mistaken as "2"	Use "and"
+	Plus or and	Mistaken as "4"	Use "and"
°	Hour	Mistaken as a zero (e.g., q2° seen as q 20)	Use "hr," "h," or "hour"
Ø	zero, null sign	Mistaken as the numerals 4, 6, or 9	Use the number "0" or the word "zero"

**These abbreviations are included on The Joint Commission's "minimum list" of dangerous abbreviations, acronyms, and symbols that must be included on an organization's "Do Not Use" list, effective January 1, 2004. Visit www.jcaho.org for more information about this Joint Commission requirement.

Permission is granted to reproduce material for internal newsletters or communications with proper attribution. Other reproduction is prohibited without written permission. Unless noted, reports were received through the ISMP Medication Errors Reporting Program (MERP). Report actual and potential medication errors to the MERP via the web at www.ismp.org or by calling **1-800-FAIL-SAF(E).**

Glossary

ABA number Appears as a fraction on the upper edge of all printed checks; identifies the geographic area and specific bank on which the check is drawn.

abandonment Charge when a health-care professional stops patient care without providing an equally qualified substitute.

abuse A practice or behavior that is not indicative of, or in line with, sound medical or fiscal practices.

accounts payable Money owed by a business; the practice's expenses.

accounts receivable Income or money owed to a business; the practice's income.

accreditation The documentation of official authorization or approval of a program.

active file The file for an active patient or for one who has been seen by a member of the practice within two years.

active listening Part of two-way communication, such as offering feedback or asking questions.

acupuncturist A practitioner of acupuncture; an acupuncturist uses hollow needles inserted into the patient's skin to treat pain, discomfort, or systemic imbalances.

add-on code ACPT code that indicates that this code is usually done in addition to a primary procedure (code) and is only reported in addition to the primary code.

advance scheduling Booking an appointment several weeks or even months in advance.

affiliation agreement A contract between the school and externship site stating the responsibilities of both parties.

age analysis The process of clarifying and reviewing past due accounts by age from the first date of billing.

agenda The list of topics discussed or presented at a meeting in order of presentation.

agent One who acts on the behalf of another, such as an employee acting on behalf of the employer.

aggressive Imposing one's position on others or trying to manipulate them.

alcohol hand disinfectant (AHD) Gels, foams, and liquid rubs that are used when running water is not readily available.

allergist A specialist who diagnoses and treats physical reactions to substances including mold, dust, fur, pollen, foods, drugs, and chemicals.

allowed charge The amount that is the most the payer will pay any provider for each procedure or service. The payer's payment is based on this allowed charge.

alphabetical order A filing system in which the files are arranged in alphabetical order, with the patient's last name first, followed by the first name and middle initial.

Alphabetic Index One of two ways diagnoses are listed in the ICD-9-CM. They appear in alphabetic order with their corresponding diagnosis code(s).

American Association of Medical Assistants (AAMA) The professional organization that certifies medical assistants and works to maintain professional standards in the medical assisting profession.

American Board of Medical Specialties (ABMS) An organization of different medical specialty boards. Its primary purpose is to maintain and improve the quality of medical care and to certify doctors in various specialties. This organization helps the member boards develop professional and educational standards for physician specialists.

American Medical Technologists (AMT) The registering organization for medical assistants that provides online continuing education, certification information, and member news.

Americans with Disabilities Act (ADA) Passed in 1990, this federal act is sometimes referred to as the civil rights act for the disabled since it forbids discrimination based on physical or mental handicaps.

anaphylaxis A severe allergic reaction with symptoms that include respiratory distress, difficulty in swallowing, pallor, and a drastic drop in blood pressure that can lead to circulatory collapse.

anesthetist A specialist who uses medications to cause patients to lose sensation or feeling during surgery.

annotate Underlining, highlighting or commenting in documents or letters to draw attention to certain portions of the document.

antivirus software Provides protection for your computer by scanning your system for viruses automatically and manually. If it finds a virus, it either destroys it automatically or alerts the user to respond by "cleaning" the file, thus destroying it.

arbitration The process in which the opposing sides choose a person or persons outside the court system, often with special knowledge in the field, to hear and decide the dispute.

asepsis Utilizing techniques to prevent the spread of, reduce, or eliminate pathogens.

assault The open threat of bodily harm to another, or acting in such a way as to put another in the "reasonable apprehension of bodily harm."

assertive Being firm and standing up for oneself while showing respect for others.

assignment of benefits Written consent from the patient allowing the insurance company to directly pay the practitioner.

attitude A disposition to act in a certain way.

audit To examine and review a group of patients' records for completeness and coding correctness.

authorization Document to be signed by patient, after being fully informed of all consequences, giving permission for treatment or release of medical information.

authorized prescriber (AP) A health-care professional who is legally allowed to order prescription medications; includes physicians,

nurse practitioners, and physician assistants.

automated external defibrillator (AED) A computerized defibrillator programmed to recognize lethal heart rhythms and deliver an electrical shock to restore a normal rhythm.

autopsy The examination of a cadaver to determine or confirm the cause of death.

balance billing Billing the patient for the difference between a higher usual fee and the lower allowed charge.

battery Any action that causes bodily harm to another person.

benefits Payment for medical services.

bioethics Ethical issues that arise related to medical advances.

biopsy The removal and examination of a sample of tissue from a living body for diagnostic purposes.

bioterrorism The intentional release of a biologic agent with the intent to harm individuals.

birthday rule A rule that states that the insurance policy of a policy-holder whose birthday comes first in the year is the primary payer for all dependents.

body The main portion of a letter.

body language Nonverbal communication, including facial expressions, eye contact, posture, touch, and attention to personal space.

body mechanics Proper body movement to prevent injury and enhance physical capabilities.

bookkeeping The systematic recording of business transactions.

boundaries A physical or psychological space that indicates the limit of appropriate versus inappropriate behavior.

breach of contract Charge if either party in a contract fails to comply with the terms of a legally valid contract.

budget The predicted expenses and revenues to operate over a given period of time.

bundled code Any CPT code that includes more than one procedure in its description.

burnout The end result of prolonged periods of stress without relief; energy-depleting condition that can affect one's health and career.

capitation A payment structure in which a health maintenance organization prepays an annual set fee per patient to a physician.

cardiologist A specialist who diagnoses and treats diseases of the heart and blood vessels (cardiovascular diseases).

cardiopulmonary resuscitation (CPR) A series of ventilations and compressions used on a person who has stopped breathing or whose heart has stopped beating.

carrier A person who is reservoir host and does not exhibit symptoms yet spreads the disease to others.

cash flow statement A statement that shows the cash on hand at the beginning of a period, the income and disbursements made during that period, and the new amount of cash on hand at the end of the period.

cashier's check A check issued from the bank's account and signed by a bank representative. Funds are withdrawn from the requester's account at the time the check is written.

categories The 3-digit codes subdivisions of ICD-10.

CD-ROM A compact disc that contains software programs; an abbreviation for "compact disc—read-only memory."

Centers for Disease Control and Prevention (CDC) Agency that studies the transmission and control of diseases. It serves as the foundation for determining effective interventions for the public's health in combating illnesses and promoting preventive medicine.

Centers for Medicare and Medicaid Services (CMS) A congressional agency designed to handle Medicare and Medicaid insurance claims. It was formerly known as the Health Care Financing Administration.

central processing unit (CPU) The central processing unit or microprocessor, is the primary computer chip responsible for interpreting and executing programs.

certification Confirmation by an organization that an individual is qualified to perform a job to professional standards.

certified check A personal check written and signed by the payer and stamped "CERTIFIED" by the

bank, guaranteeing funds will be available.

Certified Medical Assistant (CMA) A medical assistant whose knowledge about the skills of medical assistants, as summarized by the 2008 AAMA Occupational Analysis, has been certified by the Certifying Board of the American Association of Medical Assistants.

chain of command Began in the military to demonstrate how each rank is accountable to those directly superior and how the authority passes from one link in the chain to the next, or from the top to the bottom.

CHAMPVA (Civilian Health and Medical Program for Veterans Administration) A type of insurance that covers the expenses of dependents of veterans with total, permanent, service-connected disabilities. It also covers the surviving dependents of veterans who die in the line of duty or as a result of service-connected disabilities.

chapters Divisions of ICD-10 named either for a body system or specific disease type.

charge A debit to an account.

charge slip The original record of services performed for a patient and the charges for those services.

check A bank draft or order for payment.

CHEDDAR Chief complaint, History, Examination, Details of problems and complaints, Drugs and dosages, Assessment, and Return.

chief complaint (CC) The patient's primary reason for seeking care.

chiropractor A physician who uses a system of therapy, including manipulation of the spine, to treat illness or pain. This treatment is done without drugs or surgery.

chronological résumé The type of résumé used by individuals who have job experience. Jobs are listed according to date, with the most recent being listed first.

civil law Involves crimes against the person. Lawsuits come under the heading of civil law.

clarity To be clear in meaning.

class action lawsuit A lawsuit in which one or more people sue a company or other legal entity that allegedly wronged all of them in the same way.

clearinghouse A group that takes nonstandard medical billing software formats and translates them into the standard EDI format.

Clinical Laboratory Improvement Amendments of 1988 (CLIA '88) A law enacted by Congress in 1988 that placed all laboratory facilities that conduct tests for diagnosing, preventing, or treating human disease or for assessing human health under federal regulations administered by the Health Care Financing Administration (HCFA) and the Centers for Disease Control and Prevention (CDC).

closed file A file for a patient who has died, moved away, or for some other reason is no longer treated by the medical practice.

closed posture A position that conveys the feeling of not being totally receptive to what is being said; arms are often rigid or folded across the chest.

cluster scheduling Groups similar appointments together on a specific day or for a specific block of time during the day or week.

codes In the Tabular List, subsets of subcategories consisting of up to 7 characters. Those that contain a 7th character must be reported at the 7th character level to be considered a valid code.

coinsurance A fixed percentage of covered charges paid by the insured person after a deductible has been met.

communication Giving and receiving accurate information.

compactible files Files kept on rolling shelves that slide along permanent tracks in the floor and are stored close together or stacked when not in use.

compensation time Time-off given for working extra without pay.

compliance plan A process of finding, correcting, and preventing illegal medical office practices.

complimentary closing The formal close of the letter such as *Sincerely* or *Very truly yours*.

comprehension Learning, retaining, and processing information.

concise Direct and to the point.

concurrent care Similar care being provided by more than one physician.

conflict An opposition of opinions or ideas.

consent The patient has given either expressed or implied permission for texts, physical exam, treatment, etc.

constructive criticism A type of critique that is aimed at giving an individual feedback about his or her performance in order to improve that performance.

consultation Care provided at the request of other health-care providers.

consumer education The process by which the average person learns to make informed decisions about goods and services, including health care.

continuing education Education and training that occurs after you have entered a profession that promotes professional development and meets requirements of your certification or registration.

continuing education units (CEU) Credits given by a professional organization for participating in approved educational offerings to maintain membership.

contract A voluntary agreement between two parties in which specific promises are made for a consideration.

controlled substance A drug or drug product that is categorized as potentially dangerous and addictive and is strictly regulated by federal laws.

conventions A list of abbreviations, punctuation, symbols, typefaces, and instructional notes appearing in the beginning of ICD-9. The items provide guidelines for using the code set.

cooperation Working with others in the best interest of completing the job.

coordination Integration of activities.

coordination of benefits A legal principle that limits payments by insurance companies to 100% of the covered expenses.

copayment A set amount of money determined by the patient's insurance company that must be paid by the patient at every visit.

corporation A body formed and authorized by state law to act as a single entity.

counseling Codes used when discussing with the patient and family questions or concerns regarding one or more of the following: diagnostic results and recommendations; prognosis; risks and benefits of options; instructions for treatment and/or follow-up; importance of compliance; risk factor reduction; and patient/family education.

counter check Special bank check that allows the depositor to withdraw funds from his account only.

courtesy title A person's formal title: Mr., Mrs., Dr., etc.

cover sheet A form sent with faxed information providing details about the transmission and disclaimer regarding faxes received in error.

covered entity Any organization that transmits health information in an electronic form that is related in any way with a HIPAA-covered entity.

crash cart A rolling cart of emergency supplies and equipment.

credentialing The process of establishing qualifications for organizations or licensed professionals.

credit An extension of time to pay for services, which are provided on trust.

credit balance A negative balance on an account that occurs when more money than is owed is paid to the practice.

credit bureau A company that provides information about the credit worthiness of a person seeking credit.

crime Any offense committed or omitted in violation of a public law.

criminal law Law involving crimes against the state.

critical care Care provided to unstable, critically ill patients. Constant bedside attention is needed in order to code critical care, so the physician's documentation must be explicit regarding the time spent with the patient.

critical thinking Purposeful judgment resulting from analysis and evaluation.

cross-reference The notation within the ICD-9 using the directions *See* or *See also* after the main term in the index. Notes that another term may be more appropriate when coding the referenced diagnosis.

cross-referenced Filed in two or more places, with each place noted in each file.

cross-trained The acquisition of training in a variety of tasks and skills.

cultural diversity The variety of human social structures, belief systems, and strategies for adapting to situations in different parts of the world.

Current Procedural Terminology (CPT) A reference with the most commonly used system of procedure codes; the HIPAA- required code set for physician procedures.

cursor A blinking line or cube on a computer screen that shows where the next character that is keyed will appear.

cycle billing A system that sends statements to groups of patients every few days, spreading the work of billing all patients over the period of a month, while billing each patient only once.

cycle of infection Also known as the chain of infection; the manner in which pathogens are spread.

daily log The sheet that records and calculates the total charges and payments received by the patient for the day.

damages Money paid as compensation for violating legal rights.

database A collection of records created and stored on a computer.

dateline The date the letter was written.

deductible A fixed dollar amount that must be paid (yearly) by the insured before additional expenses are covered by the insurer.

defamation Damaging a person's reputation by making public statements that are both false and malicious.

dependent Persons who depend on the employee for financial support.

dermatologist A specialist who diagnoses and treats diseases of the skin, hair, and nails.

diagnosis (Dx) The condition for which the patient is seeking care.

diagnosis code The alphanumeric designation used to communicate the diagnosis to the third-party payer on the health-care claim form.

digital subscriber line(DSL) A type of modem that operates over telephone lines by using a different

frequency than a telephone, allowing a computer to access the Internet at the same time that a telephone is being used.

disability insurance Insurance that provides a monthly, prearranged payment to an individual who cannot work as a result of an injury, illness, or disability.

disclaimer A statement of denial of legal liability or that refutes the authenticity of a claim.

disclosure Information is disclosed when it is transmitted between or among organizations.

disclosure statement A written description of agreed terms of payment; also called a federal Truth in Lending statement.

disk cleanup A computer maintenance utility designed to free up disk space on a computer user's hard drive.

disk defragmentation A computer program designed to increase access speed by rearranging files stored on a disk to occupy contiguous storage locations, a technique commonly known as defragmenting.

doctor of osteopathy A doctor who focuses special attention on the musculoskeletal system and uses hands and eyes to identify and adjust structural problems, supporting the body's natural tendency toward health and self-healing.

doctrine of informed consent The legal basis for informed consent (or denial of treatment) and is usually outlined in a state's medical practice acts.

doctrine of professional discretion Under HIPAA, a patient's right to see or copy his or her medical record is protected. The doctrine of professional discretion protects the physician if he or she feels it will be harmful for a patient to access the medical record.

documentation Recording information in the medical record.

dot matrix printer An impact printer that creates characters by placing a series of tiny dots next to one another.

double-booking system Two or more patients are scheduled for the same appointment slot.

downcoding Term used when the insurance carrier bases reimburse-

ment on a code level lower than the one submitted by the provider.

durable item Refers to a piece of equipment that is used indefinitely.

durable power of attorney Part of the Advance Directive, in which the patient names someone who will make decisions regarding medical care on their behalf if the patient is unable to do so.

E code A type of ICD-9 code that identifies external causes of injuries and illnesses such as accidents and poisonings.

editing Checking a document for factual accuracy, logical flow, conciseness, clarity, and tone.

elective procedure A medical procedure that is not required to sustain life but is requested for payment to the third-party payer by the patient or physician. Some elective procedures are paid for by the third-party payers, whereas others are not.

electronic data interchange (EDI) Transmitting electronic medical insurance claims from providers to payers using the necessary information systems.

electronic health record (EHR) A computerized system of the patient's medical record allowing tracking and transmission of documentation of histories, care, orders, results, reports, and administrative functions. Also, medical records kept in an electronic format, which <u>are</u> available to providers outside of the medical office that has ownership.

electronic mail (e-mail) Any transmissions that are physically moved from one location to another through the use of magnetic tape, disk, compact disk media, or any other form of digital or electronic technology.

electronic media Any information stored on a computer storage device.

electronic medical records (EMR) Medical records kept in an electronic format that <u>are generally not</u> available to providers outside of the medical office that has ownership.

electronic transaction record The codes and formats used for the exchange of medical data.

E/M codes The codes used to describe the wide range of time, effort, and skill and locations used by physicians for different patients to diagnose conditions and plan treatments.

emergency medical services (EMS) A network of qualified emergency services personnel who use community resources and equipment to provide emergency care to victims of injury or sudden illness.

empathy Feeling and understanding another's experience without having the experience yourself.

employee handbook A synopsis of an organizations policies, procedures and expectations for all employees.

employment grade Category of employment based on specific criteria such as job requirements and duties and associated salary range.

enclosure Letter notation signaling the receiver that documents are included with the letter.

endocrinologist A specialist who diagnoses and treats disorders of the endocrine system, which regulates many body functions by circulating hormones that are secreted by glands throughout the body.

endorse To sign or stamp the back of a check with the proper identification of the person or organization to whom the check is made out, to prevent the check from being cashed if it is stolen or lost.

enunciation Clear and distinct speech.

epidemiology The study of the transmission and control of diseases.

e-prescribing Entering prescription medication orders electronically and transmitting them directly to a pharmacy to be filled.

ergonomics The science of adjusting the work environment to the human body.

established patient A patient who has been seen by the physician within the last three years; an important determination when using E/M Codes.

ethics A standard of behavior and a concept of right and wrong beyond what the legal consideration is in any given situation.

etiology Cause of disease or condition.

etiquette Good manners.

exclusion An expense that is not covered by a particular insurance policy, such as an eye exam or dental care.

expendable item An object that is used and then must be replaced.

explanation of benefits (EOB) Information that explains the medical claim in detail including the amount billed, amount allowed, amount of subscriber liability, amount paid, and notations of any noncovered services with explanations. Also called *remittance advice (RA)*.

exposure control plan Describes personal protective equipment and other safety engineering devices and processes; it provides instructions for handling an exposure.

expressed contract A contract clearly stated in written or spoken words.

externship A period of practical work experience performed by a medical assisting student in a physician's office, hospital, or other health-care facility.

externship coordinator (practicum coordinator) The representative of the school who generally ensures that affiliation agreements are in place and the responsibilities of all parties are met which includes scheduling, monitoring, problem solving, and facilitating students.

factual teaching Method of teaching that provides the patient with details of the information that is being taught.

family practitioner A physician who does not specialize in a branch of medicine but treats all types and ages of patients; also called a general practitioner.

Federal Insurance Contributions Act (FICA) Social Security and Medicare taxes are withheld from employee paycheck and combined with employer matching contributions.

Federal Unemployment Tax Act (FUTA) Requires employers to pay a percentage of each employee's income, up to a certain dollar amount, to cover unemployment compensation.

fee-for-service Formerly a major type of health plan, it repays policyholders for the costs of health care due to illness and injuries.

fee schedule A list of common services and procedures (performed by a physician) and the charges of each.

feedback Verbal and nonverbal evidence that a message was received and understood.

felony A crime such as abuse, fraud, and practicing medicine without a license. These crimes are punishable by imprisonment in a state or federal prison for more than 1 year or in some cases, death.

file guide A heavy cardboard or plastic insert used to identify a group of file folders in a file drawer or shelf.

firewall A system that protects a computer network from unauthorized access by users on its own network or another network such as the Internet.

first aid The immediate care given to someone who is injured or suddenly becomes ill, before complete medical care can be obtained.

fomites Inanimate objects that transmit diseases.

Food and Drug Administration (FDA) An organization of the government that sets standards for all new drugs to be approved and sold.

Form I-9 Employment Eligibility Verification certifying the employee's United States citizenship, legal alien status, or legal authorization to work in this country.

formulary An insurance plan's list of approved prescription medications.

fraud Deceitful practices in depriving or attempting to deprive another of his or her rights, usually for the gain of another.

full-block letter style Letter format where all information within the letter begins at the left margin.

functional résumé A résumé that highlights specialty areas of a person's accomplishments and strengths.

gastroenterologist A specialist who diagnoses and treats disorders of the entire gastrointestinal tract, including the stomach, intestines, and associated digestive organs.

generic name A drug's official name.

gerontologist A specialist who studies the aging process.

global period The period of time after many procedures for follow up care that is considered included in the payment for that procedure.

grievance process A specific, formal procedure to address employee dissatisfaction on a certain topic or event.

gross earnings The total amount of income earned before deductions.

group practice A medical practice model in which three or more licensed physicians share the collective income, expenses, facilities, equipment, records, and personnel for the practice.

growth An ongoing effort to learn and improve.

gynecologist A specialist who performs routine physical care and examinations of the female reproductive system.

hard copy A readable, paper copy or printout of information.

hard skills Specific technical and operational proficiencies.

hardware The physical components of a computer system, including the monitor, keyboard, and printer.

HCPCS Level II codes Codes that cover many supplies such as sterile trays, drugs, DME; also referred to as national codes. They also cover services and procedures that may not be found in CPT.

health-care acquired infections (HAI) Diseases that are a result of exposure in a health-care setting.

Healthcare Common Procedural Coding System (HCPCS) A coding system developed by the Centers for Medicare and Medicaid Services that is used in coding services for Medicare (and some other payers') patients.

Health Insurance Portability and Accountability Act (HIPAA) A set of regulations whose goals include the following: (1) improving the portability and continuity of health-care coverage in group and individual markets; (2) combating waste, fraud, and abuse in health-care insurance and health-care delivery; (3) promoting the use of a medical savings account; (4) improving access to long-term care services and coverage; and (5) simplifying the administration of health insurance.

health maintenance organization (HMO) A health-care organization that provides specific services to individuals and their dependents who are enrolled in the plan. Physicians who enroll with an HMO agree to provide certain services in exchange for a prepaid fee or capitation payment.

hierarchy A term that pertains to Abraham Maslow's hierarchy of needs stating that human beings are motivated by unsatisfied needs that must be satisfied before higher needs are met.

homeostasis A balanced, stable state within the body.

hospice A system of caring for terminally ill patients and their families in preparation for death.

icon A pictorial image on a computer screen; a graphic symbol that identifies a menu choice.

identification line The initials of the person dictating or writing the letter as well as the initials of the typist with a colon or forward slash separating the two.

immunocompromised or immunodeficient The inability to effectively fight off an infectious disease.

implied consent Permission for treatment, physical exam, and so on, is understood through the patient actions (such as making an appointment, rolling up the sleeve for venipuncture, etc), rather than by written permission.

implied contract Contracts in which the conduct of the parties, rather than expressed words, indicates acceptance and creates the contract.

inactive file A file of a patient not seen by the medical practice in a given time period, usually two years.

incident report A special form required by a facility when an adverse outcome or event with risk of liability occurs; also referred to as an *occurrence report*.

indexing The naming of a file placed in an established order.

indexing rules Rules used as guidelines for the sequencing of files based on standard business practice.

individual identifiable health information Information such as patient SSN or insurance policy number that easily reveals patient identity.

infection control Stopping the spread of or reducing or eliminating pathogens through use of aseptic technique.

informed consent The patient's right to receive all information relative to his or her condition and to make a decision regarding treatment based upon that knowledge.

informed consent form Document signed by the patient to verify that the patient understands the treatment offered and the possible outcomes or side effects of the treatment.

ink-jet printer A nonimpact printer that forms characters by using a series of dots created by tiny drops of ink.

in-service Education and training conducted in the facility.

inside address The name and address of the person to whom the letter is addressed.

integrity (honesty) Adhering to the appropriate code of law and ethics; trustworthy and honest.

interactive pager A pager designed for two-way communication. The pager screen displays a printed message and allows the receiver to respond by way of a mini keyboard.

International Classification of Diseases, Ninth Revision, Clinical Modification (ICD 9-CM) Code set based on a system maintained by the World Health Organization. The use of ICD-9 codes is mandated by the Department of Health and Human Services for reporting patient diseases, conditions, and signs and symptoms.

International Classification of Diseases, Tenth Revision, Clinical Modification (ICD-10-CM) Code set based on a system maintained by the World Health Organization. The use of ICD-10-CM codes will be mandated by the Department of Health and Human Services for reporting patient diseases, conditions, and signs and symptoms, replacing ICD-9-CM as of October 1, 2013.

Internet A global network of computers.

internist A doctor who specializes in diagnosing and treating problems related to the internal organs.

interpersonal skills Attitudes, qualities, and abilities that influence the level of success and satisfaction achieved in interacting with other people.

inventory List of supplies currently on hand.

invoice Bill for supplies or services.

itinerary A detailed travel plan listing dates and times for specific transportation arrangements and events, the location of meetings and lodgings, and phone numbers.

job description An overview of the position duties with the necessary qualifications and requirements; also referred to as a *job analysis*.

journalizing Recording in the daily journal services provided, the fee charged, and any payment received.

judgment Coming to an appropriate conclusion and acting accordingly; critical thinking.

key The act of inputting or entering information into a computer.

knowledge Understanding gained through study and experience; associating theory with practice.

labor relations Issues between employees and management.

LAN Abbreviation for local area network.

laser printer A high-resolution printer that uses a technology similar to that of a photocopier. It is the fastest type of computer printer and produces the highest-quality output.

lateral file A horizontal filing cabinet with shelves where files are arranged with sides facing out.

law A rule of conduct or action prescribed or formally recognized as binding or enforced by a controlling authority, such as local, state, and federal governments.

law of agency Law that states that an employee is considered to act as the agent of the employer

lease To rent an item or piece of equipment.

letterhead Formal business stationery on which the practice name and address are printed.

liability insurance A type of insurance that covers injuries caused by the insured or injuries that occurred on the insured's property.

liable One person being responsible for another's actions.

libel Publishing in print damaging words, pictures, or signed statements that will injure the reputation of another.

lifetime maximum benefit The total sum that a health plan will pay out over the patient's lifetime.

limited check Checks that are stamped as being negotiable only for specific amounts or limited time frames.

locum tenens A substitute physician hired to see patients while the regular physician is away from the office.

maintenance contract A contract that specifies when a piece of equipment will be cleaned, checked for warn parts and repaired.

malpractice claim Lawsuit by a patient against a physician for errors in diagnosis or treatment.

managed care organization (MCO) A health-care business that, through mergers and buyouts, can deliver health care more cost effectively.

massage therapist An individual who is trained to use pressure, kneading, and stroking to promote muscle and full body relaxation.

Material Safety Data Sheets (MSDS) Forms that address the potentially hazardous substances used and provide workers and emergency personnel with the procedures for handling or working with these substances if a spill or other accident occurs.

matrix The basic format of an appointment book, established by blocking off times on the schedule during which the doctor is not available to see patients.

mediation A process in which a third-party assists in resolving a disagreement between two or more parties.

Medicaid A federally funded health cost assistance program for low-income, blind, and disabled patients; families receiving aid to dependent children; foster children; and children with birth defects.

medical identity theft When a person seeks health care using another person's name or insurance.

Medicare A national health insurance program for Americans aged 65 and older; as well as some patients under age 65 who meet specific criteria.

Medicare Advantage plans PPOs, HMOs, private fee-for-service plans, and Medicare medical savings accounts that provide Medicare beneficiaries with plan coverage choices in addition to the traditional Medicare plan.

Medicare Improvements for Patients and Providers Act of 2008 (MIPPA) Law enacted in 2008 that among other things provides positive incentives for physicians to use e-prescribing.

Medigap Private insurance that Medicare beneficiaries can purchase to reduce the gaps in Medicare coverage; the amount they would have to pay from their own pockets after receiving Medicare benefits.

microbes Living organisms too small to see with the naked eye.

microfiche Microfilm in rectangular sheets.

microfilm A roll of film stored on a reel and imprinted with information on a reduced scale to minimize storage space requirements.

middle digit A small group of two to three numbers in the middle of a patient number that is used as an identifying unit in a filing system.

midlevel provider A medical caregiver who is not a physician but is licensed to diagnose and treat patients, usually under the supervision of a licensed physician.

minors Persons under the age of majority

minutes A report of what happened and what was discussed and decided at a meeting.

misdemeanor Crime that is less serious than a felony, such as attempted robbery. Misdemeanors are punishable by fines or by imprisonment in a facility other than a prison for 1 year or less.

modeling The process of teaching the patient a new skill by having the patient observe and imitate it.

modem A device used to transfer information from one computer to another through telephone lines.

modified-block letter style Similar to block letter style, except that the dateline, complimentary close, and signature block all begin at or slightly to the right of center.

modified-wave scheduling A scheduling system similar to the wave system with patients arriving at planned intervals during the hour, allowing time to catch up before the next hour begins.

modifier One or more two-digit alphanumeric codes assigned in addition to the five digit CPT code to show that some special circumstance applies to the service or procedure performed by the physician.

money order A type of guaranteed payment; it must be purchased in cash and includes a small fee to the vendor (post office, bank or some convenience stores).

moral values Serve as a basis for ethical conduct. Moral values are formed through the influence of the family, culture, and society.

morbidity Causes and severity of illnesses.

mortality Causes of death.

motherboard The main circuit board of a computer that controls the other components in the system.

mouse A pointing device that can be added to a computer that directs activity on the computer screen by positioning a pointer or cursor on the screen. It can be directly attached to the computer or can be wireless.

multimedia More than one medium, such as in graphics, sound, and text, used to convey information.

multitasking Running two or more computer software programs simultaneously.

National Association for Health Professionals (NAHP) An organization dedicated to assisting students in the health-care field to obtain a credential in the most proficient manner possible.

National Center for Competency Testing (NCCT) An independent, third-party organization that certifies individuals through examination and avoids any allegiance to a specific organization or association.

National Healthcareer Association (NHA) An organization that provides certification and continuing education services for health-care professionals as well as curriculum development for education institutions.

negligence Charge when a health-care practitioner fails to exercise ordinary care and the patient is injured.

negotiable Legally transferable from one person to another.

nephrologist A specialist who studies, diagnoses, and manages diseases of the kidney.

net earnings Take home pay. Gross Earnings − Total Deductions = Net Earnings.

network A system that links several computers together.

neurologist A specialist who diagnoses and treats disorders and diseases of the nervous system, including the brain, spinal cord, and nerves.

networking Making contacts with relatives, friends, and acquaintances that may have information about how to find a job in your field.

new patient Patient who, for CPT reporting purposes, has not received professional services from the physician within the last 3 years.

noncompliant A medical term used to describe a patient who does not follow the medical advice he or she is given.

no-show Patient who does not come to the appointment and does not call to cancel.

notations Information at the end a letter including enclosures and carbon copy notations.

Notice of Privacy Practices (NPP) Document consisting of HIPAA-compliant communication of patient rights.

numeric filing system A filing system that organizes files by numbers assigned to a name instead of by the name.

objective Data from the physician examination and from test results.

Occupational Safety and Health Administration (OSHA) The agency of the federal government responsible for safety in the workplace.

oncologist A specialist who identifies tumors and treats patients who have cancer.

open-book account An account that is open to charges made occasionally as needed.

open-hours scheduling Patients arrive at their own convenience with the understanding that they will be seen on a first-come, first-served basis unless it is an emergency.

open posture A position that conveys a feeling of receptiveness and friendliness; facing another person with arms comfortably at the sides or in the lap.

optical character recognition (OCR) The process or technology of reading data in printed form by a device that scans and identifies characters.

organization Planning and coordinating information and tasks in an orderly manner to efficiently complete the job in a given time.

organizational chart A model showing the supervisory structure and reporting relationships between different functions and positions in an organization.

Original Medicare Plan The Medicare fee-for-service plan that allows the beneficiary to choose any licensed physician certified by Medicare.

orthopedist A specialist who diagnoses and treats diseases and disorders of the muscles and bones.

osteopathic manipulative medicine (OMM) A system of hands-on techniques that help relieve pain, restore motion, support the body's natural functions, and influence the body's structure. Osteopathic physicians study OMM in addition to medical courses.

otorhinolaryngologist A specialist who diagnoses and treats diseases of the ear, nose, and throat.

out guide A marker made of stiff material and used as a placeholder when a file is taken out of a filing system.

overbooking Scheduling appointments for more patients than can reasonably be seen in the time allowed.

overpayment Payment made that is more than the amount billed; results in a credit balance.

over-the-counter (OTC) drugs Drugs that can be bought without a prescription.

packing slip List of items and quantity of each shipped.

palliative care Care that provides comfort only. Care is not meant to be curative in nature. Hospice services are palliative in nature.

pandemic Widespread disease or outbreak that affects populations throughout the world.

panel Lab tests frequently ordered together that are organ or disease-oriented.

participating physicians Physicians who enroll in managed care plans. They have contracts with MCOS that stipulate their fees.

participatory teaching Method of teaching that includes demonstrations of techniques that may be necessary to show that a something has been learned.

partnership Two or more physicians decide to practice together, based on a legal contract that specifies the rights, obligations, and responsibilities of each partner.

passive listening Hearing what a person has to say without responding in any way.

pathogen Disease-causing organism.

pathologist A medical doctor who studies the changes a disease produces in the cells, fluids, and processes of the entire body.

patient advocacy The act of speaking and acting on behalf of the patient's needs and well-being.

patient ledger card Individual patient financial record containing patient's name, address, telephone numbers, guarantor name, insurance information, and any special billing instructions.

patient record/chart Documentation of important information about a patient's medical history and present condition serving as both a communication tool and legal record.

pay schedule How often an employee is paid (weekly, biweekly, etc.).

payee The person to whom the check is written.

payer The person who writes the check.

pediatrician A specialist who diagnoses and treats childhood diseases and teaches parents skills for keeping their children healthy.

pegboard system A bookkeeping system that uses a lightweight board with pegs on which forms can be stacked, allowing each transaction to be entered and recorded on four different bookkeeping forms at once; also called the write-it-once system.

persistence Continuing in spite of difficulty; determined; overcomes obstacles.

personal protective equipment (PPE) Disposable gloves, mask, eye shields, and gowns worn to protect health-care personnel from contamination with blood and body fluids.

personal space A certain area that surrounds an individual and within which another person's physical presence is felt as an intrusion.

petty cash Set amount of cash kept for incidental office expenses.

philosophy The system of values and principles an office has adopted in its everyday practice.

physiatrist A physical medicine specialist, who diagnoses and treats diseases and disorders with physical therapy.

pitch The varying highs and lows of your voice.

plastic surgeon A specialist who reconstructs, corrects, or improves body structures.

podiatrist Physician who specializes in the study and treatment of the foot and ankle.

policies and procedures (P&Ps) Incorporate the organization's philosophy or mission, the expectations, and the correct method for performing the topic of the individual policy.

POMR Problem-oriented medical record.

portfolio A collection of an applicant's résumé, reference letters, and other documents of interest to a potential employer.

power of attorney Legal document giving a person the legal right to handle financial matters for another person who is unable to do so.

practitioner One who practices a profession.

preauthorization The process of the provider contacting the insurance plan to see if the proposed procedure is a covered service under the patient's insurance plan.

preceptor A teacher or mentor.

precertification See *preauthorization.*

preferred provider organization (PPO) A managed care plan that establishes a network of providers to perform services for plan members.

premium The basic annual cost of health-care insurance.

prescription A physician's written order for medication.

primary care physician A physician who provides routine medical care and referrals to specialists.

primary diagnosis The first diagnosis listed for outpatient claims as the *primary* reason for the patient's visit.

principal diagnosis The first diagnosis listed for inpatient claims as the *principal* reason found, after study, for the patient's hospitalization.

prioritizing Sorting and dealing with matters in the order of urgency and importance.

Privacy Rule Designed to provide strong privacy protections that do not interfere with patient access to health care or the quality of health-care delivery.

probationary period An allotted period of time when a new employee may be terminated without cause; a trial period.

procedure code Codes that represent medical procedures, such as surgery and diagnostic tests, and medical services, such as an examination to evaluate a patient's condition.

proctologist Physician who diagnoses and treats disorders of the anus, rectum, and intestines.

professional A member of a vocation requiring specialized educational training.

professional development The skills and knowledge attained for both personal development and career advancement.

professionalism Exhibiting the traits or features that correspond with some model of that profession.

pronunciation Saying words correctly.

proofreading Checking a document for grammatical, spelling, and formatting errors.

protected health information (PHI) Individually identifiable health information that is transmitted or maintained by electronic or other media, such as computer storage devices.

punctuality Showing up on appointed days and times.

punitive damages Money paid as punishment for intentionally breaking the law.

quality assurance (QA) Ensuring that the services meet or exceed the requirements and standards.

quarterly return The Employer's Quarterly Federal Tax Return; a form submitted to the IRS every three months that summarizes the federal income and employment taxes withheld from employees' paychecks.

qui tam From Latin, meaning to bring an action for the king and for one's self, allows individuals to bring civil actions on behalf of the U.S. government for false medical claims.

radiologist A physician who specializes in taking and reading x-rays.

random-access memory (RAM) The temporary or programmable memory in a computer.

rapport A harmonious, positive relationship.

read-only memory (ROM) The permanent memory of a computer, which can be read by the computer but not changed. It provides the computer with the basic operating instructions it needs to function.

reception The area where patients enter the office, inform the staff of their presence by "signing in," receive a greeting, and wait to be seen.

receptionist The employee who greets people, checks them in, directs them, and answers the phone.

reconciliation Comparing the office's financial records with the bank records to ensure that they are consistent and accurate.

records management system An established process for creating, filing, maintaining, and destroying files.

recovery position The position a person is placed in after receiving first aid for choking or cardiopulmonary resuscitation.

Red Flags Rule August 1, 2009, law requiring certain businesses including most medical offices and other health-care facilities to develop written programs to detect the warning signs or red flags of identity theft.

reference A recommendation for employment from a facility or a preceptor.

referral An authorization from a medical practice for a patient to have specialized services performed by another practice; often required for insurance purposes.

Registered Medical Assistant (RMA) A medical assistant who has met the educational requirements and taken and passed the certification examination for medical assisting given by the American Medical Technologists (AMT).

registration Granting of a title or license by a board that gives permission to practice in a chosen profession.

remittance advice (RA) See *Explanation of Benefits (EOB.)*

requisition A formal request from a staff member or doctor for the purchase of equipment or supplies.

reservoir host An insect, animal, or human that has been invaded by a pathogen and is capable of sustaining its growth.

res ipsa loquitur Latin term meaning "the thing speaks for itself"; refers to a case in which the doctor's fault is completely obvious.

resource-based relative value scale (RBRVS) The payment system used by Medicare. It establishes the relative value units for services, replacing the provider consensus on usual fees.

respondeat superior "Let the Master Answer"—the employer is responsible for the employee's actions or inaction.

résumé A typewritten document summarizing one's employment and educational history.

retention schedule A timeframe that details how long to keep different types of patient records in the office after they have become inactive or closed and how long the records should be stored.

return demonstration Participatory teaching method in which the technique is first described to the patient and then demonstrated to the patient; the patient is then asked to repeat the demonstration.

risk management (RM) A plan and processes that continually assess, identify, correct, and monitor functions of the medical office to prevent negative outcomes and minimize exposure to risk.

salutation The greeting of a letter.

scanner An optical device that converts printed matter into a format that can be read by the computer and inputs the converted information.

screening Performing a diagnostic test on a person who is typically free of symptoms.

screen saver A program that automatically changes the monitor display at short intervals or constantly shows moving images to prevent burn-in of images on the computer screen.

Security Rule Specifies how patient information is protected on computer networks, the Internet, disks, and other storage media, and extranets.

self-confidence Believing in oneself; assured.

sensory teaching Method of teaching that provides patient with a description of the physical sensations they may have as part of the learning or the procedure involved.

sentinel event An unexpected occurrence involving death or serious physical or psychological injury, or the risk thereof.

sequential order One after another in a predictable pattern or sequence.

service contract A contract that covers services for equipment that are nor included in a standard maintenance contract.

sexual harassment Unwelcome verbal, visual, or physical conduct of a sexual nature that is severe or pervasive and affects working conditions or creates a hostile work environment.

sign Objective or external factor such as elevated BP, rash or swelling that can be seen, felt by the physician, or measured by an instrument.

signature block The writer's name and title, following the complimentary closing, leaving space for the writer's signature.

sign-in The process in which an arriving patient lists his or her name and other information on a form in the registration area; also refers to the registration area.

simplified letter style Block letter style with elimination of the salutation and courtesy title, with a subject line placed between the address and body of the letter (in all caps). Complimentary close is omitted and the writer's name is again typed in all caps.

single-entry account An account that has only one charge, usually for a small amount, for a patient who does not come in regularly.

skips People who move and leave no forwarding information in the hopes that they will not be found.

slander Speaking damaging words intended to negatively influence others against an individual in a manner that jeopardizes his or her reputation or means of livelihood.

SOAP Subjective, Objective, Assessment, and Plan.

soft skills Personal attributes that enhance an individual's interactions, job performance, and career prospects.

software A program or set of instructions that tells a computer what to do.

sole proprietorship A physician practicing alone assumes all the benefits for and liabilities of the business.

SOMR Source-oriented medical record.

standard precautions Techniques for health-care personnel to minimize the risk of catching or spreading an infection.

State Unemployment Tax Act (SUTA) Taxes withheld by some states; these taxes are filed along with FUTA taxes.

statement A form similar to an invoice; often contains a courteous reminder to the patient that payment is due.

statute of limitations A state law that sets a time limit on when a collection suit on a past-due account can legally be filed.

stroke A condition that occurs when the blood supply to the brain is impaired. It may cause temporary or permanent damage.

subcategories In the Alphabetic Index, subdivisions of the ICD-10 chapters containing a clinical description of the code range and the guidelines for coding; in the Tabular List, the codes consisting of four or five characters specifying the level of complexity of the diagnosis.

subclinical case The symptoms of a disease are so slight that they may go unnoticed.

subject line Sometimes used in a letter to bring the reader's attention immediately to the purpose of the letter.

subjective Data from the patient describing history of symptoms; usually in his or her own words.

subpoena A written court order addressed to a specific person requiring that person's presence in court on a specific date at a specific time.

subpoena duces tecum A court order to produce specific, requested documents required at a certain place and time to enter into court records.

subpoena ad testificandum Subpoena which requires the person to provide testimony in court under penalty.

superbill (encounter form) Form used to list services and charges for the patient's visit.

Surescripts The national clearinghouse for e-prescribing. This company electronically connects physicians, pharmacists, and payers nationwide, enabling them to exchange health information and prescribe without paper. Surescripts collaborates with national EHR vendors, pharmacies, and health plans to support physicians using EHR software.

surgeon A physician who uses hands and medical instruments to diagnose and correct deformities and treat external and internal injuries or disease.

susceptible host An individual has little or no immunity to that specific organism.

symptom Subjective or internal condition felt by the patient (such as a headache) that generally cannot be seen or felt by the physician or measured by instruments.

tab A tapered rectangular or rounded extension at the top of a file folder.

tablet PC A laptop or slate-shaped mobile computer, equipped with a touch screen or graphics tablet to operate the computer with a digital pen or fingertip instead of a keyboard or mouse.

Tabular List One of two ways that diagnoses are listed in the ICD-9-CM. In the tabular listing, the diagnosis codes are listed in numeric order with additional instructions regarding the use of the code for each diagnosis.

targeted résumé A résumé that is focused on a specific job target.

tax liability accounts Accounts where money is deposited and which is used to pay taxes to appropriate government agencies.

telecommunication device for the deaf (TDD) Formerly known as a TTY; a specially designed telephone that looks very much like a laptop with a cradle for the telephone receiver.

telephone triage Deciding the nature of a phone call, to whom the call should be routed, and the action to take regarding each call.

template Standard pre-set formats within many software programs.

terminal digit Groups of two to three numbers used as patient identifiers in a filing system and read left to right.

third-party check Check made out to the patient rather than to the practice.

third-party payer The entity that pays for a service received from one party but provided by another party.

tickler file A reminder file for keeping track of time-sensitive obligations.

time management Utilizing time in an effective manner to accomplish the desired results.

time-specified scheduling Assumes a steady stream of patients all day long at regular, specified intervals. Also called *stream scheduling.*

tort A civil wrong committed against a person or property that causes physical injury or damage to

someone's property or that deprives someone of his or her personal liberty and freedom.

touch pad   A type of pointing device common to laptop and notebook computers that directs activity on the computer screen by positioning a pointer or cursor on the screen. It is a small, flat device or surface that is highly sensitive to the touch.

touch screen   A type of computer monitor that acts as an intake device, receiving information through the touch of a pen, wand, or hand directly to the screen.

tower case   A vertical housing for the system unit of a personal computer.

trackball   A pointing device with a ball that is rolled to position a pointer or cursor on a computer screen. It can be directly attached to the computer or can be wireless.

tracking   Watching for changes in spending so as to help control expenses.

trade name   A drug's brand or proprietary name.

transcription   Transforming spoken notes into accurate written form.

transfer   With patient consent, giving PHI to another party outside the treating physician's office.

traveler's check   Preprinted checks in established denominations of $10, $20, $50, and $100; these checks MUST be signed at the location where they were purchased, and when being used, they MUST be signed in the presence of the payee.

treatment, payment, and operations (TPO)   HIPAA allows for sharing of PHI without specific consent, if it is for the reasons of treatment, payment, or normal business operations such as quality improvement.

triage   A process of determining the level of urgency of each incoming emergency and how it should be handled.

TRICARE   A program that provides health-care benefits for dependents of military personnel and military retirees.

troubleshooting   Trying to determine and correct a problem without having to call service supplier.

tutorial   A small program included in a software package designed to give users an overall picture of the product and its functions.

unbundling   Listing services or procedures separately instead of using an applicable, available code that includes all services provided in order to receive higher reimbursement.

underbooking   Leaving large, unused gaps in the doctor's schedule; this approach does not make the best use of the doctor's time.

uniform donor card   A legal document which states one's wish to make an anatomical gift such as organs or skin, upon death.

unit   A part of an individual's name or title used in filing.

upcoding   purposely choosing a code of a higher level than that of the service provided in order to achieve higher reimbursement.

urologist   A specialist who diagnoses and treats diseases of the kidney, bladder, and urinary system

use   Information is used when it moves within an organization.

utilization review   Ensures that the treatment plan and services are appropriate and cost effective.

V code   An ICD-9 code used to identify health-care encounters for reasons other than illness or injury, such as annual physical exams, immunizations, and normal childbirth.

ventricular fibrillation (VF)   abnormal heart rhythm.

vertical file   A filing system that usually contains a metal frame or bar in hanging file folders.

voice mail   An advanced digital form of an answering machine that allows a caller to leave a message if the phone line or person requested is busy.

void   Contract or situation which is not legally enforceable.

voucher check   Business checks with perforated stubs attached for record keeping.

VPN   Abbreviation for virtual private networks, which are used to connect two or more computer systems.

vulnerable populations   Groups considered at risk for coercion and exploitation; generally, children, the elderly, and groups with special needs.

walk-in   A patient who arrives at the office without an appointment and expects to see the physician.

WAN   Abbreviation for wide area networks.

warranty   A contract that specifies free service and replacement of parts for a piece of equipment during a specified period of time, often a year.

wave scheduling   A system of scheduling in which the number of patients seen each hour is determined by dividing the hour by the length of the average visit and then giving that number of patients appointments with the doctor at the beginning of each hour.

W-2 tax form   The employer states how much gross income the organization paid the employee for the year and the taxes withheld.

W-4 tax form   Form stating the number of deductions the employee wishes to claim.

World Health Organization (WHO)   A specialized agency of the United Nations (UN) that acts as a coordinating authority on international public health.

work ethic   A set of values of hard work held by employees.

work quality   Striving for excellence in doing the job; pride in one's performance.

written contract account   An agreement between a service provider and the receiver of services stating exactly what service will be provided and the fee that is agreed upon for that service.

X12 837 Health Care Claim   An electronic claim transaction that is the HIPAA Health Care Claim or Equivalent Encounter Information.

zip drive   A high-capacity floppy disk drive developed by Iomega®. Zip disks are slightly larger and about twice as thick as a conventional floppy disk. Zip drives can hold 100-750 MB of data. They are durable and relatively inexpensive. They may be used for backing up hard disks and transporting large files.

Photo Credits

UNIT OPENERS
1: © Tom Grill/IPN Stock RF; 2: © Upper Cut Images/Getty RF; 3: © Banana Stock/Picture Quest RF; 5: © Steve Cole/Getty RF; 4: © Ryan McVay/Getty RF; 6: © Eric Audras/Photoalto/PictureQuest RF; 7: © SuperStock RF.

CHAPTER 1
Figure 1-1a: Courtesy American Medical Technologists; 1-1b,1-1c: Courtesy Total Care Programming, Inc.; 1-2: © Royalty-Free/CORBIS; p. 18: © Silverstock/Digital Vision/Getty RF.

CHAPTER 2
Figure 2-1: © Ryan McVay/Getty RF; 2-2: © Jupiterimages/Imagesource RF; 2-3: © Getty Images/Digital Vision RF; 2-4: © BananaStock/PictureQuest RF; 2-5: © Blend Images/Alamy RF; 2-6: © Thomas Hartwell RF; p. 34: © Asian Images Group/Getty RF; 2-7: © McGraw-Hill Companies, Inc./Gary He, photographer.

CHAPTER 3
Figure 3-1: © Don Thompson/Getty Images; 3-2: © Royalty-Free/CORBIS; 3-3: © Lester Lefkowitz/Getty Images; 3-4: © Javier Larrea/age fotostock RF; 3-5: © David Kelly Crow; 3-6: © Will and Deni McIntrye.

CHAPTER 4
Figure 4-2: © Keith Brofsky/Getty Images RF; 4-4: © Tim Pannell/Corbis RF; 4-5: © Sean Justice/Getty Images; p. 78: © Jupiterimages/Getty RF; 4-6: © Richard Shock/Getty Images; 4-7: © Keith Brofsky/Getty Images RF; 4-8, 4-9: © Cliff Moore.

CHAPTER 5
Page 98: © Digital Vision/Getty RF; 5-3: © Jeff Greenberg/PhotoEdit, Inc.; 5-4: © Image Source/Getty Images RF.

CHAPTER 6
Page 156: © Comstock/Getty RF; p. 158: © Adam Gault/SPL/Getty RF.

CHAPTER 7
Page 175: © Rana Faure/Photo Disc/Getty RF.

CHAPTER 8
Figure 8-1: © Royalty-Free/Corbis; 8-2: © Terry Wild Studio; 8-3: © Don Farrall/Getty Images RF; 8-4: © Cliff Moore; 8-5: © Altrendo Images/Stockbyte/Getty RF; 8-6: © David Kelly Crow; 8-10: © Purestock/Getty RF; p. 193: © PhotoDisc/Getty RF; 8-11: © 2009 Jupiterimages RF.

CHAPTER 9
Figure 9-2: Courtesy of the Centers for Disease Control and Prevention; 9-3: © David Allan Brandt/Getty Images; 9-4: © Zia Soliel/Getty Images; 9-5: © The McGraw-Hill Companies, Inc./Jill Braaten, photographer; p. 210: © Sheer Stock, Inc./Getty RF.

CHAPTER 10
Figure 10-1: © The McGraw-Hill Companies, Inc./Jill Braaten, photographer; 10-2: Courtesy of Total Care Programming, Inc.; 10-3: © The McGraw-Hill Companies, Inc./Jill Braaten, photographer; p 223: © Jupiterimages/Getty RF; 10-6: Courtesy of Total Care

Programming, Inc.; p.231: © beyond goto/Getty RF; p. 232: © Adam Gault/SPL/Getty RF; p. 236: © Comstock/Getty RF; 10-8: Courtesy of Total Care Programming, Inc.; 10-9: © Tim Flach/Getty Images; 10-10: © PhotoDisc Collection/Getty Images RF; 10-11: © Duncan Smith/Getty Images RF; p. 244: © Stockbyte/Getty RF; 10-13: © Comstock Images/Alamy RF; 10-14: Courtesy of Total Care Programming, Inc.; 10-16: © Terry Wild Studio; 10-17: © David Kelly Crow; 10-18: Courtesy of Total Care Programming, Inc.; 10-19: © Terry Wild Studio; 10-20: © PNC/Digital Vision/Getty Images RF; p. 257: © Rana Faure/PhotoDisc/Getty RF.

CHAPTER 11
Figure 11-1: © Thomas Barwick/Getty Images RF; 11-2: © Javier Pierini/Getty Images RF; p. 271: © David Neil Madden/Flickr/Getty RF; 11-3: © Robyn Beck/AFP/Getty Images; p. 278: © BrandX Pictures/Getty RF; 11-5: Courtesy of Total Care Programming, Inc.; 11-7: © Digital Stock/Corbis RF.

CHAPTER 12
Page 312: © Digital Vision/Getty RF; 12-8: © Terry Wild Studio.

CHAPTER 13
Figure 13-1: © The McGraw-Hill Companies, Inc./Jill Braaten, photographer; 13-14, 13-15: © Cliff Moore; p. 357: © Silverstock/Digital Vision/Getty RF.

CHAPTER 14
Figure 14-1: © Image Source/Jupiter Images RF; 14-2, 14-4: Courtesy Bibbero Systems, Inc. Petaluma, CA, 800-242.2376, www.bibbero.com; 14-5: © Image Source/Jupiter Images; p. 378: © Image Source/Getty RF; 14-6: © Jon Feingersh/Getty Images.

CHAPTER 15
Figure 15-1: © Hank Morgan/Photo Researchers, Inc.; p. 398: © Jupiterimages/Getty RF; 15-8: © UpperCut Images/Getty Images; 15-9: Courtesy of Total Care Programming, Inc.; 15-10: © David Kelly Crow; p. 407: © Adam Gault/SPL/Getty RF.

CHAPTER 16
Figure 16-1: © Sheer Stock, Inc./Getty RF; p. 438: © Jupiterimages/Getty RF.

CHAPTER 17
Figure 17-3: © David Kelly Crow; p. 492: © Rana Faure/PhotoDisc/Getty RF; 17-13: © Stockbyte RF; p. 504: © Stockbyte/Getty RF.

CHAPTER 19
Figure 19-1: © Danilo Calilung/Corbis; p. 552, 19-8: © PhotoDisc/Getty RF; 19-9: © Digital Vision.

CHAPTER 21
Figure 21-5: Courtesy of Bibbero Systems, Inc., Petaluma, CA, 800-242-2376, www.bibbero.com; p. 617: © Sean Justice/Stockbyte/Getty RF; 21-10: Courtesy Total Care Programming, Inc.; p. 626: © Jupiterimages/Getty RF.

CHAPTER 22
Figure 22-1: © Pixtal/age fotostock RF; 22-5: © Doug Menuez/Getty RF; p. 661: © Sheer Stock,

Inc./Getty RF; 22-10: © Banana Stock/Picture Quest RF; 22-11: © Ryan McVay/Getty RF.

CHAPTER 23
Figure 23-1: Courtesy Total Care Programming, Inc.; 23-2: Photo Courtesy of Laerdal Medical; 23-3: © Leesa Whicker; 23-4: Courtesy of Total Care Programming, Inc.; p. 679: © The McGraw-Hill Companies, Inc./Jan L. Saeger, photographer; 23-5: © David Kelly Crow.

CHAPTER 24
Figure 24-1: © Thinkstock/Getty RF; 24-3: © BananaStock/PunchStock RF; p. 702: © Rana Faure/Photo Disc/Getty RF; 24-4: © Creatas/PictureQuest RF.

Text Credits

Chapter correlations to CMA Standards: Reprinted with the permission of the American Association of Medical Assistants.
Chapter correlations to RMA and AMT Standards: Reprinted with permission of American Medical Technologists.
ABHES competencies throughout the book: © Accrediting Bureau of Health Education Schools.
CAAHEP competencies throughout the book: 2008 Standards and Guidelines for the Accreditation of Educational Programs in Medical Assisting, Appendix B, Core Curriculum for Medical Assistants, Medical Assisting Education Review Board (MAERB), 2008.

CHAPTER 1
Pages 8–9, AAMA Creed and Code of Ethics: Reprinted with permission of American Association of Medical Assistants.

CHAPTER 3
Table 3-2: © The Joint Commission, 2010. Reprinted with permission.

CHAPTER 4
Figure 4-1: From Booth: *Medical Assisting*, 4e. © The McGraw-Hill Companies.; 4-3: From Booth: *Medical Assisting*, 4e. © The McGraw-Hill Companies.;

CHAPTER 5
Figure 5-1: From Hamilton: *Electronic Health Records*, 2e. © The McGraw-Hill Companies; 5-2: From Hamilton: *Electronic Health Records*, 2e. © The McGraw-Hill Companies.; 5-5: From Booth: *Medical Assisting*, 4e. © The McGraw-Hill Companies.; 5-6: From Booth: *Medical Assisting*, 4e. © The McGraw-Hill Companies.; 5-7: From Hamilton: *Electronic Health Records*, 2e. © The McGraw-Hill Companies.; Fig. 5-8: From Hamilton: *Electronic Health Records*, 2e. © The McGraw-Hill Companies.

CHAPTER 6
Figure 6-2: Caitlin Palm, Caring for Massachusetts Youth: Legislative Reform for Homeless Minors (a Collaborative Project: Justice Resource Institute and the Northeastern University School of Law [NUSL], Legal Skills in Social Context, Social Justice Program (fall 2002 on file with NUSL). Reprinted with permission.; Table 6-1: Reprinted with permission of the American Medical Technologists.; 6-3: From Booth: *Medical Assisting*, 4e. © The McGraw-Hill Companies.; 6-4: From Booth:

Medical Assisting, 4e. © The McGraw-Hill Companies.;

CHAPTER 9
Figure 9-1: From Booth: *Medical Assisting,* 4e. © The McGraw-Hill Companies.

CHAPTER 10
Figure 10-3: From Booth: *Medical Assisting,* 4e. © The McGraw-Hill Companies.; 10-4: From Booth: *Medical Assisting,* 4e. © The McGraw-Hill Companies.; 10-5: From Booth: *Medical Assisting,* 4e. © The McGraw-Hill Companies.; 10-7: From Booth: *Medical Assisting,* 4e. © The McGraw-Hill Companies.; 10-12: From Booth: *Medical Assisting,* 4e. © The McGraw-Hill Companies.; 10-15: From Booth: *Medical Assisting,* 4e. © The McGraw-Hill Companies.; 10-21: From Booth: *Medical Assisting,* 4e. © The McGraw-Hill Companies.; 10-22: From Booth: *Medical Assisting,* 4e. © The McGraw-Hill Companies.

CHAPTER 11
Figure 11-4: From Booth: *Medical Assisting,* 4e. © The McGraw-Hill Companies.; 11-6: From Booth: *Medical Assisting,* 4e. © The McGraw-Hill Companies.; 11-8: From Hamilton: *Electronic Health Records,* 2e © The McGraw-Hill Companies.

CHAPTER 12
Figure 12-1: From Booth: *Medical Assisting,* 4e. © The McGraw-Hill Companies.; 12-3: From Booth: *Medical Assisting,* 4e. © The McGraw-Hill Companies.; 12-4: From Booth: *Medical Assisting,* 4e. © The McGraw-Hill Companies.; 12-5: From Booth: *Medical Assisting,* 4e. © The McGraw-Hill Companies.; 12-9: From Booth: *Medical Assisting,* 4e. © The McGraw-Hill Companies.

CHAPTER 13
Figure 13-2: From Booth: *Medical Assisting,* 4e. © The McGraw-Hill Companies.; 13-3: From Booth: *Medical Assisting,* 4e. © The McGraw-Hill Companies.; 13-4: From Booth: *Medical Assisting,* 4e. © The McGraw-Hill Companies.; 13-5: From Booth: *Medical Assisting,* 4e. © The McGraw-Hill Companies.; 13-6: From Booth: *Medical Assisting,* 4e. © The McGraw-Hill Companies.; 13-7: From Hamilton: *Electronic Health Records,* 2e. © The McGraw-Hill Companies.; 13-8: From Hamilton: *Electronic Health Records,* 2e. © The McGraw-Hill Companies.; 13-9: From Booth: *Medical Assisting,* 4e. © The McGraw-Hill Companies.; 13-10: From Booth: *Medical Assisting,* 4e. © The McGraw-Hill Companies.; 13-11: From Booth: *Medical Assisting,* 4e. ©The McGraw-Hill Companies.; 13-12: From Booth: *Medical Assisting,* 4e. © The McGraw-Hill Companies.; 13-13: From Booth: *Medical Assisting,* 4e. © The McGraw-Hill Companies.

CHAPTER 14
Figure 14-3: From Booth: *Medical Assisting,* 4e. © The McGraw-Hill Companies.

CHAPTER 15
Figure 15-2: From Booth: *Medical Assisting,* 4e. © The McGraw-Hill Companies.; 15-3: From Booth: *Medical Assisting,* 4e. © The McGraw-Hill Companies.; 15-4: From Booth: *Medical Assisting,* 4e. © The McGraw-Hill Companies.; 15-5: From Booth: *Medical Assisting,* 4e. © The McGraw-Hill Companies.; 15-6: From Booth: *Medical Assisting,* 4e. © The McGraw-Hill Companies.; 15-7: From Hamilton: *Electronic Health Records,* 2e. © The McGraw-Hill Companies.; 15-11a: From Hamilton: *Electronic Health Records,* 2e. © The McGraw-Hill Companies.; 15-11b: From Hamilton: *Electronic Health Records,* 2e. © The McGraw-Hill Companies.; 15-12: From Hamilton: *Electronic Health Records,* 2e. © The McGraw-Hill Companies.; 15-13: From Booth: *Medical Assisting,* 4e.

CHAPTER 16
Screenshots: Screen captures of Springcharts® Electronic Health Records Software are reprinted with permission from Spring Medical Systems, Inc. All rights reserved.; Figure 16-1: From Booth: *Medical Assisting,* 4e. © The McGraw-Hill Companies.; 16-2: From Hamilton: *Electronic Health Records,* 2e. © The McGraw-Hill Companies.; 16-4: From Booth: *Medical Assisting,* 4e. © The McGraw-Hill Companies.; Table 16-1: Please visit www.pdrhealth.com for drug and disease information.; 16-5: From Booth: *Medical Assisting,* 4e. © The McGraw-Hill Companies.; 16-6: From Booth: *Medical Assisting,* 4e. © The McGraw-Hill Companies.; 16-7: From Booth: *Medical Assisting,* 4e. © The McGraw-Hill Companies.; 16-8: From Booth: *Medical Assisting,* 4e. © The McGraw-Hill Companies.; 16-9: From Hamilton: *Electronic Health Records,* 2e. © The McGraw-Hill Companies.; 16-12: From Booth: *Medical Assisting,* 4e. © The McGraw-Hill Companies.; 16-13: From Hamilton: *Electronic Health Records,* 2e. © The McGraw-Hill Companies.; 16-14: From Hamilton: *Electronic Health Records,* 2e. © The McGraw-Hill Companies.

CHAPTER 17
Figure 17-2: From Booth: *Medical Assisting,* 4e. © The McGraw-Hill Companies.; 17-4: From Booth: *Medical Assisting,* 4e. © The McGraw-Hill Companies.; 17-5: From Booth: *Medical Assisting,* 4e. © The McGraw-Hill Companies.; 17-6: From Booth: *Medical Assisting,* 4e. © The McGraw-Hill Companies.; 17-7: From Booth: *Medical Assisting,* 4e. © The McGraw-Hill Companies.; 17-9: From Booth: *Medical Assisting,* 4e. © The McGraw-Hill Companies.; 17-12: From Booth: *Medical Assisting,* 4e. © The McGraw-Hill Companies.; 17-13: From Booth: *Medical Assisting,* 4e. © The McGraw-Hill Companies.; 17-14: From Booth: *Medical Assisting,* 4e. © The McGraw-Hill Companies.; 17-15: From Booth: *Medical Assisting,* 4e. © The McGraw-Hill Companies.; 17-16: From Booth: *Medical Assisting,* 4e. © The McGraw-Hill Companies.; 17-17: From Booth: *Medical Assisting,* 4e. © The McGraw-Hill Companies.; 17-18: From Booth: *Medical Assisting,* 4e. © The McGraw-Hill Companies.

CHAPTER 18
Figure 18-1: From Booth: *Medical Assisting,* 4e. © The McGraw-Hill Companies. 18-5:

From Hamilton: *Electronic Health Records, 2e.* © The McGraw-Hill Companies.; 18-6: From Hamilton: *Electronic Health Records, 2e.* © The McGraw-Hill Companies.

CHAPTER 19
Figure 19-3: © World Health Organization.; 19-4: © World Health Organization.; 19-6: © World Health Organization.; 19-7: © World Health Organization.; Table 19-6: Reprinted with permission from Contexo.

CHAPTER 20
Figure 20-1: Reprinted with permission of the American Medical Association.; 20-2: Reprinted with permission of the American Medical Association.; 20-4: From Booth: *Medical Assisting,* 4e © The McGraw-Hill Companies.; 20-5: From Hamilton: *Electronic Health Records,* 2e. © The McGraw-Hill Companies.; Table 20-1: Reprinted with permission of the American Medical Association.; Table 20-2: Reprinted with permission of the American Medical Association.

CHAPTER 21
Figure 21-1: From Booth: *Medical Assisting,* 4e. © The McGraw-Hill Companies.; 21-2: From Booth: *Medical Assisting,* 4e. © The McGraw-Hill Companies.; 21-3: From Booth: *Medical Assisting,* 4e. © The McGraw-Hill Companies.; 21-4: From Booth: *Medical Assisting,* 4e. © The McGraw-Hill Companies.; 21-6: From Booth: *Medical Assisting,* 4e. © The McGraw-Hill Companies.; 21-7: From Booth: *Medical Assisting,* 4e. © The McGraw-Hill Companies.; 21-8: From Booth: *Medical Assisting,* 4e. © The McGraw-Hill Companies.; 21-13: From Booth: *Medical Assisting,* 4e. ©The McGraw-Hill Companies.; 21-14: From Booth: *Medical Assisting,* 4e. © The McGraw-Hill Companies.: 21-15: From Booth: *Medical Assisting,* 4e. © The McGraw-Hill Companies.

CHAPTER 23
Figure 23-6: From Booth: *Medical Assisting,* 4e. © The McGraw-Hill Companies.; 23-7: From Booth: *Medical Assisting,* 4e. © The McGraw-Hill Companies.; 23-8: From Booth: *Medical Assisting,* 4e. © The McGraw-Hill Companies.; 23-9: From Booth: *Medical Assisting,* 4e. © The McGraw-Hill Companies.; 23-10: From Booth: *Medical Assisting,* 4e. © The McGraw-Hill Companies.; 23-11: From Booth: *Medical Assisting,* 4e. © The McGraw-Hill Companies.; 23-12: From Booth: *Medical Assisting,* 4e. © The McGraw-Hill Companies.; 23-13: From Booth: *Medical Assisting,* 4e. © The McGraw-Hill Companies.; 23-14: From Booth: *Medical Assisting,* 4e. © The McGraw-Hill Companies.; 23-15: From Booth: *Medical Assisting,* 4e. © The McGraw-Hill Companies.; 23-16: From Booth: *Medical Assisting,* 4e. © The McGraw-Hill Companies.; 23-17: From Booth: *Medical Assisting,* 4e. © The McGraw-Hill Companies.

CHAPTER 24
Figure 24-2: Reprinted with permission from Maricopa Community College.

Index

Page numbers in **boldface** indicate figures or illustrations. Page numbers followed by b indicate box features, p procedures, and t tables, respectively.

A

AAMA. *See* American Association of Medical Assistants
AAMAS. *See* American Association of Medical Audit Specialists
AAPC. *See* American Association of Professional Coders
Abandonment, 133, 138
ABA number, 610
Abbreviations
  appointment book, 300–302
  ICD-9-CM, 525–526
  ICD-10-CM, 551, 552t
  medical
    error-prone, 727–730
    in medical records, **403**
    in notations, 724–725
  prescription, 436, 437t
  telecommunication device for deaf, 273, 274t
ABC assessment, 673
ABHES. *See* Accrediting Bureau of Health Education Schools
ABMS. *See* American Board of Medical Specialties
ABN. *See* Advance Beneficiary Notice of Noncoverage
Abuse, in practice or behavior, 242
Abuse cases, reporting of, 137
Acceptance, in stages of dying/grief, 81
Acceptance of criticism, 29–30, 177–178
  definition of, 27t
  rubric for evaluating, **36**
Accepting, as communication skill, 72
Accessibility, of office, 184–185, **185**
Account(s)
  open-book, 499
  past-due
    age analysis of, 500–501, **502,** 517p
    collection of, 499–505
    quality of work and, 641
  single-entry, 599
  tax liability, 625, 629
  written-contract, 499
Accounting
  accuracy of, importance of, 598
  establishing procedures for, 598–599

forms and records, 600–606
patient, methods of, 599–608
pegboard system of, 495–497, 599, **606**
posting charges, payments, and adjustments, 635p
single-entry system of, 599
software for, 229
Accounts payable (A/P), 493, 603
  management of, 618
  setting up system of, 639p–640p
Accounts receivable (A/R), 493, 603
  age analysis of, 500–501, **502,** 517p
  collection of, 499–505
  insuring, 505
  quality of work and, 641
Accreditation, 11, 12, 14–15
  AAMA standards for, 15
  benefits of programs with, 15
  definition of, 14
  topics covered in programs with, 14
Accrediting Bureau of Health Education Schools (ABHES), 11, 12, 13, 14–15, 697
Accuracy
  of bookkeeping and banking, 598
  of medical records, 402, 404
ACP. *See* American College of Physicians
Acquired immune deficiency syndrome. *See* HIV/AIDS
Active files, vs. inactive or closed, 378
Active listening, 71, **71**
Active voice, in writing, 332
Activity-monitoring systems, 236
Acupuncturists, 49
Acute condition, in ICD-9-CM, 534
ADA. *See* Americans with Disabilities Act of 1990
Addendum, to electronic health record, 408, **409,** 416p
Adding machines, 248
Add-on codes, of CPT, 571
Address(es)
  change, and payment collection, 510
  delivery, 348, **348**
  format on envelope, 350–351
  inside, 334–335, **335**
  placement on envelope, 349–350, **350**
Address books, computerized, 232b
Address labels, 331–332
Adjustment, billing, 468, 600, 635p
Administrative duties
  advanced, 7
  after patient discharge, 173–177
  entry-level, 6

and law, 137–141
  non-patient related, 176–177
  overview of, **176**
  patient-related, 175–176
  simplification of, HIPAA and, 143, 152–153
Administrative supplies, 188, 189t
Administrator, 349p, 649. *See also* Medical practice, management of
Admissions clerk, hospital, 316b
ADNs (associate degrees in nursing), 53
Adolescent(s), minor status of. *See* Minor(s)
Adolescent medicine, 47
Advance Beneficiary Notice of Noncoverage (ABN), 470, **471**
Advanced duties
  administrative, 7
  clinical, 7t
  laboratory, 7t
Advance medical directive, 140
Advance scheduling, 306
Adverse effects
  in ICD-9-CM, 538
  in ICD-10-CM, 559
Advice, telephone requests for, 281
Advocacy, patient, 31
  cautions on, 32t
  definition of, 31
  guidelines for, 31t
AED. *See* Automated external defibrillator
Affective domain, of learning, 95–96
Affiliation agreement, 697, **697**
Age analysis, of past-due accounts, 500–501, **502,** 517p
Age Discrimination in Employment Act, 659
Agency, law of, 134–135
Agenda, for meeting, 320, 652, **653,** 664p
Agent, 134
Aggressive behavior, in communication, 75, 75t
Aging. *See* Elderly patients
Agreement
  in communication, 73
  in contracts, 123
  on externship, 697, **697**
AHA. *See* American Hospital Association
AHD. *See* Alcohol hand disinfectant
AHDI. *See* Association for Healthcare Documentation Integrity
AHIMA. *See* American Health Information Management Association
Airborne transmission, 204t
Airmail supplies, 352
Airway assessment, 673

Electronic mail. *See* E-mail
Electronic media, HIPAA and, 236
Electronic media claims (EMCs). *See*
    Electronic claims
Electronic medical records (EMRs), 405. *See*
    also Electronic health records
Electronic remittance advice (ERA), 478
Electronic scheduling system, 322p
Electronic telephone log, 284
Electronic transaction(s), 229–231
Electronic transaction records, 153
E-letters, 339–341, **342,** 359p
Eligibility for services, patient, 472–473
E-mail, 230, 289
    appointment scheduling via, 311
    consent for communication via, 289, **290**
    correspondence with patient via,
        339–341, **342,** 359p
    etiquette for, 230
    HIPAA and, 230, 231b
    management of, 289, **289**
    managing, 230
    physician "mouse calls" via, 318
    professional, composition of, 293p
    résumé sent via, 707
    sending and receiving, 232b
    staff communication via, 652
Emancipated minor, 496
E/M codes, 567, 578–582, 578t–579t
EMCs. *See* Electronic claims
eMedicineHealth, 231t
Emergency(ies)
    medical, 670–676
        documentation of, 675–676
        evaluating patient in, 673–674
        handling of, 671–676
        patient stress in, 674–675
        personal protective equipment for,
            672, 672–673, 673t
    office emergencies and disasters, 680–683
        assisting in, 680t
        evacuation and shelter-in-place plans
            for, 682–683
        triage in, 680, 690p
    patient, 676–679
    telephone, 285, 286t, 672
Emergency appointments, 311, 312b
Emergency codes, 673, 675t
Emergency medical services (EMS),
    contacting, 670–671, 684p
Emergency medical technician (EMT), 55
Emergency medicine, 45
Emergency preparedness, 669–693
Emotionally disturbed patient,
    communicating with, 80
Empathy, 72
Employee(s)
    benefits of, 663
    orientation and development for, 662
    participation by, 661b
    payment to. *See* Payroll
    probationary period for, 663
Employee handbook, 662, 662t
Employee records, retention of, 378
Employee's Withholding Allowance
    Certificate (Form W-4), 623, **624,** 663,
    663
Employer identification number (EIN),
    620–621
Employer's Quarterly Federal Tax Return
    (Form 941), 629, 630, **631,** 633

Employment contract, 124
Employment Eligibility Verification, 621, 663
Employment laws, 161
Employment search, 701–713
    interview in, 709–712
    job application in, 703, 713p–716p,
        714–715
    networking in, 702–703
    reasons for not being hired, 712
    references in, 703
    resources for, **702**
    résumé and cover letter in, 703–709,
        716p–717p
Employment services, 702–703
Employment verification, in credit check,
    506
EMRs. *See* Electronic health records
EMS system, 670–671, 684p
EMT. *See* Emergency medical technician
Enabling, 30
Enclosures, in business letter, 336–337
Encounter forms (superbills), 474, **475,** 494,
    498, 601
    coding for/with, 532–536, **582,** 582–583,
        589b
    customized, creating, **589,** 589b
    procedure for completing, 516p
    use of, 172, 308, **309**
Endocrine system
    CPT coding for, 585
    ICD-10-CM coding for, 554–555
Endocrinologists, 45
Endocrinology, 45
Endorsement, check, 612
End-state renal disease (ESRD), ICD-10-CM
    coding for, 557
English grammar and usage manuals, 344
Entrance, means of, for infection, **203,**
    204–205
Entry into medical practice, 169–172
Entry-level duties
    administrative, 6
    clinical, 7t
    general, 6
    laboratory, 7t
Enunciation, in telephone calls, 270
Envelopes, 331
    address format on, 350–351
    address placement on, 349–350, **350**
    for overnight delivery services, 352
    preparation of, 349–351
Environment, medical office, 181–201
EOB. *See* Explanation of benefits
Epidemiology, 206
Epinephrine autoinjector, **677,** 677–678
Epocrates, 426–427
Eponym, in CPT coding, 587
E-prescribing, 438, 439b
Equal Credit Opportunity Act (ECOA), 503t,
    505, 506, 510
Equal Employment Opportunity
    Commission (EEOC), 659, **661**
Equal Pay Act, 659
Equifax Inc., 506
Equipment, 219–266
    communication, 240–247, **241,** 268,
        288–291. *See also specific types*
    inventory of, **258,** 258–259
    mailing, 249–252, 261p–262p, 352
    office, 188, 219–266. *See also* Office
        equipment

purchasing of, 253–256
ERA. *See* Electronic remittance advice
Ergonomics, 195–196, 195t–196t
Erikson, Erik, 66
Errors
    abbreviations, symbols and dose
        designations prone to, 727–730
    insurance claim, common, 490t, 491
    written, proofreading for, 345–348
E-scheduler, 307
ESRD. *See* End-state renal disease
Established patient
    appointment for, 308
    in CPT coding, 579, **579**
Esteem needs, 67, **68**
Ethics, 157–160
    code of
        AAMA, 9
        AMA, 58–59, 157–159
    definition of, 121
    issues of, 121, 157
    law vs., 121
    of mandatory disclosure, 154–155, 156b
    social issues (bioethics), 157–160
    understanding of, importance of, 121
Etiology, 556
Etiquette
    for e-mail, 230
    for telephone calls, 269–272
Evacuation plan, 682–683
Evacuation route, planning, 682
Evaluation and management services, in
    CPT, 567, 578–582, 578t–579t
Examination(s). *See* Certification,
    examinations for; Physical examination
Excludes
    in ICD-9-CM coding, 527, 533
    in ICD-10-CM coding, 553t
Exclusions, in insurance, 453
Exit, means of, for infection, **203,** 203–204
Expanded problem-focused history, 579
Expanded problem-focused physical exam,
    580
Expendable item, 188
Expense statement, 620
Experience, on résumé, 704–706
Explanation, requesting, in communication,
    74
Explanation of benefits (EOB), 478,
    517–518
Exploring, in therapeutic communication, 73
Exposure control plan, 657
Exposure guidelines, 142
Expressed contract, 123
Express Mail, 353
External audit, 411–413
External causes
    in ICD-9-CM, 524, 525t, 529, 530–531,
        537–539, 543p
    in ICD-10-CM, 558–559, **559**
Externship, 15, 697–701
    affiliation agreement for, 697, **697**
    definition of, 15, 697
    HIPAA and, **699**
    professional behaviors for, 34, 699, 703b,
        717
    responsibilities in, 697–699
    site for, 697–699
    success in, 699–701
    thank-you note for, 700, 713p
Externship coordinator, 698

Eye(s)
   care and treatment of (ophthalmology),
      46–47
   CPT coding for, 585
Eye contact, 70

F

Face shields, 207, 672, **672**
Facial expression, 69–70, **70**
Facility, management of, 655–657
Facsimile machine. *See* Fax machine
Fact sheets, 98–99
Factual teaching, 96–97
Fair Credit Reporting Act (FCRA), 503t
Fair Debt Collection Practices Act of 1977
      (FDCPA), 502–503, 503t
Fair Labor Standards Act, 623, 659
Falls, 676
False billing claims, 141
False claims, federal legislation on, 141–142
False imprisonment, 122
Families
   communication with, 81–82
   telephone calls from, 281–282
Family Medical Leave Act (FMLA), 661
Family practice, 43–44
Family practitioners, 43–44
Fasting patients, scheduling appointments
      for, 312
Fax machine, 245–247, 290–291
   in all-in-one printer, 226, **226**
   benefits of, 245
   cover sheet for fax, 245–246, **246**, 260p
   information received via, in medical
      records, 399
   messages on, 242–243
   receiving fax, 246–247, **247**
   security for, HIPAA and, 151, 242–243,
      290–291
   sending fax, 260p
   thermal vs. plain paper for, 245–246
   turning on and off, 194
Fax modem, 222
FCRA. *See* Fair Credit Reporting Act
FDA. *See* Food and Drug Administration
FDCPA. *See* Fair Debt Collection Practices
      Act of 1977
Fears. *See* Anxious patient
Federal Express, 356
Federal False Claims Act, 141–142, 377
Federal legislation, affecting health care,
      141–142
Federal regulations, 12
Federal Tax Deposit Coupon (Form 8109),
      630, **630**
Federal Unemployment Tax Act (FUTA),
      625, 630–633, **632**
Feedback, in communication circle, 65, **65**
Fee-for-service plans, 455–456, 460,
      461–462
Feelings
   communicating in telephone calls, 272
   minimizing, in communication, 74
Fee schedules, 466–470, **467**
   contracted, 468
   Medicare, 466–467
Felony, 122
Female genital system, CPT coding for, 585
Fetal tissue transplant, ethics of, 157
FICA tax, 625, 629–630
File(s)

active vs. inactive or closed, 378
compactible, 370
   lateral, 370
   maintaining and protecting, 376–377
   misplaced, locating, 376, **376**
   retention of, 377–379, 388
   security of, 371, 376–377
   storage of, 377–381
      computer, 379
      facilities for, 379, **379**
      options for, 379–380
      paper, 379, **379**
      safety of, 380–381
   tickler, 375, 381p–382p
   vertical, 370
File folders, 371
File guides, 371
Filing cabinets, 370
Filing equipment, 370–371
Filing supplies, 370–371
Filing systems, 371–376
   alphabetic, 372, **372**, 373t–374t
   color coding in, 375–376, **376**
   numeric, 372–375, **375**
   sequential order, 371–372
   tickler, 375, 381p–382p
Finance charges, 504
Finances, overall, management of, 655
Financial records
   retention of, 377–379, 388
   separation from medical records, 392–393
Financial responsibility information,
      169–172, **171**, 177p
Financial summaries, understanding, 620
Fire(s), 680t, 681
   prevention of, 681
   safety equipment for, 258, 681–682, **682**
Fire extinguishers, 258, 681–682, **682**
Firewalls, 237
First aid, 670
First-aid kit, 671, 671t
First-class mail, 353
First party, in health insurance, 453
Five Cs of communication, 269
Flash drive, 379
Flatbed scanner, 224
FMLA. *See* Family Medical Leave Act
Focusing, in therapeutic communication, 73
Folding and inserting machines, 248–249,
      249
Folding letters, 248–249, **249**, **351**, 351–352
Follow-up, in medical records, 396, 401
Follow-up letter, after job interview,
      711–712, 713p
Follow-up statements (billing), 500
Fomites, 204–205, **205**
Food, Drug and Cosmetic Act of 1938, 429
Food and Drug Administration (FDA), 429
Foodborne transmission, 204t
Ford, Henry, 712
Foreign body airway obstruction, 676
   in responsive adult or child, 684p–685p,
      685
   in responsive infant, 685p–686p, **686**
Forensic pathologist, 47
Form 41 (Registrants Inventory of Drug
      Surrender), 434, **435**
Formatting errors, proofreading for, 345
Form I-9, 621, 663
Formulary, 453–454
Four Cs of malpractice prevention, 136

Four Ds of negligence, 133–134
Fourth-class mail, 353
Fractures
   CPT coding for, 583–584
   ICD-10-CM coding for, 556–557,
      557, 558
Fraud, 122, 141, 143, 462–463
   coding compliance and avoiding, 590–593
   insurance, 591–592
Friendliness, 72
Friends
   communication with, 81–82
   telephone calls from, 281–282
Front desk. *See* Reception area
FTD. *See* Federal Tax Deposit Coupon
      (Form 8109)
Full-block letter style, **337**, 339
Full-Scale Burnout Phase, 86
Furnishings (furniture)
   ergonomics of, 195–196, 195t–196t
   in reception area, 183–184
FUTA. *See* Federal Unemployment Tax Act

G

GAF. *See* Geographic adjustment factor
Gastroenterologists, 45
Gastroenterology, 45
General duties, entry-level, 6
General ledger. *See* Daily log
General practitioners, 43–44
General supplies, 188, 189t
General surgeons, 48
Generic name, of drug, 422–423
Genitourinary system
   CPT coding for, 585
   ICD-10-CM coding for, 557
Genuineness, 72
Geographic adjustment factor (GAF), 467
Geriatric patients. *See* Elderly patients
Gerontologists, 45
Gerontology, 45
Glossary, 731–742
Gloves, 207, 672
   contaminated, removing, 211p–212p
   use of, 209
Goal-setting, 5, 6t
Google, 231
Government health plans, 454, 457–466. *See
      also* Medicaid; Medicare
Gowns, 207, 672
Grammar, 333, 344
Graphical user interface (GUI), 227, **227**
Greed, and malpractice, 136
Green practices (recycling), 18b
Grief, stages of, 81
Grievance process, 663
Gross earnings, 623
Group practice, 160
Growth, 29, **30**
   definition of, 20, 27t, 29
   new computer system and, 263
   professional development, 17–18
   rubric for evaluating, **36**
GUI. *See* Graphical user interface
Gynecologists, 45
Gynecology, 45

H

Habits, healthy, 102–103
Haemophilus influenzae type b, 204–205

HAIs. *See* Health-care acquired infections (HAIs)
Handbook, employee, 662, 662t
Handheld computer. *See* Personal digital assistant
Handheld scanner, 223
Hands-free devices, 270, **270,** 271b
Hand washing, 208, **208,** 673
   alcohol hand disinfecting, 208, 211p
   general, 208, 210p–211p
   medical aseptic, 208
   sterile or surgical, 208
Harassment, sexual, 662
Hard copy. *See* Paper claims; Paper medical records
Hard disk drive, 224
Hardship cases, 510
Hard skills, 25
Hardware, computer, 221–226
   functions of, 221
   input devices, 221–224
   output devices, 225–226
   processing devices, 224
   selecting and upgrading, 234–235
   storage devices, 224–225, 238
Hazardous Communication Standard, 207
HBV. *See* Hepatitis B/hepatitis B virus (HBV)
HCPCS. *See* Health Care Common Procedure Coding System
HCQIA. *See* Health Care Quality Improvement Act of 1986
Heading, on résumé, 704
Health and Human Services, U.S. Department of, 548, 591
Health and safety compliance, 657
Health care
   changes in, 5, 8, 17–18, 121
   federal legislation affecting, 141–142
   multiskilled professionals in, 17–18
   reducing costs in, 17–18
   rising costs of, impact of, 121
Health-care acquired infections (HAIs), 206
Health-care administrator, 349p, 649. *See also* Medical practice, management of
Healthcare Common Procedure Coding System (HCPCS), 153, 523, 588–590
   Level I codes, 588
   Level II codes, 588–590
   locating code, 594p
Health-care proxy, 140
Health Care Quality Improvement Act of 1986 (HCQIA), 141
Health-care team, 42–62
   billing and insurance specialist on, 511b
   certified medical reimbursement specialist on, 555b
   clearinghouse claims representative on, 608b
   compliance officer on, 155b
   cooperation on, 29, **30,** 60
   coordination of, 29
   CPR instructor on, 679b
   electronic claims professional on, 592b
   hospital admissions clerk on, 316b
   medical assisting educator on, 33b
   medical chart auditor on, 411b
   medical coder, physician practice on, 541b
   medical librarian on, 102b

medical office or health-care administrator on, 349p
   medical specialties on, 43–49
   medical transcriptionist on, 250b
   pharmaceutical representative on, 428p
   physician assistant on, 652b
   public health nurse on, 207b
   registered health information technologist on, 380b
   specialty career options on, 54–56
   working with other allied health professionals on, 49–54
Health-care workers. *See specific occupations*
Health information. *See also* Medical records
   disclosure of, HIPAA and, 145, 398b
   individually identifiable, 144–152, 398b
   managing/storing, HIPAA and, 145–147
   release of
      without authorization, situations for, 149
      authorization for, **148,** 148–150, 154–155, 162p–163p, 169, **171,** 177p, 377
      improper, preventing, 154
      verbal, agreement form for, **310,** 310–311
   security of, HIPAA and, 150
   sharing, HIPAA and, 148–149
   use of, HIPAA and, 145, 398b
Health information technologist, registered, 380b
Health insurance
   assignment of benefits, 169–172, **171,** 177p, 469–470
   billing claims under. *See* Insurance claims
   copayment with, 186
   drug coverage under, 422–423
   enrollment, by type of plan, 456, **456**
   fee-for-service, 455–456
   fraud in, 591–592
   government plans, 454, 457–466
   identity theft and, 187–188
   lack of, 454
   managed care, 11–12, 313b, 453, 455–456
   portability of, 143
   private plans, 454–457
   reform of, 454
   terminology of, 453–454
   third-party payers in, 169
Health Insurance Portability and Accountability Act (HIPAA), 141, 142–154
   and administrative simplification, 143, 152–153
   compliance with, 172–173, 183
   and computer, 235–236, 236b
   definition of, 14
   and disclosure of health information, 144, 398b
   and electronic health records, 152b
   and e-mail, 230, 231b
   as examination topic, 14
   and externship, **699**
   and faxing, 151, 242–243, 290–291
   frequently asked questions about, 153–154
   and identifiers, 144–152, 398b
   and identity theft, 187–188
   and insurance claims, 480–481, 491p, 492, 492b

and management of medical records, 145–147, 369, 377
   and medical coding, 153, 523–524, 567
   Notice of Privacy Practices under, 107, 145, **146,** 149–150, 161p–162p, 398b
   and ownership of medical records, 138
   and paper shredding, 253
   patient information on, 107, 308
   and patient registration, 185–186
   Privacy Rule of, 144–152, 153
   purposes of, 143
   and recycling, 18b
   and retention of files/records, 379
   and security measures, 150–151
   Security Rule of, 150
   and sharing health information, 148–149, 162p–163p, 398b
   and storage of medical records, 145–147
   and telephone calls, 242–243, 275, 282
   Title III of, 143
   Title II of, 143
   Title I of, 143
   Title IV of, 143
   Title V of, 143
   and use of health information, 144
   and verbal release of information, **310,** 310–311
   violations and penalties of, 147, **147,** 152, 162p, 175b, 591–592
Health maintenance organization (HMO), 159, 453, 456, **456**
Health Professions Network, 57t
Health-promoting behaviors, 104
Health promotion, 102–104
Health records. *See* Medical records
Health system, contact with
   in ICD-9-CM (V codes), 524, 525t, 529, 530–531, 537
      health screening, **540,** 540p
      locating, 542p–543p
   in ICD-10-CM, 559–560, **560**
Healthy habits, 102–103
Hearing aids, patients wearing, 88p
Hearing loss, patients with
   communicating with, 79, **79,** 88p
   office accommodations for, 184
   telecommunication device for, 273, **273,** 274t, 291p
Heart attack, 678
Hemic system, CPT coding for, 584
Hemorrhaging, 676–677
Hepatitis B/hepatitis B virus (HBV), 142, 207, 657
Hierarchy of human needs, 66–68, **68**
High-complexity medical decision making, 580, 581t
High-severity complaint, 581
HIPAA. *See* Health Insurance Portability and Accountability Act
Hippocrates, 157
Hippocratic oath, 157
Hiring process, 659–661
History, patient. *See* Medical history, patient
History of present illness (HPI), 579–580
HIV/AIDS
   ICD-10-CM coding for, 554
   OSHA regulations on, 142
   reporting of, 137
HMO. *See* Health maintenance organization
Hold, telephone call on, 270–271
Homeostasis, 67